Internet Comedy Television Series,
1997–2015

Internet Comedy Television Series, 1997–2015

VINCENT TERRACE

McFarland & Company, Inc., Publishers

Jefferson, North Carolina

Library of Congress Cataloguing-in-Publication Data

Names: Terrace, Vincent, 1948– author.
Title: Internet comedy television series, 1997–2015 / Vincent Terrace.
Description: Jefferson, North Carolina : McFarland & Company, Inc.,
Publishers, 2016. | Includes index.
Identifiers: LCCN 2015051016 | ISBN 9780786497607
(softcover : acid free paper) ∞
Subjects: LCSH: Internet television—Encyclopedias. |
Television comedies—Encyclopedias.
Classification: LCC PN1992.2 .T53 2016 | DDC 791.45/617—dc23
LC record available at http://lccn.loc.gov/2015051016

British Library cataloguing data are available

ISBN (print) 978-0-7864-9760-7
ISBN (ebook)978-1-4766-2393-1

Front cover photograph of *Destroy the Alpha Gammas* by Eilene
Beniquez from a poster designed by Sara Fletcher (courtesy Leah
McKendrick); background image of tablet © 2016 Halfpoint/iStock

Printed in the United States of America

*McFarland & Company, Inc., Publishers
Box 611, Jefferson, North Carolina 28640
www.mcfarlandpub.com*

TABLE OF CONTENTS

PREFACE

Internet Comedy Television Programs, 1997–2015, is the fourth volume in a one-of-a-kind series that covers various genres of Internet television programming. Like the prior books (*Internet Horror, Science Fiction and Fantasy Television Series, 1996–2013*; *Internet Drama and Mystery Television Series, 1996–2014*; and *Internet Lesbian and Gay Television Series, 1996–2014*), this volume is also the only book to date that presents a history of television programs produced exclusively for the worldwide web.

Internet television programs are produced like a broadcast or cable TV series but *without* the big budget and, in most instances, *minus* name performers. When it comes to comedy programming available on the web, the viewer has a variety of choices of which show to watch. This book is not only a guide to those comedy series, but a detailed account of what they are about with story lines, casts, credits, episode lists, dates, and web addresses. (Keep in mind that web addresses listed in this volume reflect those where program information can still be found at the time of publication and are not necessarily the official websites, as many have closed since this book was first begun.) There are also accompanying photographs and a complete index.

In the arena of Internet-based comedy series, there are entries about bartenders who love you (*Bar Flies*) and those who detest you (*The Bartender Hates You*). There are enjoy-able TV spoofs of shows like *Charlie's Angels* (with *Chico's Angels*) and movie parodies like *BabeArella* (a send-up of *Barbarella*). There is a very elderly, still active secret agent (*Agent 88*), and even an obnoxious, talking piece of fruit (*Annoying Orange*). When it comes to odd couple roommates there are such entries as *Bigfoot Roommate*, *Grape's Roommate* (a guy living with a store-bought bunch of grapes) and *American Blob* (a talking rock). There is a program about an infant who fights crime (*Baby Mentalist*), an animal detective (*Llama Cop*), and a gorilla who helps humans (*Gorilla Therapy*). *My Life with Sock* finds a woman falling in love with a tube sock that comes to life, there is a man who believes his son's plush toy is real (*Delphis*), and a husband struggling to cope with his wife's come-to-life plush toy monster (*A Guy, a Girl and Their Monster*). If the latter's premise were not strange enough, there is a bizarre mother just trying to raise her children (*Brain Eatin' Zombie Babies*), a snake who runs a company (*Dennis the Office Cobra*), an alien TV talk show host (*The Gorburger Show*), and rampaging animals (*Possum Death Spree*). We also have ghost hunters (*Ghost Ghirls*, *Giving Up the Ghosts*), health spa spoofs (*Trainers*, *Venus Spa*), and personality and character spoofs with *Kam Kardashian* (the lesbian sister of Kim Kardashian), *Adult Wednesday Addams* (the daughter of Gomez and Morticia Addams), and *Very Mary-Kate* (the twin sister of Ashley Olsen). *Shelf Life, Sassy Batman, Sweethearts of the Galaxy*, and *Vexika* present super hero spoofs while *Cowgirl Up* and *DareDoll Dilemmas* offer beautiful women in a whole new light. These are only a very small sampling of what other amusing oddities are contained in the pages of this book.

The Internet has and is presenting a whole new world of television-like entertainment that, while still in its infancy, is continually growing and maturing. With this series of books about genres of web TV series, you will have the only printed record presently available of its pioneering, intriguing history.

The author would like to thank James Robert Parish for his assistance on this project.

THE SERIES

1 *Abel.* webserieschannel.com. 2013.

Abel Crane is a man who had it all until his bride-to-be left him at the altar for another man. Devastated and lost without her, he begins a downward spiral with drugs "helping" him cope with what has happened. As time passes he realizes he must let the past go and move on. The program chronicles what happens when Abel sets out to find a new love and somehow achieve a better understanding of life.

Cast: James Tucci (Abel Crane), Grant Austin O'Connell (Trever Mercer), Leann Pulvermiller (Katherine Pierce), Courtney Case (Whiskey), Cory Sharpe Haynes (Riley), James Walters (Dean), Audrey Hayner (Tatum). **Credits:** *Director:* Kenneth Price. *Writer:* Kenneth Price, James Tucci, Ansley Thaler. **Comment:** A bit dramatic at times (adult situations) although the acting and production are very good.

Episodes: *1.* Reckoning. *2.* Consequence. *3.* Choices.

2 *About Abby.* aboutabby.tv. 2011.

Abby is a young woman who believed she had the perfect life until the man she thought was her one true love (her high school sweetheart) leaves her for another woman. Seeing that Abby is hurting, her best friends (Caroline and Micah) convince her to get back into the dating scene and find that special someone. The dates Abby acquires in her quest to find her true love ("and maybe a little fun too") are chronicled.

Cast: Keghan Hurst (Abby Freeman), Ashley Reign (Caroline LeDeux), Gabe Pasillas (Micah Acosta), Eric Lloyd (Xander Falls), Lisa Younger (Theo), Jeff Whitlatch (Patrick), Will Barker (Christian), Patrick Blakey (Lloyd), Ashley Gomes (Raine), Nathanael Theison (Riley). **Credits:** *Producer:* Sassy Mohen, Matthew Stubstad. *Writer-Director:* Sassy Mohen. **Comment:** Charming series with very good acting and production values.

Episodes: *1.* Test. *2.* About Abby and the Aussie. *3.* About Abby and the Ex. *4.* About Abby and the Musician. *5.* About Abby and the Dead Fish. *6.* About Abby and the New Guy.

3 *Act Naturally.* webserieschannel.com. 2012.

Nick and Kelsi are a couple who appear to be perfect for each other. Nick, however, has become displeased with Kelsi's often strange behavior and loud sexual dreams (not necessarily about him) and is seeking to break up with her. Just when he thinks the moment is right, Kelsi receives a phone call informing her that her Grandpa Teddy has passed away. Seeing that Kelsi is upset Nick postpones telling her and the program follows Nick's efforts to continue living with Kelsi with Kelsi clueless that she will be the cause of their breakup (which is never actually seen as happening).

Cast: Kelsi Roberts (Kelsi), Yassir Lester (Nick), Tony Baker (Tony), Chase Bernstein (Chase), Megan McMillan (Nurse), Daniel Roy (Boss), Jarrod Harris (Dr. Goodman). **Credits:** *Producer-Writer-Director:* Nick Cervantes. **Comment:** The program begins well then quickly turns into a morbid comedy when Nick discovers he has cancer. Medical issues are simply not funny and it becomes uncomfortable to watch at times.

Episodes: *1.* Dream Nick. *2.* Pretty Normal Activity. *3.* The Boy Who Cried. *4.* Fine for Now.

4 *Acting Out.* youtube.com. 2012.

Believing that he must hide his true sexual identity in order to acquire jobs in the acting field, a young man (Bogie) pretends to be straight hoping to acquire the roles that will make him a household name. The program chronicles what happens as he attempts to lead two different lives and contend with friends who want to help but just complicate what he is trying to do (all of which is heard through his internal thoughts as situations progress).

Kyle, Bogie's boyfriend, wishes Bogie would be true to himself and not pretend to be what he is not. Bridge and Sadie, Bogie's lesbian friends, try to be helpful and offer advice that is more tailored to being gay than being straight. Owen is Bogie's best friend, a deliveryman who is more concerned about the economy and his well being than Bogie's problems.

Cast: Brennan Hillard (Bogie), David Tolemy (Kyle), Victoria J. Myers (Bridge), Molly Schrieber (Sadie), Justin Giddings (Owen), Cary Adams (Jackson Powers), John Moschitta, Jr. (Ramshackle), Emily Churchill (Candy Hart), Frank Birney (Warner). **Credits:** *Producer:* Jeff Parke, Shane Houston. **Comment:** Enjoyable saga of a confused young man with good acting and production values. The fast-talking John Moschitta, Jr., as Bogie's agent adds to the amusement (as he will not only confuse Bogie, but viewers as well with advice that is hard to comprehend [the intent] due to his speedy delivery).

Episodes: *1–4.* The Manager.

5 *Acting School Academy.* youtube.com. 2009.

"What we do here is real acting," says Maryin De-Witt, the head of Acting School Academy which strives to go beyond what other schools call acting classes. Maryin is strict and feels that his years as an actor have taught him what is needed to succeed in the business. As Maryin tries to instill "the real" spirit of acting into his students, the program focuses on the students, in particular Laura and Mike, who find romance with each other, and Ivan and Seregi, Russian criminals who use the school as a cover for their illegal activities.

Cast: Nina Fehren (Laura Peterson), Kris Sharma (Mike Lipschitz), Mo Darwiche (Sergei), Arick Salmea (Ivan), Dennis Haskins (Maryin DeWitt), Michael Mayorga (Gary Lopez), Gwen Hollander (Katie Pierce), Michael Mullen (Damien Foster), Amber Marie Bollinger (Gwendolyn Ravenwood), Joy Darash (Flower Higgens), Dylan Hobbs (Jason Stackhouse). **Credits:** *Producer:* Mo Darwiche, M. Ian Smith. *Director:* M. Ian Smith. *Writer:* Michael Mayorga. Kris Sharma. **Comment:** Interesting take on programs dealing with acting schools by adding the nefarious dealings of two criminals. Dennis Haskins, who plays Maryin may be recognized by some as playing Richard Belding on NBC's *Saved by the Bell.* The overall production is well acted and produced.

Episodes: *1.* Partners. *2.* Self Discovery. *3.* Relationships. *4.* Real Emotions. *5.* Personalize Things. *6.* Personalize People. *7.* The Business. *8.* The Showcase. *9.* Ivan & Sergei: Crime Clean Commercial. *10.* Ivan & Sergei: Cooking Show. *11.* Ivan and Sergei: Cribs.

6 *An Actor Unprepared.* webserieschannel. com. 2014.

Gianmarco is a young man whose life revolves around the word "no." He is a New York–based actor struggling to achieve fame but is hampered by his inability to properly prepare for the roles for which he auditions. Gianmarco constantly faces rejection and hearing phrases like "you are not right for the role" are just a part of his life. But he is not dismayed and has set his goal to acquire the top roles no matter how many degrading parts he must endure before that big break.

Cast: Gianmarco Soresi (Gianmarco), Remy Germinario (Ross). **Credits:** *Producer:* Stephen Ditmer. *Director:* Gia McKenna. *Writer:* Gianmarco Soresi. **Comment:** The program is well produced and acted. The use of split screens (allowing two people in two different locations to appear in the same frame) is very good and its only drawback is the use of vulgar language (which is really not needed).

Episodes: *1.* An Actor Unprepared. *2.* An Actor Under the Bus. *3.* An Actor Under Pitched. *4.* An Actor Unemotional. *5.* An Actor Undressed.

7 *The Actors.* webserieschannel.com. 2011.

Nathan, a young filmmaker hoping to make his mark on the world, finds that accomplishing that goal is much harder than he imagined. When he learns of a competition being held wherein filmmakers will compete for a cash prize, he quickly registers and becomes one of the contestants. Nathan is full of hope until he finds that others are much more experienced than he is and the prize will be much harder to achieve. Now, as the least experienced member of the group, but with an unrelenting enthusiasm, Nathan assembles a group of actors and the program charts all the mishaps Nathan encounters as he sets out to make an outstanding film and not only net the first prize but see his vision become a reality.

Cast: Ryan Booth (Nathan), Kristy Nadine (Anna), Melissa Hartzel (Belinda), Rob Plumbly (Andy), Max Hutchinson (George), Hanna Barel (Waitress), Matt Brewer (Peter). **Credits:** *Producer-Writer-Director:* Dave Connors. **Comment:** British produced program that is well presented once you adjust to what is happening. It begins in the middle of a scene and can leave one wondering what is going on. Other than that, the acting and production values are good, typical of most American produced web series.

Episodes: *1.* Nathan's Mum. *2.* The Agent.

8 *The Actress.* theactressseries.com. 2010–2014.

Hannah is a woman hoping to become an actress. But Hannah, with a temp job at Rockefeller Center in Manhattan, falls into what is called "the bottom-feeding" syndrome (hopefuls who spend countless years seeking something that will never happen in the way they envision it). Hannah is a bit older than others seeking stardom, has "clawed and scrapped and sacrificed" but has yet to realize she will soon have to settle for what she has become and readjust her thinking. Even though it appears pointless, Hannah is full of enthusiasm and the program follows her efforts to work, attend auditions, put on little no-nothing plays and climb that ladder to stardom. Brian is her unmotivated, stoner boyfriend; Claire is her sister.

Cast: Ann Carr (Hannah Kennon), Mike Still (Brian), Margot Leitman (Claire). **Credits:** *Producer:* Ann Carr, Warren Holstein, Amanda Hammett. *Director:* Tim Bierbaum, Jim Turner. *Writer:* Ann Carr, Warren Holstein. **Comment:** Ann Carr as Hannah is especially good as she truly gets across to the viewer the frustrations such people feel. The acting is very good and the overall production is one of the better of the struggling actor series.

Season 1 Episodes: *1.* Hannah. *2.* Sisters. *3.* The Day Job. *4.* The Seminar. *5.* The Crazy Maker.

Season 2 Episodes: *1.* Worst Day Ever. *2.* Meet Brian. *3.* Fraternal Humor. *4.* Denise. *5.* The Cab Ride. *6.* The Teacher. *7.* The Scene Partner. *8.* The Photographer.

Season 3 Episodes: *1.* The Dermatologist. *2.* No Broadway. *3.* Kate. *4.* Mom. *5.* The Agent. *6.* The Wedding. *7.* Unemployment. *8.* One Too Many.

9 The Actress Diaries. actressdiaries.com. 2013–2014.

Vancouver, Canada, provides the setting for a look at the outrageous lengths two aspiring actresses, Lisa (Australian) and Kate (Canadian), engage in to make their mark on the world. Lisa and Kate work as waitresses with season one episodes focusing on their job-related experiences and acting pursuits. The second season combines aspects of their personal lives with their continual efforts to balance work and capture that elusive acting career. Lisa and Kate are seen as the hosts of an on-line show called *Lisa and Kate Know Better Than You* and through their vlogs introduce viewers to the world of auditions with tips on what to do and what to avoid.

Cast: Kate Bateman (Kate Bateman), Lisa Hughes (Lisa Kimberly Hughes), Matt Hamilton (Matt), Simon Baush (Simon), Sean MacLean (Joel), Ken Lawson (Bruce Richards), Melanie Crystal (Joan Baker), Lauren Donnelly (Joan's assistant), Kris McRonney (Jackson Davis), Brynn Peeles (Delilah Deluca), Jennifer Pielak (Harper Parker), Aliyah O'Brien (Nikki Evans), Lisa Oives (Cassandra Carpenter-Wells), Arianna McGregor (Maggie Deluca), Henry Mahr (Solomon Feng). **Credits:** *Producer:* Jackie Massar, Lisa Hughes, Kate Bateman, Megan Russell. *Director:* Lisa Hughes, Jackie Massar. *Writer:* Matt Hamilton, Lisa Hughes, Mike Mitton, Megan Russell. **Comment:** The program is a well acted and produced spoof (a "mockumentary") of the auditioning process actors endure before getting a role.

Season 1 Episodes: *1.* Pilot. *2.* Tip 2. *3.* Tip 3. *4.* Tip 4. *5.* Tip 5.

Season 2 Episodes: *1.* YouTube Sensation. *2.* Going Postal. *3.* Wanted: Roommate. *4.* Red Carpet. *5.* The Milano Method. *6.* Muffin Pants. *7.* The Lucky Jacket. *8.* It's a Celebration. *9.* The Date. *10.* Get the Role.

10 Adult Wednesday Addams. youtube. com. 2013–2015.

Wednesday Addams, the solemn, gothic girl-like daughter of Gomez and Morticia Addams (from *The Addams Family* TV and movie series) has decided, now that she is a young woman, to move out of her family home and find her place in the world. She chooses to live in Los Angeles and with Spanish doubloons from her late grandmother Wednesday acquires an apartment and a new life. Wednesday possesses an air of gloom, sets her hair in long braids (her hair is sensitive and doesn't like to be separated), wears her great great Aunt Libby's black dress and has an uncanny ability to avoid being photographed (a blinding white light appears around her in pictures). Wednesday is, in essence, an outsider who refuses to fit in. She wants to remain herself and the program relates the events that spark her life as she navigates the world on her own for the first time.

Cast: Melissa Hunter (Wednesday Addams). **Credits:** *Producer:* William Cubbon. *Director:* Mike Bernstein. *Writer:* Melissa Hunter. **Comment:** Melissa Hunter is outstanding as Wednesday. She encompasses the look of Lisa Loring (from the TV series) and Christina Ricci (from the feature film versions), all of which are based on the comic strip by Charles Addams. Whether Wednesday is attempting to baby sit, learn how to drive, or even walk a dog, it is all seen in a different perspective and makes for a truly enjoyable program.

Season 1 Episodes: *1.* The Apartment Hunt. *2.* Job Interview. *3.* Internet Date. *4.* Dog Walker. *5.* One Night Stand. *7.* Planned Parenthood.

Season 2 Episodes: Baby Sitting. *2.* Driver's Ed. *3.* Wednesday vs. Catcallers. *4.* The Haircut. *5.* The Reality Star. *6.* The Flea Market. *7.* True Love.

11 Adventures in Assisting. webserieschannel.com. 2012.

Alice is a young woman with one goal: to become a successful artist. But her artwork has yet to catch on and her income is virtually zero. To supplement her income, she applies for and receives a job as the personal assistant to Gabriella Maitland, a demanding, neurotic entrepreneur. Alice is the girl next door type; Gabriella is a woman like Alice has never encountered and the program charts her efforts to deal with all the demands required of being a personal assistant.

Cast: Andie Karvelis (Alice Hamilton), Suzanne Rydz (Gabriella Maitland), Christopher Newell (Jason). **Credits:** *Producer:* Andie Karvelis, Suzanne Rydz, Sacha Iskra, Rene Ruiz. *Director:* Ken Grant.

Writer: Andie Karvelis. **Comment:** All episodes and virtually all text information have been taken off line. It is not possible to provide a further detailed story line or even present a comment based on what is available.

12 *The Adventures of Barry Baz.* barry baz.com. 2012.

Barry Baz, an Australian-based delusional actor, music performer, playboy and champion boxer, yearns for more than his home-based fame. He seeks glory in Hollywood and become an actor "Just like Errol Flynn." To begin his quest he hires a filmmaker (Hu Wang) to document his journey and bring it to life for everyone to see. Barry, however, is obnoxious, chases women and only out for what he wants no matter who he offends or hurts in the process. As Hu Wang documents the many stories Barry has to tell about his life in Australia (which are seen in flashbacks), his rather unethical pursuits to achieve stardom are also chronicled.

Cast: Nicholas Coles (Barry Baz), Alfred Hsing (Hu Wang), Larry Hankin (Joe the Bum), Amanda Aday (Amy), Jackie Monohan (Aussie Sheila). **Credits:** *Producer:* Nicholas Coles, Albert Brocca. *Director:* David Brocca. **Comment:** Those familiar with Australian comedian Paul Hogan will find that Barry is his evil twin, a man with no redeeming social values. The program comes off as quite sleazy with sexual jokes, adult situations and a hard-to-fathom character as actually existing. But because of those unsavory aspects, the program can be viewed as a well paced comedy with the lead as an over-the-top personification of an Aussie Outback character.

Episodes: 3 untitled episodes, titled "Chapter 1," "Chapter 2" and "Chapter 3."

13 *The Adventures of Chadwick Periwinkle.* webserieschannel.com. 2011.

It is the year 4010 A.D. and the world looks upon slackers like Chadwick Periwinkle as an abomination to the universe and deems that such trash must be eliminated from society. As the termination begins Chadwick manages to escape and the program charts his adventures as he attempts to avoid the Universe Hit Men who are out to get him.

Chadwick, a once a happy-go-lucky young man, is now a futuristic hoodlum—eager to steal from anyone and use his ill-gotten gains on hookers, booze and drugs. His reputation has grown from nice guy to incompetent drug smuggler to guilty-by-association mass murderer. But Chadwick doesn't see himself as a good guy or bad guy; he's an "indifferent guy."

Hal-E is the artificial female intelligence attached to Chadwick's ship, the *Deus Ex-Machina.* She is constantly abused by Chadwick, suffers from paranoia and plagued by the numerous viruses that have infiltrated her system and trying to take over her thought processes. Although she is not human, she has feelings for Chadwick.

The Dream Girl is the gorgeous imaginary woman that haunts Chadwick's dreams. But is she just a dream vision or is she a mysterious foreshadower (in Chadwick's dreams, she appears to have a message to relay).

Baron Von Nazty-Kins is a cyborg bounty hunter that has been programmed in the image of a World War II Nazi. He calls himself "A Nazi-Cyborg-Bounty-Hunter-Serial Killer from Space." He pilots the ship *The Donkey Punch* and is dead set on capturing Chadwick.

Chevey Periwinkle is Chadwick's older brother, a renowned womanizer and adventurer whose ship, *The Feral* is his portable bachelor pad. His job appears to be copyrighting catch phrases then turning them into hits. His current "hit" is "You've been Periwinkled."

Cast: Stimson Snead (Chadwick Periwinkle), Shayla Keating (Hal-E), Wonder Russell (Dream Girl), Charissa Adams (Li'l Red), Bjorn Whitney (Chevey Periwinkle), Gene Thorkildsen (Baron Von Nazty-Kins), Marty Krouse (Jack Manly), Lizzie Officer (Madame Bubala), Ian Lindsay (Johnson J. Jackson), Parker Mathews (Hacifert), Bryan Bender (Big Dog). **Credits:** *Producer:* David Purdy. *Writer-Director:* Stimson Snead. **Comment:** Comically played space adventure that, despite its absurd premise is amusing with good acting and production values. The Dream Girl is especially appealing and Hal-E's issues add to the fun.

Episodes: *1.* Chadwick Periwinkle, the Inaction Hero. *2.* Chadwick Periwinkle and the A.I. from Hell. *3.* Licensed to Slack. *4.* I've Had Worse Days *5.* Chadwick's Ugly Little Mind. *6.* If Your Problems Don't Include Nazi Cyborgs. *7.* The Cursed Planet of Cursed Doom. *8.* Chaddy O'Periwinkle an' Da Little People. *9.* Oh Ricky!

14 *The Adventures of Lewis and Clark.* adventuresoflewisandclark.com. 2013.

Lewis and Clark, not the famous explorers, but two slackers, and one pretty (and responsible) but unfortunate girl (Charese, Lewis's sister), embark on a journey of fulfillment—to find not only love, but money by any means they can, usually through the unconventional methods they devise. The program follows what happens when they enact their warped ideas only to discover what they thought was brilliant has turned into a nightmare.

Cast: Mark Elias (Lewis Meriwether), Jus Reddick (Clark Wallace), Charese Mongiello (Charese Meriwether), Hidekun Hah (Sweet Liu), T.J. Slaughter (T.J.), Karli Rae Grogan (Carly), Aryn Wuthrich (E-Wuth), Gary Casey (Crazy Gary), Thomas F. Evans (Karl Meriwether), Michele Karpel (Marge Meriwether), J.J. Nolan (Jessica). **Credits:**

Producer-Director: Jus Riddick, Charese Mongiello, Mark Elias. *Writer:* Mark Elias. **Comment:** If "dude jokes" and slacker humor is your cup of tea, then *Lewis and Clark* will be a delightful surprise. While the situations are just what they are meant to be—preposterous, the acting and production values are good enough to make it an enjoyable experience.

Episodes: *1.* Gutter Balls. *2.* Get Real Laid. *3.* I Wanna Get Highered. *4.* Casting for the Couch. *5.* To Sketch a Thief. *6.* Undercover Brothers. *7.* Seeing Stars. *8.* Downward Dogs. *9.* Taser Tag. *10.* Nuns n' Roses. *11.* Everybody Get Dangerous. *12.* Birthday Package.

15 *The Adventures of Suzy Boon.* suzy boonwebseries.com. 2014.

Suzy Boon is a young woman desperately trying to find her place in the world. She is working a trial period at the New Zealand Immigration Service and is eagerly trying to impress her boss (Linleigh) in the hope of being asked to fill one of the two permanent positions that are available. She is also without a man and has turned to Internet dating to find a soul mate. The program follows Suzy as she desperately tries to balance her work life with her love life and not make them more comp   l i c a t e d than they already are.

Suzy, half Chinese and half Maori, is a bit awkward and struggling to figure out the important "stuff" in her life: love, happiness and her identity. She lives with her father, a retired businessman who relocated to New Zealand when he was in his early twenties. He was married to a Maori girl and had

only one child, Suzy, before she passed away, leaving Mr. Boon to raise Suzy by himself. Denise, eight months pregnant, has been working at the immigration service for three years. Lisa is another veteran of the service who, like Denise, was trained by the stern Linleigh. Paul and Mitch are trainees also vying for one of the openings that will soon become available.

Cast: Kura Forrester (Suzy Boon), Yvette Parsons (Linleigh Turnbull), Liesha Ward Knox (Denise), Charles Chan (Mr. Boon), Scott Cotter (Paul), Genevieve Cohsn (Lisa). **Credits:** *Producer:* Roberto Nascimento, Roko Antonio Babich. *Director:* Cristobal Araus Lobos. *Writer:* Roberto Nascimento, Louis Mendiola, Thomas Sainsbury. **Comment:** Nicely produced New Zealand program that actually presents characters as people you may know. They appear natural (no excessive makeup or other frills) and its subject matter is something that has not been done before.

Episodes: *1.* The Trial. *2.* Hooked on a Feeling. *3.* Warrior Princess. *4.* The Beach. *5.* Leonardo DiCapriano. *6.* Confucius Says.

16 *Adventures of the Hunky Pipe-Fitter.* webserieschannel.com. 2011.

Adrian is an actor who believes he has it made as part of the cast of the successful daytime TV soap opera *The Old and the Useless* (a title switch on TV's *The Young and the Restless*). His world suddenly falls apart when he is fired and replaced by Peter Smeader in the role of Joe Strong. Adrian has an agent (Dusty) but finds there are no acting jobs due to the economy and declining soap opera ratings. With mounting bills and no other choice, Adrian returns to his former profession as a plumber (which got him the acting job when he auditioned and fixed the casting director's leaky sink). Work is not the only thing Adrian has to contend with: his father (Arthur) married his ex-lover (Marcie) and wants to start a family. The situation sounds logical only Arthur wants Adrian to impregnate Marcie as a medical condition prevents him from doing so. The program chronicles the life Adrian now leads with situations making him feel like his real life is just like the soap opera he worked on.

Cast: Adrian Colbert (Joe #1), Kevin Sloan (Dusty), Peter Smeader (Joe #2), Mersiha Musovic (Fran), Rafael Pellerin (Howard), Tijana Popovic (Marcie), Megan Lightle (Liza), Marcel Perro (Arthur). **Credits:** *Producer:* Jennifer Pitcher, Megan Lightle. *Writer:* Salvatore Stefanile. **Comment:** A unique idea that is well acted and produced and different.

Episodes: *1.* First Job. *2.* Who's Your Daddy? *3.* Maybe He's Having a Baby.

17 *The Adventures of Velvet Prozak.* vel vetprozak.com. 2014.

The Adventures of Suzy Boon. Series poster art (used by permission of Roberto Nascimento).

Bartholomew Fogglehorn believes becoming an actor is his calling. It began when, at the age of five, he performed as a Michael Jackson impersonator, but his parents quickly put an end to it as they felt their son was heading down the wrong path. But Bartholomew believes he was meant to be a star and has vowed to pursue that goal. Bartholomew, now 22 years old, lives in Florida with his parents and feeling that the time is right, leaves home to pursue his dream in Hollywood. His parents believe he is delusional but cannot stop him. It is a year later when the program begins and Bartholomew has not yet become the star he hoped. He works as a French fry (dressed in a rubber suit for Happy Fries, a fast-food store), has small acting roles and something he hadn't counted on—bad luck as anything that can go wrong happens to him. Bartholomew appears a bit nerdy (unruly hair, large glasses), has a controlling manager (Sandra), a girlfriend (Jacqueline) who is only dating him for a chance at an acting job through Sandra and a feeling that his parents may have been right. As his downward spiral continues to increase, he hits on a plan to change his look and personality and re-invent himself as Velvet Prozak. The program follows what happens as Bartholomew, now as Velvet, seeks to become the star he set out to be.

Cast: Saige Walker (Bartholomew Fogglehorn), Jason Boegh (Jack), Allie Meixner (Sandra Greene), Andy Milonakis (Zack), Ron Rogge (Tom Goodman), Karen Sedgley (Bartholomew's mother), Steve Gorlin (Bartholomew's father), Gary Sievers (Stan Levi), Sasha Neboga (Shay), Knight Davison (Molly), Tanisha Guity (Stephanie), Gabrielle Nevins (Jacqueline Sweet), Isabella Sanchez (Maria), Katie Sokoien (Kat). **Credits:** *Producer:* Pamela Armstrong, Nash Ron, Rachel Ryling, Stefan Sacks, Gary Sievers, Sydney Silver, Saige Walker, Michael Wallet. *Director:* Saige Walker. *Writer:* Steve Gorlin, Saige Walker. **Comment:** Part of the fun is the way Bartholomew is presented—a real nerdy-looking character that can't see that his looks are his downfall. While the subject matter has been done countless times before, there can always be a twist, and *Velvet Prozak* has found a good one as one lost soul seeks a dream.

Episodes: *1.* The Wrong Side of the Bed. *2.* Ballz 2 the Wall. *3.* Game Over. *4.* Zack Attack, Andy Milonakis. *5.* Poody Tang. *6.* Summer's Coming. *7.* Line Wars. *8.* Bong Off, Andy Milonakis. *9.* Bon R Pop, Andy Milonakis. *10.* Party Bus. *11.* Hollywood.

18 *After Forever.* aterforeverwebseries.com. 2014.

Cade appears to be a young woman but in actuality is centuries old. She is an immortal and has spent her life destroying evil wherever it exists. She dresses as a medieval warrior, carries a bow and arrow and her mission is "to impose good on the

likes of evil." For centuries Cade lived for the thrill of the hunt and triumph but as she is about to celebrate her 623rd birthday, she has become disillusioned. Dragons and evil creatures are no longer a threat and fighting the bad guys in a modern day world has gotten her nothing but lawsuits for her reckless behavior against people she often mistakes for being criminals. Cade believes enough is enough and it is time for her to lead her own life and become a mortal. Cade lives in a room above the Pepper Sisters Southeast Cuisine Restaurant and has a talking horse named Theodious (Ted for short). Having battled evil for such a long time Cade cannot just quit cold turkey and, during a scuffle with a thief who stole a candy bar, she injures an innocent bystander named Tucker (a patron of the restaurant). Tucker is impressed by Cade while Cade fears another lawsuit. She is surprised when Tucker tells her he will not sue her if she makes him her sidekick. With no other choice, Cade agrees and the program follows Cade and Tucker's efforts to foil evil with Cade seeking to find the mysterious Sorceress and the key to becoming mortal.

Cast: Natalie Fedak (Cade), Will Homel (Tucker), Evan Christopher (Voice of Ted), August Browning (Rich), Charlotte Guyette (Sorceress), Natlaie Nelson (Tammy), Leon Charbonneau (Narrator). **Credits:** *Producer-Writer-Director:* Natalie Fedak. **Comment:** Cade insists she is not quitting, "just retiring" although that may not be an easy task to accomplish. The program is charming from beginning to end with very good acting and production values. Adding a narrator adds a feeling of an ancient story being told in modern times (captures in a way, the feeling of the TV series *Zena: Warrior Princess*).

Episodes: 6 untitled episodes, labeled "Episode 1" through "Episode 6."

19 *Agent 88.* agent88films.com. 2013.

"Killing just gets better with age" is the tag line that describes an 88-year-old British woman (real name not revealed) that is not only the country's top secret agent and its most deadly assassin, but an elderly woman who also suffers from bouts of memory loss and hasn't changed her wardrobe since the 1970s. Agent 88, as she is called, currently lives in Los Angeles and although she should have retired 23 years ago, she is still active and the program follows her less-than-daunting exploits as she uses everything—from martial arts to the latest in weapons to keep the world safe from evil doers.

Cast: Kay D'Arcy (Agent 88), Ricardo Mamood-Vega (Manolo). **Credits:** *Producer:* Demian Lichtenstein, Digger Mesch. *Director:* Digger Mesch. *Writer:* Digger Mesch, William O'Neill. **Comment:** Unusual to say the least, with a most unlikely hero. The program is well acted and produced and the use of special effects greatly helps to make an elderly woman appear more agile than she really is. Such an idea (using an elderly woman as a hero) is not actually original as a British TV series called *Super Gran* used the same idea, a grandmother in this instance, as a super hero.

Episodes: *1.* Agent 88 Pilot.

20 *Agents of Cracked.* cracked.com. 2009–2011.

Cracked.com is real humor website where Daniel O'Brien and Michael Swain are its most popular writers. Adapting that website as the program's setting, an exaggerated look at how such a website operates is seen through the writing assignments of Daniel (who prefers to be called D.O.B.) and Michael, who work for a sinister boss (The Chief) who is only seen in a shadow and speaks with an electronically altered voice.

Cast: Daniel O'Brien (Himself), Michael Swaim (Himself), Oren Katzeff (The Chief), Lisa Marie King (Mandy Manderson), Soren Bowie (T-Bone). Credits: *Producer:* Randall Maynard, Matt Barrs. *Director:* Abe Epperson. *Writer:* Joel Farrelly, Daniel O'Brien, Michael Swaim, David Wong. Comment: Exaggerated is not used lightly here as Michael is so annoying that unless you can stand his loose cannon attitude you will not continue to watch. How Michael ever became the assistant editor is a mystery but his being paired with the nerd-like D.O.B. makes for a strange Odd Couple situation.

Season 1 Episodes: *1.* The End of the Beginning. *2.* The Trial of Dr. Baby. *3.* The Revenge of Roboface. *4.* The Tragedy of Fightin' Hogs. *5.* The Web of Sites. *6.* The Algorithm of Alan Rickman. *7.* The Curse of the Idol. *8.* The Parable of the Pumping Stallion. *9.* The Secret of Rainbow Bridge. *10.* The Battle of H-Town. *11.* The Case of the Sodomized Corpse. *12.* The Mystery of the Ladies Room. *13.* The Beginning of the End. *14.* The End.

Season 2 Episodes: *1.* Ding. Dong. Dead! *2.* A Chili Day in Hell. *3.* Molotov Shock-Tale. *4.* Defamation of Character: With a Vengeance. *5.* Proof That Facebook Could Be Waaay Creepier. *6.* Some People Take Prank Wars a Little Too Seriously. *7.* The Secret Service Apparently Can't Take a Joke. *8.* Bad Idea: Hanging Out with Work Friends Outside the Office. *9.* Best Santa Ever.

Season 3 Episodes: *1.* Worst Wingman Ever. *2.* Friendly Fire Marshall. *3.* F.U.B.A.R.—King Up the Wrong Tree. *4.* Hoorah!shomon. *5.* Apocalypse Now. *6.* A Chilling Tale of Drugs in the Workplace. *7.* Cooking for Six (of the Deadliest People in the World). *8.* Most Poorly Planned Heist Ever. *9.* Why Two Cracked Editors Have to Die. *10.* The Plot Twistingest Finale in the History of Final Episodes.

21 *Aim High.* webserieschannel.com 2011–2013.

Nicholas Green, a student at Fairview High School in Chicago is very special: he has been recruited by the U.S. government as a special agent for sensitive, top secret missions. For Nicholas it began in the seventh grade when he joined a fitness program called DEPP (Department of Education Pilot Program) and took first honors. Little did he (or apparently anyone else) know that DEPP was a training program for future U.S. government spies. When Nicholas reached the age of 16, he was asked to join "the team." Believing it would be something different he did and now regrets it as it has totally changed his life. Nick, as he is called, may not be able to attend all his classes, pass all his tests or even complete all his homework assignments, but he is an effective, clever and deadly agent. As a student Nick has a crush on Amanda, the beautiful "wickedly cool rocker" who, unfortunately for him, is dating Derek, the captain of the school's swimming team. As an agent Nick is an underage version of James Bond and stories follow Nick as he struggles to keep his two worlds separate, maintain his grades and save the world from evil.

Cast: Jackson Rathbone (Nick Green), Aimee Teegarden (Amanda Miles), Natalie Dreyfuss (Dakota), Devon Bostick (Marcus Anderson), Chris Wylde (Terry), Tony Cavalero (Deuce), Natalie Lander (Marcy), Steve Kim (Sukarno), Johnny Pemberton (Marcus Anderson), Jonathan McDaniel (Derek), Jonathan Avigdori (Goombah), Matthew Moy (Scott Winelin), Greg Germann (Ockenhocker), Michelle Glavan (Trish), Ray Corasani (Goombah Gordon), Massi Fulan (Joey). Credits: *Producer:* McG, Richie Keen, Lance Sloane. *Director:* Thor Freudenthal. *Writer:* Richie Keen. Comment: Although not an original idea (the Fox TV series *The New Adventures of Beans Baxter* used the same teenage government agent idea), it is charming, well acted and produced.

Episodes: 6 untitled episodes, labeled "Episode 1" through "Episode 6."

22 *Alex and Jane.* alexandjanewebseries. com. 2014.

Alexandra, called Alex, and Jane are girlfriends but not lesbians or romantically involved with each other. Alex married young, had kids and "never sowed her wild oats." Jane is single and looking to settle down but hasn't found the right man. Jane is prettier, fashion conscious and outgoing; Alex is pretty (but plays it down), a bit laid back and looks to have settled into a dull life as a housewife and mother. Jane feels Alex needs to lighten up and add excitement to her life and the program follows Alex as she attempts to sow some of those oats she neglected when she was younger.

Cast: Julie Rosing (Alex), Rachel Rosenthal (Jane), Taylor Newhall (Jay), Bill DiPiero, Colin Longstaff, Jenn Roman, Will Cooper. Credits: *Director:* Beth Miranda Botshon. *Writer:* Beth Miranda Botshon, Maria Stasavage. **Comment:** Delightful program that hooks you in from the first episode with very good acting and production values.

Episodes: *1.* Friday Night. *2.* Online Dating. *3.* Awkward Coffee Date. *4.* Lion Face.

23 The All-For-Nots. blip.tv. 2008.

The All-For-Nots is a rock band seeking to make their mark in the music world. Johnny, Shirley, Caleb and Paul comprise the band and the program follows their road tour from their home in Brooklyn, New York, to their ultimate goal: Los Angeles and music stardom.

Cast: Brian Cheng (Larry), Erica Harsch (Shirley), Kevin Johnston (Johnny), Thom Woodley (Paul), Michael Moravek (Caleb), Vanessa Reseland (Farrah), Marielle Heller (Heather). **Credits:** *Producer:* Jane Hu, Kathleen Grace, Melissa Schneider, Thom Woodley, Steve Cohen. *Director:* Kathleen Grace. *Writer:* Andrew Wagner, Thom Woodley, Matt Yeager. **Comment:** Each episode relates what happens as the band tours. It is well acted, has some tender moments and is well produced.

Episodes: *1.* Brooklyn. *2.* Providence. *3.* Boston. *4.* Woodstock. *5.* The Headliners. *6.* Philadelphia. *7.* Jersey City. *8.* Queens. *9.* East Village. *10.* Washington, D.C. *11.* Cleveland. *12.* Chicago. *13.* St. Mary's. *14.* Detroit. *15.* Madison. *16.* Minneapolis. *17.* Odessa. *18.* Kansas City. *19.* Boulder. *20.* Cheyenne. *21.* Salt Lake City. *22.* Reno. *23.* Olympic Valley. *24.* L.A.

24 All in the Method. allinthemethod.com. 2012–2013.

There are many people seeking to fulfill a dream and become an actor. Each has his or her own method to achieve success and two young men, Luke and Rich are no exception. They are brothers who share the same apartment and have devised what they believe is their key to success: become a character they have been hired to play 24/7. Will it work? Will they impress producers? The program chronicles what happens when becoming a character begins to take charge of your life and who you really are is becoming a thing of the past.

Cast: Rich Keeble (Rich), Luke Kaile (Luke). **Credits:** *Producer-Writer:* Luke Kaile, Rich Keeble. *Director:* Chris Chapman. **Comment:** For some the program will become an immediate turn-off as the leads take the concept of living a character way beyond what is normal (an example being their wearing women's bikinis or sitting naked in a kids' pool of plastic balls). Some scenes are just unpleasant to watch; the acting is just passable and the production just something that seems to be looking for an audience that thrives on the really absurd.

Episodes: *1.* The Heartbreak Kid. *2.* The Acting Guru. *3,4.* The Resting Actor.

25 Almost a Turkish Soap Opera. youtube. com. 2011.

Best friends Adel and Kamil are young men living in Turkey but seeking to become part of the American Dream. When his Grand Uncle Emre, known as "The Godfather of Istanbul," seizes control of the money and land left to Adel and his family by their late grandfather, Adel opts to escape the poverty that now surrounds him and, with Kamil by his side, journeys to the United States to begin a new life. The program charts what happens when Adel and Kamil soon discover that what they heard and read about that American Dream is simply not handed them to them on a silver platter and their journey to reinvent themselves almost becomes a Turkish soap opera. Yonka is Emre's obnoxious granddaughter (who Adele later marries when he is caught as an illegal alien and moves to Canada); Nora is the English teacher (at the English Language Institute in Canada) who captures Adele's heart; Michael is the Academic Program Director at the school; Mirwan is Emre's underhanded right-hand man; Mehmet is Kamil's friend; Sami is Adel's brother; Ayca is Kamil's wife.

Cast: Jon Welch (Adel), Fatih Turan (Kamil), Kim Bennett (Nora), Donna Bonastella (Yonka), John Samaha (Uncle Emre), Seyhan Demir (Adel's father), Victoria Vice (Adel's mother), Sam Mansouri (Mirwan), Sera Malazi (Ayca), Tony Hoare (Michael), Farshad Taghizadeh-Roudposhti (Mehmet), Arif Guler (Sami). **Credits:** *Producer:* Jospeh Khalil. *Writer-Director:* Anne-Rae Vasquez. **Comment:** Episodes unfold in the manner of a daily TV soap opera and are well acted and produced.

Episodes: *1.* The Arrangement. *2.* The Wedding. *3.* Hollywood Here We Come. *4.* Bad News. *5.* Welcome to Beverly Hills. *6.* Training Day at LA Airport. *7.* Adel's Lessons in Money Making. *8.* Adel Meets His Hollywood Dream Girl. *9.* Adel Is Arrested.

26 The Amazing Gayl Pile. gaylpile.com. 2013–2014.

SAHC (Shop-At-Home Channel) is a QVC-like program that allows viewers to shop from the comfort of their homes. Gayl Pile, the son of big game hunter Gayl Pile, Sr. (a woman) is the host of *The Ladies' Power Hour*, a program that presents products geared to women. Gayl appears to be gay and inherited the position as host after his mother's passing. Along with the pitches, Gayl upstages his guests, relates anecdotes and tells (bad) jokes all in a misguided effort to become the ultimate home shopping icon ("The Amazing Gayl Pile, Pitchman Extraordinaire").

J.D. Castlemane is the self-proclaimed Australian "female beauty virtuoso" that co-hosts Gayl's show; Renee is the channel's popular model who believes that Gayl's dorky image is definitely hindering her on-air appearance and is determined to change that by seeing to it that he gets fired; Reverend Dave is the self-righteous man that sells shoddy religious items on the channel; Darron, the lowest status member of the Shunt crime family, is the producer who tries to shun as much responsibility as possible (just too much paper work).

Cast: Morgan Waters (Gayl Pile), Andy King (J.D. Castlemane), Inessa Frantowski (Renee Le-Mans), Brooks Gray (Reverend Dave), Leo Scherman (Darron Shunt). **Credits:** *Producer*: Andrew Ferguson, Brooks Gray, Matt King, Morgan Waters. *Writer-Director:* Brooks Gray, Morgan Waters. **Comment:** Canadian produced program where nothing is fully spelled out. There are strong hints that Gayl (and possibly J.D.) are gay (with J.D. also leaning toward bisexual). That aside, it is a well crafted spoof of home shopping channels with very good acting and production values.

Episodes: 10 untitled episodes, labeled "Episode 1" through "Episode 10."

27 *Amber's Show.* ambersshow.com. 2013.

Amber and Michelle are struggling actresses and friends living in Los Angeles and sharing a small apartment together. Each does acquire roles, although small, and Amber is taking a screen writing course hoping for the best—"I swear if I could come up with a good concept I'd write a script myself and make my own movie." Later, when Amber and Michelle begin talking about their lack-luster dating lives, Amber hits on an idea for a movie based on their dating experiences—"But it's going to be edgy and funny and be about a group of friends who date and talk about their dates." Michelle likes the idea and agrees to help by securing a crew—Trent (a bumbling P.A. [Production Assistant]) and Tim, a somewhat clueless cameraman. However, a suggestion by the crew that they make a web series inspires Amber to do just that—something that can be done with little money and quickly. The program is sort of a behind-the-scenes look at what happens as Amber and Michelle set out to make a web series.

Cast: Julie Birke (Amber), Michelle Campbell (Michelle), Mike Bissonette (Alex), Trent Busenitz (Tim). **Credits:** *Producer-Writer-Director:* Adam Krayvo. **Comment:** A very well acted and produced program with female leads that are most appealing.

Episodes: *1.* The Concept. *2.* Meet the Crew. *3.* Ready for Production.

28 *American Blob.* webserieschannel.com. 2014.

Mike is 28 years old and working at an architectural firm. Sounds normal until you enter his apartment and meet his roommate—the Blob, a living and talking chunk of what looks to be a rock. Blob, as Mike calls him, is nasty, has sharp teeth and something Mike doesn't have—a gorgeous human girl-friend (Misty). And if Mike should even look at Misty in passing, the Blob becomes rather jealous and upset. The program chronicles brief events in the daily lives of two unusual roommates.

Cast: Arian Adams (Mike), Emily Buckener (Misty), Karl Hess (Blob's voice). **Credits:** *Producer:* Sonja Mereu. *Writer-Director:* William Luke Schreiber. **Comment:** The Blob is a nicely created whatever it is supposed to be. The acting and production is good but it would be nice to know how Mike acquired his roommate and where it came from.

Episodes: *1.* Pilot. *2.* The Blob on Politics. *3.* The Blob Gets a Package. *4.* The Blob and Misty vs. Mike. *5.* The Blob Is Bad. *6.* The Blob Gets an Itch. *7.* The Blob Does It Himself. *8.* The Blob Did It Again. *9.* The Blob Gets Hungry. *10.* The Blob Takes the Stairs. *11.* The Blob and the Pants. *12.* The Blob Never Sleeps. *13.* The Blob Is a Good Listener. *14.* The Blob Is the Smell. *15.* The Blob Likes What the Blob Likes. *16.* The Blob Makes Out.

29 *America's Next Top Girl Scout.* web serieschannel.com. 2014.

A spoof of the CW series *America's Next Top Model* that seeks to find the one woman who personifies the leadership qualities necessary for her to be crowned "America's Next Top Girl Scout." It is Cycle 7 of the program when it begins and Ira Shanks, the program's host and lead judge, must choose, with her fellow judges, the one young woman who not only possesses talent, survival abilities, beauty but Girl Scout qualities to receive the coveted crown and its associated prizes: a $50 contract with the Girl Scouts and a two box picture spread on Girl Scout Cookies.

Cast: *Host-Judge:* Cynthia Silver as Ira Shanks. *Judges:* Melissa Mahoney (Mr. Robin), Lexi Langs (Robin Cloneman). *Contestants:* Caroline Aimetti (Charity), Andrea Angove-Volb (Accident), Alisha Bhaumik (Drew), Michelle Bocanegra (Vicki), Erin Brownett (Grace), Jennifer Carlson (Grace 2.0), Savannah Des Ormeaux (Eloise), Caitlyn Ziobro (Gwenyth), Kate Falk (@*&#!). **Credits:** *Producer-Writer-Director:* Abbey Glasure. **Comment:** Exceptionally well done program. Fans of *America's Next Top Model* will immediately notice the similarities: the opening theme, the girls speaking into the camera to relate what is happening, the challenges, the eliminations and the final competition. It can be seen that time and effort went into the making of this series and it has paid off in a very enjoyable spoof.

Episodes: 4 untitled episodes, labeled "Episode 1" through "Episode 4."

30 *Amy Kidd, Zombie Speech Pathologist.* webserieschannel.com. 2013.

It is the near future and a zombie apocalypse has changed the world, destroying most humans but most importantly, leaving speech therapist Amy Kidd without patients. Amy, however, is resilient and revises her practice to help zombies. Since zombies are unable to speak, Amy feels she can help them and opens a zombie charm school. The program charts Amy's progress as she attempts to help zombies adjust to society.

Cast: Audrey Noone (Amy Kidd), Brooke Solomon (Look Out Girl), Curtis Reid (Joey), Chris Estes (Arnold Milquetoast), Talli Clemons (Look Out Man). **Credits:** *Producer-Writer-Director:* Audrey Noone. **Comment:** Played strictly for laughs, but presenting zombies in a new light, the potential series looks good from the pilot presentation but could suffer from monotony as to how far can the concept be stretched.

Episodes: *1.* Pilot.

31 Andy and Kirk's Beer Ramblings. web serieschannel.com. 2012–2014.

Beer, specifically Budweiser, is the most important thing in the lives of friends Andy and Kirk. However, when they overindulge they see the world in a different light and begin discussions on issues that matter most to them (like Tacos, BBQ's, YouTube videos). Those ramblings form the basis of each episode.

Cast: Andy Pettit (Andy), Kirk A. Paulson (Kirk). **Credits:** *Producer-Writer:* Andy Pettit, Kirk A. Paulson. **Comment:** For the kind of program that it is, episodes are just too long (15–30 minutes each) and one quickly tires of hearing two drunks ramble. Season 2 titles are an indication that not everything makes sense and the program becomes rather unpleasant with drinking, ramblings and foul language. If beer and drunks are funny, then this is the program for you.

Season 1 Episodes: *1.* Taco Bell's Loco Tacos: The Pros and Cons. *2.* The Pabst BBQ Recap. *3.* The Most Epic YouTube Video. *4.* Beard Trimmers. *5.* We Have No Agenda. *6.* Massage Tables. *7.* Our Special Olympics Show. *8.* R.I.P. Lisa and Corey Taylor. *9.* Train Wrecks and City of Heroes. *10.* Boner Bucks and Here's the Thing.

Season 2 Episodes: *1.* Aluminum Bats and Paul's Taking Over. *2.* Art Gets Drunk at Kenny's Birthday. *3.* Rule 34 and Stinky Dee. *4.* VooDoo and Too Much Cough Syrup. *5.* Anchovies and Dick Punches. *6.* Al Shallal and Harlem Shake. *7.* Doober Flankes and Channel Locks. *8.* Poor Derek and Creepy Mimes. *9.* We're All Paul Stanley and Kenny Strikes Back. *10.* The Season Finale and Halloween.

32 Angelica Y Roberta. anjelicayroberta.com. 2012–2013.

Angelica and Roberta are the type of girls people grow up with but never really notice. They keep to themselves, always sit in the back of the classroom and just become a part of the scenery. It happened to them as children and it has happened to them as adults. The passing of Angelica's grandparents changes the course of their lives when Angelica inherits a rural home and she and Roberta decide to leave home and move in together. A challenge has been presented and the program chronicles the mishaps they encounter as they face a world in which their comfort zones no longer exist.

Cast: Sandra Lesta (Angelica), Sonia Mendez (Roberta), Xlio Abonjo (Edu), Alberto Rolan (Edu's Cousin). **Credits:** *Producer-Writer:* Sandra Lesta, Sonia Mendez. *Director:* Xacio Bano. **Comment:** Spanish produced program with English subtitles. Like virtually all Spanish-produced Internet series, the acting and production is high caliber.

Season 1 Episodes: *1.* Do You Know Us from Something? *2.* Earning a Living. *3.* The Party. *4.* The Neighbor, Edu. *5.* The Friend. *6.* Edu's Cousin. *7.* Christmas Eve. *8.* New Year's Eve.

Season 2 Episodes: *1.* I'm Glad That You Have Fallen Into the Black Hole. *2.* Remember Me, I'm Looking Chinese. *3.* Papa Smurf Was the Queen Bee. *4.* There Are May People Living Bored and Not Lesbians. *5.* Having a Common Translator So You Do Not Want to Get Too Cool.

33 The Angry Video Nerd. youtube.com. 2004–2013.

Reviews of video games presented in a style like never before: by a nasty, foul-mouthed, alcohol-addicted video game fanatic through straight commentary or skits.

Cast: James Rolfe (Angry Video Nerd). **Credits:** *Producer-Director:* James Rolfe. *Writer:* James Rolfe, Mike Matei. **Comment:** Although the program is geared to video game users, its presentation allows for it to be enjoyed by anyone as the Nerd is truly outrageous.

Season 1 Episodes: *1.* Castlevania II: Simon's Quest. *2.* Dr. Jekyll and Mr. Hyde. *3.* The Karate Kid. *4.* Who Framed Roger Rabbitt? *5.* Teenage Mutant Ninja Turtles. *6.* Back to the Future. *7.* M.C. Kids. *8.* Wally Bear and the No! Gang. *9.* Master Chu and the Drunkard Hu. *10.* Top Gun. *11.* Double Dragon 3. *12.* Friday the 13th. *13.* A Nightmare on Elm Street. *14.* Power Glove. *15.* Movie and Video Game Sequels. *16.* Rocky. *17.* Bible Games.

Season 2 Episodes: *1,2.* Teenage Mutant Ninja Turtles 3. *3.* Atari 5200. *4.* Ghostbusters. *5.* Ghostbusters: Follow-Up. *6.* Ghostbusters: Conclusion. *7.* Spider-Man. *8.* Sega CD. *9.* Sega 32X. *10.* Silver Surfer. *11.* Die Hard. *12.* Independence Day. *13.* The Simpsons. *14.* Bugs Bunny Birthday Blowout. *15.* Atari Porn. *16.* Nintendo Power Memories. *17.* Fester's Quest. *18.* Texas Chainsaw Massacre. *19.* Halloween. *20.* Dragon's Lair. *21,22.* An Angry Nerd Christmas Carol.

Season 3 Episodes: *1*. The Legend of Zelda Timeline *2*. Rambo. *3*. Virtual Boy. *4*. The Wizard of Oz. *5,6*. Double Vision. *7*. The Wizard and Super Mario Bros. 3. *8*. N.E.S. Accessories. *9*. Indiana Jones Trilogy. *10*. Star Trek. *11*. Superman. *12*. Superman 64. *13,14*. Batman. *15*. Deadly Towers. *16*. Battletoads. *17*. Dick Tracy. *18*. Dracula. *19*. Frankenstein. *20*. Hotel Mario. *21*. Zelda Wand of Gamelon. *22*. Faces of Evil and Zelda's Adventure. *23*. Bible Games 2.

Season 4 Episodes: *1*. Michael Jackson's Moonwalker. *2*. Milton's Secret Castle. *3,4*. Jaguar 64 Bit. *5*. Metal Gear. *6*. Odyssey. *7*. X-Men. *8*. Terminator. *9*. Terminator 2. *10*. Transformers. *11*. Mario Is Missing. *12*. Plumbers Don't Wear Ties! *13*. Bugs Bunny's Crazy Castle. *14*. Super Pitfall. *15*. Godzilla. *16*. Wayne's World. *17–20*. Castlevania. *21*. Little Red Hood. *22*. Winter Games.

Season 5 Episodes: *1*. Street Fighter 2010. *2*. Hydlide. *3*. Ninja Gaiden. *4*. Swordquest. *5*. Pong Consoles. *6*. Action 52. *7*. Cheetahmen. *8*. Game Glitches. *9*. Zelda II: The Adventures of Link. *10*. Back to the Future Trilogy. *11*. Dr. Jekyll and Mr. Hyde Re-Revisited. *12*. Lester the Unlikely. *13*. How the Nerd Stole Christmas.

Season 6 Episodes: *1*. Day Dreamin' Davey. *2*. Star Wars Games. *3*. R.O.B. the Robot. *4*. Spielberg Games. *5*. The Making of an Episode. *6*. Kid Kool. *7*. Nintendo World Championships. *8*. Dark Castle. *9*. Bible Games III.

Season 7 Episodes: *1*. Schwarzenegger Games. *2*. Ghosts N' Goblins. *3*. Atari Sports. *4*. Ikari Warriors. *5*. Toxic Crusaders. *6*. Bill and Ted's Excellent Adventure. *7*. Tiger Electronic Games. *8*. Alien 3. *9*. AVGN Games. *10,11*. Wish List.

Season 8 Episodes: *1*. Big Rigs: Over the Road Racing. *2*. Desert Bus. *3*. E.T. Atari 2600. *4*. Beetlejuice. *5*. Tagin' Dragon. *6*. ALF. *7*. Crazy Bus. *8*. Ren & Stimpy: Fire Dogs. *9*. Rocky and Bullwinkle. *10*. Mary-Kate and Ashley: Get a Clue. *11*. V.I.P. with Pamela Anderson. *12*. Lethal Weapon. *13*. Porky's. *14*. HyperScan. *15*. Universal Studios Theme Parks Adventure. *16*. LJN Video Art Entertainment System.

Season 9 Episodes: *1*. Hong Kong 97. *2*. Darkwing Duck.

34 *Annoying Orange.* youtube.com. 2009–2014.

When one buys fruit or vegetables one expects that they will be just that—fruit or vegetables. One piece of fruit, however—Orange—is quite different. He is alive, possesses the ability to speak and, through his eyes, other fruits, vegetables and objects in his environment (a kitchen shelf) also come to life. But what is different about Orange is his tendency to annoy others—funny to him, but often insulting to anyone or anything else. A view of life, though limited to the kitchen, as seen through the insulting remarks of a piece of fruit that has been deemed "Annoying Orange."

Other Characters: Passion, a female passion fruit (who is also Orange's female fruit friend, but also sought by Grapefruit); Pear, a Bartlett pear; Grandpa Lemon (an elderly, forgetful lemon); Grapefruit (Orange's arch enemy); Marshmallow (a genderless soft confection that loves puppies, kittens and rainbows); Chef's Knife; and a small Red Delicious apple called Midget Apple although he prefers Little Apple.

Note: Four spin offs were produced:

1. *Ask Orange* (2011–2012). Annoying Orange responds to questions asked of him by viewers.

2. *The Juice* (2013). Characters from the parent series (Orange, Marshmallow, Grapefruit, Pear and Midget Apple) answer questions sent in by viewers.

3. *The Misfortune of Being Ned* (2013–2014). Cartoon mishaps of Ned (voice of Steve Zaragoza), a crudely drawn man who encounters mishap in everything he does. *Other voices:* Megan Camarena (Wendy), Kevin Brueck (Greg).

4. *The Marshmallow Show* (2014). Using the same technique as its parent show with the Marshmallow character interviewing (with his co-host, Joe the Coffee Mug) celebrity guests (including Felicia Day, Miranda Sing, Weird Al Yankovic, Hannah Hart and Brittani Louise Taylor).

Voice Cast: Dane Boedigheimer (Orange/Pear/Midget Apple/Marshmallow), Robert Jennings (Grapefruit), Justine Ezarik (Passion Fruit), Kevin Brueck (Grandpa Lemon), Kevin Nalty (Knife).

Credits: *Producer-Director:* Dane Boedigheimer. *Writer:* Dane Boedigheimer, Spencer Grove, Bobby Jennings, Aaron Massey, Zack Scott, Andy Signore.

Comment: The program uses a system called "Syncro Vox" that was developed in the 1960s for the cartoon series *Clutch Cargo* (wherein a human mouth was superimposed into where the character's mouth would be). The technique is advanced one step further too also include the voice provider's eyes. The program is also a good example of taking a concept that works at first but not knowing when the time is right to end it. As the series entered its latter years, it simply lost its charm with repeated material and stale jokes.

2009 Episodes: *1*. Hey Apple! *2*. Plumpkin. *3*. Toe-May-Toe. *4*. Sandy Claus. *5*. More Annoying Orange. *6*. Wazzup. *7*. Hey, YouTube! *8*. Super Bowl Football. *9*. Annoying Saw. *10*. Passion of the Fruit. *11*. Passion of the Christ. *12*. A Cheesy Episode. *13*. Luck o' the Irish. *14*. Tanning Salon. *15*. Super Mario. *16*. Muddy Buddy. *17*. Excess Cabbage. *18*. Annoying Trailer. *19*. Cursed Onion Ring Tape. *20*. Onion Ring. *21*. Wassabi. *22*. Pain-Apple. *23*. Pacmania. *24*. Picture Contest. *25*. Grapefruit's Revenge. *26*. Grandpa Lemon. *27*. Picture Contest Winners. *28*. Back to the Fruiture. *29*. Mystery Guest. *30*. Annoying Orange vs. Fred. *31*. Orange of July.

2010 Episodes: *1*. Orange Cup. *2*. Teenage Mutant Ninja Apples. *3*. Lady Pasta. *4*. Cruel As a

Cucumber. *5.* Crabapple. *6.* Million Clones. *7.* Close Encounters of the Annoying Kind. *8.* The Sitcom. *9.* Going Walnuts. *10.* Bonsai Tree. *11.* Saw 2: Annoying Death Trap. *12.* No More Mr. Knife Guy. *13.* Happy Birthday, Orange. *14.* Exploding Orange. *15.* Frankenfruit. *16.* Theme Song Attack. *17.* Annoying Pear. *18.* Viral Vote. *19.* Orange after Dentist. *20.* Kitchen Intruder. *21.* Sneezing Baby Marshmallow. *22.* Annoying Orange Meets Charlie the Unicorn. *23.* Equals Annoying Orange. *24.* Kitchen Intruder Song. *25.* Mystery of the Mustachios. *26.* Japapeno. *27.* Wishful Thinking.

2011 Episodes, 1–30: *1.* Amnesiac Orange. *2.* Rap-Berry. *3.* Food Court. *4.* Wazzup Blowup. *5.* Best Friends Forever. *6.* Annoying Valentines. *7.* Annoying Valentines Surprise. *8.* It Takes Two to Mango. *9.* Annoying Orange vs. Gecko. *10.* Zoom. *11.* Orange Through Time 1. *12.* Kung Fruit. *13.* Fortune Cookie. *14.* April Fruit's Day. *15.* Kitchen Carnage. *16.* Rolling in the Dough. *17.* Nya Nya Orange. *18.* Comedy Clubbing. *19.* Orange Through Time 2. *20.* Mommy and Me. *21.* Fruit for All. *22.* Juice Boxing. *23.* Flower Power. *24.* Be a Star. *25.* First Person Frutier. *26.* Meteortron. *27.* You Tubers. *28.* Trollin'. *29.* Orange Potter and the Deathly Apple. *30.* The Voodoo You Do.

2011 Episodes, 31–60: *31.* Orange Goes Hollywood. *32.* Previously On. *33.* Orange Takes on VidCon. *34.* In the Dark. *35.* Naval Orange. *36.* Orange Through Time 3. *37.* Gumbrawl. *38.* Pet Peeve. *39.* Souper Dooper. *40.* Ask Orange 1. *41.* Fake 'n' Bacon. *42.* Orange Through Time 4. *43.* Annoying Orange vs. Angry Birds. *44.* Microwave Effect. *45.* Ask Orange 2: Toast Busters. *46.* Chiller. *47.* Magic Clam. *48.* Jumping Bean. *49.* Party Rock. *50.* Epic Peel of Time. *51.* Epic Rap Battles of Kitchenry. *52.* Go! Bwaaah! *53.* Talking Twin Baby Oranges. *54.* Friday. *55.* Ask Orange 3: Toy-ing Orange. *56.* Grapefruit's Totally True Tales: Bigfoot. *57.* Xmas Card Xplosion. *58.* Midget Rudolph. *59.* FPS Orange. *60.* 1 Billion Kills.

2012 Episodes, 1–25: *1.* Once Upon an Orange. *2.* Annoying Orange Comedy Roast. *3.* Fruitbowl. *4.* The Dating Game. *5.* Poison Apple. *6.* He Will Mock You. *7.* Annoying Orange vs. Mortal Kombat. *8.* Ultimate Marshmallow Tease. *9.* Dr. Bananas. *10.* Leprechaun Trap. *11.* Hungry Games. *12.* Annoying Orange 2.0. *13.* Easter Island. *14.* Marshmallow's Favorites: Doggie Videos. *15.* Ask Orange 4: Master Chef. *16.* WazZoom. *17.* Buddy Cops. *18.* Bacon Invaders. *19.* U Can't Squash This. *20.* Tough Enough. *21.* Big Top Orange. *22.* Avocado. *23.* Behind the Seeds. *24.* Ask Orange 5: Once in a Blew Moon. *25.* OMG.

2012 Episodes, 26–55: *26.* Going Donuts. *27.* Fruitrix. *28.* Mac and Cheese. *29.* Animated. *30.* Fruits vs. Zombies. *31.* Summer Vacation. *32.* Marshmallow Pic Contest Winners. *33.* Orange Nya Nya Style. *34.* Buddy Cops 2: Stachehouse. *35.* Monster Burger. *36.* Clam's Casino. *37.* Pit Rommey Presi-dential Campaign Video. *38.* Broccoli Obama Presidential Campaign Video. *39.* Kitchen Decision 2012. *40.* TV of Terror. *41.* Leek of Their Own. *42.* New Kitchen President. *43.* Time to Burn. *44.* Ask Orange 6: Fart Ship. *45.* Ask President Marshmallow. *46.* Wazzup Video Game Style. *47.* Saw: Animated. *48.* Lady Pasta Animated. *49.* Kitchen-Mon. *50.* Christmas Is for Giving. *51.* Annoying Ways to Die. *52.* Garret the Parrot. *53.* Weird Al Holiday Duet. *54.* Cheesy Salesman. *55.* 2012 Kills.

2013 Episodes, 1–20: *1.* Ask Orange 7: Fus Ro Dah. *2.* Yo Yo. *3.* Annoying Orange vs. Slender Man. *4.* Pickleback. *5.* Harlem Shake 9000. *6.* Random Cuts. *7.* Annoying Orange vs. Pong. *8.* Weenies. *9.* Annoying Orange Subscribe Trailer. *10.* No More Mr. Knife Guy. *11.* Popeye Yeah. *12.* Annoying Orange vs. Minecraft. *13.* Annoying Marshmallow. *14.* Annoying Orange vs. Duck Hunt. *15.* Aril Fool's Gold. *16.* Top 5 Ways to Get Out of a Speeding Ticket. *17.* Beauty and a Beet. *18.* Earth Day. *19.* Iron Apple Teaser Trailer. *20.* Iron Apple.

2013 Episodes, 21–40: *21.* Ask Orange 8: Evil Robot Twin. *22.* Despicable Me 2: Choose Your Villain. *23.* Epic Trailer. *24.* Honey I Shrunk the Fruits. *25.* Snack Attack. *26.* Monster Truck. *27.* Bored. *28.* Blow Bubbles by Draft Lunch. *29.* Despicable Me Too. *30.* Grapefruit vs. Donkey Kong. *31.* Man of Peel. *32.* Picnic Massacre. *33.* Orange Approved: Chainy the Chainsaw. *34.* Nude Dude. *35.* The Juice #1. *36.* Out of the Blue. *37.* Arnold Schwarzen-Egger. *38.* Annoying Orange vs. Mario Kart. *39.* Grumpy Old Fruits. *40.* Mystery of the Sasquatch.

2013 Episodes, 41–77: *41.* Orange Approved: Meteor Sandwich. *42.* Random Cuts #2. *43.* Asteroranges. *44.* Grape Expectations. *45.* Annoying Orange vs. Tiny Wings. *46.* Epic Rap Battles of Kitchenery. *47.* Annoying Orange vs. Street Fighter. *48.* Wasabi Goaee Party. *49.* Food-splosion 1. *50.* Easy As Pi. *51.* 5 Ways to Get Out of Your Homework. *52.* Insta-Graham. *53.* The Juice 2: Goose-Moose. *54.* The Sock. *55.* Food-splosion: Wanda Watermelon. *56.* Breaking Bad Eggs. *57.* Shocktober. *58.* Barewolf. *59.* Top 5 Ways to Survive a Zombie Apocalypse. *60.* Dead and Berried. *61.* The Juice: Biggest Fear. *62.* The Deviled Egg. *63.* Food-splosion: Halloween Edition. *64.* The Dining. *65.* Horrorscope. *66.* Angry Orange. *67.* Gut Wrenching. *68.* Ask Orange 9: Orange Is a Brony? *69.* The Juice: Emo Knife. *70.* Goat Carts. *71.* Food-splosion: Pablo the Pepper. *72.* Black Hole Donut. *73.* The Juice: Bat-Pan & Robinero. *74.* Icicle Insanity. *75.* Coal for Christmas. *76.* Infinity Snowball. *77.* Food-splosion: Pineapple Goes Batty.

2014 Episodes, 1–20: *1.* Montage and Marsmallow Announcement. *2.* How to Make the Annoying Orange. *3.* Teenage Mutant Ninja Turnips. *4.* Ask Orange: 2 Million Knives. *5.* Vine Compilation: Bacon Strips & Twerky Jerky. *6.* Directed by Michael Bygle. *7.* Emmett the Lovin' Mitt. *8.* Fan Boy. *9.* Sacrifice Play. *10.* Sour Rangers. *11.* Rage Sage. *12.* Bad

Apple. *13.* 2 Billion Views. *14.* Dumb As a Brick. *15.* Crappy Captioned. *16.* Puns of Anarchy. *17.* Tea'd Off. *18.* Annoying Orange vs. Flappy Bird. *19.* Buddy Cops 3: Blue Detective. *20.* Rump Roast.

2014 Episodes, 21–47: *21.* Double Rainbow Trout. *22.* Rubik's Cube. *23.* Ask Orange 11: Flappy Bird Returns. *24.* Orange Coin. *25.* Crappy Captioned 2. *26.* Kriss Kut. *27.* Food-splosion: Coconut Ukulele. *28.* Teenie Weenie. *29.* TMI Podcast. *30.* Feel the Burn. *31.* Briquet. *32.* Ask Orange: Break Dance Lessons. *33.* Mini Shark. *34.* Limes. *35.* Cruel Middle School. *36.* Ice Bucket Challenge. *37.* Totally Dental. *38.* Control Freak. *39.* Seinfood. *40.* Annoying Sister. *41.* Crappy Captioned 3. *42.* Haunted Leaf Pie. *43.* Headless Horseplay. *44.* Gourdzilla. *45.* Deadline at Daneco. *46.* Minecraft Puns 1. *47.* Turducken.

35 *Antique America.* webserieschannel. com. 2012.

Spoof of the PBS TV series *Antiques Road Show* that follows the trail of supposed antiques expert Cicily Von Trapp as she travels across the U.S. appraising relics from the country's past but not always appraising them as the antiques they really are.

Cast: Christina Waterman (Cicily Von Trapp). **Credits:** *Producer:* Kelli Blissard, Chris Rubalcaba. *Director:* Morgan J. Steele, Kelli Blissard, Chris Rubalcaba, Megan Brotherton. **Comment:** From the "This program is made possible in part by" to the treasure chest logo and money amount on the left side of the screen, a well done take off on *Antiques Road Show* has been created. The people Cicily encounters, however, are greatly exaggerated profiles of people seen on the PBS series. Here, for example, items up for appraisal are anything but spectacular (like a ragged board game or tarnished tea pot) but the reactions—whether positive or negative, provide the fun when the person hears what his treasure is worth.

Episodes: *1.* The Great Teapot. *2.* Asses in Assassination. *3.* Little Miss Kansas. *4.* Made in China. *5.* Best Friends Forever. *6.* Pages from Someone Else's Book. *7.* Mrs. White with the Lead Pipe. *8.* Really Close Encounters.

36 *AP Life.* webserieschannel.com. 2014.

Aubrey, Sadie, Ocean, Reagan, Ellie and Piper are students at Central High School in Massachusetts that have little in common with each other but somehow manage to remain friends. Aubrey, a bit shy and awkward is a transfer from Minnesota and desperately trying to fit into a new environment (something she finds difficult to do). Ocean, who claims her Hippie parents gave her a name that would embarrass her all her life, is not going to let that or anything else stand in her way of becoming whatever she chooses. Sadie feels she is destined for

greatness ("I wanna be a celebrity bombshell") and yearns to be the center of attention ("If you've got it, flaunt it"). Reagan is the school's Queen Bee and believes she is the best at everything, including riding horses, modeling, boys and dating. Ellie is a bit snobbish and considers herself above everyone else. Piper, a drama enthusiast, is hoping to become an actress. Six very different teenagers and what transpires as each tries to be who she is but what also happens when each is there for the other when it matters.

Cast: Taylor Kudalis (Aubrey Hassel), Alexandra Jordyn (Sadie Champagne), Ava Serene Portman (Ocean Fine), Katie Sour (Reagan Desjournais), Kallie Tabor (Piper Vinton), Chris Dubrow (Grayson Cooper), Elizabeth Percy (Ellie O'Grady), Chelsea Armstrong (Mila Kline). **Credits:** *Producer:* Lee Ann Giordano-Silletti. *Writer-Director:* Jace Paul. **Comment:** Although the program is fun to watch, and the acting and directing very good, it is a bit difficult to understand at times due to acoustic problems at filming locations (like the school's gym).

Episodes: *1.* Minnesota: The Show Me State. *2.* The Backwards Cowboy Hokey Pokey. *3.* The Varsity Creeper Team. *4.* That Embarrassing Incident with Chamomile in the Bedroom. *5.* Going to Cooper Market. *6.* The Barbie Dream House of Backstabbing and Drama. *7.* Ketchup on Cheesecake (Halloween Special). *8.* Bitch-Smacked by Vonnegut. *9.* The Plattah with the Sawsauge.

37 *Apartment 102.* youtube.com. 2013.

Prince George's County was once a quaint little town in Maryland but has changed with the times and become an urban-like jungle replete with crime and corruption. It was the birth place of Doug and, hoping to find the serenity of his childhood, he and his wife, Jen, decide to leave the big city and make the county their new home. Doug is shocked at what has become of his home town and his and Jen's effort to enjoy their new life is depicted in direct-to-the-camera storytelling through their experiences.

Cast: Reba Corrine (Jen), Insight Seeker (Doug), Louis Davis (Earl "Big Boy" Savoy). **Credits:** *Producer-Writer-Director:* Marcus V. Simon. **Comment:** A very well done spoof of small town life and how two "city slickers" try to become a part of that life—even with their self-proclaimed friend, Earl (a plumber) at their side. The acting and overall presentation is very good.

Episodes: *1.* The Newlyweds. *2.* Neighbor Earl. *3.* Roommate Earl. *4.* Started from the Bottom. *5.* Attack of Angry Jen.

38 *Apocalypse Boyz.* webserieschannel.com. 2010.

There has been an apocalypse. Life as we know it has been, for the most part, wiped out. There are survivors but there are also zombies on the prowl. Matt and Ozzie are two such survivors and have thus far managed to stay alive by battling their undead enemy. But Matt and Ozzie are also not like ordinary people as getting stoned helps them get through each day. The program chronicles what happens as they battle zombies and become involved with a deranged scientist attempting to build a robot he calls Z.E.D. (Zombie Eradication Device).

Cast: Bruce Blauer (Ozzie), Taylor Girard (Matt), Slake Counts (Scientist), Courtney Foxx, Andrew Racker, Thelma Duff. **Credits:** *Producer:* Kevin Hoag, Juan Carlos Millan. *Director:* Kevin Hoag. *Writer:* Juan Carlos Millan. **Comment:** Very good special effects dominate a comically violent take off on the AMC TV series *The Walking Dead* (or any other zombie-related film). Ozzie is somewhat hot-headed and flies off the handle without thinking first. Since there are zombic children also about, Ozzie has come up with an ingenious way to dispose of them—ride around in an ice cream truck, draw the children to him then machine gun them down.

Episodes: *1–3.* Meet the Boyz. *4–6.* Z.E.D.

39 *Around the World in 30 Lays.* youtube. com. 2009–2010.

Seth, Quentin (called "Q"), Ryan and Bradley are college students sharing the same dorm room. Like most college guys depicted on TV and in movies, they have only two things on their mind: drinking and girls, but not necessarily in that order. With the focus on girls, the roomies decide on what they consider a unique competition: see who can first sleep with thirty different girls from thirty different countries. The chaos that results as each sets out to "conquer the world" through sex is chronicled.

Cast: Adam Goldhammer (Seth), Connor MacKenzie (Ryan), Simon Box (Quentin), Rudyard Olejnik (Matt), Dayle Mcleod (Bradley), Jennifer Polansky (Dora). **Credits:** *Producer-Writer:* Jason Palter. *Director:* Craig Chambers. **Comment:** The program, well acted and produced, does contain adult themes (sexual situations) that are provocative but well within decency standards as it highlights the dates the guys endure.

Episodes: 10 untitled episodes, labeled "Webisode 101" to "Webisode 110."

40 *Ask a Slave.* askaslave.com. 2013.

Lizzie Mae is an African-American woman, representing a slave, who lived and worked on a farm owned by President George Washington in Mount Vernon. She served as the housemaid (one of twelve) to George and his wife Martha in the main mansion house while 316 slaves worked to maintain the President's five farms. Lizzie Mae, seated in a room of the main house, answers questions of present-day

people (seen as cutaways) curious about slaves and how one such person acquired the position (according to Lizzie Mae, she saw an ad in the newspaper: "Wanted: One Housekeeper. No Pay. Must Work 18 Hours a Day, 7 Days a Week. No Holidays." She applied, got the job and its "benefits," "You get to wear pretty dresses and if you're lucky you just might carry a famous white man's bastard child").

Cast: Azie Mira Dungey (Lizzie Mae). **Credits:** *Producer-Writer:* Azie Mira Dungey. *Director:* Jordan Black. **Comment:** Although Lizzie Mae is a fictional character, Azie Mira Dungey based her on several real women when she portrayed a character interpreter providing museum education in Mount Vernon. The concept works and Lizzie Mae's refreshing point of view adds much to the program's overall charm.

Season 1 Episodes: *1.* Meet Lizzie Mae. *2.* Abolitioning. *3.* You Can't Make This Stuff Up. *4.* New Leaf, Same Page. *5.* Two Sides of Every Coin. *6.* I Love That Boy.

Season 2 Episodes: *1.* True Story. *2.* Caught in the Web. *3.* What About the Indians. *4.* Kids. *5.* House and Field. *6.* Sound Advice. *7.* The Christmas Special.

41 *Assisted Living.* viralfilmvideo.com. 2009.

The world of a down-on-his luck man named Dustin is explored. It begins with his getting thrown out of his apartment by his girlfriend and having to beg his sister, Sarah, to let him live with her (something she is reluctant to do as they are not close). Dustin's efforts to get back on his feet are charted when he befriends a homeless man (Bob), buys a pet guinea pig (Swayze) and with the help of his friend Darius attempts to jump start his stand-up comedy career.

Cast: Dustin White (Dustin), Grace McPhillips (Sarah), Bob Farster (Bob), Heather Mingo (Josephine), Joette Waters (Marge), Nicole Arroyo (Doreen), Casey Larwood (Donna), Charles Harris (Arnie), Darius Kennedy (Darius) Mouzam Makkar (Mahiki), Sara Nitz (Heather), Patty Wu (Emma), Kristin Johnson (Becky), Katie Dorn (Betty), Justin R. Jackson (Andy), Iris Kohl (Rebecca Saint), Mike Lebovitz (Bosco), James Pusztay (Tiny), JD Robertson (Bianca). **Credits:** *Producer:* David J. Miller, Michelle DeLong. *Writer-Director:* David J. Miller. **Comment:** In addition to Dustin's attempts to get back into comedy, many episodes focus on the girls he encounters and the sexual situations that arise. While the overall series is well acted and produced, it is a bit suggestive for its sexual content.

Season 1 Episodes: *1.* In the Butt. *2.* The Vibrator. *3.* The Girl's a Whore. *4.* Shell Shock. *5.* An Acquired Taste. *6.* Money for Prostitutes. *7.* Happy Ending.

Season 2 Episodes: *1.* I Need Sex. *2.* Shaving My Pubes. *3.* A Long Talk. *4.* Free Food. *5.* What's a

Queef? 6. The Blind Dates. 7. Sexually Transmitted Disease. 8. Sexy Doctor. 9. The Stripper.

Season 3 Episodes: 1. St. Peter and the Pearl Necklace. 2. Money for Nothing, Chicks Aren't Free. 3. Sister Swap. 4. Deluxe Apartment in the Sky. 5. D-bags with Money Are Hilarious. 6. Red Hot Annie Comes Lately. 7. Limp As a Sponge. 8. Wham Bam Thank You Pam.

Season 4 Episodes: 1. What About My Eggs. 2. The Muffin Muncher. 3. Three Way Advantage. 4. Bad Advice. 5. Performance Anxiety. 6. The Last Supper.

Season 5 Episodes: 1. Sour Puss. 2. Pity the Fool. 3. Comedians Are A-Holes. 4. Gun Shy. 5. Fringe Benefits. 6.C**k Blocked. 7. The Cold Shoulder. 8. Make-Up Sex. 9. Coffee, Tea or Me? 10. Sweet 16. 11. Addicted to Sex.

Season 6 Episodes: 1. Breast Feeding. 2. Lethal Weapons. 3. Coma Sex. 4. Dear Diary. 5. Purity Ring. 6. Re-Populate the Earth. 7. Anal Probation. 8. Awakenings. 9. Stealing the Spotlight. 10. Earth Girls Are Easy. 11. Pressing Question. 12. Girl Fight.

42 *At the Counter.* youtube.com. 2012.

"Where everybody knows your name" is the most familiar part of the theme song from the TV series *Cheers.* Incorporating that aspect, the viewer becomes a voyeur (the bartender) and in varying stories about people who find solace in bars, becomes a part of their lives as they talk about everything and anything, from their love life to their daily problems. **Cast:** Kimberley Robinson, Samuel Robinson, Christina Sewell, Aurelien Laine, Vickie Eisenstein, Annette Taehyang Kim, David Oxenbridge, Pat Hann, Yann Le Bail, Daria Krutova, Carlos Pavao, Troy Zitzelsberg, Seulki Heo, Michael Jones, Christina Sewell, David Oxenbridge, Jessica Yoon, Edward Burgos. **Credits:** *Producer-Writer-Director:* Aurelien Laine. **Comment:** An anthology-like program that is well done and acted with cast members playing different roles in different stories. Some of the episodes derive laughs from foreign-speaking characters whose dialogue is hard to understand— but the reactions of the person (or persons) overhearing that conversion is the actual focus of attention.

Episodes: 1. Silence Is Golden. 2. Over the Top. 3. Garcon. 4. Not Too Much for Everyone. 5. Tourists. 6. Doggy Style. 7. Road Works. 8. A Kind of Magic. 9. Live Up. 10. Naked Women in Public Bath. 11. That's What She Said. 12. Running Short. 13. Coffee Break. 14. Geeking Out. 15. Draw Something on Google Glasses. 16. Subway Rush. 17,18. Size Doesn't Matter. 19. Tuesday Night Special. 20. Ladies Night. 21. Musical Stretch. 22. Shazam. 23. The Peanut. 24. Economic Crisis. 25. Positive Energy. 26. Tourettes? 27. Memory Loss. 28. On Sale. 29. Han Han.

43 *At the Shop.* attheshop.com. 2012.

A neighborhood barber shop provides the setting for a look at a group of barbers who share the space and their interactions with each other as they talk about the things that matter most to them.

Cast: Nelson J. Davis (Reggie), Tajaron Lewis (Michelle), Johnray Jones (Scott), Davin Artis (Lance), Saqenda Dallas (Jessica), David Jones (Lee), Ariel Little (Alissa), Michael Harts (Kelly). **Credits:** *Producer:* Donaty Artis, Johnray Jones. *Writer-Director:* Donaty Artis. **Comment:** The concept is not new as the TV series *That's My Mama* and *Barber Sop* also had the same backdrop. But here, a slight change in concept with the attention focused totally on the staff does make a difference as the "whacky customers" are absent (as are the numerous situations that could occur because of them).

Episodes: 1. The Invite (Pilot).

44 *Augie, Alone.* augiealone.com. 2014.

Literally a one-man production wherein Lee August ("Augie") Praley does everything—the comedy bits, the acting, producing, writing, directing, etc. **Cast:** Lee August Praley (Augie). **Comment:** Unusual program that is quite humorous as Augie deals with anything and everything that can creep in and spoil the comfortable life he is leading.

Season 1 Episodes: 1. Flirting. 2. Boogers. 3. Healthy. 4. Affirmation. 5. Nostalgia. 6. Bachelor. 7. Hurry. 8. Book Club. 9. Fame. 10. Cooking. 11. Comedy. 12. Dear Diary. 13–17. Break-In. 18. A Career in the Arts. 19. Hover. 20. Beautiful. 21. Bird Watching. 22. Dad. 23. E-mail. 24. Sequel. 25. Friends. 26. Job Interview. 27. Mirror. 28. New Friend. 29. New Neighbors. 30. Orson. 31. Notes. 32. Message.

Season 2 Episodes: 1. Celebrate. 2. #TBT. 3. Charity. 4. Day After Mother's Day. 5. Doctor. 6. Echo. 7. Fame Rebooted. 8. K2. 9. Late. 10. Learning. 11. Workin' Out. 12. Love. 13. Lookin' Good. 14. Monologues. 15. Vines. 16. One-a-Day. 17. Poison Control. 18. Records. 19. Rejection. 20. Results. 21. Secret. 22. Sixty-Nine. 23. Stomach Virus. 24. Takin' a Break. 25. Augie, Alone: The Video Game. 26. Upgrades. 27. Weight Watchers. 28. Weed. 29. Wednesday. 30. Weird. 31. #TBT 2.

45 *Average Joe.* webserieschannel.com. 2012.

Before becoming that average guy with little money and no girlfriend, Joe seemed to have what most guys would like—a gorgeous girlfriend (Annie) and a sweet living arrangement. However, with a website designed to make money with a 75-year-old ventriloquist and no hits and Annie becoming fed up with what she believes is his non-commitment to their relationship, she dumps him, leaving Joe to fend for himself. Now, without a girl or a steady relationship, Joe joins the ranks of others like him, especially his best friend Andy. Rather than wallow in self-pity, Joe has vowed to get over his ex and move on—something that is not as easy as it sounds as Joe fails to realize that he needs to change his prior ways. With Andy's help, Joe's efforts to re-invent his life are chronicled.

Cast: Joe Flanders (Joe), Andy Biersack (Andy), Nikiva Dionne (Kim), Lee Page (Lee), Graham Bowlin (Greg), Christian Coma (Clarence), Nick Perdue (Daryl), Maude Bonani (Beth), Matt Rolfe (Danny), Emma Sleath (Diner waitress), Alexandra Marian Hensly (Annie). **Credits:** *Producer:* Lee Page. *Writer:* Joe Flanders. *Director:* Joe Flanders, Patrick Fogarty. **Comment:** When first seen Joe seems anything but average as he has a home and a gorgeous girlfriend. But once she throws him out, he does becomes that "Average Joe" and the pro-gram, containing adult sexual situations, is very well acted with good production values.

Season 1 Episodes: *1.* Dumped. *2.* Was That Too Rough? *3.* I'm Pretty Sore. *4.* Don't Blow the Rape Whistle. *5,6.* The Sex Tape Therapist. *7.* The Christ-mas Special.

Season 2 Episodes: *1.* New Year, Same S**t. *2.* Gay. *3* .The STD Test. *4.* Day Trip to MILF Town. *5.* Girl, Woman or Lady? *6.* The More You Know. *7.* The Birthday Blowout. *8.* Who Are You? *9.* One of These Days. *10.* Cabin in the Woods. *11.* New Be-ginnings. *12.* Carried Away.

46 *Awkward Embraces.* youtube.com. 2010.

Three young women (Jessica, Candis and Lynd-sey) living together in a Los Angeles apartment are billed as "being hot." The notion is that such sexy and alluring women can attract any man and pick from a wide variety of potential suitors. Is it a myth or is it the truth? With "hot" not the magnet it is presumed to be, events in the lives of the girls is pre-sented as they seek that ideal man but encounter men who are anything but perfect.

Cast: Jessica Mills (Jessica), Lyndsey Doolen (Lyndsey), Candis Phlegm (Candis). **Credits:** *Pro-ducer-Writer:* Jessica Mills. *Director:* Adam Jason Finmann. **Comment:** The leads are average, pretty young women living in a dream world wherein they believe they have more potential to attract men than other women on the same level. The acting and pro-duction is good but the concept is something that has been done numerous times before (an example being the movie and TV series *How to Marry a Mil-lionaire*).

Episodes: *1.* The IT Guy. *2.* The Geek Date. *3.* The Bulge. *4.* The Morning After. *5.* The Party. *6.* The Favorite Episode. *7.* The Rescue. *8.* The Blind Date. *9.* The Run. *10.* The Advice. *11.* The Confes-sion.

47 *Axis of Action.* webserieschannel.com. 2014.

"Ever feel like your life is like a movie? Amy and I (Kyle) feel like that a lot. It's like the littlest things sends us into some crazy action adventure" is the in-troduction that is heard as a young married couple (Amy and Kyle) attempt to solve their relationship problems through high-adventure fantasies as de-picted in feature films. Each episode presents a prob-lem and how, through fantasy sequences, they enact a film's characters and through that experience re-solve that particular problem.

Cast: Kelly Park (Amy), Kyle Cowgill (Kyle). **Comment:** Amy and Kyle do live in the real world but need that fantasy film reenactment to solve their problems. The idea is good as is the acting and pro-duction.

Episodes: *1.* The Man with the Golden Pen. *2.* The Good, the Bad, the Pizza.

48 *B-Roll.* youtube.com. 2014.

Chris is a young filmmaker who hopes to make his mark in what is called "The Indie" (Independent) Film Industry. To accomplish his goal, Chris enters a 48-hour film contest that requires a commercial to be produced about duct tape. Now with an idea but no team Chris posts flyers that read "Let's Make a Movie. Wanna Be Famous? Join the Crew" and through it acquires his team: Ingrid, the writer; Joanne, the producer; and James and Mike, the cam-eramen. The program, billed as "a story about film-makers by filmmakers," charts all the problems Chris encounters before, during and after shooting as he struggles to get his commercial made within the two-day deadline. The commercial fails to win the contest and Ingrid becomes the focus of season two episodes. When she comes across a banner boasting of a film competition ("The 25th Annual Spring Film Festival") she decides to enter it and produce a film based on the lines of a Spanish television soap opera called "Telenovela." Ingrid is followed as she re-connects with her former crew from the failed duct tape commercial to produce a unique, award winning film.

Cast: John Griswold (Chris Henson), Luz Lopez (Joanne Jacobs), Jerry Hsu (James Cromwell), Crys-tal Liu (Ingrid Leigh), Brian Li (Mike Song), Marvin Qian (Joe), Alexi Sargeant (Carl), Mona Cao (Gab-rielle), Nicole De Santis (Roxanne), Samantha Lig-ato (Maxine), Elliott Meyers (Andrew Williams), Chris Henson (John Griswold). **Credits:** *Producer:* Katie Stoops, Ginny Maceda, Travis Gonzalez. *Direc-tor:* Will Heffner. *Writer:* Travis Gonzalez, Deandra Tan, Brian Li, Ilana Strauss. **Comment:** At first the program has the feeling that it just begins in the mid-dle of nowhere as a man (Chris) just address the au-dience. Stick with the program as it becomes a well acted and produced satire of film making.

Season 1 Episodes: *1.* Meet the Crew. *2.* Auditions. *3.* Lights, Camera CUT! *4.* The Editing Room. *5.* That's a Rap.

Season 2 Episodes: *1.* The Reunion. *2.* Ay Dios Mio, Telenovela. *3.* What's Your Favorite Scary Movie? *4.* The Experimental Film. *5.* Let's Make a Musical. *6.* Behind-the-Scenes Stuff.

49 *BabeArella.* vimeo.com. 2012.

Barbarella is a 1968 science fiction movie starring Jane Fonda as Barbarella, a sexual woman of the 41st century who has been assigned the task of bringing to justice an evil villain (Durand Durand) based in the City of Sogo. The time has come for a remake of the film and a struggling young actress named Jane Fondue is cast as the lead opposite Johnny Depp (who will play Durand Durand). All is progressing well for Jane until she learns she is pregnant (by her husband Roger) and now fears she will not be able to play the part (especially since it requires revealing costumes and several nude scenes). The program follows Jane as she ponders what to do—give up the role of a lifetime or have the baby.

Cast: Kate Rees Davies (Jane Fondue), Monique Kalmer (Marion, her agent), Valmike Rampersad (Roger Fondue), Naina Michaud (Rachel Welsh, Jane's competition). Credits: *Producer:* Kate Rees Davies, Monique Kalmer. *Director:* Kate Rees Davies. Comment: Although Jane Fondue has a similar name to Jane Fonda, she doesn't appear to be as sexy or even right for the role. But that doesn't stop a producer from hiring her and while there are no actual scenes regarding the film that is to be made, the time spent with Jane auditioning for the role, being granted the role and then discovering she is pregnant (and what to do) are all very well done and do make for a very well presented series.

Episodes: *1.* Results. *2.* I'm Pregnant. *3.* Going Home.

50 *Baby Mentalist.* webserieschannel.com. 2013.

George Chung is a plainclothes detective with the Los Angeles Police Department. He is divorced from Barbara and the father of Ruby (with whom they share custody). But Ruby is no ordinary infant. She possesses psychic abilities and is called "Baby Mentalist" by George. He also incorporates her in his investigations and stories follow Ruby as she uses her facial expressions (through which her abilities are released) to unnerve suspects (who fall under her spell) and allow George to solve cases. Subplot of the series is George's efforts to reconcile with Barbara and become a happy family again.

Cast: Randall Park (George Chung), Jae Suh Park (Barbara Chung), Ruby Louise Park (Ruby Chung), Larry Hankin (Chief Bernard Briggs). Credits: *Producer-Writer:* Randall Park. *Director:*

Tim Wilkerson. Comment: Clever spoof of the CBS TV series *The Mentalist* with excellent action and production values. Some may recognize actor Larry Hankin as the inspiration for the Kramer character on the TV series *Seinfeld*.

Episodes: 6 untitled episodes, labeled "Episode 1" through "Episode 6."

51 *Baby Time!* funnyordie.com. 2013.

Richard and Anna are a happily married Chicago couple expecting their first child. Anna is experiencing labor pains (thirty minutes apart) and all is progressing smoothly until Richard gets a phone call from his mother-in-law (Chelsea), who needs to be picked up and united with Anna. Richard obliges and the program charts what happens when Anna goes into serious labor and Richard, desperate to get back for the birth, encounters numerous obstacles that appear to prevent him from doing so.

Cast: Brian Boland (Richard), Cassandra Bissell (Anna), Sara Sevigny (Thelma), Barbara Robertson (Chelsea), Dan Kenney (Max). Credits: *Producer:* John Gallegos, John Berger. *Writer-Director:* Dan Gorski. Comment: Although similar concepts have been done before it is always refreshing to see a new take on the idea. The acting and entire production is very good and a rather enjoyable program to watch.

Episodes: *1.* Labor Pains. *2.* The Soccer Mom vs. the Pit Bull. *3.* Cursed. *4.* The Disillusionment Express. *5.* Der Fundenaissers. *6.* Leggo My Preggo.

52 *Back to Reality.* backtorealityseries.com. 2014.

Cassandra, Jackson, Samantha and James were ordinary people who became famous when they were chosen to star on the reality TV series *Rise to the Top*. Encompassing a show within a show format, the program relates events in their lives as they try to adjust to their new status as stars.

Cast: Shelby Bartelstein (Samantha), John Hollingsworth (Jackson), Laura L. Thomas (Cassandra), Jacob Green (Aidan), Roderick Lawrence (Travis), Mat Leonard (James), Carlton Tanis (Chris). Credits: *Producer-Writer:* Shelby Bartelstein, John Hollingsworth. *Director:* Alex Forstenhausler.

Comment: An obvious spoof of the numerous reality shows that dominate both network and cable TV to show what happens when ordinary people suddenly become famous and how they react to what has suddenly happened to them.

Episodes: *1.* The Interview. *2.* Shark Attack. *3.* Bromantic. *4.* The Way of the Future. *5.* The Photo Shoot. *6.* Dinner Party.

53 *Backseat Bitches.* youtube.com. 2014.

Best friends Jinny and Mimi may not be the crème

de la crème of society but they are determined to become a part of the social scene by attending all the lavish Hollywood parties to which they have not been invited. Without a vehicle of their own they hire cars to take them to where the celebrities are and the program is a look at the backseat conversations that transpire between the two friends. **Cast:** Melissa Hunter (Mimi), Jessica Lowe (Jinny). **Credits:** *Producer:* Marissa Gallant. *Director:* Noam Bleswell. *Writer:* Melissa Hunter. **Comment:** Although the girls are not actually seen crashing parties, the conversations they hold are lively, well written and the overall production well done.

Episodes: *1,2.* Britney's Bitches. *3,4.* Bridesmaids. *5,6.* Macaulay Culkin's Birthday Jam.

54 *Backwash.* crackle.com. 2010.

A free toaster being given away as a bank promotion to attract new customers arouses the curiosity of three slacker friends (Jonesy, Val and Fleming) who feel they must have one. Based on available information, Jonesy is mistaken for a thief, handed $100,000 and, with police believing he and his accomplices (Val and Fleming) are bank robbers, begin a desperate effort to evade police (in an ice cream truck) and somehow prove their innocence. **Cast:** Michael Panes (Jonesy), Joshua Malina (Val), Michael Ian Black (Fleming). **Credits:** *Producer:* Daniel Schnider, Danny Leiner, Joshua Malina. *Writer-Director:* Danny Leiner, Joshua Malina. **Comment:** All episodes have been taken off line and existing text information is quite sketchy. It is just not possible to provide a more comprehensive story line or assess the program.

Episodes: *1.* Val and Jonesy. *2.* Meat Snack. *3.* Meet Nick Fleming. *4.* The Fuzz. *5.* The Topsy Turvey Diner. *6.* Number 9. *7.* Sharks. *8.* Lake Pupik. *9.* Survival. *10.* Clark Attack! *11.* Travel Games. *12.* First Dates. *13.* The Beginning of the End.

55 *Backyard Science with Bob.* youtube. com. 2013.

While hunting, a rather unpleasant looking hillbilly (Bob) stumbles upon a young scientist (Debbi) who has trespassed on his land to conduct an experiment (a not-so-funny cure for AIDS). Upset that the woman is on his property, Bob fires several shots and scares her off. While examining the equipment Debbi left behind Bob becomes intrigued and the program chronicles what results when a man without scientific knowledge begins conducting his own experiments. **Cast:** Ryan Connor (Bob), Jessica Wilkolak (Debbi). **Credits:** *Director:* Ryan Connor. *Writer:* Todd Wilkolak. **Comment:** Bob is simply a hard character to enjoy because of how grotesque he looks (bad teeth and unshaven). It is simply not a program for everyone.

Episodes: *1.* Bob Discovers Science. *2.* Lava Lamp. *3.* Explosions, Deer and the Government. *4.* Bob's Green Discovery. *5.* Where Is It? *6.* 15 Minutes of Fame. *7.* Bob's First Christmas.

56 *Bad Date.* webserieschannel.com.2012.

Branson and Francine are friends and roommates seeking to find romance but not with each other. With little luck on their own they decide to help each other by setting up blind dates: Branson with guys he knows for Francine and Francine with girls she knows for Branson. The program is simply a look at those blind dates and what results. **Cast:** Adam Armstrong (Branson), Megan Brown (Francine). **Credits:** *Producer:* Timothy O'Halloran, Brittany Cole, Kristofer Brandow, Adam Armstrong, Brad Riddell. *Writer-Director:* Timothy O'Halloran. **Comment:** "Warning. This Webisode contains foul language, sexual content, vicious date hunting and two very narcissistic individuals that may hurt your feelings in their quest to true love. Viewer discretion is advised" opens each episode in a well acted and produced program that despite the long warning is no more "harmful" than dozens of such series that contain unsavory language and sexual situations.

Episodes: *1.* Date Hunt. *2.* Patchouli and Don. *3.* Peter and Johanna. *4.* Tyler.

57 *Bad Eulogy.* webserieschannel.com. 2013.

An anthology presentation that explores what happens when loved ones attempt to honor the deceased and everything that can go wrong does. **Cast:** Will Storie, Keisha Zollar, Lucas Hazlett, Krista Worby, Joe Bonacci, Betsy Stover, Michael Canfield, Alexandra Gjerpen, Deirdre O'Keefe, Jamie Matson, Shyda Hoque, Frank Courter. **Credits:** *Producer-Writer-Director:* Michael Canfield, Joe Bonacci. **Comment:** A rather morbid concept with acceptable acting and production values but not something everyone will enjoy as it can make one feel uncomfortable watching it.

Episodes: *1.* The Undead. *2.* The Salesman. *3.* The Psychic. *4.* The Wife. *5.* The Holy Man. *6.* The Best Friend.

58 *Banana Boys.* webserieschannel.com. 2011–2012.

Wilson and Billy are friends who have just graduated from college. Although they have degrees they are unable to find jobs and see nothing positive in the near future. The only thing they seem to have in common is their love of bananas and what they do to amuse themselves with bananas—from playing jokes to just eating them is the focal point of the program.

Cast: June Sabatine (Wilson Vango), August James (Billy Martian), Mike Jones ("The Funk"). **Credits:** *Producer:* August James, June Sabatine. *Director:* August James. **Comment:** A disgusting, truly annoying program that is also badly acted and produced. Without a doubt, the worst of the Internet comedy series—unless you like seeing extreme close-ups of two idiots munching on bananas, playing banana jokes on people and doing other distasteful things then check this series out. If not, avoid it completely.

Episodes: *1.* Testify. *2.* Where's the Funk? *3.* Banana Abuse. *4.* Eggs in a Basket. *4.* The Good, the Bad and the Best. *5.* Dumpster Dandy.

59 *Bar Flies.* webserieschannel.com. 2012–2013.

The Brass Rail Lounge is a bar that is typical of bars seen on many TV series, especially *Cheers*. It has the supposedly all-knowing bartender (Chad) and its share of off-the-wall regulars: Evan, a drunk; Dan, the awkward romantic; Eve, the girl whose romantic life is in a shambles; Sherri, her best friend; Wayne, a conspiracy theorist; Nykki, the bitchy girl; and Jackson, the wingman. The program follows Chad as he becomes involved in and attempts to solve the problems presented to him by his customers (Bar Flies) who are also his friends.

Cast: Blake McNamara (Chad), Stephanie Schumacher (Eve), David Scott (Dan), Christine MacCarthy (Sheri), Stephen Farrugia (Jackson), Kevin MacCarthy (Evan), Rena Patrick-Watters (Nykki), Jeremiah Arnett (Wayne), Terrell Gray (Geoff). **Credits:** *Producer:* Laura Scott. *Writer-Director:* David Scott. **Comment:** "The following program has not been rated by the MPAA, ESRB, FCC or NIMH. It contains adult language and situations as well as simulated alcohol use and may not be suitable for persons under the age of 18. Rest assured that had this content been rated we would have promptly been shot, locked up, shot again and left for dead. We at *Bar Flies* did not bear feed or raise your children and do not take responsibility for what they find on the Internet. Thank you and enjoy responsibly" opens each episode of a program that will remind anyone who has seen *Cheers* that it too has its charming side, outrageous characters, an all-knowing bartender and situations that are often funny.

Season 1 Episodes: *1.* Pilot. *2.* Nice Glass. *3.* Starved. *4.* Dreamy Nightmares. *5.* The Geoff. *6.* Wayne's Brain. *7.* Closing Time.

Season 2 Episodes: *1.* Familiar Faces. *2.* Big News. *3.* Best Laid Plans. *4.* Breaking Up. *5.* Memories, Memories. *6.* Being Chad. *7.* Wedding Blues.

60 *Barbie: Life in the Dream House.* barbie.com. 2012–2014.

The Mattel series of Barbie fashion dolls come to life via computer animation to relate events in the life of a beautiful teenage girl (Barbie) who lives in a fantasized version of Malibu, California, with her younger siblings (Skipper, Stacie and Chelsea) in the Dream House, a large pink mansion.

Barbie, the iconic doll created in 1959, has remained a bright, charming role model for young girls. She is personable, well-mannered and, although she is considered a Malibu celebrity, she tries to be just a regular girl. Ken is her boyfriend; Teresa, Nikki, Midge and Summer are her girlfriends; Raquelle is Barbie's "frenemie," the girl seeking to steal Ken away from her; and Ryan is Raquelle's vain twin brother who is secretly in love with Barbie.

Voice Cast: Kate Higgins (Barbie), Sean Hankinson (Ken), Paula Rhodes (Skipper/Stacie), Laura Gerow (Chelsea), Katie Crown (Teresa), Nakia Burrise (Nikki), Haviland Stillwell (Raquelle), Ashlyn Selich (Midge), Charlie Bodin (Ryan), Tara Sands (Summer). **Comment:** The computer animation is very good and it captures the images of the dolls with Barbie's physical attributes altered somewhat (smaller breasts and a larger waist) to make her more realistic. The voice match-ups are also good and the stories flow evenly from beginning to end. A real treat to girls who are, were, or still are Barbie fans.

Season 1 Episodes: *1.* Closet Princess. *2.* Happy Birthday, Chelsea. *3.* Pet Peeve. *4.* Rhapsody in Butter Cream *5.* Ken-tastic Hair-tastic. *6.* Party Foul. *7.* Day at the Beach. *8.* Sticker It Up. *9.* Oh How Campy. *10.* Bad Hair Day. *11.* License to Drive. *12.* I Want My BTV. *13.* Gifts Goofs Galore. *14.* The Barbie Boutique.

Season 2 Episodes: The Reunion Show. *2.* Closet Princess 2.0. *3.* Sisters Ahoy. *4.* The Shrinkerator. *5.* Plethora of Puppies. *6.* Closet Clothes Out. *7.* Accidentally on Porpoise. *8,9.* Gone Glitter Gone.

Season 3 Episodes: *1.* Playing Heart to Get. *2.* Catty on the Catwalk. *3.* Help Wanted. *4.* A Spooky Sleepover. *5.* A Smidge of Midge. *6.* Occupational Hazards. *7.* Ooh How Campy, Too. *8.* Let's Make a Doll.

Season 4 Episodes: *1.* Endless Summer. *2.* Sour Loser. *3.* Another Day at the Beach. *4.* Happy Birthday to You. *5.* Cringing in the Rain. *6.* The Ken Den. *7.* Primp My Ride. *8.* Mall Mayhem. *9.* The Closet Upgrade.

Season 5 Episodes: *1.* Doctor Barbie. *2.* Stuck with You. *3.* The Only Way to Fly. *4.* Perf Pool Party. *5.* Trapped in the Dream House.

Season 6 Episodes: *1,2.* Style Super Squad. *3.* Little Bad Dress.

61 *The Bartender Hates You.* funnyordie. com. 2009–2012.

The setting is an unnamed bar where its principal bartender is not a Sam Malone (*Cheers*), but a rude, obnoxious man who has little patience for anything, including patrons, all of whom he finds quite annoying. It is definitely not a bar "Where everybody knows your name" and the program is simply a very quick look at how the bartender handles each patron who approaches him.

Cast: Alan Stephens (The Bartender), Natalia Fedner (Sara), David Martel (Ari), Bert Rotundo (Arman), Susannah Hillard (Monica). **Credits:** *Producer-Writer:* Bert Rotundo, Alan Stephens, Greg Young, Noah Applebaum, D.P. Davis. *Director:* Greg Young. **Comment:** Anyone familiar with the reality series *Bar Rescue* would immediately expect bar rescuer Jon Taffer to turn up and fire this bartender on the spot as he is costing the business money by being rude and obnoxious. But Jon has not yet found him and the program's short videos are quite amusing to watch.

Season 1 Episodes: *1.* Ice. *2.* Taste Test. *3.* Water. *4.* Salt. *5.* My Hiney. *6.* Know It All. *7.* Cell Bath. *8.* Episode #1.8. *9.* The Laugh. *10.* Change. *11.* Patron.

Season 2 Episodes: *1.* The Snapper. *2.* Birthday Shots. *3.* Enough with the Mojitos. *4.* For the Ladies. *5.* Bubbles. *6.* Minty Fresh. *7.* That's for You. *8.* On the House. *9.* The Buffet. *10.* The Hold Up. *11.* The Squeeker. *12.* The Man Glass. *13.* Coat Check. *14.* The Tapper. *15.* Two Cubes. *16.* Frisco Tickler. *17.* The Searcher. *18.* Blah Blah Blah. *19.* Drunk Shots. *20.* The Waver. *21.* Separate Ways.

Season 3 Episodes: *1.* The Moocher. *2.* Never Change.

62 *Bath Roomies*. bathroomies.com 2013.

Brigette is a gorgeous young woman who, for reasons known only to her, agrees to become roommates with Patrick, Ryan and Ronnie, three men who live in the apartment's bathroom. The situation doesn't seem to faze Brigette and the program follows what happens as the guys literally eat, work and sleep in the bathroom and try to share their home away from home with a girl who now lives with them.

Cast: Brigette Davidovici (Brigette), Patrick Cavanaugh (Patrick), Ronnie Khalil (Ronnie), Ryan P. Shrime (Ryan). **Credits:** *Producer-Writer:* Ronnie Khalil, Ryan P. Shrime. *Director:* Snehal Patel, Nicholas Brandt, Gabriel Cullen. **Comment:** While not a totally original idea (fans of the TV series *Happy Days* may recall that Fonzie had his "office" in the boys room at Arnold's Drive-In) but adding the feminine touch makes for a whole new feel and, with good acting and production values, an unusual, if not interesting series emerges.

Episodes: *1.* Porn Is Expensive. *2.* Rape Face. *3.* Sleep Stalking. *4.* The Date-Me Game. *5.* Shower Together.

63 *Bayberry Hall*. webserieschannel.com. 2013.

Because college officials believe its student body

cannot always be trusted and need supervision, a system called RA (Resident Adviser) has been instituted. Cho, Darcy, Jamie and Scott are four such RA's assigned to the Bayberry Hall dormitory and the program follows their efforts to keep students in check and maintain the dignity of Los Angeles State University.

Cast: Narisa Suzuki (Cho), Bonnie Sludikoff (Darcy), Matt Lara (Jamie), Nikolai Fernandez (Scott), Beskett West (Jack), Christian Guerroro (Sam), Ronnie Loaiza (Lena), Tiffany Oliver (Courtney), Lesley Marshall (Ivy), Jesse C. Boyd (Simon). **Credits:** *Producer-Writer:* Bonnie Sludikoff, Christoper Schamber. **Comment:** A rarely tackled topic that is based on the writer's personal experiences with very good acting and production values.

Episodes: Although 15 episodes are mentioned as being produced only four are on line: *1.* Pilot: Taking the Floor. *2.* The Housing. *3.* Textbook Case. *4.* Easy Like Plato.

64 *Be Here Nowish*. beherenowish.com. 2014.

At a party thrown by a mutual friend, two young women (Samantha [called Sam] and Nina) meet and become friends. Sam is straight and works as a dating consultant; Nina, a lesbian, is a courier who delivers prescription pills to eccentric clients. Although Sam can advise men about dating techniques, she cannot seem to hold a boyfriend. Nina, unable to make a commitment, has been living a bit recklessly, hooking up with a different girl each night. Despite the world of differences that define them, they each inspire the other and impulsively decide to leave New York for Los Angeles to seek a plant medicine ceremony with a Shaman for the guidance needed to redirect their lives. The program follows their rather outrageous experiences as they experiment with various spiritual practices, attempt to shed their old lives and become a part of each other's new life.

Cast: Alexandra Roxo (Sam), Natalia Leite (Nina), Adam Carpenter (Clay), Victoria Haynes (Victoria), Christina Jeffs (Christina), Daniella Rabbani (Dabiella), Ry Russo-Young (Zoe), Risa Sarachan (Risa), Karley Sciortino (Aurora). **Credits:** *Producer:* Dennis Mykytyn, Natalia Leite, Alexandra Roxo. *Director:* Natalia Leite, Alexandra Roxo. *Writer:* Natalia Leite, Alexandra Roxo, Liz Armstrong. **Comment:** An expertly acted and produced program. There are intimate scenes and partial nudity and the doorway has been left open for Nina and Sam to encounter new adventures.

Episodes: *1.* Pilot. *2.* Bob. *3.* GPO. *4.* Viva Placenta. *5.* The Fish Is Fresh. *6.* Liquid Gold. *7.* Jacqui the Bear. *8.* I Love the Universe. *9.* Kale Syrup. *10.* There and Back Again.

65 *Because I'm Me.* youtube.com. 2011.

Tre (actor), London (socialite), Destiny (model), Robbie Q (comedian) and Undre (gay fashion designer) are hopeful entertainers seeking to achieve fame. Believing that Atlanta holds the greatest opportunity, they move to Georgia but find that they not only have no idea of what they are doing but each has an ego problem that becomes another obstacle that stands in their way. Life changes for them when they are cast on a *Big Brother*–like reality series and must not only share the same house and their lives with the viewing audience but compete against others in talent competitions to win their chance at fame. Figuring this is their only hope, each sets out to prove his or her worth with the program charting how, while seeking to overcome their individual obstacles, they inadvertently help each other achieve fame.

Cast: Lamar Scott (Tre Jackson), Alina Lia (London Hampton), Thesiha McClashie (Destiny Sky), Raymond Horton (Robbie Q), Jermaine Blackburn (Undre Lamar). **Credits:** *Producer-Writer:* Deanna Rachelle, Lamar Scott, Raymond Horton. *Director:* Deri Tyton. **Comment:** Dream seekers, ego clashing and strangers sharing the same house on reality shows is nothing new as it has been seen on broadcast and cable TV in many incarnations. It is somewhat different seeing it on the Internet and it can go either way—a direct copy or something different. Here a mostly African-American variation is presented and, with the varied goals being sought, comes off as a well acted and produced program.

Episodes: *1.* Tre. *2.* London. *3.* Destiny. *4.* Undre. *5.* Robbie. *6.* Auditions. *7.* The Mansion. *8,9,10.* Untitled episodes.

66 *Becoming Batman.* webserieschannel. com. 2010.

A young man (Wayne) living in England in an apparently unfulfilled life (not made clear) discovers, while reading the newspaper that the village of Chalfont St. Peter has advertised for a Batman to battle the crime that exists. Having had a fascination with Batman since he was a child and believing that he can now fulfill a fantasy, Wayne applies for and acquires the job. Donning the guise of the movie version of the Caped Crusader (as opposed to the TV series), acquiring a gorgeous sidekick (Robin, in the person of a girl named Stephanie) and, with his friend acting as Batman's butler and advisor (Alfred) Wayne begins a quest to stamp out crime and protect the village of Chalfont St. Peter—even though he lacks the abilities of the real Batman.

Cast: Stuart Laws (Wayne/Batman), Amy Kwolek (Stephanie/Robin), Alistair Clayton, David Boydon, Chris Boyd. **Comment:** Impoverished man's version of the Batman legend with only adequate acting and production values. Many scenes are dark, characters, with the exception of Stephanie (as a Robin no movie or TV Batman ever had) are just not interesting or even very likeable. There is foul language (bleeped; possibly done after the episodes were made) that was unnecessary to begin with. There is no denying that *Becoming Batman* is totally different; but for die hard Batman fans, not what they would want to see.

Season 1 Episodes: *1.* Pilot. *2.* Batman Begins. *3.* Blind Justice. *4.* It's How You Play the Game. *5.* #38. *6.* Batman and Robin. *7.* Introduce a Little Anarchy. *8.* Identity Crisis. *9.* There Is No Hope in Crime Alley. *10,11.* Finale.

Season 2 Episodes: *1.* The Dark Knight Returns. *2.* Not Yet He Ain't. *3.* The Man Who Would (n't) Be Bat. *4.* Death in Slow Motion.

67 *Becoming Ricardo.* webserieschannel. com. 2014.

Crime, Law and Justice is a top-rated television series that has just put out a casting call for a macho-Latino male lead. Feeling that this is the opportunity of a lifetime, Jesenia Cruz, a struggling young actress, decides to audition for the role—as a man named Ricardo Montalban. With help from her cousin Sofia, a make-up artist, and some practice, Jesenia actually begins to emulate masculine traits and acquires the role. The program explores what happens to Jesenia as she struggles to live two lives and deal with the problems the situation has created—from a crazy ex-boyfriend (Jorge), a female co-star (Vivian) who has fallen in love with her (not knowing she is really a woman), meddling parents (Lydia and Hector) and a cast and crew who are not always sure that Ricardo is the macho Latino he appears to be.

Cast: Jesenia (Jesenia/Ricardo), Sofia Rodriquez (Sonia Cruz), Lisa Velez-Mello (Lydia Cruz), Roman Suarez (Hector Cruz), Junio Teixeira (Steve Castillo), Giorfona Aviv (Vivian Vox), Ron Rivera (Jose Rivera), Nasser Metcalf (Bruce Edwardson). **Credits:** *Producer:* Jesenia. *Director:* Jesenia, Tony Clomax, Davis Wright. *Writer:* Jesenia, Jenni Ruiza. **Comment:** Enjoyable gender-bender sitcom that not only borrows its format from *Tootsie* but most obviously from the TV series *Bosom Buddies*. It is a non-offensive, well acted and produced program that spotlights Latin American performers in a format that is sometimes difficult to sustain if the setting is just not right.

Episodes: *1.* Snap. *2.* Kicking. *3.* Roof Jumper. *4.* Falling. *5.* Pole.

68 *Beenanas.* webserieschannel.com. 2013.

Comical clip program that highlights what it calls "funny, strange and crazy fails."

Host: Blanche Spalding. **Credits:** *Producer:* Reali Robinson, Miki Ariyama. *Writer-Director:* Reali Robinson. **Comment:** An Internet version of the ABC TV series *America's Funniest Home Videos* that highlights people doing crazy things, but only in very short segments (under 2 minutes each).

Episodes: *1.* Snap. *2.* Kicking. *3.* Roof Jumper. *4.* Falling. *5.* Pole.

69 *Beg. Borrow. Steal.* begborroworsteal-webseries.tumblr.com. 2013.

Kat, Drake and Austin are young filmmakers with an idea for what they hope will become a block-buster feature film (*Super Godzilla vs. Rape Gorilla*). At least they think so even though the major studios refuse to back them. Although they have raised funds and acquired the services of a loan shark to see them through the project, life changes for them when their loan shark is arrested for charging excessive interest and sent to jail. Now, left out in the cold and without the resources needed to even begin their film, Kat, Drake and Austin begin their quest to acquire the money they need—by begging, borrowing or even stealing it if that becomes the case.

Cast: Shay Revolver (Kat Walker), Gabe Vinals (Austin McGee), Geoff Moonen (Drake Anderson), Stephen Wagner (Steve). Credits: *Producer:* Andrew Harrison. *Writer:* Shay Revolver, Andrew Harrison. *Director:* Shay Revolver. Comment: The movie devised by the trio has a deceiving title as it is about life in a prison with the main character, a rapist called "Rape Gorilla." It is rather talkative, uses excessive foul language and, unfortunately, missed an opportunity to be something better than it is. The writer, Shay Revolver, makes an attractive lead (also the smarter of the two guys she has working with her) but chose a laid back attempt at making a film as opposed to a more adventurous comical attempt at acquiring funds. Granted there are only three people, but with Kat as the leader and Austin and Drake as her stooges, a lot of opportunities were missed.

Episodes: *1.* The Break In. *2.* Trapped. *3.* Fire Breathing Zombie Slayer. *4.* Super Bigfoot Vs.

70 *The Beginning of Something Good.* webserieschannel.com. 2012.

At first glance Paul and James, young men who work in a funeral home, appear to be just that, young men holding down a job. But a closer look reveals they are junkies, addicted to alcohol and drugs and have been called "good for nothing idiots." As Paul and James try to keep their addictions under control the program relates their involvement with drug dealers, hippies and the low life's of conventional society.

Cast: Jose Puig (Paul), Jose Isoard (James), Jose Saucedo (Peter), Pia Gomez (Jefita), Carlos Muriel (Judas), Pablo Lanzagorta (Jesus). Credits: *Producer:* Jose Isoard, Rodrigo Murillo, Jose Puig, Carlos Muriel. Comment: The Australian produced program is a bit hard to understand due to the ac-

cents. While the setting of a funeral home is not new, adding drug and alcohol addicted morticians is a different twist.

Episodes: *1.* Blackmailin'. *2.* Travelin'. *3.* Diggin'. *4.* Pushin'. *5.* Adoptin'. *6.* Dyin'.

71 *Behind the Music That Sucks.* youtube.com. 1998–2009.

A spoof of the VH-1 series *Behind the Music* that incorporates cutout animation (uses celebrity photographs and stock images) to mock celebrities, singers and musicians who may have or have never appeared on the parent program.

Credits: *Creator-Producer:* Dave Carson, Simon Assaad. A voice cast is not credited. Comment: Truly enjoyable parodies of the people and groups profiled—from their birth and early years to where they stood at the time of production. The animation is a bit stiff but it becomes easily accustomed to as episodes are watched.

Episodes: Episodes appear to have no actual titles. The following is a list based on the more prominent celebrities and groups that have been lampooned: Tina Turner, Barbra Streisand, Ted Nugent, Tom Jones, Billy Joel, Bon Jovi, Britney Spears, Celine Dion, Cher, Christina Aguilera, Courtney Love, David Hasselhoff, Jewel, John Denver, Kenny Loggins, Lionel Richie, Mariah Carey, LL Cool J, Ted Nugent, Eric Clapton, Garth Brooks, Marilyn Manson, Melissa Etheridge, Van Halen, Will Smith, William Shatner, Shania Twain, Avril Lavigne, Hilary Duff, Jessica Simpson, Gwen Stefani, Justin Bieber, Kayne West, Katherine McPhee, Lindsay Lohan, Paula Abdul, Taylor Hicks, AC/DC, Backstreet Boys, Guns N' Roses, Hootie and the Blowfish, Dixie Chicks, KISS, Smashing Pumpkins, 'N Sync, The Black Eyed Peas, Igg Pop, Sting.

72 *Behind the Scene.* youtube.com. 2012.

How a web show is made is seen through the experiences of a "rich kid" (Travis) and two struggling and broke producers (Toby and Chad) as they delve into the world of Internet television to make a show to end all reality shows but finding that accomplishing that goal is a lot more involved than just having the funds and an idea.

Cast: Travis Bentor, Chad Gordy, Toby Weber, Kyle Hughes, Steven Abbott. Credits: *Producer-Writer:* Chad Gordy, Toby Weber, Steven Abbott. Comment: A potentially good idea that is poorly produced. It is rather talkative, has bad sound and only the planning stages of the reality show have thus far been presented.

Episodes: *1.* Artistic Values. *2.* The Black Star.

73 *Bernard and Knives.* youtube.com. 2014.

Knives, a show business knife-thrower, finds himself being interned at USK Prison in Wales (England) for ten years after assaulting a rival performer (Sasha Molatov) for having an affair with his wife. Time passes and Knives is released. He moves into the apartment of his best friend Bernard, a former strong man, and sets his goal to rebuild his life. The program chronicles what happens when everything that can go wrong does—from their accepting work from a shadowy wrestler and wannabe gangster (Big Dog) to Knives becoming a porn star to their involvement in the theft of rare *Doctor Who* TV series memorabilia.

Cast: Bill Bellamy (Knives), Ieuan Rhys (Bernard), Kirill Smolyakov, Dave Stewart (Big Dog), Chris Cox (Wendy). Credits: *Producer:* Adam Nicholas, Thomas Ries. *Director:* Adam Nicholas. *Writer:* Alex Nicholas, Thomas Ries, Bill Bellamy. Comment: A bit difficult to understand due to the British accents. Other than that it is well, acted and produced.

Episodes: *1.* Monday. *2.* Tuesday. *3.* Wednesday. *4.* Thursday. *5.* Friday. *6.* Saturday. *7.* Sunday.

74 *Bernie Says So.* webserieschannel.com. 2014.

Bernie is a Muppet-like character. He is 90 years old, a World War II veteran, married to Ethel but mostly a man with common sense who speaks his mind (although some people say he is nasty, mean to others and crabby). Seated in his reclining chair and "armed" with a laptop computer, Bernie relates his views on life drawing from his vast experiences and the wisdom and wit he possesses and still remembers.

Cast: T.C. DeWitt (Voice of Bernie), Linda Cieslik (Voice of Ethel). Credits: *Producer:* Ryan Brooks, Colin Wilcox, Doug Vojtko. *Writer:* Beverly Brooks. Comment: If Bernie says it is so, it is, as he has been around a long time and knows what to expect from life. Although a puppet is encompassed, it is not a children's show and aimed at adults. It has a Muppets-like feel to it and is not only expertly produced but very enjoyable to watch.

Episodes: *1.* Kindly Bernie. *2.* Hunger Games. *3.* The First Question. *4.* Political Choice. *5.* What About My Wife? *6.* Taking Life In.

75 *The Best Friend.* thebestfriend.com. 2010.

Sooze (27-years old) and Millie (30) have been friends since grammar school. Sooze is a perfectionist while Millie lacks confidence and is full of neuroses. Sooze also has a better romantic life than Millie and it is that aspect that becomes the focal point of the program. It is what happens in Sooze's life as seen through Millie's eyes (who is longing for a romance but often takes a back seat when it comes to finding the right man).

Cast: Marilyn Anne Michaels (Millie), Allie Smith (Sooze), Eric Loya (Dr. Joey Thompson), Jeanette O'Connor (Betsy), Jed Bernard (Rick). Credits: *Producer:* Marilyn Anne Michaels, Allie Smith, Michael Elias. *Director:* Tarique Qayumi, Wednesday Standley, Daniela De Carlo. *Writer:* Marilyn Anne Michaels, Allie Smith, Dominic Conti, Krystel Schley, Jay Coughlin, Eric Loya. Comment: Interesting take on friends and their romantic life with very good acting and a well-structured plot.

Episodes: *1.* The Ugly Friend. *2.* Cleaning House. *3.* Stalkers. *4.* Wing Woman. *5.* Girls' Day Out. *6.* Working Girls. *7.* The Big OMG. *8.* In the Ring. *9.* A Day Without. *10.* The Perfect Woman.

76 *Best Friends for Life.* vimeo.com. 2014.

Charlene, called Charlie, and Calvin have been friends since high school. They not only share an apartment together but a platonic relationship. Though it appears they do not have romantic inclinations toward each other, Calvin does care deeply for Charlie and his world changes for the worse when Charlie's relationship with her boyfriend (Dean) takes a turn for the better (for her) when Dean and Charlie decide to marry. The program follows what happens when Calvin realizes he loves Charlie but is about to lose her to another man.

Cast: Brendan Prost (Calvin), Cami Mohn (Charlie), Kane Sewart (Dean). Credits: *Producer:* Brendan Prost. *Director:* Jeremy Cox. Comment: Very talkative program with short episodes and good acting.

Episodes: *1.* Best Friends' Weekend. *2.* Family Friends. *3.* Boomer Bro Adventures! Nae Nae Edition. *4.* Boyfriends. *5.* Best Dressed Friends. *6.* Best Friends' Party.

77 *Best Laid Plans.* webserieschannel.com. 2010.

Tom, Skip, Alex and John are best friends struggling to navigate the daily rituals of life—from seeking ways to make ends meet to finding girlfriends. The program charts what happens when each attempts to help the other and disastrous results occur.

Cast: Jesse Groth Olson (Tom), Ben Seaward (Skip), Joshua Adam Snyder (Alex), John Mellies (John), Kate Hackett (Katie), Southey Blanton (Dirk), Saie Kurakula (J.D.), Katie Ryan (Jade), Brian Flaccus (Zach), Chris Pentzell (Mickey), Clint Morrison (Clint), Nicole Monet (Cherry), Bonnie Charette (Leslie), Paige Hiskey (Bridget), Ericka Zepeda (Veronica). Credits: *Producer:* Joshua Sikora, Jesse Grotholson. *Director:* Chris Hartwell, Joshua Sikora. *Writer:* Kevin Christensen, Joshua Sikora. Comment: A totally improvised program that uses a plot outline but no written dialogue. It is well done with good timing and adlibbing.

Episodes: *1.* Dashboard Confessions. *2.* Breaking and Entering. *3.* The Breakup. *4.* With Friends Like These. *5.* Best Pool Party Ever. *6.* A Perfectly Legal Adoption. *7.* Tom's Big Date. *8.* Surprise, Surprise. *9.* Date-and-Switch. *10.* Alex the Menace. *11.* The Interview. *12.* Everything's Amazing, No Worries.

78 *The Better Half.* thebetterhalfseries. com. 2013.

During a typical ride on a New York subway train two young lesbians (Amy and Lindsay) make eye contact and instantly fall in love. They date and later became roommates. Although both are self suffi- cient, they are working in dead-end jobs, stuck in the same old grind and losing the spark that united them. To add some excitement in their dull lives they decide to embark on a series of adventures (experi- encing things they have never done before) and the program charts what happens as they begin their quest and attempt to overcome all the hurdles they feel are preventing them from enjoying a lasting re- lationship.

Cast: Lindsay Hicks (Lindsay), Amy Jackson Lewis (Amy), Adriana DeGirolami (Angel), Katie Hartman (Diane), Todd Briscoe (Sandy), Leah Rudick (Cherry). Credits: *Producer:* Christine Ng, Leyla Perez. Director: Leyla Perez. *Writer:* Lindsay Hicks, Amy Jackson Lewis. Comment: Enjoyable program with very good acting and production qual- ities. The leads are a real-life couple and the prob- lems they face are some that can be experienced by almost anyone,

Episodes: *1.* Going Out. *2.* Sunny Side Up. *3.* Les- bifriends. *4.* Pure Camp. *5.* Early Retirement.

79 *Between Two Ferns.* funnyordie.com. 2008–2014.

Zach Galifianakis is the host of a TV talk show called *Between Two Ferns.* He is seated on the right side of the screen next to a potted fern while his guest sits on the left side also next to a potted fern. It looks to be a normal talk show until Zach, who has little knowledge about his guests, begins inter- viewing them with rather crude, inappropriate or ridiculous questions. The program focuses primarily on the guest and how he or she reacts or responds to the questions Zach poses.

Cast: Zach Galifianakis (Host). Credits: *Pro- ducer:* Will Ferrell, B.J. Parker, Chris Henchly, Zach Galifianakis. Comment: A very well done satire of celebrity talk shows.

Episodes: All titles begin with "Between Two Ferns with Zach Galifianakis" followed by the guest. *1.* Michael Cera. *2.* Jimmy Kimmel. *3.* Jon Hamm. *4.* Natalie Portman. *5.* Bradley Cooper and Carrot Top. *6.* Chalize Theron. *7.* Conan O'Brien and Andy Richter. *8.* Ben Stiller. *9.* Steve Carell. *10.* Sean Penn. *11.* Bruce Willis. *12.* Jennifer Aniston and Tila Te-

quila. *13.* Will Farrell and Jon Hamm. *14.* Oscar Buzz Edition (with Jennifer Lawrence, Naomi Watts, Christoph Waltz, Anne Hathaway and Amy Adams). *15.* Oscar Buzz, Part 2 (with Sally Field, Bradley Cooper, Jessica Chastain and Emmanuel Lewis). *16.* James Franco, *17.* Justin Bieber. *18.* Happy Holiday's Edition (with Tobey Maguire and Samuel L. Jackson). *19.* Pres. Barack Obama. *20.* Brad Pitt and Louis C.K.

80 *Big Ass Agency.* bigassagency.com. 2013.

B.A.A. (Big Ass Agency) is a top Hollywood tal- ent agency whose staff is anything but normal (in- cluding Benjamin, the delusional senior agent, and new hires Alice, a talented girl who knows her job, and Zack who knows very little about what an agent does). The program charts the numerous problems that befall the agency—from auditioning difficult clients to maintaining sanity within their own ranks.

Cast: Reshaun Jones (Benjamin Silver), Arthur Charles (James Simmons), Katie Amess (Alice Evans), Tommy Lukasewicz (Zack Harrison), Barika Croom (Flo'Landra). Credits: *Producer-Writer:* Re- shaun Jones. *Director:* Reshaun Jones, Barika Croom. Comment: African-American themed pro- gram that is more annoying to watch than anything else as the production is simply horrible. Not only is the unsteady (shaky) camera used but when char- acters speak the camera quickly pans back and forth from one to the other making for even more un- steady images (cutting from one character to the other would play a whole lot better). It appears, by the episodes that have been presented, that acts will be seen as they perform for the agency head (whose decisions are final on whether he will represent them or not). The idea is good although it can also be seen as a rip off of *American Idol* (the audition segments); it's just the presentation that suffers.

Episodes: *1.* Harassment and Waffles. *2.* The Helpless.

81 *Big City.* youtube.com. 2014.

Josie is a young woman, newly arrived in Brook- lyn, New York, from a small town in Oregon. She shares an apartment with a new friend (Dan) and her attempts to adjust to life in a big city form the basis of stories.

Cast: Lauren Ruff (Josie), Zane Carney (Dan). Credits: *Producer-Writer:* Lauren Ruff. *Director:* Erick Fix. Comment: Well acted and produced pro- gram that is just the right length to present a story that is straight to the point without unnecessary filler material.

Episodes: *1.* New Bike. *2.* Insults. *3.* Run-In. *4.* Fast Food. *5.* Cab Ride. *6.* A Big City Christmas. *7.* Surprise Party. *8.* Busker Battle. *9.* Delivery Guy. *10.* Day Date. *11.* Taxi Fight. *12.* Yoga. *13.* Sublet. *14.* Vacation. *15.* Boroughs. *16.* VIP. *17.* Cloudy with a

Chance of Love. *18.* Frantic (features guest star Fran Drescher). *19.* Session. *20.* Directions. *21.* Taco Truck. *22.* Jay Walking. *23.* Everyone's an Actor. *24.* Club.

82 *Big Ed Barnham's One of a Kind Big Find of the Week.* bigedbarnham.com. 2013.

Big Ed, the owner of Big Ed Barnham's Bauble Barn and Garden, is also the host of a web program called *Big Ed Barnham's One of a Kind Big Find of the Week.* Each episode begins with Ed entering a backyard setting and approaching an item on a table. He then begins talking about it (anything from old road maps to garden gnomes) and soon after offers it up for sale. The program concludes with "Not all finds are guaranteed to be one of a kind or be unsold at the time of viewing. But there's always another find next week."

Cast: Scott Rogers (Ed Barnham), Holly Wigmore (America Barnham, Ed's wife). **Credits:** *Producer-Writer:* Scott Rogers. **Comment:** Very enjoyable program for those who are fans of such TV shows as *American Pickers* and *Pawn Stars.* The idea is good and the production and acting top rate.

Episodes: *1.* Dutch Immigrants. *2.* Art Craft. *3.* Vintage Paper. *4.* Labor Day. *5.* Ed's Own Artwork. *6.* Rummage Sale. *7.* Technical Problems. *8.* Cast Iron. *9.* Hans Trinker. *10.* German Bubbly Opener. *11.* Country Music.

83 *The Big Time.* webserieschannel.com. 2012.

Gabe, a young man hoping to become an action star, and Dave, his cousin, a less enthusiastic young man with musical abilities, relocate to Los Angeles to pursue their dream jobs. Their experiences as they attempt to make their mark on the world are chronicled.

Cast: Gabe Michael (Gabe), David West (Dave). **Credits:** *Producer-Writer:* Gabe Michael, David West. *Director:* Gabe Michael. **Comment:** The format has been done countless times before (on television as early as 1951 with the ABC series *Two Girls Named Smith*) and the only difference here is that the cousins are totally unconventional and their off-the-wall antics form the basis for the comedy. For that reason, it is worth watching for a different take on an old format.

Episodes: *1.* Moving to L.A. *2.* Kissing Cousins. *3.* Why Do Puppies Cry? *4.* Mile-High Club. *5.* Actor Headshot Fail. *6.* Barely Legal. *7.* Threesome Homecoming Queen Supreme.

84 *Big Yellow A-hole.* bigyellowahole.com. 2014.

At one point in his life an actor named Steve played LaLa, the yellow Teletubbie on the British TV series *Teletubbies.* But after 116 episodes he was let go and replaced by a younger actor. Although depressed Steve feels he needs to reclaim his fame as an actor and, dressed in his LaLa costume, leaves England for the United States, first arriving in Hollywood then relocating to Texas when he finds no one will hire an actor dressed as LaLa. Life is becoming increasingly difficult for Steve until a documentary film maker, who feels people want to know what happened to the original LaLa, approaches him to become the subject of his film. Steve agrees and the program charts Steve's somewhat ridiculous efforts to again become famous.

Cast: John Venable (Steve), Frank Mosley (Richard), Larry Randolph (Ebenezer), Andrew Taylor (Film Maker), Jeff Swearingen (Tink), Ginger Goldman (Inga). **Credits:** *Producer:* Adgie Lou Davidson, John Venable. *Writer-Director:* John Venable. **Comment:** Embarrassing program with a grown man wearing a yellow Teletubbie costume and trying to act as an adult but unable to shed the boy in him. There are sexual jokes, an abundance of foul language and unsteady (shaky) scenes. Such programs always find an audience with people seeking something that is truly unbelievable but here it goes into the absurd and is difficult to even get through the first episode.

Episodes: *1.* An Introduction. *2.* Hello, Richard. *3.* The Audition. *4.* They Call Me Tink. *5* Did You Just Johnny Depp Me?

85 *Bigfoot Roommate.* webserieschannel. com. 2013.

Joe is a young man who, while strolling through the woods crosses the path of the legendary man-beast, Bigfoot. Finding that Bigfoot is friendly but saddened because progress has left him no place to stay, Joe decides to let him share his apartment. The mishaps that occur as Joe and Bigfoot become the most unlikely of roommates are depicted.

Cast: Joe De Witt (Joe), Cody Ruch (Bigfoot), Joe Martino (Voice of Bigfoot). **Credits:** *Producer-Writer-Director:* Joe De Witt. **Comment:** A *Harry and the Henderson's* movie and TV parody that is well done. Joe is likable as the Felix Unger–like roommate with Bigfoot as his sloppy Oscar Madison counterpart (from *The Odd Couple*). Production qualities are excellent and the voice syncing for Bigfoot is perfect.

Episodes: *1.* Rent. *2.* Razor. *3.* Toilet Paper. *4.* Clothes. *5.* Pillow Fight. *6.* Shower. *7.* Shoes. *8.* Sleepover. *9.* Jerky. *10.* The Y Word. *11.* Hot Dogs. *12.* Party.

86 *Bilbo Pope.* youtube.com. 2013.

Bill Pope is an enterprising, mean-spirited man who devises unique ways to fleece people. To those who know him he is called Bilbo and he has established himself as a self-proclaimed business guru with offices in the men's room of an office building. Christian Malone is a young man who dreams of becoming a playboy billionaire but thus far he only has dreams. When he learns that Bilbo is seeking an apprentice, Christian applies for the job hoping to learn from Bilbo how to become rich. With Christian as his aide, the program charts Bilbo's efforts to become rich through his "business acumen" video blogs.

Cast: Matt Dixon (Bill "Bilbo" Pope), Liam Thomas Burke (Christian Malone), Lisa Preston (Candy Pope; Bill's daughter). **Credits:** *Producer-Writer:* Matt Dixon, Liam Thomas Burke. **Comment:** The first episode purposely avoids showing Bilbo's face although his foul-mouthed voice is heard as Christian meets with him for the first time. With the second episode Bilbo is seen as a middle-aged, uncouth man with a face only a mother could love (the actor appears in an exaggerated face mask that presents Bilbo as a bit unsettling to look at). It is a British production with good acting and production values but be prepared for an outrageous character (Bilbo) and a most unusual base of operations (a bathroom) from which he conducts his activities.

Episodes: *1.* When Christian Malone Met Bill Pope. *2.* Bilbo Explains How to Get Famous Online. *3.* How to Pick Up Girls. *4.* The Original Fresh Prince of Bel Air? *5.* Arnold Schwarzenegger Interviewed by Bilbo Pope. *6.* Arnold Schwarzenegger Won't Leave. *7.* Bilbo Joins Twitter. *8.* Bilbo's Guide to "The Walking Dead" [TV Series]. *9.* Is Malone Plotting to Kill Bilbo Pope!? *10.* Bilbo Pope Hires Duncan Construction. *11.* Popeing Iron. *12.* Bilbo Pope Interviews Bane. *13.* Is Comedy Bane's Ally? *14.* Bill and Bane Remake Four Candles (Fork Handles) Comedy Sketch. *15.* Money in the (Sperm) Bank? *16.* Bilbo Pope's "Taxi Driver" Audition Footage. *17.* Bilbo and Malone Make a Porno!?

87 *Bill and Sons Towing.* billandsonstowing.com. 2013–2014.

At age 64 Bill Vanderchuck believes it is finally time to retire and turn over his business (Bill and Sons Towing) to his four thirty-something sons (Dave, Eric, Jon and Tony) to run. The idea sounds good and Bill feels his business will carry on until he discovers that the only things his sons have in common are their vastly differing opinions. The program charts the chaos that ensues as Bill's four sons attempt to run the business as a team and, in the process, keep the family together.

Cast: The Imponderables (as credited as Dave, Eric, Jon and Tony), Nicholas Campbell (Bill Vanderchuck), Angela Asher (Bill's wife). **Credits:** *Producer:* Mark DeAngeli, Vivieno Caldinelli. *Writer:* Mark DeAngeli, Eric Toth. *Director:* Vivieno Caldinelli. **Comment:** An enjoyable series with good acting and production values (while several reality series have used aspects of towing, *Bill and Sons Towing* does not venture into the reality field and is strictly a scripted comedy venture).

Season 1 Episodes: *1.* The First Meeting. *2.* Angry Customer. *3.* Job Switch. *4.* Bikini Calendar. *5.* Guard Dog.

Season 2 Episodes: *1.* Cleaning House. *2.* Sutherland Pays a Visit. *3.* Fire in the Hole. *4.* Tony Meets His Mom. *5.* Cup of Sugar. *6.* Let's Make a Deal. *7.* Jon's Mommy. *8.* Stripper for Dave. *9.* Charlie. *10.* Heavy Load. *11.* BBQ Fight. *12.* The Finale.

88 *Bill Weiner: High School Guidance Counselor.* youtube.com. 2013.

An unnamed high school provides the setting. It is here that improv actor Bill Weiner has secured a job as the school's new guidance counselor. Felling that he can make a difference, Bill incorporates his knowledge of improvisation to help his students overcome their problems. Episodes are set up as a counseling session with what happens during and after the counseling being explored.

Cast: Bill Arnett (Bill Weiner), Gregory Hollimon (Jay Cox), Lauren Walker (Stephanie Cox), Maggie Gottlieb (Dolores), Irene Marquette (Holly Kraft), Stephen Tobiasz (Robbie). **Credits:** *Producer:* Patrick Michalak, Steven Tobiasz. *Director:* Jack Newell. *Writer:* Patrick Michalak. **Comment:** The acting and production are good but the subject matter has been done numerous times before.

Episodes: *1.* Second First Impressions. *2.* 37 Nickels. *3.* Black Magic.

89 *A Bit Much.* webserieschannel.com. 2014.

Camp Messina is a summer retreat for teenagers but the focus is not on the campers but the adult counselors: Haley, a pretty but naïve young woman whose uncle (Leo) owns the camp and who only took the job to get away from her parents' on-going divorce proceedings; and Bridget, her cousin (Leo's daughter), the head girls counselor, who has set her goal to win over Pedro, an over confident Yale graduate, while trying to avoid her former love, Ben, the head boys' counselor (who has set his sights on winning over Haley). It's "a summer full of sex, lies and maybe (just maybe) love" as the program relates all the jealousy, deceit and awkwardness that ensues as the adults act more like children in their efforts to hookup with one another.

Cast: Addie Weyrich (Haley), Liv Benger (Bridget), David Dimitruk (Ben), Mike Rinere (Pedro), Jason Toledano (Corey), Colleen Scriven (Margaret), Patrick Grizzard (Leo), Rory James (John), Ben Horwitz (Ben). **Credits:** *Writer-Director:* Colleen Scriven. **Comment:** TV series using summer camp formats just do not work (an example being NBC's 1966 series *Camp Runamuck*). *A Bit*

Much is more adult-in nature and is well acted and produced (especially in mixing indoor with outdoor scenes).

Episodes: *Scene 1:* Return to Camp. *Scene 2:* Pop a Squat, It's Time for the Schpeel. *Scene 3:* Counselors Only Campfire. *Scene 4:* Pedro Hatches a Plan. *Scene 5:* Bridget and Ben Hear the Truth. *Scene 6:* Spooky Story Saturday. *Scene 7:* Pedro Confronts Bridget. *Scene 8:* Bridget and Ben Get Closer. *Scene 9:* Haley Humiliated. *Scene 10:* It Ain't Over Till It's Over.

90 *Bit Parts.* blip.tv. 2012.

BIT (The Binary Investigative Team) is a newly established organization that maintains stability in video games by overseeing the behind-the-scenes operations that are a part of each game. Agent Zero is BIT's top operative, a woman who believes that gamers are "an unexplained phenomenon" and can be affected by game playing; so much so that they can become criminal-like (Zero has also begun a series of questionable investigations based on her theory). Agent One, a by-the-books recruit, is teamed with Agent Zero to investigate crimes and/or strange happenings that may be linked to video game players. One, however, believes Zero's theories are totally unfounded and the program charts what happens during investigations when One slowly begins to realize that Zero may not be as delusional as he previously thought.

Cast: Jolyn Janis (Agent Zero), Brian Villalobos (Agent One), Shannon McCormick (Debug), Bobby Ray Cauley, Jr. (Corporal Jackson), Sam Eidson (Michael), Jacob Watson (Jeremy Eagles). **Credits:** *Producer:* Rachel Moody. *Writer-Director:* Ben Moody. **Comment:** An unusual premise that is well acted and presented, especially with the weird video game-like characters Zero and One encounter.

Episodes: *1.* Halo. *2.* Grand Theft Auto 3. *3.* Paperboy. *4.* Metal Gear Solid. *5.* Red Dead Redemption. *6.* Tomb Raider.

91 *The Bitchlorettes.* thebitchlorettes.com. 2012.

Spoof of the ABC series *The Bachelor* (and *The Bachelorette*) wherein an eligible young man (here Ben, heir to a vineyard) encounters the biggest challenge of his life: face a group of eligible but unconventional women and choose one to become his wife.

Cast: Lisa Alvarado (Latina C*ntney/Sarah Palin), Sara McClain (Heather), Ashlee Williss (Laura), Juliette Jackson (Blonde), Marquita Brookins (Token), Danny T (Ben), Zach Stiegler (Jacke), Matt Dillier (Cameraman). **Credits:** *Producer:* Lisa Alvarado, Sarah LaSpisa. *Writer-Director:* Lisa Alvarado. **Comment:** All the drama of the ABC series with a fine touch of comedy encompassing the final six women of the competition and a concluding Rose Ceremony (wherein Ben must present a rose to the girl of his choice) that surpasses anything presented on ABC. The program is well acted and smartly produced and is thus far the best spoof of *The Bachelor.*

Episodes: *1.* Group Date. *2.* The Blonde's Date. *3.* C*ntney's Date. *4.* Sarah Palin's Date. *5.* Sarah Palin Tells All. *6,7.* The Rose Ceremony.

92 *Bitter Lawyer: Living the Dream.* bitterempire.com. 2008.

Although he has graduated from Yale Law School, passed the bar and acquired a position with the prestigious law firm of Sullivan & Moore, Nick Conley is a man lost in the legal world. While it appeared easy in school, Nick now finds he has great difficulty comprehending the legal issues of the cases assigned to him. The program, based on an actual website (BitterLawyer.com) that is a sounding board for disgruntled lawyers relates incidents in Nick's life as he struggles to put to use what he learned and move up the ladder form his current rookie status.

Cast: John T. Woods (Nick Conley), Edward Kerr (Philip Atkins), Rick Eid (Senior Partner). **Credits:** *Producer:* Rick Eid, Mark Thudsum. *Writer-Director:* Rick Eid. **Comment:** Well acted and produced program that actually makes you feel Nick's frustration. It is one of the earlier Internet programs to deal with lawyers and could be considered a spoof a shows like *L.A. Law.*

Episodes: *1.* The Interview. *2.* Connotative/Derivative. *3.* Typo. *4.* Red Wine. *5.* Gayholm Syndrome. *6.* Yale. *7.* Rope. *8.* Halloween. *9,10.* Punching the Clown.

93 *Blabbermom.* youtube.com/momcave 2014–2015.

Real mothers, facing the camera, relate actual incidents regarding their children that are now more comical as compared to when they actually happened (when they were more embarrassing than funny).

Credits: *Creators:* Jennifer Weedon, J. Sibley Law, Valisa Tate, Stephanie Faith Scott. **Comment:** Interesting approach to the problems mothers face in raising children. The women, though amateurs, are quite personable and do a good job in relating their stories in short time spans.

Episodes: *1.* Kathy Blabs About Breastfeeding. *2.* Naomi Blabs About the Emergency Room. *3.* Mel Blabs About Urban Nature Walks. *4.* The Topless Heat Wave. *5.* Mika Blabs About Farting. *6.* Kathy Blabs About Her Missing High Schooler. *7.* Donei Blabs About the Zoo Disaster. *8.* Alixx Blabs About Peeing. *9.* Mia Blabs About Letting Yourself Off the Hook. *10.* Caroline Blabs About Piranha Nursing. *11.* Naomi Blabs About MacGyver Diapers. *12.*

#blabbermom
#MomCave

blabbermom
Real moms. Real stories. Real laughs.

Blabbermom. Series poster art (used by permission of Jennifer Weedon 2015).

Naomi Blabs About How Hard It Is. *13.* Mia Blabs About Restaurant Poop. *14.* Victoria Blabs About Penis Status. *15.* Jenny Blabs About Breastfeeding. *16.* Naomi Blabs About a Mother's Bond. *17.* Caroline Blabs About Car Seat Nursing. *18.* Midge Blabs About Kids Cursing. *19.* Regina Blabs About a Naked Kid Falling Out of a Window. *20.* Mariela Blabs About Cimemax. *21.* Erna Blabs About Quickies. *22.* Alyssa Blabs About Being Broke. *23.* Erna Blabs About the Counterfeit Handbag Sting.

94 *Black and White.* webserieschannel. com. 2012.

Peter Black (who is white) is a young man whose life seems serene. He gets along with and shares an apartment with a Scottish roommate (not named). His world suddenly changes when he returns home one day and finds that he has a new roommate—Jamaal White (who is black). Jamaal explains that his friend, Peter's roommate, left suddenly for Scotland and gave him the key to the apartment to become Peter's new roommate. Jamaal is anything but normal; Peter is a nervous wreck and the program relates Peter's efforts to adjust to the fact that his comfort zone must now be shared with someone who appears to need psychiatric help.

Cast: Anthony Begeron (Peter Black), Tory Smith (Jamaal White). **Credits:** *Producer:* Anthony Bergeron, Steev J. Brown, Faye Begeron. *Writer-Director:* Anthony Begeron. **Comment:** While the TV series *The Odd Couple* exclaimed "Can two divorced men share an apartment without driving each other crazy?" *Black and White* touts "Will these two opposites find middle ground and live together peacefully?" It is a good variation on the odd couple theme and interesting just to see how Jamaal, who believes he is normal, tries to adjust to Peter, whom he thinks is a bit of a loon.

Episodes: *1.* Knock-Knock, Who's There? *2.* The Scariest Doll Ever (refers to Jamaal's favorite doll, Tabitha). *3.* Message to Grandma Betty. *4.* Pickles. *5.* Peter and Jamaal Watch a Movie. *6.* Driving Mr. White.

95 *Blind Date.* funnyor die.com. 2010.

A year after Gina and her boyfriend ended their relationship Gina decides it is time to get back into the dating game. She begins by joining a dating service (Blind Date) that appears to be "the new craze for daters who need to mix it up a little." Stephanie, Gina's best friend, is a realist and feels Gina is being blindsided by all the hype and needs to realize that Blind Date does nothing but match one person with another with no pictures or background information. Gina doesn't seem to care and simply wants to explore a new world. The program chronicles that journey as it profiles Gina and the less-than-desirable blind dates she acquires.

Cast: Jessica Shelby (Gina), Melanie Hamilton (Stephanie). **Credits:** *Producer:* Camille Davis, Melanie Hamilton. *Director:* Ryan Penington. *Writer:* Melanie Hamilton. **Comment:** Nicely produced African-American program with attractive female leads who are down-to-earth, non-offensive (not made bitches as in some black produced Internet programs) and involved in stories that while exaggerated are enjoyable.

Episodes: *1.* Dirtball. *2.* Sloppy Joe. *3.* Basement Condo. *4.* Almost Perfect.

96 *Blockhead.* youtube.com. 2013.

The program is billed as "a live-action parody of Charlie Brown and the Peanuts gang." The performers are made to resemble the Charles Schulz characters as adults rather than children. They share the same names and, in most cases, the same mannerisms as their cartoon counterparts (as they are based on the *Peanuts* TV series of specials). The gang now lives in Los Angeles and each episode is a look at incidents in the lives of selected characters (see cast) encountering problems as they did in their youth but attempting to solve them (if they can) as adults.

Cast: Mike Summer (Charlie), Amanda Carneiro (Lucy), T'Lane Balue (Sally), Andy Stewart (Linus). **Credits:** *Producer:* Andy Stewart, Mike Sumner, Mitch Yapko. *Director:* Mitch Yapko. *Writer:* Andy Stewart, Mike Sumner. **Comment:** The acting is good and the overall production well done but is difficult to associate the cast as adult versions of the beloved cartoon characters.

Episodes: *1.* Charlie and the Date. *2.* Sally and the Cab Ride. *3.* Lucy and the Fat Kid. *4.* Linus and the Landlord.

97 *The Bloody Mary Show.* bloodymary show.com. 2012.

The American urban legend of "Bloody Mary" states that if one says the name Bloody Mary three times in front of a mirror her ghost will appear to tell your future. The British legend is quite different: Bloody Mary is a demon and only out to kill those who summon her—whether intentionally or not. Adapting the less violent version, Bloody Mary and her friends (Abdabs, Samantha, Malevolent and Viscera) are kind ghouls who share their experiences at a pub called Hemingway's while helping the humans who summon them.

Bloody Mary is a sweet girl who wants only to help people who are facing a difficult choice to make. Chris is a musician with a drinking problem whose life changed when he summoned Bloody Mary and fell in love with her. Viscera is Bloody Mary's best friend, a girl with mood swings who thinks nothing of telling people what she thinks of them. Abdabs, Viscera's brother, is a Grim Reaper who, despite his horrifying appearance, is "a cherry and happy fellow who accepts his role with joy." Malevolent is a banshee who had a sheltered upbringing and is now a bit naïve and a bit ditzy. Samantha, a succubus, is a rich, self-confident and aloof. Amicus is an incubus (the male version of a succubus—a creature that, through a kiss, draws the life spirit out of a person).

Herzog is the mysterious owner (a Wraith) of the Hemingway's Bar and appears to know the secrets people possess. Bloofer and Bathory are Samantha's equally beautiful succubus friends who idolize her. Rutherford and Cadinot are friends who are considered the Other Realm's "Eurotrash" as they have no respect for anyone. Carabosse is Malevolent's mother, a woman of pure evil and a threat to anyone who crosses her. The Wraith patrols the world seeking those succumbing to an addiction or pain to feed off their energy.

Cast: Hollie Taylor (Bloody Mary), Elizabeth Webster (Viscera), Craig Daniel Adams (Chris), Thomas Coombes (Abdabs), Erica Emm (Samantha), Jenny Fitzpatrick, Tanya Duff (Malevolent), Richie Hart (Amicus), David McGillivray (Herzog), Shinead Byrne (Bloofer), Cristina Lazaro (Bathory), Robert Feldman (Rutherford), Antonio Piras (Cadinot), Judith Rosenbauer (Carabosse), Tim Frost (The Wraith). **Credits:** *Producer:* Darren Chadwick-Hussein, Timur Charles. *Director:* Victoria Howell. *Writer:* Darren Chadwick-Hussein. **Comment:** British produced series that captures the flavor of the urban legend as opposed to the actual legend. The cast is creepy enough to convey that ghoulish look and the acting, writing and directing are very good. Well worth watching for something different.

Episodes: 7 episodes, labeled "Halloween: The Bloody Mary Show, Episode 1" through "Halloween: The Bloody Mary Show, Episode 7."

98 *Bloomers.* bloomerstheseries.com. 2013.

Francesca, an intelligent and confident bilingual girl from Brazil; Joanna, a devout Muslim raised by two lesbian mothers; Karen, a gorgeous girl who has made a career out of her looks; and Ross, raised by an alcoholic mother who feels he has to try harder to get what he wants, are friends and employees of Moxie, a hip Los Angeles–based underwear (or bloomers) company. The program chronicles the events that affect their lives (and those of their friends, Brooke, Clarissa and Vaughn) as they deal with the personal relationships that will change the course of each of their lives.

Francesca, the intimate apparel designer, is the material figure of the group; Brooke is gay and married to Ross, a heterosexual and works for the magazine *Wild America*. Ross, an accountant at Moxie is, although married to Ross, a womanizer who falls for impossible women (like Joanna). Joanna wears a hijab, prays five times a day and will not consume alcohol or engage in sexual activities (hence she is always trying to avoid Ross's advances).

Karen, the sexy girl with a vulgar vocabulary, is the lingerie model; Clarissa is Karen's estranged sister whose marriage ended when it was learned she could not have children. Vaughn is the bartender at the local pub hangout.

Cast: Fernanda Espindola (Francesca Rosa Tutu), Kirstin Barker (Clarissa Goldberg-Zimmerman), Jay Ali (Vaughn Daldry), Nathan Frizzell (Ross Buchanan), Holly Holstein (Karen Goldberg), Swati Kapila (Joanna Ali-Karamali), Matt Palazzolo (Brooke Matsumoto), Lisa Debra Singer (Yolanda Pissors), Tracey Verhoeven (Dr. Gail Vale), Calico Cooper (Lila Black), Rebecca Brooks (Miranda McNeil), Elizabeth Goldstein (Lisa "Boitano" Tutu), Sean Hemeon (Ken Turnage). **Credits:** *Producer:* Matt Palazzolo, Fernanda Espindola. *Director:* Henryk Cymerman, Tim Russ. *Writer:* Matt Palazzolo. **Comment:** While there is a gay and lesbian mix there is nothing objectionable and the program plays well with a good story line and excellent acting and production values.

Episodes: *1.* L.A. Baby! *2.* Have a Little Faith in Me. *3.* Sister. Sistah. *4.* Yoko Ono Homo. *5.* Hard to Be a Woman. *6.* Being Brave. *7.* Tiny People. *8.* Instinct. *9.* Unexpecting. *10.* You're So Hot. *11.* Clarissa Explains It All. *12.* The Whole Truth. *13.* On Thin Ice. *14.* Demons in the Night. *15.* The Uncertainty Principle. *16.* Mum's the Word. *17.* The Book of Bro. *18.* The Heart Is Lonely Hunted. *19.* Hard to Speak Easy. *20.* Yolanda Get Your Gun. *21.* What on Earth Are We Doing Here?

99 *The Blue Line.* webserieschannel.com. 2013.

A show within a show that follows the on-and-off screen lives of the cast of the fictional television series *The Blue Line*, a gritty crime drama about detectives with the Boston Police Department.

Cast: David C. Yee (Johnny Wang/Det. Mak), Wes McGee (Wesley Lite/Det. Briggs), Jorge-Luis Pallo (Fidel Rico/Det. Torres), Shawn Lockie (Stephanie Lynn/Det. Fitzpatrick), Tasha Ames (Chelsea/Barbie), Amy Paffrath (Amber Kneel), Tom Fisco (Justin "JB" Nieber), Jennifer An (Abbey Briggs). **Credits:** *Producer-Writer:* David C. Yee, Kevin Boston. *Director:* Kevin Boston. **Comment:** The idea is not new as many television programs used the same show within a show format with the 1977 CBS series *The Betty White Show* encompassing the same cop show scenario. Here, however, there is considerable vulgar language and more attention is paid to the cop show than personal lives.

Episodes: *1.* Rat. *2.* Method Addict. *3.* Bad Transition. *4.* Art Imitating Life.

100 *Board.* youtube.com. 2014.

Mel, Samantha and Campbell are friends who endlessly watch what they call "dreary daytime television" with an occasional movie thrown into the mix. Their landlord is trying to figure out why they waste their time glued to the TV and stories relate the reason why—to provide an ongoing critique about life and television culture.

Cast: Lauren Wigmore (Mel), Melody Schroeder (Samantha), Samuel Datactor (Campbell), Ian Alexander (Landlord). **Credits:** *Producer-Writer-Director:* Eddie Saint-Jean. **Comment:** While the program is basically the friends clicking from one channel to another it is well done and acted (and it is just not seeing the friends watching TV; clips of what they are viewing are also seen).

Episodes: 5 untitled episodes, labeled "Board Episode 1" through "Board Episode 5."

101 *The Bomb Shelter.* thebombshelter. com. 2011.

"It is the not-so-distant future. The world is no longer as it once was. The lucky died quickly. The not-so-lucky died a little less quickly" is stated as the program begins. But there are also those that have survived an unexplained apocalypse and have taken refuge in well-stocked bomb shelters that were created when fear spread that "the end was coming." Five people, Frank, a bachelor, and two married couples (Lisa and Bill; and Tanya and Jeff) have found safety in one such shelter. The program pokes fun at the circumstances that now surround them as they attempt to recreate a life like they previously enjoyed.

Cast: Mindy Montavon (Lisa), Brielle Batino (Tanya), Marcus Kiehl (Bill), Corey Landis (Frank), William Cannon (Jeff). **Credits:** *Producer:* Mindy Montavon. *Director:* Marcus Kiehl. **Comment:** Imaginative production with the dramatic license being taken to extremes that could never really happen in a bomb shelter. The entire program is well acted and produced and worth watching just for the situations that develop as one group of survivors wait for the time when they can return to the outside world.

Episodes: *1.* Lisa Leaves Bill. *2.* Someone Rode Bill's Bike. *3.* Bill Has a Surprise Party. *4.* Frank Starts a Book Club. *5.* Bill Runs a News Station. *6.* Jess Runs a Swim Club.

102 *The Book Club.* thebookclubseries. com. 2012.

Danny, Parvesh, Thomas and Chris are friends and members of The Book Club, a gathering of local people who enjoy reading and sharing their experiences about what they have just read. But for the friends, meetings are not normal as anything that can go wrong does and involves them in dangerous situations that they must somehow find a way to overcome and return to their beloved meetings. Whether it is finding a cursed relic to illustrate a point or battling a rival team of bookworms, the program charts all the chaos encountered as four guys just want to enjoy reading.

Cast: Danny Pudi (Danny), Parvesh Cheena (Parvesh), Thomas Fowler (Thomas), Chris Marrs (Chris), Gillian Jacobs (Penelope), Cristela Alonzo, Jaya Subramanian (Cobra Chai), Shalin Agarwal (Agent B), Dan Bakkedahl (The Author), Josh Drennen (Steve Hines), Daved Wilkins (Agent A). **Credits:** *Producer:* Justin Lin, Timothy Kendall, Chris Marrs, Danny Pudi. *Director:* Timothy Kendall. *Writer:* Chris Marrs. **Comment:** Well thought out program that presents a totally different approach to series about book clubs—from competitions between rival clubs, an evil villain (Cobra Chai) and even encounters with the supernatural.

Episodes: *1.* Letter of the Dragon. *2.* Enemies of the State. *3.* Dirty Jobs. *4.* The Cabin. *5.* All Valley. *6.* The Warrior Reads On

103 Boomerang Kids. youtube.com. 2013.

"You throw your children out and they come back home to live with you" opens the program. A group of friends, each just graduating from college but unable to find work due to the poor economy are forced to move back in with their parents—thinking it will be an easy life until they realize they need to find some kind of work or get out. The program charts what happens with each of the friends (Bob, Hollis, Leo and Kevin) as they face the adult world and responsibilities—even if it is from their parents' homes.

Cast: Karl Kwiatkowski (Bob Gillis), Kasey Elise (Hollis Mason), Jon Oswald (Leo Tanzi), Maxwell Towson (Kevin Jenkins), Meredith Thomas (Shannon Gillis). **Credits:** *Producer:* Narineh Hacopian. *Director:* Ryan Prows. *Writer:* Jake Gibson, Tim Cairo, Shaye Ogbonna, Ryan Prows, Maxwell Towson. **Comment:** The program, which appears to be filmed in soft focus (not as sharp as HD) to minimize harshness, is well acted but encompasses a needless use of foul language to achieve its comedy.

Episodes: *1.* Welcome Home, Get a Job. *2.* Mom's New Friend. *3.* Meat Lover's Pizza. *4.* Jazz Cigarettes. *5.* Cool Dad. *6.* Pimps Up, Leo Down. *7.* No. 1 Rob. *8.* Nonna's Grappa. *9.* White Man's Burden. *10.* Monkey Kevin. *11.* The Valley Warriors. *12.* Under Siege 2: Dark Territory 2. *13.* Michael Mann. *14.* Set It Off, Again. *15.* Foreverer Summer.

104 Boomerangs. boomerangsweb.com. 2013.

Alize, Rod and Yajaira, friends since high school and now college graduates discover, that due to the poor economy, they cannot find jobs and are forced to move back home with their parents in Oakland, California. The program relates what happens when the life they once knew at home no longer exists and they must make it on their own in the world—although until they can secure permanent jobs, from the comfort of their former childhood homes.

Cast: Kam Mendes Robinson, Andrea Garcia, Alysha English, Frederick McPherson, Sonia Whittle, Wendy Tremont King, Angela Vereau. **Credits:** *Producer:* Hadiyah Dache. *Writer:* Chas Jackson. **Comment:** Why the producer chose not to match up the character with the performer is unknown. The cast does a good job and the production, which is a bit talkative, is also well done.

Episodes: *1.* Welcome Home? *2.* How We Got Here. *3.* Job Insecurity. *4.* Test-os-terone. *5.* Enough Is Enough.

105 Bootleg Video. webserieschannel.com. 2014.

Jess is a young woman, born and raised in Iowa, who is seeking to begin a new life as a graphic designer. Her hopes are quickly shattered when she finds there are no available jobs and she is now desperately in need of money. While there are other options (like a supermarket checker) she decides on what she figures will be a more lucrative job—selling bootleg DVD's out of the back of her friend's (David) Volkswagen van. Jess's mishaps are charted as she begins her new career—not only by breaking the law but dealing with the strange people who become customers.

Cast: Karen Kobliska (Jess), Beau Batterson (David). **Credits:** *Producer-Writer:* Beau Batterson, Karen Kobliska. **Comment:** A good idea coupled with good acting and production values.

Episodes: *1.* Official #Bootleg Trailer for @BootlegVideo! *2.* #Customer Service. *3.* #Jess Rage. *4.* #Black Tar Kenny. *5.* #The Weedy Supercut. *6.* #Neighborhood Watch. *7.* #Freeze! Neighborhood Watch. *8.* #AniMating. *9.* #Sexual Pretension. *10.* @BootlegVideo: #BootlegBloopers.

106 Box of Crayons. boxofcrayonsweb series.com. 2013.

A spoof of the feature film *50 Shades of Grey* that told the story of Anastasia Steele (Dakota Johnson), a 21-year-old undergraduate who, for her college newspaper is assigned to interview Christian Grey (James Dornan), a wealthy 27-year-old entrepreneur. Grey appears normal at first glance but is anything but and Anastasia is soon seduced by him and swept into his depraved world of sexual experimentation. Encompassing that concept, *Box of Crayons* introduces Valaysia Veele, a college student who, for her school newspaper is assigned to interview Tristian Blue, a wealthy but mysterious entrepreneur. Valaysia has taken the place of her roommate (Blonde) who fell ill and was unable to conduct the interview. Blue was expecting Blonde (who is a blonde) and appears a bit disappointed at first because Valaysia is a brunette. But when Valaysia is compelled to keep repeating that she is a virgin, Blue becomes fascinated with her, so much so that he seduces her and through that seduction, the program relates what happens when Valaysia becomes a part of his depraved world of sexual experimentation (not to mention that he is also a vampire).

Valaysia's life is rather drab. She dresses like a Goth girl, is said to be a graduate of Miss Field's Beauty Academy and is employed by a button factory. It can be seen why she becomes infatuated with Blue and is swept off her feet. Blue mentions that his "crack-whore mother" turned him into a vampire when he was a child and now his world is like a box of crayons.

Cast: Stacy Ayn Price (Valaysia Veele), Zachary Spicer (Tristan Blue), Lara Clear (Blonde), Patrick Cann (Slave Boy), Alex Coehlo (Raul Ramiro), Nannette Deasy (Evil Bitch Mother), Stephanie LaCapra (My Inner Goddess). **Credits:** *Director:* David Rey. *Writer:* Stacy Ayn Price. **Comment:** Unlike the feature film, which is an erotic thriller, the series is anything but as Stacy Ayn Price plays her role as Valaysia with such naivety that you are attracted to her and drawn right into the plot. The acting is very good and the production, although a comedy, is dark and a bit eerie at times.

Episodes: *1.* Pilot. *2.* The Seduction. *3.* The Date. *4.* Nostromo. *5.* Walk of Shame. *6.* The Apocalypse. *7.* Hamlet.

107 *Boy Friends.* boyfriendswebseries.com. 2014.

Benny, Evan and Danny, along with a girl named Sam, are best friends living in New York City. They are in their early twenties and have been together since high school. The program interweaves the incidents that effects each of their lives as they seek relationships, work and face the challenges that lie ahead.

Cast: Keith Rubin (Ben), Claudine Quadrat (Sam), Charlie Covey (Danny), Adam Levinthal (Evan). **Credits:** *Producer-Writer:* Jon Steinfield, Andrew Hartman. *Director:* Jon Steinfield. **Comment:** While the program sports good acting and production values it is simply a look at the interactions between the friends.

Episodes: 2 untitled episodes, labeled "Episode 1" and "Episode 2."

108 *Boychicks.* youtube.com. 2013.

Ethan, Josh and Julian are friends who share an apartment. They are rather lazy, have little money and zero motivation to do anything outside of their apartment. While they seem content in their comfort zone, they do encounter "adventures"—the mishaps that only they can find in an apartment (and the program charts those less-than-spectacular encounters). Their one "great" idea to become rich is to invent an app and get the brother of actress Jennifer Lawrence to back them).

Cast: Josh Margolin (Josh), Julian Silver (Julian), Ethan Dawes (Ethan). **Credits:** *Producer-Writer:* Ethan Dawes, Josh Margolin, Julian Silver. *Director:* Ethan Dawes. **Comment:** Shows about slackers have appeared not only on the Internet but on network and cable TV as well as in syndication. While the production and acting is good, it differs only slightly from others of its kind in that virtually all the action is set in the apartment (venturing more "into the outside world" would have helped elevate it to a slightly higher level).

Episodes: *1.* Pilot. *2.* Fart Real Estate. *3.* Ethan Loves Jennifer Lawrence. *4.* Spring Breaker Taker. *5.* Ethnicity Mystery. *6.* Back to School.

109 *Boys Are Stupid, Girls Are Mean.* youtube.com. 2013.

"Boys are stupid. Girls are mean. That is all you need to know about high school relationships" exclaims a female narrator as she introduces viewers to a look at high school life that explores just how mean girls can be because the boys they know "are so stupid." Is it because boys "are just born that way" or is it because pretty girls can make them do anything just by smiling at them? The mystery is explored through three very pretty girls, Cady, Holly and Karen as they tackle relationships, help each other through the travails of teenage dating and use boys for their own means. It is boys like Jack, who didn't realize he was a boyfriend until he discovered he had a girlfriend (Karen), who seem to strengthen the theory that boys (possibly blinded by love) are just stupid.

Cast: Lindsay Bushman (Cady), Caroline Heinle (Karen), Megan Albertus (Holly), Noah Grossman (Jack), Laurel Brewer (Alex), Sam Wyatt (Alan), Emily Heaps (Beth), Juliette Frette (Ms. Monroe), Sam Gasch (Eugene), Michele Moreno (Ms. Stewart), Vanessa Marano (Narrator). **Credits:** *Producer-Writer-Director:* Johnny Severin. **Comment:** While the teen high school comedies *Saved by the Bell* and *Sweet Valley High* may come to mind, dismiss them as this show is not a copy and is more adult in nature. The girls are just as pretty as those in *Saved* and *Sweet* and some of the boys just as dumb, but how the dating situations are handled here is done in a humorous, adult way with problems explored and how they are resolved. The acting is good and production values outstanding (akin to the TV series that were mentioned).

Season 1 Episodes: *1.* Throw Like a Girl. *2.* Boyfriend? *3.* With Tongue. *4.* Dumbest Life Form on the Planet. *5.* Second Base. *6.* Friends? *7.* Know When to Stop Digging. *8.* From F Minus to C Minus. *9.* Worst She Can Do Is Say No. *10.* Just Like a Baby Seal. *11.* Jesus and Judas.

Season 2 Episodes: *1.* Things I Do. *2.* Perfectly Perfect Boobs. *3.* It Never Ends and You Can Never Win. *4.* Landscaping. *5.* Bikini. *6.* Swallow. *7.* IndieGoGo Campaign 8. Have I Taught You Nothing? 9. Dumbest Idea Ever.

110 Brain Eatin' Zombie Babies. youtube. com. 2010.

Baby, as he is called, is one of three children of a very pretty woman. Baby, and his infant one-year-old sister, Daisy, are zombies, while her teenage son (no name given) is a normal human. There is no background information on how a normal woman acquired her zombie babies (which are hand puppets) but even as infants Baby (but no so much Daisy yet) crave human brains for nourishment. The program follows the mother's efforts to raise her three children and how Baby seeks to secure his brain food.

Cast: Alyson Court (Mother). **Comment:** While baby is ravishingly disgusting, the program does come with a warning: "This Video Not Suitable for Small Children." Alyson Court as the mother is perfectly cast as she sees her zombie babies as just normal kids. The short sequences play very well and seeing what Baby does is just fun to watch. It is also the first time baby zombies where placed front and center—even if they are hand puppets.

Episodes: 30 episodes were produced but only the following are still on line: 1. Swing Time. 2. Snack Time. 3. Subway. 4. The Salesman. 5. The Big Burp. 6. Happy Birthday.

111 Break a Leg. breakaleg.tv. 2006.

Groommates, a television series about three ex-roommates, has been created by David Penn, a writer who finds himself in a most precarious situation: his sitcom will be produced but he must die "for the good of the network" when it ends its run. David is first seen being held captive with a gun pointed to his head and through his narration, the incidents that led to his predicament and what happens as *Groommates* progresses is charted.

Cast: Yuri Baranovsky (David Penn), Erik Bergmann (Andy Corvell), Hillary Bergmann (Jennifer John Bradley), Alexis Boozer (Amber Turnipseed), Daniela Dilorio (Francesca Scala), Skip Emerson (Sebastian Windlethorpe III), Daniel George (Humphrey Archibald), Justin Morrison (Chase Cougar). **Credits:** *Producer:* Justin Morrison, Vlad Baranovsky, Yuri Baranovsky, Dashiell Reinhardt. *Director:* Yuri Baranovsky. *Writer:* Vlad Baranovsky, Yuri Baranovsky, Justin Morrison. **Comment:** Sort of like an Internet version of what are called "Snuff" films (wherein someone is supposedly killed). While the program ends unresolved, it is none-the-less well acted and produced and a most unusual behind-the-scenes look at how networks are desperate for ratings and what they will do to achieve them.

Episodes: 1. Pilot. 2. Bad Press. 3. High Treason.

4. Back to School. 5. Detention. 6. Sex Ed. 7. Courting 101. 8. Cutting Class. 9. Sex and Violence. 10. Road Trip. 11. Drug Trip. 12. My Surreality. 13. Ghosts, Mimes and Partridges. 14. War Games.

112 Bricktown. webserieschannel.com. 2010.

With all episodes off line and only scattered text information available, the program appears to be a comical take off on the network reality shows *Big Brother* and *The Amazing Race*. A group of six young people (Nikki, Lisa, Kel, Split, Rich and Sam) are assembled by a director (Cain) to participate in a reality show first by agreeing to live in the same house then competing against each other in various challenges to emerge the winner at the show's conclusion.

Cast: Torey Byrne (Nikki), Ty Dickson (Kel), Martha Corkum (Lisa), Ann-Lisette Cavney (Split), Taylor Harris (Sam), Aaron Wertheim (Rich), Brett Garrett (Cain). **Comment:** The program states that this show "Could be the youngest comedy cast on a network, other than the director character, the main cast is age 19 to 24." The statement, even for 2010 is totally incorrect as TV series produced prior to this date, like *A Date with Judy*, *Meet Corliss Archer* and *Dobie Gillis* (1950s), *Gidget (1960s)* and *Saved by the Bell* and *Sweet Valley High (1990s)* used teenagers, even younger than 19, as the principal cast.

Episodes: 8 untitled episodes, labeled "Episode 1" through "Episode 8."

113 Broad City. youtube.com. 2014.

Internet version of the Comedy Central series of the same name that charts events in the lives of two very pretty young women (Abbi and Ilana) as they navigate life in New York City.

Cast: Abbi Jacobson (Abbi), Ilana Glazer (Ilana). **Credits:** *Producer:* Tony Hernandez, Dave Becky, Ilana Glazer, Lilly Burns. *Director:* Lucia Aniello, John Lee, Nicholas Jasenovec, Amy Poehler. *Writer:* Ilana Glazer, Abbi Jacobson, Tami Sagher, Lucia Aniello, Paul W. Downs, Chris Kelly. **Comment:** Perfect complimentary program with very good acting, production values and great situations that involve Abbi and Ilana with their off-the wall friends as well as the outrageous situations they encounter as they attempt to make ends meet.

Episodes: 1. What a Wonderful World. 2. Pu$$y Weed. 3. Working Girls. 4. The Lookout. 5. Fattest Asses. 6. Stolen Phone. 7. Hurricane Wanda. 8. Destination Wedding. 9. Apartment Hunters. 10. The Last Supper.

114 The Brodio. youtube.com. 2012.

Drew, Jon and Matt are roommates by accident when a dubious lease agreement forces them to live together. With no choice but to share the apartment, which they call "The Brodio," the program charts their efforts to live with one another, despite their vastly differing personalities and efforts not to kill each other in the process.

Cast: Matthew Schumacher (Matt Marino), Jonathan Acosta (Jon Jacot), Drew Gibadlo (Drew Dumass). **Credits:** *Producer:* Jonathan Acosta, Drew Gibadlo. *Director:* Jonathan Acosta. *Writer:* Jonathan Acosta, Drew Gibadlo, Matthew Schumacher. **Comment:** An "Odd Couple"-like program with three instead of two mismatched roommates. While the acting and production values are good, it is difficult to devise new situations that have not been done in one way or another on the many other such programs that use the same concept. Presenting a little mystery about who Matt really is (he is hiding something) adds a somewhat different twist.

Episodes: *1.* Pilot. *2.* In the Army Now. Again. *3.* Facebook Cancer.

115 *Brooklyn Is for Lovers.* youtube.com. 2008–2009.

A search for love as depicted through the experiences of five loosely connected friends living in Brooklyn, New York: Annie, a bi-sexual web TV show host; Ashley, a butch-type lesbian coffee shop waitress; Dee, Annie's boyfriend; Casey and Riggles (gay roommates) and Ashley, Annie's friend (who introduces Annie to a whole new world where "black girls are delicious").

Cast: Anne Mistak (Annie), Chris Riggleman (Riggles), Ashley D. Brockington (Ashley), Paul Case (Casey), James Rich (Dee). **Credits:** *Producer:* Zachary Ludescher, James Rich. *Writer-Director:* Shandor Garrison. **Comment:** The program is well-acted and produced but is adult in nature with strong language and sexual situations.

Episodes: *1.* Ass-Trology. *2.* Losing It. *3.* Third Eye Technique. *4.* Male Features. *5.* Gay Seinfeld. *6.* Boner's Owner. *7.* Frisky Business.

116 *Brooklynites.* youtube.com. 2013.

Brooklyn, New York, provides the backdrop for a look at the comical events that befall a group of friends (see cast) navigating life in a large city, whether they are alone or together.

Series producer Sarah Stockton requested that the program's official blurb be included: "Like the borough itself, *Brooklynites* is sexy, fun, a little dirty, and full of heart. From the cast, crew and locations, to the indie-heavy soundtrack, it's Brooklyn through and through. A show that according to *NYLON* magazine, 'manages to out-Girls Girls itself.'"

Cast: Sarah Stockton (Sarah), Keith Hamilton (Keith), Katherine Freeman (Kat), Zach Glass (Zac), Karen Rockower Glass (Karen), Aaron Knauer (Aaron). **Credits:** *Producer-Writer-Director:* Sarah Stockton, Keith Hamilton. **Comment:** Well acted and produced program that is simply a brief glimpse into the lives of the friends.

Episodes: *1.* Breaking Up Is Hard to Do. *2.* Back on the Horse, Hombre. *3.* Kicking and Swinging. *4.* Parlez-vous Passions Peak? *5.* Small and Safe or Big and Scary? *6.* Soap Stars and Stinky Chi. *7.* Two Worlds Collide.

117 *Bros.* youtube.com. 2013.

Watching the trailer will give you "From the guys who watch HBO... A show no one asked for" (being

Brooklynites. Series poster art (used by permission).

that *Bros* is a parody of the HBO series *Girls*). Here four friends, Drew, John, Mike and Tyler, living in New York City, are profiled as they struggle with all the emotional stress in their lives—from career challenges to relationship problems to just trying to survive each day on the streets of Manhattan.

Cast: John Michael Hastie (Mike Oberlander), Peter Hourihan (Tyler McCullen), Steve White (John Sullivan), Matthew Jacques (Drew Winterfield), Emily Droody (Michelle). **Credits:** *Producer:* Anthony DiMieri, Lindsay Copeland. *Director:* Anthony DiMieri. *Writer:* Anthony DiMieri, Joseph Lombardi. **Comment:** Although it is a show no one asked for, it is quite well done with good characterizations, acting and production values.

Episodes: *1.* Williamsburg. *2.* Murray Chill. *3.* Santa Conned.

118 The Brothers Russell. webserieschannel.com. 2013.

James and Phil are brothers. But is James better than Phil or is Phil better than James? Through a series of outrageous competitions, the brothers set out to discover who is the superior sibling with the program following the competitions they devise—from swivel chair racing to playing board games to eating the hardiest breakfast.

Cast: Phillip Russell (Philip), James Russell (James), Daniel Mazariegos (Daniel), Tom Capps (The Drunken Scholar), Charlie Desjardin (Charlie), Terence Krey (The Butler), Klement Tinaji (Klement). **Credits:** *Producer:* James Russell. *Director:* Phillip Russell. **Comment:** Adding a female presence would have helped make the program more interesting. It was meant to be ridiculous and works up to a point. But just how far can the competition be stretched before an outcome is determined? The ten episodes that were produced are quite outrageous and if you can accept swivel chair racing, the program is right up your alley.

Episodes: *1.* The Competition Begins. *2.* Chair Chase. *3.* Breakfast of Champions. *4.* Five Finger Fillet. *5.* Kick. *6.* Bored. *7.* Polishing a Turd. *8.* Blenders of Doom. *9.* Arm Wrestle Z. *10.* Brodown.

119 Brothers with No Game. brotherswithnogame.com. 2014.

London, England, provides the backdrop for a look at the lives of four twenty-something friends (Dorian, Junior, Marcus and Theo) as they face "a quarter-life crisis" while attempting to come to terms with responsibilities, family, work, friendships "and most notably women," but, although each has a distinctive personality, each also has a common trait—"they have no game."

Cast: David Avery (Marcus), Jay Marsh (Theo), Isaac Sosanya (Junior), Zephryn Taitte (Dorian), Magdalene Mills (Nicole), Natalie Duvall (Lisa), Dani Moseley (Simone), Venetia Twigg (Charlotte), Daniel Rusteau (Leon). **Credits:** The producers, writers and directors are all credited as "Brothers with No Game." **Comment:** Virtually every country that has produced an Internet series about 20, 30 or 40-somethings a bit confused about life have all portrayed them as it relates to their particular countries. *Brothers with No Game* is a bit more universal and has a broader appeal as what is portrayed here, especially with female relationships (mishaps) is something any one, from any country, can relate to.

Episodes: *1.* The Heskey Role. *2.* Domestics. *3.* Who's Got Game? *4.* Recession Dating. *5,6.* The House Party. *7.* The Interviews.

120 Bruce Goes Hollywood. youtube.com. 2013.

Bruce Dickinson is a young man with a "great" idea for a TV reality series called "World's Greatest Prom Date." The title is totally deceiving as the concept calls for high school participants to believe they will be attending a dream prom (with Lady Gaga as their guest singer). In reality, it will be a true nightmare with cameras catching all the chaos that occurs as the program sets situations up to be the worst night of their lives. But for the moment, it is only an idea. Life changes suddenly for Bruce when he is fired from his job at Target and, with his mother's encouraging, decides to pursue his TV idea. Through a connection from a friend, he contacts an agent, explains his idea and finds that the agent, Steve Winwood, is in real estate, not entertainment. Though surprised, but not discouraged, he persuades Steve to back him and the program charts what happens when an idiot with an idea meets a moron with no idea as to how to produce a TV show put their heads together and set out to make what each considers will be an Emmy-winning reality show.

Cast: Daved Wilkins (Bruce Dickinson), Chris Pentzell (Steve Winwood), Karen Chase (Viriginia). **Credits:** *Producer:* Sam Kimbrell, Loris Lora, Nick Jackman. *Writer-Director:* Sam Kimbrell.

Comment: A good idea that is well played out as two amateurs attempt to sell a TV show. The idea about intentionally bad reality shows has actually been done before but seeing how one goes about achieving such a goal is different. There is some vulgar language and the production itself and acting are good.

Episodes: *1.* The Pitch. *2.* The Transformers Auditions. *3.* Not Working. *4.* The ABC Pitch. *5.* Bruce's World's Greatest Prom of All.

121 The 'Bu. funnyordie.com. 2008.

Malibu Beach, California, is the setting for a look at four young people (who call it "The 'Bu" to indicate that they are still young and hip) as they navigate life in the beach resort community.

Cast: Pamela Fenton, Roger Croke, Jesse Miller, Daniel Merritt. Credits: *Creator:* David Eckford.

Comment: The video quality is a bit poor and the story is purposely made ridiculous as it has an animated rabbit (Frazzers) appear in a scene to tell viewers to put on their special red/blue glasses so they can see that segment in 3D. The cast are aware of such scenes and use props and motions to make the effect pop.

Episodes: Eight untitled episodes, labeled "Episode 1" through "Episode 8."

122 *Bubala Please.* blip.tv. 2011.

Two would-be gangsters (Jaquann and Luis) about to engage in a street fight suddenly become the best of friends when each sees (through medals that they wear) that they are both Jewish. With Jaquann being black and Luis Hispanic they decide they need to spread the word about Jewish traditions and present their versions of those traditions as each was brought up to observe.

Cast: Marcus Wayne (Jaquann), Rick Mancia (Luis). Credits: *Writer-Director:* Jacob Salamon.

Comment: A very good idea that is laden with vulgar language. The acting is good and the program is simply the two friends preparing Jewish meals or talking about Jewish traditions.

Episodes: *1.* Making Latkes. *2.* Hanukkah Bush. *3.* Game Day. *4.* We Doin' Purim Rap. *5.* Passover Munchies. *6.* Make Your Own Passover Haggadel. *7.* Gangster Bits. *8.* Shabbit. *9.* Finding a Jewish Girl.

123 *Bumps in the Night.* youtube.com. 2009.

"No Ghost" is a company run by Emmett, Greg and John, bumbling paranormal enthusiasts who are pool cleaners by day (for Senor Aqua Pool Cleaners) and ghost hunters by night. Their efforts to debunk ghostly happenings in a spoof of the Syfy TV series *Ghost Hunters* are presented.

Cast: Emmett Furey (Emmett), Greg Benevent (Greg), John Reha (John). Credits: *Producer:* Emmett Furey, John Reha, Greg Benevent. *Director:* Stuart Davis, Rudy Jahchan, Taryn O'Neill, Samuel Proof, Alethea Root, Greg Benevent, Emmett Furey, John Reha. *Writer:* Greg Benevent, Emmett Furey, John Reha, Ian Abrams. Comment: A comical paranormal spoof and nothing more with competent acting and adequate production values.

Episodes: *1–4.* Ghost in the Pool. *5.* The Haunted Apartment. *6.* Evil Parking Garage of Evil. *7.* Anti-Love Seat. *8.* Evil Whisperers. *9.* An Exorcise in Futility? *10.* Why Can't They All Be Psychic Girls? *11.* The Pink Scare. *12.* Too Much Chicken and Waffles Presents the Inaugural All Valley Ghost Hunting Tournament.

124 *Burning Love.* youtube.com. 2012.

Comical spoof of reality dating series (ABC's *The Bachelor* being the best example) that features an elimination competition wherein a man must choose one girl from a number of eligible women or a woman must decide which man from an equal number of possibilities is the right one for her (a later format changed the concept somewhat wherein those that found a compatible mate won money instead of love). The program can become a bit confusing because three versions (seasons) of the program do not exist but are mentioned in various other season episodes. The actual seasons are listed below (in bold) with the non-existent seasons (in italics) placed where they would have aired if they were produced.

Cast: Michael Ian Black as Bill Tundle, the Host. Credits: *Producer:* Ben Stiller, Jonathan Stern, Stuart Cornfeld, Michael J. Rosenstein, Ken Marino, Erica Oyama. *Director:* Kim Marino. *Writer:* Erica Oyama. Comment: The program is a well acted and produced matchmaking spoof. The actual season programs are listed in bold below.

Episodes:

1. *Burning Love with Joe Rutherford.* First of the non-existent seasons (Ben Stiller supposedly played the bachelor, Joe Rutherford).

2. **Season 1 Cast: Burning Love with Mark Orlando.** *Bachelor:* Ken Marino as Mark Orlando. *Contestants:* Kristen Bell (Mandy, a devout Christian), Jennifer Aniston (Dana, the girl of mystery), June Diane Raphael (Julie Gristlewhite, a psychotic woman), Ken Jeong (Ballerina, an exotic dancer), Malin Akerman (Willow, a homeless woman), Natasha Leggero (Haley, a gorgeous sex addict), Abigail Spencer (Annie, the personification of perfection), Carla Gallo (Tamara P, the blind woman), Janet Varney (Carly, a lesbian), Deanna Russo (Tamara G, a woman with medical issues), Beth Dover (Lexie, the woman obsessed with Mark), Morgan Walsh (Vivian, the pregnant girl), Helen Slayton-Hughes (Agnes, the mature woman), Noureen DeWulf (Titi, the woman of wealth).

3. *Burning Love: Hot for Teacher.* The non-existent second season (Abigail Spencer was said to play the bachelorette Annie).

4. **Season 2 Cast: Burning Love with Julie Gristlewhite.** *Bachelorette:* June Diane Raphael (Julie Gristlewhite). *Cast:* Jerry O'Connell (Henry, a contractor), Adam Scott (Damien, a psychologist), Joe Lo Truglio (Alex, a single father), Paul Scheer (Robby Z, a party planner), Rob Huebel (Simon, a prince), Nick Thune (Teddy, a musician), Brandon Johnson (Trevor, a bonus bachelor), Adam Brody (the Jewish bachelor), Colin Hanks (Allison, the dapper bachelor), Micael Cera (Wally, the hopeless romantic), Martin Starr (Leo, the child-like bachelor), Ryan Hansen (Blaze, a "bad boy"), Nick Kroll (Khris, a professional babysitter).

5. *Burning Love: A Fantasy Tale with Hathwell Granger Crisping.* The non-existent third season.

6. **Season 3 Cast: Burning Love: Burning Down the House.** Contestants compete for money. *Cast:* Natasha Leggero (Haley), Leslie Bibb (Beverly), June Diane Raphael (Julie), Joe Lo Truglio (Alex), Rob Huebel (Simon), Ryan Hansen (Blaze), Abigail Spencer (Annie), Alex Anfanger (Noah), Carly Craig (Felicia), Kumail Nanjiani (Zakir), Helen Slayton-Hughes (Virginia), Arman Weitzman (Hathwell), Morgan Walsh (Vivian), Rob Delaney (Kirk), Janet Varney (Carly), Beth Dover (Lexie), Ken Marino (Mark).

125 Bus People. funnyordie.com. 2012.

The program states "Nobody rides the bus in L.A. ... But if they did, it might be said like this." An anthology presentation that looks at brief incidents in the lives of people who actually ride buses (mostly their interactions with the other bus passengers). **Cast:** Carl Owens, Peter Elbling, Adrian Daz-Chapan, Khira Thomas, Judith Wilson, Thales Correa, Tara Kim, Savy Brown. **Credits:** *Director:* Stephen Thomas. *Writer:* Carl Owens, Stephen Thomas. **Comment:** Although only two episodes were made, the producers hit on a good idea (sort of an expanded idea of a taxi cab ride) with good acting and production values. **Episodes:** *1.* Wo-Man. *2.* Cuffs.

126 By the Book. blip.tv. 2013.

If nothing else members of the Buffalo (New York) Police Department's Organized Task Force are dedicated to one thing: bringing criminals to justice—just as long as it is not overly taxing and can be done within a reasonable amount of time. It has been 18 months and team leader Sergeant P.J. Rafferty believes he has finally gotten the goods on Big Sal, the head of a notorious crime family. The final step is to coordinate a raid and capture him. It sounds easy but for Rafferty's team (Rhonda, Kathleen, Chris and Dale) it is anything but a typical bust. The team is positioned to grab Big Sal once he returns home. A problem arises when Big Sal is late (not following his normal routine). The program charts what happens (and what the team members do) as they begin a stakeout and wait and wait (and wait) for Big Sal to come into their sights. **Cast:** Andre Colon (P.J. Rafferty), Angel Izard (Rhonda Ives), Arlynn Knauff (Kathleen Hanna), Michael J. Morel (Steve Womack), Will Mutka (Chris Callahan), Aleksander Ivicic (Jay Donovan), Juston R. Graber (Dale Grayden). **Credits:** *Producer-Director:* James Renzi. *Writer:* James Renzi, Will Mutka, Nigel Mahoney. **Comment:** The idea, while good, can only be stretched so far as the team attempts to amuse themselves by doing whatever they can to relieve boredom. It just becomes too stale too fast and can deter viewers from watching.

Episodes: *1.* 22 minutes. *2.* Personnel Problems. *3.* Alpacas and Hobbits. *4.* The Sitting Bored. *5.* Drunk and Disorderly. *6.* Big Bro. *7.* The Deep End. *8.* Snuggie Up. *9.* Finally, Finale.

127 The Cabonauts. youtube.com. 2009.

It is the 22nd century and travel from planet to planet has been accomplished. Rocket-powered taxi cabs have also become a part of the system. There are countless outposts and colonies in space and simply by calling Cabonauts, your destination is assured. Two such cabbies are Cyril, a cynical, veteran driver, and Harry, his young, naive partner (who is training to get his hack license). While acquiring passengers and bringing them to their destination begins each episode, the story quickly becomes a musical with an original song and video to depict the trip. **Cast:** Hayden Black (Cyril), Norm Thoeming (Harry), Monica Young (Lolita), Nichelle Nichols (CJ). **Credits:** *Producer-Writer-Director:* Hayden Black. **Comment:** A good idea that is, in a way, a futuristic version of the TV series *Taxi.* The addition of former *Star Trek* regular Nichelle Nichols (Lt. Uhura) adds to the fun but being that the pilot was made in 2009, it appears unlikely any additional episodes will be made. **Episodes:** *1.* Pilot.

128 C.A.K.E. The Series. youtube.com. 2013–2014.

Darryl (black) and Jan (white) are activists who have joined together to fight the world's biggest problem—racism with their belief that everyone should love one another. They have formed an organization called Color Friends and their mission is to wipe out racist behavior and make the world a non-prejudiced family. They have recruited several members (Justice, Misfit and Slice) and the program relates the missions the organization tackles to change how certain people view others. **Cast:** Ericka Harden (Justice), Daryl Anthony Harper (Slice), Kendra Hill (Misfit), Ayo Sorrells (Muscle), Joshua Denhardt (Adam), Bethany Blackwell (Jan). **Credits:** *Producer-Writer-Director:* Ericka Harden. **Comment:** The program, with its attractive cast is well done and produced and lives up to a statement released by the producer: "Created to promote a system of justice by educating what racism is and how it affects non-white people all over the world. We believe black entertainment [an African American production] can be constructive, witty and funny." When searching the program, the title above should not be shortened or it will bring up a CBS program called *Cake* (about three craft-making friends). **Episodes:** 11 untitled episodes, labeled "Episode #1.1" through "Episode #1.11."

129 Callbacks. callbackswebseries.tumblr. com. 2014.

The White/White Casting Agency is a Hollywood firm run by M.J. (Mary Jane) White and her husband Thom. M.J.'s only desire is to cast a role and have that person win an Oscar. Thom, on the other hand, only cares about money and will cast anybody in any type of role that is required. Also a part of their lives is Jan, M.J.'s cousin, who works as their assistant and is just looking to have the best time he can in Hollywood. The program is somewhat of a behind-the scenes look at what happens at a casting agency and the people who are its clients (especially when M.J. lands a movie script called *Country Retreat* and the agency must scramble to cast it).

Cast: Toks Olagundoye (M.J. White), Michael Scovotti (Thom White), Matt Jones (Jan), Mimi Chan (Claire, the office assistant). **Credits:** *Producer-Writer:* Toks Olagundoye. *Director:* Jon Michael Kondrath. **Comment:** For some unknown reason the program has no opening theme song and begins only with a warning "Some language and content may not be suitable for children." While that may discourage some viewers, the program is a top notch production and should not be missed. Toks Olagundoye (from the ABC series *The Neighbors*) is outstanding as M.J. and involves herself with a well-chosen cast that makes the show work.

Episodes: *1.* Pilot: Loo(m). *2.* Millipede vs. the Sun King. *3.* We Got Her. *4.* Person of Color.

130 CandyLand. candylandseries.com. 2012–2013.

Pacific Palisades Preschool is not just an ordinary educational institution in Southern California. With its motto, "Where the Top One Percent Get Their Smarts," it is a grammar school for the privileged children of wealthy parents. Children who do not meet its standards are simply not welcomed. Ema is such a young girl, newly enrolled at the school, and through her experiences, a view of school life as few children ever experience is depicted.

Kale, the vegetarian (called a Vegan) is Ema's friend; Pear is the school heartthrob; Bethany #1 and Bethany #2 (sometimes called "The Bethany's") are the super rich, spoiled young girls who are also the school's "back-stabbing bitches"; Lucy, the ultra snob (the school's Queen Bee), leads the Bethany's (all members of the school clique, The Toddlers Tiaras Crew); and Beckham is the spoiled rich kid.

Cast: Tatum Hentemann (Lucy), Katherine Manchester (Ema), Mikey Effe (Pear), Mma-Syrai Alek (Bethany #1), Gracie Hall (Bethany #2), Wes Watson (Beckham), Shayna Brooke Chapman (Kale), Olivia Choate (Ema's mother). **Credits:** *Producer:* Win Bates, Damian Horan, Ali Scher. *Director:* Win Bates, Samian Horan, Ali Scher. *Writer:* Win Bates,

Jeremy Cohen, Damian Horan, Jonathan Langager, Ali Scher, Courtney Thomas. **Comment:** A pre-teen version of most notably *Beverly Hills, 90210*, although aspects of *Saved by the Bell* and *The O.C.* can also be seen. The production is top rate and the child performers all handle their roles quite well. It is also a bit of a shock at first glance to see such young children dress and act beyond their years—as it is something that is rarely seen on television in the manner presented here. While Ema is sweet and innocent, the Bethany's are real "adult" bitches and Lucy the ultimate, nasty snob—a unique depiction not even seen on the shows it copies.

Episodes: *1.* The New Girl. *2.* Beckham's Bash. *3.* Keep Your Friends Close. *4.* Confessions of a Bethany. *5.* Mad, Bad and Dangerous to Know. *6.* The Real Lucy. *7.* Oops, I Did It Again.

131 Canvassing. funnyordie.com. 2011.

Thom is a recent college graduate with no ambition, no applicable skills and absolutely no job prospects. As boredom sets in and he feels that he needs to find some meaning to life, he joins a team of somewhat bizarre yet passionate political idealists. While seriously doubting what he has done at first, he soon finds that these are his people and actually involved in caring about something other than himself. Thom is followed as he matures in the world of canvassing.

Cast: Casey Schlosser (Thom), Rebecca Ribich (Laiken), Will Spagnola (Jon), Stephanie Moise (Dylan), Nicole Honore (Tessa), Darri Ingolfsson (Marcos), Alex Sanborn (Josiah), Darrel Cherney (Danny), Jon Cahill (Chad), Sara Weinshenk (Jessica), Matt Black (Larry). **Credits:** *Producer:* Stephanie Moise. *Director:* Nicholas Collenti. *Writer:* Katrina Albright, Nicholas Collenti, Stephanie Moise. **Comment:** Something different when it comes to politically themed programs that is well cast and played. A shot above others of its kind although its roots can be traced back to network series of the past. Episodes: *1.* Pilot. *2.* Stalin. *3.* Bill, Bill. *4.* Elbow Tap. *5.* James Franco. *6.* Party Down. *7.* Mitch. *8.* Assistant, Assistant. *9.* Them's the Rules. *10.* It's Larry.

132 Capital Culture. youtube.com. 2014.

Wellington, New Zealand, provides the setting for a look at the lives of a group of young, creative women as they navigate life: Lennon, 27, works in a vintage clothing store and runs an Internet fashion blog; Imogen, 24, is a mixologist whose life revolves around devising the next great drink while working as a bartender; Willoughby, 25, an aspiring singer/songwriter who currently works as a café waitress and D.J. but hopes for that one gig that will change her life; and Frankie, 23, an aspiring actress and filmmaker who yearns to produce her own films.

Cast: Miriam O'Connor (Lennon Mackenzie), Isobelle Walton (Imogen Garcia), Martine Harding (Willoughby Stone), Virginia O'Connor (Frankie Mackenzie). **Credits:** *Creator-Writer:* Isobelle Walton, Martine Harding, Miriam O'Connor, Virginia O'Connor. **Comment:** A very well acted and produced New Zealand series that may have a drawback for some: getting use to the foreign accents. The subject matter is interesting and it does take a few minutes to adjust to the dialogue. A nice touch is showing the leads as real people as they talk to the camera to relate what is happening to them.

Episodes: *1.* Capital Culture Teaser. *2.* Frankie: The Filmmaker. *3.* Willoughby: The Coffee Snob. *4.* Imogen: The Mixologist. *5.* Lennon: The Fashion Blogger. *6.* Oriental Bay. *7.* Jakey. *8.* Fashun. *9.* Anahera. *10.* Scar: The Ex Boyfriend. *11.* Saturday Afternoon. *12,13.* The Gallery.

133 *Capitol Hill.* youtube.com. 2014.

In a small hillbilly-like town in Portland, Oregon, lives Roses Smell, a not-so-pretty woman (bald, beard, moustache, no figure) who has a dream of traveling to "the greatest, most beautiful city in the world," Seattle, Washington. Roses had been raised by her two mean sisters since the death of her mother (who took her own life by drowning when Roses "was a wee child"). After confiding in her pet goat that she is about to embark on the greatest challenge in her life, Roses departs for Seattle. Immediately after arriving a thief steals Roses' luggage, leaving her without money, clothes or a place to stay. Seeing what has happened, a television producer (Tanya) comes to Roses' aid and allows her to stay with her until she can find a job. The following day, life changes for Roses when Tanya finds her a job—as the host of a TV talk show called *Women in the Workplace*. The program charts Roses' adventures as she attempts to follow the words her mother once told her: "No point in living unless you follow every dream."

George is the chauvinistic TV station owner (harasses female employees); Dottie is the TV show host who despises Roses for taking the spotlight away from her; Helen Pen Poison is the mystery writer-forensic detective; and Mother Terisha is Roses' nemesis, the nun who hates gays (responsible for "aborting nine gay babies") and on a mission to destroy the gay population of Seattle. **Cast:** Waxie Moon (Roses Smell), Robbie Turner (Dottie Pearl), Alexandra Cramer (Tanya), Mark Siano (George), Aleksa Manilla (Helen Pen Poison), Brian "Mama Tits" Peters (Cookie), Miss Indigo Blue (Poops), Hannah Victoria Franklin (Sluttonia), Jonathan Crimeni (The Mayor), Syndi Deveraux (Sheriff Johnson), Kaleb Kerr (Cousin Rocky), Nettie Ann Snickle (Mother Terisha), Jennifer Jasper (Sister Malvita), Jewcy That (Michelle). **Host:** Ben De La Crème. **Credits:** *Producer-Writer-Director:*

Wes Hurley. **Comment:** While no one is exactly sure what Roses is (a he or a she, but is treated like a she), the program, which encompasses drag queen performers, is not only enjoyable from the first episode, but the acting and production values are top rate.

Episodes: 10 untitled episodes, labeled "Episode 1" through "Episode 10."

134 *Car Jumper.* channel101.com. 2012.

A man, known only by his code name of Car Jumper, is a skilled acrobat whose death-defying job involves jumping from one moving car (or motorcycle or truck) to another to apprehend escaping criminals. He is also an agent of The Secret Government Force, a U.S. organization whose only function is to apprehend criminals who attempt escape through vehicles. Colonel Theodore Drax heads the unit; his other team members are Kharizma (espionage expert), Bricks (demolition expert), MCX3 (a rapper), Cups (the world's fastest cup stacker), Querty (computer expert; "can type 80 words a minute"), and Soggy Biscuits ("can eat six saltine crackers in one minute"). The program follows the missions that are called for when some nefarious, dastardly villain attempts to escape the clutches of the law by car.

Cast: Jim Klimek (Car Jumper), Brady Novak (Colonel Drax), Whitey Avalon (Querty), Michael Marshall (MCX3), Bobby Miller (Soggy Biscuits), Erni Walker (Kharizma), Emmet Shoot (Cups), Todd Wright (Bricks). **Credits:** *Producer:* David Seger, Spencer Strauss. *Director:* David Seger. *Writer:* David Seger, Spencer Strauss. **Comment:** Exceptionally well done (if not wacky) program with actual car jumping scenes. The agents are a bit-off-the wall (perhaps the only recruits the government could find) and the mix of action and comedy works well here.

Episodes: 23 untitled episodes, labeled "Episode 1" through "Episode 23."

135 *Care-y About You with Evan and Mariah.* webserieschannel.com. 2014.

She is very pretty and very talented and singer Mariah Carey has "teamed" with comedian Evan Zelnick to co-star on a web series to relate their wisdom to all who view their program. While "their" wisdom is only the words spoken by Evan, Mariah does "check in" with clips from her songs that relate to the topic at hand. Mariah's absence is always explained as the episode begins and the program relates Evan's views on what he believes should be the views of everyone else. Also known as *I Care-y About You.*

Cast: Evan Zelnick (Evan/Various Other Characters). **Credits:** *Writer-Director:* Evan Zelnick. **Comment:** "Uplifting, motivating and wildly vulgar, you won't want to miss a moment of this wacky web series" is stated in the on-line program description. Evan Zelnick is a most unusual host and his deadpan presentation does make the show (despite the fact that Mariah is not present). The overall concept is well done and entertaining—even if you find yourself totally disagreeing with what Evan has to say.

Episodes: *1.* Inner Strength. *2.* Lust. *3.* Religion. *4.* Friendship. *5.* Perseverance. *6.* Anytime You Need a Friend. *7.* Make It Happen. *8.* Outside. *9.* Fly Like a Bird.

136 The Carla Critical Show. webseries channel.com. 2012.

"Hello friends I haven't met, I'm Carla Critical and I wear red from head to toe so you don't have to" is the program's opening that introduces viewers to a woman who is critical about everything and, through a selected topic (and clips from various sources) sets out to prove why it is necessary to be critical.

Cast: Colleen Hubbard (Carla Critical). **Credits:** *Producer-Writer:* Colleen Hubbard. *Director:* Larry Bograd. **Comment:** Something different with a good presentation and acting. Carla, acting as a moderator, is always dressed in red and her comments and observations on the social scene are well thought out and presented—with guests sometimes appearing to give their own opinions.

Episodes: *1.* In a Better Place. *2.* Head, Shoulder, Knees and Toes. *3.* Just Don't Look. *4,5.* That Tingly Feeling. *6.* Interview with a Vampire. *7.* Women of a Certain Age. *8.* Stop with the Goat Cheese Already.

137 The Casting Room. thecasting room.com. 2011.

How an actor approaches a casting call is showcased with a look at the scene he is asked to perform and how he goes about doing it. Based on the experiences of one of Canada's top casting directors, the program was devised to show actors in the industry how to prepare for and what to expect from auditions.

Cast: Stephanie Gorin (Casting Director), Naomi Snieckus (Casting Assistant). **Credits:** *Producer-Writer:* Stephanie Gorin, Naomi Snieckus. *Director:* Matt Baram, Brett Blackwell. *Writer:* Stephanie Gorin, Naomi Snieckus. **Comment:** While virtually all the actors listed as the episode titles are Canadian and will most likely be unfamiliar to American viewers, the program is still quite amusing and different as

it gives the onlooker an insight into what really happens (the mishaps) at casting calls.

Season 1 Episodes: *1.* Eric Peterson. *2.* Marty Adams. *3.* Jayne Eastwood. *4.* Jesse Bostick and Demetrius Joyett. *5.* Charlotte Arnold. *6.* Lori Alter. *7.* Ed Robertson. *8.* Al Sapienza.

Season 2 Episodes: *1.* Ennis Esmer. *2.* Joseph Motiki. *3.* Debra McGrath. *4.* Devon Bostick. *5.* Peter Keleghan. *6.* Aislinn Paul. *7.* Anand Rajaram. *8.* Allana Harkin and Ava Preston. *9.* Joe Bostick.

Season 3 Episodes: *1.* Colin Mochrie. *2.* Matt Baram. *3.* Scott Thompson. *4.* Sheila McCarthy. *5.* Dan Redican. *6.* Jonas Chernick. *7.* Suresh John. *8.* Ron Pederson. *9.* Aunt Ethel.

Season 4 Episodes: *1.* Sean Cullen. *2.* George Strombo. *3.* Ron James. *4.* Kari Skogland. *5.* Munro Chambers.

138 Castle Siege. youtube.com. 2011.

There are groups of people who have become obsessed by certain characters (whether from history,

Castle Siege. Series poster art (used by permission).

motion pictures, comic books or TV) and gather to live their fantasies through role playing. For those that participate the fantasy ends when their little game ends. But for some, the game never ends. Such is the case of a group of medieval role players who believe it is not a game and they are really living in the Middle Ages and need to right wrongs and defeat the evil that exists in their imaginary world. The program follows a group of modern-day people who begin a wacky quest to save the world in a manner consistent with their medieval way of thinking (having to defeat the evil Mage Zarcon and acquire the magic "Sword of Silence" to do so).

Cast: Stephen Folker (Lord Parsley), David Goodloe (Lord Darkness), Sarah Garvey (Lady Lisa), Bri Kinney (Castle Member), Thomas Ely Sage (Patrick the Peasant), Paul Berge (Mage Zarcon), Trena Penson (Wendy the Witch), Jim Plovanich (Gary Shire). **Credits:** *Producer-Writer-Director:* Stephen Folker. **Comment:** The program immediately captures your attention with a nicely produced antiquated opening theme song. The program is meant to be silly and it lives up to that goal with a cast of role players encountering various adventures in modern times but seeing what they encounter as evil from their medieval disillusions.

Episodes: *1.* For the Alliance. *2.* Castle Siege: Episode 2. *3.* Parting Ways. *4.* The Long Journey. *5.* A New Beginning. *6.* Maiden Stew. *7.* A Wizard's Fury. *8.* Epic Battle.

139 Castlehassle. webserieschannel.com. 2013.

Queendom is a medieval kingdom ruled by the Queen and her friend and advisor, the Countess. All was peaceful in the kingdom until a group of rogue knights, the Tobedoos, arrived and, believing Queendom was easy pickings, now want to overthrow it and establish their own rule. Now, with their kingdom threatened, the Queen and the Countess must protect it and the program follows their various attempts to thwart the Tobedoos and retain control of Queendom.

Cast: Iulia Nastase (Queen/Mr. Pink Pig), Marlene Bearden (Countess), Jason Lantz (Watt the Goblin/Tobedoo 2), Cheryl Fowle (The Cherie), Lynn West (Frosty Witch), Tina Lee Johnson (Giggly Witch), Ross Hammond (Tobedoo 1), Tyler Lantz (Henry), Kelly Young (Desdemona), Neva Howell (The Nanny), Jeffrey McBath (The Messenger), Mike Menart (Gray Knight). **Credits:** *Producer-Writer-Director:* Iulia Nastase. **Comment:** Trying to find the story line by watching the episodes may be a bit difficult as the presentation is quite confusing. Characters, using a medieval style of speech are hard to understand at times and talk directly into the camera. There is virtually no action and the talkative scenes can be become quite boring. The cinematography is very poor and the acting can

be seen as people just trying to act. There are puppets thrown into the mix with a ridiculous sub story line about crows with the ability to carry off kingdom residents and take them into the future (as happens here with the Queen who too easily adjusts to the 21st century). The knights are wimpy, witches are seen with poor special effects and the Queen, in medieval times, has braces on her teeth.

Episodes: *1.* It's Us of Course. *2.* Dragon Farts. *3* Kidnapped by Crows. *4.* The Yearly Bath at Hammam. *5.* Party in Medieval Style.

140 Cat Chiropractor. funnyordie.com. 2009.

One man: Dr. Charlize Therond. One mission: Rid the world's cats of their feline problems. Because he cannot adjust to people but can to cats, Therond has come to the conclusion that it is his duty to help cat owners solve their pet's problems (from a cat with a twisted tail to a cat that lost its meow). Delusional as he is, he begins his quest with the program chronicling his meowing experiences in a world where no sane person has gone before.

Cast: Bobby Tisdale (Dr. Charlize Therond). **Credits:** *Director:* John Allison. *Writer:* Bobby Tisdale.

Comment: A bit far out but enjoyable. Luckily for the audience, Therond's treatments are, for the most part, not shown as what he does to those poor felines would constitute cruelty to animals.

Episodes: 4 untitled episodes, labeled "Episode 1" through "Episode 4."

141 Cataclysmo and the Battle for Earth. cataclysmo.com. 2008.

The time travelers (Johnny and Bucky) from *Cataclysmo and the Time Boys* (see entry) are reunited and placed on present-day earth with their companion, Samantha, in a tale that has them attempting not only to save Earth from an army of ravaging gorillas from the future but stop the evil Dr. Crankshaft from his efforts to rule the universe.

Cast: Brian Walton (Johnny Zanzibar), Erin Evans (Samantha), Chris Hartwell (Bucky Stallion), Nate Bell (H.G. Welles), Kal Bennett (Queen of Atlantis), Jai Khalsa (Ameila Earhart), Jesse Grotholson (Dr. Crankshaft). **Credits:** *Producer:* Joshua Sikora, Nathan Jeffers, Chris Hartwell. *Director:* Anthony Parisi. *Writer:* Kevin Christensen, Anthony Parisi, Joshua Sikora. **Comment:** With all episodes taken off line a comment is not possible.

142 Cataclysmo and the Time Boys. itunes. com. 2007–2008.

In a futuristic time a war has broken out and scientists theorize that it can be stopped from happening if it never occurred. To accomplish the task, a time machine is built (by H.G. Welles) and two young men (Johnny, a soldier, and Bucky, a chef) are chosen to return to the earth of 2007 and prevent a mad scientist (Dr. Crankshaft) from setting in motion the events that will lead to war in the future. Johnny and Bucky are sent back in time and, in 2007, they immediately befriend a girl of the time, Samantha, who agrees to help them after she is convinced they are who they say—people from the future (when Bucky demonstrates his ray gun). The program follows the trio as they try to stop a disaster before it happens. See also *Cataclysmo and the Battle for Earth*, the spin off series.

Cast: Brian Walton (Johnny Zanzibar), Erin Sullivan (Samantha), Chris Hartwell (Bucky Stallion), Jesse Groth Olson (Dr. Crankshaft), Kenlyn Kanouse (Mildred Crankshaft). **Credits:** *Producer:* Joshua Sikora. *Director:* Kevin Christensen. *Writer:* Kevin Christensen, Anthony Parisi, Joshua Sikora. **Comment:** Although the special effects are minimal and the gorillas from the future that use a force field to travel to present-day Erath are obvious as actors in costumes, the program, with its mix of science fiction and comedy is well done and amusing to watch.

Episodes: *1.* Under Crimson Sky. *2.* They Died with Their Pants On. *3.* In the Land of the Blind. *4.* Men Like Gods. *5.* The House at the End of the World. *6.* Strangers in a Strange Land. *7.* The Day the Internet Stood Still. *8.* Meanwhile, in the Underwater Lab... *9.* Across the Stars. *10.* Gorillas in the Midst. *11.* Monkey Bar Skirmish. *12.* A Close Call. *13.* Trapped Under the Tide. *14.* The Underwater Demise. *15.* Forget Me Not. *16.* Sands of Chaos. *17.* The Origin of the Species. *18.* The Food of the Gods and How It Came to Earth. *19.* The Shape of Things to Come. *20.* Blockade Runners. *21.* The Last Stand. *22.* Heart of Darkness. *23.* The Good, the Mad and the Ugly. *24.* There's No Place Like Home.

143 Catherine: A Story in 12 Parts. youtube.com. 2013.

Catherine appears to be a woman who encompasses the style of another time but lives in the present. Her appearance, attitude and work ethics are simply old fashioned and there is an air of mystery about her. The program begins with Catherine being rehired from a company that she left for unknown reasons and relates how she deals with office politics and the world that surrounds her.

Cast: Jenny Slate (Catherine), Chris Johnen (Ian), Autumn Withers (Jean), Marshall Givens (Jerome), Dan Wingard (Philip), Nelson Cheng (Richard), Raquel Bell (Robin), Brandi Austin (Samantha). **Credits:** *Producer:* Daniel Kellison, Doug Deluca, Mickey Meyer, Debbie Chesebro. *Director:* Dean Fleischer-Camp. **Comment:** Enjoyable program from the moment Catherine is introduced. There is something about her and keeping the viewer in the dark works. The acting and production are top rate.

Episodes: 12 untitled episodes, labeled "Chapter 1" through "Chapter 12."

144 CaucAsian. youtube.com. 2013.

Joe and Karen are a young married couple who have a most unusual baby. A freak of nature has occurred and while they are Caucasian, the baby (whom they name Marie) looks Asian. With only the best intentions for Marie, Joe and Karen decide to "Asianize" her and raise her in an Asian culture of her choice. The program chronicles their odyssey from Chinatown and Bryant Park to the West Village and Little Manila as they immerse themselves in another culture for the sake of their child.

Cast: Melisa Breiner-Sanders (Karen), Joshua Levine (Joe), Kana Conroy (Marie). **Credits:** *Producer:* Melisa Breiner-Sanders. *Writer-Director:* Joseph Patrick Conroy. **Comment:** A unique idea that really works. The acting is very good and, while not meant to be offensive, there are always those that will find it just that.

Episodes: *1.* Pilot: The Birth. *2.* The Chinatown Connection. *3.* When All Else Fails, Go Online. *4.* Dating Games. *5.* Big Trouble in Manila. *6.* No Need to Talk.

145 The Cavanaughs. youtube.com. 2010–2012.

CaucAsian. **Series poster art (used by permission).**

The Cavanaughs. Cast photograph (copyright © 2010 OAPCA Productions).

In 2008 a TV pilot film called *The Cavanaughs* was produced starring drag queen Noreen Cavanaugh. It was rejected by the networks and placed on the shelf until 2010 when Noreen decided to revise the project (about a group of offbeat actors seeking unconventional ways to keep their small theater in Hollywood operational). The program charts the process that goes into making a TV series with a particular focus on the cast and how they slowly create a family of their own.

Noreen Cavanaugh, the "woman" for whom *The Cavanaughs* was written, is a flamboyant drag queen actress (man pretending to be a woman) and takes great pride in everything she does.

Bryan, the program's exasperated writer, is gay and has the uneasy job of retooling the program and its characters.

Maddie, Brian's writing and producing partner is a confident woman who cares deeply for her friends and watches over them like they were her own family. She is also a lesbian and cares deeply for an actress on the show (Charley).

Charley, best friends with Maddie, is a chain-smoking actress and secretly a lesbian (she fears revealing her secret will tear her family apart).

Sarah and Mark are actors on the show who share a love-hate relationship. Sarah is a bit quirky and became known through her work in TV commercials; Mark is a successful working actor but too confident as his actions make him appear a bit off-center to those he meets.

Scott, Sarah's best friend is, like Sarah, a good person at heart and hopes to embark on a singing career.

Hope is the producer hired by Noreen to make *The Cavanaughs* happen no matter what it takes to do it.

Beverly is Noreen's drag queen friend and confidante.

Cast: Grant Landry (Mark), Cwennen Corral (Maddie), Deborah Estelle Philips (Charley), Adrian Morales (Bryan), Michael Womack (Noreen Cavanaugh), Amanda Broadwell (Sarah), Daniel Rhyder (Scott), Percy Rustomji (Dumas), Mikey Lamar, Ryan Kibby (Shea), Camille Bennett (Hope), Carla Marie (Charlotte), Lars Slind (Cary), Nathaniel Vincent (Bingo), Emily Sandack (Rebecca), Katie Caprio (Kirsten), Dina Martinez (Herself), Kimberly Fox (Hope), Georgan George (Marlena), Eric Van (Beverly Fairfax), Matthew Trbovich

(Zack), Kevin Makely (Justin), Patrick O'Sullivan (Chris). **Credits:** *Producer:* Cwennen Corral, Adrian Morales, Bryon MacDonald, Ryan Kibby, Joshua Gollish. *Director:* Bryon MacDonald, Adrian Morales, Cwennen Corral, Nicole Olmsted, Ryan Kibby. *Writer:* Ryan Kibby, Adrian Morales. **Comment:** A bit of everything: lesbians (Maddie and Charley), gays (Mark, Brian and Dumas), drag queens (Noreen and Beverly) and straights in a well tuned program that captures the feeling of what goes into the making of a TV sitcom.

Season 1 Episodes: *1.* Think of Me. *2.* Woman in White. *3.* If Only. *4.* Half a Moment. *5.* Stop! Wait! Please! *6.* Don't Know How to Love Him. *7.* Memory. *8.* Dice Are Rolling. *9.* Seeing Is Believing. *10.* Likes of Us. *11.* Let Me Finish. *12.* Point of No Return.

Season 2 Episodes: *1.* The Wine and the Dice. *2.* If Not For Me. *3.* Beautiful Game. *4.* So Much to Do. *5.* Poor Fool. *6.* Dear Old Friend.

Season 3 Episodes: *1,2.* Toast of the Town. *3.* I Remember. *4.* Let's Talk About You. *5.* Wrestle with the Devil. *6.* Surrender. *7.* Memory of a Happy Moment. *8.* Heaven by the Sea. *9.* Unsettled Scores. *10.* Twisted Every Way.

Season 4 Episodes: *1.* With One Look. *2.* Try Not to Be Afraid. *3.* The Arrest. *4.* Too Late for Turning Back. *5.* Nothing Like You've Ever Known. *6.* Getaway with Anything. *7.* Forgive My Intrusion. *8.* Damned for All Time. *9.* Dead Zone. *10.* An Angel in Heaven. *11.* Once Upon Another Time.

146 *Cc':d.* blip.tv. 2013.

Segal and Reinhold is a mid-size Madison Avenue advertising agency that is surviving through the acquisition of small accounts. Denise Barrows is its manager and life not only changes for her, but for her group of creative minds (as she calls her employees) when Budz Beer, a Fortune 500 account becomes a client—a client so big that it can put Segal and Reinhold on the New York advertising map. The only problem—the client wants a campaign pronto (within two days). The program follows Denise and her team (in particular Jason and Lawrence) as they set out to break a record and come up with a campaign that will not only impress the client but become a stroke of marketing genius.

Cast: Charlie LeGrice (Denise Barrows), Jordan Turchin (Jason Rhodes), Eric Loscheider (Lawrence Booth), Ingrid Vollset (Caroline Schaffer), Michael Marcel (Malcolm Reed), Ryan Dacalos (Maynard Dacalos). **Credits:** *Producer-Writer-Director:* Henry Rembert. **Comment:** Programs concerning advertising are nothing new. 1980 saw *Bosom Buddies* and 2012 gave us *The Crazy Ones*. *Cc':d* is more like the Robin Williams–Sarah Michelle Gellar series *The Crazy Ones* in concept (going to extremes to devise campaigns) but is a far cry from its production values. The cast and story line is good but (and it is un-

fortunate) the picture itself suffers through a nauseating use of bobbing the picture up and down and from side to side (too much use of the unsteady [shaky] camera). It is simply not needed especially when the entire program is set in the ad agency.

Episodes: *1.* Just Ping Me. *2.* Channeling. *3.* The Hovercraft. *4.* The Presentation. *5.* This Is the Remix. *6.* For Placement Only.

147 *Chad Vader Day Shift Manager.* youtube.com. 2006–2012.

A spoof of *Star Wars*. Chad Vader is a young man who leads two separate lives. He is the day shift manager of Empire Supermarket and supposedly a Sith Lord, the brother of the evil Darth Vader. Chad (also called Lord Vader) wears at times, a black life support suit and helmet given to him by Darth. Like his brother who yearns to control the universe, Chad has set his goal to make Empire Market the dominate food retailing industry by crushing the competition.

First season episodes establish the overall premise with Chad interacting with his co-workers: Clarissa, Jeremy, Lloyd, Clint and Weird Jeremy. Randy is their boss. Conflict is added in the second season when Empire is taken over by a large corporation (Red Leader Foods) and Maggie McCall becomes the corporate liaison and acting general manager. Third season episodes find Maggie promoting Chad as the general manager while the concluding season finds Chad becoming unstable and realizing he must step down to again become the day shift manager.

Cast: Aaron Yonda (Chad Vader), Matt Sloan (Chad's Voice), Paul Guse (Jeremy Wickstrom), Craig Johnson (Weird Jimmy), Karen Moeller (Maggie McCall), Rob Matsushita (Lloyd), Brad Knight (Randy), Christina LaVicka (Clarissa), Kate Sprecher (Libby), Bill Bolz (Lionel), Sean Moore (Marshmallow Bandido). **Credits:** *Producer:* Matt Sloan, Aaron Yonda, Courtney Collins. *Director:* Matt Sloan, Aaron Yonda. *Writer:* Matt Sloan, Aaron Yonda, Tim Harmston, Craig Johnson, Rob Matsushita. **Comment:** While the program is enjoyable to watch (even if you are not a *Star Wars* fan) there are numerous twists and turns as the story progresses. The acting and production are good although some of the earlier episodes have poor video quality that is instantly noticeable.

Season 1 Episodes: *1.* A Galaxy Not So Far Away. *2.* The Date. *3.* The Night Shift. *4.* Dog in the Store. *5.* Drunk. *6.* New Job. *7.* Trapped in the Trash. *8.* Chad Fights Back.

Season 2 Episodes: *1.* The Takeover. *2.* Laser Trouble. *3.* Into the Basement. *4.* The Basement Strikes Back. *5.* The New Employee. *6.* First Kiss. *7.* Goodbye, Chad. *8.* Bandito Beat Down. *9.* Showdown. *10.* Somebody Dies.

Season 3 Episodes: *1.* Surveillance Assistant. *2.* Rockets and Chaos. *3.* Lloyd Town. *4.* Nothing

Happens. *5.* The Return of Clint. *6.* Vampire Market. *7.* Sick Day. *8.* The Improvised Episode. *9.* Duel to the Death. *10.* Six Ways to Die.

Season 4 Episodes: *1,2.* The Return of Weird Jimmy. *3.* The Return of Commander Wickstrom. *4,5.* The Return of Brian. *6.* Vader vs. Vader. *7.* Chad Vader Makes Me Want to Cry. *8.* Surprise Inspection. *9.* Martial Law. *10.* Chad Vader Dies.

148 *Chad's Angels.* webseriestoday.com. 2012.

"A long time ago in a galaxy far away there were three little girls who appeared on YouTube: one from the 1920s (Flapper), one from the 1980s (Nancy) and one from ... an era yet to be determined (Stormy)" is heard by a man named Chad, the owner of a private detective agency who somehow crossed their paths, united them and hired them as his team of private detective (his "Angels"). Like the TV series *Charlie's Angels*, each of the girls had "very hazardous duties": Flapper was a night club dancer; Nancy, an aerobics instructor and Stormy, who wears an eye patch, a futuristic warrior fighting for right. The girls receive an assignment from the unseen Chad and the program charts their rather haphazard means of solving cases (here to solve a series of mysterious killings that appear to be related to a vampire cult).

Cast: Angie St. Mars (Flapper), Leilanie Giordmania (Nancy), Sophie Chic (Stormy), Chris Greenway (Chad Baker). Credits: *Producer-Writer-Director:* Chad Greenway. Comment: Enjoyable spoof of *Charlie's Angels* that even uses the same silhouette images for the girls as well as the same incidental music that is used to transition from a closing scene to a commercial break. While the original *Charlie's Angels* (Sabrina, Jill and Kelly) were quite sophisticated, Chad's girls are rather flamboyant with few

scruples and likely to show cleavage. The acting and production are very good. See also *The McCaingels* and *Chico's Angels*.

Episodes: *1.* Twilight Angels. *2.* Venus Spa. *3.* New Moon. *4.* Eclipse. *5.* Breaking Dawn, Part 1: Vampire/Werewolf Dance. *7.* Breaking Dawn, Part 2: Electric Boggaloo.

149 *Chaos Theory.* phoebetv.com. 2004.

Although Jessica Fletcher, called Jess, views life as "an odd but exciting adventure," she is a New York girl whose life revolves around her friends, co-workers (at the Farnsworth, Mills and Russell marketing company) "and the various men she dates, sometimes successfully, sometimes disastrously." Each looks out for the other and the program relates the events that sometimes come between them and how they always come back as the best of friends. Monica is Jess's mother, the woman who believes Jess is a bit naïve and idealistic; Owen is her co-worker; Michelle is Jess's self-absorbed best friend; Sarah is Owen's no-nonsense wife; Stewart is Jess's co-worker; Suzette is a self-licensed life coach.

Cast: Lauren Cook (Jess Fletcher), Bari Biern (Monica), Rufus Tureen (Owen), Cara Greene (Sarah), Emily Allyn Barth (Michelle), Jessica Elaina Eason (Dena), Rachel Hamilton (Suzette Monticedllo), Paul Caiola (Stewart). Credits: *Creator:* Mike Stickle. *Writer:* Paul Bastel, Lauren Cook, Brenda Dargan, Emily Isler, Kate Schweitzer, Mike Stickle. *Supervising Editor:* Jim Isler. Comment: A nice chemistry exists between the main characters that is not overplayed and gives you the feeling they are friends off the set as well as on. The acting and production are very good and one of the better (and pioneering) Internet sitcoms. Episodes: *1.* Cupcake. *2.* Dinner Parties. *3.* Jess Grows a Pair. *4.* Office Politics. *5.* Promoting the Coach. *6.* City and

Chaos Theory. Series poster art (used by permission).

the Sex. *7.* Shrinkage. *8.* Spa Day. *9.* Old Married Couple. *10.* Dill Weed. *11.* I Can Has Candy. *12.* The Couch. *13.* The Pregnant Shirt. *14.* Christmas and the Hard Luck Kid. *15.* Shoot the Homeless. *16.* Waiting for Jess. *17.* Spare a Dime. *18.* Monica Dearest. *19.* Peaches and Herb. *20.* Fate: It's All Happening. *21.* The Fallout. *22.* Exposed. *23.* Team Bonding. *24.* O Brother. *25.* Season 1 Gag Reel.

150 The Charlie Feldon Show. youtube.com. 2013.

Although it has a human name, Charlie Feldon is a small, yellow plastic duck that lives in the shower of its owner, a man named Kevin. Charlie speaks, is nasty and constantly complains about where he has to live. The program, which is basically a conversation between Charlie and Kevin, relays those conversations with Charlie always coming out on top, no matter what the topic may be.

Cast: Brent Teclaw (Kevin). Charlie's voice is credited as "Charlie Feldon: Himself." **Credits:** *Producer-Director:* Brent Teclaw. *Writer:* Dale Selby. **Comment:** There is no explanation given as to how Charlie can talk or how Kevin acquired him (a childhood "rubber ducky?," something he found?, something he just bought?). Charlie is just that—a plastic duck and no real attempt (like computer animation) is made to make him anything more. Overall it is just another "Odd Couple" variation and despite an annoying laugh track, it is different and well produced.

Episodes: *1.* Pilot.

151 Checked Out. youtube.com. 2012.

Trader Jack's appears to be an ordinary small town grocery store where two of its most valued employees, Jamison and Marissa, are not the workaholics they are believed to be (as most of their time is spent in the store's stock [break] room to not only not work, but get paid for it). The program, set mainly in the break room, follows Jameson and Marissa as they "work" for that pay check—by relaxing for five of their eight hour shifts. Lisa is the oldest of the employees, a woman who is overly fond of animals (especially cats), very emotional, easily upset, and actually does work; Rajit, the other featured employee, also works but is hampered somewhat by his inability to deal with the stress of the situation as he has a fear of cardboard and unpacking boxes just adds to his distress. **Cast:** David Greenman (Jameson), Zelda Williams (Marissa), Arjun Gupta (Rajit), Vicki Lewis (Lisa), Gabriel Long (Billy). **Credits:** *Producer:* David Greenman, Gabriel Long. *Director:* Gabriel Long. *Writer:* David Greenman. **Comment:** The comedy is a bit subtle as situations are more geared to conversation than actual customer or boss confrontations. Zelda Ritter is the daughter of John Ritter and handles her role quite well. Jameson is the personification of the perfect slacker while Lisa and Rajit represent the people who do work but will not snitch to the boss.

Episodes: 4 untitled episodes, labeled "Episode #1.1" through "Episode #1.4."

152 Chic. webserieschannel.com. 2013.

Gwen and Margo are women working in the adult film industry (for a studio called Slink Productions). It is the present day and such films are literally wall-to-wall sex with little or no storyline or actual romance. Gwen is an actress (kind and sweet) and Margo, her director (domineering and feisty). Each of the women believes that it was during the 1970s, when adult-themed films were at their best and feel they need to recapture those times by striking out on their own (as owners of Chic Studios) and making a film that marries sex with substance. The program chronicles their mishaps as they set out to capture a time in Triple XXX rated films when there was a story, character development and also sex.

Cast: Alissa Kulinski (Gwen Angel), Sarah Hesch (Margo Divina), Tim Towne (Cyrus Stone), Brandon Grinslade (Harry Lance), Kevin O'Heron (Brad McCallum). **Credits:** *Director:* Chris Snapp. **Comment:** While the 1970s did produce adult films with a story-sex merge (like *The Devil in Miss Jones*) it was actually in 1980 with the Kay Parker film *Taboo* that changed the way adult films were made to pay just as much attention to the story as to sex. Several additional *Taboo* films followed that featured the top porn stars but as the decade progressed, producers began making films that leaned more toward sex and less toward story; this eventually became the norm with a story (if you can call it one or find it) somewhere in the movie. *Chic* is rather sexy and provocative as it tries to recapture the past (many films from the 1970s, like *Teenage Fantasies*, *The Sex Boat* and *Deep Throat* are being re-distributed). *Chic* also tries to recapture a time when there were adult stars like Traci Lords, Ginger Lynn, Loni Sanders, Candy Samples, Christy Canyon, Ron Jeremy, Peter North and Annette Haven whose names were used to sell movies; current films have their stars but it is largely not a selling point—only the sex is). Overall the program is very well done with good acting and a behind-the scenes look at the making of such films (and just like with real "XXX" films, mishaps occur and even that aspect has been released as Blooper DVD's).

Episodes: *1.* Chic Pilot. *2.* Fallout. *3.* The Script. *4.* Downtown Abby. *5.* Cattle Call. *6.* The Morning After. *7.* Fund Raising. *8.* Betrayal. *9.* The Rehearsals. *10.* Victor Snag. *11.* The Curse. *12.* First Shoot. *13.* Shut Up and Roll.

153 Chico's Angels. youtube.com. 2010.

Kay, Chita and Frieda (drag queens) are police

academy failures that have been hired by a mysterious man named Chico to become his "Angels," private detectives who tackle the cases Chico acquires. To conceal is true identity Chico only communicates with his staff via a telephone; he has hired Bossman to oversee his operations and keep an eye on the Angels. The program, a spoof of *Charlie's Angels*, charts the cases acquired by Chico and how his Angels, using a style more "feminine" than Charlie's original Angels (Jill, Sabrina and Kelly) attempt to solve crimes—in heels, elegant gowns and a bit of sass.

Kay, born in Tijuana, was a police academy drop out turned fashion model whose stylish good looks and charming personality brought her to Chico's attention when he saw a girdle ad she did for the *Penny Saver* magazine. Kay is self-absorbed, high maintenance and believes she is not only the prettiest Angel, but the most voluptuous.

Frieda, born in Ciudad Juarez Mexico, was abandoned as an infant and left under the door mat of a convent. She was raised by the convent nuns and was being groomed to join the order until she had an affair with "a handsome churro salesman" and realized she loved sex. She left the convent and set out to make a life for herself in society. When she turned to prostitution and was arrested by a vice cop, she was sent to jail. After a sexual encounter with a guard, the guard set her up for enrollment at the police academy but her failure to become a rookie set her on a path to re-establish herself in Los Angeles—where she was discovered by Chico and hired as an Angel.

Chita, born in East Los Angeles dreamed of becoming a ballerina but living in the ghetto shattered those hopes as gangs ruled and fighting them took precedence over dancing. She eventually joined a gang (the Mariposas) but her inability to conform to the rules of society got her arrested. At a police station she saw an academy recruitment poster and decided to become a police officer. Her fiery temper caused her expulsion from the academy six months later but she came to the attention of Chico and was hired as an Angel.

Bossman, as he is called, is a long time friend of Chico's ("an old spy buddy"). He was born in Pacoima, California, and had the unique ability to contort his body and escape from anything. He joined the circus, hoping to become a star, but the FBI required his skills and recruited him. He trained to become a Navy SEAL but only rose to the rank of Penguin. Shattered that he could not achieve a higher ranking, he turned to booze and women and one night became so intoxicated that he slipped off an apartment building roof and lost his contortionist abilities when a fire escape broke his fall. When Bossman re-connected with Chico they decided to establish the company with Bossman becoming the liaison between Chico and the Angels (as did John Bosley on *Charlie's Angels*).

Cast: Danny Casillas (Frieda Laye), Oscar Quintero (Kay Sedia), Ray Garcia (Chita Parol), Alejandro Patino (Bossman), Gabriel Romero (Voice of Chico). **Credits:** *Producer:* Danny Casillas, Maria Quintaro, Jerry A. Blackburn. *Director:* Kurt Koehler. *Writer:* Danny Casillas, Kurt Koehler, Oscar Quintero. **Comment:** If *Bosom Buddies* could sustain itself for two years on ABC in the 1980s, *Chico's Angels* could achieve the same heights as it is TV series worthy. For those familiar with the *Charlie's Angels* theme song you will find that it has been adapted, in part, for the program here (even using, in a way, the same type of opening theme silhouette visuals).

Episodes: *1.* Missing Chihuahua. *2.* Steak-Out. *3.* Get Ready for Rumba. *4.* A Sparkling Finish. *5.* Ransom and Then Some. *6.* The Price Is Wrong. *7.* Mexican Baby. *8.* Little Churros.

154 *Child of the '70s.* theofficialchildof the70s.com. 2012–2015.

Carlo Perdente is a 40-year-old man who believes he is a total loser. He has been fired from his job for a sex chat line, lost his New York City rent-controlled apartment and has no choice but to move in with his over-bearing Italian mother. But life soon changes for Carlo when he is offered the job of a lifetime: working as the personal assistant to KiKi Lawrence, a washed-up 1970s television star (and his idol). The program charts what happens when Carlo finds his dream job becoming a nightmare as he caters to Kiki's every whim. Third season episodes find Carlo acquiring a role on the daytime TV soap opera *The Bridge Across Tomorrow* with a focus on the cast, crew and Carlo's experiences as an actor.

Cast: Michael Vaccaro (Carlo Perdente), Ann Walker (Kiki Lawrence), Leo Forte (Joe Rivera), Terry Ray (James Hunter), David Zimmerman (Bernie Steinberg), Geri Jewell (Herself), Chuck Saculla (Cousin Alfonso), Bruce Vilanch (Larry Lawrence), Greg Lucey (Albert Perdente), Duane Boutte (Weezy), Claysey Everett (Bonita Lawrence), Carole Ita White (Aunt Connie), Susan Olsen (Nickel), Sheena Metal (Siobhan McKay), Natalie Toro (Brenda). Laura Harden (Teresa). **Credits:** *Producer:* Michael Vaccaro, David Schellenberg, Amy Ruskin, Annie Price, Paul Belsito, Steven Roche, Michael Summers, Bruce L. Hart. *Director:* Eric Scot, Gary Lamoin, Michael Vaccaro, Tom Pardoe. *Writer:* Geri Jewell, Terrence Moss, Michael Vaccaro, Steven Wishnoff. **Comment:** The program is a bit depressing and not very appealing at first as the first three episodes are not in the same caliber as the rest of the series (as they are just too much focused on Carlo's woes. It picks up speed with the fourth episode when Kiki is introduced and sets the pace for the rest of the series).

Season 1 Episodes: *1.* You're Doing It Wrong. *2.* Merry Christmas, Darling. *3.* Happy Darling. *4.* KiKi Lawrence. *5.* New York, This Was Your Last Chance.

Season 2 Episodes: *1.* It Never Rains in Southern California. *2.* Lonely People. *3.* I Love You. *4.* The Bonita Triangle. *5.* Pop Goes the Question. *6,7.* The Wedding.

Season 3 Episodes: *1.* Welcome Back, Carlo. *2.* The Bridge Across Tomorrow. *3.* Mama's Jewels.

155 *Childrens Hospital.* tv.com. 2008 (web run).

A look at the bizarre staff of Childrens Hospital, a medical center named after its founder, Dr. Arthur Childrens: Blake Downs, the surgeon who wears clown makeup and believes in the power of laughter to heal, not medicine (he also believes he is a member of the Clown Race and his real name is "Mr. Bojiggles"); Cat Black, a doctor (and the show's narrator) who has lesbian tendencies, practices nudism at home and had a bizarre relationship with Little Nicky, a six-year-old boy stricken with an advanced aging disease; Glenn Richie, the ladies' man who once dated Cat; Owen Maestro, the dim-witted former cop turned dim-witted doctor; and Chief, the crippled head of the hospital staff (she is of Choctaw Indian heritage and her mother had originally intended to name her "Whore" but chose Chief when she saw it on a Scrabble board).

Web Cast: Rob Corddry (Dr. Blake Downs/Cutter Spindell), Lake Bell (Dr. Cat Black/Dixie Peters), Megan Mullally (Hospital Chief/Lady Jane Bentic-Smith), Ken Marino (Dr. Glenn Richie/Just Falcon), Rob Hiebel (Dr. Owen Maestro/Rob Huebel), Nick Kroll (Little Nicky), Nathan Corddry (Dr. Jason Mantzoukas), Ed Helms (Dr. Ed Helms), John Ross Bowie (Dr. Max von Sydow), Kulap Vilaysack (Nurse Kulap). **Credits:** *Producer:* Rob Corddry, Rich Rosenthal, Jonathan Stern, David Wain, Keith Crofford. *Director:* Rob Schrab, Rob Corddry. *Writer:* Rob Corddry, Jonathan Stern, David Wain. **Comment:** After ten episodes the program moved to the Cartoon Network in 2010 and its showcase for mature comedies on Adult Swim. Although there have been medical spoofs prior to this, the program does manage to do a good job with an attractive cast, good acting and excellent production values.

Web Episodes: 10 untitled episodes, labeled "Episode 1" through "Episode 10."

156 *Chip and Nick.* funnyordie.com. 2012.

Chip and Nick are best friends employed by the same company but are not seen within the confines of that company. Instead, they are seen in their car during their lunch break eating fast food and the program focuses on that aspect of their lives as they discuss matters that are important to them, but seemingly less important to anyone else.

Cast: Chip Godwin (Chip), Nick Paliokas (Nick). **Credits:** *Producer-Writer:* Chip Godwin, Nick Paliokas. *Director:* Chip Godwin. **Comment:** Although set away from their actual business, the program works with likeable leads, good acting and production values.

Episodes: *1.* Drugs. *2.* Harper's Bizarre. *3.* Marathon Man. *4.* Misfortune Cookie. *5.* Buyer's Remorse. *6.* Be Specific. *7.* Rhode Island Reds. *8.* Turnabout.

157 *Chloe and Zoe.* chloeandzoe.com. 2012.

Two best friends, Chloe and Zoe, and how they simply try to adjust to the world in which they live—a world no different from the world everyone faces, but for Chole and Zoe, a world that presents "serious" problems as making plans to do something always turns out better when they break them and choose not to do them.

Cast: Chloe Searcy (Chloe), Zoe Worth (Zoe). **Credits:** *Producer:* Kim Leadford, Daniel McCarney, Tim Nye. *Director:* Charlie Alderman, Emma Berliner, James Gallager, Chloe Searcy, Melanie Shaw. *Writer:* Chloe Searcy, Zoe Worth. **Comment:** Enjoyable romp with two young women who simply cannot agree on anything or what to do. There is a nice chemistry between the leads and it includes good production values but there is vulgar language used on occasion.

Season 1 Episodes: *1.* Job Search. *2.* Dinner. *3.* Astrology. *4.* Stoned. *5.* Beaver. *6.* Bully. *7.* Chloe 2. *8.* Dance. *9.* Performance. *10.* Finale.

Season 2 Episodes *1.* Evicted. *2.* Job Search. *3.* The Pitch. *4.* Brainstorm. *5.* Charlie. *6.* Paint Store. *7.* Camille. *8.* Nightmare. *9.* Revelations. *10.* Chloe 2 2. *11.* Killer GPS.

158 *Chop Socky Boom.* chopsockyboom.com. 2012–2014.

Final Zodiac Warrior is a Kung Fu web series produced in Seattle. The five major roles have been cast (Rat, Pig, Rabbit, Rooster and Dragon) and each of the actors who acquired the role had to overcome numerous obstacles to secure that role. With the cast set and the production ready to roll the program follows the mishaps that plague the cast (struggling to overcome personal demons and deal with mistreatment from the show's leading stars), its misunderstood director and less-than knowledgeable crew as they do their best to produce a very low budget web series.

Cast: Khanh Doan (Khanh), Dan Humphrey (Charlie), Jay Irwin (Scottie), Andrew McMasters (Trick), Jennifer Page (Paige), Brandon Ryan (Max), Darlene Sellers (Daisy), Shawn Telford (Jerry), S. Joe Downing (Dillon), Cliff Lee (Bruce), Eric Stevens (Ty), Lisa Coronado (Eva). **Credits:** *Producer-Director:* Darlene Sellers, Heath Ward. *Writer:* Mark Price, Darlene Sellers, Heath Ward.

Comment: Very well acted and produced program. It is literally a spoof of martial arts feature films with well developed characters (like members of *The Power Rangers* TV series as each character has a unique costume and personality).

Episodes: *1.* Auditions. *2.* Callbacks. *3.* Day One on the Set. *4.* The Nude Scene. *5.* The Day Job. *6.* The Table Read. *7.* The Divas Episode. *8.* The Thunder Dome Episode.

159 The Chronicles of a Man Child. you tube.com. 2012.

Amanda is a very attractive woman who could have any man she chooses for a lover. Her strange choice, however, is an adult male (only called Man Child) who has not matured and has the intelligence of what appears to be a toddler. The program charts their rather strange relationship as seen through Amanda's eyes as she puts up with all the juvenile antics of a "man" who has no idea what an adult relationship is or what it means to have a girlfriend.

Cast: Justin Schollard (Man Child), Dana Rosendorff (Amanda), Taryn Southern (Sarah), Jessica Rose (Dana), Ashley Avis (Kira), Tomi Townsend (Stephanie), Mara Klein (Chloe), Cara Fleming (Nicole). Credits: *Producer:* Dana Rosendorff, Richard J. Lee. *Director:* Richard J. Lee. *Writer:* Dana Rosendorff, Jenna Kruiskamp. Comment: While the idea has several "what were they thinking here" undertones, the overall presentation is just unsettling. Man Child is simply disgusting and an instant turn off. You just don't want to watch him. The series *Mork and Mindy* used the concept of a man child with Jonathan Winters portraying such a character in comic genius. If truly unusual scenarios amuse you, you will be in seventh heaven here.

Episodes: *1.* For the Bible Told Me So. *2.* Toilet Training. *3.* The Birds and the Bees.

160 Chuggers. vimeo.com. 2014.

Chuggers are, in British terminology, "awareness enhancers, street fund raisers and charity muggers" Chuggers for short, the people who annoy the heck out of other people through their fund raising efforts. Darryl and Ian are two such people and the program presents a look at the comical side of their lives—the mishaps they encounter as they attempt to raise money for what they consider worthy causes.

Cast: Matt Ralph (Darryl), Lee Griffiths (Ian). Credits: *Director:* Marcus J. Richardson. *Writer:* Matt Ralph, Lee Griffiths. Comment: British produced program that is easy to understand (not burdened by thick accents although there is some foul language), well acted and produced and something different as a series about people begging for money.

Episodes: *1.* Hooves for Horses. *2.* The Rival Chugger. *3.* Tiny Tim. *4.* #Awkward. *5.* Mario's Magic Words. *6.* Help the Homeless. *7.* CATch 22. *8.* Sob Story. *9.* The New Guy.

161 City of Dreams. cityofdreams.com. 2012–2013.

Music blends with comedy to present the struggles of three talented singers and dancers (Jamie, Julie and Julian) as they seek to make a name for themselves on Broadway by acquiring roles in the production of *The Ballad of Ofagina*.

Cast: Justin Anthony Long (Jamie Carmel), Jee Young Han (Julie Wong), Jonathan Lee, Jr. (Julian Wong), Christopher DeProphetis (Chris), Kelvin Moon Loh (Kelvin), Joanna Burns (Becky), Joe Conti (Spencer), Dayna Grayber (Gypsy Friend), Jon Fletcher (Arthur Birmingham), Sheila Head (Maggie), Victoria Casella (Carolee Carmel), Clifton Lewis (Greg Carmel). *Ballad of Ofagina Cast Members:* Sam Arlen, Mike Liscio, Mike McNulty, Desiree Rodriquez, Calvin M. Thompson, Dwight Trice, Victoria Huston-Elem, Desiree Justin, Elizabeth Owens Skidmore, Amanda Trusty. Credits: *Producer-Writer-Director:* Jee Young Han, Jonathan Lee, Jr., Justin Anthony Long. Comment: Surprisingly well performed program with a talented cast of performers. Musical comedies are a rarity on the Internet and even a difficult sell on network TV. Combine the right formula and the right cast and a hit emerges (like Fox TV's *Glee*) and the same can be said for *City of Dreams* as it has all the elements needed to become a hit.

Episodes: *1.* Pilot. *2.* Unexpected Song. *3.* You're the One That I Want. *4.* Finishing the Hat. *5.* I Hope I Get It. *6.* A Summer in Ohio. *7.* Nice Work if You Can Get It. *8.* Anything You Can Do (I Can Do Better). *9.* Don't Rain on My Parade. *10.* Not for the Life of Me. *11.* The Ballad of Ofagina.

162 Clark: A Gonzomentary. gonzomentary.com. 2011–2012.

"Gonzomentary" is a term that was created specifically for this program (combined from the words "gonzo" and "documentary"). It can be produced either on film or video "and combines objectivity with pre-scripted fictitious events." It also "creates fictitious characters but presents them through outside means as realistic in order to obscure a distinction between reality and fiction within the story." The program also encompasses aspects of the word "mocumentary" (using the documentary format to portray fictitious characters or events). With the terminology explained, the program now encompasses the format of a reality show as a documentary crew are assigned the task of capturing the life of a controversial (but penniless) artist (Clark) as he goes from bad (homelessness) to good (an art gallery exhibit).

Cast: William Clark (Clark), James Curcio (J.C.), Jazmin Idakas (Jazmin), Daniel D.W. (Daniel). Credits: *Producer-Writer-Director:* Daniel Warwick. Comment: Although billed as a comedy it is also depressing at times. It appears that satirizing depression was meant to be funny, but it may not appear like that to everyone. The acting is acceptable but the annoying unsteady (shaky) camera method of filming is really not needed and steady scenes would have been more acceptable and less irritating.

Episodes: *1.* Clark: A Gonzomentary Pilot. *2.* Clark's Art Encapsulated. *3.* Sin'optic Changes. *4.* The Drunkards Have Fallen Asleep. *5,6,7.* Unmasking the Artist Within. *8.* Clark: A Gonzomentary: The Movie (all the episodes edited together with added footage that runs 1 hr., 45 min).

163 *Classholes.* youtube.com. 2011–2012.

Benjamin Tavish is a brilliant educator who has devised what he believes is the next great step in the educational process: OYM (One Year Masters) a series of sped-up classes that allow college honor roll students to complete their Masters degrees in one year. As the program is set into motion, a computer glitch overlooks the sought students and, instead, selects students who may be high (on drugs) but are also the bottom dwellers in the school system. As the semester begins, Professor Tavish discovers what has happened and the program follows Benjamin as he struggles to find a way to rectify the situation before he is actually stuck teaching a class of undesirables.

Cast: Adam Stephenson (Prof. Benjamin Tavish), Matt Chiaramonte (Patrick), Darryl Villacorta (Nixon), Mackenzie Wiglesworth (Kate-Lyn), Mat Labotka (Kevin), Carissa Casula (Helena), Noah Applebaum (Chris), Lindsey Scalise (Holly), Kate Lane (Penelope), Greer Bishop (Felicia), Kevin Williamson (Danny), Christian Gray (Officer Rodney), Jennifer Papsujevic (Anya), Emily Tichawa (Amanda), Neil O'Callaghan (The Dean). **Credits:** *Producer:* Grant Pollard, Richard Smith. *Director:* Grant Pollard, Richard Smith, Matt Chiaramonte. *Writer:* Matt Chiaramonte. **Comment:** Finally, you may think, school kids who are really rotten and not the sugary-sweet characterizations that are so prominent on some series. While it becomes obvious that Benjamin will become stuck with his class of undesirables, the students also realize that they have come to respect the professor and, if the series were to continue, it would no doubt establish a different student-teacher relationship as well as situations that reflect their efforts to actually pass his classes.

Episodes: *1.* Intro to Introductions. *2.* Psychoology. *3.* Human Anatomy. *4.* Twas the Night Before Classholes. *5.* There's a Me in Team. *6.* Danny vs. Holly. *7.* Lights on, Intelligence Out.

164 *Classic Alice.* classicalice.com. 2014.

Alice Rackham is a college student at Valeton University with an uncontrollable desire to succeed. She is majoring in English and has always achieved the highest grades possible. One day, after receiving a "B minus" on a term paper, Alice's world begins to fall apart—"I failed a paper that was in my major" (although with Alice's record, her GPA could absorb two "F's" and still let her retain her valedictorian ranking). Alice's paper contains the professor's remarks ("Your writing is consistently dull and unimaginative") and to prove to her professor that she does understand what she reads, she decides to live her life as characters from books (her first choice being, for Season 1 episodes, *War and Peace*; *Pygmalion* is her choice in second season episodes). And to document what happens, Alice creates video blog wherein she shares her experiences with viewers. Andrew, her friend, a film major, seizes upon the opportunity to film her vlog as an assignment for his film class; he is replaced in second season episodes by Alice's friend, Cara, a music student, who films her vlog (Alice mentions that Andrew is still in school and that she sees him on campus with his camera in hand; it is assumed class commitments prevent him from helping Alice).

Cast: Kate Hackett (Alice Rackham), Tony Noto (Andrew Prichard), Elise Cantu (Cara Graves), Chris O'Brien (Ewan McBay), Reid Cox (Reagan Starkie). **Credits:** *Producer:* Kate Hackett, Lex Edelman, Clare O'Flynn. *Writer:* Kate Hackett. *Director:* Clare O'Flynn. **Comment:** Captivating program with excellent acting and overall acceptable production values (noticeable editing is quite obvious). Although the series is mostly just Alice relating what happens, it is not boring to watch as Kate Hackett is appealing and can keep an audience tuned in.

Season 1 Episodes: *1.* Down the Rabbit Hole. *2.* Just a Little Peril. *3.* (A Lot of) Battle Plans. *4.* Terror Sets In. *5.* To Siberia. *6.* Punishment.

Season 2 Episodes: *1.* Why Can't the English? *2.* Wouldn't It Be Lovely. *3.* With a Little Bit of Luck. *4.* On the Street Where You Live. *5.* I Could Have Danced All Night.

165 *Clean Livin'.* webserieschannel.com. 2009.

Vinnie and Bobby are long-time friends and secretly hit men and considered the most deadly contract killing duo in Rhode Island. Vinnie is a bachelor, seemingly unable to find a girl who will put up with his craziness, who lives in the basement of his mother's home. Bobby, a devoted family man and loving husband, conceals his true occupation as the legitimate owner of a small business. With their clean living covers established and no one the wiser to who they really are, the program charts the hits they are hired to do (eliminate the less-desirable members of society) but also on their efforts to balance their two distinctive lives.

Cast: Greg Paul (Vinicio "Vinnie" Viviani), Joe Siriani (Robert "Bobby" Barcarelli), John Cleary (Joey Fernowe), Chuck Doherty (The Mark), Tim

Goff (Tony), Bernard Larrivee, Jr. (The Boss). Credits: *Director:* Dave Borges. *Producer-Writer:* Dave Borges, Eric Lebow. **Comment:** It's nothing like the 1990s Fox TV series *Vinnie and Bobby* (about clean living friends) but a dark comedy about the underbelly of society as experienced by two ruthless hit men. The acting is good and the production itself well executed to present the darker picture of life.

Season 1 Episodes: *1.* About Last Night. *2.* Almost Done There? *3.* New Hope. *4.* Family Thing.

Season 2 Episodes: *1.* The Call. *2.* Short and Stout. *3.* Run Down. *4.* Hits and Mrs. *5.* Sister, Sister. *6.* Industrial Complex.

166 The Clean-Up Crew. tv.com. 2008.

There has been a gruesome crime and it has to be cleaned up. But who do the police call? Frank's Crime Scene Steam-N-Clean Service. No matter how gruesome, Dan Dahler, the company's Operations Manager, and his crew have one goal: make the scene as clean as it was before the crime. Unfortunately, Dan and his crew are anything but totally competent as Dan appears more interested in sensitivity training and teaching his staff the value of getting along with the crime scene investigators. He is also yearning for the day its clueless company founder (Frank) will retire so he can take over. Candace is the office secretary; Ofato doesn't (or is unable to) talk; and Phil is actually the only team member with an associate degree in criminal investigation and actually knows what he is doing (or at least he thinks he does). Using a "mockumentary" style of presentation, the program spoofs TV series like *C.S.I.* and *Law and Order* with a look at what happens after a crime has been committed and things need to be cleaned up. **Cast:** Dale Midkiff (Dan Dahler), Richard Riehle (Frank), Matt Bettinelli-Olpin (Phil Hornacek), Chrissy Leigh Anderson (Candace), Jessica McClendon (Brooke Branson), Travis Willingham (Investigator Harris), Tyler Tuione (Ofato). **Credits:** *Producer:* Scott Rickels, Timothy Kolesk. *Director:* Scott Rickels. *Writer:* Scott Rickels, Tim Dragga. **Comment:** While the show is well acted and has all the production values of a network TV series, it is laden with racist jokes and offbeat (at times) dark humor. **Episodes:** 6 untitled episodes, labeled "Episode 1" through "Episode 6."

167 Click It!: Silicon Alley Reality. webserieschannel.com. 2013.

CPXi, a global digital media company with the slogan "What's Now, What's Next" is located in California's Silicon Valley and run by a man (Mike) with a vision for the future (unlike his colleagues who feel comfortable just the way things are and do not readily accept change). Life changes at CPXi when Mike believes all TV reality shows are fake but his idea for one (*Click It*) will be as real as possible and put his company on the map. Since computers are the backbone of his company and clicking (on computers) is the norm (hence the "Click It" title) he sets in motion the wheels to begin the reality series. The program charts what happens when his somewhat reluctant board members refute the idea when they feel an upcoming trade show will better benefit the company and the chaos that results when they attempt to mix the two together and salvage both avenues of publicity. **Cast:** Mike Seiman (Mike, CEO and Company Founder), David Shay (David, SVP Marketing and Communication), Jonathan Slavin (Jonathan, Chief Revenue Officer), Michael Zacharski (Michael, Chief Operations Officer), David Zapletal (SVP Media Optimizer). **Comment:** Michael Zacharski is outstanding as the guy with ideas—his acting alone makes the program worthwhile. The overall production and acting are very good and the program itself is something that has not been done numerous times before. **Episodes:** 3 untitled episodes, "Webisode 1," "Webisode 2" and "Webisode 3."

168 Cliff Notes. webserieschannel.com. 2011.

Cliff Notes is a bookstore just struggling to survive in a changing economy. Management realizes that people are simply not reading books like they once did and selling books is becoming a much more difficult job. The program relates the problems the staff encounters, not only from customers, but from each other, as they tend to the daily business operations. **Cast:** Christian Taylor (E.G.B. Bankhead), Matt Thurston (Dan Barry), Marcus Stimac (Gomez), Martha Harms (Candice Pantaloni). **Credits:** *Producer-Director:* Michael Johnson. *Writer:* Michael Johnson, Jeremy Nichols, Christian Taylor. **Comment:** Shades of the Fox TV series *Stacked* (which starred Pamela Anderson) may come to mind as it too dealt with the antics of workers at a bookstore called Stacked. Here, however, vulgar language is incorporated and is actually not needed to make for an effective program. **Episodes:** *1.* Brave New Guy. *2.* The Lurker, 1,001 Feet from the Threshold. *3.* The Compleat Baggler. *4.* The Origin of the Flondorphs by Means of Bowdlerization.

169 The Club. theclubseries.com. 2012.

Sarah, a young woman expelled from college and cut off from her parents' financial support finds that she must make it on her own and secure a job. Dana and Alison, women in their thirties and working in the posh White Ridge Country Club, become

Sarah's immediate friends when she applies for and receives a waitress job. Dana and Alison realize that Sarah has reluctantly taken the job and the program follows Sarah as she learns to not only become responsible, but an adult, through the guidance of Dana and Alison when they take her under their wing (although Dana and Alison, with their drinking and tendency to use drugs, are not the best influence in Sarah's life).

Cast: Misti Patrella (Alison), Amy Hunt (Dana), Christine O'Keefe (Sarah), Neil Maloney (Peter), Joe Orednick (Dr. Mac.), Christopher Meister, Les Rorick, Melissa Cline, Tina Renee Grace, Tommy Martin, Gene Rachinsky. Credits: *Producer-Writer-Director:* Susan Athey. Comment: While several TV series have dealt with waitresses (such as *Alice, It's a Living* and *2 Broke Girls*), *The Club* can stand on its own as being different; the acting and the chemistry between the three leads is also very good.

Episodes: *1.* Whiskey Fight. *2.* Triangle. *3.* Reward. *4.* Smoky Treat. *5.* Rotgut. *6.* The Smart Decision.

170 Club Swim. clubswimshow.com. 2013.

The Flounders are a team of amateur swimmers hoping to become professionals and compete in national contests. They are coached by a man named Charles and have a rivalry with a team called the Barracudas. The program is a look at the team members and the problems they encounter as Coach Charles goes about conditioning them to become great swimmers.

Cast: Eric Henninger (Coach Charles), Anna Phillips (Jessie) Bear Grider (Timmy), Alex Heath (Nathan), Hezekiah Crocker (Warren), Jane Brannen (Kayla), Merry Moore (Catherine), Andrew Hunter (Devin), Nick Crockett (Dave), Luke Kidwell (Mer), Rebecca Robles (Ranay), Lucy Allen (Madison), Shannon Baker (Francine), Brady Parks (Brady). Credits: *Producer:* Daniel Bowman, Jennifer Silver, Hannah Black. *Director:* Kyle Thiele, Zack Brewer. *Writer:* Zac Cooper, Hezekiah Crocker, Kyle Bailey, Luke Kidwell, Anna Phillips, Isaac Blade. Comment: Although there are no actual swimming competitions to see and the girls not the *Sports Illustrated* swim suit model type, the program is different with good acting and production values.

Episodes: *1.* Goal Meeting. *2.* Flounders Court. *3.* Quarantine. *4.* Personal Trainers. *5.* Play Date. *6.* Motivational Speaker. *7.* Game Night. *8.* The Investor.

171 Clued-Less. cluedless.com. 2012.

Stevie Hart is a young woman facing a sudden crisis. Her boyfriend has just ended their relationship; she has been fired from her low-paying internship job and she has been evicted from her less-than-desirable apartment. With no money and no job

prospects Stevie is forced to move back into her parent's home. As depression begins to get the better of her, Stevie figures that she needs to get out and do something. That something is a job as a party entertainer at The Clue Club, a company run by Scott that performs the board game "Clue" at social functions; the only problem: Stevie is not an entertainer and she must not only pretend to be something she is not, but work with a crew of misfit performers (Leo, Noah and Jon). The program charts the mishaps that befall Stevie as she tries to regain control of he life—even if it means being "Clued-less" about what she is currently doing.

Cast: Renee Dorian (Stevie Hart), Ben Begley (Noah), Kevin Thompson (Leo), Jonathan Flanagan (John), Matt Lusk (Scott), Victoria Ortiz (Melinda). Credits: *Producer:* Renee Dorian, Ben Begley, Warner Davis, Andy Palmer. *Director:* Dave Cain, Andy Palmer. *Writer:* Renee Dorian. Comment: Very enjoyable saga of a young woman just trying to find herself and fit into a situation where she feels completely out of place. The acting and production values are also very good.

Episodes: *1.* Dial M for Mystery. *2.* Murder She Didn't Write. *3.* The Unusual Suspects. *4.* South Central L.A. Confidential. *5.* The Man Who Screwed Too Much.

172 The Coasters. webserieschannel.com. 2013.

Three close friends (Raven, Rocco and Colton), living in Los Angeles and having grown up together, are now adults and facing the world for the first time on their own. Without the financial support of their families, and with an enthusiastic approach to achieve their dreams, the program relates the various mishaps they encounter as they navigate "the mean streets of Los Angeles."

Cast: Tamara Dhia (Raven), Rocco Rosanio (Jason), Stephen Buchanan (Colton), Ben Whitehair (That Dude), Cherie Daly (Kristen), Amber Hubert (Melissa), Alexander Garville (Dante), Josh Heine (Mark). Credits: *Producer-Director:* Tamara Dhia, Rocco Rosanio, Tim Dowlin. *Writer:* Tamara Dhia, Rocco Rosanio. Comment: Typical buddy-buddy comedy with all the pitfalls that can happen presented front and center. Although the concept has been done countless times before, there are always twists and turns evident and adding a girl to the concept always makes for a better presentation.

Episodes: *1,2.* That Dude. *3.* The Ex-Factor. *4.* Bra Menace. *5.* Hug Life. *6.* FMZ.

173 Coco and Ruby. webserieschannel. com. 2012.

It is 1941 and two young women, Coco and Ruby are struggling singer-dancers hoping to make a name for themselves. One night after rehearsing a routine

Coco notices the time as 11:11 p.m. and immediately tells Ruby. Together they make a wish: "to get out of this town (Newark, New Jersey) and become famous in Los Angeles, California—where everyone appreciates hard work and a decent living." Unknown to them, mysterious forces are about to grant that wish. Upon awakening the next morning Coco and Ruby find they have somehow been transported to Hollywood but are unaware, at first that it is the Hollywood of 2012, not 1941. Once realizing that they are in the future and with no idea how to return to their own time, they must now become a part of a new world (which begins when they stumble upon an apartment for rent and start their transition from the past to the present). A wish has been granted; a whole new world of opportunities lies before them and the program follows their efforts to become the stars that they had hoped to become in 1941.

Cast: Courtney Freed (Coco), Rebecca Johnson (Ruby), Sara Gray Schilling (LaRue, their agent). **Credits:** *Producer-Director:* Steve Brian, Rachel Roderman. *Writer:* Rachel Roderman. **Comment:** The program is seen in black and white for its 1941 scenes and switches to color when Coco and Ruby find themselves in the future. The idea, acting and production is very good and the program well worth watching. Most programs (even feature films) that deal with time travel all make the same mistake: the characters adjust much too quickly to their new surroundings and accept what has happened. Making the characters feel uneasy and frightened as they attempt to understand what has happened is a much more powerful weapon and should be taken into account for future filmmakers contemplating a time traveling concept. A nice touch is the musical numbers that appear in the episodes.

Episodes: *1.* The Leap Year. *2.* Letters Home. *3.* Find a Man. *4.* Draft Dodgers. *5.* Just Like Us. *6.* Acting Out. *7.* Ginger Honies. *8.* Agent Knows Best.

174 *Co-Ed the Web Series.* youtube.com. 2013.

Scott and Natalie are friends who live together but are not dating or romantically involved with each other. The program relates the experiences each has as two people stuck in the middle—dating others but not making a connection and dealing with friends who are a couple.

Cast: Steve Holbert (Scott), Jamie Walsh (Natalie), Erica Sanders (Emily), Kane Lewis (Josh), Lyssa Hoganson (Leaf), Jami Terracino (Beth), Troy Hencely (Mic), Zack Pursley (Jagger). **Credits:** *Producer-Director:* Troy Hencely. *Writer:* Steve Holbert. **Comment:** The program tries hard to be good but it is hampered by poor audio (difficult to understand what is being said) and dark lighting giving the production an overall unappealing look and feel.

Episodes: *1.* House Guests. *2.* Parents' Day. *3.* The

Breakup. *4.* Ouija Board. *5.* Home Cooking. *6.* Breaking and Entering.

175 *The Cold Read.* youtube.com. 2013.

"What it is like to be an actor in New England" is the program's tag line and through the experiences of group of aspiring actors, especially best friends Tom and Seth, a behind-the-scenes look at the world of film making in Boston is presented.

Tom is dedicated to and takes his craft seriously. Seth appears more interested in pursuing girls than achieving success as an actor. Nancy is Seth's girlfriend; Kat is Tom's friend, a girl seriously dedicated to pursuing her acting career; Brittany is the fun-loving girl who, like Seth, does not take acting seriously and believes it is all about enjoyment and no work; Shannon is Kat's talented but talkative sister who is also seeking an acting career.

Cast: Curtis Reid (Tom), Brian Farmer (Seth), AnGe Borges (Kat), Jeanna McGowan (Shannon), Anna Rizzo (Nancy), Valerie Hines (Brittany). **Credits:** *Producer:* Curtis Reid, Brian Farmer. *Director:* Jeffrey Buchbinder. *Writer:* Brian Farmer. **Comment:** Although the first episode is a bit talkative, the pace picks up with the following episode and presents an interesting look at the film industry in markets other than Los Angeles and New York.

Episodes: *1.* Pilot. *2.* Makeover. *3.* Agent. *4,5.* The Bah. *6.* Call. *7.* Recast. *8.* Student Film. *9.* Finale. *10.* Gag Reel #1. *11.* Season 1 Promo Video #2. *13.* Behind the Scenes of "The Bah." *14.* Trailer for "The Bah."

176 *Cold Turkey.* funnyordie.com. 2013.

Vincent Voss is a young man headed for a devastating future. He simply does not take care of himself and is a pre-diabetic and "a stone's throw away from liver and heart disease." His doctor has reprimanded him for his drinking and frivolous lifestyle and has strongly suggested that he change his ways or suffer the consequences. Phil, his brother, has heard the diagnosis and demands that Vincent listen to what he has been told—even if he has to do it cold turkey. Although reluctant at first, Vincent listens to Paul and the program chronicles what happens when one tries to do something cold turkey.

Cast: Brent Alan Henry (Vincent Voss), Phil Kimball (Phil Voss), Michelle Renee Allaire (Dr. Hotsin). **Credits:** *Writer-Producer:* Patrick O'Keefe. *Director:* Jason Roberts. **Comment:** Although only a pilot episode has been made, it is well done but story lines can only go so far on such an idea. The acting is good but there is foul language spread throughout the episode.

Episodes: *1.* Pilot: Beancan.

177 *The Collectible*s. youtubc.com. 2011.

The Power Posse is an organization of super heroes dedicated to righting wrongs. However, unlike other such characters (for example, Batman, Spider-Man and Wonder Woman), The Power Posse are controlled by a corporation (CorpCo, Inc.) and must contend with office politics to appease their sponsors (who own their rights and merchandising potential). While crime and corruption is rampant the team is only responsible for battling the evil CorpCo, Inc. assigns them. With conflicts among the team members, corporate heads who can only see profits and defeating evil somewhere down the line, the program follows a somewhat intrepid group of super heroes who argue more than do what they were hired to do.

The Super Heroes:

Super Star, alias John White, is the team leader. He has a hero rating of 5.0, super strength, the ability to leap and "exceptional charisma." Super Star first realized he was different when an altercation in grammar school led him to discover his super strength. On the bad side, Super Star fears his career as the team leader is in jeopardy as team favorite Crimson Pike suffered a pelvic injury under his command (this is the recurring series theme as Crimson's Pike's injury has forced him to retire and a search has begun to find a replacement).

Ultrafemme, alias Dana Stavros, is the team's executive officer. She has a hero rating of 4.6, possesses super strength, martial arts abilities and is proficient with a bullwhip. Ultrafemme is the daughter of Lina (the Greek Goddess of Weaving) and Polyphemus (better known as the Blind Cyclops). Although Ultrafemme was trained by Amazon warriors on a mystical Greek island, she chose to use her beauty, rather than her abilities and ventured into the U.S. to compete in beauty pageants. A confrontation with F.U.G.L.Y. (The Federation of Under-Good-Looking Youth) led her to join The Power Posse when she realized beauty isn't everything. Ultrafemme is the most complacent team member, always accepting company policy without question or complaint. CorpCo has some reservations about Ultrafemme as she appeals to most people but can't capture the under 12 male crowd and the over 40 female market.

The Quick, has an unknown alias and identity. He possesses hypersonic speed and an enhanced metabolism. Apparently a scientist, The Quick invented an energy drink that not only gave him his abilities but wiped out his long-term memory. His enthusiasm has pleased CorpCo and they consider him a breakout intellectual property (especially since their $10 million investment in the Quick Café has paid off generously for them).

Shield Maiden, alias Freya Wagner, has an low hero rating (2.8) and can produce kinetic energy fields. Freya is descended from a long line of super humans created "when a Valkyrie mated with a Danish prince." Shield Maiden suffers from back pain and was at one time a member of the company's board of directors and had a hero rating of 5.0. However, when she chose to have breast reduction surgery, her male fans lost interest, her

EVEN THE GOOD GUYS HAVE BAD DAYS.

THE COLLECTIBLES

The Collectibles. Series poster art (copyright © Despot Media).

rating fell to 2.8 and she was dismissed from her board duties. As a further result, she has a lower self esteem about herself and is prone to insubordination.

Death-Wish, with a secret identity and an unknown alias, holds the position of surveillance and recon expert. He is an electronics expert and of Korean heritage. He was adopted and raised in Virginia and at the age of eight witnessed a Mafia hit murder; two years later he was a witness to a Russian Mafia murder. Perhaps it was his horrific childhood experiences that led him to become a master in martial arts and his being recruited by the Power Posse.

Aguaman, alias Jesus Batista Cruz, Jr., has a 2.6 hero rating. Although he can breathe under water, communicate with aquatic life and has ordinary strength, his position is filing clerk. Almost identical to "Aquaman," Aguaman was born of a human fisherman and a lost city of Atlantis princess. Being a prince, he was raised in exile while a mad sorcerer ravaged Atlantis. When he became of age, Prince Cruz formed an army of dispossessed Merfolk and defeated the sorcerer. After turning over the government to his cousin Pablo, Aguaman joined the Power Posse to continue his battle against evil. He was regulated to filing chores after an unfortunate accident involving commercial albacore fishermen cost him his right eye. He is also insubordinate and drinks while on the job.

Receiver, alias Oona Marsden, has a hero rating of 3.5 and is the team's receptionist. She is a telepathic and hates loud thoughts. She was born in the American Mid-West and is the offspring from a family of Meda-Humans. Because it is undetermined how useful (or powerful) a telepath would be in the field, Receiver has been assigned inside duty and is under consideration to replace Crimson Pike.

Cast: Brian Sutherland (Super Star), Lisa Skvarla (Ultrafemme), Dan Humphrey (The Quick), Wonder Russell (Shield Maiden), S. Joe Downing (Death-Wish), Frank Aye (Aguaman), Trish Loyd (Receiver), Elizabeth Daruthayan (Ennui), Paul Eenhoorn (Dr. Flaming Skull), Lisa Coronado (Evil Hand), Josh Traux (Choking Hazard), Jim Demonakos (Joel Bradavky), Kyle Stevens (Rob Schufeld), Jessica Hendrickson (Deborah Lang), Conner Marx (Graviator), Darlene Sellers (Daisy), Ben Andrews (Dale), Trin Miller (Mighty Girl), Angela DiFiore (Brain Pain), Devielle Johnson (Shrink Ray).

Credits: *Producer:* Dan Heinrich, Todd Downing, Landon Salyer, Cherelle Ashby, Jonelle Cornwell, Trish Loyd. *Director:* Dan Heinrich, Todd Downing, Landon Salyer. *Writer:* Dan Heinrich, Todd Downing.

Comment: The Power Posse, despite their ties to a ruthless corporation, are committed to excellence but it appears that only if circumstances permit they will actually battle evil. While most of the action is set at CorpCo, the character costumes are well done, the acting is good and the overall production is pleasing.

Episodes: *1.* Pilot to Co-Pilot. *2.* Tool Time. *3.* The Views Expressed. *4.* Location, Location, Location. *5.* Ninja Please. *6.* With Grrrl Power Comes Grrrl Responsibility. *7.* How Does That Make You Feel. *8.* Hostile Takeover. *9.* In the Bored Room. *10.* In Case of Emergency Press Here.

178 *Coma, Period.* blip.tv. 2009.

Following a car accident a young man (Dan Humford) is diagnosed as being in a coma. While he appears to be unaware of anything that happens, his subconscious is very active and it is through the thoughts that live in his mind that a view of his life is presented as he relives memories of his past— "This is my life, or whatever this is."

Cast: Rob Delaney (Dan Humford). **Credits:** *Producer:* Doug Spice, Jesse Vigil, Sean E. Williams, J. Rick Castaneda. *Writer-Director:* J. Rick Castaneda. **Comment:** Interesting presentation that uses a total white background with no sets to show the emptiness of Dan's life as it now stands. The acting and production are very good.

Episodes: *1.* Marking the Days. *2.* Do Not Open the Door. *3.* Re-enactment. *4.* Fetus. *5.* Candy Bar. *6.* P*ssing. *7.* Coma, Coma. *8.* Push Button. *9.* Fighter. *10.* Mail Room.

179 *Comedians in Cars Getting Coffee.* crackle.com. 2012–2015.

Simplistic format, adapted from the British series *Carpool* that finds comedian Jerry Seinfeld in a vintage car with a guest comic embarking on a mission to chat and have a cup of coffee together.

Cast: Jerry Seinfeld (Himself). **Credits:** *Producer:* Jerry Seinfeld. *Director:* Jojo Pennebaker, Larry David. *Writer:* Jerry Seinfeld, Larry David. **Comment:** The program has television quality production values and one hopes that older classics, from the 1930s and 1940s would also become a part of the series. The program itself is filmed in New York, California, and New Jersey and features Jerry first explaining the characteristics of the car he is driving, then picking up his guest and driving to a restaurant for talk and coffee.

Season 1 Episodes:

1. Larry Eats a Pancake. Larry David (guest); 1952 Volkswagen Bettle (car).

2. Mad Man in a Death Machine. Ricky Gervais (guest); 1967 Austin-Healey 3000 (car).

3. A Monkey and a Lava Lamp. Brian Regan (guest); 1970 Dodge Challenger T/A (car).

4. Just a Lazy Shiftless Bastard. Alec Baldwin (guest); 1970 Mercedes-Benz 280 SL (car).

5. A Taste of Hell from on High. Joel Hodgson (guest); 1963 Volkswagen Karmann Ghia (car).

6. Unusable on the Internet. Bob Einstein (guest); 1970 Mercedes-Benz 300SEL 6.3 (car).

7. You Don't Want to Offend a Cannibal. Barry

Marder (guest); 1966 Porsche 356 SC Cabriolet (car).

8. I Hear Downtown Abbey Is Pretty Good. Mario Joyner and Colin Quinn (guests); 1976 Triumph TR 6 (car).

9. I Want Sandwiches, I Want Chicken. Mel Brooks and Carl Reiner (guests); 1960 Rolls Royce Silver Cloud II (car).

10. It's Bubbly Time, Jerry. Michael Richards (guest); 1962 Volkswagen Bus (car).

Season 2 Episodes:

1. I'm Going to Change Your Life Forever. Sarah Silverman (guest); 1969 Jaguar E-Type Series 2 (car).

2. I Like Kettle Corn. David Letterman (guest); 1995 Volvo 960 (car).

3. No Lipsticks for Nuns. Gad Elmaleh (guest); 1950 Citroen 2 CV (car).

4. You'll Never Play the Copa. Don Rickles (guest); 1958 Cadillac Eldorado (car).

5. Really?! Seth Myers (guest); 1973 Porsche 911 Carrera RS (car).

6. Kids Need Bullying. Chris Rock (guest); 1969 Lamborghini Miura P4000S (car).

Season 3 Episodes:

1. Comedy, Sex and the Blue Numbers. Louis C.K. (guest); 1959 Fiat 600 Jolly (car).

2. How Would You Kill Superman? Oswalt Patton (guest); 1981 DeLorean DMC-12 (car).

3. Comedy Is a Concealed Weapon. Jay Leno (guest); 1949 Porsche 356/2 (car).

4. So You're Mellow and Tense? Todd Barry (guest); 1966 MGB (car).

5. Feces Are My Purview. Tina Fey (guest); 1967 Volvo 1800S (car).

6. The Over-Cheer. Jason Alexander and Wayne Knight (guests); 1976 AMC Pacer (car).

7. The Last Days of Howard Stern. Howard Stern (guest); 1969 Pontiac GTO (car).

Season 4 Episodes:

1. A Little Hyper-Aware. Sarah Jessica Parker (guest); 1976 Ford LTD Country Squire (car).

2. Two Polish Airline Pilots. George Wallace (guest); 1965 Buick Riviera (car).

3. Opera Pimp. Robert Klein (guest); 1967 Jaguar Mark 2 (car).

4. It's Like Pushing a Building Off a Cliff. Aziz Ansari (guest); 2012 Prevost X3-45 VIP (car).

5. The Sound of Virginity. Jon Stewart (guest); 1968 AMC Gremlin (car).

Season 5 Episodes:

1. You Look Amazing in the Wind. Kevin Hart (guest); 1959 Porsche RSK Spyder (car).

2. I'm Wondering What It's Like to Date Me. Amy Schumer (guest); 1971 Ferrari Daytona (car).

180 Comedy Rainbow. youtube.com. 2010.

A collection of skits, jokes and parodies presented under an umbrella title.

Cast: Michael Jamieson, Phil Morley, Jonny Borders, Claire Ash. **Credits:** *Director:* Michael Jamieson. *Writer:* Phil Morley, Michael Jamieson, Jonny Borders. **Comment:** An evaluation is not possible as all episodes have been taken off line.

Episodes: 31 untitled episodes, labeled "Episode 1" through "Episode 31."

181 Comfort Food. youtube.com. 2013.

Liyana and Luke are introduced as a young couple who are attempting to maintain a long distance relationship. They lived in the same town but Liyana has recently relocated to a different city. While each fears that in the long term new loves will enter their lives, for the time being they are still together. To maintain that togetherness, they have devised a somewhat unusual plan: not only will they talk about what happens in their lives over the telephone but they will prepare meals as they do so. The program begins by establishing a phone call and what happens as they each prepare the same dessert.

Cast: Jenny Harrold (Liyana), Edward Mitchel (Luke). **Credits:** *Producer:* Nick Williams. *Director:* Will Scothern. *Writer:* Sandy Nicholson. **Comment:** The British produced program is charming, well acted and produced. Even though it does have an unusual premise, Jenny Harrold as Liyana is very enjoyable to watch.

Episodes: *1.* Apple Crumble. *2.* Peach Cobbler.

Comfort Food. **Jenny Harrold (used by permission).**

3. Arctic Roll. *4.* Baked Alaska. *5.* Banofee Pie. *6.* Soufflé.

182 *Comics Open.* funnyordie.com. 2012.

Milt is a standup comedian who owns a combination golf course and comedy club. He also has Nadia, a Russian mail order bride who has not only become his soul mate but his partner. The program, literally a spoof of golf, shows what can happen when the game gets a bit out of hand and everything that can go wrong—from "golficide" to hooked drives that send the ball into top secret military installations—does.

Cast: Paul Rodriquez (Milt), Maria Zyrianove (Nadia), Karl Anthony, Bobby Parker. **Credits:** *Producer:* Ken Dalton. *Director:* Paul Madden. **Comment:** Wild and silly are the best two words to describe the program. Comic Paul Rodriquez is especially good and the incidents surrounding the golf-addicted stand up comedians who engage in the game are slapstick in nature making for a program that should have been pitched to basic cable (even the Golf Channel).

Episodes: *1.* The Cheater. *2.* Milt vs. Military. *3.* The Funeral. *4.* The Crash. *5.* Jake vs. Varmint. *6.* V*AGRA G*LF. *7.* Golf Course.... Or Intercourse?

183 *The Common Room.* webserieschannel.com. 2011.

Faith, Lyla, Rosie and Beatrice (who demands to be called Happy Ray of Sunshine) share an apartment in Los Angeles. Lyla and Faith are cousins and Happy Ray of Sunshine (a hippie) and Rosie (a loudmouth) are Lyla's friends, girls who resent the fact that Faith, a much too religious girl has moved in with them. The apartment is crowded and Rosie and Happy Ray of Sunshine are forced to restrict their unconventional ways to accommodate Faith and make Lyla happy. The program charts what happens when Rosie and Happy Ray of Sunshine try to change the stuck up Faith and make her one of the girls—something that is not that easy due to her strict religious upbringing. But with alcohol as their secret weapon, the situation begins to change with Faith loosening up and experiencing life as she has never known it before.

Cast: Amanda Bauer (Lyla), Heather Harvey (Faith), Danna Maret (Happy Ray of Sunshine), Melanie Leanne Miller (Rosie). **Credits:** *Producer:* Amanda Bauer, Justin Pastryk, Jordan James Smith. *Writer-Director:* Amanda Bauer. **Comment:** Although the series is described as "a slightly vulgar female web series," it does have vulgar language but the leads are so appealing and the acting so good that the negative aspect can be overlooked.

Episodes: *1.* The Unity Is Broken. *2.* No Fussy, No Pussy. *3.* The F-Word. *4.* Trippin' Balls. *5.* Who Ordered the Stripper?

184 *Community Service.* funnyordie.com. 2014.

As Dwayne Tate stands before a judge, he is ordered to perform 50 hours of community service in Los Angeles County for a crime that he committed. Being that he has a background in psychology he is to offer that time in free counseling although not from an office, but from his car, traveling to where people need help. Dwayne's efforts to help people with their emotional, social, educational and health-related concerns are chronicled.

Cast: Slink Johnson (Dwayne Tate). **Credits:** *Producer:* Van Elder, Renard F. Young. *Writer-Director:* Van Elder. **Comment:** The "crime" for which Dwayne was accused is not stated. Although Dwayne complains about giving his services away for free, he begrudgingly tackles his community service with the program highlighting aspects of the people seeking his help. The production and acting are also very good.

Episodes: *1.* Freaky Fetish. *2.* Bye Sexual. *3.* Political Office. *4.* Reality Check. *5.* Painful Pleasure.

185 *Compiling.TV.* youtube.com. 2012.

Six TV programmers working in one small office is the basic setting. The program shows what happens as they attempt to do their job as getting on one's nerves and backstabbing are only a small part of the problems each faces on a daily basis.

Cast: Francois St-Maurice (Frank), Jonathan Poirier (Jo), Celinka Serre (Cel), Louis Allard (Louis), Maxime Bélanger (Max), Pier-Luc Comeau-Tremblay (Pier-Luc), Karl Bessette (Karl), Sydney Roc (Boss). **Credits:** *Producer:* Francois St-Maurice, Celinka Serre. *Director:* Celinka Serre. *Writer:* Francois St-Maurice, Celinka Serre, Sydney Roc, Jonathan Poirier. **Comment:** The program, although well acted and produced, is basically set in the office with the daily happenings of the staff profiled.

Season 1 Episodes: *1.* Noodles. *2.* Compiling Studio. *3.* Yoga. *4.* Police Rescue. *5.* Down Time. *6.* Taking a Build. *7.* Lorem Ipsum. *8.* The List. *9.* A Boss's Ego. *10.* A Close Call. *11.* Not What I Asked For. *12.* The Hideout. *13.* Much Ado About Compiling. *14.* Disco(m)piling. *15.* The Rant. *16.* The Alibi. *17.* Textual Foursome. *18.* Getting the Third Degree. *19.* Low-Fi. *20.* PrOn. *21.* Bubbles. *22.* Smoked. *23.* Aging Method. *24.* Eliminating the Eliminator.

Season 2 Episodes: *1.* Critical Elimination Failure. *2.* The F.N.G. *3.* Equivocal Pursuit. *4.* Get Off My Case. *5.* Must Merge Code. *6.* DeCSS. *7.* High Efficiency. *8.* Compilations and Codes. *9.* Double Compile. *10.* The Code Cracker. *11.* Big Compiler. *12.* The Contest. *13.* Code Block. *14.* Going Nuts. *15.* Auto-Compile. *16.* Network Denied. *17.* Compiling Build. *18.* 3 Is the Denominator. *19.* Easy As Pi. *20.* Little Trigger. *21.* The Eliminator.

186 *The Complex (2012)*. youtube.com. 2012.

"My heart hasn't found a home. No one ever told me life would be so complex" are the opening words spoken by Johanna Smith, a young woman who, after losing her job as an executive at WFMH-TV in Florida, decides to return to her home town of Atlanta to begin a new life. She begins by moving in with her twin sister Rhianna (whom she calls "RiRi") and the program charts the road Johanna takes as she faces the complexities of life—from fulfilling her dream of finding a job within the entertainment industry to her relationship with Rhianna to the men who also become a part of her life.

Cast: Sue-Ann Marie Hines (Johanna), Candace E. Hines (Rhianna), Tracy E. Tart (Theresa), Kristy Butler (Blonde Kelly), James Luckett (Joe). **Credits:** *Producer-Writer:* Sue-Ann Marie Hines. **Comment:** Real life sisters Sue-Ann Marie and Candace perform their roles well in a program that does not glamorize life but tries to show just what obstacles one encounters as she tries to begin a new one. The production values are also very good and the program flows smoothly from episode to episode.

Episodes: *1.* The Big Move. *2.* The Search. *3.* Roommate. *4,5.* The Dating Game. *6.* The Detour. *7.* The Sticky Situation. *8.* The Moment of Truth. *9,10.* Merry Christmas from the Cast.

187 *The Complex (2013)*. youtube.com. 2013.

After dating James for four months, Greta feels that he is not the man of her dreams and dumps him. For Greta, that man is kind, handsome, generous and a well-established provider. Because James is not motivated, cares only about himself and provides little to pay expenses, Greta ended their relationship by handing him her "We're Breaking Up Manuel," a thorough description of what she considers to be the perfect mate. With no place to go, James finds temporary shelter at he home of his friends Lauren and Hannah and with their help becomes determined to win Greta back by becoming the man in her manual. The program chronicles the journey James takes—with everything that can go wrong happening as he finds re-inventing himself is not as easy as it sounds.

Cast: James Edward (James), Greta Jung (Greta), Lauren Smerkanich (Lauren), Hannah Louise Miller (Hannah), Katie French (Katie), Jeffrey Addiss (Boris, the Super), Laryn Stout (Madame Lisette), Han Nah Kim (Kim) **Credits:** *Producer:* Laryn Stout, Katie French, Lauren Smerkanich, James Edward Shippy. *Director:* Laryn Stout. *Writer:* Laryn Stout, Lauren Smerkanich, Katie French. **Comment:** Like the above title, it is an African-American production and well done with a simple but effective twist on the guy trying to win back the girl of his dreams with good acting and production values.

Episodes: *1.* The List. *2.* We Never Do Anything Exciting. *3.* You've Let Yourself Go. *4.* Your Job Is Ridiculous. *5.* You're Sexually Unadventurous. *6.* You Don't Care About Anything But Yourself. *7.* You Have No Style. *8.* You Don't Get Along with My Friends. *9.* Your Friends Suck. *10.* You Always Hang Out with Your Ex.

188 *Compulsive Love*. compulsivelove. com. 2013.

Aaron is a young man who hopelessly and continually falls in love but always with the wrong kind of girl. He is seeking his one true love and each episode depicts his encounter with a different girl and the inane situations he encounters in his quest to find that special girl—who is out there somewhere, but where?

Cast: Alex Anfanger (Aaron), Laura Ramadei (Zoey), Amy Staats (Melissa), Travis York (Travis), Allison Altman (Janice). **Credits:** *Producer:* Aaron Edell, Timothy C. O'Neill, Kevan Tucker. *Director:* Kevan Tucker. *Writer:* Adam Szymkowicz. **Comment:** Pleasant program with good acting and production values. There are some mild adult situations but nothing offensive.

Episodes: *1.* Love At First Bike, Maria. *2.* Mamma Mia! Lily. *3.* The Godmother, Linda. *4.* Lesbian Experience, Marge. *5.* Sister Act, Leena, Lucy and Lyssa. *6.* Role Pay. *7.* A Stolen Heart, Vicki. *8.* Friends with Benefits, Season Finale.

189 *Concerned Citizens*. youtube.com. 2013.

Felix Hancock is a man on a mission to re-educate the public as to what is happening in the world: a powerful criminal network is controlling the U.S. and manipulating world events. Although Felix is exercising his First Amendment rights of free speech, he always neglects to get the necessary permits and becomes a constant nuisance to those he protests as he is continually dismissed as a nut case. Letting nothing defeat him, Felix continues his lone crusade with the program showcasing what happens as he preaches "Resist Tyranny" but accomplishing nothing but trouble for doing so.

Cast: Patrick Hune (Felix), Mariella Jacqueline, Aaron Goold, JR Ritcherson. **Credits:** *Producer-Writer-Director:* Lee Lovino. **Comment:** While only a pilot episode appears to have been produced, it is well acted and presented. Slight computer animation presents the characters in a cartoon-like appearance that just adds to the program's charm. If you know someone who stands up for causes, you will love this series; if not, you will get an insight into what some people really believe and what they go through to spread the word.

Episodes: *1.* This Country Is Being Used.

190 Confessions of the Munchies. confes sionsofthemunchies.com. 2013.

Andy Long is a young man who dreams of a life of fame and leisure. He has moved to Los Angeles but soon finds that dream is not possible as he must get a job and make money just to survive. The program relates events in Andy's life as, not being a 9 to 5 (or 8 to 4) type of guy, he navigates a world he particularly doesn't like. **Cast:** Andy Long (Andy), Eric Semple, Tom Gregory, Dan Tirman, Brendan C. Kelly. **Credits:** *Producer-Writer:* Andy Long. **Comment:** All episodes have been taken off line thus an evaluation is not possible.

Episodes: *1.* Pilot: Cocked and Loaded.

191 Connections. youtube.com. 2013.

Survive is a dramatic serial about a young man's angst, torn between passion and duty "in a winding story of love, art, sex and disease." *Never Do Business with Friends* is a sitcom detailing the mishaps that abound as the drama is being produced. The program itself combines two separate series under one title to bring viewers both a dramatic story as well as a sitcom related to the drama (the making of that program). **Cast:** Michael Knowles, Sigrid von Wendel, Hunter Wolk, Arden Rogow-Bales, Kyle Clark, Julia Myers, Sean McCusker, Kalyan Ray-Muzambar, Edward Delman, Julie Shain, Shannon Riccio, Lindsey Pearsall, Kyle Eisenberg, Murray Biggs. **Credits:** *Producer:* Julia Myers, Sean McCusker. *Director:* Julia Myers. *Writer:* Julia Myers, Sean McCusker, Alex Lin, River Clegg. **Comment:** A rarity in Internet programming as combining two different concepts under one title has its challenges, the biggest being, who are the producers hoping to attract— those interested in a drama or those in a comedy? It is a hard concept to sell on broadcast television and is rarely produced. Here a group of Yale University students have attempted the idea and, although the episodes (especially in *Survive*) are a bit long (over 20 minutes; Internet users prefer short episodes and producers are becoming more aware of that) and can deter one from sticking with the program.

Survive **Episodes:** *1.* One Year Apart. *2.* The Evidence of Things Not Seen. *3.* In My Unbelief. *4.* As I Lay Dying. *5.* All the World's a Stage.

Never Do Business with Friends **Episodes:** *1.* Jake Quit. *2.* Action! *3.* This Is the Moment? *4.* Take the Risque. *5.* 'Tis the Season. *6.* It's Supposed to Be Funny.

192 Consequences. youtube.com. 2012.

Barbara, Jesus, Hari, Monisa, Martha, Thorah, Ray and Billy are strangers who have one thing in common: They are ex-convicted felons who have been assigned to a court-ordered support group (led by Melody) in order to hopefully rehabilitate them and make them law-abiding citizens. What sounds good is anything but as the ex-cons struggle to shed their criminal pasts and, if at all possible, become decent citizens. **Cast:** Jill Czarnowski (Melody), Shaun Landry (Martha), Amanda Ohly (Barbara), Misa Doi (Monisa), Ashley Knaysi (Thorah), Tilt Tyree (Ray), Sashen Naicker (Hari), Ronnie Karam (Jesus), Marco Tazioli (Billy). **Credits:** *Producer:* Darrin Yalacki, Michael May, Lindsay Harbert, Katie Bogart Ward. *Director:* Michael May. *Writer:* Darrin Yalacki. **Comment:** Talkative but interesting at times profile of eight ex-cons as they delve into the personal aspects of their lives and what led them down the wrong path.

Episodes: *1.* Pilot. *2.* Barbara. *3.* Billy. *4.* Martha. *5.* Thorah. *6.* Ray. *7.* Jesus. *8.* Monisa. *9.* Hari. *10.* Everyone and Everything.

193 The Contractors. youtube.com. 2012.

Max and Bernie are contractors that hire out their services as hit men for a price. Bernie is somewhat unbalanced, skittish and shoots at anything he fears. Max, more down-to-earth, fears Bernie's quirks will get them noticed, and is forever trying to resolve the situations that arise due to Bernie's actions. While they seem to be in demand, they also have numerous problems and the program relates their escapades as they perform hits—and try not to get caught in the process. **Cast:** Tom Murphy (Max), James Wainwright (Bernie). **Credits:** *Producer-Writer-Director:* Ben Johnson. **Comment:** British produced program that tackles a subject most often seen involving American hit men. Bernie's actions do provide the comedy, especially in the third episode when he kills a prostitute, brings her body into his and Max's apartment and presents Max with a problem: how to dispose of her without getting caught. The acting and production values are good but the program just ends in the middle of nowhere with a possibility that additional episodes will be produced.

Episodes: *1.* Pilot. *2.* This Isn't the Matrix. *3.* Whore Corpse.

194 A Conversation While... youtube.com. 2011.

Jasper and Horace are brothers and criminals who, before engaging in a crime debate the merits of what they are about to do. Those conversations form the basis of stories. **Cast:** Kevin Joiner (Horace St. Jake), Jason McMahan (Jasper St. Jake). **Credits:** *Director:* Stephen Boatright. *Writer:* Jason McMahan, Kevin Joiner. **Comment:** Unusual bad guy saga (complete with vulgar language) that, for the most part, is well produced but incorporating an audience laugh track in some episodes, especially in outdoor scenes, really doesn't work.

Episodes: 10 untitled episodes, labeled "Episode 1" through "Episode 10."

195 *Convos with My 2-Year-Old.* youtube. com. 2011–2013.

Actual conversations between a father (Matthew) and his two-year-old daughter (Coco) are re-enacted by two grown men—one as the father (Matthew) and the other as the daughter (David, Matthew's friend).

Cast: Matthew Clarke (Himself), Coco Frances Harrison-Clarke (Herself), David Milchard (Coco impersonation), Leila Harrison (Herself, Coco's mother, Matthew's wife). **Credits:** *Producer:* Matthew Clarke. *Director:* Darshan Rickhi. **Comment:** While the concept is unique in presentation (and well done) it can be seen as a take off on Art Linkletter's 1950s TV series *House Party* wherein children were asked questions with their answers providing the comedy.

Season 1 Episodes: *1.* Pilot. *2.* Episode 2. *3.* The Cookie. *4.* The Check. *5.* Playtime. *6,7.* The Pants. *8.* Come on, Let's Play.

Season 2 Episodes: *1.* Dinner Time. *2.* Make the Bed. *3.* The Princess Dolls. *4.* Fashion. *5.* Bath Time. *6.* Leaves. *7.* Doctor. *8.* The Slide.

Season 3 Episodes: *1.* The Crack. *2.* Mother's Day Special. *3.* The Day After Tomorrow. *4.* Dreams. *5.* Big/Small. *6.* Electricity. *7.* The Elevator. *8.* Coffee Table.

196 *Cool Justice.* youtube.com. 2012.

Tom Martin and Helen Wheels, two male detectives living in 1973 are pursuing felons when they are shot and left for dead. But all is not lost. They are cryogenically frozen by a scientist and stored in a warehouse. It is 2012 when the scientist passes and his will leaves everything to his granddaughter Zoe—provided she can unravel clues that will lead her to a fortune. Zoe's ability at deciphering puzzles leads her to a warehouse where she finds her childhood bicycle. As Zoe mounts the bike and begins to peddle it, she activates a computer that brings up a pre-recorded image of her grandfather on a TV monitor. As her grandfather speaks, she learns of a vast fortune awaiting her and something else—the frozen detectives. It is learned that Zoe's grandfather had some nefarious dealings (that actually led to Martin and Wheels being shot) and with their help, she can uncover the hidden fortune by deciphering cryptic clues left by the billionaire scientist. The program concludes with Zoe finding the detectives (in a secret room) and them slowly defrosting.

Cast: Brian Grosh (Helen Wheels), Todd Rulapaugh (Tom Martin), Camila Greenberg (Zoe Ben-

Effron). **Credits:** *Producer:* Luke Elliott. *Director:* Jeff Hodsden. *Writer:* Todd Rulapaugh, Brian Groh. **Comment:** Martin and Wheels are an extreme exaggeration of TV series detectives *Starksy and Hutch* and Zoe is a pretty girl who will no doubt become involved in their crime-busting efforts while seeking to clean up her grandfather's mess and find her inheritance (assumed to be as no additional episodes have been produced). The acting is very good and meant to be as corny as it appears.

Episodes: *1.* Pilot.

197 *Cooler Than You.* youtube.com. 2012.

Shelley Buttman is a very pretty aspiring actress hoping to make her mark on the world. She has an agent (who is also her boyfriend) and feels that success is just around the corner. Her world changes when her boyfriend tweets her that he is dumping her for another woman. Devastated but not defeated, Shelley bounces back and through her video blogs the program presents her efforts to not only establish herself as an actress but venture into the often awkward world of dating. Her cousin, Larry assists her as her vlog cameraman while her roommate and fellow actor, Blake, also lends a hand as she navigates through both worlds.

Cast: Megan Minto (Shelley Buttman), Rocky Conly (Cousin Larry), Ray Rosales (Blake), Christy Decker (Christina R.), Ben Tovar (Sweet Poppa Bill), Richard C. Jones (John Wall), Jenny Keto (Audrey Rose), Kristyl Tift (Ruth Bush), Jason Erick Taylor (Jean Pierre-Paul). **Credits:** *Producer:* Ray Rosales, Megan Minto, John Erick Taylor, Matthew Hardesty, Olive Sancho. *Writer-Director:* Ray Rosales, Olive Sancho. **Comment:** Shelley calls herself "A super star waiting to happen" and as she vlogs, flashbacks are used to show what happened that created those vlogs. Megan Minto is captivating as Shelley and handles her role expertly with the rest of the cast well chosen to support her. The production values are also good and while the subject matter has been done before, it is presented here in a slightly different and enjoyable manner.

Episodes: *1.* All My Exes Live in Texas. *2.* No One Can Eat Fifty Eggs. *3.* Bye Bye Birdie or Singles Group Magic. *4.* Le Headshots. *5.* Occupy (John) Wall Street. *6.* Uranus, Buttman and Yoga.

198 *Co-Op Stories.* youtube.com. 2012.

Santa Monica, California, provides the backdrop for a look at the happenings at a local supermarket co-op with a particular focus on the somewhat unusual patrons that are drawn to shop there.

Cast: Janet Lee Rodriquez, Zachary Ray Sherman, Ronald Menzano, Scot Nary, Jimmy McHugh, Julien Amorosi, Jeremiah Bryant, Smyth Campbell. **Credits:** *Writer-Director:* Ben Wolfinson. **Comment:** Programs set in supermarkets or grocery stores are quite rare as they are just not done. The acting is very good and the overall production pleasing to watch.

Episodes: *1.* Cell Phone Checkout. *2.* Celebrity Sighting. *3.* Juggle Complex. *4.* Juice Fight. *5.* Just Try a Sample. *6.* All I Want Is Gum. *7.* Who Took My Cookie? *8.* Changing States. *9.* Fixed Pricing. *10.* The Sex Talk. *11.* Empty Returns. *12.* The Job Interview. *13.* Could You Be My Doctor? *14.* The Stick Up. *15.* Don't Eat the Cake. *16.* The Promo Video. *17.* Gluten Free Pick Up.

199 Copy and Pastry. youtube.com. 2009.

Roommates Tory and Scott have a dream to begin their own pastry business. They begin by selling their home made pastries on the street but competition from bakeries forces them out of business. But they are not defeated. Without a permit and illegally turning their Berkeley, California, apartment into their place of business, Tory and Scott begin an on-line pastry delivery service (Copy and Pastry) and the program chronicles all the problems that ensue as Tory and Scott launch their newest enterprise.

Cast: Tory Stanton (Tory), Scott McCabe (Scott) Casi Maggio (Penelope Nicholls), David Weise (Lesley Lindsay), Rana Weber (Patty Plumbopple), Nathaniel G. Fuller (Peter Plumbopple), Matt Gunnison (Health Inspector Vick). Clive Chafer (Narrator). **Credits:** *Producer-Writer:* Tory Stanton, Scott McCabe. *Director:* JK Pincosy. **Comment:** A bit off the wall at times but well acted and produced.

Episodes: *1.* The One Where a Business Gets Started. *2.* The One Where the Business Tries to Attract Customers. *3.* The One Where the Business Discovers the Benefits of Having an Employee. *4.* The One Where the Business Gets Sidetracked. *5.* The One Where the Business Makes a Special Delivery. *6.* The One Where the Business Receives a Thorough Probing. *7.* The One Where...

200 Corporate. webserieschannel.com. 2014.

Alice is a young woman employed as a Human Resources Representative in an unnamed company. Life changes for her when she is assigned the task of compiling her company's exit reviews (interviewing people who retire, quit or are fired). Although the new position is not to her liking, Alice sees it as an opportunity to advance her position and the program, while focusing mostly on her interviewing people, also shows how she begins manipulating the system to become head of the HR department.

Cast: Chrissy Swinko (Alice), Darrin Yalacki (Dave), Adalgiza Chermont (Mrs. Catalano), Sheila Grenham (Judith), Jonathan Chase (Chad), Caitlin Muelder (Monica), Parvesh Cheena (Dave), Nancy Friedrich (Bonnie), Ryan Gowland (Keith), Kale Hills (Mikey). **Credits:** *Producer:* Chrissy Swinko,

Darrin Yalacki. *Director:* Anne Brashier. *Writer:* Chrissy Swinko. **Comment:** Alice is a woman who tells it like it is and doesn't care who she hurts doing so. The premise really hasn't been done before and comes off as rather good (due for the most part by Chrissy Swinko as Alice, who is perfect in the role). The production as well as the performances by the other cast members is just as good.

Episodes: *1.* Pilot. *2.* Chad. *3.* Monica. *4.* Judith. *5.* Nate. *6.* Bonnie. *7.* Keith. *8.* Mikey. *9.* Dave.

201 Cost of Living. costoflivingseries.com. 2014.

Marisa is a young woman who, to please her boyfriend, became a vegan. But enough is enough and Marisa misses the life of eating (especially cheese) she once enjoyed and dumps him when he refuses to change his ways ("One can only go so long without eating cheese"). Jules, Marisa's best friend, is a career woman with a successful corporate job but feels she needs to follow her dream of opening a rubber stamp company and is struggling over what to do (she later quits to pursue her dream). Hamilton (a girl), called Hammy, is their friend, a "once cool woman" (gave up her law practice for a marriage license). She is married to Timothy, a technician who wants to quit his job to become a bar tender. Dylan is Jules' boyfriend, "an eternal dreamer" who is unaware that Jules has quit her job and is now broke; Ezra, although a bisexual and always in a struggle over it, is the most stable member of the group and the glue that holds the friends together. A group of friends and the problems each faces, whether alone or together, form the basis of each episode.

Cast: Kate Elston (Marisa), Meg Hayes (Jules), Julianne Fawsitt (Hammy), Eric Bryant (Ezra), Sean McQueen (Dylan), Daniel Martinez (Timothy), Tess Bellomo (Cecily), Matt Nelson (Ben), Alec Kaplan (Josh), Vince Faso (Mikael). **Credits:** *Producer:* Dave Binegar. *Writer-Director:* Shannon Bowen. **Comment:** Very well acted and presented program that may have you wondering why this is not on regular TV.

Episodes: *1.* Bathroom Not Included. *2.* Lady Date. *3.* Lady Bits. *4.* Indian Summer. *5.* Victorian Bride. *6.* Jesus' Baby. *7.* $TD. *8.* Virtual Happy Hour. *9.* Oregon Trail. *10.* Friendsgiving.

202 Couch Surfers. webserieschannel.com. 2012.

Travis, a man without a job or an apartment; Nick, a rolling stone (a person with no job, no home and no ambition) and Armen, Travis's uncle, a sex therapist whose TV show *Intercourse Discourse* is on hiatus and has no income, solve their homeless problem by logging on to couchers.com, an on-line hospitality network wherein people open their homes to people in a bind. The program charts the mishaps the trio finds as they take total advantage of the site but encounter people who are anything but normal. Shelby is Travis's girlfriend, a journalist who becomes involved in all his shenanigans.

Cast: Chase Green (Travis Cundell), Jason Peter Kennedy (Nick Walsh), Clint Carmichael (Armen Cundell), Kelsey Glasser (Shelby Lewis). **Credits:** *Producer:* Sean Mier, Stuart Arbury, Joseph McPhillips. *Director:* Sean Mier. *Writer:* Sean Mier, Stuart Arbury. **Comment:** Although the idea has been done numerous times before, a nice twist is presented making the subject, especially with the off-the-wall characters the trio encounter, interesting. The program is also known as *Couchers*.

Episodes: *1.* The Get By Guys. *2.* The Aspiring NFL Cheerleader Guy. *3.* The Babysitter Bully Lady. *4.* The Immigrant Smuggler Guy. *5.* The Threesome Lover Lady. *6.* The Christian Science Guy. *7.* The Chronic Masturbator Lady. *8,9.* The Mall Walker Lady. *10.* The Legally Dead Guy. *11.* The Paranormally Active Lady.

203 *County Sheriff.* webserieschannel.com. 2012.

Rick, an incompetent and illiterate police officer, and Jim, his best friend and partner, are members of the County Sheriff's Office. In an effort to profile the crime-solving abilities of the police department and present a better image, the local TV news channel has been granted permission to accompany Rick and Jim as they patrol and protect. The program relates all the mishaps that occur as Rick and Jim patrol and attempt to deal with all the deranged criminals that are on the loose.

Cast: Ryan Webber (Lt. Rick Riverson), Ryan Mey (Lt. Jim Johnson), Brett Christiansen (Deputy Burt Reynolds), Katherine Cheslek (Deputy Jill Jameson), Rob Antor (Douglas Newton), Andrew Tiberio (Sheriff Joe Jenkins). **Credits:** *Producer:* Ryan Webber, Ryan Mey, Brett Christiansen. **Comment:** During the 1940s there was a radio series called *The Police Recorder* wherein a reporter rode with two police officers and recorded what happens for the radio audience. *County Sheriff* not only encompasses that aspect but elements from the TV series *Reno 911* to present a spoof of law enforcement. It works but the episodes are much too long (23 to 30 min. each) to sustain interest for an Internet series (under ten minutes is ideal as the viewer's attention span will not be lost).

Season 1 Episodes: *1.* Pilot. *2.* Routine Traffic Stop. *3.* Wherein the World is Jim Johnson? *4.* A Big Accident. *5.* I, Remember. *6,7.* The Deal. *8.* The Interrogation. *9.* Distraction. *10.* The Return, Part 1.

Season 2 Episodes: *1.* The Return, Part 2. *2.* Mission Impossible. *3.* Wrong Place, Wrong Time. *4.* Restoration of Power. *5.* All Quiet on the County Front. *6.* Someone Stole My Boat. *7.* The Ride Along. *8.* Domestic Dispute. *9.* A Night with Gary.

204 *Cowgirl Up.* onemorelesbian.com. 2011–2013.

"Just a stone's throw away" from the resorts, restaurants and shopping centers of a large city in California is Cochella Valley, home to the Double D Ranch where gorgeous young women gather to "play cowgirl" and engage in activities from trick shooting to trick riding. The program charts their experiences as cat fighting and making love to each other are also part of the activities.

Cricket and Lu are the ranch owners. Among the sexy cowgirls are Savannah, Cricket and Lu's adopted daughter; Dakota, the girl out to win every competition; Maddie, Dakota's best friend, a lesbian with a mean streak; and Robbie, the star of a western TV series called *Spur* who has come to the ranch to learn how to be a real cowgirl and do her own stunts. Rusty and Dee are ranch wranglers; Coon-Ass Kate is the girl who can't see "the lesbian thing" at the ranch and prefers "real dudes." Babe and her associate, Bitsy (a man in drag) are the local law enforcers and, adding intrigue to the story are Maeve and Snapper, con-artists who have secretly learned the ranch sits on top of oil and are now out to acquire the property for themselves.

Cast: Mandy Musgrave (Dakota), Bridget McManus (Babe), Marnie Alton (Abby), Kodi Kitchen (Dee), Melissa Denton (Lu), Linda Miller (Cricket), Shannan Leigh Reeve (Rusty), Kate McCoy (Coon-Ass Kate), Nicole Travolta (Eager Beaver), Niki Lindgren (Jo), Maribeth Monroe (Meredith), Treisa Gary (Sunny Trails), Aasha Davis (Robbie), Butch Jerinic (Chief Morning Wind), Brandy Howard (Snapper), Valery M. Ortiz (Maddie), Maeve Quinlan (Buckshot Betty), Hannah Madison Taylor (Savannah), Matt Cohen (Sheriff Bitsy Calhoun), Pam Pierce (Hooch McCarthy), Nancylee Myatt (The Boss). **Credits:** *Producer:* Nancylee Myatt, Paige Bernhardt, Matt Cohen, Christin Mell, Nicole Valentine. *Director:* Paige Bernhardt, Matt Cohen, Nancylee Myatt, Christin Mell, Courtney Rowe. *Writer:* Paige Bernhardt, Nancylee Myatt. **Comment:** "Wanna see funny and hot girls ridin' horses, shootin' guns and playin' Cowgirl?" is the tag line for an enjoyable series. The girls really appear to be doing their own stunts and the competition sequences, though somewhat campy, are fun to watch. The acting and production values are first rate.

Episodes: Episodes are available only through a pay subscription service. The following episodes are available for free on the official website. *1.* Season 1, Episode 1: The Good, the Bad and the Pretty. *2.* Girls Gone Wild: Meredith and Dakota. *3.* Girls Gone Wild West: Jo and Eager Beaver. *4.* Girls Gone Wild West: Dee and Abby. *5.* Girls Gone Wild West: Wrangler Fight.

205 Craft Ladies. webserieschannel.com. 2012.

Karen and Jane are best friends who not only share a love of crafting but wine. Although the women lead totally different lives, their crafting interest bonds them. With an idea to share their abilities (drinking and crafting) with the world, they decide to begin a web series (from Karen's garage) and with their motto "Craft Up Nice Things" offer advice and demonstrations on how to craft. **Cast:** Tiffany Anne Price (Karen), Lauren De Long (Jane). **Credits:** *Producer-Writer:* Tiffany Anne Price, Lauren De Long. *Director:* Ambika Leigh. **Comment:** Although wine was not incorporated, the children's television series *Cake* presented the craft idea in a well produced series. *Craft Ladies* is like an adult version of that show with very good acting, production values and humorous take-offs on crafting ideas. Karen and Jane often wear cleavage-revealing outfits and the camera is there for close-ups of that aspect of their wardrobes.

Episodes: *1.* Toilet Paper Roll Owls. *2.* Sewing. *3.* Friendship Bracelets. *4.* Vision Boards. *5.* Tie Dye. *6.* Corking. *7.* Baking. *8.* Esty.

206 Craig and the Werewolf. blip.tv. 2009.

One day a young man (Craig) returns home earlier than expected to see that his roommate, Brett, is a werewolf and feasting on a victim. Once overcoming the shock, Brett admits to the fact and Craig sort of accepts it as he doesn't want to move and lose his security deposit. Complications ensue when Craig is bitten, becomes a werewolf and both must now try to live two lives—ordinary people and werewolves when the moon is full. Haley is Craig's girlfriend (secretly a vampire). **Cast:** Craig Frank (Craig), Brett Register (Brett), Haley Mancini (Haley), Katy Stoll (Katy), Angie Cole (Angie), Daniel Norman (Daniel). **Credits:** *Producer-Writer-Director:* Brett Register. **Comment:** Comical parody of the werewolf legend with a focus on how a werewolf adjusts to everyday life. The acting and production values are good but the werewolf eating people aspect is so badly presented (and so obviously overplayed) that it distracts from the overall intention of the program.

Season 1 Episodes: *1.* I, Roommate. *2.* While Grown Men Sleep. *3.* I'm Going Through Changes. *4.* What Beautiful Eyes You Have. *5.* Requiem for a Werewolf.

Season 2 Episodes: *1.* Worst Werewolf Ever. *2.* This Sucks. *3.* The Intervention. *4.* When Trojan Horses Collide. *5.* Let's Face the Music and Slay.

207 Crash Pad. crashpad.tv. 2012–2013.

The Crash Pad is an airport rooming house where flight attendants live together between assignments.

The program, which incorporates improvisation, focuses on twelve such attendants (see cast) and how they spend time in the crash pad as opposed to their experiences on airplanes with passengers. **Cast:** Tatum Langton (Rebecca), Ashley Campbell (Molly), Christopher Lars (Stewart), Joshua Cameron (Kevin), Adrienne Hartvigsen (Sara), Aline Andrade (Angela), Jaclyn Easton (Kristen), Chantel Flanders (Julia), Jesse Peery (Brad), Lee Fobert (Jimmy), Brenden Whitney (Louis), Antonio Lexerot (Gregory). **Credits:** *Producer:* Antonio Lexerot, Chris Henderson, Cathy Tidwell. *Writer-Director:* Antonio Lexerot. **Comment:** Television series dealing with airlines never become a success. *Flying High*, *From a Bird's Eye View*, *San Francisco International Airport*, *LAX* and *Pan Am* are examples; *Wings* is a rare exception as it became the only such hit. *Crash Pad*, with its quirky (and sometimes hard to believe as being real) characters would fall into the realm of the non-successful airline based series and is a candidate for being the least desirable to watch of them all as it is simply unappealing.

Episodes: *1.* F.N.G. (Fairly New Guy). *2.* Cleaning Day. *3.* Homeless. *4.* White Water. *5.* Rule #1. *6.* Jewelry. *7.* Allen. *8.* I Never. *9.* Punch. *10.* Meds. *11.* The End?

208 Creepy Priest. webserieschannel.com. 2011.

Father Joseph Leahey is a Catholic priest with St. Felicitas Parish who is a "good friend with God" and talks to him all the time. Being a priest, Father Leahey also takes an interest in his parishioners' lives, seeking to help where he can. But there is a creepy side to Father Leahey—his uncontrollable urge to especially help children. The program explores what happens as Father Leahey attempts to get too close to the children of his parish. **Cast:** Jeff Hatz (Father Joseph Leahey). **Credits:** *Producer:* Arik Cohen, Jared Bauer. *Director:* Jared Bauer. *Writer:* Jeff Hatz. **Comment:** Father Leahey is not only a bit creepy but the overall concept appears to be a satire on the problems the Catholic Church has faced regarding priests and their inappropriate association with young boys. While nothing is shown that it is offensive, the program is witty and well acted and produced.

Episodes: *1.* Cowboy Roundup. *2.* Younger Brother. *3.* Suicidal. *4.* The Son Came Out.

209 The Crew. thecrewwebseries.com. 2007–2009.

The future has many changes in store, one being the ability to travel through space. The United States is still exploring the vast regions of space and has a number of vessels that can travel great distances into the atmosphere and to other planets. One such vessel is the *Azureas*. Unfortunately, the ship is not equipped with the most intelligent or effectual crew (sort of its misfits) and the program relates the missions undertaken by the *Azureas*, missions that are accomplished more by accident than anything else.

Cast: Philip Bache (Tom Wilkerson), Ariel Lazarus (Andrea Lee), Craig Frank (Patrick Fargent), Amy Kline (Jennifer Parker), Michael Hart (Stewart Kobbler), Michelle Exarhos (Sarah Clauson), Cathy Baron (Dr. Talia), Brett Register (Tim Waterson), Angie Coe (Amber), Taryn O'Neill (Corrine), Daniel Norman (Evil Patrick), Robin Thorsen (Agule), Jessica Rose (Map), Payman Benz (Laurent). **Credits:** *Producer-Writer-Director:* Brett Register. **Comment:** Enjoyable space spoof with good acting and production values. The special effects, while limited, are good for an Internet series.

Episodes: *1.* Pilot. *2.* Last Romantics. *3.* Ghost Ship. *4.* Poop Deck. *5.* An Explanation of Sorts. *6.* Departed. *7.* No Escape. *8.* Barfly. *9.* Verdict. *10.* Call the Doctor. *11.* Break Ups and Make Ups. *12–14.* Clones. *15.* The Signal. *16.* Survival. *17.* Pirates. *18.* A Pirate's Life. *19.* Misguided. *20.* Baby on Board. *21.* Rendezvous.

210 *Crisis PR.* webserieschannel.com. 2012.

Richard, Susan, Tim and Traj are the owners of a struggling public relations firm called Crisis PR. For a nominal charge and with their slogan, "You Know Where Your Money's Going," they attempt to rebrand tarnished reputations and restore a positive image. The program chronicles several of those people and firms Crisis PR attempts to rehabilitate.

Cast: Brenden Gallagher (Tim), Alison Levering (Susan), Zhubin Parang (Richard), Will Stone (Traj). **Credits:** *Producer-Director:* Stiv Brown, Brenden Gallagher. *Writer:* Zhubin Parang, Alison Levering. **Comment:** Standard Internet comedy with acceptable story, acting and production.

Episodes: *1.* Strong and Hamill. *2.* Christian Day Evangelical Church of Holy and Righteous Ascension. *3.* Mothers Against Chilling. *4.* Merqks Candy Bar. *5.* Daisy.

211 *Crumbs in the Bed.* youtube.com. 2012–2013.

A bedroom is the setting. Here a young African-American newlywed couple rarely sleeps or have sex but discuss all the problems that have entered their lives. The bed has become their comfort/war zone and the program relates their conversations as they deal with anything and everything from their bed.

Cast: Lynn Andrews III, Robyn K. Sapenter. **Credits:** *Producer:* Adam Scott Thompson, Ezra James, Stephanie Hall, Rusty Hall. *Director:* Solomon Onita, Jr. *Writer:* Adam Scott Thompson. **Comment:** The program has no real introduction to who the characters are (not even names) and assumes the viewer will know they are married (and

not just two people living together). The acting and production values are good and, even though it all takes place in a bedroom, the format does work.

Episodes: *1.* Oh Crumby Night. *2.* Groggy Froggy. *3.* Yo Mama. *4.* Tokehouse Cookies. *5.* Book Club vs. Fight Club. *6.* Bust a Nap. *7.* From Another Mother. *8.* Why Did I Get Summoned? *9.* Dirty Jobs. *10.* He Said, She Said.

212 *Crusaders.* youtube.com. 2012.

Sally, Meg, Ant, Dev, Ryan and Duck, friends since high school, reconnect years later after each had gone their separate way. Each had dreams at the time but has each fulfilled that destiny? The program follows each of the friends as they reveal what has happened to them and what they believe the future holds (all in a comedic way as they were "wild and crazy" in high school and for most, that hasn't changed; it is said to be "based on true events that have been blown out of proportion").

Cast: Brittny Gonzales (Sally), Marcis Hammer (Dev), Magnus Chan (Ant), Steve Olson (Ryan), Bri Pasely (Meg), Nick Haas (Duck). **Credits:** *Producer:* Nick Haas. *Director:* Matthew Miranda, Josh Ricci. *Writer:* Josh Ricci, Nate Follen, Matthew Miranda, Chris Cruz, Matt Sahatdjian. **Comment:** The program kind of starts in the middle of nowhere but is easy to figure out as the first episode progresses. The acting and production is good and the program did seem to have potential but only two episodes were produced.

Episodes: *1.* Homecoming. *2.* Circumcised Crusader.

213 *CSU: Crime Stoppers Unit.* blip.tv. 2013.

The CSU (Crime Stoppers Unit) is a volunteer group of citizens who like a neighborhood watch (but with more authority) is designed to help the police battle crime. The unit is run by Chief Pierson and her team includes JJ, Karl, Brick and Addison. The primary action is set in the unit's headquarters and focuses mainly on the activities in which they become involved as opposed to taking to the streets and patrolling to keep their community safe.

Cast: Granison Crawford (JJ), Melinda Lee (Martha Pierson), Gregory Nelson (Brick), Karli Kaiser (Addison), Sebastian Fort (Karl Cooper), Corey Roberts (Nelson), Christopher O'Brien (Trent Summers). **Credits:** *Producer:* Granison Crawford, Sebastian Fort. *Director:* Granison Crawford.

Comment: The acting is acceptable although the constant bickering makes one wonder what kind of people the CSU accepts as volunteers. That point is really never made clear but as long as one wants a job without any pay, then the CSU wants you.

Episodes: *1.* New Guy. *2.* Case Closed. *3.* Field

Day. *4.* Hard Times. *5.* Lady Problems. *6.* New Developments. *7.* Big Day.

214 *CTRL.* webserieschannel.com. 2008.

A spilled glass of Nestea changes the life of Stuart Grundy, an ordinary guy working at an ordinary, boring office job, when the liquid reacts with his computer keyboard and allows him to use the CTRL key to do amazing things (for example, CTRL+B to confront his immature boss; CTRL+Z to return to his past; CTRL+Y to return to the present). The program, based on the short film *CTRL Z* by Robert Kirbyson, relates what happens as Stuart experiments with the various key combinations.

Cast: Tony Hale (Stuart Grundy), Emy Coligado (Elizabeth), Steve Howey (Ben Piller), Zaden Alexander (Jeremy), Richard Karn (Arthur Piller). **Credits:** *Producer:* Thomas Bannister, Tony Hale, Robert Kirbyson, Barney Oldfield. *Director:* Robert Kirbyson. *Writer:* Robert Kirbyson, Bob Massey. **Comment:** Enjoyable comical fantasy program that is well produced and acted. The first stand alone web series to be produced by a major broadcast network (NBC and its digital studios division).

Episodes: *1.* Pilot: CTRL. *2.* CTRL B. *3.* CTRL Z. *4.* F1. *5.* CTRL C, CTRL V. *6.* CTRL Home. *7.* CTRL X. *8.* CTRL Zzzzzz. *9.* CTRL Y. *10.* CTRL, AlT, Del.

215 *Cup of Joe (2011).* youtube.com. 2011.

Benny is a young man who just lost his best friend and co-worker (Joey) through a tragic accident. As Benny returns to work, he finds that it is not the same as Joey is not there—that is until the office coffee maker begins talking to him (seen as the blinking red "on" light) and tells him that he is Joey, who has been reincarnated as a coffee maker. Benny has a job he really doesn't like, a boss who is forever on his back and co-workers who do not appreciate him. Now, with Joey again by his side (although Benny is the only one who can hear Joey speak), the program follows what happens as Joey, in his ghostly manner, helps Benny navigate life at work.

Cast: Ben Warner (Benny), Patrick Rolls (Voice of Joey), Valerie Armin (Bianca), Don Hampton (Mr. Schwapp), Erin Howell (Carli), Agatha Raleigh (Tamara), Jason Sweatt (Rod). **Credits:** *Producer:* Jack Tomas, Ben Warner. *Director:* Jack Tomas. *Writer:* Joey Milillo. **Comment:** While the subject matter is not new (the TV series *My Mother the Car* perhaps exemplifies the reincarnation scenario) there is always a twist that can be made to make it something different. Although only a four-part pilot has been produced, it is well done and an interesting program to watch.

Episodes: *1–4.* The Pilot.

216 *Cup of Joe (2013).* vimeo.com. 2013–2014.

Joey is a 25-year-old with no ambition, little motivation and currently living at home with his mother. When Joey's mother sees that her son is simply wasting his life away, she kicks him out in an effort to make him a man and face the real world. Still not motivated, Joey finds shelter at the home of his estranged sister, Nikki, an actress contemplating taking a job within the adult film industry, who is not thrilled about having Joey living with her and putting a cramp on her lifestyle. Seeing that Joey is totally useless, she arranges an interview that actually nets him a job for a company wherein he becomes the personal assistant to demanding boss (Bill). The program charts the path Joey takes and the circle of people that soon become his friends: Wolly, an ex hockey player "with fabulous hair"; Freezz and Lil' $hit, rappers; Kelly, Joey's girlfriend, and Galen, an office worker.

Cast: Joey von Haeger (Joey), Nikki von Haeger (Nikki), Wolly Wolcott (Wolly), Wynn Reichert (Bill), Chris Feaster (Freezz), Nathan Ruff (Lil $hit), Galen Milender (Galen), Kevin Reed (Kevin). **Credits:** *Producer:* Joey von Haeger, Wes Powers, Michael Beatty. *Writer:* Joey von Haeger, Wes Powers. **Comment:** Joey comes off as a person who is so stupid that it is hard to believe that he can accomplish anything. The show cannot be taken seriously and that is were the fun lies—seeing just how annoying Joey is to others and how they put up with his nonsense. The program does contain foul language (usually spoken by the characters Joey annoys).

Season 1 Episodes: *1.* The Interview. *2.* The Grind. *3.* The Secretary. *4.* The Party. *5.* The Freeez Frame. *6.* The Date. *7.* The Noise. *8.* The Foursome. *9.* The End.

Season 2 Episodes: *1.* The One in Los Angeles. *2.* The One Where Wolly Actually Plays Hockey. *3.* The One with the Lil Private. *4.* The One in Wisconsin. *5.* The One with the Roller Girls. *6.* The One with the Baby.

217 *Cut to the Chase.* webserieschannel. com. 2012.

Chase Fountaine is an aspiring young film producer-writer-director who shares an apartment with Josh Wood, a young filmmaker also. The friendship, however, becomes a thing of the past when creative differences get in the way of a movie project ("a futuristic space opera of epic proportions" called *Odyssey Through Time*) and Josh moves out, opting to make the movie on his own. Chase, now on his own, decides to document his life as he attempts to make that space opera with the help of his girlfriend (Natalie) and a film student he hires (Jason) as his assistant. The program follows Chase as he sets out to create a diary of his life and what happens when virtually everything that can go wrong does.

Cast: Owen Roth (Chase Fountaine), Christina Aceto (Natalie), Mena Massoud (Jason), Evan Bellam (Josh Wood). **Credits:** *Producer:* Owen Roth, Evan Bellam, Devin Knowles. *Writer-Director:* Owen Roth, Evan Bellam. **Comment:** Very well acted and produced series. Owen Roth is especially appealing as Chase and expertly handles the role. Some of the comedy is very subtle and what is happening around the main action needs to be watched; the best example being a cable news station sticking with an interview with Josh while headlines that report numerous disasters are run as a ticker across the bottom of the screen. The opening is also unique for its use of green screen technology to show Chase walking in a position that is not humanly possible.

Episodes: *1.* Pilot. *2.* The Sidekick. *3.* The Number. *4.* The Producer. *5.* The Professor. *6.* The Audition. *7.* The Investor. *8.* An Evening with Josh Wood.

218 *Cynic.* funnyordie.com. 2014.

Ted is a stand up comedian who, because of his having to live with cerebral palsy, has become "a disabled deviant." Rachel is Ted's domestic assistant (support worker) and the program follows Ted as he not only struggles to live with what he has, but somehow learn to control his nasty attitude for the benefit of all those who surround him.

Cast: Ted Shiress (Ted), Rachel Helena Walsh (Rachel), Laura Ramona Kendrick (Laura), Aisling Bell (Cassandra/Janine), Dan Mitchell (Dan), Gareth Brand (Gareth), Karen Steadman (Karen), Clint Westwood (Kim). **Credits:** *Producer:* Ted Shiress, Paul Hunt. *Director:* Hugh Griffiths, Geraint Knott. *Writer:* Ted Shiress. **Comment:** A show that is definitely not for everyone as some will find it is quite offensive for making fun of a disability. It is simply a very difficult program to watch unless seeing a person with cerebral palsy trying to navigate daily life doesn't bother or offend you.

Episodes: *1.* Coffee. *2.* Date. *3.* Evening. *4.* Metaphorically Speaking. *5.* Kim. *6.* Kerb Your Enthusiasm. *7.* Gags. *8.* Spastic Dating

219 *The Cynical Life.* webserieschannel. com. 2012.

Harper Hall, the author of a children's book called *Oko the Bear* is in New York on a book signing tour while her boyfriend Benny, a rocker with a small band, remains at home in Los Angeles. When Harper's tour ends earlier than expected and she returns home, her world begins to crumble when she catches Benny with another woman. Harper ends their relationship and finds comfort (and advice) from Rajit, a therapist based in Pakistan she consults via Skype (at $25 an hour). Having left the home she and Benny shared and with no place to stay, Harper moves in with her younger sister Nettie (a stage performer who prefers to be called by her professional

name of Sparrow) and her two roommates, Jessica and Plum. With advice from not only Rajit, but from her new roomies, Harper must now come to terms with what has happened and the program follows her efforts—aided (or hindered) somewhat by her addiction to drinking (straight from the bottle).

Cast: Ashley Avis (Harper), Camille Cregan (Sparrow), Gerry Bednob (Rajit), Chelsea Rae Bernier (Plum), Janna VanHeertum (Jessica), David Ballam (Benny). **Credits:** *Producer:* Amed Khan, Ashley Avis, Colin Day, Paul Harrison Daggett. *Director:* Matthew Sullivan. *Writer:* Ashley Avis. **Comment:** Well cast program with excellent acting and production values. While there is some vulgar language, the scenes with Harper and Rajit are well done and one can see (and hear) Rajit's frustration over Harper as he attempts to help her.

Episodes: *1.* David Hasselhoff's Illegitimate Daughter. *2.* Break-Up Sale. *3.* Intro Fertilization. *4.* Do You Play Sims? *5.* How's Your Salad? *6.* My Reason for Drinking. *7.* Separation of Assets.

220 *The DaddyMan.* thedaddyman.wee bly.com. 2009.

"DaddyMan, DaddyMan, does whatever a DaddyMan can…" opens the program to introduce the DaddyMan, a supposed supernatural entity that is constantly reborn to take on new identities and intervene in human destiny. While the DaddyMan enjoys a drink and smoking his pipe, he also rants and raves about what he is and how he is meant to change destinies. Each episode is a look at one of the DaddyMan's rebirths and how his intervention changes the lives of people (his vessels) that are selected by a means known only to him.

Cast: Matt Wright (DaddyMan), Nick Ford, Christopher Blodgett, Erin Williams, Kelsey Houser, Hayleigh Albers, E.J. Tangonan. **Comment:** The DaddyMan appears a bit deranged when first introduced as his ranting does make him seem peculiar. His ability to project his image through TV and mirrors makes him mystical while "his humble home in heaven" is nothing more than a chair in what appears to be a living room or den. The program is a bit unusual, sort of a satirical spoof of programs like *Touched by an Angel* with good acting and production values.

Episodes: 12 episodes with a titled pilot ("The DaddyMan Commeth") and 11 additional untitled episodes, labeled "Episode 2" through "Episode 12."

221 *Damien's Quest.* webserieschannel. com. 2012.

Damien Johnson is an advertising executive living in Los Angeles. He is not an out-going or flashy person and lives a quiet unconventional life. Damien believes that time should never be wasted and that if life throws an obstacle your way, you need to push back and get yourself back on track. His philosophy is a bit out-of-the-ordinary, but it suits him and he enjoys being who he is. However, sometimes pushing back at life does not always net the same results and what you had hoped for does not happen. The program charts those instances that change Damien's outlook on life when Fate throws a monkey wrench into the works and Damien must learn how to deal with it, being, most often unsure as what to do. **Cast:** Ernest Pierce (Damien Johnson), Anita Davenport (Clara Johnson), L.A. Dillard (Michelle), Eric Dean (Juan Valdez), Christeen Gordon (Philip), Tasha Biltmore (Aunt Brutrishia). **Credits:** *Producer:* Ernest Pierce, Lloyd Stephen Knight. *Director:* Ernest Pierce. *Writer:* Ashlee Elfman, Ernest Pierce. **Comment:** Not only does Damien have to deal with work and friends, but a bit off-the- wall family as well. The acting and production is good but there are adult sexual situations and a needless use of foul language. **Episodes:** *1.* What Damien Wants, Damien Gets. *2.* Mama's House. *3.* Meet Damien's Family. *4.* Therapeutic Tendencies. *5.* Friends and Therapeutics. *6.* Treava the Diva.

222 *Dancing in Small Places.* webseries channel.com. 2014.

Olivia Tennet is a very pretty young woman who is also a very talented dancer. Her expertise in various dance styles is combined in comic vignettes that explore dancing in very small places (as can be seen by the episode list). **Cast:** Olivia Tennet (Herself). **Comment:** Filmed in black and white and, while not a laugh-out loud comedy, it is just a pleasant, humorous look at how dancing can be performed anywhere and in any situation. **Episodes:** *1.* Shower. *2.* Car. *3.* Pantry. *4.* Park Bench. *5.* Toilet. *6.* Bath. *7.* Phone Booth.

223 *Danger 5: The Diamond Girls.* you tube.com. 2011.

The Australian television series *Danger 5* is set in a fantasy-like World War II era wherein a team of spies (Danger 5) have been assigned to stop Adolf Hitler from achieving world domination. *The Diamond Girls* aired as a prequel to the TV series and begins by establishing that Hitler has discovered a rare black diamond whose dust (when turned into makeup) can transform ordinary women into super fighters (and impervious to bullets) called She-Nazis. Danger 5, an Australian-based unit of fearless spies (Ilsa, Claire, Jackson, Pierre and Tucker), led by Colonel Chestbridge, are assigned the task of recovering the diamonds and stop another devious plot by Hitler as he slowly gains inroads on his ultimate goal (here to infiltrate the Allied command of the World President, Massimiliano Importanta).

Cast: Natasa Ristic (Ilsa), Amanda Simons (Claire), David Ashby (Jackson), Aldo Mignone (Pierre), Sean James Murphy (Tucker), Tilman Vogler (Chestbridge), Carmine Russo (Adolf Hitler), Anna Cashman (Nazi Hostess), Ryan Cortazzo (Gunther), Susanna Dekker (Madam Julietta), Caitlin McCreanor (Nazi Priestess), Cameron Pike (Hein), Peter Powell (Gibraltar). **Credits:** *Producer:* Kate Croser, Dario Russo. *Director:* Dario Russo. *Writer:* David Ashby, Dario Russo. **Comment:** Enjoyable World War II spoof that presents Hitler in a totally new light (a megalomaniac with ways of defeating the Allies the real Hitler never imagined). The acting and production values are outstanding and the use of miniature sets to establish outdoor scenes is very well done. **Episodes:** 5 untitled episodes, labeled "Episode 1" through "Episode 5."

224 *Danger! Relax, Please.* dangerrelax-please.blogspot.com. 2011.

Angry J is a very pretty Japanese woman who is called Angry J for a reason: when something upsets or disturbs her, she becomes very agitated. Angry J does not speak English (her speech is seen in subtitles) but understands the English language as the people she encounters speak English. As Angry J just navigates daily life, her encounters with the people who eventually annoy her are profiled—and what she does to dismiss them from her life are showcased. **Cast:** Jenny Hou (Angry J), Malachi Rempen (Various roles). **Credits:** *Writer-Director:* Malachi Rempen. **Comment:** Exceptionally well done program that is truly enjoyable. The special effects are well done and the use of sound effects to highlight what Angry J does adds to the program's charm (it is sort of like the sound effects that are seen on *The Three Stooges*; without them, it just wouldn't be as funny). The end credits move at lightning fast speed—but by pausing here and there, some comedy gems can be found. **Episodes:** *1.* Water Worries. *2.* Citrus Casbotage. *3.* Postal Puns. *4.* Fatherly Falderal. *5.* Baguette Brawl. *6.* Regulation Rukus. *7.* Duel Debacle. *8.* Orbicular Outrage.

225 *Dare Doll Dilemmas.* dyna-flix.com. 2007–2010.

A city that appears to be like any city is under the protection of the Dare Dolls, a group of ultra sexy, spandex clad super heroines who do battle the bad guys but often do not always come out the victor. The Dare Dolls (see cast) endure many perils as they seek to stop Larry and Chad Peeper, villainous brothers who devise ingenious traps to capture them and ultimately destroy them as they stand in their way of dominating the city. "If you like beautiful women, tight and shiny costumes, you are home," exclaims an announcer as the Dare Dolls not only risk their lives to battle evil, but display their bodies for camera shots that explore every inch and curve.

Cast: The Dare Dolls are only credited as follows: Apple, Athena, Aura, Baby, Blaze, Blu, Boots, Cherry, Diana, Dusk, Ice, Jade, Juice, Kiki, Kitt, Lash, Leather, Legs, Lila, Lotus, Mint, Minx, Onyx, Pippi, Puss, Pyro, Rio, Soleil, Sweets. **Credits:** *Producer-Writer-Director:* Dynahunk Productions. **Comment:** While the program is a spoof of the TV series *Batman, Wonder Woman* and *Electra Woman and Dyna Girl* not even Lynda Carter as Wonder Woman, sexy as she is, is as alluring as the Dare Dolls. It's like seeing fetish porn for the way the girls dress and how they manipulate themselves in their attire. There is a parental warning for "lurid dialogue and situations" and, although episodes cannot be viewed for free (as of July 2015), they are available for purchase on DVD. Clips from each episode can be seen on the official website and several sharing sites like YouTube. The clips are a bit racy and do give the viewer the idea that the actual episode is a lot sexier than the clip. Any attempt to call up an actual episode from any site will redirect you to Amazon.com for purchase.

Episodes: 99 episodes have been produced as 33 three-part chapters.

Chapter 1: *1.* Puss and Boots Are a Desired Taste. *2.* Puss and Boots Are Much Desired. *3.* Puss and Boots Make Their stand.

Chapter 2: *1.* Puss Gets Goosed. *2.* Leather Gets Tethered. *3.* Blaze Is Taken Aback.

Chapter 3. *1.* Blaze in a Daze. *2.* Lash Has an Evil Twin. *3.* Puss Is Taken Aback.

Chapter 4. *1.* Legs Walks on Shells of Eggs. *2.* Puss Is a Real Doll. *3.* Leather's Tether Is a Bad Guy's Pleasure.

Chapter 5. *1.* Ice and Mint Can't Take a Hint. *2.* Minx Thinks Something Stinks. *3.* Can Jinx Straighten Their Kinks?

Chapter 6: *1.* Puss Is Abed in a Web. *2.* Mint in a Bind with a Rapacious Vine. *3.* Barbecued Minx.

Chapter 7. *1.* It's the End for Jinx, Methinks! *2.* Minx Shall Now Get Poked. *3.* A Taste of Mint in Winter.

Chapter 8. *1.* Jinx and Rio, Served with Brio. *2.* Jinx Is Ripe for the Plucking. *3.* Rio Is a Regular Riot.

Chapter 9. *1.* Ice Is for Bloodthirsty Buds. *2.* Minx and the Overly Phallic Power Tool. *3.* Mint and Lila Are All Tied Up.

Chapter 10. *1.* A Mint-and-Lila Sandwich. *2.* Puss Is All Wound Up. *3.* Jade Faces Destiny's Blade.

Chapter 11: *1.* Mummified Minx. *2.* Keep Smilin' Lila. *3.* Ice and Jade Are in the Soup.

Chapter 12. *1.* Mint Is Going to Be So Totally Screwed. *2.* Jinx Is on the Brink of Being Eaten. *3.* Jade and Ice Are Fish Out of Water.

Chapter 13. *1.* What's on Your Mind, Puss? *2.* Mesquite-Flavored Minx. *3.* Minx vs. Puss.

Chapter 14: *1.* Kiki Makes Such Great Taffy. *2.* Apple's Roasted Over an Open Fire. *3.* Blu's Quest Is Fruitless/Bootless.

Chapter 15: *1.* Apple and Blue Are Stuck in the Mud. *2.* Pinx and a Snake That Slinks. *3.* Pop Goes the Puss Doll.

Chapter 16. *1.* Kiki and the Kinky Day. *2.* Lotus Meets a Lethal Susan. *3.* Puss and Boots Are Brainwashed Beauts.

Chapter 17. *1.* Minx Gets Sliced in Thrice. *2.* Soleil Finds a Needle in the Hay. *3.* Kiki's Stuck on Some Thorny Horns.

Chapter 18. *1.* Kitt Tries on a New Belt. *2.* Pinx Beneath the Pendulum. *3.* Kiki Out in the Cold.

Chapter 19. *1.* Exit Kiki/Enter Diana. *2.* Soleil and the Sticky Stick. *3.* Kitt Meets Her Mousetrap.

Chapter 20. *1.* A Lovely Lotus Wrapped in Silk. *2.* Soleil, the Human Parfait. *3.* Pinx Within a Dream.

Chapter 21. *1.* Let's Roast Blue and Lila. *2.* Blue vs. Lila. *3.* Lila vs. Blu and Soleil.

Chapter 22. *1.* Pinx Within a Dream Within a Dream. *2.* A Taste of Cherry. *3.* Juice and Onyx Are Pearls Before Swine.

Chapter 23. *1.* Juice and Onyx Are Hot and Cold. *2.* Soleil Fights Her Tights. *3.* Introducing Dare Doll Aura.

Chapter 24: *1.* Exit Aura, Enter Cherry. *2.* Attack of the 50-Foot Pyro. *3.* Lotus Finds Cherry Fit to Be Tied.

Chapter 25. *1.* At the End of a Rope with Lotus and Cherry. *2.* Aura and the Really Big Borer. *3.* Introducing Dare Doll Athena.

Chapter 26. *1.* Aura and the Human Fly Trap. *2.* Pyro's Inferno. *3.* Introducing Dare Doll Dusk.

Chapter 27. *1.* Introducing Sweets, or When Blu Met Dusk. *2.* Lotus and the Curse of the Pharaohs. *3.* In the Clutches of the Silver Seductress.

Chapter 28. *1.* Cherry Gets Eaten. *2.* Sweets Might Gum Up the Works. *3.* The Human Pin Cushion.

Chapter 29. *1.* The Devil Eyeballs Dare Doll Dynamo. *2.* Cherry Sliced. *3.* Bringing Down Baby.

Chapter 30. *1.* Lotus vs. Dynamo. *2.* Cherry, Juiced. *3.* Cherry Juiced 2.

Chapter 31. *1.* Dynamo Walks the Plank. *2.* Cherry, Juiced 3. *3.* Aura Gets Processed.

Chapter 32. *1.* Attack of the Viewer Mail. *2.* Attack of the Viewer Mail 2. *3.* Attack of the Viewer Mail 3.

Chapter 33. *1.* Dynamo Is a Real Knock-Out. *2.* The Cake Takes Dynamo. *3.* Pyro's Last Pose.

226 *Darren Has a Breakdown.* darren-has-abreakdown.tumblr.com. 2014.

Darren and Steph are a couple and life couldn't be better for Darren—until they break up and Darren begins to fall apart (it was so bad that three policemen had to break down Steph's bathroom door to remove Darren from her home). Due to his actions, Darren has been court-ordered to attend therapy in an effort to get over Steph, the love of his life. Helping Darren (or attempting to) is his best friend Tony, who figures that Darren needs to move on and find another girl or try and find a way to get back with Steph. The program follows Darren who, with Tony's help, seeks a way to escape the life of depression he has created for himself.

Cast: Matt Houston (Darren), Daniel Cech-Lucas (Tony), Louise Williams (Steph). **Credits:** *Writer-Director:* Menelik Simpson. **Comment:** British produced program that is well acted and produced. It actually captures the distress Darren feels as he tries to get over Steph and move on with his life.

Episodes: *1.* Therapy. *2.* Big Sister. *3.* Threesome. *4.* Blind Date. *5.* Moving On. *6.* Stakeout.

227 *Date A Human.com.* youtube.com. 2010.

In an unspecified future time humans and outer space aliens can live side by side and marry if they so desire. The alien population, however, outnumbers the human population and human women are now expected to have as many children as possible to increase the human aspect. Allie is a young human woman who, after getting her heart broken by a human male "for the last time" takes the advice of Ruthie, her roommate, and begins a quest to find an interspecies romance. Episodes follow Allie and her experiences with what she meets on DateAHuman.com.

Cast: Anne Griffin (Allie), Brooke Lyons (Ruthie), Cathy Shambley (Allie's mother). **Credits:** *Producer:* Amber J. Lawson, Joy Gohring, Lauren Schnipper. *Director:* Joy Gohring. *Writer:* Joy Gohring, Paul Malewitz, William Weissbaum. **Comment:** Interesting reversal on dating and matchmaking programs with good acting and amusing stories.

Episodes: *1.* Pilot. *2.* Space Dumped. *3.* Alien Filth. *4.* Lava Lips. *5.* Total Rip-Off. *6.* The Love Bug Dating Blues.

228 *Dates Like This.* dateslikethis.com. 2012–2013.

Alicia (straight) and Meg (lesbian) are friends seeking the love of their lives but not romantically involved with each other. The program relates their quest but in two different ways. While Alicia follows a normal dating routine, Meg has devised a scheme called "30 Dates in 30 Days" to hopefully find the woman of her dreams. With Meg's 30 Dates system not producing any positive results and Alicia also unable to find a mate, each sets out on a new course to find their special someone in Season 2. Alicia, hoping to reignite her career as a dancer (while working as a bartender) has found romance with a

co-worker (Zachary) but a girl named Blake may have awoken feelings in her that she may be bisexual; Meg has several issues to deal with, including a girlfriend from her past (Vera) and her relationship with an older woman (Danielle), a boutique owner.

Cast: Hannah Vaughn (Meg), Leigh Poulos (Alicia), Kathy McCafferty (Danielle), Jessie Barr (Nikki), Rebecca Robles (Blake), Matthew Robert Gehring (Zach), William G. Kean (Scott), Natalie Fehlner (Gwen), Colin Aarons (Owen), Kristen Lazzarini (Vera), Johnny O'Malley (Dave), Keiko Green (Theresa), Jess Ritacco (Lindsay), Katie Hammond (Claire), Jillian Green (Amber), Brittany Anne Oman (Allison), Katie Rose Spence (Jessie), Jill Wurzburg (Norah), Rachel Sussman (Melody). **Credits:** *Producer-Writer:* Leigh Poulos, Hannah Vaughn. *Director:* Hannah Vaughn, Leigh Poulos (Season 1), Jessica Solce (Season 2). **Comment:** Meg and Alicia are smartly cast in a well-acted and produced program. There are several kissing scenes but nothing objectionable and the story flows smoothly from beginning to end.

Season 1 Episodes: 8 untitled episodes, labeled "Episode 1" through "Episode 7."

Season 2 Episodes: *1.* Happy Birthday Bitch. *2.* Mona Lisa's. *3.* Not So Happy Hour. *4.* Sorry Ladies. *4.* The Good, the Bad and the Boring. *5.* Fork and Field.

229 *Dating on Mars.* datingonmars.com. 2012.

David and Nova, astronauts, and Karl, a NASA engineer, were scheduled to be part of a space flight destined for Mars. When the project is delayed they are let go. Nova and Karl have made new lives for themselves but David, unemployed and divorced, has a difficult time adjusting and even more problems getting back into the dating scene. With help from Karl and Nova the program charts the situations that occur as David ventures forth into the world of dating. Complications arise when Karl, who had appropriated (stolen) NASA equipment, is discovered to have technology he should not have and is pursued by two government agents (Men in Black) who seek to retrieve NASA's equipment.

Cast: David Conklin (David), Christopher Fitzgerald (Karl), Jaclyn Walsh (Nova), Lauren Hart (Barbara; Karl's wife), Carl Wormer, Geoffrey Henderson (Men in Black), Gilda DeMartino (Helen), Wendy Tiburcio (Maria). **Credits:** *Producer-Writer-Director:* Carl Wormer. **Comment:** When the mystery surrounding Karl is exposed (creating weapons from items he stole from NASA) the program takes on a different perspective (running from the law) as opposed to David attempting to create a new life. The acting and production are good and the program interesting for its twists and turns.

Episodes: *1.* Karl and Nova. *2.* Barbara. *3.* For Your Eyes Only. *4.* In the Beginning: Dave's First

Date. *5.* When World's Collide. *6.* Close Encounters. *7.* Men in Black. *8.* Kinky Aliens. *9.* Meeting M. *10.* Mars Ain't the Kind of Place.

230 *Dating Pains.* youtube.com. 2014.

Lucy and Alex, best friends but not dating each other, are each seeking their soul mate. But neither has had any luck and each believes that the people they meet are, for the most part, losers and not someone they would want to settle down with. The program charts their efforts to find that perfect someone by plunging into the dating world, not realizing that fate had intended them to be perfect for each other.

Cast: Darielle Deigan (Lucy), Baker Chase (Alex). **Credits:** *Producer:* Baker Chase, Darielle Deigan. *Director:* Marc Cartwright. *Writer:* Baker Chase, Darielle Deigan, Aaron Lee Harvey, Ryan Stockstad. **Comment:** Amusing twist on dating scene programs. The acting and production values are good and, although the program's episodes seem to progress from under two minutes to over twelve minutes, there is no resolution and the doorway is left open for further episodes to appear.

Episodes: *1.* The First Date. *2.* Party for Two. *3.* Cat-astrophe. *4.* Deal Breakers. *5.* Spoiler Alert. *6.* Unofficially Invited. *7.* The Jig Is Up!

231 *Dating Rules from My Future Self.* alloyentertainment.com. 2012–2013.

Lucy Lambert (Season 1) and Chloe Cunningham (Season 2) are young women with good jobs and good friends but a love life that is anything but desirable as they seem to have little luck finding the right man. One day Lucy (then Chloe) receives a text message from ten years in the future—from their future selves. It is accomplished through an app that allows a person to reconnect with that same person as they were ten years earlier. That future person has already made the decisions and choices that the present person has not and knows what lies ahead. The program follows the choices the women make through the guidance of their future selves.

Season 1 Cast: Shiri Appleby (Lucy Lambert), Mircea Monrow (Amanda), Alison Becker (Kelcy), Bryce Johnson (Brenden), Taylor Kinney (Dave), Candace Accola (Chloe Cunningham), Leah Rachel (Olivia), Lindsay Karft (Tara), Toby Meuli (Scott). **Season 2 Cast:** Candace Accola (Chloe Cunningham), Lindsey Kraft (Tara), Toby Meuli (Scott), Leah Rachel (Olivia), Reid Ewing (Andrea). **Credits:** *Producer:* Leslie Morganstein, Joshua Blanl, Josh Schwartz, Bob Levy, Tripp Reed, Shiri Appleby. *Director:* Elizabeth Allen. *Writer:* Wendy Weiner, Sallie Patrick. **Comment:** Interesting concept with very good acting and production values. Chloe is the more flirtatious girl, playing the field and not taking love seriously while Lucy is more laid-back and not

so much a player but someone who truly wants to find the man of her dreams.

Season 1 Episodes: *1.* Who R U? *2.* What Is Luv? *3.* Change Ur World. *4.* Heal Urself. *5.* Be Ur Own Woman. *6.* Open Ur Eyes. *7.* Keep Calm and Carry On. *8.* Time 2 Intervene. *9.* U Can Get It if U Really Want It. *10.* Luv Yourself.

Season 2 Episodes: *1.* Time to Get Ur S**t Together. *2.* The Sexy Black Cat. *3.* Ruiner. *4.* The Jimmy Song. *5.* Kool-Aid. *6.* The Last Shrimp.

232 *Dating Savannah Love.* datingsavannahlove.tumblr.com. 2013.

Savannah Banks is a very pretty African-American woman whose adult life has been focused on achieving success. Her career came first (editor of a bridal magazine) and a social or love life was the furthest thing from her mind. But now, at the age of thirty, she begins to realize what she has missed, especially finding a man and starting a family. Seeing that Savannah has expressed an interest in dating, Valerie, her best friend and assistant, convinces her to venture forth into the world of on-line dating. The program follows Savannah as she takes the plunge and must now juggle a career with a dating life with her intent being to find her perfect soul mate.

Cast: Donna Cerise (Savannah Banks), Mandalyn Meades (Valerie), A.J. Davis (Derrell), Gayla Johnson (Pamela). **Credits:** *Producer:* Pentene Monique, Brandon Kyle. *Writer-Director:* Brandon Kyle. **Comment:** A pleasant diversion from many African-American productions as it strays from tough bitch-like characters, foul language and unpleasant sexual situations. Donna Cerise is charming in her role and the producer has done a great job in exploring incidents in the life of a young black woman.

Episodes: *1.* Pilot. *2.* The First Date. *3.* Casa de Juanita. *4.* Mama's Boy. *5.* Beggars Can Be Choosers. *6.* Savannah in Training. *7.* 30 is the New Savannah. *8.* Savannah, Falling. *9.* A Pleasant Surprise Or Two.... Or Three. *10.* Brand New.

233 *The Daughters of POP.* webserieschannel.com. 2014.

Chloe Valentine and Beth Henley are very special young women: they are the daughters of rock star legends. They grew up together and had an upbringing like no one else as they toured the world with their mothers. It was an exciting life for Chloe and Beth until the tours stopped and they were thrust into the real world. They are now unsure of who they are and where they stand in the world. Through serialized 15-second episodes the program shows how Chloe and Beth attempt to find out via social media. The program is also known as *The Real Daughters of POP.*

Cast: Heather Lee Moss (Beth Henley), Anna

Borchert (Chloe Valentine), Meg Schaab (Shelley Mason), Charlie Merlo (Josh Cooper), Logan Loughmiller (Seth Anderson), Phillip Daniel (Liam Worthington), Chad Layman (Mo Newman). **Credits:** *Creator:* Heather Lee Moss. *Co-Creator:* Anna Borchert. *Producer:* Anna Borchert, Heather Lee Moss, Anne Woods. *Director:* Chad Layman, Richard Carroll. *Writer:* Heather Lee Moss. *Story By:* Anna Borchert, Heather Lee Moss. **Comment:** Very fast moving program with a lot happening in a very short span of time. While four episodes can be watched in a minute, viewing episodes back-to-back does not become a chore and it is literally the only way to enjoy the program.

Season 1 Episodes: *1.* Gossip Girls. *2.* Mommy Issues. *3.* Meet The Assistant. *4.* How Would We Survive. *5.* Josh Hangs Out. *6.* This Is Gonna Be a Problem. *7.* Shelley the Ex-Chaser. *8.* Meditation Moment. *9.* Chloe-tinis. *10.* Stairwell Surprise. *11.* Caught in the Act. *12.* And We're Off! *13.* Meet Our Driver. *14.* Backseat Driver. *15.* Get Out!! *16.* Stranded. *17.* Oh the Horrah. *18.* We're Never Gonna Make It. *19.* Yeah Yeah Yeah.... Get In! *20.* Shelley Takes Care of Everything. *21.* Mo Lays Down the Law. *22.* Primp, Prep, Perfect!

Season 2 Episodes: *1.* Door Drama. *2.* That Guy. *3,4.* Shots of Shame. *5.* Mission. *6.* Where's Shelley? *7.* Ring Pops. *8.* Girl Fight! *9.* Shelley Goes Off. *10.* Tradition. *11.* No Twirling. *12.* Mama Drama. *13.* Is That Your Friend? *14.* Meet Seth. *15.* Last to Leave. *16.* Let's Get In-N-Out. *17.* My Hero. *18,19.* What Was That? *20.* I Can't Sleep. *21.* Couch Buddies. *22.* Girls Love This Stuff. *23.* Shh! He's Sleeping! *24.* I'm Gonna Need Those Keys Back. *25.* Outside Now!! *26.* Winner!! *27.* Let's Call It What It Was. *28.* Life After Liam.

Season 3 Episodes: *1.* Sex Tape Aftermath. *2.* Mo Solves Another Problem. *3.* The Meltdown Begins.

4. The Meltdown Continues. *5.* Now It's on TV?!?! *6.* Hamptons Bound.... Finally! *7.* Can't You See I've Helped You. *8.* Beth, I'm Handling it. *9.* Lose Her Number. *10.* I Knew You'd Be Back. *11.* Escape from L.A. *12.* This Is Not the Hamptons. *13.* Settling In. *14.* Shelley Sucks. *15.* You Say Dubai, I Say Brunei. *16.* Let's Make the Best of It. *17.* In-Room Amenities. *18.* Josh, You're the Best. *19.* Room Service. *20.* Can We Talk? *21.* Shots of Shame. *22.* Dancing on the Ceiling. *23.* Catnap Canoodling. *24.* Chloe Confesses All. *25.* Midnight Madness. *26.* Sealed with a Kiss. *27.* Everybody Needs to Calm Down. *28.* No, I'm Leaving. *29.* The Party's Over. *30.* Are You Sure You Want to Leave? *31.* I Have Good News. *32.* No, I'm Sorry. *33.* I've Got Some Good News. *34.* More Good News. *35.* Shelley Out.

234 *Day Drinking.* youtube.com. 2014.

Quentin Day is a radio disc jockey for alternative rock station WKAH who finds his life changing when he is moved from the Afternoon Drive Time Show to overnight disc jockey playing music he detests. Following his first graveyard shift he finds a bar that caters to night shifters and befriends a group of people who are in the same situation: Georgina (an E.M.T.), Ray (a janitor) and Aggie (tech support girl). The group meets each morning after work and the conversations they have are the focal point of stories.

Cast: Brit Belsheim, Jason R. Chin, Geoff Crump, Melissa R. DuPrey, Erin Rooney, Dave Urlakis. **Comment:** While the bar remains nameless and the only employee seen is Janet the waitress, the program manages to pull off a format that is hard to accomplish: people just sitting around a table and talking. The characters are believable (it would have been a nice gesture if the producer matched the performer with the player) and their conversations quite interesting.

Episodes: *1.* Dumped or Fired. *2.* Invisible Bear. *3.* Rough Night. *4.* Robots. *5.* Phones.

235 *A Day in the Life of Death.* webserieschannel. com. 2009.

Bob, otherwise known as the Grim Reaper, has become bored with his job and decides to quit and experience life as an ordinary human being. His experiences are shared with on-line viewers.

Cast: Julian Byrne (Death), Andrew Kines (God). **Comment:** A comical fantasy that has potential as Bob attempts to figure out the human side of life.

Episodes: *1.* Pilot. *2.* The Grim

The Daughters of Pop. Series poster art (used by permission of www.daughtersofpop.com).

Reaper Makes a Vlog. *3.* Cereal Confession. *4.* Deadly Procrastination. *5.* What's in the Grim Reaper Bag? *6.* Grim Reaper Fails. *7.* The Grim Reaper Caught on Tape. *8.* What Happens When You Read the Light.

236 *Dead Grandma.* vimeo.com. 2011.

Not-Pasadena Junior College, not located in Pasadena, California (hence its name) is a university where a young man (Andy) has just begun classes. He is in the school's library, spying on a girl over a row of books when he is started to see the ghost of his late grandmother appear to him—to help guide him through his next stage in life. Dead Grandma, as Andy calls her, can only be seen by Andy and his actions (influenced by Dead Grandma's words and actions) make him appear a bit strange to the other students who can only see him. The program relates what happens as Dead Grandma attempts to help Andy find the right girl and Andy's efforts to lead a life that has now become anything but normal.

Cast: Matt Heder (Andy), Beverly Welsh (Dead Grandma), Shannon Mary Dixon (Judy), Nicholas Zaharias (Meathead), Umbero Riva (Fabrizio), Jon Heder (Host). Credits: *Producer:* Will Kindrick, Matt Heder, Tom Morrill. *Writer:* Will Kindrick, Courtney Branning, Matt Heder. *Director:* Will Kindrick, Courtney Branning. Comment: While web site information states that Dead Grandma is senile, she doesn't appear so in the program. The concept of a ghost helping the living is nothing new (dates back to *Topper* on early 1950s TV) but each case can be different, as it is here. The ghostly effect surrounding Dead Grandma is well done and the acting and production is top rate. The use of a host to introduce the episodes is simply done for what looks like a filler and really not needed.

Episodes: *1.* Library. *2.* Ice Cream. *3.* The Jacket. *4.* The Wrong Crowd. *5.* Dirty Burlesque Tramp. *6.* Foreign Exchange Student. *7.* Job Interview. *8.* Drive-in-Movie. *9.* Pool Party. *10.* Finale.

237 *The Deadline.* webserieschannel.com. 2012.

Nicholas, Gareth and James are amateur filmmakers who hit on an idea to make a web series. The only problem is—what should it be about? With a deadline approaching to make the series, they decide that the perfect plot would be to film a web series depicting themselves thinking of an idea to make a web series. The idea sounds logical and the program depicts how the web series is accomplished—by the filmmakers building a time machine and going back in time when they had an idea to make series but no idea as to what it would be about.

Cast: Nicholas Anscombe (Nicholas), Gareth Turkington (Gareth), James Parsons (James), Harriet Catchpole (Karen), Leigh Gill (Luthor). Cred-

its: *Producer-Writer-Director:* Graeme Willets. Episodes: Only 3 short teasers are on line and a fair assessment of the series cannot be made.

238 *Dealership.* dealershiptheseries.com. 2012.

Barkley Automotive is a large used car dealership that is owned by Charles Barkley. Only male employees appear to work for Charles and it is under the condition that they sport a moustache. "Barkley Auto—Home of the Car" is the company slogan and the program charts the company employees (Marty, Grant and Russell) as they attempt to sell cars, but are usually too busy doing other things to worry about making sales. Otis is the company's rather unsavory mechanic.

Cast: Roger Johnson (Charles Barkley), Todd Spence (Marty Freebrook), Shawn Kohne (Grant Kind), Danny Barton (Otis), Paul Goetz (Russell Rimshot). Credits: *Producer:* Dan Gartner. *Director:* Sean Gartner, Zak White. *Writer:* Todd Spence, Roger Johnson, Zak White. Comment: The main focus of episodes is what you are not supposed to be doing (goofing off) when you should be selling cars. The moustache requirement is a bit different but the concept of selling cars has been done numerous times before. There is foul language and the acting and production just standard for an Internet series.

Episodes: *1.* Power Blinds. *2.* Cursed. *3.* Drew Carey. *4.* Sales Contest. *5.* The Lemon. *6.* Chapped. *7.* The Election. *8.* The Trip. *9.* Season 1 Finale.

239 *Debt Collectors.* debtcollectorsthe series.com. 2012.

Dead Beats, as they are often called, are people who incur debts but can't or refuse to repay them. Tired of numerous complaints from people owed money the government decides to do something about the situation and creates the Federal Debt Collection Agency (FDCA), an organization dedicated to finding, capturing and imprisoning those who fail to repay debts. A young woman named Sabrina Rollins is in debt; she has a college degree, aspirations of achieving greatness but she is not easily motivated. Her life has been characterized by mediocre choices which have led her nowhere. When Sabrina was twelve years old she purchased a CD called "That's What I Call Music, Volume 1" from the Columbia House of Music CD Club. It cost $22.50 but Sabrina never paid the bill when it arrived. Eventually she just forgot about it—but the FDCA didn't. The bill, with compounded interest has risen to $14,622.19 and the agency wants their money. Sabrina is found and captured and brought to FDCA headquarters where she faces the wrath of Lieutenant/Sergeant/Captain Melania Gibbs, the dedicated leader of the agency who offers her a choice when she learns Sabrina cannot pay the debt:

be sent to Debtors Prison or work for them as an agent. With the only logical choice possible, Sabrina elects to join the ruthless agency and stories chart her experiences as she and her partner (Lana Stone) become bounty hunters seeking those who refuse to repay their debts. Enzo Malone is the agency's Wonk (technician and computer expert) with an uncanny knack for appearing from out of nowhere; Kim Turner is Sabrina's cousin, with whom she lives; Greg is Kim's live-in boyfriend.

Cast: Jahmela Biggs (Sabrina Rollins), Caitlin Talbot (Lana Stone), Puja Mohindra (Melania Gibbs), Chris Hampton (Enzo Malone), Jamila Webb (Kim Turner), Alex Cantry (Greg). **Credits:** *Producer:* Christina Martin, Jahmela Biggs, Caitlin Talbot. *Director:* James Bland. *Writer:* Christina Martin. **Comment:** A rather slow-moving start (should have been edited) before anything really happens. But after several minutes, the story line is presented and an enjoyable, if not far-fetched program emerges (sort of a spoof of the TV series *She Spies*).

Episodes: *1.* The FDCA. *2.* Debt Relief.

240 *Decisions, Decisions.* vimeo.com. 2011.

Roger and Patrick, office workers for Generic Products, are often so bored with their job that they devise hypothetical question-and-answer games to pass the time. As they ponder the merits of each question, such as living life as a cartoon or a live action movie character, a fantasy sequence is seen that explore the merits of both sides of the coin.

Cast: Brendan Countee (Roger Ponders), Adam Countee (Patrick Shruggs). **Comment:** The idea is quite good (although the topics a bit ridiculous as the comparisons are not always equal). The acting and production are also good.

Episodes: *1.* Wheelbarrow or Ewoks? *2.* Masturbation or Drunkest Moments? *3.* Al Gore or Controversy? *4.* Civil War or Press Conference? *5.* Pooparazzi or Asshole? *6.* Dikembe Mutombo or Purple Gatorade? *7.* Tennis Ball Machine or Ski Boots? *8.* Cartoon or Bourne Identity? *9.* Chuck Norris or Pink Dildo. *10.* Salty Old Sea Captain or Doc Holliday? *11.* Tin Man or Studio Audience? *12.* Make Your Own Clothes or Gentleman Dandy? *13.* Napoleon or Larry King? *14.* Pants Peeing or Poetry Slam. *15.* Satellite Delay or Nose Drinking.

241 *Delphis.* vimeo.com. 2013.

Charles is married, the father of a young son and best friends with Delphis, his child's plush dolphin. Charles is so immersed in the plush toy that he actually believes it is real and can communicate with him. The program charts a rather strange relationship between Charles and Delphis, taking it to a point where Charles eats and sleeps with it, takes a bath and sings to it and even has tea parties with it and the other plush animals in his child's room.

Cast: Scot Michael Walker (Charles), Christi Michael (Angel), Gail Cronauer (Sophie), Sarah Kate Allsup, Tom Marcantel, Christi Michael, Billy Blair II. **Credits:** *Writer-Director:* Scot Michael Walker. **Comment:** *Delphis* has to be seen to be believed. Fortunately "no toy plush animals were harmed" in the making of the series and for something completely different, *Delphis* holds the record.

Episodes: *1.* Tea Party. *2.* Don't You Want Me? *3.* Let's Talk About S**t. *4.* Sophie, the Bitch. *5.* Jack Is Cray Cray.

242 *Dennis the Office Cobra.* webseries channel.com.desert patrol 2012.

For as long as there have been jobs and bosses, employees have always been told what to do. Edgar is one such man. He works in an office and for the most unusual boss in the world—Dennis, a cobra (represented by a snake hand puppet). How Dennis managed to achieve his position of authority (or even how a snake came to be employed) is not explained but Dennis rules with an iron fist. The program relates what happens when Edgar tries to please Dennis but is apparently unable and receives Dennis's retaliation—a bite to the head or neck.

Cast: Steve Lattery (Edgar), Chris Johnson, Shanan Custer, Gary Denbow, Stephanie Denbow, Tristan Jonks, Andre Cavan. **Credits:** *Producer-Writer:* Steve Lattery. *Director:* James Snapko. **Comment:** Dennis is a well crafted puppet that doesn't speak but nods his head when asked a question and bites when he gets annoyed. The idea is truly original with very good acting and production values.

Episodes: *1.* The Promotion. *2.* The Supervisor. *3.* The Small Talk. *4.* The Team Building. *5.* The Gift.

243 *Desert Patrol.* funnyordie.com. 2011.

Sarge and Dan are a two-man team that forms The Desert Patrol, a unit that is part cop and part park ranger designed to protect the wilderness, here the desert. Sarge and Dan operate out of (and live in) a trailer in the desert and in their own world. Littering is the most offensive crime one can commit and if caught by the patrol, one is in for a steep fine—maybe even imprisonment. The program chronicles the cases Sarge and Deputy Dan investigate with the people who encounter them learning that the desert is their world and it would have been a wiser decision not to enter it in the first place as they have lost touch with reality.

Cast: Joseph Brock (Sarge), Travis Morris (Deputy Dan). **Credits:** *Producer-Writer:* Joseph Brock, Zach Wood, Chris Sullivan. *Director:* Joseph Brock. **Comment:** Take a bit of the TV series *CHiPs* (for its motorcycles) and throw in *Reno 911* (for its outlandish police officers) and what emerges is a spoof of TV crime programs that is well acted and produced. Dan and Sarge live in bubble, fight crime that is really not a crime (like a youngster riding a bike without a helmet) and how they react when they spot, chase and capture felons provides the comedy.

Episodes: *1.* Just Got a Call. *2.* A Dangerous Game. *3.* Lessons Learned. *4.* Domestic Disturbance. *5.* Mandatory Vacation Day.

244 *Destroy the Alpha Gammas.* destroy theeags.com. 2013.

The Alpha Gamma House is a college sorority that accepts only the most beautiful young women as its members; women who are stylish, rich and snobs. It is run by Autumn and her vice president Lauren. The Delta Pi Sorority, a less popular sorority house, consist of young women (Carrie, the president, and sisters Jen, Mary, Arlie, Ling, Bex, Stacey, Marty and Britney) who are not as popular nor hot but are caring and responsible. Although there is a rivalry between the two sororities, the situation changes drastically when Carrie catches her boyfriend cheating on her with Autumn and all she can see is revenge. Taking on the format of a romantic musical comedy, the program follows the sisters of Delta Pi as Carrie "declares war" determined to bring down The Alpha Gammas.

Cast: Leah McKendrick (Carrie), Anastacia McPherson (Autumn), Sara Fletcher (Jessie), Lindsay Morgan (Lauren), Anna Roberts (Jen), Christie Ann Burson (Mary), Cara Manuele (Stacey), Julina Creamer (Marty), Michelle Martinez (Ling), Karma Stewart (Bex), Cindy Derby (Britney), Lisa Marie Summerscales (Arlie), Judy Norton (Mrs. Andrews), Dennis Haskins (Officer Glen), Rachel Amanda Bryant, Alexandra Fatovich, Lee Karis (Alpha Gamma Sisters), Jen Fiskum, Lee Laris (Delta Pi Sisters). **Credits:** *Producer:* Leah McKendrick, Anna Roberts, Shintaro Shimosawa, Aerienne Booker, Scott Brown, Brigida Santos. *Director:* Scott Brown. *Writer:* Leah McKendrick. **Comment:** Exceptionally well done series. The cast can not only act but sing and dance as well making it appear as good or better at times than the Fox series *Glee.* Sharp-eyed viewers will most likely spot Judy Norton (Mary Ellen on *The Waltons*) and Dennis Haskins (Mr. Belding on *Saved by the Bell*) as appearing on the program.

Episodes: *1.* A Declaration of War. *2.* The Sausage Festival. *3.* Liar, Liar, Panties on Fire. *4.* Are You Calling Me an Aniston? *5.* There Will Be Blood. *6.* Black Swan Dive. *7.* Bitch.

Destroy the Alpha Gammas. **Series poster art (photograph by Eilene Beniquez, poster design by Sara Fletcher).**

245 *Development Hell.* you tube.com. 2013.

Death Waltz is a film released by Apollo's Chariot Pictures and directed by Damien Lockwood. The film is immediately and harshly criticized and brings disgrace not only to its releasing company but Damien as well when it becomes a commercial failure (the only movie to gross a negative amount of money). Damien, however, believes he has the ability to make the ultimate movie ("a musical sextacular") and convinces Chariot Pictures to give him one more chance to prove his abilities. Having not really learned a lesson from what just happened, Damien recruits the same people who helped him create a disaster: Blake Montana, his shirtless leading man; Archie Something (his last name appears to be unpronounceable and people call him Something), his droll assistant and Scott Wondolowski, his child-like producer. He decides on the ultimate stage musical for his project and the program follows Damien and his less-than-talented cast as they go about making the film to end all films.

Cast: Aria Ithavong (Damien Lockwood), Devon Henry (Archie Something), Max Sjostrand (Blake Montana), Rich Rubin (Scott Wondolowski), Tenere Williams (Tom Robinson), Isidro Lopez (Miguel Angel Torres), Nicola Barber (Narrator). **Credits:** *Producer-Writer:* Devon Henry, Aria Ithavong. *Director:* Carla Dauden. **Comment:** Vulgar language, which is really not needed here, is incorporated in a standard acted and produced program to present a behind-the-scenes look at what desperate measures are taken to produce a movie and regain one's reputation.

Episodes: *1.* Don't Mail Poop. *2.* Uno Mother-Fu***r. *3.* It Was My Goat. *4.* You Are Tearing Me Apart, Damien! *5.* A, Que?

246 *Devil's Couriers.* devilscouriers.com. 2013.

A spoof the TV series *The Sons of Anarchy*. The Devil's Couriers are a motorcycle gang that earn money by selling Viagra pills. They ride motorcycles, look mean and tough and carry guns. The Hipsters on Scooters (ride pink and red scooters) are their enemies and, although it hasn't happened yet, a turf war appears to be in the making. The Hipsters on Scooters also carry guns but their appearance is far less threatening than the Devil's Couriers. Although the rival gangs have their little skirmishes, nothing has gotten out of hand and things are usually settled peaceably. However, when the Hipsters on Scooters acquire a new male performance drug called Bonera and its sales start to cut into the Devil's Couriers business, all hell breaks loose with both sides seeking control of the drug trade. The program relates the conflict between the two gangs as each strives to make inroads in their town of Gobbler Creek and the lucrative retirement community that seeks their product.

Cast: Shane Cibella (Tristan), Tim Aslin (Max), John Charles Meyer (Richie), Kovar McClure (Frank), John Walcutt (Henry), Heidi James (Grace), Amanda Hall (Sara), Brian Ibsen (Dillan), Max Faugno (Gregory), Max Wolf (Adrian), Jacob Magas (Jake the Kid), London Vale (Barb), Paula Fins (Gertrude), Amanda DePover (Stacey), Brock Wilbur (Trevor). **Credits:** *Producer:* Tim Aslin,

Winston Abalos, Kovar McClure. **Comment:** Well done program with very good acting and production values. The two gangs are vastly different and attention was paid to detail in their depictions. Because of the type of program it is it does contain foul language.

Episodes: *1.* Pilot. *2.* Hipsters. *3.* Mount My Steel Horse. *4.* The Triple Lindy. *5.* Crispy Bacon. *6.* Fresh Diapers. *7.* Not the First. *8.* Outlaw Love. *9.* Bonera.

247 *Dial-A-Ranger.* youtube.com. 2012.

Dan Gerbil is a young man who leads a pretty ordinary life as the owner of a company called Dan's Pooper Scooper. "It's not glamorous," Dan says, but he likes to think he is helping people out. Since a kid, Dan has been fascinated by the TV series *The Mighty Morphin Power Rangers* and believes he has a calling to be a super hero. After much thought he decides to don a Power Ranger costume and creates "Dial-A-Ranger," a service people can call if they need help. He begins by posting flyers around the neighborhood and the program chronicles the adventures of an ordinary man, dressed in a red Power Ranger suit, as he tries to live out his fantasy and help people—even if they do not want his help.

Cast: Seth Jones (Dan Gerbil). **Credits:** *Producer:* Stephany Keller. *Writer-Director:* BJ Lewis. **Comment:** As crazy as the story sounds, the program is really fun to watch. It incorporates good acting and production values and rather obscure crimes for Dan to solve.

Episodes: *1.* My Calling. *2.* Overtime. *3.* This Is It! *4.* Hello, Destiny? *5.* The Call!!! *6.* The Questioning. *7.* Rededicated. *8.* A New Guy? *9.* Going Big! *10.* Cold Shock. *11.* Red Again? *12.* Season Finale.

248 *Diary of a Job Seeker.* vimeo.com. 2012.

Jacob Dunin is a man without a job and few to no employment opportunities. Until the time comes when he can re-establish his footing in the business world, he decides to start a video blog and relate his life as it unfolds. He possesses a degree in music composition and dreams of scoring the music for an epic Hollywood blockbuster film. Jacob resides in Chicago, lives with his sister (Liz) and the program relates that video blog as the events in his life unfold.

Cast: Jeremy Lee Cudd (Jacob), Quetta Carpenter (Liz). **Credits:** *Producer-Director:* Jeremy Lee Cudd. *Writer:* Jeremy Lee Cudd, Quetta Carpenter. **Comment:** While there are numerous programs that use the video blog format (normally one or two people facing the camera and talking), Jacob strays from that aspect at times and really changes the aspect of such series; hence, with its good acting and production, a more watch-able type of program is presented.

Episodes: *1.* Pilot. *2.* Routine. *3.* The New Normal. *4.* Book of Job. *5.* How to Pass a Piss Test.

249 *The Diary of an Assistant Bookkeeper.* youtube.com. 2013.

The program, set during the latter 1880s and based on a story by Anton Chekov, depicts the plight of an assistant bookkeeper seeking a job promotion, but knowing it can only be accomplished following the demise of the current head bookkeeper.

Cast: Luca Negroni (Assistant Bookkeeper). **Credits:** *Producer-Director:* Roberto Pacini. **Comment:** All episodes have been taken off line and it is not possible to present an evaluation.

Episodes: *1.* Glotkin 1863. *2.* Lethal 1865. *3.* Cholera 1867. *4.* Omen 1870. *5.* Plague 1878. *6.* Dying 1883. *7.* Buried 1883. *8.* *Wives 1886.*

250 *Dick Doblin, Private Eye.* dickdobin.com. 2013.

Dick Doblin has been a private detective for over twenty years (as he states in the first episode) and he has figured it is time to share his vast knowledge and experiences via an Internet video blog. He is assisted by his friend (and cameraman) Randy but disaster strikes shortly after he begins his first vlog when a thief steals his camera. Dick is not the type of person to stand by and do nothing and elects to catch the dastardly culprit himself. With Randy by his side, and with his limited knowledge of what real life is all about (Dick appears very naive at times) the program follows the clues Dick uncovers as he attempts to retrieve his stolen camera.

Cast: Lucas Whitehead (Dick), Tyler G. Hall (Randy). **Credits:** *Producer-Writer-Director:* Ross Brunetti, Tyler G. Hall. **Comment:** Dick works out of Pittsburgh, Pa. and appears much too young to have been working the private eye racket for twenty years. That discrepancy aside, the program is entertaining due mainly from Dick's failure to fully comprehend what is going on. The acting is good and had the series produced more episodes it would have involved Dick in cases other than finding his camera.

Episodes: *1.* Acting Natural. *2.* Interrogating. *3.* Staking Out. *4.* Car Chasing. *5.* Finding Your Man.

251 *Dick Dribble: Pro-Baller/Private Eye.* blip.tv. 2012.

Dick Dribble's family history boasts of detectives. His father and his grandfather were detectives and it was only natural that Dick would follow in their illustrious footsteps. It happened in a tragic way. Dick's father was killed in a traffic accident and Dick had to relinquish a promising career as an Australian basketball player to take over the family business—but he chose to take the "gumshoe business" as he calls it in a totally different direction—battle the crime that exists in the world of basketball (he believes if you knew the crime that exists there it would make your head spin). The program chronicles his lone crusade against the strange criminals that are associated with the profession (or those that only exist in his mind). As the program states: "Basketball crime has a new enemy—Dick Dribble." Ray is Dick's neighbor and assistant; Irene is Dick's mother and office administrator (she answers the phone with "Dick Dribble, P.I. How may I direct your call?"). She is also the founder of a local newsletter she named "The Kensington Towners Gazette."

Scout is a private detective whom Dick believes is trying to muscle in on his territory. She is arrogant and ignorant about basketball and Dick claims, "If it means I have to commit basketball crimes so I can still have a job, so be it. Also, I love her. What of it?"

Andrew "Drewy" Gaze was Dick's team mate and considered the Australian Hoop God of Melbourne. They are friends and Dick seeks his help when he is troubled.

The Nasty, Villainous Basketball Criminals: Grug Pfister is a teenager who is known for cheating and lying and bringing disgrace to the game of basketball.

Greg Pfister, age 28, is Grug's older brother, a dim-wit who follows what his brothers do because he does not possess the sense to tell right from wrong.

Cregg Pfister, the youngest of the brothers (10), is believed by Dick to be an evil genius and the most dangerous of the brothers.

Mr. Pfister, age 56, is the leader of the clan and accomplishes evil by being a bully and intimidating people by his gravel voice.

Graig Pfsiter is the first criminal Dick busted ("I blew his fake basketball tube sock racket wide open"). He is serving time in jail but plotting his revenge when he gets out.

Craig Pfister, age 5, cannot be counted out as an evil basketball villain because, due to age and tiny arms, he is not skilled at basketball. Dick believes Craig may one day follow in the footsteps of his evil brothers.

Tiny Man, age 35, sports a flared corduroy suit and appears to be a fun guy. "But guess again," Dick says, "Tiny is rotten to the core."

The Sniffer, as Dick calls him, is a dastardly, evil fiend who steals basketball sneakers to satisfy his urge to sniff sweaty feet.

Cast: Daniel Cowan (Dick Dribble), Matthew C. Vaughan (Ray Gertner), Madeleine Jackson (Irene Dribble), Dave Jackson (The Sniffer), Pierre Lioga (Graig Pfister), Michael Vaughn (Greg Pfister), Hunter Vaughn (Cregg Pfister), Armando (Mr. Pfister), Djovan Caro (Grug Pfister). **Credits:** *Producer-Writer-Director:* Greta Harrison, Matthew C. Vaughan. **Comment:** Australian-produced program that, despite its bizarre concept, is really quite enjoyable. It is well acted and produced and easily understandable (not hampered by thick Australian accents).

Episodes: *1.* White Men Can't Sniff. *2.* Erin Basketballovich. *3.* Slam Dunce. *4.* Badminton as I Wanna Be. *5.* Double Dribble. *6.* High Top Noon.

252 The Digressions. thedigressions.com. 2012.

"Almost adults almost discussing what's important" is the tag line for a look at five young people (Michelle, Preston, Theo, Kenley and Spencer) as they discuss the issues that affect them in their daily lives—from politics to the dating scene.

Cast: Aubrey Saverino (Michelle), Winslow Corbett (Kenley), Jordan McArthur (Spencer), Eric Pargac (Theo), Andrew Dahl (Preston). **Credits:** *Producer:* Andrew Dahl, Jordan McArthur, Aubrey Saverino, Eric Pargac. *Director:* Andrew Dahl, Eric Pargac. *Writer:* Andrew Dahl, Jordan McArthur, Eric Pargac. **Comment:** With an attractive cast, good acting and production values, a nicely presented program emerges.

Episodes: *1.* People Sounds. *2.* Smiling More. *3.* Interrupting Prison Rapist.

253 Dillon Jones: Former Child Star. youtube.com. 2014.

Dillon Jones, an adult with a fading acting career, was once a famous child star. He had it all but as he grew out of kid roles the acting profession just abandoned him. Dillon managed to survive and through his agent (Harold) has acquired small roles in non-monumental productions. But as time passes he feels he must let his fans know he is still alive and chooses to write his own screenplay—something no one wants to produce. Frustrated but not giving up, Dillon elects to use the Internet and relate aspects of his life to YouTube viewers ("I've been on YouPorn, why not YouTube?"). The program chronicles the life of a has-been as he seeks to make a comeback—even if it is over the Internet.

Cast: Price Lindsey (Dillon Jones), Paula Gilbert (Stephanie), Max Obertelli (Harold). **Credits:** *Producer:* Ryan Claffey, Peter Somogyi. *Writer-Director:* Ryan Claffey. **Comment:** Australian produced show that is well done. Dillon is a likeable character (who sounds American) and is supported by a good cast.

Episodes: *1.* Media Whore. *2.* Return of the Roomie. *3.* Ending Up with Paper Cuts. *4.* Stalker, Stalker, Midnight Walker. *5.* Brother of Mine. *6.* Cottaging.

254 The Diner. webserieschannel.com. 2011.

Rick and Louis are friends who frequent a diner wherein their friend Beth is a waitress. They consider the diner "a great place to chew the fat" and episodes are simply their daily gathering wherein matters that are important to them are discussed.

Cast: Griff Kohout (Rick), David Lyman (Louis), Sarah Morris (Beth). **Credits:** *Producer:* Griff Kohout, Micah Goldman, David Lyman. *Writer:* Griff Kohout, Micah Goldman. **Comment:** Simplistic plot, effective outcome with likeable characters, non-world threatening conversations and good acting and production values.

Season 1 Episodes: *1.* Somebody's Somebody. *2.* Duffle Bag. *3.* The Redhead. *4.* Hedging. *5.* The Big Wig. *6.* Complain Bragging. *7.* Meatball Hero.

Season 2 Episodes: *1.* Cupid. *2.* The Asshole. *3.* Occupy the Diner.

255 Dirk and Canon: Insurance Detectives. dirkandcanon.com. 2012.

Is an accident covered by insurance? Are fires covered by insurance? Is this or that covered by insurance? Dirk and Canon are insurance detectives assigned to determine just what is and what is not covered by an insurance policy. But unlike normal investigators who tackle the problem after a claim has been issued, Dirk and Canon seek to discover the answer before something happens by creating the claim themselves. The program charts what results from their misguided actions (and at the end of each episode reveal whether or not such claims would be honored or not). Mr. X, their mysterious boss, appears as a holographic image that emanates from a sphere on their office desk.

Cast: Brandon E. Berning (Dirk), Alex Vaughn Meierdierks (Canon), Sonny Burnette (Mr. X). **Credits:** *Producer:* Jack Thomas. *Director:* Brandon E. Berning, Mark A. Hill. *Writer:* Brandon E. Berning. **Comment:** Dirk and Canon are dim-wits and their approach to creating the claims are truly comical. This, coupled with good acting and production values makes for an enjoyable (if not silly) series.

Episodes: *1.* Arson. *2.* Power Surge. *3.* Throw Aunt Mildred Down the Stairs. *4.* Jet Plane Lands on Car. *5.* Wrecking Ball Accident.

256 Disconnected. funnyordie.com. 2010.

A sweet Midwestern woman (Sandy) either makes or receives a telephone call. The conversation that results with the weird people on the other end of the line forms the basis of each episode.

Cast: Meryl Hathaway (Sandy Donaldson). **Credits:** *Producer-Writer-Director:* Meryl Hathaway. **Comment:** Meryl Hathaway is delightful as Sandy, who appears somewhat nerdy as she gets excited about everything. The acting and production are top rate.

Episodes: *1.* Debbie the Telemarketer. *2.* Tammi—

a Sexpot with Feelings. 3. Phyllis, the Easy-to-Please Sister-in-Law Who Loves and Hates You. 4. Lala the Latina Spitfire. 5. Kendall—Her Mom Is a Democrat. 6. Nat—The Gym Membership. 7. Brenda, Guess What You've Won. 8. Karen Passed Out.... For Holiday Stress Worth Getting Hammered Over.

257 *The Discount Therapist.* webseries channel.com. 2013.

Dr. Sanjay Goldberg is a graduate of the Harvard School of Psychology. While he possesses his Ph D. and appears to be a man of reason, he believes in the Mayan Calendar and that the world would end in 2011. Fearing the worst, Dr. Sanjay experimented with LSD "to get himself in a better place." It is 2013, the world has not ended and Sanjay has turned rogue. He abandoned conducting sessions in an office, replaced it with a park bench and cut his therapy sessions to ninety-nine cents. The program follows a most unusual therapist and the people who come to him seeking help with their problems.

Cast: R.G. (Dr. Sanjay Goldberg). **Credits:** *Producer:* Brick Rucker, R.G., Mark Rybarczyk. *Writer-Director:* R.G. **Comment:** Interesting take off on the feature film *The Cheap Detective* that does a good job of showing how, in most cases, a fortune need not be spent for professional help. The acting and production values are good and the program is something different to watch.

Episodes: 3 untitled episodes, labeled "Episode 1" to "Episode 3."

258 *Disguntled.* webserieschannel.com. 2013.

The IT department of an advertising firm provides the backdrop for a look at a new hire (Randy) and his co-workers (Jessica and Mike) as they navigate the daily pressures of their less-than-exciting jobs.

Cast: Bryant Tarpley (Randy), Kiry Shabazz (Mike), Claire Fischer (Jessica), Wade Lucas (Mr. Holloway), Janelle Murphey (Missy), Brittany Hall (Jessica's Girlfriend), Chad Meisenheimer (Chad). **Credits:** *Producer:* Chester Finney, Chad Meisenheimer, Roberto Berrios, Jr., Steven Ng. *Director:* Chad Meisenheimer. *Writer:* Chad Meisenheimer, Leo Zuniga. **Comment:** The program does capture the feeling of workers who are displeased with their jobs and only doing so because nothing better has come along. The acting and production is typical of a low budget Internet series: generally good.

Episodes: 1. Randy's First Day. 2. Jessica's Breakup. 3. A New Place. 4. Jessica Likes the Ladies. 5. Randy and Jessica Find a New Place.

259 *Dr. Conard.* drconard.com. 2014.

Borrowing elements from the feature film *Irma*

La Duce wherein a man (Jack Lemmon), to keep a beautiful hooker off the streets of Paris (Shirley MacLaine) pretends to be someone else (a British Lord) to win her over. Here Bryan Mallard is a young man who has recently lost the love of his life (Pam) and desperately wants to win her back. Bryan works as a secretary to Janey Mount, "a cougar therapist," and learns through her that Pam is seeking a therapist to help her get over the breakup. Bryan hatches a plan: pretend to be a French therapist (Dr. Pierre Conard) and become her doctor. The program relates what happens when Bryan, with no experience on how to be a therapist, tries to win back Pam through devious means.

Cast: Shawn Telford (Bryan Mallard), Jessica Martin (Pam Saunders), Tracey Conway (Janey Mount), Kevin Darley (Jeremy Reef), Yoni Jung (Victoria). **Credits:** *Producer:* Chris Oliver. *Director:* John Jacobsen. *Writer:* Bill Abelson. **Comment:** While only a pilot episode has thus far been produced it can be seen as well done and interesting. Further than that it is hard to predict how long Bryan can fool Pam and how long before she figures out that Dr. Conard is really Bryan.

Episodes: 1. Pilot.

260 *Dog Park.* youtube.com. 2014.

Simple premise about a group of dog lovers who meet each day at the local dog park to discuss their home lives, jobs, marriage and anything else that comes up during their conversations.

Cast: Aaron Takahashi (Neal), Collin Christopher (Carl), Tony Rago (Matt), Gianna Burke (Leslie), Marianne Davis (Jamie), Jill Klopp (Kara), Kevin Williams (Tim), Helenna Santos (Lynn), Chris Fisher (Freeman), Tony Evangelista (Ken), Dj Sauceda (Paul), Hanna Margulies (Amy), Armando Vasquez (Greg), Susie Hillard (Holly), Jackie Fogel (Jackie), Russ Davis (Hank), Phil Martin (Brian), Ross Butler (Scotty) Katie Bogart Ward (Janelle). **Credits:** *Producer:* Tony Tago, Tim Harrington, Marianne Davis. *Writer-Director:* Tony Rago. **Comment:** Just the friends discussing matters in the dog park while watching their canine pets. The show is a bit talkative but well acted and produced.

Episodes: 1. Ruff. 2. Leave It. 3. Bad Dog. 4. Drop It. 5. Wait. 6. Roll Over. 7. Stay. 8. Gimme Paw. 9. In Heat.

261 *Dogs and Me.* dogsandme.com. 2012.

Matt is a young Hollywood actor struggling to make his mark on the movie industry. He has no social life, although his friend Megan has offered to help him find a girl as he appears unable to find one on his own. Besides Megan trying to run his life, Matt has two dogs, Jerry and Scarlet who can not only talk to him, but also try to run his life. Matt's conversations with the dogs as he tries to get his life in order and look for that big break are showcased.

Cast: Matt Rocklin (Matt), Samantha Gutstadt (Megan), Petra Areskoug (Voice of Scarlet), Ray Plumb (Voice of Jerry), Karen Strong (Laura), Jani Blom (Fred), Christine Moore (Stacey), Christopher Gehrman (Chris). **Credits:** *Producer-Writer-Director:* Matt Rocklin. **Comment:** The talking dog idea goes back to the 1950s and the TV series *The People's Choice* (wherein a dog related her feelings to the audience as opposed to talking to her owner). *Dogs and Me* uses voice-over speeches for the dogs; it is like Matt can hear what they think. Computer animating the dog's mouth would be expensive and that has to be taken into account. Accepting the dogs as they are and following Matt's efforts to deal with his crazy life do make for an interesting twist on series that cover the out-of-work young man (or woman) seeking to reinvent his (or her) life.

Episodes: *1.* Boss Balls. *2.* I Heart Megan. *3.* Booger Finger. *4.* Muffins. *5.* Poop Hands. *6.* Friend Test.

262 *Donksvile's Ghost.* youtube.com. 2009.

A child, called only Donksvile, was bullied for being Asian. It didn't appear to bother him because he thought he was cool and part of "the in-crowd" at school. However, when he attempted to join "a cool school club" and was rejected, the bullying took full effect and Donksvile committed suicide. But he has not moved on. He has remained earth bound and apparently "living" the same miserable life he had previously lived. He was misadventure prone then and he is misadventure prone now. Episodes relate brief incidents in the "life" of a ghost who can't seem to do anything right (and who has seemed to have grown from child to adult).

Cast: Dee Jacobs, Jr. (Donksvile). **Credits:** *Producer-Writer-Director:* Matt Bowie. **Comment:** Amusing gem that is lost amid the influx of Internet series. The acting and production values are very good and the only "special effects" are placing the star in a sheet with eye cutouts and drawn on eye brows. His speech is that of a ghost howling, but it all works for an enjoyable change of pace—but be warned, there is foul language—both in the captions used for Donksvile and the speaking characters.

Episodes: *1.* Phone Whore. *2.* Humungous. *3.* Black Magic. *4.* Gay Rapist. *5.* Batman's Revenge. *6.* Farm vs. Zoo. *7.* Surprise Porno. *8.* Batman Attacks. *9.* Gay Rapist Returns. *10.* Bestiality Beatbox.

263 *Donna's Revenge: Confessions of an Ex-Contestant.* facebook.com. 2011.

Artist Andy Warhol once claimed "that everyone will be famous for 15 minutes." Donna Wickland is a young woman who became a contestant on a *Survivor*-like TV show called *So You Think This Is Your Island* where she not only came in second, but

achieved her 15 minutes of fame—or so it seems. Donna had become accustomed to the cameras rolling and the notoriety she achieved that when the show ended she could not let the thought of that experience end with it. She has convinced herself that the cameras are still rolling and everything that she does is being filmed. Donna is seeing a therapist (Dr. Wanglang) who is trying to convince her that cameras are not filming her, but her subconscious refuses to listen to him or anyone else. As Donna goes about her daily life, turning her head sideways on occasion to speak into that camera, the program follows what happens as a girl with her head in the clouds simply tries to regain something she will never have again: fame (although she does have three personal goals: find love, a steady job and spiritual fulfillment).

Cast: Seana Kofoed (Donna Wickland), Eddie Jemison (Dr. Wanglang), Suzy Nakamura (Janet), Scott Lowell (Steve), Rusty Schwimmer (Dr. Skinner). **Credits:** *Producer:* Seana Kofoed, Meghan Schumacher, Jeff Peters. *Director:* Oliver Oertel. *Writer:* Seana Kofoed. **Comment:** Seana Kofoed is so good as Donna that she will have you believing there are cameras filming her. The overall production is very well acted and produced.

Episodes: *1.* The Sixteenth Minute. *2.* Let the Training Begin. *3.* Love Is Blind: Sometimes Literally. *4.* Keeping Kosher Every Now and Then. *5.* Donna Wickland, Agent to the Stars. *6.* Game On, Dr. Wanglang. *7.* For All Life's Moments, Real or Imagined. *8.* The Great American Shrink-Off.

264 *Don't Do It, Do It.* facebook.com. 2013.

Chandy, Travis and Chandler are friends with completely different outlooks on life. While they do like each other and put up with each other, they inevitably always differ about something the other one does. The program relates the experiences each faces as "friends who shouldn't be friends" simply try to live the life that he or she feels best fits his or her style.

Cast: Chandy Burke (Chandy), Travis Braxton (Travis), Chandler Strang (Chandler). **Credits:** *Producer-Writer:* Chandy Burke, Travis Braxton, Chandler Strang. **Comment:** The acting is good, the production well paced and the program quite interesting to see how one's activities can get on another's nerves and how one attempts to deal with it.

Episodes: *1.* Pennies. *2.* Party. *3.* Giant.

265 *Doobie Nights.* doobienights.com. 2013–2014.

Jim and Jam are friends who live for only one thing—smoking marijuana and getting high. Their individual experiences, while high are related to the viewer—from seeing "sex ghosts" to uncontrollable hunger to a skewed view of reality.

Cast: Jim Vlahopoulos (Jim), Rohan Mirchandaney (Jam). **Credits:** *Producer-Writer-Director:* Jim Vlahopoulos, Sam Warren. **Comment:** Spotlighting drug use is not the best way to present a program, especially when it glorifies drug use and any one, even children, can view it, giving some the wrong idea about drugs. If you enjoy seeing two potheads and their warped view of life, then you will enjoy the show; if not, it will be a complete turnoff.

Episodes: *1.* The Munchies. *2.* Green Out. *3.* Spark in the Bath. *4.* Traffic Jam. *5.* Cosmina. *6.* Pot Head. *7.* Cheezy Ghost. *8.* Holy Smokes.

266 Door-to-Door (2012). webserieschannel.com. 2012.

Andy Porter is a young man who cares about his Chicago neighborhood. He was raised in it but it has deteriorated over the years. With a plan to do something about it, Andy decides to run for the office of Alderman of the 51st Ward. The qualifications appear to be simple—just acquire 100 signatures that endorse him. With the help of his brother, Evan, Andy begins his quest—knocking on doors but encountering the strangest people ever known to live (without supervision) in his neighborhood.

Cast: Tommy Reahard (Andy), Ben Cook (Evan), Derrick Aguis, Jesse Case, Sarah Dell'Amico, Lauren Dowden, Lindsey Finn, Emily Fitzpatrick, Micah Philbrook, Kelly Reilly. **Credits:** *Producer:* Leonardo Adrian Garcia, Tyler Dean Kempf, Tommy Reahard, Ryan Taylor. *Director:* Tyler Dean Kempf. *Writer:* Tommy Reahard, Tyler Dean Kempf. **Comment:** Delightful program made enjoyable by the array of very strange people Andy and Evan encounter as they go door-to-door seeking signatures.

Episodes: *1.* Phillip. *2.* Stephanie. *3.* Antonio Garza. *4.* Yard Sale. *5.* Nobody. *6.* Lil' Madison. *7.* Seth.

267 Door-to-Door: The Web Series (2013). vimeo.com. 2013–2014.

At Your Door Service Enterprises is a company that literally sells anything they believe the consumer may need through its traveling door-to-door salesmen in particular new hirers Bryan Cooper, the socially confused Cynthia Patterson and the fitness freak Ed Phuket. The company is managed by Klaus Schlegle and the program chronicles the mishaps that occur as the people you do not want to see at your front door appear to annoy you. Mildred Mortimer is the bitter receptionist that maps out the routes the salesmen must follow.

Klaus, who just "ran away from home" a year ago, enjoys peanut butter and jelly sandwiches with pop rocks. He always dots his "i's" with little hearts and his dream is to vacation in Jurassic Park.

Bryan Cooper, whose favorite food is an Easy Mac made with Gatorade hopes to one day host his own radio program. He has had six jobs in the past year and in his spare time, writes a comic book about a vitamin that produces super human powers.

Cynthia Patterson not only loves creatures "great and small—but mythical." She also hosts a video blog with its only viewer—her mother.

Ed Phucket, who thrives on protein bars, believes any activity is a fitness challenge and it is his way of keeping in shape.

Mildred Mortimer simply hates everyone. She has a degree in Library and Information Studies and a fascination with the Harry Potter stories.

Cast: Pat Dortch, Justin Xavier, Rachel Woodhouse, Paul Freeman, Ana Shaw, Thom McKinnes. **Credits:** *Producer-Writer:* Rachel Woodhouse, Justin Xavier. *Director:* Rachel Woodhouse, Justin Xavier, Joe Chiazza. **Comment:** A bit kooky but fun to watch with good acting and production values.

Episodes: *1.* Pilot. *2.* Costume Party. *3.* Deter Dry. *4.* The Cherry Tree. *5.* Closing Ceremonies. *6.* Edpocalypse. *7.* Piñata. *8.* The Candy Funnel. *9.* Candace. *10.* The Dirt Sucker. *11.* The Prepper. *12.* Blind Date. *13.* Invitations. *14,15.* Pool Party. *16.* The Sunburn. *17.* Uncle Finkelstein.

268 Dorks. webserieschannel.com. 2010–2011.

Delta Omega Rho Kappa Sigma is a college sorority that has just rebound from a terrible fire that destroyed its former housing. Jane, a third year business major, has become Delta's West Coast Sorority President and believes, to avoid a repeat of what previously occurred, she and her sisters need to document what happens each day. The program relates events in the lives of each sorority sister as they speak directly to the viewer in a confessional-like room where they can vent what also bothers them.

Bethany is a second year philosophy major (and a bit dense); Plex, a third year theater major, talks with a lisp and is simply a nerd (pretty, but a nerd); Gaby, a business/economics and Spanish language major also has minors in German, music and basket weaving. Amelia, who has taken a vow of silence (communicates through written notes) is a communications major; and Sharon is a political science major.

Cast: Caitlyn Larimore (Jane/Plex/Sharon/Amelia/Bethany/Mary/Gaby). **Credits:** *Producer-Writer-Director:* Caitlyn Larimore. **Comment:** Superbly acted and produced program. It may take an episode or two before you realize that Caitlyn Larimore plays all the roles (and in such a convincing manner that it really doesn't dawn on you that they are all played by the same actress). While the concept is basically the girls speaking directly to the camera, the characterizations are so well executed that it becomes passé and you get the impression that more is happening than just what the girls report (like what they actually experienced on campus).

Episodes: *1.* In the Beginning. *2.* The Visit. *3.* Huntgertine's Day. *4.* Judgment Day. *5.* Holiday Party. *6.* Sharon's Revenge. *7.* Mother Dearest. *8.* The Visit. *9.* President Plex. *10.* History Lesson. *11.* Plex's Plan. *12.* Fund Raiser. *13.* Homecoming. *14.* The Green Machine. *15.* The Happiest Sorority on Earth.

269 *Dorm Life.* hulu.com. 2008–2009.

Events in the lives of a group of college students who live in the campus dorm (floor 5 South) and presented as a "mocumentary" of life as young adults begin living on their own for the first time (usually presented through the web cam each student possesses).

Mike is thoughtful and happy and trying to continue a relationship with his high school girlfriend, Emily. He hosts "The Mike Sanders Show" on his webcam (where he interviews various people he finds of interest). Shane is the party animal and president of 5 South and rarely attends classes (and placed on academic probation for doing so).

Gopher is Shane's best friend and roommate (and a party animal). Josh is Mike's roommate, a somewhat eccentric drama student. Danny, a pre-pharmacy student, shares a room with Shane and Gopher. He hosts the web cast called "Fun Facts with Daniel Benjamin." Marshall is the competitive but abusive resident assistant of 5 South.

Stephanie, who shares a room with Abigail, is a fun girl who would like everyone to enjoy life. Courtney, who had a romantic fling with Mike, is roommates with Brittany. She is a talented singer and recorded an album called "Four Leaf Clover." But she also loves to party and drink. Brittany began life at college as a shallow person who matured as the program progressed. Abby is the shy girl from a conservative upbringing who frowns on anything that will disrupt her way of thinking.

Cast: Chris W. Smith (Mike Sanders), Jack De-Sena (Shane Reilly), Jim Brandon (Gopher Reed), Zachary Maze (Josh Morgan), Jordan Riggs (Daniel Benjamin), Brian Singleton (Marshall Adams), Jessie Gaskell (Stephanie Schwartzman), Hannah Pearl Utt (Brittany Wilcox), Nora Kirkpatrick (Courtney Cloverlock), Anne Lane (Abby Brown), Andy Gardner (Andy), Jamison Lingle (Jayme, "The Mystery Hot Girl"), Keye Chen (Paul Chen), Valentina Garcia (Lacey), Sidney Brtown (Derrick Johnson), Aadit Patel (Aadit), Allen Loeb (Dean Tomlinson), Gracie Lane (Emily). Credits: *Producer:* Peter White, Garrett Law. *Director:* Mark Stewart Iverson, Chris W. Smith. *Writer:* Jim Brandon, Jack DeSena, Jessie Gaskell, Mark Stewart Iverson, Jordan Riggs, Brian C. Singleton, Chris W. Smith. Comment: A somewhat exaggerated look at college life although the acting and production are very good. Each of the students was given a web camera "to keep the audience up-to-date and what is going on."

Season 1 Episodes: *1.* Roommates. *2.* Game Night. *3.* The Smell. *4.* Campaign. *5.* Pranks. *6.* I.M. Football. *7.* Date Party. *8.* Halloween. *9.* Talent Show. *10.* All Nighters. *11.* Tissues. *12.* Alarmed. *13.* Recon Mission. *14.* Come (Out) Today. *15.* Turkey Drop. *16.* Teamwork. *17.* Marshall's New Hat. *18.* Group Shot. *19.* He's Back. *20.* Finals.

Season 2 Episodes: *1.* Welcome Back! *2.* The Screening. *3.* Markers. *4.* Selling Out. *5.* A Capella. *6.* Valentine's Day. *7.* Traumatic Event. *8.* The Camp Out. *9.* Parents' Weekend. *10.* The List. *11.* The Frat Party. *12.* March Madness. *13–17.* Spring Break. *18.* Tour de 5-South. *19.* Marshall's New Plan. *20.* Abby's Party. *21.* Blood, Sweat and Tears. *22.* SpoOoOoky Adventure. *23.* Floor Dinner. *24.* Quiz Owl. *25.* Dormal. *26.* Moving Out.

270 *Double Leche.* youtube.com/doubleleche 2013–2014.

An anthology presentation that explores the rather sensitive yet awkward situations mothers face while nursing their babies in public.

Cast: Jennifer Weedon, Stephanie Scott, Valisa Tate, Norm Golden, Sage Suppa, Michael Nixon, Jacqueline Sydney, Ashley Wren Collins, Duncan Murdoch. Credits: *Producer:* J. Sibley Law, Jennifer Weedon, Stephanie Scott. *Director:* J. Sibley Law. Comment: The issue of breast feeding in public is sensitively handled in short comedy skits. There is no nudity and stories simply relate what happens when one encounters such a situation with a particular focus on the mother's reaction.

Episodes: *1.* Trailer. *2.* Breast Feeding at Work. *3.* Pervy Wervy. *4.* Peek-a-Boo. *5.* Aren't You Worried About Your Breasts? *6.* Am I an Exhibitionist? *7.* Boobs at Work.

271 *Downers Grove.* webserieschannel.com. 2008.

Downers Grove is a small town where four friends (Alden, Brett, Jodi and Pudge) attended grammar and high school together but when others their age left for college, they remained behind believing that once you leave, you can never go back. So rather than leave and try to come back they chose to stay and continue living the only life they have ever known—one filled with mischief, partying and literally avoiding the responsibilities of life. The program charts what happens when real life does dawn on them and four slackers must deal with all its reality—even if it means growing up and becoming adults.

Cast: Michael Blaiklock (Brett), Justin Becker (Jodi), Dave Horwitz (Alden), Elisha Yaffe (Pudge), Heidi Heaslet (Becca), Anne Gregory (Maybe Ellen). Credits: *Producer:* Anne Kenny, Eric J. Wilker. *Director:* Bob Walles. *Writer:* Dave Horwitz, Elisha Yaffe, Michael Blaiklock. Comment: All episodes have been withdrawn but being pro-

Double Leche. Series poster art (used with permission of Jennifer Weedon 2015).

Cast: Eric Messner (Stephen Wunder), Peter Stray (Max Templeton), Kimberly Gilbert (Gemima Curtis), Andrea Honeycutt (Sibu), Frank Britton (Godfrey). **Credits:** *Producer:* Alexandra London-Thompson. *Writer-Director:* Peter Stray. **Comment:** Not so talented better describes the actors. The program, which is just standard for an Internet series, is sort of a behind-the-scenes look at how regional theater works as opposed to actual plays being produced.

Season 1 Episodes: *1.* Dumpage. *2.* Wunderkind. *3.* Maximus. *4.* Accentricity. *5.* Crystalized. *6.* Attenboroughed. *7.* Nesesises..es-. *8.* Kumquattery. *9.* Heat-ed. *10.* Soliloquizer.

Season 2 Episodes: *1.* Cedric. *2.* Ndugu. *3.* Topher. *4.* Cassandra. *5.* Magnus. *6.* Saffron. *7.* Bernardo.

duced by the WB network it no doubt had outstanding acting and production values.

Episodes: *1.* Pilot. *2.* Independent Brett. *3.* Just Like Say Anything. *4.* Open Season. *5.* Flowers for Pudge. *6.* Heist School Party. *7.* Classy Drink Night. *8.* Wedding Bells. *9.* Road to Nowhere.

272 *Downstage Confessions.* funnyordie. com. 2011.

The regional theater scene in Washington, D.C., provides the backdrop for a look at the frustrations faced by a group of struggling actors (called stupid actors on the website) as they encounter mishaps seeking and auditioning for roles.

273 *Downtown Girls.* thedowntowngirlsseries.com. 2013.

Sam, Abney, Alex and Zora are young women who attend NYU (New York University) and share a campus dorm room. The women are dissatisfied with their dorm room and yearn to move into an apartment away from campus in Chelsea. Their problem: no money to do so. With initiative and determination the women plot to acquire the money they need with the program charting the mishaps that inevitably come with harebrained schemes. "Welcome to Adulthood! Now, How Will You Survive" is the tag line that accompanies the program when its second season begins to explore what happens after the girls graduate and impulsively decide to start their own business—despite their do nothing, partying lifestyle. But reality eventually sets in and the friends are now determined to make something of themselves and leave their mark on their generation by incorporating their lifestyle into an app called "House Party Finder"—to "bring the party back to the people and away from nightclubs." And to do so, they transform their apartment (acquired from season 1) into that party house with the program again charting all the mishaps that can occur and do.

Samantha "Sam" Soloman is a stylish hustler who gets what she wants because she knows what strings to pull. She claims, "I am an aspiring fashion magazine editor, social media junkie and shopping aficionado.... I love to have a good time. I am where the party is at and if you play your cards right you just might get invited!"

Me Ilamo Zora James, called Zo is part of a family connected to the Midwest Mafia and plans "to become king among sound engineers (in the music industry)"; but for the time being, acquires money "by making art." She feels music keeps the world in check and despises girls who take endless "selfie" pictures of themselves in the same outfit but from different angels.

Alexandria Johnson, called Alex, is the daughter of Colonel Samuel Alexander Johnson III and Yvonne Letellier Johnson. Although born in the South, Alex considers herself a New York girl as she has been bedazzled by the bright lights, architecture and countless boutiques that are a part of Manhattan. She is a political science major and "lives for art gallery opening nights, the scintillating installations at Bergdorfs' and the annual UN summits that I hope to one day work for." She hasn't found a boyfriend yet. "I pound the pavement daily in search of my northern prince charming and a brownstone on the upper east side."

Abney Amber Anderson is the sixth child of "Harold, the baby maker." She also hates her name ("my family likes alliteration") and "you can call me Abney the Revolutionary." Abney admits she has a potty mouth but will refrain from using it at school. Abney hates people who have settled for who and what they are and have not pushed beyond their blind spots to see what could lie ahead.

Cast: Emebeit Beyene (Sam), Crystal Boyd (Abney), Chivonne Michelle (Alex), Chandra Russell (Zora). **Credits:** *Producer:* Emebeit Beyene. Crystal Boyd, Chivonne Michelle, Chandra Russell. *Director:* Kevin Walker. *Writer:* Jessica Lamour. **Comment:** A bit different from shows that tackle the same subject matter (college students) in that most of the action (in season 1) is set away from classrooms, books and studying and more of a focus on how the girls need to acquire money. The acting is very good and the production well done.

Season 1 Episodes: *1.* Spring Break. *2.* Dressing the Part. *3.* Sam Turns.... Um, 21? *4.* Prada Cakes. *5.* A Star Is Born. *6.* Race to the Flop. *7.* Behind Door Number 1. *8.* Just Got to Fake It.

Season 2 Episodes: *1.* The Inception. *2.* We Poppin Bottles. *3.* One Word: Drugs. *4.* Dancers! *5.* Wait, What?

274 *Draculette.* youtube.com. 2012.

Draculette, Morbidelia and Victoria are misfit vampires who have been shunned by the normal vampire clans. Although they have shortcomings (like Draculette having a fear of blood), they have banned together and established their own little covet. The program follows the trio as they attempt

to deal with and overcome their problems to one day return to the Colony from which they have been expelled.

Cast: Jennifer Lauer (Draculette), Amanda Troop (Morbidelia), Ivana Shein (Victoria), Alec Tomkiw (Thurston). **Credits:** *Producer:* Jennifer Lauer, Chris Lauer. *Writer:* Jennifer Lauer. *Director:* Chris Lauer. **Comment:** While the presentation and acting are good, only a pilot episode has been produced.

Episodes: 1. Pilot: Moonbathing (wherein Draculette, "The Vampire with a Eating Disorder," seeks professional help to overcome her fear of blood).

275 *Drama Queen.* webserieschannel.com. 2013.

Spanish produced program about Elena, a woman in her thirties, who to relieve the frustration she feels, has begun seeing a therapist (Andres) who presents her with an unusual way to deal with and hopefully overcome her problem: combining psychological training with his acting skills to create an exotic form of role play therapy. The program follows Elena as Andres teaches her how to handle her problems, the most severe being her inability to deal with men (others include anger issues and loneliness).

Cast: Josefina Rubio (Elena), Jesus Villega (Andres). **Credits:** *Producer-Writer-Director:* Gabriel Amiel. **Comment:** The program is in Spanish with English subtitles. The acting and production is well done and there are mild sexual situations.

Episodes: *1.* The Oral Spelling. *2.* The Living Space. *3.* The Capitalist Jacuzzi. *4.* The Therapy of Art.

276 *Drama Queenz.* dramaqueenztheseries. com. 2008–2012.

Three gay friends (Jeremiah, Davis and Preston) living in Manhattan and their often misguided attempts to not only further their careers as actors but find love. Jeremiah is the most enthusiastic friend, full of hope and dreams but plagued by continual bad luck. Davis, the perfectionist, has set his standards for a starring role on Broadway just a bit too high and, despite all the efforts he puts into what he does, he always finds others cannot meet his demands; Preston, the most sensible one of the group, is a realist and knows that the road ahead is a tough one and even more so for gays.

Cast: Dane Joseph (Jeremiah Jones), Kristen-Alexander Griffeth (Davis Roberts), Troy Valjean Rucker (Pareston Mills III), Jaylen Sansom (Tristan), Kevin Martinez (Mike), Fred Ross (Donovan), Benjamin Fischer (Trevor). **Credits:** *Producer-Writer:* Dane Joseph, Kristen-Alexander Griffeth, Troy Valjean Rucker. *Director:* Ryan Balar. **Comment:** A well-constructed story that genuinely attempts to explore the problems encountered by three like-able friends. Using black and white sequences during narrated scenes, then switching to color for what happens is different and a nice touch.

Season 1 Episodes: *1.* I Dreamed a Dream. *2.* Unexpected Song. *3.* Small World. *4.* A Little Fall of Rain. *5.* By the Sea. *6.* Simple Little Things. *7.* There's Gotta Be Something Better Than This. *8.* Ain't No Party.

Season 2 Episodes: *1.* And the World Goes Round. *2.* That's the Way It Happens. *3.* Money. *4.* Operating Doors. *5.* Make Them Hear You. *6.* Merrily We Roll Along. *7.* In My Own Little Corner. *8.* Tomorrow.

Season 3 Episodes: *1.* Everything's Coming Up. *2.* Don't Tell Mama. *3.* Something's Coming. *4.* My Favorite Things. *5.* Ease on Down the Road.

277 *Driver's Ed.* youtube.com. 2009.

The U.S. American Driving School in San Bernardino California is dedicated to not only teaching Americans how to drive but foreigners as well. Mohammed "Ed" Parsa and his adopted Caucasian son, Smitty, are its instructors; Ed is very reckless while Smitty is a bit more concerned about safety on the road. The program charts how the father-son team prepares their students for their final goal of taking a driving test with the most unconventional (if never heard of) methods ever devised.

Comment: A cast and credit listing is not given. Ed has his own ideas as to what his students need to learn and believes that what he teaches is right—no matter how wrong it is (that is breaking traffic rules). How he manages to retain his teaching school license is a mystery (especially when he has confrontations with traffic sops and is always ticketed) but watching Ed teach what he does is the fun part of the program (with students' reactions also adding to the amusement).

Episodes: *1.* California Stop. *2.* Double Lines. *3.* Psyche. *4.* My Space. *6.* Pole Position. *7.* Changing Lanes.

278 *Drunk History.* funnyordie.com. 2007.

A look at history that would make any teacher cringe as it is seen through the retelling of an intoxicated narrator while guests, portraying historical figures, reenact what is happening (with total accuracy not guaranteed).

Credits: *Producer:* Derek Waters, Jeremy Konner, Will Ferrell, Adam McKay. *Writer:* Derek Waters, Jeremy Konner. *Director:* Jeremy Konner. Comment: In 2010 the series moved to the Comedy Central cable network and only those episodes remain on line. While the web series version has been withdrawn, its charm has been carried over to the cable version which too has the same misconception of historical events with good acting and production values.

Episodes:
1. The Burr-Hamilton Duel. Michael Cera (Alexander Hamilton), Jake Johnson (Aaron Burr), Ashley Johnson (Elizabeth Schuyler), Derek Waters (Thomas Jefferson).

2. Benjamin Franklin's Kite Experiment. Jack Black (Benjamin Franklin), Clark Duke (William Franklin).

3. Benjamin Franklin's Relationship with Annabelle. Jack Black (Benjamin Franklin), Jayma Mays (Annabelle), Derek Waters (Annabelle's Husband).

4. Oney Judge's Escape from the Washington's. Danny McBride (George Washington), Marianna Palka (Martha Washington), Tymberlee Hill (Oney Judge).

5. Harrison's Presidency and Death. Paul Schneider (William Henry Harrison).

6. Lincoln and Douglass Friendship. Will Ferrell (Abraham Lincoln), Don Cheadle (Frederick Douglass), Zooey Deschanel (Mary Todd).

7. Tesla Meeting and Working for Edison. John C. Reilly (Nikola Tesla), Crispin Glover (Thomas Edison).

8. A Visit from St. Nicholas (a.k.a. 'Twas the Night Before Christmas). Ryan Gosling (Narrator), Jim Carrey (St. Nicholas), Eva Mendes (Ma), A.J. Culp, Ellie Culp (Children).

279 *Duder.* duder.com. 2006.

Borrowing the format established by the TV series *Seinfeld* (where there is no actual story but what you do as the day progresses becomes your life) a look at two best friends is presented: Glen, who is gay, and Ricky, who is straight. They are recent college graduates, living in Brooklyn, New York, but not eager to embark on a life's goal. As press information states, "It's a show about a bunch of duders who just, you know, duder around a bit. It's not the size of the plot that counts, it's how you avoid it at all costs."

Cast: Matt Kirsch (Glen), Alden Ford (Ricky Paulson), Julie Lake (Judy Cakes), Daniel Levine (Paul Gruff), Gregory Kennedy (Gregory), Libby Winters (Lorraine), Justin Noble (Bill), Dru Lockwood (Zev Abrams), Satya Bhabha (Stephen). Credits: *Producer-Writer:* Matt Kirsch. *Director:* Katrina Whalen, Ben Kegan, Gregory Kennedy, Jeremy Robbins, Ricky Price, Ryan Iverson. Comment: Likeable characters, good writing, acting and directing and stories that are fun to watch.

Episodes: *1.* Pilot. *2.* If Balls Could Talk. *3.* The Third Sneeze. *4.* Lil' Help. *5.* Cat People. *6.* The Fountain. *7.* Nice Place. *8.* Gregory. *9.* Who's Paul Gruff? *10.* Welcome Home, Paul Gruff. *11.* Sex Dreams. *12.* Lick Thing. *13.* How Are Your Lives Duder? *14.* The Toothpaste Incident. *15.* Glen's Lisp. *16.* Monks Are Hot. *17.* Lost His Swipe. *18.* Haircut. *19.* The Epileptic Cat. *20.* More Gregory. *21.* Another Door Note. *22.* Glen and Gruff. *23.* Duder Announcement. *24.* Gray Hairs. *25.* The Spoon Revisited. *26.* Facebook Faux Pas. *27.* The Other Glen.

280 *Dumbass Filmmakers.* dumbassfilm makers.com. 2012.

Harrison DeWinter is a young writer who has just completed a film script called "Abandoning Our Hopes: A Life Renewed and Lost and Forgotten." It is about saving the environment, battling injustice and promoting bisexuality. Harrison, however, is not a producer or knowledgeable in any aspect of filmmaking and is, even in the eyes of his own mother (Brenda), a loser. But Harrison does have a partner, Vicki Moretti, an overly organized but lonely young woman who latches onto the film project with the hope that it will fill the void in her life and win Harrison's love, despite the fact that he is also drawn to men. Enter Bobby Tulane, a handsome ingénue who is the first person to actually understand Harrison's script at a core level, leaving Harrison hopeful, but Vicki feeling threatened and even more alone. The program charts what happens when production begins on a film nobody understands and nobody knows what they are doing. Ricky is Harrison's vain ex-boyfriend; Scott is a casting director who knows how to play both sides of the fence; Amalia and Nancy are actresses vying for the film's leading female roles; Wanda is Harrison's talent manager.

Cast: Hunter Lee Hughes (Harrison DeWinter), Elizabeth Gordon (Vicki Moretti), Jimmy Dinh (Scott Fleischman), Justin Schwan (Bobby Tulane), Erwin Stone (Omega), Eric Colton (Ricky Blaine), Denise D. Williamson (Wanda Jones), Dale Raoul (Brenda DeWinter), Barbara Costa (Amalia Sousa), James Lee Hernandez (Rick Rameriz), Melinda Hughes (Nancy Smith), Jared Winkler (Drew Tompkins), Adrian Quinonez (Marco Lorenzo), Ben Wells (Ned Draper). **Credits:** *Producer:* J. Parker Buell, Jason Fracaro, Elizabeth Gordon, Hunter Lee Hughes, Melinda Hughes. *Writer-Director:* Hunter Lee Hughes. **Comment:** A well acted and filmed and an enjoyable fantasy look at producing a film—mostly depicting all the problems that are encountered rather than actually getting it made.

Episodes: *1.* What's the Story? *2.* Do Something. *3.* The Rise of Bobby Tulane. *4.* Amalia Makes Magic. *5.* Scott Stuck in the Middle. *6.* Destruction. *7.* Vicki's Power Play. *8.* The Fall of Bobby Tulane. *9.* Cappuccino Day. *10.* Kung Fu Connection. *11.* Bobby, Harrison, a Credit Card and a Sea Turtle. *12.* Known Quantities.

281 *Dummy.* youtube.com. 2014.

Donny is a ventriloquist with a dummy named Sammy. Donny's act is not very funny and if one looks closely you can see that Donny's lips move when speaking for Sammy. When on stage or in public Sammy is simply a wooden dummy; however, when alone, Sammy becomes real to Donny and comes to life to offer his opinions on what is happening to them as an act (sometimes criticizing Donny for what he does). The program relates what occurs during the times when Sammy becomes real and how Donny attempts to cope with what he is being told.

Cast: Joe Dalo (Donny), Izzy Diaz (Sammy). **Credits:** *Producer:* Renee Dalo, Julianna DiMaggio. *Writer-Director:* Joe Dalo, Izzy Diaz. **Comment:** The idea of a dummy coming to life for its owner is not new and has been done before (as on the TV series *What a Dummy* and *Victorious*). Aspects of Donny's act are seen and the program is acceptable in acting and production.

Episodes: *1.* One Joke at a Time. *2.* Socky Was a Hack. *3.* Meet, Greet, Repeat.

282 *Dungeon Bastard.* dungeonbastard. com. 2011–2012.

"I'm here. I'm Bill Cavalier, Adventure Coach" is the introduction viewers hear when they log on to see a man, seated in a chair and claiming to be the world's greatest gamer coach. The program explores his techniques as he not only gives people wanting to learn how to play video games but in the process make them a better person.

Cast: Tom Lommel (Bill Cavalier). **Credits:** *Producer-Director:* Cindi Rice. *Writer:* Tom Lommel. **Comment:** Although Bill is mostly seen seated in a chair and just talking to the viewer, his presentation is well done and, although it appears to be directed to people interested in mastering video games, it does have an appeal to others (as a curiosity to those who may want to see what gaming is all about).

Season 1 Episodes: *1.* Adventure Coach. *2.* Clerical Duties. *3.* Gen Con. *4.* Campaign Confusion. *5.* Best Axe. *6.* Halflings. *7.* Elves. *8.* Gnomes. *9.* Half Elves. *10.* Half Orcs. *11.* Humans. *12.* Dwarves. *13.* Girls and Dungeons and Dragons. *14.* Stuck in a Pit. *15.* Halloween Tips. *16.* Monks. *17.* Alignment Change.

Season 2 Episodes: *1.* Holiday Special 2011. *2.* The Trouble with Success. *3.* The Other Side of the Screen. *4.* Edition Wars. *5.* DM Role Playing Tips. *6.* The Paladin. *7.* Staff of the Magi. *8.* The Evil Campaign. *9.* Sonics. *10.* A Late Start. *11.* Inter Party Conflict. *12.* Hard Times as the Table.

Season 3 Episodes: *1.* Coffee vs. Beer. *2.* Theater of the Mind. vs. Battlemat. *3.* Jerky vs. Pasta. *4.* Ennie Awards Voting. *5.* Stingy DM. *6.* The 5 Commandments of Gen Con. *7.* WWSP? *8.* Costume Badass #1. *9.* Wolfgang Baur. *10.* Costume Badass #2. *11.* Bill Cavalier. *12.* Kids Korner. *13.* Ultimate Beatdown. *14.* Home vs. Office. *15.* Dwarf Style.

283 *Dusty Peacock.* youtube.com. 2009.

Dusty Peacock is a disillusioned young man who dreams of becoming the world's greatest illusionist. His ambitions are high but he is short on talent. He does have his "Team Peacock" consisting of Naomi, his money-hungry girlfriend; Stu, his brother, an incompetent lawyer; Burt, his manager; and Nick, his agent. The program follows Dusty as he attempts (but always fails) to perform illusions, hoping for that one that will put him in the record books.

Cast: Gary Valentine (Dusty Peacock), Melissa Peterman (Naomi Flood), Nick Turturro (Stu Peacock), Nick Bakay (Burt Reynolds), Bas Rutten (Nick Hoogaboom). **Credits:** *Producer:* Kevin James. Jeff Sussman, Rock Reuben. *Director:* Rob Schiller. *Writer:* Rock Reuben. **Comment:** Although episodes have been removed, it is an obvious take-off on the Bob Einstein character Super Dave who sought fame by performing dangerous stunts. Kevin James from *The King of Queens* TV series oversees the project.

Episodes: *1.* The Amazing Breath of Death. *2.* The Death Defying Bullet Catch Trick. *3.* The Kiss Kiss Boom Boom Couple. *4.* The Crazy Crane. *5.* The Incredible Insomniac. *6.* The Magic Fire Walk. *7.* The Grape Escape. *8.* The Giant Cheese Pizza Situation.

284 *E-Commando.* webserieschannel.com. 2011.

Leon Green is an ex-Navy SEAL who, after his girlfriend leaves him (driving off in his motor home) is forced to take a job protecting the environment as a U.S. government Eco-Warrior. Leon, however, is environmentally clueless and possibly the least qualified person on the planet to protect Mother Nature from evil. But he is broke and homeless and now has a job and with his talking car, Bro, begins a crusade to protect the environment—no matter how much disaster he causes doing it.

Cast: Jason Nash (Leon Green), David Cross (Voice of Bro). **Comment:** All episodes and virtually all information, including its website, have been taken off line thus an evaluation is not possible.

Episodes: 3 untitled episodes, labeled "Episode 1," "Episode 2" and "Episode 3."

285 *Early Birds.* funnyordie.com. 2014.

Early Birds is a British TV morning television show (called Breakfast TV) that is similar to American programs like *The Today Show* and *Good Morning America.* Brian, Michelle and Alan are its hosts; Bethany, the news anchor; Dani, the sportscaster and Steve, the entertainment reporter. It is produced by Brian's friend Tony and the program is a behind-the-scenes look at how each show comes together and the conflicts that exist within the cast and crew (especially with Brian, who is seeking a higher position as anchor of the channel's six o'clock news program).

Cast: Paul Cattunar (Brian), Ned Law (Tony), Justine Kacir (Michelle), Brett Garland (Alan), Michele Mattiuzzi (Dani), Bianca Raess (Bethany), Peter Mack (Steven). **Credits:** *Producer-Writer-Director:* Drew Pearson. **Comment:** The program is a British production that, like some American series, feels the need to encompass foul language (simply not funny here). The acting is good and it does give a glimpse of what could happen between the cast and crew of such a show.

Episodes: 5 untitled episodes, labeled "Episode 1" through "Episode 5."

286 *Easy to Assemble.* easytoassemble.tv. 2008–2011.

Illeana Douglas is an actress who believes she needs to get out of show business (and start leading a normal life) and begins by taking a position in a Burbank, California, IKEA (do it yourself furniture store) as an entertainer to raise company morale, team spirit and actually work in the store. All is progressing well until her actress friend, Justine Bateman sees this as an opportunity to jump start her career (famous for her role as Mallory on *Family Ties*) and sets up her own Internet talk show (*40 and Bitter*) on the floor of Illeana's store. The program, funded by IKEA (and letting you know with the numerous logo placements) follows Illeana's efforts to escape a life she now finds is nearly impossible once her store becomes a haven for celebrities and she learns that once show business is in your blood, it is there forever.

Cast: Illeana Douglas (Herself), Justine Bateman (Herself), Michael Irpino (Lance Krapp), Tom Arnold (Himself), Eric Lange (Manager Erik), Robert Mailhouse (Paul), Sean Durrie (John), Todd Spahr (Pete), Ogy Durham (Karin), Jane Lynch (Manager Swenka), Mia Riverton (Sam), Roger Bart (Howard Friske), Craig Bierko (Jebedehia Bateman), Greg Proops (Ben), Ed Begley, Jr. (S. Erland Hussen), Michael Panes (Spazzy Sheraton), Hannah B. Campbell (Hannah), Wallace Langham (Bjorn Epperstein). **Credits:** *Producer:* Illeana Douglas, Justine Bateman, Magnus Gustafsson, Alia Kemet, Barney Oldfield, Warren Chao, Peggy Robinson, Thomas Bannister, Raymond Simanavicius. *Director:* Greg Pritkin, Michael Kang, Chris Bradley, Kyle LaBranche, Melanie Mayron. *Writer:* Illeana Douglas. **Comment:** Third season episodes change the setting slightly when Illeana and her fellow IKEA employees journey to Sweden where Illeana is to be awarded her "Co-Worker of the Year" award. It is here that Justine meets her long-lost brother Jebedehia and Illeana encounters the ghost of S. Erland Hussan, the famed IKEA designer. With its distinctive blue and yellow colors IKEA takes total advantage of what is called Product Placement (getting a sponsor's product seen as much as possible—whether it is straight out hit you in the face or in subtle background scenes or a combination of both). There are numerous guest stars that appear throughout the series and the production itself is television quality with excellent acting. The comedy, however, is not as straight forward; it may appear as obvious, or what just happened and even quirky or weird. It all depends on the viewer's perception.

Season 1 Episodes: *1.* Training Day. *2.* Actors Anonymous. *3.* Gotcha. *4.* Co-Mingling. *5.* The Justine Bateman Show. *6.* Personal Shopper. *7.* How Swede It Is. *8.* You Can't Be Somebody Else. *9.* Celebrity Bull Riding. *10.* Art Is Where You Make It. *11.* Training Video: Greeting the Customers. *12.* Training Video 2: Your Allen Wrench and You. *13.* Training Video 3: Meatball Preparation. *14.* Training Video 4: Swedish Phrases. *15.* Training Video 5: Self Service Warehouse.

Season 2 Episodes: *1.* What's in Store? *2.* The Team Building Event. *3.* Bitter Is Better. *4.* Taking Stock. *5.* Celebrity Intervention. *6.* People Skills. *7.* Meet Sparhusen. *8.* Gotcha Covered. *9.* S. Erland Hussen #76. *10.* Co-Worker of the Year. *11–13.* Flying Solo.

Season 3 Episodes: *1.* We're in Swedenland. *2.* Finding North. *3.* Good Morning Stockholm. *4.* The Third Bateman. *5.* The Road to Uppsala. *6.* Almost Happy. *7.* 48 Hours of Daylight. *8.* Chasing Windmills. *9.* A Very Heavy Package. *10.* Scorpio Rising. *11.* Taxi to Trosa. *12.* Mrs. Hullestaad. *13.* You're Never Alone. *14.* Co-Worker of the Year. *15.* Sammy Salt. *16.* Now I'm Black Mailing You. *17.* Bjorn Borg Is Not a Celebrity in America. *18.* I'm Literally Out of Material.

Season 4 Episodes: *1.* Bossy Lady. *2.* IKEA's Got Talent. *3.* You're My Producer? *4.* Married to My Work. *5.* The Friske Touch. *6.* Good with Names. *7.* The All-Nighter. *8.* We're Finished. *9.* Will You Be My Partner? *10.* I'm Gonna Love You Through This. *11.* What's Happening?

287 *Easy Way Out.* webserieschannel.com. 2014.

Easy Way Out is an online company that has only one goal—to intervene in situations where a couple are on the verge of a breakup and send them to therapy to make the breakup as easy as possible. Nolan heads the company with Sane, Breana, Alli and Seth as his counselors.

Cast: Matt Kessler (Nolan Puppers), Ben Griesse (Shane Mitchell), Eric Larsen (Marc Markopoulis), Sophie Leonard (Alli Espinoza), Kristina Hess (Breana Neilsen), Michael Johns (Seth Black), Kristin Ige (JJ Jones), Brittany Ortiz-Nelson (Dr. Ryan Fusck), Sean Mount (Dr. Ashley Fusck). **Credits:** *Producer-Writer-Director:* Logan Cross. **Comment:** Although the program has a TV sitcom-like laugh track (which is totally not needed) the episodes, es-

pecially the first one, are not laugh-out funny but amusing. The acting and production is very good and for a series dealing with breakups, it is something different.

Episodes: *1.* The Commercial. *2.* The Meeting. *3.* Pie Charts. *4.* Lingerie. *5.* Sorry. *6.* Kobe. *7.* The Chippendale. *8.* A Small Part. *9.* The Transceiver. *10.* Toddy. *11.* War of the Flies. *12.* Doublemint Case. *13.* Crossing Over. *14.* Staring Contest. *15.* Behind the Mask. *16.* Hole Punch. *17.* Zarnon X. *18.* It's All Greek. *19.* Pooh Bear.

288 *Eat Our Feelings.* vimeo.com. 2014.

Two young women, Emma and Sasha claim, "We're just a couple of hip Brooklyn gals, making food, eating food, and exploring the harrowing depths of our emotions. We laugh, we cry, we put avocado on everything. So please, eat our feelings." A comical situation is established that in some way relates to food. Emily and Sasha then turn to their cooking expertise to make a meal that is linked to the prior encounter with food.

Cast: Emma Jane Gonzalez (Emma), Sasha Winters (Sasha). **Credits:** *Producer:* Doug Anderson. **Comment:** The plot doesn't really grab you by words alone as it appears to just be a variation on some Food Network cooking show. But watching will surprise you. Comedy is interspersed with actual cooking and the combination of the two pays off in a well produced and acted program that some watchers may link to a 1970s TV series called *The Galloping Gourmet* wherein chef Graham Kerr mixed comedy with cooking.

Episodes: *1.* Sandwich Time. *2.* Vegetable Meal.

289 *Elevator.* sidereel.com. 2007–2010.

Short segments (usually under one minute) that relate brief encounters people have in elevators. The program incorporates what is called locked-frame (one steady image) and one-take (hopefully everything will be come off as planned without redoing scenes). Being as short as they are, production allows for shooting multiple episodes in a single day.

Cast: Ben Pace (Harold, the Janitor), Kate Micucci (Lily, the IT Girl), Woody Tondorf (Chris), Brendan Bradley (Brendan), Genevieve Jones (Intern Jane), Angie Cole (Britney from R&D), Andrew Zilch (Jacob), Craig Frank (Craig), Annemarie Pazmino (Anna), Paul Guylas (Paul), Maxwell Glick (Tyler), Eric Spiegelman (Mr. Grant). **Credits:** *Producer:* Woody Tondorf. *Director:* Woody Tondorf, David Nett, Derek Housman, Scott Brown, Brett Register, Bernie Su. *Writer:* Woody Tondorf, Ben Pace, Bernie Su, Derek Housman, Brett Register. **Comment:** The program was originally an HBO Labs production that was later sold to its original hosting site, Break.com (available episodes can only be seen on YouTube). Based on what is available, the acting is good, the story fast-moving and, although confined to the space of a typical elevator, humorous little tales unfold.

2007 Episodes: *1.* Enter the Ninja. *2.* Music. *3.* Pranksters. *4.* Lights Out. *5.* Universal Health Care. *6.* Police Line. *7.* Super Hero. *8.* Tower of Terror. *9.* Badly Times Jokes. *10.* Don't Fear the Reaper. *11.* Killer Joke Man. *12.* Cringe Singer. *13.* Corporate Raiders. *14.* Oriental. *15.* Always Be Prepared. *16.* Chick in a Box. *17.* Power to the People. *18.* Highway to Hell. *19.* Twisted Twister. *20.* Sabbath. *21.* Guy Talk. *22.* Pranksters 2. *23.* Jacob Goes Green. *24.* Kitty Smackdown 2. *25.* That'll Teach 'Em. *26.* Leverage.

2008 Episodes, 1–20: *1.* Elevator. *2.* Green Ball of Doom. *3.* Accelerated Cure Project for Multiple Sclerosis. *4.* Son of the Boss. *5.* Hazing. *6.* Breakfast Buffet. *7.* The Cable Guy Must Die! *8.* Morning Wood. *9.* Vote for the Future. *10.* Beyond the Palin. *11.* Elevator Halloween–Zombie American. *12.* Elevator Halloween–Zombies. *13.* Elevator Halloween–13th Floor. *14.* Elevator Halloween Theme Week! *15.* Pet Cemetery. *16.* Theme Party. *17.* Mentoring Bobby. *18.* Take It Outside. *19.* Hero Worship. *20.* Keep It to Yourself.

2008 Episodes, 21–40: *21.* Joust Do It. *22.* The Squeeze. *23.* Don't Be a Drip. *24.* Don't Be A Drip. *25.* Don't Taze Me, Bro! *26.* Plan B Isn't Good Enough. *27.* Obama-rama! *28.* What's In A Name? *29.* Smash And Grab. *30.* Quit Clowning Around. *31.* Whatthebuck vs. Woody–Who Gives a %^&* About The Olympics? *32.* Intern Jane Needs Our Help! *33.* Girls Night Out. *34.* College Buddies. *35.* Just Dropping In. *36.* The Final Ritual. *37.* Live Chat Tuesday! *38.* Pledging. *39.* Big Pimpin. *40.* Elevator Vlogtacular!

2008 Episodes, 41–60: *41.* Cereal Killers. *42.* Pet Peeves Bloopers. *43.* Pet Peeves. *44.* Comments. *45.* Give Me Back My Spud! *46.* Choose Our Reward Video! *47.* Re: Rich Sommer Comes Out of the Closet. *48.* Chemical Warfare. *49.* Buck vs. Jason. *50.* Jedi Jacob Bloopers! *51.* Jedi Jacob. *52.* Access Denied. *53.* Game Face. *54.* The Elevator Cast Serves the 3rd Street Promenade. *55.* Imaginary Girlfriend. *56.* Lily's Diet. *57.* April Fools on Genevieve! *58.* Clone Wars. *59.* Picture of Success. *60.* Vote Elevator For Best Series!

2008 Episodes, 61–84: *61.* Strip Club. *62.* Sibling Rivalry 2. *63.* A Boy and His Cat. *64.* Playing With Your Balls. *65.* Need Hannah Montana Tickets. *66.* Intern Shawn Pyfrom Is Not A Puppy. *67.* Terminator Is A Web Of Lies. *68.* The Office Song. *69.* Melora Hardin Super Fan. *70.* Nanny Cam. *71.* Run-a-way-box Kablamo! *72.* Rejected! *73.* Sibling Rivalry 2. *74.* To Have And To Hold. *75.* Middleman. *76.* Woody's Valentine's Day Date Advice. *77.* Woody's Penguin Incident. *78.* Sibling Rivalry 3. *79.* Crushin' on Shawn Pyfrom. *80.* Ewf 2. *81.* Eulogy for the Patriots Season. *82.* Live Chat with Woody. *83.* Love Ballad. *84.* That's What She Said.

2009 Episodes, 1–20: *1.* Drunk Dial. *2.* Telemar-

keter. *3.* Corporate Raiders 2 with Dave Days. *4.* Secret Agent Thrash with Charles Trippy. *5.* Corporate Raiders 2 With Dave Days. *6.* Bank O' Harold. *7.* Eavesdropping with Ryan Higa. *8.* Ewf Grudge Match with Mr. Safety. *9.* The TV Set with Kev Jumba. *10.* A Familiar Face with Laura Silverman. *11.* Boy Band with Mr. Safety. *12.* Kev's Think Tank. *13.* Harold's Pitch with Laura Silverman. *14.* Who's Your Daddy with Dave Days. *15.* Face The Music with Kev Jumba. *16.* A Second Opinion with Laura Silverman. *17.* Lily's Bailout (in Hd!). *18.* I, Harold (in Hd!). *19.* The Resistance. *20.* You Can't Take It With You.

2009 Episodes, 21–40: *21.* Trading Places. *22.* Ace's Hookup. *23.* Let's Rage. *24.* Chivalry Is Dead. *25.* EWF 3. *26.* Intern Jane's Roommates. *27.* Getting High. *28.* Do Not Touch. *29.* Enter the Matrix. *30.* Prom. *31.* Dance Like Nobody's Watching. *32.* What Could Possibly Go Wrong? *33.* Harold's on Twitter. *34.* Open Mike Night. *35.* You Had To Be There. *36.* Want to Know How I Got These Scars? *37.* Secret Admirer. *38.* Heel Hath No Fury. *39.* Never Forget. *40.* Woody vs. Shaycarl: GI Joe–The Rise of Cobra review.

2009 Episodes, 41–59: *41.* Harold the Janitor's Nemesis. *42.* The Thief. *43.* Food Fight. *44.* Harold's Ultimate Weapon. *45.* Wookie Mating Call. *46.* Kissing Intern Jane. *47.* 40s and Drive Bys. *48.* Hater Hitman vs. Tobuscus. *49.* Oh Oh Oh It's Magic. *50,51,52,53.* Harold the Vampire. *54.* Infestation. *55.* Omerta. *56.* Support Desert Bus For Hope. *57.* The Death of Mr. Grant. *58.* Harold Hates Santa Claus. *59.* Nominate Elevator for the 2010 Streamys!

2010 Episodes: *1.* Streamys 2010 for Your Consideration. *2.* Ace's Sex Tape. *3.* XBOX 360 Achievements In Real Life! *4.* War Stories. *5.* Hot Chick Zone Defense. *6.* The Bad Touch with Jessica Rose. *7.* Elevator got Nominated in the Streamy Awards! *8.* One More Chance to Vote Elevator in the Streamy Awards. *9.* The Last Ride.

290 *Elinor and Marianne Take Barton.* elinorandmarianne.wix.com. 2014.

Barton University is a prestigious school where Marianne Dashwood has just begun her freshman year. She is 18 years old and an English Lit major. Her 19 (going on 20) year-old sister, Elinor, a sophomore studying math and physics, also attends the university but lives off campus while Marianne shares a dorm room with a girl named Charlotte. Marianne is thrilled to be attending college and feels it will be the greatest experience of her life. To see that there is a record of what happens, Marianne begins a video blog, and with Elinor's help, records what transpires as both girls navigate college life.

Cast: Bonita Trigg (Marianne Dashwood), Abi Davies (Elinor Dashwood), Sophia Pardon (Charlotte Palmer), Joshua Allsopp (Brandon Palmer), Gareth Roberts (Edward Ferrars), Georgie Wedge (Lucy Steele), Craig Nannestad (Will Johnson).

Credits: *Producer:* Emily Nabney. *Director:* Olivia Cole. *Writer:* Olivia Cole, Emily Nabney. **Comment:** Very well acted and produced series (said to be based on Jane Austen's *Sense and Sensibility* novel). While it is just the main characters talking to the camera, they are very appealing and personable and make the program worth watching.

Episodes: *1.* Introducing the Marvelous Marianne. *2.* Marianne's Guide to Freshers. *3.* Holding Out for a Hero. *4.* The Most Romantic Day of My Life. *5.* Awkward Canary. *6.* Lucy in the Sky with Tequila. *7.* Flirting Ridiculousness. *8.* Escaping My Flat Mate. *9.* Live from the Big Barton Diary Room. *10.* The Fallout. *11.* Will and Marianne Do a Vlog Episode. *12.* Clean Cup! Move Down. *13.* Complications in Relations. *14.* Lack of Communication. *15.* Silence Is Louder Than Text. *16.* Girl Talk. *17.* Princess Preparation. *18.* S**t Goes Down. *19.* My Life Is Terrible. *20.* Drama in the Rain. *21.* The Truth. *22.* Revelation. *23.* Post Mortem. *24.* Goodbye and Hello. *25.* Reflection.

291 *Eli's Dirty Jokes.* youtube.com. 2007–2015.

Eli is an animated older gentleman with an apparently endless supply of sex-themed jokes. As Eli tells a joke (and provides all the voices) an animated scenario accompanies each joke that visualizes what happens.

Cast: Eli Buchalter (All characters). **Credits:** *Producer-Writer:* James T. McFadden, Tyler McFadden. *Director:* Doug Bresler. **Comment:** Eli is drawn to represent an old man with decent animation throughout. There is no parental warning and while some of the jokes are funny, others are stale and the punch line can be guessed on others.

Season 1 Episodes: *1.* BBQ Booty. *2.* Moose Hunting. *3.* Rawr! *4.* Five Birds. *5.* Nice to Meet You. *6.* Piano Man. *7.* The Farmer's Daughters. *8.* Track Team. *9.* Monkey Love. *10.* Hoshimota. *11.* The Shepherd and His Boy. *12.* Loving Remembrance. *13.* The Three Fugitives. *14.* Recovery Roses. *15.* The Key to the Bedroom. *16.* Arabian Justice. *17.* The Sloppy Drunk.

Season 2 Episodes: *1.* Peanut Ear. *2.* Nosy Neighbor. *3.* Yukon Ho. *4.* Ugly Baby. *5.* Sunset Island. *6.* Bedroom Burglar. *7.* Prime Mates. *8.* Face Lifted Spirit. *9.* Son of a Beech. *10.* The Drunk's Dry Cleaning. *11.* Manic Moms. *12.* Wild Ski Trip. *13.* Lucky Leprechaun. *14.* Whale of a Good Time. *15.* Hot Mic. *16.* Costume Party. *17.* Pirate Barrel. *18.* Cougar Hunting. *19.* Health Hazard. *20.* Ladies Night. *21.* Schedule Conflict. *22.* Genie in a Bottle. *23.* Gator Boots. *24.* Christmas Cop. *25.* First Drunk. *26.* Funky Flatulence. *27.* Golden Gals. *28.* Serious Situation.

Season 3 Episodes: *1.* Switchblade Girlfriend. *2.* Badass Mice. *3.* Down By the Docks. *4.* Talking Dog for Sale. *5.* The Donation Station. *6.* Rocktopus. *7.*

The Elephant and the Ant. *8.* Wedding Night Woes.

292 *The End.* theendwebseries.blogspot. com. 2010.

It is a time when a robot apocalypse has befallen the earth. There are survivors and few areas that are safe. Two young men, Duke and Johnny are survivors, but are currently trapped in a city where danger lurks around every corner. Their one goal is to reach Columbus, Ohio, a human city of safety. Each episode begins with Duke escaping from a KillerBot and approaching Johnny: "Johnny, there is a KillerBot just around the corner ... if we take off now we might be able to make it to Columbus ... if it still exists." Johnny, however, is always pre-occupied with something (the "Of" in the episode list) and Duke soon becomes so involved in Johnny's activity that he forgets the approaching danger and joins him. The program charts those activities that deter Duke and Johnny from escaping and making it to the safety of Columbus.

Cast: Bryan Mayer (Johnny), Justinh Avery (Duke). **Credits:** *Producer:* Bryan Mayer, Peter Harmon, Justinh Avery, Rick Bickerstaff, Ian Becker. *Director:* Rick Bickerstaff. *Writer:* Peter Harmon, Bryan Mayer. **Comment:** While only a brief glimpse of a KillerBot is seen, it is not a program about battling the enemy. It is simply two guys discussing a topic amid the danger that lurks all around them. While each episode's opening is an attention getter, most of the episodes do hold their own as a conversation program goes.

Episodes: *1.* Of Gossip. *2.* Of Marshmallows. *3.* Of Contacts. *4.* Of Thanksgiving. *5.* Of Peeing. *6.* Of Girlfriends. *7.* Of Expletives. *8.* Of Santa. *9.* Of Countdowns. *10.* Of Love. *11.* Of Botulism. *12.* Of Cannibalism. *13.* Of Batteries. *14.* Of Upbringing. *15.* Of Comedic Situations. *16.* Of Paradox. *17.* Of Predictability. *18.* Of Ignorance. *19.* Of Pseudonyms. *20.* Of Spoiler Warnings. *21.* Of the End.

293 *The End Is Nigh.* youtube.com. 2011.

While taking a math test, high school student Jason Wurther has a revelation. He believes the end of the world is coming and rushes out of the classroom "to spread the word." Jason, however, is not sure how the world will end and theorizes it could be the sky will fall, the earth will implode or "killer bunnies will eat everybody" (or could it be that high school is ending and the prom is approaching and Jason fears what the future holds). As he tries to convince others that what he is saying is the truth, he finds that no one will take him seriously as he has no proof. The program follows Jason as he tries to convince others "that the end is near" and find the evidence he needs to prove what he is saying is the truth (but needing to face his fears and realize that when high school ends life will go on).

Cast: Marc Silverman (Jason), Heather Ursaki (Chloe), Style Dayne (Duncan), Nina Winkler (Angie), Greigh Laschuk (Mr. Knave), Brittany Vesterback (Clara). **Credits:** *Producer-Director:* Quinn Spickler, David Manuel. *Writer:* Brittany Vesterback. **Comment:** Literally a different approach to a high school-set comedy. While the plot is a bit out there, the casting is well done and represents what most high school kids are really like (not only in looks but actions and does not copy shows like *Saved by the Bell*). The acting is surprisingly good and the overall production is very well done.

Episodes: 10 untitled episodes, labeled "Episode 1" through "Episode 10."

294 *Englishman in L.A.* webserieschannel.com. 2014.

After an appearance on a U.K. television interview series hosted by Bridgette and Rupert, British best selling author Tom Dingle announces that he is heading to the United States, Hollywood in particular, to make his dream of getting his book (*The Lonesome Dove*) turned into a movie become a reality. Tom figures to begin by starring in a reality show based on an author—something that has not been done before and something that could get him the exposure he needs to get backing for his movie. Tom is rather naïve when it comes to Hollywood and, although he acquires an agent (Cassidy) he is like a fish out of water. As Tom begins adjusting to his new lifestyle and he and Cassidy begin shopping the idea, trouble enters the picture—from people wanting to take advantage of his recent success, to a crazed fan (Molly) to his mentor (William) who has become jealous and seeks to steal his spotlight.

Cast: Cameron Moir (Tom Dingle), Tamela D'Amico (Cassidy Clark), Eddie Jemison (William Willy), Ashley Fink (Molly Summers), James Meehan (Rupert), Wendy Johnson (Brigette), Julia Max (Candy). **Credits:** *Producer:* Jennifer Stang, David Vendette. *Director:* Cassandra Clark. *Writer:* Cameron Moir. **Comment:** Interesting to see how someone from England views Hollywood. The acting is very good and the production, which contains bleeped foul language, is also very well done.

Episodes: *1.* Prelude. *2.* The Arrival. *3.* Cassidy Clark. *4.* Mother Sunshine. *5.* Candy. *6.* William Wiley. *7.* I Think You Should See My Therapist.

295 *Eric Finley: Comment Counselor.* youtube.com. 2012.

"100 Impressions in 5 Minutes" is a video made by Eric Finley, a junior guidance counselor at Filmore High School, and posted on YouTube. While Eric believes his video is good, YouTube trolls immediately criticize the video and anger Eric. Hoping to teach the trolls a lesson, Eric acquires their IP addresses (through the help of a computer-whiz student) and plans his revenge: ambush them with a surprise counseling session to make them see what they are doing is wrong and make the Internet a happier place by posting that session on-line. The program charts each of the trolls Eric tracks down and the counseling session that follows.

Cast: Aaron Eisenberg (Eric Finley). **Credits:** *Producer:* Ashton Kutcher, Anthony Batt, Brin Lucas, Michael Lewen. *Director:* Will Eisenberg. *Writer:* Will Eisenberg, Aaron Eisenberg. **Comment:** An unusual concept that is very well done. Excerpts from Eric's video are presented and it is indeed a bad presentation as his celebrity impressions are quite awful.

Episodes: *1.* The Troll Hunt Begins. *2.* Don't Psychoanalyze a Therapist. *3.* Finley Don't Give a S**t. *4.* How Can People Be So Mean?

296 *Eris.* webserieschannel.com. 2014–2015.

A spoof of the 1970s CBS TV series *Isis* (also known as *The Secrets of Isis*). Several years ago, while on an archeological dig in Egypt, a young science teacher named Harmony Papadopoulos uncovers an ancient ring, made in the symbol of a golden apple that endows her with the powers of the Greek goddess Discord. The ring was made "by the Royal Jeweler and presented to some ancient lady" that when worn not only transformed that ancient lady into Eris but endowed her with special abilities (so the legend states). Now 3,000 years later, Harmony becomes a modern-day Eris and acquires abilities to battle evil when she places the ring on her finger. Harmony, however, does not acquire powers that are all that helpful as hers are more in line with what discord means—creating havoc. Like the *Isis* TV series wherein Isis wore a white tunic-like costume, Harmony is similarly dressed and has a best friend, Dick Mason (Rick Mason on *Isis*) and Mindy Ree (Cindy Lee on *Isis*) her student helper. While Isis faced danger that was not meant to be funny, Eris encounters dangers that are—from naughty students to bad guys who just can't seem to do anything right—all of which is complicated by Eris and the discord she creates in attempting to right wrongs.

Cast: Cady Zuckerman (Harmony/Eris), Pete Cross (Dick Mason), Emily Faris (Mindy Ree), Scott Hamby (Principal). **Credits:** *Producer:* Pete Cross, Mark Leasor. *Writer-Director:* Pete Cross. **Comment:** One of the best TV spoofs made for the Internet. The program is a direct rip-off of *Isis* with good acting and production values. Cady Zuckerman as Harmony (JoAnna Cameron played the character as Andrea Thomas on *Isis*) is the only one without a similar sounding name. The opening theme is also very similar to the *Isis* theme narration (that explains how Isis acquired her magic amulet, not a ring). If you remember *Isis* or have seen the reruns on Retro TV, then you should check out *Eris* to see just how something new is like something old again.

Episodes: *1.* Fat Girl. *2.* Just a Girl. *3.* Bigot. *4.* Doyle Honeysuckle. *5.* A Pretty Special Halloween Episode. *6.* Sir Isaac Newton's Circle Jerk. *7.* The Unaired Pilot.

297 *Escape My Life.* youtube.com. 2013.

Skylar is a very pretty, thirty-something year old woman who works as a wardrobe designer in Hollywood. She needs a car but refuses to consider one because, "Buying a car freaks me out." Skylar feels she is doing just fine, having others drive her where she needs to go until her friend and co-worker Scarlet, tells her about a Ford Motor Company placement program where they lease their cars and trucks to people in the entertainment industry as part of a "buzz-gathering" strategy (people will talk and word about Ford cars will spread). Skylar appears to be just what Ford is looking for and, after meeting with the company representative is given a Ford Escape and Barry. "And what is a Barry?" as Skyler asks. Barry is not a what but a who and he comes along with the car ("I'm Barry. I came from Detroit. I come with the car"). Sklyar accepts the deal, has a new car—and a Barry—and the program chronicles what happens to Skylar as she tries to live a normal life despite that fact that she has extra baggage—Barry, a man who is with her 24/7 and putting a cramp on her personal and professional life.

Cast: Natasha Leggero (Skylar), Joe Lo Truglio (Barry). **Credits:** *Producer:* Luke Ricci. *Director:* Ben Zlotuchi, Ruben Fleischer. *Writer:* Ben Zlotuchi. **Comment:** The merits of the Ford Escape are related and praised throughout the series as a perfect example of Product Placement (see also *Easy to Assemble*). Barry represents the Ford Motor Company and constantly extols the merits of the car. Natasha Leggero is delightful as Skylar and the program itself is very well produced and acted.

Episodes: *1.* What's a Barry? *2.* Yesterdead. *3.* Mimsy. *4.* Cheerio. *5.* The Two Escapes. *6.* Powdered Milk. *7.* World of Boxes. *8.* Finale.

298 *Evergreen Surgery.* youtube.com. 2013.

Evergreen Surgery is a small health care office run by Dr. Marty Phillipson in the quaint English village of Retford. Marty appears to be a qualified doctor but often acts childish giving the impression that seeking his assistance may not be a good idea. The program, a spoof of TV series like *Marcus Welby, M.D.* is simply the conversation Marty has with the patients who come to see him.

Cast: Jon Corr (Dr. Marty Phillipson), Russ Smith, Dave Bomley. **Credits:** *Producer-Writer:* Jon Corr, Russ Smith. **Comment:** A bit difficult to understand at times due to the British accents. While several comedy pilots were produced for American TV about small town doctors, none really made it to an actual series (an exception could be the series

Doc, although the setting was New York). The acting and production are good but it is a bit talkative.

Episodes: *1.* Pilot. *2.* Beat-Boxing. *3.* Porn. *4.* I'm in Love. *5.* Thief. *6.* Fitness. *7.* Proving Fitness. *8–10.* Finale.

299 *Everyone's Famous.* everyonesfamous. com. 2014–2015.

As a child Donald Farmer dreamed of one day becoming famous. But his father, being a practical man, shattered those dreams when he said, "Fame is for famous people." Donald believed him and lost interest in that dream. He is now an adult, has a job at a call center, a girlfriend (Judy) and looks to have settled into a normal life. But after he sees an Internet video go viral (a cat playing a piano) his childhood memories come back and he decides to become famous by creating viral videos. He quits his job and with his friend Richard begins a quest to become famous. The program chronicles Donald's efforts to create that one special video but encountering anything but success in his quest. Judy is a writer whose Internet stories acquire hits in the hundreds of thousands while Donald's number in the low hundreds. Eric is Donald's co-worker.

Cast: Ryan Beil (Donald Farmer), Kayla Lorrette (Judy Michael), Pat Thornton (Richard), Kyle Hickey (Eric). **Credits:** *Producer:* Walter Forsyth, Angus Swantee. *Writer-Director:* Andrew Bush. **Comment:** Is Donald just going through a phase? Or can he actually become famous by posting a video that will score hundreds of millions of hits? That is a question that arises but is never really answered. The idea, acting and production is very good and makes for worthwhile watching (more to see what failure happens as opposed to any successes).

Episodes: 4 untitled episodes, labeled "Episode 1" to "Episode 4."

300 *Evie (Has a Spare Room).* vimeo.com. 2012.

Evie is a critical care nurse living in England. She is a social butterfly and has no sense when it comes to personal boundaries. She also has a spare room in her home for rent and the program follows Evie as she seeks a boarder and how she reacts to situations when she pushes the rules of polite personal conversation and actions into an uncomfortable zone.

Cast: Evie Jones (Evie), Yannick Lawry (Jamie), Ben Brunnekreef (Zach). **Credits:** *Producer:* Christopher Beeson, Debra Waters, Andrew Deane. *Writer-Director:* Christopher Beeson. **Comment:** *Evie* is one of the few foreign produced programs that do not cross channels very well. While it may be humorous in its homeland, to other countries the program is a bit difficult to fathom (exactly what is going on) and not humorous (very talkative). There are a number of reasons for this, but the main problem appears to be in the casting. The cast are total unknowns in the U.S. and just not as appealing as they may be elsewhere. This coupled with its subtle humor is tailored to people who really appreciate something different (like opera and Shakespeare) as opposed to the general masses who crave Three Stooges like comedy.

Episodes: *1.* The Breakup Party. *2.* I Love You Zach.

301 *Ewoks Don't Blink.* funnyordie.com. 2012.

Carl and Mac are clerks in a video store and earn $7.25 an hour. Carl is a *Star Wars* fan while Mac, a very pretty girl, is a *Star Trek* fanatic (so much so that she wears Mr. Spock Vulcan ears and considers herself a Trekker, not a Trekkie. A Trekkie, according to Mac, lives at home and in the basement of his mother's home; a Trekker is someone who has moved out and beginning life on his own). While the program is about two nerds, all the action takes place in the video store and what happens when a thief enters, attempts to rob the store and encounters Mac's wrath when he calls her a Trekkie.

Cast: Justin McFarlane (Carl), Grace Kinser (Mac), Ajay Lee (Jamison). **Credits:** *Producer-Writer:* Beau Batterson, Anthony Mitchell. **Comment:** While only one story line has been produced it is well produced and acted.

Episodes: 3 untitled episodes, labeled "Episode I," "Episode II" and "Episode III."

302 *The Ex-Box.* blip.tv. 2012.

Allie, a young woman with dreams of becoming a leading lady in movies, and Nate, her boyfriend, a young man with high ambitions to become a famous film director, have recently moved in together and rented an apartment at 405 Hollywood Way in Los Angeles. Their first time living together appears to work well until three months later when they find they can no longer stand each other. But they also find that if they break their lease they will be responsible for paying off what time is left on it (nine months). Financially unable to do so, Allie and Nate decide to remain together and continue sharing the apartment. Allie divides and labels everything ("Allie" or "Nate") and the program explores their living situation as they seek their dreams but also shows that, in an "Odd Couple" like environment ex-lovers can not really be friends—or can they?

Cast: Adam Kitchen (Nate Reed), Emily Brownell (Allie Burke), Richard Riehle (Mr. Reed), Laura Sheehy (Laura), John Forest (Dave), Juliette Hing-Lee (Jezebel), Brad Lee Wind (Jerry Antoni). **Credits:** *Producer:* Kristyn Macready, Emily Brownell. *Director:* Annie Lukowski. *Writer:* Emily Brownell. **Comment:** Ex-lovers living with each other has been done numerous times before—on TV, in the movies and even on the Internet. Each has their own take and *The Ex-Box* holds up as one of the best. Not only are the leads very like-able, but the acting and production values are excellent.

Episodes: *1.* This Is Yours, This Is Mine. *2.* How to Get Over Your Beotch. *3.* The Breakup Rules. *4.* Devil in Disguise. *5.* The Seduction. *6.* It's Broke, Fix It! *7.* The Proposition. *8.* Threesome. *9.* Happy Ending.

303 *The Ex-Girlfriend.* theexgirlfriend. net. 2000.

Madison is a young woman living what she considers an ideal life. She has a good job as a beautician, a nice apartment and a boyfriend (Josh). Unknown to Madison, Josh had secretly been dating her sister, Sabrina, and all comes to light when Sabrina and Josh breakup and Sabrina accidentally reveals to Madison that she dated Josh at the same time Josh was dating her. Madison is not only shocked and upset but now wonders if she can date a guy whose ex-girlfriend is her sister. Madison's struggles to overcome what happened, date other guys but somehow find a way to forgive Sabrina and Josh and reconnect with him are presented.

Cast: Madison Gorman (Madison), Nicole Galiardo (Sabrina), Josh Randall (Josh). **Comment:** An early Internet program on which all information has now been taken off line thus commenting is not possible.

Episodes: *1.* Meet Madison. *2.* Madison, the Ex. *3.* Madison Moves on.

304 *Excuse You!* webserieschannel.com. 2012.

An unnamed Italian restaurant in England provides the setting. It is here that service is anything but fast or competent, the silverware may be a bit dirty and checks encompass fees in addition to the food ordered. The program focuses primarily on one customer (unnamed) who enters the diner and what results when he tries to order his food, is finally served and his reaction to a bill that is anything but typical. Filmed at the Forge and Foundary in Camden Town, London.

Cast: Dexter Pickett (Customer), Claire Austin (Maria), Joanna Finata (Waitress), Sunil Goswami (Manager), Roberta Goodheart (Waitress), Dory LeSand (Nadia), Jason Tasker (George), Ken Birk (Creepy Guy). **Credits:** *Producer-Director:* Sunil Goswami. **Comment:** Enjoyable program that takes all the good aspects of diner-themed TV series and transposes them into what could happen if things were reversed. Well acted and produced and really something different to see.

Episodes: *1.* Excuse Me, Excuse You. *2.* May I Please Order? *3.* Money Matters. *4.* We'll Bill You Later. *5.* The Real Manager. *6.* The Price You Pay. *7.* Love Is Creepy.

305 Experi-Mates. experimates.com. 2013.

Eric and Shelli are a newlywed couple who find that the spark they had when they dated has vanished as their sex life has become rather uninteresting. Hoping to change the situation the couple seeks professional advice and the program charts what happens when they follow the advice of their therapist (from swinging to using techniques found in the *Kamasutra*) to spice up their love life.

Cast: Steve White (Eric), Elizabeth McIntire (Shelli), Zeshan Bhatti (Dr. Fingerling, the Therapist). **Credits:** *Producer:* Zeshan Bhatti. *Writer-Director:* Bobby Chase. **Comment:** While there is adult content, it is, for the most part discreetly handled and the program shines as a pleasant diversion from other programs that deal with a floundering love life.

Episodes: *1.* Swing and a Miss. *2.* The Relationship Savior. *3.* Kamasutra. *4.* Improv. *5.* The Rapist.

306 The F-List. vimeo.com. 2013.

Hollywood is known as a town for breaking hearts and spoiling dreams. But for two young hopefuls, Gracie and Bobby, Hollywood is a challenge they are willing to accept. Although they do have acting abilities they are considered unprofessional and placed at the bottom rung of the ladder, the F-List. The program chronicles their endless and seemingly fruitless efforts to break into show business through auditions they acquire. Gracie appears to be the more ambitious of the two with a role on the TV cooking show *Once Upon a Thyme* and a theory that she feels is her best weapon—"If you want the part become the part."

Cast: Sean Edwards (Bobby), Beth Triffon (Gracie), Jared Ward (Cliff), London Vale (Jenny), Clint Brink (Abs), Lynn Freedman (Sandy), Nija Okoro (Jane). **Credits:** *Producer:* Ken Cooper, Mary Beth Searls, Donna Morong. *Director:* Donna Morong, Lorne Hiltser. *Writer:* Giorgis Despotakis, Andy Lee. **Comment:** Well acted and produced program that comically depicts the struggles young actors face as they try to break into show business.

Episodes: *1.* Once Upon a Thyme. *2.* Networking. *3.* Breaking In. *4,5.* Fake It 'Til You Make It.

307 Fagney and Gaycey. youtube.com. 2009–2010.

Ron Fagney and Walter Gaycey are, even if their names do not define them, gay detectives with the Los Angeles Police Department. In a spoof of the 1980s CBS series *Cagney and Lacey* (which dealt with the investigations of N.Y.P.D. detectives Chris Cagney [Sharon Gless] and Mary Beth Lacey [Tyne Daly]) Ron and Walter are profiled as they attempt to solve unusual crimes in the gayest-like manner possible.

Cast: Mike Rose (Ron Fagney), Drew Droege (Walter Gaycey), George McGrath (Lt. McGrath), Andie Bolt (Off. Andie), Amy Procacci (Off. Amy), Brennan Campbell (Off. Brennan). **Credits:** *Producer-Writer-Director:* Mike Rose. **Comment:** Anyone familiar with the CBS series will immediately recognize that the show's musical theme ("The Theme from Cagney and Lacey") has been used here with similar opening visuals. *Fagney and Gaycey* is a clever take-off with good acting and production values but an over-abundance of gayness to replicate the friendship that existed between Chris and Mary Beth (who were straight).

Episodes: *1.* Flasher. *2.* Baby, Baby, Baby. *3.* Black and Blue. *4.* Episode 4. *5.* Episode 5.

308 Fail: The Web Series. youtube.com. 2011.

Alicia is a college freshman looking forward to a prosperous and rewarding education. Her hopes are shattered when she finds the work much harder than she imagined. But all is not lost when Hope, her cousin, offers her a solution—join a study group, preferably hers. Alicia is somewhat relieved and chooses not to join with Hope but with a group who are less than studious and on the verge of academic probation for their non conformity to the rules. The program follows Alicia and her study mates as they become more interested in indulging in each other's social circles than in books.

Cast: Vanessa Baden (Hope Love), James Bland (Jones Jenkins), Tristin Mays (Alicia Lopez), Andrew Bachelor (C.K.), Whitney Reed (Billie Jean Goldberg), Jeryn Mays (Jet). **Credits:** *Producer:* Christopher "Play" Martin, James Bland, Vanessa Baden, Adam Mack, Ed Voccola. *Writer-Director:* Vanessa Baden. **Comment:** *Fail* has its own twist on college life as seen through Hope, Alicia, Jones, Billie Jean, Jet and C.K.: they are African-American and the producers try to avoid all the clichés and present a program that can have its comedic moments but not lose track of what it set out to do: show that sometimes life lessons can be learned outside of a classroom.

Episodes: *1.* Teach Me to Study. *2.* B.J. Finds Herself. *3.* Hoe to Get the Answers. *4.* Desperate Measures. *5.* Where the Party At? *6.* One More Chance. *7.* Rock the Vote. *8.* Cereal Killa on Trial. *9.* 106 & Park. *10.* Ain't Gone Hurt Nobody. *11.* Blame It on the Justice. *12.* Mo Money, Mo Problems.

309 Fake It Till You Make It. youtube.com. 2010.

As a kid, Reggie Caulkin was the star of the hit television series *I Got Dibs.* But as Reggie grew, the kid-like charm of the series dwindled and the program was cancelled. Reggie apparently returned to a normal life but, now in his thirties, has become an agent for future stars. Even though his calling card reads "Reggie Caulkin, Celebrity Trainer" and Reggie is not the success he once was, he puts on airs to make everyone believe he is a big-time Hollywood agent. The program follows Reggie as he sets out to recapture a time of his youth through the people he handles as clients. **Cast:** Jaleel White (Reggie Culkin), Betsy Rue (Kathy Buttram), Christopher Nicholas (Darren Kernin), Elaine Tan (Leela). **Credits:** *Producer-Writer:* Jaleel White. **Director:** Todd Pellegrino. **Comment:** Jaleel White (Steve Urkel from the TV series *Family Matters*) shines as the former child star turned agent. He is no Urkel and anyone familiar with how Urkel looked and acted will be in for quite a surprise to see the two are nothing alike. The acting and production are excellent but there are some (really not needed) suggestive sexual situations. **Episodes:** *1.* Power Breakfast. *2.* Talk to My Agent. *3.* Residual Income. *4.* Never Sleep with the Fans. *5.* You Are What You Drive. *6.* Midnight Negotiations. *7.* Dine and Ditch. *8.* Wayne Brady Tweets.

310 *Fame and Fidelity.* youtube.com. 2013.

Yusuf Malik is a young man struggling to fulfill his dream of becoming an actor. His efforts, however, are not easy, as he is subject to being typecast, has a senile agent and there are many actors who are much better. But also affecting Yusuf is his religion, which often contradicts what he is doing. In a different twist on struggling actors, the program follows Yusuf as he seeks his dream but also tries to remain faithful to his religious beliefs (fame and fidelity). **Cast:** Yusuf Zine (Yusuf Malik), Nigel Irwin (Miguel), Brian Hayden (Noal Emmerich). **Credits:** *Producer:* Kevin Young, Jamaal Azeez, Derek Wong. *Writer-Director:* Yusuf Zine. **Comment:** A simple twist on struggling actors that mixes religious beliefs with what life is really about and what has to be done to succeed. Aspects of Yusuf's auditions are seen (seemingly always cast as a terrorist or some Muslim extremist) with his eagerness to break the type casting mold that he now finds a curse. The acting and production are well done. **Episodes:** *1.* Pilot. *2.* Via Con Dios. *3.* The Zipper. *4.* Scottish Play. *5.* Self-Represented. *6.* Lost Horizon. *7.* Method. *8.* Picture Wrap.

311 *Famous Farrah.* famousfarrah.com. 2013–2014.

Farrah Satrapi is 26-years old and facing her quarter-life crisis. She is engaged to John, a Wall Street "big shot," works a boring job in a lab and has little to no excitement in her life. It is the night of her twenty-sixth birthday when Farrah is stood up by John, who has failed to remember it is her big day. Ava, Farrah's vivacious sister, comes to the rescue and takes her out for a night on the town. The eve-ning brings a dramatic change in Farrah's life when she has a chance encounter with Mac Illa and Greg Greasy, crew leaders of The Cake Boyz, a floundering rock group who are seeking a gimmick to spice up their band. Mac and Greg see something in Farrah and believe they can transform her into the image they need and offer her the change she has been seeking. With Farrah accepting and her life changing from dull to exciting the program chronicles the mishaps Farrah encounters as she embarks on an uncertain road that could lead to a new career (if she can be taught to Rap) and new loves. **Cast:** Kathleen Khavari (Farrah Satrapi), Mike Ivers (John), Giselle Vazquez (Ava), Lamar Cheston (Mac Illa), Eden Marryshow (Greg Greasy), Ashley Zuger (Sharon), Leigh-Ann Rose (Leslie), Jeremy Burnett (Cease), Jill Durso (Hanna), Lil Bob Mc-Call (Steve), Shara Ashley Zeiger (Lucy), Andrew Planter (Derek), Mike Ivers (John). **Credits:** *Producer:* Khaliah Neal. *Director:* Talibah Newman. *Writer:* Chuck Neal. **Comment:** Somewhat of a rags-to riches back to rags saga as it charts Farrah's less-than sensational climb up the music ladder. The acting is good and the production flows smoothly from episode to episode. **Episodes:** *1,2.* Pilot. *3.* The Next Day. *4.* She Can't Rap. *5.* Hands Like Feet. *6.* Management. *7.* Sorry Guys. *8.* Unemployment.

312 *Far from the Tree.* youtube.com. 2011–2012.

Reggie and Sarah are a married couple and the parents of Liz, Martha and Mark. As time passed and the children grew, Sarah and Reggie also grew apart and eventually divorced. Sarah gained custody of the children and Reggie found a new love interest (Katy). Mark is never seen or heard; Liz is a young woman trying cope with her dysfunction family; Martha, the preferred daughter by Sarah, is a struggling actress and Sarah is a woman living in the dark ages as she is not even aware of an Internet or what it is. While the website claims "It's *Mama's Family* meets *The Office*," the program is not as outrageous as either but does, in its own way, present a humorous glimpse into the lives of the family and how each copes with the situations that surround them. **Cast:** Joanna Churgin (Sarah), Robin Shelby (Liz), AnnaLisa Erickson (Martha), Jeffrey Markle (Reggie), Alex Rose Wiesel (Katy), Barry Pearl (Barry), Henry LeBlanc (Nick). **Credits:** *Producer:* Robin Shelby, Sean Spence. *Director:* Sean Spence. *Writer:* Sean Spence, Lorne Cooke. **Comment:** The acting, situations and production are good and Liz's facial expressions as she often finds herself in the middle of a Sarah and Martha thing make those episodes even more enjoyable. **Season 1 Episodes:** *1.* Coffee. *2.* Frosty. *3.* Birthday. *4.* Internet Date. *5.* Game Day. *6.* Makeover. **Season 2 Episodes:** *1.* Issues and Tissues. *2.* Acting Up. *3.* Is This Real Life? *4.* Sell, Sell, Sell. *5.* Made of Honor. *6.* The Secret.

Season 3 Episodes: *1.* Sexy, and I Know It. *2.* Poker Night. *3.* Close Up. *4.* Missed Again. *5.* True or False. *6.* No Other Hand.

313 *Fat Guy.* fatguyshow.com. 2011.

DrastiSlim is a new diet pill that promises big things. It claims it can make overweight people slim again but its manufacturers conceal the fact that it can cause brain cancer. Caskey, a young gay man in his twenties, is the poster image for the product. Caskey was born in the Midwest and came to New York City to further his career as an actor. Through his agent (Susan) Caskey becomes the model for DrastiSlim and a before and after image of him appears on billboards and in magazine ads. The program, while following Caskey's mishaps as he attempts to acquire acting jobs, also chronicles what happens when he finds himself embroiled in a scandal over DrastiSlim when a before shot of him is used with an after shot of a faked slim him—and word of the side effects leak out.

Cast: Caskey Hunsader (Caskey), Eva Shure (Eva), Andrew Wehling (Greg), Kelly Shoemaker (Kelly), Kristin Maloney (Susan), Lauren Kadel (Kim), Sari Schwartz (Melissa Mendoza), Jacob Bressers (Susan's assistant). **Credits:** *Producer-Writer-Director:* Caskey Hunsader. **Comment:** "Welcome to the Biggest Series on the Web" is an appropriate tag line for a very enjoyable program with good acting and production values.

Episodes: *1.* The Offer. *2.* The Shoot. *3.* The Show. *4.* The Date. *5.* The Billboard. *6.* The Aftermath. *7.* The Audition. *8.* The Scandal. *9.* The End.

314 *Faux Baby.* hulu.com. 2008.

Madeline is a young woman, married to Harry, and wanting to start a family but is fearful of having a baby. Hoping to ease her anxiety, Madeline visits a psychologist (Dr. Greenfield) to overcome her fear of "breaking a baby." Seeing that Madeline lacks self confidence when it comes to babies, the doctor prescribes her taking care of a faux baby, a doll that acts like and needs to be cared for like a real baby. Although reluctant at first, Madeline slowly begins to think of the doll (Adam) as a real baby and the program follows Madeline as she (and Harry) care for Adam and face all the same situations parents do when caring for real babies.

Cast: Missy Yager (Madeline), Lucas Bryant (Harry), Laura Jane Salvato (Allyson), Lauri Hendler (Carrie), Susan Rudick (Lisa), Carolyn Almos (Ellen), Robert Chapin (Elliot), Leslie Hope (Dr. Greenfield). **Credits:** *Producer:* Laura Brennan, Rachel Leventhal, Jennifer Maisel, Patty Cornell, Michael Franks. *Director:* Charlie Stratton. *Writer:* Jennifer Maisel, Laura Brennan, Rachel Leventhal.

Comment: The subject is not new (it has even been done with eggs and sacks of flour substituting as babies) but it is taken to the extreme here with Madeline believing Adam is real especially when she befriends of group of mothers (Ellen, Lisa, Carrie and Allyson) while taking Adam for a stroll. It is very well acted and produced and well worth watching.

Episodes: *1.* Birth of a Faux. *2.* Bringing Up Faux Baby. *3.* There Will Be Milk. *4.* The Boob Ultimatum. *5.* Super Dad. *6.* Valley of the Fauxs.

315 *Fauxtography.* vimeo.com. 2014–2015.

Jeff is a young man in his twenties who has decided to become a photographer when he feels his liberal arts degree is useless and he becomes tired of working odd jobs. Jeff's introduction to photography came in high school when he bought a disposable instant camera and enjoyed taking pictures of his friends. But it seemed like only a phase and he abandoned it when he entered college. Recalling the fun he had with that camera, Jeff decides to make photography his career. But is it his true love or calling? "Probably not," Jeff says, "but it will do for now" and the program follows all the mishaps Jeff encounters as he tries to not only figure out his personal life, but how to fit in with the ever increasing Instragram revolution.

Cast: Alex Zuko (Jeff), Amy LoCicero (Laura), Daniel Baldock (Ken). **Credits:** *Writer:* Sam Kantrowitz. *Director:* Justin Connors. **Comment:** *Shutterbugs* (see entry) was the first Internet series to comically deal with photographers and like that program, presents a nice twist on the topic with good acting and production values.

Episodes: 4 untitled episodes, labeled "Episode 1" through "Episode 4."

316 *FCU: Fact Checkers Unit.* webseries channel.com. 2010.

What is actress Pauley Perrette's (*N.C.I.S.*) natural hair color? Is Luke Perry's (*Beverly Hills 90210*) house haunted as he believes? Is Donald Faison (*Clueless*) afraid to fly? These are just some of the many mysteries (or myths) surrounding celebrities and the magazine *Dictum* is dedicated to uncovering the facts—no matter who they embarrass in the process. Dylan and Russell are the magazine's top fact checkers and the program chronicles the outrageous lengths they take to prove obscure celebrity facts "for accuracy's sake."

Cast: Brian Sacca (Dylan), Peter Karinen (Russell). **Credits:** *Producer:* Thomas Bannister, Robert Fernandez, Tatiana Derovanassian, Barney Oldfield. *Director:* Dan Beers. *Writer:* Dan Beers, Peter Karinen, Brian Sacca. **Comment:** While the program does sound intriguing, it cannot be watched ("This Video Is Private") and commenting is not possible.

Season 1 Episodes: *1.* Paranormal Activity. *2.*

Fear of Flying. *3.* SPF 125. *4.* Gilfonator. *5.* Turn Up the Heat with Jon Heder. *6.* The Rider. *7.* Blonde on Blonde. *8.* Fact Master.

Season 2 Episodes: *1.* Moby's Grammy. *2.* Three-Pain. *3.* Excessive Gas. *4.* Fly Like a Buttress. *5.* Party in My Mouth.

317 *Felix Blithedale.* webserieschannel.com. 2014.

It is the dawn of the Industrial Revolution and life is changing drastically. One man, an inventor named Felix Blithedale, is determined to change the world by creating something that will put his name in the history books. But what? His prior inventions have not been spectacular; his family and friends have little faith in him, but Felix believes that the world needs that special something. Through his steam powered "meta-photo-cinema-graph" (a camera that is capable of video and speech recording) Felix decides to chronicle his experiments and those of other inventors of the early 20th century. The program, which is produced in black and white and has the look of a lost film from the early 1900s, chronicles Felix's efforts as he seeks to take advantage of steam power and bring progress to the world through his inventions.

Felix is the son of Gerald and Katherine, the owners of the Blithedale Coal Company. When the company folded, Felix moved to San Francisco where he found work with Dr. Haddington, his former professor at Oxford. Now, based in Haddington's basement, Felix seeks that one invention that will restore his family's good name and fortune.

Dr. Sylvester Haddington is a renowned chemist but somewhat of a skeptic when it comes to the changing times. Life changed for Sylvester when he offered a course called Chemical Engineering at Oxford and no one signed up for it; he went on a sabbatical, returned to San Francisco and hired Felix to assist him.

Elizabeth Blithedale, called Lizzy, is Felix's sister, a medical student who was forced out of school when her family lost its fortune. She works as a nurse at the local hospital and is struggling to prove that women are just as capable as men in the work place.

Edward "Eddy" Rockridge was born in Nebraska, is a veteran of the Spanish American War and journeyed to San Francisco to gamble, drink and womanize. He has befriended Felix and together they share adventures (mishaps) apart from inventing.

Jane Haddington is Sylvester's daughter and the apple of Felix's eye. She is being tutored by Felix and is literally bored with his teachings and the basement lab; she rather cut class and enjoy the grandeur and beauty of the Opera House.

Cast: Erik MacRay (Felix Blithedale), Clive Ashborn (Dr. Sylvester Haddington), Meredith Shank (Elizabeth Blithedale), Edward Rockridge (Adam Mayfield), Mary Loveless (Jane Haddington), Scott

King (W.T. Colbridge). **Credits:** *Producer-Writer:* Erik MacRay. *Director:* Beau McCombs. **Comment:** Very well done program that stands on its own as not only unique, but quite enjoyable. The costumes and settings are also antiqued and very believable as it ushers you into another time period.

Episodes: *1.* Felix vs. the Introduction. *2.* Felix vs. the Dynamo. *3.* Felix vs. the Foreclosure. *4.* Felix vs. the Broken Maverick. *5.* Felix vs. the Letter. *6.* Felix vs. the Leyden Jars. *7.* Felix vs. the Lesson. *8.* Felix vs. the Feces. *9.* Felix vs. Validation. *10.* Felix vs. Current Events. *11.* Felix vs. the Field Test. *12.* Felix vs. Alcohol. *13.* Steam Finale.

318 *Fen's Friends.* vimeo.com. 2011.

"It's a cartoon, but it's not for kids" is a tagline that explores the rather adult world of Fen, a late night TV talk show host, his best friends, Robbie and Dean, and Roosevelt, Fen's less-than-effectual agent. They meet at Abby's Diner and the discussions about what happened during the week, coupled with a special guest for Fen's show, provide the story lines.

Voice Cast: Chris Riddle, Stuart Hildebrandt, Travis Nagy, Lee O. Smith, Jessica Counts, Josh Stout, Rozlyn Stanley, Perry Odom. **Credits:** *Creator-Writer:* Chris Riddle. **Comment:** Although the animation is a bit stiff it is well presented and stories follow the format of a live action sitcom.

Season 1 Episodes: *1.* The Woodsman. *2.* Lovely Rita. *3.* The Bouncer. *4.* The Cleaning Lady. *5.* The Stage Manager. *6.* The Yoga Instructor. *7.* The Guitar Guy. *8.* The Mormon. *9.* The Doctor. *10.* The Targets. *11.* The Megazord. *12.* Mary Mary.

Season 2 Episodes: *1.* Mary Had a Little Lamb. *2.* The Host. *3.* The House Sitter. *4.* The Daughters. *5.* The Brother-in-Law. *6.* The Prospect. *7.* The Journalist. *8.* The Guests. *9.* The Cute Kid. *10.* Mom's New Boyfriend.

319 *Fetching.* aol.com. 2009.

Fetchings is a Doggie Day Care business owned by an independent woman named Liz. Although Liz had both a boyfriend and a job as a lawyer she was simply not happy and gave up both to follow her dream and open Fetchings. Liz soon discovers that running a small business is not all it is cracked up to be and the program charts the difficulties she encounters, how deals with them and how she attempts to overcome them (all of which begin when she hires Matt as her assistant and David, a washed-up celebrity hair stylist, as her groomer).

Cast: Colette Wolfe (Liza), Levi Fiehler (Matt), Sandra Vergara (Adi), Elaine Hendrix (Sheila), Brian Titchne (David), Dave Annable (Blake), Robert Bagnell (Jack), Josh Casaubon (Mitch). **Credits:** *Director:* Jason Reilly. *Writer:* Amy Harris. **Comment:** The official website and all its episodes have been taken off line thus an evaluation is not possible.

Episodes: *1*. A Girl's Best Friend. *2*. Old Dog, New Tricks. *3*. Two Dog Night. *4*. New Dogs in Town. *5*. Yappy Endings. *6*. Doggiversary. *7*. Party Animal. *8*. Animal Attraction. *9*. Two Sides to Every Tale. *10*. Heavy Petting. *11*. Let Sleeping Dogs Lie. *12*. Heel Boy. *13*. Downward Facing Dogs. *14*. Welcome to the Dog House. *15*. Puppy Love.

320 *59 Days in New York.* youtube.com. 2014–2015.

Amy is a small town girl with a dream to move to New York City and achieve fame as a singer-songwriter ("I want to be the next Dolly Parton"). Amy felt that her chance for achieving success at home would not happen ("I don't want to sing at local farmer's markets") and scrimped and saved and now has enough money that she calculates will last her 59 days in the Big Apple. Amy takes that first big step and buys a ticket, acquires an apartment from Craigslist and through musical numbers and songs the program charts Amy's efforts to find her dream, something that has been eight years in the making.

Cast: May-Elise Martinsen (Amy), Keri Acer (Boss Woman), Sam Benedict (Andy), Caitlin Graham (Director). **Credits:** *Producer-Writer:* May-Elise Martinsen. *Director:* May-Elise Martinsen, Justin Rogers. **Comment:** May-Elise Martinsen is absolutely delightful as the wide-eyed, innocent girl-next door type who seeks stardom. May-Elise is also a very good singer and performer and the entire series is a new way of retooling an old idea.

Episodes: *1*. New York, New York. *2*. Nice Little Home. *3*. The Lobe Letter. *4*. Thirty. *5*. The Internship. *6*. Oatmeal and Paper Cuts. *7*. The Great Dolly Parton. *8*. Dream. *9*. Almost.

321 *Fifty Shades of Blue.* disparrowfilms. com. 2013.

Frederico and Arnoldo are would-be hoodlums who believe they are gangsters and living in the 1950s. Frederico loves the color blue and everything associated with him is in blue (even his gun); Arnoldo appears to thrive on bananas and even incorporates them as weapons. Jia and Katja are a lesbian couple who are not only lovers, but their friends. The program follows the disillusioned gangsters as they become involved in a plot to retrieve a mysterious suitcase from the real underworld; unknown to them, Jia and Katja are only friendly with them to help them achieve their goal—the suitcase for themselves.

Cast: Lukas DiSparrow (Frederico Blue), Jordan Adriano Brown (Arnoldo), Suan-Li Ong (Jia), Taly Vasilyev (Katja), Ricky Rajpal (Banana Dealer). **Credits:** *Producer-Writer-Director:* Lukas DiSparrow. **Comment:** Although living disillusioned lives,

Frederico and Arnoldo are not afraid to do what it takes to achieve a goal. Based on the two episodes that have been produced, the program shows signs of being a real change from the typical gangster-themed programs of the past. Throwing in beautiful lesbians, their kissing scenes and some comical action, *Fifty Shades of Blue* could easily become a fan favorite.

Episodes: *1*. The Pilot. *2*. The Stranger.

322 *Filmmaker Wannabes.* webserieschannel.com. 2014.

Tyler and Rich are not your average indie (independent) filmmakers (competent people seeking to make a statement through their films); they are total morons and can't seem to produce anything with substance. Life changes for them when they begin work on a grind house film called *Black Lincoln* and the program charts what happens when production begins and anything that can go wrong does.

Cast: Jerred D. Adams (Tyler Sebert), Aaron J. Smith (Rich Cornell), Erin Mills (Vincent Polk), Lynsey Pavlik (Rebecca), Shayne Knepper (Herb Brighton), Elijah Kimball (Timmy Bugg), James Camarillo (Combs), Tyler Miller (Dale Pepper), Shao-Line Adams (Desdemona), Lisa Adams (Apple). **Credits:** *Producer-Director:* Jerred D. Adams. *Writer:* Jerred D. Adams, Aaron J. Smith.

Comment: It takes a few minutes to overcome the absurd silliness of the program. What follows is a standard acted and produced program that basically focuses on the chaos that arises when the leads have only one week to produce their film.

Episodes: *1*. 3 Months Later. *2*. A Troma Production.

323 *Finding Normal: The Web Series.* webserieschannel.com. 2013.

Ashley is a young woman whose quirkiness makes it difficult for her to become a normal part of society. She has become somewhat of a loner and forced herself into seclusion, so much so that she cannot face the prospect of attending college and has resorted to taking on-line screen-writing classes. Ashley, who is also fearful of leaving her apartment, believes that she needs "to find normal" and begins an Internet video diary of her various attempts to fit in (hoping that it will help her observe her own behavior in an objective way and teach her how to become "more normal" for the sake of social acceptance; she does try to fit in, but is rather awkward and things just do not go her way). All is progressing well for Ashley until she is assigned to work with a partner (Devin) and her world again comes crashing in around her. Although faced with bouts of anxiety and awkwardness, she agrees to accept Devin and soon discovers that she and Devin share similarities, although he has a higher level of confidence. The program follows Ashley as she attempts to come out of her self-imposed shell and not only find romance but become a functioning part of society.

Cast: Lisa Coombs (Ashley), Rich Prugh (Devin), Angel Fajardo (Jose), Yuka Takara (Kim), Delia Farizath (Maria). **Credits:** *Producer:* Lisa Coombs, Faizah Griggs. *Director:* Cooper Griggs. *Writer:* Lisa Coombs. **Comment:** Charming program with good acting and production values.

Episodes: *1.* Welsh. *2.* Devin. *3.* How to Ski in the Antarctic. *4.* Penguin Marriage Counseling. *5.* Awkward Pass. *6.* Cat Whisperer.

324 *First Day.* alloyentertainment.com. 2010–2011.

Cassie is a teenage girl starting her first day of high school. From what to wear and how to present herself has been carefully planned and now all Cassie has to do is make that good first impression. Unfortunately, for Cassie, everything that can go wrong does as she tries to impress a boy (Ryan) and her first day becomes a total disaster. That night, while talking to her plush dog Max, Cassie wishes what happened today never did—"I just wish I could just erase today and start over." The following morning Cassie finds that her idle wish has come true as she begins to relive events of the prior day all over again. Cassie had humiliated herself in front of the perfect guy but now she has been given a second chance. But can she undo what already happened? Cassie believes that knowing in advance what will happen and avoiding those hazards to impress Ryan will be the key that ends her repeating each day as that first day. The program chronicles what happens each day that Cassie relives and how, even when knowing the future, one cannot change what has already happened.

Cast: Tracey Fairaway (Cassie Mitchell), Elizabeth McLaughlin (Sasha Mitchell, Cassie's sister), Courtney Rackley (Cassie's mother), Jesse Kove (Ryan), Erik Stocklin (Gregg), Martha Brigham (Curly Haired Girl), Jazz Raycole (Paige), Alanna Masterson (Abby), Bailey Noble (Rosie Rovello), Ron Butler (Vice Principal Lewis), Kara Crane (Taylor Weller), Alexandra Rodriquez (Whitney), Brandon Jones (JT Fox), Molly McAleer (Miss Harvey). **Credits:** *Producer:* Tripp Reed, Joshua Bank, Bob Levy, Leslie Morganstein. *Director:* Sandy Smolan. *Writer:* Alyssa Embree, Jessica Koosed Etting, Benjamin Oren, Melissa Sadoff Oren. **Comment:** Although the idea has been done before, it is very well presented here in a different take with excellent acting and production values.

Season 1 Episodes: *1.* The Boyfriend Plan. *2.* If at First You Don't Succeed. *3.* Wherefore Art Thou Romeo? *4.* Must Love Punk and Pets. *5.* Sister Act. *6.* Repeat Offender. *7.* Kiss Me You Fool. *8.* I Want to Love.

Season 2 Episodes: *1.* First Dance: Totes Adorbs. *2.* First Dance: Deja Boo. *3.* First Dance: Friending the Enemy. *4.* First Dance: More Like Honesty. *5.* First Dance: Pretending Sucks Way More. *6.* First Dance: Never Saw It Coming.

325 *Firsts the Series.* facebook.com. 2013–2014.

Sally and Chuck are friends who have decided to take the next step and become a couple. They are inexperienced in many aspects of a relationship but feel they can overcome any obstacle they may encounter. Those firsts (the obstacles) are chronicled with the program relating how Sally and Chuck react to them. The conversations Sally has with her girlfriend, Amanda, as she relates what happens during all those firsts, are also featured.

Cast: Courtney Rackley (Sally), Troy Ruptash (Chuck), Rebecca Larsen (Amanda), Dave Shalansky (Dave), Anthony Backman (Tim), Henry Dittman (Allen), Whitney Dylan (Melissa), Gretchen German (Colleen). **Credits:** *Producer:* Courtney Rackley, Matt Crabtree, Troy Ruptash, Cassandra Shalansky, Dave Shalansky. *Director:* Vicky Jenson, Dave Linstrom, Andrew Miller, Kevin Wade, Ben Rock, Alicia Conway, Brian Groh, Michael A. Hammeke, David Marmor, Scott Schofield, Peter Alton, Miranda Bailey, Andrea Fellers, Mark W. Gray, Tom Magill, Alex Rotaru, Andrew Treglia. *Writer:* Courtney Rackley, Brian Groh, David Radcliff, Abi Wurdeman, Philip Wurdeman, Debora Cahn, Kathleen Dennehy, Bob DeRosa, Julie Mullen, Adam Stein, Kevin Berntson, Brett Greenberg, Jude Roth, Jenelle Roth, Vanessa Claire Stewart, Casey Venseventer. **Comment:** Very well done program with excellent acting and production values There are some adult sexual situations although no parental warning is posted before episodes begin.

Season 1 Episodes: *1.* First Night of the Rest of Your life. *2.* First Kiss. *3.* First Date. *4.* First Game Night. *5.* First F**k. *6.* First Running Into Your Ex. *7.* First Phone Sex.

Season 2 Episodes: *1.* Meet Chuck and Sally. *2.* First Meet His Best Friend. *3.* First Trip. *4.* First STD. *5.* First Threesome. *6.* First Embarrassing Moment. *7.* First Double Date. *8.* First Meet the Parents. *9.* First Proposal. *10.* First I Do. *11.* First Temptation.

326 *Fishbowl of Love.* webserieschannel.com. 2011.

Beverly Stevens is a young twenty-something woman who leaves the comfort zone of her home in the Midwest to seek a new life and career in Hollywood. But what she thought would be an easy adjustment is anything but and she soon finds herself all alone with her only contact her Indian neighbor Danjit. To solve her dilemma Beverly joins an Internet dating site hoping to meet people and explore

Los Angeles. The program relates the experiences Beverly encounters when the hoped-for normal dates become more like Holly-weirdo dates.

Cast: Brittany Samson (Beverly Stevens), Jorge Luis Abreu (Danjit). **Credits:** *Producer:* Chris Darkes, Brittany Samson. *Writer:* Adam Brodsky. **Comment:** Enjoyable little program with the best scenes being Beverly's sharing her before dating strategy and after results with Danjit (who really listens and attempts to help her). The sharing aspect sets it apart from other series dealing with a single woman looking for love and it is also well acted and produced.

Episodes: *1.* Poetic Justice. *2.* Captain Hollywood. *3.* Red Flag. *4.* Suave Maga. *5.* The Best Date Ever. *6.* The Checklist.

327 *The Fitness Center.* webserieschannel. com. 2013.

Derek Pearson is a young man who enjoys his time at a gym called The Fitness Center. Derek is happy the way he is, enjoying what he does without any romantic involvement at the present. He does have a woman friend, Michelle, whom he does not see in a romantic light, but as his workout partner, best friend and someone to talk to when things get tough. Michelle respects Derek for his choices but feels he needs a girl in his life even though it isn't her. One Friday night life changes for Derek when a new member, Zao, enters the center and Michelle sees her as the perfect girl for Derek. Derek is not looking for a girl nor is he too happy when Michelle announces that she is now his wingman and sets her sights on making the perfect match. Michelle's efforts to bring two people together, especially when one (Derek) is quite reluctant to begin a new romance, are chronicled.

Cast: David Spearman (Derek), Carole Kaboya (Michelle), Amy Chiang (Zao). **Credits:** *Producer-Writer-Director:* David Spearman. **Comment:** The first episode establishes the story line in a totally narrated manner that is well done and quite captivating. The remaining episodes, which use character dialogue continues the mood that was previously set but is a bit disappointing as it ends unresolved.

Episodes: *1.* Derek. *2.* Bygones. *3.* Ice Breaking 101. *4.* Zao.

328 *5-A.* webserieschannel.com. 2010.

Ritesh is a 21-year-old man who has just moved from India to New York to begin a new life. While it is not established as to how, he lives with Eddy, an obsessive neat freak (in Apartment 5-A) and has made two friends: Roberto, "a dumb-ass playboy" and Jesse, a sociopath method actress. Ritesh appears to have quickly adjusted to his new life style but anything that can go wrong does for him. The situations that befall Ritesh and his friends as they simply try

to live their lives with as little conflict as possible are presented.

Cast: Ritesh Rajan (Ritesh), Anni Weisband (Jesse), Eddie Vona (Eddy), Roberto Aguirre (Roberto). **Credits:** *Producer-Director:* Matt O'Brien. *Writer:* Colin Hunt, Isaac Loftus. **Comment:** Surprisingly well produced program considering the plot has been done numerous times before. *5-A* has found its own niche with good acting and very like-able characters.

Episodes: *1.* Welcome to the Party. *2.* Tesh Meets Eddy. *3.* I Know What You Did Last Night. *4.* Prostitute No. 4.

329 *Flat 3.* flat3series.com. 2013–2014.

Flat 3 is an apartment in Australia that is shared by three friends (Jessica, Perlina and Lee). They are living on their own for the first time and haven't quite figured out what they are doing or where they are headed. The program, which spoofs the cultural scene, follows the flat-mates as they just try to keep their heads above water, find love and net the perfect jobs.

Lee is a quiet and reserved girl (some call her "Mousy") who is smart, has an off-beat sense of humor and is a bit socially awkward (she doesn't have the courage to fully express herself). She is not aggressive and always finds comfort in following someone else's lead. As long as she doesn't have to make difficult decisions she is fine. She has yet to decide what she wants to be and is literally searching for answers.

Jessica, who is a bit of an airhead, has a big heart and will always give of herself to help others, although her good intentions make it look like she is helping herself and is perceived as being a bitch (which she is not). She feels she has her two feet planted firmly on the ground and is hoping to become an actress (she does acquire small roles but she is never taken seriously at auditions).

Perlina is outspoken and holds nothing back; she says what she thinks (or tells it like it is without thinking of the consequences). Jessica is her best friend and her biggest fear is having to eat alone.

Katrina is Perlina's co-worker and mate in the band SuperSisters in the SuperCity. Simon is an accountant (called "The Accountant") and friends with Lee, Perlina and Jessica. Nic is Perlina's ex-boyfriend. Hweiling is Jessica's nemesis, a fellow actor who has a knack for rubbing Jessica the wrong way. Jackie Chan (not the real one), is a friend to the flat mates; Aidan, an actor, is Jessica's current boyfriend.

Cast: J.J. Fong (Jessica), Perlina Lau (Perlina), Ally Xue (Lee), Katrina Weeseling (Katrina), Simon Ward (Simon), Nic Sampson (Nic), Hweiling Ow (Hweiling), Mike Ginn (Aidan). **Credits:** *Producer:* Roseanna Liang, Kerry Waskia, J.J. Fong, Perlina Lau, Ally Xue. *Writer-Director:* Roseanna Liang.

Comment: Australian produced program that has a soap opera like feel to it but is also well acted and produced.

Episodes: *1.* Lee. *2.* Jessica. *3.* Perlina. *4.* The Flat Warming. *5.* The Speed Date. *6.* The Home Intruder. *7.* Blind Date. *8.* The Promo Girl. *9.* In the Bedroom. *10.* Wasted, *11.* Team Building. *12.* On the Road. *13.* Carper Diem. *14.* Teacher. *15.* Man Talk, Baby. *16.* Sale Now On. *17.* The White Album. *18.* The Game. *19.* The Xmas Special.

330 *Flicks.* webserieschannel.com. 2014.

Peppy, Jack, Herb and Chuck are not only best friends, but aspiring filmmakers (idiotic filmmakers, but non-the-less, filmmakers). They reside in Brooklyn, New York, and the program charts their efforts to produce films, all of which are hampered by their narrow thinking and inability to agree on anything that is best for the overall scheme of things.

Cast: Carson Alexander (Peppy), Mark Greene (Jack), Paul Kropfl (Herb), Steve White (Chuck), Crystal Arnette (Gwen, their friend). Credits: *Producer:* Brian Dodd. *Director:* Rich Wojcicki. Comment: Nothing out of the ordinary, just another take, although well produced and acted, on the struggling actor syndrome.

Episodes: 8 untitled episodes, labeled "Episode 1" through "Episode 8."

331 *Floaters.* youtube.com.2006.

Megan, Kaitlyn and Nisha are friends sharing an apartment and working as temps for a company called Effortless. While the girls appear content with their jobs, they are each hopeful that a brighter future is just around the corner. Kaitlyn and Nisha are seeking careers that are seemingly impossible to acquire at present while Megan has no real idea as to what she wants to become. Although it was not meant to be the center of attention, Megan's breakup with her boyfriend Jake overpowered the program's real focus to make her representative of young women facing adulthood and trying to find their place in the world. These episodes, while also focusing on the home and working lives of the friends, relate how Kaitlyn and Nisha attempt to get Megan out of the depression she is now suffering by making her see that she needs to let Jake go and move on.

Cast: Lauren Cook (Megan Gallagher), Erika Appleton (Kaitlyn Black), Punan Bean (Nisha Rampal), Ephraim Lopez (Cameron Diaz), Tonya Canada (Andi Weiss), Lisa Adams (Pippa Bunting), Mike Stickle (Matthew Warfield), Jamie Cummings (Roland Bart). Credits: *Producer-Creator:* Mike Stickle. *Producer:* Karen G. Jackovich, Pamela Canales. *Director:* Paul Batsel, Mike Stickle. *Writer:* Brooke Berman, Lauren Cook, Paul Batsel, Mike Stickle, Elizabeth Angell, Caitlin Morris, Jennifer Morris. Comment: One of the earlier series on

Floaters. Series poster art (used by permission of Mike Stickle).

which episodes can still be watched. The acting and production is comparable to a network TV series. The characters, especially Megan, are well executed and very believable and really do represent what many young women face as they begin their adult lives.

Episodes: *1–5.* Look Who's Stalking. *6–10.* Doctrine of Opposites. *11–15.* The Winds of Fate. *16–20.* Change—It's Not Just What Happens When You Break a Dollar. *21–25.* Good Impressions. *26–30.* Self Improvement. *31–35.* Harasser? I Hardly Know Her! *36–40.* The Jake-a-like. *41–45.* Hollywood Confidential. *46–50.* Poetry. *51–55.* Erika's Bad Day. *56–60.* Everybody Loves Roland. *61–65.* Just Like Me. *66–70.* Shannon Frasier's Comin' to Town. *71–75.* The Big Break.

332 *Floored.* youtube.com. 2011.

Boston Hill 8 Cinema is a relic. It was once a glamorous British movie theater but, like most such establishments in England, it has fallen on hard times due to the latest technology and the unwillingness of people to go to a theater to see a feature film. Jennifer is the theater manager; Alex and Trevor the ushers and Blake the trainee. While all is not progressing well, it gets even worse when Jennifer announces that, due to finances the theater may close. Unable to see their livelihood disappear, Alex seeks ways to make the theater once again profitable and stories relate his various attempts, with his best idea being to sell pirated movies to customers with their ticket purchase.

Cast: Carolyn Masson (Jennifer Crown), Mike Salisbury (Alex McDonald), Duncan Bruce (Trevor Murphy), Genevieve Brock (Blake Hartley), Will

Weatheritt (Jake Ward), Jarrod Sandells (Tim Porter), Emma-Louise Buck (Casey Cowan), Rowenia Wong (Sandy Zhao). **Credits:** *Producer:* Jessica Gulasekaram. *Director:* Justin Brewster. *Writer:* Michael Salisbury. **Comment:** A bit slow moving when compared to American series that dealt with the same situation (like *The Popcorn Kid*). The comedy is a bit subtle and the program is not hindered by thick British accents.

Episodes: *1.* It's Not Just Ripping Tickets. *2.* Boyz & Girlz. *3.* That's What She Said. *4.* She Kissed a Girl and She Liked It. *5.* Austin Hasn't Used That Maneuver in Years. *6.* Things Have Changed for Me (But That's Okay). *7.* Return of the MAC (Donald). *8.* Kristen Stewart Should Be Happy She's Even in *Twilight*.

333 Florence and Evelyn. funnyordie.com. 2012.

Florence, a bit mishap prone, and Evelyn, her confident best friend, have unknowingly been dating the same man (Gavin), a handsome politician. Life changes for them when each discovers the other is dating "her" man. Rather than get even with each other, Florence and Evelyn decide to extract their revenge on the man who put a wedge in their relationship—Gavin. The program follows what happens when they kidnap him for two-timing them and suddenly become criminals—with little knowledge at being such or how to get out of the situation they just created.

Cast: Carissa Casula (Evelyn), Elena Rossi (Florence), Tomek Kosalka (Gavin), Circus-Szalewski (Dan), Keira Ward (Young Evelyn), Allyssa Bainbridge (Young Florence), Shae Smolik (Ashley), Tammy Felice (Karen), Jake Bucher (Dale). **Credits:** *Producer-Writer:* Carissa Casula, Elena Rossi. *Director:* Patrick Hunter. **Comment:** Although it appears that only a pilot will be produced, it is well done but comes off as a rather dark comedy with the passive Florence and the aggressive Evelyn at odds with each other as they go about paying back (through torture) Gavin for what he has done. The chemistry between Florence and Evelyn makes the program and its only fault would be the continual use of vulgar language.

Episodes: *1.* The Pilot: Accidental Criminals.

334 Flour Girls. flourseries.weebly.com. 2012–2014.

Violet Flour is a responsible young woman who owns Flour Bakery and is living in a comfortable apartment with her boyfriend Tristan. Tulip, her sister, is carefree, free-spirited and has little or no direction in her life. It doesn't seem to faze her until she breaks up with her latest boyfriend (Liam) when she believes he is gay. Liam's explanation that he is bisexual and has chosen her over men, leaves Tulip devastated and sends her into a whirlwind of uncertainty. With no place to live, Tulip moves in with Violet and an "Odd Couple" situation is born. The program follows Violet as she and Tristan seek to live a normal life despite Tulip's crazy antics and equally crazy friends who have also invaded her life. As the program progressed, Violet and Tulip became stars on the reality TV series *Sisterly Love* but as that ended, so did the series. Violet and Flour returned for one final episode in 2014 called "The Next Chapter: Series Finale" wherein it is learned that the sisters have acquired a new show on Oprah Winfrey's Own Network called *Violet and Tulip: The Next Chapter*.

Cast: Deirdre McCullagh (Tulip), Jeni Miller (Violet), Michael Conolly (Tristan), Brianna Tillo (Madison), Loren Lepre (Clay), Jeff Orens (Liam). **Credits:** *Producer:* Deirdre McCullagh, Jeni Miller, Keisha Thorpe. *Director:* Keisha Thorpe. *Writer:* Deirdre McCullagh. **Comment:** Charming program with engaging leads, especially Deidre McCullagh as Tulip whose breakup is priceless but whose efforts to get back on track really make the program. Some outdoor scenes (like the protest in season 2) are a bit difficult to understand as the microphone appears to be just too far away from certain characters as they speak. Other than that it is a worth while program to watch.

Season 1 Episodes: *1.* Why Does Tulip End Up Moving in with Her Sister. *2.* The Commercial. *3.* The Engagement. *4.* Is That a Dog? *5.* The Bake Sale. *6.* 5 More Minutes. *7.* What Makes for a Good Reality Show Audition? Drama! *8.* What Type of Halloween Party Is This?

Season 2 Episodes: *1,2.* The Protest. *3.* The Next Chapter: Series Finale.

335 Flyboy. youtube.com. 2013.

He is known only as Flyboy and with his only super human ability, to fly through the air, he considers himself a super hero—"Defender of the Truth; Lord of the Air." Unfortunately he has not made a name for himself and criminals are oblivious to who or what he is. While no background information is given on how Flyboy acquired his abilities, he chose to become an orange-costumed hero to bring criminals to justice. Unfortunately being able to fly is not a good defense against the bad guys and Flyboy's confrontations always find him getting the worst end of the deal (like being beaten up). Flyboy has an uncanny sense to pick up on criminal activity and the program charts his less-than-spectacular encounters as he tries to become Ireland's only super hero.

Cast: Desmond Daly (Flyboy), Sharon Clancy (His wife), Aidan Corrigan, Amy Kelly, Stephen Thompson, Keith Jordan, Seamus Connolly. **Credits:** *Producer:* Seamus Connolly. *Writer-Director:* Keith Jordan. **Comment:** Super heroes from other countries are a rarity and patterning Flyboy after Superman is well done (as are the green screen effects to produce his flying sequences). The acting is good but the production suffers a bit as there is no background information on the characters or any real setup as how he became Flyboy.

Episodes: *1.* Forced Entry. *2.* Flyboy: Episode 2. *3.* Flyboy: Episode 3. *4.* Flyboy: Episode 4.

336 *Fodder.* webserieschannel.com. 2012.

A parody of TV cooking shows, restaurants, cafes, bars and diners that explore America's obsession with literally anything that is edible. Short comedy skits are incorporated to show that obsession (from out-of-control chefs to shopping in a supermarket).

Cast: Brandon Gulya, Mamrie Hart, Grace Helbig, Geoff Lerer, Gabe Liedman, Jim Santangeli, Laura Willcox, Sasheer Zamata. **Credits:** *Producer:* Carly Duncan, Chris Vivion. *Director:* Matthew C. Mills. *Writer:* Sasheer Zamata. **Comment:** How not to prepare meals could best sum up the program based on the only video that remains on line—a teaser. It is difficult to judge the entire series but viewing the teaser will net you how to shop for food, how to (and not to) prepare meals; chefs with attitude issues and people just too out-of-control to be handling sharp kitchen utensils.

Season 1 Episodes: *1.* Trend Alert. *2.* Dude vs. Food. *3.* Hot or Not? *4.* Side of Standup. *5.* The Klingon Word for Blew It? *6.* The Most Average Thing I Ate. *7.* Fantasy Food Draft. *8.* Agonizing Food Show Wait.

Season 2 Episodes: *1.* Insano Grub Fest. *2.* You'll Never Look at "Iron Chef America" the Same Way Again. *3.* The Hippest Speakeasy Bar You've Ever Seen. *4.* Really Depressed Cooking. *5.* The Colondator. *6.* What's in the Basket? *7.* Gruel Off. *8.* Lindsay Lohan's Great Haul. *9.* Gwyneth Paltrow's Bodega Haul. *10.* Abe Lincoln in a Bar. *11.* Chef Detective. *12.* Food Channel News Googa Mooga. *13.* What Hobbits Do.

337 *Fools for Hire.* youtube.com. 2012–2013.

Corporate entertainment is a little known aspect of show business wherein actors provide entertainment for corporate functions. Janet is the event coordinator; Anderson is the booking agent; Nick and Mike are two such actors and Eric is the self-professed God of Corporate Entertainment. With Florida as the program's setting and with a desperate desire to get out of corporate entertaining Nick and Mike feel that it can only happen if they can rise above what they do and produce their own play. With Eric behind them Nick and Mike create a pirate play and the program charts what happens as they seek to take Florida by storm.

Cast: Nick Harrison (Nick), Mike Cavers (Mike),

Eric Breker (Eric Von Huffington), Barbara Kozicki (Rochelle), Jennifer McClean (Janet Clarkson), Pearce Visser (Anderson Wyzbinski), Victoria Davidson (Victoria), Brianna Loop (Bianca). **Credits:** *Director:* Neil Every. **Comment:** Corporate Entertainment is brought to light in an unusual but well acted look at show business.

Season 1 Episodes: *1,2.* Piracy. *3.* Family. *4.* Look Into My Eyes.

Season 2 Episodes: *1,2.* The Hungry Game. *3.* Homeless. *4.* Wahid. *5.* Whores. *6.* The C-Word. *7.* This Is Gonna Go Viral. *8.* Bianca.

338 *A Fool's Parade.* webserieschannel.com. 2013.

Jake and Cooper are roommates who find their lives changing when Jake's cousin, Paul has his heart broken when his fiancé leaves him for another man (an astronaut) and moves in with them. Seeing that Paul needs to get over what happened, Jake and Cooper take matters in their own hands and attempt to get him back in the dating scene. The program focuses on what happens during those attempts (although actually focusing on the life lessons each learns).

Cast: Nick Pupo (Paul), Tom Feeny (Jake), Ben Kampschroer (Cooper). **Credits:** *Producer-Writer-Director:* John Yehling. **Comment:** The above story line is based on the pilot episode. Being it was the only episode thus far produced the plot could change (as often happens from pilots to actual series). It is often difficult to judge a program's merits based on just a pilot because it was a first attempt. The acting is good but it is rather talkative and not much happens.

Episodes: *1.* A Fool's Parade Pilot

339 *For the Love of My Sistas.* youtube.com. 2012.

Vanessa, Halle, Tori, Brandy, Nicole and Paul are siblings who must learn to work together and keep their house in order after their mother falls ill. Halle, the second oldest sister, becomes like her mother and takes charge of the situation; Vanessa, the oldest, has moved out of the house and in with her boyfriend; Tori, the third oldest sister, is somewhat irresponsible and considered the life of any party; Brandy is a college student who places herself in stressful situations trying to succeed; Nicole, the youngest sister is literally a bitch with an attitude and, being the only sibling with a different father, looking for acceptance; and Paul, the only male, is simply "a lazy good-for-nothing" who just won't get his life together. While the program's description reads like a drama it is actually a comedy with the siblings clashing with one another while trying to come together for the sake of each other.

Cast: Karla Waymman, Rashon Murph, Shawna

Sykes, Wanda-Marie Carey, Chloe Brooks, Steven Davis, Shomari Bullard, Latisha Hardee, Jean Bevins. **Credits:** *Producer-Writer-Director:* Jean Lu Bevins, Joyce Eli Bevins. **Comment:** An African-American production that needs a bit of an attitude adjustment as the characters are not only difficult to understand at times but not very appealing (more of a turn-off than an attention getter). The idea is there but the presentation lacks good acting and production values. It would have also been nice if the performers were matched with the characters they play.

Episodes: *1,2.* Pilot. *3,4.* Ways Around It. *5,6.* All Together Now.

340 For Your Entertainment. webseries channel.com. 2012.

Jackson, Shep and Tyler are uncouth actors who work for an acting company called For Your Entertainment. Here, people with little or no talent who think they can act, dress as cartoon characters and entertain at various functions (like children's birthday parties). But Jackson, Shep and Tyler not only hate their jobs, but their lives and the dorky costumes they must wear. To take the edge off they use drugs and the program follows what happens when they begrudgingly perform for whatever functions they are hired to do by their boss, Janis. **Cast:** Aaron Markham (Shep), A.J. Chiodini (Jackson), John Ashley Owens (Tyler), Hannah Lundy (Janis), Brian Kreitner (Karl), Ian Thomas Hardin (Randolph). **Credits:** *Producer:* Aaron Markham, Kevin Harmon. *Director:* Brian Kreitner. *Writer:* Brian Kreitner, Aaron Markham. **Comment:** Why Janis, their boss doesn't fire the friends is a mystery as she knows they are on drugs and like to party all the time. A parental warning accompanies each episode for the vulgar language and adult situations that are a part of the program. The production is just passable and the acting not always convincing as it looks amateurish at times.

Episodes: *1.* Life of the Party. *2.* Children and Weapons and Pant-zings, Oh My! *3.* Better Holmes and Gardeners.

341 The 40s Guys. webserieschannel.com. 2011.

It is the year 2011 but for three men, it is the 1940s. They see the world through the black and white motion pictures of that era and not only encompass the dress style men wore at the time, but their speech also reflects a by-gone era. With a production presented in black and white and scenes reminiscent of film noir movies, the program is simply the men, consuming alcohol and smoking cigars discussing current world events. **Cast:** Toby Johnston (Guy #1), Mike Coulter (Guy #2), Will Shivers (Guy #3). **Credits:** *Producer:*

Blue Spark Studios. *Writer-Director:* David Brzozowski. **Comment:** The program does capture the feeling of a 1940s movie and flows smoothly although it is just basically the three leads talking. A nice touch is the use of film scratches to represent flaws that some older films possess.

Episodes: *1.* Osama's Porn Stash! *2.* Something About Buddha! *3.* I Don't Often Drink Beer.

342 40 and Leroy. 40andleroy.com. 2012–2013.

Reginald, called "40 oz" and Leroy are cousins living in New York City. Leroy is a dreamer and always looking to make money without really working for it. 40, on the other hand, is not as bright as Leroy and more of a screw-up, always following Leroy's lead and not really thinking for himself. Their attempts to not only navigate life in an urban jungle, but find the right scheme that will lead them to the road to easy street are profiled. **Cast:** Lorenzo Eduardo (40), Horace Glasper (Leroy), Ma Barker (Cee Cee). **Credits:** *Producer:* Neema Barnette. *Director:* Reed R. McCants. **Comment:** Billed as "in the tradition of the great New York comedic duos like Abbott and Costello and Seinfeld and Costanza" the program is more like the team of Bud Abbott and Lou Costello with Leroy the straight man and 40 the fall guy (here though, African-American). The idea, acting and production are very good and the program not only humorous but enjoyable.

Season 1 Episodes: *1–4.* Hudson Water. *5.* Leroy's Harlem Stories.

Season 2 Episodes: *1.* Occupy Leroy. *2.* Halloween Godfather. *3–5.* Cable Apocalypse. *6.* Just Listen to the Case. *7.* Hot Ass Summer. *8–10.* The Case of the Stained Towel. *11.* Bro Love. *12.* Out-Take Week. *13.* Crime Pays Less. *14.* Smoke On. *15.* Mini Doc (Documentary). *16,17.* Out-Worked Workout.

Season 3 Episodes: *1.* In Search of Leroy. *2.* Found But Still Lost. *3.* Who Are These Guys? *4.* What's So Funny About the Name Leroy? *5.* The Fro Must Go. *6.* The Illuminatrix. *7.* Run 40 Run. *8.* Fit in or Fall Out. *9.* Slow Down Baby. *10.* 40 Meet Seven. *11.* Operation Save Leroy. *12.* Leroy is the Key. *13.* Cee Cee to the Rescue.

343 Four Minute Ordeals. webserieschannel.com. 2014.

Jimmy and Rich are young men stuck in a rut. They never do anything exciting and just accept life as it is. One day, after both apply for a job and are rejected, they decide it is time to make a change by doing things they have never done before. The program follows their bucket list of things to accomplish—from drinking coffee for the first time, shooting guns and, most importantly to them, impressing "and sleeping with hot black women; or in Rich's case, any woman at all." The title refers to episode lengths, which are just seconds above four minutes each.

Cast: Montana Bertoletti (Jimmy), Eric Rivera (Rich), Kimberly Vaughn (Stacey, "The Hot Black Girl"), Stephanie Leigh Rose (Shilf), Ben Ross (Officer Buckley). **Credits:** *Producer:* Montana Bertoletti, Eric Rivera. *Director:* Montana Bertoletti. *Writer:* Eric Rivera. **Comment:** The program starts a bit slow but progresses into a well acted and produced comedy.

Episodes: *1.* Done Being Losers. *2.* Coffee Shop. *3.* Hard Time. *4.* Pump Time. *5.* The iGlass. *6.* Gameboy. *7.* I'll Take You to the Gun Shop. *8.* The Purge. *9.* Sure Thing. *10.* The Shilf!

344 *The 4 to 9ers: The Day Crew.* hulu. com. 2014.

Jeremy and Samantha, a young couple sustaining themselves by working at Subway, find rent is becoming a problem until Jeremy hits on an idea to split the rent three ways by inviting his life-long friend, Charlie to move in with them. The problem: Samantha once dated Charlie. Samantha, although against the idea (as Samantha considers Charlie Jeremy's roommate) reluctantly agrees and the program follows what happens as three unlikely roommates try living together.

Cast: Devin Crittenden (Charlie), Nick Jandl (Jeremy), Stephanie Koenig (Samantha), Asif Ali (Joe), David H. Lawrence (Sgt. Doyle), Tara Holt (Brianna), Doris Roberts (Mrs. Doyle), Amy Yasbeck (Sylvia), Ted McGinley (Ray). **Credits:** *Producer:* Peter Isacksen, Stuart McLean, Tim O'Donnell, James Widdoes. *Director:* James Widdoes. *Writer:* Michael Langworthy, Tim O'Donnell. **Comment:** A "Three's Company"-"Odd Couple" situation with a good story line, acting and production values.

Season 1 Episodes: 5 untitled episodes, labeled "Episode 1" through "Episode 5."

Season 2 Episodes: *1.* The Art of the Deal. *2.* Mama Mia! *3.* Dancing with the Subs. *4.* Nobody Likes a Lark. *5.* Seth We Hardly Knew Ye.

345 *4 Villains.* webserieschannel.com. 2012.

It is a time when heroes are adored and villains have become the outcasts of society. Shadowsnake, Psynapse, Evil Hidden and Dr. Don't are villains who want to change all that and get some respect. To accomplish their goal, they establish 4 Villains, a guild where the downtrodden, unworthy and unwanted villains of the world can become as one and create their own presence in the world's villainous community. The program follows "our heroes" as they establish their organization and seek to make names for themselves. Although the setting is Vik-

tem City, common citizens know it as Victoria City; heroes maintain that it is called Victory City; villains know it as Viktem [Victim] City. While heroes and villains continue to argue over a proper name, the common citizens see them both as more of a danger to their safety than the vigilantes who are also commonplace. There is no government regulation and because of that both factions are accepted.

Cast: Jeff Saamanen (Shadowsnake), Laura Lapadat (Psynapse), Devin Douglas (Dr. Don't), Justin Guthrie (Evil Hidden). **Credits:** *Producer-Writer:* Lucas Erskine. *Director:* Jeff Saamanen. **Comment:** While only a pilot has been released, it is an intriguing, comical twist on organizations that hold only superheroes in esteem (like The Justice League of America). The production values and acting are good and there is potential for some intriguing stories if the villains are allowed to perhaps, once achieve some villainy and recognition as opposed to always remaining downtrodden.

Episodes: *1.* Pilot: Crucifired.

346 *Freckle and Bean.* blip.tv. 2010.

Emma and James, two pretty young women called Freckle and Bean, live in Los Angeles and each hold down two jobs as personal assistants and waitresses. They are also hopeful actresses and each is seeking a steady romantic relationship with a man who can respect their dreams. Billed as "A younger *Sex and the City* meets a modern-day *Friends*," the program relates all the heartaches Freckle and Bean encounter as they navigate the often difficult road to travel to stardom. Joie is their best friend; Chase is their roommate.

Cast: Elena Crevello (James), Heather McCallum (Emma), Bailey Conway (Joie), Bobby Gold (Chase), Betsy Cox (Skye), Paul Preiss (Gavin), Brad Rowe (Devin), Meghan Strange (Andrea). **Credits:** *Producer:* Elena Crevello, Heather McCallum. **Comment:** With the exception of some foul language, the program is well acted and produced.

Episodes: Of the 13 episodes that were produced, only the following remain on line: *9.* The Runaway Holloway. *10.* Lizard Eyes. *11.* Misrepresented. *12.* Finding the Courage. *13.* Lucky Break.

347 *Fred.* youtube.com. 2006–2011.

Fred Figglehorn is a six-year-old boy (portrayed by an adult) with a high-pitched voice (digitally altered audio). Fred's life is anything but normal. He has been a victim of child abuse, lives with his alcoholic mother and his grandmother (Fred's father is mentioned as being in prison and on Death Row. Mr. Figglehorn deserted the family when his wife was pregnant with Fred and thus Fred has never seen him). Fred is always six years old and the first three seasons have Fred relating what happens in his life with references to other characters (who remain off stage). Season four changes the production a bit as other characters are seen as Fred continues to experience life. It is summertime when the first season begins and Fred's activities during that time are explored. When Fred's mother goes into rehab, the second season focuses on Fred falling in love for the first time with a girl in his class named Judy and running against the school bully, Kevin, for class president. Season three continues to depict Fred's activities in school while Season Four relates Fred's adventures as he tackles various occupations.

Cast: Lucas Cruikshank (Fred). **Credits:** *Writer-Director:* Lucas Cruikshank, Michael Tidde. **Comment:** How did such a program garner millions of YouTube hits will not be the only thing that astounds you. Just attempting to watch a grown man playing a child with a sped-up Chipmunk-like voice is not only ridiculous but after a few minutes the concept becomes totally annoying with the repeated lunacy and nauseating facial close-ups becoming just too much to fathom. It is literally an adult making a total fool of himself (for more detailed descriptions of just how bad *Fred* is, check the "Viewer Reviews" section in "Explore More" on IMDB.com). For some unknown reason, a feature film was also made called *Fred the Movie* and it can be considered one of the worst movies ever made.

Season 1 Episodes: *1.* Fred on Halloween. *2.* Fred on St. Patrick's Day. *3.* Fred Goes to the Park. *4.* Fred on the 4th of July. *5.* Fred Gets Babysat. *6.* Fred on Christmas. *7.* Fred on Valentine's Day.

Season 2 Episodes: *1.* Fred on May Day. *2.* Fred Loses His Meds. *3.* Fred Gets Bullied. *4.* Fred Goes to the Dentist. *5.* Fred Stalks Judy. *6.* Fred on Father's Day. *7.* Fred Goes Swimming. *8.* Fred Meets Bertha. *9.* Fred's Mom Is Missing.

Season 3 Episodes: *1.* Fred's Grandma Has a Secret. *2.* Fred Goes Camping. *3.* Fred Auditions for a Play. *4.* Fred's Mom Returns. *5.* Fred: A Star in His Own Mind. *6.* Fred Sneaks Into Judy's Party. *7.* Fred Tries to Ride a Bike. *8.* Fred Runs for President. *9.* Fred Faces a Dirty Campaign. *10.* Fred on Election Day. *11.* Fred on Thanksgiving. *12.* Fred Wants to Be a Star.

Season 4 Episodes: *1.* Fred on *iCarly* (the Nickelodeon TV series). *2.* Fred Rescues the Neighborhood Squirrels. *3.* Fred Cooks for Judy. *4.* Fred on April Fool's Day. *5.* Fred Goes to the Doctor. *6.* Fred Throws a Party. *7.* Fred Gets Dissed at Bible School. *8.* Fred Works Out. *9.* Fred Tries Dancing. *10.* Fred Sees a Therapist. *11.* Fred Goes on a Date with Judy. *12.* Fred Has a Vocal Lesson. *13.* Fred Goes Fundraising. *14.* Fred Gives Advice. *15.* Fred Finds a Creepy Doll. *16.* Fred Has a Snow Day. *17.* Fed Goes to the School Dance. *18.* Fred Gets a Letter from His Father. *19.* Fred's Top Secret New Project.

348 Fresh Off the Plane. youtube.com. 2012.

Brianna (Canadian), Jake (American), Caleb (Australian), Nikolai (Russian) and Lillian (British) all have one thing in common—they share an apartment in Los Angeles and have a neighbor in common, a young man named Larry. Each episode is a look at the incidents that befall the friends as they not only try to adjust to a new environment, but each other (the episode titles relate the person to whom the mishaps befall).

Cast: Alexandra Harris (Brianna Evans), Brandon Morales (Jake Jacobson), Adz Hunter (Caleb Mackey), Heather Wilds (Lillian Sugars), Sasha Francis (Nikolai Pushkin), Sasha Feldman (Larry Bird). **Credits:** *Producer:* Alexandra Harris, Ryan Turner. *Director:* Ryan Turner. *Writer:* Adz Hunter. **Comment:** Billed as "Think *Friends* meets *The Office* but swap in immigrants from all over the world." Unfortunately all the episodes (with the exception of a very short teaser) have been taken off line. It is not really possible to judge the program (other than the cast is attractive) based on so little video information.

Episodes: *1.* Canada. *2.* Australia. *3.* Next Door. *4.* Russia. *5.* United Kingdom.

349 Friends Helping Friends. webseries channel.com. 2012.

There are friends who are friends and there for each other and there are friends who are friends for reasons known only to them. Mark and Brand are long time friends who are a combination of both of the above statements. They tolerate each other but are, in a way, terrible to each other. The program sort of deviates from the terrible aspect to focus on the buddy-buddy aspect as Mark, the more outrageous, not clearly thinking friend finds help in dealing with all the complex situations he becomes involved with through Brand's intervention.

Cast: Brand Rackley (Brand), Mark Potts (Mark). **Credits:** *Producer-Writer:* Mark Potts, Brand Rackley. *Director:* Mark Potts. **Comment:** Typical comedy with Mark being the most annoying of the two. Each episode presents a situation with Brand and Mark taking turns helping the other out of a jam. Like many such comedies, the acting ranges from good to bad depending on how you personally accept the characters.

Episodes: *1.* Brand Helps Mark Back His Car Out of the Garage. *2.* Mark Helps Brand Break Up with His Girlfriend. *3.* Brand Helps Mark Feel Better. *4.* Mark Helps Brand Balance His Checkbook. *5.* Brand Helps Mark Prepare for a Date. *6.* Brand Helps Mark Get Hard Drugs.

350 Friendship Is the Best Ship. webseries channel.com. 2014.

There is an old song called "Friendship" ("Friendship, friendship, just the perfect blendship, when other friendships have been forgot, theirs will still be hot") that fits perfectly here (it was also used as the theme to the 1950s TV series *My Friend Irma*). Willa and Laura are those best friends, young women navigating the world wherein most of their time is spent looking for work and seeking ways to make ends meet.

Cast: Willa Song (Willa), Laura Reich (Laura). **Credits:** *Producer-Writer:* Willa Song, Laura Reich. **Comment:** An embarrassingly silly program that may come off to some as just plain stupid (especially the first episode wherein the leads are truly ridiculous and with eating scenes and close-ups of their mouths that is anything but funny or pleasing to look at). The remaining two episodes are just as ludicrous with truly unflattering images of two supposedly grown women. The idea was there, but something happened from paper to film.

Episodes: *1.* Friendship Is Orgasmic. *2.* Friendship Is an Identity Crisis. *3.* Friendship Is an Adventure.

351 *Full Nelson*. blip.tv. 2011.

The Nelson Alliance of Wrestling is a small, struggling Fresno, California, wrestling promotional company owned by Jake Nelson, a single father (of Alexis) who hopes for bigger and brighter things. Jake inherited the company from his late father, "King Cole" and is trying to hold onto the tradition he established: "Every family needs a home and Nelson Alliance will always be a home for the wrestling family." The times have been hard with little money and little attendance until Jake discovers Dylan Cole, a teenager with the potential to become a huge wrestling star. Dylan, however, is skinny and shy and the program relates what transpires as Jake struggles to make Dylan see his potential and realize his own dreams of becoming a top notch promotion company.

Cast: Adam Paul (Jake Nelson), Danielle Soibelman (Alexis Nelson), Mike Mauloff (Mike Millstein), Eric Allan Kramer (Erik the Viking), Lisa Donovan (Shelley Woslyencki), Derek Carter (Dylan Cole), Ric "The Equalizer" Drasin (Ric Pearl), Carlos Bernard (Chachin). **Credits:** *Producer:* Keith Richmond. *Writer-Director:* Andy Bobrow, Adam Paul. **Comment:** Strictly geared to wrestling fans although the concept is quite good. The syndicated 1980s wrestling-themed TV series *Learning the Ropes* had a problem similar to this one and that was its inability to appeal to a wider audience. Not everyone is a fan of this or that sport and producers should take that into account when they produce a series with a sports theme.

Episodes: *1.* The Sport of Kings. *2.* Blood Is Thicker. *3.* The Son Also Rises. *4.* The Warm Embrace of a Headlock. *5.* The Man with a Missing Pinky. *6.* Matches Made in Heaven. *7.* A Home for the Wrestling Family.

352 *Funemployed*. youtube.com. 2009–2014.

Chicago provides the setting for a look at a recent group of college students as they navigate life and seek employment, but finding only less-than-desired sporadic jobs and their associated mishaps. Later episodes focus in particular on Ted and Amy, hopeful actors, as they seek a role in *Forrest Gump: The Musical*.

Cast: Ted Evans (Ted), Kate Carson-Groner (Amy), Michael Lippert (Jay), Dan Hale (Bill), Alex F. Harris (Lockwood), Alix Klingenberg (Beth), Keith Habersberger (Dex), Stevi Baston (Callie), Jackelyn Normand (Jackelyn), Katherine Schwartz (Katherine), Ashley Bates, Sarah Hildreth, Ellen Girvin (Actress), Lindsay Bartlett (Erica). **Credits:** *Producer:* Ted Evans, Michael Lippert, Emily Cooper, Adina Kwasigroch, Lindsay Bartlett, Chris T.K. Coyne, Dan Hale, Alex F. Harris, Tim McGuide, Katey Selix. *Director:* Michael Lippert, Brigg Bloomquist, Brett Sechrist, David Schmudde, Ted Evans, Chris T.K. Coyne. *Writer:* Kate Carson-Groner, Ted Evans, Dan Hale, Alex F. Harris, Michael Lippert. **Comment:** The program progresses from college life to post graduate life for the students in a well produced and acted series (even the thought of turning the film *Forrest Gump* into a musical is well done).

Season 1 Episodes: *1,2.* The End of the World As We Know It. *3,4.* Oui Need Jobs. *5.* There Will Be Beards. *6.* Lockin' It Down. *7.* Doomsdate. *8.* The Rise of Dark Ted. *9.* True Colors.

Season 2 Episodes: *1.* Lord of the Flies. *2.* Ball Traps. *3.* The Return of Bill. *4.* Mashed Potatoes. *5.* Dopplegangs. *6.* Nuts to the Guts.

Season 3 Episodes: *1.* Prologue/Mama Always Told Me. *2.* True Theater. *3.* Just a Taste. *4.* Role Play. *5.* The French Tickler. *6.* Look Out, Ladies. *7,8.* The Big Problem with Bill. *9.* Fat, Naked Chicken. *10.* Breaking Up Is Hard to Do. *11.* The Margaritas of Misery. *12.* All for Love. *13.* Man Up. *14.* Facing the Truth. *15.* Showtime. *16.* The Feel Good Episode. *17.* Series Finale: Getting Into Character.

353 *The Further Adventures of Cupid and Eros*. cupidanderos.com. 2010–2011.

Most people believe that only Cupid is the ancient Greek God of Love and are unaware that he is assisted by Eros (a woman), both of whom reside on Mt. Olympus. Cupid, considered "the original nice guy," is sweet, charming and "a mortal's best friend." Eros is just the opposite, a sex-crazed goddess who believes she is irresistible to any god, mortal or anything in between. Cupid is thus the ultimate romantic while Eros is thus the ultimate personification of sexuality. Cupid and Eros have only one goal: to make matches and stem the tide of divorce and infidelity. There are times, however, when they become confused by what they create. The program follows their efforts to really understand what they do and what happens when their matches are not always "made in heaven."

Cast: Jo Bozarth (Eros), Josh Heine (Cupid), Aliza Pearl (Isis), Kiera Anderson (Jo), Bradford Anderson (Achilles), Sheila Thiele (Lacey), Jeffrey Cannata (Apollo), Kaathleen Curran (Psyche), Dexx Hillman-Sneed (Thoth), Taryn O'Neill (Athena). **Credits:** *Producer:* Avi Glijansky, Andy Wells. *Writer-Director:* Avi Glijansky. **Comment:** Amusing series with good acting and production values that attempts to show that gods are people too—and have the same problems.

Episodes: *1.* I'm Fine. *2.* Two Gods Walk Into a Bar... *3.* Hopeless Romantics. *4.* Good Idea/Bad Idea. *5.* Hello, My Pantheon Is. *6.* Dueling and Diapers. *7.* Will You Be My...

354 *The Future Machine.* youtube.com. 2012.

After a night of drinking, roommates Matt and Tom begin arguing over who owns a bear costume that hangs in their apartment. Without a normal way to settle their differences, they decide to transform a German-built microwave oven into a time machine and travel into the past to discover who bought the bear suit and thus determine its rightful owner. The program charts their harebrained attempts to build a time machine—and what happens when they actually succeed in doing so.

Cast: Matthew Okine (Matt), Andrew Ryan (Tom), Cariba Heine (Katie Hill). **Credits:** *Producer-Writer:* David Barker, Matthew Okine, Tom Sheldrick. *Director:* David Barker. **Comment:** While comedy overpowers the science fiction aspects of the program, it does attempt to explore what could happen if time traveling were developed, although the approach here is a bit far-fetched.

Episodes: *1.* That's My Bear Suit. *2.* The Rules of Time Travel. *3.* How to Get Rid of a Body. *4.* Phantom Limb. *5.* Building a Time Machine. *6.* Boys Become Men. *7.* Return Trip. *8.* Our Friends Are Animals.

355 *The Gaga Experiment.* webserieschannel.com. 2012.

Does entertainer Lady Gaga hold the secret to unlocking the mysteries of what scientists call String Theory (a mathematical theory that attempts to explain certain phenomena that are not able to be explained by what currently exists). Theater director Cal Vin honestly believes that Lady Gaga's repertoire holds the key to proving the theory. He begins by assembling a group of less-than-accomplished actors (who possess an "Inner Gaga"), devising a musical that encompasses the true essence of Lady Gaga's

mystique and once and for all prove that what he believes is correct. The program charts what happens as a disillusioned man attempts to prove something that has stumped the greatest minds in science.

Cast: Vanessa Cole, Edmund Finegan, Tamara Gourley, Erica Gribova, Rod Lara, Paolo Lolicata, Stephanie Lillis, Aili Storen, Christopher Talbot, Luke Western. **Comment:** Although amusing at times, it also tends to drag at times. The acting and production is acceptable but portions are a bit hard to understand due to acoustics at filming sites.

Episodes: 7 untitled episodes, labeled, "Episode 1" through "Episode 7."

356 *Game of Bros.* webserieschannel.com. 2013.

Each year four friends (Tell, Touchberry, Wilbanks and Burdick) reunite to play a board game to determine where they will spend their summer (as decided by the game's champion). The summer is approaching and the friends choose the game of Monopoly as the determining factor for their vacation. The program follows the game the friends play with each seeking to become the winner by achieving the right to sit atop The Foam Throne and the power it affords—to determine their summer activity.

Cast: Eli Tell (Tell), Jackson Touchberry (Touchberry), Aaron Wilbanks (Wilbanks), Alex Burdick (Burdick), Austin Goven (Tell's advisor), Kim Robinnson (Touchberry's advisor), Devin Heiss (Wilbanks' advisor), Sean Timbs (Burdick's advisor). **Credits:** *Writer-Producer:* Eli Tell, Jackson Touchberry, Aaron Wilbanks, Alex Burdick. *Director:* Alex Burdick. **Comment:** After watching the first episode you come off feeling that it is just a bunch of guys having fun playing a game. They do go to extremes with the game but the acting and production are just acceptable and nothing else.

Episodes: *1.* Monopoly. *2.* Strategy. *3.* Antebellum. *4.* The Battle of House Touchberry. *5.* The Package. *6.* The Battle of Five Kings.

357 *Gary Saves the Graveyard.* webserieschannel.com. 2014.

Gary is the newly hired groundskeeper for a local graveyard. On his first night on the job Gary is shocked to see the ghost of Andy, his friend from high school who passed away 20 years ago. But that is not Gary's only problem: 235 living corpses have risen and have left the cemetery seeking to complete an unfulfilled desire. One additional ghost, Abe, a Civil War soldier, has, like Andy, remained by Gary's side to help him complete a seemingly impossible mission: return the ghosts to the cemetery within five hours by helping each of them fulfill that non-completed desire.

Cast: Jim Santangeli (Gary), Tallie Medel (Andy), Nicole Byer, Michael Delaney, Nate Dern, Shannon

O'Neill. Credits: *Director:* Todd Bieber. *Writer:* Todd Bieber, Kristy Lopez-Bernal, Laura Grey, Zack Phillips, Avery Monsen. **Comment:** A little strange at first but the program holds its own as it progresses and you accept the fact that these ghosts are solid (not transparent) and act and look like ordinary people (with the exception of their eyes, which give them a somewhat eerie look). The acting, story line and production are very good.

Episodes: *1.* Pilot. *2.* The Living Dead.

358 *Gay Nerds.* gaynerds.tv. 2014.

There are people, whether straight, gay or bi-sexual who have learned to accept who they are. Lana, Ralphie and Sam are gay friends who do not fit the typical definition of what their sexuality means. They are literally unable to accept the world in which they live and use pop culture to make sense of everything that surrounds them. The program relates what happens as the world of pop culture becomes all too real to them and they find themselves unable to distinguish fantasy from reality.

Cast: Robert Keller (Ralphie), Alexandra Wylie (Lana), Ryan Kerr (Sam). **Credits:** *Producer-Writer-Director:* J.P. Larocque. **Comment:** Well acted and produced parody of not only gay and lesbian characters, but TV shows and movies as well. Although the characters may appear a bit off center, it has to be remembered when watching that their lives have been influenced by pop culture and the only way they can handle reality is to associate it with a movie or TV show that parallels what they are experiencing.

Episodes: *1.* Tyrannosaurus Ex. *2.* The Bat, the Cat and the iPhone. *3.* Gayliens. *4.* The Fellowship of Sarah Michelle Gellar. *5.* Canada's Next Top Bottom. *6.* Rise and Shining.

359 *Gay Town.* tv.com. 2008.

Owen is a young man caught in a most unusual situation. He is straight but lives in Gaytown, which is populated by gays and lesbians. There are other straights (but still in the closet) and Owen must keep his sexuality a secret and pretend to be gay. From as early as he can remember, Owen felt there was something wrong with him ("I never fit in with the other guys"). While boys his age went out for ballet and figure skating, he yearned to play basketball with the girls—and took a beating from other boys for being a non-conformist. As time passed, Owen figured that to live in Gay Town he must pretend to be gay and has a pretend boyfriend named Pierce (who actually loves Owen while Owen's attentions are drawn to Lina, a lesbian who is only his friend because she believes he is gay). As Owen says, "I've always tried to fit in, but you can't hide who you are. I'm an outsider. I'm a straight man living in Gay Town" and stories follow Owen as he tries to

do just that—be himself while circumstances just won't permit him to do so.

Cast: Owen Benjamin (Owen), Payman Benz (Pierce), Brooke Lenzi (Jen), Jordy Fox (Herbert), Lina Miller (Lina), Brody Stevens (Mayor Stevens), Andrea Kelley (Annie). **Credits:** *Producer:* Owen Benjamin, Jesse Shapiro. *Director:* Jesse Shapiro, Todd Strauss-Schulson, Owen Benjamin, Payman Benz, Sam Becker, Greg Benson. *Writer:* Owen Benjamin. **Comment:** Well acted and produced role reversal with a straight person being "the outcast." The program can be watched by anyone although there is some sexual tension between the characters but nothing objectionable.

Episodes: *1.* Welcome to Gay Town. *2.* Assume the Position. *3.* The Rain-bros. *4.* Born Sinners. *5* I'm Different. *6.* Straight Pride Parade. *7.* Season Recap. *8.* What Happened. *9.* Gay Town on Fire. *10.* The Man. *11.* Community Service. *12.* Small and Bald. *13.* Zip Me Up. *14.* Back on Track. *15.* A New Start. *16.* Finale.

360 *The Gaye Family.* youtube.com. 2010.

Parents Pervis and Tina and their children Laura and Billy have the last name of Gaye but insist they are not gay "but as straight as they come." Pervis is a fashion stylist and sounds gay; Tina holds a job with a demolition company; Laura loves sports and dresses like a butch lesbian; and Billy acts like a feminine gay male but is a diva (a ladies' man). The program relates the events that befall the family, situations made a bit more complex to resolve as the images they present to the public has them perceived as something they are not.

Cast: Anthony Boyd (Pervis Gaye), Brun Alexandra Drescher (Tina Gaye), Cole (Laura Gaye), Marc J. (Billy Gaye), La Tee (Grandma). **Credits:** *Producer:* Brian Anthony Butler, Norris Young. *Writer-Director:* Norris Young. **Comment:** A surprisingly well acted and produced program that compares to such current syndicated African-American TV series like *Are We There Yet* and *Tyler Perry's House of Payne.* It is a non-offensive and well thought out program that should be expanded upon and pitched as a syndicated TV series.

Episodes: *1.* Introducing the Gaye Family. *2.* Episode 2. *3.* Grandma's Arrival. *4.* Pervis vs. Grandma. *5.* Laura Goes to the Dentist. *6.* Billy Comes Home. *7.* A Very Gaye Vacation. *8.* The Gaye Family Bloopers.

361 *Gay's Anatomy.* youtube.com. 2009.

Three young urologists are profiled in a spoof of the ABC-TV series *Gray's Anatomy.* Mark is a lovesick gay who seems unable to find the perfect man; Jim is a nervous, stressed-out doctor who relieves tension by "giving colonoscopies to the homeless" and Marc finds that dealing with the situations that surround him can only be accomplished by "using cocaine responsibly."

Marc (with a "c") is a graduate of Harvard Medical School and yearns to do his internship in a large New York City hospital. He met Mark (with a "k") during the hospital's interview process and is looking to bond with him.

Jim, a graduate of UC Berkeley, is an eager doctor who dresses in frilly outfits but is eager to "get his hands dirty in the exam room."

Casey is Marc's roommate, a butch lesbian who is on the prowl for a lady lover.

Amy is a neurotic hospital radiologist who seeks to become the best doctor there is. She believes that "her love of cripples" is her proof of leadership qualities.

Eddie is the shy and overly observant doctor's colleague who looks for male and female eye candy.

Robin is the mysterious, cocaine-addicted girl who feels like Mark that drugs and good times go together.

Cast: Wil Petre (Mark Weston), Max Jenkins (Jim Gable), Bobby Hodgson (Marc Merriman), Beth Hoyt (Robin Starr), Becca Blackwell (Casey Blunt), Amy Kersten (Amy Campbell), Jim deProphetis (Eddie DeGrazio), Joe Currnutte (Brad Johnson), Meghan Hemingway (Esme Cunkle), Jess Barbagallo (Dyque Vander Goose), Drae Campbell (Shelley Lopez). **Credits:** *Director-Writer:* Karina Mangu-Ward, B. Hodgson. **Comment:** Although the annoyingly unsteady (shaky) camera is used, the program is well done and acted and once viewing it, you will never see medical dramas produced on network TV in the same light.

Episodes: *1.* New Positions. *2.* Come Out Tonight. *3.* Taking It All In. *4.* Unexpected Foursome. *5.* Please Be Gentle. *6.* Bottoms Up. *7.* A Lot to Swallow. *8.* Deep Deep Inside. *9.* Who's Coming Now? *10.* Urine-vited. *11.* Gynosaurus Rex. *12.* Partner Up.

362 Geeks vs... youtube.com. 2013.

MacReady, Loomis, William and Blair are friends hooked on horror movies. They know the legends of zombies, werewolves and vampires and everything else Hollywood filmmakers have created. Not thinking much of it at first, the friends soon realize that what they have seen on the screen is not fiction, but based on fact as those movie monsters really exist. The program follows what happens when the friends suddenly begin to encounter the unnatural and how they use their knowledge of horror films to dispense of it (or at least deal with it). **Cast:** Josh Evans (Loomis), Thor Reese (William), James Kopp (MacReady), David Rock (Blair). **Credits:** *Producer:* James Kopp, Andrew Price, Robert DelTour, Aaron Mauldin, Matt Kieley. *Director:* James Kopp. *Writer:* James Kopp, David Rock. **Comment:** While the idea has been done before, it is always interesting to see what movie mon-

sters will come out of the screen and who will tackle them. The monsters are typical and the guys a bit nerdy but the acting and overall production is good.

Episodes: *1,2.* Zombie. *3.* Vampire.

363 Geez Louise. geezlouiseshow.com. 2012–2014.

COBB is an all-girl gym owned by a voluptuous, sexy and alluring lesbian named Victoria. She lives with Cairn, her sister, and their friend Louise, both of whom are lesbians but less attractive. Cairn is a bit scatterbrained while Louise is often mistaken for a man. The animated program relates the problems life throws at them and how, mostly through Victoria, they resolve them.

Voice Cast: Angela Adams (Cairn/Victoria/Santa/Shmadam), J. Adams (Louise/Maureen/CB/Lady Cabindish/Louise's mother/Irlene/Victoria's mother). **Credits:** Producer: J. Adams, Angela Adams. *Writer-Director:* Angela Adams. **Comment:** Delightful, non-offensive lesbian-themed program that has no sex, no vulgar language and no intimate scenes. It does have well developed stories, intriguing characters and an animation style that becomes increasingly appealing as the episodes play. The stiff-like animation does take getting use to, but that is part of the series charm, especially in the rendition of Victoria (and Maureen, Victoria's equally gorgeous rival) who are the ultimate lesbians while Cairn and Louise are more boy-like (in figure) and even more child-like (especially the mischievous Louise).

Episodes: *1.* Bird in the Hand. *2,3.* Cairn on the COBB. *4,5.* Car Tunes & Annie Mae. *6,7.* SpaNtaneous. *8,9.* Bowled Over 'n' Out. *10.* In Front of Everybody? *11.* Swimmin' with Wimmin. *12.* It's Somebody's Birthd Eh? *13.* Get Yaaargh Sweat On! *14.* I Can Fix That. *15.* The Winery. *16.* A Liege of Their Own. *17.* Battle of the FemmeBots. *18.* Sittin' with Louise. *19.* Chip's Ship. *20.* Victoria's Secret. *21.* LGBT BBQ. *22.* Halloween Special. *23.* LeadFoot Louise. *24.* It's the Thought That Counts. *25.* The 7th Map. *26.* Desire's Unfurling Patience. *27.* Maybe It's French Toast.

364 GenEd. webserieschannel.com. 2011.

Sara, Hillary, Hunter and Grey, friends since high school, are beginning their sophomore year at college. It appears, at first, they have adjusted to college life (especially with Grey checking out all the freshman babes) but seeing through Sara that each semester is different and each semester should hold a special place in their lives. The mishaps that befall each of the friends as they experience the trials and tribulations of college life are explored. **Cast:** Ty Fanning (Grey Fletcher), Callie Nichols (Sara Bayer), Emily Feldman (Hillary Townely), Benjamin Richardson (Hunter Bayer), Ayssette

Munoz (Macy). **Credits:** *Writer-Producer:* Brian Lawes, Candace Robinson. *Director:* Brian Lawes. **Comment:** Overall a very good depiction of college life with a genuinely honest look at what some students may experience. The acting is very good and the production is also well executed.

Episodes: *1.* The Election. *2.* The Swedish Fish. *3.* The Jeggings.

365 Generation Black. youtube.com. 2013.

A look at a select group of African-Americans as they navigate through life by attempting to embrace what they have rather than suppress it to fit into their individual environments.

Cast: Tarra Denise Jackson (Lalah), Michael Vazquez (Cory), Michael Bruins (Kellen), Crystal West (Dana), Louis Davis (Mandela), Tonja Robinson (Grace), Whitney Shepard (Patience). **Credits:** *Producer:* Tena Veney. *Writer-Director:* Michael Bruins. **Comment:** A good idea but with episodes running over 35 minutes each they are much too long for a web series. It is very difficult to sustain attention when web episodes run past ten minutes (unless exceptionally well done) not alone more than a half-hour. Although the program's description reads like a drama, it is a comedy with all the mishaps that can happen do, but the mood is somewhat spoiled by the use of an obviously fake laugh track.

Episodes: *1.* Birthday Woes. *2.* Divide and Conquer.

366 Generic Girl. genericgirl.com. 2012.

Gillian and Pete are friends who idolize comic books (more so with Pete as he envisions himself as the super hero Captain Freelance). Their lives change when a package, meant for the evil and diabolical Dr. Mascalzone, is delivered to Gillian by mistake. As Gillian opens the package she discovers it to contain a rather beat-up looking box that is able to speak and proclaims itself to be god. Meanwhile, when the doctor learns what has happened to his package, he instructs his gorgeous, but dense daughter, Hildy, to get him that box (as he needs it in his harebrained plans for a death ray). Hildy finds Gillian but when she is unable to get the box, she kidnaps Pete as a bargaining chip for the box. Adapting the heroics of her comic book heroes (but considering herself a Generic Girl hero) Gillian begins her quest to save the world—and Pete from Dr. Mascalzone, his dim-witted henchmen and Hildy (whose ability to seduce any man appears to be her only ability).

Cast: Alexandra Olson (Gillian Romero), Matthew Bohrer (Pete Kirby), Sarah Ho (Brunhilda "Hildy" Mascalzone), Robert Amico (Deus Ex Machina), Matthew Farhat (Sgt. Catarsis), Richard Hawkins (Dr. Mascalzone), Christy Keller (Angelika Doom), Kristin McCoy (Miss Mayhem), Jordan Preston (Major Thunder), Jade Nicole (Lexis), Darcell Hoover (Mercedes), Nataly Pena (Candy), Sarah Roberts (Persia), Rochelle Roepke (Charity). **Credits:** *Producer-Writer-Director:* Steven Itano Wasserman, Aaron Hartley, Victor Solis. **Comment:** Gillian is adorable; Hildy is sexy; Pete is a nerd and Dr. Mascalzone is stark raving mad. All the ingredients needed for a comical story about good defeating evil (well, it has to be assumed so as the series ends without a resolution).

Episodes: *1.* Exposition. *2.* Requiem for a Henchman. *3.* A Barrage of Bosom Burning Fire. *4.* Gillian's Love Box. *5.* Peter Envy. *6.* Scent of a Henchman. *7.* Teabags for Two. *8.* The Last Meow. *9.* One More Into the Breeches. *10.* Generic Girl Climaxes.

367 Gentleman's Dwelling. funnyordie.com. 2012.

Donald and Louie are brothers who share a Manhattan apartment. The brothers could be considered a bit dysfunctional as they each have different views on life, personal hygiene and morality issues but somehow manage to get along with each other without killing one another. As if there were not enough conflict already, additional friction enters their lives when they encounter financial problems and decide to take in a third roommate. Their choice: Crantz, "the lovable moron from upstairs." The program relates what happens as a moron and two different as night and day brothers not only attempt to navigate life, but live together.

Cast: Ben Leasure (Donald), Joe Lankheet (Louie), Zach Stasz (Crantz). **Credits:** *Producer:* Lindsey Timko. *Director:* Giles Sherwood. **Comment:** Louie is a disgusting slob; Donald is no better and Crantz puts up with the two of them but the audience shouldn't have to. Between the bathroom "humor" and the food eating scenes, the program is totally unpleasant to watch. For some, repulsive humor is delightful but for most it isn't and should only be viewed if this type of comedy appeals to you.

Episodes: *1.* The Roommate. *2.* Sherry Baby. *3.* Stratford Upon Harlem. *4.* Roommate Contracts. *5.* The Cold Wars. *6.* Green Card Marriage. *7.* Pitching a Tent. *8.* Rescue Mission.

368 Georgian Way. georgianway.com. 2012.

Steven is a mild-mannered young accountant who enjoys but rarely gets the sedate life he cherishes. He lives with his freeloading, obnoxious brother (Skippy) and is constantly annoyed by his neurotic neighbors, his nagging mother and the various friends (especially Paul and his Internet purchased wife Sasha) that are also a part of his life. The program chronicles the situations Steven encounters as he reluctantly becomes involved in the situations created by all those who surround him and whom he just wishes would go away and leave him alone.

Cast: John A. Gurtshaw (Steven), Daniel Thorp (Skippy), Paul Sulsky (Paul), Mytem Lenz (Sasha), Bill Kelsey (CoCo), Marlene Zechman (Steve's mother), Lam Rivere (Chris), Pugs-Lee McKoy (Pugs, Skippy's dog). Credits: *Producer:* T.L. McKoy, Sharin Nelson, Cooki Karriem. *Writer-Director:* T.L. McKoy. Comment: A somewhat "Odd Couple" paring with a responsible man (Steven) and a degenerate (Skippy). At first glance, the Skippy character appears to be an annoying low life who just plagues Steven's life. As you watch you will see that Skippy is a low life who not only plagues Steven but honestly tries to help him with the limited abilities he appears to have.

Episodes: *1.* Here Comes the Bride. *2.* Oh Baby. *3.* Don't Turn Your Back on CoCo. *4.* Where to Put a Hooker. *5.* Peer Pressure Hurts. *6.* Don't Mess with Russia. *7.* 127 Minutes. *8.* Special People Cause Fights. *9.* I've Been Reborn. *10.* Tonight's the Night.

369 *G.H.O.S.T.* webserieschannel.com. 2013.

Guys Helping Out Ghosts Together (G.H.O.S.T. for short) is a ghost-busting agency run by Jake, Mark, Dan and Sammi, college students who believe they have found an answer to their money problems by helping people haunted by the unnatural. The program follows the rather misfit ghost busters as they seek to help restless spirits move on. Jake is the team leader and founder; Sammi is a medium who can communicate with ghosts; Dan is the cameraman; and Mark is the skeptic who joins them to prove that ghosts do not exist.

Cast: Jake Mattern (Jake Schneider), Mark Kazor (Mark Raider), Dan Foster (Dan White), Sammi Begelman (Sammi Lockhart). Credits: *Producer:* Jack Mattern. *Director:* Connor Griffin. Comment: Clever spoof of the numerous ghost related series on channels such as Destination America and Syfy. The situations are a bit bizarre (like a ghost who haunts the bathroom of his former girlfriend) but the acting and production is top rate.

Episodes: *1.* The Pilot. *2.* The Sleepover. *3.* Lost in the Library. *4.* The Exorcism of Dan.

370 *Ghost Catchers.* dailymotion.com. 2012.

"Won't Get Ghouled Again" is the slogan of Ghost Catchers, a spook-busting business that makes house calls to rid one's life of ghosts "and other pesky spirits." Cassandra is the company's blind medium (but she claims she can "see" the spirit world) and she is assisted by Stuart, Bonequeef and Jones.

Cast: Kerri Van Auken, Collin Lindo, Josh Baillon, Zeke Nicholson, Anne Clark, Pearson Jenks, Kelly Ehrler, Chris Milliken. Credits: *Producer:* Kerri Van Auken. *Director:* Pearson Jenks. *Writer:* Pearson Jenks, Kerri Van Auken. Comment: While

only a pilot has been made it does show potential for being a good spoof of ghost hunting movies and TV series. If future episodes are made it would be a good idea if the producer matched the performer with his or her character.

Episodes: *1.* Pilot.

371 *Ghost Ghirls.* yahoo.com. 2013.

Ghost Ghirls is a company run by Angelica and Heidi, two very pretty ghost hunters who each believe they have the ability to detect spiritual activity and that ability can make them money. Stories follow their efforts to help people threatened by ghosts. Heidi is a bit off-the-wall while Angelica is more down-to-earth. They have disagreements as to how a case should be handled and often feel each has the better solution when in reality neither one does; it is when they put their heads together and work as one that they achieve their goal.

Cast: Amanda Lund (Heidi), Maria Blasucci (Angelica). Credits: *Producer:* Maria Blasucci, Amanda Lund, Jack Black, Sheila Stepanek. *Director:* Jeremy Konner. *Writer:* Amanda Lund, Maria Blasucci, Jeremy Konner, Ryan Corrigan. Comment: Charming mix of comedy and horror with excellent acting and production values. Heidi and Angelica are perfectly matched and the stories are well written and directed.

Episodes: *1.* Home Is Where the Haunt Is. *2.* Hooker with a Heart of Ghoul. *3.* Field of Screams. *4.* Will You Scarry Me? *5.* Ghost Writer. *6.* I Believe in Mira-Ghouls. *7.* Comedy of Terrors. *8.* School Spirit. *9.* The Golden Ghouls. *10.* Something Borrowed, Something Boo. *11,12.* Spirits of '76.

372 *Ghostfacers.* webserieschannel.com. 2010.

Ed, Maggie, Harry, Ambyr and Spruce are amateur ghost hunters who consider themselves professionals and capable of doing what the real ghost hunters do—help people threatened by spirits. The program, a proposed spin off from the CW series *Supernatural* relates their rather fumbling methods to investigate unnatural occurrences (as in the only story line presented: the mystery of a theater haunted by a ghost).

Cast: A.J. Buckley (Ed Zeddmore), Travis Wester (Harry Spangler), Brittany Ishibashi (Maggie Zeddmore), Mircea Monroe (Ambyr), Austin Basis (Kenny Spruce), Kelly Carlson (Janet Meyers). Credits: *Producer:* Peter Johnson, Jeff Grosvenor, Eric Kripke, Phil Sgriccia. *Writer:* A.J. Buckley, Patric J. Doody, Chris Valenziano, Travis Wester. Comment: Played more for laughs than horror, the program is well produced and acted and encompasses Kelly Carlson (from the series *Nip/Tuck*) as its guest star (Janet Meyers). The original series concept was to have the cast investigate a real haunted house; this was dropped in favor of the haunted theater.

Episodes: *1.* Meet the Facers. *2.* The Grand Showcase. *3.* The Big Break. *4.* CSI: Maggie. *5.* Dead Time. *6.* Finishing the Job. *7.* The Comeback. *8.* Cutting Room Floor. *9.* Shattered. *10.* Why We Fight.

373 *Ghouls.* webseriestoday.com. 2010.

During the 1930s and 40s Frankenstein, Dracula, the Wolfman and the Mummy reigned as fright creatures on the silver screen. But as time passed and America's fascination with them grew less, they blended into the background and became unnoticed for decades. But that was then. They have returned to the modern world and, having lived a sheltered existence now face a world that is totally unfamiliar to them. Stories follow their efforts to recapture the glory of their pasts by again becoming the screen's greatest monsters. Jason is their agent.

Cast: Dan Merket (Frankenstein), Julian Martinez (Dracula), Bryce Wissel (Wolfman), Sweet P. (Mummy), David Hall Page (Phantom of the Opera), Jose Rosete (Jason), Geoffrey Dwyer (Royce McCutchens), Patrick Waller (Michael Myers). Credits: *Producer:* Alisa Allen, Sandy Haddad, Shelby Sexton, Mathew Lancaster. *Director:* Benjamin T. Ross. *Writer:* Benjamin T. Ross, Kris Simonian. Comment: The idea has been done on TV before with the live action *Monster Squad* and the animated *Drak Pack.* Even *The Munsters Today* conceived of such an idea. Here, however, the monsters are anything but convincing and are horribly depicted (Frankenstein, for example, has a green face and a bad toupee; Dracula looks normal; and the Mummy has a bad case of loose bandages). The program begins with no introduction as to how the monsters came to be (in the present) or how they acquire their friend Jason. Had some time been taken to present the monsters as they should look and couple that with a decent story line, *Ghouls* would have made a good series. As it stands now *Ghouls* is ghoulish.

Episodes: 6 untitled episodes, labeled "Episode 1" through "Episode 6."

374 *Gigahoes.* gigahoes.com. 2014.

In the year 2024 scientists created the first full functional robot with human level artificial intelligence. Ten years later the robots were developed even further and became so life-like that they were impossible to tell apart from real humans. To capitalize on the robots an escort company called Artificial Intercourse is created and, instead of using real humans to satisfy the sexual needs of its clientele, it replaces them with Sexbots. Steven is the owner of Artificial Intercourse; Sarah is his office manager; Jessica and Charlie (a girl) are HP Generation 6 Sexbots; Branden is a model 700104 robot and

Gigahoes. Series poster art (used by permission).

Adam is an HP Generation 5 Sexbot. To publicize the new technology, a film crew has begun documenting how the company operates and how the Sexbots function and it is through that filming that a look at a fantasized future escort service is depicted.

Cast: Kevin Gilligan (Steven), Marjorie Bryant (Sarah), Jessica Park (Jessica), Daniel Florio (Branden), Kimberlee Walker (Charlie), Adam Lash (Adam). Credits: *Producer:* Adam Lash, Kevin Gilligan. *Director:* David Wright. *Writer:* Adam Lash, Kevin Gilligan. Comment: Interesting concept that literally takes the Japanese Love Doll creations and transforms them into robots. There is blurred nudity, mild sexual situations and strong adult content all of which is presented without any rating or parental warning. The acting and production is very good but the program is intended for mature audiences only.

Episodes: *1.* Welcome to Artificial Intelligence. *2.* Branden, Baker's Man. *3.* Amber Alert. *4.* Jessica Goes Into the Woods. *5.* Mother Knows Best. *6.* The Photo Shoot. *7,8.* Synth-Skin Is the New Black. *9.* Charlie and the Porn Factory. *10.* Double Date. *11.* Salacious Sal's Sexbot Emporium. *12.* Thanksgiving.

375 *Gigi: Almost American.* gigialmost american.tumblr.com. 2010.

Gigi is a foreigner on American shores who just wants to fit in. He cannot speak or understand English, is unfamiliar with American customs and yearns to become an average U.S. citizen. Gigi is very naïve but determined and the program follows the road he takes to achieve his dream, made all that more comical when he does teach himself to speak English but putting what he has learned and understanding what others say provide the stumbling blocks he must overcome.

Cast: Josh Gad (Gigi), Tyler Moore (Hank Goldberg), Ida Darvish (Didi), Amy Hiller (Amy). Credits: *Producer:* Ty Clancey, Warren Chao, Rob Nennett, Jane Tranter, Daniel Tischler, Courtney B. Conte. *Director:* Ty Clancey. *Writer:* Ty Clancey, Ida Darvish, Josh Gad, Kevin Larsen, Tyler Moore. Comment: Although it is not an original idea, Josh Gad makes the program work with a stellar performance as Gigi (not to be confused with a movie about a French mute named *Gigi*). The program is produced by the BBC (British Broadcasting Corporation) as one of its first Internet endeavors.

Season 1 Episodes: *1.* Speak Learn English. *2.* Donate Good Cause. *3.* Pocket Access. *4.* For a Good Time. *5.* Gigi Sings for Gigi. *6.* Gigi's Book Club. *7.* Sorry Lady Lady. *8.* Space Cowboy. *9.* Teach Learn English. *10.* Didi.

Season 2 Episodes: *1.* Nice Home. *2.* Cavity Search. *3.* Judging Gigi. *4.* Yogi. *5.* Date Night.

376 GiGi Eats Celebrities. gigieatscelebrities.com. 2012.

GiGi is a woman who loves to mock celebrities and what they do (like how they stay in shape and what they eat). Through short video sequences, GiGi takes on a celebrity (somewhat in the manner of an *Entertainment Tonight* TV series host) and goes about ripping apart what she believes is either fact or fiction about that person.

Cast: GiGi Dubois (GiGi). Credits: *Producer:* Idalis de Leon, Armen Atoyan. *Director:* Idalis de Leon. *Writer:* GiGi DuBois. Comment: Very fast-moving program with visuals to backup who and what GiGi decides to rip apart. The pace is good and the acting and production top rate.

Episodes: *1.* A Ridiculous Diet Plan Involving Cookies. *2.* Bogus Baby Food Bodies. *3.* In the Zone. *4.* Victoria's Other Secret. *5.* Exclusive! Baby Makes Weight Loss. *6.* Eat Fat, Lose Fat? *7.* Erotic Fitness Dancing Starring Martha Stewart. *8.* Clear Your Skin By Eating Right. *9.* Britney Spears Coffee Drink Disaster. *10.* Oprah vs. Janet Jackson: Yo-Yo Battle. *11.* Paris Hilton Is Not Having Sex in This Video.

377 Girl Parts. blip.tv. 2011.

Ashley "Ash" Jennifer Barlow is a former child actress who now works as a talent agent and lives with three hopeful actresses (Ava, Katie and Sam). As a child, Ash was probably best known for her starring roles on the Fruity Fruit Juice TV commercials and for her role in the feature film *Bright Lightning, Big Thunder*. But as she grew kid roles became scarce and her acting career was over. But show business was still in her blood and she acquired a job with UTA (Uger Talent Agency) where "We represent actors who rarely ever book a job." The events that befall Ash as she attempts to cope with her roommates, her job, and a boss who doesn't seem to care about acquiring aspiring actors roles are chronicled.

Cast: Kelsey Robinson (Ash Barlow), Meagan Gordon (Sam), Corinne Becker (Katie), Melanie Molnar (Eva), Matthew Montgomery (Pete). Credits: *Producer-Writer:* Kelsey Robinson. *Director:* Mike Drobinski. Comment: Simply charming with very good acting and production values.

Episodes: *1.* The Flareup. *2.* 6 Days Later and a Dollar Short. *3.* The Child Star/Den Mother. *4.* The Wake Up Call. *5.* Hot Is Always Right. *6.* Blatant Crashers. *7.* The One with Jason Horton. *8.* When to Cut a Bitch. *9.* We Are the Lucky Ones. *10.* A Walk of Shame and Triumph.

378 Girls Will Be Girls. funnyordie.com. 2007.

Evie Harris, once a C-List actress, but no longer in demand, has turned to alcohol for comfort. It was during the 1970s that her career took off with the low budget disaster film *Asteroid*, the television series *Court TV: Celebrities Who Kill* and a stint as the spokesperson for Dr. Vim's Miracle Elixir. During this time Evie had a rival, Marla Simonds, a woman who tried to upstage her at every opportunity (her claim to fame was starring as Chesty on *Fill Her Up*, a spin off [that never actually occurred] from the 1970s actual TV series *C.P.O. Sharkey*). Marla also has a daughter, Varla, who is seeking to follow in her mother's footsteps and become an actress. Life changes for Evie when Marla dies and Varla, desperately in need of money, turns to Evie for help. Although unable to support her, Evie invites Varla to live with her and her roommate, Coco Peru, a not-so attractive spinster who carries an unrelenting torch for the young doctor who performed her abortion several years ago. The program, which encompasses men in drag as women, follows the three roommates as they attempt to live together with the principal focus on Evie and her relentless efforts to reignite a show business career that never had an illustrious moment.

Cast: Jack Plotnick (Evie Harris), Clinton Leupp (Coco Peru), Jeffrey Roberson (Varla Simonds). Credits: *Producer:* Michael Warwick, Jack Plotnick. *Writer-Director:* Richard Day. Comment: Excellent acting and production values make for an enjoyable drag queen series where the guys as girls are very convincing assuming female roles. The series is adapted from the feature film of the same title and is as good as other series that use the drag queen format (like *Have You Met Miss Jones?*, *Capitol Hill* and *Chico's Angels*; see titles for information).

Episodes: *1,2.* Girl Stalker. *3.* The Jizz Party. *4,5.* Delivering Coco.

379 Giving Up the Ghosts. webserieschannel.com. 2011.

Ghost Stalkers is an amateur group of paranormal investigators that have set out to rid their commu-

Giving Up the Ghosts. Series poster art (copyright 2011 Road Apple Productions).

nity of ghosts. Anton and Ed, co-workers in a me-dieval-themed liquor store, founded the organiza-tion and Regina, a wealthy girl addicted to the new age spirituality (and wine) is their assistant. Ghost Stalkers is also a member of The Paranormal Society and to maintain their membership they must suc-cessfully prove the existence of ghosts or paranormal happenings. Anton, Ed and Regina have yet to prove anything the society requires and have been put on a six month probation status: If they do not provide sufficient evidence of the unnatural they will be ex-pelled from the society. The program charts their desperate attempts to find a ghost and live their dreams of becoming professional ghost busters.

Cast: Jared Moore (Anton), Kristofer James (Ed), Monica Reichl (Regina), Tony Riech (Roy). **Cred-its:** *Producer:* Tony Riech, Nick Hartman, Maurice Wyble. *Director:* Nick Hartman. *Writer:* Tony Riech. **Comment:** The program is a well-done spoof of ghost busting TV and movie series with good act-ing and production values (especially the ghost hunting scenes which will be familiar to fans of the Syfy TV series *Ghost Hunters*). The situations en-countered by the group are meant to be corny and that goal has been achieved.

Episodes: *1.* Liquor Fools. *2.* Cooler, We Have a Problem. *3.* All That Glitters. *4.* Tormented by Spir-its. *5.* Hostage Negotiations. *6.* Light's Out. *7.* T.N.T.

380 Glitch. youtube.com. 2012.

Glitch, as he is called, is a nerd, totally devoted to video games. He is a video game tester and eats, sleeps and dreams them, so much so that, as he enters a quarter-life crisis, he makes an idle wish that his life could be more like a video game. Unseen forces sort of grant his wish. Instead of making it awesome and full of action he finds that his life is now plagued by video game glitches. But Glitch is not alone. An Old Man, who is seen as a different video game char-acter in each episode, becomes Glitch's somewhat ineffectual guide as he navigates life in a whole new perspective—with the help of his two best friends, Samantha (a nerdy girl who prefers to be called Samus) and Wyatt, a fellow video game enthusiast employed by a construction company.

Cast: Jesse Lee Keeter (Glitch), Tessa Archer (Samus), Conner Marx (Wyatt), Thomas Brophy (Neville), Brian J. Sutherland (Old Man), Brian

Lewis (Lars), Curtis Eastwood (The Boss), Trin Miller (Erica). **Credits:** *Producer:* Tyler J. Hill, Josephine Hoy, Brian Sutherland. *Writer-Director:* Tyler J. Hill. **Comment:** While the program is directed to video game enthusiasts it is a well done and acted comedy that can be enjoyed by anyone despite its target audience. Outsiders (non-video game players) may enjoy the concept but much of the humor involves video game-playing knowledge as jokes do revolve around their characters and premises.

Episodes: *1.* OMG Pilot. *2.* Game Night. *3.* The Day of Fail. *4.* Nerd Lent. *5.* The Crazy One. *6.* The One Where Everybody Loses Their Job.

381 The Goddamn George Liquor Program. youtube.com. 1997–1998.

Events in the life of George Liquor, a very patriotic American and Jimmy the Idiot Boy, his incredibly stupid teenage nephew. Sody Pop is a 15-year-old girl who has fallen for Jimmy; Cigarettes is Jimmy's cat; Dirty Dog is the neighborhood watchdog; bullies Slab and Ernie are Jimmy's cousins. Merle is Sody's older sister; George's late wife, Mabel is also seen (after her passing, George preserved her torso and legs on a trophy stand and now, with her butt facing you, she adorns the living room).

Cast: Michael Pataki (George Liquor), John Kricfalusi (Jimmy), Wendy Balomben (Sody Pop). **Credits:** *Producer:* Kevin Kolde, John Kricfalusi. *Director:* John Kricfalusi. *Writer:* John Kricfalusi, Richard Pursel. **Comment:** The program is the second animated Internet series (*Whirl Girl* [see entry] was the first premiering in March of 1997; *George* premiered in October of that year). The animation is a bit more sophisticated here and the program is quite amusing.

Episodes: 8 episodes were produced that have been edited to form a 15 minute and 47 second episode.

382 Gold Stars. vimeo.com. 2014.

Anna and Cassie are young lesbians (but not lovers) who share a two bedroom apartment in Brooklyn, New York. Cassie is the more ambitious of the two and each rely on odd jobs to survive. While Cassie is just as attractive as Anna, Cassie often wonders why women are more attracted to Anna than her. The events that spark their lives—from trying to find that right girl to the increasingly bizarre odd jobs that come their way are chronicled.

Cast: Lane Moore (Cassie), Molly Knefel (Anna), Katie Compa (Carol), Hilary Warburton (Ghost Girl), Brittany Connors (Elyse), Chen Drachman (Yael). **Credits:** *Producer-Writer-Director:* Lane Moore. **Comment:** Delightful comedy with the only problem being the last episode wherein background noises make dialogue difficult to understand. There is no nudity or foul language and only the last three episodes deal with the lesbian aspect of the series.

Lane Moore and Molly Knefel are nicely cast as each plays well off the other (sort of like a female "Odd Couple" but without the neatness or untidiness).

Episodes: *1.* The Foot Job. *2.* The Couch Guy. *3.* S**T Job. *4.* Craigslist Roommate Search. *5.* Housewarming Party. *6.* But You Don't Look Gay Enough to Be a Lesbian. *7.* Cool Girls. *8.* Awkward Date.

383 Golden California. youtube.com. 2013.

Travel Channel spoof that follows Herb Hendricks as he travels around California seeking to interview people and hoping to discover what their particular communities have to offer in the way of fun and excitement. Naturally, he encounters all the eccentrics and, not being a truly informed host, must make do with what he can come up with in a moments notice.

Cast: Ron Hanks (Herb Hendricks). **Credits:** *Producer:* Ron Hanks, Megan Brotherton, Christopher Rubalcaba. *Writer-Director:* Morgan J. Steele, Megan Brotherton. **Comment:** Herb is a befuddled host and his efforts to tackle the various areas and sights of California do come off as quite amusing, especially when he gets himself into a predicament and must scramble to find a way out.

Episodes: *1.* Fields of Gold. *2.* Where There's Smoke. *3.* Summer in the City. *4.* The Desert Has Turned to Sea. *5.* Herb Hendricks on Ice. *6.* Pineapple Milk Shakes. *7.* Erectile Dysfunction. *8.* Valley Girls.

384 Gone Hollywood. webserieschannel. com. 2014.

Lola and Natalie are young women who have moved to Hollywood to pursue their dreams of becoming actresses. Sounds simple, but as Lola and Natalie soon discover, it is anything but. Their attempts to audition for roles, acquire jobs and somehow make their dreams come true are profiled.

Cast: Lulu Fotis (Lola), Madeleine Johnson (Natalie). **Credits:** *Producer:* Ashim Ahuja. **Comment:** Short sequences that simply place the women in a situation and let them comment on it. It is not set in a studio and thus the commentary-like production works well as it goes on location to document a situation.

Episodes: *1.* #Runyon. *2.* #Seth Rogen. *3.* #Master Cleanse. *4.* #Coffee Girl. *5.* #Sugar Daddy. *6.* #Tinder. *7.* #Chosen. *8.* #Rich Guys.

385 Good God (2006). tv.com. 2006.

The setting is the heavenly office of God. It is here that his office employees ("Angels") assist him and do his bidding. While the overall concept is just a day at the office and what happens, it also showcases God in a light where he is learning to encompass the new world (like signing up for a MySpace page) and his Angels being just like ordinary mortals—trying to outdo each other and always facing the wrath of a "boss" like no other.

Cast: Bryan Michael McGuire (God), Kurt Braunohler (Jesus), Jenna Jolley (Heidi, Angel of Heavenly Affairs), Kelly AuCoin (Michael Archangel), Henry Afro-Bradley (Angel of Death), Julian Reyes (Associate Archangel Gabriel). **Credits:** *Producer:* Jeffrey Sikaitis, Jeff Stamp, Jake Wheeler. *Director:* Jeffrey Sikaitis. **Comment:** While the program does sound interesting, all episodes and trailers have been taken off line making a comment based on viewing not possible.

Episodes: *1.* Tech Upgrade. *2.* Business Pitch. *3.* Office Pool. *4.* Status Meeting. *5.* Jesus Bails.

386 Good God (2012). themovienetwork. ca. 2012.

George is a man who appears to be in his late thirties. He has recently been dumped by his live-in girlfriend (Claire) and life is looking dim until he reconnects with his old flame, Virginia, the socialite daughter of Mike Hailwood, a media mogul who loves horses "and is a right wing whacko." At a meeting arranged by Virginia to meet with Mike, Mike offers George the position of running the Canadian branch of his American news network Right Wing. George feels the station is a right wing version of Fox news "and I wouldn't take it (the job) if someone held a gun to my head. But then he (Mike) held money to my head." Now George is running Right Wing and the program charts all the problems he faces (not being right wing) as he tries to deal with his staff and the problems associated with presenting a fair position on the news stories they broadcast.

Cast: Ken Finkleman (George Findlay), April Mullen (Kathy Duncan), John Ralston (Danny McClure), Lolita Davidovich (Virginia Hailwood), Jason Weinberg (Doug), Stephanie Anne Mills (Christine Adams), Janet van de Graaf (Brenda Duke), Samantha Bee (Shandy Sommers), Doug Murray (Charlie Kuntz), Steve McCarthy (Allen), Jud Taylor (Troy), Brendan Gall (Elliot Mooch), Alex Poch-Goldin (Bill Callum), Christopher Shyer (Tony Cassano), Tamara Hope (Becky). **Credits:** *Producer:* Ken Finkleman, Scott Garvie, Christina Jennings. *Writer-Director:* Ken Finkleman. **Comment:** Well defined characters and an interesting concept merge to present what is called a "mockumentary" to not only spoof a right wing view of the news but the television workplace environment.

Episodes: *1.* One Station Under God. *2.* Elliot Big Balls. *3.* I've Never Met a Disease I Didn't Catch. *4.* Old Friends Never Die, Unfortunately. *5.* Solidarity for Never. *6.* The Naked Truth. *7.* Cheese and Cops with Holes in 'Em. *8.* Two Treadmills. *9.* God, Nation and the Kung Pao Chicken. *10.* Dead Dogs Don't Lie.

387 Goodnight Burbank. goodnightburbank.com. 2011.

A behind-the-scenes look at the workings of a TV station (Channel 6 in Burbank, California) and in particular its nightly news program, "Goodnight Burbank," where putting on the news is a news story in itself.

Gordon Winston-Smythe, the co-anchor, was born in Manchester, England, and in 1997 relocated to the U.S. to try his hand at producing a home shopping network. He had performed with the 1990s band "The The The" that had only one hit—"I'd Love It If You Loved Me." When that failed he worked his way into radio and eventually to Burbank and Channel 6.

Whitney Appleby, the co-anchor, was born in Orange County, California, and previously worked as a newscaster in Arizona (as the newsreader of the radio program "Good Morning AZHoles" goof gang) and in North Carolina on the TV series *Nice to See You, Huh*. She is a devout Christian and embellishes herself in "The Three C's": Charity, Children and Church.

Elizabeth Chivers, the entertainment reporter, is the sister of station owner Chilton (how she got the job) and suffers from Asperberger's Syndrome.

Genevieve Nigwua, the field reporter, has five master's degrees, a doctorate in psychology and awards in track and field. In her spare time she volunteers at the Burbank Stray Animal Shelter and transports the elderly and handicapped to hospitals.

Paul Lynch, a field reporter, is also from Manchester, England, and originally worked for the BBC before accepting a job at "Goodnight Burbank."

Terri Blake, a field reporter, graduated Magna Cum Laude from the University of Burbank and enjoys giving back to the community. She also loves hanging out at parks and libraries.

Paisley Parker is the weathergirl and has been with the station since 2000 (right after she graduated from high school), is married and the mother of four children. She has also won numerous awards for her accurate forecasting.

Yan Bobek is the news director. He spent most of his life in Communist Estonia directing adult (porn) films that were sanctioned by the government. He escaped in 2008 and managed to find a job at Channel 6.

Holly Johnson is the lighting director (she majored in studio lighting at Burbank Community College).

Nadira Farhad, the station makeup artist, was born in Orange County, and is from a large second generation Muslim family (her grandparents escaped from Iraq during World War II and came to America fearing Hitler may kill Muslims if the Jews weren't enough).

Chilton Chivers is the station owner and a hero of sorts. In 2010, Channel 6 burned down in what has been recorded as a gruesome, horrible fire that took the lives of many of the stations established personalities. In 2011 he rebuilt the station and returned Channel 6 to the airwaves.

Cast: Hayden Black (Gordon Winston-Smythe), Laura Silverman (Whitney Appleby), Dominic Monaghan (Paul Lynch), Camden Toy (Yan Bobek), Adrienne Wilkinson (Paisley Parker), Miracle Laurie (Elizabeth Chivers), Cameron Bender (Chilton Chivers), America Young (Holly Johnson), Hadeel Sittu (Nadira Farhad), Diahnna Nicole Baxter (Genevieve Nigwua). **Credits:** *Producer:* Hayden Black, Laura Silverman, Alexis Nelson, Phil Ashcroft. *Director:* Canyon Prince, Tracie Laymon. *Writer:* Hayden Black, Tracie Laymon. **Comment:** While not an original idea (the CBS series *Goodnight, Bean Town* may come to mind) it does go a bit overboard than others of its kind with the cast and crew experiencing all the worst that can possibly happen covering the news. The writing and direction are good and the characters, some of the best spoofs of real TV journalists.

Episodes: *1.* What Goes Up. *2.* Car Quake. *3.* The Phantom of the Garage. *4.* Demon Seed. *5.* Lesbians on Acid. *6.* The Casting Couch.

Note: In 2006, the original version of the program aired with the following cast. All other information, including a synopsis, episodes and trailers have been taken off line.

2006 Cast: Hayden Black (Gordon Winston-Smythe), Shulie Cown (Kelly Jones), Rich Fulcher (Dane Rivers), David H. Lawrence (Frank Warfield), Monica Young (Autumn Stanton), Wendy Rosoff (Zoe Travis), Angela Espinosa (Trisha Sakamoto), John F. Schaffer (Kenny Schickler), Carly Craig (Taylor McCall), Mary Pat Farrell (Kitty Robinson), Jamie Denbo (Susan Jones).

388 *Goodstein.* webserieschannel.com. 2013.

Jonathan Goodstein is a successful New Jersey attorney, married to Suzy and, because of his charm and charisma he has been chosen to represent a group of liberal politicians. Jonathan's life, however, is not all cozy as the country's most powerful conservative news network (Ace News) is seeking to destroy him for his liberal views. At home, life is not much better: Fern, Suzy's high school best friend, has married Jonathan's high school enemy, Vinny, a plumber who resented Jonathan then and resents him even more now as he must put up with Jonathan's antics (knowing he is putting out a false image, especially since he likes to get high on pot). Fern also believes Jonathan is a phony and has set her goal to expose him. Entering the picture is Andrew, Jonathan's brother, who has decided to write a book based on his brother and his own experiences as a newsman. The program charts what happens as Jonathan becomes more of a center of attention then he would like and how he manages, with that charm

and charisma, to exonerate himself before he can be exposed as a fraud.

Cast: Lee Navlen (Jonathan Goodstein), Connie Romano (Suzy Goodstein), Alice Weber (Fern Mazzilli), Joe Romby, Jr. (Vinny Mazzilli), Sean Klenert (Andrew Goodstein), Elijah Navlen (Sheldon Carson), Suz Stone (Linda Lane). **Credits:** *Producer:* Debra Johnson. *Director:* Carlos Garcia. *Writer:* Lee Navlen. **Comment:** Foul language is (needlessly) used in an okay story with acceptable acting and production values.

Season 1 Episodes: *1.* Goodstein. *2.* The Conservative. *3.* The Salon.

Season 2 Episodes: *1.* Basket Ballin. *2.* Hash Brownies. *3.* The Drug Test.

389 *The Gorburger Show.* youtube.com. 2012.

Gorburger is a large, blue, fierce-looking alien from outer space with a fondness for Earth musicians. One day he invades a Japanese TV news network, takes over and acquires his own talk program (*The Gorburger Show*) wherein his interviews with musicians as well as celebrities are comically presented. Hiroku is Gorburger's on stage sidekick; Tokyo Fever 1 and 2 are the show's game show segment ("The Laser Round") assistants (where guests are challenged to answer three questions—two simple and one near impossible).

Cast: T.J. Miller (Gorburger), Tsubee U (Tokyo Fever 1), Chihiro Kawamura (Tokyo Fever 2), Marisa Tayui (Hiroku). **Credits:** *Producer:* Sean Boyle, Josh Martin, Ryan McNeely, Kathleen Fay Magee, Nicolas Plotquin, Betsy Koch. *Writer:* Andy Kadin, Josh Martin, Ryan K. McNeal, T.J. Miller. **Comment:** Granted, an outrageous plot but an enjoyable program with Groburger as a most unusual talk show host.

Season 1 Episodes: *1.* Tegan and Sara. *2.* Mariachi el Bronx. *3.* The Mars Volta. *4.* 3OH!3. *5.* Le Butcherettes. *6.* Dum Dum Girls. *7.* Health. *8.* Fool's Gold. *9.* La Sera. *10.* Andrew W.K.

Season 2 Episodes: *1.* Flea. *2.* Grouplove. *3.* MelloHype. *4.* Carson Daly. *5.* Wayne Coyne. *6.* Bleached.

390 *Gorgeous Tiny Chicken Machine Show.* youtube.com. 2007–2008.

Kiko is a very pretty Japanese woman who hosts her own web series. She begins each program with a song then proceeds to interview a guest. All is typical of a normal TV talk show until Kiko speaks and not only mispronounces her guests names but other words as well (in typical stereotyped Japanese fashion) with the guest not only trying to comprehend what she is saying but also give her the correct way of saying their name. Because her English is not very good, her producers have chosen to subtitle what she says—and also misspelling the guest's name to reflect Kiko's pronunciation. Following the interview Kiko and her guest participate in a game-like segment where even more confusion reigns as they become involved in outrageous activities. Kiko is assisted by Go-Go Dancer, UniCow (a cow with a Unicorn head) and Cowincorn (a cow that is part Unicorn).

Cast: Kim Evey (Kiko), Payman Benz (UniCow), Michele Gregory (Paula), Sean Becker (Cowincorn), Julie Wittner (Go-Go-Dancer). **Credits:** *Producer-Writer:* Kim Evey. *Director:* Greg Benson. **Comment:** Not even Charlie Chan, the famed Oriental detective spoke with such a stereo-typed accent. Kim Evey dresses in pink, has a child-like living room set and is simply delightful as the wide-eyed, cherry host. It will take a few minutes to adjust to Kiko's accent to understand what she is saying, but once you do, you will want to see other episodes in the series.

Episodes: Of the 41 episodes produced, only the following remain on line: *1.* Lick Poop. *2.* Chicken Itchy Balls. *3.* Slumber Party. *4.* Kiko's Doorstep. *5.* Bush Baby. *6.* Lick Poop VI. *7.* C.A.R.E. *8.* Surprise Party. *9.* Talk to the Hot Dog. *10.* Garden Party. *11.* Broken Fun. *12.* Fortune Time. *13.* Global Housewarming. *14.* A Very Special Episode. *15.* Unicow Gets Laid. *16.* Costume Party. *17.* Political Party. *18.* The Taming of Unicow. *19.* Dancing. *20.* Unicow Gets Pregnant. *21.* The Future Is Now.

391 *Gorilla Therapy.* vimeo.com. 2014.

A gorilla has risen far beyond the ranks of others like him. He has the intelligence to become a therapist and has even set up his own office. He has human patients and, through three arc episodes, the patient meets with Gorilla to discuss his or her problem (episode 1), while the second episode sees the problem progressing with the third episode finding a resolution.

Cast: Philip Hersh (Gorilla). **Credits:** *Producer:* Missy Hauser. *Director:* Nathaniel Dueber. *Writer:* Tanner Sawitz. **Comment:** If there can be a product called Gorilla Glue (and Gorilla Tape) why not a Gorilla therapist. While the gorilla suit is a bit cheesy looking, the idea is good and the program itself quite enjoyable—where else will you see people seeking help from a gorilla?

Episode List: *1,2,3.* Complimentary Tourettes (a man with a compulsion to compliment people) *4,5,6.* Mafioso Kindergarten Teacher (a kindergarten teacher who moonlights as a Mafia boss).

392 *Goth Girl.* watchgothgirl.com. 2009–2012.

Selena Ravenvox is the alias of Susan "Suzie" Anderson, a pretty 17-year-old girl who feels that her parents hate her—"They just had me so they could come home and make someone as miserable as they are." She also feels she has only one true friend—Asteroth: "His parents hate him too which is why we get along so well." Suzie also has anger management issues and has encompassed the Goth world where she is known as Selena ("an Internet blogging Gothic Goddess"). Selena's world totally revolves around being Goth—not just a member, but its Queen. Selena would also like to find someone who would come along "and take me from this hellish existence ... a dashing gentleman who will sweep me off my feet—a vampire. We would sleep all day and go out at night and feed upon all the cheerleaders at my school." Selena believes her parents and sisters (Erica and Taylor) do not understand her; her teachers are amazed at her personality change and she has encompassed friends who are only Goth—"Welcome to my world—Biatches!" Stories relate events in the life of a girl who wants things done her way, but also a girl desperately trying to discover who she is in a world she feels she does not truly belong. Sadisto is Asteroth's cousin; Desiree is Sadisto's controlling girlfriend; Malicia is Selena's nemesis, the girl seeking to dethrone her; Trinity Divinity is Selena's rival in later episodes; Charlie is Selena's creepy uncle.

Cast: Vera VanGuard (Selena Ravenvox), Joel Reed (Asteroth), Emily Yetter (Taylor), Lauren Bennett (Erica), Darth Schuhe (Sadisto Ameroth), Mister Marco (Selena's father), Laura Renee James (Selena's mother), Alex Cartana (Malicia), Marcus Langston (Bobby), Jacelyn Schutte (Desiree Angelripper), Hana Lash (Wynter), Cara Manuele (Trinity Divinity), Scott Blugrind (Uncle Charlie), Cosmoe Tayson (Mortalis), Joe Filippone (Quill Cadaver), Mariah Pasos (Aluna), Kristal Luna (Vulvet), Dave Max (Dan the Man), Audrey Cain (Tormentra), Anne Arreguin (Devianna), Elspeth Weingarten (Rosey Hips). **Credits:** *Producer:* Nick Griffo, Vera VanGuard. *Writer-Director:* Nick Griffo. **Comment:** An enjoyable, well-acted program with Vera VanGuard (Selena) really capturing the feel of a Goth Girl. The other performers play their roles just as well and the only negative aspect would be its occasional use of vulgar language.

Episodes 1–18: *1.* The Dream Killers. *2.* Half-Ass Pool Party. *3.* Sisters, Neighbors and Twilight. *4.* Meltdown in the Bedroom. *5.* Get Out of My Face. *6.* The Lecture. *7.* I Have a Dream. *8.* Vlad. *9.* Apologies = Enslavement. *10.* Avenge My Nuts. *11.* Pubic Pizza. *12.* Operation Erica. *13.* Who's Shrinking Who? *14.* Sibling Promiscuity. *15.* Be Edward for Me. *16.* The Night Ends Prematurely. *17.* Stockings Stomp Down. *18.* Halloween Magic.

Episodes 19–38: *19.* Gothic Smack Down. *20.* Twilight by Selena. *21.* Selena's Fan Mail. *22.* Know Your Place, Biatch! *23.* The Joke's on You. *24.* Handle My Light Work. *25.* Taking Out the Trash. *26.* I Know You're Not Back-Talking Me, Monkey Bitch! *27.* Just When You Thought It Couldn't Get Any Creepier... *28.* Asteroth Fail. *29.* Shrinks, Strippers, and One, Big, Happy Family. *30.* Selena's Relationship Device. *31.* Dad's Internet Victory. *32.* Asteroth Moves On. *33.* '70s Martial Arts Cinema Duel. *34.* Uncle Charlie's Fantasy. *35.* Dad vs. the Po-Po. *36.* This Is Burbank. *37.* Selena's Big Break. *38.* Epic Goth Brawl.

393 *Grapes Roommate.* funnyordie.com. 2014.

Andy appears to be an ordinary young man. Although one may not think so when his choice for a roommate is a talking bunch of grapes. The grapes act human (even eat and apparently have sex with female humans) and how Andy puts up with his choice for a roommate (and vice versa) comprises the heart of each episode.

Cast: Andy Zou (Andy), Justin Daniel Fischer (Grapes), Eve Del Prado (Harmony), Nick Packard (Uncle Jerry), Andrew Farmer (Uncle Barnaby), Katie Eisenberg (Sister), Jon Fusco (Cousin), Hudson Rhotenberry (Jeff). **Credits:** *Producer-Writer-Director:* Andy Zou. **Comment:** There are no special effects—the grapes roommate is literally a supermarket purchased bunch of red grapes with a voice over for his speech. It is a strange take on "The Odd Couple" theme with the comedy stemming from the grapes acting as a human with Andy (and everyone else) oblivious to the fact that grapes can actually be human.

Episodes: *1.* Milk. *2.* Break Up. *3.* Walking In.

394 *Gregory Way TV.* webserieschannel. com. 2011.

As a child Tom Gregory dreamed of becoming a movie star. Although he never achieved that fame he did dabble in the entertainment industry and become successful and seems to have it all—charisma, a home, cars, clothes and even his own art gallery (Gregory Way Art Gallery) in Beverly Hills. But nothing seems to make Tom content. He needs to always be involved in something new and when his friend Dan and his personal assistant, Andy, suggest that he produce a web series he seems to take an interest, especially when it is decided they do a new version of *The Wizard of Oz*. The problem: who to play Dorothy? With the assist of Andy and Dan, the program strays from the art gallery aspect and follows, for the most part, Tom, Andy and Dan's travels across America as they seek the perfect girl to play Dorothy.

Cast: Tom Gregory (Tom), Andrew Espinoza Long (Andy), Dan Tirman (Dan), John Chaney (John), Mary Shriver (Mary), Damon Mininni (Damon), George Bugatti (George), Brendon deVore (Brendon), Jenny Gulley (Jenny), Christian Quiroga. **Credits:** *Producer:* Andrew Espinoza Long. *Director:* Brendon deVore, Andrew Espinoza Long, Raymond Griego, Bart Miller. *Writer:* Tom

Gregory, Raymond Griego, Andrew Espinoza Long, Dan Tirman. **Comment:** While "The Dorothy Project" is the predominant aspect of the series, several sub stories are also presented (such as Tom's adventures in the various cities he visits). Overall, the series is well acted and produced.

Episodes: *1.* World on a String. *2.* Breakdown. *3.* Networking. *4.* What Are You Wearing? *5.* Caught in a Mousetrap. *6.* The Main Event. *7.* Leave the Gun, Take the Cannoli. *8.* Gigi's Night Out. *9.* Memory Lane. *10–22.* The Dorothy Project. *23.* Closing Time. *24.* She's a Mess. *25.* A Visit from Mom. *26.* The Good Life. *27.* Story Time. *28.* Tom's Bad Hair Day. *29,30.* Meet Me on the Mountain.

395 *Grumble.* youtube.com. 2013.

If the world was without computers, camera phones, Facebook and other social media, it would be the ideal world for a man named Grumble. Although he accepts the latest technology (as everyone around him encompasses it) he longs for the time of audio cassettes and the Walkman and the less-confused world of that time. But Grumble cannot stop time and he tries to accept the modern-day world. He is married to Penny, a woman who puts up with him because she truly loves him. Grumble has an unnatural fear of celebrity chefs, a bad habit of only reading newspaper headlines and not the accompanying article and CDs and DVDs are still a technological mystery to him. Whether he likes it or not, Grumble is a member of the human race and the program charts how he learns to live in a world where he wants to talk to people over a beer, not a computer and honestly believes that if everyone is equal enough to pay taxes, everyone should be equal

Grumble. **Constance Washington and Soren Jensen** (used by permission of Danny Matier).

enough to be paid for the same job and marry whomever they please.

Cast: Soren Jensen (Grumble), Constance Washington (Penny), Chloe Gavin (Stacey), David Hugh Mcrae (Father Fitzpatriuck/Harold). **Credits:** *Producer-Writer-Director:* Danny Matier. **Comment:** Australian produced program that is very well done with easy to understand dialogue (the performers do not have thick accents).

Episodes: *1.* Baby. *2.* A Night Out. *3.* Nicknames. *4.* A Bucks Night. *5.* Gyno. *6,7.* Bank Manager.

396 *The Guild.* youtube.com. 2007–2012.

Cyd Sherman is a very pretty young woman whose life revolves around on-line video games. She is socially awkward and retreats to a fantasy world to avoid facing the complexities of life. In one such (unnamed) game, she envisions herself as Codex, the Priestess of a guild called the Knights of Good (which also includes Bladezz, Clara, Tinkerballa, Vork and Zaboo) as they battle the evil Axis of Anarchy. The program was originally a look at Cyd as she used the game to retreat from the responsibilities of the real world but eventually evolved into a profile of her life when she does face the world and acquires a job at a video game company called The Game.

The Knights of Good: Cyd, as Codex is not as brave as she pretends to be and does panic under stress. In the real world Cyd is a concert violinist although she was dismissed for setting fire to her boyfriend's cello.

Zaboo, real name Sujan Goldberg, is the Warlock, and considers himself a "HinJew" (son of a Jewish father and a Hindu mother). He is skilled with computers and has a secret crush on Codex.

Vortex, real name Herman Holden, is a warrior and leader of the Guild. He believes in obeying the rules and logic. He works in the real world as a Notary Public but it pays little and lives off his late grandfather's Social Security, food stamps and has free WiFi (stealing it from his senile neighbor).

Bladezz, real name Simon Kemplar, is the Rogue, a high school student who is rather crude and rude to the other Guild members (although he constantly hits on the female Guild members). He earns money by modeling which he puts toward his college education (under which he uses the name Finn Smulders).

Clara, real name Clara Beane, is the Frost Mage who is not only a stay-at-home mother but a college partier and an ex-cheerleader. Although she is the mother of three children, she is somewhat irresponsible as she puts gaming before their needs. She uses her real name as her Avatar name because her old game name, "Momin-a-Trix," presented the wrong image to her children.

Tinkerballa, real name April Lou, is the Ranger of the Guild. She is very secretive and even keeps her real name and personal life a mystery. Tink, as she is called, was a pre-med student who switched majors to become a fashion designer. She is adopted, has two sisters and can be cold and manipulative when she has to be to get what she wants.

Mr. Wiggly, real name George Beane, is Clara's husband and a Hunter in the Guild.

The Axis of Anarchy: Fawkes is the leader. Venom, the only female member, is a substitute high school teacher. Bruiser, the Healer is a corrupt police officer. Kwan speaks only Korean and is accompanied by his female companion Nik, who translates for him. Valkyrie is the comedian of the group, whose jokes appear to be funny only to himself.

Cast: Felicia Day (Codex), Sandeep Parikh (Zaboo), Jeff Lewis (Vortex), Vincent Caso (Bladezz), Amy Okuda (Tinkerballa), Robin Thorsen (Clara), Brett Sheridan (Mr. Wiggly), Wil Wheaton (Fawkes), Viji Nathan (Zaboo's mother), Michele Boyd (Riley), Gaby Gantvoort (Gaby), Mike Rose (Valkyrie), Tara Caso (Dena), Alexander Yi (Kwan), Teal Sherer (Venom), Alexandra Hoover (Theodora), Toni Lee (Nik), J. Teddy Garces (Bruiser). **Credits:** *Producer:* Felicia Day, Kim Evey, Jane Selle Morgan. *Director:* Jane Selle Morgan, Sean Becker, Greg Benson, Christopher Preksta. *Writer:* Felicia Day, Jeff Lewis, Kim Evey. **Comment:** While the main characters are involved in gaming, the program also focuses on their quirks and mishaps as well as the situations they encounter as a consequence of their social ineptitude. While some jokes will not be understood by the non-gamer, the acting and production values are good and the program well worth watching.

Season 1 Episodes: *1.* Wake-Up Call. *2.* Zaboo'd. *3.* The Macro Problem. *4.* Cheesybeards. *5.* Rather Be Raiding. *6.* Total Wipe. *7.* Home Invasion. *8.* Tipping Point. *9.* Owning Bladezz. *10.* Boss Fight.

Season 2 Episodes: *1.* Link the Loot. *2.* Block'd. *3.* Quest Accepted. *4.* Heroic Encounter. *5.* Sacking Up. *6.* Blow Out. *7.* Panic Attack. *8.* Emergency! *9.* Grouping Up. *10.* Socializing Sucks. *11.* Collision Course. *12.* Fight!

Season 3 Episodes: *1.* Expansion Time. *2.* Anarchy! *3.* Player Down. *4.* Get It Back! *5.* Application'd. *6.* Newbtastic. *7.* Coping and Stuff. *8.* +10 to Bravery. *9.* Wit's End. *10.* The Return! *11.* Lan Off. *12.* Hero.

Season 4 Episodes: *1.* Epic Guilt. *2.* Strange Allies. *3.* Supportive'd. *4.* Moving On! *5.* Loot Envy. *6.* Weird Respawn. *7.* Awkward Birthday. *8.* Busted. *9.* Pirate Paddy. *10.* Festival of the Sea! *11.* Hostile Takeovers. *12.* Guild Hall.

Season 5 Episodes: *1.* Road Trip. *2.* Crash Pad. *3.* Megagame-o-ranacon. *4.* Ends and Begins. *5.* Focus Problems. *6.* Revolving Door. *7.* Downturn. *8.* Social Traumas. *9.* Invite Accepted. *10.* Strategy Timez. *11.* Costume Contest. *12.* Grande Finale.

Season 6 Episodes: *1.* Dream Questine. *2.* New Party Members. *3.* Makeshift Solutions. *4.* Raid Timez. *5.* Strange Frenemies. *6.* Into the Breach. *7.*

Occupy HQ. *8.* Dialogue Options. *9.* The Case of the Game Leak. *10.* Tripping Points. *11.* Raid HQ. *12.* End Game.

397 A Guy, a Girl and Their Monster. web serieschannel.com. 2013.

Jenn and Phil are a married couple with a most unusual house guest: a plush toy named Henry Monster. As a young girl Jenn had a best friend, a monster (whom she called Henry Monster) that lived under her bed. As she grew, Monster became less important and gradually disappeared from her life. But when Jenn becomes nostalgic and recalls her childhood, she decides to readopt Monster. Unfortunately for Phil, he too can see Monster and the three must now share the apartment. Stories follow Jenn and Phil—and their Monster (who has a craving for bacon) as they struggle to live together.

Cast: Jenn Daugherty (Jenn), Philip Hughes (Phil), Matt Zunich (Henry Monster). **Credits:** *Producer-Writer:* Jenn Daugherty. *Director:* Philip Hughes. **Comment:** A unique production with very good acting and, of course, Henry, an annoying (to Phil) likeable plush doll come to life.

Episodes: *1.* Bacon. *2.* Steve. *3.* Hollywood Monster. *4.* A Monster's Revenge. *5.* Henri Le Monstre.

398 Guy Eating Cereal. webserieschannel.com. 2010.

All Guy wants to do is enjoy his bowl of morning cereal (as the show's tag line says, "He came to America with a bowl, a spoon and a dream. This is his journey. What's not to get?"). However, enjoying that bowl of cereal is anything but easy when everything that can happen to interrupt his favorite time of day and his favorite activity happens. The program charts Guy's relentless efforts to just sit down and enjoy his cereal wherever he can (not oatmeal, though, "Who would want to watch a show called 'Guy Eating Oatmeal?'").

Cast: Tamir Kapelian, Renata Rose, Nicole Smith, Madilyn Smith, Alex Pappas, Jacqueline Rosenthal, Brigitte Buny. **Credits:** *Producer:* Tai Fauci. *Director:* Jack Monroe. **Comment:** Interesting concept that is as silly as it sounds. There is comedy and it comes from Guy's efforts to enjoy that daily bowl of cereal, even if he can't have it for breakfast.

Episodes: *1.* Cerealization. *2.* Playground. *3.* Evil Clones. *4.* Rejected Network Pilot. *5.* Karate. *6.* Bikini Dreams. *7.* Special Delivery. *8.* Oral Hygiene. *9.* Happy Hour. *10.* Laundry Day.

399 The Hairdos. funnyordie.com. 2010.

Jenn and Em, best friends and hopeful actresses, figure that in order to get noticed in Hollywood they have to be different and to achieve that they must be quirky. The program relates what happens as quirkiness does not always pay off and being such can cause more embarrassment than hopeful acting jobs.

Cast: Jennifer DeFilippo (Jenn), Emily Maya Mills (Em). **Credits:** *Producer-Writer:* Jennifer DeFilippo, Emily Maya Mills. *Director:* Matt Manson. **Comment:** Amusing program with good acting and production, likeable leads and an interesting take on the struggling actor syndrome.

Episodes: 8 untitled episodes, labeled "Episode 1" through "Episode 8."

400 Halls Web Series. webserieschannel.com. 2014.

A prestigious British university provides the setting for a look at a group of freshmen as they begin the next phase of their lives with the program focusing more on the out-of-class antics the students encounter as they become a part of college life. Marie is called "The Fake Tan Addict"; Mo, "The Pot Head"; Anya, "The One with Issues"; George, "The Jock," Lily, "The Virgin," Steve, "The Stud" and Alan, "The Old Fart."

Cast: Robyn Bennett (Marie), Amelia Birrell (Lily), Leonie Turner (Anya), Gavin Bruce (Alan), Ben Dunne (Steve), Jack Hopkins (George), Brad St. Ledger (Mo). **Credits:** *Producer:* Joanna Gordon. *Director:* David Allain. *Writer:* David Allain, Joanna Gordon, Caroline Lees. **Comment:** British produced program that is well acted and produced but suffers from a continual use of vulgar language (even American produced programs feel the filthier the language, the funnier the program is). If the language factor can be overlooked, a different twist on college freshmen can be seen.

Episodes: 7 untitled episodes, numbered as "Episode 1" through "Episode 7."

401 Handsome Police. blip.tv. 2012.

It is the present-day and Stacey Valentine and Johnny Babe are 1970s-styled detectives with the Los Angeles Police Department. They perform their duties well, investigating cases and capturing the bad guys, but they are totally different in that they not only love themselves, but women can't resist them and other men want to be like them—handsome and irresistible. But beneath the surface, Valentine and Babe are not the personification of good they project as their case investigations take on questionable (and illegal) aspects and the program charts those investigations (like, busting a drug dealer then testing the stash to make sure it is real; pulling over a gorgeous woman and figuring out a way to discover if she is a cold-blooded killer).

Cast: Nicholas S. Biron (Johnny Babe), Derek Weston (Stacey Valentine), Rachel Alig (Miss Leone), Andrew Bachelor (Mr. Santiago), Brian Zinda (Freddy). **Credits:** *Producer:* Nicholas S.

Biron, Matt Devino, Derek Weston. *Director:* Matt Devino. *Writer:* Nicholas S. Biron, Charlotte Derby, Matt Devino, Derek Weston. **Comment:** The program's concept reads much better than it plays. There is an over abundant amount of foul language and the paper-to-video transformation of the detectives begins well then just falls apart as they are just too unrealistic to be even taken comically. The idea is there but the extreme over-acting just spoils the intent

Episodes: *1.* The Case of the Cocaine Birthday. *2.* The Case of the Wonder Woman Drag Queen. *3.* The Case of Whiskey, Lemon Drops and Titties.

402 *Hanging with Wolfie.* funnyordie. com. 2013.

Wolfie, as he is called, is a very different young man. He is a wolfman but not the vicious type portrayed in feature films. He does have a hairy face, but no sharp fangs or claw-like fingernails. In fact he shares an apartment (with humans Mike and Doug), has a human girlfriend (Luna) and would like only one thing else—just live a normal life even if he is a bit different. Wolfie's efforts to deal with all the problems of being a wolfman and trying to live as a human are chronicled.

Cast: Andrew Burnell (Wolfie), Michael Stringer (Mike), Cory Stocks (Doug), Kristin Sanchez (Luna). **Credits:** *Director:* Andrew Burnell. *Writer:* Andrew Burnell, Michael Stringer.

Comment: There is no background information on how Wolfie became what he is, how he became roommates with Mike and Doug, how he found Luna or anything else regarding his past. The concept tries to humanize the wolfman idea that dates back to the Lon Chaney, Jr., feature film of the 1940s (*The Wolfman*) but it is hard to get those original concepts out of your mind when you see *Wolfie*.

Episodes: *1.* Pilot.

403 *Hansford.* webserieschannel.com. 2012.

Arnold Shaworski is a man on a mission: raise the funds he needs for a trip to Greenland to train snow dogs. As Arnold begins his quest, traveling from town-to-town doing odd jobs, he stumbles across the town of Hansford, a seemingly normal town that he soon finds is anything but. When he saves the life of a man (Dilby) from an attack by a wolfcat beast, he is hailed as the town hero and asked to stay and protect them from the strange phenomena that plague the bizarre and unusual town. The program follows Arnold as he struggles over a decision: remain in a town that has welcomed him as their hero or leave, after raising the money he needs, to pursue his dream job in Greenland.

Cast: Jim Scannapiece (Arnold Shaworski), Bill DeBiase (Laleen Dinkwher), Ed McGuire (Eye-Patch Man), Troy Pepper (Mayor Blendel Wigits).

Credits: *Producer:* Brad Riddell, Andrew Stulck. *Writer:* Brian Reilly, Andrew Stulck, Bryan Kastelan. **Comment:** A small, less populated and more isolated town would have been the ideal setting— not the busy city-like locale that is depicted. The illusion of strange things happening and no one can stop them until Arnold comes along to become a hero stretches the concept too far. As it stands now, the idea is there but the presentation is lacking.

Episodes: *1.* Welcome to Hansford. *2.* Will Work for Wonga. *3.* Deerly Departed. *4.* Horse Cents. *5.* Hey, Arnold!

404 *The Happy Mommy Hustle.* webseries channel.com. 2012.

Sophie is a stay-at-home housewife, married to Rob and the mother of twins (Cameron, diagnosed with ADHD, and Maddie). Lisa is a working mother with a tween daughter (Lexie). Sophie and Lisa are also sisters but as different as night and day. They each have their issues, know their limitations and each believes that whatever they do they are not doing it right. The sisters feel they are constantly being judged by others but neither sister realizes just how much each judges the other. The program follows Sophie and Lisa as they navigate a life that appears to get more complex with each passing moment.

Cast: Rebecca Louise Miller (Sophie), Tiffany Bartok (Lisa), Jenna Laurenzo (JJ, their younger sister), Jayce Bartok (Rob), Jessica Blank (Katie), Famecia Ward (Angela), Emma Lesser (Lexie). **Credits:** *Producer:* Debra Kirschner, Sherese Robinson, Roxana Petzold. *Writer-Director:* Debra Kirschner. **Comment:** The program originally aired as *Mom, Enough for Ya?!* and is very well written, acted and directed. The format is nothing new but the characterizations make the format work.

Episodes: *1.* M-Words. *2.* ADHD. *3.* Kids on Facebook. *4.* Take Our Daughters to Work Day. *5.* All the Good Mom Names Are Taken. *6,7.* Bad Seed.

405 *Harry Potter and the Ten Years Later.* furiousmolecules.com. 2012.

A parody of the stories by J.K. Rowlings. Harold "Harry" James Potter, orphaned when his parents are killed by the evil Dark Lord Voldemort, discovers on his eleventh birthday that he is a wizard and must attend the Hogwarts School of Witchcraft and Wizardry (where he befriends fellow wizards Hermione and Ron) to develop his abilities to battle the evils of dark wizards and witches. It was a battle royal (as depicted in the various *Harry Potter* feature films) but times have changed and Harry has apparently vanquished Lord Voldemort although he is still a member of the British government's Auror Division. It is ten years later when the series begins and Harry has married his sweetheart, Ginny. Hermione, a successful barrister, and Ron, an endlessly failing entrepreneur, have also married. The present is nothing like the past and Harry is bored with his job, just sitting at a desk and filing reports. Life changes for Harry when he is fired by the Ministry when they realize there is a lack of evil to battle and the Auror Division is no longer needed. Now, without a job for the first time, a wife who is eager to have children and no income, Harry feels his life has hit a downward spiral until he is contacted by Magical Enforcement, a private contracting company whose agents (Enforcers) capture evil witches and warlocks and erase their memories of the crimes they have committed. As Harry settles into his new job cleansing the minds of demons as a Wiper, the program chronicles all the drama that is also a part of Harry's life—from a wife who wants to start a family to Ron and Hermione's marital woes to dealing with Hermione's seducing him and Ginny's efforts to deal with the aftermath of her catching Harry and Hermione in bed together.

Cast: Matt DeNoto (Harry Potter), Dana DeRuyck (Hermione), Aryiel Hartman (Ginny), Marti Matulis (Stretch), Jonica Patella (Squat), Tucker Matthews (Ron), Kate O'Toole (Malfoy), Lamont Webb (Shacklebolt), Andrew Graves (Andrew). **Credits:** *Producer:* Matt DeNoto, Dana DeRuyck, Bob J. Quinn. *Writer-Director:* Matt DeNoto. **Comment:** For a low budget production, the program is very well done and acted and incorporates special effects that far surpass many other Internet series that attempt to use them. The actors are all American but speak with British accents and overall, it is one of the better *Harry Potter* spoofs and well worth watching even if you are not a true *Harry Potter* fan.

Episodes: 8 untitled episodes, numbered "Episode 1" through "Episode 8."

406 Hat Fulla Beer. fun nyordie.com. 2014.

Hat Fulla Beer is a local pub owned by a woman named Roxie. It appears to be a neighborhood bar where, like the TV series *Cheers*, "everybody knows your name." While not a copy of *Cheers* it is a look at the bar patrons, their troubles and how Roxie becomes a part of their lives.

Cast: Bobbie Breckenridge (Roxie), Kinga Phillips (Sydney), Kylie Contreary (Jamie), Todd Hansen (Spin), Michael Raif (Corey). **Credits:** *Producer:* Peter Giambalvo, Brenden Clark. *Director:* Lew Abramson. *Writer:* Lew Abramson, Peter Giambalvo. **Comment:** Shows about bars date back to 1940s radio with *Duffy's Tavern* and the concept hasn't changed since: a bar owner or bartender and how he or she becomes involved in the problems of his or her patrons. Although only a pilot has been made, it does

Harry Potter and the Ten Years Later. Series poster art (used by permission).

show potential for being a bit different than others that preceded it with good acting and production values.

Episodes: *1.* Pilot.

407 *Have You Met Miss Jones?* blip.tv. 2012–2013.

Angelina (man in drag) is a woman on a mission: find a husband to become a father figure for her gay teenage son Joe. Angelina is a somewhat unstable widower in her thirties and figures that the best way to catch a man is to join Miss Lolly's, a dating service. The program charts all the mishaps Angelina encounters—not only from off-the-wall dates, but from the seemingly unstable people that are also a part of her life: Connie, her foul-mouthed, married-to-the mob mother; Jake, the devout Atheist; Christian, the recovering heroine addict; Kelly, a deviant who believes Angelina may be a transgender; and Double D, the celebrity transsexual mafia hit man now a part of the FBI's Witness Protection Program.

Cast: James Di Giacomo (Angelina Jones), Patty McCormack (Connie Campolitarro), Dot-Marie Jones (Miss Lolly), James Kyson (Jake), Art LaFleur (Limo Lou), Ilia Yordanov (Joe Jones), Greg Bryan (Double D), Bunny Levine (Minnie LaValla), Ugo Bianchi (Father Gallo), Cleo Anthony (Kelly), Louis Trent (Christian Glam Rocker). **Credits:** *Producer-Writer:* James Di Giacomo, David D. Mattia. *Director:* James Di Giacomo, Tom Shell. **Comment:** From the catchy opening theme vocal to the closing scene in the last episode, the program flows smoothly from beginning to end. The acting and production values are very good and accepting the fact that a man plays Angelina and that devilish kid (Patty McCormack) from the 1956 feature film *The Bad Seed* has grown and now has a potty mouth should not deter anyone from enjoying something truly different when it comes to comedy programs.

Episodes: *1.* Versatile. *2.* Atheist. *3.* Cakes and Cookies. *4.* Area 51. *5.* Who's Troy Donahue? *6.* All About That Gay Stuff. *7.* Smoke and Vodka. *8.* You'll Get Yours. *9.* The Housekeeper. *10.* Drano "The Finale."

408 *He Don't Got Game.* youtube.com. 2014.

Orlando Florida is a young man desperate to find "female companionship in his daily life." Orlando, however, has no real idea or plan on how to accomplish that goal. Using his own strategy and that of advice from friends (even strangers he asks on the street) Orlando begins his quest with the program showcasing what can and does go wrong for Orlando.

Cast: Justin Shenkarow (Orlando Florida), Adam Wylie, Veronica Alicino, David Cowgill, Jason Davis, Lara Hickman, Irina Maleeva. **Credits:** *Pro-ducer-Writer:* Justin Shenkarow. *Director:* Jason Safir. **Comment:** A video blog type presentation is seen with Orlando relating what happens. Orlando mentions that he has degrees in computer science and engineering "but still hasn't done the dirty deed." The idea is not new but the presentation is well done.

Episodes: *1.* Hello World. *2.* Picking Up Chicks at the Gym. *3.* The Hot Tub. *4.* Orlando Is a Momma Bear. *5.* How to Pick Up a Cougar. *6.* The Biggest Mistakes Men Make in Bed with Women. *7.* Pick Up Lines That Don't Work!

409 *Heartbreak High U.S.A.* youtube.com. 2013.

Kate, Lindsay, Amber and Tanya are high school cheerleaders who believe they have the answer to everything. Everything that is, except love and that it can come in many forms. Because only a pilot film has thus far been released, it appears that episodes will focus on how a boy comes into each of the girl's lives and how they attempt to make a relationship work. In the pilot, it is Kate's turn as she falls for the new kid in school—Trevor, a teen who dresses as a clown (complete with makeup and big red nose).

Cast: Elizabeth Hirsch-Tauber (Kate), Kimberly Jo Howard (Lindsay), Ksenia Delaveri (Amber), Emily Clibourn (Tanya), Steve Brian (Trevor), Robert Hallak (Kate's father). **Credits:** *Producer:* Tracy Chitupatham. *Director:* Noah Weisel. *Writer:* Elizabeth Hirsch-Tauber. **Comment:** Strange to say the least. With Trevor attending school dressed as a clown (and not getting ridiculed by other students) is just odd to begin with. But his going out on a date with Kate in the same clown attire is even stranger (it seems that only Kate's father can see that there is something not right with Trevor). It is just impossible to tell where the series is headed based on what has been released.

Episodes: *1.* The New Guy.

410 *Heaven's Gate.* webserieschannel.com. 2013.

"Welcome to Heaven's Gate. It's real. You're not in a coma" is the sign posted above as people wait in line to meet with St. Peter to be judged whether or not they are worthy to enter Heaven. Episodes depict how St. Peter treats each of his subjects and how he must not anger "the boss" with the decisions he makes.

Voice Cast: Simon Goodway, Holly Powis, Sam Powis. **Credits:** *Writer:* Simon Goodway, Holly Powis. **Comment:** Animated program that is well executed with a slightly different twist on what happens at Heaven's Gate and how easily God can become angered when the right choices are not made.

Episodes: *1.* The God Collusion. *2.* Welcome to Paradise. *3.* Whiter Than White. *4.* Blind Faith. *5.* Regret Nothing. *6.* Contract Void.

411 Hei and Lo. heiandlo.com. 2014.

Heidi and Lola are friends living in Sydney, Australia. They are actresses seeking roles that will change the course of their lives. At the present, Heidi works a multitude of jobs between plays while Lola, who also works as a wedding singer and substitute teacher, has set her sights on moving to Los Angeles once her career gets off the ground. To relieve the drudgery of non-monumental parts, Heidi and Lola indulge in their favorite pastime—drinking and the program relates their mishaps as they navigate "the craziness of their chosen industry." Birdy is Heidi's long-time boyfriend.

Cast: Hayley Flowers (Heidi Rose), Lucy Kate McNabb (Lola Green), Jackson Davis (Birdy). Credits: *Producer-Writer-Director:* Hayley Flowers, Lucy Kate McNabb. Comment: Typical of Australian-produced series with very good acting and production values. It takes a minute or so to adjust to the accents, which is made a bit more difficult here due to poor room acoustics in several scenes.

Episodes: *1.* Reunion. *2.* Gount. *3.* Frogs. *4.* Commercials. *5.* Decisions. *Note:* Episode 2 refers to finding out what it would be like for Heidi and Lola to date male equivalents of themselves.

412 Held Up. webserieschannel.com. 2008.

Life is anything but enjoyable for a man named Ray. He is a bank teller and extremely bored. Life changes drastically not only for him but all concerned when two different groups of bank robbers, dressed in character disguises (like Batman and Robin) hit Ray's bank on the same day and at the same time. Ray feels that his life has suddenly changed for the better and the program follows the chaos that results as a spoof of the Stockholm Syndrome takes effect with robbers not sure what to do, hostages lives at stake and police and SWAT teams ready to strike at a moment's notice.

Cast: Jon Dore (Ray), Hason Sklar (Batman), Randy Sklar (Robin), Cyrus Farmer (Rocky 1), Kaitlin Olson (Rocky 2), Samm Levine (Hector Stiffman), Jessica Chaffin (Sharon), Eddie Pepitone (Martin), Aja Evans (Dancer), Maria Bamford (Rachel Gonzales), Sean Tillman (Phil), Chris Cox, Vincent Cerone (Police officers), Jennie Floyd, Bob Rickard, Lauren Christie, Jaime Soria, Lani Nishiyama, Jimmy Schulman, Christopher Raff (Hostages). Credits: *Producer:* Jason Sklar, Randy Sklar, Jamie Tarses, Jason Taragan, Inman Young. *Director:* Arthur Mulholland. *Writer:* Randy Sklar, Jason Sklar.

Comment: Programs dealing with hostage situations are not rare, but throw in confusion, panic, thieves who are anything but competent and a group of police officers just as dumbfounded as what to do, and the end result is something different with good acting and production values.

Episodes: *1.* Pilot. *2.* Food Order. *3.* A List Can Be Demanding. *4.* Mastermind Masturbator. *5.* Tweeter Dee Tweeter Dum. *6.* I Am the News. *7.* Ray Breaks Through. *8.* Negotiate This. *9.* Pocket Deuce. *10.* Bad Lady. *11.* Don't S**T Where U Eat. *12.* Get Your Phil. *13.* Ray vs. Rocky. *14.* Lordy Look Who's 40. *15.* The Final Countdown.

413 Hellbenders. youtube.com. 2012.

Zach and Chris are not only roommates but rather dense friends who always try to do the right thing—but what they think is right is never so. The animated program follows the mischief they create and their efforts to fix what they broke.

Cast: Zach Hadel (Zach), Chris O'Neil (Chris). Credits: *Writer-Creator:* Zach Hadel, Chris O'Neill. Comment: The animation is a bit off center as characters have large round heads with small eyes and mouths. Stories are also highly exaggerated as the situations Zach and Chris encounter can only happen in a cartoon.

Episodes: *1.* Ice Cream. *2.* Appaloosa. *3.* A Hellbenders Christmas.

414 Hello Cupid. youtube.com. 2013–2014.

On-line dating mishaps are explored as two young women, Whitney and Hayley, enter a world in which they have little experience as they search for the perfect man.

Cast: Ashley Blaine Featherson (Whitney), Hayley Marie Norman (Robyn), Brandon Scott (Cassius), Janora McDuffie (Milan). Credits: *Producer:* Dennis Dortch, J. Christopher Hamilton, Brian Ali Harding. *Director:* Dennis Dortch. *Writer:* Dennis Dortch, Numa Perrier, Lena Waithe, Ashley Blaine Featherson, Jozen Cummings. Comment: The program, which contains vulgar language, is simply a look at the friends as they find a perspective date and what happens with that date.

Season 1 Episodes: 10 untitled episodes, labeled "Episode 1" through "Episode 10."

Season 2 Episodes: Episode #2.1. *2.* Birthday Party. *3.* Cassius. *4.* Robyn. *5.* Whitney. *6.* The Date. *7.* Hello Roomie. *8.* Milan. *9.* Episode #2.9.

415 Hell's Kitty. hellskitty.com. 2011–2014.

Nick, single and living in Hollywood, is seeking to write that one screenplay that will make his career. He has a girlfriend (Lisa, an actress that runs a dog walking side business called Walking with the Dog Stars, LLC) and a best friend, Adam, who considers himself a professional slacker (although he does work on occasion as a movie extra). Angel is a seemingly normal and adorable cat that lives with Nick. She is happiest when she is around Nick and loves him but Angel was not always a cat; she is an evil girl from another lifetime that was cursed to endure life as a feline. Nick is unaware of Angel's secret but is concerned that Angel literally attacks the girls he becomes close to (Angel feels she is the only girl for Nick). Although Nick's love life is suffering due to Angel, he won't abandon her. Lisa hates Angel and wishes Nick would get rid of her; Adam feels Angel is possessed by the Devil and seeks to exorcise her. With a focus on Angel the program chronicles the chaos she causes as Nick, Lisa and Adam just try to live normal lives and somehow figure out a way to get along with the demon cat.

Cast: Nicholas Tana (Nick), Lorrie Rivers (Angel's voice), Adam Rucho (Adam), Lisa Younger (Lisa Ashen), Nina Hartley (Ms. Rommel), Michael Berryman (Det. Pluto), Jaime Cesarz (Jaime), Nina Kate (Dr. Laurie Strodes), Lee Meriwether (Grandma Kyle), Adrienne Barbeau (Mrs. Carrie), Ashley C. Williams (Lindsay), Barbara Nedeljakova (Natalya). **Credits:** *Producer:* Denise Acosta. *Writer-Director:* Nicholas Tana. **Comment:** In addition to a good story line and special effects, three stars from the past make guest appearances: Adrienne Barbeau (from *Maude*; episode 11), Lee Meriwether (from *Barnaby Jones*; episode 8, although the title refers to Lee's portrayal as Catwoman in the 1966 feature film based on the TV series *Batman*) and Nina Hartley (an adult film queen of the 1980s; episodes 4 and 5). While one could see that the idea of a possessed cat could have been borrowed from the ABC series *Sabrina the Teenage Witch* (wherein Sabrina's cat, Salem, was once a warlock who was turned into a cat for attempting to take over the world), Angel has her own take and is much more frightening than Salem ever was as Angel is a real cat and the voice over provides the sinister themes (while a real cat was used for Salem in non-talking scenes, a mechanical feline was used for his interactions with Sabrina [Melissa Joan Hart]). The acting is very good and for a low budget series, it is well produced and quite enjoyable.

Episodes: *1.* Cujo Cat. *2.* Nightmare Visitor. *3.* Pentagram Pet. *4.* Pussy Whipped. *5.* Tongue Tied. *6.* Heart Breaker. *7.* Hell Hound. *8.* Catwoman vs. Hell's Kitty. *9.* Blood Bath. *10.* Fingered. *11.* Phasmophobia. *12.* Burned. *13.* Valentine's Day Massacre. *14.* Cat's Eye.

416 *Henchpeople.* webserieschannel.com. 2012.

Buford, who insists he be called Ford, is a young man who believes his future is set. He has a girlfriend (Evelyn) and has just graduated from college with a degree in Early Edwardian Literature. His world changes drastically when Evelyn breaks up with him (believing that his life is not going anywhere) and he realizes that his degree is totally useless. All is not lost, however, when he sees a recruitment sign for a company called M.A.L.I.C.E. ("See the World.

Work Abroad. Change Your Life. Achieve Your Potential"). Believing that Mal-ice (as it is pronounced) is for him, he joins, not realizing at first that the company employs disposable people who do the dirty work as employees of super villains. Ford is sent to the forests of Latvia, the nefarious company's headquarters, where he is trained and placed in charge of a small group of recruits once supervised by a woman named Columbia (who is not all that happy that she has been replaced). The program follows Ford as he becomes one of the Henchpeople and is now stuck in an organization that he really despises but cannot leave due a very large contract that he signed without reading that literally states M.A.L.I.C.E. owns him.

Cast: Chris Schonfeldt (Ford), Fiona Revill (Columbia), David Quast (Liebowitz), Andrey Summers (Nikolai), Katherine Gauthies (Evelyn). **Credits:** *Producer-Writer-Director:* Andrey Summers. **Comment:** Intriguing idea coupled with good acting and production values. Like many other comedy programs, it is believed that adding foul language really makes a program funny. It doesn't and is simply not needed.

Episodes: *1.* Pilot. *2.* Mutual Respect. *3.* New Management. *4.* Mole People. *5.* Away Mission. *6.* Bottled Birthday. *7.* See the Wizard. *8.* Captive Audience.

417 *Henry: A Web Series.* henrywebseries.com. 2013–2014.

Henry is what one could call a poor soul. He is unemployed, broke and feels that his life is going nowhere. He is trying to figure out what to do next but only finds himself being involved in situations that present more problems than solutions. The program follows Henry as he tries to rise above his current situation and find his true calling in life (or as close as he can come and find some happiness).

Cast: Jaime Fernandez, Michael Diaz, Kumiko Konishi. **Credits:** *Producer:* Alain Alfaro, Juan Caceres, Cecilia Greco. *Writer-Director:* Alain Alfaro. **Comment:** A well done program that unfortunately has no cast and performer match-up.

Episodes: *1.* The Bicycle Thief. *2.* The Married Life. *3.* The List. *4.* Prescilla with an "E."

418 *Herbert: A Web Series.* herbertseries.com. 2014.

Caleb, Rex and Herbert are roommates living in Canada. Caleb and Rex are what you would consider normal while Herbert is a bit eccentric and holds his own theories about everything. To Caleb and Rex Herbert is just plain odd (knows nothing about anything) and their efforts to "educate" him as they see fit (make him see life as it really is) is the focal point of stories.

Cast: Stephen Vani (Herbert), Mark Matechuk

(Caleb), Evan Rissi (Rex). **Credits:** *Producer:* Scott McIntyre. *Writer-Director:* Evan Rissi. **Comment:** Herbert is a queer duck, like someone who just fell off the turnip truck and wandered into the lives of Caleb and Rex. The idea is good and the program flows smoothly from episode to episode as Caleb and Rex attempt to show Herbert an unbiased view of everything that is not familiar to him.

Episodes: *1.* The Chase. *2.* The Girl. *3.* Talking to Girls. *4.* The Greatest Fighting Techniques of All Time. *5.* The Bet.

419 *Here All Week.* vimeo.com. 2013–2014.

The Last Laugh is a U.K. comedy club that presents a different show each night featuring stand-up comedians. The club is managed by Greg with Jenny as its emcee. Senthil is its tech wizard; Sophia, the new hire; Amy, a waitress; Walt is Greg's assistant; and Josh, a bartender who yearns to perform on stage. The program is a behind-the-scenes look at a comedy club with most of the drama centered around Greg (a man with little vision as to how to run a club); Senthil, a man perceived as racist (perhaps due to his Indian heritage) and struggling to make shows happen with always failing equipment; and Jenny, who yearns to become the host of her own TV talk show but can't convince Greg to let her use the club to make her pilot film.

Cast: Hari Sriskantha (Senthil), Rachel Timney (Jenny), James Stewart (Greg), Tom Pseudonym (Walt), Clarisse Loughrey (Amy), Richard Hanrahan (Josh), Olivia McNulty (Sophia). **Credits:** *Producer-Writer:* Hari Sriskantha. **Comment:** Interesting look behind the scenes of a comedy club. The British-produced program is a bit talkative at times, but does present some stand-up routines with generally good acting and production values.

Episodes: 6 untitled episodes, labeled "Episode 1" through "Episode 6."

420 *Hero Envy.* vimeo.com. 2005–2009.

Four off-the-wall friends (J.D., Orson, Wally and Dekker) and how they deal with the situations they encounter as they just go about their daily activities. J.D. acts like a three-year-old but is actually 30 and lives for babes, beer and cartoons. He is also very irresponsible and has little respect for the law (or even people). Dekker, a clerk at the local comic book store (Fly on the Wall Comics), is not as out-going as his friends and is considered a loner. He loves "Blood, guts and horror" and keeps abreast of all the latest "Internet geek news." He also has an unusual hobby: e-mailing nasty letters to the studios who remake his favorite horror movies. Wally is the level-headed considerate friend who looks for the good in everybody.

Cast: John Cimino (J.D. Fields), Keith Gleason (Dekker), Mike Hopta (Wally North), Kurt Loether (Orson H. Cochrane). **Comment:** Ridiculous characters, foul language and not very convincing acting. Despite the ludicrous production a spin off was created called *Hero Envy: The Swass Adventures* that aired in 2009. Here, Dekker's further adventures were chronicled but in an alternate universe where he now lives with a man known only as the Toy Dealer. His efforts to return to his own time while dealing with his current situation were the focus of the program.

Episodes: *1.* Saturday Morning. *2.* J.D. is a Dick. *3.* Cat Woman Sucked. *4.* Internet Fad. *5.* Science Fiction. *6.* Geek Games. *7.* Cartoonathon. *8.* Hero Envy: Live. *9.* Contest of Champions. *10.* Orson Comes Home. *11.* Who Is Cochrane? *12.* Enter: El Diablo! *13,14.* Realistically Speaking. *15.* Smoked. *16.* Never Meet Your Heroes Penciller. *17.* Astro Train Spotting. *18.* Requiem for an Autobot. *19.* It Started on Yancy Street. *20.* Interlude. *21.* Hero oreH (Hero backwards). *22.* The Game Is Afoot. *23.* The Man Who Knew Not Much.

421 *Heroes of the North.* heroesofthenorth.com. 2009.

In an alternate universe to the Earth there exists a legion of super heroes that protect Canada. It is led by The Canadian and he is assisted by Fleur-de-Lys, 8 Ball, Nordik, Black Terror and The Canadian Shield. The program charts their adventures as they battle Canada's most evil super villains (see "Villains" below).

Heroes: Christopher Adam Newman, alias The Canadian, is a descendant of Canada's first super hero The Canadian Shield (Charles Alfred Newman). He was raised from his childhood to become a killer and is now the field leader of the Eastern Division of the Canada Organization.

Natalie De Verscheres, known as Fleur-de-Lys, was a research scientist who became a super hero after developing a high tech weapon. She often takes chances and puts her life in jeopardy.

Tony Falcon, alias 8 Ball (for his wizardry at the game of pool) was recruited from prison for his skills after he was arrested for seeking justice (killing the thugs who attacked and killed his girlfriend, Bronwyn).

Manon Desches, called Nordik is a girl with an inner strength she acquired from a Shaman. She was recruited from the Canadian Arctic to Montreal after she risked her life to apprehend Russian soldiers trespassing in her territory.

Robert "Bob" Benton, alias The Black Terror, has connections to the underworld and is struggling to break his addiction to drugs.

Villains: Dr. Joseph Mengele (the evil commander of Medusa) is a World War II Nazi scientist who found a way to revive the dead as Zombots.

Madame Doom, real name Dominique Ophelle

Martin, was a 1990s beauty queen whose face was partially disfigured when acid was thrown at her by a feminist who disagreed with her beliefs. She now covers the scars with a partial mask.

Diana Adams was a socialite who, to find excitement in her dull life, became the vigilante Masquerade; she now works for Madame Doom.

Hornet, real name Hortense Netter, is the Executive Vice President of Medusa Industries and the intelligence officer to the Medusa Commander.

Crimson is a gorgeous hired assassin who often works for Medusa.

Cast: Larry Vinette (The Canadian), Edith Labelle (Fleur-de-Lys), Vanessa Blouin (Nordik), Anderson Bradshaw (8 Ball), John Fallon (Black Terror), Constantine Kourtidis (Medusa Commander), Bianca Beauchamp (Crimson), Anne-Marie Losique (Madame Doom), Pia Metni (Masquerade), Yann Brouillette (Alpha Q), Michel Brouillette (Canadian Shield), Marie-Claude Bourbonnais (Hornet). **Credits:** *Producer-Director:* Christian Viel. *Writer-Director:* Tann Brouillette, Michel Brouillette. **Comment:** Canadian produced program with gorgeous heroines coupled with gorgeous villains that adds to the enjoyment of a well produced super hero saga. The costumes, especially for the females, are striking and special effects, though limited are well done.

Episodes: *1.* The Canadian: Origins. *2.* Fleur-de-Lys: Origins. *3.* 8 Ball: Origins. *4.* Nordik: Origins. *5.* Black Terror: Origins. *6.* Canadian Shield: Origins. *7.* Kiss of Death. *8.* Brothers-in-Arms. *9.* Secret Lives. *10.* Cold Turkey. *11.* All That Masquerade. *12.* Crimson. *13.* Fashion Statement. *14.* Enter the Zombots. *15.* Wardrobe Malfunction. *16.* Operation Rock and Roll. *17.* Past and Present. *18.* Brave New World. *19.* Falling Masks. *20.* Hornet's Nest.

422 Heroic Daze. webserieschannel.com. 2012.

Nottywood is a city in turmoil. Criminals rule, citizens live in fear and its corrupt government does nothing to stop it. Two rather lame-brained stepbrothers, Bryan and Matthew decide to do something about it. Having dreamed of becoming superheroes, Bryan dons the guise of The Redd Robbyn and Matthew becomes his sidekick, Mr. Nyce Guy. The villains believe they have nothing to fear but Bryan and Matthew think differently and wage a war against the city's nefarious bad guys—Big Boss and Me-No Black—as the JustUs League. Episodes chart their rather inept efforts to bring an end to crime in Nottywood.

The Redd Robbyn and Mr. Nyce Guy are two of 48 adopted step brothers (their rich parents, Donny and Marie, adopted one child from every state). Bryan and Matthew became close due to their interest in comic books. They also asserted themselves as the law enforcers of the family thus alienating them from their other siblings. Having only each other for companionship, they soon began to fantasize about becoming superheroes. The Redd Robbyn has styled himself after heroes such as Batman, Superman and Spider-Man while Mr. Nyce Guy has chosen heroes who looked like him (like Green Lantern, Black Panther and Shadow Hawk).

Cast: Bryan Lugo (The Redd Robbyn), Matthew McKinley (Mr. Nyce Guy), Harold Stancle (Me-No Black), Neil Brown, Jr. (Oliver), Joshua D. Lewis (Repo), Derrick White (Big Boss), Marlon Bivens (Bishop). **Credits:** *Producer:* Bryan Lugo, Anthony Soriano, Matthew McKinley. *Director:* Bryan Lugo. *Writer:* Harold Stancle, Matthew McKinley. **Comment:** An African-American themed program that needlessly incorporates foul language and violence. The acting and production values are somewhat amateurish and the costumes rather pale in comparison to other such superhero series. The program tries to be street smart but fails when reality clashes with hero mythology. Adding a sexy female superhero or villain would have helped to keep viewer attention.

Episodes: *1,2.* Rise of Me-No Black. *3.* You Repo What You Sow. *4.* The Glow.

423 Hey Girl. viralfilmvideo.com. 2013.

Julie and Becka are best friends living in Wisconsin. When Julie feels she needs to re-invent her life, she moves to Chicago but doesn't break ties with Becka. Soon Julie learns that re-inventing herself is not as easy as she thought and her friendship with Becka (via telephone) helps her navigate life as she holds dear the advice Becka gives her. As the weeks pass and Julie finally begins to adjust to her new life (and lecherous landlord, Mr. Willis), she gets a shock when Becka and her boyfriend, Jason, decide to relocate to Chicago to escape their boring lives. With no place to stay they move into Julie's cramped apartment and while it's not Chrissy, Janet and Jack from the TV series *Three's Company* it's a similar situation with the program focusing on three friends and how they each try to find a new life for themselves.

Cast: Alli Urbanik (Julie), Deneen Melody (Becka), Kevin Wunder (Jason), Danny Glenn (Mr. Willis). **Credits:** *Producer:* Michael Forsythe, David J. Miller. *Writer-Director:* David J. Miller. **Comment:** Pleasant program that shows how maintaining a friendship, even a long distance one, can be beneficial. Although the first episode basically shows Julie preparing for a date (with several lingerie shots) it picks up from the second episode on.

Season 1 Episodes: *1.* Sexting. *2.* Propositioned. *3.* Orgasmic. *4.* Another Chance. *5.* Walk of Shame. *6.* Another Satisfied Customer. *7.* Rent Check. *8.* Some People Never Die.

Season 2 Episodes: *9.* I Want Candy. *10.* Breast Exam. *11.* One Broke Girl. *12.* Horsing Around. *13.* Lobster Town. *14.* Sexercise. *15.* Country Boys and Dixie Chicks. *16.* Sunbathing Sleepover.

Hey Girl. Series poster art (used by permission).

424 Hey Guy! webserieschannel.com. 2011.

Guy and Guy (as they call themselves) are middle-aged men who meet often to bicker about everything. Guy, without a shirt, is the one whose negative attitude about everything has Guy (with the shirt) always finding fault with what (shirtless) Guy has to say. With the premise established the program relates the conversation that ensues as a topic is brought up and Guy and Guy present their points of view.

Cast: David C. Roberson (Guy; shirtless), Jeffery Hunt (Guy). **Credits:** *Producer-Writer:* David C. Robertson, Jeffrey Hunt. **Comment:** While the premise doesn't sound like something that constitutes a series, it does have its own unique sense of charm and does work—even if Guy is shirtless through all the episodes and the action is basically the Guys talking.

Episodes, 1–20: *1.* Chemical Spill. *2.* Female. *3.* In the Dictionary. *4.* An Honest Living. *5.* Rabbit's Foot. *6.* Piano Bars. *7.* $0.35 Cigarettes. *8.* Hairballs and Feathers. *9.* Word of the Day. *10.* Revolver. *11.* Three Degrees. *12.* Eight Babies. *13.* Brain Rot. *14.* Organ Thieves. *15.* Pop Quiz. *16.* The Darkest Irishman. *17.* Bye Guy. *18.* The Lucky Ones. *19.* Gold Diggers. *20.* Job Opening.

Episodes, 21–40: *21.* Yale Midgets. *22.* Diff'rent Strokes. *23.* Gamma Globulin. *24.* Syphilis Is a Whore. *25.* Geography. *26.* Travel Companion. *27.* Manacle! *28.* Piano Man. *29.* Brain Rest. *30.* The Definition of Fumble. *31.* The Business. *32.* Drinkin' a Lot of Scotch. *33.* Clown Shoes and Immigrants. *34.* A Fecal Matter Between Friends. *35.* Michael Jackson Was Albino. *36.* The Weather Outside Is Frightful. *37.* A Way with Words. *38.* So You Think You Can Dance. *39.* Fat Cat. *40.* Puppy Chow.

Episodes, 41–60: *41.* Cocaine. *42.* Word of the Day, Part 2. *43.* Occupy. *44.* Under the Weather. *45.* Indian Toilet Paper. *46.* Nam. *47.* Humping Jack Frost. *48.* Racketeering. *49.* Acid Trip. *50.* Mating and Money. *51.* The Light At the End of the Tunnel. *52.* Pimp. *53.* Burning One. *54:* Diaper Days. *55.* Football Players. *56.* The Borrower Is Slave to the Lender. *57.* Retirement Plan. *58.* Acute Rental Failure. *59.* It's Your House. *60.* What's Shakin', Backin.

Episodes, 61–80: *61.* The Etiquette of Playing with Your Food. *62.* How to Date Despite House Guests. *63.* A Suspicion Arises. *64.* Suspicion Becomes Accusation. *65.* A Confession Confided. *66.* You Say At Your House I Say in Your House. *67.* Clarity Is the Issue. *68.* Foreign Matter in Food. *69.* Anatomically Incorrect Elephants. *70.* Are You Drinkin' Again? *71:* What's on the Story Board? *72.* A Man of Many Faces. *73.* Hypo-gamma-glob-ulinemia. *74.* Little Punk Tablets. *75.* Chimichanga of Choice. *76.* People in the Walls. *77.* Gibberish. *78.* How to Be a Leisurely Gentleman. *79.* People Like You and Me. *80.* A Bucket of Bottom Feeders.

425 Hi, This Is Me, John. webserieschannel.com. 2012.

John is a young man who lives with two friends, Vlad and Billy Bob. While they are as different as night and day, they each have one thing in common: They are entrepreneurs and looking for that million dollar idea. The problem: they are lazy and completely lack skills of any kind. The program is set in their apartment and relates the events that befall each of the characters as they wait (and wait) for that million dollar idea.

Cast: Ralph Baumann (John Branon/Billy Bob MacDonald/Vlad Beletsky). **Credits:** *Producer-Writer-Director:* Ralph Baumann. **Comment:** Ralph Baumann plays all three roles in a convincing production that almost makes you believe there are three different actors.

Episodes: *1.* Procrastination vs. Entrepreneur. *2.* First Job Interview with Vlad. *3.* The Dream Team. *4.* Cleaning vs. Hamster. *5.* The Types of Pole Players.

426 *High Maintenance.* vimeo.com. 2012–2015.

His name is not revealed but his job is: delivery man for stressed out people living in Brooklyn, New York, who need their daily "medication" (drugs). The program encompasses the format of an anthology wherein the delivery man is like a catalyst that sets things in motion with the consequences being what happens to the people who use his product (depicted in a comical vein).

Cast: Ben Sinclair (The Guy). **Credits:** *Producer-Writer:* Katja Blichfeld, Ben Sinclair. *Director:* Sarah-Violet Bliss, Thomas DiNapoli, Katja Blichfeld, Ben Sinclair. **Comment:** The program is similar to the 1950s TV series *The Millionaire.* The Guy is like Michael Anthony (Marvin Miller) who delivered a check for $1 million and what happened to the recipient of the check was seen. Here, what happens to the recipient of the drugs is profiled with The Guy (like Michael Anthony) taking a back seat. The acting and production values are good and *High Maintenance* is a worthwhile look for something different.

Season 1 Episodes: *1.* Stevie. *2* Heidi. *3.* Jamie.
Season 2 Episodes: *1.* Olivia. *2.* Helen. *3.* Trixie. *4.* Dinah.
Season 3 Episodes: *1.* Jonathan. *2.* Elijah. *3.* Brad Pitts.
Season 4 Episodes: *1.* Qasim. *2.* Matilda. *3.* Rachel.
Season 5 Episodes: *1.* Geiger. *2.* Genghis. *3.* Ruth.

427 *Highlighters.* highlightersseries.com. 2013.

Jeremy, a publishing company employee, is the embodiment of Murphy's Law (what can go wrong will go wrong). He tolerates his job but is annoyed by the fact that he cannot always use yellow highlighters as his boss prefers that employees use various colors. The program relates all the chaos that ensues as Jeremy simply tries to lead a normal life, but finds that no matter what he does, nothing every goes right for him.

Cast: Danny Ward (Jeremy), Patrick Saxe (Nick), Anna Brodd (Jennifer), Emmeli J. Stjärnfeldt (Simone), Sara Burnett (Juliette), Jeff Glickman (The Super). **Credits:** *Producer-Writer-Director:* Danny Ward. **Comment:** With the only a pilot produced (that runs 29 minutes and 46 seconds) it drags in places and is just too long for an Internet series. Attention is easily lost and it feels like scenes were dragged out to make the presentation longer (like Jeremy constantly complaining about the color of highlighters).

Episodes: *1.* Highlighters Pilot.

428 *Hipsterhood.* blip.tv. 2012.

Silver Lake is a California community where two people, called Hipster Girl and Hipster Guy live. They are unknown to each other but wherever they go they always run into each other. Both appear to be attracted to the other, but neither one has the courage to approach the other and break the actual meeting ice. The program chronicles their continual accidental meetings with the situations that develop as they admire each other from afar.

Cast: Elizabeth Ferraris (Hipster Girl), Kit Williamson (Hipster Guy). **Credits:** *Producer-Writer-Director:* Shilpi Roy. **Comment:** Charming, well acted and produced program. A majority of the dialogue appears in the form of voice-over thoughts as the hipsters continually encounter each other. For something that is amusing and different, *Hipsterhood* fills the bill perfectly.

Season 1 Episodes: *1.* Hipsters Buy Cereal in Silver Lake. *2.* 2 Hipsters, 1 Street Corner and a Hooker in Silver Lake. *3.* Hipsters Jogging in Silver Lake Run Into Each Other. *4.* Hipster Catastrophe at Silver Lake Coffee Company on Glendale Blvd. *5.* Hipsters Go to the Dry Cleaners. *6.* Hipster Girl Spots Hipster Guy At the Awesome 99 Cent Store. *7.* Part 2 At the 99 Cent Store. *8.* Shopping At Hipster Boutique Myrtle on Sunset Blvd. *9.* Hipster Dog's Birthday Party in Silver Lake.

Season 2 Episodes: *1.* Hipsters with Hangovers. *2.* Hipster Run-in At the Pharmacy. *3.* Hipster Date. *4.* Hipster Texting. *5.* Sometimes a Hipster Just Needs a Drink. *6.* Flashbacks! Hipster Ping Pong. *7.* Hipsters Jogging Again. *8.* The 99 Cent Store Revisited. *9.* Hipster Mecca: The Silver Lake Farmer's Market. *10.* Hipsters in Nature.

429 *His and Hers.* youtube.com. 2014.

It was at a Renaissance Fair that two people (Matt and Maggie) met and fell in, for lack of a better term, instant like. They dated, moved into together and now share an apartment where they try to get along together, but each has a view and opinion on just about everything. The program relates the clashes that arise when Matt and Maggie simply try to live together but need to explore all the issues that arise as they are now a couple (for example, "Where do I put my stuff?," "Can I have friends over?" and "Are you going to pay for that?").

Cast: David Scott (Matt), Kate Bowen (Maggie), Rebecca Zamolo (Beth), Matt Cordova (Brian), Drew Seeley (Jason), J. Kristopher (Phil). **Credits:** *Producer-Writer:* Kate Bowen, David Scott, Ken Scheffler. *Director:* Ken Scheffler. **Comment:** Surprisingly well done program as such couple concepts do not always work. The his and her conflicts are also interesting and very well presented.

Episodes: *1.* Matt and Maggie Pilot. *2.* A Little Bit More. *3.* Clear Thinking. *4.* We Met at the Ren Faire. *5.* All Your Friends Are Men. *6.* Bathroom Wars.

430 Hits. hitstheseries.com. 2014.

Is Pinky Sweeps the innocent looking chimney sweeping company that it appears or is it something more sinister? It is the latter at it is actually a front for an exterminating company that does away with those people you do not want in your life for a hefty price. Pinky is the man who runs the assassination business and his hit men are Beth, a sassy young woman who prefers the term "hit people" and is determined to prove that she is as good as any man when it comes to taking out a client. Rocco is socially awkward and feels more comfortable not using his gun to kill a client by shooting him (the gun's handle will do the job just as well and leave little evidence). The A, as he is called, is ruthless and selfish and is only in the business for the money he can make. Billy V, as he is known, is offensive, opinionated and gets the job done no matter what it takes. The program charts the lives of a group of assassins as they not only do their job but clash with one another over anything and everything.

Cast: Bill Van Tholen (Billy V), Johnny Perkins (Rocco), Joshua Aldis (The "A"), Jules Reid (Beth), Jonathan Peletis (Pinky). **Credits:** *Producer-Director:* Johnny Perkins. *Writer:* Joshua Aldis. **Comment:** There is the assignment, the planning and the actual hit. But there is also foul language and just a bit too much talking about how a hit should be handled. Other than that, the acting and production is good.

Episodes: *1.* The Circle of Life. *2.* A Night Wasted. *3.* Workplace Variety. *4.* Billy V, the A and the Bethany Hallows. *5.* Hazed and Confused. *6.* The Ninja. *7.* Don't Forget to Brush. *8.* Arbitration in the Ashes. *9.* Between a Rocco and a Hard Place. *10.* Trouble.

431 HOA Police. blip.tv. 2012.

Officers Steve and Jeff are men hired by a Home Owners Association to patrol and protect their suburban Arizona housing complex. They are dedicated but the power they possess has gone to their heads

and they are mostly feared by the complex's residents. As Steve and Jeff patrol, they take everything too literally and try to bust residents for the most inconsequential actions. The HOA doesn't seem to mind but the residents do and the program follows two swell-headed HOA code enforcement officers as they do what they believe it takes to keep their complex safe and crime free—even if it means busting a man for not carrying his HOA lease with him at all times or arresting a little girl for standing too close to the complex's outdoor swimming pool.

Cast: Jeff Breuer (Officer Jeff), Steve Mastin (Officer Steve), Michelle Merriman, Jeff Watson, Esteban Valverde, Sam Mastin. **Credits:** *Producer:* Steve Mastin, Jeffrey J. Watson. *Director:* Jeff Breuer. *Writer:* Jeff Breuer, Steve Mastin. **Comment:** An original idea depicting HOA officers and well done with the over dedication to work by Jeff and Steve making the whole program work. The acting is also meant to be a bit stiff as Jeff and Steve are just that—straight-laced "cops" too dedicated to work and nothing else.

Episodes: *1.* Pilot. *2.* NASCAR Isn't America. *3.* Recycling Justice. *4.* Suburban Gangland. *5.* Soliciting B!$#@$. *6,7.* Weed Bust, Parts 1–2. *8.* The Mexican Passat. *9.* In the Closet. *10.* Smoking Hot. *11.* Madam President. *12.* Doggy DNA. *13.* Doggy DNA Number Two. *14.* Extra Judicial Prisoners and Enhanced Torture Techniques. *15.* Tea Time. *16.* Halloween Special. *17.* Border Crossing. *18.* Stay Classy Ma'am. *19.* Smooth Criminal Behavior. *20.* The Triangle. *21.* Smorgasbord. *22.* Propaganda. *23.* Thanksgiving Special. *24.* Preemptive Christmas. *25.* Indecent Proposal. *26.* Money for Deceptions. *27.* The Board. *28.* Mom's Red Shirt. *29.* Dearly Departed. *30.* Christmas Special. *31.* HOA Habeas Corpus. *32.* Grand Day for a White Trash Wedding.

432 Hollywood Girl. funnyordie.com. 2010.

Quinn Monroe is a young woman with a big dream: acquire success as an actress and her name on the Hollywood Walk of Fame. Until that time comes, Quinn auditions for roles by day and works as a waitress by night. Quinn is talented but a dark cloud appears to hover over her as she encounters numerous obstacles that always put a damper on and often cost her acting roles. Quinn, however, is never defeated and the program charts her continual efforts to make her mark on Hollywood—no matter how tired, broke and frustrated she becomes until that time happens.

Cast: Courtney Zito (Quinn Monroe), Shawn Ashley (Lauren Taylor), Clarissa River Harlow (Callis Davis), Kelsey Scott (Madison Carroll), Robert Grant (Michael Grant), Johnny Wactor (Shane Hudson), Caitlin Biship (Sarah), Danielle Bisutti (Pascha Maneer), Jenni Cardone (Betthany). **Credits:** *Producer:* Courtney Zito, Taryn Teigue, Melissa Teigue, Jon Santos. *Director:* Courtney Zito. *Writer:*

Courtney Zito, Kelsey Scott, Sean Beatty, Macklen Makhloghi. **Comment:** Courtney Zito is delightful as Quinn and, although such projects have been done before, *Hollywood Girl* manages to put its own spin on the topic.

Season 1 Episodes: *1.* Pilot. *2.* Prophyl-what? *3.* Say a Little Prayer. *4.* Code Red Carpet. *5.* Limp of Shame.

Season 2 Episodes: *1.* Curves Ahead. *2.* Boot Camp Bitch. *3.* The Curvy Girl Revolution. *4.* Minus a Plus One. *5.* Scary-Go-Round.

433 *Home Schooled.* watchhomeschooled. com. 2011.

Mickey is a teenager heading down the wrong path. He hates high school and his delinquent ways appear to be guiding his life until he gets expelled (caught using drugs) and finds that he must be home schooled—a situation that becomes his personal nightmare when he discovers that everything he despised about a regular high school is front and center in his own home—from a queen bee step-sister (Audrey), a nerdy brother (Abel) and even a strict teacher (his mother, a former kindergarten teacher for 20 years). The program follows Mickey as he attempts to deal with a situation that he can't believe is occurring in his own home.

Mickey is 17 years old and has little ambition (as his main things are hanging out, smoking pot and playing Xbox). He does have dreams of becoming a video game designer and constantly blames the world for his problems.

Audrey is a promising tennis star and is being home schooled so she can devote time to her career. She is a master at manipulating boys and flaunts her body and promiscuousness in front of Mickey to have fun (her sick way of torturing him) as she really doesn't like him.

Abel, a 10-year-old genius, has never attended a regular school and has been home schooled all his life. He is a master at math, can play the guitar and is currently preparing to take his SAT tests.

Jeannie is Mickey and Abel's mother and, although she previously taught only kindergarten, she teaches high school subjects through illustrated text books. Although she is now a part of a blended family and should treat all her children equally, she adores Audrey and Abel but is not too fond of Mickey. She considers herself a "selfless, hardworking mom" and is determined to turn Mickey's life around.

Ed, Jeannie's much older husband, is the stern "principal" of the house and also saddened by Mickey's attitude and lack of ambition. He considers him a screw-up and, despite his age, taunts Mickey with the fact he is having sex with his mother.

Juan is the family's gardener, an ex-addict who prides himself as being the best outdoor landscaper he can possibly be. He considers the backyard "his

turf" and has littered it with his less-than desirable artwork.

Dulce is the family's housekeeper, a woman who is somewhat mysterious, loves hardcore punk music and is the apple of Mickey's eye (he has a secret crush on her and would rather not let that fact be known). She is Juan's second cousin and appears to hate the family she works for.

Cast: Franklin Killian (Mickey), Katy Foley (Audrey), Jennifer Christopher (Jeannie), Jacob Bertrand (Abel), Amanda Westlake (Dulce), Eric Chavaria (Juan). Jack Gilroy (Ed). **Credits:** *Producer:* Matthew Morgenthaler, Maura Kelly, Kellye Carnahan. *Writer-Director:* Matthew Morgenthaler. **Comment:** With the exception of the WB TV series *The O'Keefe's* which dealt with a home schooled family, there have not been any other series totally devoted to home schooling and *Home Schooled* hits the jackpot for being a delightful twist on high school-themed programs. While the Mickey character reads like a degenerate he is not when seen. He appears as a regular guy just dealt a bad blow by fate (as he says about his present situation, "I thought I was done with high school but high school followed me home"). His thoughts about what is happening to him are also wisely presented as Mickey directs those thoughts to the audience.

Episodes: *1.* Home School Sucks. *2.* The Bully. *3.* Ready, Willing and Abel. *4.* So Wrong But So Right. *5.* Mickey vs. Ed vs. the SAT. *6.* The Missing Stash.

434 *Home Work.* webserieschannel.com. 2012.

Angela and Todd, a young couple laid off from their former professions believe they have found a solution to their financial woes by beginning a home shopping network from their small apartment. With the site launched and Angela and Todd now being together all the time, their efforts to not only contend with each other but the customers they must deal with becomes the focal point of stories (beginning with their first sale item—X-rated garden gnomes).

Cast: Sarah Burkhardt (Angela Pfeiffer), Drew Bell (Todd Pfeiffer), Gil Christner (Vic), Helen Wilson (Roz). **Credits:** *Producer:* Andrea Kikot. *Director:* Boris Damast. *Writer:* Boris Damast, Mike Bednar. **Comment:** Delightful program with a good story line, acting and production values. Angela and Todd have an unusual home shopping site wherein through the Internet they can see and communicate with their customers. Vic is Todd's friend, a guy with numerous connections who can apparently get them merchandise (although not always top rate) and Roz is Angela's mother, who becomes an active part of their new venture.

Episodes: *1.* Bear Ass Gnomes. *2.* Sensuality Wear. *3.* Candles in the Wind.

435 Home Wrecker Houseboy. youtube. com. 2007.

The world has changed to a point where bad things happen to good people and villains thrive on the rewards of their treachery. Being good is a strike against you and such people find that becoming evil is the only way to survive. Spoofing those who are good and achieve their wealth through legitimate means, the program incorporates a gay theme and charts the lives of several less-than-desirable bad people: Morgan, "a snake" who lies, cheats and destroys anyone who gets in his way of getting what he wants; Steve, a good apple "with a rotten past" who betrayed his true love to save his own hide; Derek, the town's most prestigious businessman who is now "the village chum"; and Benny, the man who had the perfect life until he turned into a junkie.

Cast: Cameron Zeidler (Benny), Jeremy Lucas (Steve), James Masotto (Derek), Tyler Kamerman (Morgan). **Credits:** *Producer:* Tim Dumas, Kevin Richey. *Writer-Director:* David LeBarron. **Comment:** Very well acted and produced but geared totally to a gay male audience. Strong sexual situations prevail throughout the series and, for reasons that are known only to the producer, episodes do not contain cast or credit information. A special cast video exists that gives such information "in response to viewer requests to see the cast." Although the producer claims this video is really not to his liking (production) it is well done.

Episodes: 50 untitled episodes, labeled "HH 1" through "HH 50."

436 Homo Thugs. youtube.com. 2012.

They can say they are not gay but the actions of Big Thug and his sidekick, Little Thug prove them otherwise. Big and Little are African-American homophobic, closeted gangsters who will not admit they are gay (even though they are turned on by men of any color). They talk about how they are not gay, but can't refute the fact that they even dream about men. Stories follow Big and Little as they go about their daily lives commenting on this and that but their actions, especially when it comes to not admitting they are gay, makes you realize they are—even if they will not admit it.

Cast: Kevin Barnett (Big Thug), Jermaine Fowler (Little Thug). **Credits:** *Producer:* Bodega Cat Sanchez. *Director as credited:* Kenji. **Comment:** There is vulgar language, Big and Little perform their roles expertly and the program is meant to be nothing more than a deliberate exploration of the stereotyped male black gay-would-be gangster. Enjoyable, well written and produced program that is worth watching just for something different when it comes to a portrayal black gay men.

Episodes: *1.* Soft in the Paint. *2.* Tip Drill. *3.* Fet Dick or Dis Tryin.

437 Honorable Mention. webserieschan nel.com. 2014.

Ryan, Danni and Cat are best friends who possess their own opinions on life and thus do not fit the typical mold of fitting in. The program charts what happens as each of the friends attempts to change their positions and become a part of the everyday scene.

Cast: Christina Jones (Ryan), Anna Christie (Danni), Lissa Danshaw (Cat). **Credits:** *Producer-Writer-Director:* Christina Jones, Anna Christie. **Comment:** Only a teaser for the first episode remains on line. It is difficult to assess the program based on that but it appears to be well acted and produced.

Episodes: *1.* Drunk Olympics 2014.

438 Horrible People. blip.tv. 2008.

It is the night of the engagement party for Margaret and Carter. Friends and family have been invited, including Carter's best friend, Michael and his fiancée, Danielle. Shortly after the party begins, Carter kills Danielle and hides her body. Soon Danielle is missed and Michael begins looking for her. With a killer loose and a mystery established, the program takes on the aspects of a typical daytime TV soap opera as it explores each of the party guests and what motivated Carter to kill Danielle.

Cast: Kristen Schaal (Margaret), Mather Zickel (Carter), Joy Franz (Meredith), Joe Lo Truglio (Billy), A.D. Miles (Michael), Israel Hernandez (Arturro), Sylvianne Chebance (Josephine DuPont), Jean Brassard (Leon Landouille), Rachael Robbins (Amanda), Ginger Kroll (Danielle), Edmund Guest (Rex). **Credits:** *Producer:* Rob Barnett, Joe Lo Truglio, Jonathan Stern. *Writer-Director:* A.D. Miles.

Comment: Diehard TV soap opera fans will be shocked to see what can happen to their beloved characters when they are spoofed. While the program does play like a soap opera the writing is purposely made ridiculous to highlight the quirks such characters have but are never really seen on legit soaps.

Episodes: 10 untitled episodes, labeled "Episode 1" through "Episode 10."

439 The Ho's on 7th Avenue. youtube.com. 2012.

The Ho's are a Chinese-American family that live on 7th Avenue in Manhattan. The home has recently been taken over by two of the three family siblings, Lily and Regan; John has left the family nest to enter the business world on his own. But when the unfortunate happens and John loses his wife and job he finds it necessary to move back home and the program chronicles what happens when three siblings try to share a house wherein two have never left. Megan is Reagan's girlfriend.

Cast: Robert Wu (John Ho), Elaine Kao (Lily Ho), Chuck David Willis (Reagan Ho), Giselle Rodriquez (Megan Brookes). **Credits:** *Producer:* Robert Lee. *Director:* Dom Magwili. *Writer:* Michael Hornbuckle, Robert Lee. **Comment:** Interesting take on siblings moving back home, this time into a house owned by John's brother and sister. The acting and production is top rate and the program quite enjoyable.

Episodes: *1.* Homecoming. *2.* My Room, My Stuff. *3.* Working Girl. *4.* Booty Time. *5.* Listen! *6.* The Test. *7.* Family Dinner.

440 Hot Mess. sheamess.com. 2013–2014.

Just because a girl is beautiful does not mean she is perfect. Encompassing an anthology-like presentation, stories of women who may look fabulous but possess the ability "to screw up, fall down, cause a scene and make a mess" of a situation "and live to tell the tale" are performed by an ensemble cast.

Cast: Amy Kersten, Cheri Paige Fogleman, Mary Catherine Green, Molly Anne Coogan, Miranda Childs, Julia Granacki, Yasha Jackson, Chad Callaghan, Jim DeProphetis, Bobby Hodgson, Fil Vocasek. **Credits:** *Producer:* Amy Kersten. *Writer:* Amy Kersten, Cheri Paige, Molly Anne Coogan, Megas Sass, Chad Callaghan. *Director:* Amy Kersten. **Comment:** Very well acted and produced series that features cast members playing different roles in stories that range from that has happened to me to I hope that never happens to me.

Season 1 Episodes: *1.* Dog Day Afternoon. *2.* Elevator. *3.* War Craft. *4.* Fire. *5.* Robbed. *6.* Party. *7.* Keys.

Season 2 Episodes: *1.* Fruit Flies. *2.* Splash. *3.* Powder. *4.* Skinny Jeans. *5.* Butter My Bread. *6.* Spit. *7.* Mugged. *8.* Zipper. *9.* Angel of Harlem.

Season 3 Episodes: *1.* A-List Fail. *2.* Whatever Lola Wants. *3.* Men from Last Night. *4.* No Bra, No Shoes, No Service. *5.* Someone. *6.* Neti Polish. *7.* FU. *8.* Power Walk. *9.* Flip Tease. *10.* Dropping Anchor. *11.* Catastrophe Waitress. *12.* Grandma's Spoon. *13.* Lipstick. *14.* Whiskey Sour.

441 Hotel Reject. webserieschannel.com. 2012.

Sisters Jacklyn and Jordan Jensen have been chosen as contestants on the TV reality series *Marry F*** Kill* (sort of an exaggerated version of ABC's *The Bachelor*). The sisters, however, are not the luckiest of contestants as they are the first ones to be kicked off the program. With that strike against them they also learn that due to program secrecy they will not be permitted to return to their normal life until the competition is over. In the mean time they cannot make contact with the outside world and are placed by the show's producers in an undisclosed location called Hotel Reject. The program follows Jacklyn and Jordan as they reluctantly become hotel guests and attempt to enjoy their new surroundings until they are permitted to leave.

Cast: Scarlett Bermingham (Jacklyn Jensen), Christine Bullen (Jordan Jensen), Grant O'Brien (Gregory), Joie Bauer (Joie), Rachel Cipriano (The Maid), Anthony Bowden (Dylan). **Credits:** *Producer:* Matt McBrayer. *Writer-Director:* Andrew Rhymer. **Comment:** Interesting concept as to what happens to the participants of reality shows when they are eliminated before the competition ends. While even winners of reality shows are not "jailed" but must not reveal the outcome of the show until after it airs, they are free to go about their daily lives. Scarlett and Christine play their roles well as what happens to them could likely happen to any such contestant if they were kept out of the public eye to avoid unnecessary spoiler leaks. The acting and production values are also very good.

Episodes: *1.* Pilot. *2.* The Substitute. *3.* Loud Sex. *4.* Foursome.

442 The House on South Bronson. you tube.com. 2012.

Sketch comedy program set at the House on South Bronson where a group of eccentric housemates attempt to live together without driving each other crazy.

Cast: Daisy Alvarez (Daisy), Eric Salazar (Eric), Ali Naqvi (Ali), John Flores (John), Chris Menown (Chris), Andrew Cudzilo (Andrew), Paul Davila (Paul). **Credits:** *Producer-Director:* Ali Naqvi. *Writer:* Chris Menown, Andrew Cudzilo. **Comment:** The program does have its unpleasant moments (especially episode number two) and it can come off as ridiculous to some and just impossible to believe to others. It is also a poor way to begin a program with the entire first episode becoming very boring as it deal's with an actor's audition.

Episodes: *1.* The Audition. *2.* Bean Dip. *3.* La Telenovela. *4.* Pakistani Alarm Clock. *5.* Last Chance Dating. *6.* Clip Show.

443 HOV. webserieschannel.com. 2011.

Billed as "From the guys who brought you ... well, nothing, comes a new web comedy series about life in a High Occupancy Vehicle." And the billing is right on—the experiences shared by three guys who apparently live in a HOV are depicted: The Suit (James; always attired as such), The Mascot (Jim; dressed in a yellow chicken outfit) and The Contractor (Ford).

Cast: James Brannon (James), Jim Stanek (Jim), Ford Seeuwas (Ford), Frankie McGuire (Frankie), Adam Johns (Albert). **Credits:** *Producer-Writer-Director:* Adam Johns, Ford Seeuws. **Comment:** All the action is set in the HOV and while it would not seem likely it does work (although never on network or cable TV) because the episodes are short and right to the point. ABC attempted a similar idea with the series *Carpool* but it was cancelled before the car ran out of gas.

Episodes: *1.* Chicken Suit for the Soul. *2.* Sixty-Two Thousand, Fur Hundred Repetitions. *3.* The Name Is Bond, Ford Bond. *4.* Pirate Treasure. *5.* Giga What. *6.* All Good Things. *7.* The Five Rs.

444 *How Men Become Dogs.* howmenbe comedogs.com. 2013.

Cameron, Julian and Mario, friends since college, have been playing the field but not finding much success with the opposite sex. Their lives suddenly change when Cameron discovers that his girlfriend is cheating on him; Julian is left flat when his girlfriend leaves him for someone she feels is more suited to her tastes; and Mario, left in the cold when his girlfriend deserts him when she feels he needs to get his act together and become a responsible adult. Although the friends are seeking those special girls and have exchanged their "dating secrets," they feel that perhaps they need professional advice and seek the help of Hamlin, "a master of all things" who offers a course that teaches men how to become womanizers (dogs). The program follows Cameron, Julian and Mario as they take the advice of their "Alpha Male" and set out on a possibly disastrous course to become the victor (the man no woman can resist) and find that one special girl.

Cast: Marc A. Cunningham (Cameron Pierce), Brian Isom (Julian Ford), Corey Gaddis (Mario Irvin), Bechir Sylvain (Hamlin), Yazmin Monet Watkins (Brandy Ellis), Lourdes Gonzalez (Lisa Romero), Kalilah Harris (Krista Davenport), Crystal-Lee Naomi (Jessica Harris), Wayne Bowser (Julian Ford), Tiffany Snow (Samantha Rutherford). **Credits:** *Producer:* Yvette Foy, Issa Rae, Benoni Tagoe, Harold Sylvester. *Director:* Marc A. Cunningham, Bechir Sylvain, Harold Sylvester. *Writer:* Marc A. Cunningham, Yvette Foy, Shannon B. King. **Comment:** Women, just as well as men, have encountered situations where they are dumped and sometimes can't understand why. Most just take it in stride and move on, hoping the next person they find will be different. Here, three guys take drastic steps to change their way of impressing women. The idea, although done before, is still good especially when you have guys desperate enough to go to ridiculous extremes to achieve that goal. Good acting and production values and something different when it comes to the guy seeking girl saga.

Episodes: *1.* A Dog Is Born. *2.* Right vs. Wrong. *3.* The Perfect Woman. *4.* Hamlin Let the Dogs Out. *5.* Doggie Style. *6.* Pit Bulls and Terriers. *7.* Two Bones in a Bowl. *8.* Beware of Dog. *9.* Loyalty Bites. *10.* Bury the Bones.

445 *How to Be an Actor.* webserieschannel.com. 2012.

Dylan is a young man who is determined to become an actor. Glenn is a top agent who skipped the acting route and just established himself as a representative. Dylan believes Glenn is the agent for him, but Glenn believes Dylan is just not the type of client he wants to represent as he feels his talent is not up to the standards of his other clients. Dylan knows Glenn is totally mistaken and has set his goal to convince him otherwise. The program charts Dylan's outrageous efforts (through acting) to prove to Glenn that he not only has super talent but would be his perfect client.

Cast: Devon Ferguson (Dylan Master), Jason Mckinnon (Glenn Harrison). **Credits:** *Producer:* Devon Ferguson. *Writer-Director:* Devon Ferguson, Jason Mckinnon. **Comment:** Glenn is just a guy who wants no part of Dylan but Dylan's persistent (and totally embarrassing) attempts to prove he is an actor provides the basis of the program which, despite Dylan's lunacy, is well produced and acted. Numerous movies and TV series have tried the idea—and the twist here is Dylan.

Episodes: *Lesson 1:* Getting an Agent. *Lesson 2:* Branding Yourself. *Lesson 3:* Acting Class. *Lesson 4:* Auditions. *Lesson 5:* Eliminating the Competition.

446 *How to Be Dead.* webserieschannel.com. 2012.

With the official website closed, very little text information available and only a pilot episode produced, it is difficult to figure out exactly what the program was about. According to available information, the living (called "the undead") are administrative errors that Death "and his staff" must protect from "ghosts, zombies, vampires and medium-sized apocalypses." By watching the episode, a young man (Dave) meets Death after a near-death experience (a car accident) with Death trying to explain to Dave that he is not dead. It ends with Dave recovering and Death going on his merry way. It appears by the episode that the people Death encounters would be the focus and what results chronicled.

Cast: Mark Oosterveen (Death), Ben Wigzell (Dave). **Credits:** *Producer:* Lara Greenway, Dave Turner. *Director:* Lara Greenway. *Writer:* Dave Turner. **Comment:** As previously stated, what the program is all about is a mystery. It appears to be a British production (by Death's accent) with acceptable acting and production values.

Episodes: Pilot. The on-line description is also not very helpful: "Dave has a near Death experience. Death has a near Dave experience."

447 *Howard Gets an Interview.* blip.tv. 2012.

Howard is a young man seeking a job in digital marketing. He possesses the necessary skills but he just can't seem to catch a break. The program charts Howard's relentless pursuit of that dream job and what happens when he resorts to a last desperate measure—using an alumni contact to secure the position. **Cast:** Timothy Hornor (Howard Zitter), Jason Banks (Theodore Rose), Patrick Hancock (Mr. Coverdale), Elisabeth Kiernan (Jamie), April Brooks (Receptionist), Christian S. Anderson (Competitor), Melissa Strauss (Marketing V.P.). **Credits:** *Producer:* David Salzberg. *Director:* Jon Polansky. *Writer:* Jonathan F. Cohen. **Comment:** While not an original idea the project flows smoothly as Howard desperately seeks a job.

Episodes: *1.* Competition. *2.* The Firing. *3.* The Date. *4.* The Phone Call. *5.* The Alumni.

448 *Human Food*. humanfood.com. 2014.

Human Food is a public access cable show hosted by a man named Zach. Being public access cannot guarantee even one viewer, not alone the large audience Zach would like. The program follows what happens when Zach tries to improve ratings by interviewing the most bizarre people he can find. **Cast:** Zachary Zweifler (Zach). **Credits:** *Producer-Director:* Zachary Zweifler, Spencer Perrenoud. *Writer:* Zachary Zweifler, Michael Gerstein. **Comment:** Interesting concept with scenes in color and black and white but the production as well as the acting are somewhat amateurish and not as good as it could have been.

Episodes: *1.* Hot Dogs. *2.* Pizza Rolls. *3.* Sushi. *4.* The Finale.

449 *The Hunted*. youtube.com. 2001–2014.

Several people, bitten by vampires, have not yet turned and have formed a group to prove that such creatures of the undead really exist. The vampires, however, have developed immunity to the time-honored methods that normally destroy them (a cross, holy water, daylight) and it is now only by beheading with a sacred sword that can destroy them. The vampires are now planning to wipe out the entire human race. Combining humor, martial arts, sword fighting and sexy female vampires, the program follows the survival group (who has curtailed their thirst for human blood) as they set out on a dangerous but comical quest to destroy the undead before they can accomplish their goal. **Cast:** Robert Chapin (Bob), Kendall Wells (Kendall), Elisha Patterson III (Eli), Audrey Wells (Audrey), Ned Donovan (Ned), Jochen Repolust (Mikey), Kerry Glover (Kerry), Derek Conley (Derek), Charlie Forray (Charlie), Mitchell Murdock (Mitchell), Anthony De Longis (Vincent), Patti Pelton (Wren), Andrew Helm (Evil Kevin), J. Hunter Ackerman (Jeff). **Credits:** *Producer:* Kendall Wells, Derek Conley, Chris Fields, Robert Chapin, Brett D. Jones, Mark Bedell, Kevin Inouye, Jaclyn Marshall. *Director:* Robert Chapin, Kendall Wells, Ned Donovan, Derek Conley, Chris Fields, Kirsten Foe, Kevin Inouye, Brett D. Jones, Steven Vargas, David Kessler. *Writer:* Robert Chapin, Kendall Wells, Devala Rees, Ned Donovan, Derek Conley, Chris Fields, Andrew Helm, Mark Bedell, Max Lorn-Krause, Kirsten Foe, Kerry Glover. **Comment:** Aspects of the TV series *Buffy the Vampire Slayer* can be seen (but in a comical fashion) with acting that varies from good to very good (based on what is available to see). The production also varies but overall the idea is good and, while the cast lists the performers who appear in 5 to 18 episodes, the program has no official cast as it relies on user content (which fans upload and it is linked to the main show). This interaction was intensified by contests for cash prizes with entries judged by a panel of industry professionals. Hence, anyone could become a part of the show (and the producers took full advantage of this as money was tight and long commitments to actors would have not been possible).

Episodes: 50 episodes were produced but only Season 1 episodes remain on line: *1.* Breaking Up, Part 1. *2.* Two for One. *3.* Tough Love. *4.* Blade in Training. *5.* Breaking Up, Part 2. *6.* Dance of the Undead. *7.* The Stalker. *8.* That's Show Biz. *9.* Class Ritual. *10.* Rendezvous. *11.* Con Job. *12.* Faire Warning. *13.* Return of the Stalker. *14.* Film at 11. *15.* Star Power. *16.* The New Guy. *17.* Breakthrough. *18.* Slay Me in St. Louis.

450 *Hunter and Hornet*. webserieschannel.com. 2014.

What does it take for a guy to become a pickup artist? That is the question friends Cade and Sade want to know. They like the ladies but have no luck with them. They are awkward, appear to be fearful of even approaching a pretty girl and have vowed to change all that by becoming "pickup gurus." The program charts what happens when Cade and Sade seek all the advice they can about picking up girls (even asking strangers on the street) and proceed to test those theories. **Cast:** Sonny Vrebac (Sade/Hunter), Aljin Abella (Cade/Hornet), Emily Rose Brennan (Rhonda), Laura Dundovic (Anna). **Credits:** *Producer-Writer-Director:* Sonny Vrebac. **Comment:** The program is well acted as the friends seek to impress the girls they have set their sights on.

Episodes: 21 episodes were produced but only the following are on line for free (others require a fee to watch): *1.* Zygote. *2.* Sunbathing. *3.* Awkward Turtles. *4.* Bookstore. *5.* Post Code. *6.* PUG. *7.* Birth of HnH (Hunter and Hornet).

451 Hurricane Bonnie. webserieschannel. com. 2011.

Joel and Anthony are quarrelsome adult brothers who have put their issues aside to attend the funeral of their mother, Bonnie, a woman, married to "a nasty man" and left to raise her sons alone. Her one enjoyment was her annual trip to Wonderland in Lake Wakabeka with Joel and Anthony and her brother Bob. Here, she cherished riding the Big Woody, a legendary wooden roller coaster that was the thrill of her life, and eventually she received the nickname "Hurricane." Following the memorial service Joel and Anthony learn that Bonnie's last wish was to have her ashes scattered at Wonderland. The program follows their efforts to do just that (with everything that can go wrong happening).

Cast: Dusty Vollmer (Joel), Jordan Gwiazdowski (Anthony), Jocelyn Dawson (Amanda), Linda Cieslik (Hurricame Bonnie), Steve Golla (Uncle Bob). **Credits:** *Producer-Writer:* Linda Cieslik. *Director:* Linda Cieslik, Quinn Hester. **Comment:** With the exception of a poorly-produced teaser (that doesn't explain a lot) all the episodes have been taken off line. It is just not possible to make a statement of what the actual series was like based on what is available.

452 Hurtling Through Space at an Alarming Rate. blip.tv. 2009.

In a future era people who live in apartments have the ability to travel through time and space. The only drawback is that apartment residents cannot leave although visitors can enter and depart. Roommates Mike and Stuart are two such people who are using their apartment for a secret mission (but for whom and what is unknown). Mike and Stuart are often in a daze about what is happening and the program charts their mishaps as they land on various planets and attempt to deal with the alien inhabitants who often find them anything but amusing.

Cast: Michael Davies (Mike), Stuart Paap (Stuart), Stephanie Thorpe (Elizabeth), Taryn O'Neill (Michelle), Jacob D. Smith (Gary), Barry Alan Levine (Kalm, Master of the Universe). **Credits:** *Producer:* Amber J. Lawson, Taryn O'Neill, Stephanie Thorpe. **Comment:** With elements of the TV series *Doctor Who*, *Hurtling...* tries to be different by using a traveling apartment, ignoring every law of physics (not to mention science in general) and present something different (and when the apartment chooses to touch down, it does so with an impact so intense that only the land on which it sets down suffers damage). The producers have succeeded on that point and the program itself is good for a few laughs.

Episodes: *1.* The Planet of Tons of Dirty Laundry. *2.* The Planet of Extremely Sticky Floors That Make It Impossible to Do Anything. *3.* The Planet of Eventually Exploding Time Bombs and Calamitous Proportions. *4.* The Planet of Fairly Attractive Women with Terrible Fashion Sense. *5.* The Pizza Man Cometh/The Episode of Mostly Exposition. *6.* The Wrath of Kalm.

453 Husbands. husbandstheseries.com. 2011–2014.

Cheeks, a well-known actor and Brady, a major league baseball player are a gay couple, who, after becoming intoxicated during a Las Vegas party, unintentionally marry and soon realize they were not ready to make such a commitment. The marriage is legal and Cheeks and Brady must stay married as a public divorce would not only disappoint their fans but could destroy their careers. While the program focuses on the problems the newlyweds face, it explores some problems that could also enter any marriage by showing that whether the union is gay, lesbian or straight, it takes two people, working together as a team to make the marriage work.

Cast: Brad Bell (Cheeks), Sean Hemeon (Brady Kelly), Alessandra Torresani (Haley). **Credits:** *Producer:* Brad Bell, Jane Espenson, Jeff Greenstein. *Director:* Jeff Greenstein, Eli Gonda. *Writer:* Brad Bell, Jane Espenson. **Comment:** The characters are very like-able and the program flows smoothly from episode to episode. Although it has been stated that *Husbands* is the first such program to focus on a gay married couple, it is not so as the concept dates back to television in 1974 when the ABC series *Hot L Baltimore* presented a gay couple (although not married as an amendment did not exist) as well as a lesbian character long before any other show.

Episodes: *1.* Waking Up in Vegas. *2.* We Can't Be Married. *3.* Being Britney. *4.* A Decent Proposal. *5.* IDEHTW. *6.* Haley, the Life Coach. *7.* Normal People. *8.* The Together Thing. *9.* Instant Love. *10.* Return of the Zebra. *11.* Winky Face. *12.* Appropriate Is Not the Word. *13.* The Straightening. *14.* A Better Movie of What We're Like. *15–17:* I Do Over. *18–20:* I Dream of Cleaning.

454 The Hustler. youtube.com. 2009.

Travis Hustleberg is a man who now goes by the name The Hustler. He rides a motorcycle and is seeking to extract revenge on those who ruined his life. It was the year 1983 when Travis attended Hamilton Middle School. He was on the school's football team and was about to go into the school's record books for making the most touchdowns to win a game when the coach of the opposing St. Luke's school team brought in a ringer (a professional player) that cost Travis his dream. Now, in the year 2009, Travis has begun his quest and the program charts his efforts to get even with that opposing team, one member at a time.

Cast: Mark Feuerstein (The Hustler), Chris Fernandez Lizardi (Danny), Lindsey Smith-Sands (Anna), Al Brown (Bernie), Zach AImen (Meat). **Credits:** *Producer-Director:* Mark Feuerstein, Sam Friedlander. *Writer:* Mark Feuerstein, Sam Friedlander, Mike Sikowitz. **Comment:** While most of Travis's encounters are on the comical side, his encounter with the coach of that opposing team turns it into a dark comedy when his revenge turns deadly. Overall though, the program is well acted and presented.

Episodes: *1.* Piñata Hustler. *2.* Hustle and Bustle. *3.* You Gotta Hustle. *4.* Hustle and Throw. *5.* McDonnelly's Surprise. *6.* Handicapped Hustle. *7.* Stake Out on Meat's House. *8.* Can't Knock the Hustler. *9.* The Forgotten Hustle. *10.* Huslin' Hands. *11.* The Drop.

455 *I Am Tim.* webserieschannel.com. 2010–2012.

The Van Helsings are a noted family of vampire hunters that have devoted their efforts to destroying creatures of the undead. The family origins date back centuries and it appears that Timothy Ronald Van Helsing, called Tim, is the last of the family bloodline. Tim was just an ordinary guy enjoying life with two ordinary friends (Anna, a charity shop manager; and Pancho; occupation: sidekick) in England but has now inherited a mission (from Abraham Van Helsing): battle the forces of evil that lurk in the darkness. The program charts those efforts with Tim, Anna and Pancho never quite sure how to handle the various situations they encounter. Stories are introduced by Richard Timmons, the creator, in a comical version of Rod Serling's hosting chores on *The Twilight Zone* (Richard also involves himself in the plots to help move things along).

Cast: Jamie Simcox (Tim Helsing), Jennifer Jordan (Anna Elena Mondragon), Tom Cockram (Poncho de la Cruz), Richard Massara (Hannibal King), Richard Timmons (Himself). **Credits:** *Producer:* Richard Timmons, Peter Crump. *Director-Writer:* Jamie McKeller. **Comment:** The characters are likable, the plots unbelievable, the production values above many other web series but it suffers at times from difficult to understand British accents.

Episodes: *1.* York, England, Planet Earth. *2.* The Total Cycle Path. *3.* Romance Is Deadified. *4.* It Is Pitch Dark. *5.* The Thing About Poncho. *6.* Sparkle Free Vampires. *7.* Don't Fear the Red Shirt. *8.* Fan Service. *9.* Sibling Rivalry. *10.* The Daily Grind. *11.* A Staple Diet of Violence. *12.* The Fork in the Road. *13.* What a Wonderful World. *14.* For the Viewers at Home. *15.* 110% Epic. *16.* Out with the Old. *17.* Nothing Like Doctor. *18.* Not So Fresh Meat. *19, 20.* Tim vs. the Sheeple. *21.* Back to the Daily Grind. *22.* Night of the Living Bread. *23.* Return of a King.

456 *I Hate Being Single.* blip.tv. 2012.

Rob is a young man living on his own and struggling to find his place in the world. He lives in Brooklyn, New York, has friends, dates, attends parties but in the overall scheme, finds everything that is now a part of his life is a bit overwhelming (and at times confusing). He has recently broken up with a girl, has two a bit-off-the wall friends (Shannon and Dom), an uphill road to achieve his dream of becoming an actor and how he manages to navigate all the issues that surround him form the basis of each episode.

Cast: Rob Michael Hugel (Rob), Shannon Coffey (Shannon), Dom Manzolillo (Dom). **Credits:** *Producer-Writer-Director:* Rob Michael Hugel. **Comment:** With situations that parallel the life of the series creator (Rob Michael Hugel), the program plays well as it depicts the actual incidents that can happen to a single man. The acting and production values are good and, while the second season sort of slacks off from the concept of first season episodes (the same feeling is just not there) it is still enjoyable.

Season 1 Episodes: *1.* That's Love. *2.* I'm Mature. *3.* The Banker. *4.* Wouldn't Wanna Be You. *5.* Do You Like Me? *6,7.* Season 1 Finale.

Season 2 Episodes: *1.* Nap Time. *2.* You Over-Instagram. *3.* You Don't Watch *Homeland* (cable TV series). *4.* It'll Take a Second.

457 *I Hate My Roommates.* roommate hate.com. 2013.

Justin, Jessica and Kenny share an apartment only out of desperation as each loves to hate the other. Believing they are in a unique situation, they decide to make a web series about hating each other and how to deal with such a predicament. The program follows the roomies as they begin their web program and explain how and why to hate your roommate.

Cast: Justin Tuttle (Justin), Jessica Coburn (Jessica), Kenny Wilcoxon (Kenny). **Credits:** *Producer-Writer-Director:* Justin Tuttle. **Comment:** Some vulgar language can be heard but that aside the program comes off as one of the better odd couple-roommate efforts. They not only have to deal with hating each other, but the personal issues that each one faces.

Episodes: *1.* Webshow. *2.* Let's Make Dinner. *3.* Panties on the Doorknob. *4.* Kenny Quits Smoking. *5.* Mystery of the Subway Sandwich.

458 *I Love Dick.* outlicioustv.com. 2013.

It is 1955 and a young gay couple, Mickey and Dick, have just rented an apartment from their female landlords, Fran and Edy. Mickey is the "man of the house" and Dick, his more girly-like lover, yearns for a career in show business but is regulated to caring for the apartment while Mickey (an actor) works. It is also a time when gays and lesbians were not readily accepted and for Mickey, being gay could be a strike against him. Rather than spoil his chances at acquiring acting jobs, Mickey pretends to be straight with Dick being just a guy with whom he shares an apartment. Fran and Edy happen to be lesbians and are unaware that Mickey and Dick are gay (and vice versa). The program, a spoof of the TV series *I Love Lucy* relates the events that befall a gay couple in a time when being gay is not accepted and how they deal with the situations that could expose their "secret."

Cast: Jeremy Lucas (Mickey), Michael Ciriaco (Dick), Sarah Gaboury (Edy), Patricia Villetto (Fran). **Credits:** *Producer:* Tony Jeris, Brian Pelletier. *Writer:* Tony Jeris. *Director:* Brian Pelletier. **Comment:** Amusing spoof with very good acting and production values. The program is filmed in black and white and even has a laugh track to represent a live studio audience. The program is also squeaky clean (nothing objectionable) and worth checking out for a modern take on an old TV sitcom. **Episodes:** 12 untitled episodes, labeled "Episode 1" through "Episode 12."

459 I Love My Annoying Spouse. meritage pictures.com. 2013–2014.

Bobby and Susan met as singles on an airplane. Now, married for five years they have discovered that each has a number of annoying habits. The program relates those annoying habits and how each deals with it.

Cast: Ann Tierney Kelly (Susan), Jonny Loquasto (Bobby). **Credits:** *Producer-Writer-Director:* Jane Kelly Kosek. **Comment:** Susan and Bobby simply talk to viewer and explain how they deal with a situation that arises. It is sometimes difficult to maintain this type of series due to its presentation. Some do not make it due to poor camera work, others because the stars are just not appealing or simply cannot act. Here, those obstacles have been overcome and an enjoyable program has resulted with an appealing cast and good production values.

Season 1 Episodes: *1.* Bobby and Susan Meet in the Not-So Friendly Skies. *2.* Susan Thinks She's a Good Listener. *3.* Bobby's Romantic Proposal to Susan. *4.* Susan and Bobby Plan a Trip for Their 5th Year "Wooden Anniversary." *5.* Is That My Toothbrush? *6.* What's That Smell? *7.* What's the Problem? *8.* That's for My Tart. *9.* Itsy Bitsy Spider. *10.* You Dirtied My Sink. *11.* I Want Your Cookie. *12.* Are You Watching "Mad Men" Without Me? *13.* Apology Accepted. *14.* Get Lucky Flowers Equals Hotness.

Season 2 Episodes: *1.* Getting Up Is Hard to Do. *2.* You Really Are Pregnant? *3.* How to Work Out During Pregnancy.

460 I Love the '30s. tv.com. 2005–2008.

A look back at some of the historical events that sparked the 1930s as seen through minor celebrities of the 1940s who recall, in a comical manner, what "actually" happened.

Cast: John Mulaney, Nick Kroll, Brain Huskey, Rob Huebel, Sarah Burns. **Credits:** *Producer:* Brendan Colthurst, Will Hines, Nick Kroll, John Mulaney. *Director:* Brendan Colthurst. *Writer:* Brian Donovan, Nick Kroll, John Mulaney, Conrad Mulcahy, Brendan Colthurst. **Comment:** Virtually all information has been taken off line thus a comment is not possible.

Season 1 Episodes: *1.* The Lindbergh Baby. *2.* The Legend of Babe Ruth. *3.* Lightning Round.

Season 2 Episodes: *1.* War of the Worlds. *2.* The End of Prohibition. *3.* The 1936 Olympics. *4.* Monopoly. *5.* The Hindenburg. *6.* Decade of the Dictators. *7.* Bonnie & Clyde. *8.* The Great Depression.

461 The Ice Queen. icequeenweb.tumblr. com. 2014.

A psychiatrist (Dr. Brittany) heads a super villain rehabilitation center wherein three evil villains (Mel, Magda and Jack) are housed along with a normal woman (Irena) who was kidnapped when Jack destroyed her laboratory and research work. It appears that Mel, Magda and Jack are quite reluctant to be reformed and Irena, being held against her will, quite eager to escape. Based on what has been released, the program will follow Irena as she attempts to escape, later assisted by Magda and Mel, who also want out to continue their evil ways.

Cast: Deanna Noe (Irena), Nikki Glick (Dr. Brittany), Maya Sayre (Mel), Jasmine Kaur (Magda), Gavin Lee (Jack). **Credits:** *Producer-Writer-Director:* Pricialla Spencer. **Comment:** Assumptions have to be made as the pilot episode leaves the doorway open for anything to happen. The acting is very good and the plot could become intriguing depending on what path the characters take.

Episodes: *1.* Pilot: The McGuffin.

462 The Iceman Chronicles. hulu.com. 2009.

In Blythe, Arizona, a small desert town with buried secrets, one has come back to haunt them: the Iceman Killer. It began in 1967 when a killer, using an icicle as a weapon, evaded police capture leaving them with only one clue: the word "Iceman" scrawled in blood on a wall. The killings suddenly stopped but the case was never solved. It had been considered a cold case until 2009 when the Iceman Killer returned (as the sheriff says, "There's a killer on the loose. Head for the hills. Forget the elderly"). Spoofing the ABC TV series *Twin Peaks* the program chronicles the fear faced by a small town with a killer on the loose and how the clueless law enforcement figures, especially veterinarian/corner Russell Coldpalm, set out to capture him.

Cast: David Fickas (Russell Coldpalm), Christine Lakin (Barbie Pedderson), Lee Arenberg (Buttonwillow McKittrick), Ric Barbera (Young Winston Fairchild), Stephanie Barnes (Janie Doe), Michael Cornacchia (Tommy Chubbs), Alex Fox (Saul Miller), Stephen Heath (Judd Kemp), Andy Hungerford (Mike Binkmeyer), Mark Kelly (Stan Smith), Beth Kennedy (Mrs. Cominicci), Mickey Meyer (Joey Doe), Rick Overton (Chief Winston Fairchild), Leonora Gershman (Off. Charlie Left), Kirk Ward (Pappy DeKiller). **Credits:** *Producer:* Brice Beckham, David Fickas, Josh Uranga. *Director:* David Fickas. *Writer:* Brice Beckham, David Fickas. **Comment:** With all episodes being withdrawn a comment based on viewing is not possible.

Episodes: 6 untitled episodes, labeled "Episode 1" through "Episode 6."

463 ICU Dating Service. icudatingservice. com. 2013.

People who may be clumsy; people who may be undesirable and those that are simply insecure have a new way to find a mate—through the services of ICU Dating, an on-line dating company that promises to find a mate for anyone regardless of who or what they are. Incidents in the lives of those "special" people who have chosen to incorporate the services of ICU are profiled.

Cast: Chrissy Cannone (Ginny MacGyver), Michael Cannone (Lazer Torpedo), Emily Dahm (Nora Rumple), Danielle Dutton (Goldie Hawk), Hunter Johnson (Clear Bear Marigold), Katie Jo Riordan (Angelica Godfried), Beau Smith (Shane Brighton), Jason Stafford (Nigel Humphries). **Credits:** *Producer:* Chrissy Cannone, Michael Cannone. *Writer-Director:* Michael Cannone. **Comment:** A different take on dating services that works with good acting and production vales. Catering to the less fortunate seeking a mate has been done a few times before and each has a unique way of dealing with the matter, so each series does not copy or become the same old thing.

Episodes: *1.* The Laws of Love. *2.* Bugpocpalypse. *3.* Mistaken Identity.

464 Iguana Man. iguanam.com. 2014.

Colin Kincade is a recent college graduate, living in Manhattan and earning money as an artist but hoping to break into the TV industry as a cameraman. Colin is also a unique individual: he has the ability to transform himself into an Iguana and battle crime as Iguana Man. Although he has only the ability to disable villains by biting off their feet, he also has trouble battling crime as he is considered an outlaw and must do it as a vigilante. Although N.Y.P.D. police cars are seen on the streets, the series is set in the city of Greenville and Colin's efforts to battle the crime of the city are depicted. In the only story line that was presented, Colin battles the evil Maynard Arthur Nelson, a criminal that hates his first name (he wants to be called Arthur) and has vowed to get even with Iguana Man for biting off his feet.

Cast: Chris Cashon (Colin Kincade), Shane Willimon (Maynard Arthur Nelson), Lauren Paige Wilson (Samantha Black), Wallace Krebs (Robert Wolfrom), Evan Harris (Grant Knight), Jessie Kuipers (Candi Hart), Brian Coker (Dr. Saul Clavell), Tiffany Morton (Jessica Rayne), Morgan Monnig (Veronica Onya), Peter Lupu (Mike Bateman), Silas James Rowland (Aaron Carpenter), Bethanna Pistolis (Sally Mander), Bill Kennedy (Off. George Grande), Charles Poore (Det. Nick Striker), Elizabeth Gray (Brandi Owens), Delvin Choice (Smitty Jones), Vonda Skelton (Mayor Martha Stone), LeRoy Kennedy (Commissioner Alexander Fratz). **Credits:** *Producer-Writer:* Dean Ferreira, Wofford Jones. *Director:* Dean Ferreira. *Writer:* Dean Ferreirs, Chris Cashon. **Comment:** Colin has the partial face of an Iguana when he transforms and his tongue is like Spider-Man's "Spidy Senses." The idea, although played for laughs, is good but there is no background information on how Colin acquired his powers or scenes of him actually transferring (understandable due to the money it costs for special effects). The program ends unresolved but could pick up the story if additional episodes are made.

Episodes: *1.* The Alley. *2.* Investigations. *3.* Doctor's Orders. *4.* Transformations. *5.* Instincts.

465 Imaginary Bitches. imaginarybitches. com. 2008–2009.

Eden is a beautiful, slightly self-conscious young woman who feels neglected as all her friends are in a relationship. When loneliness overcomes her, she creates three imaginary friends who can only be seen and heard by her: Catherine (mean, greedy and selfish), Heather (a bisexual who is perky, rather nice but too promiscuous) and Jennifer (a down-to-earth girl who is also a lesbian). Eden's dream of having someone to confide in soon becomes more than she bargained for when Jennifer, Catherine and Heather evolve into "Imaginary Bitches" who not only become more real to her but begin to take charge of her life, causing her more problems than she had before she created them. Lizzie, Brooke and Connie are Eden's closest friends while Jessalyn, a friend to Eden at first, becomes more of her nemesis as stories progress (especially when it is revealed that she is a lesbian).

Cast: Eden Riegel (Eden), Brooke Nevin (Brooke), Elizabeth Hendrickson (Lizzie), Connie Fletcher (Connie), Jessalyn Gilsig (Jessalyn), Angela Trimbur (Angela), Michael Daniel (Cassady), Megan Hollingshead (Shannon), Brittany Ishibashi (Brittany), Sam Page (Riley). **Credits:** *Director:* Andrew Miller.

Writer: Andrew Miller, Nichole Millard, Jeffrey Poliquin, Bo Price, Kathryn Price, Sam Riegel. **Comment:** Enjoyable program with very good acting, writing and production values, made especially appealing with Eden Riegel as Eden as she is so natural that she makes you believe she is really talking and reacting with someone as opposed to speaking into thin air (the "bitches").

Episodes: *1.* It's Not Easy Making Imaginary New Friends. *2.* The Dirtier Isn't Always Better. *3.* Where Were You When Eden Got Drunk and Puked All Over Me and Lizzie. *4.* A New Leper in the Colony. *5.* It's Totally What You Think. *6.* Help Dr. James Help You. *7.* A Spiritual Bitch Bath. *8.* Sexy Secret Santa. *9.* Porn Star Priest. *10.* Imaginary Bridezilla. *11.* Only Crazy Girls Quife. *12,13.* Three Bitches Is an Imaginary Crowd.

466 The Importance of Being Mike. blip. tv. 2013.

Ali, like all people, dreams. For most people a dream is just that—something that is soon forgotten. One night, however, Ali has a dream so vivid that she is unable to forget it or get it out of her thoughts. In it she met a man named Mike and soon afterward married him. The problem is she did not see his face or even learn anything about him. Believing that it was an omen that she will marry a man named Mike, Ali begins a quest to find that man. The program chronicles her quest by dating only men named Mike and what results as she has no idea what he looks like but believes once she dates him she will know.

Cast: Shona Kay (Ali Olsen), Melanie Gardener (Gwen), Michael Birkeland (Doug). **Credits:** *Producer-Director:* Brian Brough. *Writer:* Brian Brough, Brittany Wiscombe. **Comment:** An original idea that is well executed with good acting, stories and production values. Shona Kay is just perfect as Ali as she follows a dream and seeks that unknown Mike while her too-focused quest could prevent her from actually finding the man (not named Mike) of her dreams. The program ends unresolved with the doorway left open for Ai to date more Mikes but also the possibility of adding a non-Mike to challenge the validity of her dream.

Episodes: *1.* I Had a Dream. *2.* Outdoorsy Mike. *3.* Disco Mike. *4.* Personal Space Mike. *5.* Hypochondriac Mike.

467 In English, Please? youtube.com. 2014.

A high school in Western Australia provides the backdrop for a look at incidents in the lives of three English teachers (Hammond, Dobson and Christina) and how they deal with student problems, school issues and their own personal insecurities. It is, in essence, a look at high school from the teacher's point of view.

Cast: Sarah Harris (Hammond), Olivia Darby (Dobson), Kiran Wilson (Christina), Daniel Maddox (Mr. Denny). **Credits:** *Producer:* Kiran Wilson. Sarah Harris. *Writer-Director:* David Harris.

Comment: While such ideas have been done before (focusing more on the teacher than the student) it is different to see how similar situations are handled in foreign countries. The Australian-produced program is well produced and acted and worth watching for a different look at high school life.

Episodes: *1.* Parent/Teacher Night. *2.* Photocopier. *3.* Yard Duty. *4.* Marking. *5.* School Dance. *6.* Muck Up Day.

468 In Gayle We Trust. nbc.com. 2009–2011.

Maple Grove is Midwestern town and home to many colorful characters, one of which is Gayle Evans, an insurance agent who, for reasons she does not quite understand, has become sort of a counselor, helping people with needs other than insurance. Seasons one and two capture this aspect with Gayle becoming more like a psychologist than an insurance agent (although most of those seeking help are her clients). Third season episodes change the format to focus on Gayle becoming involved with a producer (Rafael) and his efforts to turn her story into a Broadway musical called *Policies, Policies* (the story of a lovable small town insurance agent who helps her clients solve problems other than insurance).

Cast: Elisa Donovan (Gayle Evans), Sarah Taylor (Mrs. Anderson), Todd Waring (Mr. Anderson), Sarah Baker (Smith), Dan Donohue (Rafael), Kirk Fox (Jack Stumpfl), Ginger Gonzaga (Kim Kaminski), Jeremy Rowley (Drake LaBouche), Brian Palermo (Mike Evans), James McCauley (Mr. Monroe), Grace Bannon (Harper Simone Chanteuse), Gary Anthony Williams (Zeke Robinson), Shane Cambria (Charlie Evans), Jennifer Chang (Anna), Jonathan Spencer (Andrew Stillman). **Credits:** *Producer:* Brent Forrester, Elisa Donovan, Ryan Noggle, Tatiana Derovanessian, Jason Farrand, Sheridan Thayer, Farzin Toussi. *Director:* Brent Forrester, Sandy Smolan, Jason Farrand. *Writer:* Anthony Q. Farrell, Brent Forrester, Timothy McKeon, Kevin Seccia. **Comment:** Elisa Donovan, co-star of the ABC TV series' *Clueless* and *Sabrina the Teenage Witch* shines here just as she did on ABC. The production values are network quality and while stories are complete in themselves, some have recurring characters (like Mr. and Mrs. Anderson) who require additional help beyond their first meeting with Gayle.

Season 1 Episodes: *1.* Gayle and the Rival. *2.* Gayle and the Plumber. *3.* Gayle and the Teen Driver. *4.* Gayle and the Report Card. *5.* Gayle and the Hypnotist. *6.* Gayle and the Birthday Call. *7.* Gayle and the Fender Bender. *8.* Gayle and the Newlyweds. *9.* Gayle and the Soccer Lesson. *10.* Gayle and the Dog.

Season 2 Episodes: *1.* Gayle and the Salon. *2.* Gayle and the Accident. *3.* Gayle and the Tow Truck. *4.* Gayle and the New Parents. *5.* Gayle and the Changes. *6.* Gayle and the Coach. *7.* Gayle and the Rock Star. *8.* Gayle and the White Whale. *9.* Gayle and the Chili Cook-off. *10.* Gayle and the New Technology.

Season 3 Episodes: *1.* Gayle and the Shadow. *2.* Gayle and the Investors. *3.* Gayle and the Auditions. *4.* Gayle and the Table Read. *5.* Gayle and the Car Washer.... And Rafael. *6.* Gayle and the Notes. *7.* Gayle and the Breakdown. *8.* Gayle and the Pep Talk. *9.* Gayle and the Opening Night. *10.* Gayle and the Musical.

469 *In Her Shoes.* youtube.com. 2011.

Beatrice, Dolores, Martina, Miriam and Letizia are presumably very beautiful young women who turn to each other for advice as they navigate the working world and dating life. The women appear to be always fashionably dressed and wear the latest in footwear. The program, produced in Spain, charts the situations the women encounter—as seen from a shoes-eye view as they talk gossip, discuss intimate secrets, relate relationship problems and in general, just chat. It has been said, "You can recognize a woman by her shoes," and *In Her Shoes* sets out to prove it.

Cast: Liliana Olivieri (Beatrice), Sharon Fryer (Dolores), Marianne Hasley (Miriam), Rachel Roberts (Letizia), Audrey Sadleir (Martina). Credits: *Producer:* Lorena Adami, Alessandro Perrone. *Director:* Lorena Adami, Alessandro Paci. Comment: Clever idea wherein the shoes the ladies wear are the actual "stars." Based on the shoes seen, it is assumed the women are gorgeous (their faces are never seen) and always fashionably dressed. Although the program is in Spanish (an English translation is available) it can be enjoyed by anyone whether they speak Spanish or not as the focus is on the shoes and how the women who wear them manipulate them as if they were alive.

Episodes: *1.* Monday Morning. *2.* The Feminine Touch. *3.* The Context of a Woman.

470 *In Pursuit of Nothing.* webserieschannel.com. 2011.

Jacin is a former recording star who has fallen on hard times. He hasn't made an album or had a hit in years and now lives with his second cousin (Jonah), both of whom are also struggling to just pay the rent. Jacin is optimistic and believes that life will soon change for the better as he believes people still love him and it is only a matter of time before he becomes famous. His spirits are lifted when a documentary film crew offers to chart his life—only to make Jacin realize in the end that nobody (his fans) ever loved him and he just doesn't fit the mold for being famous.

Cast: Jacin Shrives (Jacin), Johanna Huston (Jonah), Ruby Kemp (Rebecca), Peter Miedema (Peter), Tyler Campbell (Tyler). Credits: *Producer-Writer:* Jacin Shrives, Ruby Kemp. Comment: All video information has been taken off line and it appears that only one episode has been produced ("This Video Is Private" will appear on attempts to watch it). By text information, the word "flat" and "flat-mate" is used indicating that it may have been a British produced program.

Episodes: *1.* The New Roommate.

471 *In Real Life.* youtube.com. 2012.

Things happen. We can't control them and most are just unwelcome situations that we must endure. For five friends (Elaine, Michael, London, Cassie and Terrence) who live in Sacramento, California, the unwelcome continually happens and the program follows their efforts to overcome them by the only means they know how—through each other although being friends is the only thing they have in common.

Cast: Asia Rey (London), Christa Quinn (Cassie), Robert Shiple (Terrence), Romann Hodge (Michael), Vanita Johnson (Elaine). Credits: *Producer-Writer:* Patrick Harris. *Director:* Patrick Harris, Christa Quinn. Comment: Although tagged as a comedy, the program has its dramatic moments and is well acted and produced.

Episodes: *1.* The Break-Up. *2.* The B**** Is Back. *3.* A Little Late. *4.* The Long Day.

472 *In the Key of Z.* webserieschannel.com. 2012.

During the 1990s a rock band called Noah's Park (Noah, Cassie, Len and Parker) ruled and just as fast as they rose to fame, they quickly fell into obscurity. Although they sold six million albums, all the band mates, except Noah, knew there was no going back (Noah believed he will one day recapture the glory of his past). When a documentary film maker believes there is a story in Noah, he reorganizes the band for a 10 year reunion concert. It is the night of the concert and fans are beginning to commence when it is learned that the fans are anything but fans, but zombies, the by-product of a recent apocalypse and for those unaffected, it has become a battle for survival. The program follows the band members as they join forces to battle an evil that exists and find a safe haven.

Cast: Keith Cooper (Noah), Saffron Cassaday (Cassie), J.R. Digs (Len), Dave Thomson (Parker), Jacob Allen (P. Quivers), Bob Charters (Bob), April Morgan (Roxy), Derek Sunderland (Chance). Credits: *Producer:* Saffron Cassaday, Keith Cooper, April

Morgan, Derek Sunderland, Dave Thomson. *Director:* Keith Cooper, Jeffrey P. Nesker, Melanie Orr. *Writer:* Keith Cooper. **Comment:** Literally a dark comedy that centers around a zombie apocalypse. The acting and production values are good but the program ends unresolved.

Episodes: *1.* Pilot. *2.* It Gets Real. *3.* What Now? *4.* While My Guitar Gently Bleeds. *5.* Lullaby. *6.* Divided We Fall. *7.* Olive Branches. *8.* Oh Brother. *9.* Family.

473 *In the Motherhood.* youtube.com. 2007–2008.

Kim, Kelly and Heather are women who are also mothers (and supposedly representative "of mothers we all know"). Kim and Heather are sisters (each is also divorced); Ashley is Kim's daughter; Joyce is Kim and Heather's mother. True life incidents faced by mothers are re-enacted from stories written by actual mothers and submitted to the show's website (created by its sponsors Sprint and Suave). In 2009 ABC adapted the program to TV in a version that featured Megan Mullally (Rosemary), Cheryl Hines (Jane) and Jessica St. Clair (Emily) as mothers in stories "inspired by real life experiences of real life mothers."

Cast: Leah Remini (Kim), Jenny McCarthy (Kelly), Chelsea Handler (Heather), Alina Foley (Ashley), Lainie Kazan, Jane Curtin (Joyce), Eileen Galindo (Maria; Kim's friend), Kylee Anderson (Kelly, age 6), Dannika Liddell (Jenny), Liberty Lubran (Kim's daughter), Taylor Pigeon (Kelly, age 3). **Comment:** Professionally acted and produced with a name cast (a rarity in Internet series). While the program has been taken off-line and its television version also gathering dust in some storage unit, both versions were amusing depictions of the problems faced by mothers and how, with the help of friends and family, they attempt to not only cope with them, but also solve them.

Episodes: *1.* The Mother of All Days. *2.* Nightmare on a Plane. *3.* Bedtime, Dreadtime. *4.* The Birds and Bees Talk. *5.* The Ex Becomes Your Doctor. *6.* Just Shoot Me, Cupid. *7.* The Preacher, the Panties and the Policeman. *8.* The Infamous Third Date. *9.* All's Fair in Love and War Sibling Rivalry. *10.* Mother Dearest.

474 *In Transit.* youtube.com. 2012.

A group of six friends, four men (Caesar, Marcus, Arj and Matt), and their two female companions, Maya and Yvonne and how, now that they are in their twenties, they will find their place in the world.

Cast: John Gomez Goodway (Caesar), Thulaisi Sivapalan (Arj), Alex Millwood (Marcus), Nicholas Richard (Matt), Maddy Butler (Maya), Jorja Brain (Yvonne). **Credits:** *Producer:* Haris Kruskic, Azi Wallmeyer. *Director:* Alastair Wharton. **Comment:**

Australian produced program that is basically the friends exploring their options. The acting and production is good but there is the use of vulgar language.

Episodes: 7 untitled episodes, labeled "Episode 1" through "Episode 7."

475 *In Your Dreams.* youtube.com. 2014.

Lisa and Sammi are friends who have one very unusual trait in common: they play out their fantasies to cope with their realities. Each episode establishes a specific situation, first showing the fantasy solution to the problem then returning to reality to let the friends actually deal with what is facing them.

Cast: Lisa McGurn (Lisa), Sammi Cains (Sammi). **Credits:** *Director:* Tyler Newhouse. *Writer:* Lisa McGurn, Sammi Cains. **Comment:** Well done program that is a bit different than other buddy-buddy programs with good acting and interesting situations for the girls to face.

Episodes: *1.* Grow a Pair. *2.* Work It Out. *3.* Just One Beer. *4.* The Run In. *5.* Gain Some, Lose Some.

476 *Indie.* webchannelseries.com. 2012.

Josh, Chad, Roland and Lowell are young men attempting to live their dream of achieving rock music stardom. But they live in the real world and must face real life situations, beginning with accepting the fact that fame and fortune can be had but struggles must be overcome first. As the friends begin that rocky climb to the top, they are followed by a crew of amateur filmmakers who have chosen to document their activities (which are explored, at least in the only episode filmed, the pilot).

Cast: Stephen Andrew, Tyler Gianesini, Travis Blood, Levi Gable, Paul Macs, Jon Floyd, Sidney Jayne Hunt, Spencer Baldwin. **Credits:** *Producer-Writer:* Tyler Gianesini, Stephen Andrew, Spencer Baldwin. *Director:* Tyler Gianesini. **Comment:** It is difficult to predict where future episodes would take the band based on only the pilot episode. While the acting and production are okay, it does have bleeped foul language and an unsatisfying conclusion as nothing is really resolved.

Episodes: *1.* Lockdown.

477 *Infinite Issues.* mongrelstudios.com. 2013.

The Alter Egos is a comic book shop that employs a young woman named Becca, perhaps the only person who is not a geek like her boyfriend (Tom) or the shop regulars. Becca is hoping for a normal relationship with Tom but Tom is, like his friends, totally into comic books and their related mystique. The program explores what happens when Tom and others like him attempt to mix their fantasy lives with their social lives and what happens to Becca when, in the only story presented, she sees life through Tom's eyes when she is forced to host a midnight release party for a popular trading card game at the shop.

Cast: Rebecca Teran (Becca), Quinn Allan (Tom), Matt Voisine (Arlo), Jacob Bean-Watson (Cormac), Jonah Weston (Barry), Lindsae Klein (Sativa), Joshua Stenseth (Chris), Aparna Brielle (Lylyth), Jeffrey Janoff (Zazreal), Ethan Reed McKay (Kevin), Brynn Baron (Annie). **Credits:** *Producer:* Jared Yanez, Quinn Allan. *Writer-Director:* Jared Yanez. **Comment:** Somewhat talkative program that has an idea but drags out the premise. The acting is good but there are adult themes (mostly sexual related) that may offend some viewers.

Episodes: *1.* Right Hand of Diva. *2.* Seduction of the Innocent. *3.* Blackest Night. *4.* Go Eat a Beat. *5.* Directing Barry.

478 *Inside the Legend.* webserieschannel. com. 2012.

Was Lizzie Borden the famous ax murderer history records? Did Jack and Jill (from the nursery rhyme) start their own business when they grew up? Is St. Peter, Keeper of the Pearly Gates, really in God's Inner Circle? Is William Shakespeare the real Bard as history makes him out to be? These are just a few of the many questions Chaz Hannigan and Rhonda Kokopele would like answered, and their efforts to get those answers by interviewing the people (real and fictional) behind the legend are showcased.

Cast: Phil LaMarr (Chaz Hannigan), Vanessa Ragland (Rhonda Kokopele). **Credits:** *Producer:* Phil LaMarr, Cindi Rice, John Frank Rosenblum. *Director:* Jason Axinn. *Writer:* Tony Wallace, Jason Axinn, Phil LaMarr. **Comment:** A great idea with very good acting and production values. While there are both male and female guests, for some reason the producers chose to have the male host (Chaz) interview the female guests while Rhonda interviews the male guests (depending on who is hosting, he or she explains why his or her co-host was unavailable for a particular episode). The guests who appear are not like you pictured or have seen before. Lizzie Borden, for example, is a hip-talking modern-day Valley-like girl (who still wields an ax); John Henry, the famous strong man who engaged in a railroad rail spiking contest against a machine, reveals that he also created that rail spiking machine; and Jill (from Jack and Jill) is now a wealthy woman who started a water hauling business with Jack but must now "suffer" alone as Jack was killed in an accident.

Episodes: *1.* Lizzie Borden. *2.* John Henry. *3.* Shakespeare. *4.* Saint Peter. *5.* Jill. *6.* Beowulf. *7.* Musashi (Japanese Swordsman). *8.* Joan of Arc. *9.* Lancelot. *10.* Jezebel. *11.* Freud. *12.* Pandora.

479 *Insourcing.* webserieschannel.com. 2012.

James and Travis are customer service representatives for United Family Products. Supposedly they have been hired to help customers over the phone, but that appears to be the farthest thing from their mind as texting and talking to one another are more important. With that thought (and perhaps showing what people think is happening when they try to get customer support from a company) the program is simply a look at what James and Travis accomplish each day.

Cast: Fabian Lopez (Travis), Daniel Bokor (James), Greg Vestal (Dicklan). **Credits:** *Writer:* Stephnay Keller. *Director:* B.J. Lewis. *Writer:* Billy Mau. **Comment:** A talkative, no action program that has standard acting and Internet production values (acceptable but cannot compare to a broadcast or cable series).

Episodes: 15 untitled episodes, labeled "Episode 1" through "Episode 15."

480 *The Institute.* webserieschannel.com. 2010.

The Institute is an acting school run by four friends (Bambi, C.J., Edwina and Jackie) that has declared itself a non-profit educational institution. While legitimate schools can claim that for tax purposes, The Institute has just claimed it to avoid taxes as it is a school for students to learn the art of adult (porno) films. It offers a six week course and a starring role for each student in their own film upon graduation (directed by adult film expert Jackie Fitzgerald). CJ, a former adult film star (of such classics as *Ding Dong You're Dead* and *Fist Cop*), concocted the idea and the program, set in the 1970s in the San Fernando Valley at the breakout era of such films, relates how students learn to make and star in triple XXX rated films. See also *Porno School.*

Cast: Mo Mandel (C.J.), Gena Shaw (Jackie), Danny Lampson (Edwin), Annie McCain Engman (Samantha), Clifford Banagale (Bambi), Nir Assayag (Dan), Shawn Kathryn Kane (Patricia), Will Hawkes (Tim), Kelly Landry (Sarah), Anna Moon (Ling Ling), Stefany Mandap (Mei Lie), Jennifer Lynne (Debbie), Gina Torrecilla (Ronda), Cindy Trometer (Jackie), Laura Waddell (Liz). **Credits:** *Producer:* Jeff Anderson, Michael Anderson, Nate Cardoza, David Coxxolino, Brett Mortenson, Elizabeth Bicholson, Robert Shannon. *Director:* Tyrone Huff. *Writer:* David Martin Cohen. **Comment:** While there is no nudity, there are suggestive sexual situations and the program should (but doesn't) have a parental warning. The acting feels a bit forced at times (just not natural) and the production itself tries hard to depict the golden age of adult film making (when future stars like Candy Samples, Ron Jeremy, Kay Parker, Annette Haven and Seka were just getting started).

Episodes: *1.* Dirty Sanchez. *2.* The Blumpkin. *3.*

C.J. vs. Paul. *4.* The Rusty Trombone. *5.* Donley Punch. *6.* Dog in the Bathtub. *7.* The Perfect Ending. *8.* First Base. *9.* Tea Bagging. *10.* Pearl Necklace. *11.* First Interracial Scene Ever.

481 Interactive Sex: The Arcade Game. webserieschannel.com. 2012.

As an episode begins, primitive characters from a vintage eight-bit video game transform into live action personalities and are presented with a comical dilemma: what to do when faced with a tough decision (as listed in episodes). The program was originally interactive and allowed the viewer to choose one of the two characters (that appear in each episode) then select one of six choices that were available (hence, the outcome is determined by the viewer's selection).

Cast: Gabe Michael, Sophia Monti, David Wuest, Alexis Jones, Brittany Rohm, Hannah Townsend, John Charles Meyer, Ryan Holloway. **Credits:** *Creator:* Gabe Michael, David Wuest. **Comment:** Episodes are now under two minutes each as each one ends unresolved. When originally presented, the interactive aspect allowed each episode to run about six minutes. It can still be seen that the program was well conceived with good acting and production values.

Episodes: *1.* Donkey Punch Country (Player Meets a Lady of the Night). *2.* Call of Booty (Player Must Decide between Helping an Injured Jogger or Taking a Phone Call). *3.* Womb Raider (Player Must Decide Between a Jogger and His Ex). *4.* Street Walker (Player Meets a Friendly Woman on the Street). *5.* Beards of War (Player Tries to Get Into a Party).

482 Internet Affairs. blip.tv. 2012.

Erica, April and Jodi, three young women living in New York City, have reached the end of their rope when it comes to finding the perfect man. Their dating experiences have been anything but satisfactory and to resolve their dilemma they hit on a plan to use Internet dating. The program, based on "real-life dating disasters and romantic ups and downs," charts what happens when they are matched with a man chosen by a computer.

Cast: Johanny Mota (Erica), Chantal Ngwa (Jodi), Heather Cambanes (April). **Credits:** *Producer:* Johanny Mota. *Director:* Katie McHugh. **Comment:** Charming program with very good acting and production values. The program, although ending unresolved, leaves the doorway open to continue the dating mishaps of the three leads.

Episodes: *1.* Setting Up a Profile. *2.* The Dog Walker. *3.* Caps. *4.* The Actor. *5.* You're Not on My Path. *6.* The Birthday. *7.* Oh Mother! *8.* Thimble Robin. *9.* Manage Anyone? *10.* Bad Service. *11.* New Friends.

483 Internet Famous. webserieschannel.com. 2014.

Andy Palumbo is thirty years old and living in Pittsburgh. He has always yearned to be something—artist, filmmaker or writer; what he has is a job as a copy editor of the "Celebrity Corner" column on the city's second worst newspaper. One night frustration gets the best of Andy and he gets drunk. Unknown to him, his roommate records an obscene rant with his video camera and posts it on line. The video ("Assdick Andy") immediately goes viral (with over two million hits) and Andy becomes an Internet sensation—but it is not the kind of fame Andy had dreamed about. Andy's world has now changed and the program follows what happens due to all the fallout that results from that posted video.

Cast: Trent Wolfred (Andy), Matthew Robison (Dave), Lish Danielle (Kim), Cori Shetter (Emma), Elyse Alberts (Gabby), Richard Eckman (Tom). **Credits:** *Producer:* Justin Manna, Robert Simpson. *Writer-Director:* Tom Williams, Chris Lee. **Comment:** There is an over abundant use of vulgar language and stories that are, for the most part, just Andy seeking to do what he wants to do most—become a writer for something better than his newspaper job.

Episodes: *1.* What Kind of Day Has It Been? *2.* The Word. *3.* Not Another Catch Phrase Sitcom? *4.* The Gang Goes for a Night Out. *5.* The One with the Flashback. *6.* Episode 6. *7.* Internet Famous.

484 Introverts. youtube.com. 2014–2015.

Susan, Amy and Waltra are young women who have one thing in common—each is an introvert. They have difficulty communicating with others (even females) and even more trauma making decisions (like, wanting to order pizza—but who will make the call). The program charts the situations the girls encounter and how they deal with the issues when coming out of their shells is not as easy as it sounds.

Cast: Abby Dillion (Susan), Aina Dumlao (Waltra), Rachel Tucker (Amy). **Credits:** *Producer:* Rachel Tucker, Nick Lawrence. *Director:* Nick Lawrence. *Writer:* Rachel Tucker. **Comment:** Exceptionally well-done program that flows smoothly from episode to episode. The leads are very appealing and the program is both well acted and produced.

Season 1 Episodes: *1.* The Extrovert. *2.* The Pizza. *3.* The Meet Cute. *4.* The Party.

Season 2 Episodes: *1.* The Magic Bullet. *2.* The Nazi. *3.* The Scarf. *4.* The Christmas Special.

485 Involuntarily Single. vimeo.com. 2012.

Maggie, Vanessa and Faye are three young women living in Los Angeles. Although they date, they have each learned that finding Mr. Right is seemingly impossible as all the men they meet are losers. In an effort to solve their dilemma, they hit on an idea to engage in Internet dating. The program chronicles what happens as they embark on a new way of dating and encounter more disasters than dream dates.

Cast: Jessee Foudray (Maggie), Vanessa Bednar (Faye), Sonya T. Evans (Jackie), Mickaelle Bizet (Mimi), Briana Kennedy (Dora), Yumi Ishibashi (Yumi), Martha Jameson (Brittany), Karina Wielgosz (Lois). **Credits:** *Producer:* Loretta Clay, Louis McGruder, Sonya T. Evans. *Director:* Sonya T. Evans, Louis McGruder. *Writer:* Sonya T. Evans, Louis McGruder, Tyme Rison. **Comment:** Charming little program depicting the ups and downs women encounter trying to meet Mr. Right. Like the program *Internet Affairs*, it is an interesting look at the joys and sorrows of Internet dating.

Episodes: *1.* Hitting a Brick Wall. *2.* Frog Extractions. *3.* Love vs. the Heart. *4.* It's Decision Time. *5.* Challenge Accepted. *6.* Molded from Fire. *7.* Sizzle Reel.

486 *Is It Me?* webserieschannel.com. 2010–2012.

A look at the romantic ups and downs of six close friends in their early twenties as they help each other navigate the dating scene: Alana, Julian, Melanie, Nick, Brandon and Olivia.

Cast: Andrea Cortes (Alana), Justin Jones (Julian), April Ronquillo (Melanie), Philip Renard (Nick), Londale Theus, Jr. (Brandon), Sheree Swanson (Olivia), Otto Tony Graham (Randy), Giovanni Watson (Xavier), Allen English (David), Yumarie Morales (Amanda), Noel Gibson (Rebecca). **Credits:** *Producer:* Rudy Murillo, Holly McGuinn. *Director:* Sean Patrick Cannon, Charles Clemmons, Holly McGuinn, Tim Daniel, Gary LeRoi Gray. *Writer:* Holly McGuinn. **Comment:** Likeable cast coupled with good acting and production values.

Season 1 Episodes: *1.* Pilot. *2.* Twitter Fail. *3.* Love Me Not. *4.* Text Talk. *5.* One on One. *6.* Fork in the Road. *7.* Like At It's Finest. *8.* Dirty Little Secrets. *9.* Surprise. *10.* What's Going to Happen Next?

Season 2 Episodes: *1.* Illusions. *2.* New Friends.

487 *Is This Thing On?* youtube.com. 2013.

Stand-up comedy is the dream of a young man named Stan. Unfortunately, his material is simply awful and not at all funny. His life, however, is just the opposite—as the incidents that happen to him can make people laugh, but Stan has not made the connection to turn his life into his stage act. Believing that he has no purpose in life, he seeks help by joining a support group to hopefully turn things around. As Stan tells of his woes, flashback sequences are used to relay aspects of his life and how missed opportunities could have made all the difference.

Cast: Kyle Bondeson, David Fabozzi, Paulina San Millan, Rebecca Whiteman, Olinka Clay, Justin Bondeson, Ian Troy. **Credits:** *Director:* David Higgins. *Writer:* Kyle Bondeson, Patrick Bowler. **Comment:** Only a pilot episode has been produced and based on that alone, the program appears very talkative and uninteresting. The acting and production are just acceptable.

Episodes: *1.* Pilot.

488 *Issues (2011).* webserieschannel.com. 2011.

Ever since he can remember Ted wanted to become a psychologist and help the world's greatest super heroes with their problems. His dream becomes more of a nightmare when he receives his degree and acquires the clients he yearned for—who appear to him in animated form and saddled with numerous neuroses that are slowly driving him to see his own psychologist to deal with the issues they are implanting in him (that in a world of super heroes he is just un-super). Ted's clients include Captain Magnificent, The Dark Kodiak, Side Car, K-9, The Nothing and The Incredible Flame.

Captain Magnificent, although invincible and handsome, has identity issues and feels he needs to reveal his real self to the public. The Dark Kodiak is a vigilante by night who in his true identity is a billionaire. Although he is a martial arts expert, can speak 15 languages and uses out-of-this world gadgets to battle evil, he is burdened by insecurities. Side Car, Kodiak's sidekick, is fed up with being just a sidekick and wants to become his own super hero; the problem: Kodiak won't let him leave. K-9 is a blind super hero who is never quite sure he has actually stopped crimes due to his disability. He also has issues as to what he looks like in his super hero costume and whether he actually punched out a bank robber or was it some innocent by-stander. The Nothing is invisible and, because nobody can see him, he is never held responsible for his actions but constantly worries that because of his condition, he may be considered a pervert for what he can do. The Incredible Flame has issues about everything because he is constantly on fire and has nothing, including friends, sex or clothes.

Cast: Josh Cooke (Ted), Joanna Canton (Lisa), Seth Green (Side Car), Greg Grunberg (The Dark Kodiak), Ron Livingston (The Nothing), Rob Riggle (Captain Magnificent), Eric Stonestreet (K-9), Eddie Kaye Thomas (The Incredible Flame). **Credits:** *Producer:* Matt Oates, Josh Cooke, Clio Tegel. *Director:* Matt Oates. *Writer:* Josh Cooke, Matt Oates. *Animation Producer:* Ben Kalina. **Comment:** Clever super hero take off that is set in Ted's office with Ted on one side and the animated super hero seated opposite him. Using animation for the super heroes is also something different and blending it with live action works well. Only one episode, "Side

Car" is still on line and, although it may not pertain to the other episodes, be prepared for Side Car's continual use of vulgar language.

Episodes: *1.* Captain Midnight. *2.* Side Car. *3.* K-9. *4.* The Dark Kodiak. *5.* The Nothing. *6.* The Incredible Flame.

489 Issues (2014). youtube.com. 2014.

Kate is a young woman who has numerous issues (as depicted in the episode titles below) and having a somewhat difficult time handling them. Each episode is a focus on one particular issue and how Kate attempts to deal with it.

Cast: Richelle Meiss (Kate), Nate Weisband, Shawn Allen Robinson, Aaron Shand, Kate Kugler. Credits: *Producer-Writer:* Richelle Meiss. *Director:* Lorin Becker, Eric Davis. Comment: Rather than become a program of discussion it wisely chose to present Kate's issues through scenes of her actually confronting them with the viewer seeing what starts it off, how it progresses and how Kate tries to deal with it (but always falling short of conquering it). Richelle Meiss can actually make you believe that she has issues beyond those that were presented.

Episodes: *1.* Insecurity. *2.* Paruresis (a fear of using a public restroom). *3.* Baggage. *4.* Desperation. *5.* Loneliness. *6.* Catestrophizing (automatically assuming a worst case scenario). *7.* Paranoia.

490 It Could Get Worse. itcouldgetworse. tv. 2013–2014.

For a young actor named Jacob Gordon, there appears to be no hope of acquiring starring roles as he feels his being gay has closed those doors. He is also in a floundering relationship with Philip and finds that his parents (Judy and Leo) simply cannot accept his life choices. To make matters worse, Judy and Leo have just separated and Leo has moved in with him. But there is a light at the end of the tunnel: he has been asked to audition for a starring role in a Broadway musical called *The Ice Queen.* The jubilation, however, is short-lived when he discovers that his co-star is Veronica Bailey, a notoriously temperamental stage star who is not only difficult to work with, but known for being a diva that gets her way or it's no way at all. A struggling actor about to land the role of his dreams and what happens as he not only deals with Veronica, but all the other annoyances that happen to be a part of his hectic life.

Cast: Wesley Taylor (Jacob Gordon), Gideon Glick (Philip Klein), Alison Fraser (Veronica Bailey), Adam Chanler-Berat (Ben Farrel), Mitchell Jarvis (Sam Atkinson), Brennan Brown (Rich), Richard Poe (Leo Gordon), Nancy Opel (Judy Gordon), Bryce Ryness (Hank), Hannah Nordberg (Sadie), Blake Daniel (Colin), Jennifer Damiano (Stacy). Credits: *Producer:* Paula Marie Black, Jesse Stalnaker, Mitchell Jarvis, Wesley Taylor, Paris

Remillard. *Writer-Director:* Mitchell Jarvis, Wesley Taylor. Comment: Well acted and produced look at a young gay man and what surrounds him.

Episodes: *1.* Give 'Em Hell for Me, Kid. *2.* He Sounds Like a Girl. *3.* Lighten Up. *4.* Let Down Your Hair. *5.* Terrible People. *6.* Uncharted Territory. *7.* Straight Offer. *8.* Too Much Candy. *9.* Fate.

491 It Gets Betterish. itgetsbetterish.com. 2011.

An obsession with singer Lady Gaga, flamboyance and immaculate attire are some of the attributes people associate with gay men. Eliot and Brent, two such men, are friends not lovers, and detest those labels society has placed on them. But they are a part of society and emulate a stereotypical gay life style to fit in (and encounter all the annoyances that attach themselves to gay men, like orgies and straight women who seek that perfect "gay best friend"). In essence, the program profiles two gay men who could be perceived as odd and the complications that arise when Brent, a closeted transgender, reveals that he is pregnant.

Cast: Eliot Glazer (Eliot), Brent Sullivan (Brent), Nicole Byer, Michael Hartney, Ann Carr. Credits: *Producer:* Seth Keim. *Director:* Randy Foreman. *Writer:* Eliot Glazer, Brent Sullivan. Comment: Although the program ends unresolved regarding the pregnancy issue (other than Brent dreaming of giving birth) it is still enjoyable to watch. Although episode 8 is the most offensive (excessive amounts of vulgar language—although it is bleeped) other episodes have such words left untouched. Why? The acting is good and the overall production well executed.

Episodes: *1.* Drag Queen. *2.* Lady Gaga. *3.* Gay Republican. *4.* Pregnant. *5.* Karaoke. *6.* Party Monster. *7.* Orgy. *8.* Fag Hag. *9.* HIV AIDS Test.

492 It's Mel. youtube.com. 2014.

Putaruru is a small town in New Zealand and home to Mel, a man who feels he needs to get out of his predicament, move to the big city and find his calling in life. He takes the first step and moves to the city of Auckland but is totally unprepared for what he has done. With no place to go, he turns up at his cousin, Lisa's home but is not all that welcome as Paul, Lisa's husband, simply does not like Mel. Soon after, and with the help of his friend Alisha, Mel establishes an Internet business called Spy Mel (wherein he is a detective of sorts and will help people find things) and future episodes (if produced) appear to focus on his spy adventures. Lisa is a writer; Paul a college anthropology professor.

Cast: Mark Scott (Mel), Lisette de Jong (Lisa), Paul Paice (Paul), Alisha Lawrie-Paul (Alisha), John Palino (Himself). Credits: *Producer-Writer:* Lisette de Jong. Comment: If you had Mel as a relative you may want to hire a hit man to take him out as he can be that annoying. That characteristic works well here in a well acted and produced New Zealand series.

Episodes: *1.* You, Me and Mel. *2.* Auckland. *3.* Business Time. *4.* The Palino Job. *5.* Alisha. *6.* Spy Me.

493 It's Not You. vimeo.com. 2013.

Julia and Laura are roommates who each have a knack for what they call "bad dating" (not only meeting losers in person but also through hook ups on the Internet). The program is a look at the not-so-great dates each of the women has as seen through their conversations following such a disastrous date.

Cast: Cristina Lark (Laura), Anna Elena Pepe (Julia), Alex Roseman (The "Princess" Guy), Zac Gabriel (The "Man" Guy), Mark Nunnington (Adrian), Barry McStay (The "Married" Guy), Masafumi Yamaguchi (The "Sushi" Guy), Jaz Bailey (The "Phone" Guy), Ruggero Dalla Santa (The "Office" Guy), William Alexander (The "Moon" Guy), Matthew Cosgrove (The "German" Guy), Craig Daniel Adams (The "Dazzled" Guy), JP Lord (The "Milano" Guy) **Credits:** *Producer-Writer-Director:* Cristina Lark. **Comment:** How two such pretty girls as depicted through Cristina and Julia always manage to pick losers can only happen on TV (now on the Internet too). The program is well acted and tightly woven to present the dates, which begin with Cristina and Julia talking about what happened and brief flashbacks being incorporated to illustrate their points.

Episodes: 7 untitled episodes, labeled "Episode" 1 through "Episode 7."

494 It's Still Real to Us. funnyordie.com. 2013.

Mikey, Harry, Dan and Naitch are life-long friends and devout wrestling fans. Following their high school graduation, the friendship loses one of its members when Dan and his family move to another city. As happens in such situations, touch is lost and each accepts the fact that they must move on. It is years later when Mikey, Harry and Naitch hatch a plan to recapture what they once had with Dan by organizing a high school reunion. They believe it is going to be like old times until, at the reunion they not only see that Dan has become a corporate stooge (working for Fine Crescent Enterprises) but he has married the boss's daughter (Nikki), a girl who takes an instant dislike to them and forbids Dan from associating with them (as she thinks watching wrestling is for idiots). The program charts Mikey, Harry and Naitch's efforts to retrieve their old friend by making him see that what he once had is what he still needs, despite his job position and wife.

Cast: Liam Thomas Burke (Harry), Matt Dixon (Mikey), Karl Davies (Naitch), Tom Robb (Dan), Lisa Rohnagan (Nikki), Alan Watton (Mr. Hickenbottom), Maura Judges (Mrs. Parker), Jamie Attril (Jimmy). **Credits:** *Producer:* Matt Dixon, Liam Thomas Burke, Karl Davies. *Director:* Matt Dixon, Liam Thomas Burke. *Writer:* Matt Dixon. **Comment:** Although the program comes off as a bit sleazy-looking when first begun, it does improve in appearance and becomes a program that would most likely appeal only to wrestling fans as the three main buddies are overly possessed fans of the sport and what's worse they believe wrestling is real (and no one can convince them otherwise). Dan's transition from what he was to what he has now become is well done with him yearning to become that kid again but encountering a fierce stumbling block—Nikki.

Episodes: *1–3.* The Reunion.

495 It's Temporary. itstemporary.wix.com. 2013.

Sasha, Robin, Jessica, Dan and Argo are tenants at the Easy Point Apartments, a California complex managed by a woman named Marjory. Although strangers to each other when they first moved in, Robin, Sasha and Argo (the older of the three) have since become friends and the program charts what happens as they navigate the world that surrounds them—from their individual romantic pursuits to the pressures of work to just trying to find some alone time away from the hectic situations that surround them.

Sasha, "The Angel," is a first grade foreign language teacher who hopes to become a Yale professor. She is an intellectual (loves reading and art galleries) and dreams about finding her Prince Charming. Sasha, very proper and modest, despises people who use foul language and prefers not to engage in small talk.

Marjory is the building manager and is the town gossip. While she is cheerful and fun to be around, she is also loud and talkative. Marjory has a good heart and even though she appears bossy, kind words can melt her heart and soften her up.

Robin, called "The Heart Breaker," is outspoken and feels comfortable dating more than one guy at a time. She is very friendly, likes to party and hopes to become an interior designer (she currently works as a kids' party decorator).

Argo, "The Artist," is a painter although he works as an usher in a small theatre and still receives a monthly allowance from his family. He enjoys the company of younger women and has avoided marriage because he fears growing old with anybody. Those who meet Argo believe he is an intellectual but in reality he isn't as he knows just enough to give people that impression.

Dan is an animal lover (works at Pet Hotel) who dreams of owning a five star hotel. He is a movie buff, smug, opinionated, sarcastic and blunt. Dan is also insecure (although he is able to hide this from his friends) and appears charming but his reserved personality gives women the impression that he is a bit weird.

Jessica, a perfectionist, is Robin's half sister. She works as an editor for a small newspaper and is competitive and bossy. She dreams of becoming a news editor for CNN (Cable News Network) and, although she doesn't realize it, she is a workaholic. Jessica is also a bit neurotic and rarely dates because she feels no man is good enough for her (thus she has only short-fling relationships).

Cast: Svetlana Islamova (Sasha), Desi Ivanova (Robin), Anthony Montes (Argo), Valorie Hubbard (Marjory), Kika Cicmanec (Jessica), Tony Evangelista (Dan). **Credits:** *Producer:* Svetlana Islamova, Desi Ivanova. *Director:* Sebastiano Olla. *Writer:* Sebastiano Olla, Desi Ivanova, Joshua Martin. **Comment:** Smooth-flowing, well acted program that manages to make its own statement—from an annoying landlady (Marjory) to a sweet and innocent girl (Sasha) to a much older artist (Argo) who paints beyond what he sees (an example being Sasha posing for him fully clothed but being painted nude).

Episodes: *1.* Temporary Stranger. *2.* Temporary Bug Sitting. *3.* Temporary Nudity. *4.* Temporary Boyfriends. *5.* Temporary Egg Hunt. *6.* Temporary Friends. *7.* Temporary Attack. *8.* Temporary Dare. *9,10.* Temporary Farewell.

496 Itty Bitty Liddy. tv.com. 2007.

G. Gordon Liddy, a real-life FBI agent and Watergate scandal organizer provides the basis for Liddy, an six-inch high man created by government scientists to implicate left-wing political figures. It is assumed Liddy was once a normal size human and through experimentation was reduced to his current size. With their goal accomplished, Liddy's superiors, the Right Brothers, now plan to use Liddy as a secret agent to infiltrate the government and expose corruption. Liddy, however, finds that the conservative Right brothers are not what they profess to be and their assignments not only put his life in danger but constantly require him to change his course of action to survive. The dangerous and sometimes seemingly impossible to accomplish missions Liddy tackles are profiled.

Cast: Troy Hitch (Liddy), Matt Bledsoe, Troy Hitch (The Right Brothers). **Credits:** *Creator-Writer:* Matt Bledsoe, Troy Hitch. **Comment:** The program is filmed in black and white and actually quite intriguing. There are minimal special effects to make Liddy appear small but when Liddy performs a mission a plastic doll is used for the perilous action. In 1959 the syndicated TV series *World of Giants* used a similar concept with a government agent performing missions that could only be accomplished by a miniature agent.

Episodes: 3 untitled episodes, labeled "Episode 1," "Episode 2" and "Episode 3."

497 Jack and Emma. jackandemmashow. com. 2014.

With dreams of stardom, high school graduates Jack and Emma leave their small town (and its quirky residents) behind. They never thought they would ever return but after twelve years of chasing dreams (Jack as a writer; Emma, an actress) they decide enough is enough and return to their roots. Their homecoming is more than they expected as the whole town is aware of their return and for Jack and Emma it is life as it was when they left—a time capsule where nothing seems to have changed. Jack and Emma's experiences as they seek new lives but find that may not be as easy as they thought are chronicled.

Cast: Kati Lightholder (Emma), Blake Lightholder (Jack), Aaron Kleiber (Fender), Claire Chapelli (Marie), Joseph James (Daan; pronounced "Dane"), Jennie Bushnell (Jen), Klase Danko (Kirsten), Julie Beroes (Maddie), Krish Mohan (Krish), Jim Donovan (Greg the Mailman). **Credits:** *Producer:* Kati Lightholder. *Writer:* Kati Lightholder, Blake Lightholder. **Comment:** All episodes have been taken off line thus an evaluation is not possible.

Episodes: *1.* Premiere. *2.* Fender. *3.* Super Excited. *4.* Twelve Years Ago. *5.* They Don't Know We're Coming Back. *6.* Mailman Surveillance Agency. *7.* Talk Blocker. *8.* FLOA. *9.* Worst Pick Up Line at the Gym. *10.* Don't Put That in Your Mouth. *11.* Scrapbook. *12.* Rain Stick.

498 Jack in a Box. jackinaboxsite.com. 2009–2012.

Being gay and having a difficult time pursuing his dream of becoming an actor, a man named Jack settles for a job as a seller at Ticket Universe, a service whereby theater patrons can purchase tickets by telephone for their favorite shows. Jack possesses a BFA degree in acting but has no life skills and took the job as it involves no physical activity but keeps him in touch with the theatrical world. He is often mistaken for a woman over the phone ("I'm a sir, not a ma'am") and his patience has worn thin over the years dealing with people who are even more unstable than he is. The job has left Jack with anger issues and the program follows Jack's efforts to navigate the life he now leads, made bitter by the fact that he is growing older and no longer the mild-mannered, easy-going, theater-loving person he once was.

Cast: Michael Cyril Creighton (Jack), Beth Cole (Becca), Katina Corrao (Suzie), Lusia Strus (Gloria), Desiree Burch (Jill), Becca Blackwell (Kris), Paul Thureen (Drew), Mary Testa (Jack's mother), Alison Frazer (Aunt Heidi), Cole Escola (Drew). **Credits:** *Producer:* Michael Cyril Creighton, Jim Turner. *Writer:* Michael Cyril Creighton. *Director:* Jim Turner, Marcie Hume. **Comment:** A very good program that is ruined by truly annoying and bad camera work. Not only is the unsteady (shaky) camera method used, but it is coupled with unsteady back and forth panning (from character to character as they speak) and just as unsteady in-and-out zooming on characters' faces. What effect the director was seeking is unknown as the whole production is more of a turn off than something to watch. If you can overlook the camera work, the acting and writing are excellent and the program quite enjoyable as Jack just struggles to survive each day.

Episodes: *1*. The Receiver. *2*. The Alpha Actor. *3*. The Evaluation *4*. The Student. *5*. The Rave. *6*. The Mother. *7*. The Co-Worker. *8*. The Friend. *9*. The Change. *10*. The Agent. *11*. The Lunch. *12*. The Family. *13*. The Roommate. *14*. The Interview. *15*. The Buzz. *16*. The Reunion. *17*. The Return. *18*. The Victim. *19*. The Visit. *20*. The Surprise. *21*. The Testosterone. *22*. The Advice. *23*. The Date. *24*. The Breakup. *25*. The Compromises. *26*. The Staff Meeting. *27*. The Pest. *28*. The Snake. *29*. The Grilling. *30*. The Bonding. *31*. The Future.

499 Jailbait. tv.com. 2011.

Ozzie O'Connor is a young man with a positive attitude on life until his world is turned upside down. He accidentally purchases drugs in a sting operation and is arrested on two felonies: possession and intent to sell. Unable to prove his innocence, Ozzie is sentenced to nine months in Kilmer State Prison and stories chart his attempts to adjust to prison life—not only to fit in but deal with all the issues associated with his fellow convicts—from serial killers, skin heads, rapists, arsonists and "pen pals of indeterminate gender."

Cast: John Lehr (Ozzie O'Connor), Candace Kita (Officer Earnshaw), Evie Peck (Nurse Lawrence), Paul Renteria (El Rey). Credits: *Producer:* Nancy Hower, John Lehr, Keith Raskin. *Director:* Nancy Hower. *Writer:* Nancy Hower, John Lehr. Comment: Why Ozzie was sent to a hard core prison for only buying drugs is not really explained. Through Ozzie's more hilarious than dramatic experiences, it is shown what prison is like and why they were built—"to make you wish you weren't here." The lead character is very likeable, the acting very good and overall an enjoyable alternative to other prison-themed dramas.

Episodes: *1*. How to Survive State Prison. *2*. Funniest Prison Extraction Video. *3*. Chain Gang. *4*. Sex with a CPR Dummy. *5*. Erection Pill Gone Wrong. *6*. Prison Pen Pal. *7*. Anger Management. *8*. Rape in Prison.

500 Jan. webserieschannel.com. 2012.

Jan is a young woman, very pretty but very clumsy and unsure of herself, who yearns to become a professional photographer. When Jan enters and wins a national competition to become the assistant to world-renowned photographer Melanie (Mel) Karpova, her life appears to change for the better until she begins her internship and realizes she is anything but helpful to Mel. While Jan's bumbling does complicate her chances of branching out on her own, Mel is a patient woman and puts up with Jan's shenanigans (often questioning how she won the competition) with the program chronicling her experiences, especially when she meets a client (Gerald) and a budding romance seems to also be in Jan's future.

Cast: Caitlin Gerard (Jan), Virginia Madsen (Mel), Laura Spencer (Vanessa), Stephen Moyer (Gerald Noth), Kyle Gallner (Robbie), Jaime Murray (Andie), Andreea Damaris (Vera). Credits: *Producer:* Jacob Avnet, Jon Avnet, Rodrigo Garcia, Marsha Oglesby. *Writer-Director:* Jon Avnet. Comment: Caitlin Gerard is just adorable as Jan and her sweet innocence just makes the program work. The acting is very good and the production values are comparable to a network TV series.

Episodes: *1*. First Job. *2*. Almost Fired. *3*. Fired? *4*. Uncanned. *5*. Mace. *6*. M9P. *7*. Robbie (Ex). *8*. Dunce. *9*. Last Stop. *10*. No Camera. *11*. Cass. *12*. Fight??? *13*. Trust. *14*. Wine Bar. *15*. Afterglow.

501 Jared Posts a Personal. jaredpostsapersonal.com. 2013.

AlrightyAphrodite.com is an on-line dating site that offers men and women an opportunity to meet people with whom they have something in common. Jared, a young man with numerous dating problems, is convinced by his friends Nick and Tim to join and meet women the modern way. As Jared posts his profile the program charts the dates Jared acquires—women who are anything but normal, having little or nothing in common with Jared and in situations where deciding what to do becomes more involved than an actual date.

Cast: Jared Warner (Jared), Nick Ciavarella (Nick), Tim Dean (Tim). Credits: *Producer:* Adam Wirtz, Samantha Stubbs-Wirtz. *Director:* Adam Wirtz. Comment: It's all about a date, what to do and what not to do—and it all comes off as an amusing twist on other dating-themed shows.

Season 1 Episodes: *1*. Pilot. *2*. Netflix. *3*. Blind Date. *4*. Long Night. *5*. Casual Encounters. *6*. Bushwick (Brooklyn, N.Y.) Dating Game.

Season 2 Episodes: *1*. Missed Connections. *2*. Speed Date. *3*. The Boys Are Rich. *4*. Personal Crisis. *5*. Threesome! *6*. The Sad and True Story of John Moreno and Moby.

502 Jason Gets a Bomb Strapped to Him. webserieschannel.com. 2014.

As he is returning home from the supermarket, a young man named Jason is attacked by a person wearing black and immobilized when a bomb is placed around his chest. Perhaps due to the trauma of the situation, Jason runs to his friend Dan's home and, rather than call the police, decide to handle the matter themselves. As Dan figures out a way to remove the bomb without blowing himself and Jason up, the program also charts their efforts to find out who placed the bomb on Jason and why.

Cast: Jason Meagher (Jason), Dan Rogers (Dan), Mike Kall (Jerry), Rachel Kilcoyne (Carey), Mike Gormino (Kevin), Jeff Kall (Barry), Tommy Wiseau (Mike R.). **Credits:** *Writer:* Jason Meagher, Dan Rogers. **Comment:** While the bomb-strapped-to-the-chest idea is old hat, it is always interesting to see how a person winds up in such a situation. If the authorities were called there would be no series so the best solution is to let Jason and Dan solve the mystery. The program, which is well acted, does become a comical mystery as the culprit is sought.

Episodes: *1.* Trinity. *2.* Memory Frags. *3.* Defusing the Situation. *4.* Reinforcement. *5.* Carey on My Wayward Bomb. *6.* Bug Bomb. *7.* Before the Bomb. *8.* Searching for Shrapnel. *9.* Raptor 1 Glide Bomb.

503 *Jenifer Lewis and Shangela.* youtube. com. 2012.

Shangela is a drag queen who comes to the notice of actress Jenifer Lewis when she sees her on the TV series *RuPaul's Drag Race.* Believing there is potential in Shangela, Jenifer takes her under her wing and the program follows Jenifer as she mentors the up-and-coming performer (who, until she becomes a star, resides in the basement apartment of Jenifer's Hollywood mansion).

Cast: Jenifer Lewis (Herself), D.J. Pierce (Shangela Wadley). **Credits:** *Producer:* Jenifer Lewis. *Director:* Mary Lou Belli. *Writer:* Mark Alton Brown, Dee LaDuke. **Comment:** An enjoyable program with Jenifer and Shangela playing perfectly off each other as the teacher and the student. Jenifer's "potty mouth" actually adds to the comedy as Shangela can get on anyone's nerves and Jenifer is no exception.

Episodes: *1.* Pilot. *2.* Recognition. *3.* Gold Earring. *4.* Mouse.

504 *Jess Like Me.* webserieschannel.com. 2013.

Jessica Jordan, a young aspiring actress and singer living in Los Angeles, was born in Georgia and left home to pursue her career. Jessica, like all star-struck young women, soon found that what she hoped to find was not handed to her on a silver platter and she must struggle for what she wants. The program chronicles Jessica's journey, with friends Lisa and Jason in tow, as she seeks her dream of stardom.

Cast: Heather Paige Cohn (Jess), Amasha Alexandra Scott (Lisa), Pauline Mark (Gwen), Shane Singleton (Janet), Ammy Nando h(Jason). **Credits:**

Producer-Director: Amasha Alexandra Scott, Taviysha White. *Writer:* Amasha Alexandra Scott. **Comment:** Acceptable acting and production values that needlessly incorporates a laugh track (something, especially on the Internet, that is not needed to tell the viewer when he or she should laugh).

Season 1 Episodes: *1.* Call Me Maybe? *2,3.* Help Is on the Way, Parts 1–2. *4.* The Wedding Singer. *5.* Battle of the Sistah's. *6.* Make-Up. *7.* Meet the Parentless. *8.* Star Struck. *9.* Say's the B****. *10.* Moving Up, Moving On.

Season 2 Episodes: *1.* Homo for the Holidays. *2.* Big Time Crush. *3.* Just the Three of Us. *4.* Law and Ordained. *5.* Extra, Extra, Read All About Her. *6.* Reality Check.

505 *Jesse and Jesse.* webserieschannel.com. 2012.

Jesse is an African-American reporter for a money-losing newspaper called the *Daily Times Tribune Gazette.* While he believes he is doing a good job, his boss (Larry) feels his stories are all fluff and need some grit and photographic content. He is given an ultimatum—find a photographer or face termination. At this same time, Jesse's uncouth landlord (Harry) has raised his rent leaving Jesse in a bind as how to pay the increase. Figuring that a roommate is the answer, Jesse advertises for one over the Internet and gets several responses, only one of whom shows any potential, a white male named Jesse—a guy who just happens to have a camera and whom Jesse talks into pretending to be a photographer. The boss is satisfied, the sexy but ditzy office secretary (Olivia) can't see that Jesse (black) pulled the wool over her eyes and the program charts the stories the Jesse's cover to not only keep their jobs, but keep the paper from going under.

Cast: W. Ben Jackson (Jesse; black), Jesse Griffith (Jesse; white), Shawn Erickson (Larry Sturd III), Olivia Sedak (Olivia), Sean Flanagan (Dan), Brian Chang (Harry). **Credits:** *Producer-Writer-Director:* Michael Mizov, Shawn Erickson. **Comment:** Programs about newspaper reporters date back to the early days of cinema, most notably with *The Front Page.* Male-male, female-female and male-female teams have also been done but what makes such concepts work are the people who play the roles. Get that right and the idea becomes new. *Jesse and Jesse* has achieved that and an enjoyable program results basically from the mismatched Jesse's: Jesse (black) is neat and sophisticated while Jesse (white) is more of a slob and less intelligent (sort of an "Odd Couple" set at a newspaper office).

Episodes: *1.* Enter the Jesse. *2.* Publicity. *3.* Missed Connections. *4.* A Decimal Thing. *5.* /b/Real.

506 *JewFro.* youtube.com. 2013.

Darryl Levy is a young man caught between a rock

and a hard place: he is African-American but he is also Jewish. He was adopted by a Jewish family and has all the personality traits of a Jew; but he also has all the physical attributes of a black. Darryl has managed to combine both aspects and is doing just fine until his biological family comes back into his life and a crisis erupts when his family objects to what he has become. Is Darryl black or is he a Jew? The program follows Darryl as he finds he must make a decision and decide who he is on the inside and who he is on the outside.

Cast: Evan Raynr (Darryl Levy), Alain Azoulay (Harold), Genevieve Glass (Carly), Crystal Lane Swift (Caryl). **Credits:** *Producer:* Alexander Familian, Devin Glass. *Writer-Director:* Devin Glass. **Comment:** The TV series *Welcome Back, Kotter* had a Puerto Rican Jew (in the character of Epstein) so why not an African-American Jew? Although the concept is not really absurd, it does depict a situation that could happen and what could result. It is well acted and produced and, although religion is being satirized, it is not offensive.

Episodes: *1.* Pilot. *2.* Black Cracker. *3.* Teach Me How to Dreidel. *4.* Romeo and Jewilet. *5.* The Surprise. *6.* Challah at Me. *7.* The Lookout. *8.* Drop Thy Beat. *9.* Ba Donka Donk. *10.* Darrell. *11.* Raising Hell. *12.* Black on Black. *13.* Lenny. *14.* Key Kay's Challenge. *15.* Embrace the JewFro.

507 *JewVangelist.* jewvangelist.com. 2014.

Leah Levy is a Rabbi with a small congregation and a serious problem: her synagogue is in financial straits and is facing closure. Determined not to be defeated and save her temple, Leah devises a unique plan: convert people to Judaism by encompassing the conversion methods of other religions. As Leah embarks on her holy mission, accompanied by her

Jewvangelist. Behind the couch: Michael Saltzman, Jayme Bell. On the couch: Terrence Colby Clemons, Becky Kramer, Willem van der Vegt. In front of the couch: Alex Trugman (copyright Adam Hendershott, 2014).

cantor, Jay (a wannabe rock star), she encounters a stumbling block when her twin brother, Asher, also a Rabbi, objects to what she is doing as he feels it is unethical. Leah defies Asher and the program charts Leah's efforts to continue with her plan despite Asher's efforts to put a stop to what she is doing.

Cast: Becky Kramer (Leah Levy), Alex Trugman (Jay Katz), Jayme Bell (Tripp Hopley), Michael Saltzman (Asher Levy), Willem van der Vegt (Perry Lovejoy), Terrence Colby Clemons (Pastor Price). **Producer:** Becky Kramer, Kaitlin Walsh, Christian Ayres, Aaron Milus, Jason Moss. *Director:* Aaron Milus. *Writer:* Christian Ayers. **Comment:** Leah is compassionate and considers herself a father, mother and friend to those she serves. While religion is the butt of the jokes, it is not offensive and is well acted and produced.

Episodes: *1.* The JewVangelist. *2.* Leah Goes to the Mormons. *3.* Leah Goes to the Evangelicals. *4.* Leah Revamps the Music. *5.* Leah Goes Viral. *6.* The Finale.

508 Jeza and the Belles. youtube.com. 2011.

Eusta, Drag Queen of the Galaxy, has become dissatisfied with the crime and violence on planet Earth and has made plans to destroy it before it spreads throughout the galaxy. But she also believes there may be hope for the backward planet. She transports the drag queen Belle sisters (Jeza, Badora and Sue-She) to her realm and offers them the opportunity to save Earth by eliminating evil. If they succeed, the planet will be spared; if not, it will be destroyed. To help, Eusta presents each of them with a special piece of jewelry. Badora receives a bracelet that allows her to move swiftly through time; Sue-She possesses a necklace that makes her fierce and agile; and Jeza is awarded a ring that makes her a sorceress and able to control minds. Making their mission even more difficult, is an evil villainous named Smelva, a (real) woman who emits a fish odor, surrounds herself with her army of legal male prostitutes and has defied Queen Eusta to conquer the universe. The Belle sisters are returned to Earth to rid the world of evil before Smelva defeats them and Queen Eusta destroys the planet.

Cast: Jeza Belle [Billy Canyon] (Jeza Belle/Queen Eusta), Sir Honey Davenport [James Clark] (Badora Belle), Tara Miso Rice [Danart Ros] (Sue-She Belle), Gina Jarrin (Smelva). **Credits:** *Producer:* Billy Canyon, Cee Canyon. *Writer-Director:* Billy Canyon. **Comment:** Very well acted, television-quality production that even incorporates a sitcom-like laugh track. The sisters are outlandish (especially in their hair styles) and the program is enjoyable from beginning to end.

Episodes: *1.* Drag Queen Heroes. *2.* Uhhh.... No Fishy. *3,4.* The Boy Is Mine.

509 Jill and Jenny. youtube.com. 2013.

Jill (blonde) is a young woman working in a florist shop when Jenny (brunette) enters the store looking for a plant to brighten up her new apartment. By coincidence, when the women begin talking, they each discover a similar need: Jenny is seeking a roommate and Jill is looking for someone to share an apartment. Jenny invites Jill to share her apartment and the program relates events in the lives of two women who are not totally compatible: Jill is somewhat socially awkward and has a knack for losing jobs; Jenny is quirky and feels she is under a dark cloud as she cannot maintain a steady romance.

Cast: Jessica Kennedy (Jill), Jessica Lafrance (Jenny), Rob Norman (Bryan). **Credits:** *Producer:* Vivienne Au Yeung, Jessica Kennedy, Jessica Lafrance. *Director:* Vivienne Au Yeung. *Writer:* Jessica Kennedy, Jessica Lafrance. **Comment:** The program is charming, well acted and produced.

Episodes: *1.* Friend or Foe? *2.* A Lesson in Flirting. *3.* Ready, Set, Aim. *4.* Wanted! A New Best Friend. *5.* Box of Broken Dreams and Carriages. *6.* Liza Minnelli and Inner Peace. *7.* Tutus and Tea.

510 JJDD Super Heroes. webserieschannel.com.2014.

JJ and DD are super heroes in a league that apparently encompasses only them and their unique, self-proclaimed mission: recycle items instead of throwing them away. Encompassing a pair of ordinary scissors and what they call their "Up-Cycling Powers," JJ and DD set out on a journey where no super hero (or even super villain) has ventured: solve the problems of people in trouble through "up-cycling." JJ and DD take what they are doing to heart (even wearing "up-cycled" clothes) and the program relates their re-purposing adventures as they help the citizens of their fair city.

Cast: Janie Fontaine (JJ), Dianne Freeman (DD). **Credits:** *Producer:* Janie Fonatine. *Director:* Matt Watterworth. **Comment:** "Reuse, reduce, recycle ... or run" is the series tag line. Unfortunately only one episode, "Red Monster" remains on line and judging by it, it appears unique and well acted and produced.

Episodes: *1.* Potato Potahto (how to reuse a potato chips bag). *2.* The Magic Bottle (reusing a soda bottle). *3.* Serial Cereal (using a cereal box as a gift box). *4.* Pajama Party (recycle paper into a wallet). *5.* More Milk Please (reusing an empty milk container). *6.* Red Monster ("up-cycle" shirts).

511 Job Hunters. youtube.com. 2013.

It is a futuristic time and jobs are extremely scarce, so much so that for college graduates to secure employment by the MAEWIN Corporation, they must become Job Hunters—fight (even to the death) candidates seeking the same positions. Candidates for MAEWIN jobs are placed in company-owned safe houses where, from 9 a.m. to 5 p.m. they battle in an arena with the remaining time their own. MAEWIN has established the Job Hunters as a means of population control as well as acquiring the best candidates for jobs. The program follows a group of Job Hunters as they deal with the situation that confronts them—from roommate issues to life in the MAEWIN community with impending doom uppermost on their minds as only through the arena can their skills be tested.

Cast: Tara Theoharis (Tiffany), Kristina Horner (Avery), Forest Gibson (Devon), Joe Homes (Max), Steve Minor (Phil), Jana Hutchinson (Charlotte), Meagan Naser (Paige), Brian Sutherland (Dr. Monroe), Meredith Binder (Commissioner Ashleigh), Liz Leo (MAEWIN Announcer). **Credits:** *Producer:* Forest Gibson, Tara Theoharis, Liz Leo, Kristina Horner. *Director:* Alexander JL Theoharis. *Writer:* Alexander JL Theoharis, Rob Whitehead, Forest Gibson, Kristina Honer, Liz Leo, Tara Theoharis. **Comment:** The program focuses mainly on the activities the house members encounter rather than the actual arena fights (although snippets of such action are seen). The acting and production values are good as well as character development over the six episode run.

Episodes: *1.* Safe House. *2.* Rules of Engagement. *3.* Shell Shock. *4.* Tactical Assessment. *5.* Evasive Action. *6.* Friendly Fire.

512 The Job Interview. webserieschannel.com. 2012.

A person about to enter a room for a job interview is seen. Just before the interview is to begin several options as to how to approach the interview appear on the screen. Each has a different outcome and the viewer can choose one or watch all three.

Cast: Joe Bonacci, Michael Canfield, Alexandra Gjerpen, Zachary Wade, Janet Skim, Shyda Hoque, Karen Sneider, Norah Yahya, Gabrielle Gundelfinger, Lance Baker, Emily Petrone, Mike Tomczyk. **Credits:** *Writer-Director:* Michael Canfield, Joe Bonacci. **Comment:** A very good idea but unfortunately only the trailer remains on line. It is difficult to judge a series by something that runs only 56 seconds, but it does appear to be an intriguing program that allows for the viewer to choose the outcome.

Episodes: *1.* Game Intro.

513 Joe and Buzz. joeandbuzz.com. 2011.

An office provides the setting for the humorous exchange of talk that occurs between three friends—Joe, Buzz and Amy Ann.

Cast: George Kenyon (Joe), Coby Toland (Buzz), Monica Kenyon (Amy Ann). **Credits:** *Producer:* George Kenyon, Coby Toland, Monica Kenyon. *Writer:* George Kenyon. **Comment:** Very simplistic program that establishes a topic and finds the cast

expressing their thoughts and opinions on it in short, under two-minute segments.

Episodes: *1.* Chorizo. *2.* Elephant. *3.* Hammock. *4.* Burglar. *5.* Pawned! *6.* Fries. *7.* Darth Vader. *8.* Shark vs. Lion. *9.* Man Cave. *10.* The Beard. *11.* Sherlock Holmes. *12.* Cheating. *13.* Six-Pack. *14.* Booty Call. *15.* Dilwonk. *16.* Cold Shower. *17.* White on Rice. *18.* Ole Miss vs. MSU. *19.* Crosswalk. *20.* Under the Bed. *21.* Space Program. *22.* Junior. *23.* Secretariat. *24.* Oh Boh. *25.* Late Night. *26.* All Nighter. *27.* Popcorn Party. *28.* Street View. *29.* Fifth of July. *30.* Banter. *31.* Fog Machine. *32.* Pillow Talk. *33.* Magic. *34.* Jury Duty. *35.* Smell It. *36.* Packing. *37.* Step-dad. *38.* Caller ID. *39.* Stupid Questions. *40.* Middle Seat. *41.* Freedom. *42.* States. *43.* Tarzan. *44.* De-friended.

514 Joe and Nancy Mysteries. joeandnancymysteries.wordpress.com. 2012.

Joe and Nancy are friends and graduate students who have one thing in common: they are in need of finances to continue their education. To solve their dilemma they decide to become detectives and solve crimes for money. With the assist of their friends Bess, Dave, Ned and Callie, Joe and Nancy set out to solve crimes that are sometimes not only intriguing, but also deadly as murder is also involved.

Cast: Germain Choffart (Joe), Teresa Moore (Nancy), Betsy Tremmel (Bess), Matteo Gilebbi (Dave), Jesús Hidalgo (Checho), Aude Dieudé (Callie). **Credits:** *Producer:* Teresa Moore, Jesus Hidalgo. *Director:* Jesus Hidalgo, Teresa Moore. *Writer:* Teresa Moore. **Comment:** Without even seeing the program's website it can be figured out that Joe is one half of the Hardy Boys and Nancy is Nancy Drew, the famous teen detectives created in the 1930s. The program might also bring to mind the TV series *The Hardy Boys-Nancy Drew Mysteries.* There are comical twists and turns in the mysteries Joe and Nancy investigate and the program itself is well acted and produced.

Episodes: *1.* Picnic of Death. *2.* The Chapel Rescue. *3.* The Book with Flaps. *4.* The Stolen Dissertation. *5.* Paper Masked Silence. *6.* Death in the Shadows. *7.* The Beach House Murder Mystery.

515 John and Kyle Do Everything. youtube.com. 2012.

John, Kyle and Brad are best friends who also share an apartment. Brad is the more level-headed, down-to-earth roommate while John and Kyle have their heads in the clouds and dream of things they would like to accomplish. One night they devise an "ingenious" plan and create a list of things they would like to do. Now, with a purpose to their otherwise mundane lives, John and Kyle set out to accomplish the items on that list. The program chronicles their pursuit of that lists' goals—with Brad becoming the recipient of the fallout from their harebrained attempts to conquer them.

Cast: John Horan (John), Kyle Vorbach (Kyle), Erikas Chesonis (Brad), Helene Weiss (Rachel), Blaize Hall (Shannon). **Credits:** *Producer-Writer:* John Horan, Kyle Vorbach, Erich Westfield. *Director:* Erich Westfield. **Comment:** Amusing program that portrays John and Kyle as two somewhat less-than-competent guys who would have trouble tying their shoe laces while Brad, appearing a bit nasty at first, attempts to keep his cool living with them. The acting is good and production values are also good.

Episodes: *1.* We're Live. *2.* Spread the Word. *3.* Drinks on the Table. *4.* Cut, Cut, Cut!

516 *Jon and Jen Are Married.* jonandjen aremarried.com. 2013.

Jon and Jen are a married couple who are in a rut. They have become too use to each other and feel their marriage is now just boring. The program follows their efforts to spice things up by going beyond what is normal and experiencing the unknown—like Jen teaching Jon how to be a man; Jon getting a hooker; the couple adopting a son.

Cast: Jackie Geary (Jen), Jamison Haase (Jon), Mike Rock (Toby), MacKenzie Marsh (The Hooker), Kristen Miller (Constance), Keri Safran (Tammy), Shon Little (Wendell), Kiva Jump (Lucy). **Credits:** *Producer-Writer-Director:* Gregory Fitzsimmons. **Comment:** The program does manage to convey the message that Jon and Jen need to add something to their lives even though what they attempt is a bit

Jon and Jen Are Married. Jamison Haase (left) and Jackie Geary (used by permission).

bizarre. The acting is very good and the program well executed.

Season 1 Episodes: 8 untitled episodes, labeled "Episode 1" through "Episode 8."

Season 2 Episodes: 8 untitled episodes, labeled "Episode 1" through "Episode 8."

517 *Jon Davis Gets a Sex Robot.* youtube. com. 2013.

For fans of the TV series *The Honeymooners* it will be recalled that the only reason Ralph Kramden did not buy his wife Alice a TV set was that he was waiting for 3-D TV. That was 1955—but today there is 3-D TV and Ralph would have to spend the money and buy one. Layla is a young woman who is sort of in the same position: before she married Jon, she promised that if perfectly formed human sex robots were created, she would allow him to have one to fulfill his life-long dream. The day has come and, true to her word, she allows Jon to purchase one. Was it a good idea? The program relates what happens when a gorgeous sex robot moves in with and becomes a part of Layla and Jon's life (and how a jealous Layla gets her revenge when she orders a male sex robot). The program opens as follows: "Warning: This show is called *Jon Davis Gets a Sex Robot.* It features sex, robots, Jons, Davises and all kinds of perversion. Please don't watch it if you are sensitive to such things (actually watch it but turn off the volume and leave the room. We need the view count").

Cast: Michael McMillian (Jon Davis), Rikki Lindhome (Layla Davis), Nikki Soohoo (Sex Robot), Chris Jericho (Rob). **Credits:** *Producer:* Jeff Balis, T.J. Sakasegawe, Rhoades Rader. *Director:* Rob McKittrick. *Writer:* Matt Allen, Josh A. Kagan, Jonathan L. Davis, Rob McKittrick, Caleb Wilson. **Comment:** While not soft-core porn, it is rather blunt with language and sexual situations (although nothing objectionable is seen). It can be offensive to some viewers but overall it is a well acted and produced program.

Episodes: 6 untitled episodes, labeled "Ep 1 of 6" to "Ep 6 of 6."

518 *Joni and Susanna.* after ellen.com. 2008.

Joni and Susanna are best friends and seeking that ideal mate—but in different ways. Joni is a lesbian and Susanna is straight but they are not romantically involved with each other. Joni and Susanna also have a problem: difficulty in connecting with the right person. The program follows their efforts to help each other find that special someone and what happens when their efforts often sabotage what they are trying to accomplish for the other.

Cast: Joni Lefkowitz (Joni), Susanna Fogel (Susanna), Bridget McManus (Bridget), Stephanie Escajeda (Stephanie), Ginger Haggerty (Ginger), Terrie Haggerty (Terrie), Julia Miranda (Julia), Jaime Reichner (Jaime), Dave Richman (Dave), Mariah Robinson (Mariah). **Credits:** *Producer:* Susanna Fogel, Joni Lefkowitz, Erica Kraus. *Director:* Susanna Fogel. *Writer:* Susanna Fogel, Joni Lefkowitz. **Comment:** Well acted and produced with Joni and Susanna appearing like "frenemies" as their good intentions always back fire and cause more innocent harm than good.

Episodes: *1.* Party. *2.* Gym. *3.* Comedy. *4.* Stable. *5.* Brunch. *6.* Mall. *7.* Joni and Susanna Go to Jack-in-the-Box. *8.* Joni and Susanna Look for a Parking Space.

519 *Judith: My Quest for Judaism.* youtube.com. 2009.

At the age of 15, Judith, a Jewish girl living in New York City, believes she had an epiphany when God appeared before her to tell her to stop consuming alcohol. But Judith just dismissed it until she reached the age of 21 and, having become bored with drinking, vowed to stop using alcohol. As she recalled what happened six years ago, she decides to change her life by traveling to Israel to re-connect with her lost faith. Judith believes she is now in the presence of God and the problems she encounters as she attempts to produce a documentary—to show others the light—are chronicled.

Cast: Lior Landau (Judith), Evgeny Gertzenstain, Orianne Partem. **Comment:** Judith is very pretty, very aggressive and nasty. She also uses too much vulgar language and that is where the program begins to fall apart. For one who believes she made a connection with God she doesn't appear at all sincere in what she is attempting to do. Her addressing the viewer via her video blogs is a nice touch, but even there she uses unsavory language and, until producers learn that cursing is not funny, they'll have to take their chances on who will watch and who will be turned off.

Episodes: *1.* Pilot: No Time for Double Penetration. *2–4.* Untitled.

520 *Just Moved In.* youtube.com. 2013.

Camila and Max are a young unmarried couple who have decided to begin the next phase of their relationship by moving in together. The program charts their various experiences—from acquiring their first apartment to simply adjusting to each other as they now live together.

Cast: Natalia Reyes (Camilla), Andrew Ruth (Max). **Credits:** *Producer:* Clementine Cayrol. **Comment:** Short, right to the point stories that are well acted and produced. The episodes are in fact too short as the characters are very likeable and a bit more time peeking in on their lives would have made the program better than it already is.

Episodes: *1.* Apartment Hunting. *2.* Settling In. *3.* The Bathroom. *4.* Comfortable Together. *5.* Sharing the Bathroom. *6.* Being Sick. *7.* Still Pretty? *8.* Shake Shack?

521 *Just Passing Through.* justpassingthrough.ca. 2013.

Terry and Parnell are cousins living on Canada's Prince Edward Island. When they feel they need to better their lives they head to Alberta for jobs in its oil fields. En-route their car breaks down outside of Toronto and with no other choice they invite themselves to stay with their cousin, Owen, a man of culture and refinement. Terry and Parnell could be considered backwards people while Owen is upper class. The program relates what happens when Terry and Parnell soon make their stay permanent and a triple odd couple roommate type situation is created with Owen seeking a way to rid his life of his annoying cousins and Terry and Parnell attempting to adjust to city life. To sustain themselves Terry and Parnell, with their friend Alex (a girl) establish a roadside stand that sells PEI (Prince Edward Island) Moonshine, Garlic Fingers, PEI Potatoes and PEI Erotica (X-rated DVD's).

Cast: Tyler Seguin (Owen Stevens), Dennis Trainor (Terry Gallant), Robbie Moses (Parnell Gallant), Bridget Tobin (Alex), Sydney Dunitz (Vanessa). **Credits:** *Producer-Writer:* Jeremy Larter, Geoff Reid, Jason Larter, Robbie Moses. *Director:* Jeremy Larter. **Comment:** Interesting production that has its comic moments with Terry and Parnell attempting to sell their products, especially moonshine (homemade alcohol) on city streets. Bridget Tobin is especially good as Alex, a city-bred girl who takes an instant liking to the uncouth cousins and becomes their business partner.

Episodes: *1.* Alberta Bound. *2.* Pogey and Pubes. *3.* Charlotte Town. *4.* The Handy Clam. *5.* We're All God's Creatures. *6.* Turning Toronto. *7.* The Call.

522 *Just Playing with Jason.* webseries channel.com. 2012.

At the age of twenty-five Jason could be considered a late bloomer as he hasn't gotten much attention in the dating world. Realizing that something must be done, he gets himself into shape by researching YouTube fitness videos. Now, feeling that he is ready to meet the ladies, Jason uses his love of research to find women on the Internet and hopefully convince them to date him ("It was time for a change in my life. I'm gonna find a girl"). But Jason is not alone. His brother Dante and their friend Rei have agreed to help him and episodes relate a date Jason acquires, his attempts to impress her and what happens as the end result.

Cast: Maleek Griffith (Jason), Curtis Hamilton (Dante), Vasha Narace (Rei). **Credits:** *Producer:* Talya Adams, Kateem Brown. *Writer-Director:* Talya Adams. **Comment:** The program is presented mostly as a video blog with Jason relating what happens. The acting and production are okay but it is not much different form other shows that use the same blog format.

Episodes: *1.* Pilot. *2.* Dance Lessons. *3.* Drop It Low Jason, Drop It Low. *4.* The Bad Chick. *5.* Swag Out Jason, Swag Out. *6.* Speed Dating.

523 *Just Us League.* youtube.com. 2014.

Bruce, Barry, Hal and Clark run a marginally successful company that sells "strangers junk" over the Internet. They are not super heroes, but they believe they have a persona that parallel's a comic book super hero. The program relates aspects in both their business operations and their private lives as they try to make each balance the other out.

Cast: Nathan Guerra (Bruce), Shashank Maruvada (Barry), Jeffrey Jay (Hal), Spencer Harlan (Clark). **Credits:** *Director:* Nathan Guerra. *Writer:* Nathan Guerra, Shashank Maruvada. **Comment:** Rather disjointed series that is not very interesting although the idea is good but the execution poor.

Episodes: *1.* Point of No Return. *2.* Racing Hearts. *3.* Batman Returns. *4.* Last of the Jehoviant. *5.* Crisis. *6.* Hal Sized Hole. *7.* Thanksgiving Day. *8.* It's a Wonderful Christmas Carol.

524 *Justice and Control: Cop City Blues.* welcometotripcity.com. 2013.

Cop City is a city like no other. It is ravaged by crime and corruption and, although it has a police department, its less-than-effective officers are anything but successful (although they are diligent) when it comes to halting the rising crime rate. The program follows a select group of detectives as they do what they do best (foul up) as they try to keep citizens safe and somehow put an end to the unsavory elements that have taken over their city.

Cast: Paul Coughlan (Det. Chandler Ashton St. John), Chris Miskiewicz (Det. Wagner Murdoch), Alexander Martin Jones (Det. Thomas Mabeline), Paul Bosche (Insp. Marcus Garvey), Jacob Declement (The Shirtless Man). **Credits:** *Producer-Writer-Director:* Chris Miskiewicz. **Comment:** Interesting spoof of cop programs. The detectives presented here are rather tough, foul-mouthed and always with their drawn guns in hand (as apparently, they never know when they will be confronted by

criminals). The production is well paced and the acting very good.

Episodes: *1.* Season 1 Trailer. *2.* The Shirtless Man. *3.* Practice. *4.* Get Santa.

525 *K & A.* karlyandalex.com. 2014.

Two dysfunctional friends (Karly, who is straight; and Alex, a lesbian) living in Brooklyn, New York, and the problems they encounter—co-dependent on the other and each seeking to find the perfect mate—but not with each other.

Cast: Audrey Claire Johnson (Karly), Ashley Elmi (Alex). **Credits:** *Producer:* Audrey Claire Johnson, Katie Shannon, Mike Madden. *Writer-Director:* Katie Shannon. **Comment:** Enjoyable comedy with good acting and production values. The characters are very like-able and the sexual situations acceptable; the use of vulgar language is really not needed as gutter talk does not enhance scenes.

Episodes: *1.* The Herpes. *2.* K & A Do Nice Stuff for People. *3.* DeTox. *4.* 50 Shades of K & A. *5.* Intervention.

526 *Kaitlin and Nacho.* funnyordie.com. 2012.

Kaitlin (a girl) and Nacho (a girl dressed as a man complete with moustache) are friends who observe life from a city park bench. Their observations on what they see are presented in short video segments.

Cast: Kaitlin Smith (Kaitlin), Hannah Hafey (Nacho). **Credits:** *Producer-Writer:* Kaitlin Smith, Hannah Hafey. **Comment:** Both girls are very pretty (even through the moustache you can see that Nacho is pretty) and the concept is so simple it is literally brilliant. While virtually all the episodes run under 30 seconds each, they do make you wish they were a bit longer as what the duo encounter is just presented in too short a time frame. The acting is excellent as are the production values. It's not a laugh-out loud comedy, but a subtle look at life.

Episodes: *1.* Kaitlin and Nacho See a Squirrel. *2.* Kaitlin and Nacho Understand a Concept. *3.* Kaitlin and Nacho Split a Sandwich. *4.* Kaitlin and Nacho Experience Spring Allergies. *5.* Kaitlin and Nacho Ignore an Animal. *6.* Kaitlin and Nacho Take a Nap. *7.* Kaitlin and Nacho Make a Friend. *8.* Kaitlin and Nacho Play Hide and Go Seek. *9.* Kaitlin and Nacho Reach an Agreement. *10.* Kaitlin and Nacho Respect Aquatic Life.

527 *Kam Kardashian.* kamkardashian. com. 2012–2014.

Kameron, called Kam, is a member of the infamous Kardashian family but the disowned sister of Kim, Khloe and Kourtney (booted out of the family when a sex tape scandal involving Kam and Marcia Clark, the prosecutor in the O.J. Simpson murder trial, revealed that Kam was a lesbian). Cut off financially and evicted from the family home, Kam had no choice but to fend for herself and now survives mostly through petty crimes. Kam is proud of the fact that she is a lesbian, has a girlfriend (Mary) and one ultimate goal: to once again become a part of the Kardashian family. The program charts her attempts, assisted by the slightly unbalanced Mary, as she finds re-inserting herself into the Kardashian brand is not as simple as just claiming she is a Kardashian. (It is revealed that the Kardashian family had knowledge of the sex tape and when it was learned that Kim became pregnant by a man named Tom Greene and not her husband, they leaked the tape to the media to take attention away from Kim and place it on Kam.) Later episodes find Kam becoming associated with GLAWD (Gays and Lesbians Achieving World Domination), a top-secret gay rights organization wherein Kam becomes the face of a gay revolution; it concludes with Kam attempting to establish her own fashion line.

Cast: Fawzia Mirza (Kam Kardashian), Mary Hollis Inboden (Mary Hollis), Joel Kim Booster (Joel), Beth Stelling (Agent Stone), Mark Raterman (Himself). **Credits:** *Producer:* Fawzia Mirza. *Director:* Ryan Logan. *Writer:* Fawzia Mirza, Brittany Ashley, Joel Kim Booster, Mary Hollis Inboden, Mia Horberg, Ryan Logan, Jackie Migliore. **Comment:** An enjoyable spoof the Kardashian family, especially Kim, with very good acting and production values. Fawzia Mirza is very convincing as Kam and can make you believe that she could actually be a Kardashian and not just an actress playing a role.

Episodes: *1.* The Gay One. *2.* Haircut. *3.* BFF. *4.* Hustling. *5.* Xmas Special. *6.* Orange You GLAWD. *7.* First Date. *8.* One Night Stand. *9.* Internment. *10, 11.* Fan Faction. *12.* Therapy. *13.* Fashion Forward.

528 Kate and Joe Just Want to Have Sex. youtube.com. 2013.

The mood is set. The time appears to be just right. Kate and Joe are about to make love when anything (and everything) that can destroy the moment happens. The program chronicles what happens each time the moment appears to be right and how the couple attempts to adjust to what just happened to ruin the mood.

Cast: Kate Hackett (Kate), Joe Starr (Joe). **Credits:** *Producer:* Kate Hackett. *Writer:* Kate Hackett, Joe Starr. *Director:* Chris Yule. **Comment:** Enjoyable program that is presented in short segments with very good acting and production values. There are adult situations and suggested nudity (for example, Kate seen in a situation suggesting she is naked) as the couple, who do not live together, attempt to get together for sexual encounters.

Episodes: *1.* Migraine Sex. *2.* Phone Sex. *3.* YouTube Sex. *4.* Clean Sex. *5.* Sorry Sex. *6.* Sex Sex. *7.* Quickies.

529 Kate and Kula. kateandkula.tumblr. com. 2012.

The Polanis Group is a drug company that offers doctors the latest in meds. Friends Kate (white) and Kula (black) are two of its pharmaceutical representatives who often find themselves having to coerce nefarious doctors into ordering their company's product. When the company's unethical selling practices come to light and budget cuts force the company to slash salaries, Kate and Kula find they cannot survive on what they now make and decide to seek work elsewhere—as paid test subjects for a new medication, Fem A, which is designed to curb women with Type A personalities (their emotions and reactions). The program charts what happens when Kate and Kula become affected by the drug's side effects and exhibit "comically violent, darkly deviant and psycho sexual behavior."

Cast: Katie Hyde Lewars (Kate), Namakula Mu (Kula). **Credits:** *Producer-Writer:* Katie Hyde Lewars, Namakula Mu. *Director:* Namakula Mu. **Comment:** The program begins with Kate arriving at Kula's apartment to find her splattered with blood. As Kate looks inside she sees something and asks Kula what happened but before going any further Kate tells Kula maybe we should let the audience know what happened and a flashback is used to back date the story six months, just when they quit their jobs. While the story is good and a mystery is begun it is never concluded as the series ends with episode six and previews a seventh episode but it has thus far not appeared. The sixth episode suggests that Kula, affected by Fem A, may have killed or seriously wounded her boyfriend.

Episodes: *1.* Pilot. *2.* Fem A Advert. *3.* Happy Beepday. *4.* Subway. *5.* Stephen. *6.* Surrogate.

530 Keanu and Nic's Excellent Adventure. youtube.com. 2013.

Keanu Reeves appeared in such films as *The Matrix*, *The Day the Earth Stood Still*, *The River's Edge* and the movie and TV versions of *Bill and Ted's Excellent Adventures*. Nicholas Cage can be seen in such films as *Ghost Rider*, *Ghost Rider: Spirit of Vengeance*, *Amos and Andrew* and *Leaving Las Vegas*. Using a documentary-like format, the rise-to-fame of the two actors is presented (in a comical tone) with a look at their heartaches, mistakes, relationships and other events that span thirty plus years.

Cast: Ken DuBois (Keanu Reeves), David Loker (Nicholas Cage), Lola Slimenteva (Svetlana). **Credits:** *Producer:* David Loker. *Director:* Ken DuBois. *Writer:* Ken DuBois, David Loker. **Comment:** While the program is mostly talkative (the leads addressing the camera) it is well done and for those interested in the two actors being portrayed you will not be disappointed as an interesting look at their struggles as well as their accomplishments are presented.

Episodes: *1.* Welcome to L.A. *2.* The Auditions. *3.* Nicholas Cage in "Fast Times at Ridgemont High." *4.* Cool Breeze Over the Mountains. *5.* Oh Bitchin' Is This 3D? But Your Face Is. *6.* Nicholas Cage: Laying Down the Lines. *7.* Keanu Reeves in "Youngblood." *8.* Nicholas Cage's New Habit. *9.* April in L.A. *10.* Who Is Keanu Reeves? *11.* The Call. *12.* Nicholas Cage in "Rumble Fish." *13.* Introducing Svetlana. *14.* Svetlana vs. Superman. *15.* Movie Night. *16.* "Bill and Ted's Excellent Adventure."

531 Keeping Up with the Kartrashians. blip.tv. 2011.

A parody of the real-life Kardashian family. Kris, the mother of Kim, Khloe, Kourtney and Robbie, was married, but is now divorced and, after losing her job as a stripper at a Hooters-like club, had to turn to public assistance to survive as her children are anything but ambitious, especially Robbie. But the government help has run out and now the family must fend for themselves with the program focusing on how they use schemes to survive, the most ludicrous of which is starring Kim in a fake sex tape scandal and hoping to cash in on all the publicity it generates.

Cast: Angela Landis (Kim/Kourtney/Kloe), Taylor Ashbrook (Kris), Billy Noon (Robbie), Dylan Vox (Bruce), William Morse (Scotty). Credits: *Producer:* Angela Landis, Whitney Houser, Rebecca Roberts. *Director:* Whitney Houser, Dave Sussman. *Writer:* Angela Landis, Rebecca Roberts. Comment: Angela Landis is delightful as the three sisters (if you did not know in advance that she plays all three roles you would never realize it). The program is a bit dated as a lot has happened to the real family since 2011 but overall is a well acted and presented parody.

Episodes: *1.* Parole Party. *2.* Gone Viral. *3.* Preggo My Eggo. *4.* Drinking While Kartrashians. *5.* Mom Agent.

532 Kelly and Lindsey Do New York. kellyandlindsey.com. 2013.

Kelly and Lindsey are friends who do not believe in working for a living although they do hold down jobs they detest as waitresses. They are quite happy leading mediocre lives although they are constantly in need of money just to get by. If something can be gotten with not actually working for it, Kelly and Lindsey will find a way to get it. The program chronicles all the fallout (although not always bad) as Kelly and Lindsey use scams, cons and whatever devious methods that can think of to live the life they want to live, not a life dictated by society.

Cast: Kelly Wallace-Barnhill (Kelly), Lindsey Gentile (Lindsey), Gabe Pacheco (Landlord), Chris Harbur (Crusty Tom). Credits: *Producer-Writer:* Kelly Wallace-Barnhill, Lindsey Gentile. *Director:* Ross Anthony Evans, Hugh Scully. Comment: Two slacker girls is a welcome change from the slacker guy sagas of so many movies and TV series. Add that both girls are pretty and quite devious makes for a pleasant diversion on an old theme. The acting and production qualities are also top rate.

Episodes: *1.* Kelly and Lindsey Get a Job. *2.* Kelly and Lindsey Get a Boyfriend. *3.* Kelly and Lindsey as Drag Queens. *4.* Kelly and Lindsey Have People. *5.* Kelly and Lindsey Get Outta Town.

533 Kentuckiana. webserieschannel.com. 2012.

Life in Southern Indiana as seen through the antics of Eddie and Jimmy, two uncouth friends who believe they were meant for the finer things in life. With no actual plan to improve their situation, they set out on a mission with the program charting their harebrained efforts, which always fail and remind them they must endure life in a town in which they are hopelessly stuck.

Cast: Eddie Payton (Eddie Allen), Jimmy Rager (Jimmy Knives), Chris Elbert (Chris Moon), Marria Baisch (Ninja Tits). Credits: *Producer-Writer-Director:* Eddie Payton, Jimmy Rager. Comment: Billed as "extremely low budget and campy" and the program lives up to that statement. The performers look like they are just rehearsing scenes as opposed to acting. The production values are quite bad and there is a considerable amount of vulgar language. The program does fall under the "schlock" category and will appeal to those seeking such programs

Episodes: *1.* No Beer on Sunday. *2.* Kemp vs. Bird. *3.* Culmination. *4.* Chips and Tits. *5.* The Spread. *6.* The Ray Lawrence Massacre. *7.* Girlz in da Hood. *8.* Moon Goes to Mexico. *9.* Fruit Pie and Anus. *10.* Point of Impact. *11.* Cast Out. *12.* Rise of Cougar Mouth. *13.* Chic-Cru-Sades. *14.* Breaking Is Bad. *15.* Two Guys, One Gift Card. *16.* System Update. *17.* Against Some Odds. *18.* Episode Off Line. *19.* Why Did You Kill Me For?

534 Kevin and Phebe. kevinandphebe.com. 2012.

Kevin and Phebe are twenty-something singles who share an apartment. Brief incidents that affect their lives are presented as the couple simply deals with whatever they encounter.

Cast: Graham Halstead (Kevin), Saskia Maarleveld (Phebe). Credits: *Producer:* Kailee McGee, Rich Costales. Comment: It is actually like the TV series *Seinfeld* which was considered a show about nothing. Anything that came into Jerry Seinfeld's field of vision became a subject for an episode. The same type of concept is presented here. Whatever Kevin and Phebe encounter becomes the subject of the episode (although all too brief as the concept is really good). The characters are likeable and the acting and production values very good.

Episodes: *1.* Buzzer. *2.* Roof. *3.* Bed. *4.* Bag. *5.* Rat. *6.* Blue Chair. *7.* Balloon. *8.* Box. *9.* Bucket. *10.* Notebook. *11.* Spoon. *12.* Sky. *13.* Shower. *14.* Toothbrush. *15.* Rose Petal. *16.* Water. *17.* Pizza Box. *18.* Toast. *19.* Cake. *20.* Television. *21.* Ballet Shoes.

535 *King Bachelor's Pad.* bachelorspad.tv. 2012.

King Bachelor, as he is called is apparently very wealthy and lives a life of luxury surrounded by a flock of beautiful women he calls "Batches." King, is in a way, an African-American version of Hugh Hefner and his Playboy Bunnies image. Here, however, King is like a story teller with him appearing as the protagonist in each tale that he relates (seen as short skits).

Cast: Andrew Bachelor (Host/Protagonist). *Guest Performers:* Robert Ri'card, Tamala Jones, Bree Olson, Neil Brown, Jr., Iman "Alphacat" Crosson, Skye Townsend, Lyman Johnson. Credits: *Producer:* Andrew Bachelor, Jonathan Lesane, Adam Bradshaw. *Director:* Matei Dima. Comment: The immediate impression you get is that King is a black Hugh Hefner. The program is well done and the skits well acted and produced.

Episodes: *1.* Mr. Sherlock Homeboy. *2.* Hot Zombie. *3.* Last Wish. *4.* Hunger Games.

536 *King of Fitness.* kingoffitnesstv.com. 2012.

Graham Tyler is publicist for the Dooey Agency whose life begins to fall apart after he returns from a two week vacation. His employers feel his work is not up to their standards and he is fired; his girlfriend, Emma, has become fed up with his complaining (mostly about her and what she doesn't do) and leaves him. Although heartbroken over Emma's leaving him, he knows he must get on with his life, but is having a difficult time until his friends Maddy and Heath intervene and set their goal to get Graham out of his funk. They are partially successful when Graham attempts to finish a movie project he started called *King of Fitness.* The downside: Graham still longs for Emma and the program charts the ups and downs Graham (and Maddy and Heath) encounter when all of Graham's energies are directed toward Emma and not his film.

Cast: Shawn M. Smith (Graham Tyler), Kiera Capitanio (Maddy), Dawn Collet (Emma), Matthew Bayer (Heath), Mark Parker (Carter). Credits: *Producer:* Jon Santos, Shawn M. Smith, Andrew Thomas Pitkin, Jon Saltzman, Jonathan Widro. *Director:* Jon Santos. *Writer:* Andrew Thomas Pitkin, Shawn M. Smith. Comment: A bit depressing at times as Graham relents about losing Emma (but it can be seen that Graham had no respect for Emma and her decision to leave him was justified). Although the lamenting over a lost love has been done

countless times before, each scenario can be different, as it is here; it is also well acted and produced.

Episodes: *1.* Hello. *2.* Good to See You. *3.* Doomed to Sink? *4.* Special Kind of Way. *5.* Word by Word. *6.* Too Far Away. *7.* Chance Encounter. *8.* Precious Equipment *9.* Perseverance and Humility.

537 *Kip Perry: Adventures in the Unknown.* studentfilms.com.webserieschannel.com. 2010.

It appears that Australia is not only called "The Land Down Under" but it is also home to mysterious creatures and strange phenomena. Kip Perry, a monster hunter and crypto-zoologist, is aware of such oddities and has devoted his life to uncovering them. But Kip is rather unsuccessful at what he does and most people would consider him a failure as he never gets what he goes after. While this would discourage anybody, Kip only becomes more enthused to prove to everyone that they are wrong. Assisted by Francis and Kate, Kip ventures into the world of the unknown and stories relate his efforts to just stay alive while he investigates strange phenomena.

Cast: Michael Robert Kelly (Kip Perry), James Hess (Francis), Amy Funder (Kate). Credits: *Producer-Writer-Director:* Michael Robert Kelly. Comment: Enjoyable spoof of the real-life monster hunters with just the right amount of humor. The program is well cast, written and directed and the stories interesting to watch. The creature special effects are done on the cheap side, but passable here as it is not meant to be taken seriously (especially with the kind of creatures Kip seeks).

Episodes: *1.* The Monobaboso. *2.* Kip vs. Zombies. *3.* Kip vs. the Werewolf. *4.* Kip vs. the Aquapig. *5.* Kip vs. Survivorman. *6.* Kip vs. the Landsquid.

538 *Klaus.* youtube.com. 2012.

Klaus is a mysterious man who wonders about many things—not things that are out of this world but things as simple as bicycles, trees, playing catch and even sweeping out a garage. Stacy is his friend, a young man who is always by his side and who becomes involved in the wonders Klaus experiences. As Klaus encounters something, a story is presented as told from his point of view.

Cast: Gregory Hoyt (Klaus), Brian Girard (Stacy), Stephanie Nelson, Heather Pasternak, Mila Vayntrub, Eric Lim, San Dolan. Credits: *Producer-Writer:* Gregory Hoyt, Andy Schlachtenhaufen. *Director:* Andy Schlachtenhaufen. Comment: Filmed in black and white with a surrealistic feel to it. It will appear strange at first but sticking with it will present a most unusual program that will make you curious about all the episodes. The acting and production values are excellent.

Episodes: *1.* That Bike. *2.* Down from the Tree. *3.* Lollipops. *4.* Sweet Dreams. *5.* Go Fish. *6.* Puzzled. *7.* Blueberries. *8.* Spotted. *9.* Santa. *10.* New Day. *11.* Typewriter.

539 *Knockin' on Doors.* webserieschannel.com. 2012.

Dana and David are twins who believe they have found their own niche when it comes to business. Being entrepreneurs they feel that the only way money can be made is to figure out what America needs and produce that product. Dana and David establish their own marketing research method by literally going door-to-door and asking home owners what they think the country needs. The program follows their rather unusual procedure and what results from the people they interview.

Cast: Devon Weigel (Dana), Anthony Fanelli (David). **Credits:** *Producer:* Kevin Kocsis, Anthony Fanelli. *Director:* Eric Golowski. **Comment:** Interesting concept that is well acted but hampered somewhat by overpowering background music (makes it difficult to understand the dialogue at times). The program just ends in the middle of nowhere and it appears additional episodes will not be produced.

Episodes: *1.* Scalping. *2.* The Bet. *3.* Make-out Town.

540 *Kole's Law.* youtube.com. 2010.

Terrence Kole, a recent law school graduate who hates to be called Terry, is currently unemployed. His applications to law firms have all been rejected but he has an idea to begin his own legal practice—from his apartment. His shares the apartment with Dan, an ex-football star who inherited a great deal of money and chooses to live the life of a slacker, and his sister, Samantha (kicked out her parents' home and with no place to go moved in with Terrence and Dan; she works at the Print Shanty). Terrence establishes his law office and acquires clients through a newspaper ad: "Need Legal Help on a Budget? Call Terrence Kole at the Law Office of Terrence Kole: 958–565–3529. Free Pizza." The program follows Terrence's efforts to conduct his business—with the help and hindrances of Dan and Samantha.

Cast: Pete Kosmal (Terrence Kole), Jennifer Schuler (Samantha Kole), Rick Schuler (Dan Jansen), Rachel Kosmal (Colleen Lipinsky). **Credits:** *Producer-Director-Writer:* Branden Johnson. **Comment:** Interesting spoof of TV lawyers that is well acted and produced.

Season 1 Episodes: *1.* Pilot. *2.* Brasuit. *3.* Love and War. *4.* Talking Shop. *5,6.* Guilty As Charged.

Season 2 Episodes: *1.* Dick Kole. *2.* Livin' Large. *3.* The Terrence Kole Affair. *4.* Tri-Curious. *5,6.* Partying Is Such Sweet Sorrow.

Season 3 Episodes: *1.* Kole Lawrence. *2.* Sister Act. *3.* The Bachelor.

541 *Kristy.* webserieschannel.com. 2012.

Kristy is a young woman, quite attractive and well-dressed who appears to be just an ordinary woman. But get on her bad side or do anything to upset her and she becomes a bit psychotic if something doesn't go her way. The program chronicles what happens when Kristy encounters the people who annoy her to a point where she just has to let them have a piece of her mind.

Cast: Dawn Davis (Kristy). **Credits:** *Producer:* Dawn Davis, George Fivas. *Writer-Director:* George Fivas. **Comment:** Episode 1 deals with Kristy becoming outraged when she believes a woman, walking her dog, will not clean up after it. Episode 6 has Kristy trying to enjoy a leisurely ride in her car. The producers' state: "Oh, and what about Episodes 2, 3, 4 and 5? Well, we decided that if George Lucas can release Episode 4 first (referring to the *Star Wars* saga) then we can release Episode 6 second.... But don't worry, you won't have to wait 28 years to see the preceding episodes." While Kristy is delightful and the concept unique and well presented, only two episodes have thus far appeared.

Episodes: *1.* Episode 1 (The Very First One, There Is a Dog). *2.* Episode 6: The Convertible.

542 *L.A. Bitches.* webserieschannel.com. 2013.

Tajma and Heather are very attractive young women who are not only best friends but a bit ditzy. They live in Los Angeles and have several goals: frequent the hottest clubs, meet celebrities and become famous. The program follows their efforts to achieve those goals, all of which are hampered by the fact that they are not that bright and just getting from one place to another poses a real challenge.

Cast: Katy Colloton (Tajma Hall), Katie O'Brien (Heather Mills). **Credits:** *Producer-Writer:* Katy Colloton, Katie O'Brien. *Director:* Brendan Kelly. **Comment:** From a catchy theme song to good acting by the leads an enjoyable (but much too short) program is presented. Although Tajma and Heather are presented like Valley Girls and similar concepts have been done before, Katy Colloton and Katie O'Brien put their own spin on the project to make it unique.

Episodes: *1.* Chicken. *2.* Coyote. *3.* Chateau Marmont.

543 *L.A. Famous.* webserieschannel.com. 2014.

Jack is a young man with a big heart and insane ideas. After his best friend Albert falls into a deep depression when his girlfriend dumps him, Jack hits on an idea to make Albert, a struggling actor in Los Angeles, famous as a YouTube sensation. Albert and Jack share an apartment with Jacob, a documentary filmmaker and rope him into their project. Each episode is a look at a video the group produces in an effort to make Albert famous; unfortunately, the three could be considered idiots as they create videos that are anything but believable, not alone worthy of viral standings.

Cast: Albert Huber (Albert), Jack Lawrence Mayer (Jack), Jacob Hurwitz-Goodman (Jacob), Johanna Middleton (Johanna). Credits are not given. **Comment:** Intriguing program as it explores the really insane ways people go to become Internet sensations. The acting is good and the production acceptable.

Episodes: *1.* Getting Famous. Episodes 2 through 6 are untitled and labeled "Episode 2" through "Episode 6."

544 *L.A. Girls.* webserieschannel.com. 2013.

Shoshana, a level-headed girl with a heart of gold; Hannah, an unemployed actress struggling to make ends meet; Marnie, a girl who dates men but is thought to be bisexual; and Jessa, adjusting to being a mother after adopting a child, are friends attempting to navigate life in Los Angeles. Adam is Hannah's friend, an adult film star extra; Elijah is a male model.

Cast: Tiffany Ariany (Shoshana Shapiro), Rya Meyers (Marnie Michaels), Kylie Sparks (Hannah Horvath), Victoria Bullock (Jessa Johansson), Carl Gambino (Adam Sackler), Zachary Haven (Knick Knack), Kyle Colton (Ray Ploshansky), Michael Collins (Elijah Krantz), Erich Lane (Charlie Dattolo). **Credits:** *Producer:* Tiffany Ariany, Matt Blessing, Kylie Sparks. *Director:* Matt Blessing. *Writer:* Tiffany Ariany, Matt Blessing. **Comment:** A spoof of the HBO series *Girls* that is very well acted and photographed although story lines abruptly end without resolving issues. There is a bit of foul language but nothing else objectionable.

Episodes: *1.* Judaism Nepotism. *2.* I've Got Knick Knack in My Pants. *3.* Is Everyone Gay? *4.* This Isn't Breaking Bad. *5.* Mirrors. *6.* L.A. Girls Blooper Reel.

545 *Lady Business.* funnyordie.com. 2012–2013.

Lady Business: News on the Rag is a feminist news program dedicated to covering issues that affect women in a humorous vein. It is co-anchored by Rebecca (who is conservative) and Jenny (who is liberal). While not as high caliber as broadcast news programs, it is informative and the program chronicles what happens as Rebecca and Jenny clash over issues when their viewpoints differ greatly.

Cast: Rebecca Whitehurst (Rebecca Whitehurst), Jenny Grace (Jenny Grace), Arturo Castro (Tyler). **Credits:** *Producer:* Jenny Grace, Rebecca Whitehurst, Michael Cervieri. *Director:* Rebecca Whitehurst, Jenny Grace, Bill Hopkins, Candy Kugel. *Writer:* Jenny Grace, Rebecca Whitehurst.

Comment: Commenting is not possible as all episodes have been taken off line.

Episodes: *1.* Pilot. *2.* New in the Newsroom. *3.* The Intern. *4.* Marcy. *5.* Gloria Steinman.

546 *Lady Cops.* youtube.com. 2008.

"Meet Roxie and Margo.... They're lady cops.... They're good-for-nothing, but they sure are pretty" is the tag line used to describe Roxie DeJour and Margo Kildare, Special Police with The Lady Cop Precinct of an unidentified city. They are very pretty and they are a bit off-the-wall and take orders from a photograph (with a voice over) of Reginald Vel Johnson (in police uniform from his role on the TV series *Family Matters*). Roxie and Margo half-heartedly follow his instructions and the program charts their efforts to solve crimes as best they can, which is not saying much as they approach everything as if it were a joke—but if pretty can solve a crime, then Margo and Roxie are the best weapons against crime the precinct has.

Cast: Amy Harper (Off. Roxie DeJour). A girl, credited only as Erin, plays Officer Margo Kildare and an actor, credited only as Reuben provides the voice of their superior (the photograph). **Comment:** There are numerous possibilities for the program, especially with attractive leads and improbable stories. Unfortunately, only two short episodes were made and it appears unlikely any additional episodes will follow. The acting, meant to be corny, is very good and the production values just standard for an Internet program.

Episodes: *1.* At the Office. *2.* Undercover Crack Whores.

547 *LARPs.* larpsseries.com. 2014.

People who live in the real world but engage in fantasy role playing are called LARPs ("Live Action Role Playing"). Will, Shane, Brittany, Arthur and Evan are five such people and the program explores various aspects of their two worlds (real and imaginary) with a particular focus on how they live and play out their game fantasies.

Cast: Scott Humphrey (Will), Elizabeth Neale (Shane), Charlotte Rogers (Brittany), Jonathan Silver (Arthur), Jon Verrall (Evan). **Credits:** *Producer:* Benjamin Warner. *Director:* Julian Stamboulieh. *Writer:* Jon Verrall. **Comment:** By focusing more on the fantasy world than the real world, the program presents an interesting look at what such people experience when they indulge in their fantasies. It may not be as vivid as it is here, but it is a well acted and produced look at such role playing.

Episodes: *1.* Episode 1. *2.* GM. *3.* Episode 3. *4.* IC. *5.* XP. *6.* Loot. *7.* OCC. *8.* Meta-gaming. *9.* Encounter. *10.* Broken.

548 Laura Sweeney's The Mothership.
webserieschannel.com. 2013.

Mrs. Tate (no first name given) is a housewife and mother whose only time away from her demanding family is when she is in her "mothership" (the family Volvo station wagon). Each escape from the house Mrs. Tate makes is brought forth for the viewer to see as she relates, from her car, what is happening in her life and how she deals with it.

Cast: Laura Sweeney (Mrs. Tate). **Credits:** *Producer-Writer-Director:* Laura Sweeney. **Comment:** While virtually all the "action" is set in the Volvo, where Mrs. Tate even exercises and pole dances to illustrate a point, the show itself is very well done and acted. It is interesting to watch and Mrs. Tate is quite appealing.

Episodes: *1.* Mom's Burning Rubber. *2.* Pole Position. *3.* Need a Lift? *4.* Holiday Maniac. *5.* Power Steering. *6.* Manual De-frost. *7.* Anti-Lock Brakes. *8.* Car Wash. *9.* Earth Day.

549 Leap Year. youtube.com. 2012.

Aaron, Olivia, Jack, Derek and Bryn, employed by a company called Gemini Corp, face an uncertain future when they are suddenly laid off and find themselves with no income and no job prospects. The friends, however, are enterprising and to solve their financial woes enter an entrepreneurial contest, hoping to win the $500,000 first prize. The program follows their efforts to win the contest and what happens when they do and with the seed money create C3D, a cutting-edge holographic video conferencing platform based in San Francisco. But the win also brings additional problems as they still face an uncertain future launching a new enterprise and competition from a company called Livefye, whose deceitful practices could destroy them.

Cast: Wilson Cleveland (Derek Morrison), Yuri Baranovsky (Aaron Morrison), Daniela Dilorio (Olivia Reddox), Drew Lanning (Jack Sather), Alexis Sterling (Bryn Arbor), Rachel Risen (Lisa Morrison), Craig Bierko (Andy Corvell), Kim Fitzgerald (Scarlett Lane), Eliza Dishku (June Pepper). **Credits:** *Producer:* Vlad Baranovsky, Yuri Baranovsky, Wilson Cleveland, Justin Morrison, Dashiell Reinhardt. *Director:* Yuri Baranovsky, Justin Morrison. *Writer:* Vlad Baranovsky, Yuri Baranovsky, Wilson Cleveland. **Comment:** Subtle comedy presentation that is well acted and produced.

Season 1 Episodes: *1.* All Hands. *2.* Released. *3.* A Simple Contest. *4.* Used People Salesman. *5.* Nothing Personal. *6.* That Kind of Day. *7.* Corporate Cupid. *8.* Five Roads. *9.* Kind of a Genius.

Season 2 Episodes: *1.* A Train Wreck. *2.* One of Those Nights. *3.* Of All the Gin Joints. *4.* Just Trying to Survive. *5.* The Very Idea of Loving Love. *6.* What It Takes to Win. *7.* A Moment of Weakness. *8.* Behind the Hologram. *9.* What We're Capable Of. *10.* How to Bite.

550 Least Favorite Love Songs. leastfavoritelovesongs.com. 2012.

"I'm a writer and I've temporarily run out of inspiration," says Molly Mueller, a struggling writer hooked on drugs and in an uneasy relationship with her rocker boyfriend Eddie. Molly lives in New Orleans and, after a trip on drugs, becomes inspired to write a story about "the amorous underbelly" of the city, the people hooked on drugs and sex. Molly suddenly finds a boost to her career and the program charts Molly and Eddie's encounters (tagged "misadventures") with the least desirable people as she interviews them for a story "that has to be told."

Cast: Helen Kreiger (Molly), Chris Trew (Eddie), Joseph Meissner (Tim John), Ali Arnold (Calliope), Leslie Monteyne (Juliet), Tami Nelson (Anne). **Credits:** *Producer:* Patrick Francis, Dwayne Rodney Washington, Helen Kreiger. *Director:* Todd Ritondaro, Joseph Meissner, Andrew Larimcr, Michael Domangue. *Writer:* Helen Krieger, Joseph Messner, Cyrus Cooper, Tami Nelson, Maurice Carlow Ruffin, Chris Trew. **Comment:** The program doesn't read like a comedy nor does it play like a typical sitcom (although it is tagged as one). There are adult situations, not so-likeable characters and stories that border more on drama than comedy (especially on the subject that it tackles). The acting is good and for those interested in seeing a dark comedy, *Least Favorite Love Songs* will fill that bill.

Season 1 Episodes: *1.* Tim John the Sketchy Dealer. *2.* Stoned Job Interview. *3.* Eddie the Sort-of-Boyfriend. *4.* Sex Club Orientation.

Season 2 Episodes: *1.* Juliet. *2.* Molly. *3.* The Band. *4.* Fight.

551 Left Over the Series. youtube.com. 2014.

A spoof of reality TV cooking programs as seen through the experiences of a young man (Jon) who is chosen to be a contestant on *Cooked*, a show hosted by Mo Morrison, and the competitions he endures hoping to win the first prize: his own restaurant.

Cast: Andrews Cope (Jon Baker), Dave Little (Mo Morrison), Chad Cline (Kermit Van Dyke), Kristin McCollum (Shay Gwenvarro), Mollie Milligan (Britney Gambit), Leslie Patrick (Tawny Butane), Chris Caligari (Chris Rager), Christopher Nash (Gregor). **Credits:** *Producer:* Brian Fabian, Mollie Milligan. *Writer-Director:* Jim Kuenzer. **Comment:** The program does capture the feeling of a network competition series with a different twist: Jon relating his feelings that he will be sent home as no one talks to him, no one pays any attention to him and the cameras do not follow him like they do with other contestants.

Episodes: *1.* Introduction. *2.* Audition. *3.* Flash Feast. *4.* Finale.

552 *The Legend of Sprada.* facebook.com. 2011.

When Sprada, a drag queen living in England feels she cannot achieve her dream of becoming a super star in her homeland, she journeys to the United States in an attempt to change all that. She chooses to live in Chicago, where she acquires her first friend (Dixie Lynn, a drag queen) and an agent, Walter Bastardman ("the 'd' is silent") and a new hope to become a mega super star. The program charts Sprada's adventures as becoming that international super star takes more than just being talented, beautiful and eager especially when her agent specializes in casting females in movies and TV series that require corpses (only seen covered in a sheet).

Cast: Spencer Gartner (Sprada), Dixie Lynn Cartwright (Herself), Bill Larkin (Walter Bastardman), Dave Camp (Oscar), Claire Kander (Lizzie), Brandon Vejseli (Landon Skankefski). **Credits:** *Producer-Director:* Brandon Vejseli. *Writer:* Brandon Vejseli, Steve Macy, Spencer Gartner, Dixie Lynn Cartwright. **Comment:** *Chico's Angels* (see entry) is one example where programs about drag queens work. *The Legend of Sprada* is another one. It is very enjoyable with good acting and production values.

Episodes: *1.* Coming to America. *2.* Box of Hair. *3.* Tops and Bottoms. *4.* I Know What I'm Doing. *5.* Really Proud. *6.* Paycheck. *7.* Short a Waitress. *8.* Hello World. *9.* Nailed It. *10.* Rock Your World. *11.* Some Other Bimbo. *12.* Grand Slam.

553 *Leidy's New Boyfriend.* youtube.com. 2009.

Leidy is a young woman who believes, like some people, that if you see something you like, you should have it. One day Leidy sees something she must have—a man (Charlie) sitting on a park bench who immediately strikes her as the man of her dreams. Leidy, brazen as she is, approaches Charlie, begins a conversation and soon has Charlie asking her out on a date. Charlie is okay at first until he slowly gets to know Leidy and feels something is just not right with her. Leidy is a girl living in her own dream world and the program charts what happens as her attempts to pursue Charlie make her appear like a psychopath (especially when she gets him alone for the first time and he discovers her "playful" activities include pain and torture).

Cast: Susan Spano (Leidy), Ryan Reyes (Charlie). **Credits:** *Producer:* Frank Tobin. *Director:* Jake Barsha. **Comment:** Intriguing concept, good acting and good production values but not a typical comedy series. It is more of a dark comedy with Charlie becoming the victim of a young woman whose public life is nothing like the life she leads behind closed doors.

Episodes: *1.* She Stalks Her Prey. *2.* Erotic Date.

3. First Kiss. *4.* She Is Always in Control. *5.* She Feeds Him a Juicy Piece of Meat. *6.* She Takes Care of Her Man.

554 *Lesbian Space Invaders.* onemorelesbian.com. 2010.

On the feminine-ruled planet Femgina, located in an unknown galaxy, travel through time and space has been accomplished through estrogen-powered ships. Its citizens, presumably all lesbians as men do not appear to exist, are living a peaceful existence until it is learned that the Queen desires a new source of pelvic devises to please herself. The Scientific Council deems it is necessary to explore other planets to fulfill the Queen's request. Exploratory groups are formed with each party assigned to study a specific planet. One such group consists of Zelda (the captain), Lou Lou (the medic), Tawny (maintenance engineer) and Blurfy (navigator). The program charts what happens when they land on the planet Earth and encounter men for the first time.

Cast: Kathy Betts (Zelda), Tierza Scaccia (Tawny), Jessica Londons (Lou Lou), Cameron Esposito (Blurfy), Marsha Mars (Avery), Nicki Shields (Crazy Cat Lady), Kerry Norton, Rosemary C. McDonnell, Jen Bullock. **Credits:** *Producer-Writer-Director:* Christine Collins. **Comment:** There are no special effects; there is no nudity, no kissing, no foul language and no graphic sexual encounters—but it is produced in black and white! The acting and production values are good but some will be disappointed in the lack affection between the space invaders and their encounters with Earth women.

Episodes: *1.* Caught Between a Rock and a Hot Spot. *2.* You Know They Do Aliens, Don't You? *3.* And I Thought They Were Crazy on Planet Femgina.

555 *Lesbros.* youtube.com. 2012.

Luis, who is straight, and Vickie, a lesbian, are best friends ("lesbros") who try to help each other navigate the world of dating, relationships and the daily stresses of life.

Cast: Luis M. Navarro (Luis), Vickie Toro (Vickie). **Credits:** *Producer:* Erika Cervantes, Linda Yvette Chavez, Emily McGregor. *Director:* Emily McGregor. *Writer:* Luis M. Navarro, Vickie Toro. **Comment:** A charming, well-acted and produced series that is well worth watching. Vickie and Luis are into each other, but not in a romantic way and each story is just a look at a brief incident in their daily lives.

Episodes: *1.* Sex Ed. *2.* Our Gang. *3.* Exercise. *4.* Doma. *5.* Haircut. *6.* Butchest. *7.* Comic-Con. *8.* Spooning. *9.* Secret Handshake. *10.* Threesome. *11.* Dooplebros. *12.* Marriage Equality. *13.* Muffins. *14.* Happy Movember Love, Lesbros.

556 Let's Kill John Stamos! youtube.com. 2012.

John Stamos is perhaps most famous for his co-starring role as Jesse on the TV series *Full House*. Matt, Aaron and Josh are three less-than-intelligible friends who hatch a plan to achieve notoriety by killing the actor. Matt has come up with a plan to not only make money but become famous by creating a web series and killing John Stamos live on the Internet. The plan goes as follows (but intentional technical problems prevent the viewer from seeing or hearing the details). With the technical problems resolved and the program resuming, it is learned that all the details have been worked out and all that remains is to trick John into becoming a guest on their show. The program chronicles their plotting of what they believe with be "the crime of the century" and make them infamous.

Cast: Matthew Dressel (Matt), Joshua Kinne (Josh), Aaron Ruby (Aaron). **Credits:** *Writer-Producer:* Matthew Dressel. *Director:* Joshua Kinne. **Comment:** Rather than give anyone ideas, the actual plotting is blocked through technical problems. While the acting is good, the annoying unsteady (shaky) camera is coupled with panning back and forth as characters speak making for swiftly moving (and sometimes blurry) images. Panning is okay but should not be used to extremes as it is here (cutting from character to character would be a lot more acceptable). The program is also not that original as an ABC series called *The Knights of Prosperity* used a similar concept wherein a group of friends plotted to steal from celebrities, not kill them.

Episodes: *1.* Pilot. *2.* The Convincing. *3.* Things Get Weird. *4.* Dead Al Yankovich. *5.* How to Move a Couch. *6.* The Inside Stamos. *7.* I'm No Racist, That's What So Insane About This. *8.* The Fake John Stamos. *9.* Penultimatocity. *10.* Teaser.

557 Let's Make Lemonade. youtube.com. 2012.

Sketch comedy series that pokes fun at situations people encounter in everyday life.

Cast: Steve Cohen, Marie Faustin, Will Brennan, Chris Dougherty, Errol Toulon III, James Newman, Jackie Bello, Justin Toulon, Mike Vespa, Michael Crowe. **Credits:** *Producer:* James Newman, Justin Toulon. *Director:* James Newman. *Writer:* James Newman, Justin Toulon. **Comment:** The little girl seen in the opening theme setting up a table outdoors to sell lemonade sets the stage for well acted and produced vignettes that attempt to tackle life's problems.

Episodes: *1.* It's All Part of the Plan. *2.* Now That We Have Your Attention.

558 Life as We Blow It. webserieschannel.com. 2012.

Natalie, Marissa, Blake, Conner and Nissi are recent college graduates seeking to establish themselves in the business world. The post recession economy, however, has deterred those ambitions and left the friends with little hope of acquiring their dream jobs. With determination, but few prospects, the program charts their efforts to make the best of the circumstances that surround them as they seek to find what work they can to survive.

Cast: Adrienne Marquand (Natalie), Evan Thomas (Blake), Michele Lyn Vasile (Nissi), Johnny San Martin (Conner), Kelsey Christie Knight (Marissa). **Credits:** *Producer:* Stuart Gold, John W. Wells III, Ryan Echols. *Writer-Director:* John W. Wells III. **Comment:** The program opens in the middle of nowhere and expects you to know who and what the characters are with no introduction. The acting and production values are good and the story can be followed if you stick with it (although episodes are over 20 minutes long, making it difficult for some viewers to watch as Internet series need short, right to the point stories to grab attention).

Episodes: *1.* You Can Have a Salad. *2.* Unexpected. *3.* Fascist Zombies.

559 Life at Large. webserieschannel.com. 2012.

Avery Kaplan is a young man who rarely leaves his house. He is addicted to the Internet and not only runs his business through it (creating apps) but attends school and even orders food—anything to avoid going in public. One day the unthinkable happens—his computer crashes and Avery is literally stopped in his tracks. What to do? He begins by ordering a replacement computer but again finds his world in chaos when the package, delivered by a girl named Paula, contains a microwave oven. While Avery begins to panic, Paula sees him as a challenge and immediately attaches herself to him (although Avery sees her as a nuisance and someone who has invaded his comfort zone). The program charts the decisions Avery must make as Paula, a girl with few social boundaries, becomes a part of his life and he must now face the world he has for so long abandoned. Diane and Alan Kaplan are Avery's parents. Diane is, as Avery describes her, "a hippy high priestess" with an addiction to spending money while Alan, an alcoholic, struggles to contend with Diane's spendthrift ways. Dr. Katz is Avery's web therapist.

Cast: Avery Bargar (Avery Kaplan), Megan Rosati (Paula), Tawny Kitaen (Diane Avery), Alan Blumenfeld (Alan Avery), Chris Gore (Dr. Katz). **Credits:** *Producer:* Chris Sibley, Kevin J. Foxe, Jason Blagman. **Comment:** The program is, in a way, a take off on the character Adrian Monk (from the TV series *Monk*) as Avery is just as neurotic. Paula, is in a way, like Monk's nurse, Sharona (and later Natalie) as she re-introduces him to the world he has left behind. The acting and production values are good although the sound dips (low at times) and is hard to understand.

Episodes: *1.* The Crash. *2.* Special Delivery. *3.* The Date. *4.* Ravi the Thief. *5.* Bliss Kiss. *6.* WTF Dad. *7.* Kobe Beef. *8.* The Finale.

560 *Life on Camera.* webserieschannel.com. 2011.

April Rayborn is a 16-year-old girl just trying to survive life as a high school student. But April is no ordinary girl. She is an apprentice witch, has her own Japanese reality TV series (on JBC, the fourth rated network) and a nemesis named Lena Sears, who has been charged to see that April keeps her powers in check. The animated program follows the events that spark April's life—all of which are captured on camera and broadcast via her program.

Voice Cast: Patty Leigh (April), Rina Adachi (Lena), Lucia Reed (Chloe), John Walker (Rich), Ross Bushman (Mr. Takeda). **Credits:** *Writer-Director:* Ross Bushman. **Comment:** Rather still-like animation with only slight mouth movements to define the characters. It becomes acceptable as you watch and the stories are well done.

Episodes: *1.* April vs. the Camera. *2.* April vs. the Agent. *3.* April vs. the Green Fire. *4.* April vs. the Ex. *5.* April vs. the Ninja Paradox. *6.* April vs. the Premiere.

561 *Life with Kat & McKay.* blip.tv. 2009–2014.

Katherine "Kat" Steele is the daughter of a rich father (Will Steele) and socialite-cougar mother (Sharyn Quest). While she is a "Daddy's Girl" she does work as an interior decorator. McKay Dunn, a waiter at Robano's Pizza Kitchen is the mama's boy son of middle-class parents Doyle and Belinda. While at the pizza parlor with her friend Tiffany, Kat meets McKay and it is a love at first sight. All is progressing well until Kat learns that McKay is tied to his mother's apron strings and that his mother is not too fond of her; and Will is not too happy with Kat dating someone on a lower social scale. The program follows the rocky relationship that develops between Kat and McKay and how it becomes even more so when a prenuptial agreement is brought up.

Cast: Jenna Finley (Katherine "Kat" Steele), Paul Haitkin (McKay Dunn), Marie Del Marco (Belinda Dunn), Dean Gosdin (Doyle Dunn), Jim Garrity (Will Steele), Ryan Parniez (Gabe), Angee Hughes (Cora), Pamela Walworth (Tiffany Anderson), Gabrielle McCrossin (Sharyn Quest). **Credits:** *Producer-Writer-Director:* Sandra J. Payne. **Comment:** Enjoyable saga of lovers who may not be right for each other. The acting and production are excellent.

Season 1 Episodes: *1.* Pilot. *2.* Hello, Princess! *3.* You're Too Young to Say Things Like That. *4.* No Dessert for You. *5.* Goodness Gracious, No! *6.* It's Nothing. Or Is It? *7.* I Love Nature. *8.* I'm Sooooo Happy for You! Yeah. *9.* Ooo, It's the Good Stuff. *10.* No Good Deed Goes Unpunished. *11.* The Cat's Out of the Bag. *12.* Are You Sure You Want to Do This? *13.* Telling Mother. *14.* Cocoa and Jammies. *15.* Lights! Camera! Oh My Stars! *16.* Is This Thing On? *17.* OMG, I Can't Say That! *18.* And the Beat Goes On... *19.* Come Here You Sexy Kitten. *20.* What Did You Say Is in These Cookies? *21.* A Penny Saved.... Doesn't Go Very Far.

Season 2 Episodes: *1.* You Want Fries with That Prenup? *2.* I'll Have the Prenup with a Side of Aspic.

Season 3 Episodes: *1.* Bunco Me This!

562 *Life with Say.* youtube.com. 2012.

While an age is not given, Saquan appears to be a man in his forties. Child Support is his son, a man in his twenties that apparently only he can see and hear (a reason why is not given). But Child Support doesn't appear to be a ghost as he does things real people do, like eating. Saquan is trying to lead a normal life but is burdened by Child Support's continual meddling in it. The program follows Saquan as he tries to ignore his imaginary son and just lead a normal life (or as normal as can be expected with Child Support always budding in).

Cast: Dave Lester (Saquan), Simeon Goodson (Child Support). **Credits:** *Producer-Writer-Director:* Saquan Jones. **Comment:** Rather confusing program as nothing is explained regarding Child Support. Other than that, the program is typical of a low budget web series with acceptable acting.

Episodes: *1.* You Can't. *2.* The Dinner Whore. *3.* I Hate You. *4.* My Name is Saquan. *5.* The Conservative Mind. *6.* The Weight Watcher. *7.* Did You Call? *8.* We.... A Team???

563 *Life with Zombies.* lifewithzombies.com. 2013.

An apocalypse has devastated the earth and zombies are roaming the streets seeking human brains on which to feed. Survivors are confined to their homes until authorities can figure out a way to destroy the menace. The program focuses on seven people who now live together as they figure out how to survive the situation that surrounds them.

Cast: Gary Rolin (Barry), Jennifer Losi (Sara), Julia Carpenter (Cathy), Michael Perrick (Lester), Tim Sands (Banks), Perry Daniel (Megan), Robbe Henke (Floyd). **Credits:** *Producer-Writer-Director:* Gary Rolin. **Comment:** Played strictly for laughs with a cliff hanger ending. Worth watching for a few chuckles but do not expect much horror (basically only in the last episode).

Episodes: 5 untitled episodes, labeled "Episode 1" through "Episode 5."

564 *LifeS Anonymous.* youtube.com. 2012.

Karen, Jane and Al have joined, with Heaven, Susan, Aretha and Jonis, LifeS Anonymous, a therapy group that appears to be just an ordinary therapy group. But once enrolled you are imprisoned until your fear, addiction or whatever is overcome. The program follows the new inductees as they become prisoners and find there is no escape until they are cured.

Cast: Sarah X. Hernandez (Karen), Gayla Johnson (Aretha), Davina Joy (Susan), Tara Oslick (Jane), Jash Salazar (Al), Lenka Svobodova (Heaven), Rolando Zee (Jonis). **Credits:** *Director:* Mitch Lamoureux, Mark Blaise Fallon. **Comment:** The therapy session is seen with flashbacks relating the incidents that led a specific person to seek therapy. The idea has been done before but the acting and production are good.

Episodes: *1.* Dumb Phone. *2,3.* The Hell of Heaven. *4.* Take One for the Team.

565 *Lindsey Lou: Urban Cowgirl.* lindsey louurbancowgirl.com. 2012.

Lindsey Lou is a young woman with a dream: travel to Memphis, Tennessee, and sing with the greatest stars of country and western music. Lindsey Lou is a talented singer and songwriter and lives in Edinburgh, Scotland (although she shows no signs of a Scottish or British accent). Dolly Parton is her heroine and Lindsey Lou, while not as busty, dresses and acts like Dolly. The program charts her journey and the adventures she encounters along the way, not only in attempting to adjust to a new country but the sometimes quirky people she meets along the way.

Cast: Lindsey Lou (Herself). **Comment:** To enjoy the program you have to adjust to Lindsey Lou. Her overly perky personality and bright and cherry outlook on life takes a bit of getting use to; but once you do you will be treated to something totally different. Lindsey Lou does a very good job of acting like her heroine and the production values are quite good. There are purposely staged "booty shots" of Lindsey as sings (a message appears during the songs to say "gratuitous booty shots") and the overall attempt to spoof country and western music has been achieved.

Episodes: *1.* Hi Y'all! *2.* Anything Can Be an Instrument. *3.* Boats 'N Things. *4.* Ghostbustin' Cowgirl. *5.* A Very Lou Christmas. *6.* The Edinburgh Festival. *7.* Halloween Special. *8.* Olympic Torch Rally in Edinburgh.

Note: Episodes 1, 2 and 3 feature Lindsey Lou performing a song. Episode 4 is presented like a movie trailer and made to look like a pilot for a new series as it features Lindsey Lou as "The Ghostbustin' Cowgirl," a lovely young woman who risks her life to save a city gripped by a fear of demons (most notably The Mad Monk and Street Wolf).

Episode 5 features Lindsey Lou promoting her holiday album, "A Very Lou Christmas" (with short video song highlights). Episode 8 finds Lindsey Lou back in Scotland running with the Olympic Torch (which turns out to be an ice cream cone that she proceeds to eat).

566 *LIPS.* flovinger.com. 2012–2013.

LIPS, a band organized by its lead singer, London, has a lesbian following but it has been unable to achieve the recognition London envisions. The program chronicles all the mishaps that occur as London and her best friend and band mate, Didi, travel the rocky road to musical stardom. Fiona, then Gino, manage the band; Helen and Doris are the band's backup singers/eye candy; Rousaura is the sexy dancer who rocks London's world; Bubba is the man infatuated with London (despite the fact that he has a jealous girlfriend named Endora).

Cast: Flo Vinger (London), Vivi Rama (Didi), Marlyse Londe (Helen), Elaine Hendrix (Herself), Ashley St. Pierre (Doris), Hana Mae Lee (Endora), Christine Lakin (Rocker Chick), Sheetal Sheth (Rousaura), Debra Wilson (X-Girlfiend), Brian Jay Ecker (Bubba), Lita Lopez (Barista), Bernardo Verdugo (Armondo), Catherine Waller (Snaps), Amber Tisue (Amber). **Credits:** *Producer:* Flo Vinger, Brian Jay Ecker, Kate Tobia. *Director:* Flo Vinger, Chad Callner. *Writer:* Flo Vinger, Brian Jay Ecker. **Comment:** A well acted and produced program with a slightly different approach to series encompassing lesbian characters. There is plenty of eye candy and kissing and comical mishaps as the band struggles to achieve their dream.

Episodes: *1.* Chicks with Licks. *2.* Dinah or Bust. *3.* The Love Itch. *4.* Trickery. *5.* Working for Tips. *6.* Audition This! *7.* Lips or Bust. *8.* Elaine Hendrix Won't Take No for an Answer. *9.* Debra Wilson Faces Off with London. *10.* Snaps and Gino. *11.* Swept Off Her Combat Boots. *12.* Rousaura Rocks London's World. *13.* Lip Locked. *14.* Dreadlock Lap Dance. *15.* Ur the Opposite of That. *16.* Love Hurts. *17.* You're in My Personal Space. *18.* Barbie's a Lesbian. *19.* R.I.P. Fiona. *20.* The Ultimate Kiss. *21.* Here Today, Gone.... Today.

567 *Living the Dream.* webserieschannel. com. 2013.

The program, created "For Moms by a Mom" takes a satirical look at the lives of three such women: Andi, Marissa and Sara, friends who are trying to be creative (as actresses) while at the same time tending to a house and family in Los Angeles.

Cast: Monica Torres (Marissa), Sabrina Hill (Andi), Laura Pursell (Sara), David Carrera (Sam), David S. Jung (Jason). **Credits:** *Producer-Creator:* Monica Torres, Efren Muro. *Director:* Beth Dewey. *Writer:* Monica Torres. **Comment:** The program does have a different feel to it and is a well acted and produced effort to show how some women attempt to pursue a career while raising a family.

Episodes: *1.* Say What? *2.* I'm Not a Believer.

568 *Living Together.* webserieschannel.com. 2012.

Just as a young man (Luke) feels he has made a successful adjustment leaving the family nest, he finds his life turned upside down when his father (Albert), facing a mid-life crises after losing his job as well as divorcing his wife, decides to move in with him. The program follows Luke and Albert as they attempt to get along with one another with Luke trying to lead a life of his own, without the influence of his father (although Albert finds the situation reversing: him becoming the son and Luke, the father for all the rules he must follow). Alex is Luke's girlfriend.

Cast: Paul Arnold (Albert), Max Flisi (Luke), Sarah Schreiber (Alex). **Credits:** *Producer-Writer-Director:* Israel Grajeda. **Comment:** Television quality acting and production. While the idea is not original (TV series like *Foot in the Door* used the same concept) it is enhanced here by the role reversal with Albert finding he is becoming the son and Luke now controlling his life.

Season 1 Episodes: *1.* Introducing Bros. *2.* Big Bro Break In. *3.* Role Playing. *4.* Goth Sign-Up. *5.* A Goth's Sacrifice. *6,7.* Qute Qittens. *8.* Intrusion of the Stars. *9.* Acorn Adventure. *10.* Sexually Induced Stroke. *11.* Fever Dreams. *12.* The Youth Trap.

Season 2 Episodes: *1.* Season 1 Recap. *2.* Rescue Mission. *3.* Signs of a Visitor. *4.* New Brodder, a Breader Brotha. *5.* Love from the Past/Love from Today. *6.* Beyond Desktops. *7.* Stand By Your Friends. *8.* Ringtones. *9.* Lady Killers. *10.* Survival Camp. *11.* Lift Warz.

569 *Living with Daniel.* webserieschannel.com. 2013.

Daniel and Greg are young men who share a small apartment in New York City. Greg is a man who likes things orderly while Daniel is quite irresponsible and a constant source of aggravation to Greg. The program charts their efforts to get along with one another with a particular focus on Greg as he finds putting up with Daniel's nonsense a most difficult task to accomplish.

Cast: Greg D. (Greg), Daniel H. (Daniel). **Credits:** *Producer:* Lou Fong, Cam Dunbar. *Director:* Keenan Thompson. **Comment:** Simplistic stories (like Greg reading a book or getting up in the morning) that are each under 30 seconds and right to the point (basically how Greg attempts to adjust to something stupid that Daniel has done).

Episodes: *1.* Milk. *2.* Toothbrush. *3.* Reading. *4.* Cupcake. *5.* Couch. *6.* Good Time. *7.* April Fool's Day. *8.* Rise and Shine. *9.* Girlfriend.

570 *Living with Frankenstein.* livingwithfrankenstein.com. 2012.

Frankenstein, the novel written by Mary Shelley in 1818, was apparently based on an actual creature created by Percy Shelley (her now ex-husband) by bringing the dead back to life. Mary, the creature (called Frank), Percy and their friend, Lord George Gordon Byron have survived the decades by injecting themselves with Frank's blood. After living in England for nearly 200 years, Mary believes she needs a change of scenery and moves to Los Angeles, hoping to find the atmosphere she requires to write a second book. But it is not as Mary deemed it would be as she, Frank, Percy and Lord Byron have aroused suspicions, especially with a reporter (Ernestine) who has uncovered their secret and has vowed to expose them. The program follows Mary as she tries to protect her family from becoming a major news story.

Cast: Jennifer Neala Page (Mary Shelley), Matt Kelly (Frank), Tatjana Bluchel (Ernestine), Patrick Thompson (Percy Shelley), Steve Brian (Lord Byron), Laura Waddell (Claire). **Credits:** *Producer-Writer-Director:* Deborah Baxtrom. **Comment:** Horror spoof that places the actual Frankenstein monster in the modern world in a well produced story that, although it ends unresolved, is a new approach to the legend with Mary Shelley herself involved in Frank's plight.

Episodes: *1.* The New Romantics. *2.* Temper, Temper. *3.* Mary Shelley. *4.* PB Shelley. *5.* Lord Byron. *6.* Frank Grows Up. *7.* Dangerous Decisions.

571 *Living with Friends.* youtube.com. 2010.

Brothers Zak and Aaron and their friend Efehan are roommates sharing a small apartment. They do not always get along, act impulsively at times and for the most part do not take life seriously. The program relates the events that spark their lives as it slowly dawns on them that they are getting older and must deal realistically with the world that surrounds them, including trends, sexual identity and their own inner demons.

Cast: Zachariah Tatham (Zak), Aaron Manczyk (Aaron), Efehan Elbi (Efehan), Leon Hui (Leon), Bradford Wilson (Bradford), Selam Yohnnes (Selam). **Credits:** *Producer-Writer-Director:* Zachariah Tatham, Aaron Manczyk. **Comment:** The program opens with three people dancing (or attempting to). With this taking 2 minutes of the 7 minute and 43 second episode, it then focuses on their attempts to sing. It is now 4 minutes and 8 seconds into the episode and you have no idea who these people are or what the series is about. With the remaining time left, the three begin talking and acting a bit crazy. It ends without revealing who they are or establishing anything by way of a story line. The following episode is just as bad, spending most of its time watching the three playing with Slinky toys. By the third episode the storyline is somewhat revealed. But by this time most people will have not bothered to even venture that far. The producers wrongly assume the craziness presented will just make you stick with the show no matter what. If attention isn't grabbed almost immediately, the audience will be lost. The acting is just passable and the production itself suffers for its lack of establishing (at least) the characters or a storyline. How the show went for two seasons is a mystery as the program is not funny, just embarrassingly awkward.

Season 1 Episodes: *1.* Introducing Bros. *2.* Big Bro Break-In. *3.* Role Playing. *4.* Previously On... (a recap of the first 3 episodes). *5.* Goth Sign-Up. *6.* Intrusion of the Stars. *7.* Acorn Adventure. *8.* Sexually Induced Stroke. *9.* Fever Dreams. *10.* The Youth Trap.

Season 2 Episodes: 1. Season 1 Recap. 2. Rescue Mission. *3.* Signs of a Visitor. *4.* Beyond Desktops. *5.* Stand By Your Friends. *6.* Ringtones. *7.* Lady Killers. *8.* Survival Camp.

572 *Living with Uncle Charlie.* youtube.com. 2012.

Sixteen-year-old twin brothers Evan and Ethan, left orphaned following the death of their mother (their father abandoned them when they were born) find their life changing for the worse when they are taken in by their Uncle Charlie, an irresponsible man who can barely take care of himself. Uncle Charlie appears to survive by taking odd jobs, is being pursued by his wacky neighbor, De De and finds that becoming a parent is not a job he was cut out to do. The program follows Evan and Ethan as they struggle to not only care for each other but become a "parent" to their Uncle Charlie as well.

Cast: Monte James (Charlie Hawkins), Joel Harold (Evan Hawkins), Joseph Harold (Ethan Hawkins), Molly Hanson (D.D. Williams), Nick Leland (Pete). **Credits:** *Producer:* Joel Harold, Joseph Harold. *Director:* Jonathan W. Cypress II. *Writer:* Joel Harold. **Comment:** Well produced and acted African-American program that has traces of the feature film (and TV series) *Uncle Buck* but can stand on its own as kids trying to live with an irresponsible guardian.

Episodes: *1.* Meet the New Modern Family. *2.* Life As We Know It. *3.* Unexpected House Guest. *4.* The Money Maker. *5.* Vengeful Old Man Jenkins.

573 *Llama Cop.* webserieschannel.com. 2014.

Buddy Llama is a maverick police officer. He does what he wants when he wants as long as it is in the cause of justice. Buddy is not fast on the draw and loves to use disguises when he investigates cases.

Buddy is also a Llama (not a guy in a costume, but a real Llama) and has been partnered with Detective Joe Bauer, a by-the-books cop who just doesn't understand Buddy's continual defiance of the rules. How Buddy even managed to become a cop and why Police Captain Foley would consider hiring him are not stated—but the series does portray Buddy's relentless efforts to investigate cases and bring the bad guys to justice (the storyline presented relates Buddy and Joe's efforts to stop a drug cartel from taking over the city).

Cast: Walter Masterson (Joe Bauer), Antonio D. Christy (Capt. Foley), Brad Lee Ward (Gregor), Michael Edelstein (Pavel), John Pirkis (Father Robler). **Credits:** *Producer:* Louie Torrellas, Stephen Brown. *Director:* Charlie Zwick. *Writer:* Walter Masterson, Maximillian Clark. **Comment:** Buddy "is a tough rookie cop" and "the last hope" the city has and the presented story is well acted and produced.

Episodes: *1.* Badass Llama Goes Undercover. *2.* Llama Exposes Its Dark Side. *3.* Llama Gunfight Surprise. *4.* Llama's Ex-Wife Is Very Naughty.

574 *Loch Ness: The Web Series.* lochnesswebseries.com. 2013.

Donna, Joey, Kyle and Steve are teenagers living in Omaha, Nebraska. They have been friends for years, attend the same high school and share a love of folk metal music, so much so that they have formed their own band, Loch Ness. The program charts their mishaps as they deal with the problems they now face—disapproving parents, a lack of funds, off-key musicians and a town where such music is not appreciated or readily accepted. Donna's views on life have thus far been the only episodes released (called "The Donna Diaries" and are listed below).

Donna, although pretty and popular, never felt she fit in with girls and considered herself more as "one of the guys" ("just prettier and better smelling"). Although her father somewhat approves of her choice (her mother doesn't) Donna parlayed her talent with her keyboard into the beginnings of the band.

Joey, although more off-key than musically correct, is the band's drummer (he considers himself one of the world's best such musicians; he just needs to convince the world that it is so). He has the enthusiasm that could propel Loch Ness into greatness.

Kyle, the lead guitarist, is the youngest member of the group (17) and yearns for the day he can buy cigarettes (to prove he is a true metal head).

Steve, depicted as a pot smoking, video game player, is 18 years old and causes more problems than solutions (although he writes "killer bass lines")

Cast: Christina Marie Leonard (Donna), Josh Saleh (Kyle), Mishone Feigin (Steve), Chris Muckey

(Joey), Lindsey Jean Routzel (Alex), Acyil Yeltan (Martha), Jim Hanna (Richard), Nick Uzarski (Chad), David Quane (Thorvald), Roger Lawrence Goff III (Peter), Tom Spath (Tony), Claudia Voloma (Olga). **Credits:** *Producer:* Christina Marie Leonard, Mijoe Sahiouni, Rachel Gunnerson, Melanie Recker. *Writer:* Christina Marie Leonard. *Director:* Graham Shiels, Mijoe Sahiouni. **Comment:** The program is based on a real folk metal band called Loch Ness that actually existed in Omaha (Christina Marie Leonard, a member of the real band, created the series). While actual episodes have not yet been released, a series of video diaries have and feature Christina as Donna expressing her comments on life.

Donna Diaries Episodes: *1.* Why My Mom Wants to Ruin My Life. *2.* Girls Just Want to Have Fun. *3.* Why My Mom Is a CockBlock. *4.* Why Guys Are A-Holes. *5.* Why Ren Faire Guys Are Sexy. *6.* Why James Hertfield Is a Pilaf. *7.* You Should Always Lock Your Door. *8.* Why Taylor Swift Is Anti-Metal. *9.* How To Get Along with Your Mother. *10.* Don't Judge a Book By Its Cover. *11.* What Should the Loch Ness Band Be for Halloween? *12.* 5 Reasons Why I Slept with Nick Jonas.

575 *Log Jam.* youtube.com. 2012.

The Log Jam, a gay Republican bar in Chicago, is a hangout for Arnold, Betsy and Phil, gay conservatives seeking love and understanding in a liberal gay world. Arnold, currently unemployed (dismissed from his job as a government contractor for the Blackwater project) is seeking what he calls "Mr. Hard Right." Betsy, an investment banker, considers herself a power lesbian and has set her goal to get the Republican Party to recognize that she and others like her have the right to choose the lovers of their choice without the backlash that same sex relationships cause. Phil, a powerful CEO, is a man with a passion for family values but tormented by his inner demons—his lust for exotic fetish play. As the friends meet each day at the bar, Nancy Reagan, the drag queen bar owner, dispenses advice regarding life and love and the program relates the incidents that befall Arnold, Betsy and Phil as the advice given is not always the right advice to follow when it comes to their love lives.

Cast: Andy Eninger (Phil), Becca Levine (Betsy), John Loos (Arnold), David Cerda (Nancy Reagan), Katy Colloton (Linda the Moderate), Lisa Linke (Gillian), Brett Mannes (Rich). **Credits:** *Producer-Writer:* John Loos. *Director:* Ward Crockett. **Comment:** While most of the action takes place within the bar, the stories are well plotted and nicely acted. The production values are good and the only objection would be the use of foul language, which was not really needed.

Episodes: *1.* Minority Outreach. *2.* The Billionaire. *3.* Ladies' Night. *4.* The Liberal.

576 *Long Distance.* youtube.com. 2014.

At an out of town party two strangers, Colby and Breanne, meet and immediately find an attraction to each other. As the evening progresses and the party ends, Colby, who lives in Chicago, and Breanne (from San Diego) believe what they have just experienced is like a ship passing in the night until each decides to keep in touch and carry on a long distance relationship. Will it work, or will it be like so many who have tried and failed? The program relates how Colby and Breanne attempt such a relationship and how it not only affects them, but their friends as well.

Cast: Jeff Allen (Colby), Taylor Cloyes (Breanne), Jonathan Biver (Steve), Veronica Mannion (Robin), Claire Gordon-Harper (Amy), Katie Seeley (Annabelle), Victoria Levine (Jules), Adrian Bustamante (Joe), Miriam Korn (Rebecca). **Credits:** *Producer:* Ted Barnes, Jeff Allen, Paul Hart-Wilden, Earl Bolden, Jr. *Director:* Paul Hart-Wilden. *Writer:* Ted Barnes. **Comment:** While such plots have been done before, the acting here is quite good and the production itself well done.

Episodes: *1.* Pilot. *2.* Limbus. *3.* After the Math. *4,5.* Visiting Hours. *6.* Changes.

577 *Long Story, Short.* longstoryshortseries.com. 2009.

Kristen is a 21-year-old woman who is attractive, bright and ambitious but without a clue as to what she is doing with her life. She had a dream to move to New York and attend art school but when she was unable to make the cut, she quit and has now returned to her home in Toronto where she has reconnected with her friends Carson (cynical and unconventional) and Lucy (a reserved school teacher seeking a job). Kristen has a knack for dating "bad men" and finds relief from her woes in alcohol. Together, however, Kristen, Carson and Lucy are like the Three Musketeers and stories relate all that happens as each seeks to overcome their failures and experience the good things in life.

Cast: Katie Boland (Kristen Harvey), Tommie-Amber Pirie (Carson), Lauren Collins (Lucy), Adam Butcher (Andrew), Michael Seater (Dave). **Credits:** *Producer:* Katie Boland, Gail Harvey. *Writer:* Katie Boland. **Comment:** With all episodes off line a comment is not possible.

Episodes: *1.* The Summer I Lost My Mind. *2.* Taken. *3.* The Lies We Tell Ourselves. *4.* Hard to Get. *5.* Nothing to Lose. *6.* Where's This Going? *7.* Lonely. *8.* Crutches. *9.* The Hangout. *10.* The Morning Light. *11.* What's Next.

578 *Look No Further.* webserieschannel.com. 2010.

Jeffrey and Drew, friends with degrees in journalism believe that people need to read about the stories they write. But the economy is tough and they are unable to find the kind of jobs they would like for that to happen. Until that time comes, they have turned to the Internet and begun a news blog. Unfortunately, the blog receives no hits. Frustrated but not defeated, Jeffrey devises what he calls a "Flog" (filming news stories and presenting them as a blog). Jeffrey believes it is the latest technology and perfect for the social media (as you can optimize what you have for the most exposure possible). The world "has never had a good flogging" (as Jeffrey says) and the program charts their escapades as they deliver the hard hitting news stories that have fallen though the cracks and are overlooked by the major broadcast and cable news stations.

Cast: Jeffrey Loucks (Jeffrey), Andrew Dergousoff (Drew), Laura Hope, Chris Coolie, Timothy Loucks, Stu Cawood, Leighton Garfield, Rory McClure, Ross Lockhart, Jenny Fremlin, Erin Hoyt, Carly Ramsey. **Credits:** *Producer:* Jeffrey Loucks. **Comment:** Nicely paced, well acted and produced program that attempts to be no more than it is—a simple look at two journalists acquiring stories and the troubles they encounter.

Season 1 Episodes: 13 episodes, titled Scene 1, Part 1 to Scene 1, Part 13.

Season 2 Episodes: Follows the same format: Scene 1 (Second Series) to Scene 9 (Second Series).

Season 3 Episodes: Encompasses the same labeling: Scene 1 (Third Series) to Scene 8 (Third Series).

579 *Lords of Mayhem.* webserieschannel.com. 2010.

Michael, David and Angus are dysfunctional young men who are members of The Lords, street fighters who compete in underground fight clubs. While their lives seem to revolve around their gang association, they have not really come to terms with the real world that surrounds them. The Lords are there for each other in times of need and the program follows each of the friends as they deal with the world beyond fighting—from relationship problems with girls to discovering who they really are and what they the future holds for them away from the world of club fighting.

Cast: Dru Moores (Michael), Gleb Gorine (David), Sammy Allouba (Angus), King Yeung (Martin), Paquito Hernaci (Arnold), Julia MacPherson (Abigail), Shailene Garnett (Nancy), Cassie Nadeau (Cassie), Johnny Quinn (Terrence). **Credits:** *Producer-Writer-Director:* King Yeung. **Comment:** Although tagged a comedy, it is more action oriented than comical. There is foul language, abundant fighting scenes and situations that are hard to accept as comical. The producer appears at the beginning of the first episode to introduce the story and characters and sets the tone for the entire series. The acting and production values are good, but do not expect a comedy in the typical sense of the word.

Episodes: Episodes 1–5 are untitled. *6.* The Art Party. *7.* School Daze. *8.* Even the Odds.

580 *Los Feliz Blvd.* youtube.com. 2012.

Los Feliz Boulevard in Los Angeles provides the backdrop for a look at the lives of several people: Fig, Stanford, Shelly and Hannah. Fig and Stanford have been friends for some time and each has had their share of romantic problems. Fig has just broken up with a girl and Stanford has become engaged to Shelly. Just as Stanford believes Shelly is the girl of his dreams, he meets DK, a girl that sweeps him off his feet and implants doubts that Shelly may not be the right girl for him. As a friend to a friend, Stanford asks Fig's help in keeping his affair with DK a secret while he still remains engaged to Shelly. Fig reluctantly agrees and stories follow what happens as both Fig and Stanford attempt a cover up with everything that can possibly go wrong happening.

Cast: Bernard Badion (Fig), Stephen Avitabile (Stanford), Wendy McColm (DK), Eugenie Coetzee (Shelly), Hannah Johnson (Hannah), Jake Regal (Atticus). **Credits:** *Producer:* Kevin Hinman. *Writer-Director:* Bernard Badion. **Comment:** The program immediately captures your attention as the plot is presented right away and does not drag out the story line. The acting and production values are very good and the story flows smoothly from episode to episode.

Episodes: *1.* Paper Towles. *2.* Cupid. *3.* Cake.

581 *Lost in L.A.* lostinlaseries.com. 2013–2014.

Billed as "2 Broke Girls meets Romi and Michelle" as it explores the lives of Candace and Bridgett, close friends, working as waitresses, who are lost in their dreams of pursuing a better life in Los Angeles. Each episode is a look at a predicament that affects Candace and Bridgett and how they manage to handle it, all the time hopeful of achieving that dream of success.

Cast: Sascha Raeburn (Candace Benson), Laura Hughes (Bridgett Dunn), Abby Kammeraad-Campbell (Abby Townsend), Katie Oliver (Judy Freeman), Kristie Munoz (Alex Richards). **Credits:** *Producer-Writer-Director:* Sascha Raeburn. **Comment:** With the exception of Season 1 episodes 1, 2 and 9, which are a bit adult in nature (copying the sexual comedy of *2 Broke Girls*), the remaining episodes are a bit tamer and more in line with what the series is. It is charming, well acted and produced.

Season 1 Episodes: *1.* Crabs/Itchy Pussy. *2.* Having a Dick. *3.* Hollywood Sign. *4.* Caneage. *5.* Hollywood Hustle. *6.* Gauging. *7.* Happy Endings. *8.* Pool Hopping. *9.* How to Pick a Hollywood Name. *10.* Pros and Cons of Becoming a Slut.

Season 2 Episodes: *1.* Wanna F**k? *2.* Maybe He's a Weed Muncher. *3.* Lost in Joshua Tree. *4.* Hollywood Connection. *5.* Meeting with Aggy. *6.* A Week with Aggy. *7.* The Truth About Aggy. *8.* Get Shaggy with Abby. *9.* Bridgett Left Town. *10.* Welcome to Hollywood.

Season 3 Episodes: *1.* Hollywood Manager. *2.* Runyon with Jude. *3.* Kick the Tour Guide. *4.* In Hollywood There's Always Tomorrow. *5.* Hollywood Works. *6.* Be Like Caterpillar. *7.* The Masturbator. *8.* Avatar Self Test.

582 *Louis Grant.* webserieschannel.com. 2012.

Louis Grant is a young man and the father of a nine month old daughter (called "Baby"). He is single and lives in the attic of the home of the woman (called "Mommy") he got pregnant. Louis has no money, little ambition and devises somewhat ingenious (but always back-firing) methods to just get by. Because Mommy is strict and Louis not man-enough to stand up to her, he is forced to care for Baby while Mommy works. The program charts the adventures Louis shares with Baby as he seeks to better his life (through scams) and get out from under the iron rule of Mommy.

Cast: Damien Blackshaw (Louis Grant), Aiyana (Baby), Manuela Feris (Mommy), Robin Dalea (Vanessa), Rebecca Abraham (Paige), Glen Anthony Vaughan (Joey), Jaime Parker Stickle (Jenny). **Credits:** *Producer:* Todd Louis Green, Damien Blackshaw. *Director:* Todd Louis Green. *Writer:* Damien Blackshaw, Todd Louis Green. **Comment:** Very well constructed program with good acting and production values. The final episode establishes that Mommy has been away on business (in Hong Kong) but has returned to tell Louis that she has taken a job oversees, is taking Baby with her and selling the house, leaving Louis to now fend for himself.

Episodes: *1.* The Date. *2.* The Negotiation. *3.* The Interview. *4.* A Sure Thing. *5.* Another Time Around. *6.* The Return of the Prodigal Mother.

583 *The Louise Log.* thelouiselog.com. 2007–2014.

Louise is a housewife and mother living in New York City. She is also overcome by the world that surrounds her and it could be said she is a bit insecure as well as an emotional train wreck. While everyone has to deal with the issues that surround them, for Louise it is more of a challenge and she is determined to overcome those challenges. Through Louise's inner voice, her feelings about a situation are related to the viewer coupled with her actual approach to solving that situation. Louise is married to a high maintenance man (Phineas) and her efforts to deal with him as well as her controlling sister Ava and niece Monique are also a part of the program (with second season episodes primarily focused on Louise and Ava's efforts to produce a web series).

Cast: Christine Cook, Morgan Hallett (Louise), Kenneth B. Goldberg, Joe Franchini (Phineas), Jenifer Sklias-Gahan (Ava), Mathilde Dratwa (Monique), Snezhana Chernova (Svetlana), Mohammad Akmal (Raj), Talulah Mei Barni (Liza), Aidan Brogan, Bruno Zero (Charles), Senemi d'Almeida (Cica). **Credits:** *Director:* Anne Flournoy. *Writer:* Anne Flournoy, Sandra Vannucchi. **Comment:** A different approach to people dealing with confrontation that is well acted and produced. The inner thought gimmick has been used numerous times before but it is presented here as a major aspect of the series with Louise sort of whispering her lines as she relates her feelings to the viewer. Because episodes are short, it does not become an annoyance to constantly hear that whispering; had episodes been longer, it could get on one's nerves and become a turn-off rather than an attraction.

Season 1 Episodes: *1.* How to Face Mortality. *2.* How to Talk to Men. *3.* How to Live on the Edge. *4.* How to Take It Like a Girl. *5.* How to Wreck Your Reputation. *6.* How to Make a Perfect Cup of Coffee. *7.* How to Have Fresh, Radiant Skin. *8.* How to Interview Babysitters. *9.* How to Get a Woman Excited. *10.* The Revenge of the Minivan. *11.* The New Babysitter. *12.* How to Meet Your Child's Principal. *13.* How to Deal with a Cute Repairman. *14.* How to Set Up a Menage-a-Trois. *15.* How to Become a Belly Dancer. *16.* How to Chair Wrestle. *17.* How to Wreck Your Marriage.

Season 2 Episodes: *18.* How to Kill Your Husband. *19.* How to Make Matters Worse. *20.* How to Be Free of Envy. *21.* How to Welcome a Witch Doctor. *22.* How to Lose Weight. *23.* How to Light Your Inner Firecracker. *24.* How to Cope with Your Inner Cat. *25.* How Not to Make a Web Series. *26.* How to Flirt. *27.* How to Be a MILF. *28.* How to Be Cool. *29.* How to Cope with War on a Video Set. *30.* How to Be a Woman. *31.* How to Fake It. *32* How to Tap Into Your Power.

Season 3 Episodes: *33.* How to Be Where You Are. *34.* How to Bully a Bully. *35.* How to Fire Things Up with Your In-Laws. *36.* How to Get What You Want. *37.* How to Get There by Subway. *38.* How to Get Out of Crazy Town. *39.* How to Re-enter the Work Force. *40.* How to Ruin a Hot Date. *41.* How to Shake N' Bake a Marriage. *42.* How to Be Chill. *43.* How to Fix Your Family (Not). *44.* How to Go Rogue.

584 *Love and Other Mishaps.* youtube.com. 2011–2013.

Stella is a young woman burdened not only by mishaps but by an unrequited love (someone she yearns for but cannot have). Rather than see her wallow in self pity, her best friend and roommate, Paul, urges her to move on and find someone new. The program charts what happens when Stella re-enters the dating scene and encounters men who are anything but desirable, not alone what she is looking for.

Cast: Ferin Petrelli (Stella), Paul Case (Paul), Nicole Zeoli (Patty), Lauren Middleton (Lauren), Max Middleton (The Boss), Mariel Martinez (Juanita). Credits: *Producer-Writer:* Ferin Petrelli. *Director:* Josef Geiger, Ferin Petrelli. Comment: The program opens with Stella telling her audience, "This is the story of my life ... and I'm stuck in the friend zone." While attractive but never really having a boyfriend Stella has settled in what appear to be fantasy love affairs. Through Paul's urging Stella's life changes and the well acted and produced series presents the humorous incidents that befall Stella, a girl who wants only to be left alone, eat chocolate and dream about the love she can never have.

Episodes: *1.* Pilot. *2.* The Blind Date. *3.* The Cheater. *4.* The Assistant. *5.* The Workout Partner. *6.* The Birthday Surprise. *7.* The Fifth Wheel. *8.* The Crappy Day. *9.* The House Guest. *10.* The Wedding Nightmare.

585 *Love Bytes.* youtube.com. 2013.

Jade, a 26-year-old videographer, is a lesbian and seeking as much fun as possible before settling down with the woman of her dreams. Jade, attracted to girls for as long as she can remember, is a Virgo and a bit picky when it comes to dating and prefers women who are more eccentric than normal. Michael, a strong believer that money can often spoil relationships, is gay and looking to become a trophy husband by finding a man who is rich and will spoil him. He is 27 years old, has the astrological sign of Leo and works as a receptionist. Stacey, 28 years old and single, is straight and dreams of settling down, having a family and living in a cottage in the country. She is a Pisces, works as an artists' representative and finding the man of her dreams is much more difficult than she imagined as she has a tendency to meet men who are anything like what she pictures. The program follows their mishaps as they venture into the world of dating with each seeking that special someone that appears impossible to find.

Cast: Emily Rose Brennan (Stacey), Billie Rose Pritchard (Jade), Adriano Cappelletta (Michael), Bec Irwin (Samantha Fox), Dave Halalilo (Adam). Credits: *Producer:* Tonnette Stanford, Emma McKenna. *Writer-Director:* Tonnette Stanford. Comment: British produced, delightful lesbian-gay mix series. The characters are very well executed and like-able with excellent writing and directing. There are sexual situations, kissing (mostly girl/girl) and a well thought out and executed program.

Episodes: *1.* Herpes of the Lips. *2.* Justin Beaver. *3.* Experimenting. *4.* The Sex Bet.

586 *Love Handles.* youtube.com. 2014.

Leeza and Derek are lovers but Leeza's gaining weight has upset Derek who feels she has let herself go and has chosen to end their relationship. The breakup does not go well for Leeza as it has begun to affect her mind and body. Seeing that she needs help, her best friends, Charlie and Jade step in and the program chronicles how Leeza (and Charlie and Jade) take on the world of health and fitness when they join a "man magnet" fitness group that not only tests their friendship, but physiques as well.

Cast: Erica Nicole Robinson (Leeza), Skye Marshall (Jade), Leilani Smith (Charlie), Mustafa Shakir (Derek). Credits: *Producer:* Benjamin Hurvitz, Gary Woods, Angela Burris. *Writer-Director:* Carlton Jordan, Crystle Clear Roberson. Comment: Unusual format for a sitcom that is well acted and produced.

Episodes: *1.* Bootyboo. *2.* Be Aggressive. *3.* Watch Your Back. *4.* Africanized Yoga. *5.* Drive By. *6.* Sweet Dreams. *7.* Leeza and Derek.

587 *Love Hurts.* webserieschannel.com. 2013.

When Josh Hurts, a school teacher breaks up with his girlfriend (Tiffany) because he feels they are not right for each other, he gets a taste of what that feels like when he discovers she cheated on him and he was totally unaware of it. Now, more depressed than he was before the breakup, Josh feels that getting back into the dating scene will help him forget what happened. Tiffany may have been the best thing that has ever happened to him as finding a girl to replace her becomes his greatest challenge. The program follows Josh as he begins dating but hooks up with women who are anything but normal (from an insane Internet date to a fanatical feminist to a day release mental patient) and learns, along the way that love hurts.

Cast: Chris Hembury (Josh Hurts), Joanne Dawn (Tiffany), Lauran Boddy (Amy), Zuzana Garaiova (Anna), Bianca Rudman (Rosie), Cat Iddon (Rachel), Dale Bowkett (Timmy), Phillip Ciokowski (Billy), Nathan Lee (Rick), Sue Evans (Edna), Owen Herbert (Karl). Credits: *Producer-Director:* Chris Hembury. *Writer:* Chris Hembury, Steve Collins. Comment: It's not the ordinary break-up find a new mate story. It's breaking up then trying to find a girl who is not out to destroy you. The premise, acting and production are all very good.

Episodes: *1.* Breaking Point. *2,3.* Surprise. *4,5.* What Makes Britain Great. *6,7.* You Can't Buy Love. *8,9.* Cinema Date. *10,11.* All Men Are Bastards.

588 *Love Kabob.* lovekabobusa.com. 2012.

Elle is an American Catholic. Kamal is a Pakistani Muslim. They have been married for four years and live in New York City. The marriage has been a success because each respects the other's religion and their sometimes quirky ways. Each believed that before they married, they negotiated all their major theological differences and their union would be a blissful one. But over time slight discrepancies have crept into their marriage and have each seeing the other in a different light. The program charts the problems Elle and Kamal encounter when they literally attempt to readjust to each other while at the same time deal with a group of off-the-wall friends and opinionated in-laws who have their own views on how their children should live. Alex and Jamie are Elle and Kamal's married friends; Khadija and Saleem are Kamal's parents; and Hank and Faith are Elle's parents.

Cast: Lindsay Levesque-Alam (Elle), Gerrard Lobo (Kamal), Matthew Rini, Jarret Karlsberg (Alex), Risa Rini (Jamie), Daniel Blatman (Matt), Katie Murphy (Skyler), Jyoti Singh (Khadija), Rahoul Roy (Saleem), Deb Trouche (Faith), John Carlton (Hank), Jeff Green (Father Bobby). **Credits:** *Producer-Writer-Director:* Lindsay Levesque-Alam. **Comment:** Delightful, well-acted and produced sitcom-like comedy. While mixed marriages have been tackled on TV numerous times, they can stand on their own if the right mix is found. Such is the case here and the end result is something familiar but with a whole new twist.

Season 1 Episodes: *1.* Sending Our Love. *2–4.* The Confession. *5,6.* Drinking Games. *7.* Dancing with the Goldfarbs. *8,9.* Fashion Statement. *10–13.* Mother's Day. *14–16.* Simka.

Season 2 Episodes: *1,2.* The Karate Lesson. *3,4.* What the Goat Started. *5–7.* When Everyone Met Sally. *8–10.* The E-mails. *11,12.* Inspired by Sandy and Some Other Bitches.

589 *Love, Period.* youtube.com. 2013.

Love Evolve is a prestigious match-making company that claims to find matches that last a lifetime. That is the image the staff of Love Evolve want you to believe. In reality, they are a bit insecure, argumentative and often offend clients with questions that go beyond the norm. But they do have their good days (but mostly bad) and the program follows the staff as they attempt to match the right man with the right woman and what happens when their attempts are anything but successful.

Cast: Jeannette Woolf (Paula Sharpe), Daryl Ferrara (Scott Powder), Kate Forsatz (Michelle Baker), Lauren Hooper (Jasmine Johnson), Erick Szentmiklosy (Dan McCallister), Daniel Spencer (Henry Chang). **Credits:** *Producer:* Daryl Ferrara, James Lindsay, Jeannette Woolf. *Director:* Robert Tagliareni. *Writer:* James Lindsay. **Comment:** Television has presented a number of series built around a match-making service and none were a success. It could be the casting, the stories, the premise or a combination of things. *Love, Period* tries to be different and it achieves that goal with off-the-wall

characters, especially Michelle (who feels she needs to probe clients with questions that are way too personal) and Paula, a young woman struggling to not only deal with her unpredictable staff, but sometimes eccentric clients as well. The acting and production values are good and the premise is there, but only three episodes were produced.

Episodes: *1.* Love Is in the Air. *2.* What She Say? *3.* Eddie's Lament.

590 *Love's a Bitch.* loves-a-bitch.com. 2014.

Allison and Wes were very much in love. But over time circumstances have changed the way they feel for each other and each agrees that it is time to end their union. They knew it was coming and they have no one to blame but themselves. It is the aftermath that is the most difficult to overcome and the program chronicles what happens as they attempt to move on with their lives but still have a connection to each other.

Cast: Jamie Lee (Allison), Josh Rabinowitz (Wes), Charlie Hankin (Tim), Matt Porter (Matt), Ann Valia (Julie). **Credits:** *Producer;* Jeff Schwartz. *Director:* Matt Kazman. *Writer:* Eric Ian Goldberg, Matt Kazman, Timothy Moran, Anu Valia. **Comment:** A look at marriage from a different angle— the sometimes dramatic and comic things that happen after Allison and Wes decide to end their relationship. The acting, story and production are very good.

Episodes: *1.* Happy Birthday, By the Way. *2.* The Mutual Friend. *3.* The New You. *4.* Ex-Factor. *5.* Winter Is Coming. *6.* Seeing Other People. *7.* About Last Night. *8.* Is There Someone Else? *9.* The Truce. *10.* She's Having a Baby. *11.* Family Time. *12.* In Your Dreams.

591 *Lovin' Lakin.* lovinlackin.tumblr.com. 2012.

Christine Lakin is a real life actress who began her show business career as a child (as a regular on ABC's *Step by Step*, 1991–1998) and has appeared on such television series as *Touched by an Angel*, *Promised Land, Veronica Mars, Third Rock from the Sun* and *Melissa and Joey*. While Christine's career has not actually floundered (as she has been active to date), Christine presents herself as a child actress who has grown into an adult and needs to re-establish herself in Hollywood. In between roles she teaches an acting class for children and, in a "mocumentary" style presentation, shares her experiences as she attempts to once again shine as a television and movie star (which she feels can only be accomplished by her theory that "it is not who you are, but who you know").

Cast: Christine Lakin, Kristen Bell, Patrick Duffy, Kristen Chenoweth, Seth MacFarlane. **Credits:** *Producer:* Andy Fickman, Betsy Sullenger, Christine Lakin, Dave Mahanes. *Writer:* Christine

Lakin, Ross Patterson. **Comment:** Christine is as delightful now as she was on *Step by Step*. She is bright, bubbly and full of determination to jump start her career. It is a nice touch adding stars such as Kristen Chenoweth (who welcomes Christine into her home for singing lessons) and Kristen Bell (who, although she worked with Christine before, has a hard time recalling who she is). The documentary style spoof works with good acting (everything appears unscripted and natural) with TV-like production values. If you remember Christine from her ABC series and would like to see her now (or just curious to see who Christine Lakin is) *Lovin' Lakin* will fill that bill.

Episodes: *1.* Lakin Teaches an Acting Class. *2.* Lakin Takes a Voice Lesson from Kristin Chenoweth. *3.* Lakin Gets an Agent. *4.* Lakin Visits Her Dad. *5.* Lakin Goes to an Audition. *6.* Lakin Runs Into Kristen Bell. *7.* Lakin Films a Commercial. *8.* Lakin Goes on a Date. *9.* Lakin Impresses a Director. *10.* Lakin Finds Her Voice with Seth MacFarlane.

592 *Low Boys.* thelowboys.net. 2014.

Hammersworld is a New York City bar styled after a medieval pub. It is managed by Mr. Overstreet, a mixology expert known for crafting unique drinks. Steven Stephens is the general manager, a man who provides impeccable service but is somewhat anti-social. Tony McKeve is the head chef, a man who aspires to prepare only the perfect meals, despite its somewhat mediocre clientele. Leslie is a young woman who works as a waitress but is rather clumsy and just not suited for such work (but she's pretty and that affords her the job). The program, somewhat like a spoof of the TV series *Cheers* relates the mishaps that occur as all attempt to work together for the benefit of the bar.

Cast: Kevin Kelly (Mr. Overstreet), Michael S. Galligan (Steven Stephens), Allison Frasca (Leslie), Kevin Ricche (Tony McKeve). Credits are not given. **Comment:** The idea and acting are good but the continual use of shaky side-to-side scenes coupled with scenes bobbing up and down can easily turn people off. Had steady scenes been used the program would be much easier to watch; right now it can make you sea sick.

Episodes: 6 untitled episodes, labeled "Episode 1" through "Episode 6."

593 *The Lumber Baron of Jasper County.* lumberbarontheseries.com. 2012–2014.

Jasper County is a small town where the lumber industry once ruled. But times have changed and with the economy in the state it is in, the lumber business has been suffering. One man, however, the owner of a lumber supply store, devises a way to improve business. He wears a mask and a crown and dresses in a cape and overalls and calls himself "The

Lumber Baron." A series of newspaper ads prove successful and business begins to pick up but things go to The Lumber Baron's head and not only does he actually think he is the king of lumber but his actions make him appear like he is a complete idiot. He actually may be and the program follows a man as he lives out his delusions (beliefs) that he is actually The Lumber Baron of Jasper County.

Cast: Dave R. Watkins (Lumber Baron), Candace Mabry (Ashley), Grant Garlinghouse (Mike), Michael D. Friedman (Pete), Matt Nielsen (George), Nate Hill (Frog), Chris Burns (Mickey Bob). **Credits:** *Director:* Dave R. Watkins. *Writer:* Michael D. Friedman, Dave R. Watkins. **Comment:** Embarrassing program as it makes you just feel uncomfortable watching a complete idiot make a fool of himself. It is not so much how he looks but his actions lead you to believe he has mental issues and needs to seek medical help. While the production values are good, the acting on the part of the lead is just awful and if acting unbalanced is funny, then the producers have achieved their goal; if not you will have to decide for yourself.

Season 1 Episodes: *1.* Gator George. *2.* Maple Oak Luv 69. *3.* Jon From Elljay. *4.* Jon from Elljay Tries Again. *5.* Jolly Sam 1225. *6.* Maple Oak Luv 69 Returns. *7.* Sexy Lumber Jack Lady 4U. *8.* Pete Calls In. *9.* King Mickey Bob.

Season 2 Episodes: *1.* Jackalope Hunt. *2.* High as an Asteroid. *3.* Loose Screw. *4.* Temporary Employment. *5.* Acai Madness. *6.* Mr. Fixer. *7.* Bronco Buck. *8.* Buzz Words. *9.* High as a Kite. *10.* Business End Push. *11.* Ally's Gator Brew. *12.* Gator George.

Season 3 Episodes: *1.* Scorned Hot Chick. *2.* Lumber Extraordinaire Ryan. *3.* Dillo Caulk Commercial. *4.* Lumber Baron's Halloween Special. *5.* It's Christmas Ned, In July. *6.* The Trouble with Dave. *7.* Dark Times. *8.* Hangover Blues. *9.* As the Lumber Chicken. *10.* Shark Jumin'. *11.* We're Taking a Break.

Season 4 Episodes: *1.* Jackalope Hunt. *2.* Things to Do in Jasper County After Surviving an Imaginary... *3.* Zombies, Moonshine and Heartbreak. *4.* Get Purple. *5.* The Negotiation Situation. *6.* No Chicken in Yer Lumber. *7.* Free Hot Dogs. *8.* Operation Tier One: Lumber Chicken. *9,10.* St. Patrick's Day Special, Parts 1–2. *11.* Fertalizin' the Cornfield. *12.* Skiiin! *13.* Lost in the Woods in New Zealand. *14.* Knock on Wood. *15.* Arbor Day. *16.* Alepus Maximus.

Season 5 Episodes: *1.* Location Scout. *2.* Poltergeist Extreme. *3.* Fixer It. *4.* They're Coming. *5.* Tom Jenkins Strikes Again. *6.* Conversion. *7.* Boxed In. *8.* #Hastaggin' *9.* Festerin' Splinters. *10.* Aunt Betsy, Yardman. *11.* Gator Brew Askew. *12,13.* Purple Juice Day. *14.* The Pumpkin Man's Lair. *15.* Headspace. *16.* Collection Time. *17.* Ashley, Store Manager. *18.* Character Study. *19.* Dillo Man.

594 *Madden Girl Web Series.* youtube. com. 2013.

Madden is a high school girl who is not typical of such girls as they are usually depicted on TV (at least not in starring roles). She is, like other girls her age, bright, bubbly and pretty, but unlike the image presented on TV, she is addicted to food and overweight and constantly lamenting on the fact that "I'm fat." Madden lives with her father (divorced) and brother Stevie. At home her father allows her to eat what she wants without really taking a serious interest that she needs to go on a diet; Stevie, also not supportive, is rather unkind and lets Madden know she is fat. The program relates the events that befall Madden—from her rejection by the "Cool Girls" (led by Bambi) to her relationship with Rach, her best friend since the sixth grade.

Cast: Britt Elexandria (Madden), Shantiel Vazquez (Rach), Lindsay Bushman (Bambi), Chelsea Vale (Savvy), David Mamminga (Jay), Tyler Shamy (Noah), Taylor Watts (Stevie), Keonna Evans (Vanessa), Eric Keyes III (Daz Money), John Vazquez (Dad), Myke Wilken (Ginsen III). **Credits:** *Producer-Writer-Director:* Britt Elexandria. **Comment:** Don't expect gorgeous girls like Kelly, Lisa or Jessie from *Saved by the Bell* or characters as quirky as Rosalie "Hotsy" Totsie on *Welcome Back, Kotter.* Expect the other side of the coin—a portrait of real girls, represented by Madden, who are not cool or with the school in-crowd but who face ridicule and bullying. Nerds are also represented (by Ginsen III), jocks (Jay) and even the token black student (Daz)—all of which comes together to present a teenage version of, in a way, the ABC series *Ugly Betty* to show that among "the beautiful people of the world," there are also those who feel they are the unnoticed, underbelly of society, the forgotten.

Episodes: *1.* Who I Am. *2.* Bronze Buns. *3.* I Like Stevie. *4.* It's Party Time.

595 *Madi to the Max.* madi2themax.com. 2013.

One actress, numerous characters (Goth girl, Valley girl, geek, fashionista, cat, dog, guy, robot, Brit, hand puppet, librarian, sports girl, prom queen, Anime Chick, Face Maker, and nerd) and how each perceives life—with each having a different (strange at times) point of view.

Cast: Madison Brunoehler (All Characters). **Credits:** *Producer-Writer-Director:* Madison Brunoehler. **Comment:** Very intriguing program that is not only well acted and presented but to see how one woman can be so many different people.

Episodes: *1.* Freezing Pudding. *2.* Talk Twilight. *3.* Ramona. *4.* Not Your Mother's Robot. *5.* Who Is Your Role Model? *6.* The Many Functions of Friends. *7.* Backdrops. *8.* And Then There Was Sucy. *9.* Zombies! What Could Go Wrong? *10.* Food. *11.*

What's the Difference Between Britain and America? *12.* Diary of a Dog and Diary of a Cat. *13.* Mr. Chico. *14.* TV Shows. *15.* Do You Believe in Aliens? *16.* The Avengers and Poppy.

596 *Madre Mía.* youtube.com. 2012.

Spanish produced program that follows Mother Conchita, a Catholic nun who, after a vision she believes is God, devises a unique way to raise money to save her financially strapped convent: offer online confessions in return for donations. With the help of her mentally handicapped nephew Tito, Mother Conchita masters the mysteries of a computer and the Internet and begins her crusade to save her convent.

Cast: Soledad Lopez (Mother Conchita), Alfredo Huereca (God), David Vega (Tito), Esther Montero (Agripina), Laura Termini (Frances Telamente), Juan Villarreal (The Pope). **Credits:** *Producer:* Robert Gates, Francisco Fuertes, Franciso Lupini Basagioti. *Writer-Director:* Francisco Lupini Basagoiti. **Comment:** TV series dealing with nuns are rare with *The Flying Nun* (the only successful one), *In the Beginning* and even two failed pilots *Sister Michael Wants You* and *Sister Terri.* Although the program is in Spanish with English subtitles, it is something different with good acting and production values.

Episodes: *1.* Conchita's Ecstasy. *2.* Conchita and the Holy Object. *3.* Cyber Conchita. *4.* Hebemus Nun. *5.* The Flying Cat. *6.* The White Haired Man. *7.* The Holy Screw-Up. *8.* Appetite's Underworld. *9.* Symbiosis of Bodies.

597 *Maggie.* blip.tv. 2013.

Gaspar is an Accidentally Deceased Spiritual Guide (the powers that be took him before his time) who has been assigned to watch over Adam, a young man who was killed in a tragic car accident. Maggie is a young woman (an artist) who was best friends with Adam and now has the ability to see and speak to Adam, who has returned as a spirit to reconnect with her and watch over her. Although Maggie accepts Adam as her ghost friend, she finds her life changing even more when Gaspar appears to her to tell her that she can help Adam—but what she is told is not heard by viewers (as the scene becomes a long shot with the two of them talking; it apparently has something to do with helping Adam solve a series of riddles that can help him move on). With that unknown information (to continue the series, which did not occur) the program relates Maggie's experiences with Adam prior to meeting Gaspar as she struggles to conceal the fact that she has a ghostly roommate.

Cast: Emily Rued (Maggie), Joe Bearor (Adam), James Lontayao (Errol), Cooper Gillespie (June), Jorge Garcia (Gaspar). **Credits:** *Producer-Writer:*

Emily Rued. **Comment:** Although the idea is not new with such concepts dating back to *Topper* in movies and on TV, good acting and production make for an enjoyable twist on the subject.

Episodes: *1.* The Reveal. *2.* Ice Cream. *3.* Ghost Clothes. *4,5.* Dennis. *6.* Move In. *7.* Art Show. *8.* Having Him Gone. *9.* Gaspar, the Friendly A.D.S.A. *10.* Gaspar the Ambiguous.

598 Making New Friends. peachesandhotsauce.com. 2013.

Some people have an easy time making friends while others are just the opposite. Zack and Pat are two friends who yearn to make new friends. Each episode is a look at how they make those new friends and what results during and after the meeting.

Cast: Patrick O'Rourke (Pat), Zack Mast (Zack), Michael Gau, Charles Pettitt, Mo Gibbins, Jack Pelzer, Jennifer Burns (Friends). **Credits:** *Producer-Writer:* Patrick O'Rourke, Zack Mast. *Director:* Eric Richter. **Comment:** A simplistic program with good acting that shows the interactions that occur as new friends become a part of Pat and Zack's lives.

Episodes: *1.* Charlie the Milkman. *2.* Mo and Jack. *3.* Mickey the Barber. *4.* Yogi Sri Shangat.

599 The Making of Jane D. Smith. webserieschannel.com. 2012.

Jane D. Smith is a young woman, possessing a degree in Russian Literature, who, because of her degree ("I have a degree in Russian Literature; who uses that for anything?") constantly finds herself being fired from the jobs she is able to acquire. But Jane is not defeated. She feels she needs to take a new approach and creates the "Board of Possibilities," a chart of jobs and a determination to not only find a suitable job but reinvent herself. The program chronicles her pursuit of those jobs (from magician to baker to figure skater) and what happens as she tackles them.

Cast: Melissa Blue (Jane D. Smith). **Credits:** *Producer:* Melissa Blue. *Writer:* Melissa Blue, Taylor Casey. **Comment:** Although only one character is seen and she talks directly to the viewer, it is effectively done with Jane somewhat involved in the job she is tackling (as opposed to her just sitting in a chair and relating what happened). Such formats are chancy as the lead needs to set the pace and keep the viewer interested. Melissa Blue accomplishes that goal in episodes that are just the right length so as not to become a chore to watch.

Episodes: *1.* Fired. *2.* Cupcake Queen. *3.* Cold as Ice. *4.* Songbird. *5.* Feel the Burn. *6.* Abbra Cadabra.

600 Man-Teen. youtube.com. 2010–2012.

Laz, as he is called is 35 years old but has the men-

tality of a teenager. While he can think and do things for himself, he acts rather foolishly and what happens when he tries to become a part of adult situations is profiled.

Cast: Andy Lazarus (Laz), Terryn Westbrook (Claire), Kirk Zipfel (Sam). **Credits:** *Producer:* Andy Lazarus, Brian Spitz. **Comment:** Laz is made to be a foul-mouthed obnoxious character and placed in situations that make him look ridiculous. The production suffers somewhat because of that as it can become just too stupid to watch. The program was revised in 2014 but no cast or credits were released.

Episodes: *1.* A Celebration of Life. *2.* Cleanin' the Kitty. *3.* Honest Talk. *4.* Thanks for Lunch. *5,6,7.* Game Night.

601 ManDate. webserieschannel.com. 2011.

A ManDate, according to the program is when two guys get together to talk about their relationships, experiences and sexual encounters with women. Sam and Leon, friends living in Manhattan, are two such friends and their ManDate is explored as they discuss their problems—but not only with each other, but anyone who cares to watch.

Cast: Steve White (Samuel), Zeshan Bhatti (Leon), Kristen Seavey (Alex), Amy Wilson (Jessica), Kristin Muri Roman (Sara), Moe Yehia Hamdy (Lanny). **Credits:** *Producer:* Sheraz Bhatti, Bobby Chase, Alycia Schenkman. *Director:* Zeshan Bhatti, Ian James Ortiz. *Writer:* Zeshan Bhatti. **Comment:** The title can be misleading and make you believe it is a series about gays. Far from that as it is just guys bonding (say over a drink) to discuss matters. The acting and production are good.

Episodes: 5 untitled episodes, labeled "Episode 1" through "Episode 5."

602 The Maria Bamford Show. youtube.com. 2007–2008.

Maria Bamford is a stand up comedienne with a talent for impersonation, especially mocking friends and family to make humorous observations about the world in which she lives. Maria is performing her act at a Friars Club gathering in Hollywood when she suffers from a nervous breakdown and simply disappears. Three months later she was found by a homeless fan of hers selling clock radios on the streets of Detroit. Her parents were contacted and Maria was brought to their home in Minnesota to recover. Maria suffers from various mental health issues and needs to take medication and, while she recuperates, incidents that befall Maria are shared with the viewing audience.

Cast: Maria Bamford (All Characters). **Credits:** *Producer:* Dan Pasternack, Bruce Smith. *Director:* Damon Jones. *Writer:* Maria Bamford. **Comment:** Maria Bamford has a great talent for impersonation and it shows here. Although the program is basically just Maria talking to the camera as different characters, it is edited in such a way that it flows smoothly from one impersonation to the other.

Season 1 Episodes: *1.* Dropout. *2.* Maria Gets a Job. *3.* Kicked Out. *4.* Search for Meaning. *5.* Ready for Love. *6.* Mother's Day. *7.* Showtime. *8.* Crevasse. *9.* Bread. *10.* Dark.

Season 2 Episodes: *1.* Will. *2.* Faith. *3.* Oh, CD. *4.* Death and Happiness. *5.* Boredom. *6.* Acting Out. *7.* Horror. *8.* Moving. *9.* Replacement. *10.* Exit.

603 The Marriage Counselor. webseries channel.com. 2012.

He is a marriage counselor but doesn't appear to take his patients seriously as he tends to laugh at their problems or play games (like office golf) if he becomes bored. Yet, people come to him seeking relief from their marital woes. Such is the situation and the program explores how The Marriage Counselor (as he is called) deals with his patients and how the patients, who appear to have normal relationship issues, deal with the methods of a man who might just need psychiatric counseling.

Cast: Matthew St. James (The Marriage Counselor), Amanda Dawn Harrison (Francesca), Kyle J. Mattocks (Brandon), Allison Hammond (Ali), Dane White (Scott), Rebecca Catalano (Madame Tug), Taylor Piedmonte (Lance), Meg Duell (Katie), Brian Swinehart (Jerry), Lena Thomas (Amanda), Kelley Teeple (Anna), Matthew Godfrey (Alex). Credits: *Producer:* Misty White, Rachel Janine Lyon. *Director:* Jerry J. White III. *Writer:* Raymond Creamer. Comment: With the exception of a short teaser all episodes have been taken off line and it is just not possible to judge the series by it.

Episodes: *1.* Jerry & Amanda Case #421. *2.* Ali & Scott Case #666. *3.* Lance & Katie Case #123. *4.* Matt & Anna Case #999.

604 Married Young. youtube.com. 2012.

Jake and Maggie are like many people—young, in love and recently married. But did they do the right thing? Or did they rush into marriage before the time was right? The program explores what happens when young people, who have not weighed the pros and cons of being together, tie the knot and now have to figure out how to live with each other and accept both their good and bad faults.

Cast: Paul McLalin (Jake), Taylor Orci (Maggie). Credits: *Producer:* Paul McLalin, Jason Levinson. *Director:* Jason Levinson, Paul McLalin. Comment: Mostly under one minute episodes that are well acted and produced although laughter can be heard in the background, most likely from the crew as opposed to a laugh track.

Episodes: *1.* Movie Night. *2.* Gaining Weight. *3.* Monogamy. *4.* Til Death Do Us Part. *5.* Hanging Out. *6.* Pets. *7.* 401-K. *8.* Television Shows.

605 Mars: The Web Series. youtube.com. 2014.

Alana and Jake are people who live in Australia but on its opposite sides. Alana is a graphic artist who hates her job; Jake is a struggling writer who hopes for greatness but has doubts that will ever happen. By chance they meet on line, become friends and agree to use Skype to visually communicate with each other (and unexpectedly, fall in love with each other). But it is a long distance relationship and the program relates what happens as two people attempt such a situation.

Cast: Melody Lynn (Alana), Mark Isaacson (Jake). Credits: *Producer-Writer-Director:* Mark Isaacson. Comment: The program varies in presentation from bad to good. Too many facial close-ups, the leads typing messages to one another and the viewer having to read them is not the way to begin a program. This becomes less as the program continues and a rather interesting story emerges with a good production resulting.

Episodes: *1.* Pilot. *2.* Episode 2. *3.* Episode 3. *4.* Episode 4. *5.* The Game of Waiting. *6.* Work Day. *7.* A Story. *8.* The Incident Contract.

606 Marvelless Martan. youtube.com. 2014.

The Martan Show is a talk program hosted by the narcissistic Martan and staffed by a crew who are less than stellar. Choosing to encompass a behind-the-scenes look at a television talk show, the program reveals what happens when you mix a narrow-minded host (who is obsessed with singer Taylor Wayne) with a misfit staff and a network that would like a normal talk show but does not know how to remedy the situation (in the episode "Street Talk" the network discharges Martan and his wacky crew which leads Martan to do *On the Street with Martan*, a show wherein Martan approaches strangers for unrehearsed conversations). The title is derived from Martan's catch phrase "That's Marvelless."

Cast: Martin Joseph (Martan), Henriette Mantel (Wendy), Dierdra McDowell (Sandra), Connor Griffin (Jerry), Meghan Griffin (Agnes), Verlon Brown (Scotty). Credits: *Director:* Martin Joseph. Comment: Martan can become somewhat annoying to watch as episodes progress as he is simply too stereotyped. The overall idea is good though.

Episodes: *1.* The Wrong Taylor. *2.* Backstage Blunder. *3.* Going Viral. *4.* Driver's Ed. *5.* Talking Staff. *6.* Backstage Blunder. *7,8.* Going Viral. *9.* Locked Out. *10.* Only in His Dreams. *11.* Street Talk.

607 Mary Pillard. webserieschannel.com. 2014.

In 2008 Mary Pillard, a young woman from Great Stone, Missouri, and a member of its City Council,

Mary Pillard. Series poster art (used by permission).

put in her bid for President of the United States. She received four votes. As the 2012 Presidential election neared, Mary again put in her bid. She received 13 votes. With the 2016 Presidential election approaching Mary has again decided to run for office, this time with a different strategy: hit the campaign trail. Accompanied by her husband, Daniel Pillard (he took his wife's last name), her sister-in-law Cindy Pillard (also taking Mary's last name) and her assistant and loyal follower, Nicole Pritchard, Mary's travels across the country (beginning in New York) are chronicled as she tries to win votes the old fashioned way—meeting her public.

Cast: Noelle Stewart (Mary Pillard), Sam Reeder (Daniel Pillard), Michelle Marie Trester (Cindy Pillard), Maria Freda (Nicole Prichard), Andreas Damm (Tom), Jacob-Sebastian Phillips (Jason). Credits: *Director:* Daliya Karnofsky. *Writer:* Noelle Stewart. Comment: Enjoyable program with an attractive cast and good production values.

Episodes: *1.* Pilot. *2.* Let's Take a Tour of N.Y.C. *3.* The Speech. *4.* Presidential Debate. *5.* Try Again.

608 *Masters of the House.* webserieschannel.com. 2011.

Robert Delaney is a mega Hollywood producer who is not only ultra famous but filthy rich. He lives in a mansion and has a staff to attend to his every need. Robert is also a mega ladies' man and after a night of wild passion dies of a heart attack. But what about his staff; what will happen to them? When they realize their jobs will be terminated they devise an ingenious plan to remain as they are: conceal Delaney's death and make it look like he is still alive. The program charts all the problems that arise as the staff (see cast) continues in their normal jobs but what also happens when Delaney is needed, ex-wives appear, excuses are made and investigations begin.

Cast: John Mawson (Baxter), Rachel Rath (Maura), Jon Abrahams (Jerry), Kevin Marron (Danny), Carlos Antonio (Cesar), Kim Estes (Vincent). Credits: *Producer:* John Mawson, Rachel Rath. *Director:* Rachel Rath. *Writer:* John Mawson. Comment: While the idea is not new, the program is well done and enjoyable as the employees, called the Masters, attempt to keep their secret and proceed with life as if nothing has happened.

Episodes: *1.* Credit Crunch. *2.* Desperate Ex-Wives. *3.* Deal or No Deal. *4.* Suddenly Last Summer. *5.* Silence of the Hams. *6.* Deus Ex Machina.

609 *Matchstick McCoy.* matchstickmccoyweebly.com. 2012.

A spoof of the 1970s Kung Fu theatrical feature films as well as the Chuck Norris TV series *Walker, Texas Ranger.* Matchstick McCoy, nicknamed as such for his having to strike a match to light his cigarettes (which he is never seen without) is a cop skilled in the martial arts. While McCoy does have a gun, he prefers to tackle each criminal with his hands (deadly weapons) but if that doesn't work, shooting them will also do the job. Each episode presents a case handled by McCoy—and the reluctant partner the Chief assigns to accompany him (as no one apparently wants to accompany the reckless McCoy, who has contempt for authority and doing it his way is the only way).

Cast: Benjamin Watts (Matchstick McCoy), Mark Berry (The Chief), David Chan (Sum Yung Guy/Shing), Ben Seton (Rod Steele/Hugh G. Richard), Cassius Willis (Julius Axsomebody Jenkins/Willie Moses), David Hughes (Lawrence Bergenstein/D.A. Draggins). Credits: *Producer:* Benjamin Watts, Ben Seton. *Writer-Director:* Benjamin Watts. Comment: Although the photography is a bit pale compared to other programs and the sound a bit low here and there, the idea is good and Benjamin Watts as McCoy captures the look and feel of a cheap version of Chuck Norris (and other Kung Fu heroes of the day).

Episodes: *1.* The Oriental Express. *2.* The English Connection. *3.* Big and Black. *4.* Eye for an Eye.

610 *Matumbo Goldberg.* matumbogold berg.com. 2011.

Mark is a senior marketing executive. He is 33 years old and lives in Bellflower (its exact location is not stated). Mark's company downsizes and he is let go but all is not lost. In an idiotic plan, he logs onto the African Adoption Agency web site and enters his name as Matumbo, a four-year-old orphan living in Nairobi. Meanwhile, a slightly dense Jewish couple, called only Mr. and Mrs. Goldberg, had contemplated adopting a baby but chose not too because it was too depressing. However, when Mrs. Goldberg reads a story about Hollywood celebrities adopting children from foreign lands, she convinces her husband that they need to do the same thing. While searching the Internet for adoption agencies, Mrs. Goldberg comes across the African Adoption Agency and applies for that four-year-old Matumbo. Several days later there is a knock on the Goldberg's door and Mark, smoking a cigar and pretending to be Matumbo, appears. The Goldbergs are stunned—as what they expected is not four years old but perhaps, as Mrs. Goldberg says, sixteen years old. They welcome Matumbo into their home and the program follows what happens when the world's oldest "baby" must endure all the aspects of being treated like a child (including a Bar Mitzvah) in order to maintain his new standard of living.

Cast: Anthony Anderson (Mark/Matumbo), Rob Pearlstein (Mr. Goldberg), J. Robin Miller (Mrs. Goldberg), Jenna Elfman (Matumba, Matumbo's sister). **Credits:** *Producer:* Anthony Anderson, Thomas Bannister, Brian Dobbins, Barney Oldfield, Rob Pearlstein. *Writer-Director:* Rob Pearlstein. **Comment:** A very good idea that is literally spoiled by the continual use of foul language (especially on the part of Anthony Anderson). The acting and production is good and if you are not offended by numerous four-letter words, then the Goldberg family will log on another viewer hit.

Episodes: *1.* Pilot. *2.* Tribesmates. *3.* Bar Mitzvah. *4.* Sex-Ed. *5.* Matumba.

611 *Max & Melvin's Mortuary Madness.* vimeo.com. 2012.

Max and Melvin are brothers and out of work. Their parents are fed up with them and have threatened to throw them out if they do not get a job. But the brothers are lazy and not easily motivated—that is until they devise an ingenious plan where they can live and work at home by opening a mortuary in their basement. Thus is born The M&M Mortuary and the program chronicles what happens when two morons attempt to operate an illegal business with no knowledge of what being a mortician is all about.

Cast: London Homer-Wambeam (Melvin Marvin), Rory Eggleston (Max Marvin), Ali Briere (Molly B. Mittins), Audrey Hansen (Melanie Mar-

vin), Rodney Wambeam (Moe Miller). **Credits:** *Creator:* London Homer-Wambeam, Rory Eggleston. **Comment:** While not a totally original idea (such themes have been tackled on TV and in the movies) it is different in that the leads are so incompetent that it adds a twist to what has been done before.

Episodes: *1.* Pilot. *2.* Caribbean Escape. *3.* Diced Tomatoes Spooktacular. *4.* A Royal Funeral. *5.* Happy Christmanukkahdanzaa.

612 *The McCaingels.* vimeo.com. 2008.

A spoof *Charlie's Angels* wherein three gorgeous young women (Whitney, Heidi and Tze Lan) solve crimes for the mysterious head of a private detective agency from orders they receive by a telephone by the never-seen John McCain. As the Angels try to solve each case with as little fanfare as possible, they are watched over by Boslow (John's associate) and the program charts what happens as three young women battle evil—using their sexuality, beauty—and fighting skills to solve cases for their clients.

Cast: Natasha Leggero (Whitney), Carrie Wiita (Heidi), Kulap Vilaysack (Tze Lan O'Reilly), Ron Lynch (Boslow). **Credits:** *Producer:* Julie Trampush. *Writer-Director:* Michael Addis. **Comment:** The earliest of the Internet *Charlie's Angels* spoofs (see also *Chad's Angels*) with very good acting and production values. Natasha Leggero is especially good as the sexy Whitney.

Episodes: 3 untitled episodes, labeled "Episode 1," "Episode 2" and "Episode 3."

613 *McManusLand.* onemorelesbian.com. 2011.

Bridget McManus, the host of *The Bridget McManus Half-Hour Comedy Hour* on the "low rent" gay TV network ICON, is a comedienne with expectations of reaching great heights in the entertainment world. Thus far, however, her only claim to fame has been her low rated television series (which airs on the second Wednesday of every month at 3:30 a.m.). While the show does give Bridget some hope of achieving fame, her world comes crashing down around her when she receives a cancellation notice and finds her dreams are shattered.

Bridget is a lesbian and married to Karman, a level-headed woman who has supported her through her numerous efforts to become a star. While losing her show is a blow, Bridget has not been defeated. She has her own ideas about how to play "the fame game" and the program follows her slightly delusional efforts to achieve her dream—no matter how many times she encounters rejection.

Cast: Bridget McManus (Bridget), Karman Kragloe (Karman). **Credits:** *Producer:* Bridget McManus, Adriana Torres. *Director:* Adriana Torres. *Writer:* Bridget McManus. **Comment:** Bridget Mc-

Manus is a delight and her scenes pampering her dog (Taffy) are truly comical. The entire program is well acted and produced and, while there are brief moments of tenderness, the program's focus is on Bridget and the setbacks she encounters trying to reignite her career. While season one is available for free, season two is available only through a paid subscription system at the program's website.

Season 1 Episodes: *1.* I Am Oprah. *2.* Fat Action. *3.* Secret Agent. *4.* The End of a New Beginning.

Season 2 Episodes: Continues the story line with Bridget determined to achieve her dream and Karman, inspired by Bridget's enthusiasm, rekindling a dream of her own (from high school): starting her own rock band, Peg Leg.

614 *Me + U.* webseriesnetwork. com. 2012.

A young couple not identified by names (but called "Your Girlfriend" and "Your Boyfriend" in text information) live in New York City. Whether married or not, they share an apartment and face all the problems that befall not only couples, but virtually everyone else, whether single or married. The program is a glimpse into their private lives and how they face and deal with the challenges that confront them each day.

Cast: Carter Roy (Your Boyfriend), Megan Hill (Your Girlfriend), Amy Staats (The Neighbor), Woody Boley (Andrew, the Delivery Guy), Geneva Carr (Friendly Stranger). **Credits:** *Producer-Writer:* Kantarama Gahigiri, Megan Hill, Carter Roy. *Director:* Kantarama Gahigiri. **Comment:** Episodes are well done, acted and amusing. Rather than set all the action in their apartment, they are seen outside of their "battle zone" and doing things other than just talking or arguing.

Season 1 Episodes: *1.* Cereal. *2.* Pen. *3.* Insult. *4.* Booger. *5.* Joint. *6.* Selfish. *7.* Muffed. *8.* Neighbor. *9.* Guest. *10.* Zombie.

Season 2 Episodes: *1.* Exes and Ohs. *2.* Even. *3.* Status. *4.* Sacred. *5.* Delivery. *6.* Party. *7.* The Spat. *8.* Snap. *9.* The Baby.

615 *Me and Zooey D.* youtube.com. 2013.

Zooey Deschanel is the star of the Fox TV series *New Girl.* She is also the sister of Emily Deschanel

Me + U. Series poster art (© Circus Productions [Kantarama Gahigiri]).

(of the TV series *Bones*) and the idol of Alex Bernstein, a young woman who has recently moved to Los Angeles with two friends but yearns only to become best friends with Zooey. While her friends Chris, a hopeful director, and Haley, an actress, pursue their careers, Alex sets out on a path to find Zooey and the program charts her wild enthusiastic endeavors to make a dream come true. Alex doesn't know if she will ever meet Zooey or if Zooey will ever be friends with her. She only wants to tell Zooey how much she means to her.

Cast: Ari Berkowitz (Alex Bernstein), Brittany Belland (Haley), Ben Smith (Chris). **Credits:** *Producer:* Carina Sposato. *Director:* Hunter Wolk. *Writer:* Ari Berkowitz. **Comment:** A rather enjoyable program that is well acted and produced.

Choosing a then lesser-known star makes for an interesting variation on "ordinary" people seeking to meet celebrities. Here nothing can deter Alex from meeting Zooey and that enthusiasm, no matter how much it dims, makes the program.

Episodes: 6 untitled episodes, labeled "Episode 1" through "Episode 6."

616 Medium Rare—Viewer Discretion Is Not Advised. blip.tv. 2010.

Helga was a Hollywood legend who has since faded from the celebrity scene. She is married to Harry, a B-movie director and is overly devoted to her French poodle, Fifi. Trouble enters their lives when an ambitious producer (Mitch) threatens to expose Helga's unsavory past and in turn, ruin Harry's career. Recalling an incident wherein Helga attempted to dry Fifi in her microwave oven after giving her a bath (but killed the dog) Harry devises a most bizarre way to rid his life of Mitch: bake his brain in a microwave oven. It didn't work for the dog and it didn't work for Harry as Mitch emerges from the ordeal as a deranged killer with weird superpowers. The program follows Mitch as he becomes deranged and Harry as he seeks a way to stop him from going on a killing spree.

Cast: Burt Young (Harry Costas), Brad Dourif (Mitch Malone), Lainie Kazan (Helga), Brenda Bakke (Rosie), Al Ruscio (Det. Hill), Timothy Leary (Dr. Kyle), Alex Winter (Timmy), Sy Richardson (Marv), Frances Bay (Gertrude), Larry Storch (Willie). **Credits:** *Producer-Writer-Director:* Paul Madden. **Comment:** The story plays as crazy as it sounds. It is a comedy-horror mix and features singer Laine Kazan and TV actors Burt Young and Larry Storch. It has its truly unbelievable moments (like the baking of Mitch's head) and, despite all the silliness, plays like an episode of a typical silly TV sitcom.

Episodes: 9 untitled episodes, labeled "Episode 1" through "Episode 9."

617 Meeting Hard Blowz. youtube.com. 2013.

Cash and Mouth are wannabe rap artists who have formed a group called Hard Blowz. They have encompassed a theme called "Gangster Rap" and want to introduce it in their native homeland of the U.K. But is England ready for them? To spread their message, they engage a documentary film crew (headed by Clive Gregson) and the program follows the path Hard Blowz takes to establish themselves in a land where their type of music appears not to be acceptable (although they do have Jonathan, a possessed fan).

Cast: Danny D'Anzieri (Cash), David R. Roberts (Mouth), Alastair Greener (Lewis), Christian R. Allan (Jonathan), Justin Noel Agabi-Keyamo (Clive),

Wesley Gilbert (Mark). **Credits:** *Producer:* Danny D'Anzieri. *Director:* Alex Lloyd. **Comment:** Naturally, an abundant use of foul language is incorporated as it deals with rap music (it is just uncomfortable to listen too here). It is also slow moving and the idea, which is good, too dragged out.

Episodes: *1.* The First. *2.* 2 Guys, 1 Gang. *3.* David the Hamster. *4.* Jonathan. *5.* Internet Rapping. *6.* The Last.

618 Megan and Meghan. webserieschannel.com. 2012.

Megan and her friend Meghan are young women living and working in Chicago. Megan (long blonde hair) and Meghan (shorter blonde hair) love vodka, Diet Coke and seek what appears to be only fun. But are they gay? Megan feels she may be a lesbian (or bisexual) as she kissed a girl and really liked it. Meghan, on the other hand, believes she is straight although she has a knack for falling for men who are gay. The events that befall Megan and Meghan as they navigate life in a big city are chronicled.

Cast: Kiley B. Moore (Megan), Leah Raidt (Meghan). **Credits:** *Producer-Writer:* Joseph W. Reese. *Director:* Joseph W. Reese, Colin Sphar. **Comment:** It doesn't matter if you can't tell which Megan is Megan and which Meghan is Meghan as the program is delightful either way. The episodes are very short (under three minutes) and being as such makes you wish they were somewhat longer as Kiley B. Moore and Leah Raidt are a delight to watch.

Episodes: *1.* Katy Perry. *2.* Serenity. *3.* RuPaul. *4.* Bastian. *5.* Lost Phone. *6.* D.I.Y. *7.* Kesha. *8.* Bears.

619 Melbourne Girls. melbournegirlstv.wordpress.com. 2014.

Comical stories about various young women who live in Melbourne, Australia, but who are not friends or related to one another.

Cast: Danielle Carlo, Lucy Hawkins, Madeleine Ryan, Isabelle Bertoli, Emily Deague-Hall, Andy Wheeler, Nores Cerfeda. **Credits:** *Producer-Writer-Director:* Kim Miles. **Comment:** While vulgar language is used and can be overlooked in favor of the female leads, it is also well acted and produced.

Episodes: 4 untitled episodes, labeled "Episode 1," through "Episode 4."

620 Mermates. youtube.com. 2012.

Chris and Michelle are a young couple who seem to live for only one thing—watching the TV series *Breaking Bad* together. One night, when Michelle fails to show up for their TV date, Chris does the unthinkable and watches an episode alone. The situation so upsets Michelle when she finds out that she breaks off her relationship with Chris and throws him out of her apartment. Now, with no place to live, Chris sees an ad for an apartment ("Please move in with me. Must be tolerant of Mermaids") and decides to check it out. There he meets William and learns that he is a Mermaid (should actually be a Merman as Mermaid refers to a female) but one of a rare breed—an "Inside Outie" (the outward appearance of a human but the innards of a fish. William claims its scientific name is "Everted"). While the situation might send some people running, Chris figures that for only $500 a month and having a Mermaid as a roommate is a good deal and accepts. The program charts a real "Odd Couple" situation with Chris attempting to live a normal life with William (especially when he hogs the bathroom and needs to constantly sit in the bathtub to remain wet) trying to live as normal life as he can being what he is.

Cast: Alex Aschinger (William), Chris Yule (Chris), Tina Huang (Michelle), Katie Conway (Sasha). **Credits:** *Producer-Director:* Michael Jonathan Smith, Chris Yule, Alex Aschinger. *Writer:* Michael Jonathan Smith. **Comment:** Tales of Mermaids date back to feature films (such as *Miranda*, *Mr. Peabody and the Mermaid* and *Splash*), on television in series such as *H2O: Just Add Water* and in over 50 Internet series (such as *A Splashy Tale*). All portray such creatures as beautiful females. *Mermates* is deceiving in that it would lead one to believe a beautiful "fish out of water" story is about to be told. While the "Mermaid" here is a man, it is a good idea and presented well.

Episodes: *1.* The Apartment. *2.* The Blind Date. *3.* The Girlfriend.

621 *The Message Board.* youtube.com. 2009.

Broadway Universe is an Internet sounding board where people who log on can discuss matters with other users on anything that interests them or on any topic that is posted. The program follows a group of such people, each with unique personas, who log on and then express their often differing opinions on topics with one another.

Cast: Mark Eugene Garcia (Cubby), Jason Barker (Phantom69), Caroline Clay (Aquarius Dawn), Margaret Curry (Cat Golightly), T.J. D'Angelo (Applause 64), Julia Frey (Legally Elphie), Tim Howard (Daddy Danger), Molly Moore Lehmann (Aunt Daffy), Jared Pike (Coo Velvet), Paul P. Robilotto (SS Singer), Scott Wisniewski (WWRD). **Credits:** *Producer-Writer-Director:* John Raymond Baker. **Comment:** Rather boring program unless you like listening to people chatting about this or that. The acting and production are just fair.

Episodes: *1.* Getting to Know You. *2.* What Makes a Legend Least? *3.* Love's a Bitch. *4.* Mass Debating. *5.* I Love You, You're Perfect, Now Get Off the Computer. *6.* When It Cliques. *7.* Meltdown. *8.* Return to Sender. *9.* Behind the Scenes Special.

622 *Metalhedz.* metalhedz.com.uk. 2014.

Ginge (male) and Tails and Beki (females) are not only best friends but roommates living in Scotland. Ginge has no morals, prefers one night stands with girls and doesn't appear to be looking for a mate until he meets Chloe, a girl who is his complete opposite, but a girl who appears reluctant to date him due to his unsavory reputation. Tails, described as a "geeky, gay gamer girl," has feelings for Beki, but is hesitant to express them, fearing that a girl who is her complete opposite will never fall for her. Rounding out the friendship is Skull, a sleazy guy who sees each night as one big party. Adapting a more adult-themed version of the British TV series *Man About the House* (seen in the U.S. as *Three's Company*) the program charts the events that spark their lives, especially the developing relationships between Ginge, Chloe, Tails and Beki and how each must deal responsibly with the situations they now encounter.

Cast: Felicity Allen (Tails), Jess Butler, Emma Burgess (Beki), Simon Fox (Ginge), Jamie Melrose (Chloe), Graeme Strachan (Skull). **Credits:** *Producer:* Simon Fox, Graeme Strachan. *Writer-Director:* Simon Fox. **Comment:** A British produced program that does, at least, warn the viewer that "The following program contains crude humor and bad language." It is a bit hard to understand at times due to accents but is well acted and produced.

Season 1 Episodes: *1.* Intervention. *2.* Party

Metalhedz. **Series poster art featuring Felicity Allen (copyright Simon Fox 2015).**

Hard. *3.* Girls, Girls, Girls. *4.* Dude Looks Like a Lady. *5.* Redefine. *6.* Make a Move.

Season 2 Episodes: *1.* Creeping Death. *2.* Calling All Skeletons. *3.* The Crow and the Butterfly. *4.* Haunting Me. *5.* All the Small Things. *6.* The End Is the Beginning Is the End. *7.* Tears Into Wine. *8.* Separate Ways.

623 *Middleton.* youtube.com. 2013.

Middleton is a picturesque English village located on the moors of North Yorkshire. It had everything going for it until the year 2011 when the horrific Flood Fiona resulted from a storm and devastated it. Adapting the "mockumentray" style of filming, the program follows the village residents as they attempt to rebound and upgrade their status from village to town, causing a non-violent-like civil war from those who approve and those that want to keep Middleton a village.

Cast: Jim McMaster (Terry Coombs), Danny Ward (Danny Coombs), Richard Little (Dave McReed), Helen Coverdale (Bella Armstrong), Ree Collins (Denise Fowler), Glen Fawcett (Clive Sturgeon), Richard Clare (Ned Riley), Jack Bandeira (Keith Tate), Gemma Whiteley (Judge Reynolds), Lynne Lawson (Judge Andrews), Spencer Vale (Judge Pascale), Dee Sadler (Janice). **Credits:** *Producer:* Lydia-Grace Pitts. *Director:* Martin Davies. *Writer:* Martin Davies, Glen Fawcett, Adrian Phipps. **Comment:** Each episode is like a visit to a small English village with post card-like scenery and colorful people. The idea, somewhat like the movie *The Mouse That Roared* is a worthy endeavor that is well acted and produced.

Episodes: 15 untitled episodes, labeled "Episode 1" through "Episode 15."

624 *A Mid-Semester Night's Dream.* you tube.com. 2014.

The William Shakespeare comedy *A Midsummer Night's Dream* transplanted to modern times and a college campus to focus on a group of students, styled to represent the play's characters, experiencing an academic career totally set apart from reality although presented with the comedy (from romance to back-stabbing) of normally set college-themed series.

Cast: William Harrington (Theseus), Cate Jo (Hippolyta), Sam Dressler (Egeus), Lauren Mandel (Hermia), Christopher Kessenich (Lysander), Ryan Medlock (Demetrius), Julia Seales (Helena), Sydney Waitz-Kudla (Quince), Mara Bloomfield (Snug), Nick Brovender (Bottom), Nick Mecikalski (Flute), Tommy Pruchinski (Snout), Tara Ptacek (Starveling), Rachel Brittain (Titania), Cameron Williams (Oberon), Sadie Andros (Puck), Kelsey Janser (Peaseblossom), Sylvana Lewin (Mustardseed). **Credits:** *Producer:* Julia Seales, Rachel Brittain, Lau-

ren Mandel. *Director:* Lauren Mandel, Julia Seales. *Writer:* Julian Seales. **Comment:** The performers do a decent job (even professional actors sometimes have difficulty performing the Bard's material) but the idea, while intriguing at first, rapidly becomes tiresome listening to the dialogue when all you want them to do is speak normal English.

Episodes: 5 episodes, listed as "Act 1" through "Act 5."

625 *Mild Mannered.* webserieschannel. com. 2012.

Joey and Eric are friends who work at a comic book store in Beacon City. Joey is infatuated with a girl named Michelle, while his roommate, Eric is smitten with a girl named Lucy. Beacon City, however, is different as it is like a comic book and littered with super heroes and villains who are making life a bit uncomfortable for its citizens. Eric and Joey have super hero abilities but rarely use them as impressing girls comes first; battling evil (even when the city's number one super hero, Captain Justice, is out of town) is somewhere down the line. The program charts the chaos that exists in the city (seen through television news reports) while Eric and Joey to do everything in their power to avoid dealing with it.

Cast: Peyton Clark (Eric), Travis Lincoln Cox (Joey), Whitney Morgan Cox (Lucy), Mary Emfinger (Michelle), Linden King (Captain Justice), Mark Mushakian (Richard), Herman Randle (Alfred). **Credits:** *Producer-Writer-Director:* Nick Reiber. **Comment:** It is a bit difficult to figure out exactly what powers Eric and Joey have and if they have ever used them to help Captain Justice. The production is a bit talkative but does incorporate action scenes of the chaos that befalls the city.

Episodes: *1.* Secret Origins. *2.* Party Monster. *3.* Villains.

626 *Millennial Parents.* millennialparents. com. 2014.

Annie and Kurt are married and the parents of an infant named Tanner. Annie is the strict worry all-the-time mother while Kurt is a bit more relaxed and feels Annie overreacts to everything that has to do with their marriage but especially their son. The program is a look at their lives and what happens mostly when it comes to Tanner's upbringing.

Cast: Laura Eichhorn (Annie), Lea Coco (Kurt), Alyshia Ochse (Morgan), Michael Cassidy (Leo), Amrita Dhaliwal (Jasmine), Ana Free (Samantha), Sarah Hollis (Jennifer), David Greene (Mark), Andy Goldenberg (Max). **Credits:** *Producer:* Jake Greene, Natalie Irby, David Greene. *Director:* Jake Greene, Natalie Irby. *Writer:* Jake Greene. **Comment:** Humorous program with very good acting, especially Laura Eichhorn as Annie, whose anxieties can be felt by anyone—whether a parent or not.

Season 1 Episodes: *1.* Inappropriate Lullabies. *2.* Be Honest. *3.* Rollercoaster World. *4.* Civilized Meals. *5.* Special Lingerie. *6.* The Embargo. *7.* Part Parents (Pet Peeves). *8.* The Last And... *9.* Naked Pictures. *10.* Are We Cooler Than Our Parents? *11.* Vegas Parenting. *12.* Sex & Pizza. *13.* Vacay Dismay. *14.* Pick One. *15.* Pros and Cults. *16.* 40 Is the New 26. *17.* Will Power.

Season 2 Episodes: *1.* Stripper Babysitter. *2.* Tamed in the Man Cave. *3.* Not Ready for Romance. *4.* Stolen Premiere. *5.* We're Pregnant.

627 *A Minority Report.* aminorityreport. com. 2012.

Actors, whether talented or those who think they are, appear at auditions. It doesn't matter what sex or what nationality you are, auditioning for roles is part of the procedure. For some it is a breeze, but for others, especially minorities, it is a bit more difficult because of what they are. The program, which takes liberties, explores the pitfalls minority actors face working in the entertainment industry as seen through three women, who are also friends: Chriselle, Zoey and Sai.

Cast: Zoey Martinson (Zoey), Chriselle Almeida (Chriselle), Sai Rao (Sai), Johnson Chong, Jacob Burstein-Stern, Margaret Blakeman, Gina Manziello, Isaiah Johnson, Brandon Gardner, Jon David Martin, Adam McNulty, Chris Ruth, Karen Murray, Court Wing, Paul Gosselin, Seril James, Steve Ruddy. **Credits:** *Director:* Zoey Martinson. *Writer:* Zoey Martinson, Brandon Gardner. *Producer:* Smoke & Mirrors Collaborative. **Comment:** The program, presented like a reality series, is well done and acted. It shows that while there are sometimes numerous open auditions for roles, minorities have the most difficult time acquiring them. It is not a lambasting of the industry (it is just the way things are) but an attempt to make (possibly casting agents) see that people are treated differently because of who they are.

Episodes: *1.* Urban Musical. *2.* Paging Dr. Patel. *3.* The Last Egg Role.

628 *The Misadventures of Awkward Black Girl.* awkwardblackgirl.com. 2011.

A first-person narrative look at the life of a very pretty African-American woman (J) as she navigates life in New York City, most often encountering its uncomfortable side (like meeting people in unfamiliar places, dealing with an obnoxious co-worker [Nina] and the two men [White Jay and Fred] who have become infatuated with her).

J, as she is called, is employed at the call center at Gutbusters, a company that produces a weight-loss pill. CeCe is J's best friend, a somewhat kooky girl who works in the company's Human Resources division. Nina is J's nemesis at the company, a girl, just

promoted to a higher position, whose goal is to make J's life miserable.

Boss Lady is the head of Gutbusters; Fred is one of J's lovers and a fellow employee; A, as he is called, is J's nerdy co-worker (she calls him her "awkward mistake" as she slept with him at the company's annual holiday party); Patty, nicknamed "Germy Patty" (due to the fact that she is continually sick), is a former employee who was fired but continues to attend the company's social events.

Amir and Darius are employees of Gutbusters. Darius is distinguished as being a "low talker" and his whispers can apparently only be understood by Fred. Dolores, a Human Resources employee, had a recent enlightening and has become a born-again Christian named Sister Mary; Jesus, a former sensitivity trainer, becomes the new company manager when Boss Lady resigns; White Jay is the anger management counselor and the man who eventually becomes J's choice for a hopefully lasting relationship; Jerry is the company's temporary employee; D is J's former boyfriend.

Cast: Issa Rae (J), Sujata Day (CeCe), Tracy Oliver (Nina), Hanna (as credited; Boss Lady), Madison T. Shockley III (Fred), Andrew Allan James (A), Kiki Harris (Patty), Fahad (as credited, Amir), Tristen Winger (Darius), Leah A. Williams (Dolores), Michael Ruesga (Jesus), Lyman Johnson (White Jay), Ricky Woznicak (Jerry), Mike Danger (D). **Credits:** *Producer:* Issa Rae, Deniese Davis, Tracy Oliver. *Director:* Shea William Vanderpoort, Dennis Dortch, Issa Rae. *Writer:* Issa Rae, O.C. Smith, Amy Aniobi, Tracy Oliver. **Comment:** J's life is seen in several ways, from straight forward narration to dream sequences to voice-over narration as scenes unfold. It is quite witty and its portrayal of an African-American woman is quite realistic (as her character can be seen like a simple, down-to-earth girl you may actually know, not a TV stereotyped girl who is hard to fathom as actually existing). The program is also known as *Awkward Black Girl* and searching either title will bring up the series.

Season 1 Episodes: *1.* The Stop Sign. *2.* The Job. *3.* The Hallway. *4.* The Ice Breaker. *5.* The Dance. *6.* The Stapler. *7.* The Date. *8.* The Project. *9.* The Happy Hour. *10,11.* The Unexpected. *12.* The Exes. *13.* The Decision.

Season 2 Episodes: *1.* The Sleepover. *2.* The Visit. *3.* The Jingle. *4.* The Search. *5.* The Interview. *6.* The Waiter. *7.* The Group. *8.* The Friends. *9.* The Check. *10.* The Call. *11.* The Apology.

629 *Misdirected.* misdirected.com. 2013–2015.

Through a series of flashing scenes when the program begins, a young woman is seen in an automobile accident (its exact cause intentionally left vague) then on a hospital gurney and being examined by doctors. When next seen, the woman is seated in the

Misdirected. Series poster art (copyright Lauren Mora 2013).

hospital's waiting room and holding a potted plant. A young man (Josh) enters the room but the woman fails to recognize him as her best friend. When Josh realizes that what he has been told by doctors, that the woman (Fredericka) has lost her memory, is true, he introduces himself to her and gains her confidence by telling her how they met (in college), her name (that she hates her formal name and uses Freddie) and her address (East 45 Washington, #12). Although a bit reluctant, but realizing she has no other choice, Freddie allows Josh to take her home. The surroundings, however, are not familiar to her, nor are her two other friends, Cameron and Gerald, when she is introduced to them. Freddie has no recollection of her past or even who she is. She is now facing a life that is totally unfamiliar to her and relies on her friends to help her become the woman she once was. Though, for reasons of their own, they are not being entirely truthful, and by the end of Season 1, Freddie starts to suspect that she has been *Misdirected.*

Cast: Lauren Mora (Freddie), John T. Woods (Josh), Joel Kelley Dauten (Cameron), Ross Philips (Gerald), Erika Ishii (Melanie). **Credits:** *Producer:* Lauren Mora. *Writer-Director:* Marion Kerr. **Comment:** Lauren Mora is charming as Freddie and the idea, acting and production values are very good.

Season 1 Episodes: *1.* Pilot. *2.* Random Dude. *3.* Birthday. *4.* Seal the Deal. *5.* Freddium. *6.* Labyrinth. *7.* Nuh-uh. *8.* The Time When…

Season 2 Episodes: *1.* Operation. *2.* One Minute. *3.* Time's Up. *4.* Listen. *5.* Lost. *6.* Cool. *7.* Woo. *8.* The Office. *9.* A Is For… *10.* Problem.

630 Misery Loves Company. vimeo.com. 2010.

Barb and Helen are best friends in life and in business. They also have one serious fault in common: neither has been lucky in the romantic arena. Frustrated but not defeated, Barb and Helen come up with a way to turn their sorrow into profit: begin an on-line dating service called Misery Loves Company to help others in the same position overcome their problems by using a computer to make perfect matches. The program shows not only the profiles clients make but how Barb and Helen operate their company and what happens with the matches that are made.

Cast: Tiffany Price (Helen McLellan), Alecia Claxton (Barb Bicchione), Brian Maples (Logan), Tom McDonald (Rich the Greek). **Credits:** *Producer:* Tiffany Price, Christina Marie Price, Amy Marie Price, Alecia Claxton. *Director:* Caleb Claxton. *Writer:* Alecia Claxton, Caleb Claxton, Tiffany Price. **Comment:** Tiffany Price and Alecia Claxton are delightful and however Barb and Helen became friends is a mystery. Overall, the acting and production is very good.

Episodes: *1.* Genesis. *2.* Promercial. *3.* Cybilism. *4.* JillSmash! *5.* Bizzy. *6.* Interdate. *7.* BUM-mer. *8.* Docu-peater. *9.* Trumped! *10.* Finally. *11.* Halloween.

631 Miss Holland. missholland.com. 2012–2013.

Miss Holland, as she is called, is Dutch and loves

her fatherland (Sweden) but has disillusions that her beauty alone can earn her the title of "Miss America"; she doesn't realize that a girl has to be a U.S. citizen to earn the coveted title. But Miss Holland loves the U.S. and wants something more in her life—that crown and nothing will stop her from getting it (or so she thinks). The program relates what happens when Miss Holland comes to America, learns the harsh reality then begins a quest to become a U.S. citizen by learning all she can about the American way of life.

Cast: Eline Van der Velden (Miss Holland), Cameran Surles (Brooke Hollister). **Credits:** *Producer:* Eline Van der Velden, Cameran Surles, Daniel Healy. *Director:* Eline Van der Velden. *Writer:* Eline Van der Velden, Carmen Surles. **Comment:** Very enjoyable program that is quite original and is not only well acted but well produced.

Season 1 Episodes: *1.* CraigsList. *2.* Immigration Lawyer. *3.* Miss Minsk. *4.* Venice. *5.* Straight Outta Compton. *6.* Election Day. *7.* Backseat. *8.* An Interview with a D.J.

Season 2 Episodes: *1.* London. *2.* Dutch Swearing. *3.* Brick Lane. *4.* The Brazilian Make Up.

632 Missing Connections Live. missedconnections.com. 2010.

A missed connection, when referring to romance occurs when two people meet then exchange contact information but that information is somehow misplaced or lost. To hopefully reconnect with one another, such people will use newspapers or the Internet to post ads. Real such postings are re-imagined and presented as satirical short stories on how people hope to make a reconnection. Melissa Center appears in various roles as sort of a host who relates stories of "Missed Connections."

Cast: Melissa Center (Various characters). **Credits:** *Producer:* Melissa Center. *Director:* Melissa Center, Rachel Connors, Brent Rose, Dutch Doscher, Benjamin Salley. *Writer:* Melissa Center, Brent Rose. **Comment:** Melissa Center is charming in each of the women she plays. The series itself is interesting and well produced.

Episodes: *1.* Where Are You Economist Man? *2.* Hipster Chick. *3.* Lonely Girl Channels Alicia Keys. *4.* Cougar at the Safeway. *5.* Tits Meets Acapulco. *6.* The Missed Connection. *7.* Moustaches Are Neat. *8.* Fat F**k. *9.* Les Cutie. *10.* Ode to Audrey. *11.* When Morty Met Esther.

633 Missing Something. missingsomething.tv. 2013.

Rachel is a young woman who works as a designer for a London-based game company called Chaos Games. She is in her twenties and is facing a quarter-life crisis that has her becoming a bit neurotic as she tries to adjust to a turning point in her life. She is trying to deal with what is happening and is receiving help from her friends Aaron and Freddie, but more problems than she already has from her roommate Annie, a hypochondriac of the worst kind (constantly acquiring some illness). The program relates events in Rachel's life as she attempts to adjust to what is happening to her (and "not go bonkers" as the program states).

Cast: Leila Sykes (Rachel), Yaz Al-Shaater (Aaron), Scott Wilson-Besgrove (Pete), Francesca Binefa (Annie), Ashlea Kaye (Claire), Lee Drage (Freddie), Amr El-Bayoumi (Earl), David Blackwell (Andy). **Credits:** *Director:* Yaz Al-Shaater, Haz Al-Shaater. *Writer:* Leila Sykes, Tom Crawshaw. **Comment:** Quarter-life crisis programs have been done before and each has its own take (usually dealing with more than one person). Here the use of a single person works well as it is easy to follow and, coupled with good action and production, enjoyable to watch.

Episodes: *1.* A New Something. *2.* A Something Named Desire. *3.* In the Name of Something. *4.* Bohemian Something. *5.* Something for Art's Sake. *6.* Something Outside the Box. *7.* Something's in the Water. *8.* Taking Two to Something. *9,10,11.* Season Finale.

634 Mission: Rebound. onemorelesbian.com. 2010.

Cloie, a lesbian, and Vera, straight, are friends but not romantically involved with each other. Vera accepts Hayley as Cloie's lover and Cloie accepts Malcolm as Vera's boyfriend. Hayley and Malcolm also know each other and life changes when Cloie catches Malcolm having sex with Hayley. The couples separate and, while they have been burned by their respective lovers, Cloie and Vera plot to get even. The program follows two scorned women and the path they take when they attempt to rebound.

Cast: Vera Miao (Vera), Cloie Wyatt Taylor (Cloie), Malcolm Barrett (Malcolm), Thea Brooks (Hayley), Adalgiza Chermont (Ada), Jesse Torrilhon (Jesse), Karey Dornetto (Heather). **Credits:** *Producer:* Vera Miao, Cloie Wyatt Taylor, Micki Poklar. *Director:* Gigi Nicolas. *Writer:* Vera Miao. **Comment:** The program, while well acted, is a bit hard to see at times due to poor lighting. There are adult situations and vulgar language is used but overall it is an amusing series and different when it comes to lesbian and straight mix series.

Episodes: *1.* Ho-Mates. *2.* Cuddle Ditch. *3.* Astro Stalker. *4.* Tour de Pants.

635 MisSpelled. thewitchesofmisspelled.tumblr.com. 2014.

In the modern-day world there are covens of witches that still exist but who have cleverly concealed themselves from the outside world. Stella,

Emma, Quinn, Nina and Gladys comprise one such coven, but unlike other covens, these witches are a bit clueless when it comes to what they should do and how to handle their powers. The program relates only one incident that threatens to expose them: their efforts to help Gladys cover up her accidental killing of her boyfriend when her emotions got out of control during an argument.

Stella is a bit quirky and wants to be friends with everyone but no one appears to want to be her friend. She is very kind and understanding and always looks out for her sisters' best interests.

Emma is a female version of Adrian Monk from the series *Monk* as she is germ phobic and takes her repulsion at germs to the extreme. She embraces her powers but really doesn't like to associate with people.

Quinn is a mystic and always wanted to be a part of something bigger than herself. When her powers developed she was granted her wish and has now found her place in the universe. She has also made herself the coven leader.

Nina is a very competitive person and feels her powers are a burden as they prevent her from what she really wants to do. Although she has no choice, she reluctantly joins with her sisters.

Gladys's powers are a bit different as they are tied to her emotions and can cause great harm if she does not learn to control them. She is, in fact, the glue that holds the coven together.

Cast: Gabriela Banus (Nina), Chelsea Jones (Quinn), Lindsey McDowell (Gladys), VyVy Nguyen (Emma), Carina Perez (Stella), Nick Bender (Ian). **Credits:** *Producer:* Lindsey McDowell, Joseph Ruggieri. *Director:* Joseph Ruggieri. *Writer:* Lindsey McDowell. **Comment:** Well done witch series spoof with good acting and production. While series like *Charmed* and *Sabrina, the Teenage Witch* may come to mind, *MisSpelled* can stand on its own as being different.

Episodes: *0.* Promologue. *1.* #Witch Bitch. *2.* #Creepin'. *3.* #Murkin' *4.* #What the Heka.

636 Mister French Taste. webserieschannel.com. 2012.

Leon Wong is the unruly and only son of a prosperous but conservative Hong Kong family. He has become a constant source of aggravation and embarrassment to the family and to hopefully resolve their problem they hire Mister French, a French etiquette coach to transform a brat into a respectable, perfectly groomed young gentleman. Mister French has his job cut out for him but complications ensue when Lily Lee, the beautiful young heiress to a Hong Kong fashion empire crosses their path and both fall instantly in love with her. The program follows Mister French as he attempts to refine the crude Leon and romance Lily despite the fact that he has competition from Leon, who is also seeking to court her.

Cast: Olivier Malet (Mister French), Osric Chau (Leon Wong), Sarah Lian (Lily Lee). **Credits:** *Producer:* Veronique Grima, David Guillon. *Director:* Jennifer Thym. **Comment:** An enjoyable transposition of the Pygmalion tale (most familiar as the motion picture *My Fair Lady*) with good acting and production values. Mister French may bring to mind the character of Mr. French from the TV series *Family Affair* due to their nearly identical mannerisms. Text information that appears on line makes Leon sound like a young mischievous child, not a teenager and that age difference does make a difference as what could have been a real brat turns out to be a young man with identity issues.

Episodes: *1.* The Job Interview. *2.* Meeting Leon. *3.* Fashion Sense. *4.* The Language of Love. *5.* Taichi, Dreams of Love and French Kiss. *6.* The Secret of Etiquette. *7.* The Unfortunate Fortune Teller. *8.* The French Art of Seduction. *9.* Cuisine de Terror. *10.* Chateau Decadence.

637 Mr. Wang Goes to Hollywood. mrwanghollywood.com. 2013.

Mr. Wang (as he is only called) is a wealthy gentleman living in China and supporting his nephew, Jonathan, a college medical student living rent-free in a West Hollywood condo purchased by Mr. Wang for his estranged daughter, Emily. While it would seem, with virtually no bills to pay, Jonathan would have an easy life. But it is not so. He is deeply in debt and must now contend with his uncle when Mr. Wang retires and decides to move in with him and Emily. Mr. Wang is not only "super rich" but privileged and seeks to be treated that way even in America. Mr. Wang is not all that happy with the way Jonathan is living his life, but he is even more dismayed by Emily, when he learns she is dating someone well beneath her social scale—Jerome, a black comedian who can barely support himself. While Mr. Wang must deal with Emily, he must also contend with Jonathan, a schemer who is seeking to end his financial woes by out thinking and out maneuvering his uncle—a situation that he finds most difficult as Mr. Wang is as wise as he looks and "squeezing blood out of a stone," as the old saying goes, is literally a challenge for Jonathan. Karen Chen, Jonathan's fiancé, immediately takes a disliking to Mr. Chang, and has set her mission to make Jonathan stand up to his uncle and be a man (something Jonathan, at age 25, simply cannot due). Liping is Mr. Wang's ex-wife, a long-suffering woman (being married to Mr. Wang) who moved to Los Angeles several years ago to escape her nightmarish world with him. Ryan and Marcus are Jonathan's interracial gay neighbors, who constantly face Mr. Wang's blatant homophobia and racism. Maria is the house maid (and perhaps the only sane one in the Wang home).

Cast: Jesse Wang (Mr. Wang), Jimmy Tang (Jonathan Wang), Jani Wang (Emily Wang), Peggy Lu (Liping), Drea Castro (Karen Chen), Darrel Davenport (Jerome Martin), Sheila Korsi (Maria), Rajiv Shah (Marcus), P.J. Ochlan (Ryan). **Credits:** *Producer:* Christina Zhao, Robert Berg, Jesse Wang. *Writer:* Robert Berg, Jesse Wang. *Director:* Michael Regalbuto. **Comment:** The story, while not totally original (shades of the ABC TV series *Mr. T and Tina* can be seen) it is well acted and produced.

Episodes: *1.* Pilot. *2.* Life Saver. *3.* Science in the Hood. *4.* Yaowen.

638 Mister Wiskers. mrwiskers.com. 2013.

Richard Wiskers is a brilliant police detective with the N.Y.P.D. He was born in Luton, England and is the son of Charles (a carpenter) and Annabelle ("a filthy prostitute"). Richard was raised by Charles and inherited a strange condition from him: unusual hair growth. While large swaths of hair grew from Charles's ears, Richard's condition became an embarrassment when large amounts of hair began growing from his nostrils. Cutting it was fruitless as it would grow back overnight. As time passed, Richard kept to himself and emerged himself first in comic books then drugs and prostitutes. Although Richard's condition forced him to become a loner, he soon discovered that his large whiskers gave him the ability to sense things that no one else could. Soon his ability became known to the police, who incorporated it to help them solve crimes. As his reputation grew, the Queen of England commissioned him as her personal detective. But it was not the life Richard sought, as the Queen regulated him to minor tasks around the castle (like finding her missing reading glasses). As Richard grew bored (the excitement he sought was just not there) he returned to his old ways and soon became an embarrassment to the Royal Family. Outraged, Her Majesty banished Richard to Brooklyn, New York, which she considered the most evil place that existed. Richard soon experienced the harsh realities of a big city when he was stabbed and shot days after arriving in the Bedford Stuyvesant section. Feeling the need to find better accommodations, Richard moved to nearby Greenpoint where he met Rodney Hammock, a rouge detective seeking a roommate. The two not only became friends, but a team. While Richard is a stickler for rules, Rodney is just the opposite. He was suspended (lost his badge) eight times when he was with the Miami P.D. for what he claims was getting too close to uncovering police corruption. Rodney knows only one thing and that is being a cop; Richard has unique abilities and with crime everywhere around him, he knows what he must do: solve them. As Richard takes on the appearance and mannerisms of Sherlock Holmes the program chronicles his and Rodney's efforts to solve crimes of the most deadly nature: murder.

Cast: Mike Diaz (Richard Wiskers), Blake Babbit (Rodney Hammock), Jonathan Kim (Hotaru), Zoe Sloane (Sodapop), John Conor Brooke (Blanc Black), Harvey Dareff (Sam Sockcucker). **Credits:** *Producer:* Brett Ziebarth. *Director:* Brett Ziebarth, Jason LeMaster, Joe Bandelli, Mike Walls. *Writer:* Brett Ziebarth. **Comment:** Strange to say the least but well acted and produced.

Episodes: *1.* The Old Racist %$#@. *2.* The Curious Case of the Golden Goldfish. *3.* Attack of the Crohn's. *4.* The Glorious Mystery Hole. *5.* Romancing the Foreskin Stone. *6.* As I Lay Crying.

639 Mr. Wong. youtube.com. 2000.

Mr. Wong, a Chinese-American, enjoyed his life as a butler to singer Bing Crosby for 37 years. But Bing's passing has saddened Mr. Wong in a number of ways as he dearly misses the man with whom he has spent most of his life. Now, at 85 years of age, he has become the butler to a spoiled socialite named Miss Pam, who inherited Bing's home. The animated program follows Mr. Wong, depicted as a racist Asian-American, as he begrudgingly performs chores for Miss Pam while struggling to get over the loss of Bing Crosby (whom he cries over while listening to his recordings).

Voice Cast: Kyle McCulloch (Mr. Wong), Pam Brady (Miss Pam). **Credits:** *Producer:* Dave Andrews. *Writer:* Pam Brady, Kyle McCulloch. *Theme Vocal:* Davy Jones. **Comment:** Like the movie series *Charlie Chan* which was criticized for its portrayal of a Chinese detective (using a non Asian actor) and the TV series *Amos 'n' Andy* (blasted for its stereotyped portrayal of African-Americans), *Mr. Wong* has been criticized for its blatant racism by Asian-American groups as well as the mainstream media. It did, however, obtain a cult following and still survives on YouTube where, if the racist aspect is overlooked it can be enjoyed as just an old Chinese gentleman working for a young socialite with too many demands for him to handle.

Episodes: *1,2.* Urine Trouble. *3,4.* Yellow Fever. *5,6.* Meet the Creep. *7,8.* Treasure Cat. *9,10.* Gary Peterson's Wonder Wand. *11–13.* Stand Up for Mr. Wong!

640 Mob on the Run. mobontherun.com. 2013.

Mick the Quick, the alias of Michael "Mickey" Costavento, is a small-time mobster arrested for book making and sentenced to five years in the Lewisburg Federal Penitentiary in Philadelphia. Mickey has several unethical business operations and, before beginning his prison term, stashed a considerable amount of money, which he planned to use to restart operations once he is released. Unknown to Mickey, his two less-than-intelligent associates, Dominic "Dom the Bomb" Delegino and Tony (Anthony "Two Ton Tony") Martin, have squandered that money and now, as Mickey is nearing his release, are fearful for their lives. To hopefully recoup the money they spent they establish On the Run, a travel agency front for a book-making operation. Mickey, released from prison, returns to his base of operations but instead of being angered accepts what Dominic and Tony (with the assist of Mickey's girlfriend Vivienne) have done and plans to actually make On the Run legitimate to further conceal its true nature. The program follows Mickey as he attempts to run a book-making business, keep the Feds from discovering the true nature of his operations and please "The Family," the New York City–based head of the organization who often worry that Mickey's activities could expose them.

Cast: Michael Belveduto (Mickey Costavento), Barry Tangert (Dominic Delegino), Rob Misko (Tony Martin), Carrie Leigh Snodgrass (Vivienne Longetti), Joseph D'Onofrio (Sonny Falco), David Giordano (Lorenzo Locatelli), Analise Traficante (Angelica "Angel" Mistro), Albert Gomez (Nico "Steady Nick" Luchessi), Mark "Madcat" Capone (James "Crowbar" D'Angelo), Paul Dudrich (Patrick "Paddy" McGonegal), Mike Adler (Frankie Santori), Anthony Romano, Jr. (Vito "Big Man" Toscano), Michael Shands (Agent Gerry Jackson), Matt Duffin (Agent Michael Sandusky), Antonia Menta (Geanna Russo), Rick Romano (Vincent "Iceman" Moretti), Joe Gawalis (Nino "Babyface" Scalini), Carlo Bellario (Carmine "The Jaw" De Rossi), Eddy Privitzer (Franco "Double D" DeLuca), Steven Bongiovanni (Bobby "Loops" Victorio), Johnny G. Lee (Alexi Azajov), Chris Sloane (Agent Jack Grady), Karl Barbee (Johnny Kyro), Dan Eash (Gene Boner), Christopher Waite (The Squealer), Andrew Rodes (Kitty Pitty). **Credits:** *Producer:* Michael Belveduto, Barry Tangert, W. Jeff Crawford, Andrew Rodes. *Director:* Michael Belveduto, W. Jeff Crawford, Andrew Rodes, Barry Tangert. *Writer:* Michael Belveduto. **Comment:** Smartly acted, written and directed spoof of the hardcore gangster sagas. Once the initial shock of the vulgar language passes, the program becomes enjoyable with a smooth-flowing story that captures your attention from the very beginning. There is a unique viewer discretion that appears before each episode begins, stating that it has an equivalent (to a feature film) "R" rating "for situations that may contain a Whole Lotta Ass-Kicking, Friggin' FBombs, Nice and Sexy Situations and Stuff that Will Jail Ya."

Episodes: *1.* Mickey Ain't Happy. *2.* Mickey Gets Out. *3.* So Why Here and Why Me? *4.* Here Comes Trouble. *5.* Caught in the Act. *6.* Nothing but a "G" Thing. *7.* Mickey Approves Some Action. *8.* The Angel and the Devils. *9.* It's Sonny in Pennsylvania. *10.* Sonny ... with a Chance of Dead.

641 *Mock Justice*. mockjustice.com. 2012.

Before entering law school Jeff Meyers was the best prosecuting attorney in his high school's mock justice legal system. But one case, Primrose v. Parsons, destroyed his enthusiasm for mock justice when he could not solve the crime (who stole an old lady's [Mrs. Primrose] pie) and he vowed to never participate in such pretend games again. Several years have passed and Jeff has an office and a secretary (Trudy) and a problem: a student (Brett), failing in his remedial social studies class, has approached him for help in learning the justice system as his teacher has assigned him to try mock trials for extra credit. Jeff is reluctant at first until he learns that the case Brett has been assigned is Primrose v. Parsons and he now feels he can redeem himself by solving the case. The program follows Jeff, assisted by Brett (and up against defense lawyer Olivia Stone) to once and for all remove that embarrassing moment from his self-proclaimed disgrace record.

Cast: Nick Downs (Jeff Meyers), Dan Crosby (Brett McKenna), Taylor Alfano (Olivia Stone), Alex Yarnevich (Trudy), Harmoni Salisbury (Mrs. Primrose), Lily Propes (Student Judge), Penelope Green (Alexis Tesner), Andre Iadipulolo (Herb Smitty). **Credits:** *Producer:* James Madejski, Kris Wellman, Rolfe Bergsman. *Writer-Director:* James Madejski, Kris Wellman. **Comment:** Series based on high school or college mock trial sessions are nonexistent and while cases are not earth shattering (as depicted in the series) they are interesting to see how high school students handle adult situations. The acting and production is well done and for something different in lawyer shows, *Mock Justice* fills that bill.

Episodes: 6 untitled episodes, labeled "Episode 1" to "Episode 6."

642 *Moderation Town*. webserieschannel. com. 2013.

When a factory, the primary source of its revenue collapses, a small town reinvents itself by becoming a startup Internet company. As the company begins to grow it also faces the normal problems of any company but here the staff also has to deal with H8RAID, an ingenious hacker who delights in tormenting them. The program follows company founder Alex and his team as they not only deal with their personal issues but battle to keep their company going despite a hacker's attempts to shut them down.

Cast: Nick Flanagan (Alex Karpillo), Danielle Barker (Heather), Pardis Parker (Christian), Mike McLeod (Brad), Bob Mann (Darryl), Trudy Fong (Sandy), Mike Hampson (Jason), Amber MacArthur (Amber). **Credits:** *Producer:* Victoria Ha, Evan Jones. *Director:* Mark Mullane. *Writer:* Tim McAuliffe, Mike Mullane. **Comment:** Interesting approach to following the mishaps that an upstart Internet company faces. The acting and production are good although vulgar language is incorporated but really not needed.

Season 1 Episodes: *1.* What Is Moderation? *2.* Don't Feed the Trolls. *3.* The Internet Makes You an Asshole. *4.* Chocolate Fountain. *5.* Sex Tape Leaked. *6.* Getting What He Deserves. *7.* One of Those Bitch Clients. *8.* David Carradine's Genitals. *9.* Frustrating Fruit. *10.* The Zoning Problem.

Season 2 Episodes: *1.* Brand the Mooch. *2.* Frustrating Fruit. *3.* The Zoning Profile. *4.* Indiana Jones, Jr. *5.* Hulk Hogan Made It Look So Easy.

643 *Mom Cave Live.* momcave.tv. 2014–2015.

Real mothers relate real stories about childbirth and raising children—all of which has actually happened to or experienced by them.

Cast: Jennifer Weedon, Valisa Tate, Stephanie Faith Scott. **Comment:** The hosts are delightful to watch as they reveal real incidents in their personal lives. The mothers each appear to be comfortable telling their stories and the program presents them as a friend and talking to you (the viewer) on a personal level.

Episodes 1–20: *1.* Meet the Moms. *2.* Who's the Cool Mom? *3.* Moms Play "I Never." *4.* Holiday Shortcuts. *5.* My Kid Is Taking Over My Apartment. *6.* Sick Babies and Kids. *7.* The Things They Say... *8.* Childcare Chaos. *9.* Mommy R&R. *10.* Mom Cave

Mom Cave Live. Series poster art (used by permission of Jennifer Weedon 2015).

"Sort of." *11.* Ages and Stages. *12.* Bedtime Battles. *13.* Secrets of a Doula. *14.* Crap People Say. *15.* Dear Dads with the Lil Mamas. *16.* Big Kid Advice. *17.* Boys and Their.... Things. *18.* The Orange Rhino Challenge. *19.* Project Motherhood. *20.* Baby Gear and Pumping.

Episodes 21–45. *21.* The Reluctant Mom. *22.* Mommy Tips by Cole. *23.* Laughing and Lactating. *24.* Halloween Hacks Mom. *25.* Starting Your Own Business. *26.* Holiday Shopping Chaos. *27.* Weight. *28.* My Child Is Out of Control. *29.* Let It Go. *30.* Kiddie Soccer Is a Verb. *31.* Mommy Mashups. *32.* Weird and Creative Pregnancy. *33.* When Mom Is Sick. *34.* My Kid Won't Eat Vegetables. *35.* World's Worst Mom. *36.* Making Mom Friends Is Worse Than Dating. *37.* When Mom Is on the Phone. *38.* Potty Talk. *39.* How Not to Lose Your S**t. *40.* I Won't Grow Up. *41.* Martinis and Minivans. *42.* Sweat Pants for Kate. *43.* S**t Southern Moms Say. *44.* The Sex. *45.* Best of Mom Cave.

644 *Moms.* webserieschannel.com. 2013.

Shari Peters is a single mother trying to readjust to life after her divorce from Corey. She has a son (Dylan), three best girlfriends (Dee, Leslie and Melinda) and a hectic life. She also appears to be missing one element—a new romance. Dee, Leslie and Melinda (married to Lincoln and pregnant) feel Shari needs to get back into the swing of things and have set their goals to do just that. The program follows Shari as she tries to balance her life as a single mother yet still find time for romance.

Cast: Saadiqa Muhammad (Shari Peters), Keena Ferguson (Leslie Beckett), Jillian Reeves-Ortiz (Dee Landers), Marta McGonagle Cross (Melinda), Kristin Farrell (Bethany), Samuel Caruana (Dylan Young), Joel Anderson (Corey Young), Tyler Michael Brown (Glenn Beckett), Layla Boyce (Alexandra Beckett). **Credits:** *Producer:* Saadiqa Muhammad, Nika Williams, Christina DeLeon. *Director:* Saadiqa Muhammad. **Comment:** Nicely paced story of a woman just trying to rebound after her divorce. It is an African-American themed program and well acted and produced.

Episodes: *1.* Meet Shari. *2.* Oops, I Did It Again. *3.* It's Ladies' Nite. *4.* Go Take a Hike. *5.* There's Something About Aunty Shari. *6.* It's My Party. *7.* Everybody's Got That Feeling. *8.* Dirty Dancing. *9.* Just Breathe. *10.* Special Delivery.

645 *The Monday Knights*. webserieschan nel.com. 2011.

To escape the drudgery of his daily life (refurbishing computers at Electronic Emporium) Marty Collins, a young adult hooked on video games since becoming addicted to *Dungeons and Dragons* devises a way to become a hero by creating "The Game," a fantasy world wherein he is the hero of the story. But he can't do it alone and convinces his friends, most notably Sam, Ryn, Rayfax and Gordon (who becomes the enemy of the game he must defeat) to join him and the program, cleverly switching back and forth between Marty's real life and his fantasy world, relates how Marty copes with the situations that surround him; situations that in one way or another parallel the other.

Cast: Derek Mesford (Marty Collins), Jon Jolin (Sam Weisse), Carly Johnson (Ryn Salve), Brant Mickey (Rayfax), Reed Harvey (Gordon Carter), Matt Bynum (Kelly), Carter Lee Churchfield (Willie). Credits: *Producer:* Meghan Harvey. *Director:* Prescott Harvey, *Writer:* Prescott Harvey, Meghan Harvey, Reed Harvey, Loren Hall. Comment: The program mixes reality (Marty's life) with fantasy (aspects of "The Game") in a well acted and constructed program. While the medieval game action is accomplished through computer animation and green screen technology, it is quite convincing and adds to the enjoyment of the program.

Episodes: *1.* Frenemies. *2.* Sam Weisse the Brave. *3.* The Terms of Rayfax. *4.* To Catch a Thief. *5.* Game Day. *6.* The Chubby Princess. *7.* The Hunt. *8.* Gordon's Feint. *9.* Battle for the Chubby Princess. *10.* The Last Debate. *11.* Special Abilities. *12.* Last Knight.

646 *The Monogamy Experiment*. webserieschannel.com. 2011.

Amy and Edgar are a young couple who recently married but now have second thoughts about whether they made the right decision. With the most pressing problem being did they marry too young they decide to find the answer by making a documentary. The program chronicles that production as each seeks to discover if they were meant to be monogamous or not through a thirty day open relationship experiment.

Cast: Amy Rider, Edgar Morais, Tohoru Masamune, Gina Hirazumi, Shauna Dillard, Brayden Pierce, Liisa Evastina, Aarti Mann, Anne Sackmann, Eric Mourer. Credits: *Producer:* Tohoru Masamune. *Writer-Director:* Amy Rider. Comment: All episodes and virtually all text information have been taken off line thus a comment is not possible.

Episodes: *1.* Pilot: Your Sex Is on Fire.

647 *Montreal Hearts*. youtube.com. 2010.

Reg is a young man, living a seemingly quiet and uninvolved life, whose world is turned upside down when his father passes and he inherits a bar (Grumpy's) and an sleazy escort service (Montreal Hearts) that is actually a prostitution business. With a strong determination to continue running both businesses (uppermost making Montreal Hearts classy) but in a manner more in accord with who he is (honest) and not like his conniving and greedy father, Reg's efforts are explored as he becomes a Canadian businessman with unscrupulous employees and off-the-wall customers.

Cast: Adam Kelly Morton (Reg), Rob Corti (McLen), Jason McCullough (Jim), Ryan Hipgrave (Garth), Alison Vermaat (Ronnie), Rosaruby Kagan (Cameron), Sofia Banzhaf (Nana), Adrien Benn (Patrick), Adrienne McGrath, Christine Sciortino, Alexandra Valassis, Jason Eslinger, Stephanie Coco-Palermo, Victoria Kelly, Jessica Laurence, Andrew Leeke, Chris Alsop, Vanessa Brisset. Credits: *Director:* Shaun Malley, Raphael Hebert, Andrew Leeke, Elias Varoutsos. *Writer:* Rob Corti, Shaun Malley, Jason McCullough, Adam Kelly Morton. Comment: When first seen Reg appears to be one mean dude who will take nothing from anyone. As he addresses the staff of his just inherited businesses on what he plans to do, he is seen as laid back and nicer than he appears. The storyline, acting and production values are good and the characters well defined and each has that love or hate aura about them. While there are sexual situations and vulgar language is used, the program's on-line episode descriptions needlessly use foul language and go beyond the decency standards of what is normally seen on other sites. There is simply no need to offend people who may just want to read what a program is about (although its tag line is "A nasty, sexy comedy").

Episodes: *1.* Orient Express. *2.* Good Business. *3.* Girls on the Take. *4.* Vancouver. *5.* Duress. *6.* Wages. *7.* Lollipops. *8.* Beef Job Interview. *9.* Mary and Nana. *10.* Poker. *11.* Milk. *12.* V.I.P. *13.* reg@ home.

648 *Morning Wood*. youtube.com. 2013.

Events in the lives of a group of twenty-something friends (see cast) with a particular focus on Landon, JJ and Mitch, three less-than-mature adults seeking to find their place in the world (but never able to find it as their child-like antics prevent them from achieving success of any kind).

Cast: Mikey Anthony Velez (Landon), Tom Anello (JJ), Jason Edelstein (Mitch), Katie Rotolo (Julie), Marissa Gould (Kate), Natasha Waisfeld (Sasha), Nori Tecosky (Lara). Credits: *Director:* Omar Carrion. *Writer:* Tom Anello, Ryan Didato.

Comment: Characters are not defined and the story is a bit difficult to understand as everything is just thrown into the mix. The main male characters are downright disgusting; annoying flashing inserts are used to go from one scene to another; and scenes that involve too many characters at one time need to be reworked (as constant cutting back and forth between them just makes things confusing). Adult situations are encompassed and nudity is censored. There is also an attempt for the male leads to find romance, but what girl in her right mind would even want to begin a relationship with a guy who seems unable to grow up and mature?

Episodes: *1.* Pilot. *2.* Trailer.

649 *Mother Eve's Secret Garden of Sensual Sisterhood.* mother eves.com. 2011.

Eve is a charming woman who is also a schemer and con artist. If there is a way to make money without actually working for it, she will find that way. Adapting the name Mother Love and calling her apartment the Secret Garden, Eve hatches a plan to help women who feel "frumpy, dumpy, lumpy, crappy and unhappy" by offering them her exclusive and expensive exercises and treatments. Assigning each woman a flower name and calling her group her Divine Petals, Eve's story is told in music and song.

Cast: Ashley Wren Collins (Mother Eve), Maitely Weismann (Mustard Plant), Anne Barry (Daisy), Alena Acker (Rhododendron), Amy Dannenmueller (Rose), Uma Incrocci (Snap Dragon), Donna Lobello (Violet), Danielle Montezinos (Bird of Paradise), Kirk McGee (Practice Boy). Credits: *Producer:* Maitely Weismann, Alena Acker, Anne Barry, Ashley Wren Collins, Amy Dannenmueller, Uma Incrocci, Erica Jensen, Donna Lobello, Kirk McGee, Danielle Montezinos, Dan Remmes. *Director:* Erica Jensen. *Writer:* Uma Incrocci, Kirk McGee, Dan Remmes. Comment: All episodes have been taken off line. A trailer does remain and while it does look good, it is not really possible to judge the series based on that.

Episodes: *1.* Pity Party. *2.* MAN-euvering Without Him. *3.* Pussy. *4.* Unleash Your Inner Skank. *5.* Clothes Swap. *6.* Abundance.

650 *Movie Night.* youtube.com. 2014.

Each Friday night a group of friends (Ashley, Blake, Kevin and La'Sarah) attend their friend, Esther's weekly movie night gathering. The group simply enjoys watching a film and Esther, the stickler that she is, always keeps the event as complacent as can be. One Friday the situation changes when an outsider (Jaynee, a friend of Kevin's sister) invites herself to the gathering and immediately sets Esther on the warpath. Stories follow Esther as she attempts

Movie Night. Clockwise, beginning with the girl in front: Beth Crudele, Kerrington Fier, Oriana Nudo, Rance Collins, Rachel Wolf, Justin Scarelli (© 2014 By-Law Production. Used with permission).

to deal with an outsider invading her movie night and how each gathering affects each of the friends, especially when Jaynee becomes a part of their lives.

Cast: Oriana Nudo (Esther Woolf), Rance Collins (Kevin Brooks), Beth Crudele (Jaynee Smithe), Kerrington Fier (Blake Adams), Oriano Nudo (Esther Woolf), Justin Scarelli (Ashley Gray), Rachel Wolf (La'Sarah Levinski). Credits: *Producer:* Rachel Wolf, Justin Scarelli, Oriana Nudo, Beth Crudele, Kerrington Fier, Rance Collins. *Director:* Rance Collins, Kerrington Fier, Justin Scarelli. *Writer:* Rance Collins, Beth Crudele, Kerrington Fier, Oriana Nudo, Justin Scarelli, Rachel Wolf. Comment: Very well acted and produced program that is enjoyable to watch.

Episodes: *1,2.* This Is Your Oz. *3,4.* La'Sarah's Choice. *5,6.* Who's Afraid of Esther Woolf? *7,8.* Breakfast at Jaynee's. *9,10.* The Man Who Didn't Want to Get Away. *11,12.* Whatever, Sera, Sera.

651 *Moving In.* webserieschannel.com. 2012.

Michael Jones is a first year student at the University of Portsmouth in England. He suffers from Asperger's Syndrome (autism) and has been assigned to a student house run by a law-breaking landlord and paired with three less-than-socially acceptable roommates: Callum, a party guy; Poppy, an obsessed artist who believes she can predict the future; and Amy, a writer who loves to procrastinate. The program follows Michael as he not only has to deal with his disability, but life at school, made all the more complicated by Callum, Poppy and Amy.

Cast: Paul Goldthorpe (Michael), Kelly Gardiner (Amy), Charlotte Cloud (Poppy), David Lewis (Callum). **Credits:** *Producer-Writer:* Mark Lever. *Director:* Gary Thomas. **Comment:** A British produced program that, based on the only episode released, appears to be rather talkative (but this could change as pilots only sets the stage). The acting and production is good.

Episodes: *1.* Pilot: The Freshers Week.

652 *Moving Numbers.* webserieschannel.com. 2011.

A political spoof that follows the campaign of Senator Robert Sanders, a man running for re-election but who is quite clueless about what he should actually be doing as a state representative. But he has supporters and the people love him and through the less-than-honorable methods of his campaign manager, Jason Mahoney, a behind-the-scenes look at the making of a candidate is shamefully exposed.

Cast: Peter McCain (Jason Mahoney), John Colton (Robert Sanders), Jon Briddell (Bob Sinclair), Jennifer Field (Alicia). **Credits:** *Producer:* Leslie Baker. *Writer-Director:* John Brabender. **Comment:** All episodes, with the exception of a trailer titled "Fourth and Ten" have been taken off line. It is difficult to judge an entire series by the short trailer, but it does appear to have been a well produced and acted political satire.

653 *Ms. Vampy.* msvampy.net. 2009.

She believes the HBO TV program *True Blood* is a reality series and dreams of joining its cast. She indulges on Godiva chocolates, Bloody Mary drinks and enjoys playing Xbox. She has not yet married (she's only 110 years old) or had children but she is sexy, young (for her age) and funny. Such describes, in part, Ms. Vampy, now a gorgeous vampire who was once a normal woman. She was born in Transylvania in 1899 and was shy and sweet until her eighteenth birthday when she had a bit too much to drink, unknowingly hooked up with a vampire and was bitten. While a creature of the undead, she suddenly became voluptuous and developed an insatiable sex drive ("I went from being a brainy bookworm to a blood-loving, vampire sexpot in just minutes"). It was during the 1920s that Ms. Vampy fell in love with New York and made her home in Brooklyn. A short time later, after tumultuous affair with a Wall Street banker-vampire, Ms. Vampy de-

cided to move to Hollywood and begin a new life. Now, as the owner of Ms. Vampy's Villa and just as alluring as she always was, Ms. Vampy opens her home to her friends each evening and the program chronicles what happens during those ghoulish get-togethers.

Cast: Brooke Lewis (Ms. Vampy). **Credits:** *Writer-Director:* Brooke Lewis. **Comment:** Although she does show cleavage and has fangs (and talks well with them) she has, without a doubt, been inspired by Cassandra Peterson's "Elvira, Mistress of the Dark" character. While the program does appear to be interesting in text information, actual episodes have been taken off line. See also *Ms. Vampy Bites* and *Ms. Vampy's Love Bites.*

Episodes: *1.* Coffin Tawk. *2.* Twilight??? *3.* Six Degrees of Mutilation. *4.* Dahmer.

654 *Ms. Vampy Bites.* msvampy.net. 2013.

Ms. Vampy, the alluring vampire, in a spin off from *Ms. Vampy* wherein she attempts to give advice to on-lookers about the issues that not only affect vampires, but the living as well.

Cast: Brooke Lewis (Ms. Vampy). **Credits:** *Writer-Director:* Brooke Lewis. **Comment:** Brooke Lewis is charming as the sexy vampire and her advice is meant to be more humorous than clinical.

Episodes: *1.* Texting Etiquette. *2.* Dating a Younger Man. *3.* Gay Male Model Looking for Love. *4.* Changes in Your Life and Career. *5.* Having the "Right" Success.

655 *Ms. Vampy's Love Bites.* msvampy.net. 2013.

A second spin off (in the same year) from *Ms. Vampy* wherein a sexy vampire (Ms. Vampy) offers her viewers humorous advice relating to the opposite sex and dating.

Cast: Brooke Lewis (Ms. Vampy). **Credits:** *Writer-Director:* Brooke Lewis. **Comment:** Enjoyable companion program to the prior two titles that showcases the alluring Ms. Vampy while offering helpful dating advice.

Episodes: *1.* Online Dating. *2.* Sex on the First Date. *3.* Who Pays on the First Date? *4.* Dating a Friend's Ex.

656 *MsLabelled.* youtube.com. 2015.

Label is a fashion magazine where Ella, the assistant to the fashion editor (Percy) believes she has found her place in life. But *Label* is somewhat behind the times and its editor, Jeanne, sees potential in Ella to bring it up-to-par with other fashion magazines (especially since the industry gossip rag *Mirror Mirror* ["The ruthless Page 6 of Fashion"] has been attacking it). With the help of her best friend Anna, a fashion designer, and Gus, her tech guy, Ella

Now Available on YouTube at Vervegirl
T U E S D A Y S + T H U R S D A Y S

MsLabelled poster featuring Rebecca Liddiard (courtesy Shaftesbury/ Smokebomb).

begins a fashion blog—the niche for finding her own voice but also a challenge as she must now bring *Label* into the "real" world. Rumi, Andy, Duke and Janice are *Label* fashion designers; Xander runs Xander Vintage, a blog for the fashion community.

Cast: Rebecca Liddiard (Ella), Sara Hennessey (Anna), Sydney Kondruss (Janice), Marni van Dyk (Bee), Jeanne Beker (Jeanne), Alanna Durkovich (Xander), Spencer Robson (Andy), Richard Young (Percy), Adamo Ruggiero (Duke), Shawn Ahmed (Gus), Nykeem Provo (Luke), Barbara Mamabolo (Rumi). **Comment:** Charming inside look at a fashion magazine and how it attempts to survive in a rapidly changing world. The acting is very good and the program flows smoothly from episode to episode.

Episodes: *1.* How to Ruin Everything. *2.* How to Get Mentored by Jeanne Freakin' Beker in One Day. *3.* How to Get Fired By Your Competition, Showgirls-Style. *4.* How to Ruin a Gown in One Night. *5.* How to Fix a Dress at 4 a.m. *6.* How to Bring a Sense of Humor to Style. *7.* How to Be an Evil Cheerleader at the End of the World. *8.* How to Get Unfired at *Label* Magazine. *9.* How to Put Modelizers in Their Place. *10.* How to Create DYI Denim, Pearls and Creepo MacDiddies. *11.* How to Design Sweaty Bulls*h*t. *12.* How to Storm in Like a Kardashian. *13.* How to Delete a Blog in One Second. *14.* How to Gain a Following from a Vicious Troll. *15.* How to Dress a Socialite for the Blue Footed Booby Ball. *16.* How to Find a Vintage 80s Sweaters Haul. *17.* How to Design Formal Wear and Spot the Lesbians. *18.* How to Sniff Out a Mole at a Magazine. *19.* How to Alter a Collection to Save a Reputation. *20.* How to Investigate Your Best Friend's Girlfriend. *21.* How to Win a Walk-off and Ruin the Party.

657 *Mugs: The Web Series.* mugsthefilm.com. 2013.

Kevin is the son of a single mother whose addiction to alcohol placed his upbringing in the hands of their cross-dressing housekeeper, Ramon. While it appears Ramon had no effect on Kevin, Kevin finds his world spinning out of control when he acquires a summer job at a local coffee house (Mugs) and finds its patrons are anything but normal (all a bit quirky). His fellow employee, Charlie, is openly gay and their boss (Rosie) is an eccentric. Suddenly, taken out of his comfort zone and introduced to a world that he has never known before, Kevin realizes that how he was brought up was not normal and he is now unsure of who he is or who he wants to be. Kevin's efforts to navigate a world he cannot fully comprehend and discover who he really is are charted.

Cast: Brian Kane (Kevin), Michael Howell (Charlie), Gio March (Ramon), Mamie Morgan (Rosie), Laina Burgess (Darcy). **Credits:** *Producer:* Zac Underwood. *Director:* Mckenzie Figueiredo. *Writer:* Kyle Taylor, Z.T. Underwood. **Comment:** For some reason, producers believe that using abundant amounts of foul language makes for good comedy. It doesn't. The acting and production values are very good and the story, although unresolved (it appears Kevin will follow a gay path) leaves the doorway open for the series to continue.

Episodes: *1.* Kevin Gets a Job. *2.* Kevin Gets Accused of Thieving. *3.* Kevin's Play Date. *4.* Kevin Gets Into a Fight. *5.* Kevin Gets Involved in Drama. *6.* Kevin's Discovery. *7.* Kevin Sees Something Crazy.

658 *Murder Squad.* murdersquad.net. 2009.

Ryan and Greg are low level agents with the Center for Homicide Control, Washington, D.C. Division who yearn for and have delusions of becoming top notch crime scene investigators. Delusional, but not defeated, they have teamed with Samantha, the office secretary, to work their way up the department ladder with the program charting their less-than-professional efforts to solve crimes that require the skills of real CSI detectives.

Cast: Jayson Blair (Ryan Newcombe), Adam Jennings (Greg Kirsch), Tristen MacDonald (Samantha), Bob Rummock (Chief Malcolm), Gerald Downey (Agent MacFarlane), Frank Krueger (Agent Goodman), Jennifer Riker (Captain Cabrera). Credits: *Producer-Director:* R. Chett Hoffman, Matt Quezada. *Writer:* R. Chett Hoffman, Will Phillips, Matt Quezada. Comment: While not heavy on crime scene investigations, the program is a decent spoof of shows like *C.S.I.*. The acting is good and the cases are typical of any cop show.

Episodes: *1.* Field Trip. *2.* Sex Offenders. *3.* Testosterone Test. *4.* The Blend. *5.* Andy Lee's Hot Wife. *6.* Malcolm's Office.

659 *Muscle United.* webserieschannel.com. 2013.

Muscle United is a super hero organization led by Captain Speedman that has been established for only one purpose: defeat the diabolical enemies of the earth (which include such fiends as the power-mad Francis Lubealotsi; Tormentus the Sorcerer; Pedro the blood-thirsty alien; and the Bun Maker). But that was some time ago and the unit now consists of a ragtag band of old men and high school dropouts, but its purpose has not changed. With the assist of Kitten Girl, Tangleweb, Aqua Queen and Dr. CrippleCracken, Captain Speedman leads the battle against the evil that threatens the lives of decent citizens.

Cast: Geoff Oxland (Captain Speedman), Elliot Jackson (Tangleweb), Hannah Pitchford (Kitten Girl), Kerry Davies (Aqua Queen), Alan Webdale (Dr. CrippleCracken), Kim Oxland (President of the World). Credits: *Producer-Writer-Director:* Owen Lightburn. Comment: For a first-time attempt at a web series Owen Lightburn did a remarkably good job. The super hero spoofs are well done and acted and include decent special effects for a limited budget series.

Episodes: *1.*Buttocks and Budgets. *2.* The Spawn.

3. The Bun Maker. *4.* The Queer Second Coming. *5.* Episode 5. *6.* The Torment.

660 *My Alibi.* youtube.com. 2008.

Marley, Rebecca, Cy, Scarlet and Jonah are students at Wheeler High School. They are best friends and do everything together including, by coincidence, coming late to class on the day someone pulled a prank that has upset Principal Tuckerman. In retaliation, and believing the late students are responsible, Tuckerman sends them to detention and will only release them when one of them confesses. As each student sits in detention, literally in a fog as to why they have been sent there, the program relates the story each has to tell as to why they were late to school.

Cast: Cyrina Fiallo (Marley Carabello), Julianna Guill (Scarlet Hauksson), Adam Chambers (Cy Woods), Alison Brie (Rebecca Fuller), Marque Richardson (Justin Walker), Zachary Burr Abel (Jonah Madigan), Gabrielle Carteris (Principal Tuckerman). Credits: *Director:* Oren Kaplan. *Writer:* Julie Restivo. Comment: Gabrielle Carteris, from the TV series *Beverly Hills, 90210* plays the principal in a program a bit reminiscent of the Molly Ringwald movie *The Breakfast Club* as it too was set in a school detention room. But that is where the similarity ends as here it is a matter of discovering each student's secret of the morning in question with good acting and production values.

Episodes: *1.* Busted. *2.* First Period. *3.* Out of the Bag. *4.* Cat-astrophe. *5.* Picture Perfect.

661 *My Bitchy Witchy Paris Vacation.* bitchywitcythefilm.com. 2010.

Diane, a middle-aged woman and the mother of 24-year-old Ashley and 15-year-old Miranda, has just separated from her husband; Ashley is pregnant; and Miranda, not quite 15 ("14 and 363 days old") is "desperate for her first period to come while she is on vacation." The vacation is in Paris and the program follows their efforts to cope with everything that surrounds them—from their relationships with each other to Ashley and Miranda bonding to all the anxiety they encounter as they deal with their own personal issues.

Cast: Kate Michaels (Diane), Esmee Buchet-Deak (Miranda), Pelham Spong (Ashley), Alyssa Landry (Belle), Sebastian Galluci (Ferdinand). Credits: *Producer-Writer:* Alexis Niki. *Director:* Katrik Singh. Comment: Enjoyable program that is well acted and produced. It was filmed on location in Paris and presents both a comical and moving look at the lives of three women who have grown apart but try to come together during a vacation that is anything but typical.

Episodes: *1.* It'll Never Be Over. *2.* A Deal with Santa. *3.* Baby Pictures.

662 My Cousin Dakota. youtube.com. 2013.

Simplistic premise wherein a young woman appears before the camera, attempts to do something and evoke laughs as she struggles to do it. **Cast:** Colleen Hennessy (Dakota). **Credits:** *Creator:* Thomas John Hayes. **Comment:** Strange presentation that is simply sort videos of a woman who doesn't speak and tries to get laughs. Doesn't quite work as the woman has very little appeal and the episodes make little or no sense.

Episodes: *1.* What's Your Sign? *2.* A Mother's Prayer. *3.* Bad Girl. *4.* Started. *5.* The In Crowd. *6.* The Review. *7.* Revlon Red. *8.* Exciting. *9.* Dancing with a Star. *10.* The Search.

663 My Friend Blashe. myfriendblashe.com. 2014.

Blashe, Denny and Sal have been friends since childhood. While Denny and Sal had a normal upbringing with a mother and father, Blashe was raised by his off-the-wall single father (Simon). Now as adults, Sal has come to realize that Blashe is annoying, hangs out to much with him and has become too dependent on him and Denny. Denny, however, appears to be oblivious to this and his relationship with his girlfriend, Julie, appears to hang in the balance because she sees exactly what Sal sees in Blashe. While Jill and Sal would simply like to get Blashe out of their lives and make Denny see what he is truly like, they can't and the program charts the mishaps that befall them as Blashe is (and apparently always will be) a part of their lives. **Cast:** Bentley Potter (Blashe Richter), T. George McArdle (Denny Brown), Summer Corrie (Jill Martin), Frankie Witowski (Sal Mastriano), Andrew Austin (Herm Dunbar), Guy Seligman (Simon Richter), Trinka Lee Whitaker (Cindy the Bartender). **Credits:** *Producer:* T. George McArdle, Bentley Potter, Michael Habernig. *Director:* T. George McArdle. *Writer:* T. George McArdle, Bentley Potter. **Comment:** Annoying best friends who do not realize they are such has been done countless times before. But no matter how tired the concept, new life can be brought to it if the right mixture is found. Such is the case here and with good acting and production values to match. The drawback would be that it incorporates an annoying laugh track—

something today's comedies simply do not need, whether it is on broadcast, cable or Internet TV.

Episodes: *1.* The Visit. *2.* Double Date. *3.* Peaches. *4.* Therapy.

664 My Gimpy Life. youtube.com/My GimpyLife.com. 2014.

Teal is a very pretty young woman who yearns to be an actress. She has all the qualifications but is hampered by the fact that she is disabled (uses a wheelchair) and roles in her situation are not plentiful. Despite all the drawbacks, Teal is never discouraged and has set her goal to be the best at whatever role she acquires (usually through her agent Charles). "Hi, I'm Teal, like the color. I live in Hollywood, the place where dreams supposedly happen

My Gimpy Life. Series poster art (copyright Rolling Person Productions, 2014).

and I'm an actress," says Teal as she opens each episode. But she continues: "You probably noticed I'm in a wheelchair but I never let my disability define me." The program presents a view of life from Teal's perspective as she just tries to lead a normal life, or as she says, "This is my gimpy life." Second season episodes change the format somewhat when acting jobs become scarce and Teal acquires a position at a marketing company to help make ends meet.

Cast: Teal Sherer (Teal), Gary Anthony Williams (Charles), Brent Bradshaw (Brent), Teale Sperling (Teale), Felicia Day (Felicia), Amy Okuda (Amy), Mindy Sterling (Maggie), Marissa Cuevas (Marissa), Patricia Tallman (Casey), Eric Acosta (Milo). Credits: Producer: Steven Dengler, Gabe Uhr, Teal Sherer, Russell Winkelaar. Director: Sean Becker. Writer: Gabe Uhr. Comment: A very well done and acted program to make viewers aware of what such people go through just to live a normal life. It is loosely based on the life of actress Teal Sherer who is also a disability advocate and combines comedy with light drama to satirize show business and the social struggle disabled people face "from inaccessible auditions to patronizing head shots and beyond." Familiar TV and movie names like Mindy Sterling, Gary Anthony Williams, Felicia Day and Amy Okuda are also a part of the program.

Season 1 Episodes: 1. Accessible. 2. Two Shades of Teal (introduces a "mini-me" version of Teal named Teale). 3. Inspirational. 4. Crowded. 5. The Commercial.

Season 2 Episodes: 1. Day Jobs. 2. Also Teal Too. 3. The Morning After. 4. Viral Superstar.

665 (My) Immortal: The Web Series. myimmortalseries.com. 2013.

Hogsmeade is a magical high school that teaches future wizards how to embrace their abilities. Enoby Darkness Dementia Raven Way is one such student, a not-too-bright girl who even has trouble pronouncing her own name. She encompasses the Goth look and believes she is the number one Goth girl and will stop at nothing to prove it. Students like Harry, Hermione and Ron have become victims of her misguided efforts and stories follow Enoby as she turns the fantasy world of Harry Potter, including the Hogwarts School, upside down.

Cast: Justine Cargo (Enoby), Joseph Bradley (Harry Potter), Eli Terlson (Draco Malfoy), Justin Kosi (Ron Weasley), Jennah Foster-Catlack (Hermione Granger), Jen Matotek (Bellatrix Lestrange), Tanya Casole-Gouveia (Narcissus), Richard Chuang (Yaxley), Jeff Stone (Snap), Brian McLellan (Loopin), Dani Alon (Millicent Bulstrode), Amie Everett (Pansy Parkinson), Michael Demski (Viktor Krum), Gabriel Mansour (Vlad). Credits: Producer: Calotta von Ahn, Candace Meeks. Director: Cameron McLellan. Comment: A delightful parody of Harry Potter with an unlikely heroine, songs, dances, very good acting and even aspects of the Goth world.

Episodes: 4 untitled episodes, labeled "Episode 1" through "Episode 4."

666 My Lesbian Friend. youtube.com. 2013.

Keara, straight, and Kathleen, a lesbian, are roommates but not lovers. Society, however, sees such a situation as two young women living together as not just friends, but lovers. Keara and Kathleen are each seeking that special someone and the program tackles a situation that has often been played in gay-themed series, but infrequently on lesbian-themed programs: a best friend situation (with all the highs and lows that Keara and Kathleen encounter as they navigate a dating life but not with each other).

Cast: Keara Doyle (Keara), Kathleen McKeown (Kathleen). Credits: Producer-Writer: Thyna Catamara, Keara Doyle, Kathleen McKeown. Director: Thyna Catamara. Comment: The program is very well acted and produced. Keara and Kathleen are both quite attractive and the story line is very well constructed. Other than the one episode on YouTube there is virtually no other information on line to explain the series concept or the number of episodes produced. It appears that even though the available episode is labeled number seven, it could actually be the pilot and made to look like more episodes were produced but have been taken off line.

Episodes: 1. Barbecue.

667 My Life with Sock. webserieschannel.com. 2014.

Hugh is a sock puppet that believes it is human. It all begins when a young woman named Mia meets Hugh, a white tube sock, at a restaurant (apparently a blind date). Before she knows it, Mia falls in love with Hugh and the two begin living (and having sex) together. Mia becomes pregnant, has a sock puppet child but their life together ends when Mia catches Hugh watching "sock porn" on the Internet (even shown for the audience) and realizes she can longer please him and ends the marriage. That meeting, courtship, birth and divorce form the basis of the program.

Cast: Mia Pinchoff (Mia/Hugh), Chris Riggi (Hugh's frat brother), Anni Weisband (Mia's ex girlfriend), Mary Grace Hinkle (Mia's friend), Christina Shipp (Mia's friend), Joseph Calleri (Hugh's father), Theresa Falco-Calleri (Hugh's mother). Comment: Despite its title and use of a sock puppet, it is not a series for children. It is adult in nature with sexual situations and bleeped foul language. There is no parental warning given and for something really different, My Life with Sock is truly different.

Episodes: 1. First Date. 2. First Kiss. 3. Laundry Day. 4. The–. 5. First Time. 6. Beach Day. 7. Bromance. 8. The Ex. 9. Meet the Sock Parents. 10.

Vows. *11.* Sock Birth. *12.* Sock Baby. *13.* Sock Porn. *14.* Sock Divorce. *15.* Blind Date.

668 My Long Distance Relationship. tv. com. 2008–2009.

Samantha and Sam are high school sweethearts whose lives change when they graduate and each decides to pursue a different educational future: Samantha at South Southern East State in Florida and Sam at Far West University in Oregon. The Internet helps the couple continue their relationship but meeting new people (and possible new loves) threaten to break them up. The program relates what happens as Samantha and Sam struggle to find out whether their love can endure all the pitfalls of a long distance relationship.

Cast: Rachel Specter (Samantha), Dan Levy (Sam), Randy Wayne (Cody), James Kirkland (Eddie).

Credits: *Producer:* Dan Levy, Jonathan Levy, A.J. Tesler. *Director:* Ramsey Mellette. *Writer:* Dan Levy, A.J. Tesler. **Comment:** With all episodes off line a comment is not possible.

Episodes: *1.* Who the F%*k is Cody? *2.* Cyber Sex. *3.* Intense Incense Bust! *4.* LDR-GF Stealer. *5.* Support Group. *6.* Boo Boo. *7.* The Break Up. *8.* I Vlog U 4 Evr. *9.* Sight for Sore Eyes. *10.* Sam Lights Up Cody. *11.* LDR Remix.

669 My Not So Sub-Conscious. youtube. com. 2013.

Dani is a young woman who seemed to have everything—a good life, perfect job, a great boyfriend (Jim) and great friends. Dani has always liked Jim but never really told him that she loves him. On the day she feels she needs to express her feelings for Jim, doubts enter her mind and she begins to wonder who she really is—and why she has a male-sounding inner voice. That inner voice, her thoughts, is seen by viewers but not Dani and as she wonders what to do, the inner voice relates those feelings to the audience. As the day progresses Dani comes to realize that her sub-conscious has a life of its own and the program follows Dani as she struggles to find a way to control it before it takes over her life.

Cast: Jennifer Betit Yen (Dani), Kamran Khan (Sub-Conscious) Marissa Carpio, Andy Baldeschwiler, Mami Kimura, Veronica Dang, Jim Chu.

Credits: *Producer:* Kamran Khan, Jennifer Betit Yen. *Director:* Kamran Khan, Jason Wong. *Writer:* Kamran Khan. **Comment:** This is one of those programs where each person will see it differently. To some Dani's inner voice will appear annoying as it is not feminine. Her actions will also be judged as she does not stop to analyze what is happening. Inner thoughts being heard by the viewer is nothing new, but the presentation here is.

Episodes: *1.* Monday Morning at the Office. *2.*

The Engagement Party. *3.* The–. *4.* Hello, Doctor. *5.* A Proposal? *6.* The Breakup.

670 My Olde Roommate. webserieschannel.com. 2014.

Zale, 75 years old, and Jerry, fifty years younger, share an apartment (how they came to be roommates is not stated). Each has a differing opinion about life and each episode is a look at a topic and how each reacts to it.

Cast: Jerry TerHorst (Jerry), Zale Kessler (Zale). **Credits:** *Producer-Writer-Director:* Jerry TerHorst.

Comment: The old-young man situation has been done before but it is always interesting to see how different producers handle the topic and what they will use as the topics of conversation. The acting and production are very good.

Episodes: *1.* Cold Vegetable Salad. *2.* Star Wars. *3.* Sleep-Talking. *4.* Motor Trend. *5.* Cross Fit Thing. *6.* The Big C.

671 My Pal Satan. funnyordie.com. 2009.

Donna is a young woman facing an immediate problem: how to pay the rent. Believing that taking in a roommate is the answer, she places and ad and almost immediately gets a response from a man who is literally Satan. Donna is kind and loving; Satan, with his red-like skin and glowing red room, is what he is—the Devil. The program relates what happens as Donna and Satan attempt to live together and adjust to each other's quirky ways with the unforeseen happening—each finding an attraction to the other, proving that opposites do attract.

Cast: Rachel Wilson (Donna), Jefferson Brown (Satan). **Credits:** *Producer:* Bryce Mitchell. *Director:* Vivieno Caldinelli. *Writer:* Dennis Heaton. **Comment:** One of the few, if not only program to make Satan appear as a likeable human. The acting and production are good and had additional episodes been produced it would have most likely showed a most unusual marriage—that of Donna to the Devil.

Episodes: *1.* No Apologies. *2.* Cheaters Never Perspire. *3.* Slaughterhouse and Home. *4.* Miss Popular. *5.* Possession Is 9/10th of the Fun. *6.* Making Out Is Hard to Do.

672 My Roommate the Cylon. myroommatethecylon.com. 2009.

Cylons, first coming into focus on the 1978 TV series *Battlestar Galactica* have actually invaded Earth and integrated one of their own into society. A young woman (Jessica) believes that one of her three friends (Bennett, Dale or Peter) is a Cylon (a human-looking robot). But she is unsure and to find out whom and save the Earth from an invasion, she devises a series of gruesome, subhuman and outlandish tests that each must endure with the hope of humiliating the Cylon into revealing himself and saving humanity.

Cast: Dorien Davies (Jessica Yarborough), Alex Enriquez (Bennett Jacobs), Tyson Turrou (Peter Odama), Kenny Stevenson (Dale McKinney). **Credits:** *Producer-Writer-Director:* Robert Gustafson, Alec McNayr. **Comment:** Do not expect a serious story, in fact do not expect a story based on scientific fact. What you can expect, even if you are not a *Galactica* fan is comic tale of what could happen if android technology created something so real that it is indistinguishable from an actual human.

Episodes: 6 untitled episodes, labeled "Episode 1" through "Episode 6."

673 *My Screaming Neighbours.* webseries channel.com. 2012.

A home in England provides the setting (and hence spelling of the title) where a young woman (not named) tries to live a quiet life but is constantly disturbed by the loud vocal exchanges of her next-door neighbours (also unnamed). But as the neighbours become louder and louder and their arguments intrigue the woman, she becomes fascinated by what she hears and makes it a point to listen. The program simply focuses on the woman as she eavesdrops.

Cast: Emily Schooley (The Woman), Suzanne Bernier (Mother), David Kinsman (Father), Gloria Adora (Little Girl), Matthew Sarookanian (Teenage Boy), Scott Clark (Teenage boy's friend). **Credits:** *Producer-Writer-Director:* Becky Shrimpton. **Comment:** Short, right to the point episodes (under two minutes each) that join a vocal argument in progress and how the woman is intrigued to listen. Unusual presentation that is well acted and produced.

Episodes: *1.* In Which We Learn the Importance of Using Your Indoor Voice, Outdoors. *2.* In Which We Learn That Math Is a Privilege, Not a Right. *3.* In Which We Learn Proper Etiquette for Table Settings and the Consequence of Failing to Adhere to Those Rules. *4.* In Which We Learn Not to Meddle in the Ways of Neighbours. *5.* In Which We Learn a Valuable Lesson—If You Can't Out Scream Her, Join Her.

674 *My Secret Sexy: The Life of an Undercover Sex Toy Reviewer.* vimeo.com. 2012.

Lillian Fischer appears to be a very pretty young woman leading a seemingly normal life. Looks can be deceiving as Lillian, under the name Evelyn Fearless, hosts a live web program called *Odyssey-X.com* wherein she reviews the latest in sex toys. Each episode is a look at one of Lillian's programs with her describing an item and taking calls from people who seem to not playing with a full deck. It also focuses on what happens to Lillian when she attempts to use a sex toy and it malfunctions.

Cast: Erin Nicole Cline (Lillian Fischer/Evelyn Fearless), Laura Sommer Raines (Female Callers), Michael Jacobson (Male Callers). **Credits:** *Writer-Director:* Cherie Sanders. **Comment:** The program should but doesn't have a parental warning for its adult language, sex toy visuals and suggestive situations. The atmosphere created for the set is somewhat reminiscent of red bordello rooms featured in moves and the overall production, including the wacky phone callers, is original, different and well done.

Episodes: *1.* Odyssey-X.com. *2.* Happy Halloweenie. *3.* Pole Dancing Queen. *4.* Juicy Snatch Patch. *5.* More Than Pubes. *6.* The Jerk Off. *7.* Closet Freak. *8.* Super Snatch. *9.* Devil's Fart. *10.* XXX Friends.

675 *My Super Overactive Imagination.* mysuperoverativeimagination.com. 2013–2014.

Kat and Olivia are best friends living in Los Angeles but each sharing a different perspective on life. Kat has a rather negative outlook as she is continually looking for a mate but can't find one that lives up to her fantasized expectations. Olivia, although frustrated by the lack of dates she has, accepts the fact that what she may be seeking in terms of a relationship may also be beyond her reach (she fails to realize that her flaws are the problem as she subconsciously refuses to acknowledge them). Through the events that spark Kat and Olivia's lives a lampoon of the single girl psyche vs. L.A. culture is presented.

Cast: Cat Rhinehart (Kat), Maria Shehata (Olivia). **Credits:** *Producer:* Cat Rhinehart, Maria Shehata, Aleah Lauchlan, Jonathan Salem, Jacob Whitney. *Director:* Cat Rhinehart, Stephen Anthony Bailey, Jonathan Salem, Jeff Feazell, Steven Lemorte, Maria Shehata, Kerri Feinsworth. *Writer:* Cat Rhinehart, Maria Shehata. **Comment:** Charming program with a good story, good acting and fine production values. The leads are very appealing and grab viewer attention throughout the series run.

Season 1 Episodes: *1.* Design for Dreaming. *2.* Facebook Friend. *3.* The Professor. *4.* Paleo. *5.* Therapy. *6.* The Musician. *7.* The Cross-Dresser. *8.* Drunk. *9.* Paddle Board. *10.* Playlist.

Season 2 Episodes: *1.* Babies. *2.* Lifeguard. *3.* Brodown. *4.* Chipotle. *5.* Bukowski. *6,7.* Showcase Showdown, Parts 1–2. *8.* The Promise. *9.* Dating Coach. *10.* Big Day. *11.* Apples to Apples.

Season 3 Episodes: *1.* Work Day. *2.* Free Couch. *3.* Happy. *4.* Friday Night. *5.* Runyon. *6.* Botox. *7.* Double Date. *8.* Olivia's Over. *9.* Earl vs. Wess. *10.* Missed Connection.

Season 4 Episodes: *1.* Plan B. *2.* Special Delivery. *3.* The Chocolate Scene. *4.* Cheaters. *5.* About Face. *6.* But Why Not? *7.* I Scream, You Scream.

676 *My Two Fans.* mytwofans.com. 2009.

Kate, like many people, has social network

friends. She is single, currently unemployed and having trouble finding a boyfriend. Feeling low and without really thinking first, Kate invites two such friends, Teddy and Franklin, to become part of her life as fans to cheer her on each day. As Teddy and Franklin become too much a part of Kate's life, Kate finds she must deal with all the embarrassing situations that arise as wherever she goes, trouble (Teddy and Franklin) follows.

Cast: Barret Swatek (Kate Maxwell), Bill Escudier (Teddy), Todd Felix (Franklin). **Credits:** *Producer:* Max Goldenson, Samantha Deane, Lauren Iungerich. *Writer- Director:* Lauren Iungerich. **Comment:** Does Kate really need her fans? That is the question that will come to mind. It is not a situation where someone is haunted by a ghost (for example, *Topper*) and only he can see it; here those "ghosts" can be seen by everyone. The opening theme is quite impressive (a mini version of a Broadway musical number) and the acting and production are just as good.

Episodes: *1.* Bittersweet. *2.* Going Under Covers. *3.* Damage Control. *4.* Brad-Cipation Proclamation. *5.* Back in the Saddle Again. *6.* Katezilla. *7.* One Plus None. *8.* Book Club. *9.* Take One for the Team. *10.* Fans' Fan. *11.* Breaking Up Is Hard to Do. *12.* Don't Call Us, We'll Call You. *13.* Feng Shui Away. *14.* The Rules. *15.* Better Than Therapy. *16.* New Beginnings.

677 Myles to Go. mylestogo.com. 2013.

Myles More Shoes is an "empire" run by two middle-aged brothers (Myles and The Kid, as he is called) from their mother's basement. What makes the company even more unique is that the stock consists of used running shoes. With the help of Grace, Myles' girlfriend (a science nerd) and Carla, their investor, the program charts their uphill battle to not only establish themselves, but become a profitable business.

Cast: Larry Hoffman (Myles), James D. Hopkin (The Kid), Shelley Mahon (Grace), Suzanna Cardellini (Carla), Teddy G. Alexander (Dr. Natron Diamond), Angy Stimson (Gladys), Michelle Warkentin as Rose), Tony Norman (Bruce), Barb Mitchell (Jenniver), Beau Barker (J.D.). **Credits:** *Producer:* Teddy G. Alexander, Shelley Mahon, Larry Hoffman. *Director:* Smita Acharyya. *Writer:* Larry Hoffman. **Comment:** The program has no formal introduction as it begins with the brothers already established in their basement business. While the acting and idea is good it falls flat by incorporating Dr. Diamond as an evangelist-like character who opens each episode with a spiritual-like message that seems to be nothing more than a time filler rather than an essential part of the stories.

Episodes: *1.* The Brotherhood. *2.* What You Pay For. *3.* Mightier Than the Sword. *4.* Piece of Mind. *5.* A Couple of Deep Breaths.

678 Naked in a Fishbowl. nakedinafishbowl.com. 2010.

The set is bare. There is no scripted dialogue. A basic plot outline is used and everything else is improvised. The setting is New York City and the relationship between six friends is showcased as they experience life—from dating to what the future holds.

Cast: Katharine Heller (Sara), Lauren Seikaly (Bonnie), Brenna Palughi (Sophie), Daliya Karnofsky (Chloe), Molly Knefel (Alice), Rachel Axelrod (Ruby), Lynne Rosenberg (Jean), D'Arcy Carden (Lucy), Valerie Smaldone (Kara), Joy Browne (Gay). **Credits:** *Producer:* Lauren Seikaly. *Director:* Hugh Sinclair, Erica Gould. **Comment:** "Life Improvised" is the program's tag line and it rises above some TV series that attempt the same thing (for example, *Whose Line Is It Anyway*) as a much truer perception of what can happen in life.

Season 1 Episodes: *1.* Now That's an Education. *2.* Good Mom/Bad Mom. *3.* Pride and Prejudice. *4.* Reconcilable Differences. *5.* Dog Day of Summer. *6.* Who's Your Daddy? *7.* Born to Run. *8.* Alice's Closet. *9.* Mistrust Fund. *10.* Picnic on the Wagon. *11.* Old Habits Die Hard. *12.* A Face for Radio.

Season 2 Episodes: *1.* The Treasured Chest. *2.* Into the Woods. *3.* Sudafed Up. *4.* Staying Abreast. *5.* Trick or Cheating. *6.* Can't Buy Me Love. *7.* Slumberless Party. *8.* S**t Happens. *9.* Ring in the Holidays. *10.* Do You Hear What I Hear. *11.* Super Santa.

Season 3 Episodes: *1.* Smooth Moves. *2.* Rolling Stones. *3.* Surprise. *4.* Blossom Barney Crystal Healer. *5.* Let's Talk About Sex. *6.* Let Them Eat Cake. *7.* Beach Bodies. *8.* Celebrity Apprentices. *9.* In Harmony. *10.* The Bold and the Bucious. *11.* Juvie Jen. *12.* The Scottish Play.

Season 4 Episodes: *1.* The Fringe Fantasy. *2.* Ruby's Revenge. *3.* Dude, Where's My Phone? *4.* Runaway Bridesmaids. *5.* The Quest for Zestra. *6.* My Man T.

679 The Nanny Interviews. webseries channel.com. 2013.

Brook, married to Brandon, is a young woman who has just become pregnant. While most women dream of raising their child, Brook also has that dream—but with the full time help of a nanny. But not just any nanny will do as Brook has a specific type in mind and the program chronicles her journey to find that one special nanny before the big day arrives.

Cast: Beth Shea (Brook), Jason Harris (Brandon), Pasquale Cassalia (The Manny), Georja Umano (Juanita), Seila Korsi (Maria). **Credits:** *Producer:* Nicole Sacker, Clea Frost, James Tuverson. *Director:* Nicole Sacker. *Writer:* Nicole Sacker, Lin Kwan. **Comment:** The program captures your attention from the very beginning and flows smoothly from episode to episode. Beth Shea is delightful as Brook and her efforts to find a nanny and the interviews that follow are quite amusing. Season 2 episodes are more of a prequel, showing how Brook and Brandon met, married and established housekeeping.

Season 1 Episodes: *1.* The First Interview. *2.* The Manny Interview. *3.* The Post Baby Shower Interview. *4.* The Marathon Interviews. *5.* The Nanny Fantasy. *6.* The Final Interview.

Season 2 Episodes: *1.* The Drop-Off. *2.* The Business Plan. *3.* Cocktails. *4.* Dirt. *5.* Brandon Meets Manny. *6.* The Real Asian Nanny.

680 *The Neighbors (2013).* onemorelesbian.com. 2013.

Samantha (called Sam) and Alex are straight girls and friends who find an ideal apartment but then discover it is a residence for gays only. In an attempt to keep the apartment they pretend to be lovers and the program, a spin off from *Roomies* (see entry) chronicles all the mishaps that occur as Sam and Alex try pull off a charade to keep their apartment. Tammy and Tami are their neighbors.

Cast: Julie Goldman (Sam), Brandy Howard (Alex), Kelly Beeman (Sally), Hannah Aubry (Tammy), Emily Peterson (Tami). Credits: *Producer-Director:* Christin Mell. *Writer:* Julie Keck, Jessica King. Comment: The program retains all the charm of the original series and although shades of the TV series *Bosom Buddies* can be seen, it is well acted and produced.

Episodes: *1.* The Thinnest Walls. *2.* The Laundry Room. *3.* Being the Baguette.

681 *Neighbors (2014).* youtube.com. 2014–2015.

Jackie is a young woman who has just moved into what she believes is a dream apartment. All is progressing well until she discovers she is surrounded by a group of eccentric (if not crazy) neighbors who do nothing but plaque her with their endless nonsense. The program follows Jackie as she tries to maintain her cool while dealing with people who are a bit out of touch with reality.

Cast: Jackie Jennings (Jackie). Credits: *Director:* Hayley Kosan. *Writer:* Jackie Jennings. Comment: It is just Jackie answering a knock at her door and dealing with a neighbor. It is well done and acted and really something different when it comes to annoying neighbors.

Episodes: *1.* Amber Alert. *2.* Offender. *3.* Keys. *4.* California. *5.* Salesman. *6.* Cat. *7.* Shower. *8.* FYI. *9.* The Vegan. *10.* Good Stuff.

682 *Neil's Puppet Dreams.* youtube.com. 2012–2013.

Neil Patrick Harris is an actor who, when asleep, dreams about puppets—puppets that are alive and representative of "people" he encounters in his daily life. Neil also has the "ability" to fall asleep anywhere at anytime and it is through those sudden sleep experiences that the viewer sees first hand what happens when one dreams of puppets. Neil lives with his life partner David Burtka and opens each episode with "Hi, I'm Neil. I sleep a lot and when I dream, I dream in puppet."

Cast: Neil Patrick Harris (Himself), David Burtka (Himself). *Voices:* David Massey, Colleen Smith, Allan Trautman, Donna Kimball, Nathan Danforth, Victor Yerrid, Brian Henson, Brian Clark, Spencer Liff, Mykell Wilson. *Drag Queens:* Willam Belli, Matthew Sanderson. Credits: *Producer:* Janet Varney, Neil Patrick Harris, Chris Hardwick, David Burtka. *Director:* Kirk R. Thatcher. *Writer:* David Burtka, Brian Clark, Neil Patrick Harris, Michael Serrato, Kirk R. Thatcher, Janet Varney. Comment: The program is produced in association with Muppet creator Jim Henson's company "Alternative Henson." It is a television quality production with excellent writing and acting.

Episodes: *1.* The Lullabye. *2.* Doctor's Office. *3.* The Restaurant. *4.* To Catch a Puppeteer. *5.* Dream Bump. *6.* Alien Abduction. *7.* Bollywood.

683 *Never Ever Land.* webserieschannel.com. 2015.

Zoey is a 17-year-old starry-eyed girl who has been conditioned by her mother (Claire) to become a big Hollywood star. It has to be assumed Zoey has graduated from high school as she and Claire have left their home in Detroit to pursue their goals in Hollywood after a regional casting director saw potential in Zoey. While Claire appears to be more enthused than Zoey over the move, they soon realize that stardom is not handed to them and one must earn it. To sustain themselves, they open a children's birthday party business and the program relates Claire's continual efforts to make Zoey a star in what turns out to be crushed dreams in Never Ever Land.

Cast: Jennifer Levinson (Zoey Simone), Marisa O'Brien (Claire Simone), Chris Game (Ricky Dismer). Credits: *Producer:* Steven Kanter, Jennifer Levinson. *Writer-Director:* Steven Kanter. Comment: The program is well acted and produced but site information differs from actual episode information. It is clearly established in the first episode that Zoey is 17 and she and Claire have just arrived in Hollywood (site information states Zoey is 14 and has been in Hollywood for two years). It is also leads you to believe that Chloe has had no auditions, although she does audition for a commercial in the first episode.

Episodes: *1.* Welcome to Hollywood. *2.* The Audition. *3.* The Worst Audition Ever.

684 *The New Adventures of Peter and Wendy*. newpeterandwendy.com. 2014–2015.

An adaptation of the J.M. Barrie story *Peter and Wendy*. Never Land is a small town in Ohio where Peter Pan, the boy who never wants to grow up, is now in his twenties and still determined to remain a boy for as long as he can (although he is a slacker he does work as an illustrator). Wendy Darling, the girl with whom Peter shared adventures in a fantasy Never Land battling evil pirates, is now a vlog advice columnist and a girl who did grow up. Peter and Wendy are also friends whose relationship has blossomed into a romance. Hindering that romance is Peter and his refusal to face the reality of the world in which he lives. The program follows what happens as two worlds collide with Peter struggling to remain who he is and Wendy seeking to make him face reality.

Cast: Paula Rhodes (Wendy Darling), Kyle Walters (Peter Pan), Brennan Murray (Michael Darling), Graham Kurtz (John Darling), Lovlee Carroll (Lily Bagha), Jim Beaver (George Darling). **Credits:** *Producer:* Shawn DeLoache, Adam Laupus, Jenni Powell. *Director:* Matthew Breault. *Writer:* Shawn DeLoache. **Comment:** Unfortunately, and for reasons that are not stated (perhaps copyright infringement) all episodes, with the exception of a Kickstarter campaign video, have been taken off line. The video is simply the producer asking for financial support and providing any further comment is not possible.

Season 1 Episodes: *1.* Prologue. *2.* Growing Up. *3.* Fudgeopolis. *4.* The Bossman Cometh. *5.* Git 'Er Done. *6.* Pre-Game. *7.* Post-Game. *8.* Never Land Hath No Fury. *9.* Rejected. *10.* Drag Racing. *11.* When I Grow Up. *12.* The Hits Keep Coming. *13.* Fear and Loathing in Never Land. *14.* No Fly Zone. *15.* Boys Are Stupid. *16.* Never Trust a Fairy. *17.* Forgot Is Such a Strong Word. *18.* Gift of the Pan-Gi. *19.* Torn. *20.* Boom Goes the Dynamite. *21.* No More Secrets. *22.* Lost Boy. *23.* Lost Girl. *24.* The Question. *25.* To Grow Up or Not to Grow Up.

Season 2 Episodes: *1.* The Wendy City. *2.* Life Goes On. *3.* Mad Women. *4.* P-4. *5.* Chronicle. *6.* Date Night. *7.* Just Like Dad. *8.* Homeward Bound. *9.* Hooked. *10,11.* Wow.... This Is Awkward. *12.* House of Cards. *13.* The Times They Are a Changin' *14.* Hearing vs. Listening. *15.* Bully. *16.* Daddy's Girl. *17.* The Lost Boys. *18.* Darlings. *19.* Give Peace a Chance. *20.* Double Date. *21.* Knocked Out. *22.* We're The Fairy Best of Friends. *23.* Rise and Fall. *24.* Gentlemen Callers. *25.* Father and Son. *26.* The Tiger and the Bear. *27.* He's the Pan with a Plan. *28.* Three Words.

685 *New VHS*. webserieschannel.com. 2012.

Digital recording has replaced the analog recording abilities of VHS (and the even earlier Beta recording system). Although some still encompass VHS (just like some people prefer vinyl records over CDs for music) it is virtually an element of a bygone era (late 1970s through the mid 1990s). Using VHS recording techniques, a collection of comedy shorts are presented along with all the problems encountered by people who used such equipment (such as sometimes poor video quality, glitches [steaks or silver like interference] and color rainbows resulting from editing).

Cast: Hudson Rhotenberry, Mickey Vantaggi, Pete Clendening, Jordan Paul Miles, Kevin R. Wright, Spencer Starnes. **Comment:** Although the problems with VHS are somewhat exaggerated it is a well done reminder to anyone who had a home VHS recorder and the problems that did exist (including tape wrinkling when the cassette was not properly loaded).

Episodes: *1.* Unbearable: The Last Urban Kodiak. *2.* Mime Brother and Me. *3.* The Unaired Pilot of "Valley Boys High." *4.* Come to Philadelphia!

686 *Next Time on Lonny*. maker.tv. 2011–2014.

Lonny is a young man that appears to have problems that most young men face—from dealing with the opposite sex to just navigating everyday life. But unlike virtually everyone else, Lonny's life is presented first as a pleasant blog wherein he relates certain aspects about his life then in a nightmarish situation where he must extricate himself in order to survive (anything from dealing with a crazed friend to an invasion from space). Several short segments are presented in each episode with an announcer relating things like "Next Time on Lonny" to "Now Back to Lonny" as a means of integrating the segments.

Cast: Alex Anfanger (Lonny), Aaron Schroeder (Garrett), Lannon Killea (Gustav), Anna Greenfield (Bethany), Jessica Rothe (Stephanie), Nick Kocher (Chet), Beck Bennett (Eddie Velour). **Credits:** *Producer:* Alex Anfanger, Dan Schimpf, Stuart Cornfeld, Deborah Liebling, Michael J. Rosentein, Ben Stiller. *Director:* Dan Schimpf. *Writer:* Alex Anfanger, Dan Schimpf. **Comment:** Although first season episodes are set in Brooklyn, New York, and the second in Los Angeles, the quirky format is carried through and makes for a most unusual program with good acting, stories and production values.

Season 1 Episodes: *1.* Lonny's Next Step. *2.* Lonny's Disastrous First Date. *3.* Lonny Goes Big Time. *4.* Lonny Jerks Off. *5.* Lonny Throws a Bachelor Party. *6.* Lonny Gets Revenge.

Season 2 Episodes: *1.* Welcome Back, Lonny. *2.* In Lonny We Trust. *3.* Lonny, the Dog Whisperer. *4.* Lonny Is Famous. *5.* Lonny's Best Friend. *6.* Lonny Brings Peace. *7.* The Lonny Experiment. *8.* Choose Your Own Lonny. *9.* Lonny Goes for Broke. *10.* The End of Lonny.

687 The Nextnik. webserieschannel.com. 2012.

After twenty-five years at the same management job Larry Zimmerman is abruptly fired. The dismissal came as quite a surprise and Larry is, for the first time in his life, without a job. Realizing that he will never get a similar job, he decides to start from scratch and explore his personal growth and professional career opportunities. Emma, his girlfriend, doesn't understand his reasoning and questions why he doesn't use his abilities and experiences to search for a job suited to him; Mark, his best friend, is all for what Larry has chosen to do and has set his goal to help him find what Larry calls his "Nextnik." The program explores all the pitfalls Larry encounters as he seeks to find that one job that will set the course for the rest of his life.

Cast: Rick Kain (Larry Zimmerman), Connie Bowman (Emma), Paul Fahrenkopf (Mark), Allison Howard (Kim Zimmerman), Janice Gallant (Ann), Emily Morrison (Julie). **Credits:** *Producer:* Mike Kravinsky, Liza Kravinsky. *Writer-Director:* Mike Kravinsky. **Comment:** With all episodes off line, a comment is not possible.

Episodes: *1.* Out of the Blue. *2.* Tambourine Man. *3.* The Search Begins. *4.* Spill the Wine, Take That Pearl.

688 Nice Girls Crew. nicegirlscrew.tumblr.com. 2012.

Sophie, Leena and Geraldine, best friends since second grade and now living in Los Angeles, decide to diversify their lives by starting a book club called the Nice Girls Crew. Their interests range from vampires to teddy bears and the program follows what happens at each of the meetings where discussing the actual book in question leads to more thought-provoking conversations.

Cast: Lynn Chen (Sophie), Sheetal Sheth (Leena), Michelle Krusiec (Geraldine), Leonardo Nam (Donatello), Tsai Chin (Geraldine's mother). **Credits:** *Producer:* Brenda Alvarez, Lynn Chen, Michelle Krusiec, Krystel Gapasin, Donald Young. *Director:* Christine Kwon. *Writer:* Christine Kwon, Tanuj Chopra. **Comment:** Charming Asian-American program with a like-able cast, good acting, writing and production values.

Season 1 Episodes: *1.* Out of Order. *2.* Count Chocula of Venice Beach. *3.* The Bryonic Hero. *4.* Hoot 'n' Holla. *5.* Cattle in the Sky.

Season 2 Episodes: *1.* Sisterhood of the Traveling Fat Pants. *2.* The Reluctant Mixologist. *3.* Game Day. *4.* The Talented Geraldiney. *5.* Sophie and the Giant Buttcake.

689 Nigel & Victoria. webserieschannel. com. 2010.

The program is billed as "An Unromantic Comedy" that follows the awkward relationship between a marketing executive (Nigel) and a gorgeous Dutch film actress (Victoria). It all begins when Nigel is assigned to produce a series of films for the technology products produced by his company (Phillips) and meets Victoria, "a super bright, independently minded, gadget-crazy" Dutch actress. As Nigel and Victoria, who is in essence the product tester for the films, get to know each other a romance slowly develops and the program follows the unlikely match-up as Nigel attempts to not only do his job but impress Victoria and win her love.

Cast: Ben Willbond (Nigel), Victoria Koblenko (Victoria). **Comment:** Very well acted and produced program that appears to have had a second season of episodes that were planned but apparently not produced as only a promotional video for it appears on line.

Episodes: *1.* Boyfriend? *2.* It's My Film. *3.* Subdued. *4.* Cup of Ti... (Nigel sees Victoria topless). *5.* Hello, I'm Nigel Williams. *6.* Would You Have Dinner with Me? *7.* Get a Room. *8.* The Departure.

690 Night of Reality: The Web Series. youtube.com. 2014.

Marcus is a hopeful actor who believes that he can be catapulted to fame by appearing on the reality TV series *Who Wants to Be a Celebrity?* With his acceptance on the series and the taping completed, Marcus invites his best friends over to watch the first episode as it airs. What Marcus hadn't expected was to see all his embarrassing antics as well as his infidelities as he hit on his female co-stars. The program takes place in one night and depicts Marcus's efforts to cover up what he did, especially from his girlfriend (Leanna) by distracting them as best he can.

Cast: Brad Bukauskas (Marcus), Lindsay Beeman (Leanna), Jocelyn Cruz (Zoe), Ron Drynan (Dereck), Katie Sherrer (Cici), Amy Amir (B.J.), Tabitha Marsden (Cthulu), Tamara Perry (Lee Lee) Owen Edinger (Reality Show Host). **Credits:** *Producer:* Amy Amir, Owen Edinger. *Director:* Lucas Bessey. *Writer:* Owen Edinger. **Comment:** The program begins with Marcus introducing himself and his roommate (Dereck) and what has happened to change his life (his appearance on the reality show). He is all excited as the show is about to premiere and from that point it because a night of horrors for Marcus as all his antics have been recorded and now made public. The idea is good and is coupled with good acting and production values.

Episodes: 4 untitled episodes, labeled "Episode 1" through "Episode 4."

691 No Answer. youtube.com. 2013.

StatNation is a marketing research company that compiles statistics on whatever a client requires. It's a boring, underpaid job; has a policy that states

"Employees are not to think" and it requires employees to ask personal questions of complete strangers. Three men and "one token woman" are the featured players (none of whom are given a name) and through their experiences, a view of work life is presented that has them questioning their own reality.

Cast: Amélie Onzon, Carlo Slats, Eryc Why, Robert Alexander. **Credits:** *Producer:* Nicola Bozzi, Catalina Iorga. *Director:* Nicola Bozzi, Francesco Greco. *Writer:* Nicola Bozzi, Francesco Greco, Marco Gagliardi, Paul Russell. **Comment:** It is unusual for performers not to have character names but it does happen here. The program is set in a badly painted yellowish-like room where the four regulars conduct their telemarketing. It is simply their exchange of conversation and brief snippets of calls they make (with Amelie Onzon, "the token female," who possesses a British or Australian accent [hard to tell] being the most appealing. If you listen carefully to the names she gives, they all come from TV series—like Rachel Green [*Friends*] and Buffy Summers [*Buffy the Vampire Slayer*]).

Episodes: *1.* Your Time Is Our Gold Mine. *2.* Life in StatNation. *3.* The Bar. *4.* Fear and Regrets. *5.* Dreaming It Through.

692 *No Class.* webserieschannel.com. 2012.

Four close friends (Paul, Dan, Spoons and Ed) and how, by pretending to be something they are not, deal with life—and all its problems, from earning a living to impressing girls. Dan lies about having a special needs brother to impress girls; Spoons is addicted to gambling and constantly in need of money; Paul pretends to date his "hot" cousin to make girls jealous; Ed has no ambition or drive and is struggling not to flunk out of college.

Cast: Drew Martin, Richard Conlen, Jake Watson, J.B. Twomey. **Comment:** All episodes have been taken off line and an evaluation is not possible.

Episodes: *1.* The Car Problem. *2.* The Special Little Brother. *3.* The Borrowing. *4.* The Cousin. *5.* The Party.

693 *No Method.* nomethodseries.com. 2013.

No one ever said Hollywood is an easy nut to crack; it is quite the opposite and for one young, twenty-something actress (Caitlin Graham) it has become a tough nut to crack. Although she is enthusiastic, full of determination and likes to have things go her way, Caitlin has found that she needs to pay her dues and the program charts how she copes with everything that surrounds her—from over-bearing parents, friends who try to help and the acting roles she acquires (Caitlin mentions she is currently working on a theater production of Lanford Wilson's *Fifth of July*).

Cast: Caitlin Graham (Herself), Isabelle Pierre

(Greer), Jackie Rivera (Jackie), Mike Indelgio (Riley), Hannah Abney (Jewel), Julia Kwamya (Adele), Sheira Feuerstein (Kristin), Garrett Paknis (Dan). **Credits:** *Director:* Caitlin Graham, Sara Zuniss. *Writer:* Caitlin Graham. **Comment:** A touch of narration by Caitlin adds just the right touch to make a well acted and produced series even the more pleasing to watch.

Episodes: *1.* The Roach. *2.* The Musician.

694 *No Strings, Please.* nostringsplease. com. 2013.

Charley Parker ("that's Charley with a 'y' and not 'ie,'" she says) is a young woman who likes to break the rules to make her own rules. She lives in Brooklyn, New York, but feels the time has come for her to leave home and start her own life (or as she says, "search for myself"). She begins by moving to Washington, D.C., where she takes up residence with her friend from college (Megan) and acquires a job as an analyst. The events that spark Charley's life as she seeks to discover who she really is and what her destination in life is are chronicled.

Cast: Naima Ramos-Chapman (Charley Parker), Ann Turino (Megan), Clayton LeBouef (Dr. James Riley), Pei Pei Lin (Kit), Dennis Blackmen (Sean Cook). **Credits:** *Producer:* Gemal Woods, Dawn Hall. *Writer-Director:* Gemal Woods. **Comment:** Charley is a young African-American woman who is not stereotyped as a foul-mouthed, sex hungry bitch (as had been done in other Internet series). She is well educated, very pretty and dedicated to a single goal. The acting and production values are very good and the program enjoyable.

Episodes: *1.* Goodbye Brooklyn. *2.* Welcome to D.C. *3.* Connections. *4.* Never Judge a Book. *5.* My Effin Job. *6.* Criminal Contemplation. *7.* Brooklyn Keeps Takin' It. *8.* Beautiful Crutch. *9.* Things Are Looking Up. *10.* The Case for the Case.

695 *No Way.* webserieschannel.com. 2014.

Anne is a young International Student (as she is called) who has just arrived in Tromso (Norway) to begin classes at University. She has reunited with Sophie, her best friend from childhood, who is also attending the same school. Although Anne is Norwegian, she has left the comfort of her hometown and now appears a bit unsure of herself and exactly where she is heading. As Anne begins classes the program chronicles her experiences as she seeks to find her place in the world.

Cast: Hanca Spickova (Anne), Irina Emalianova (Sophie), Lila Gleizes (Mia), Florian Lebret (Alan), Mat Mot (Rob). **Credits:** *Writer-Director:* Mat Mot. **Comment:** Norwegian produced series that was made with (as stated in the opening) no budget and no professional equipment. It also asks that for a better understanding to switch on the sub-titles.

Although the actors speak in English, accents take a few seconds to adjust to and the sub-titles are really not needed. For a no budget show it is very well acted and produced and Hanca Spickova is simply delightful as Anne.

Episodes: 5 untitled episodes, labeled "Episode 1" through "Episode 5."

696 *Non-Essential Personnel.* vimeo.com. 2010.

Mercury Systems is a private defense contractor located in Portland, Oregon. It does for the people what the government can not do—provide corporate solutions to military problems. It has also instituted a new rule: "All non-essential personnel have been opted into a mandatory twelve per-cent pay cut—the full amount of which will go directly toward additional training and combat material for our international security teams (to help reinvent democracy)." The company's employees, especially non-essential document specialist Jonathan Clark are non-too happy as a choice was made for them without their approval. As Jonathan continues working his lone cubicle but resenting what has happened, the program follows the plan Jonathan creates to strike back for the injustice he has experienced.

Cast: Joe Ballman, Stephen Lisk, Alicia Tolman, Leif Norby, Jim Craig, Melissa Kaiser, Chris A. Bolton. Credits: *Producer:* Matt Knapp, Joe Ballman. *Writer-Director:* Matt Knapp. Comment: Like so many other comedy series that use vulgar language when it does nothing to enhance the comedy, *Non-Essential Personnel* does the same needless thing (it also encompasses the annoying habit of not matching performers with their characters). That aside, the idea is rather intriguing with good acting and production values.

Episodes: *1.* Corporate Solutions. *2.* The Why Documents. *3.* Leaks. *4.* Military Problems. *5.* TBA.

697 *Non-Union.* youtube.com. 2010.

Detroit provides the backdrop for a look at two struggling actors (Will and Corey) and how they attempt to maintain full time jobs while encountering all the pitfalls of the area's independent film industry.

Cast: Alex Bozinovic (Will), Brandon Bautista (Corey). Credits: *Producer-Writer:* Alex Bozinovic, Brandon Bautista. Comment: Detroit is not depicted as a buzzing film community but filmmakers have begun to take advantage of it and Will and Corey must seize upon every opportunity to become a part of it. It is well acted and produced and a somewhat different approach to the plight of struggling actors.

Episodes: *1.* Brody Evans' Acting Secrets. *2.* Getting a "B." *3.* Action. *4.* Just Cos. *5.* Corey's Christmas Card. *6.* IMDb Pros. *7.* The Flys. *8.* The Boof. *9.* American Bad Acts. *10.* The Scrooge.

698 *Not!* notshow.net. 2011–2012.

A couple, a date and what happens before, during and after that date. Using the anthology style of presentation (different stories and casts) *Not!* is exactly that—what not to do or expect on a first date. Each story explores, from the male and female perspective, how they hook up with one another and how if it looks too good to be true it probably is (for example, on-line profile pictures that are faked; sexy girls who reveal more than you want to hear; people plagued by bad advice and people with weird sexual desires).

Cast: Liv von Oelreich, Randy Tobin, Griffin Kohout, Jackie Koppell, Nandini Iyer Donovan, Marco Infante, Annie Bakke, Cristina Sasso, AJ Gentile, Ralph Lopez, Katie Rich, Ron Lehmann, Kathy Goral, Greg Roudebush, Mary Ann Biewener, Ellen Clifford, Jim Hayes, Daryl Kane, Derrick Tuggle. Credits: *Writer-Director:* Tim Devitt. Comment: The program is quite adult in nature (sexual situations) although no parental warning is given. There are eight different stories and casts and each is well acted and produced.

Episodes: *1.* Trevor & Heidi & Roger & Sam. *2.* Head Department. *3.* Big Mitch. *4.* Body Fat. *5.* Shannon's Late. *6.* Over Her. *7.* Flash. *8.* Parental Units.

699 *Not by Choice.* youtube.com. 2012–2013.

Dave Choice is a cable technician whose life is suddenly thrown into turmoil when his company folds and he finds himself without a job in a tough economy. As Dave searches for a job a window of opportunity opens when the Dolla Company offers him a position as a cable installer. Dave is reluctant to take the job as the company is unethical but does so when he realizes he must support his family: his fiancée Angie and their children Dallas and Diego. Life again changes for Dave when Angie acquires a higher-paying job with the police department and Dave feels he must be the bread winner, not Angie. Although the Dolla Company insists it is not selling illegal cable but "black market cable," Dave takes the job and the program relates Dave's experiences as an illegal cable installer while seeking another job that will earn him more money than Angie.

Cast: Dave Lewis (Dave Choice), Lorren Cotton (Angela), Sasha Matthews (Dallas), Rashard Hunter (Diego), Solomon Hoilett (Dolla Stacks), Pentene' Monique (Niecy), Deon Sams (Issac), Courtney Richards (Trent), Glenn Davis (Grady), Wilma Morris (Grandma Verna). Credits: *Producer:* Brandon Kyle, Pentene' Monique Woolen. *Director:* Brandon Kyle. *Writer:* Brandon Kyle, Eric Montgomery, Redd Kaiman. Comment: The program honestly depicts how difficult acquiring jobs are in a hard economy and what some people will do when a job opportunity comes along. The program depicts an African-American protagonist in a positive light with good acting and production values.

Episodes: *1.* Pilot. *2.* A Technical Difficulty. *3.* A Wire Made for Tapping. *4.* A Law Not Abiding Technician. *5.* A Technical Malfunction. *6.* A Too Warm Welcome.

700 Not Looking. funnyordie.com. 2014.

Parker, a gay young man living in Los Angeles for the past three years, has accomplished nothing that is worth talking about and feels his life is just unrewarding. His gay friends, Colby, Danton, Shayne and Rodrigo all seem to be progressing well in the dating game and Parker believes he should stop looking for Mr. Right and just settle into the life he is now leading. The program, a spoof of the HBO series *Looking,* follows events in the lives of the friends, especially Parker when a girl enters his life (Tina) and gives him a new outlook to seek that perfect man.

Cast: Jason Looney (Parker), Justin Martindale (Colby), Jeremy Shane (Shayne), Drew Droege (Danton), Jai Rodriquez (Rodrigo), Jes Dugger (Tina). **Credits:** *Producer:* Jason Looney, Karen Liff, Jon Robert. *Director:* Jason Looney. *Writer:* Jason Looney, Drew Droege, Justin Martindale, Jeremy Shane. **Comment:** Simple, non-offensive tale of five gay friends with good acting and production values. There is nothing offensive and the program flows smoothly from beginning to end.

Episodes: 5 untitled episodes, labeled "Episode 1" through "Episode 5."

701 Not My Department. webserieschannel.com. 2012.

John and Lou manage Floor 5 of Wycotes Industries. Jen is the girl that works for them but longs for something more than just a gopher-like position. To make matters worse, John and Lou are not only inept, but childish, treat Jen like dirt and get their kicks by constantly teasing her. The program relates the antics of the inept bosses as Jen seeks to contend with them while at the same time improve her position within the company.

Cast: Victoria Youngman (Jen), Johnny Whiting (John), Louis Coates (Lou), David Durie (Creepy Simon), Richard Glenn (Mr. Wycotes), John Youngman (Himself). **Credits:** *Producer-Director:* Victoria Youngman. *Writer:* Victoria Youngman, Harry Huddart. **Comment:** Embarrassing program that makes you cringe when you see how unbelievable John and Louis act (not only child-like but people who literally belong in a mental institution). Jen, who is very pretty and bright, is also made to look like a fool for putting up with what she does. She has all the ammunition necessary for a sexual harassment suit but fails to go to HR (Human Resources) and report anything. Work place comedies are a

dime a dozen and for one to succeed it must have a gimmick. *Not My Department* does have its own unique gimmick but it is so absurd that it borders on "what were they thinking when they made this."

Episodes: *1.* Pilot. *2.* Lou's Birthday. *3.* Finale.

702 Not Quite Fabulous. youtube.com. 2013.

Victoria, Maggie, Holly, Alexa and Dalton are the subjects of the title, young women who work behind-the-scenes in the Hollywood film industry. Although only classified as assistants they feel it is the first step in that long climb to the top and the program charts not only their struggles and mishaps on and off the job, but their efforts to figure out their own lives and if what they are doing is the right career choice.

Cast: Margaux Mireault (Holly), Courtney Stewart (Victoria), Danielle Argyros (Maggie), Shannon Stacey (Dalton), Kim Cooper (Alexa). **Credits:** *Producer:* Danielle Argyros, Kim Cooper, Margaux Mireault, Courtney Stewart. *Director:* Danielle Argyros. *Writer:* Danielle Argyros. Kim Cooper, Margaux Mireault, Shannon Stacey, Courtney Stewart. **Comment:** With the exception of the second episode and a short teaser all episodes have been taken off line. Judging by the available episode, the program appears to be quite humorous, well acted and produced.

Episodes: *1.* #Pilot. *2.* #Are You Okay? *3.* #Baby Love. *4.* #PMS. *5.* #Is This Seat Taken? *6.* #Preggo. *7.* #That's a Wrap.

703 Not So Super. webserieschannel.com. 2012.

Prime City is now a decent community in which to live. But it wasn't always so as it was overrun with criminal activity. It took the courage of one man (Vince, called Hero), seeking a place to settle down, to change all that and rid the city of evil. But that was fifteen years ago. Vince is married (to Genevieve) and the father of Hannah and now a middle-aged super hero. But being a super hero did have its benefits (fame) but it also has its faults: he is now struggling to make ends meet and feels he has lost his purpose in life as Prime City no longer needs his services. As life for Vince further spirals downward, a glimmer of hope appears when criminal activity again surfaces but does Vince have the ambition to once again become a hero? The program follows Vince as he contemplates what to do—sit back do nothing and complain about the misery that surrounds him or get back in shape and save Prime City from the dark forces that will soon destroy it.

Cast: Christophor Rick (Vince Ible/Hero), Rob Mass (Ben/Scandal), Trish Hundhausen (Genevieve Ible), Hannah Schmidt (Hannah Ible), Taylor Klaustermeier (Odile), Tommy Balistreri (Archon Anders). **Credits:** *Producer:* Christophor Rick, Jeff

Garbarck. *Writer-Director:* Christophor Rick. **Comment:** Interesting twist on the super hero genre focusing instead on what happens to a super hero when he has done his duty and feels he is no longer useful.

Episodes: *1.* Pilot.

704 *Not the Sharpest Crayon.* notthesharp estcrayon.com. 2011.

Robyn is pretty, brunette, slightly overweight and has a noticeable New York Jewish accent; Nicole is blonde, beautiful and witty and Robyn's best friend. Life appears to go well for Nicole but for Robyn, it is a different story—if something can go wrong it will go wrong for her. The women are roommates and live on Long Island (in New York) and stories explore the situations the friends, both unemployed, encounter, especially Robyn, as she reacts to what happens around her.

Cast: Robyn Schall (Robyn), Licia Zegar (Nicole). **Credits:** *Producer-Director:* Richard Schall, Robyn Schall. *Writer:* Robyn Schall. **Comment:** Enjoyable program that is well acted and produced. The leads are perfectly cast and make for a perfect "Odd Couple"-like combination. Each season of episodes has a color distinction and that color needs to be activated to watch the episodes on its website.

Season 1 "Pink" Episodes: *1.* Jewish Jeremy. *2.* Loose Lips. *3.* Big Booty. *4.* Fat Frank. *5.* Second Rate Star. *6.* Wacky X Wedding.

Season 2 "Blue" Episodes: *1.* F***ing Fatty. *2.* Life Lessons. *3.* Scamming the Stupid. *4.* Deaf Dave. *5.* My Mother's Mistakes. *6.* Driving Mr. Daddy.

705 *Nut House.* blip.tv. 2014.

A half-way house (a stopover between a hospital and the real world) for the mentally insane provides the setting. It is here that a caretaker (Bobby) and two patients (Robert and Jeremy) have become friends with the program charting all the mishaps that occur as Bobby tries to help Robert overcome his penchant for stealing and Jeremy, a fragile soul, face the world.

Cast: Alec Balas (Robert and Bobby), Chris Smith (Jeremy). **Credits:** *Producer-Writer:* Alec Balas, Chris Smith. **Comment:** Feature films and TV series have tackled the same topic, both in serious and comic lights. *Nut House* is more of a dark comedy (with few humorous moments) and often just plain depressing. Whatever appeared on paper as being funny just didn't translate well to film.

Season 1 Episodes: *1.* The Thief. *2.* The Intruder. *3.* The Prank War. *4.* The Ghost. *5.* The Explosion. *6.* The Doctor. *7.* The Plan. *8.* The Treasure Map.

Season 2 Episodes: *1.* Tax Man. *2.* Gifts All Around. *3.* Prince's Palace.

706 *Nwar Mysteries.* webserieschannel. com. 2014–2015.

Nwar, as he is called, is a private detective with no friends and a somewhat miserable life. He yearns for the days of yore when crime was a bit more prevalent and solving them kept him busy. While he now spends most of his time sulking, a bright light often enters his life when a case comes his way. The program charts, through black and white animation and Nwar's narration, the cases he acquires and how he (and his sometimes partner Blanche) solve crimes.

Cast: Dan Markowitz (Narrator). **Credits:** Producer-Writer-Animator: Dan Markowitz. **Comment:** Intriguing animated gem that uses almost still-like animation coupled with narration to tell stories. The stories are good and the program enjoyable to watch.

Episodes: *1.* Graveyard Shift. *2.* High Stakes. *3.* String Theory. *4.* Match Point. *5.* Loose Cannon. *6.* Watered Down. *7.* Heist Ashes. *8.* Speed Demons. *9.* Total Reboot. *10.* Vision Quest. *11.* Trench Warfare. *12.* Dirty Dozen.

707 *NYC Glitters.* youtube.com. 2011.

Feeling that his life in Philadelphia is just too depressing, a young gay man (Joe) impulsively decides to leave and heads for Manhattan to start over. When the series begins Joe has since made several friends (gays Steven and Josh; and Taylor and her boyfriend, Michael) and the program charts their experiences as they seek to fulfill their hearts desires, especially focusing on Joe "as my real adventures begin."

Cast: Joe Harris (Joe), Sarah Pribis (Taylor), David McEniry (Seth), Kevin Beckett (Josh), Graham Halstead (Steven), Christof Lombard (Marcus). **Credits:** *Producer-Writer-Director:* Joe Harris. **Comment:** Only a pilot film has been produced and it is not only well acted and produced but cleverly written (has a nice witty touch to it). While nothing major has been established (like what the friends do for a living or how they met) the doorway is left open for that and many other issues to be addressed should the program continue (it is hinted that Taylor is a dancer and Josh is pursuing a musical career).

Episodes: *1.* Pilot: Deal Breakers.

708 *O-Cast.* youtube.com. 2009.

After 1600 years of taking a backseat to life in the modern-day world, 12 gods of Greek Mythology decide to change their lives for the better and live in the 21st century. They begin by renting (and sharing a New York City apartment "with only one bathroom") and, appearing as twenty-somethings, begin their own Olympian telecasts ("The O-Cast") to convince mortals of their modern relevance and save themselves from extinction.

Cast: Leah Johnston (Athena, Goddess of Wisdom), Kate Kuen (Hera, Queen of the Gods), Jon Riddleberger (Poseidon, God of the Seas), Peter Coleman (Hades, God of the Underworld), Andrews Landsman (Zeus, King of the Gods), Anne Richmond (Hestia, Goddess of the Hearth), Melissa Klein (Demeter, Goddess of Nature), Heather Parcells (Aphrodite, Goddess of Love), Alex Goode (Ares, God of War), Preston Martin (Apollo, God of the Sun), Arielle Hader (Artemis, Goddess of the Hunt), Tim Reinhart (Hephaestus, God of Metal Working). **Credits:** *Producer-Writer:* Anne Richmond, Bryan Dechart. *Director:* Bryan Dechart. **Comment:** Programs dealing with the ancient gods, whether Greek or Roman, have appeared in movies and on television with a fair amount of success. Taking the ancient gods and placing them in modern times has been done before, but not in the manner as portrayed here (especially with making Zeus an alcoholic). The broadcasting twist adds a nice pace to a well-acted and produced series.

Episodes: *1.* Meet the Olympians. *2.* Speed Dating. *3.* Derailed. *4.* Occupational Hazards. *5.* The 13th Wheel. *6.* The Pledge.

709 Octane Pistols of Fury. octanepistols.com. 2011.

A spoof of the motion picture *The Maltese Falcon.* There is a priceless and mysterious porcelain Buddha that has been stolen and its owner, a crime boss (Mr. Johnson), wants it back. His thugs, Vinny and Rufus are hot on the trail, but also are rival gang members who want it. The principal focus is on Vinny and Rufus and it is best if Vinny explains their plan: "First we go to see The Russian. He lets us see Fat Ronnie. Fat Ronnie knows where to find Buzzsaw Magee. His good buddy is Gerry the Gigolo. A client of his is Betty Hotsauce whose landlord is Filthy Paddy. His cousin is the Dirty Irishman and he can get us the number of one Jimmy Pancakes who knows where the porcelain Buddha is."

Cast: Andrew Pifko (Vinny), Greg Stees (Rufus), Chris Pine (The Russian), Aldous Davidson (Fat Ronnie), Trevor Williams (Jimmy Pancakes), Jennifer Rubins (Betty Hotsauce), Jeremy Westphal (Dirty Irishman), Tom Silverstro (Buzzsaw McGee), Jon Higgins (Gerry the Gigolo), Stefanie Grassley (Tina Turnpike), Juan Crouch (Cuban Rodriquez), Mitch Magee (Mr. Johnson), Charles Jeffreys (Filthy Paddy), Dan Schimpf (Wise Tommy), Rachel Laforest (Mystery Woman). **Credits:** *Producer-Writer-Director:* Chris Pine, Greg Stees. **Comment:** With a parade of colorful characters and the feel it has for being like a gangster movie, the program is an enjoyable romp as two dim-wits seek the Buddha. There is some foul language but overall the acting and production are good.

Episodes: *1.* Turnpike. *2.* Fat Ronnie. *3.* The Russian. *4.* Vinny and Rufus.

710 Odd Ducks. webserieschannel.com. 2013.

Five friends gather each week at a diner and their random exchange of conversation as they discuss what happened since their last meeting forms the basis of each episode. The friends are Howard (lists occupation as "Geek"), Dwight (professional trainer), Helen (family counselor), Paige (writer/actress) and Bernard (the diner owner).

Cast: George Zanta (Howard), Daniel Snyder (Dwight), Candace Goodheart (Helen), Victoria White (Paige), Kenny Rogers (Bernard). **Credits:** *Producer-Writer-Director:* Kenny Rogers. **Comment:** A good cast (interact well with each other), a good story and very good production values. While the idea is not totally original (the movie and TV series *Diner* will come to mind) it is different for its diverse choice of characters. The Kenny Rogers listed above is not the famous country and western performer, but a young African-American filmmaker.

Episodes: *1–3.* Odd Ducks.

711 Off-Awful. offawful.com. 2014.

Revenge of the Nerds: First Blood is literally an Off-Off-Broadway play that has its roots in other such distant from Broadway plays as *A Streetcar Named Wanda* and *Mars Attacks Cats.* But to Sarah Jane Sutton it is her dream job as she seeks that actual Broadway spotlight. The program chronicles Sarah Jane's experience in a world where far from Broadway is just that—far away with less superior plays, actors and directors.

Cast: Sarah Jane Marek (Sarah Jane Sutton), Leah Dashe (Leah), Anthony Mead (Bad Director), Christina Roman (Crystal), Marek Sapievski (George), Alex Dunbar (Jeff), Tiffany Sims (Starla), Katie Sullivan (Jessica). **Credits:** *Producer:* Sarah Jane Marek, Leah Dashe, Adam Tullis. *Writer-Director:* Leah Dashe. **Comment:** There have been programs about Broadway and even Off-Broadway but few have combined far Off Broadway with bad play ideas. The acting and production is good and the program interesting to watch.

Episodes: *1.* Pilot. *2.* Agent Night. *3.* Head Shots. *4.* Mob Apartment. *5.* Cocktail Hour.

712 Off Her Meds. youtube.com. 2014.

Jade and Shannon (referred to "Gutta" and "Yutta") are middle-aged women dependent on their prescription medication and medical benefits. With the economy as bad as it is, Jade and Shannon not only lose their jobs but their insurance benefits leaving them in a quarry as what to do. After much thought they decide to cut expenses by only taking their psych meds when they believe they need it. The program charts what happens when the idea sounds good but the end results are not so desirable (their plan to look out for each other is for one to take her medication one week while the other does not and vice versa).

Cast: Angela Wilson (Jade), Lisa Hassler (Shannon). **Credits:** *Producer-Writer:* Lisa Hassler, Angela Wilson. *Director:* John Carstarphen. **Comment:** With the basic premise established in the first episode it is difficult to predict how long it will work before it becomes repetitive. The idea, acting and production are good but the program has limited appeal as it demographic is geared to an older audience than virtually all other Internet comedy series.

Episodes: *1.* Off Her Meds.

713 The Off-Season. youtube.com. 2010.

Don McGriff is a seasoned head college football coach who, like his three assistant coaches (King, Nailon and Stewart) is not only dysfunctional but hoping to jump-start a crumbling career by instituting a strength-and-conditioning program called Firecat Football (to replace his old and out-dated methods). While Don hopes the program will not only make his team better players he also fears that one of his assistants is seeking his job when his contract expires. The program charts the mishaps that result as Don begins his program, seeking to build the best college football team that he can, win games and ensure that his contract will be renewed.

Cast: Tom Buttel (Don McGriff), Adam Ward (Coach King), David Greene (Coach Nailon), Jake Greene (Coach Stewart), Matt Buttel (Terry Garfield), Paula Buttel (Don's wife), Andy Buttel (Nick "The Needle"), Brett Buckles (Gene). **Credits:** *Producer:* Jake Greene, Barry Simmons. *Director:* Sebastian Davis. *Writer:* Jake Greene. **Comment:** While not as charming as the ABC series *Coach*, aspects of it can be seen here as Don tries to whip his team into shape. Don is a hothead and does not want anyone on his staff to move on; he prefers being the head man and will not let anybody become better than he is. While geared to sports fans, it can be enjoyed by anyone.

Episodes: *1.* Attacking Defense. *2.* Firecat Pride. *3.* Stare-roids. *4.* Hot Prospect.

714 Office Problems. youtube.com. 2013.

A work place environment and the problems office workers face are explored in various stories that are presented as an anthology.

Cast: Colby Katz, Abraham Ntonya, Eric Banzon, Stephanie Harris, Audrey Starr, Michael Sosnowski, Anthony Bentrovato, Megan Lester, Chris Pentzell, Albert Stroth, Trip Langley, Levi Petree, Scott Christopher, George Buczek, Anthony Miller. Julie Montoya. **Credits:** *Producer:* Brandon Buczek, Colby Katz. *Writer-Director:* Brandon Buczek. **Comment:** While some of the episodes are a bit slow moving and talkative the overall production is well

acted and produced. It does attempt to expose some of the many problems workers actually face but in a much more satirical light.

Episodes: *1.* Forgetting a Name. *2.* Long Hallway. *3.* Leaving on Time. *4.* The Last Piece of Cake. *5.* Loud Pooper. *6.* Sexual Harassment. *7.* Forgetting a Fork. *8.* Trying to Surf the Internet. *9.* Annoying Cubicle Neighbor. *10.* Exposed Underwear. *11.* Depressed Co-Worker. *12.* Stealing Breast Milk. *13.* Boss Watching Porn. *14.* Late Night Partying.

715 Olanzapine. vimeo.com. 2013.

It is the not-too-distant future and one woman based in the Netherlands (country of production) has stepped forward as the super hero Olanzapine to battle evil. The Prime Minister has been kidnapped by the diabolical Dr. Scarlett and her accomplices, the evil Precious Twins (Jade, with her hypnotic eye, and Sapphire, with her flowing, deadly hair) and the program relates Olanzapine's efforts, accompanied by her sidekick, Captain Tilburg, to rescue the Prime Minister with as little fanfare as possible.

Cast: Madeline Harms (Olanzapine), Zoë Wijnsouw (Prime Minister), Lana Panfilow (Jade Precious), Astrid van Stijn (Sapphire Precious), Pauline Elvira Weijs (Dr. Scarlett), Ingmar Sauer (Captain Tilburg), Lars Wettmann (The Wonder Kid), Max van Pelt (Dr. Pelt). **Credits:** *Director:* William Lu. **Comment:** The program was made in two days for "The 48-Hour Film Project." Entrants were given a character and virtually nothing else and had to make a pilot-like episode. Considering the restraints under which the program was made, it is very well done. Olanzapine, as well as the female villains are quite attractive and the fight scenes are well choreographed for a rushed project.

Episodes: *1.* Olanzapine Pilot.

716 On Empty. youtube.com. 2010.

Vince, born in North Carolina, and Tyler, from Syracuse, New York, were strangers who met and befriended in Los Angeles. Each has a dream to become a movie star but thus far neither has had any success. Determined to change life for the better, they hit on a plan to pretend to be working actors and film a documentary about themselves to show the world just how great they are. Their experiences as they attempt to create their own futures are chronicled.

Cast: Vince Foster (Vince), Tyler Haines (Tyler), Money B, Kyle Cowgill, Noah Sife, Stuart McClay Smith, Alice Hunter, Laura Steigers, Nehemiah Clark, Brandon Drozd, Sy Ozcan, Tim Morales, Jeremy Gilbert, Melody Jackson, Pat Mateos Ballestero, Alex Perez, Dave Lehan, Suave X. Dugais. **Credits:** *Producer-Writer:* Vince Foster, Tyler Haines. *Director:* Vince Foster. **Comment:** The program is presented as a "mockumentary" as Vince and Tyler struggle to create a false impression of themselves. It is a bit rough around the edges (especially in some of the outdoor scenes) but nicely acted with a smooth-flowing progression of their attempts to become famous.

Episodes: *1.* Street Cred. *2.* Middle Man. *3,4.* Training Day. *5.* Team Yellow. *6.* Finding Matthew McConaughay. *7.* Personal Business. *8–10.* Donut Contacts.

717 *On Set.* watchonset.com. 2014.

A satirical behind-the-scenes look at the making of a low budget movie as seen through the eyes of Ryan, the writer (who is trying to impress Laura, the quirky, head-strong assistant director), the director (Albert) and the crew and cast from its inception through the wrap party.

Cast: Ryan Redmond (Ryan), Victoria Swilley (Laura), Stan Madray (Albert), Matt Einhorn (Jeff), Alexis Buck (Shelly), Ruben Mercado (Jay), Jamie Davenport (Charlie), Matt Conners (Ryan 2), Vanessa Aranegui (Rachel), Zarius Suiraz (Gerald). **Credits:** *Producer:* Jamie Davenport. *Director:* Juan Soto. *Writer:* Ryan Redmond. **Comment:** While not an original idea, as TV series and movies devoted to the making of a project have been done numerous times before, each puts a different spin on the concept, here being Ryan's infatuation with Laura. The acting and production are good and the program concludes with the tenth episode.

Episodes: *1.* Action. *2.* Love. *3.* Hot. *4.* Jealous. *5.* Rumors. *6.* Creamer. *7.* Spite. *8.* Fire. *9.* Wrap. *10.* Party.

718 *Once Upon a Time in Brooklyn.* you tube.com. 2010.

Malik and Rigo are friends and roommates who live in an apartment in Brooklyn, New York. With bills to pay and no money to do so, Malik and Rigo decide to take in a roommate. A situation that seems like an easy solution until Reg rents the room to Lindsay, and Malik, not knowing what Reg has done, rents the room to Emily. Four roommates, little personal space and the problems that occur as four people attempt to not only live together, but get along with each other.

Cast: Alec Stephens III (Malik), Isis King (Emily), Michael Navarro-O'Brien (Rigo), Lindsay Hicks (Lindsay). **Credits:** *Producer-Writer:* Nick Blake. *Director:* Alan Smithee. **Comment:** The program is well acted and produced with a new twist on the roommate scenario.

Episodes: *1.* The New Roommate. *2.* The Situation. *3.* The Sauce. *4.* The New Place. *5.* The Bromance. *6.* The Break-In.

719 *One Die Short.* onedieshort.com. 2014.

Rob, Sam, Howie and The DM (Dungeon Master) are friends who could be considered geeks as they escape the pressures of daily life by delving into the fantasy realm of tabletop Role Playing Games (RPG). The program mixes their real life experiences (dealing with careers and loves) with those of their RPG counterparts (battling to save the world).

The Dungeon Master, as he is called, is the son of an unwed teenage mother and at an early age fell into a world of fantasy and delusion. His father abandoned his mother before his birth and, having never seen his father, believes that he was conceived by pan-dimensional alien beings. He holds a job in a bookstore and his only goal appears to be to write his RPG guide.

Sam, who considers herself to be like a Jedi (from *Star Wars*) was raised by a schizophrenic mother after her father died when she was seven years old. She was born in the Mid-West and before graduating from high school she left for New York City when she felt she had to get away. It was when she befriended Howie that she discovered the world of RPG.

Rob is the quirkiest of the friends. He was raised as a Christian but rebelled against it early on and has since alienated himself from the family. He has become openly Satanic, wears kilts and will admit to only one geeky thing: RPG.

Howie, raised in a Catholic family, possesses a degree in computer science and works as a programmer, delighting in the fact that he has success and money. Although he enjoys RPG, he denies admitting that he is a nerd.

Thelema is Rob's fantasy character. She is part Dark Elf and was cast aside for rejecting their god. After having a vision of the end of the world she set out on a quest to stop it before it happens by finding those who will be responsible for it. She travels with Matilda, the alcoholic half Demon Monk, and Soren (both of whom she believes are idiots).

Soren, Howie's fantasy character, is the realm's only Agnostic Paladin who is on a quest to find truth and meaning in the world while having to deal with petty and arrogant gods. He has turned his back on his destiny and has been stripped of all his Paladin abilities; thus he is considered a useless traveling companion.

Matilda, Sam's fantasy character, is "a raging alcoholic" who was raised in a monastery until she was 17 years of age (at which time she left it to seek fun and excitement). Being a half-breed she became the target of prejudice and nearly lost her life to a lynch mob until Soren stepped in and saved her. She derives pleasure in tormenting Soren but will do anything for him.

Cast: Matthew Forcella (Dungeon Master), Pallas Ravae (Sam), Erich Harbowy (Rob), Will Moritz (Howie), Risa Scott (Matilda), Cody Dermon

(Soren), Marina Michelle (Thelema), Roger Norquist (Lester), Kileigh Hammond (Kristin), Joel Janssen (Jonathan). **Credits:** *Producer:* Lester Ward, Matthew Forcella, Pallas Ravae. *Director:* Pallas Ravae, Matthew Forcella. *Writer:* Matthew Forcella. **Comment:** The Role Playing Game has been done several times before and each has its own way of doing things. Here the fantasy costumes and sequences are well done with good acting and production values.

Episodes: 6 untitled episodes, labeled "Episode 1" through "Episode 6."

720 101 Ways to Get Rejected. webseries channel.com. 2013.

Samantha Spenceley, called "Sam," is a pretty high school junior who can't seem to find a steady boyfriend. She has tried everything she can think of to impress boys—from opening her blouse and exposing her breasts to begging for a date, but only embarrassing herself when all such efforts fail. Determined to be like other girls and have a boyfriend, Sam begins a rather badly planned quest to find that one elusive boy of her dreams.

Cast: Susie Yankou (Sam), Taylor Dearden (McKenzie), Alyssa Overbeck (Becky), David Mandell (Smith), Grady Northrop (Westley), Hayley Keown (Weird Brenda). **Credits:** *Producer:* Dylan Visvikis, Michael Effenberger, SusieYankou, Kerry Mohnike. *Director:* Michael Effenberger, Susie Yankou. *Writer:* Susie Yankou, Morgan Lutich, Alden Derck, Emily Kuperman, Sara Monge. **Comment:** Quite different from other school set shows in that the characters are much more believable in how they act and how they attempt to shed their feelings of being strange or squares.

Season 1 Episodes: *1.* Pilot. *2.* The Morning After. *3.* Cheerloser. *4.* Model Behaviour. *5.* Something Unexpected. *6.* Bonfire. *7.* Opposites Attract. *8.* Powderpuff. *9.* Give No F***s. *10.* Prom.

Season 2 Episodes: *1.* Aftermath. *2.* Cheer Up. *3.* Man Up. *4.* Dare Night. *5.* Mommy Dearest. *6.* Closure. *7.* The Break-In Party. *8.* Finale.

721 A 1-UP Kind of Life. the1uplife.com. 2012.

Trey Stevens, called "Triple Kill" for his expertise at video games, is a recent college graduate who wants to turn that skill into a career as a video games professional player. Trey works at GamerDoc and is a member of the Konami Code team, but his friends, and especially his parents believe that he is heading in the wrong direction and needs to see a clear path to the future—one that does not involve video games. The program charts all the mishaps that Trey encounters as he seeks to fulfill a dream that is becoming more of a challenge to achieve than he previously imagined. He feels that if he can win an up-coming Pro Gamers Live Tour it will be the first step as it will net him a contract and instant fame.

Cast: James Ward (Trey Stevens), Brandy Blackmon (Angel Woods), Timothy Corbett (Mark Stevens), Charlene Jones (Sarah Stevens), Brandon Oakley (Jordan Mitchell), Tom Goreas (Mike Jeffries), Donnell Goss (Eric), Dean Allen Jones (Dr. Sanders), Reid Meadows (Lil' Vipa), Jon Karnofsky (Brad "The Noob Slayer" Walsh), Jonathan Perryas (Jason "J-Dex" Campbell), Zach Buckler (Chuck Stone), Jocelyn Rose (Stacey "Big Red 1" Taylor), Michelle R. Woods (Kelly), Lisa Rademacher (Tina). **Credits:** *Producer-Writer-Director:* Matthew Bussey. **Comment:** Such shows find more success on the Internet than they do on network or cable TV and *A 1-Up Kind of Life* is perfectly suited for the medium. It is well acted and produced and can find its own little niche without the worry of being cancelled by networks before it achieves its goal.

Season 1 Episodes: *1.* About a Game Boy. *2.* Achievement Unlocked. *3.* Headshot Thru My Head. *4.* Respawn. *5.* Power Pad the Pounds Away! *6.* Choose Your Destiny.

Season 2 Episodes: *1.* Back in the High Life.... Again? *2.* Side Missions Suck! *3.* The Reboot.

722 The Online Diary of Jackson, Virtual Artist. webserieschannel.com. 2013.

"I'm Jackson. I'm an artist who uses Microsoft Painter. Buy my art" says a young man only identified as Jackson. Jackson, along with Mary and Randy are members of the Virtual Painters Club. Jackson believes that no one can surpass the art he creates (not even Randy, whose paintings are literally much better) and it is through the works of art that Jackson creates that a view of life as he sees it is presented.

Cast: Joshua Michael Payne (Jackson), Elisha Lawson (Randy), Jesse Krebs (Mary). **Credits:** *Producer-Writer-Director:* Joshua Michael Payne. **Comment:** The program does a good job in establishing a premise but after a while the unsteady (shaky) camera method of filming becomes annoying as you simply do not need scenes bobbing up and down to watch a person talk. A steady camera would have been much better as the only person you hear speaking is Jackson (as he talks to the camera and narrates what is happening). Jackson is rather emotionless to begin with and the shaky camera simply does not make a director statement due to that aspect.

Episodes: *Entry #1:* Pilot. *Entry #2:* Dinosaurs and Newspapers. *Entry #3:* Art Duels and Black Eyes. *Entry #4:* Exhibits and Red Bulls.

723 Ortho and His Remote. snootyrobot. com. 2011.

Ortho Peters is a middle-aged man who has no pleasures in life. He lives in the basement of a home owned by a man named Mr. Wilkens and his only enjoyment seems to be watching television. But it's not normal television. Ortho possesses a magical remote control that allows him to become a part of a program he watches. The program, although set in England and using British TV series as its basis, shows what happens as Ortho presses that remote control button and becomes part of the show he is watching. **Cast:** Scotty Fusion (Ortho Peters), Amy Hoerler (Martha), Marc C. Zatorsky (Mabel), Steve Cohen (Voice of Mr. Wilkens), Glenn Alexander (Dick Rogers), Jackie Turner (Nell). **Credits:** *Producer:* Shawn Lewis, Scotty Fusion. *Writer-Director:* Marc C. Zatorsky. **Comment:** A comment based on viewing is not possible as all episodes have been taken off-line.

Episodes: *1.* Pilot. *2.* It's Only Rock and Roll. *3.* Women Have You-Know-Whats?

724 Orville vs. Pedro. youtube.com. 2012–2014.

Orville and Pedro are friends. Orville believes he is better than Pedro while Pedro contends he is better than Orville when it comes to anything and everything. To finally settle the dispute and prove who is better Orville and Pedro begin a series of competitions with the program relating the result of each competition. **Cast:** Matthew Landon (Orville), Jordan Imiola (Pedro). **Credits:** *Producer-Director:* Jordan Imiola, Matthew Landon, DeWalt Max. *Writer:* Jordan Imiola, Matthew Landon. **Comment:** Short (under 60 seconds each) right-to-the-point stories that present a competition and what happens as each tackles it.

Season 1 Episodes: *1.* Basketball. *2.* Drinking Contest. *3.* Crushing. *4.* Knife Trick. *5.* Water Fight.

Season 2 Episodes: *1.* Election. *2.* Homeless. *3.* Christmas. *4.* Stealing. *5.* Holding Breath.

725 Our Cultural Center. webserieschannel.com. 2013.

The Craft Family Cultural Center, overseen by Victoria and Katee Craft, is a family-owned arts center that is now facing its most difficult challenge: It has lost its public funding and is on the verge of closing. It is saved when Randall Vandeburg, Vickie's ex-husband, a profit-driven businessman who has his own vision as to how the center should operate, takes over. The center has been saved, the owners and staff (Pete and Louie) are happy in one aspect but disappointed in another and the program, a spoof of the arts and the arts community, relates Randall's efforts to reinvent the center against everyone's wishes. **Cast:** Julia Kessler (Victoria Craft), Kurt Ehrmann (Randall Vandeburg), Eric Feltas (Peter Bomba), Katie Hunter (Katee Craft), Andy Hager (Louie). **Credits:** *Producer:* Martin Jon. *Director:* Dan Findley. *Writer:* Martin Jon, Mandy Rogers.

Comment: Entertaining and well done with the only problem being an echoing sound problem at times that makes it a bit hard to understand.

Episodes: *1.* Randall Arrives. *2.* The I in Team. *3.* Day Sleeper. *4.* Should. *5.* Flu. *6.* That Damn Tsan. *7.* Fries. *8.* The Coffee Run. *9.* Paperless. *10.* Dluzen Confusion. *11.* Randall's E-Mails. *12.* On a Different Level. *13.* Black Friday. *14.* Pete's Job Search. *15.* Friday the 13th. *16.* Merry Christmas. *17.* Flowers. *18.* Walter Fydrick Flip. *19.* Louie's Slump. *20.* Domestic Monument. *21.* Money Talks. *22.* Valentine's Day.

726 Out of Place. funnyordie.com. 2013.

It is 1951 and a double murder has occurred at the home of Sylvester Martin, a local resident who was known to be an inventor. While examining the murder scene, Detective Boone finds a music box, turns its handle and, as the song "Twinkle, Twinkle Little Star" plays, he is transported to the year 2013. Due to the unavailability of episodes to explain exactly how the story progresses, it is revealed that Boone meets a girl (Claire) who, while helping him adjust to the modern world, also seeks a way to help him return to his own time. **Cast:** Marco Salerno (Det. Boone), Amanda Rodriguez (Claire), Mark Pezzula, Chris Masih, David Picariello, Ali Sarnacchiaro. **Credits:** *Producer:* Jacqueline Bono, Jay Ruzicka. *Writer-Director:* Jay Ruzicka. **Comment:** With the exception of the first episode, all other episodes and teasers have been taken off line. Judging by the first episode, the program needlessly incorporates foul language and is rather lame in explaining how the detective is transported through time. The acting is acceptable as is the production itself.

Episodes: *1.* The Martin House. *2.* Claire. *3.* The Plan. *4.* Newsman.

727 Out of State. youtube.com. 2013.

Josh, newly enrolled in a New York City college has been assigned to share a dorm room with a freshman named Matt. Josh, born in Connecticut, and Matt, a native of Los Angeles, are now, what Josh calls out of state roommates. Life at college, as experienced by Josh and Matt are the focal point of episodes. **Cast:** Josh Lovell (Josh), Matt Giudice (Matt), Deanna Giulietti (Deanna). **Credits:** *Writer-Director:* Matt Giudice. **Comment:** Programs about grammar school, high school and college are plentiful and all have one thing in common: the mishaps that befall the principal players. *Out of State* is well acted and produced but not much different in what has been done before.

Season 1 Episodes: *1.* Someday. *2.* Last Nite. *3.* Life Is Simple in the Moonlight. *4.* Machu Pikachu (The Pokemon One). *5.* Under Control. *6.* Is This It?

Season 2 Episodes: *1.* Gone for Good. *2.* For a Fool. *3.* September. *4.* Caring Is Creepy. *5.* Girl in Form.

728 *OutTerns.* webserieschannel.com. 2014.

Roxanne and Kip appeared to be a happy couple until Kip just couldn't take her argumentative ways and ended their relationship. The breakup devastates Roxanne, who moves in with her best friend Diana and her roommates, sisters Maddie and Millie. Kip, with no place to go, moves in with his friends Luke, Harry and Cristoph. Eight friends and a look at how each experiences life: Roxanne, Cristoph, Kip and Luke are hospital interns; Diana and Harry are nurses; Maddie, a "professional" private dog grooming intern; and Millie, a girl who likes to walk around topless, is a free spirit and art intern.

Cast: Nicklaus Von Nolde (Kip), Aimee Shultz (Roxanne), Darrin Bush (Harry), Lauren Patrice (Diane), Nathan Stephenson (Cristoph), Haly Etlantus Schaeffer (Millie), Samuel Hernandez (Luke), Christal Hartley (Maddie). **Credits:** *Producer:* John Delbarian. *Director:* Elle Stempe. *Writer:* Samuel Hernandez. **Comment:** An interesting mix of personalities although they do not all live together. The story, acting and production are good and the program flows smoothly from episode to episode.

Episodes: *1.* Getting the Hell Out of Dodge. *2.* Getting to Know Your Inner Platypus. *3.* Getting the Beast Out of His Cave. *4.* Getting Rid of the Fat. *5.* Getting to the Bottom of the Dick.

729 *Overly Attached Andy.* overlyattached andy.tumblr.com. 2013.

Andy is a seemingly like-able young man who, at first glance, appears to have his life all together. But once you get to know Andy it becomes obvious that he is nothing like he appears. Andy is a man who so attaches himself to the girls he meets that, when they break up (simply because she can't have her space) it is always she that ends the relationship ("It's you, not me"). Andy becomes deeply depressed after such breakups and is drawn to tears but doesn't realize that his obsessive tendencies are to blame. Andy is seeking one thing: his one true love and feeling that he needs help seeks the advice of his friends. The program charts what happens as Andy sets out to find that elusive girl—"I know she's out there" and he will, by hook or crook, find her.

Cast: Andy Gates (Andy), Emily Button (Emily), Virginia Collins (Virginia), Deborah S. Craig (Deborah), Taryn Horacek (Taryn), Jason Pickar (Jason), Nicole Serrat (Nicole). **Credits:** *Producer:* Leena Pendharkar, Jane Kelly Kosek. *Writer-Director:* Leena Pendharkar. **Comment:** Although programs with a dysfunctional man or woman seeking a mate has been done before, it can always be different when the cast is good and the story well presented. Such

Overly Attached Andy. Series poster art (used by permission).

is the case here and Andy's search for that unknown girl is a good comical portrayal of such a search.

Episodes: *1.* It's Definitely You. *2.* Makeover Time. *3.* DTF? What's That? *4.* Too Many Compliments. *5.* Friends, Just Friends. *6.* Hunter S. Thompson on Crack. *7.* Chemistry or Just Sex? *8.* No Such Thing As Perfect.

730 *P.O.P: Puppets of Porn.* youtube.com. 2010.

They look a bit like the Muppets from *Sesame Street* but these puppets are not kid friendly. They are crudely made "porn puppets" and work for POP (Puppets of Porn), an "adult video" producing company located in Chatsworth, California (to where such companies have set up a base as Hollywood "no longer accepts creative people"). With partial puppet nudity, puppet on puppet (as well as puppet and human) sex and a small smattering of foul language, a spoof of the adult entertainment industry is presented with a mostly behind-the-scenes look at what happens in the making of those triple rated "X" films (without the hardcore sex or total nudity).

Voice Cast: Luke Gibleon (Gib), Brooke Cusmano (Kim), Jackie L. Virgo (Jax), Johnny James (Jimmy). **Credits:** *Writer-Director:* Jackie L. Virgo, Luke Gibleon. **Comment:** Don't expect the sophistication of the Muppets but do expect a well done human-puppet mix that while it does have suggestive sexual situations, it does stray from being too raunchy. There is a warning about what to expect before each episode begins and, although the puppet-human mix is not an original idea (Fox attempted it *Greg the Bunny*) it is something totally different and enjoyable here.

Episodes: *1.* First Day. *2.* Jazmyn Rice. *3.* Lost Package. *4.* Kim's Sex Tape.

731 Pageantry. webserieschannel.com. 2012.

Markham College is not only a university dedicated to educating its students but it is famous for its annual beauty pageant, The Miss Markham College Queen. Only the most beautiful girl holds the prestigious title and with the crown comes not only honor but prestige. A new school year has begun and five of the most beautiful women on campus have been chosen to compete for the coveted crown. The program charts what happens as personalities and egos clash with each of the candidates seeking to become the next Miss Markham College Queen.

Cast: Joi Fletcher (Cheyenne), Vashti Powell (Daniella), Ebone' Johnson (Crystal), Britney Abrahams (Brichelle), Bashira Shamsid-Deen (T'Kya), Shanice Spencer (Aisha). Credits: *Producer:* Airelle McGill. *Director:* Airelle McGill, Keenan Carver. *Writer:* Keenan Carver. Comment: African-American produced program that is well acted and presented. While the pageant is the overall focus of the program, it also shows how the chosen candidates deal with life around campus and their interactions with other students.

Episodes: *1.* Pilot: The Unveiling. *2.* Platforms and Intros. *3.* Dance Lessons. *4.* Walk. *5.* Q&A. *6,7.* The Pageant.

732 Pale Force. funnyordie.com. 2005–2008.

A web spin off from a series of animated skits that aired on the NBC TV series *Late Night with Conan O'Brien*. Host Conan O'Brien and his side kick, Jim Gaffigan are a team of super heroes that battle evil with the power of paleness. Jim is the tall, muscular super hero while Conan is the wimpy, scrawny and always needing Jim's help to accomplish something side kick. Although mismatched and possessing the power of paleness, the duo, members of the League of Pale, believes they are saviors and episodes depict their comical efforts to battle evil villains.

Voice Cast: Jim Gaffigan (Conan/Jim), Eartha Kitt (Lady Bronze). Credits: *Producer:* Jim Gaffigan, Paul Noth. *Director:* Paul Noth. *Writer:* Jim Gaffigan, Patrick Noth, Paul Noth. Comment: Well produced and amusing fantasy that pokes fun at a network and the celebrities associated with it.

Episodes: *1.* Meet Pale Force. *2.* Pale Force Begins. *3.* Pale Impostor. *4.* Sidekicks. *5.* Miss Massa-

chusetts. *6.* Charlie Rose. *7.* Conan and the King. *8.* Conan in Love. *9.* Pale Christmas. *10.* Pale Force: The Movie. *11.* Law and Order: Pale Force. *12.* The Cliffhanger. *13.* Carnival Conan.

733 Palisades Pool Party. blip.tv. 2009.

It is the summer of 2009 and for Cassidy Flowers, a popular Pacific Palisades High School girl, it means throwing the biggest summer bash imaginable. With her parent's permission and the help of her close-knit friends (Bianca, Tori and Mischa), arrangements are being made and all is progressing well until Cassidy succumbs to temptation and sleeps with Josh, an unpopular student (and her next-door neighbor). As word leaks out, the backlash threatens to ruin Cassidy's party and the program follows what happens to Cassidy and her friends when she tries to make up for what she did and continue with her party plans.

Cast: Ashley Schneider (Cassidy), Karen Austin (Desiree), Katie Seeley (Bianca), Mary Kasnias (Tori), Francesca Fauci (Tiffani), Ronnie Alvarez (Mario), Joseph Lee Fields (Antwon), Philip Marlatt (Chad), Andrew Pandaleon (Scott), Whitmer Thomas (Josh), Danny Zaccagnino (Mischa). Credits: *Producer:* Tai Fauci. *Director:* Jack Monroe. *Writer:* Jack Monroe, Tai Fauci. Comment: Ashley Schneider shines as Cassidy as she struggles to overcome the numerous obstacles that threaten her party. The acting and production values are very good and the story flows smoothly from beginning to end.

Episodes: *1.* Sex with Neighbor Boy. *2.* I'm Out of Her Top 8. *3.* Heroine Kills People. *4.* The Dirty Little Secrets Girls Keep in Their Makeup Bags.

734 Pants on Fire. funnyordie.com. 2014.

Encompasses the last half of the saying, "Liar, liar, pants on fire" and aspects of Baron Von Munchausen and from old time radio, Fibber McGee, two world-renowned liars. Dr. Felix Sebring is a 43-year-old psychiatrist who works out of the home of his mother (Mum), a woman obsessed with anything British. He has an unrelenting crush on his assistant, Monica, and is a pathological liar. Felix can not help what he does, normally bragging about himself as he deals with his eccentric patients. The program chronicles the situations that develop when Felix's lies come back to haunt him. Only one storyline was presented. Here Felix attempts to deal with a patient, Mrs. Mendelbaum, who has developed an unnatural attachment to her lap dog Hubert, after her husband, Stanley's passing (even going so far as to make Hubert wear Stanley's toupee). The case becomes complicated when Philomena, Mrs. Mendelbaum's mentally unstable granddaughter, kidnaps Hubert and sets Felix on a path to rescue him.

Cast: Jim McCaffree (Felix Sebring), Jamie Lou

Moniz (Monica), Carol Kline (Mum), Karen Forman (Mrs. Mendelbaum/Philomena Mendelbaum). **Credits:** *Producer:* Laura McLaughlin, Frank McLaughlin. *Writer:* Laura McLaughlin. *Director:* Jamie Lou Moniz. **Comment:** The first impression you get is that the program is British as Felix's mother (called Mum) is first seen and singing "Rule Britaina." The acting, story and production are good and the doorway has been left open for future episodes to be produced.

Episodes: 4 untitled episodes, labeled "Episode 1" through "Episode 4."

735 *Pappy's Pizza.* youtube.com. 2014.

Pappy's Pizza is a pizzeria and pasta restaurant that, if one could see what happens in the kitchen, one would not step foot in the door not alone eat there. A behind-the-scenes look at how a pizza parlor operates is the focal point with a look at a staff of uncouth individuals that only a deranged person would hire as they have no respect for customers and no idea of sanitary meal preparation.

Cast: Josh Pudliener (Kyle), Nate Beals (Matt), Erik Bremer (Bobby), Cameron Britton (Randal), Ryan Mcgivern (Charles). **Credits:** *Writer-Director:* Kyle Mixon. **Comment:** If you are a fan of the TV series *2 Broke Girls* and are disturbed over how Oleg, the diner cook, prepares meals, then you will be appalled here. It is okay to make fun of food servers and diners (for example, *Alice*) but taking the concept to where it becomes just too ridiculous happens here.

Episodes: *1.* Lunch Shift. *2.* Order for Wesley Snipes.

736 *ParaAbnormal.* paraabnormal.com. 2009.

Ken Livingston, a self-proclaimed supernatural investigator, believes the stories he hears or reads about relating to strange phenomena are real and has decided to do something about it. Operating from his grandmother's garage and with his assistants, Wendy, Bunky and Tony the program relates their efforts to uncover the truth behind ghostly occurrences.

Cast: Ken Livingston (Ken), Wendy Donigan (Wendy) Alexander "Bunky" Hunt (Bunky), Joe Schmidt (Tony). **Credits:** *Producer:* Demetrea Triantafillides. *Director:* Jamie Nash, Eduardo Sanchez. *Writer:* Jamie Nash. **Comment:** Somewhat amateurish take off on ghost hunting series that is interesting for the unusual cases the team handles.

Episodes: *1–6:* Case 1: Ghost on a Sex Tape. *7–12:* Case 2: Haunted Motel Room. *13–18.* Case 3: Haunted City Morgue. *19–22.* Case 4: The Succubus.

737 *Parker and Steve: A Bromcom.* parkerandsteve.com. 2012.

Parker and Steve are best friends and living in New York City. They have each reached the age of thirty and their life, for the most part, has not improved over the past ten years. They have trouble meeting girls (even dating) and constantly face financial problems. The program charts their reactions to the situations they encounter as they not only attempt to meet girls, but get ahead in their career choices: Parker, a writer and Steve, a rapper.

Cast: Brennan Taylor (Parker), Tim Intravia (Steve). **Credits:** *Producer:* Alyson Leigh Rosenfeld, Tim Intravia. **Comment:** Interesting stories coupled with good acting and production values.

Episodes: *1.* Pilot. *2.* Idiot! *3.* Flirt Booking. *4.* Each Other. *5.* Aaaaaah! *6.* Are You? *7.* $20 Dollar Bill. *8.* Leave It Alone. *9.* Look, Find, Dispose. *10.* Same Old New. *11.* Loyalties Lie. *12.* Hello, Goodbye. *13.* Forgive and Recover. *14.* Silver Lining. *15.* Suppose I Love You Too. *16.* The Next Day. *17.* Fat Chance. *18.* The Reveal. *19.* Happy Ending.

738 *Partners in Pretension.* youtube.com. 2011.

Angel and Dorian have graduated from college but are faced with both unemployment and graduate school rejection. Circus great P.T. Barnum once said "There's a sucker born every minute" and Angel and Dorian come up with a unique idea: make how-to videos that can create revenue through the ignorance of the common man. The program relates their efforts to post their videos (see episode list) and the mishaps that occur after doing so.

Cast: Fernando Noor (Angel), Tristan Scott-Behrends (Dorian), Kate Hackett (Eden), Clayton Farris (Everett). **Credits:** *Producer:* Claire Wasmund, Fernando Noor. *Writer-Director:* Claire Wasmund. **Comment:** The program is basically a look at a client and what results when he or she is faced with the cold hard facts. The idea is a bit different than other shows that attempt to defraud people and is well acted and produced.

Episodes: *1.* How to Co-Exist with the Common Man. *2.* How to Ask for Money. *3.* How to Handle Adversity. *4.* How to Ask Someone Out on a Date. *5.* How to Have a Bad Day. *6.* How to Stab a Friend in the Back.

739 *Part-Time Fame.* parttimefame.com. 2012.

Patrick ("Friendly neighborhood bouncer"), Zen (landlord), Mavis (suicide hot line operator), Clifford (assistant manager of Bobo's Day Care Center and Clown Fill-In) and Missie (professional food mascot) are friends and roommates with only one thing on their minds: to become rich and famous. While they each care for the other, they each have an idea how to achieve fame—from unusual schemes like dumpster diving in Beverly Hills hoping to find gold (here the panties of actress Pamela Anderson to sell on e-bay) to inventing a time machine, go back one day in time and change their destinies. The program explores the avenues the friends take to become famous—and the always disastrous situations that result.

Cast: Romel De Silva (Patrick "Picard" Lee), Matthew Jennings (Zen), Bethany Koulias (Mavis Featherstroke), Levi Austin Morris (Cliff Nixon), Sascha Vanederslik (Missie McDowell). **Credits:** *Producer:* Jennifer Hall. *Writer:* Haeli Dunstan. *Director:* Saul Phriver. **Comment:** An interesting mix of friends as they seek to better their lives and achieve their dreams of fame. The acting and production values are good and while roommate TV series and movies are a dime a dozen, *Part Time Fame* manages to find its own little gimmick to be a bit different.

Episodes: *1.* The Time with the Panties. *2.* The Time We Online Dates. *3.* The Time We Time Traveled. *4.* The Time We Mid-Summered on Mars.

740 *Party Girl Plus One.* partygirlplusone.com. 2009–2011.

"I may be a party girl but that's not what I am," says Jen, a young woman working as a bartender who pretends to be something she is really not in an effort to date as many men as she can until she finds Mr. Right. For the moment that man is elusive and the program chronicles Jen's various dates—from her preparation to the actual date and what happens afterwards.

Cast: Jennifer Dawson (Jen), Vince Pavia (Vic), Jake Pavelka (Bryce). **Credits:** *Producer:* Jennifer Dawson, Lyndon Chubbuck. *Writer-Director:* Jennifer Dawson, Daniel Doherty II. **Comment:** Every program, whether on broadcast TV, cable or the Internet that deals with a young woman seeking the right man, needs to have that something special to survive. Zooey Deschanel achieved that success on her Fox series *New Girl* and Jennifer Dawson accomplishes that same charm here. The character is very likeable, has her flaws and overall, the program is well acted and produced

Episodes: *1.* Party Girl. *2.* Sir Smells a Lot. *3.* Extreme Measures. *4.* Frequent Flyer. *5.* Wonder Women. *6.* The Big Squeeze. *7.* The World Is Mine. *8.* The Talented Mr. Somebody. *9.* Three's Company. *10.* My Own Private Freakdom. *11.* Booty Calls.

741 *Pat and Andy.* blip.tv. 2012.

Best friends Pat and Andy enjoy playing video games together, watching TV together but most importantly discussing various aspects of life together. The program relates the topics they explore with each giving his opinion about it.

Cast: Patrick Mulvey (Pat), Andrew Scott-Ramsay (Andy). **Credits:** *Producer-Writer:* Patrick Mulvey, Andrew Scott-Ramsay. **Comment:** Simplistic program with the two leads simply discussing matters.

Episodes: *1.* Shh, Jen? Maybe. *2.* Pick, Peck. *3.* My Power, My Pleasure, My Pain. *4.* Pat and Andy and Wine. *5.* Boom Ba Boom Boom. *6.* Turn Me Around So I Can See. *7.* She's a Little Low Set. *8.* Just Droopy. *9.* I Took the Weight Right Off. *10.* A Very Big Night. *11.* When I Start to Get Angry. *12.* 5 Letters?

742 *Pat and Myra Kill Somebody.* killsomeboy.tv. 2013.

When Energreen, the power company that supplies energy to their community, goes beyond what it is supposed to do (creating discount energy whose process could be detrimental to the environment), Pat and Myra, two social misfits, attempt to stop them but run into numerous blocks (like no one signing petitions) and are unable in the conventional manner. To achieve their goal and bring down Energreen and its head, "the evil" Angela Deering-Downey, Pat and Myra believe that if they kill somebody it will bring attention to their cause and foster an investigation into the power company's tactics. The program charts the elaborate disguises the pair use (and seen in fantasy sequences) to find a victim and pull off their foul deed.

Cast: Tim Fairley (Pat), Libby Schap (Myra), Becky Schap (Angela Derring-Downey), Tina Marie Sheehan (Trish). **Credits:** *Producer:* Tim Fairley, Libby Schap. *Director:* Seth Halko. *Writer:* Dan Schap. **Comment:** Very well acted and produced program that is sure to hit a nerve (at getting angry) for what energy companies do. Libby Schap, pretty as she is, wears an eye patch which is really not needed (explaining that she fell asleep on the beach and a sand crab scratched her eye) but does give her that sinister look for the scheme she concocted.

Episodes: *1.* Completely Evil. *2.* I Could Be Interested. *3.* Ideas Worth Streaming. *4.* Getting Closer. *5.* Finished. *6.* Really Messed Up. *7.* Getting Busted. *8.* Bad for You. *9.* Mutual Friend. *10.* Dealing with It. *11.* It's Done.

743 *Patrick and Molly and All the Small Things.* sidereel.com. 2010.

The small things that enter people's lives and how they deal with them forms the basis of a program that focuses on a young couple (Molly and Patrick) as they discuss those small things—like dreams, movies, taking vitamins and even exchanging gifts that can create a bigger picture.

Cast: Nellie Barnett (Molly), Ryan Reyes (Patrick). **Credits:** *Producer-Writer-Director:* Jade Brookbank. **Comment:** Although the program is basically Molly reacting to something Patrick has done, it is very well acted and produced.

Episodes: *1.* Werewolves. *2.* Testosterone. *3.* Secrets. *4.* I Love Ewe. *5.* Broken Laptop. *6.* Big Ass. *7.* Dreams. *8.* Nudie Photos. *9.* Meteoroid. *10.* Porcupine. *11.* The Fist. *12.* Outtakes.

744 *Paul the Matchmaker.* webserieschannel.com. 2011.

Paul, an attractive, super-likeable and happy person (in his own estimation) is married to Teri, a wealthy woman who buys him whatever he wants. Life suddenly changes for Paul when he inherits his Aunt Cathy's matchmaking company and must now run it. Paul has his own warped theories on how the company should be run and implements his policy of being brutally honest with clients—no flattery and no embellishing the truth. The program relates what happens when Paul reopens the business but finds his totally honest approach to what a client looks like and how they act becomes more of a nightmare than a dream when the backlash causes more problems than he can handle.

Cast: Paul Bartholomew (Paul), Darcy Shean (Ruth), Teresa Ganzel (Rosemarie), Ann Ryerson (Renee), Alyssa Bartholomew (Rachel), Larry Clarke (Rick), Nadia Dajani (Maureen), Julie Dretzin (Sally), Jean Louisa Kelly (Darla), Michael Linstroth (Bob), Romy Rosemont (Daphne), Erik Van Wyck (Bruce). **Credits:** *Director:* Paul Bartholomew. *Writer:* Paul Bartholomew, Liz Tuccillo. **Comment:** The program incorporates TV actress Teresa Ganzel, probably best known as Greedy Gretchen on the series *Three's Company.* Unfortunately all the episodes have been taken off line and providing a comment based on viewing is not possible.

Episodes: *1.* First Impressions Are Everything! *2.* Know When You're Not Ready. *3.* Do What It Takes. *4.* Don't Be a Meanie. *5.* The Experts. *6.* Know When You're Simply Too Old. *7,8.* Know How to Cook. *9.* Fear Can Make Someone Love You. *10.* Never Give Up on Love.

745 *Paulie Pastrami: King of Illegal Meats.* webseriescannel.com. 2013.

In New Jersey a virtually unknown battle is raging between rival dealers to become king of the illegal deli meat pastrami business. Paulie Pastrami, a man who has been conducting such activities for so long that he knows nothing else, operates out of Newark, and has set his goal to become the only illegal meat dealer on the East Coast. He is married to Paula and the father of Paulette and Paulie, Jr. Paulie, assisted by his bodyguard, Big Pasta, is a member of the notorious Pastrami crime family. In New York City, there operates Sammy the Salami, the man who is seeking to do away with Paulie and thus prevent him from expanding into the city and encroaching on

his business of illegal meat selling. Sammy is not the only enemy Paulie has. A police detective, Susan Swallows, is determined to end Paulie's operations as her mother nearly died from his illegal meat. The program follows the battle that wages between Paulie and Sammy and how Susan's determination could put an end to both of their careers.

Cast: John William Larkin (Paulie Pastrami), Mike Beaury (Big Pasta), Rebecca Lieberman (Paula Pastrami), Samantha Glovin (Paulette Pastrami), Frank Paris (Paulie Pastrami, Jr.), Leigh Ann Rose (Susan Swallows), Robert Minutoli (Vinnie Veal Cut). **Credits:** *Director:* Rodney Reyes. *Writer:* Steven Williams. **Comment:** A most unusual concept to say the least. It captures the feel of real gangsters, especially in the guise of Big Pasta. There is foul language, some mild violence and overall a well acted, produced and enjoyable program to watch.

Episodes: *1.* Pilot. *2.* Meat in the Streets. *3.* Chasing Paulie. *4.* You the Man! *5.* The Meeting.

746 *Pay Up.* payup.tv. 2013.

"Are you in debt? Do you have some sort of mental problems that you spend more money than you have? Are you tired of people like me calling people like you? Want to do something about it? I'm here to help" claims a collection agency caller who operates from a company called Pay It Back. Each episode is a look at the after-effects such calls have on the people to whom they are directed.

Cast: Richard Glen Lett (Jack), Jason Weinberg (George), Kristina Agosti (Lisa), James Kirchner (Hugo), Jeanie Calleja (Kassie), Zoe Cleland (Shawna), Ash Catherwood (Mitch), Carl Bauer (Chad), Frank MacLeod (Oliver). **Credits:** *Writer-Director:* Craig MacNaughton. **Comment:** Only the teaser episodes remain on line and are simply the contacted person relating his or her feelings. They are well done and judging by them, the actual episodes would have probably begun with the phone call and other information relating to why the person incurred the debt.

Episodes: *1.* The Deal. *2.* It Won't Start. *3.* Put Him On. *4.* Call Me Anytime. *5.* Half by Friday. *6.* Did You Get It?

Episode Teasers: *1.* Are You in Debt? *2.* Jack. *3.* George. *4.* Lisa. *5.* Hugo. *6.* Chad. *7.* Mitch. *8.* Oliver. *9.* Shawna. *10.* Kassie.

747 *PB and J with the H.O.A.* webserieschannel.com. 2013.

Gateway Greens is a well-cared for housing community with very strict H.O.A. (Home Owners Association) rules and regulations. Break any of them and fines are as high as $800 for each violation. Peter Browman is the Vice Chief Deputy of Public Affairs for Gateway Greens and a man totally dedicated to his job. Javier Jimenez is a new resident and immediately incurs the wrath of Peter when someone litters his home with advertising fliers and he faces the prospect of a large fine. Although Peter and Javier do not hit it off at first, Peter sees potential in Javier as an H.O.A. officer and persuades the unemployed young man to join his team. Although reluctant at first, Javier falls prey to Peter's pressure and the program charts the mishaps the duo encounter as they attempt to patrol, protect and uphold the rules and regulations of Gateway Greens.

Cast: Eddie Sanchez (Javier Jimenez), Jason Young (Peter Browman), Maryam Cne (Jessica Porter), Marcus Murray (Gene Waterson), Doree Seay (Gizel Wellington), Chris Labadie (Carter Carter), Cheldea Samuelson (Patricia Bodwell), Chris Sheffield (Otis O'doul), Jonathan Medina (Enrique Llamas). **Credits:** *Producer:* Hui-Vhin Yang, Phil Castro. *Director:* Eddie Sanchez, Chris Labadie. **Comment:** A convincing Odd Couple pairing with the by-the-books Peter and the less-than enthusiastic Javier becoming a team. The acting and production values are good and the program is a bit different with its H.O.A. setting.

Episodes: *1,2.* Flier Fight. *3.* An Unexpected Journey. *4,5.* Stray Cats. *6.* Sick Day—Wh-Wh-Wh-Wh. *7.* Sick Day—Rock! Rock! *8–10.* Peter's Great Green Buffalo. *11.* The Mole: Peter's Formulation. *12.* The Mole: Penetration. *13.* The Mole: Extraction.

748 *Peach Fuzz.* webserieschannel.com. 2012.

Short videos that revolve around two friends (Brooks and Kevin) and the mishaps they encounter living in a cartoon-like world. Each segment is structured like a comic strip (and presented under two minutes) with each panel building a premise and leading to a punch line.

Cast: Brooks Morrison, Kevin Eis. **Credits:** *Producer-Writer:* Brooks Morrison, Kevin Eis. **Comment:** Short and right to the point. Well acted and produced and for the simplicity of each situation (like crossing the street or preparing for a holiday) a lot happens in a short time.

Episodes: *1.* Slide. *2.* Beard. *3.* Going Out. *4.* Tattoo. *5.* Chase. *6.* Banana Peel Prank. *7.* 5:30. *8.* Knock Knock. *9.* Trick or Treat. *10.* Question. *11.* Turkey Day. *12.* Sword Fight. *13.* Band Aid. *14.* Late. *15.* We're on Vacation. *16.* Toilet. *17.* Imaginary Friend. *18.* Moustache. *19.* Bus Stop. *20.* Errands. *21.* Bad Dinner. *22.* Stain. *23.* Car Ride. *24.* Wet Paint. *25.* Lion. *26.* Crazy Day. *27.* Q-Tip. *28.* Magic Trick. *29.* Oops. *30.* Fan.

749 *Ped Crossing.* vimeo.com. 2012.

Byron is not a police officer, a high school teacher, a private detective or even a serial killer. He is a middle-aged man who is a pedophile. Byron is apparently unable to control his addiction to children and constantly stalks them, although he does not appear to have the ability to harm them. Byron is followed as he looks at children in a strange light but also as he just tries to adjust to the world that surrounds him and how he struggles to function in it (from finding a job to buying a car).

Cast: Paul Thomas (Byron), Beth Stelling, John Leadley, Chad Briggs, James Fritz, Kellen Alexander, Mark Raterman, Brian Babylon, Jim Fath, Patrick Raynor, C.J. Sullivan, Chad Wilson, Tiffany Puterbaugh. **Credits:** *Producer:* Chad Wilson. *Director:* Paul Thomas. *Writer:* Paul Thomas, Chad Briggs. **Comment:** Although dramatic TV series have dealt with pedophiles, comedy series have mostly strayed from the topic with the exception being the character of Ted on the TV series *Police Squad* where it was suggested he was a pedophile. It is a risky topic to deal with as it can only be taken so far. Here nothing shocking happens and the program is also a look at how Byron attempts to get through each day.

Episodes: *1.* Kayne. *2.* Leon of Kings. *3.* James Dean. *4.* A Close Shave. *5.* Reality Bites. *6.* Snap, Crackle and Pop. *7.* Lady and the Tramp. *8.* Parks and Wreck. *9.* The Pianist. *10.* The Seeker. *11.* All Quiet on the Eastern Front.

750 *Penelope: Princess of Pets.* youtube.com. 2007–2008.

Penelope is a young woman who loves animals. And like Dr. Dolittle, she can talk to and understand them ("I found out when I became a woman," she says). But there is a dark force that threatens to ruin everything: an evil legislator (Thomas Stone) who is bent on destroying the world (a situation she learned about from a talking cow). Accompanied by Kyle, her orphan friend, and her sarcastic puppet pet bird Ruby (who drinks, smokes, has a potty mouth and lives in her coat pocket), Penelope begins a quest to save the animal kingdom by killing Stone.

Cast: Kristen Schaal (Penelope), Kurt Braunohler (Kyle), Ali Reza Farahnakian (Senator Stone), Sam Kennard, Matt Kennard (Stone's henchmen). **Credits:** *Producer:* Kristen Schaal, Kurt Braunohler. *Director:* Ben Palmer. *Writer:* Rich Blomquist, Kurt Braunohler, Kristen Schaal. **Comment:** Enjoyable farce that has to be seen to be believed. The acting is very good and the program very campy with Penelope encountering numerous obstacles as she seeks to complete her goal. Unfortunately, the program ends unresolved with Penelope and Kyle hot on Stone's trail.

Episodes: 9 untitled episodes, labeled "Episode 1" through "Episode 9."

751 *The People That Touch Your Food.* foodservice.tv. 2012.

The Second Spoon Café is a neighborhood diner owner by Ed Danson and managed by Paige. Conrad is the chief chef; Janice, the pastry chef; Emily, a waitress; and Milo, the head server. There is also a major fast food franchise (Aunt Betty's) moving into the neighborhood and The Second Spoon Café could face extinction. The program charts the mishaps that occur within the café as Paige deals with her dysfunctional staff and customers and of all concerned to find a way to remain in business despite what is happening down the street.

Cast: Jenna Dykes (Paige Peters), Trent Wilkie (Ed Danson), Ben Dextraze (Chef Conrad), Georgia Irwin (Chef Janice), Kristen Padayas (Emily), Ben Stevens (Milo). **Credits:** *Producer:* Nathan Brown, Tito Guillen. *Director:* Chris Hill. *Writer:* Chris Hill, Ryan Byrne. **Comment:** For a series set in a diner, it is well acted and produced although hints of the TV series *Alice, Flo* and *It's a Living* will no doubt come to mind. It is really difficult to devise a concept that has not yet been tackled (even the diner facing extinction from a chain franchise has been done on *Alice*) but it is the cast and how the problem is resolved that makes the difference. Here it is not handled in one episode (as on *Alice*) but well thought out and resolved over a series of episodes.

Season 1 Episodes: *1.* The Pilot That Starts Your Show. *2.* The Decider. *3.* Be-Her-All. *4.* Women Don't Belong in the Kitchen. *5.* Milo Has a Moustache Now. *6.* The Food Critic. *7.* Milo's Got a Shameful Secret Now. *8.* Danson Strikes Back. *9.* Shark Week. *10.* Saving the Spoon.

Season 2 Episodes: *1.* Cake and Wine. *2.* Sex, Lies and Be-Her-All. *3.* Social Extortion. *4.* Milo's Got a Dictatorship Now. In these episodes the diner is saved but Paige must still deal with staff problems.

752 *Periods.* webserieschannel.com. 2010.

Short comedy productions presented in an anthology-like program that satirizes various historical periods and characters.

Cast: Alison Fyhrie, Mary Grill, Philip Quinaz, Chris Manley, Michael Lidondici, Brian Shoaf, Anna Martemucci, Damian Lanigan, Giovanni P. Autran, Lauren Weisstein, Victor Quinaz, Yamin Segal, Sian Heder, Thyra Heder, Helena Lukas, Haj Pintouck, Barnara Quinaz, Dasha Martikaien, Scott Robinson, Sean Akers, Mishka Brown, Neal Dodson, Ashley Williams, Pablo Schreiber, Zachary Quinto. **Credits:** *Producer:* Dasha Martikaien, Yamin Segal. **Comment:** A good idea that uses authentic costumes but the overall effect of trying to recreate a past time is lost through the use of modern-day dialogue (while not copying, but being truer to the time would have helped greatly). As such, the program comes off as just people in costumes pretending to be in a different time period. While the acting is good, the production suffers through its camera work (the unsteady camera method is used for scenes that should be stationery [like people talk-

ing to each other] and in spots, it appears the camera is "lost" [as it comes in and out of focus searching for what it should be filming]). CBS has attempted such an idea with a Pilgrim-set series (*Thanks*) and an unsold pilot (*1776*) and it too found such ideas just do not work.

Season 1 Episodes: *1.* Pilgrims. *2.* Edith Wharton's Ethan Frome. *3.* Forefathers (George Washington, Thomas Jefferson, Benjamin Franklin). *4.* Hags.

Season 2 Episodes: *1.* Fops. *2.* Viking Wives. *3.* Re-Creation. *4.* Dec. 26. *5.* NAM (re-imaging of the 1978 film *Deer Hunter*).

753 *Perks.* youtube.com. 2011.

Lemonjello is a coffee shop owned by Max and staffed by Natalie, Lucy and Will. Max is just trying to keep his head above water and hopefully save his business from going under as it is in financial strains. Natalie, Lucy and Will are a bit eccentric and the program follows the situations that occur as Max deals with both staff and sometimes equally as eccentric customers.

Cast: David Gries (Max), Kate Rudd (Natalie), Reid Coe (Will), Molly Michelle (Lucy). **Credits:** *Producer:* Paul Genzink, Lindsey Scott. **Comment:** Well acted and produced program that manages to find its own niche in diner-set programs and just not copy series like *Alice* and *It's a Living* .

Episodes: *1.* Everything's Broken. *2.* Hair Restraints. *3.* Weapon of Choice. *4.* Charly. *5.* Full Circle.

754 *Peter Bear's Den.* peterbearsden.com. 2013.

Peter Barrett is a twenty-something young man who believes that he is blessed with bountiful wisdom and creativity and needs to share it with the world. His friend Judy decides to help him spread the word and they create an Internet video blog called "Peter Bear's Den Online" (the premise of Season 1 episodes as it also details their efforts to deal with Matthew Saginoff, a cyber bully [uses the name SaginMeOff] who targets and torments Peter and Judy). Season 2 episodes follow Judy's efforts to reconnect with her estranged family while Peter introduces a new feature to his site: "Your Mother Jokes." Peter's efforts to produce an "epic" science fiction film called *The Battle for Creata Forest* form the basis of Season 3 episodes. The concluding Season 4 deals with Judy's efforts to come to terms with her family while Peter plans to take a trip to Los Angeles.

Cast: Joe Worthen (Peter Barrett), Breanna Foister (Judy Robertson), Justin Johnson (Matthew Saginoff), Mary Alice Adams (Cindy Barrett), Avon Stephenson, Jr. (Chuck Robertson), Ahmed Mustaf (Parker Banks), Robert Fuson (Barry), James Harvley (E. Jenkins). **Credits:** *Producer:* Alex Wroten,

Lindsay Wolfe. *Writer-Director:* Alex Wroten. **Comment:** Although each season is a bit different, the
overall feeling for the series' original concept (Season 1) is captured through the various episodes. The
acting and production values are very good and it is
one of the first Internet series to deal with Internet
bullying.

Season 1 Episodes: *1.* Peter Barrett. *2.* Oatmeal.
3. Guitar and Game. *4.* Sequels. *5.* A Real Good Person to Know. *6.* Very Upset. *7.* Open Letter. *8.* What
Can You Do? *9.* Driving to Tennessee. *10.* Angry
Guy in the Yard.

Season 2 Episodes: *1.* Pam Jenkins. *2.* Just Judy.
3. It Turns Out. *4.* The Talk. *5.* Pay Phones Are Dan-
gerous Places. *6.* Put the Camera Away. *7.* Two
Minds Are Better Than One. *8.* You Said You Were
Done with This. *9.* Driving to North Carolina. *10.*
Barry.

Season 3 Episodes: *1.* Home Invasion. *2.* This Deserves a Punishment. *3.* The Campaign. *4.* Blank
Pages. *5.* Another Dimension. *6.* Pe-Production. *7.*
And—Action! *8.* A Singular Vision. *9.* A Few Dol-
lars Short. *10.* Angry Guy at the Premiere. *11.* Battle
for Creata Forest.

Season 4 Episodes: *1.* Bad News. *2.* Staying or
Goin? *3.* Putting Down Roots. *4.* Questionable
Contents. *5.* Parker. *6.* The Tourist.

755 PIT: The Paranormal Investigative Team. vimeo.com. 2010.

Art Mack and "The" Deuce Moran are, by daytime, the owners of the Big Yellow Diner on Pico
Boulevard in Los Angeles. By night they become
ghost hunters and are assisted by Pam Duberry, a research specialist; Lear Levin, a tech wizard, and investigator Clark Dunwoody. The program follows
their activities as they investigate paranormal occurrences in and around Southern California.

Cast: Thomas Mills (Art Mack), Oscar Torre
(Deuce Moran), Heather Seiffert (Pam Duberry),
Maxx Maulion (Lear Levin), Sanford Holsapple
(Clark Dunwoody), Cara Picton (Inga Sprawler).
Credits: *Producer:* Thomas Mills, Wendy Winston.
Writer-Director: Thomas Mills. **Comment:** Enjoy-
able but not to be taken seriously Syfy Channel
Ghost Hunters take off with the PIT team out to de-
bunk supposed unnatural occurrences.

Episodes: *1.* Grant Me Asylum. *2.* Dead and
Breakfast. *3.* Ghostus Interruptus. *4.* No, No Robot.
5. You Know What They Say: Bigfoot. *6.* Something
Approaches.... It Looks Blonde. *7.* Pheromones
Gone Wild. *8.* Unzipped.

756 Places Please. vimeo.com. 2010.

Sex and the Beach is a spoof of the TV series *Sex
and the City* that is set to film in Hoboken, New Jersey, and star three working class New York actors
(Emmy, Fitz and Jack). Emmy, Fitz and Jack, friends
who have a difficult time acquiring acting roles, are
suddenly propelled into a new light when they are
chosen as the stars by Emmy's friend, Cammy
(whose Uncle Marty has put up the money for the
project). The program charts what happens when
the *Sex and the Beach* goes into production but often
dim the hopes of the friends to achieve notoriety
when numerous production problems plague the series.

Emmy grew up in a controlled religious sect and
is thus a bit naïve when it comes to the real world.
While she does hold down a job, she is most thrilled
about her potential acting career and usually takes
whatever roles come her way. While she is talented
as an actress, she is somewhat unprepared when it
comes to dating and usually falls for the wrong type
of guy.

Trevor, a former door-to-door salesman who
failed in his dream to become the greatest such person, gave it up to turn to his true love of acting (he
honestly believes he is "God's gift to Hollywood"
even though he hasn't had a single acting lesson; he
feels he just needs the right insider to discover him).

Jack is not only an actor but the program's writer
and director. He recently lost a high-paying corporate job and hopes to make it big on *Sex and the
Beach*.

Michael Fitzgerald, called Fitz, is like a throwback
to the past, searching for the East Village Arts scene,
something that has since disappeared. He is more
culturally defined than his friends and has hopes of
living life as a downtown artist but for the time being
Sex and the Beach appears to be his only source of
income.

Cammy, though a bit overweight, claims that people say she looks like Sarah Jessica Parker (as she did
on *Sex and the City*). She believes she deserves recognition as she began acting as a baby in the early
1980s. Acting is the only life she knows and she will
live it as long as she can.

Cast: Rodney E. Reyes (Jack), Rachel Skrod
(Emmy), Jonathan Weirich (Fitz), Daryl Denner
(Trevor), Nancy Pagan (Cammy), Rodney E. Reyes
(Jack). **Credits:** *Producer-Writer:* Rodney E. Reyes,
Jonathan Weirich, Daryl Denner. *Director:* Rodney
E. Reyes, Rachel Skrod, Jonathan Weirich. **Comment:** A good story, with good acting and directing
with Rachel Skrod very appealing and a standout in
the program. For whatever reason, there is bleeped
foul language (either purposely done or an after-
thought when it was decided vulgar language was
not needed).

Episodes: *1.* Sex and the Beach. *2.* Showcase
Yourself. *3.* Whose Whine Is It Anyway. *4.* Ebony
and Ivory.

757 Plant. plantwebseries.com. 2013.

Todd and Tammy Lawn are ministers who, after
twenty years of marriage, have decided to follow

through on a promise they made when they married: build (plant) a church in the heart of New York City. With virtually no funds, little knowledge as exactly what to do and facing opposition from Paulette Whack, Pastor of a "blood-thirsty mega church," Todd and Tammy venture forth into uncharted territory to build their dream church. They are assisted by Gwendolyn Jones, a former C.E.O. who has become their treasurer.

Cast: Liz Days (Tammy Lawn), Lynn Berg (Todd Lawn), Susannah Jones (Gwendolyn Jones), Peggy Queener (Paulette Whack), Marie Cecile Anderson (Amber Burke), Stephan Amenta (Matthew Lawn), Linda Elizabeth (Chloe). **Credits:** *Writer-Director:* Andrew Nielson. **Comment:** Poking fun at religion is not always easy and most TV series that attempt have failed (like *In the Beginning* and *Soul Man*). Presenting Tammy and Todd as somewhat naive as to what they are doing adds to the enjoyment and, coupled with good acting and production, makes for something different to watch.

Episodes: *1.* Pilot. *2.* Sacrifice. *3.* Joyful Noise Unto the World. *4.* Lock In. *5.* David and Goliath. *6.* Jesus Chips. *7.* Fallacy. *8.* Give It All to God. *9.* Mysterious Ways. *10.* Forgive Us Our Trespasses. *11.* Through the Looking Glass. *12.* Good Cop, Bad Cookies. *13.* Movin' On. *14.* Modesty Is Important. *15.* The Brood's All Here.

758 *Platonic (2011).* youtube.com. 2011.

Does a platonic relationship actually work? Can a man and a woman actually remain friends without intimate encounters? A young woman named Melissa would like to know the answer to that question and sets her goal to find out. With her theories that such a situation is not possible, Melissa begins her mission: to seduce men she knows and discover for herself who are her true friends and those who want her only for sex.

Cast: Leah McKendrick (Melissa), Sara Fletcher (Tricia), Brendan Bradley (Tommy), Bradley Fletcher (Jimmy), Rosalind Rubin (Voice of Reason). **Credits:** *Writer-Director:* Benny Fine, Rafi Fine. **Comment:** The program opens like a scene from *Sex and the City* (the women talking around a table) and presents a well acted and produced look at one woman's relentless efforts to find the truth. There are adult situations and foul language is too generously used.

Episodes: *1.* Friends with Benefits. *2.* Attacked! *3.* Love and Marriage. *4.* Love Thy Brother.

759 *Platonic (2014).* platonicseries.com. 2014.

Two years ago Gray and her best friend M.J. gave into temptation and had a one night stand. The encounter changed their relationship and they agreed that it was never to happen again but remain friends.

It is the present and Gray and M.J. work as servers at a bar-restaurant called The Thirsty Tuna Restaurant. It has an over-sexed bartender (Ames), a high-strung manager (Tony) and a dysfunctional chef (Barry). Although they agreed to maintain a platonic relationship they work together and the program charts their efforts to do what they promised as well as dealing with all the behind-the-scenes nonsense that occurs among the restaurant employees.

Cast: Gracie Lane (Gray), Matt Jackson (M.J.), Eamon Kelly (Ames), Navaris Darson (Tony), Kelly Morris (Maddie), Sonny Valicenti (FNG), Keri Safran (Jasmine), Patrick Daniel (Chef Barry), Dakota Greene (Bobby). **Credits:** *Producer:* Gracie Lane, Brent Findley. *Writer-Director:* Matt Jackson, Selena Lane. **Comment:** Avoid watching the promo that is available as it is badly produced and will do nothing to interest you in checking out the series. The idea of platonic relationships has been done countless times before (even in the prior title) but when it is well acted and presented, it becomes something different and, despite the foul language (really not needed) enjoyable to watch.

Episodes: *1.* Pilot. *2.* Hysterical Maddie. *3.* Injaculation. *4.* Anniversary. *5.* 86 Thirsty Tuna. *6.* Taj Mahal.

760 *Platoon of Power Squadron.* platoonofpowersquadron.com. 2009–2014.

It is a time when supernatural abilities are not just limited to comic books, movies and TV shows. It is a time when four ordinary blue-collar workers (Donald, Sebastian, Virginia, and Jonas) discover they are the only people that possess unique abilities. There are no crazed super villains, fancy costumes or spectacular weapons; there are just four twenty-somethings trying to live as normal life as possible while struggling to harness their supernatural abilities. Donald is alias Mr. Dr. Electricon; Sebastian (a girl) is Madam Generator; Virginia, Princess of the 4th Dimension; and Jonas, Prof. Synapse. Their everyday jobs, however, are quite ordinary: Donald is the mascot of a taco stand (Cuernavaca), Virginia, who loves to knit, works in a crafts store (Close Knit); Sebastian, who can duplicate herself, works as a clerk at Half-Price Books; and Jonas is a clerk in a comic book store (Dark Tower).

Cast: Craig Benzine (Donald), Eliza Toser (Virginia), Carlyn Janus (Sebastian), Jake Jarvi (Jonas). **Credits:** *Producer:* Jake Jarvi, Eliza Toser, Tim Ferrin. *Director:* Jake Jarvi. *Writer:* Jake Jarvi, Christopher Davis. **Comment:** The program explores what it is like to be someone extraordinary while having to hide who you really are. They do attempt to solve local crimes (or what they believe are crimes) and the entire production is well acted and produced.

Episodes: *1.* The Last Slice. *2.* Jobs. *3.* Transition. *4.* Identity. *5.* Fate. *6.* Barrier. *7.* Catalyst. *8.* Fight.

761 *The Player Characters.* webserieschan
nel.com. 2012.

Melissa is a young woman who feels she needs to
escape her real life for a few days. Realizing that
LARPing (Live Action Role Playing) may be the answer, she joins The Crossden LARP Group. Although the whole idea behind LARPing is to have
a character and physically act out that character's actions, she decides to make things up as she goes
along. She creates the alias Mesa and the program
follows the group as they act out their fantasies, here
to battle evil goblins in a pretend medieval forest.

Cast: Kathleen Burns (Melissa/Mesa), Phil Hart
(Sid), Michael Floria (Brighton), Michael Frank
(Rash/Goblin), Genna Schnorrbusch (Marr/Gob-
lin), Jessica Suiter (Event Producer), Al Kopka (War-
lord/Black Knight), Gabi Kenny (Warlord Fan-
girl/NPC Goblin), Alisha Moge, Steve C. Albanese,
Ed Barren (Goblins). **Credits:** *Producer-Director:*
Kathleen Burns. *Writer:* Phil Hart. **Comment:**
While the premise is geared to gamers (as people
unfamiliar with gaming terms may not understand
everything that is happening) it is also not as appealing as other programs encompassing gamers.
The characters are just not believable and the acting
is quite lame at times. The production is also just
about standard for a low budget web series.

Episodes: *1.* Assassinate! *2.* Wakeup Call. *3.*
Looking for Group. *4.* The Box. *5.* Warlord. *6.* Rescue Party. *7.* All Powerful.

762 *Playing Dead.* webserieschannel.com.
2008.

One day, while on her computer, a young actress
(Grace) receives an e-mail chain letter that states if
you forward it to 15 people within five minutes, a
wish will be granted. Grace, out of work and in need
of money, wishes for an acting job then forwards the
e-mail. Seconds later there is a knock at her door—
and it is Death, dressed in black, who has come to
grant her wish with a job offer—assisting him in es-
corting people into eternity. Believing it will be an
easy gig, Grace accepts. Stories relate what happens
as Grace begins her job as the assistant to Death (to
allow him to take some much-needed time off).

Cast: Suzanne Keilly (Grace Bass), Noel Orput
(Death), Kristen Roberts (Mona, Grace's friend).
Credits: *Producer:* Ted Raimi, Kurt Rauf. *Director:*
Ted Raimi. *Writer:* Suzanne Keilly. **Comment:**
Suzanne Keilly is delightful as Grace in a nice comedy-horror mix that moves right along. The acting
is good and the program itself is well produced with
an ending that leaves the doorway open for future
episodes.

Episodes: *1.* Curtains. *2.* Dead End Job. *3.* Rots
the Matter. *4.* Dead in the Water. *5.* Death with a
Side of Sickles. *6.* You Oughta Be in Coffins. *7.* The
Totally Dead Show. *8.* That Girl's a Reaper.

763 *Please Tell Me I'm Adopted.* indiego
go.com. 2015.

Tiffany Grant's world has just crashed. She has
been fired, dumped by her boyfriend and lost her
home. With no money or job prospects, and with
no other choice, she moves in with her sister Emma
and her husband Bob. Tiffany feels she needs to find
herself; Emma is delighted to have Tiffany with her;
Bob does feel Tiffany needs to find herself—but
somewhere else. The program follows what happens
as Emma tries to keep the peace as the tension between Tiffany and Bob simply won't go away.

Cast: Nicole Michele Sobchack (Tiffany), Andie
Karvelis (Emma), Ben Kacsandi (Bob). **Credits:**
Producer: Heather Hall, Andie Karvelis, Suzanne
Rydz, Nicole Michele Sobchack. *Director:* Larry
Soileau, Emily Moss Wilson. *Writer:* Andie
Karvelis, Nicole Michele Sobchack, Larry Soileau.
Comment: A very enjoyable outing with very good
acting and production values.

Episodes: *1.* And Then There's Tiffany. *2.* This Is
Not Tom Cruise. *3.* There Is No Tiffany, Only Zoul.
4. Walking Through Walls. *5.* Truth, Care or Oba-
macare. *6.* John@harem.com. *7.* And Now There Is
a Chicken.

764 *Plus Utilities.* youtube.com. 2012.

Three friends have begun what could be considered a "Mission: Impossible" task: find the perfect
roommate. Gary, Elliot and Sniffles are the friends
and the program chronicles what happens with each
of the perspective roommates who answer their ad,
with episode 5, "A Girl Moves In," being the most
humorous as Sadie (Anne Kathryn Parman) soon
regrets even answering the ad.

Cast: Roy Ruben (Gary), Miles Crosman (Elliot),
Jeff King (Sniffles). **Credits:** *Producer-Director:* Roy
Ruben. *Writer:* Jeff King, Miles Crosman, Roy
Rubin. **Comment:** Place an ad and review potential
roommates sounds like a simple plot and not very
interesting. However, add three odd roommates
seeking someone who is normal to them adds the
ingredient that is needed to take something ordinary
and make it different. The acting and production is
also very good.

Episodes: *1.* Todd Moves In. *2.* Ted, the Humor-
less Man Moves In. *3.* Crippin Moves In. *4.* Sock
Moves In. *5.* A Girl Moves In. *6.* Justin Moves In.

765 *Poker Night.* webserieschannel.com.
2012.

Derek, Gary, Robert and Trevor are friends who
gather for a weekly game of poker. But each gathering is not as simple as four guys just sitting around
a table and playing cards. It is what happens at each
game as the friends not only try to make each game
different but discuss what has happened to them
during the week prior to the game. Derek, a Jack of

all trades, is a poor loser, unable to hold a steady job and "lives in strip clubs." Gary, "a cheapskate extraordinaire," is the "team" leader. Robert is a narcissistic personal trainer and Trevor, a naïve teenager, is the butt of the group's jokes.

Cast: Simon Acok (Derek), Patrick Carrick (Trevor), Alex McArthur (Gary), Thomas Petrakos (Robert). **Credits:** *Producer:* Ellen Fraser. *Writer-Director:* David Cooper. **Comment:** Basically a talkative program that has most of its scenes set at the poker table with the friends simply talking about what has or will happen.

Episodes: *1.* Dating Advice. *2.* Grumpy Young Men. *3.* Interrogating Trevor. *4.* Unsuitable Santa. *5.* Bump in the Night. *6.* Man, Meat, Fire. *7.* Date Night.

766 *Ponderings.* vimeo.com. 2012.

Two men situated in a specific setting (a park or the forest as an example) simply express their views on a topic that interests them (from how Canadians play hockey to whether ghosts are real or not).

Cast: Jeremy Larter, Robbie Moses, Scott Gallant, David Phillips, Kinza Baker, Kelly Caseley. **Credits:** *Producer-Writer:* Jeremy Larter, Robbie Moses. *Director:* Jeremy Larter. **Comment:** As simple as putting two guys in one place and have them talk about something. That is the premise and it plays well provided you are interested in the topic being discussed. Some of the characters are quite unappealing and an immediate turnoff. Vulgar language is incorporated but not to a great extent. Programs of this nature are a hit-and-a-miss situation where the performers must appeal to the viewer. What may appeal to one viewer might not to another viewer and each viewer must make his or her own evaluation

Episodes *1.* Thrusting. *2.* Not a Bad Guy. *3.* Good Looks. *4.* The Point of Life. *5.* Evolution. *6.* God's Creatures. *7.* The Canadian Way. *8.* Beggars Can't Be Choosers. *9.* Heaven. *10.* Personal Hygiene. *11.* Ultimatum. *12.* Dinosaurs. *13.* Nobody's Perfect. *14.* Ghosts. *15.* Beer vs. Weed. *16.* Zoo Sexuals. *17.* One Hell of a Doctor. *18.* The Five Senses. *19.* Change. *20.* Male Extinction.

767 *Poor Me.* webserieschannel.com. 2013.

Alex, a young woman who is a roommate with Kris, sustains herself by working several part-time jobs. All is progressing well until she is fired from one of them (dog walking) and money suddenly becomes a problem. Unsure of what to do, Kris, who cares deeply for Alex, steps in and figures that Alex needs a full-time job and elects to help her find one. The program charts what happens when Alex follows Kris's advice and finds that she is only cut out for part-time jobs that require very little effort to fulfill.

Cast: Ashley Friedlander (Alex), Rachel Amanda

Bryant (Kris), Jimmy Bowman (Tommy), Brian Flynn (Ryan). **Credits:** *Producer-Writer-Director:* Ashley Friedlander. **Comment:** The program is billed as "Tales of a poor girl and her less poor roommate." It is very well done and produced and with attractive leads becomes an enjoyable program to watch.

Episodes: *1.* The Stitch. *2.* The Feet. *3.* The Food Van. *4.* The Repairwoman. *5.* The Bad Good Fortune. *6.* The Set-Up.

768 *Poor Paul.* youtube.com. 2008–2011.

Paul is a Walter Mitty–like young man who lives in a fantasy world where he is always the hero in any trying situation. He is roommates with Justin (annoyingly smart) and Clyde (a neat freak) and puts up with all their nonsense but never does anything to stop it. There is a girl in the picture, Bonnie, Clyde's sister, who likes Paul, but Paul is too blind to see that. Paul lost his mother when she died while experimenting with mushrooms in culinary school and now lives vicariously through his own Internet blog. The situations that arise to make Paul imagine he is the only person that can save the day are profiled.

Cast: Zack Bennett (Paul), Samantha Droke (Bonnie), Kevin G. Schmidt (Justin), Nicholas Braun, Wes Whitworth (Clyde), Sean Michael Beyer (Mr. Ted), Floriana Lima (Elizabeth). **Credits:** *Producer:* Sean Michael Beyer, Zack Bennett, Geoff Hoff, Steve Mancini, Kevin G. Schmidt. *Director:* Sean Michael Beyer, Kevin G. Schmidt, Zack Bennett. *Writer:* Geoff Hoff, Steve Mancini, Sean Michael Beyer, Kevin G. Schmidt, Zack Bennett, Samantha Droke. **Comment:** Episodes are not in the proper aspect ratio (images are not normal; here they are stretched to fill the screen) and this is compounded by the annoying shaky (unsteady) method of filming (normally used to express a statement— but not in every scene). There are also bad camera shots (like one actor's back totally obstructing another actor) and overall just a poorly produced program.

Season 1 Episodes: *1.* Eat Your Seaweed. *2.* You Look Good Naked. *3.* Blocked. *4.* We're Irish, Not Italian. *5.* Two Generations of Sad. *6.* You Gonna Smoke That? *7.* A Rusty Trombone. *8.* Cocha O'clock. *9.* Halloween Special: Beer Pong. *10.* Rub & Tug. *11.* Paul's Sister. *12.* Paul's BroSter? *13.* Plymouth Rock Red. *14.* Roadie. *15,16.* It's a Poor Paul Christmas. *17.* I Know a Guy. *18.* Shrooms. *19.* 'Eff Ups. *20.* From the Heart. *21,22.* Q&A.

Season 2 Episodes: *1.* Where the Hell Is Paul? *2.* Big Hands. *3.* What Did You Do, Wear His Underwear? *4.* There's a Fire Down Below. *5.* The Body's Not Even Cold. *6.* Fiesta del Amor. *7.* Women! *8.* When the Walls Come Crumbling Down. *9.* Times Are a Changin'. *10.* You're a Guy. *11.* Laissez-les Bon Temps Roulez. *12,13.* At On with Nature. *14.* Life

Goes On and On ... and On. *15.* Now and Then and Stuff. *16.* It's a Paul Poor Wedding. *17.* The Beginning of the End. *18.* You Can't Live with Them. *19.* You Can't Live Without Them. *20,21.* It's Not All About You. *22.* 'Eff Ups & Stuff. *23.* If Fred Can Do It, So Can Paul!

769 Porn School. youtube.com. 2013.

According to Philippe, the Head of Acting at Porn School, one of every twenty students that attend acting schools go onto the professional stage; one out of fifty will go into film or TV. But what about the others? That is why Porn School was created and with Jenny, the coordinator and head of physical expression, as his assistant, Philippe has set his goal to teach willing students the art of performing in adult (pornographic) films. The students of Porn School are followed as they learn how to become adult film stars. See also *The Institute.*

Cast: Tony Llewellyn-Jones (Philippe), Heather Mitchell (Jenny), Gabrielle Scawthorn (Coral), Briallen Clarke (Cindy), Paige Gardiner (Samantha). *Students:* Brenton Amies, Matthew Backer, James Buckingham, Zoy Frangos, Stefanie Jones, Katie McDonald, Tim Reuben. **Credits:** *Director:* Akos Armont. **Comment:** The program is very suggestive regarding simulated sexual situations, although there is no nudity, its presentation, while well acted, is not geared for a general audience.

Episodes: 3 untitled episodes, labeled "Episode 1," "Episode 2" and "Episode 3."

770 Possum Death Spree. youtube.com. 2007.

In Alaska scientists attached to U.S. Research Station 37–5X uncover evidence that, during the prehistoric age, killer possums roamed the earth and were in part responsible for the demise of the dinosaur. More startling than that is their discovery of frozen possums in a glacier. Unfortunately, their discovery comes on the hottest day of summer and melts the glacier containing the possums. While the possums appear to be harmless, the scientists soon discover they are anything but as they attack anything that moves. The program follows the scientists' efforts to destroy a new enemy when the ravenous possums attack—and appear virtually indestructible.

Cast: Gareth Smith, Michael Horowitz. **Credits:** *Producer-Writer-Director:* Gareth Smith, Michael Horowitz. **Comment:** Extreme amounts of violence, blood and gore mix with plush animal possums whose conversations are seen in view-able dialogue.

Episodes: 3 untitled episodes, labeled "Episode 1," "Episode 2" and "Episode 3."

771 Post Life. youtube.com. 2013.

John is a middle-aged man who has worked for the Australian post office all of his life. He is a widower and the father of Stella and thought he was set for life until he was dismissed from his job. Now John is lost and unsure of his next step. A ray of hope enters his life when he meets, by chance, Melanie, a woman from his past on whom he had a crush. As John and Melanie begin dating John is still without a job and the program charts his experiences as he navigates a world in which he now feels lost as being a postal worker is the only life he has known.

Cast: Felino Dolloso (John), Monireh Khabiri (Melanie), Kathy Luu (Stella), Michele Conyngham (Mrs. McPherson). **Credits:** *Producer:* Amin Palangi. *Director:* Rushan Dissanayake, Mike Kang. *Writer:* Rushan Dissanayake, Mike Kang, Peter Yu, Latifa Hekmat, Anika Herbert. **Comment:** Australian produced program that is well acted and produced and, with its likeable characters, enjoyable to watch

Episodes: 5 untitled episodes, labeled "Episode 1" through "Episode 5."

772 The Potstickers. youtube.com. 2012.

In virtually every high school there is one very special girl (here Fanny) that is admired afar by another student. Ben is that other student, a socially awkward 15-year-old who simply cannot build up the courage to even approach Fanny. Ben feels comfortable with the friends he has known since grade school (Alec and GK) but they are stuck in the same rut—afraid to talk to girls and hooked on video games. Alone they appear to be vulnerable but together they are mighty and devise a plan to get Ben and Fanny together. The program chronicles their plan of action: crash a party that will allow Ben to hook up with Fanny (or so they think).

Cast: Andrew Hu (Ben), Victoria Park (Fanny), Jeremy Steel (GK), Zac Wong (Alec), Jeff Bee (Broyce), Jacqueline Barrett (Emily), Doug Weng (Young-Sang), Justin Song (Hyun-Joon), Abraham Pan (Mole). **Credits:** *Producer:* Shawn Wong, Ishai Setton. *Director:* Zac Wong. **Comment:** Asian-themed program with standard acting and production values that uses a tired plot with an Asian twist.

Episodes: 4 untitled episodes, labeled "Episode 1" through "Episode 4."

773 Prepare: Zombie Apocalypse. funnyordie.com. 2013.

A zombie apocalypse has been predicted and the world is about to change. Some people are disbelieving while others, like Jonah and Conner, a rather unpleasant pair (in what they do and how they act) know it is going to happen. Jonah and Connor are making plans (mostly in their bathroom as they bathe together) with the program revealing not only those plans but what to do if water is no longer available for their bath.

Cast: Andreas Damm (Conner), Jacob-Sebastian Phillips (Jonah). **Credits:** *Producer-Writer-Director:* Jacob-Sebastian Phillips, Andreas Damm. **Comment:** Why some producers think unpleasant, truly annoying or disgusting characters are funny is something that is perhaps known only to them. As such, a program like this becomes a matter of, if you like gross, you will like *Prepare*; if not, don't touch it with a ten-foot pole. Series that attempt the unpleasant never make it on network or cable TV and, just like the broadcasters have learned their lessons on what not to do, Internet producers have to learn their lessons on what not to do also.

Episodes: *1.* How Do You Save Water? *2.* What if There's No Water? *3.* How Do You Keep Warm? *4.* What Do You Do When You're Bored? *5.* How Do 2 Men Reproduce? *6.* How to Find a Mate. *7.* Repopulation. *8.* The Panic Room. *9.* This Is Sparta. *10.* Z-Day.

774 *Pretty, Dumb.* pretty dumb.tv. 2014.

Doug DuPree, a young man living in Montana with a dream to become an actor, takes the initiative and heads to Los Angeles. With limited funds, Doug moves into an apartment that he shares with Earl and Justin, two eccentric actors who also earn money by modeling. As Doug pursues his dream the program follows what happens when Earl and Justin's antics (like preparing for a zombie apocalypse) constantly hinder his chances and what he does to overcome the damage they have caused.

Cast: Cash Black (Doug Dupree), Jackson Palmer (Justin), Parker York Smith (Earl), Travis Eller (Tony Mazda), Paul Cervenka (Mitch), Deidre Lee (Emma), Pamela Portnoy (The Chick). **Credits:** *Producer:* Joshua Vonder Haar, Jackson Palmer. *Director:* Joshua Vonder Haar. *Writer:* Jackson Palmer. **Comment:** Although the subject matter of struggling actors has been done before, each attempt can be different if it is well acted. That is the case here and an enjoyable program has emerged.

Episodes: *1.* California Crash Course. *2.* Zombies. *3.* Hiccup Pick-Up. *4.* Duck Fat. *5.* Accent Accident. *6.* Mitch Unmasked. *7.* The Ones That Are There for You. *8.* Liking a Viking. *9.* Ragnarok. *10.* California Crash Course, Part 2.

Pretty, Dumb. Series poster art (used by permission).

775 *Pretty in Geek.* youtube.com. 2012–2013.

Dani is a young woman who is addicted to video games. She has conceived her own table top fantasy game (Dani's World; but also called Elfheim), made herself the Dungeon Master and has somehow managed to convince her friends, Stacey, Erin, Anna and Jason to become a part of her game-playing world. The program charts the situations that occur over a year as Dani begins her game—and efforts to become its champion.

Dani has been obsessed with video games for as long as she can remember and has become an expert on Elfheim and has so perfected her skills that she is theoretically the best DM (Dungeon Master) in the world.

Stacey, labeled "The Flake" is not quite sure how she got roped into Elfheim. She is not really into video games, is a bit eccentric but has a good heart and unable to say no to Dani.

Anna, considered "The Power Gamer," is out to beat Dani at her own game. She has a rather strange fascination with fire and "exploding things." She has anger management issues and always holds a cigarette lighter in her hand as a means of hopefully controlling them.

Erin, called "The Cheater," does not totally understand the game's concept and resorts to cheating to achieve her goals. Although she doesn't consider what she does as unethical (she calls it "bending the rules") she is out to do what it takes to become the game's champion.

Jason, "The LARPer," the lone male player, is a bit over-the-top and has done nothing but taken a back seat to his female competition. He is dating Stacey, but only doing so as he felt it was better than having her continually stalk him.

Cast: Meghan Fritchley (Dani), Jennifer Krukowski (Stacey), Stefne Mercedes (Anna), Todd Caryl (Jason), Elize Morgan (Erin). **Credits:** *Producer:* Scott Albert, Christopher Guest, Elize Morgan, Courtney Wolfson. **Comment:** Although all the "action" is set in the room in which the game is being played, the diverse choice of characters works well and each can be seen as being involved, but only doing so because they apparently have noting better to do. It is also a change of pace to see a group of very pretty girls as the gamers and not the usual male geeks as portrayed on so many TV series.

Episodes: *1.* Zombie'd. *2.* The Riddle. *3.* Trapped. *4.* Arte-Frak. *5.* Infernadoed. *6.* Mixed. *7.* The Elf Madness. *8.* Double Knight Night.

776 Pretty the Series. prettytheseries.com. 2010–2015.

A spoof of child beauty pageants (like TV's *Toddlers and Tiaras*) that follows Michael Champagne, the father of five-year-old Annette, to win for her the Miss Star Eyes Pageant. Rabina, his wife, doesn't seem to oppose this. She works as a professional smoker ("I smoke for a living") for the United Tobacco Association of America by testing their new products full time. Michael, who is apparently a house husband, is too focused on the contest to see that Rabina is having a secret affair with her brother-in-law, Ethan. Although Annette is only five, she is played by an adult actress (it is explained that Annette "had a growth spurt") and the program charts all the drama and back-stabbing that occurs as a father, instead of the normal mother, becomes a backstage father.

Cast: Stace McQueen (Annette Champagne), Sam Pancake (Michael Champagne), Dee Freeman (Rabina Champagne), Terri Simmons (Parker Kensington Parker), Troy Conrad (Ethan Champagne), Michael Taylor Gray (Royce Adams), Kirsten Vangsness (Meredith Champagne), Denise Alexander (Louise Fitzpatrick), Madeline Long (Bernadette), Melissa Peterman (Candy), David Robert May (Patrick), Alison Quinn (Ginger Adams), Jennifer Elise Cox (Lucy Devonshire), Genie Francis (Dr. Kate), Moira Quick (Eve), Juliette Jeffers (Caviar), Anthony Anderson (Nathaniel Mink), Martha Byrne (Janice). **Credits:** *Producer:* Thordis Howard, Kirsten Vangsness, Doug Prinzivalli, Steve Silverman. *Writer-Director:* Steve Silverman. **Comment:** Splendid exaggeration of child beauty pageants with excellent acting and production values. Stace McQueen is simply delightful as Annette and, if you have seen *Toddlers and Tiaras* it will make you think that program is hiding something for all the foul play that goes on in the Miss Star Eyes Pageant.

Season 1 Episodes: *1.* A Pretty Pilot. *2.* A Pretty Day at the Pageant. *3.* A Pretty Flashing. *4.* A Pretty Night in the Hotel. *5.* A Pretty Season Finale.

Season 2 Episodes: *1.* A Pretty Return. *2.* A Pretty Illegal Sequins Dealer. *3.* A Pretty Make-out Session. *4.* A Pretty Day for a Pageant. *5.* A Pretty Secret Ex-Wife. *6.* A Pretty Twist or Two or Three. *7.* A Pretty Finale.

Season 3 Episodes: *1.* Welcome to Pretty Pageant Therapy. *2.* A Very Pretty Epiphany. *3.* A Very Pretty RV. *4.* A Pretty Hot Mess. *5.* Meet the Minks. *6.* A Pretty Dangerous Situation. *7.* Pretty Desperate Measures. *8.* The Prettiest Finale Yet.

Season 4 Episodes: *1.* A Pretty New Beginning. *2.* A Pretty Family Reunion. *3,4.* A Pretty Competition Day. *5.* Pretty Big Finale.

777 PR13STS (Priests). webserieschannel.com. 2013.

David is a young Deacon who, after completing his seminary training, moves in to a rectory with three priests to begin his internship before taking his vows. But Deacon David's journey is not a normal one as a film crew has chosen to produce a documentary based on his experiences. The program charts David's efforts to not only contend with the duties of such a person, but deal with three eccentric priests and the off-the-wall parishioners that are a part of the church community.

Cast: David Taylor (Deacon David), Steve Verhulst (Father Richard), Anton Rayn (Father Polzceky), Aston Crosby (Father McCallahan), Parvati (as credited, Mathilda), Lauren Farrell (Gwen), Steve Arons (David's father). Deborah Pautler (Shirley). **Credits:** *Writer:* Kim Rybacki, Sean Tracy. *Director:* Sean Tracy. **Comment:** Based on the only episode that remains on line (Episode 4), shades of the feature film *Going My Way* can be seen although in a far-less convincing manner. The production values are good and the acting acceptable although David appears to be a bit naïve and the priests a bit hard to accept as being real.

Episodes: 5 untitled episodes, labeled "Episode" 1 to "Episode 5."

778 *Print Models.* youtube.com. 2012.

"Every year thousands of slightly average people move to Los Angeles in pursuit of a dream. They want to be.... Print Models. They want to grace the pages of mid-level clothing magazines. They want to be the smile in the brochure that gets you to enroll in a commercial college. This is the story of two of those dreamers." Caroline and Winona, very pretty young women with a dream to become print models, are those dreamers. The program charts their experiences as they learn that dreaming about something and actually pursuing it are two different worlds, especially when hard work is also involved.

Cast: Marianne Sierk, Heather Thomson, Daisy Gardner. **Comment:** Scripted series about models have not found great success on television. *Paper Dolls*, *Living Dolls* and *Models, Inc.* are three examples that tackled both print and high fashion modeling. *Print Models* is told from a different perspective and is actually quite good. Caroline and Winona (not Carolyn and Wynona as seen in web site information) talk directly to the camera to relay what they are doing and how they feel, adding a personal touch that literally makes the whole series work.

Episodes: 13 untitled episodes, labeled "Episode 1" through "Episode 13."

779 *Professional Friend.* youtube.com. 2013.

Harper is a successful young businesswoman; Larry, her fraternal twin brother, is lazy, unemployed and living with her while he contemplates what he should do. When Harper and Larry return to their parents' home for Thanksgiving, Larry hits on a great idea: use his best asset to his benefit: being a great (but professional) friend. Harper is a bit unsure of Larry's goal but, being a businesswoman she does see potential and resigns to help create the best company possible. With Professional Friend established the program charts what Harper and Larry encounter as they deal with mostly eccentric clients and learn, in the end, what true friendship is all about.

Cast: Jonathan Biver (Larry), Sal Neslusan (Harper), Christian Blackburn (Jake), Christine Donlon (Annie). **Credits:** *Producer:* Sal Neslusan, Doug Bilitch, Paul Rocha. *Writer-Director:* Eric Bilitch. **Comment:** An unusual idea for a business but well acted and produced and, for something a bit different, interesting to check out.

Episodes: *1.* A Decent Night. *2.* The First Client. *3.* Once in a Lifetime. *4.* Pterodactyl Lemonade. *5.* Code M.

780 *The Program.* funnyordie.com. 2014.

A young woman named Peace has just graduated from college with a Ph D. in medieval studies. She also owes $200,000 in student loans. The serenity she felt in school no longer exists and she must face the real world—and find a way to cope with the situation that hangs over her head—how to repay the loan. Her solution: join Debtors Anonymous, a program similar to AA (Alcoholics Anonymous) that presents a series of steps that help people get out of debt by curbing their spending. The only requirement is "a desire to stop incurring unsecured debts." The program charts Peace's experiences, as she and an equally in-debt group of people (Alan, Kelsey, Kevin and Mike) endure the 12 steps of a program that is anything but easy to accomplish.

Cast: Maria Bamford (Peace), Melinda Hill (Kelsey), George Basil (Mike), Oscar Numez (Kevin), Jerry Minor (Newcomer). **Credits:** *Producer:* Maria Bamford, Melinda Hill, Betsy Koch, Anna Wegner. **Comment:** Thus far only two episodes have been produced and for some unknown reason, only a portion of the cast is credited (both on screen and in other sources). The idea is well thought out with good acting and production values. While only the beginnings of the 12 step program are presented, the doorway has been left open for more episodes to follow.

Episodes: *1.* Visions. *2.* Powerless.

781 *Project Hollywood.* projecthollywoodwebseries.com. 2013.

Roommates Jake, Auggie and Holden have one objective: to become part of the Hollywood film industry, even if it means starting at the bottom. The program follows the friends through their various experiences with each other and Jake's courting of his neighbor (Melanie, who has a roommate also named Melanie), his acquiring a job as the personal assistant of TV producer David Dobson; Holden's endless efforts to secure an agent (which he does with the worst of the worst, Milton Spurlock, who casts him in the 'tween mummy movie *Wrapped in Your Love*); and Auggie's friendship with the somewhat sleazy Slick the Pimp.

Cast: Mark Nager (Jake Coleman), Shaun Lavery (Auggie Pace), Jason Etter (Holden Carlisle), Amy McRoberts (Melanie), Vivian Kerr (Other Melanie), Brian Brummitt (David Dobson), Keith Gerchak (Milton Spurlock), Kristin Larson (Rachel). **Credits:** *Producer:* Scott Kieffer Johnson, Laura A. Garcia, Sam Rosenthal, Kristin Larson. *Director:* Scott Kieffer Johnson. *Writer:* Scott Kieffer Johnson, Sean Monguso. **Comment:** With an attractive cast, a good story and a well rendered production, an interesting take on climbing that Hollywood ladder to success is presented.

Episodes: *1.* The Phantom Pilot: Super Duper Edition. *2.* Back in the Game. *3.* Carousel of Progress. *4.* Jake's New Job. *5.* West Hollywood Story. *6.* The David Dobson Five Point Seduction Technique. *7.* Porn Stars Are People Too. *8.* Jake and the Terrible, Horrible, No Good, Very Bad Day. *9.* Found. *10.* Almost Famous.

782 Psychodrama: The Series. psychodra matheseries.com. 2013.

As part of their acting class, students Kimmy, Liza and Luisa are told "acting is not therapy, therapy is therapy" (as the instructor believes all actors "are neurotic messes"). Figuring that seeing a therapist may help their careers, the women decide to do so and unknowingly make appointments with the same one. As each of the women talks with the therapist the program becomes like a collection of stories with each relating humorous incidents that have befallen them as they seek to fulfill their dreams and become actresses. **Cast:** Liza Renzulli (Liza), Kimmy Foskett (Kimmy), Luisa Fidalgo (Luisa). **Credits:** *Producer-Writer:* Kimmy Foskett, Liza Renzulli, Luisa Fidalgo. *Director:* Joseph Bearese. **Comment:** Just a touch of drama can be seen as the women seek careers. But just like so many other such series, foul language seems to be the norm although the program itself is well acted and produced.

Episodes: *0* The Intro. *1.* Indecision. *2.* Sex. *3.* Jealousy. *4.* Motivation. *5.* Communication.

783 Puppet Soap Opera. puppetsoapopera.com. 2014.

They are "just regular monsters" and just trying to find their place in the world. Mary, Brona, C.J., Sophie and Alistair are not only the monsters, but Muppet-like puppet friends as well. It is a turning point in the friends' lives as they have just graduated from college and the program charts their efforts to find their place in a world where, like the family from the TV series *The Munsters*, they are normal but everyone else is weird. **Cast:** Jay Malsky (C.J.), Keith Rubin (Alastair), Kelley Quinn (Sophie), Amanda Giobbi (Mary), Robbie Chernow (Brona). **Credits:** *Producer:* Robert Gelb, Steven Hascher, Amy Wallace. **Comment:** It is an adult-themed puppet series and is enacted by The Punctual Drunks, a talented improvisational group (that uses dialogue made up as the program progresses).

Episodes: *1–6.* Strings Attached.

784 Puppy Love. lstudio.com. 2008.

Short video sequences that feature stories about people living in New York City and the dogs in their lives. **Cast:** Famke Janssen (Maya), Patricia Kalember (Gail), Kristen Johnston (Katherine), Dan Hedaya (Matthew), Sarah Paulson (Emma), Martha Plimpton (Leslie), Alicia Witt (Claire), Bruce Altman (Gary), J.T. Arbogast (Guy), Heather Burns (Ricki), Mikki Baloy (Strange Girl), Derek Cecil (Malik), Sara Chase (Margie), Nadia Dagani (Bianca), Maria Dizzia (Grace), Jason Gray-Stanford (Andy). **Credits:** *Producer:* Ron Qurashi, Grace Naughton, Amy Harris, Diane Charles. *Writer-Director:* Cindy Chu-

pack, Patrick Dinhut, Amy Harris, Jason Reilly, Julie Rottemberg, Liz Tuccillo. **Comment:** An exceptionally well-produced and acted series that comes from the same team that produced TV's *Sex and the City*. The web program has the same feel as the TV series and features a number of TV personalities, like Famke Janssen, Dan Hedaya, Sarah Paulson, Alicia Witt and Martha Plimpton.

Episodes: *1.* Puppy Love. *2.* Upstaged. *3.* Shared Custody. *4.* The Rents. *5.* Whose Dog Is This Anyway? *6.* Whose Afraid of Rosencrantz? *7.* Pretty Boy. *8.* Gone to the Dogs. *9.* Fashion Faux Paws. *10.* The Wait List.

785 Pursuit of Sexiness. pursuitofsexiness.com. 2013.

They are best friends and they are broke. Nicky and Sheer are also single women and self-absorbed. Their goal: look for a good man, easy money and free meals. It is, as the tagline states, "Life, liberty and the pursuit of sexiness." **Cast:** Nicole Byer (Nicky), Sasheer Zamata (Sheer). **Credits:** *Producer:* Aleks Arcabascio, Andrew Soltys. *Director:* Todd G. Bieber, Mitch Magee. **Comment:** African-American production with good production values as it follows the friends and the various men with whom they hook up.

Episodes: *1.* Date. *2.* Thrift Shop. *3.* Facebook. *4.* Sheer Can't Have It All. *5.* Nicky Can't Have It All. *6.* Subway Dance.

786 Quarterlife. youtube.com. 2007–2008.

Dylan Kreiger, a young woman working as the associate editor of *Attitude* magazine, shares an apartment with her friends Debra (works in her father's appliance store) and Lisa (bartender and acting school student). She also maintains a video blog on the social networking website Quarterlife and it is through that blog that a view of her life and those of her friends are presented. See also *2/8 Life*, the spin off series. **Cast:** Bitsie Tulloch (Dylan Kreiger), Michelle Lombardo (Debra Locatelli), Maite Schwartz (Lisa Herford), Scott Michael Foster (Jed Berland), David Walton (Danny Franklin), Kevin Christy (Andy Melman), Mike Faiola (Eric Greensohn). **Credits:** *Producer:* Marshall Herskovitz, Edward Zwick. *Director:* Marshall Herskovitz, Josh Gummersall. **Comment:** The program, which was adapted by NBC as a network series in 2008, was one of the first to encompass the blogging aspect and in 2007 this was something new and thus it was often given harsh reviews. While it was said to "have amateur written all over it" it was really well done when compared to what has emerged since.

Episodes: Each contain six parts. *1.* Pilot. *2.* Compromise. *3.* Anxiety. *4.* Goodbyes. *5.* Finding a Voice. *6.* Home Sweet Home.

787 *Queen Dad.* queendad.com. 2013.

Monty Ellis is middle-aged man with two different lives and jobs: by day he is a plumber; at night he performs as Flora, a drag queen at the Malebox, a gay bar in Vermont run by Betty Hunter. Monty is also gay but at one point in his life, he was straight and did marry (Susan) and had a child (Jack) that he abandoned at birth (in Texas). Years later and unknown to Monty, Jack has begun a search to find his father and meet the man who deserted him. One night, as Monty is returning home from the bar, he sees a stranger asleep on his sofa. The stranger, it turns out is Jack, Monty's 17-year-old son. The program relates a father and son's efforts to reconnect with one another and of Jack's efforts to accept Monty for who he is when he discovers the dual life he is leading. Nick is the bouncer at the bar; Henry is Monty's bisexual friend.

Cast: Sean Moran (Monty Ellis/Flora) Matt Parisi (Jack Ellis), Ethel Goldstein (Betty Hunter), Jon van Luling (Nick Dinoto), Ben Ash (Henry Collins), Vivian Jordan (Susan Ellis), Berta Briones (Dr. Briones), Marc Bouchard (Chipper). **Credits:** *Producer:* Don Bledsoe, Berta Briones, Sean Moran, Arnold Wetherhead. *Director:* Sean Moran. *Writer:* Don Bledsoe, Sean Moran. **Comment:** Good idea but the pacing is a bit slow, making the program feel like it just drags. While the acting and production values are good, foul language on Jack's part sort of ruins the overall feeling of the series.

Episodes: *1.* Drips Are a Drag. *2.* Meet Jack and Jameson. *3.* No Homo. *4.* Halloween Bashed. *5.* Testosterone Trouble.

788 *Queens.* webserieschannel.com. 2010.

Life seemed perfect for John, living in a small Midwestern town until his girlfriend left him and broke his heart. Unable to deal with the situation, John moves to New York City. But Manhattan is the big city and John is unable to handle its fast-paced life style. Unable to go home again, John moves to Queens, New York, and becomes roommates with Benjamin and Willy, gays who are living together but not involved with each other. A bit naïve about city and gay life, John must now contend with the antics of Benjamin and Willy, two off-the-wall gays who are anything but helpful as he seeks to restart his life.

Cast: Cary Mitchell (John), Andrew Waffenschmidt (Benjamin), Sam Albertsen (Willy), Meghan Sinclair (Danielle). **Credits:** *Writer-Director:* John Gebhart, Dure Ahn. **Comment:** The program, billed as "A comedy about living in Queens," is well acted but does contain vulgar language. There are no sexual situations and the primary focus is on John as he attempts to deal with Benjamin and Willy's antics.

Episodes: *1.* Spandex Party. *2.* John's Gay Date. *3.* Willy Wants an STD. *4.* Fag Hag.

789 *Queer Duck.* youtube.com. 1999–2006.

Adam Seymour Duckstein, an animated gay duck better known as Queer Duck since he revealed to the world that he is gay, works as a nurse and is the son of Jewish parents (a mother who is in denial that Adam is gay and a diabetic father). He has an older straight brother (Lucky) and a lesbian sister (Melissa). Also a part of his immediate life is Little Lucky, his seemingly bi-curious nephew and Steven Arlo Gator, Adam's significant other (who is nicknamed Openly Gator). Radio talk show host Laura Schlessinger is Adam's nemesis for her negative attitude toward the gay community. Adam would just like to live the life he has chosen without all the misconceptions and hatreds that are associated with it. Adam, however, likes to gossip about anything that interests him, intrude where he is not wanted and stories follow all the pitfalls that Adam encounters simply because he cannot mind his own business.

Voice Cast: Jim J. Bullock (Queer Duck), Kevin Michael Richardson (Openly Gator), Billy West (Bi-Polar Bear), Maurice LaMarche (Oscar Wildcat), Estelle Harris (Adam's mother), Tress MacNeille (Dr. Laura). **Credits:** *Producer-Writer:* Mike Reiss. *Director:* Xeth Feinberg. **Comment:** An early animated series that has suggestive content but strays from sexual situations and vulgar language. The program uses flash animation that is well done but is not as sophisticated as animation currently seen on broadcast and cable TV.

Episodes: *1.* I'm Coming Out. *2.* Fiddler on the Roofies. *3.* Oh Christ. *4.* Queer Duck. *5.* B.S. I Love You. *6.* The Gayest Place on Earth. *7.* Gym Neighbors. *8.* Queer As Fowl. *9.* Wedding Bell Blues. *10.* Ku Klux Klan and Ollie. *11.* The Gay Road to Morocco. *12.* Quack Doc. *13.* Oscar's Wild. *14.* A Gay Outing. *15.* Radio Head. *16.* Tales of the City Morgue. *17.* Homo for the Holidays. *18.* Bi-Polar Bear and the Glorious Hole. *19.* Santa Claus Is Coming Out. *20.* Mardi Foie Gras.

790 *Quest for an Unknown Planet.* qfaup.com. 2012–2013.

Quest for an Unknown Planet is a fictional science fiction television series created and written by Josh Pike and Ron Barrett, young men with vision but their series is far below the genius of real TV programs like *Star Trek* and *Battlestar Galactica*. While *Quest* has everything wrong with it (from below par acting and cheap special effects) it is a cult favorite and has been picked up by its hosting outlet the History Channel for a second season. The program itself, sort of a show within a show, relates how an episode is created with Ron and Josh encompassing aspects of their own lives (dealing with actors, executives and incidents in their personal lives).

The fictionalized *Quest for an Unknown Planet* begins when Dr. Quinn Crusher, a celebrated astrophysicist, conducts an experiment in trans-reality

Quest for an Unknown Planet. Series Post Art (poster by Nathan Smith, Creative Commons 3.0).

Cathryn Mudon (Cathryn), David Bluvband (Glenn)

Credits: *Producer-Director:* Curtis Retherford. *Writer:* David Bartin, Curtis Retherford. **Comment:** Scenes from *Quest* are intermixed with the story and should appeal to science fiction fans just to see how bad the fictional series *Quest* is compared to what the networks and cable have produced over the years. The special effects that highlight the *Quest* storyline are cheap and seeing how the marooned crew deal with the situations they encounter is the fun part of the show.

Episodes: *1.* EPK (Electronic Press Kit). *2* Found Footage. *3.* Ron Goes on a Date. *4.* Spoiler Alert. *5.* Commentary Tracks. *6.* Location Stalk. *7.* Wicket Syndrome. *8.* Glenn Is the #2 Fan. *9.* Plagiarism.

791 QUESTing. webseries channel.com. 2012.

Josh, otherwise known as Zargon, Langston and Garrett (Wizards), Devin (Barbarian) and Nick (Noble Dwarf) are young men dedicated to the 1980s fantasy board game "Hero Quest." Jason believes the game is real and has become the leader of a group of warriors (Langston, Nick and Devin) and has been charged with a mission: Destroy the evil but mighty warrior Felmar. Though the game appears real to Jason but just a board game to Langston, Devin and Nick, they become involved in Josh's fantasies as he sets upon a quest for him

travel that is initially a failure until he retreated to his garage and secretly built an inter-dimensional engine and incorporated it in METCIS (Multiple Earth Transportation Conveyance in Space). The ship was launched and it appeared to be a success until it crashed and seriously damaged the navigation matrix. Like the TV series *Star Trek Voyager* Dr. Crasher and his crew are marooned in space and must find a way to one day return to their home planet of Earth. Dr. Reginald T. Savonius is the Science Officer; Jasmine Ryder is a warrior; and Pharaoh is the alien ally.

Cast: Curtis Retherford (Ron Barrett), David Bartin (Josh Pike), Maegan Maes (Jasmine), Jeremy Bent (Dr. Quinn Crusher), Chris Scott (Dr. Reginald T. Savonius), Matt Mayer (Pharaoh), Dan Hodapp (Tyler Duncan), Dom Manzolillo (Ben),

and his team to become true heroes. Marian, the girl who lives down the hall from Josh and who loves the "Hero Quest" game is called "Girl from 4E."

Cast: Langston Belton (Langston), Nick Carrillo (Nick), Devin James Heater (Devin), Josh Hurley (Josh), Garrett Willingham (Garrett), Marian Brock (Marian). **Credits:** *Director:* Kevin Flinn, Greg Payton. *Writer:* Kevin Flinn. **Comment:** Although just watching a group of people sitting at a table and playing a board game would seem like nothing but a bore, it doesn't play that way here. It is actually interesting to watch (although soiled by foul language and a truly annoying opening theme) as Josh takes on a whole new persona and his friends become a part of his fantasies. The acting and production values are also good.

Episodes: *1*. The Beginning. *2*. Garrett. *3*. The Slaying of Ulag. *4*. Enter the Girl. *5*. Dark Wizard.

792 *A Quick Fortune.* youtube.com. 2014.

It appears to be the 1940s. A young woman (Kate) is near broke having lost all her money (how or how much is not stated). Archie, her friend, is also broke but a schemer who thrives on cons. With no other choice Kate teams with Archie and their attempts to make an "honest" buck are detailed through the far-fetched schemes Kate devises to work her way out of poverty.

Cast: Erin Hunter (Kate), James Silvestri (Archie). Credits: *Producer:* Paul DuBois, Haydn Pryce-Jenkins. *Writer:* Erin Hunter, James Gavigan. *Director:* Abbie Lucas. Comment: Delightful program with very good acting. The setting is reminiscent of a 1940s movie and is filmed in black and white to give it that touch of nostalgia. Whether it is trying to uncover long-lost Mafia money (episode 1) or steal a valuable painting (episode 2) the program never lets you down.

Episodes: *1*. Dead Presidents. *2*. The Painting. *3*. Guacamole Radio Jingle. *4*. Fortune Teller. *5*. The Race Horse.

793 *Rag Dolls.* webserieschannel.com. 2013.

With Los Angeles as the setting, the ups and downs of two young women, friends Laura and Olie, are profiled as they not only seek careers, but true love and happiness. Laura was recently laid off from her job as a real estate company secretary; Olie, a graduate of M.I.T. with a BA in environmental engineering, hates her job. Laura and Olie are from different cultural backgrounds but share a close and unique bond of friendship, a bond that carries them through all the happiness and disappointments they encounter. Billed as "*Sex and the City* with a spunky Latina flavor."

Cast: Melissa Rivera (Laura), Kira Hesser (Olie). Credits: *Producer-Director:* Melissa Rivera, *Writer:* Melissa Rivera, Kira Hesser. Comment: While it is just a story of two girls trying to find the right careers, it is also very well acted and produced. The leads are quite attractive and, although only four episodes were produced, it is well worth watching.

Episodes: *1*. Started from the Bottom. *2*. The Pot Shot. *3*. Undercover Date Agent. *4*. The Sexy Bra.

794 *Ramblers.* vimeo.com. 2011.

Ben (a girl), Dan, Dave and Tom are friends living in Manchester (England). While they appear just like any other twenty-somethings, they are, in fact, unique to themselves as they thrive on comic books, coffee, science fiction movies and miniature golf. Life for them has been, for the most part, one of leisure with few or no responsibilities. But their time as university students is drawing to a close and graduation is pending. A realization of what will happen next is presented as the friends must face the fact that they must soon take their place in the real world and abandoned the simple life they once led.

Cast: David Olsen (Tom), Daniel Winward (Dave), Amy Derber (Ben), Peter M. George (Dan), Zara Denney (Carrie). Credits: *Producer:* David Olsen, Paul Thorp. *Director:* Tom Oldham. *Writer:* Tom Oldham, Paul Thorp, David Olsen. Comment: The program opens with the friends (although you do not know that yet) playing miniature golf. You feel like you tuned in and missed something—like an introduction to the friends and some sort of story line. The program continues to be a bit evasive and coupled with its very talkative format is really not a comedy in the typical sense (although it is billed as one). The acting and production is good but the program needed to establish its format and characters at the very start and not wait until the writers felt it was a good time.

Episodes: 10 untitled episodes, labeled "Episode 1" through "Episode 10."

795 *RandomCreepyGuy.com: The Series.* dailymotion.com. 2011.

There is a website called RandomCreepyGuy.com that was established in 2009 and has only one purpose: post pictures of creepy guys with an open forum for users to post comments. It is run by friends Ben and Michael. The site has become so popular that people actually ditch work to post comments. Not satisfied with what they have they decide to steal a website called BACONisBOMB.com, which is run by a husky brute named Pigman. Pigman had established the site as a means of luring and torturing men through his gorgeous female associates, the D–Cups. With the site no longer his, and with vengeance on his mind, Pigman begins a quest to retrieve his domain by bringing down Ben and Michael.

Cast: Chris Arreguin (Michael), Niall Madden (Ben), Tommy Germanovich (Jake), Mike McAleer (Merv), Gian Molina (Pigman), Carrie Keranen (D–Cup Kim), Lauren Dobbins Webb (D–Cup Rachel), Charlie Gelbart (D–Cup Phee), Brenda Sanchez (Malena Hougen), Agnes Leach (Roachells). Credits: *Producer-Writer:* Chris Arreguin, Bryan Yong, Mike McAleer. *Director:* Zachary Lee. Comment: While the overall theme deals with website domination it becomes a bit confusing with so much happening at one time. Once you grasp the story line it becomes interesting, especially with the introduction of Pigman and his D–Cup girls and how some people can be manipulated by the Internet (and possibly suggests that some sort of FCC regulation needs to be implemented as to what is allowable).

Episodes: *1*. The Setup. *2*. Merv's Party. *3*. Mo

Money, Mo Problems. *4.* The Worst Interview. *5.* Worst Lawyer Ever. *6.* We Stole a Website. *7.* Merv. *8.* D–Cups Come Out to Play. *9.* Super Hot Ex-Girlfriend. *10.* Creep Off. *11.* The Kidnapping. *12.* Bacon Torture. *13.* Here Comes the Fuzz. *14.* Who's Screwing Up.

796 The Rascal. webserierschannel.com. 2010.

Sinclair Maddox is small time hood who thrives on cons. He has earned the nickname "The Rascal" and feels the time has come to upgrade his lowly status by devising a scheme that will take him into the big leagues. After much thought he offers to sell a super secret formula called Cold Fusion to the highest bidder. As word spreads the FBI takes an interest and is now seeking Maddox. Maddox's plan is to first create an interest in something (here Cold Fusion) then actually create it. In its planning stages the idea sounded fine. Now that it has been let loose, the U.S. wants it as well as foreign governments. But unknown to everyone but Maddox, Cold Fusion does not exist. The program follows Maddox as he seeks to figure out what Cold Fusion should be then acquire the money he needs to make it and sell it to the highest bidder.

Cast: Jay Rondot (The Rascal). **Credits:** *Director:* Ross Novie. **Comment:** All episodes and virtually all text information have been taken off line. It was not possible to expand upon the cast or credits or explain in more detail what Cold Fusion would actually become (sort of like the plot to the Rock Hudson-Doris Day movie *Lover Come Back* wherein scientist Hudson needs to create a product that was advertised before it existed).

Episodes: *1.* Fusion. *2.* Nigerian Nightmare. *3.* Death.... Valley. *4.* Abu Dhabi Derby. *5.* Mexican Mess. *6.* Bad Chicken. *7.* Animal Crackers. *8.* Global Conflict. *9.* A Positive Reaction. *10.* Rocky Bottom Blues. *11.* Two to Tango. *12.* Someone's Gonna Die.

797 Raymond & Lane. raymondandlane.com. 2014.

Everyone encounters something that aggravates them. For friends Raymond and Lane, encountering something that annoys them is just a part of their daily lives. They are a bit delusional and the program follows their efforts to deal with all they encounter as they just try to be themselves and lead as normal a life as possible.

Cast: Matt Cullen (Lane), Troy LaPersonerie (Raymond), Maddie White (Camille), Cailan Rose (Blair), Samantha Purnell (Monique), Joey Voccia (The Anthony). **Credits:** *Producer-Writer:* Matt Cullen, Troy LaPersonerie. **Comment:** While not outright slapstick, it is humorous but is does suffer from hard-to-understand dialogue at times due to the acoustics of the rooms in which some scenes are set.

Episodes: *1.* The Festivity Session. *2.* Delusions of Grandeur. *3.* Kristie/Kristy. *4.* Friendly Neighbors. *5.* A Crash Course in Modeling. *6.* The Pool Party. *7,8.* Employment.

798 Read the Signs. webserieschannel.com. 2013–2014.

It appears that Alicia's marriage to Jack is about to end as Jack has not been able to perform as he once did in the bedroom. Believing that therapy may be the answer, they seek out Dr. Sandi Ramesh, a relationship therapist who is has her own unique solutions to people needing sexual counseling. Alicia is a white collar professional and Jack, a traveling accountant consultant who is often away on business, feels jealous that his wife makes more money than he does. The advice given by Sandi, a liberated feminist, sends Alicia and Jack on whirlwind ride of uncertainty that any of her solutions will work, especially when she enjoys overpowering men to have sex with their wives. The program chronicles what happens when Alicia and Jack deviate from Sandi's strange suggestions and seek separate adventures outside their bedroom to hopefully find the reason for Jack's problem and solve it themselves.

Cast: Luke Anthony (Jack), Jennifer Linkous (Alicia), Ansuya Nathan (Dr. Sandi Ranesh). **Credits:** *Producer:* Michael W. Denison. *Writer-Director:* Luke Anthony. **Comment:** With the exception of a teaser, all episodes have been taken off line. Judging by the teaser, the acting and production are good and there appear to be sexual situations and adult language.

Episodes: *1.* Slippery Slope. *2.* T-Intersection. *3.* Two-Way Traffic. *4.* Sharp Turn. *5.* Crossroad. *6.* Winding Road.

799 Real Adult Feelings. realadultfeelings.com. 2012.

Ethan is a young man whose life takes a turn for the worse when he inherits his late mother's home and finds that it is deeply in debt (mortgaged to the hilt) and he is now responsible for maintaining it. Without money or any ideas as what to do, Ethan finds help from his friend Rob, who moves in with him. But even with his rent, Ethan finds that he is still lacking money. One night, after a drinking binge, Ethan and Rob place an ad on CraigsList seeking a roommate and acquire two: a young artist (Alice) and a mysterious man (Alex). The program simply relates events in the seemingly normal lives of Ethan, Rob and Alice and the somewhat secretive life Alex leads with Ethan and Rob determined to find out just who he is and what he is hiding.

Cast: Mikiech Nichols (Ethan Sanders), Sierra McKenzie (Alice), Devin Badoo (Rob Barnes), Eric Sanders (Greg). **Credits:** *Producer:* Jason Ryan, Bobby Farrington, Eric Sanders. *Writer:* Bobby

Farrington, Eric Sanders. **Comment:** Rather slow-moving program that is hampered by bad camera work (unsteady panning back and forth coupled with the up and down bobbing of the shaky camera method of filming). Using vulgar language at the drop of a hat also does not help move things along or make for comedy. Episodes are also very long (the pilot, if edited together runs over 40 minutes while additional episodes are well beyond 20 minutes each). Internet programming needs to be short and right to the point to hold viewer interest. It appears the producers became aware of this after the fact as there are two just under ten minute episodes that recap each of the seasons in a much faster paced production: "The Best of Season 1" and "The Best of Season 2."

Season 1 Episodes: *1,2.* Pilot. *3.* Rob. *4.* Ethan. *5.* Alice. *6.* Greg.

Season 2 Episodes: *1,2.* The Beach. *3.* STD: Less in Seattle. *4.* Welcome Home, Alice.

800 *The Real Zombie Hunters of America.* youtube.com. 2013.

Robert Daily is a man who virtually stands alone in a world ravaged by a recent zombie apocalypse: a big game hunter that has made his target the walking dead who have become a dangerous part of society.

The program charts his efforts—from setting elaborate traps to becoming the bait with all his great expectations rarely working out as planned.

Cast: Richard McGonagle (Robert Daily). **Credits:** *Producer-Writer-Director:* Michael J. McDonough. **Comment:** Enjoyable take on zombie hunters with a likable lead and well written and directed episodes.

Episodes: *1.* Interview with a Zombie. *2.* 4-D Zombies. *3.* Human Bait. *4.* Revenge of the Zombies. *5.* Zombies Aloha.

801 *Reasons Y I'm Single.* reasonsy.com. 2013.

Banana Splits is a therapy group for children, aged three to five, whose parents are divorced. Three girls, Doris, Gina and Joannie met and became friends at such a session and have remained so over the years. They are now in their thirties and still single. As each of the women seeks to discover the reason why she is still unmarried the program follows the paths they take to remedy that situation by finding that elusive man, settle down and begin a family.

Cast: Elaine Del Valle (Doris), Holie Barker (Joannie), Gina Tuttle (Gina), Karin de la Penha (Joannie's mother). **Credits:** *Producer-Director:* Elaine Del Valle. *Writer:* Jolie Barker. **Comment:**

The Real Zombie Hunters of America. Series poster art (used by permission).

The numbers that appear in the episode list refer to the reason number. The idea is different and is well acted and produced.

Episodes: *1.* I Tweet Jay Z. *2.* #38. *3.* #39A: The Latina Date. *4.* #40. *5.* #42.

802 Re-Casting Kyle. recastingkyle.com. 2014.

Weisberg-Hall Television is a casting company dubbed "White Hot TV" due to its method of only casting "young, white, attractive actors." When the company comes under scrutiny for its narrow-minded casting decisions, Kyle McNaughten, the shallow, driven and somewhat racist head of the company (even though she is African-American), is ordered to fix the issues and make it more diversi-fied. Kyle's efforts to change the company's casting profile as well as dealing with all the personal crises in her life are profiled..

Cast: Courtney Banks (Kyle McNaughten), Zac Currier (Ben), Shaleah Wagner (Lindsay), Ester Mira (Corrine), Nicholas Anthony Reid (D'Jmari-ous Ashley), Kyle Jones (Scott), Joseph Kibler (War-ren), Ethan Ingle (Mark), Laura Owen (Lily). **Cred-its:** *Producer-Writer:* Courtney Banks. *Director:* Robert Adams. **Comment:** The program does tread on iffy waters by profiling an African-American woman who is seemingly prejudice toward all races except Caucasian. The twist—she doesn't realize she is until *The New York Times* TV reviewer posts a col-umn in which he exposes the company's casting prac-tices. While she is very pretty, Kyle does have a vul-gar vocabulary (really not needed). The idea is very good (as is the acting and production) and the only complaint would be the over-use of actors audition-ing for roles (which interrupt the follow of the story as they are used as cutaways to show mostly the eth-nic groups that applied for a role but didn't get it).

Episodes: *1.* Pilot. *2.* Diversity Is... *3.* The Intern, the Witch and the Black Chair. *4.* Not Jewish, Defi-nitely Black. *5.* Move In Die. *6.* Candy Mountains. *7.* Fat Chicks and Crazy Chicks. *8.* Boyfriend/Girl-friend. *9.* All American Ass. *10.* Keep Your Options Open. *11.* Love? Locked Down. *12.* West Holly-wood Bull****.

803 Reception. vimeo.com. 2011.

Andrew is a young man who has just acquired a job as the receptionist for a theatrical casting com-pany. As Andrew sits at his front desk, the program simply relates what he does—from welcoming and directing visitors to texting messages when there is nothing to do.

Cast: Dean Chekvala (Andrew). **Credits:** *Pro-ducer:* Graham Ballou. *Writer-Director:* Will Slo-combe. **Comment:** The website synopsis states sim-ply "Andrew has a new Job." And that is exactly what it is about. Despite its simplicity it is well done.

Episodes: *1.* Alison. *2.* Showbiz. *3.* It's Not Just Prom. *4.* I Heart Vampires. *5.* Sushi at Ralph's.

804 Red Shirts. youtube.com. 2013–2014.

"Space, the final frontier, especially for the crew of the *I.S.C. Bechon*. Their mission: Survival" opens a program that is a spoof of the 1960s series *Star Trek*. The *I.S.C. Bechon* is a Starfleet-like space ship that explores the universe. It is captained by Lieu-tenant Davi and her crew consists of foul-up Ensigns Barry, Monroe and Garibaldi (there was a fourth En-sign, Bostwick, but he was "accidentally vaporized"). The sexy but no-nonsense Captain, Selena True-heart, oversees their assignments. Barry, Monroe and Garibaldi have just graduated from Basic Space Training and have been assigned to the *Bechon* where they accept missions that can only guarantee them a five point three percent chance of survival. Those missions are charted as the *Bechon* explores the un-charted regions of outer space.

Cast: Nick Armstrong (Ensign Barry), Heather Barr (Lt. Davi), Shannon McKain (Ensign Monroe), Arnie Pantoja (Ensign Garibaldi), Deanna Russo (Capt. Selena Trueheart), Brandon Henry Ro-driquez (Ensign Bostwick). **Credits:** *Producer:* Ryan Gowland, R. Benjamin Warren. *Director:* Ryan Gowland. *Writer:* Ryan Gowland, R. Benjamin Warren. **Comment:** You do not have to be a fan of *Star Trek* to enjoy the program. It is a well-done spoof with good acting and production values. The characters are immediately like-able and the action flows smoothly from episode to episode. The special effects, though minimal, are well done and the only drawback would be its unnecessary use of vulgar lan-guage.

Season 1 Episodes: *1,2.* Space Welcome. *3.* Space Cyrano.

Season 2 Episodes: *1,2.* Space Criminal. *3.* Space Weed. *4.* Space Amazon.

805 Red vs. Blue: The Blood Gulch Chron-icles. blip.tv. 2003–2013.

It is the near future and there exists a box canyon in the middle of nowhere. It is considered worthless but it does contain flags, something that is appar-ently valuable as two groups of Spartans (soldiers), divided into the Red and Blue forces have begun an unrelenting Civil War to acquire them. As the battle rages, the program explores the events that occur as well as profiling the soldiers who are engaged in a war they do not understand or want for acquisition of flags whose significance is unknown.

Blue Team members include Church, a soldier with an attitude; Tucker, a guy Church despises; Ca-boose, a dense recruit; and Tex, a mercenary who was paid to assist the Blues. On the Red Team, Sarge is the unbalanced drill sergeant-like leader of an equally misfit troop; Grif is absent minded but quite talkative; Simmons ranks along with Church as being his team's only sane member; Donut is a dimwit who has no idea what he is doing; and Lopez is a non-speaking robot built by Sarge.

Voice Cast: Burnie Burns (Leonard L. Church), Jason Saldana (Lavernius Tucker), Geoff Lazer Ramsey (Dexter Grif), Joel Heyman (Michael J. Caboose), Matt Hullum (Sarge), Dan Godwin (Franklin Delano Donut), Kathleen Zuelch (Tex Alison), Yomary Cruz (Sheila the Tank), Nathan Zellner (Andy the Bomb). **Credits:** *Producer:* Burnie Burns, Joel Heyman, Geoff Lazer Ramsey. *Director:* Burnie Burns, Matt Hallum. *Writer:* Burnie Burns. **Comment:** Based on the video game *Halo: Combat Evolved*, it encompasses scenes from this game and its sequel games (*Halo 2, Halo 3, Halo 4, Halo: Reach* and *Halo 3: ODST*) synchronized to prerecorded dialogue and other audio effects. Comedy does mix with science fiction as it details the not-so-heroic aspects of the war. The comedy can be related as what the viewer sees as being funny, sometimes not what the writer intended (comparable to a TV sitcom where a laugh track is used to convey the fact that this is funny, you should laugh too).

2003 Episodes: *1.* Why Are We Here? *2.* Red Gets a Delivery. *3.* The Rookies. *4.* Head Noob in Charge. *5.* The Package Is in the Open. *6.* Giga-Whats?? *7.* Check Out the Treads on That Tank.

8. Don't Ph34r the Reaper. *9.* After Church. *10.* A Shadow of His Former Self. *11.* Knock, Knock, Who's There? Pain. *12.* Down But Not Out. *13.* Human Peer Bonding. *14.* Roomier Than It Looks. *15.* How the Other Half Lives. *16.* A Slightly Crueler Crueller. *17.* Points of Origin. *18.* SPF 0. *19.* Last One Out Hit the Lights.

2004 Episodes: *20.* Red vs. Blue. *21.* The Joy of Toggling. *22.* Sweet Ride. *23.* Last Words. *24.* Nobody Likes You. *25.* Nine Tenths of the Law. *26.* In Stereo Where Available. *27.* Radar Love. *28.* I Dream of Meanie. *29.* Room for Rent. *30.* Me, Myself and You. *31.* An Audience of Dumb. *32.* Aftermath, Before Biology. *33.* What's Mine Missing. *34.* Nut. Donut. *35.* Dealer Incentive. *36.* K.I.T. B.F.F. *37.* Best Laid Plans. *38.* Visiting Old Friends. *39.* Let's Get Together. *40.* You're the Bomb, Yo. *41.* Make Your Time. *42.* We Must Rebuild. *43.* New Toys. *44.* We're Being Watched.

2005 Episodes: *45.* It's a Biological Fact. *46.* Heavy Metal. *47.* Roaming Charges. *48.* Silver Linings. *49,50.* Untitled Episodes. *51.* Have We Met? *52.* Let's Come to Order. *53.* Hello, My Name Is Andrew. *54.* Defusing the Situation. *55.* Calm Before the Storm. *56.* The Storm. *57.* Familiar Surroundings. *58.* Hunting Time. *59.* Fight or Fright. *60.* Fair Competition. *61.* Lost in Triangulation. *62.* The Hard Stop. *63.* Previous Commitments. *64.* Looking for Group. *65.* Exploring Our Differences. *66.* Setting a High Bar. *67.* Getting All Misty. *68.* Talk of the Town. *69.* Sneaking In.

2006 Episodes: *70.* You Keep Using the Word.

71. Getting Debriefed. *72.* Under the Weather. *73.* Right to Remain Silenced. *74.* Things Are Looking Down. *75.* Two for One. *76.* The Arrival. *77.* You Can't Park Here. *78.* Get Your Back. *79.* Baby Steps. *80.* Sibling Arrivalries. *81.* The Grif Reaper. *82.* In Memoriam. *83.* Strong Male Figure. *84.* Yellow Fever. *85.* Brass Tacts.

2007 Episodes: *86.* The Nesting Theory. *87.* Spelunked. *88.* The Haystack. *89.* Terms and Provisions. *90.* Missed Direction. *91.* Where Credit Is Due. *92.* Biting the Hand. *93.* Tucker Knows Best. *94.* Loading... *95.* The Wrong Crowd. *96.* Uncommicado. *97.* Same Old, Same Old. *98.* Repent the End Is Near. *99.* Why Were We Here? *100.* Don't Get Me Started. *101.* Free Refills. *102.* Visiting Hours.

2009 Episodes: (Episodes were not produced in 2008). *103.* Catching Up. *104.* Local Host. *105.* One New Message. *106.* Bon Voyage. *107.* Directions. *108.* My House, from Here. *109.* Lay of the Land. *110.* Dumb Cop, Bad Cop. *111.* Well Hello. *112.* Called Up. *113.* The Installation. *114.* Watch the Flank. *115.* Retention Deficit. *116.* Trust Issues. *117.* Hang Time. *118.* Think You Know Someone.

2010 Episodes: *119.* For Those of You Just Joining Us. *120.* Drink Your Ovaltine. *121.* Upon Further Review. *122.* Recovering One. *123.* 4th and Twenty. *124.* Towing Package. *125.* And Don't Call Me Shirley. *126.* Pursuing the Archive. *127.* Backup Plans. *128.* This One Goes to Eleven. *129.* Restraining Orders. *130.* Snooze Button. *131.* Battle of the Exes. *132.* Reconfiguration. *133.* Check Your Local Listings. *134.* Standardized Testing. *135.* Tenth Percentile. *136.* Rally Cap. *137.* Reunion. *138.* N+1.

2011 Episodes: *139.* Rounding Error. *140.* The Twins. *141.* Number One. *142.* Evacuation Plan. *143.* Realignment. *144.* Familiar Feelings. *145.* Case File 01.045. *146.* Shaking the Foundation. *147.* Captive Audience. *148.* Introductions. *149.* Lifting the Veil. *150.* Mid-Game Substitution. *151.* Planning the Heist. *152.* Son of a Bitch. *153.* The Sarcophagus. *154.* Hell's Angels. *155.* Spiral. *156.* Labor Pains. *157.* Whole Lot of Shaking. *158.* Hate to Say Goodbye.

2012 Episodes: *159.* Heavy Metal. *160.* Follow the Leader. *161.* Turbulence. *162.* The New Kid. *163.* What's the "I" Stand For? *164.* Oversight. *165.* Fall from Heaven. *166.* Fighting Fire. *167.* C.T. *168.* Out of Body. *169.* Out of Mind. *170.* Greenish Blue with Envy. *171.* New and Improved. *172.* Three's a Crowd. *173.* Happy Birthday. *174.* Remember Me How I Was. *175.* Change of Plans. *176.* Party Crasher. *177.* Reckless. *178.* True Colors. *179.* Don't Say It.

2013 Episodes: *180.* One-Zero-One. *181.* Get Your Tucks in a Row. *182.* Barriers to Entry. *183.* Heavy Mettle. *184.* A Real Fixer Upper. *185.* S.O.S. *186.* Can I Keep It? *187.* The Grass Is Greener. The Blues Are Bluer. *188.* A House Divided, Then Multiplied. *189.* Long Live the King. *190.* Worst Laid Plans. *191.* Finders Keepers. *192.* +1 Follower. Reconciliation. *193.* Neighborhood Watch. *194.* FAQ.

195. Ready.... Aim ... *196.* Fire. *197.* Lost But Not Forgotten.

806 *Redwood Time.* webserieschannel.com. 2013.

People appear to be drawn to Hollywood more than anyplace else to break into show business and Carter Redwood is no exception. While he does work as an artist he also has aspirations to become an actor and the program relates his efforts to balance his personal life with his work life and his dream life.

Cast: Carter Redwood (Carter Redwood), Wesley T. Jones (Lamont), Layla Yvonne (Keri), Michelle Veintimilla (Alise), Harron Atkins (Virgil), Veladya Chapman (Jamie). **Credits:** *Producer:* Carter Redwood, Clarence Williams IV. *Writer-Director:* Clarence Williams IV. **Comment:** The acting and production are okay but the story of struggling young actors has been done numerous times before.

Episodes: *1.* I Like You, Like You. *2.* Deluxe. *3.* Him & Her.

807 *Relationsh*t.* relationshitshow.com. 2014.

Rob and Farrah are a young couple who have moved from the dating stage to sharing an apartment together. Many couples do it; many succeed while just as many fail as they find they are incompatible. Rob and Farrah have had their problems and, based on the advice of a consultant, they have been encouraged to record personal vlogs detailing their problems and how they cope with them. While the program is a look at modern relationships and what can and does go wrong, it also relates those problems through Rob and Farrah's perspective.

Cast: Robin Dunne (Rob), Farrah Aviva (Farrah). **Credits:** *Producer-Writer:* Farrah Aviva. *Director:* Robin Dunne. **Comment:** The program is billed as "An unromantic comedy" and does contain adult language and suggestive situations. It is well acted and produced and ends without a conclusion leaving the doorway open for future episodes.

Episodes: *1.* Jim vs. Bill. *2.* Captain Tiny. *3.* Fat Mirror.

808 *Rent Controlled.* youtube.com. 2014.

After several years as lovers, but living apart from each other, Heather and Jennifer decide to move in together. In less than twenty-four hours they realize they are not compatible and decide to break up. But they also realize they have a problem: they must still live together as neither one can afford to break the lease. Jennifer appears to be fine with the arrangement but Heather is a bit more worried as she still longs for Jennifer. The program follows Heather and Jennifer as they each attempt to move on—with the help of their friends: Kyle and Lauren, and Ted and Carla, straight couples; Helga ("Likes women"), Anna ("Hot stuff"), Karen ("Mature lesbian lawyer") and Bianca ("Jail bait").

Cast: Heather Dean (Heather), Remy Maelen (Jennifer), John Loos (Ted), Abby McEnany (Carla), Dan Wenzel, Jr. (Kyle), Anji White (Lauren), Jax Turyna (Bianca), Bex Marsh (Karen), Charlita Williams (Anna), Natasha Samreny (Helga). **Credits:** *Producer:* Christin Baker. *Director:* Julie Keck, Jessica King. *Writer:* Heather Dean. **Comment:** As with all Tello Films excellent production values and top notch acting. A free on-line trailer gives a good indication as what to expect in terms of adult situations—all of which are expertly handled and sensitively presented.

Episodes: 7 episodes have been produced, all of which are only available through a paid subscription service. See also *Til Lease Do Us Part* for a similar program.

809 *Research.* youtube.com. 2013.

Grant Geffin is considered by his mother and therapist to be, as he says, "mentally retarded." He may be, but he also appears to be a man determined to win the MacArthur Genius Grant, money he plans to use to establish his own business—Geffen Genius Research and Solutioning. Being a genius (and not the mental case his mother believes) Grant wins the money, establishes his company and hires a seemingly insane scientist (Dr. Rust) and a team of researchers (David, Tim and Taylor). While the company is set up for any challenge—from running taste tests and focus groups for corporations to doing research for the individual, the program's principal focus is what happens behind the scenes as the research team attempts to deal with two psychos—Dr. Rust and Grant Geffen and an equally unbalanced receptionist (Kate).

Cast: Barry Bostwick (Dr. Rust), Gabriel Diani (Dave), Autumn Hurlbert (Taylor), Doug Jones (Denny), Kelly Huddleston (Kate), Kahle McCann (Grant), Sean Naughton (Tim). **Credits:** *Producer:* Nick Jones, Melanie Hall. *Director:* Adam Hall. *Writer:* Kahle McCann, Adam Hall. **Comment:** Enjoyable program from start to finish. Barry Bostwick is perfectly cast as the unbalanced Dr. Rust and his performance alone makes the whole program. The acting and production values are also very good and introducing the character of Kate just adds to the craziness that already exists at Geffen Genius.

Episodes: *1.* Pilot. *2.* Secretariat. *3.* Focus Group. *4.* Love Is in the Air. *5.* A Little Light Music. *6.* Puppy Love. *7,8.* Grant Geffen.

810 *The Retributioners.* theretributioners. com. 2007–2009.

Stephanie appears to be an ordinary young

woman living an ordinary life. Although she is married she is not happy as she has not yet proved herself to the world. She is also a bomb waiting to explode due to the fact that people have taken advantage of her over the years and now it is time for payback ("I have never forgotten or forgiven anybody or anything"). Now, with only a vindictive outlook on life, Stephanie sets a plan in motion to get even with all those who wronged her with the program chronicling her efforts to humiliate them as they once did her—from that ex-boyfriend, the school bully to that guy who stole her taxi cab ride.

Cast: Stephanie Faith Scott (Stephanie). **Credits:** *Producer:* Stephanie Faith Scott. *Director:* Eric Rasmussen, Corinne Fisher. *Writer:* Eric Rasmussen. **Comment:** Although similar ideas have been done before, Stephanie's talking directly to the camera to establish her victim and why that person needs to be taught a lesson makes for a more charming program. The acting and production is also very good.

Episodes: *1.* The Virginity Pact. *2.* Juanita Crack-Whore. *3.* Evicted. *4.* Drunk Dial Party. *5.* The Former BFF. *6.* The Taxi Thief. *7.* The Walk of Shame. *8.* Feeling Up Ophelia. *9.* Revenge of the Japs. *10.* Bear Therapy. *11,12.* Facebook Friend Purge. *13.* Oklahoma Xmas Smack Down. *14.* Hippie Freeloader. *15.* Debasing April. *16.* The American Dream.

811 *Return to Sender.* webserieschannel.com. 2012.

Bryan is an elementary school teacher living in Brooklyn, New York. His mother (Betty) constantly worries that he has not found the right girl to settle down with and start a family. Although Bryan has no luck with the ladies, he feels comfortable in the life he has set up for himself. It is the day of Bryan's thirtieth birthday and for her present to Bryan, Betty presents him with Svetlana, a Russian mail order bride. Bryan is not too pleased with what has happened and the program follows Bryan as he attempts to deal with all the problems that arise as Svetlana becomes a part of his life and Svetlana's efforts to cope with a world that is totally foreign to her.

Cast: Rebecca West (Svetlana), Jason Beaubien (Bryan), Therese Plaehn (Bridget), Anthony Gaskins (James), Erin Buckley (Buck), Jodie Lynne McClintock (Betty), Lisette Silva (Rosa). **Credits:** *Producer:* Jason Beaubien, Rebecca West. **Comment:** A new twist on an old theme with good acting and production values. Mail order bride stories have been done countless times before on TV, but adding the twist of a mother ordering her for her son (and the son's efforts to avoid her at all costs) is a nice twist. The program also sports a lively selection of Russian music for its soundtrack.

Episodes: *1.* From Russia with Love. *2.* A Hero of Our Time. *3.* Mothers and Sons. *4.* Nest of the Nobility. *5.* Between Dog and Wolf. *6.* Crime and Punishment. *7.* The Master and Margarita. *8.* The Irony of Fate. *9.* Anna Karenina. *10.* Doctor Zhivago. *11.* Notes from the Underground. *12,13.* War and Peace. *14.* Battleship Potemkin.

812 *Rich Girl, Poor Girl.* webserieschannel.com. 2008.

Reality combines with comedy for a "Prince and the Pauper"-like tale of a wealthy 19-year-old Pacific Palisades girl (Tarra) and a low income 19-year-old Los Angeles girl (Angie) who switch lives for a week to learn how the other half lives and what makes them different from each other. Their interactions with family and making new friends form the basis of stories.

Cast: Tarra Woolen (Tarra), Angie Riccio (Angie). **Credits:** *Producer:* Gary Auerbach. **Comment:** All episodes have been taken off line but based on what text information still remains, it was billed as a "Comedic social study experiment" designed to show how both girls find positive and negative aspects of the other's life. The subject switch is not new and had been mostly recently used as the basis of the ABC series *Wife Swap*.

Episodes: *1.* Welcome to My Life. *2.* The Swap. *3.* Initiation. *4.* Shop Til You Drop. *5.* Brand New Me. *6.* My New Man. *7.* Ain't We Got Fun! *8.* Guess What's Coming to Dinner? *9.* A Day in the Life. *10.* Let's Party. *11.* The Return. *12.* Home Sweet Home.

813 *Riddled with Anxiety.* youtube.com. 2012.

Tim and Shilly are young, free-spirited men who share an apartment. Each has his own quirks and each must learn to live with the other despite the annoying things each one does that bothers the other. The "Odd Couple"-like program relates simply the exchange of dialogue that occurs as each tries to adjust to what happens around them, mostly situations caused by their not totally being able to live with one another.

Cast: Tim Pavlacka (Tim), Nick Rubbo (Shilly), Jen Timper (Jen). **Comment:** The program uses the actual *I Love Lucy* theme for its theme and becomes nothing but a talk-a-thon between Tim and Shilly and their neighbor Jen as each reacts to a certain situation.

Episodes: *1.* Buyer Beware. *2,3.* Blind Date.

814 *Risa and Christina: Available.* webserieschannel.com. 2011.

Risa and Christina are friends who hug, often dress alike, snuggle up with each other and give each other gifts but claim "we are not lesbians." In spite of what they say, they are thought to be so by their parents (and possibly anyone else who might know them). Feeling they need to change their image, they join OK Cupid, an Internet dating site wherein women seek potential suitors. But will it prove to their mothers that they are straight? The program follows Risa and Christina as they each seek a male mate and what occurs when they do find a likely prospect but go totally overboard in attempting to impress him.

Cast: Risa Sarachan (Risa), Christina Jeffs (Christina). **Credits:** *Producer-Writer:* Risa Sarachan, Christina Jeffs. *Director:* Louis Gruber, Risa Sarachan, Christina Jeffs. **Comment:** Although only Risa and Christina appear, they handle their roles well. Not only are they attractive but the mishaps that occur as they prepare to meet never seen dates are well done and make each episode very enjoyable. Whether or not Risa and Christina are lesbians (or bisexual) is never revealed.

Episodes: *1.* A Note to Our Mothers. *2.* The CEO. *3.* The British Bloke. *4.* The Preschool Teacher. *5.* The Private Investigator. *6.* The Film Buff. *7.* The Politician. *8.* The Asian Guy. *9.* The Doctor. *10.* The Straight Man. *11.* El Guapo. *12.* The Neighbor. *13.* Southern Gentleman.

815 *Robot, Ninja and Gay Guy.* youtube. com. 2009–2010.

Following the unexpected departure of his roommate, Gay Guy (as he is called) places an ad on CraigsList seeking a new roommate to help pay the rent. Ninja, as he is called, becomes his first response but before he can say yes or no, there is a knock at the door and Robot, a human-looking android also applies for the position. Gay Guy's indecisiveness earns him two new roommates and a truckload of problems as he must deal with a gentle Ninja with a secretive past and a Robot curious to learn about the human world (exactly where Robot came from or who created him is not revealed). Three roommates, three differing lifestyles and the situations that develop as Gay Guy, Ninja and Robot each seek to lead separate lives and not intrude on the other's privacy.

Cast: Travis Richey (Gay Guy), Ryan Churchill (Robot), Brian Giovanni (Ninja), Phil Brown (Chad). **Credits:** *Producer:* Rob Wood, Travis Richey. *Director:* Rob Wood. *Writer:* Eric Loya, Travis Richey. **Comment:** A program with excellent acting and production values that flows smoothly from start to finish. The Ninja's disappearing and reappearing—and Gay Guy's reactions are well done and funny.

Episodes: *1.* The Robot Situation. *2.* Origin Story. *3.* The Party. *4.* New TV. *5.* Field Trip. *6.* First Halloween. *7.* Gay Guy's Not Here. *8.* Jealousy. *9.* Game Night. *10.* Ninja Training. *11.* Mr. Furper. *12.* Recurrence.

816 *Rock Star Café.* rockstarcafeshow.com. 2013.

Music blends with comedy for a look at the staff and management of New York City's Rock Star Café. Sam is the floor captain and Rhonda is the assistant manager. Tyler, the principal focus, is a singing waiter with a big dream: to become a rock star; Avery is a ruthless, self-proclaimed "Queen Bee"; Hilary is the unorthodox hostess-server with a dynamite singing voice; Valerie is a busty ditz; Brenda is addicted to alcohol. Moira is a short-tempered girl with a great voice, and Dexter, an easygoing slacker are also Tyler's roommates; Lily is the girl on whom Tyler has a crush.

Cast: Barry Debois (Tyler), Dasha Kittredge (Avery), Helen Highfield (Lily), Zach Miko (Sam), Markesha McCoy (Moira), John Curcuru (Dexter), Veronica Carr (Rhonda), Haley Selmon (Hilary), Kayle Blogna (Valerie), Hannah Lapuh (Brenda). **Credits:** *Producer-Director:* Brayden Hade. *Writer:* Brayden Hade, Andrew Lynagh. **Comment:** Music and songs are interspersed as the waiters perform at the restaurant. It is well performed and produced and an enjoyable change from shows set in diners, cafes or restaurants.

Episodes: *1.* Waiting on the Dream. *2.* Shopped. *3.* America's Talent Show. *4.* Elaine's Broadway Diner. *5.* Health Violations Unit. *6.* Fame. *7.* Eternity: A Play in Three Acts. *8.* One Table at a Time.

817 *Rocky Mountain Oysters.* webseries channel.com. 2013–2014.

Beats, T-Bird, Diddy and Sparks are friends who are uncouth, irresponsible and naïve. The events that spark their often dull lives are presented as the friends attempt to deal with situations that present them outside of their comfort zones.

Cast: Taylor Hibbs, David Sparks, Wally Wallace, Sean Williams, Kassi Jay, Tyfanny Shaddock. **Credits:** *Producer:* Sean Williams, Taylor Hicks, David Sparks, Wally Wallace. *Writer-Director:* Sean Williams. **Comment:** Rather unfunny start when the crude friends make fun of Michelle (Angela Delvecchio), a young woman who just had a mastectomy (as they do not know what that is or how they should act). Once the issue is dealt with (but played much too long) and the guys come to realize they are jerks, the program does improve with better acting and stories.

Season 1 Episodes: *1.* Mister Ectomy. *2.* Electroperaca. *3,4.* Woodsies. *5.* Nose Blows. *6.* Viagra Falls.

Season 2 Episodes: *1.* Antwon Thigrate. *2.* Por Flavos. *3.* Terminal. *4.* I Love You with All My Kidney. *5.* It's Me Or the Merkin.

Season 3 Episodes: *1.* Jailbird.

818 *Rods and Cones.* youtube.com. 2014.

Carole, a lesbian, and Mitzi, a bisexual, are art school graduates and out of work. They are $80,000 in debt (student loans) and desperately seeking a way to keep their heads above water. When they learn of a competition called "The Woman's Comedy Contest" they decide to enter (with their "Hot Mom Act") and hopefully win the "Big Cash Prize." While they are not the only contenders, they most fear George and Bess, called "The MILfies," performance artists in their thirties hoping to win the grand prize by pretending to be "Mommy Comics." The program charts the situations that result as Carole and Mitzi attempt to win the top prize.

Cast: Beth Lisick (Carole Murphy), Tara Jepsen (Mitzi Fitzsimmons), Erin Markey (George), Jibz Cameron (Bess). **Credits:** *Producer:* Lagueria Davis, Kurt Keppeler. *Writer:* Tara Jepsen, Beth Lisick. *Director:* Laurel Frank. **Comment:** Although the series has not been released (as of July. 2015) it appears to be an enjoyable comedy outing just by the brief video information that has been made available. The main leads (Carole and Mitzi) are delightful and play off each other quite well and their competition, George and Bess are the type of villains that you love to hate.

Episodes: *1.* Rods and Cones: A Proposal.

819 *Romantically Hopeless.* youtube.com. 2015.

Phil is a young man looking for love in all the wrong ways and all the wrong places. He really doesn't know what is wrong, but his romantic life is pitiful. But Phil opts to change all that and the program relates his efforts to do what it takes to change his situation and find that one special, elusive woman.

Cast: David Pinion (Phil), Maria Paris (Lisa), Lindsay Payne (Michelle), Matthew Orlando (Harris), Nicole Foti (Abbi), Brandy DeVault (Monica). **Credits:** *Producer:* Radical Soul Productions. *Writer-Director:* Jordan Imiola. **Comment:** Billed as "A web series about a hopeless romantic with the suckiest love life" is somewhat reminiscent of the ABC series *Love, American Style* for its offbeat look at love and its foibles. The acting and production are good but there is the use of vulgar language.

Episodes: *1.* Let's Just Be Friends. *2.* Girl Coming Over. *3.* Online Dating. *4.* Blind Date.

820 *Roomie, Friend, Lovers.* youtube.com. 2012–2014.

Timiko is a very attractive African-American woman with a close circle of friends: Calista, her first cousin (whom she calls a "Miss Goody Two-Shoes" and is always up to no good), Constance, Calista's younger sister, and Tiffany, whom Timiko calls "Lil' Bit." Timiko also rents a room in her home to a young man named Jayson and has a ritual wherein her choice of lovers is based on a sex journal she keeps (and shares with her friends) that rates their performance. Seeing that Timiko's love life is

suffering, Calista, Constance and Tiffany join forces and set out to change the way Timiko sees men. The program chronicles the dates Timiko acquires as she searches for the one man with whom she can love without grading him.

Cast: Shayla Hale (Timiko), Andra Fuller (Jayson), Yaani King (Cherisse), Caryn Ward (Calista), Billy Mayo (Sheldon), Sabrina Revelle, Raquel Rosser (Tiffany), Austen Jaye (Austen), Rockwelle Dortch (Tallulah), Crystal Cotton (Jazz), Ashley Blaine Featherson (Whitney), Hazelle Gobert (Constance). **Credits:** *Producer:* Dennis Dortch, Brian Ali Harding, Jeanine Daniels, Issa Rae. *Director:* Dennis Dortch, Andra Fuller, Shayla Hale. *Writer:* Dennis Dortch, Numa Perrier, James Peoples. **Comment:** Shayla Hale is extremely attractive and can captivate the viewer. The program is an above average production (more like a TV series), very well acted and written and overall one of the best of black-themed Internet love stories. There are adult themes and sexual situations but nothing objectionable.

Season 1 Episodes: 9 untitled episodes, labeled Episodes 1.1 to 1.9.

Season 2 Episodes: *1.* 3 Weeks Later. *2.* Training. *3.* In Her Defense. *4.* Available. *5.* Roosters and Peacocks. *6–9.* Episodes 2.6. through 2.9.

Season 3 Episodes: 9 untitled episodes, labeled Episodes 3.1 to 3.9.

821 *Roomies (2012).* webserieschannel. com. 2012.

Encompassing a line from the opening theme from the TV series *The Odd Couple* ("Can two divorced men share an apartment without driving each other crazy?") forms the basis of a program wherein three mismatched, quirky roommates, Jesse, Will and Trevor, attempt to co-exist amid the strange behavior each exhibits.

Cast: Jesse Laing (Jesse), Trevor Kristjanson (Jesse), Bjorn William Jakobson (Will). **Credits:** *Producer:* Dylann Bobei, Trevor Kristjanson. *Director:* Dylann Bobei, Bjorn William Jakobson. *Writer:* Dylann Bobei, Trevor Kristjanson. **Comment:** With numerous other programs using the mismatched roommates as its subjects, *Roomies* falls into the standard mold as roommates just struggle to live with each other.

Episodes: *1.* The Joke. *2.* Masturbatory Activity. *3.* Testosterone. *4.* Meanwhile in Russia. *5.* Pop-Ups. *6.* Turkish Lessons.

822 *Roomies (2013–1).* onemorelesbian. com. 2013.

Sam and Alex are lesbians who enjoy a plutonic relationship. They live apart from each other and each is involved with whom she believes is the girl of her dreams. Those dreams are shattered when their relationships end but Sam and Alex are not defeated and decide to help each other overcome what has happened. They choose to become roommates and fall in love with what turns out to be an apartment for gay couples only. Although they are only friends, Sam and Alex decide to pretend to be a couple to keep the apartment and the program relates the pitfalls they encounter as they attempt to find romance (with other girls) and keep their true life a secret. See also *The Neighbors*, the spin off series.

Cast: Julie Goldman (Sam), Brandy Howard (Alex), Kelly Beeman (Sally), Hannah Aubry (Tammy), Emily Peterson (Tami), Caitlin Bergh (Cait), Abby McEnany (Sue Fox), Jim Bennett (Dave), Deborah Craft (Tess), Noelle Lynn (Mallory). **Credits:** *Producer-Director:* Christin Mell. *Writer:* Julie Keck, Jessica King. **Comment:** A bit like the TV series *Bosom Buddies* (wherein two males posed as females to keep an apartment). The acting, story line, and production is top rate and worthy of a network or basic cable presentation

Episodes: *1.* Long Time No See. *2.* Waterbugs. *3.* Do You Feel Me? *4.* Sex Addiction Is Real. *5.* Strange Bedfellows.

823 *Roomies (2013–2).* youtube.com. 2013.

Alex and Allegra, currently roommates, were conceived on the same night by two different 1980s musical geniuses. They consider themselves to be twins and share their apartment with a man named Nick. All is progressing well until Nick abruptly leaves to pursue his dream of dancing on Broadway. The twins are now alone and unsure of what to do next. The program follows what happens as they seek a new roommate to get back to the comfortable, safe life to which they have become accustomed.

Cast: Bridget Renshaw, Colt Bell, Alexis Keegan, Jordan McMahon, Margaret Lee. **Credits:** *Producer-Writer-Director:* Bridget Renshaw, Colt Bell. **Comment:** A bit above the standard issue roommate concept (as it encompasses "twins") with good acting and production values.

Episodes: *1.* Goodbye Nick. *2.* Taboo Debacle. *3.* Mary the Mormon. *4.* New Old Beginnings. *5.* Gun Fun.

824 *Roomsies.* theroomsies.com. 2012–2014.

Jenny and Meagan are not only best friends but roommates. Although they constantly joke about everything and appear to be perfect for each other, they each have their own little quirks and it is becoming apparent that each is getting on the other's nerves. A situation is presented and how the women react to it forms the basis of each episode.

Cast: Jenny Donheiser (Jenny), Meagan Kensil (Meagan), Arielle Siegel, Will Payne, Andrew Farmer. **Credits:** *Producer:* Sam Sparks, Dan De-Lorenzo, Jenny Donheiser, Meagan Kensil. *Director:*

Dan Siegel, Sam Sparks. *Writer:* Jenny Donheiser, Meagan Kensil. **Comment:** Delightful "Odd Couple" pairing with Jenny and Meagan not only very pretty but somewhat outrageous (especially brazen when it comes to men) and fun to watch. The acting and production values are very good and there are some suggestive sexual situations that prevail throughout the episodes.

Episodes: *1.* Meet the Roomsies. *2.* Work It Out. *3.* Sexy Time. *4.* Jaggers Anonymous. *5.* Sick Day. *6.* The House Guard. *7.* Third Roomsie. *8.* The Bachelorettes. *9.* Dance Crying. *10.* The Grief Stages of Moving. *11.* Face Time. *12.* Weed. *13.* Cat Calls.

825 *Royal Sabotage.* royalsabotage.tumblr.com. 2012.

Royal, a master at avoiding work is twenty-years old, gay, carefree and living off money that he somehow manipulates from his wealthy family. But he supposedly has some sort of job as he does have a sexy associate named Beau Bardot (a woman). Royal lives in Las Vegas and the program chronicles Royal's playful road to self-destruction.

Cast: Kingsley Benham (Royal Stevenson), J.J. Wienkers (Vegas Smart), Lindsey Moore Ford (Beau Bardot), Alexis Victoria Bloom (Lily/Rose), Patrick Gomez (Antonio Fuentes), Grant Sloss (Grant Tucker), Fuller Huntington, Jr. (Sean Little), Granison Crawford (Jason Black). **Credits:** *Producer:* Kingsley Benham, J.J. Wienkers, Alexis Victoria Bloom, Kimberly Eaton, Patrick Gomez. *Director:* Alexis Victoria Bloom, Patrick Gomez. *Writer:* Kingsley Benham, J.J. Wienkers. **Comment:** Very fast moving program that is well acted and produced.

Episodes: Only 6 of 24 episodes are on line: *1.* Pilot. *2.* You Can Party Foul. *3.* Bruthas and Sistas. *4.* I Will Always Smell You. *5.* The Old Man and the Teeth. *6.* Arsenic and Old Lays.

826 *The Ruby Besler Show.* therubybeslershow.com. 2011–1012.

During the 1950s movie theaters would show short instructional videos before the feature film began. They tackled numerous everyday issues and were often very cheaply filmed and poorly acted. Taking that concept but spicing things up a bit, a very pretty (and sexy) host (Ruby Besler) presents a topic and proceeds to give her audience instructions on how to deal with it, but most importantly how to overcome it.

Cast: Anastasia Barnes (Ruby Besler), Christopher Pelletier (Mateo), Keenan Cahill (Himself), Hazel Fensky (Robin), Carolina Casto (Marisella Morelos), Christopher Pelletier (Spaniard). **Credits:** *Producer-Writer:* Anastasia Barnes. *Director:* Jim Senti. **Comment:** Unique idea that should be on regular television. The program is filmed in black and white and on a set made to look like the 1950s (including period clothes). The acting and production values are excellent and it is without a doubt one of the better web series.

Episodes: *1.* Beaver. *2.* Tap, Tap, Tap. *3.* Jig the Fig. *4.* Chin Spin Grin. *5.* The Art of Manipulation. *6.* Give It a Whirl. *7.* Make Sure He's a Man, Not a Boy. *8.* Buck Up and Smile, It's Been a While. *9.* From Frumpy to Fancy.

827 *Rugged Rock.* vimeo.com. 2013.

Rugged Rock is a theatre touring company based in the United Kingdom. It is run by Zara (the artistic director) and Dorothy (the tour manager) and the company creates and performs issue-based plays. They have just acquired the rights to produce an anti-drug play called *Charlton's Choice* and the program charts what happens (the mishaps) as the company (which includes Bazza, Daniel and Beth) begins rehearsals and prepares the play for its tour.

Cast: Francesca Marie (Zara), Katy Poulter (Dorothy), Helen Oakleigh (Beth), Warren Adams (Bazza), Leon Wander (Daniel). Credits: *Producer:* Francesca Marie, Carl Michael, Ryan Claffey. *Writer-Director:* Francesca Marie. Comment: While the program is basically a behind-the-scenes look at the production of a play, it is very well acted and produced. Although produced in England, the performers speak clearly and there is no problem with British accents as they are easily understandable. The episodes, however, are very long for a web series (20 to 33 minutes each) and thus require a commitment on the part of the viewer to watch them.

Episodes: *1.* Pilot. *2.* #Rugged Rock. *3.* The Rehearsal.

828 *Safety Geeks: SVI.* daveandtom.com. 2009.

P.O.S.H. (Professional Occupational Safety Hazard) is an organization that investigates situations that involve safety hazards and violations ("Keeping the world safe, one accident at a time"). Reginald, an eccentric trillionaire whose family patented the computer keyboard return key, and the team's "sugar daddy," established P.O.S.H. as something for him to do. His team consists of Randi, a gorgeous, sexy ex-stripper turned profiler who has written a bestselling book called *The Castrated Male in Marketing.* Budwin is the Safety Expert and head of the Enforcement Department. Sparks, the world's best computer hacker, uses a wheelchair (suffered a crippling accident when she performed in a circus trapeze act with her family The Flying Van Der Graafs) and is the home base computer whiz. Hopkins, who runs P.O.S.H. Control and regulated to the office, is Reginald's manservant. While the agency's intentions are good, its service is more of a hazard as its operatives are not only less-than-effectual but in polite terms, idiots. The program charts what happens when a case is acquired and everything that can go wrong does.

Cast: David Beeler (Reginald Syngen-Smithe), Tom Konkle (Budwin W. Yaker), Brittney Powell (Dr. Randi Minky), Mary Cseh (Sparky Van Der Graaf), Benton Jennings (Manservant Hopkins). Credits: *Producer-Writer:* David Beeler, Tom Konkle. *Director:* Roger Tonry. Comment: Television worthy production with excellent acting and production values. The characters are well developed and the comedy flows evenly from episode to episode.

Safety Geeks: SVI. Left to right: David Beeler, Benton Jennings, Tom Konkle, Mary Cseh, Brittney Powell (copyright 2010 Lumen Actus/Pith-e Productions).

There are some suggestive adult sexual situations but nothing that borders on being indecent.

Episodes: *1.* Sexy Lap Dance of Doom. *2.* P.O.S.H. Team Is Go! *3.* A Dangerous Blend. *4.* Host Poses and Sh*t. *5.* Okay, He's Really Starting to Smell. *6.* Yes, David Caruso. *7.* Dream On, Dream On. *8.* Mama's Sweet Love. *9.* Meatpacking: A Stripper's Tale. *10.* It's the Cheese: A Bottom's Up Mystery. *11.* Fondling the Truth.

829 Sage the Mage. webserieschannel.com. 2013.

The Arcane Order of the Great Sapphire Atom is an outer space society of magicians that is based on the planet MW6371. Simon, a Level 23 Ultra Magician has been sent to Earth (Los Angeles) to mentor an adorable and very special eight-year-old girl named Sage as a first-class magician. Sage possesses a magic wand (which she calls her "chicken bone") and has the power to bend the laws of nature and explore mystical realms. She is very curious and constantly experiments causing her numerous misadventures as she tries to undo the mischief she creates. Stories follow Sage as she works her way from Young Elementary Class Mage to an Ultra Magician like Simon. Parsley is Sage's brother; Rosemary is Simon's superior.

Cast: Grace Goodell (Sage), Sean O'Donnell (Simon), Georgia Goodell (Rosemary), Milo Goodell (Parsley). **Credits:** *Producer-Writer-Director:* Sean O'Donnell. **Comment:** Grace Goodell is captivating as Sage and stories do not lack for humor or action. There are numerous, well executed special effects as Sage creates her magic.

Episodes: *1.* Sage Rocks. *2.* Parsley's Perplexation. *3.* Let It Snow.... Indeed! *4.* Push Echo. *5.* Sage on the Evil English Ivy. *6.* Sage's Most Awesomest Ever Show. *7.* Trick or Donut? *8.* Out of the Frying Pan. *9.* Into the Fire.

830 Samantha & Samantha. webserieschannel.com. 2012.

Italian-produced program about how Roberto and Vittorio, friends unknowingly dating the same girl (Michela) are dumped then fall into the same situation again when they both meet a girl named Samantha—and again unknowingly begin dating the same woman.

Cast: Giulio Nocentini (Roberto), Andrea Atanasio (Vittorio), Giada Pusterla (Samantha), Ambra Pusterla (Deborah), Nadine Sciara (Michela). **Credits:** *Writer-Director:* Giulio Nocentini. **Comment:** A well-produced and acted program but it is not for everyone as it contains nudity and adult situations. The closed captioning feature needs to be activated for English subtitles.

Episodes: *1.* Bye Bye and Thank You. *2.* Fotting. *3.* L'arte del Rimorchio. *4.* Figli del Divorzio. *5.* Question the Feeling. *6.* The Score. *7.* Non Aprite Quella Porta. *8.* The Dreamers. *9.* Una Serata Bestiale. *10.* Pulp Night. *11.* La Donna, il Sogno e il Grande Incubo. *12.* Rotta Per Casa di Dio. *13.* Carramba! Che Sorpressa. *14.* Se Tutto Va Bene Siamo Rovinati.

831 SanFranLand. sanfranlandseries.com. 2014.

Bobbi is a young Georgia girl who sees a bright future for herself and her fiancé until she catches him paying for the services of a dominatrix. Heartbroken and no longer able to remain in town, she takes the advice of her girlfriends, Coco and Tara, who have recently moved to San Francisco, to join them and start over. As Bobbi begins to navigate a totally new way of life, the program relates what happens as she learns that she can truly be anything her heart desires.

Cast: Ashley Chaney (Bobbi Winters), Chrissy Mazzeo (Tara Walker), Liz Anderson (Coco Rocco). **Credits:** *Producer:* Ryan Lynch, Laura Wainer, Chrissy Mazzeo. *Writer-Director:* Ryan Lynch. **Comment:** Appealing characters, good acting and well produced.

Episodes: *1.* Life Ain't Always Peachy. *2.* San Francisco Dreamin'. *3.* Shake My Peachtree. *4.* Party in My Cabana. *5.* Have You Sinned. *6.* Shades Down Bottoms Up. *7.* Ring in the New. *8.* Put on Your Party Pants. *9.* Rock the Boat. *10.* Ghost of Party Past. *11.* Legalize It. *12.* Best F***ing Year Ever.

832 The Sarah Silverman Program: Animated Webisodes. imdb.com. 2007–2008.

Various aspects of everyday life are satirized through short animated segments.

Cast: Sarah Silverman, Justin Roiland Rob Schrab, Vatche Panos, Abed Gheith, Kelsy Abbott, Steve Agee, Myke Chilian, Brian Posehn, Jay Johnston, Rich Fulcher. **Credits:** *Producer-Writer-Director:* Justin Roiland. **Comment:** All episodes, including all sharing websites, have been taken off line thus a comment is not possible.

Season 1 Episodes: *1.* Steve and Brian. *2.* Sarah's Dream. *3.* Cookies Come Alive 1. *4.* Cookies Come Alive 2. *5.* Fantastimart. *6.* Cookies Come Alive 3.

Season 2 Episodes: *1.* Steve and Brian: Alien Abduction. *2.* Fantastimart 2. *3.* Magic Purse.

833 Sarahnormal. youtube.com. 2013. 2013.

Sarah appears to be just an ordinary teenage girl: pretty, smart outgoing and personable. But unlike other teenagers, Sarah has been blessed with an ability to see and talk to ghosts. Although people call her a psychic, she insists she is not; "I'm a medium." Like Melissa Gordon from the TV series *Ghost Whisperer*, Sarah feels a need to help troubled spirits move on by letting them possess her body to fulfill some wish they were denied when they were alive. The program charts what happens when Sarah, aided by her friends Tally and Brock, become involved in the rather quirky requests the spirits require before they can see the light and move on.

Cast: Ciera Angelia (Sarah), Sasha Kraichnan (Tally), Dabiel Kyri (Brock), Lindsey Bermingham (Lisa), Shariba Rivers (Dorothy), Joette Waters (Velma), France Jean-Baptiste (Thelma). Credits: Producer: Ciera Angelia, Diana Copeland. Director: Diana Copeland. Writer: Ciera Angelia. Comment: While not on the same acting ability or technical aspects of series such as Ghost Whisperer and Profiler, Sarahnormal is unique in that it presents an African-American girl as the protagonist (something that has not been done by network or cable TV). The plots are a bit bizarre and interesting but the overall effect the series is trying to achieve is somewhat ruined by incorporating a needless laugh track. The networks are literally phasing this aspect out of sitcoms but the Internet seems to be incorporating it as several series use this form of sweetening episodes.

Episodes: 1. Death of the Holy Ghost. 2. Special Agent Me. 3. He's the Man.

834 Sassy Batman. sassybatman.com. 2014.

A spoof of the Batman legend that finds the Dark Knight based in Los Angeles and sharing a home with his once nemesis Cat Woman. But Batman, as he is known, is not as daring, brave or prone to fighting crime as he once was. He has many personal issues to deal with and the program charts his efforts to somehow maintain his legend while navigating a life where he wants to be the center of attention—whether you want him to be or not.

Cast: Adam Jefferis (Sassy Batman), Amani Starnes (Jessica), Aries Sanders (Amber), Melissa Bender (Melissa), Kati Sharp (Cat Woman). Credits: Producer: Amani Starnes, Katie Pyne. Writer-Director: Xavier Burgin. Comment: Batman has the look and costume of the feature film versions of the legend but he is simply not that Batman (more of a wimp). The overall production is well acted and produced but there are no action scenes or encounters with the villains typically associated with him (like The Joker and The Penguin).

Episodes: 1. The Dark Boots. 2. It's Too Early. 3. Roomies. 4. That Cat's Out the Bag.

835 Saturday Special. vimeo.com. 2013.

Sarah and Katie are best friends and roommates who share a love of yard sales. The women appear to getting along well together until Sarah's obsession gets the better of her and she becomes too possessive of the objects she buys (especially dolls, which she feels are real and one could be her soul mate). Un-

nerved by what is happening and unable to convince Sarah that her obsession is overtaking her perspective on life, Katie believes that they need time apart and temporarily moves out, leaving Sarah to fend for herself. The program follows what happens as Sarah searches for a new roommate but is hampered by her obsessions, which makes her appear a bit unbalanced.

Cast: Suzan Mikiel (Sarah), Sarah Fraunfelder (Katie). Credits: Producer-Writer-Director: Katie Letien. Comment: A bit unusual to say the least. It is a unique idea and it is well acted and produced. The leads play off each other quite well and Sarah's obsession is so real that she makes you believe that, for example, a doll she just bought is more than just a doll, but a real person.

Episodes: 5 untitled episodes, labeled "Episode 1" to "Episode 5."

836 Saving Rent. blip.tv. 2009.

When a job opportunity comes his way Mike, a project manager moves from Boston to Los Angeles, accompanied by his girlfriend, Kelley, a young musician who hopes to further her career. With the money he had saved, Mike purchases a home. Shortly after, however, due to the worsening economy, Mike is laid off but neglects to tell Kelley, preferring to let her believe he is still working. Without an income and unable to pay the mortgage, Mike convinces Kelley they need to take in roommates to help with the expenses. She agrees and the couple acquire four house mates: Paul, a struggling actor from Canada; Tina, an aspiring actress (in the X-rated adult film industry), Suzie, a 16-year-old runaway (a diner waitress) who pretends to be 21; and Chucho, an illegal Latin immigrant who cleans a bar after closing and who makes extra money by selling liquor to his friends. The mishaps that befall six people as they attempt to live together under one roof are chronicled.

Cast: Alice Cutler (Kelley), Vincent Giovanni (Mike), Jacob Lane (Paul), Mallory McGill (Suzie), Ashley Palmer (Tina), Alex Ruiz (Chucho). Credits: Producer: Alice Cutler, Gary Teperman. Director: Gary Teperman. Writer: Alice Cutler, Gary Teperman. Comment: Despite what he is going through Mike says, "But it's not that bad. I've got my girlfriend and four best new friends" and the program address the subject in a well thought-out story line with very good acting and production values.

Episodes: 1. Roommates Wanted. 2. Finding a Job. 3. What's in the Bowl? 4. Animal Lover. 5. Love and Chronic. 6. You Better Not Snitch. 7. Ahoy Matey. 8. The Stalker. 9. I Love Brownies. 10. There's No Sex in the Champagne. 11. Those Damn Immigrants. 12. Superstar.

837 Savory Burger. youtube.com. 2014.

It has food combinations that are not appetizing;

it is run by a corporation interested in only one thing—profits and it appears to hire anyone who is willing to work for the cheapest pay possible. Paul Miller manages such a business—Savory Burger, one link in a long chain of fast food franchises. Burdened with everything that should not be associated with running a successful franchise—from employees stealing supplies to employees who seem not to know what they are doing, the program charts how Paul attempts to keep his head above water and still please corporate headquarters.

Cast: Roger Schwermer (Paul Miller), Justin Lucas (Russell), Krishna Smitha (Molly), Amira Sharif (Nina), Monica Santos-Quinones (Conchita), Delanie Bitler (Bobbi-Jo), Christian Heep (Mr. Jefferson), Ivy Opdyke (Madame Ivy). **Credits:** *Producer:* The Artist Playground. **Comment:** Nicely produced program that focuses more on the off-beat actions of the personnel rather than of the customers.

Episodes: *1.* Be My Eyes. *2.* I'm Not a Rat. *3.* Performance Evaluated. *4.* What Happened to the Music?

838 *School of Thrones.* youtube.com. 2013.

Characters based on the TV series *Game of Thrones* are transported to the 21st century and seen as teenagers and students at Westeros Valley High School. Westeros, however is not your typical high school. It is here that cliques rule and the highest honor is being crowned Prom King. It is also a school attended by the offspring of noble families and those that are beneath their social level are the outcasts.

Cast: Mary Kate Wiles (Sansa Stark), Nick Palatas (Robb Stark), Austin Rogers (Jon Snow), Ashly Burch (Dany Targaryen), Luke Morgan (Joff Lannister), Brendan Bradley (Renly Baratheon), Maxwell Glick (Stannis Baratheon), Matthew Boehm (Loras Tyrell), Marishia Ray (Melisandre), Nic Novicki (Tyrion Lannister), Joey Richter (Theon Greyjoy), Matthew Mercer (The Hound). **Credits:** *Producer-Writer:* Zach Grafton. *Director:* Matthew Mercer. **Comment:** The program is unique in its coverage and does present a view of high school life that capitalizes on the snobby cliques aspects of other high school-themed programs (like *Popular* and *Square Pegs*). The acting and production values are good and a *Saved by the Bell* it is not.

Episodes: *1.* Prom Night Is Coming. *2.* Sexposition. *3.* Targaryen Burn.

839 *Scout & Maggie.* scoutandmaggie.com. 2014.

Queens, New York, is home to Scout and Maggie, women in their early thirties who are not only best friends, but struggling to navigate the dating scene and find the perfect mate. As they wait for those events to occur, Maggie hits on a plan to start her own partying company ("Party Planning by Maggie" [although it is not set in stone as she hasn't decided on a definite title]) and drags not only Scout, but their friend David into the business. Stories follow Maggie and Scout as they not only seek mates but their efforts to turn an on-the-spot business into a successful venture (its beginnings are related as Maggie, Scout and David become involved in planning a wedding for their friends Kate and Greg).

Cast: Jessica Vera (Scout), Amy Johnson (Maggie), Amanda Johnson (Kate), Matt Barbot (David), Adam Swartz (Doc), Ann Marie Yoo (Judy), Brian Waters (Greg), Josh Hartung (Don), Lucy Sorlucco (Gladys), Elan Danzinger (Kai). **Credits:** *Producer:* Jessica Vera, Amy Johnson, Stephanie Dawson. *Director:* Stephanie Dawson. *Writer:* Jessica Vera, Amy Johnson. **Comment:** Billed as inspired by *Laverne and Shirley* (1970s ABC sitcom with Penny Marshall and Cindy Williams) and a modern update, the program does capture the craziness of the inspiration as back then only Laverne and Shirley could find chaos in the simplest of things (here the wedding being the culprit). The acting and production values are good and the doorway has been left open for additional episodes to follow.

Episodes: *1.* This Is Not a Ladies Happy Hour. *2.* How Did You Find Out About the Thing? *3.* This Is My Big Day. *4.* It's a Gala, It's a Fundraiser. *5.* Happiness and Love and Cake—Doy! *6.* The Story of Happiness—Cuz' We're All Happy Now.

840 *Scratch and Sniff.* blip.tv. 2012.

Scratch, a cat, and Sniff, a dog, are the pets of a man named Jeff. Scratch and Sniff, however, are not like any human's pet as they are animated and can think and do things no other pets can, not even Lassie. But Jeff is also not like any other human as his pets are a constant source of aggravation to him, sometimes involving his friend Kate in what transpires. Like Dave Seville, who had three singing chipmunks to contend with, Jeff is a live action figure involved in the carton-like adventures created when Scratch and Sniff decide to live like humans—from watching TV to preparing breakfast for Jeff.

Cast: Jeff Haas (Jeff), Brooke Fry (Kate), Shirlene Banks (Samantha), Jami Cullen (Pam). **Credits:** *Producer-Writer-Director:* Jeff Haas. **Comment:** All episodes, as well as teasers and trailers have been taken off-line. While it is not possible to provide an analysis based on viewing, by the photographs that are posted, Scratch and Sniff will immediately remind one of cartoon characters Tom and Jerry (although it doesn't appear Scratch and Sniff were always at each other's throats). The combined live action with animation looks good—but that is only based on still images.

Episodes, 1–20: *1.* Meet Scratch and Sniff. *2.* The Cable Bill. *3.* The Ruse. *4.* Busted. *5.* Lessons Learned.

6. A Walk in the Park. *7.* Lost. *8.* Any Port in a Storm. *9.* Sniff Trades Up. *10.* Living the Dream. *11.* Home Coming. *12.* Over the Teeth and Past the Gums... *13.* Sick Day. *14.* The House Call. *15.* Author! Author. *16.* Diagnosis Loopy. *17.* Let the Healing Begin. *18.* Story Tellers. *19.* Homely for the Holidays. *20.* Babe in Toyland.

Episodes, 21–49: *21.* Bad Santa. *22.* Yule Tied. *23.* Misfit Toys. *24.* Hum Bug! *25.* Holiday Heist. *26.* A New Friend. *27.* Acts of the Paranormal. *28.* Desperate Measures. *29.* Catch Us if You Can. *30.* The Reckoning. *31.* Pink Slip. *32.* Panic Attack. *33.* Up from the Ashes. *34.* Food for Thought. *35.* Bitter Dregs. *36.* Twist of Fate. *37.* Movie Night. *38.* Dinner Time. *39.* Now What? *40.* A Cat's Tale. *41.* Bad Kitty. *42.* On with the Show. *43.* Captains of Industry. *44.* Vacation of the Mind. *45.* The New Neighbor. *46.* Samantha. *47.* Pizza Night. *48.* Sage Advice. *49.* Fake Date.

841 *Screensters.* funnyordie.com. 2012.

Vignettes that explore the humorous idiosyncrasies of people (like devising ingenious ways to get rid of a worst enemy; what one does when driving alone).

Cast: Mike Smith, Clarissa Thibeaux, Danielle Arce, Devan Liljedhal. **Credits:** *Director:* Joel Shnowski. *Writer:* Joel Shnowski, Mike Smith. **Comment:** While such a concept could become tedious to watch, the production avoids that pitfall by producing only a short snippet of a topic. It is also well acted.

Episodes: *1.* My Worst Enemy. *2.* Bathroom Talk. *3.* Driving Solo. *4.* Yoga Time.

842 *Scribbles.* webserieschannel.com. 2013.

Ella is a seemingly normal young woman with a rather sad choice for a boyfriend: the somewhat "loopy" Frank. Their relationship is anything but normal as they continually argue. Tyler, a charming athletic young man and Alison, the girl he desires, appear to like each other but are a bit distant and rarely make contact with each other. Also a part of their lives are Maria, "a badass bitch," Javier, a suave ladies' man (or so he thinks) and Natasha, a mysterious young woman who has become a part of their inner circle. Stories are a look at the friends and how they navigate life, basically among themselves, without killing each other in the process.

Cast: Emma Rose Mailey (Ella), Charlie McElveen (Tyler), Armand Petri (Javier), Mari-Liis Userdnov (Natasha), Andrea Graces Lopez (Maria), Blake Curtis (Frank), Catherine Canillas (Kate), Anna Newell (Alison). **Credits:** *Producer:* Emma Rose Mailey, Charlie McElveen, Armand Petri. *Director:* Jeffrey Quinn. *Writer:* Emma Rose Mailey. **Comment:** The program, while nicely acted and presented, is somewhat confusing as there is no charac-

ter introduction in the first episode. It is set at a dinner table with the main characters attempting to enjoy a meal while the viewer sees just how dysfunctional this group really is. But who is who? An introductory episode would have helped to make a good series idea better to keep viewers interested, not somewhat in a daze as to what is going on and who is who.

Episodes: *1.* The Breakfast Club. *2.* About Last Night. *3.* Prelude to a Kiss.

843 *Scrubs: Interns.* youtube.com. 2009.

A web program based on the ABC TV series *Scrubs* that focuses on a group of first-year medical students at Sacred Heart Hospital who haven't quite chosen their field of expertise. Katie, Denise, Howie and Sonja are the young interns and the program is presented through a video diary created by Sonja.

Cast: Sonal Shah (Sonia "Sunny" Dey), Eliza Coupe (Denise "Jo" Mahoney), Betsy Beutler (Katie Collins), Todd Bosley (Howie Gelder), Sam Lloyd (Ted Buckland), Neil Flynn (The Janitor), Robert Maschio (Dr. Todd Quinlan). **Credits:** *Producer:* David Beebe, Zach Braff, Bill Lawrence, Randall Winston. *Director:* Eren Celeboglu. *Writer:* Melody Derloshon, Ryan A. Kemp, Devin O. Mahoney. **Comment:** The program, with episodes running between 3 and 5 minutes, aired during the eighth season of *Scrubs.* All episodes have been taken off line but based on reviews it was not an overall success. It appears the writing did not match the skill of the series as it was not as quirky. With the exception of The Janitor character from the parent series (who appeared in four episodes), other *Scrubs* members only appeared once.

Episodes: *1.* Our Intern Class. *2.* Our Meeting with J.D. *3.* Our Meeting with Broom Closet. *4.* Screw You with Ted and the Gooch. *5.* Late Night with Jimmy. *6.* Our Meeting with the Brian Trust. *7.* Legal Custodians Outtakes. *8.* Our Bedside Manner. *9.* Our Meeting with Turk and Todd. *10.* Our Final Advice. *11.* Our Meeting with Carla. *12.* Legal Custodians Episode.

844 *Season of the Villain.* youtube.com. 2012.

Big Bad is an international super villain and the most sought after felon on Interpol's most wanted list. Through some brilliant police work, Big Bad is captured but his arrest stirs a group of nefarious "bad guys" to rise from their hiding places and return to their wicked ways to replace Big Bad and become the new Number 1 on Interpol's Most Wanted List. Since villainy has virtually disappeared super heroes have begun to stop fighting crime to lead different lives. While there are still the good guys, like Interpol Agents Orange and Jogger, long forgotten criminals like Lucifera, Red Beluga, Dr. Cynic and

Minion have resurfaced. The program charts a good guy vs. bad guy scenario as evil seeks a way to become the number one sought after criminal.

Cast: Lotta Hannonen (Lucifera), Julia Salminen (Red Beluga), Noora Sarjanoja (Minion), Teija Ronni (Agent Orange), Veli-Matt- Ural (Agent Jogger), Aleksi Nikula (Dr. Cynic), Mikael Multasuo (Captain Cyber), Lauri Vakkuri (The Gallerist), Saara Sipila (The Fan), Laura Niskanen (The Ghost of Communism). **Credits:** *Producer-Director:* J.S.E. Salminen. *Writer:* J.S.E. Salminen, Julia Salminen. **Comment:** Swedish produced program that presents a slightly different view of super villains that are common to most Americans. The acting and production values are good and the actors speak English although English subtitles are presented on the screen to compensate for a hollow-like soundtrack that makes understanding dialogue a bit difficult at times. **Episodes:** *1.* Pilot. *2.* The Takeoff. *3.* The Strange Award. *4.* The Publicity Dilemma. *5.* The Criminal Craft. *6.* No Honor Among Thieves. *7.* The Grand Finale.

845 *Second-Hand New York.* youtube. com. 2012.

Three friends (Julie, Ariel and Patrick); one common thread (they are broke); and one common goal (enjoy what little pleasures life affords them). The program charts what happens when the three become roommates and try to rise above their dismal situation and find a better life. **Cast:** Julie Tran (Julie), Ariel R. Pacheco (Ariel), Al Patrick (Patrick), Xavier Pacheco (Todd). **Credits:** *Producer:* Ariel R. Pacheco, Julie Tran, Al Patrick. *Director:* Sean Abellar, Jose F. Toribio, Ariel R. Pacheco, Julie Tran, Al Patrick. *Writer:* Julie Tran, Ariel R. Pacheco, Al Patrick. **Comment:** Standard acting and production values that ends in a cliff hanger (what happened to Ariel) and leaves the doorway open for future episodes. **Episodes:** *1.* Pilot: Fly. *2.* Todd. *3.* Soggy Cereal. *4.* Peace and Love. *5.* Dinner. *6.* Ballin'. *7.* Taken. *8.* Untaken.

846 *Second Shot.* pnttvonline.com. 2013.

Dot's Hole, a gay bar in Morton, Ohio, is owned by an adventurous woman named Dot Collins. On one such adventure, a whaling expedition, Dot is killed when her ship sinks. Kat McDonald, a young woman living in Miami, and a former employee of the bar, is summoned to Morton for the reading of Dot's will. While each of the bar employees are expecting that one of them will inherit the bar, it is Kat who is the most shocked when it is revealed that she has been left the bar. Kat, who had become famous as a pro soccer player but lost that fame when she cost her team a world championship decides to continue the tradition set by Dot. The program relates the problems that befall Kat and her staff as they not only attempt to get along with each other, but run "the only gay bar in three counties." Ty, a lesbian waitress, Linda, the bar karaoke host, Jodi, the bartender, and Martin, the gay bartender assist Kat. Allison is Kat's ex-girlfriend (who is now married to a police officer named Paulie); and Krystal is Jodi's younger, flirtatious sister.

Cast: Jill Bennett (Kat McDonald), Amanda Christensen (Allison Silva), Maile Flanagan (Jodi Munson), Minnie Jo Mazzola (Ty Rosenfeld), Maia Madison (Linda Boonkowski), Matthew Scott Montgomery (Martin Honeycutt), Joe Crowley (Paulie Silva), Zoe Perry (Krystal Munson). **Credits:** *Producer:* Jill Bennett, Annie Price, Rebecca S. Katz, Maia Madison, Dara Nai. *Director:* Annie Price. *Writer:* Claudia Cogan, Yvette Foy, Maia Madison, Dara Nai, Jason Romaine, Tammy Lynne Stoner, Jill Bennett, Nancylee Myatt, Maile Flanagan. **Comment:** The program contains all that is necessary for a great TV sitcom—from acting to production values. **Episodes:** *1.* You Can't Go Home Again. So Why Am I Here? *2.* If It Ain't Fixed, Don't Break It. *3.* Heat? What Heat?

847 *Seeking.* seekingthewebseries.com. 2013.

Ella is a very pretty young woman, living in New York City and sharing an apartment with two male friends, Isaac and Nate. She asks only one thing from life: "I want a guy who is marginally attractive" and to go on a date without anything weird happening. "Is that too much to ask for," she says. She also believes that all the good men are either, married, in a serious relationship, gay or serial killers. Nate and Isaac think differently but only Isaac comes with a plan to make Ella see that she is wrong. He bets her that there is someone special out there for her—if she will give him a chance. Ella takes the bet, believing there is no such man and the story charts what happens when Ella agrees to at least one date a week with Nate as the judge—"I know normal" and his decision will be final. Isaac wins if Ella continues to find only what she considers abnormal men; Ella wins if she actually finds a man who she can actually date without any hassles.

Cast: Ronit Aranoff (Ella), Brian Cheng (Isaac), Michael Hanson (Nate), Raizy Pollak (Girl), Antoinette Henry (Har), Mark Mozingo (Luis), Johnny Ramey (Guy), Jenson Smith (K.T.). **Credits:** *Producer:* Ronit Aranoff, Nicole Payton, Camille Safadi. *Director:* Ruth Du, Quincy Morris. *Writer:* Ronit Aranoff. **Comment:** Nicely cast program with a different take on the dating scene with good acting and production skills. **Episodes:** *1.* The Bet. *2.* Are You Jewish? *3.* That's Not How Open Relationships Work. *4.* I Glued You: A Bluegrass Nightmare. *5.* Lick or Leave. *6.*

Not a Hipster. *7.* I Want You to Put a Baby Inside Me. *8.* Taco Tuesdays. *9.* Just a Girl Inside a Wiener.

848 *Self Storage.* youtube.com. 2010–2011.

Unit 4 of the Building C self storage unit is not full of junk, but home to Dana and Shoshanna, friends who have lost their jobs, have little money and pooled their resources to move into the unit as a means to get by until they find something better. While it is not the most comforting of places, the friends have made the unit as home-like as possible and the program showcases how two somewhat re-sourceful women solve their housing problem during a tough economy with everything that can go wrong plaguing their lives (second season episodes find the friends moving into Unit 1 of Building C and facing similar problems).

Cast: Julie Mann (Dana Feinberg), Kimberly Trew (Shoshanna Wolf), Gian Molina (Rafael), Eddie Jemison (Norman), Dave Holmes (Chad). **Credits:** *Producer:* T. Scott Keiner, Julie Mann, Wednesday Standley. *Director:* T. Scott Keiner. *Writer:* Julie Mann, Kimberly Trew. **Comment:** The program, with its good acting and production, is a clever take on the housing situation with somewhat exaggerated situations for the women to encounter (like throwing a party, having a friend stay with them).

Season 1 Episodes: *1.* Moving In. *2.* Let's Stay Together. *3.* Fresh Air. *4.* Dreamboat. *5.* This Detox Is Amazing.

Season 2 Episodes: *1.* The More Things Change. *2.* Burning My Way Out. *3.* Cuz We're Family. *4.* Wu Tang Forever. *5.* Shoshanna's Mom. *6.* Linens.

849 *Semi-Dead.* semi-dead.com. 2009.

It is a time when a zombie apocalypse has oc-curred but unlike other such occurrences (that have been seen) infrastructures are in tact and electricity remains on. In fact, if it were not for roaming zom-bies, cities would appear normal. But survivors like roommates Chris and Joe live in fear. Chris is living his life like nothing has happened while Joe has begun his battle against the zombies, doing what it takes to survive. Stories follow the two roommates as they plot to survive the zombie infestation.

Cast: Keith Arthur Bolden (Chris), Andrew Mc-Mennamy (Joe), Mike Danner (Sean), Wendy Douglas (Jessica), Mandy Flynn (Christina), Tom Flynn (Proto Joe). **Credits:** *Producer:* James Bond III, Josh Hodgins, Chris Wiltz. *Director:* Tom Flynn, Sean Patrick O'Brien, Will Prescott. *Writer:* Chris Wiltz. **Comment:** Slow-moving program that really leaves no interest to see what happens next. It is sort of like an "Odd Couple" paring with zombies being the catalyst that sparks Chad and Joe's lives. **Episodes:** *1.* If You Can't Beat 'Em, Eat 'Em. *2.* If You Can't Eat 'Em, Date 'Em. *3.* If You Can't Date

'Em, Live with 'Em. *4.* If You Can't Live with 'Em, Beat 'Em. *5.* Six Months Ago. *6.* Let's Get It Poppin'.

850 *Sequins of My Life.* blip.tv. 2013.

Dalton is a man with a vision: to become a fashion business guru by designing his own line of clothing. He begins by acquiring a job in a dry cleaner hoping to learn "the nuts and bolts of the fashion industry." After one week he quits and feels that he can achieve his dream by working out of his small New Jersey apartment (which he shares with Joshua, a cereal-eating, TV soap opera addict). Feeling that he can-not grow his business alone, he takes on three assis-tants: Denise and Greg and an intern, Tara (a student at the Parsons School of Design). Dalton, as it turns out is not the most ambitious man and although he has a vision it is a bit cloudy at the mo-ment. The program, a spoof of the fashion industry, follows the path Dalton takes to produce his own clothing line.

Cast: Michael Solis (Dalton), Tim Girrbach (Joshua Golden), Tara Hagan (Tara Kwan), Bridgid Ryan (Denise), Tom Lorenzo (Greg Fillman), Ting Wang (Ming Vase). **Credits:** *Producer-Director:* Tim Mattson. Michael Solis, Tom Lorenzo. **Comment:** Subtle comedy farce that is expertly acted and pro-duced. The characters, especially Dalton, are just so well presented that the program becomes very en-joyable.

Episodes: *1.* Crazy Fashion Designer. *2.* Meet Greg. *3.* What's on TV? *4.* The Whookies?

851 *The Series.* webserieschannel.com. 2013.

A Southern girl (Samantha), a die-hard New Yorker (Ethan) and a somewhat off-the-wall mili-tant-like Russian immigrant (Jayden) are roommates and how they not only try to live with each other but navigate life is the focal point of stories.

Cast: Shaun Fletcher (Ethan), Jen Bailey (Saman-tha), Jacob Frith (Jayden), Karen Maiko (Alyssa), Al Gerschutz (Jizni), Ivy Miller (Natalie). **Credits:** *Writer-Director:* Brian Merritt. **Comment:** "Differ-ent cultures. Different Problems. Same Roof" is the series tag line and while it sounds simple enough, there is no real character introduction or develop-ment and not a program that will appeal to every-one.

Episodes: *1.* The Beginning. *2.* A Funny Thing Happened at the Beach. *3.* Surprise! *4.* Peaches, Su-perstitions and Apple Pie, Oh My! *5.* Knock Knock… *6.* When in Russia. *7.* Growing Pains. *8.* "M" Is for Mystery. *9.* Independent Minus the "In." *10.* The Ex-Factor. *11.* Some of Our Fears. *12.* Never Too Early. *13.* The Pursuit. *14.* Search for Daddy. *15.* The Shot Heard Round the West Coast. *16.* The Christmas Series "It's a Wonderful Life to Die Hard Home Alone, Charlie Brown." *17.* The Final Chap-ter.

852 *A Series of Unfortunate People*. daily motion.com. 2011.

Annoying people, from those who constantly whine to those who are incredibly frugal to those who are just plain annoying are the focus of stories wherein their effects on people who are their complete opposite (normal) are parodied.

Cast: Leyna Juliet Weber, Beth Shea, Darren Sharper, Kym Whitley, Richard Riehle, Keegan-Michael Key, Randall Park, David A. Arnold, Matt Corboy, Willam Belli, Lindsay Hollister, Jean Carol, Devika Parikh, Manouschka Guerrier, Darren Capozzi, Matt Kawczynski, Leigh Hall, Jae Suh. **Credits:** *Producer:* Annie Lukowski, Leyna Juliet Weber. *Director:* Annie Lukowski. *Writer:* Annie Lukowski, Leyna Juliet Weber, Beth Shea. **Comment:** Performers play different roles in a well acted, enjoyable program. Even though only brief glimpses of such people are seen, it is enough to get the message across that with the normal people there also exist those who are just plain annoying.

Episodes: *1.* Bargain Birthday. *2.* Family Secret. *3.* Bad Seed. *4.* She's in a Better Place. *5.* Punch Line. *6.* Dangerously Clean. *7.* Mother's Day. *8.* Me, Me, Me.

853 *Set the Table*. watchsetthetable.com. 2013.

Becca and Mark are a married couple who appear to be growing apart since their daughter, Maddie, left home to attend school in Paris. When they learn Maddie has found a boyfriend (Antonio) through a video chat it upsets them (as they feel they have lost their little girl) but inspires them to reignite their passion in a most unusual way—through cooking. The program shows how their "adventures in cooking" looks to be the right answer to salvaging their relationship.

Cast: Deborah Adair (Becca Peterson), John Alston (Mark Peterson), Samantha Adair (Maddie Peterson), Charlie Merlo (Antonio). **Credits:** *Producer:* Deborah Adair. *Director:* Ryan McKinney. *Writer:* Deborah Adair, Ryan McKinney, Brian Adair. **Comment:** TV personality Deborah Adair stars with her real-life daughter, Samantha, in a well produced and acted program that deviates from the typical empty nest syndrome through cooking. The concept is different—and it works

Episodes: *1.* Hors d'oeuvres. *2.* Frites. *3.* Dishes Can Wait. *4.* Latkes. *5.* Lattes. *6.* Tea Party.

854 *7p/10e*. youtube.com. 2014.

The title refers to the west coast (Pacific) and East Coast time zones. At 7 p.m. in Los Angeles a young woman (Cora) chats over the Internet with her friend Patrick in New York, where it is 10 p.m. The two were introduced to each other by their friend Alison and it appears, through their daily conversa-tions that Cora and Patrick are developing a long distance relationship. Cora is interning to become an architect while Patrick works in construction and the program simply relates various aspects of their conversations.

Cast: Chris Alvarado (Patrick Callahan), Avital Ash (Cora Gable), Lauren Lapkus (Lauren), Walker Fannen (Walker), Caroline Macey (Caroline), Kyle McCullough (Cody Raggsdale), Marta McCullough (Marta), Phil McCullough (Phil Gable). **Credits:** *Producer:* Chris Alvarado, Avital Ash, Kyle McCullough, Sammi Cohen. *Director:* Avital Ash. *Writer:* Chris Alvarado, Avital Ash, Lauren Lapkus, Lucas Neff, Sammi Cohen, Kyle McCullough. **Comment:** There is just something so natural about the performances that it sort of draws you in and suddenly you are not watching a web series but watching two people communicating with each other over the Internet. The production is very well done and, although it is simply views of the leads talking, it is done in split-screen (both seen at the same time) and one does not "hog" the scene while talking.

Episodes: 25 untitled episodes, labeled "Episode 1" through "Episode 25."

855 *Sevvy Hounds*. youtube.com. 2012.

Trent and Melvin work for a company (GaggleCorp) but feel it is better to collect money for not working. Being the genius he believes he is, Trent devises a scheme to deliberately tank their jobs and get severance pay. With Melvin by his side, he and other office workers devise a way to move to the top of the layoff list by indulging in a war of incompetence and annoyance. But as suspicions are aroused on the corporate level, an investigation is begun to find out exactly what is happening among the office workers. The program charts what happens as Trent and Melvin scheme and try to outwit the company investigators by not getting fired but being paid to leave.

Cast: Andy Schindler (Trent Steele), Marcus Jones (Melvin Pratt), Karen Harrison (HR Manager). **Credits:** *Producer-Director:* Michael Schindler, Leor Baum. *Writer:* Michael Schindler. **Comment:** Work place comedy that unfortunately can only go so far in its presentation and the producers have taken the concept as far as it can go without becoming repetitive. The acting is good and the overall production well done.

Episodes: *1.* Severance Is the New Bonus. *2.* Dueling Jackasses. *3.* We Need Names. *4.* Out of Control. *5.* You Should Be Ashamed.

856 *Sex and the Austen Girl*. tv.com. 2010.

Courtney Stone is a sheltered young woman living in Regency, England, in 1813. Jane Mansfield is a free-spirited young woman living in Los Angeles in 2010. One morning each wakes up to discover they have switched bodies, time periods and lives with each now experiencing life as the other: Jane in the 19th century word of novelist Jane Austen; Courtney in the world of the 21st century. Jane must now learn to adjust to a life without technology while Courtney must contend with the advances of a world she never believed could exist. Whether talking to each other or to the camera, Jane and Courtney give their opinions on everything from makeup and clothes to dating and romance as they experience life as the other.

Cast: Arabella Field (Courtney Stone), Fay Masterson (Jane Mansfield). **Credits:** *Producer:* Brian Gerber, Amber J. Lawson, Thomas Rigler, Arabella Field. *Director:* Brian Gerber, Thomas Rigler. *Writer:* Laurie Viera Rigler. **Comment:** The program is based on the books *Confessions of a Jane Austen Addict* and *Rude Awakenings of a Jane Austen Addict* by Laurie Viera Riglo. While the concept is like a *Freaky Friday* feature film story, it does sound interesting but unfortunately all the episodes and trailers have been taken off line.

Episodes: *1.* Meeting Men. *2.* Women's Fashion. *3.* Technology. *4.* Eye of the Beholder. *5.* Is Clean Sexy? *6.* Concealer and Mascara. *7.* Lady in Waiting. *8.* Regency Dream Date. *9.* Is He for Real? *10.* Tell Tale of Signs. *11.* The 200-Year-Old Virgin. *12.* Love, Money & Pemberley. *13.* Wedding Dress. *14.* Sell-By Date. *15.* A Good Wedding. *16.* Snip, Snip. *17.* A Matter of Chance. *18.* The Art of Flattery. *19.* Clothes Make the Many. *20.* Regency Sports Talk. *21.* Chamber Pot. *22.* Transportation.

857 *Sex Personified.* vimeo.com. 2011.

In a bar that appears typical, two of its patrons are anything but: the God of Sex and the God of Violence. They are discussing various matters when Violence suddenly makes a bet with Sex: That he is incapable of making anyone on the planet achieve a sexual encounter. Sex accepts the bet. Just then a young man named Neil enters the bar, appears like a nerd (a neurotic paper pusher with little social skills) and Violence chooses him as the subject Sex needs "to make a man." Sex, calling himself Gary, begins by befriending Neil and the program follows what happens to Neil as Gary seeks to win his bet.

Cast: Andrew Jupin (God of Sex/Gary), Stephen Sajdak (Neil), Sean Weiner (God of Violence), Meryl Hathaway (Karen), Travis Mitchell (Alan). **Credits:** *Producer:* Andrew Jupin, Stephen Sajdak, Sean Weiner. *Director:* Sean Weiner. *Writer:* Andrew Jupin, Stephen Sajdak, Justin Case, Sean Weiner. **Comment:** The idea is good but the presentation is quite bad. The picture is very unsteady and can make you sea sick. It is really difficult to get through an episode, even if you are use to the unsteady (shaky) camera method of filming.

Episodes: 3 untitled episodes, labeled "Episode 1," "Episode 2" and "Episode 3."

858 *Sex Pose Man.* youtube.com. 2013.

Winston is a young African-American super stud who has, through his sexual prowess, the ability to change women's lives forever. There is a world full of women who are unsure of their desires or abilities to attract the opposite sex; and there is Winston, the one man who can change them. The program charts what happens to the women Winston encounters as he seeks to use his "gift" to benefit women of any race, creed and color.

Cast: David Bianchi (Winston), Rhyan Schwartz (Carl), Heather Lindell (Naomi), Stefanie Barboza (Linda), Ryan Bartley (Mimess). **Credits:** *Producer:* David Bianchi, Daniel J. Pico. *Director:* Daniel J. Pico. *Writer:* David Bianchi. **Comment:** A strictly adult comedy as there are suggestive sexual situations. The program comes off as a bit unusual in the subject matter it covers but is well acted and produced.

Episodes: *1.* The Caribou. *2.* Mime.

859 *Sexual Intercourse: American Style.* youtube.com. 2006–2007.

Short skits that focus on the martial problems faced by two couples: Beth and Clark and Fran and Tom.

Cast: Eliza Skinner (Beth), Matthieu Cornillon (Tom), Will Hines (Clark), Julie Klausner (Fran). **Credits:** *Producer:* Will Hines, Mitch Magee. *Director:* Mitch Magee, Jamey Shafer. *Writer:* Mitch Magee. **Comment:** An obvious take-off on the ABC series *Love, American Style* that, although it has a provocative title, has no nudity or intense sexual situations but does have its share of crude language

Episodes: *1.* The Hot Tub. *2.* Whipped Cream. *3.* The Wine Cellar. *4.* Incense and Candles. *5.* Pastries. *6.* November. *7.* Pottery Wheels. *8.* The Baby Birds.

860 *Shadazzle.* daffadillies.co.uk/shadazzle. 2012–2015.

Spittlegum is a town in England that is also home to two people about to embark on the most important journey of their lives: marriage. Florence is the bride-to be and Fred is the groom. Money is tight, so much so that Florence finds herself becoming an exotic dancer to make ends meet and also involved in a romantic bind when an unstable character (Trevor) sets his sights on her. To further complicate her life, Fred has hired an alcohol-consuming maid (Jemima) they can't afford and, as personal expenses get tighter and friends try to help, a parody of television soap operas begins with all the chaos, sorrows—and even some good times seen through the perspectives of the people who are close to Florence and Fred (hence their names also being the episode titles).

Cast: Helen Hall (Florence Smith), Brett Barnett

Shadazzle. Series logo (© 2015 Daffadillies / Brett Barnett).

(Fred Flagglebush), Leigh-Anne Homer (Alex), Stacey Mackenzie (Tess Collins), Jonathan Homer (Trevor Shaw), Catherine Wood (Jemima). **Credits:** *Producer:* Brett Barnett, Stacey Mackenzie, Leigh-Anne Homer. *Director:* Brett Barnett. **Comment:** Nicely woven situations that reflect the problems some people can face when those unexpected incidents just turn up like unwelcome company. The acting and production values are also good.

   Season 1 Episodes: *1.* Jemima. *2.* Tess. *3.* Alex. *4.* Fred. *5.* Robert. *6.* George. *7.* Trevor. *8.* Florence.

   Season 2 Episodes: *1.* Dazzle. *2.* George. *3.* Jemima. *4.* Maud. *5.* Alex. *6.* Tess. *7.* Florence. *8.* Fred.

   Season 3 Episodes: *1.* Tom. *2.* Florence. *3.* Jerry. *4.* Jemima. *5.* Alex. *6.* Robert. *7.* Maud. *8.* Tess

   Season 4 Episodes: *1.* George. *2.* Robert. *3.* Tom. *4.* Tess. *5.* Jemima. *6.* Alex. *7.* Maud. *8.* Florence.

   Season 5 Episodes: *1.* Jemima. *2.* Robert. *3.* Tom. *4.* Maud. *5.* George. *6.* Tess. *7.* Bill. *8.* Florence.

861 *The Shades.* funnyordie.com. 2014.

   Hailey and John are a young couple who believe they have found the perfect place to live when they move into a gated community called The Shades. Their beliefs are soon dispelled when they learn that community residents observe the doctrine of religious freedom and not only practice it but take it to exaggerated, if not inappropriate degrees. The program follows Hailey and John as they attempt to deal with the fanatics, especially Jade and Angelo who are now their friends and neighbors.

   Cast: Emily Olson (Hailey), Daniel Hartley (John), Natalie Kropf (Jade), Jacob Budenz (Angelo), Mara Hanlon (Mara), Sean Hanlon (Sean). **Credits:** *Producer:* Kevin Davis, Mike Barnett. *Writer-Director:* Kevin Davis. **Comment:** Poking fun at religious traditions then taking them to extremes can be iffy as you never know who will see it in the humorous light it was meant to be or take it seriously as an insult. Here, while only a pilot episode has been produced that mocks Easter with a focus on a Pagan tradition, it is more of an insult than anything else and is rather adult in nature with talk of reproduction.

   Episodes: *1.* Seed.

862 *Shades of Gray.* webserieschannel.com. 2013.

   It is a future time and an elderly couple is seen (Yvette and Michael). As the couple reminisce about their past, flashback sequences are presented to relate various aspects of their lives when they were young.

   Cast: Chinai Hardy (Yvette), Hayden Livesay (Michael), Laura Muschelli (Young Yvette), Wade Carter (Young Michael). **Credits:** *Producer-Writer-Director:* Michael Herl, Yvette Sanders. **Comment:** Nicely presented, somewhat nostalgic program that is well acted and produced.

Episodes: *1.* First Impressions. *2.* First Contact. *3.* Communication.

863 *The Shaman.* tv.com. 2009.

As a younger man Dan Goldblatt was influenced by the life style of legendary rock star Jim Morrison. As he grew older he adapted Jim's fashion tips and philosophy and now calls himself "The Shaman," a man of wisdom who has begun a mission to improve the lives of the people who surround him. While Dan believes he is an actual Shaman, people see his "wisdom" as total nonsense and the program relates Dan's unique take on the world that surrounds him. Erin is the unattainable girl he longs for; Matt is his friend.

Cast: Jason Nash (Dan Goldblatt), Erin Gibson (Erin), Matt Price (Matt). **Credits:** *Director:* Mike Blieden, Seth Margolin, Peter Bumgarner. *Writer:* Jason Nash. **Comment:** An evaluation is not possible as all episodes have been taken off line.

Episodes: *1.* The Visitor. *2.* The Truth and the French Girl. *3.* The Shaman Hits Venice Beach. *4.* The Shaman at Comic Con. *5.* Improv. *6.* Home Office. *7.* The Donut Shop. *8.* Old Flame. *9.* Spirits Underneath. *10.* The End. *11.* Sick Friend. *12.* The Shaman at Burning Man.

864 *Shazza.* youtube.com. 2013.

Shazza is a sassy young English woman with a library of knowledge on how to get things done, no matter what they are or how difficult they appear to be. Once a topic is established, Shazza gives her observations with the program showcasing that topic with one or all of her friends acting out the situation. Tasha is Shazza's best mate; Kevin is the ladies' man; Natalie is, according to Shazza, "a slut" (but still her friend); and Jeff, the nerd. And, to this group of people, Shazza is, as she says, "The Queen Bee."

Cast: Kerry Finlayson (Shazza), Helen Soraya (Tasha), Ewan Chung (Jeff), Jennifer Neala Page (Natalie), Kay D'Arcy (Nan), Don Donnelley (Kevin). **Credits:** *Producer:* Kerry Finlayson, Evan Marlowe. *Director:* Evan Marlowe. *Writer:* Kerry Finlayson. **Comment:** British produced program that has a quirky feel and captures your attention. It is enjoyable to watch with very good acting and production values.

Episodes: *1.* Meet the Gang. *2.* La Dee Da. *3.* Nan. *4.* Tea and Wontons. *5.* Girls Night Out.

865 *She Said What!* alecky87.wix.com. 2013.

Julia and Eric are a young couple who, in the first episode, become engaged. It is a big step for any couple but for Julia and Eric it becomes a world filled with uncertain circumstances and sexual ambiguities. The program relates the events that not only

enhance their lives but also complicate it with each sometimes doubting that they did the right thing.

Cast: Lindi Nolte (Julia), Alec Santos (Eric), Karen McKnight (Jennifer, Julia's sister). **Credits:** *Producer:* Alec Santos. **Comment:** Charming program that honestly tries to show (in a comedic way) what commitment means after it is made but also what happens when doubts may appear to make one rethink what has been done.

Episodes: *1.* Annals of Engagement. *2.* Three Way the Right Way. *3.* Rub-A-Dub-Dub! *4.* Revenge Served Sweet.

866 *Sheila and Sherry Save the World (From Solar Flares).* snobbyrobot.com. 2014.

The Mayan prediction that the world will come to an end in 2012 didn't happen and two middle-aged women, Sheila, a cynic, and Sherry, an optimist, are relieved although they had prepared for the worst. A newspaper article about approaching solar flares has the women again believing the world is coming to an end and feel they must decide to no longer put off what they had planned to do. Sherry had always dreamed of becoming a 911 dispatcher and somehow manages to acquire such a job without training. The program covers only this aspect as Sherry proves incompetence at its highest level with Sheila filming what happens as a record for the history books.

Cast: Amy Lloyd (Sherry), Christy Holy (Sheila). **Credits:** *Producer-Director-Writer:* Amy Lloyd, Christy Holy. **Comment:** How Sherry responds to the calls she receives are truly comical and makes you appreciate the fact there are competent people handling such emergencies. The acting is very good and the idea well presented.

Episodes: 3 untitled episodes, labeled "Episode 1," "Episode 2" and "Episode 3."

867 *Shelf Life: The Series.* shelflifeseries.com. 2011–2014.

Hero Man, Hero Lass, Bug Boy and Samurai Snake are toy action figures that sit on the shelf of a ten-year-old boy (called "The Kid" and "The Little Hitler"). Unknown to The Kid his action figures have come to life and accept the fact that they were once toys, made in China and sold in stores like Toys R Us and Odd Lots (which is the ultimate insult to them). While the figures only come to life when they are alone, they must contend with the devil Kid when they are in their natural form. Once coming to life, they deal with all the issues of the world from their shelf and stories, which are often adult in nature, relate their thoughts on the topics that are presented.

Cast: Travis Willingham (Hero Man), Tara Platt (Hero Lass), Yuri Lowenthal (Bug Boy), Dee Bradley Baker (Samurai Snake voice), Bryan Enk (Samurai

Shelf Life. Series poster art (used by permission).

rise to the caliber of TV quality and stories become increasingly outrageous (but delightful).

Season 1 Episodes: *1.* Quiet on the Set. *2.* Nuts. *3.* Losing My Religion. *4.* Hot or Not. *5.* Fluffer #7. *6.* Utility Belt. *7.* Man of Seduction. *8.* What Girls Want. *9.* Super Size Me. *10.* Emancipation Proclamation.

Season 2 Episodes: *1.* A New Week. *2.* Night Bear. *3.* Keepin' Up with the Jonesin' *4.* Pushing Buttons. *5.* Powers. *6.* The Paratrooper. *7.* Origin Stories. *8.* Breaking and Entering. *9,10.* The New Girl.

Season 3 Episodes: *1.* Sic Semper Tyrannosaur. *2.* Magic: The Blathering. *3.* Occupy the Space. *4.* Tiny Dance. *5.* Lost in Translation. *6.* Only the Lonely. *7.* Unreal Estates. *8.* Wigging Out. *9,10.* The Boogie Man. *11.* Oh, Canada.

Season 4 Episodes: *1.* Siss! Boom! Bug! *2.* Rub-a-Du-Dub. *3.* Night Terrors. *4.* Little Big House. *5.* Powered Up. *6.* Hero Worship, Losing My Religion. *7.* Toypocalypse. *8.* Pristine, Shiny Toys Holding Guns. *9,10.* Shelf of the Dead.

868 The Shop. vimeo.com. 2012.

Sherman Oaks, California, like any city or town, has its share of beauty salons. Tonya is the owner of one such salon and, like all the movies and TV series that used salons as their basis, has a dysfunctional staff, rival salons to deal with and customers who are anything but ordinary. And like all those shows, the program chronicles Tonya's efforts to deal with anything and everything that prevents her living a sane life.

Cast: Crystal Rogers (Tonya), Orlando Deral (Otis), Mario Mosley (Flip), Jaina Lee Ortiz (Petrona), William Guirola (Cesar), Elaine Hoxie (Frankie), Tomoko Karina (Mami). **Credits:** *Producer-Writer:* Orlando Doral. *Director:* Taja V. Simpson, Daniel Ari, Orlando Doral. **Comment:** While the concept is old hat, the acting and production values are very good.

Episodes: *1.* Help Wanted. *2.* The Break-Up. *3.* Tafari. *4.* Rivals. *5.* You Got the Text Too? *6.* Where Do We Go from Here? *7.* You Didn't See Me?

Snake performer), Laura Bailey (The Kid), Mary Elizabeth McGlynn (Kid's mother), Phil Morris (Black Velvet), Stephen Simon (Devlish Dan), Kirsten Vangsness (Freaky Squeaky), Valerie Arem (Amazona), Dave B. Mitchell (Crimson Crusher), Stephanie Thorpe (Knockoff Hero Lass). **Credits:** *Producer:* Tara Platt, Yuri Lowenthal, Stephanie Thorpe. *Director:* Paul Jenkins, Steven Calcote, Travis Stevens, Kevin Rubio. *Writer:* Yuri Lowenthal, Paul Jenkins, F.M. DeMarco, Derk Johnson, Yuri Lowenthal, Kristina Maniatis, Brendan McCreary, Ashley Miller, Travis Stevens. **Comment:** Not your average super hero program. A very well acted and produced series that should be shopped to broadcast or cable TV (although the vulgar language will have to be deleted, bleeped or over spoken). As the series progresses, the production values

869 *Shopping for Friends.* youtube.com. 2012.

Tony is a young woman living in Berlin, Germany. While she is surrounded by people, she has no close friends and no one she can call her BFF. To solve her problem, Tony decides to go out and look for one by following a complete stranger and making that person her friend. While standing on the sidewalk, Tony says, "The next person I see is going to be my best friend." A young woman riding on a bicycle becomes her target and using her bicycle, follows her to a grocery store (where Tony befriends her by telling her not to buy a particular brand of mustard). The stranger is Liev and the program charts what happens when Tony attempts to become close to Liev and make her a best friend forever. **Cast:** Vanessa Locke (Tony), Lacey Haynes (Liev). **Credits:** *Producer-Director:* Lacey Haynes, Vanessa Locke. *Writer:* Lacey Haynes. **Comment:** Although the program is produced in Germany, the actors speak English and there is no need to use the subtitles. The acting and production values are very good and the story is well thought out and presented. **Episodes:** *1.* The Mustard. *2.* In Europe. *3.* Deadlines, Family Things. *4.* Home Movies. *5.* Leanne Evelyn.

870 *Short Long Story.* youtube.com. 2013.

Long stories told in a short span of time by the people who have experienced harrowing or just plain crazy situations. **Cast:** Tom Assam-Miller (Tom), Almag Avidan Antoni (Almag), Ben Fischinger (Ben), Chase Cargill (Bernard), Hattie Smith (Samantha). **Credits:** *Director:* Almag Avidan Antoni. *Writer:* Tom Assam-Miller, Almag Avidan Antoni. **Comment:** Interesting mix of stories that are actually told in the shortest time possible. Dialogue is fast and its accompanying scenes are well coordinated to what is happening. **Episodes:** *1.* I Heard Voices. *2.* I Went Home for the Holidays. *3.* I Went for a Run. *4.* I Went to the Bathroom. *5.* We Made a Web Series. *6.* I Couldn't Fall Asleep. *7.* I Went to Boxing. *8.* I Went to the Beach. *9.* I Had a Movie Date. *10.* I Had to Write an Essay.

871 *Short Term.* shortterm.com. 2011.

Short Term is an employment agency that supplies temporary jobs to those who are willing to take the sometimes unusual opportunities that arise. Karen, the work-a-holic, Molly, the over-efficient girl and Naresh, the irresponsible agency employee are the featured representatives. There are jobs available and the need to fill them is what keeps Short Term in business. But with a troubled economy and clients who are more eccentric than normal, Karen, Molly and even Naresh find that placing the right person with the right job is not as easy as it sounds. **Cast:** Heather Horton (Molly), Emily Button (Karen), Raj Kalra (Naresh), Alison Koellisch (Caitlin), Kim Reed (Joan), Brad Leaf (Aldin Graves), Christopher Guetig (Danny). **Credits:** *Producer:* Jeffrey L. Parks, Heather Horton, Jennifer Bobiwash. *Writer-Director:* Jeffrey L. Parks. **Comment:** Well acted, produced and thought-out series. Emily Button is especially charming as Karen and she alone makes the program work. **Season 1 Episodes:** 6 untitled episodes, labeled "Episode 1" through "Episode 6." **Season 2 Episodes:** *1.* It's Garith. *2.* Cheese Cake Party. *3.* The Naresh Show. *4.* Nous Aurons Toujours Paris. *5.* The Beginning Is the End—Or Something. **Season 3 Episodes:** *1.* We're Back. *2.* The New Guys. *3.* Because We Care. *4.* Merry Christmas. *5.* And They All Lived...

872 *The Shrink in B-6.* youtube.com. 2014.

Nadia and Farrah are young women who are not only friends but roommates. Nadia had hoped to become a psychologist but dropped out of graduate school when she apparently became overwhelmed (an exact reason is not given). Realizing that she was premature in her decision, she now sustains herself by taking whatever jobs she can find. When the unexpected happens and she is fired from her job as a waitress, Nadia finds herself in a bind when Farrah demands that she pay her half of the rent or get out. After some thought Nadia feels that although she does not have a degree she can put her schooling to use by helping people. Through CraigsList, Nadia posts an ad for her services for affordable and intimate counseling from her apartment (B-6). The program chronicles the rather colorful people that seek Nadia's services and how Nadia attempts to deal with each one as an unlicensed "pseudo shrink." **Cast:** Shayla Love Washington (Nadia West), Tabby Molapo (Farrah). **Credits:** *Director:* Amber Bournett, Ebony Blandry. *Writer:* Ebony Blandry. **Comment:** An African-American production that does not stereotype Nadia as a street bitch but as a young woman desperately seeking to right the mistake she made (dropping out of college). There is foul language and there are some sound problems (too low to hear what is being said, especially by Nadia, and over-powering background music that also makes it difficult to hear what is happening). **Episodes:** *1.* Tacos and Ultimatums. *2.* Spin Gold Out of S**t. *3.* The She-Wolf of Wall Street. *4.* A Thyme of Hallways. *5.* Shrink in the Mirror.

873 *Shutdown.* youtube.com. 2007.

Events in the lives of a group of employees at Morbotech, a California-based tech company, that handles end-user complaints ranging from computers and video games to comic books and anime (Japanese animation). Particular focus is on Simon, an East Coast college graduate who has just acquired a job as a Desk Help Associate; and Hally, a new Help Desk recruit. Zedd is the most brilliant of the employees although he considers what he does "solving nerd problems." Chaz is the slacker and only able to keep his job because his Uncle Bill is a company vice president. Lise (Simon and Zedd's friend) works at Comics 'N Stuff. Mark is the employee who is oblivious to everything that is going on. Nicole is the party girl who is seeking to marry rich and settle down.

Cast: Mattzog Bellucci (Simon), Pin Chen (Hally), Ben Peterson (Zedd), Timothy Cross (Chaz), Courtney Buck (Lise), Cristyn Chandler (Alex), Jeff Hillman (Mark), David Finley (Bill Hicksley). **Credits:** *Producer:* Christopher R. Spencer, Mattzog Bellucci. **Comment:** A humorous profile of geeks and nerds with good acting, stories and production values.

Episodes: *1,2.* The New Girl. *3.* The Truth About Hally. *4.* Dramatic Measures. *5–8.* DDR Hero. *9,10.* The Job.

874 *Shutterbugs.* youtube.com. 2013.

Fitzroy, the creative heart of Melbourne, Australia, provides the backdrop for a look at five people with an interest in photography: Samantha, Chloe, Isaac, Bo and Trent, each with a specialty and each becoming involved in "wild and dangerous adventures in the name of taking pictures."

Cast: Rhona Rees, Saskig Hampele, Matt Furlani, Rowan Hills, Ben Prendergast, Liina Berry. **Credits:** *Producer:* Kate McIntyre, Lynda Mebberson, Kayne Tremills. *Writer-Director:* David Collins. **Comment:** Programs that revolve around photographers are not abundant and can always be intriguing. *Casey, Crime Photographer, Man with a Camera* and *Love That Bob* are 1950s TV series examples that tackled the topic so the idea is not really new. The acting and production is good, the accents easy to understand but the program lacks a performer-character match-up. See also *Fauxtopgraphy.*

Episodes: *1.* In an Instant. *2.* Friends & Enemies. *3.* Bo. *4.* Social Snaps. *5.* The Studio Is a Little Dusty. *6.* Sleuthing. *7.* Stakeout. *8.* People Skills. *9.* Ambush. *10.* Breaking, Entering, Partying. *11.* Fiesta. *12.* All Together Now.

875 *Sibling Rivals.* webserieschannel.com. 2012.

Jason and Grant are brothers who share an apartment. They each have their quirks and they each hate the other. The thought of living together is upsetting to both and the program relates what happens as the brothers stop short of killing each other as they simply try to live together.

Cast: Jason Grant-Henriques (Himself), Christopher Grant-Henriques (Himself). **Credits:** *Producer-Writer-Director* Jason Grant-Henriques. **Comment:** Although only two episodes have been produced, the premise is quickly established and the real-life brothers do a good job pretending to despise each other.

Episodes: *1.* Pilot. *2.* What I Hate About You!

876 *Silver Lake Detective.* webserieschannel.com. 2014.

Silver Lake appears to be a small community with more than its share of crime. Patrick Lawrence is a "hipster detective" (as described) who also appears to be the only private detective in town. As a client seeks out Patrick's help, his tackling of each case—from start to finish is chronicled along with all the mishaps that accompany them.

Cast: Aaron Toft (Patrick Lawrence), Quintin Allen Bell (Leon Florence), Malina Galabova (Miss Jennifer), Steve Ohl (McDonough), Werner Joseph Boer (The Major), Matthew Pater Murphy (Norman). **Credits:** *Producer-Writer:* Aaron Toft. *Director:* Aaron Toft, Brenda Bonney. **Comment:** The program is filmed in black and white to give it that film noir feeling (although foul language is unnecessarily added). Although some scenes with Patrick questioning suspects are a bit long, it is well acted and produced.

Episodes: *1–3:* The Professor. *4–7:* The Promiscuous Girlfriend. *8–13:* The Missing Millionaire. *14,15:* The PBR Famine.

877 *Single & Dating in Vancouver.* sadinvan.com. 2013.

Troy McMaster, an aspiring actor born and raised in rural Timmins (in Ontario, Canada) decides to spread his wings and get into the acting profession by moving to Vancouver. He also has plans to find that special someone and move to Los Angeles. Although he is full of hope and enthusiasm, he soon finds his dreams falling apart when being single and having a big heart are working against him. The program charts his efforts to navigate life in the big city and his relationship with the people he befriends: Michael, a laid back yoga instructor; Sheri, a sexy busybody; and Chad "Chadillac" Mayweather, a single father and real estate agent.

Cast: Troy Mundle (Troy McMaster), Michael Goudge (Michael Robinson), Sheri Rabold (Sheri Wilson), Chad Riley (Chad Mayweather). **Credits:** *Producer-Writer:* Troy Mundle. *Director:* Andrew Miller. **Comment:** The background music is a bit loud at times and makes it difficult to hear what is being said. Characterizations are a bit rough around the edges and needed to be more developed (it feels like they are just tossed at you without any warning).

Episodes: *1.* P.O.V. *2.* Unleash the Lions. *3.* Downward Dog. *4.* Oh, the Tangled Web We Weave.

878 *Single Dads.* vimeo.com. 2010.

Pete ("an idiot") and Brian (down-to-earth), friends since childhood are now single fathers. Pete is the father of Pete, Jr., and Theodore is Brian's infant son. Pete and Brian are, however, somewhat inexperienced when it comes to raising children and the program relates the comedic chaos they encounter as they attempt to become responsible fathers (using the film *Three Men and a Baby* as a guide) and raise their kids on their own with each helping the other cope with life (and somehow attract women who will appreciate the fact that they have children).

Cast: Peter Karinen (Pete), Brian Sacca (Brian), Madison Zumsteg (Pete, Jr.), Dakota Zumsteg (Theodore), Jim Connor (Jim, Pete's father). **Credits:** *Producer:* Sharon Tal, Jesse Staccato. *Director:* Jordan Vogt-Roberts. *Writer:* Peter Karinen, Brian Sacca. **Comment:** Think the ABC series *Full House* turned upside down with all that can go wrong with a single father attempting to raise an infant. The idea is well presented with good acting and production values.

Episodes: *1.* Meeting Girls in the Park. *2.* Changing Diapers. *3.* Classical Rock. *4.* Having Girls Over. *5.* Feeding Time. *6.* The Masters. *7.* Bath Time. *8.* Fatherly Advice. *9.* Sex Talk. *10.* Pushing Strollers. *11.* Brian Gets a Girlfriend. *12.* Birthday Party. *13.* Learning from Babies. *14.* Maternal Bond. *15.* Homeless Guy.

879 *Single_Never_Married.* webseries channel.com. 2013.

To most people a dog is just a dog. But to Deon, her dog (Violet) is like the sister she never had. Deon, a lesbian, obsesses over Violet and apparently fails to realize that her obsession is seen as just plain weird to her dates and an immediate turn off to all except Max, her male next-door neighbor who truly loves her but feels he has no chance with her as she is not interested in men. The program charts Deon's continual attempts to find the girl of her dreams (maybe even any girl at all) and Max's efforts to not only remain her friend, but possibly her lover (after five years of trying, he has not given up hope).

Cast: Lauren Hamilton (Deon), Monique Gelineau (Charlie), Tracy Mazyck (Max), Violet (Violet). **Credits:** *Producer-Writer-Director:* Angela Burris, Lauren Hamilton. **Comment:** Enjoyable program with very good acting and production values. Deon's obsession with Violet adds to the fun and, being that the series ends with Deon thinking she has found the right girl, leaves the viewer to wonder what will become of Max, but most importantly, what will become of Violet once she realizes there is a stumbling block to her finding happiness.

Episodes: *1.* Can I Get a Hug? *2.* Massage Me. *3.* Me or Your Dog! *4.* I'm in Love.

880 *Single Servings.* singleservingsseries. com. 2013.

A big day is approaching for Margo: the wedding of her best friend Renee (to Trip). Margo is just as excited as Renee until she realizes that she has no one to accompany her to the ceremony. Margo, like Renee, is a recent college graduate but she has not yet found her dream job, a home to call her own or even begun a serious relationship. In a way Margo feels she is still like a child but knows she must now face the realization that everyone must move on. With only six weeks until the wedding, Margo decides that it is now the time to find the perfect date and change her life for the better.

Cast: Christina Benedetto (Margo), Leah Bezozo (Renée), Alexander Kikis (Chase), Rebecca Tucker (Lizzi), Andreas de Rond (Trip), Josh Fielden (Josh), Aaron Mathias (Spencer). **Credits:** *Producer:* Jessica Rose McVay, Christina Benedetto, Leah Bezozo. *Director:* Jessica Rose McVay, Ryan Scott McVay. **Comment:** A well presented idea with good acting and production values.

Episodes: *1.* Pilot. *2.* When Trip Moves In. *3.* Of Course You Are. *4.* Who Said Anything About Perfect. *5,6.* Ten Years and Beyond.

881 *Singledom.* singledomseries.com. 2014.

Naomi and Xavier are a young couple who, after dating for several months believe it is time for each of their families to meet for the first time. The arrangements are made and a dinner party is planned. While the various family members are discussing matters, it is realized that Naomi and Xavier are cousins and a once promising relationship is suddenly thrown into turmoil. Naomi and Xavier end their relationship (but remain friends) and find themselves suddenly thrust back into the dating world. The program charts their efforts to once again find that perfect soul mate in a world where the search for love can lead to truly unexpected results.

Cast: Dawn Adams (Naomi Gibbs), Jesse Jenkins (Xavier Cole), William Lewis (Wayne), Carmen Diaz (Sundae). **Credits:** *Producer:* Elisa O'Keefe-Smith, Ant Horton. *Director:* Kyree Terrell. *Writer:* Kyree Terrell, Tiffany Barrett. **Comment:** Well produced and acted African-American program with a unique twist on how two former lovers are thrust back into the dating scene.

Episodes: *1.* We Are Family. *2.* Switch. *3.* Knock Knock. *4.* Got Any Change? *5.* Tendencies. *6.* 2 Night Stands. *7.* Love at First Stalk. *8.* NeverAgain. com. *9.* Double Date + 1. *10.* Game Night.

882 *Sintillate Studios.* vimeo.com. 2010.

On the outside Sintillate Studios appears to be an

ordinary film producing company. But its productions, such as *Naughty Nannies* and *Probing Felicity* are anything but ordinary as they are X-rated and marketed for "the adult connoisseur of sex." While their videos give the buyer "all the good stuff" the Internet viewer is given a peek behind-the-scenes to see what happens during the making of such films with all the backstage drama and none of that "good stuff." Felicity, Justin and Sterling are actors; Alisha is the ditzy starlet; Jizz is the eccentric director; Rose is the neurotic producer; Carly is Felicity's sister; and Brad is Carly's boyfriend.

Cast: Siobhan Novello (Carly), Karly Ann (Felicity), Craig McDonald (Justin), Marcus Hall (Brad), Kate Kelly (Alisha), Joseph O'Neill (Sterling), Christie Sistrunk (Rose), Charlie Handcock (Jizz). **Credits:** *Producer:* Bec Darling, Gary Sewell. *Director:* Gary Sewell. *Writer:* Amy Costello, Tina McKimmie, Siobhan Dow-Hall, Gary Sewell. **Comment:** *Sintilatte Studios* is a PG-rated version of an X-rated topic. While there are sexual situations nothing is really offensive. The acting is very good and placing that behind-the-scenes turmoil that occurs is something really different to see.

Episodes: *1.* The Sound of My Prick. *2.* Angry Lesbian Prisoners. *4.* Sex Education with Miss Titwank. *5.* Cockadile Cumdee. *6.* Arse-tralia. *7.* Carly the Vampire Layer. *8.* Shakespeare in Latex Gloves. *9.* Service My Pipes. *10.* Tower-In-Her-Fur-Now.

883 Sistah Did What? webserieschannel.com. 2013.

Alex is a very pretty young woman hoping to make it as an actress. The problem is that while she has talent, she only finds herself being cast in roles that portray women as sluts. Carmen and Jason, a married couple, are her friends (and advisors) while Linda, her mother, bothered over the fact that Alex is always cast as "a hoe" wishes her daughter would seek another career. The program chronicles Alex's efforts to achieve her dream (of quality roles) while also navigating a love life and attempting to cope with all the pitfalls she encounters along the way.

Cast: Shelli Boone (Alex), Dawn Noel (Carmen), Marian Michaels (Linda), Devon Stewart (Jason). **Credits:** *Producer-Writer-Director:* Michael Blackman. **Comment:** Shelli Boone is delightful as the lead in a series that is also very well acted and produced.

Episodes: *1.* The Best View Is the Rear View. *2.* Sistah's Mistake. *3.* Bad Birthday? *4.* The Duel. *5.* Sistah Did Who?

884 Sisters by Marriage. youtube.com. 2010.

Jeneane and Molly are best friends whose lives take a sudden turn for the unexpected when Jeneane announces that she wants a baby. The friends are ac-

tresses but currently unemployed and Molly, Jeneane's sister-in-law, feels Jeneane is not thinking clearly about the statement she just made. But Jeneane is insistent and places an application with an adoption agency. The program relates Molly's efforts to change Jeneane's way of thinking by showing her the normal day-to-day responsibilities of what being a full-time mother is all about.

Cast: Mitra Avani (Jeneane), Madeline Moser (Emily), Katharine Phillips Moser (Molly), Peter Mikhair (Peter), Christopher Muir (John), Rosemary Stevens (Mrs. Sanders). **Credits:** *Producer:* Thomas D. Moser, Katharine Phillips Moser. *Writer-Director:* Thomas D. Moser. **Comment:** The program does sound intriguing but, unfortunately, all episodes have been taken off line thus a comment based on viewing is not possible.

Episodes: *1.* I've Been Meaning to Tell You. *2.* Crash Course. *3.* Real Estate 101. *4.* Potty Training. *5.* The Phone Call. *6.* L.A. Adjacent. *7.* Paper Work. *8.* Blind Date. *9.* Razzle Dazzle.

885 Slacker, P.I. hulu.com. 2009.

During the 1980s the television crime drama *Derringer, P.I.* was the lowest-rated television show of the decade. Bo and Wyatt, twenty-something slackers, have recently discovered the show in reruns and have become addicted, watching every episode that airs. During a marathon presentation of the program, Bo and Wyatt are shocked to see that the show's detective, John Derringer and his sidekick, Sam Brady, have suddenly appeared in front of them. Are they real? Being stoners and having foggy but overactive imaginations, they believe they are (as no explanation is given as to how Derringer showed up). But Derringer did show up for a reason: Bo and Wyatt owe back rent, have overdue bills and are simply just a mess. Somehow Derringer knew this and appeared to help guide their miserable lives. The program relates all that happens as Bob and Wyatt get help from something that may only be figments of their imaginations.

Cast: Charlie Peccoraro (John Derringer), Edward Spivak (Sam Brady), Tanner Thomason (Wyatt Holden), Thom Sigsby (Bo Anderson). **Credits:** *Producer:* Jake Futernick, Taylor Garbutt, Eli Kooris, Noel Shankel. *Writer-Director:* Noel Shankel. **Comment:** A bit off-the-wall but still enjoyable. The acting is good and the production well done.

Episodes: *1.* Reverse Psychology. *2.* Race Card. *3.* Too Deep. *4.* Partners. *5.* Bill Me.

886 Slummy Mummy. slummymummy series.com. 2014.

Jennifer is a first time mother (of Jack). She waited until she felt the time was right to start a family and "I'm ready," she says, to go back to work as a profes-

Slummy Mummy. Series poster art (used by permission of Jennifer Weedon 2015).

sional shoe model. But what Jennifer says and what transpires are two different stories. As Jennifer deals with all the issues associated with raising a baby, she also tries to get her life back to the way it was and the program follows all the mishaps she encounters as she attempts to do just that.

Cast: Jennifer Weedon (Jennifer), Valisa Tate (Kiki), Dena Tyler (Kelsa), Seph Stanek (Guollermo), Joe Tuttle (Husband), Erin Brese (Bethany), Dina Drew (Noelle), Cathy Riva (Angela), Rebecca Kush (Kelli). **Credits:** *Producer:* Jennifer Weedon, Brigid Turner, Valisa Tate. *Director:* Ron Palazzo. *Writer:* Jennifer Weedon. **Comment:** Truly enjoyable program that will leave you chuckling as Jennifer tries to blend her life as a mother with her work life.

Episodes: *1.* Back to Work. *2.* Mom Cave TV. *3.* Stroller Friction. *4.* Scoop and Seep. *5.* Cat Food. *6.* Audit.

887 *The Slutty Years.* theslut tyyears.com. 2012–2013.

Andi, Jennah and Claire are smart girls, now in their twenties, whose entire lives were dedicated to achieving excellent academic records. Their social lives were non-existent and now, as roommates, they feel they must venture forth and enter the dating world. The program chronicles their efforts and what happens as they seek new lives, adventures and love.

Andi, 26, has been a nerd all her life. She was a drum major in high school and has a degree in engineering from Stanford. Reading the classics satisfied her and she now feels that becoming a photographer is her dream job.

Jennah, 26, befriend Andi at Stanford when they bonded over their love of Spider-Man comic books. Jennah is a true science fiction fan but very emotional,

Claire, 27, is a Harvard graduate who does not care to impress anyone and does not apologize to anyone for her intelligence. She lives with her 28-year-old cousin, Mac, a bartender, and gave up a socialite life set for her by her parents to experience life as she believes it should.

Cast: Amy Aniobi (Andrea "Andi" Black), Carolyn Jania (Claire McBright), Crystal Hoang (Jennah Cho), Akeem Smith (Mac). **Credits:** *Producer:* Amy Aniobi, Mike Stein. *Director:* Reese Avanessian, Zachary Wright. *Writer:* Amy Aniobi, Chelsea Steiner. **Comment:** Well acted and produced although it does contain suggestive sexual situations.

Episodes: *1.* How It Starts. *2.* Pill. *3.* Mourning After Pill. *4.* Dick. *5.* Try It. *6.* Party.

888 *Small Parts: A Web Series.* smallparts webseries.com. 2011.

An off-Broadway version of the musical *The Pirates of Penzance* has been funded and cast with performers who seem to possess little or no talent. Brynne, Kellie, Kevin, Kyle and Miguel are part of the ensemble and somewhat puzzled as to how the project ever got off the ground. The program, sort of a behind-the-scenes look at the making of a musical relate the friends' efforts to deal with the problems that plague the production—from leads with

Small Parts. Series poster art (used by permission of Brynne McManimie).

numerous issues to a director whose actions make him appear quite insane.

Cast: Brynne McManimie (Brynne), Kyle Cooper (Kyle), Kellie Spill (Kellie), Miguel Cardenas (Miguel), Kevin Tobias (Kevin), Kevin Cordova (Toby), Paul LeSchofs (Paul David), Lynn Reinert (Tamora), Mike Wilkins (Music Director), Jimmy Bean (Lighting Designer), Alex Bueno (Costume Designer). Credits: *Producer:* Miguel Cardenas, Kyle Cooper, Brynne McManimie, Kellie Spill, Kevin Tobias. *Director:* Paul Michael Cooper. *Writer:* Kyle Cooper. Comment: A bit out-of-the-ordinary is the first impression you will get as it looks to be an insane spoof of any TV series or movie that tackled the subject of preparing a Broadway show. But stick with it. The production and acting are meant to be as such and a delightful spoof has been accomplished. Needless to say, the acting and production is top rate.

Episodes: *1.* How Not to Succeed in Show Business. *2.* The Music Maim. *3.* Kiss Me, Kyle. *4.* Brynne Get Your Gun. *5.* Soo-Rag Time. *6.* Marrily We Roll Along. *7.* Jekyll and Hide. *8.* No Light in the Piazza. *9.* Jesus Christ Superstar. *10.* Little Show of Horrors.

889 Small Town Detectives (STD): Oddfjord. youtube.com. 2012.

Dave is New York City cop who is not only fed up with the crime of the city, but his life as a cop in general. Believing that small town police officers have a much easier life, Dave elects to change the course of his life by moving to a small community and just taking it easy. Apparently the U.S. has no such towns as Dave elects to move to Norway and become a peace officer in a town called Oddfjord. Dave's dreams are quickly shattered when he finds Oddfjord is not what he imagined as it is a festering town filled with the same type of criminal activity that he sought to flee. The program follows Dave as he once again faces the challenges of the past, this time in a town where its police detectives are a bit off-center and its most treasured object is a wooden spoon.

Cast: Dave T. Koenig (Dave), Stian Hafstad (Det. Hafstad), Christer Larsen (Det. Larsen), Arild Vestre (Det. Jable), Chris A. Black (Chief Michaels). Credits: *Producer:* Lars Borge Loge, Thomas Lamo Lokoen, Einar Loftesnes. *Director:* Stian Hafstad, Christer Larsen. *Writer:* Jim Garvey, Stian Hafstad, Christer Larsen. Comment: Greatly exaggerated (but fun) look at how crime in a small town can equal or go beyond what happens in large cities. The acting and production is top rate and the series really something different when it comes to Internet TV.

Episodes: *1.* Crazy Mob Train Robbery. *2.* Prison Murder. *3.* iTerrorist…? *4.* Epic Ninja Art Heist.

890 Smart Actress. smartactresstheseries.com. 2012.

Jane and Cheryl are best friends who are also aspiring actresses. Roles are scarce, the girls have the ability and the program charts their adventures—from agent meetings, call backs, auditions and anything else that comes their way.

Cast: Jake Lipman (Jane Whitman), Sherry

Smart Actress. Jake Lipman (left) and Sherry Locher (© 2015 Maeghan Donohue).

Locher (Cheryl Walker), Michael Edmund (Robert), Lynn Berg (Frank). **Credits:** *Producer-Writer:* Jake Lipman, Sheryl Locher. **Comment:** Jake Lipman is delightful as one of the two "Smart Actresses." Cheryl Walker also shines as her best friend and the program is a humorous look at what some lesser-known actors must endure before achieving fame.

Season 1 Episodes: *1.* Auditions Regularly. *2.* Prepares Diligently. *3.* Moves Well. *4.* Seeks Exposure. *5.* Attends Workshops.

Season 2 Episodes: *1.* Ages Gracefully. *2.* Knows the Ropes. *3.* Books the Gig. *4.* Gets the Red Carpet Ready. *5.* Picks Her Fights. *6.* Gets Assist-ants-ance.

891 Smile for the Camera. smile-for-the-camera.com. 2014.

"Watch us. Love us. Laugh with us. You know you want to" is the program's tag line for a series of short, right-to-the point skits that poke fun at everyday life.

Cast: Devin Dunne Cannon, Karl Hammerle, Moksha McPherrin, Susan Louise O'Connor, Brennan Taylor, Adrian Walther. **Credits:** *Producer-Writer-Director:* Isabel del Rosal. **Comment:** Enjoyable anthology program that is well acted with amusing stories.

Episodes: *1.* Smile. *2.* Killer. *3.* Tax Deductible. *4.* The Catatonix. *5.* Caulk. *6.* How to Avoid Sex with Your Husband: The Movie Night Chronicles. *7.* Stalker. *8.* The Vagina Whisperer. *9.* How to Avoid Sex with Your Husband: The Middle of the Night Chronicles. *10.* Switching Teams Infomercial. *11.* How to Avoid Sex with Your Husband: The Bath Time Chronicles. *12.* Beat Poet. *13.* Pregnant Papa. *14.* X.A.—Ex's Anonymous. *15.* Youth Center. *16.* Nursery Rhyme. *17.* Mombies. *18.* Juana—Entrepreneur. *19.* How to Avoid Sex with Your Husband: The Christmas Time Chronicles.

892 Smoke Break. smokebreakseries.com. 2013–2014.

The Pennidyne Corporation has, like all companies, banned cigarette smoking inside the building; outside, however, is a different story, and employees can smoke as many cigarettes as they please without repercussions. Using the building's court yard as its basic setting, the program follows a group of workers as they light up a cigarette for that office break to discuss whatever comes up in conversation.

Cast: David DeRock, Jeffrey Staab, Sally Bremenkamp, Somyia Finley, Adam French, Matt McInnis, Tucker Keatley, Jason Curtis Miller, Andy Perkins, Kapil Kumar Jain, Drew N. Martin, Madeline Smith, Joseph Anderson, Stephen Matlock, Dustin Blakeman, Chris Bylsma, Alice Pollack, Christine Courville, Claudia Copping, Sabrina Henderson. **Credits:** *Producer:* Nathan Bukowski, Kendal Sinn, Jeremy Osbern, Sally Cummings. *Writer-Director:* Kendal Sinn. **Comment:** There are a lot of episodes and there is a lot of smoking—perhaps just too much as the landscape of television and feature films has changed drastically since the 1970s and characters smoking cigarettes is something that is just not popularized any more.

Episodes, 1–20: *1.* A Little Special. *2.* The Rib. *3.* How to Properly Open a Door with Your Head. *4.* There's No Merit Badge for That. *5.* Proper ID Required. *6.* The Other 25% Is Wasted. *7.* Happy Trees. *8.* The Life Cycle of a Pink Post-It Note. *9.* How to Offend Everybody. *10.* A Civil Rights Scrabble Board. *11.* Here, Hold This Secret. *12.* Organic Pet Food. *13.* Potential Alien Organs. *14.* Scourge of the Married Man. *15.* If a Cat Falls off a Toilet. *16.* So, About the Fourth Floor. *17.* Dr. Phil and the Case of the Vanishing Husband. *18.* Do You Have Any Fruits to Declare? *19.* When in Rome. *20.* Zig Zag Doesn't Make Paper That Big.

Episodes, 21–40: *21.* Four Words. *22.* O.Arg.Pirate.Hooker. *23.* That's a Lot of Balloons to Transport. *24.* Little Black Box. *25.* That Didn't Go Where I Thought It Would. *26.* Who Are the Brain Eaters? *27.* Where Is Here? *28.* Activate the Zeta Beam. *29.* Oh Look, Interns. *30.* Don't I Look More Confident? *31.* So Cute to Watch You Try to Think. *32.* Wingman to Billy Dee Williams. *33.* No Use

Crying Over Broken Ice. *34.* What's After the Boob Line? *35.* Sound Travels? Who Knew? *36.* Amateur's Degree. *37.* A Sweet Story About Stalking. *38.* Dumb Story Buy Back Policy. *39.* Have You Heard the News Today? *40.* Think About It, It'll Be Funnier Later.

Episodes, 41–60: *41.* Fresh Air Break. *42.* Commies in the Fun House. *43.* Nola's Early Retirement Package. *44.* Do I Really Look Like I'm Kidding? *45.* The Ladies of Shark Week. *46.* Send in the Closer. *47.* We're Not Going Away Mad, We're Just Going Away. *48.* We Prefer the Term Special. *49.* The Shiny Thing in the Checkout Aisle. *50.* They Ain't All Van Gogh's. *51.* The Great Muppet Unsolved Mystery. *52.* Dead Bird. *53.* Zombie Bird Apocalypse. *54.* Knuckleheads. *55.* Joe Knows a Lot About Birds. *56.* This One's for All the Dead Birds. *57.* The Fine Art of Boob Brushing. *58.* The Room. *59.* That Just Happened. *60.* Hot Date with Bill Clinton.

Episodes, 61–83: *61.* A Different Kind of Dick Joke. *62.* Keep Doing That Thing You Like. *63.* Lollipop Knockers. *64.* Not a Nooner. *65.* The Vodka of Courage. *66.* One Ugly Dog. *67.* Being a Nicer Version of You. *68.* Kickball All-Star. *69.* What's Maggie Have to Do with It? *70–74.* Lunch Break: Jack and Katie. *75.* Lunch Break: Zach and Abby. *76.* Lunch Break: Ask for Bill. *77.* Lunch Break: Tough Nut to Crack. *78.* Lunch Break: Zach Steps In. *79.* Joke Week: Genghis Khan Was a Nice Dude? *80.* Star Wars Semantics. *81.* Luke Skywalker Was a Hard Ass. *82.* Lord of the Onion Rings. *83.* Dude Wedding Fantasy.

893 *Smoking.* smokingshow.weebly.com. 2012.

A cigarette is actual the "star" as it becomes the protagonist in the lives of a varied group of people. Each story deals with nicotine addiction and how cigarettes affect not only the smoker's life but those that are close to him (or her) whether it is at school, at home or the workplace. The featured players are Teddy (hopes to become a cabaret singer; currently operates a massage business); Kylie (a high school senior planning to study medicine; she is a gifted guitarist but prefers the drums); Al (a free-lance boom operator and sound mixer); Ellis (a slumlord and actor in sleazy adult films); Chi (a film editor and hopeful actor); and Marc (a high school singer hoping to become a rock star). **Cast:** Cat Doss (Kylie), Jemal Draco (Teddy), Richard Rey (Al), Holli Dean (Ellen), Gregg G. Lawrence (Ellis), Justin Blakely (Marc), Tommy Dorian (Chi), Emilio Palame (Conrad), Tanya Beatty (Darlene), Taylor Edwards (Amy). **Credits:** *Producer:* Jerome Berglund, Cat Doss. *Writer-Director:* Jerome Berglund. **Comment:** While not the best choice of topics to build a series around, it is well acted and produced and attempts to show that cigarette smoking is not cool.

Episodes: *1.* The Quitter. *2.* The Bum. *3.* The Rebel. *4.* The Redactor. *5.* The Ingénue. *6.* The Avuncular. *7.* The Slumlord. *8.* The Lady.

894 *So Awkward.* soawkwardseries.com. 2013.

Jeannie, young and pretty, is a bit awkward when it comes to the dating scene. Preston, a like-able young man, has nothing in common with Jeannie except that he too is awkward when it comes to dating. Each is seeking the perfect mate, unaware, even after dating each other, that fate had intended for them to be together. The program focuses mainly on Jeannie's life and dating experiences and what it takes for two people to realize that, despite all the awkwardness, they were meant to be together. **Cast:** Tarah Consoli (Jeannie), Elliot Joseph (Preston), Kate Spurgeon (Brenda), Emily Buck (Wendy), Paolo Mancini (Marco/Big Daddy). **Credits:** *Producer-Writer-Director:* Tarah Consoli, Elliot Joseph. **Comment:** Tarah Consoli and Elliot Joseph, the creators and stars, have managed to capture the awkwardness of dating in a manner that is amusing, yet sad in a way, as two people who are meant for each other, do not realize it until something is triggered to make them see the light.

Episodes: *1.* Like Intelligent People. *2.* Great Social Skills. *3.* What's Your Mantra. *4.* One Coffee Bean at a Time. *5.* Too Much Coffee? *6.* Dropping China in a Bullpen.

895 *So Much for Talent.* vimeo.com. 2013.

Kate Justin is a young woman who, after divorcing her husband, decides to leave Denver and return to her roots in Seattle to reconstruct her life. Kate reconnects with some friends, is invited to a "Welcome to Seattle Party," becomes intoxicated and wakes up the next morning to find that she is the owner of a talent agency (it appears in her drunken state that she either reconnected with or met [not clearly stated] Sybil Dahling, the former owner who found her the perfect pigeon to buy her agency, Endless Talent). Unable to break the contract, Kate, with no experience on how to run an agency, must now learn the ropes and the program charts all the chaos that results as she deals with the world of eccentric actors, agents and divas as well as her own off-the-wall employees. **Cast:** Lyssa Browne (Kate Justin), Tracey Conway (Sybil Dahling), Laura Kenny (Ruthie), Julianne Christie (Libby), Billy Gleeson (Simon), Simon Hamlin (Paulo), Gin Hammond (Veronica), Ian Lindsay (Thaddeus), Shellie Shulkin (Dolores), Mariel Neto (Yvette), Christine Salo (Frannie). **Credits:** *Producer:* Topo Swope. *Director:* Steven Fogell. **Comment:** As stated above it is unclear if Kate knew or just met Sybil. By a phone conversation between the two, it appears Kate and Sybil have known each other for some time. The program's premise is refreshing with good acting and production values. With only two episodes on line, the story just ends in the middle of nowhere and future episodes will most likely not appear.

Episodes: *1.* Dizzy. *2.* Furthermore.

896 *So Not Super.* day304.com. 2014.

The Gala of Justice is a super hero organization formed to protect the world from evil with Captain Famous as its most prestigious member. But not every super hero has amazing powers. Taking this into account, Samantha, a retired A-List super hero who mysteriously lost her powers, establishes a support group for the unknown heroes who have less than spectacular powers. Samantha believes that one day her powers will return but in the meantime mentors four people who are not quite A-List material: Hiss (has the ability to attract cats), Elizabeth (a pretty girl who can never get a word in), Papercut (controls paper) and Bob (the power to eat anything). With her ragtag group of yet-to-become real super heroes Samantha begins her process of changing their lives, hoping in the end for her and them to become members of the Gala of Justice.

Cast: Julie Wilhelm (Samantha), Mason Hunt (Hiss), Libby Hunt (Elizabeth), Mike Jordan (Bob), Peyton Mogley (Papercut), Gary Lobstein (Captain Famous). **Credits:** *Director:* Gary Lobstein. *Writer:* Julie Wilhelm. **Comment:** It's not an all-out super hero vs. super villain series but simply up-and-coming heroes struggling to follow in the footsteps of the illustrious Captain Famous. The acting is good and the production well presented.

Episodes: *1.* A Good Old-Fashioned Origin Story. *2.* A Hero By Any Other Name. *3.* My Powers Were Useless They Said. *4.* Super Hero 101. *5.* Famous. *6.* Training Day. *7.* I Know Your Secret Identity. *8.* Now, Everyone Knows. *9.* Same So Not Super Time. *10.* Same So Not Super Channel.

897 *So On and So Forth.* tv.com. 2006.

Five friends (see cast) as they navigate life, dealing with everything from their hopes, worries and fears to romantic entanglements and unrequited crushes.

Cast: Diana Gitelman (Chloe), Jake Johnson (Leland), Jon Togo (Dennis), Camille Chen (Joy), Armen Weitzman (Armen). **Credits:** *Creator-Writer:* Max Winkler, Matt Spicer. **Comment:** With all episodes being taken off line a comment is not possible.

Episodes: *1.* Dennis & Leland. *2.* Chloe & Leland. *3.* Sam & Joy. *4.* Dennis & Joy. *5.* Sam & Chloe. *6.* Sam & Leland. *7.* Leland & Joy. *8.* Dennis & Sam. *9.* Joy & Chloe. *10.* Dennis & Chloe.

898 *Social Animals.* social animalsshow.tumblr.com. 2011.

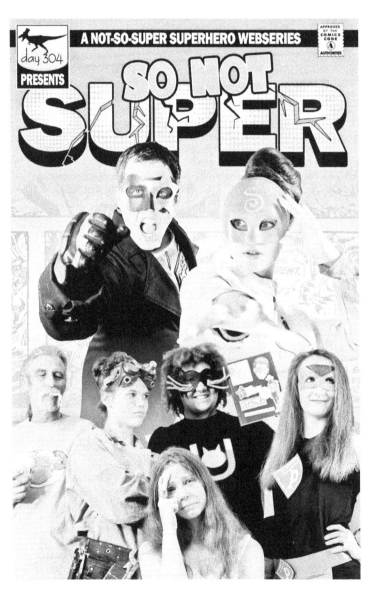

So Not Super. Series poster art (copyright Day 304, LLC).

Sarah, Riley, Kate and Tom are friends facing a dilemma: they believe they are stuck in a seemingly directionless and rather boring life. The program relates the awkward situations that develop as each tries to help the other find that unknown happiness they are seeking.

Riley is a glamorous girl who is drawn to other women but whom you would never suspect of being drawn to yard sales and involved in "dumpster diving" activities to acquire the "treasures" that someone else may have tossed away. She is also adventurous and always there for her friends in the time of need.

Kate has not moved on and lives in the same neighborhood in which she grew up. She is an only child and "hates most people, including her friends" (a result of being secretly attention starved). Because her situation has not changed since she was a child, she has settled into her uninspired life and admits that she is just too lazy to meet new people.

Thom had dated Kate, but when they realized they had nothing in common, they mutually agreed to break up but remain friends. Although Tom is straight, he contends that "dudes are boring" to hang out with and delights with his female "hangout friends."

Sarah, born in New England, is a flirtatious girl who grew up in a household with an abusive and alcoholic father. Although she hangs out with two women, she is straight but has a weakness for falling for older men in uniform. Her one principal fault is her attempt to project her outlook into the people who surround her (to make up for the lack of affection at home from her father).

Cast: Riley Rose Critchlow (Riley), Kate Heckman (Kate), Sarah Erin Roach (Sarah), Thom Shelton (Tom). **Credits:** *Producer-Director:* Erin Weller. *Writer:* Kate Heckman, Erin Weller. **Comment:** Enjoyable program with very good acting and production values.

Episodes: *1.* Perry's Party. *2.* Let's Get Physical. *3.* Adventures in Babysitting.

899 *Social Life.* youtube.com. 2011.

Wes is a graduate student seeking his degree in sociology. For his thesis Wes devises a unique concept: to understand his own social world and how he is a part of that world. With his friends, Karen and Ryan as his assistants, the program chronicles what happens as Wes begins a quest to discover who he is, how other people see him and become that person.

Cast: Adam Beauchesne, Paige Elan, Pearson Brodie, Jason Poulsen, Emily Rowed, Cameron Crosby. **Credits:** *Director:* Bryn Hewko. *Writer:* Adam Beauchesne. **Comment:** Wes talks directly to the camera making the program feel more real. The acting and production values are good and the program does conclude with Wes learning just who he is.

Episodes: 5 untitled episodes, labeled "Episode 1" through "Episode 5."

900 *Sockamamy.* webserieschannel.com. 2010.

Cassie and Bernie are not your ordinary sock puppets. They are puppets with big dreams, numerous schemes, ambition, tons of incompetence and a business called Sockamamy Enterprises. The program chronicles two sock puppets as they go about creating insane business ventures (like a Netflix service for people over 80 called Reels on Wheels) hoping that one of their ideas will hit pay dirt.

Voice Cast: Lynne Rosenberg (Cassie), Michael Solis (Bernie). **Credits:** *Producer-Writer:* Lynne Rosenberg, Michael Solis, Tim Mattson. *Director:* Tim Mattson. **Comment:** Although the thought of sock puppets means a kid show, it is geared much more to adults here. The overall production is good and while the puppets are a bit cheap and odd-looking, the story ideas are there and would have worked a lot better with real people in the roles.

Episodes: *1.* Friend Store. *2.* Energy Drink. *3.* The Next Page. *4.* Reels on Wheels. *5.* iPatch.

901 *Some Assembly Required (2011).* facebook.com. 2011–2014.

It is a future time and for women science has presented them with a unique gift: the ability to change who they are and the way they look simply by changing heads (or hands). The anthology-like presentation relates stories of women who encompass the new technology and what effect that new head presents when it is replaced with the current one in use.

Cast: Jenilyn Rodriquez, Ashley Hesse, Alison Whitney, Cara D'Aamo, Ashley Couture, Jessica L. Rodriquez, Monika Cavagno, Kari Cee, Karin Crighton, Isabkee Dungan, Nicola Fiore, Leigh Fitzjamers, Starlett Hill, Jess Joy, Despina Karakoutsis, Stephanie Katz, Melissa Nadel, Madeline Neahlen, Joycelyn O'Toole, Lisa Pincus, Karen Tanico, Catherine Cela, Johanna Finn, Melissa Ann Hardy. **Credits:** *Producer-Director:* Sameh Abdallah. *Writer:* Jenilyn Rodriquez, Sameh Abdallah. **Comment:** A unique idea that it well acted and presented. The special effects for the head changing scenes are well done and quite convincing. Would make a great candidate for a network or cable series.

Episodes: 16 untitled episodes, labeled "Episode 1" through "Episode 16."

902 *Some Assembly Required (2013).* webserieschannel.com. 2011.

Mallory is a very pretty young woman who each week faces a different situation that complicates her life. The program relates each conflict and how Mallory deals with that issue (all of which are done within mostly under 60 second episodes).

Cast: Mallory Moye (Mallory), Andrew Herrea (Andrew), Vadim Keyfes (Parker), Rachael Sondag (You're Not Emily). **Credits:** *Producer:* Kendall Sherwood. *Director:* Marisha Mukerjee. *Writer:* Mallory Moye. **Comment:** Charming series that establishes an annoyance for Mallory and tackles it completely in a very short time. The acting and production is top rate.

Episodes: *1.* Trick or Twit. *2.* Car Wash. *3.* Friendian Slip. *4.* Public Nightmare. *5.* Turkey Cam. *6.* Telescope Setup. *7.* Bang. *8.* Nativity Scene. *9.* Wind in the Sails. *10.* Mix and Metaphors. *11.* Divorce Fax. *12.* SAR Hilarious Quotes. *13.* Always Use Protection. *14.* How to Speak in an Irish Accent. *15.* Livin' the Life. *16.* Paper or Plastic. *17.* Please Hold. *18.* Down Dog.

903 Somehow I Manage. webserieschannel.com. 2013.

The University of Southern Mississippi provides the backdrop for a look at its baseball team managers as they deal with the various issues that confront them.

Cast: Brett McIntyre (Brett), Trent Walters (Trent), Jordan Burgess (Jordan). **Credits:** *Producer-Director:* Brett McIntyre. *Writer:* Brett McIntyre, Trent Walters, Jordan Burgess. **Comment:** The presentation takes a bit of adjusting to as it encompasses fading scenes (as one image fades out another comes into view over that image). The stories, acting and production values are standard for an Internet series.

Episodes: 5 untitled episodes, labeled "Episode 1" through "Episode 5."

904 Something Remote. somethingremote.com. 2009.

Neil, Matt and Eric are roommates who enjoy only one thing: watching TV. They work at dead-end jobs and have no social life. Their happiness is shattered when the remote control malfunctions and their TV can only pick up the Spanish Home Shopping Channel. The web series served as a prequel to the feature-length film of the same title and follows the friends as they struggle to get along with each other and concludes with Neil stealing the remote control devise of his ex-girlfriend, Lisa, in the hope that it will remedy his situation at home (which leads into the plot of the feature film).

Cast: C.J. Haley (Neil Trembly), Rick Desilets (Matt Highland), John Selig (Erik Goulding), Rebecca Davis (Lisa), Sarah Neslusan (Shannon), Matt Heron Duranti (Skott), Hunter Gibbs (Homeless Al), Sammi Lappin (Abby). **Credits:** *Producer:* Nick Allain, Steve DiTullio. *Director:* Alex Laferriere. *Writer:* Alex Laferriere. **Comment:** Rather silly premise that not only uses vulgar language but can

also be seen as just plain stupid. While its target audience appears to be slackers, its acting and production values are good.

Episodes *1.* Something Broken. *2.* Something Popping. *3.* Something Busted. *4.* Something Lost in Time. *5.* Something in Aisle 3. *6.* Something Tastes Like Fungus. *7.* Something Naked. *8.* Something Between Friends. *9.* Something Not Safe for Work. *10.* Boobs, Battles and Violence. *11.* Something on the Couch.

905 Sons of the Brotherhood. blip.tv. 2012.

It is a time when the face of broadcasting will be changed forever with the switch from analog to digital. KNOT is a TV station in its last days of analog broadcasting when S.O.B. (Sons of the Brotherhood) seize the station in an attempt to spread their beliefs that there are government cover-ups, mind control and other unsavory aspects affecting the world. Their plan: Begin broadcasting their self-imposed views (through "entertainment" shows like *Things I Hate and You Should Hate Too* and *Treasures of the Brotherhood*) coupled with one sided news reports and specials. The program charts what happens when propaganda is broadcast and how the TV station staff and S.O.B. members cope with all the problems that arise during the switch.

Cast: Liza Gonzalez (Smitty Kounick), Mollie Milligan (Yvonne), Shauns McLean (Rickky), Susana Gibb (Callie), Christopher Nash (Justice), Emily Ko (Gina), Kristen Sutton (Wanita), Tyler Cochran (Philipe Jones), Jerry Vizena (Jerry), Stephen Brodie (Conan), Ellen Locy (Willie Carroll). **Credits:** *Producer:* Brian Fabian, Mollie Milligan, Shauna McLean, Leslie Patrick. *Director:* Ellen Locy, Rich Levi. *Writer:* Jim Kuenzer, Emily Ko, Susana Gibb. **Comment:** Although comically depicted, the events presented could actually happen if a militant group were to take over a broadcast TV or radio station. The story is a bit far-fetched in the parodies it portrays of TV shows, but the acting and production values are good and the program very different from anything that airs on broadcast or cable TV.

Season 1 Episodes: *1.* Rogue Faction. *2.* Keep Your Eye on the Dragon. *3.* He Bobby She Bobby. *4.* Big Hair—Bigger Problems. *5.* Things I Hate. *6.* Balls with Dick Johnson. *7.* Loan Shark Pantry. *8.* Talking Pinata. *9.* Popsicle Man.

Season 2 Episodes: *1.* A Bun in the Oven. *2.* Treasures of the Brotherhood. *3.* It Takes Like Chicken. *4.* Tea Time with Olivia. *5.* Gina Gets Popped. *6.* It's Raining Possums. *7.* Around the World with Wanita. *8.* Things I Hate. *9.* Medically Speaking. *10.* The Date. *11.* The Kiss.

906 Sophomores. webserieschannel.com. 2010.

Margeaux Peters is a young woman newly enrolled at Bardell University. She is a sophomore and after a difficult first year at a prior college she is hoping to jump start her life as a student. Margeaux believes she has found the perfect school until she meets the dysfunctional students who will become her friends: Clive, a former high school jock who can't live up to his former reputation; Lizabeth, a fashion-conscious social climber who has difficulty getting along with others; Luke, a poor performing student (now in his third semester as a sophomore) who dreams of becoming a rock star; Kyla, a girl fascinated with homicide cases; and Taylor, a mean, nasty girl who believes college is all about learning and fun is something that is not in her vocabulary. With her new friends, her job as a writer for the school newspaper and a school that is anything but normal, the program follows Margeaux as she becomes involved in all the weirdness that surrounds the school (like, in the presented episodes, her involvement in a police investigation into the murder of a female student [Jessi Ann] and to prove that Kyla, convicted of the crime, is actually innocent).

Cast: Michelle Rafferty (Margeaux Peters), Nikko Pearson (Clive Jenkins), Maiya Milan Gitryte (Lizabeth Martin), Joseph Shepherd (Luke Jameson), Julianna Strack (Kyla Cane), Jennifer Mardes (Jackie Copeman), Kristy Butler (Sandra Charter), John Lee Taggart (Dorian Lang), Jessica White (Sniki Helsinki), Orly Waanounou (Renee Clark), Devin Winfield (Alexa Walton), Kaelyn Darley (Savannah Jones), Tyler Houston (Taylor Dam), Erin Rowland (Kay Anderson), Katelyn Sturdivant (Ericka Brown), John Lassiter (Det. Jay Mollock). **Credits:** *Producer-Writer:* Yones Michael, Sharon Ezra. **Comment:** Episodes are very long (29 to 31 minutes) and suited more for TV than the Internet as such productions tend to turn users off (short, right-to-the-point stories are needed to keep attention). That aside, the series, produced by Georgia State Television is well acted and produced.

Season 1 Episodes: *1.* Pilot. *2.* Add/Dropped. *3.* Moronology. *4.* I'm with the Band. *5.* Date Night. *6.* Living Condition. *7.* Dark Memory.

Season 2 Episodes: *1,2.* Murphy's Law. *3.* Mother Mary Never Married. *4.* Empty Fish Tanks. *5.* Weapon of Class Disruption. *6.* Guilty Parties. *7.* The Girl Who Cried Bluff.

907 Soup of the Day. youtube.com. 2006.

The predicament faced by Brandon Craig, a 28-year-old freelance photographer who is dating three women at the same time and struggling to keep each from learning about the other. Monique, his photo editor boss, will destroy his career if she finds out; Wendy, a tough police officer, will surely find a legal way to make him pay for deceiving her; and Franki, a manic depressant and host of the Internet show *Missleblast*, will act upon her suicidal tendencies if

she learns that Brandon has been cheating on her. The title refers to Brandon's favorite meal: split pea soup.

Cast: Jon Crowley (Brandon Craig), Catherine Reitman (Monique), Patty Wortham (Wendy), Tona Molina (Franki), Brian Palmermo (Todd), Levin O'Connor (Dr. Mitch). **Credits:** *Producer:* Marie Camuso, Christopher Berube, Paul Camuso. *Director:* Scott Zakarin. *Writer:* Bob Cesternino, Scott Zakarin. *Music:* Herman Beeftink. **Comment:** While the idea is not original (CBS had a similar series called *I Had Three Wives*) it is well acted and produced but does contain vulgar language and suggestive adult sexual situations

Episodes: *1.* Pilot. *2.* Wrong Way 4-Way. *3.* Wendy's Dog Bust. *4.* Caught in the Act. *5.* Secrets of MySpace at the Workplace. *6.* Vulcan Girl Gone Wild. *7.* Truth About Missleblast. *8.* Coupled Hypno Therapy. *9.* Missleblast Mistakes Delivery Guy for MySpace. *10.* The Ladies' Room. *11.* The Pussycat Monologue. *12.* Lo Mein Special. *13.* Sex, Lies and Viral Video. *14.* Our Exposed Private Parts. *15.* From Sex to Violence. *16.* The Suicide Girl. *17.* SOUPerman Returns. *18.* Message with a Happy Ending. *19.* The Best Finale Ever.

908 Space-Cat-Casio. funnyordie.com. 2014.

Two years ago, Casey Anthony and Tuna Cannes, members of the band Space-Cat-Casio parted ways with Casey retreating to Brooklyn, New York, and Tuna electing to live in Los Angeles. During their time together they made an album cover, but not an actual CD to accompany it. Casey and Tuna now believe the time has come to reunite and make the CD. Casey takes the biggest step, relocating to Los Angeles and with a lot of determination (but little talent as they can't sing or play musical instruments) Casey and Tuna begin a quest to break back into the music business and restart their careers (and make that CD).

Cast: Hayley Kosan (Casey Anthony), Natasha Pirouzian (Tuna Cannes), Trent Wilson (Gary). **Credits:** *Producer:* Kimberly Aiello. *Writer:* Hayley Kosan, Natasha Pirouzian. **Comment:** Casey and Tuna appear to have either Australian or British accents and they are a bit hard to understand at times. Other than that the idea is well presented with good acting and production values.

Episodes: *1.* Stoned, Tepid Pilot. *2.* Inner Rocks Gods, Out! *3.* Weekend at Space Cats. *4.* Freaky Sunday. *5.* Space Jam Session. *6.* Gave Good Face. *7.* The Social Catwalk. *8.* Feline Finale.

909 Space Guys in Space. spaceguysin space.com. 2013.

As a series of mysterious explosions begin to destroy the Earth, two morons (Carl and Stew) manage to escape the devastation in a malfunctioning space pod called *Portaterian*. Their only hope of surviving is GUSS, the ship's gorgeous female hologram support system. Episodes follow the last remaining members of the human race as they drift in space (the pod has inoperable engines) struggling to survive and hopefully find another planet with an atmosphere capable of supporting human life.

Cast: Jason Marsden (Carl), Dave Levine (Stew), Nicole Pacent (GUSS). **Credits:** *Producer:* Tony Wallace, John Frank Rosenblum, Jason Marsden. *Director:* Daniel Capuzzi. *Writer:* Tony Wallace. **Comment:** Nicole Pacent steals the show as GUSS in a comical science fiction parody of what could happen to the last survivors of a planet. The acting is good, GUSS is sexy, the special effects well executed and the overall production worth watching.

Episodes: *1.* The Podd Couple. *2.* Two Guys, One Pod. *3.* Confessional, FlurmJam. *4.* Tension. *5.* Dom Log: FlurmJam 16.5. *6.* Hole. *7.* Hunger Pains. *8.* In Dependence. *9.* Girl Gab, FlurmJam 10–3. *10.* Regrets. *11.* Confessional, FlurmJam 12.7. *12.* Albinards. *13.* Poddy Time, FlurmJam 8.6. *14.* Confessional, FlurmJam 18.2. *15.* Amazons. *16.* Girl Gab, FlurmJam 22.9. *17.* FlurmJam 60.3. *18.* Ninja. *19.* Confessional, FlurmJam 44.6. *20.* Confessional, FlurmJam 50.1. *21.* Hole Theory. *22.* Gee. *23.* Madness. *24.* Box. *25.* Hygiene. *26.* Change.

910 *Space Hospital.* spacehospital.com. 2007–2011.

The Centrality sector of outer space is owned by pan-dimensional beings called Overlords. It is here that Space Hospital, a mobile medical facility has been established. The staff is a bit off-the-wall and stories relate their antics as they attend patients and struggle to keep their facility afloat amid threats of it being closed due to its increasing financial problems. Dr. Goode is the self-medicating physician; Snead is the Chief Hospital Administrator; Ratknee is the Chief Nurse; Barbara, the gorgeous nurse; and Maggie, the zombie nurse.

Cast: Adriana Roze (Nurse Ratknee), Anne Ford Galiana (Nurse Barbara), Rich Hutchman (Administrator Snead), Tim Sullens (Dr. Goode), Robert Poe (Prince Plodd), Mary Buckley (Lindsay Long), Brett A. Snodgrass (Dr. Larry), Jodi Dybala (Nurse), Andy Hungerford (Dr. Drake), Heather Horton (Maggie Morningstar), Vanessa Vaughn (Sister Hilly), Frank Conniff (Pres. Magnavision), Tifanie McQueen (Nurse Ripner). **Credits:** *Producer:* Susan Stoebner. *Director:* Robert Poe, John Baumgartner. *Writer:* Robert Poe, Sigurd Ueland. **Comment:** Sort of a more outlandish version of the TV series *Scrubs* that is set in outer space complete with a wacky staff and patients that require the expertise of doctors and nurses that, for the most part, do not have that expertise.

Episodes: *Log 1.* Happiest Surgeon in Space. *Log 2:* I'm Pregnant. *Log 3:* Day of the X. *Log 4:* I, Manbot. *Log 5:* Save the Robots. *Log 6:* Father and Clones. *Log 7:* Boobification. *Log 8:* Reading, Writing and Reactionary. *Log 9:* Half Dozen of the Other. *Log 10:* New Organ. *Log 11:* Work Better with Svedka Vodka. *Log 12:* Omagone.

911 *Space Hospital: The Animated Series.* spacehospital.com. 2012.

The doctors and nurses of the live action series *Space Hospital* (see prior title) in an animated version that continues to relate their mishaps on an orbiting space hospital.

Voice Cast: Anne Ford Galiana, Robert Poe, Adriana Roze, Brett Snodgrass, Sigurd Ueland, Vanessa Vaughn. **Credits:** *Producer-Writer-Director:* Sigurd Ueland, Robert Poe. **Comment:** While not as outrageous as the live action series, the stories are well animated and written and an enjoyable companion series to *Space Hospital*.

Episodes: *1.* Alien Baby Birth. *2.* Lindsay Lohan Kill. *3.* Dale vs. Roach. *4.* Darth Vader vs. Space Hospital. *5.* Baba Fett in Love. *6.* Rise of the Storm-Tumors. *7.* Brangalin Gone Wild. *8.* Storm Trooper vs. Nurse Barbara. *9.* Alien Family vs. DCFS. *10.* Darth Vader Disney Make Over. *11.* The Fart of Life. *12.* Justin Bieber vs. Space Hospital.

912 *The Spirit of Adventure.* webseries channel.com. 2014.

A series of sketches performed by the Uptight Citizen's Brigade Theater, a New York based group of comedians.

Cast: Sarah Burton, Matt Dennie, Maelle Doliveux, Carrie McCrossen, Avery Monsen, Hunter Nelson, Josh Sharp, Ian Stroud, Siobhan Thompson, Joel Weidl. **Credits:** *Producer:* Matt Starr. **Comment:** Skits are rather off-the-wall with acceptable acting and production values (just nothing special to set it apart from other such series).

Episodes: *1.* Jesus Don't Let Me. *2.* Planet Earf. *3.* Frolickers. *4.* H.O.R.S.E. *5.* Tire Swing. *6.* Forest Flash Mob.

913 *Spy Queens.* youtube.com. 2014.

Three felon drag queens played by Larraine Bow (arrested for computer hacking), Britney K. O'Day (a cat burglar) and Ruby Monroe (charged with assault and battery) are recruited by the FBI and offered a pardon if they will use their unique skills to help them solve sensitive cases. Borrowing elements of the TV series *She Spies* (which used real girls released from prison to help solve crimes) *Spy Queens* cleverly combines its elements to relate their adventures as they try to become good, receive their pardons and capture the bad guys (even if they happen to be drag queens).

Cast: Larraine Bow, Britney K. O'Day, Ruby Monroe, Felicia Forrester. **Credits:** *Producer-Director:* Ephram Adamz. **Comment:** Although the TV series mentioned above may be familiar to you, you have never seen them like this before. Using drag queens puts a whole new twist on the concept (like *Chico's Angels* [see entry] did with *Charlie's Angels*) and makes for an enjoyable program to watch.

Episodes: Only a short teaser is available that barely highlights aspects of the series.

914 *Squad 85.* webserieschannel.com. 2009.

In 1985 the Los Angeles Police Department perfected time travel. Four of its finest detectives are transported 25 years into the future and establish Squad 85 at 85 Cannell Street in a home that appears to be just that—an ordinary home. Transported to the future were Toni, a young woman with a genius at disguises; Rusty, called "The Heartthrob"; Wheels, a wheelchair user and the brains of the outfit; and Bronx, the muscle. The program begins with a new recruit (Bobby) assigned to the unit and his experiences battling crime with cops from another era are comically depicted.

Cast: Milauna Jemai (Wheels), Travis Van Winkle (Rusty), Christopher Larkin (Bobby), Ceci Fernandez (Toni), Gregory Bonsignore (Bronx), Jeff Biehl (The Chief; who goes undercover as an Asian woman). **Credits:** *Producer-Writer-Director:* Gregory Bonsignore. **Comment:** An obvious spoof of the TV series *21 Jump Street* with young-looking cops and an address that uses TV producer Stephen J. Cannell's last name. Aspects of the TV series *Mod Squad* can also be seen and the program is a rather gritty version of both series with characters rough around-the-edges and not as refined as the series characters it lampoons.

Episodes: *1.* Out with the New. *2.* It's Not the Work, It's the Stares. *3.* Special Ops.

915 *Squaresville.* squaresville series.com. 2012.

Esther and Zelda are teenagers and best friends living in a small, seemingly dull suburban town. Believing that she will never venture farther than where she is, Zelda begins a quest to find adventure. With her friend Esther by her side, Zelda begins that quest with the program capturing all the mishaps that occur. Shelly is Zelda's friend, called "the hottest of messes" for all the trouble she gets into. She is also dating Esther's brother, Ozzy. Percy is the school geek and friends with Esther and Zelda. Wayne is Zelda's boyfriend; Sarah is Zelda's older sister.

Cast: Kylie Sparks (Esther), Mary Kate Wiles (Zelda), Tiffany Ariany (Shelly), Austin Rogers (Percy), David Ryan Speer (Wayne), Jim Mahoney (Ozzy), Christine Weatherup (Sarah Waring). **Credits:** *Producer:* Christine Weatherup. *Director-Writer:* Matt Enlow. **Comment:** Something different as the approach is on those who feel out of place—"If you felt strange. If you ever felt square. Spend time with Esther and Zelda" (the program's tag line). The acting and production are very good and the program quite entertaining.

Episodes: *1.* Nerds on the Run. *2.* Let's Hang Out in the Tree House. *3.* Mallscapade. *4.* Sassy Girl. *5.* The Hottest of Messes. *6.* I Don't Wanna Wait. *7.* Shelly at Large. *8.* I Know, Right? *9.* Make Out City. *10.* Tele-Marathon. *11.* Before Supper. *12.* Cougarville. *13.* Real Girl Talk. *14.* Adventure Date. *15.* Star-Crossed Action News. *16.* Too Cool for School. *17.* Back to Basics.

916 *Squatters.* youtube.com. 2010.

Hank and Alex are friends and roommates who share an apartment in Manhattan. They are in their twenties and on the month they are not able to pay the rent, they are evicted but that does mean they are homeless. While contemplating what to do, they make a bet with each other: to see who can last the longest without paying rent. The winner will pay their rent for a year when the contest is over but neither one can leave Manhattan, stay with friends or pay for housing of any kind. The program chronicles their efforts to win: Alex by camping out in his office cubicle; Hank, a ladies' man, by seducing girls and crashing at their home.

Cast: Brendan Bradley (Hank Pitman), Erik Smith (Alex Selkirk), Sandeep Parikh (Supervisor Sam), Cooper Harris (Julie), Christiann Castellanos (Ramira), Brian Ames (Jim), Marty Lodge (Larry

Squatters. Series title card (used by permission).

Stein), Casey Christensen (Lindsay). **Credits:** *Producer:* Brendan Bradley, Frank Kramer, Cooper Harris. *Writer-Director:* Brendan Bradley. **Comment:** An original idea with very good acting and production values. Based on the real-life experiences of Brendan Bradley and the first comedy series to air on Daily Motion, it does have its moments and flows smoothly from episode to episode leaving the viewer to wonder just who will win the absurd bet.

Season 1 Episodes: *1.* It Starts with a Bet. *2.* Take Me Home Tonight. *3.* In Search of a Douche. *4.* A Little Irritation. *5.* Bartering. *6.* Three's a Crowd. *7.* Rinse and Repeat. *8.* A Fresh Pair.

Season 2 Episodes: *1.* Commuters. *2.* Locked Out. *3.* Cold Spell. *4.* Party Time. *5.* The Language of Love. *6.* Borrowed Goods.

917 *Squeegees.* youtube.com. 2008.

It is a typical city with tall buildings and many dirty windows. Gil is a young man who saw a need: wash those windows and began his own window washing business, Squeegees. His staff (BC, Adam and Ronny) are slackers and foul-ups, but friends he just cannot fire. The program relates what happens as the Squeegees wash windows—and make spying on the people behind those windows their top priority.

Cast: Marc Gilbar (Gil), Brendan Countee (BC), Adam Countee (Adam), Aaron Greenberg (Ronny). **Credits:** *Producer:* Lee Ross, Craig Protzel. *Writer-Director:* Adam Countee, Brendan Countee, Marc Gilbar, Aaron Greenberg. **Comment:** Something really different as window washers have not been the subject of many movies or TV shows. The acting is good and the situations encountered by the Squeegees are a bit exaggerated but humorous. **Episodes:** *1.* Full Frontal. *2.* Shaved Ice. *3.* Dirty Money. *4.* Sex Sells. *5.* Showdown. *6.* Mile High Club. *7.* Flogging the Dolphin. *8,9.* Accidents Happen. *10.* Doody Calls.

918 *Stalker Chronicles.* stalkerchronicles. com. 2010.

Jamie and Genie are friends surfing the Internet when they stumble across a video of a young man named Ryan. Immediately they become fascinated with him and believing they are "the ying to his yang" begin stalking him. Calling themselves the Yin Ladies (or Yin Yin or Yinny) they begin using covert names to disguise their identity and each episode adapts a different theater or movie style to literally showcase how two stalkers prey on a man with whom they have both fallen madly in love with.

Cast: Jamie Lou Moniz (Yin Yin), Genie Willett (Yin Yin), Ryan Braum (Ryan). **Credits:** *Producer:* Jamie Lou Moniz, Genie Willett. *Director:* Brendan McNamara, Brigitte Erickson, Coby Garfield, Randy Kent, Jamie Lou Moniz. *Writer:* Jamie Lou Moniz, Genie Willett. **Comment:** A rather unusual and very enjoyable program that interweaves color and black and white sequences in stories that encompass both straight comedy and musical numbers depending on which style is used (from Greek Tragedy to the comedy of Neil Simon to the films of Federico Fellini).

Episodes: *1.* Waiting for Roger Braun. *2.* Wilted Daisies. *3.* The Spectacle. *3.* On the Porch. *4.* Return to Sender. *5.* Red Wire. *6.* Gutter Dolls. *7.* Toilet Troubles. *8.* Jenny.

919 *Stallions de Amor.* webserieschannel. com. 2011.

Merlinda Stallion, the incredibly wealthy Latina owner of Stallion Enterprises, is a woman with numerous enemies. Merlinda is ruthless, cares only for herself and will do what ever it takes to make her empire grow. One night, while indulging in her usual sensual bath, someone enters the bathroom and kills her, leaving the police to determine who did it and why. It appears that the killer is someone Merlinda knew and two detectives (billed as "Detective Good-Looking" and "His Asian Companion") are determined to solve the case. The program relates all the turmoil that ensues as the detectives investigate and family members, business associates and friends all become suspects.

Cast: Drew Droege (Merlinda Stallion), Chris Farah (Buffy Stallion), Pete Zias (Buck Stallion), Natalie Lopez (Esther Stallion), Shawn Parsons (Detective Good-Looking), Louise Hung (His Asian Companion), Joy Nash (Mercy), Doreen Calderon (Tia Prudencia), Melissa Camilo (Maria Guadalupe), David Pavao (Victor Sage), Andrew Carrillo (Carlos), Mikey Scott (Esteban), Raif Derrazi (Pedro), Matthew Hannon (Diego Duarte), Michael Mullen (Ricky Martinez), Dee Amerio Sudik (Augusta Valentine). **Credits:** *Producer:* Efrain Schunior, Priscilla Watson. *Writer-Director:* Efrain Schunior. **Comment:** Excellent Americanized parody of a Spanish network telenovela (soap opera). There are twists and turns in the plot; the acting is exceptional and the production very well executed. There is even a drag queen (Drew Droege) playing Merlinda.

Episodes: *1.* Oh, It's You. *2.* The Heir. *3.* That Coffee Girl. *4.* Manwoman. *5.* Flaw & Order, Part 1. *6.* Nightmares and Visions. *7.* The Equitable Life. *8.* Flaw & Order, Part 2. *9.* Building a Mr. E. *10.* The Deal of a Lifetime. *11.* Murder in the Making. *12.* Buck and Buffy Stallion Are Dead. *13.* Two Somethings. *14.* Memory Recallation. *15.* Cousin Esther. *16.* The Bullet. *17.* Into the Sunset. *18–20.* The Consequences of the Law.

920 *Stand Up Girls.* standupgirlsshow. com. 2013.

Ursula, Dolores and Harper are aspiring female

stand-up comedians. The women not only share friendship but a misguided outlook on life. For them every action has an equal and opposite reaction. The program charts their experiences as they not only deal with the problems of everyday living, but making their marks in the world of stand-up comedy. Harper is an avid collector of worthless junk and works as a magician's assistant; Ursula performs as her infamous character Louisa Franks (she prefers performing in disguise and not judged by her looks); Dolores is Australian and performs occasionally offensive routines without worrying about the repercussions. **Cast:** Jenna Brister (Harper), Hollie Lee (Dolores), Stephanie Kornick (Ursula), Jim Fath (Frederick). **Credits:** *Producer:* Blair Skinner, Amy K. Green. *Director:* Blair Skinner. *Writer:* Amy K. Green. **Comment:** Each episode begins with a short stand-up routine by one of the leads followed by their efforts to deal with a real life situation. Shades of the series *Seinfeld* can be seen as it too was built around a stand-up comedian. Here the situations are humorous, the acting good and the production enjoyable.

Episodes: *1.* Couches Don't Fit in Cars. *2.* Cut a Rug, Not a Line. *3.* The Magician, the Box and the Wardrobe. *4.* Union House Blend, 2. Splendas, 1 Pump Hazelnut. *5.* Everyone Gets Old. *6.* I Saw You. *7.* Code 60!!! *8.* The Show Must Go On.

921 Star Power. youtube.com. 2011.

Saxon is an 18-year-old with a dream to star on the Broadway stage. While talented and only a high school senior Saxon has not experienced anything beyond local community productions. He is hoping to attend the University of Michigan (but is rejected) and his audition for his first play *Seussical the Musical* also turns out to be a bust (although he does meet Gwen, an equally talented actress). Shortly after, life appears to be changing for Saxon when he acquires an agent (Max), an audition for *The Sound of Music: Revamped* (an outdoor version of the play) and a starring role on the infomercial "Zit Undo, the Acne Cream of the Future." The doorway has been opened but the road ahead is still a rocky one and the program charts Saxon's progress, stuck performing in community theater but hoping for that one big break that will get his name in lights on the Great White Way. **Cast:** Joel Swanson (Saxon Black), Keri Fuller (Gwen Kennedy), Brenna Noble (Valerie), Hannah Finnegan (Diana), Max von Essen (Max von Essen). **Credits:** *Writer-Director:* Joel Swanson. **Comment:** If there is one thing Saxon wants to relay is that he loves to sing. He believes that as an infant he was meant to be a star as his second spoken word was "star" ("pee" was his first word). Saxon immediately impresses you as a likeable chap and the program itself is an enjoyable romp as Saxon seeks his dream.

Episodes: *1.* Survivor. *2.* Wasted. *3.* Graduation. *4.* Dream. *5.* Glory.

922 Stars of the Future. webserieschannel.com. 2012.

PRAT (Performing Recording Arts Technology School) is a London (England)-based university dedicated to the performing arts. It is here that students seeking theatrical or musical training enroll with the hope of achieving their dreams. Several such students are Junior, a former American child star; Paul, a rock star (and his sidekick Malcolm), Frederick, a musical theater student; and Arthur, a young man seeking to jump start his career. With each of the students in their final year at PRAT, a documentary film crew is assigned to chart their progress and what happens directly after graduation. The program follows each of the students and their experiences, performing in a final show ("MySpace: The Musical"), before they make a name for themselves. The musical is also called in episode descriptions "MyFace: The Musical" and "Facebook: The Musical." **Cast:** Alex Evans (Steve/Malcolm), Josef Pitura-Riley (Paul/Oliver/Dan), Anthony Cahill (Arthur/Gary), Jordan Shaw (Junior), Alex McGeary (John), Nicole Holliday (Megan), Kana Gordon (Jenny), Lizzy Connolly (Ellie), David Riley (Narrator). **Credits:** *Producer-Writer-Director:* Josef Pitura-Riley. **Comment:** While not an original idea (as aspects of the TV series *Fame* can be seen), it is an interesting take on the subject matter. It is however, rather talkative and a bit slow-moving as it focuses too long on one aspect and it makes it appear that scenes that could have been edited to tighten dialogue were not.

Episodes: 10 untitled episodes, labeled "Episode 1" through "Episode 10."

923 Start Up Stories. webserieschannel.com. 2014.

London's tech scene provides the backdrop for a look at how a startup company begins and operates as seen through an investor (Alex) for a company called Startup and his employees (Claudia, Alex, Moritz and Oliver), who are more mishap prone than business sense prone. **Cast:** Dean Kilbey (Alex), Asha Lane (Claudia), Tom Borlington, Tony Hunter, Simon Walton (Moritz). **Credits:** *Producer:* Yelena Kensboro. *Director:* James Mayer. **Comment:** Produced in England and although accents make it somewhat difficult to understand at times, it does present a good idea with fine acting and production values.

Episodes: *1.* Clients and Investors.

924 Star-ving. webserieschannel.com. 2009.

Married.... With Children fans will recognize

David Faustino as playing the role of Bud Bundy, the son of Al (Ed O'Neill) and Peg (Katy Sagal) and the brother of Kelly (Christina Applegate). But that was in the past and now, with all his earnings from the series gone, David has ventured into a world of sex and alcoholism with his only source of income being a porn shop left to him by a devoted but crazed fan. Feeling that he still has that "star power" from the 1990s, David believes that he can make a comeback and sets his goal to do just that. But he feels he can't do it alone and acquires the assistance of his friend Cornin Nemec (from the TV series *Parker Lewis Can't Lose*), a down-on-his luck former star, to join him. The program charts the literally outrageous steps David takes (from stealing to killing) to once again become the star he once thought he was.

Cast: David Faustino (Himself), Corin Nemec (Himself). **Credits:** *Producer:* David Faustino, Corin Nemec. *Writer:* Todd Bringewatt, David Faustino, Sam Kass, Corin Nemec. *Director:* Sam Kass. **Comment:** All episodes have been taken offline and "This Video Is Private" will appear on attempts to call up episodes.

Episodes: *1.* Begging Ed (Ed O'Neill guests). *2.* Gilbert's Kid (Gilbert Gottfried guests). *3.* Straight Outta Compton (Coolio guests). *4.* Married with Children Movie (Seth Green and Christina Applegate guest). *5.* Starving? Literally. *6.* Just One Drink. *7.* Going O.J. *8.* Stealing Alan Thicke (Alan Thicke guests). *9.* Deliverance. *10.* El Al-Qaeda. *11.* Getting Huge.

925 *Starving in Hollywood.* youtube.com. 2014.

Various skits that satirize everything and anything: from TV game shows and newscasts to the arts and politics.

Cast: John Byford, Rebecca Honett, Lewis Brian, Jeremy Lawson, Jennifer Neala Page, Motown Maurice. **Credits:** *Producer:* Chris Honett, Rebecca Honett. *Writer-Director:* John Byford, Chris Honett. **Comment:** The presentation is very fast paced and just too much is attempted within each episode. There is no time to comprehend the first joke before another one is thrust upon you. Easing the pace would have helped greatly.

Episodes: 6 untitled episodes, labeled "Transmission 1" through "Transmission 6."

926 *Starvival.* webserieschannel.com. 2010.

Possessing a dream of becoming a star is always not as easy as it sounds. It takes a lot of hard work, some luck and sometimes taking gigs that are, for the most part absurd. The program follows Danielle Barker, a struggling actress as she belittles herself by accepting gigs that are anything but average.

Cast: Danielle Barker, Erin Empey, Markus Timothy-Schneider, Robert Nolan, Stevie Thomas, Thet

Win, Brendan Jeffers, Paul Ferguson, Erik Martin. **Credits:** *Producer-Writer:* Danielle Barker. **Comment:** The program opens with "All the footage you are about to see is real. Do not try this at home." While the situations Danielle encounters could actually happen, only starving actors would take them (as most are just embarrassing to tackle). The acting is very good and Danielle is a very like-able lead.

Episodes: *1.* Tickle for a Nickel. *2.* Trample Tootsies for Toonies? *3.* The Ploy for a Boy. *4.* The Ploy for a Boy—Continued. *5.* Pose as a Pigeon for Pennies? *6.* $7,200 to Model Clothes or $60 bucks to Model Nude? *7.* Midget Munch for Money. *8.* $100,000 to Be a Naked Geisha? *9.* My Mickey Mouse Money Slave.

927 *The State of Greenock.* youtube.com. 2012.

It is the year 2020 and 12 months have passed since Greenock, a small coastal town in Scotland became an independent state due to a political blunder. Now, free of rule by the United Kingdom, the State of Greenock, as it is called, is ruled by its first elected president Felix Crammond. A documentary film crew has been granted permission to chronicle Crammond's first year in office and the program follows, through the documentary film narrator, how Crammond and his crack (pot) staff rule and how its citizens feel about what has happened to them.

Cast: Calum Beaton (Felix Crammond), Paul Kozinski (Peter), Richard McLean (Leslie), Ryan Hendrick (Interviewer), Mark Barclay (Tam), Rowan King (Ailsa), Floss Ross (Betty), Jonathan Holt (Paul), Barry Walker (Billy). **Credits:** *Producer:* Pamela Barnes. *Writer-Director:* Gavin Grant. **Comment:** An obvious take off of the Peter Sellers feature film *The Mouse that Roared* although it has thus far not gone to that film's extremes. The documentary approach is different and the acting and production quite good.

Episodes: *1.* Greenock Pilot. *2.* A Credible Greenock. *3.* A Greener Greenock. *4.* A Healthier Greenock. *5.* A Wealthier Greenock. *6.* A Smarter Greenock. *7.* A Better Greenock.

928 *Statler and Waldorf: From the Balcony.* vimeo.com. 2005–2006.

Statler and Waldorf, the elderly Muppet curmudgeons from the 1970s TV series *The Muppet Show* review movies from the balcony of a theater, making fun of the review series *Siskel and Ebert at the Movies*. Other Muppet characters appear as guests and the hosts simply offer their opinions on upcoming movies with clips and skit parodies (Pepe the Prawn hosts the DVD release segment).

Cast: Victor Yerrid, Steve Whitmire (Waldorf), Drew Massey, Dave Goelz (Statler), Drew Massey, Bill Barretta (Pepe). **Credits:** *Producer-Director:* Ian

Hirsch. *Writer:* Jess Nussbaum, Mike Pellettieri, David Young. **Comment:** Smartly produced program that has all the charm from the series from which it originated. While somewhat dated, it is still enjoyable to watch simply for Statler and Waldorf.

Episodes: 34 untitled episodes, labeled "Episode 1" through "Episode 34" were produced along with a "Test Pilot" episode.

929 *Status Kill.* mydamnchannel.com/status kill. 2012.

It is the near future and social networking has taken on a whole new look—virtually everyone is addicted to it, especially to TweetFaceSter, the Facebook of the future. From the guy on the street to the checker in a supermarket and from the local cop to the highest ranking government official, TweetFaceSter is the premium social network. One such man, Denton "Sparky" Sparks is no exception. He is a member of TweetFaceSter and it could get him killed. Sparky is a top notch U.S. government secret agent whose assignments are compromised by TweetFaceSter (once a tweet is received a hologram appears and will not dematerialize until a response is sent). Naturally, Sparks receives tweets at the most inappropriate times and the program charts what happens when he tries to respond—and not get himself killed before he returns to his assignment.

Cast: Ayinde Howell (Denton Sparks), Julia Hoff (TweetFaceSter), Alex Sauer (Triton), Danielle Tolles (Agent Talon). **Credits:** *Producer:* Jess Cowell, Rob Barnett, Warren Chao. *Writer-Director:* Jess Cowell. **Comment:** Intriguing concept as part of that future is already here but seeing how it could (hypothetically) progress is quite amusing. Choosing an individual whose life depends on secrecy is a stroke of genius as tweets now rule his life and could either expose him or get him killed (or both).

Episodes: *1.* I Hate Invites. *2.* Don't Tag Me Bro! *3.* It's Your Birthday. *4.* Talk Is Cheap. *5.* She Needs Attention. *6.* Way Too Cute. *7.* Checking In. *8.* Trolls. *9.* Quitting.

930 *Staying in Boston.* stayinginbostontheseries.com. 2014.

C.C. is a Harvard graduate living and working in Boston as an employee of a nonprofit organization. One morning she woke up and thought becoming an actress was meant to be her life's goal. Without really thinking it through, C.C. quits her job, enrolls in an acting class then realizes she is without a job and money. C.C. loves Boston and is reluctant to leave but realizes that once she builds her resume she must move to Los Angeles or New York to pursue her career. In the meantime, part-time jobs become a part of her life and the program follows C.C. as she navigates a hectic work life while pursing her dream of becoming an actress.

Cast: Drew Linehan (C.C.), Michelle Mount (Vivian), Mario DaRosa, Jr. (Desh), Paul Ezzy (Sean), Dennis Hurley (Ben), Mikey DiLoreto (Parker). **Credits:** *Producer-Director:* Vincent C. Morreale. *Writer:* Jan Velco Soolman. **Comment:** Very enjoyable and humorous program that is very well acted and produced. Everything flows smoothly from scene to scene with Drew Linehan simply delightful as C.C.

Episodes: *1.* Pilot. *2.* Prelude. *3.* Boost. *4.* Are You Sure? *5.* Frying Pan. *6.* Driving. *7.* Twitter. *8.* Shrimp Allergies. *9.* Rooftop.

931 *Stella.* imdb.com. 2010–2015.

Pontyberry is a town nestled in the stylish countryside of the Welsh Valleys. It is here that Stella, a resourceful divorced mother of three (Luke, Emma and Ben) lives. Karl is her ex-husband and newly married to Nadine. It is a simplistic story of how Stella navigates life and how she deals with those who are also a part of her life.

Stella was born in Pontyberry and at the age of 16 became pregnant by her then boyfriend Rob Morgan (who left her for a new life in Canada to avoid a scandal). Luke resulted from the affair and Stella later married Karl, with whom she had Emma and Ben. Becoming pregnant kept Stella from pursuing her dream of becoming a nurse.

Luke is the most troublesome of Stella's children; Emma, a bit dim-witted, is studying to become a hairdresser; and Ben, the youngest, is the smartest, although his natural curiosity often gets him into trouble.

Paula is Stella's best friend (since high school) and now runs Simpson's Funeral Services with her father (who is always called "Daddy"); she is married to Stella's brother, Dai, an ex-serviceman.

Aunty Brenda is Stella's sharp-tongued aunt. Michael Jackson is Stella's next-door neighbor. Bobby is Paula's work assistant. Meg and Ken are Stella's parents.

Cast: Ruth Jones (Stella), Craig Gallivan (Luke), Catrin Stewart (Emma), Justin Davies (Ben), Elizabeth Berrington (Paula), Di Botcher (Aunty Brenda), Patrick Baladi (Michael Jackson), Aled Pugh (Bobby), Owen Teale (Dai), Maggie Stead (Meg), Michael Elwyn (Ken), Julian Lewis Jones (Karl), Karen Paullada (Nadine), Pal Aron (Jagadeesh), Sudha Bhuchar (Tanisha), Rory Girvan (Sunil), Taj Atwal (Jasminder), Steve Speirs (Alan), Daniel Gammond (Little Alan), Howell Evans (Daddy), Kenny Doughty (Sean), Mark Lewis Jones (Rob), Maxine Evans (Rhian), Deddie Davies (Marj), Daffyd Hywel (Glen), Bet Robert (Mrs. Barclay). **Credits:** *Producer:* David Peet, Josh Dynevor, Ruth Jones, Lucy Lunsden, Barry Lynch. *Director:* Ashley Way, Tony Dow, Susan Tully, Mandie Fletcher, Simon Massey, Sandy Johnson, Juliet May, Minkie Spiro, Sarah O'Gorman, David Sant, Simon

Delaney. *Writer:* Ruth Jones, David Peet, Ben Edwards, Simon Ludders, Steve Speirs, Robert Evans, Abigail Wilson. **Comment:** A New Zealand produced series with characters that are both believable and warm. While the acting and production are excellent, some of the material is hard to fathom due to its localized Welsh sense of humor. The scenery is spectacular, the stories, although bit hard to grasp at times, are still enjoyable and make for a fine viewing experience.

Episodes: 40 untitled episodes, labeled "Episode #1.1" to "Episode #4.10."

932 *Stella B. and the Busted League.* you tube.com. 2013.

The Busted League, as they call themselves, are a group of enthusiasts who love comic books. They hang out at the Titan Comics book store and the program charts the situations each of the friends face as they navigate life.

Stella, an artist is the creator of *Love in the Sky* (about a female super hero) but is facing a crisis as her comic book received good reviews but isn't selling well and could be discontinued by her publisher unless sales increase. Doc, a veteran artist, is the creator of the science fiction comic book *Bitter Technopolis*. Paul, an aspiring writer, is seeking to create that perfect comic book. Becky, a cosplayer (dresses as comic book characters at conventions), has made a slight name for herself in Japan but has yet to achieve fame in the U.S. Karin, an attractive widow (who loves to cook), is considered "the mother hen" of the group according to Stella and has set her sights on seducing Doc.

Cast: Jocelyn Everett (Stella Botticelli), Ben Bryant (Ira "Doc" Reimer), Laura Jennings (Karin Hyde), Alexis Nabors (Becky Slater), Daniel Tuttel (Paul Blunt). **Credits:** *Producer:* Stephanie Jackson. *Writer-Director:* JE Smith. **Comment:** Comic book themed series have been done before and each with varying degrees of success. *Stella B* falls into the better category with very like-able characters, good acting and production values and believable situations. The only objection would be the unnecessary use of the unsteady (shaky) camera on such a series; the viewer does not need to see scenes bobbing up and down and from side to side as characters speak. Such a filming method has been criticized many times as being truly annoying—and it holds up to that criticism here too.

Episodes: *1.* A New, Improved Hope. *2.* Rory Gilmore Is Bleeding. *3,4.* Back and There Again. *5.* Bastille Day.

933 *StepFriendz.* youtube.com. 2013.

An unusual blended family situation: Brian and Mike are best friends who grew up together but are now father (Brian) and son (Mike) when Brian marries Mike's mother. Although their connection has changed, they are still the same rambunctious "kids" and stories relate the mishaps they now encounter as father and son.

Cast: Brian Donnelly (Brian), Mike Varejao (Mike). **Credits:** *Producer-Writer:* Brian Donnelly, Mike Varejao. *Director:* Jeremiah Jordan. **Comment:** All video information has been taken off line and it appears that only a pilot episode was made. The blended family idea has been done before with *The Brady Bunch* being the best example. There are always twists and turns and *Step Friendz*, by available information, found a unique one with a best friend relationship changing to a father and son relationship.

Episodes: *1.* Pilot: Telepathic Flu Shots.

934 *Stockholm.* stockholmseries.com. 2012.

While grocery shopping an attractive young woman (Jessie) comes to the attention of a man (Danny) who appears to have become fascinated by her. As Jessie leaves the store and begins placing her groceries in the trunk of her car, she is grabbed by Danny, knocked unconscious and placed in the trunk. Jesse awakens to find herself locked in a basement with no way to escape. The dark comedy follows Jesse as she seeks to escape her situation when she realizes that Danny is not only insane but a serial killer known as "The Heartbreak Strangler."

Cast: Brittani Noel (Jesse), Zack Gold (Danny). **Credits:** *Writer-Director:* Scott Brown. **Comment:** While labeled a comedy, it is hard to find that particular aspect as the program is a tense profile of a very pretty young woman placed in an extreme and dangerous situation. The acting is very good and the program flows smoothly from beginning to end.

Episodes: *1.* Day 1: The Day She Got Kidnapped. *2.* Day 2. *3.* Day 4. *4.* Day 6. *5.* Day 9. *6.* Day 48. *7.* The Day She Was Free.

935 *The Stooges.* youtube.com. 2012.

"Help Wanted. African-American desired in order to make our company more progressive. No Experience Necessary" is a newspaper ad that a young man (George) feels he is most qualified for. George, however, finds that after the interview he is not hired and doesn't even have the "no experience" they are looking for. Frustrated and figuring the only way to survive is to do things his way, George, with the assist of his friend Princeton, decides to become a drug dealer. The program charts their rather outrageous experiences in the world of drugs when they hook up with Mikhail, their coke-addicted Russian supplier and become involved with an assortment of nasty drug buyers and pushers as they seek to deliver Mikhail's "goods."

Cast: Eric Pumphrey (George), Branden King (Princeton), Rawn Erickson (Rawn), Luke Edwards

(Mikhail), Branden King (Princeton). **Credits:** *Producer:* Luke Edwards, Natan Moss, Lee Sacks, Adam Wright. **Comment:** An amusing take on the street drug industry with two guys only trying to survive as best they can but encountering everything that could easily end their lives. The acting and production values are very good and the story flows smoothly from episode to episode.

Episodes: *1.* Better Off Dealing Drugs. *2.* Sound White. *3.* The Rabbi. *4.* A Good Excuse. *5.* Who the Hell is Rawn? *6.* Dude, Where's My Car? *7.* Do You Prefer America?

936 *Stoop Sale.* stoopsale.tumblr.com. 2011.

It is the last weekend Daisy and Brad will be together. Before moving on, however, they have decided to have a sale (on the stoop of their apartment building) to dispose of items they shared together. The program is simply a look at that sale and what happens as they deal with friends, family and buyers and slowly begin to realize they will no longer be a couple.

Cast: Devin Sanchez (Daisy), Michael Ferrell (Brad), Jamie Dunn (Jamie), D.H. Johnson (Stan), Stephanie Lovell (Mary), Josh Tyson (Dean). **Credits:** *Producer:* Michael Ferrell, Devin Sanchez. *Writer:* Michael Ferrell. **Comment:** An unusual format that is well acted and produced and is one of the few programs to deal with selling off personal items.

Episodes: 6 untitled episodes, labeled "Episode 1" through "Episode 6."

937 *Straight to Home Video.* webserieschannel.com. 2013.

To most people who see them, Joni and Lloyd are friends who appear to lead non-eventful lives. They hang out together and are constantly engaged in some sort of conversation. The program simply follows Joni and Lloyd as they go about their daily "adventures"—whether it is rummaging through trash for treasures, enjoying a trip to the supermarket or stopping to admire the items in a lawn sale.

Cast: Jonette Page (Joni), Zach Elvington (Lloyd). **Credits:** *Producer:* John Michael, Nicolle Johnson, Jason Clairy. *Writer-Director:* John Michael, Nicolle Johnson. **Comment:** Very enjoyable program that, filmed in black and white (perhaps to show the drab life Joni and Lloyd lead) is also well acted and produced. It's like a peek into the world of two people who never appear to let anything get them down. Although there is no parental warning, it does contain adult themes and language.

Episodes: *1.* Pilot. *2.* The Lawn Sale. *3.* The Parking Lot. *4.* Joni and Lloyd Go Camping.

938 *Straight Up Gay.* afterellen.com. 2014.

Some believe that a straight male cannot be friends with a lesbian and vice versa. Alison, a lesbian, has broken that mold and become friends with Brenden, who is straight. Through their eyes (singles in their twenties) a look at how each helps the other navigate the dating scene is presented.

Cast: Alison Levering Wong (Alison), Brenden Gallagher (Brenden). **Credits:** *Producer-Writer:* Alison Levering Wong, Brenden Gallagher. **Director:** Dan DeLorenzo. **Comment:** *Will and Grace* TV series parody with a lesbian twist (as *Will and Grace* focused on the gay character Will who was best friends with straight girl Grace). The acting is very good and the overall production is television series quality.

Episodes: *1.* The Barista. *2.* Brenden's Cousin.

939 *Strange Train.* strangetrain.com. 2013.

Strange Train is a magical means of transportation that is capable of traveling through time and space. Its passengers are anything but normal and appear to have destinations that are known only to the mysterious Richard Reese, a man who relates tales "of weird stuff." Those tales are seen as occurring outside the train and apparently on Earth with passengers encountering more than they bargained for when that weird stuff enters their lives.

Cast: Richard Reese (The Host). **Credits:** *Producer:* Jim Brazda. *Director:* Richard Reese. **Comment:** The program has a *Twilight Zone*–like feel to it. It is really hard to judge the program based only on two episodes because the potential is far greater and not limited to what has been produced. Thus far only comedy episodes have been produced but that could change.

Episodes: *1.* The Couch. *2.* Professor Hobbs.

940 *Striker and Swat.* youtube.com. 2009.

Their landlord likes them for only one reason: they pay their rent on time. Other than that, he (like a lot of other people) just can't stand them. They are Milo, called Striker (neurotic and aggressive) and Douglas, called Swat (mellow and gentle), friends living in a Southern California apartment complex and just trying to navigate all the complexities of everyday life—from cleaning lint out of the dryer to figuring out how a guitar works.

Cast: James Bonadio (Striker), Steve Berg (Swat), Dave Holmes (Todd), Charles Milligan (Landlord). Lainee Gram (Cassie), Dana Powell (Bonnie), Will Lupardus (Brian). **Credits:** *Producer:* Dan Redmond, James Bonadio. *Director:* Dan Redmond. **Comment:** The program tends to drag a bit and the vulgar language that is used is so obviously forced that it spoils scenes (as it is so fake). Slacker programs have been done before and there is really nothing new here to set it apart from the others.

Episodes: *1.* Lint in the Dryer. *2.* Guitar Man. *3.* Todd's Apartment. *4.* Big Jim. *5.* Cassie's Kiss.

941 Stuck. youtube.com. 2013.

Feeling that he needs to take a break from his college studies, a young man (Henry) elects to return home and just relax. Henry's expectations are short-lived when his return only rekindles memories of the situations (pitfalls) he tried to escape and is now experiencing again. As Henry realizes that returning home was a mistake, the program charts his encounters with friends and family and the slow realization that it is hopeless for him to ever try leaving again.

Cast: Joshua Mikel (Henry Robinson), Emma Elle Roberts (Joann), Andrew Melzer (Joey Robinson), Aaron Beelner (Father Doyle), Danny Williams (Craig). **Credits:** *Producer-Director:* Robert Bryce Milburn. *Writer:* Nicholas Begnaud. **Comment:** It appears that only a pilot film was produced and, judging by it, a somewhat talkative program. There are no character introductions and the plot is somewhat evasive (as it just begins in the middle of nowhere). The acting and production values are standard for a web series.

Episodes: *1.* Pilot: Guy Walks Into a Liquor Store.

942 Stuck: The Chronicles of David Rea. stucktheblog.blogspot.com. 2011.

People who feel they are stuck in a rut are the people David Rea, an Emotional Trainer, is seeking. As David begins his counseling sessions, the program chronicles what happens when David gets more than he bargained for when dealing with people who are emotional basket cases.

Cast: Riccardo Sardonè (David Rea), Ivana Lotito (Emma Diaz), Vincenzo Alfieri (Vince Ciuffo), Valentina Izumi (Ramona Wallis), Gaia Scodellaro (Lisa Durren), Mark Lawrence (Joseph Shaw), Stefano Masciolini (Luke Fraser). **Credits:** *Producer:* Emiliana De Blasio. *Writer-Director:* Ivan Silvestrini. **Comment:** Do not watch on full screen as just the normal viewing screen is overpowering when it comes to the use of facial close-ups. Just too many are used and, while the idea is good, the presentation is bad.

Episodes: *1.* The Prologue. *2.* The Observer Effect. *3.* Sex Does Not Exist. *4.* Reproduction Is Something Serious. *5.* Electra Complex Party. *6.* To Defend the Weak. *7.* Men Don't Change.

943 Stupid News in Space. youtube.com. 2014.

With December 20, 2012, approaching, the day the Mayan Calendar predicts the world will come to an end at Midnight, Ronald Grump, the billionaire owner of A.I.D.S. Broadcasting offers to fund an experiment that will place a team of reporters in space to cover the end of the world and report the news to the people below. A ship is launched and the space newscast is begun. It is the day of doom but nothing happens and Grump abandons the project but leaves the crew stranded in space. It is 2014 when the series begins and, while NASA is not even bothering to retrieve the space ship, the not-too-bright crew tries to make the best of their situation—by continuing to report the news from space.

Cast: Holly Hill (Sandy), Tone Hoeft (Intern), Arvind Mahendren (British Crew Mate), Sheldon Spanjer (Randy). **Credits:** *Writer-Director:* Holly Hill, Sheldon Spanjer. **Comment:** Why no one cares about the news crew is a mystery and why the crew doesn't seek a way out of their predicament is also a mystery. But they have the news to report and that seems more important. Similar ideas have been done before and for a different take on news casting, *Stupid News* fills the bill.

Episodes: *1.* Prequel: Stuck in Space. *2.* The World Cup. *3.* North Korea. *4.* Misogyny. *5.* Aliens.

944 Submissions Only. submissionsonly.com. 2010–2014.

Penny is optimistic, talented as a singer and dancer and hoping to become a Broadway star. As she experiences the ups and downs of what it takes to make it on Broadway, the program encompasses musical numbers to relate the events that spark her life as she auditions for plays: *Iron Dog, Intersection, Mean Girls, Piñata Party* and *Jeremy's Fort.*

Other Characters: Tim, the head of the casting agency; Steven, Penny's agent; Cameron and Aaron, actors; Gail, Tim's secretary; Linda, the flirtatious stage director; Serena, Aaron's girlfriend; Raina, a Broadway actress and Penny's roommate; Nolan, the eccentric Broadway director; Randall, Tim's reader; and Agnes, an off-the-wall actress who replaces Randall as Tim's reader.

Val is Penny's mother; Don is Val's second husband and Penny's stepfather; Donny is the uptight casting associate; Andy is the music director; Adorable Girl (as she is called) is the actress who appears to know everyone; and Eric is the actor on whom Penny has a crush.

Cast: Kate Wetherhead (Penny Reilly), Colin Hanlon (Tim Trull), Stephen Bienskie (Steven Ferrell), Lindsay Nicole Chambers (Gail Liner), Santino Fontana (Aaron Miller), Max von Essen (Cameron Dante), Anne L. Nathan (Linda Avery), Donna Vivino (Serena Maxwell), Asmeret Ghebremichael (Raina Pearl), Jared Gertner (Randall Moody), Marilyn Sokol (Agnes Vetrulli), Wade McCollum (Nolan Grigsby), Patrick Heusinger (Eric Hennigan), Beth Leavel (Val Reilly), Rick Elice (Don Martin), Andrew Keenan-Bolger (Donny Rich), Annaleigh Ashford (Adorable Girl), Jeffrey Kuhn (Andy Edmond). **Credits:** *Producer:* Joanna Harmon, Jeff Croiter, Michael Croiter, Teon Cromwell, Jen Namoff, Tom Rice, Jack Sharkey, Kevin McCollum. *Writer-Director:* Andrew Keenan-Bolger, Kate Wetherhead. **Comment:** Well acted and produced look at Broadway and the frustrations that go along with producing, auditioning and starring in a play.

Episodes: *1.* Old Lace. *2.* 165 Flies. *3.* Intersections. *4.* You're So Bad. *5.* Mean Like Me. *6.* Somethin' Else. *7.* Harness Malfunction. *8.* Gay Gardens. *9.* 2/3 Memorized. *10.* The Miller-Hennigan Act. *11.* Y'all Were Great. *12.* Woof. *13.* The Growing. *14.* Another Interruption. *15.* Petit Sweet Ending with N. *16.* Having Foresight. *17.* Box of Dirt. *18.* Expectations. *19.* Very Meta. *20.* Dangerous Anesthesia.

945 Suburbs. theshowsuburbs.tumblr.com. 2013.

Graduating from college with an arts degree but with no prospects for a job and no place to live, Scott Holmes decides to "take a few months off" and live the easy life by moving in with his sister Amy, a girl who soon wants Scott out of her pool house when his lack of ambition appears to becoming a permanent thing. Scott's lackadaisical attitude has also turned off his friends (as they have a future) and girls just do not find him a good catch. Like the ABC TV series *Suburgatory*, *Suburbs* is a mockumentary about life in the suburbs as experienced by someone who does not really fit the suburban mold.

Cast: Mike Salisbury (Scott), Julia Jones Laird (Amy), Seon Williams (Natalie), Arielle O'Neill (Sloane), Daniel Hill (Tom), Rehon Mirchandaney (Jenson), Thomas Xavier (Stan), Ellie Bricknell (Anna). Credits: *Producer:* Mike Salisbury, Justin Brewster, Jaryd Dickson. *Writer-Director:* Mike Salisbury. Comment: A talkative program that may bother people annoyed by use of the unsteady (shaky) camera method of filming. The acting is good and the production values acceptable.

Episodes: *1.* Pilot. *2.* Dine and Dash. *3.* Home Camping. *4.* Girls Day In, Boys Day Out. *5.* So Many Planes. *6.* Natalie's Party.

946 Suit Up. webserieschanel.com. 2013.

Glory University may sound like a prestigious college but it is riddled in scandal (especially within the athletic department) and is on the verge of losing a lucrative television contract with CableCorp (also called DirectTV) to cover its football games. Fearing the loss of the contract more than anything else, Jim Dunnigan, a world-famous crisis manager, is hired to "make the scandals go away" and return the university to its former glory. With the football team most involved in nefarious situations (from payoffs to steroids), dysfunctional recruits and questionable school boosters, Jim sets out on a near-impossible task to restore the school's prior pristine image (and save the TV contract).

Cast: Marc Evan Jackson (Jim Dunnigan), Barry Corbin (Dick Devereaux), Kevin McNamara (Luther Montague), Amy K. Harmon (Claire Miller), Petros Papadakis (Himself), Marco St. John (Tom Wilshire), Teri Wyble (Hannah), Christopher Severio (Beer Knight), Vernee Watson-Johnson (Coach Jan Bigsby), Beau Billingslea (Coach Wayne), Eric Nenninger (Roger Steething), Travis Harmon (Sports Announcer), Jonathan Shockley (Sports Announcer), Jesse Moore (Governor Slocum). Credits: *Producer:* Pam Duckworth, Jon Gieselman, Josh Stern. *Director:* Christopher Leone. *Writer:* Dave Canseco, Joseph Dickerson, Ralph Rodney Moon. Comment: With the exception of the NBC TV series *Friday Night Lights* virtually all sports-themed series have been failures (an example being the CBS series *Ball Four*, which ran for only four episodes in 1977). *Suit Up* is a bit different as the concentration is on the behind-the-scenes antics that can eventually close Glory University. The comedy is somewhat subtle and the acting varies from very good to just passable. The program is notable as it incorporates some TV veterans: Barry Corbin, Vernee Watson-Johnson and Beau Billingslea.

Season 1 Episodes *1.* Swine, Sports and Scandal. *2.* Glory Down. *3.* No Money, No QB (Quarterback). *4.* The Pistol Formation. *5.* The Beer Knight Rises. *6.* Cat Venom. *7.* The Investigation. *8.* Death or Glory.

Season 2 Episodes: *1.* One and Done. *2.* Who Is Roger Seething? *3.* Louisiana Vengeance. *4.* 10,000 Wayniacs. *5.* The Last Boy Scout. *6.* The Biggest Losers. *7.* Deep Throat. *8.* Time Bomb.

947 Sunday Dinner. webserieschannel. com. 2012.

Every Sunday evening a family gathers together and attempts to settle down and have a simple meal. Here a mother (called Mum), her older daughter Jen (married to Tom) and younger daughter Kate (married to Mike) are the dysfunctional family and what happens during dinner is the focal point of the program.

Cast: Angel Smith (Jen), Alynn Allman (Kate), Michele Mortensen (Mum), Jay Grove (Mike), Doug James (Tom). Credits: *Producer-Writer-Director:* Doug Blay. Comment: A not-so original idea (even in title) as CBS did the same thing in 1991 with a series called *Sunday Dinner* and NBC, in part with the 1970s series *The Montefuscos*. There are limitations to the concept (just how many ways can a Sunday dinner be profiled) but adding off-the-wall characters helps the web series with a rather loopy mother and her immediate family who can't seem to agree on anything.

Episodes: *1.* Just Dessert. *2.* A Little Chicken.

948 The Super Femmes. youtube.com. 2013.

The City, as it is called, is a sprawling metropolis with not only its decent citizens but an underbelly of criminals seeking to control it. Protecting the City are a group Super Heroines, women possessed of great abilities and who don masks, capes and go-go boots to battle whatever evil appears to keep the City safe. In the presented episodes, the heroines attempt to stop Mad Mort, who has not only threatened to destroy the City, but his principal arch nemesis, Smash Mistress.

Cat Nips, called "The Clawing Conscience of the Streets," is a martial arts master with agility and stealth. Her weapon is The Pussy Whip and she suffers from narcolepsy. Her real name is Fae Kinnit and was raised by her auto mechanic father Ray on the City's Lower East Side. When her father lost his business to the bank, Fae chose to help people facing injustice and donned a costume to fight for them. She soon became known as Cat Nips when she apprehended a sex-slave pusher called Ice Man Cometh. She often works with her roommate and partner, The Incredible Bitch.

Smash Mistress, alias corporate HR director Brandi Mends, is known as "The Patron Saint of Sassiness." She has the ability to create concussion blasts by slapping her hands together and often finds it difficult to maintain a social life with all the crime and corruption that surrounds her. Although she is skilled in acrobatics, she suffers from leg cramps.

The Incredible Bitch, called "The Champion of the Verbal Beat Down," is actually Tara Dickoff, who has the unusual power to bring up the past (when she gets angered her "bitching" reaches its boiling point and she can tap into the past of her opponents and capture them). Her weakness is that she can easily be taken advantage of. Tara is an etiquette teacher and one day, when she put food in the microwave and set the controls on "High Heat," it exploded and doused her in radiation. She didn't die but whenever she becomes angry, her inner emotions are unleashed and she is transformed into a spiteful and aggressive woman.

Iron Melons, "The Twisted Tart of Power Tools," was born Gladys Friday and is the only child of an eccentric inventor. She excelled in Shop class at school and began to adopt the alias of Iron Melons to avenge those who prey on defenseless people. She is a master with power tools and, like her father, a clever inventor (she excels in creating traps to capture villains).

Mad Mort, known as "The Evil Master of Puppets," is a skilled puppeteer and cloning master. He spent most of his childhood playing with chemistry sets and puppets and plotting revenge against the kids who teased him. He is completely unsocial and needs to create puppets and clones for companions. He has also invented the Doll Incubator, which allows him to create clones of the Super Femmes for his own evil purposes.

Galaxy Gal, "The Restless Jewel of the Stars," is actually E. Norma Snockers and has always dreamed of traveling around the world after college. On one such venture in Spain, strange beings appeared to tell her that she has been chosen to join a group of heroes (the Galactic Guardians of the Multi-Verse) that travel across the galaxy to protect the innocent from the evil forces in the cosmos. She has super strength, super breath, the ability to fly and X-Ray vision.

The Hummer, alias Mona Lott, worked with the Peace Corps to fulfill her dream of helping others. One stormy night, while returning to her camp, three men attacked her but she was able to escape by running inside the gates of a power plant. A lightning bolt hit exposed power cables that fell onto Mona. Miraculously, Mona was not killed, but endowed with the power of electricity and the ability to discharge small lightning bolts from her fingertips. She chose to leave the Peace Corps and use her powers for good (she earned her super hero name from the humming noise electricity makes). She is also called "The Vibrating Touch of Truth" (as she needs to rub her legs together to create the electrical discharges).

The Smoking Cape, alias Mike Rotch, is called "The Addictive Stench of Justice." Mike grew up watching news channels on TV and became obsessed with running for any political office he could; he eventually became the City's Mayor. Because he loves to smoke, he confuses evil doers with The Second-Hand Smoke Dart by shooting lit cigarettes at them, causing them to have concerns about their health. He has also been called "The Coughing Cancer of the Criminal Underworld" and "The Smokey Face of Night."

Cast: Vanelle Lyn Leblanc (Cat Nips), Lauryn MacGregor (The Hummer), Roger Paris (The Smoking Cape), Jacqueline Carrion (The Incredible Bitch), Leah Caruana (Smash Mistress), Dionne Johnson (Galaxy Gal), Violet Arcane (Iron Melons), Robert Gordon (Mad Mort), Lee Armstrong (Freckles the Clown), Donald Sill (Dr. Heartless), Tim Bell (Jimmy Oldson), Catherine Trail (The Golden Goddess), Don Folz (Phil McCrevice), Spencer Fox (Chest Hair Charlie), Tanner Lagasca (Pasta Fingers), Tavia Brightwell (Sharon MaBooty), Rebecca Larken (Anita Mann). Credits: Producer: Tina Bell, Dean Garris. Writer-Director: Dean Garris. Comment: Interesting spoof of super heroes with very good acting and decent special effects for a low budget production. The female heroes are quite attractive and with their unusual abilities, make for fascinating watching.

Episodes: 1. Revenge of the Doll Maker. 2. Cat and Mouse. 3. Enter the Bitch. 4. Worker Bee. 5. It Happened on West Street. 6. A Little Help from My Friends. 7. The Deception Racket. 8. The Stench of Truth.

949 Super Knocked-Up. youtube.com. 2012–2014.

Darkstar, the alias of Jessica James is a super villain

that lets nothing stand in her way of achieving her ill-gotten gains. Michael Masters, alias Captain Amazing, is America's number one super hero—and Darkstar's mortal enemy—at least when she is wrecking havoc and he is out to stop her. But Captain Amazing is also a super womanizer and Darkstar is a gorgeous woman. One day the unthinkable happens—a one night-stand results in Jessica becoming pregnant and mortal enemies become a couple to raise a baby (Matthew). Michael has continued his battle against injustice while Jessica has become torn over a decision to become good or remain evil. Becoming parents was not on either one's agenda and, as Michael and Jessica try to figure out a way to remain together for the sake of the baby, episodes follow what happens as each returns to their prior good (and so far) evil lives.

Jessica, age 28, was born in Virtue City. Although she is an independent super villain, she often takes orders from the evil Dr. Destruction. Her powers include strength, martial arts skills and energy blasts (which are discharged from her hands).

Michael is 30 years old and affiliated with the Guardians of Justice (a super hero organization). He was born in Virtue City and encompasses powers that include super strength, invulnerability and the ability to fly.

Dr. Destruction is 50 years of age and affiliated with the Sinister Society. He was born in Westhaven as Nathaniel Cross and is possessed of enhanced senses. He is extremely intelligent, skilled in technology and a master strategist.

Carol Masters, alias "Mom" (Michael's mother) is 50 years of age and was born in Starlight City. She is a doctor and affiliated with the Guardians of Justice. She appears younger than she really is and has the power of healing.

Cheery Villain, alias Katie Campbell, is 20 years old and, despite her cheery attitude, is a member of the Sinister Society. She was born in Logan, Pennsylvania, and considers herself "a sidekick wannabe" and is an expert computer hacker.

Cast: Natalie Bain, Jourdan Gibson (Jessica James/Darkstar), Mark Pezzula (Michael Masters/Captain Amazing), Yvonne Perry (Carol Masters), David Bunce (Dr. Destruction), Daniela Malave (Darcy Danger, the reporter), Catherine Mancuso (Katie Campbell/Cheery Villain). **Credits:** *Writer-Director:* Jeff Burns. *Producer:* Jeff Burns, Jourdan Gibson, Christopher Schiller, Hans Olav Bakken, Mike Feuerstein. **Comment:** Having mortal enemies trying to work together for the greater good (their child) is something that hasn't been done before and it took the Internet to bring it to audiences. The acting is good and production values comparable to a TV sitcom—The action sequences with Jessica doing battle—and holding her baby at the same time—are very well done.

Episodes: *1.* One Night Stand. *2.* Mom. *3.* Sinister Society. *4.* Dr. Destruction. *5.* I'm Taking the

Bedroom. *6.* Welcome to the Family. *7.* Super-Preggers. *8.* Super-Baby. *9.* Super-Family. *10.* Super-Battle.

950 Super Life. rhinocrateproductions. com. 2015.

Mike Mightoffski, a super hero known as Captain Might, suddenly finds himself out of work when he loses his position with the Pegasus Justice Squad, a super hero organization run by Percy Axworthy. It seems while Mike possesses super speed and strength and is good at his job, he does nothing to promote himself and thus people believe he is lame. In addition, his black mask makes him "a walking copyright violation waiting to happen." With no money and no other choice, Mike is forced to move back home with his parents and sister, Lana. Rather than feel sorry for himself, Mike continues his battle against injustice—in the same bumbling manner that got him fired in the first place.

Cast: Michael Wayne Smith (Mike Mightoffski), Kris Moreau (Percy Axworthy/Pegasus), Bailey Luthi (Lana Mightoffski), Michael Jameson (Mike's father), Jenny Gutzebezahl (Mike's mother), Kate Paulsen (Amy Athers), Shlomo Harner (Reptile Bob), Joshua Teale (Killer Cowboy). **Credits:** *Producer:* Christian Hegg. *Director:* Troy Minkowsky. *Writer:* Christian Hegg, Troy Minkowsky. **Comment:** The program has an unusual look and feel to it. It appears that characters are working against green screen technology (although not the best as backgrounds look fake). The acting and overall production, however, is good.

Episodes: Only a 50 second trailer has thus far been produced.

951 Surely Undecided. youtube.com. 2012.

Claire, a very pretty 17-year-old high school girl is enjoying her stay in a park when she is struck by a stray golf ball. A gorgeous young woman approaches Claire to retrieve the ball and instantly becomes attracted to her, believing she is a lesbian ("I'm pretty sure you're gay"). Claire's life seemed to be progressing smoothly until the girl's remark started her thinking about her sexuality. "Am I gay?" To further complicate the situation, her brother, Liem, who had witnessed what happened, tells her that he believes she is gay and sets Claire on a roller coaster of emotions—"do I like men or women?" Stories follow Claire as she seeks the answer to who she is sexually—a situation made more complicated by her parents, who, after learning from Liem what had transpired in the park, are dead set on proving she is not a lesbian.

Cast: Maddison McClellan (Claire), Lindsay Norman (Amber), Brett Hardin (Liem), Rosa Nichols (Mom), Richard Houghton (Dad). **Credits:** *Producer:* Vu Nguyen, L. Courtney Thorpe, Derrick

Granado. *Director:* Vu Nguyen. *Writer:* Vu Nguyen, Richard Houghton. **Comment:** Maddison McClellan is delightful as Claire, so much so that you not only want to see more of her, but what happens to her—is she a lesbian? Is she bisexual? Is she straight? The acting and production values are top rate and, due to the program only just establishing itself, there are no adult situations.

Episodes: *1.* Claire-Fixation. *2.* The Parents. *3.* The Blind Date.

952 Sweethearts of the Galaxy. sweetheartsofthegalaxy.com. 2013.

Trinity Infinity is a gorgeous Galactic Ranger with the Intergalactic Office of the Law. She wears a sexy purple and silver costume and has been battling evil for over 500 years. Trinity, a comic book character, is the idol of Katelyn, a caterer who earns extra money by appearing in costume as Trinity at comic book conventions. Her best friend, co-worker and roommate, Lily, appears as her sidekick Element 47. At one such convention, as Katelyn attempts to perform a stunt, she stumbles, falls and hits her head on the floor. Upon regaining consciousness, Katelyn can only recall the comic book's characters and believes she is Trinity Infinity and Lily is Element 47, together known as "The Sweethearts of the Galaxy." As her alter ego becomes more real to her, Katelyn (as Trinity) begins to wonder why she has lost her powers (like the ability to fly) but realizes that she has a mission: to find the velocity vortex (the plot of a comic book Katelyn had previously read).

Concerned over Katelyn's mental well being, Lily

Sweethearts of the Galaxy. Kit Quinn and Lola Binkerd. Photograph by Michael Premsrirat (© 2012 Michael Premsrirat. Sweethearts of the Galaxy Web series © 2013 Dexter Adriano and Michael Premsrirat).

believes that by indulging Katelyn's fantasy (by devising comic book scenarios for her to solve) it will bring her back to reality when she finds she cannot conquer them (her enemies). The situation becomes complex when Paul, their friend, is seen by Katelyn as Trinity's enemy, Necrocide and Morgan, Paul's ex-girlfriend is seen by Katelyn as Trinity's mortal foe, Wretched, the evil woman who can expose Katelyn as Trinity Infinity and reveal her true identity to the world. The program follows Katelyn as she attempts to deal with Morgan/Wretched and keep her dual identity a secret, but also risking her life when her fantasies become real to her and she sets out to capture actual villains as Trinity Infinity.

Cast: Kit Quinn (Katelyn/Trinity Infinity), Lola Binkerd (Lily/Element 47), Tallest Silver (Silvia/Dark Element 47) Megan Alyse (Morgan/Wretched), David Dickerson (Paul). **Credits:** *Producer-Director:* Dexter Adriano. *Writer:* Michael Premsrirat. **Comment:** Although Katelyn's superhero is only alive in her mind, she believes she can defeat evil and stories are well constructed around that element. Kit Quinn is charming as Katelyn and Trinity and the series is an enjoyable spoof of superheroes.

Episodes: *1.* Wish Granted. *2.* Capturing Necrocide. *3.* Becoming a Super Villain. *4.* Faking Normal. *5.* Stopping Real Crime. *6.* Hanging Out in Bars with Guys. *7.* Behold: The Committee of Evil Doers. *8.* Some Romantic Notion. *9.* Reality Bomb.

953 Swipe to the Right. vimeo.com. 2014.

With inspiration drawn from the real dating app Tinder, the program follows what happens when two people attempt to acquire dates through the system: Brooklyn and Chris, friends who have experienced nothing but failed dates and hope to improve their social life through the app.

Cast: Leigh Anne West (Brooklyn), Christian de Weever (Chris), Kate-Olivia O'Brien (Trisha), Emilly Ben Ami (Doreen/Victoria), Michael Porta (Jeff), Andrew Colford (Doug), Nathan McIntosh (Mark), Tiffany May McRae (Mia). **Credits:** *Producer:* Danny Lugo. *Director:* Raindogg (as credited). *Writer:* Rob Porta. **Comment:** Although no warnings are given, the well acted and produced program does contain adult themes and some vulgar language.

Episodes: *1.* A Tinder Diary. *2.* Coney Island. *3.* The Dinner Party.

954 Take Two. youtube.com. 2014.

Nicole, Erin, Layla and Sarah are

the children of Terri and Dexter Fazon and leading a perfectly normal life until their parents announce they are going to become a foster family and open their doors to children who need a home. With sisters Victoria and Valerie as the first children Terri and Dexter adopt, Nicole, Erin, Layla and Sarah believe it is a bad idea but must somehow welcome two strangers into their home. The program relates what happens as a family of six becomes a family of eight with what was hoped for by the parents not becoming what transpires as their children simply do not get along with Victoria and Valerie.

Cast: Jeff Rose (Dexter Fazon), Stephanie Stevens (Terri Fazon), Amanda Burnette (Erin Fazon), Ashley Burnett (Sarah Fazon), Isabel Sobrepera (Layla Fazon), Kayla Rose (Nicole Fazon) Annelyssa Destin (Victoria Janrey), Samarah Destin (Valerie Janrey), Jacob Zeigler (Cousin David Fazon), Nolan Zeigler (Cousin Corey Fazon). Credits: Producer: Aleshia Cowser, Marques Trusoul, Lana Burnette. Director: Aleshia Cowser. Writer: Shaun Mathis. Comment: A good idea that lacks an easy introduction to figure out who is who. Shades of the NBC TV series *One World* can be seen as it used the same concept (as did a number of other series, the earliest dating back to 1962 with ABC's *Room for One More*). Natural children accepting foster children is a problem in real life and perhaps the depiction of the adopted kids (Victoria and Valerie) as real stuck-up (and annoying) girls was meant to be funny, but does not come across that well (as you can feel for the Fazon kids as they just do not like them). Other than that the actresses portraying the Fazon kids do a fine job and the overall production is well acted and produced.

Episodes: *1.* The Whirlwind. *2.* The BBQ. *3.* The Blow Up. *4.* Nobody's Perfect. *5.* Different. *6.* The Let Down.

955 Tangents and the Times. tangentsandthetimes.com. 2011–2013.

Marissa, an acting school graduate, is currently earning a living as a blogger. She claims she went to acting school to learn how to become a writer but believes Los Angeles is not the right place for her. She feels there are better opportunities in New York and sets her goal to move. But setting one's goal and actually doing it are two different things as Marissa discovers with the program focusing on all that she has going on for her in Los Angeles and what may not be there for her in New York. Alexis is her best friend; Dude Friend (as he is called) is Marissa's boyfriend; Logan is her ex-boyfriend; and Torres is her nemesis.

Cast: Marissa A. Ross (Marissa), Vince Patrick (Logan), Alan Hanson (Dude Friend), Ramsey Krull (Torres), Jackie Michele Johnson (Alexis). Credits: Producer: Timothy Cubbison. Director: Bennett Smith. Writer: Marissa A. Ross, Bennett Smith. Comment: Marissa A. Ross is charming as Marissa and the entire program is well acted and produced (although there are occasional uses of vulgar language).

Episodes: *1.* Marissa Makes a Decision. *2.* Marissa Alienates Herself Per Usual. *3.* Marissa Squanders the Lead. *4.* Marissa Gets Flustered. *5.* Marissa vs. Stoned Marissa. *6.* Marissa Makes a Move. *7.* Marissa Solves Some Problems. *8.* Marissa Makes a Decision: Part Deux.

956 Teachers: A Web Series. teachersweb series.com. 2013.

Franklin Elementary School is a typical small town educational institution with its share of student and faculty problems. Rather than focus on the students and their woes, the program takes a look at the teachers and how they handle their jobs—including the sometimes inappropriate conversations they have with each other during the course of their workday.

Deb Adler, born in Ferndale, Michigan, teaches fourth grade. She feels her school needs "better protection for the bullied" and looks forward to Spring Break as that is the time she enjoys a *Twin Peaks* TV series marathon sitting on her couch with her cats. With Fishnet as her favorite fabric and the Roller Derby as her favorite sport, Deb also lives by her favorite saying, "Life sucks and then you die."

Mary-Louise Bennigan teaches second grade. She was born in Omaha, Nebraska, and to her, getting out of the house is her ideal Spring Break. She claims that the Immaculate Conception (a Catholic holy day) is her favorite holiday and the short-lived ABC TV series *Phenom* (about a girl prodigy tennis player) is her favorite 1990s sitcom. If Mary-Louise could choose between coffee, tea or vodka she would select tea and she has a celebrity crush on Neil Patrick Harris.

Sara Cannon, born in Oak Park, Illinois, teaches fourth grade. She is known for recycling Kleenex tissues and for Spring Break she would like to go to Costa Rica "to help baby turtles find the ocean." "The only recognizable feature of hope is action" are the words she lives by, Bill Clinton is her favorite President and teaching non-western math fascinates her.

Catherine Feldman, a third grade teacher, was born in Aurora, Illinois. She feels the school is too uptight and doesn't believe in a lesson plan ("We're all learning together"). "Columbus Day," she says, is her favorite holiday, "because you forget it exists and then bam, you get a three-day weekend." Her words to live by (updated from a Herbert Hoover speech): "Older men declare war, but it is the youth that must fight and die (so let's party and be real)." Adult Mornings (which combines vodka, coffee and tea) is her favorite drink and if she had a choice between soup and sandwich, she would choose "half of each and dip."

Ginger Ann Snap, born in Wilmette, Illinois, teaches fourth grade. She feels the bathroom lighting at the school needs to be improved. "If you're going to be two-faced, at least make one of them pretty," are the words she lives by (supposedly said by actress Marilyn Monroe) and her favorite "subject" to teach is "Kenny Samuelson. He is the hottest kid in my class. Like seriously."

Caroline Watson, born in Charlottesville, Virginia, teaches second grade. Christmas is her favorite holiday and the one outstanding thing her students know about her is that she is getting over a breakup. She loves the sport of figure skating, "And this, too, shall pass away" are the words she lives by. She believes "Mr. Knightly" is the perfect name for a dog and she is hooked on silk-cashmere blend fabrics.

Cast: Katie Thomas (Deb Adler), Katie O'Brien (Mary-Louise Bennigan), Caitlin Barlow (Sara Cannon), Cate Freedman (Catherine Feldman), Katy Colloton (Ginger Ann Snap), Caroline Watson (Kate Lambert). Credits: Producer: Matt Miller, Caitlin Barlow, Katy Colloton, Cate Freedman, Kate Lambert, Katie O'Brien, Katie Thomas, Matt Abramson, Alex Fendrich, David Brixton. Writer-Director: Matt Miller. Comment: A well acted and produced series with short, straight-to-the-point stories that tackle single subjects that are meant to enlighten a student or a teacher about something.

Episodes: 1. Seal's Face. 2. Hot Dad. 3. Truth or Dare. 4. Fairy Tales. 5. Kim Markley. 6. Statue Game. 7. Speak Up. 8. Baby Fever. 9. Uncle Figure. 10. Truth or Dare, Part 2. 11. Headache. 12. Cliques. 13. Jimmy Hates School. 14. Yogurt. 15. Drug Dealer. 16. Hot Kid. 17. Groupon. 18. The Burtons. 19. Monica B. 20. Ms. Butterfly. 21. Worst Nightmares. 22. Truth Talk. 23. Hot Dog Face. 24. Flesh Colored Crayons. 25. Sizzle Reel. 26. Short Sizzle Reel.

957 Team Allies! webserieschannel.com. 2012.

Reanne, Barry, Alacrity, Ruth and Profit are a close knit group of people that possess extraordinary superpowers. They have banned together and call themselves Team Allies but saving the world from its mortal enemies (like The Chef) is further most on their minds as they feel that friendship and being with their families is more important. But, deep down they each feel they need to do what is right and use their abilities to do what is expected of them. Their rather inane efforts to battle evil are chronicled.

Cast: Marchelle Thurman (Reanne Xenos), Legend Damion Simmons (Barry Sage), Noriko Sato (Ruth), Alice Dranger (Alacrity), Lotus Huynh (The Chef), Nicholas Urda (Narrator), Chad Anthony Miller (Gabe), Peter Coleman (Profit), Toby Levin (Perry Moore), Darlene McCullough (Galatea), Mickey O'Sullivan (Captain Danger), Joe Spade

(Toby), Casey Jones (General Back Story). Credits: Producer: Matthew Sheehan, Alice Dranger. Director: Dante Close, Eli Taylor, Guy Malim, Jim Tripp. Writer: Megan Shimizu. Comment: Don't expect action or fancy costumes. Expect talk and the unsteady (shaky) camera method of filming. The website claims the series was "conceived for comic book readers and geeks in general and as a high physical comedy concept anyone can laugh at and enjoy." As it stands now with only three episodes on line, that action-adventure-comedy aspect is just not present.

Episodes: 1. This Episode Doesn't Have Its Flying License. 2. Law-Abiding, Shmaw-Abiding. 3. Does Having a Sponsor Make Us Sell Outs?

958 Tease. hulu.com. 2009.

Marie is a young woman seeking to write a screenplay about the world of strip clubs. Feeling that she needs to become a part of the scene, she infiltrates a club as a waitress but soon finds herself becoming a performer, dancing on stage for a diverse crowd of men that range from college frat boys to older gentlemen seeking a thrill. Adapting the format of a prime time soap opera, the program charts Marie's not-so typical experiences as she becomes involved in the on-stage and backstage drama that is part of such a profession, especially when she discovers she has more in common with the club girls than she thought. It begins when she befriends Kat, a club dancer seeking a roommate, who teaches her how to work the stage (including pole dancing).

Cast: Lisa Jay (Marie), Samantha Cope (Betty), Cheryl Cosenza (Candy), Devin Kelley (Kat), Johnny Carnevale (Shawn), Crystle Lightning (Tina), Sarah Scherger (Marion), David Dustin Kenyon (Dustin), Mark R. Gerson (Mark), David Marion (Tony), Rene Napoli (Favorite customer), Angelique Giantonio (Sexy waitress). Credits: Producer: William Clevinger, Micah Goldman, Peter Marc Jacobson, Michael Wormser. Director: Peter Marc Jacobson. Writer: William Clevinger, Micah Goldman, Peter Marc Jacobson. Comment: Although only three episodes have appeared, it is a well acted and produced program. It is somewhat reminiscent of the Demi Moore feature film Striptease and, just like the movie, has its sleazy moments. There is no nudity but some scenes are a bit sexually suggestive, making it more adult in nature than a typical comedy.

Episodes: 1. Naked Ambition. 2. Marie's First Time. 3. Tease 'em Honey.

959 Ted & Gracie. webserieschannel.com. 2011.

Gracie and Ted appear to be an ordinary couple that are about to be married. That is they appear to be. Unknown to Gracie, Ted, an out-of-work independent masseuse, is secretly a serial killer. To bide his time between looking for work and killing, Ted creates rather strange works of art that puzzle Gracie, but do not make her aware that he is hiding something from her. The program is a look into their private lives with the events that lead up to their wedding and Gracie learning the hideous secret Ted hides. **Cast:** Jena Friedman (Gracie), Ben Kronberg (Ted). **Credits:** *Producer-Writer-Director:* Jena Friedman. **Comment:** Well done twist on a normal couple preparing for their wedding with good acting and a well plotted story line (although just by Ted's appearance you feel something is just not right with him). **Episodes:** *1.* Save the Date. *2.* The Wedding Planner. *3.* The Parents. *4.* The Fight. *5.* The Surprise. *6.* The Haircut.

960 Teddy Bear English. youtube.com. 2013.

The Teddy Bear English Language Academy in Osaka, Japan, is an educational institution named as such by its founder who believes that children can learn English from teddy bears "because everybody loves teddy bears." Don, Tim and Alice are Americans who acquire jobs at the school but must teach English to Japanese children alongside a life-size teddy bear (man in a costume). With another American, Steve, as the school manager (sort of like a principal) the program follows Don, Tim and Alice—and the teddy bear—as they attempt to perform their duties as English teachers in a foreign land. **Cast:** Edward Fricker (Don), Dan Luffey (Tim), Amanda Rollins (Alice), Trevor Ruder (Steve), Ellie Matsui (Yuki), Yuko Horsuchi (Kumiko). **Credits:** *Producer:* Dan Luffey. **Comment:** The CBS TV series *To Rome with Love* may come to mind as it also dealt with American teachers in a foreign land (Italy here). The idea is made fresher here and it is accompanied by good acting and production values. **Episodes:** *1.* Teddy Bear Uber Alles. *2.* Sex, Lies and Closets. *3.* How Could You? *4.* Fool Proof. *5.* Umbrag. *6.* It Doesn't End Well.

961 The Teddy Post. theteddypost.com. 2013.

Theodora Bayer is a talking teddy bear and the host of a television-like news program called *The Teddy Post*. Each episode is a look at a topic covered by Theodora with comical skits portraying the expose she is conducting (like the unfair treatment of Scarecrows or the secret behind robots). **Cast:** Reebie Sullivan (Voice of Theodora). **Credits:** *Producer-Writer-Director:* Reebie Sullivan, Scott Crawford. **Comment:** Theodora is always stationary and positioned on the left side of the screen. Her movement consists of her mouth and eyes and inserts on the right side of the screen are often used for the stories behind the story. The material is geared toward adults and the program itself is well

produced and a clever way of presenting comedy skits. **Episodes:** *1.* Scarecrow Hunting. *2.* When Bunnies Attack. *3.* It's Hard Out There for a Samurai. *4.* Phobias. *5.* Spy School. *6.* Hurling. *7.* Ostrich Egg. *8.* Robots. *9.* Dogs vs. Cats. Welcome to the Catsino. *10.* Alternative Careers. *11.* Man Eating Plants. *12.* Flying Pan Fandango. *13.* Sharks vs. Humans. *14.* How to Get Rid of Monsters. *15.* The Security Blanket. *16.* The Big Bad Wolf. *17.* Gnomes.

962 Telly Tips. webserieschannel.com. 2011.

On television in the 1970s Telly Savalas starred as Theo Kojak, a tough, no-nonsense N.Y.P.D. police detective on the CBS TV series *Kojak*. Kojak was a man who was set in his ways and had an opinion about people and the various situations he was forced to deal with due to the nature of his profession. He would not allow women to become a part of his team as he felt the cases were too gruesome for them to handle. While he tried to overlook what he encountered during his investigations, he could never fully dismiss the disgust he felt. As time past and if a modern-day version of *Kojak* were produced, would Lt. Theo Kojak be the same person, chatting his "Who Loves Ya Baby" catch phrase and enjoying a lollipop (his trademark) during cases? Incorporating an actor who somewhat resembles Telly Savalas as a 21st century Kojak, the program explores what such a moral person would do in a world that was a far cry from the one in which he actually lived. He is now a fish out of water and has a self-proclaimed mission: clean up a new generation of filth that is polluting his beloved city. **Cast:** Tom Dimenna (Telly Savalas), Bob Turton (Eddie Barris), Jake DeGrazia (Hipster 1), George Triester (Hipster 2). **Credits:** *Producer:* Tom DiMenna. *Director:* David C. Herman. *Writer:* Tom DiMenna, David C. Herman. **Comment:** It appears that only a pilot episode has been produced. While the idea sounds good it is unfortunate that all video information has been taken off line (no reason given; possibly due to copyright infringement using the Kojak character). **Episodes:** *1.* Pilot.

963 The Temp Life. blip.tv. 2009–2012.

Nick Cheapetta, nicknamed "Trouble," was once employed as the head of a temporary employment agency. But that was then. He has been let go, lost everything and is now back to where he started—at the bottom. Nick's lack of progress as he takes on various temp jobs with the hope of working his way back up the corporate ladder are charted. **Cast:** Wilson Cleveland (Nick Cheapetta), Mark Jude (Mark Sebastian), Rachel Risen (Aline Delores), Thom Woodley (Stormy Simonsen), Sandeep Parikh (Samel Patel), Laura Kowaloyle (Laura

Reynolds), Taryn Southern (Nancy Rodel). **Credits:** *Director:* Andrew Y. Park, Jato C. Smith, Yuri Baranovsky. *Writer:* Wilson Cleveland, Yuri Baranovsky, Tony Janning, Gabe Uhr. **Comment:** The program presents Nick with a variety of jobs to tackle and, while some are better than others, the acting and production values are good throughout all five seasons.

Season 1 Episodes: *1.* Pilot. *2.* What's in a Name? *3.* Let Them Eat Cake. *4.* Make Your Own Fun. *5.* Big Break.

Season 2 Episodes: *1.* Mergers and Acquisitions. *2.* Help Needed. *3.* DIS-orientation. *4.* Actor on Broadway. *5.* Mykrosahft. *6.* Pay It Backwards. *7.* Where in the World?

Season 3 Episodes: *1.* Dream Big. *2.* Being Glib. *3.* Nothing Personal. *4.* The Socialist. *5.* City Girls.

Season 4 Episodes: *1.* Closet Case. *2.* Office Bromance. *3.* The Interview. *4.* Donald's Mission. *5.* Touchdown. *6.* No Class Action. *7.* Going Down. *8.* The Boss. *9.* Coming Together. *10.* The Hopeful. *11.* Back in Business.

Season 5 Episodes: *1.* We're Number Two! *2.* The Sum of All Phones. *3.* The Other Roeder. *4.* Sensitivity Training. *5.* The Hungover. *6.* Law and Lunch Order. *7.* Nick's Last Stand. *8.* Return of the Eddie.

964 *Temporary Setbacks.* youtube.com. 2012.

Andre is thirty-two years of age, without a job and without a girlfriend (both of which he has just lost). Feeling he needs to get his life back on track he returns to his hometown in Tucson, Arizona, and moves in with his divorced mother (June) and her new boyfriend (Don). As Andre reconnects with his former friends he believes his life is changing for the better when his friend Bellyflap hooks him up with a job with the U.S. Census. The job is anything but pleasing to Andre and the program charts his adventures—from his return home to his job training to his first efforts as a census taker (with the worst people in the worst locations). **Cast:** Terry Clements II (Andre), Barbara MacBride (June), Steve Marmon (Don), Shawn Robinson (Bellyflap Bruce), Tenley Dene (Stacey). **Credits:** *Writer-Director:* Rock Schroeter. **Comment:** Nothing out of the ordinary until Andre acquires a job with the census bureau. The acting along with the production is good.

Episodes: *1.* Me or the Guitar. *2.* Home Too Early. *3.* By the Time I Get to Phoenix. *4.* Raised in Arizona. *5.* BellyFlop. *6.* J-O-B-L-E-S-S. *7.* Working for the Don. *8.* Mad Man. *9.* Apache Junction.

965 *Tenants.* vimeo.com. 2010.

Chris is an intellectual young man who cherishes his privacy. He lives alone and basks in the world he has created for himself. His serenity is soon challenged when Riley, an obnoxious young man shows up and claims that he has also rented the apartment. Because all video information has been taken off line and web site information is not clear, it appears that, even though Chris has a lease, it somehow allows Riley to co-inhabit the apartment. If that were not bad enough, Perry, Riley's just as obnoxious brother, also appears to becoming a part of Chris's life when he shows up for a visit and has no immediate intentions of leaving. The program presents an "Odd Couple"-like situation with the neat and perfect Chris struggling to share his apartment with people who are well beneath his social and mental status. **Cast:** Chris Reimer (Chris), James Riley (Riley), Perry Pizzolo (Perry). **Credits:** *Producer:* Chris Reimer, James Riley, Nick Denitto, Adam Tilzer. **Comment:** With episodes removed from the Internet an evaluation is not possible.

Episodes: *1.* The Uninvited Guest. *2.* The Lease. *3.* The Brother. *4.* The Blind Date. *5.* The Argument.

966 *Terjatuh in Love.* webserieschannel.com. 2014.

The Mines is a large shopping center where two people, Jay and Sofi work but have not met each other. One day while walking past a fashion shop, Jay encounters Sofi, who is admiring the dress on a mannequin. It is virtually a love at first sight and Jay and Sofi begin dating. Several months later, on the exact spot where they met, they have a falling out (Sofi believes Jay is seeing another girl) and split up. Unknown to both of them there is a witness to what just happened—the mannequin that wore the dress Sofi admired. The mannequin, named Lisa, is heartbroken over what happened and magically comes to life with a mission: reunite the lovebirds. Lisa realizes that, despite their breakup, Jay and Sofi still love each other and the program follows what happens as Lisa tries to play matchmaker but finds herself becoming the one with whom Jay falls in love. **Cast:** Syazuwan Hassan (Jay), Tash Shazleya (Sofi), Kim Low (Lisa), Afi Yamin (Maliq). **Credits:** *Producer:* Syahrul Imran. *Director:* Raymond Sekhon. **Comment:** While similar ideas can be traced back to the 1940s feature film *One Touch of Venus*, "The After Hours" episode of *The Twilight Zone* and the recent *Mannequin* movies, there is just something charming about *Terjatuh in Love.* It is produced in Korea and features a stunning actress in the role of Lisa. The acting and production is very good but there is no real explanation given as to how Lisa comes to life or why she has magical powers.

Episodes: *1.* Cupid's Touch. *2.* A Spark of Life. *3.* Love Hurts. *4.* Match Making Mission. *5.* Episode 5. *6.* The Quest Goes On. *7.* There Is Hope. *8.* Love Is So Magical.

967 *Texting with Gosling.* textingwithgosling.com. 2014.

Felix, a 27-year-old woman who earns a living as a dog walker, shares an apartment with three friends, Dana, Eden and "The Other Roommate" (as she is called). One day, while doing her job, a dog breaks lose from Felix's grip and runs into the street. Felix is able to save the dog but is hit by a car during the rescue mission. Felix appears to be okay (suffering a slight bruise) but is astounded to learn that the car's driver is Ryan Gosling, an actor she truly admires. At home, as Felix relates the story of what has just happened, she receives a text from Ryan and her life is suddenly changed as she feels she has made a connection with the actor. It is the summer of 2013 and what happens to Felix as she fantasizes about her life with Ryan Gosling is chronicled.

Cast: Claire Grasso (Felix), Hailley Lauren (Daisy), Holly Barnett (Ina), Stacey Glazer (The Other Roommate). **Credits:** *Director:* Sarah Hennigan. **Comment:** Very enjoyable saga of one girl's dream becoming a reality and how she must learn to let go of a fantasy and return to the real world.

Episodes: *1.* Pilot. *2.* Winky Face. *3.* Auto Correct. *4.* Send a Pic. *5.* Dick Pic. *6.* Blank Text. *7.* Ambiguous Text. *8.* Drunk Text. *9.* Delete It. *10.* Finale.

968 *That Guy (2012).* facebook.com. 2012–2014.

Judah, a burly heavily bearded man, Mike, his short-tempered roommate and Dionne, their "home girl" are friends in the strictest sense (no sleeping with each other). While Judah and Mike have their own share of problems, from dealing with girls to just navigating everyday life, Dionne also has problems and always stops by to sort things out, but at the most inopportune times, further adding complications to Judah and Mike's chaotic life. While incorporating filming as seen through a camcorder, the program chronicles the incidents that not only complicate their individual lives, but those problems that are also shared as a group.

Cast: Jeremy Solomon McBryde (Judah), William Catlett (Mike), Jeanine Daniels (Dionne), Lorren Cotton (Stacy), Helen Banks (Denise), Stacy Lafay (Renee), Harold Warren, Jr. (Harold), Dasha Chadwick (Keena). **Credits:** *Producer:* Brian Ali Harding, Janie Chavers, Dennis Dortch, Numa Perrier, Tina Cerin, Desmond Faison. *Director:* Jeanine Daniels, Tina Cerin. *Writer:* Jeanine Daniels, Numa Perrier. **Comment:** The filming is quite unsteady (shaky) and the dialogue appears ad-libbed at times. While it does look like a disjointed production, it somehow all comes together after watching the first and second episodes.

Season 1 Episodes: *1.* The Perfect Girl. *2.* Chill Arrest. *3.* Love & Basketball. *4.* When in Rome. *5.* Walk of Shame. *6.* That First Time. *7.* That Coldest BBQ. *8.* Jealous Bitches. *9.* The Real Hoes & Housewives.

Season 2 Episodes: *1.* Smash O'clock. *2.* Top Tier

Father. *3.* Thirsty Smurf. *4.* Dance with the Devil. *5.* The Pop Up. *6.* Catching Feelings? *7.* Clash of the Vaginas. *8.* The Ruiner. *9.* Kids R Us. *10.* That Guy. *11.* Home Wreckers of America. *12.* The Walk Through/Roll Up/Pop Up. *13.* Love and War. *14.* Episode #2.14.

969 *That Guy (2014).* youtube.com. 2014.

Time has passed much too swiftly for Daniel, as he has just hit middle age. But for Daniel, who is also gay, middle age is a crisis: he has not accomplished what he planned and now wonders if he made the right choice sexually? Adding to his frustration is his boyfriend and roommate, an unemployed, drug-addicted video game playing addict. The program depicts the chaos that ensues as Daniel tries to find meaning and balance in his life while not only dealing with his boyfriend, but the pressures of his job (working for a corporation that builds deadly weapons for the military and thrives on wars).

Cast: David Nance (Daniel), James Kazan (Boyfriend), Scott Swan (Slutty Friend), Truong Swan (Asian Friend), Rob Hamm (Shawn), Twany Arnold (Peepers), Scott O'Neill (Mr. Blakely). **Comment:** Short, right-to-the point episodes that tackle the subject facing Daniel in a well thought-out manner. The acting and production values are good and, for some unknown reason, some characters are not given an actual name.

Episodes: 4 untitled episodes, labeled "Episode 1" through "Episode 4."

970 *That's So Awesome.* youtube.com. 2011.

The Fair House Bank of Los Angeles is a financial institution managed by Chrissy. Sue, Mark and one man in particular, Asim, are her tellers. Sue is never on time (shows up for work when she pleases), Mark fears if he does something wrong he will lose his job and Asim is believed to be named "Awesome" and a Mexican with an Indian accent by Chrissy. Asim, pronounced "Ah-Sim" is also called "Aseem" and is of Pakistan descent. He recently relocated to California and has settled into a life where he longs for a girlfriend and enjoys watching romantic Bollywood films. As Asim continues to adjust to his new homeland, the program follows his efforts to navigate his work world and find happiness with that elusive girl of his dreams.

Cast: Asim Kaleem (Asim), Diego James (Mark), Kathleen Chen (Sue), Lara Ingraham (Chrissy), Chop Wigley (John), Cat Lee McGowan (Phat Ho), Chris Hampton (Creepy Customer 1), Norman DeBuck (Creepy Customer 2), Bo Youngblood (Destiny), Sarmarie Klein (Erica). **Credits:** *Director:* Asim Kaleem. *Writer:* Asim Kaleem, Erica Maeyama, Elizabeth Simonian. **Comment:** So-so program that is set in the bank and just focuses on the staff and their customers.

Episodes: *1.* Holy Cow. *2.* Getting Sued. *3.* Cook and Cleen. *4.* The Cheery Duo. *5.* Dat Knot My Naame. *6.* Sneakers. *7.* Mommy Samosa. *8.* Return of the Creepy Duo. *9.* Umrican Blue. *10.* Our Numbers Are Down. *11.* Conversations with the Creepy Duo. *12.* Party Sex. *13.* I–Fukar-Butt. *14.* Beginnings End.

971 *That's What She Said.* twssonline. com. 2010.

Five close friends (Nicole, Rae-Anne, Babette, Leslie and Shin) and their efforts to navigate life in Los Angeles.

Nicole, nicknamed "Nic," is a slightly awkward young woman, born in Ohio and making the transition to life in California after a broken romance (with another woman).

Rae-Anne, called "Rae," is Nicole's roommate, a caring girl and the glue that holds the friends together. She (and Leslie) work at a West Hollywood flower shop that is owned by Rae's family. Although she is attracted to other women, Rae prefers to be called "SGS" (Straight Girl Syndrome), as it depicts her problem of falling for women who are straight as opposed to being gay.

Babette, called "Baby," is the flirtatious, fun-loving girl who becomes overly involved in romantic situations that require the help of her friends to overcome.

Leslie, an activist who will involve herself in any cause that she feels is worthy, is an advocate for equal rights and what she calls "queer rights." Though as forceful and outspoken as she is, Leslie has a tendency to fall for gay men.

Shin is a woman whose past is unknown and who prefers to keep it that way. She is mysterious, passionate about photography and has a difficult time expressing her emotions and tends to suppress them.

Cast: Vicky Luu (Nicole Tran), Allison Santos (Rae-Anne Constantino), Claire Kim (Leslie Park), Narinda Heng (Shin Tanaka), Annigee (Babette Liu), Antoinette Reyes (Chloe), Aspen Clark (Cecilia). **Credits:** *Producer:* Pearl Girl Productions. *Director:* Vicky Luu. **Comment:** Although billed as "Queer Asian American Web Series," it is about lesbians and is better than its billing leads one to believe with good acting and production values.

Season 1 Episodes: *1.* Just Friends. *2.* Body Language. *3.* On-Line Dating. *4.* The Valentine's Day Edition. *5.* Post Holiday Stress Disorder. *6.* Self Love. *7.* How to Break Up. *8.* Losing the Relationship Weight. *9.* Episode #1.9. *10.* The Makeover Show. *11.* Five Dollar Dates. *12.* Pheromones and Attraction. *13.* Celebrity Mail. *14.* The Five Senses. *15.* Dopa-mine and Pair Bonding. *16.* Long Distance Relationships. *17.* Episode #1.17. *18.* Good Conversation. *19.* How Not to Break Up. *20.* Answering Fan Mail.

Season 2 Episodes: Only four untitled episodes (2–5), labeled "Season 2, Episode 2" through "Season 2, Episode 5" remain on line.

972 *Then We Got Help!* thenwegothelp. com. 2010.

Emily is an under-employed shoe model who has problems but believes that "You don't have to have money to get help." To prove her theory she assembles a group of cash-strapped friends in need of counseling without a therapist to solve problems by letting each give advice to the other. Feeling that she has hit on something big, she decides to video tape it and create a documentary film to show that "you don't need money to get help." The couples are Anna and Thom; Dan and Eric; Gerry and Terry; and Jenny and Kenny and the program charts what happens at the weekly therapy meetings she calls "Group Therapy Without the Therapist."

Cast: Julie Ann Emery (Emily), Kristen Shaw (Anna), Alan Campbell (Thom), Nicholas Rodriquez (Dan), Blake Hammond (Eric), Sean Mahon (Jerry), Susan Ferrara (Gerry), Kevin Earley (Kenny), Jessica Rush (Jenny). **Credits:** *Producer:* Julie Ann Emery, Kevin Earley, Janice Fields. *Writer-Director:* Julie Ann Emery. **Comment:** Take the group therapy sessions from the 1970s TV series *The Bob Newhart Show* and eliminate the psychologist (Bob) and you have an idea of what the show is like—patients helping each other. The idea is good and well presented with good acting and production skills to back it up.

Episodes: *1.* First Impressions. *2.* Like a Rabbit Out of a Hat. *3.* 8 Track Soundtrack. *4.* Truth or Dare. *5.* Cause Reading Is Fun! *6.* Someone Else's Shoes. *7.* You Are What You Eat. *8.* Your Cheatin' Heart.

973 *These 3 Girls.* youtube.com. 2013.

Three girls (Crystal, Ginger and Carla) living in New York City and how they attempt to make ends meet.

Cast: Massiel Hernandez (Crystal Martinez), Teresa Hui (Ginger Rosenberg), Joyce Laoagan (Carla Margarita), Erica DeJulio (Alexis Archer). **Credits:** *Producer:* Teresa Hui, Joyce Laoagan, Massiel Hernandez. *Director:* Jerry Skids. *Writer:* Teresa Hui, Massiel Hernandez, Joyce Laoagan, Jerry Skids. **Comment:** The program is well acted but it is not in the proper aspect ratio (as all images do not appear normal). Here the images are stretched to fill the screen, giving everything a fat look and may be a deterrent to people turned off by such images.

Episodes: *1.* Ring Check. *2.* Ninja Please. *3.* Stupid Boy. *4.* Urban Exploring. *5.* On-Line Mating. *6.* Party at Sylvia's. *7.* The Puppeteer.

974 *Thesps: The Sitcom.* vimeo.com. 2013.

The title means "Thespians," is set in London,

England, and chronicles the often difficult (and at times embarrassing) decisions a group of flat mates, all hoping to break into show business, make as they seek stardom in the competitive theater and film industry: Imogen, a recent drama school graduate who has illusions that the world is at her feet; Anna, the eldest member of the group, has become disillusioned with the profession after having suffered numerous rejections; Gareth, a method actor whose dedication makes him attempt characterizations that are near impossible to achieve; Lily, dedicated but frustrated by rejection, believes there is a role out there that will make her career (she just needs to find it); and Debbie, employed as a personal assistant to a famous actress, feels that her big break is just around the corner.

Cast: Emma Naef (Imogen), Stacey Ackers (Anna), Ellie Mayes (Lily), Kitty Withington (Debbie), Michael Dennehy (Gareth). **Credits:** *Producer-Director:* Victoria Eyton, Tiarnan O'Sullivan. **Comment:** Rather talkative program with acceptable acting and production values (although the constant use of the unsteady [shaky] camera is not needed as nothing sensational happens that needs to be expressed through that filming method).

Episodes: *1.* Moving In. *2.* The Coma. *3,4.* The Audition.

975 *The 3rd Floor.* webserieschannel.com. 2010.

Erin and Kelly, employees of the Dunder-Mifflin Paper Company (from the NBC series *The Office*) are eager to expand their horizons by breaking into show business. Their dreams become a reality when they write a horror story and convince their friend Ryan to produce it. The story, titled "The 3rd Floor," begins when a woman approaches Erin and asks to buy some paper. When Erin finds the woman cannot pay for it, she refuses to give it to her. Angered, the woman (dressed like a Gypsy) places a curse on her—to become all the serial killers who ever existed. Erin shrugs it off, but slowly she begins to change. She develops the right arm of Lizzie Borden, the left arm of Jeffrey Donner, the heart of Jack the Ripper and the legs of all the serial killers who escaped the law. Now, wielding an axe, Erin begins her rampage, killing all the third floor employees—or at least attempting to do so. Also known as *The Office: The 3rd Floor.*

Cast: Ellie Kemper (Erin Hannon), Mindy Kaling (Kelly Kapoor), B.J. Novak (Ryan Howard), Kate Flannery (Meredith Palmer), Brian Baumgartner (Kevin Malone). **Credits:** *Producer-Director:* Mindy Kahling. Writer: Kelly Hannon. **Comment:** Ellie Kemper (Erin) is a standout and just her performance as the crazed serial killer is worth the price of admission

Episodes: *1.* Moving On. *2.* Lights, Camera, Action! *3.* The Final Product.

976 *Thirty Below.* youtube.com. 2012.

Toni and Montana are friends who are approaching the age of 30 but have not yet achieved what they hoped for (like an $80,000 a year job, a marriage and two kids). Toni and Montana are made to represent many under thirty people who are in the same situation—plans made years earlier that have not yet come into fruition. As Toni and Montana try to accept what they have the program chronicles their experiences as they seek that elusive dream and what they should have had by this time.

Cast: Ajai Simone (Toni), Robert Williams (Montana). **Credits:** *Producer:* Ericka McCracken, Rahsaan Jones, Anita Jones. *Director:* Ericka McCracken. **Comment:** While the acting and characters are good you really have to be in the mood to watch such a series or else you will not go beyond the first few minutes. Nothing stands out and nothing really grabs you. It's one of those programs that tries to be high brow when Internet users are simply looking for fast-moving, short programs that require no thinking to enjoy. There is an audience for these types of shows, but they most often play on broadcast or cable television.

Episodes: *1.* Pilot: Buy You a Drank. *2.* I Thought You Knew. *3.* Thought You Were My Hommie. *4.* You Promise What? *5.* I Can Handle It.

977 *This Day Sucks.* vimeo.com. 2010.

Rudy and Rayzor are twenty-something friends sharing an apartment in New York City. Rudy appears to be cursed with bad luck while Rayzor believes he is a wild and crazy party guy. While their personalities may be as different as night and day, they do share one thing in common: seeking girls and fun. What they seek rarely happens and the program follows the friends as they deal with boring jobs, gorgeous girls they cannot have and all the miserable situations they create for themselves simply because they have no focus and believe things will never change.

Cast: Pat Bither (Rudy), Tom Schiller (Rayzor), Russell Senk (Russ Beef), James Murphy (Nigel). **Credits:** *Producer-Writer:* Pat Bither, Tom Schiller. **Comment:** The program can also be seen as another variation of "The Odd Couple" with Rayzor the slob and Rudy the neat one. Rayzor can be an annoying character (meant to be? Or he just comes off that way?) and he does take getting use to as he helps Rudy overcome the obstacles he often causes for him. The overall production is good with the acting varying from bad to good depending on how you view the characters.

Episodes: *1.* The Date. *2.* The Hot Intern. *3.* The Double Date. *4.* The Empty Apartment. *5.* The Party Pooper.

978 *This Is Mark Twain @aol.com.* you tube.com. 2013.

Novelist Samuel Clemens (better known as Mark Twain) is transported from the 19th century to the present and placed with a job in a social media company. Mark must keep his tweets to 140 characters, learn how to use items like a copying machine and keep his wits about him. While it is not explained how Mark Twain came to be in the 21st century, he does dress like he did from the past (although nobody seems to recognize him for who he is) and the program simply relates how Mark relates to and attempts to solve modern-day problems.

Cast: Bryce Wissel (Mark Twain), Levin O'Connor (Doug), Patric McIntyre (Jeff), Tracy Meyer (Denise), Marshall Givens (Jim), Lloyd Ahlquist (Himself). **Credits:** *Producer:* Ethan Cushing, Cory Jones. *Director:* Ethan Cushing. *Writer:* Mike Betette, Bryce Wissel. **Comment:** Clever idea that is somewhat convincing in the characterization of Mark Twain who is portrayed as a man younger rather than the way most people imagine him (an older gentleman). Mark is also portrayed as very helpless and how he found his way into a social media company is also not explained.

Episodes: *1.* Mark Twain Tries to Tweet. *2.* Mark Twain and the Photocopier. *3.* Mark Twain Is Racist. *4.* Mark Twain, Love Machine. *5.* Mark Twain Fights a Phone. *6.* Mark Twain Meets Epic Lloyd. *7.* Mark Twain Gives Us Perspective. *8.* Mark Twain Ruins a Birthday Party. *9.* Mark Twain Takes on Blind Dating. *10.* Mark Twain Learns the Price of Fame.

979 *Those Guys!* funnyordie.com. 2012.

The old saying "in the wrong place at the wrong time" is capitalized upon as six friends (Allen, Drew, Jake, Lou, Thomas and Tucker) are presented with a situation and simply go about trying to solve it.

Cast: Ken Napzok (Tucker), Lou Santini (Lou), Allen Rueckert (Allen), Thomas Bell (Thomas "T-Bell"), Andie Ximenes (Drew), Jake Suffian (Jake), Marilyn Valderrama (Catt), Nina Kate (Carla), Caitlin Rose Williams (Courtney). **Credits:** *Producer:* Sema Batuk, Scott R. Tomasso, Samuel Libraty, Chad Tomasso. **Comment:** Simple premise with generally good acting and production values.

Season 1 Episodes: *1–3.* Epic Battle: Tucker vs. Pizza Guy. *4,5.* The Date. *6,7.* Prius Whipped. *8,9.* The S***. *10–12.* Pretty in Pink. *13,14.* The Bitch.

Season 2 Episodes: *1.* The Girls Next Door. *2.* Abnormal Paranormal. *3.* Interview Fail. *4.* That Should Be Me. *5.* I Can't Quit You. *6.* High Noon at Pizza Creek. *7.* Chopped. *8.* Call of Duty.

980 *Three: A Web Series.* 3webseries.com. 2014.

Jason is a bisexual man who has been secretly dating his two best friends: Layla, who is straight, and Tanner, who is gay. Layla and Tanner are unaware that they are both dating the same Jason until Jason's double life is uncovered and Layla and Tanner are faced with a problem: who should give up Jason? To resolve the issue, they agree on a competition (the one who is most seductive) with the winner being chosen by Jason (the one he would rather date).

Cast: Lucas Omar (Tanner), Amber Sym (Layla), Andrew Sturby (Jason). **Credits:** *Producer:* Joshua Moody, Todd Yonteck, George Petrick, Lucas Omar. *Writer-Director:* Lucas Omar. **Comment:** The premise is good and the characters well thought out and presented. There are sexual situations but nothing that is overly offensive.

Episodes: *1.* The Proposal. *2.* Jason #1 and #2. *3.* Bloody Tampons. *4.* Avocados. *5.* I Wanna Mate. *6.* Clitoris Trophy. *7.* Spank You. *8.* Disney Jail. *9.* Creme Brulee.

981 *Three Guys and a Witch.* vimeo.com. 2013.

Val is a beautiful but evil witch who is seeking a male virgin to assist in the resurrection of a demon. Peter is that man, but he is friends with Baz and Derek, two girl-crazy morons that Val must somehow dispose of to achieve her goal. When she learns that the three friends are looking for a place to live, she makes it known that she has rooms to rent in her home. Like a magnet, the friends are drawn to Val's home and, as they settle in, only Peter seems to fear that something is not right with Val. The program focuses on those fears as Val sets out on path that could mean great destruction to the human population if she succeeds (why she needs to eliminate Baz and Derek).

Cast: Monica Nowak (Val), Edan Lacey (Baz), Oliver Ward (Peter), Clem McIntosh (Derek), Monica Nowak (Val), Alexis Maitland (Danni), Bear Schaal (Greggy), Michael Lamport (Vladik), Melody Schaal (Sophia), Lexie Galante (Michelle), Stephan Goldbach (Wolfgang). **Credits:** *Producer:* Michael Lamport. *Director:* Oliver Irving. *Writer:* Oliver Ward, Clem McIntosh, Edan Lacey. **Comment:** A bit spooky at times with good acting and production values. The program contains adult themes, foul language and a good take on witch tales making Val not only beautiful but deadly as well.

Episodes: *1.* The Hunt. *2.* The Witch. *3.* The Neighbor. *4.* The Rivalry. *5.* The Last Supper. *6.* The Great Depression. *7.* The Date. *8.* The Seduction. *9.* The Departure. *10.* The New Beginning, *11.* The Milking. *12.* The End?

982 *Three Way.* onemorelesbian.com. 2008.

Siobhan, an actress married to Dirk (an aging motion picture action idol) is the star of the TV soap opera *Young Doctors Who Cry*. Siobhan is enjoying a life of luxury until her marriage collapses and she finds herself nearly broke and retaining only her beloved dog Mojo in the divorce settlement. Although Siobhan is straight there are hints she may be bisexual as she is overly attracted to her best friend since childhood, Roxanne, whom she calls Roxie ("because she's my rock"). The divorce has left Siobhan financially strapped and emotionally scarred and Roxie becomes Siobhan's lifeline when the two move in together. Siobhan appears to be recovering emotionally until her world is again shattered when Andrea, Roxie's girlfriend (and lover) also moves in with them. Further complicating Siobhan's life is Geri, Roxie's ex-girlfriend who again wants to become a part of Roxie's life. The events that spark the lives of all four women, especially Siobhan as she seeks serenity, happiness and maybe sexual experimentation are showcased.

Cast: Maeve Quinlan (Siobhan McGarry), Jill Bennett (Andrea Bailey), Cathy Shim (Roxie Lautzenheiser), Maile Flanagan (Geri O'Flanagan), Donna W. Scott (Winter Kote), Elizabeth Keener (Celia Sanderson), Liz Vassey (Mikki Majors), Christina Cox (Lara Lancaster), Kristy Swanson (Leslie Lapdalulu), Bridget McManus (Rhonda Rapid Delivery), Gabrielle Christian (Cindy Shimms), Linda Miller (Frankie), Elisa Dyann (Jamie). **Credits:** *Producer:* Paige Bernhardt, Nancylee Myatt, Maeve Quinlan, Joey Scott. *Director:* Mary Lou Belli, Courtney Rowe, Nancylee Myatt, Robert Ben Garant. *Writer:* Paige Bernhardt, Maile Flanagan, Nancylee Myatt, Maeve Quinlan, Georgia Ragsdale. **Comment:** Maeve Quinlan is delightful as Siobhan as she tries to make sense of everything that happens around her. The production values are TV quality; there are kissing scenes and a bit of profanity but overall a charming, non-offensive program to watch.

Episodes: *1–3.* Let the Gaymes Begin. *4.* Fatal Distraction. *5.* Lady Cop. *6.* Psychodrama.

Note: The above episodes are available on line for free. Other episodes, available through a subscription service, include "Siobhan Sizzles," "Rhonda Rapid Delivery," "What's for Dinner," "Friday Night Dykes" and "The Dinah Monologues." In all, twelve episodes have been produced as well as twelve "confessional extras."

983 The 3xtremes. youtube.com. 2011.

Danielle, Sara and Vanessa, recent college graduates, decide to pool their resources and move to Los Angeles to search for Mr. Right. Sort of adapting the format of the TV series *How to Marry a Millionaire*, the program charts what each of the women encounter while they attempt to find that one perfect guy (and meet anyone but).

Cast: Sophia Zolan (Sara), Kim Burns (Danielle), Ketryn Porter (Vanessa). **Credits:** *Producer:* Kim Burns, Stefanie Motte, Dylan Stern, Sophia Zolan. *Director:* Sophia Zolan, Steven Sims, Dylan Stern. *Writer:* Sophia Zolan. **Comment:** The well acted

and produced program has the leads first talking about a date encounter and using a flashback like sequence to detail the experience. It also focuses on the women as they try to be something they are not, most often bowing to the situation they encounter to achieve a goal rather than actually being themselves.

Episodes: *1.* The Girls vs. Hollywood. *2.* The Girls vs. the DJ. *3.* The Girls vs. the Family. *4.* The Girls vs. Skit Skat Guy. *5* The Girls vs. Classy Folk.

984 Tight Quarters. viralfilmvideo. 2013.

Katie and Liam, a young couple sharing ownership of a condo, appear to have all the ingredients that are needed for a lasting relationship. They do love each other but one night they become embroiled in an argument that ends their relationship. Feeling she needs a place where she can just clear her mind (as she is not sure who broke up with whom) Katie finds help from her best friend Jamie, a Burlesque dancer who shares a small apartment with her boyfriend, Alan. While the living arrangements are a bit awkward, Katie feels she made the right decision to just get away from Liam. While the program does focus on Katie and her efforts to get her life back on track (with the help of Jamie), it also chronicles the activities of Liam and his best friend, Mick, a womanizer who is trying to make Liam see that he and Katie need to reconcile (although he feels, like Katie, that they can no longer become a couple). Patrick, the owner of an import-export company, is Liam and Mick's boss; Lily and Hailee are their co-workers.

Cast: Heather Mingo (Katie), Paul Whitehouse (Liam), Marla Seidell (Jamie), Paul Sanders (Mick), Thomas Kelly (Gary), Stacey Norgren (Lily), Brian Rooney (Patrick), Amanda Wells (Jenny), Nicole Arroyo (Hailey), Betina Gozo (Maria), Shannon Edwards (Kelly), Herman Harmann (Benjamin). **Credits:** *Producer:* David J. Miller. *Co-Producer:* Heather Mingo. *Writer-Director:* David J. Miller. **Comment:** Network-like production with a very good story line, direction and acting. The women incorporated into the production are sexy and while there are adult situations, they are handled discreetly making for an enjoyable program. Although the program ends unresolved, it appears that Katie and Liam, despite all they have gone through, may just become a couple again.

Episodes: *1.* The Breakup. *2.* Sexy Red Head. *3.* Friends with Benefits. *4.* Hairy Gary. *5.* Bro Code. *6.* Sleeping Arrangement. *7.* The Next Morning. *8.* Sexual Harassment. *9.* Foot Fetish. *10.* A Girl Named Maria. *11.* Pretty Dumb Woman. *12,13.* Sex Tape. *14.* Blonde Date. *15.* Drunk Sex.

985 Tights and Fights: Ashes. youtube.com. 2010–2012.

Ronin Force is a prestigious super hero organization based in Toronto, Canada. Fantabulous Gal,

Tight Quarters. Series poster art (used by permission of David J. Miller).

Leopard Woman, Major Faultline, Captain Euchre and The Plumber are the heroes who battle evil (namely Evil Trojan Borscht) but are personally troubled and experience problems of everyday life.

Fantabulous Gal was raised by a single mother who often had trouble making ends meet. She had hoped to become a Hooters waitress but when she realized Toronto was plagued by super villains she believed she found her calling as a super hero. But becoming a super hero, with no training and only her abundant enthusiasm as "her power," she thought it would be best to become a sidekick and volunteered her services as such. She came to the attention of Dyna Gal, who hired her as both a sidekick and personal assistant and fought along side her. When the pressure of work caused Dyna Gal to have a breakdown and be institutionalized, Fantabulous Gal lost her job. With no recourse, Fantabulous Gal reinvented herself, striking out on her own as a gorgeous super heroine with a can-do attitude, enthusiasm, business acumen—and the crime-fighting equipment once used by Dyna Gal.

Leopard Woman was born in Leopardia, the Cat Kingdom in the center of the planet. She became a Queen and had ruled in her true form as a feline until an earthquake virtually destroyed her kingdom. It was at this time that Bill Faultline, a super hero known as Major Faultline, "fell" into Leopardia and Leopard Woman became infatuated with him, but in her cat form, could only become his pet. Fate intervened when Leopard Woman found a magic amulet that gave her the power to assume the human form of a woman. To be with Bill, she relinquished her Cat Throne and journeyed to the surface to find

Bill and eventually marry him. Leopard Woman became a charter member of Ronin Force but their marriage has suffered over time with their super hero activities threatening to breakup their relationship.

Major Faultline is the scion of a wealthy and affluent family. At age 13 William "Bill" Lyon Mackenzie King Faultline joined the Canadian Army Cadets and quickly rose to the rank of Major. Life changed for him when, during an interplanetary mission he was captured by the Asparagusians and subjected to genetic experimentation. When he was returned to Earth he discovered he was endowed with strange electronic parts embedded in his chest and right hand and has the ability to create earthquakes. He also has the ability to time travel (acquired when he had a brush with a nuclear missile).

The Plumber, alias Robert Strovesco, is the son of Oscar and Lucinda Strovesco. Oscar, better known as The Electrician, is a man with the power to control electrons. At a young age, Oscar felt it was time for Robert to follow in a family tradition and began mentoring him as a super hero. But Robert failed every test his father gave him. After graduating from high school Robert attempted to become a plumber and joined his Uncle Sal's business, Strovesco Plumbing. But Robert could never really master the art and was assigned to tackle the dirtiest unclogging jobs. As time passed, Robert met his future wife (Tanya) and they became the parents of Justin. It was also at this time that Robert decided to become the super hero his father wanted him to be and took up the alias The Plumber ("Snaking the Drains of Justice"). Robert is also known as The Damp Defender, The U–Bend in the Pipe of Life and the Ronin Force's least wanted member.

Captain Euchre, an expert at the card game Euchre, was struck by a stray ray of pure energy shot out of the sky. His deck of Euchre cards absorbed its energy and now enables him to battle injustice. With a vow to bring all criminals to justice, Captain Euchre created the Ronin Force, which unites Toronto's heroes as a super-powered crime fighting force (similar to The Justice League of America).

Evil Trojan Borscht is a man of mystery, even to himself. He first came to prominence by posting videos and it soon became apparent that he was under some sort of mind control (but its source could not be determined). He considers himself to be a genius hacker although his grasp on technology is quite limited. He taunts superheroes and average citizens with videos and blogs from his hidden lair in Toronto. **Cast:** Chelsea Larkin (Leopard Woman), Jeremy Knight (Major Faultline), Melanie Hunter (Fantabulous Gal), Scott Watkins (The Plumber), Scott Albert (Captain Euchre/Evil Trojan Borscht). **Credits:** *Producer:* Courtney Wolfson, Scott Albert, Christopher Guest. *Writer:* Scott Albert, Christopher Guest, Neil James, Kristin McGregor, Conor O'Hegarty, Melanie Hunter, Scott Watkins, Chelsea Larkin. *Director:* Christopher Guest. **Comment:** Exceptional video quality; well acted, written and directed (the episodes feature the characters addressing the camera to talk about what happened).

Fantabulous Gal Episodes, 1–20: *1.* Jobless. *2.* Snail Mail. *3.* Shopping for Super Clothes. *4.* Hello, My Name is Fantabulous Gal! *5.* Turned Down. *6.* Shaken Up. *7,8.* Thank You for Calling. *9.* Name Change. *10.* Captain Euchre is in Trouble! *11.* Party All the Time. *12.* Wasn't That a Party? *13.* Stretching the Bounds of Good Taste. *14.* Fantabulous Gal Shafted. *15.* The At-Odds Couple. *16.* Learning Japanese. *17.* A Few Cars Short. *18.* Robbin' the Hood. *19.* We-ell I'm Movin' on Up. *20.* AAA Plan.

Fantabulous Gal Episodes, 21–45: *21.* Special Delivery. *22.* It Figures. *23.* The Audit. *24.* So Sue Me. *25.* Doing the Can Con. *26.* Dyna Worry, Be Happy. *27.* Ninjas, I'm Home. *28.* Straight Up. *29.* The Ninja Blues. *30.* AAA What's Going On? *31.* Down and Out.... Of Business. *32.* After the Rumble. *33.* The Package. *34.* Captain Euchre Does a Three Way.... Fight! *35.* On the Bright Side of Life. *36.* A History of PFO Letters. *37.* Power Pointed. *38.* Fantabulous Gal to the Rescue. *39.* Kiss and Tell. *40.* Visiting Hours. *41.* Liquor in the Front, Euchre in the Back. *42.* I Did What to Who Now? *43.* New—Finally Some Respect. *44.* Match Game. *45.* Reformation Party.

Leopard Woman and Major Faultline Episodes, 1–20: *1.* While the Rat's Away. *2.* The Best Laid Flans of Mice and Men. *3.* Counseling. *4.* Acting Director. *5.* Major Faultline Wants Back In. *6.* Crème of the Crap. *7.* Welcome to 1994, Chump. *8.*

Shook Me All Night. *9,10.* Counseling Redux. *11.* Puzzle, Puzzle, Toil and Trouble. *12.* A (Very) Simple Plan. *13.* Making Up. *14.* Have You Seen This Cat? *15.* Space Time Talk. *16.* Credit Where It's Not Due. *17.* Honey I'm Home. *18.* Time Travel 101. *19.* The Yoke's on You. *20.* Go Fly a Kite.

Leopard Woman and Major Faultline Episodes, 21–47: *21.* Alexander Graham Bull. *22.* Caffeine Conundrum. *23.* Cat Kingdom Come. *24.* We Love You, Simon Le Bon, Jr. *25.* Council This! *26.* Kitty Bidding. *27.* Dating Licks. *28.* Adieu and a Warning. *29.* Blogs of Future Passed. *30.* Urine for a Heck of a Future. *31.* Shoulda, Coulda, Woulda's. *32.* Digging Up the Past. *33.* Getting Ducks in a Row. *34.* Here, Kitty Kitty! *35.* Winning Is Half the Battle. *36.* Back on Top. *37.* All Day Sucker. *38.* Therapeutic Breakthrough. *39.* The Little Death. *40.* Sucker Says. *41.* That Guy Again. *42.* Funny Story. *43.* See Ya Later Sucker. *44.* New—Future Fodder. *45.* Kick You Out Before I Go-Go. *46.* Second Time's a Charm. *47.* Euchre Rising.

Evil Trojan Borscht Episodes, 1–20: *1.* Phoenix or the Cuckoo? *2.* Always During an Evil Ultimatum. *3.* My Chair, My Frenemy. *4.* Going My Way. *5.* Barry. *6.* This Ain't No Texas Hold 'Em. *7.* Trojy's Recruiting Drive. *8.* Ask a Silly Question.... Get 17051 Junk Mails. *9.* Hint: Ticking Bomb? Not Good. *10.* One Sweet Heist. *11.* Bean Bag Chairs Weigh Heavy on the Soul of Injustice. *12.* Watch Your Butter. *13.* Crazy Ultimatum Time. *14.* Barry's Big Day. *15.* The Importance of Being Thwarted. *16.* In Search of a New Barry. *17.* Sticking It to the Mail Man. *18.* Worst Rickroll Ever. *19.* Trojy Gets Fired. *20.* Lessons in Love from Elmer Fudd.

Evil Trojan Borscht Episodes, 21–42: *21.* Monsieur Popular. *22.* For Whom the Pants Tent. *23.* Confessions of a Super Villain. *24.* Transmigration of Evil Trojan Borscht. *25.* Trojy Finds Religion.... His. *26.* Boom and Greetings. *27.* Signal to Noise. *28.* Don't Cry for Me, Mississauga! *29.* The Gathering Storm. *30.* The Evil Villain's Guide to Self Love. *31.* Le Blog of Le Dead. *32.* Do Cyborg's Dream of Half-Electric Sheep? *33.* The Weird Part. *34.* Into the Woods. *35.* The Rubber Glove Procedure. *36.* This Is Why We Can't Have Nice Things. *37.* Or a Mustard and Cheese Sandwich Perhaps. *38.* The Alyssa Milano Maneuver. *39.* Stupid Cult. *40.* Le Evil Monologue. *41.* They Always Escape. *42.* ETB: The Next Generation.

The Plumber Episodes, 1–20: *1.* Blocked at Every Turn. *2.* Trickle to a Torrent. *3.* The Obligatory Groveling Episode. *4.* The Plumber's Call. *5.* Those Other Plumbers. *6.* Plumb Out of Luck. *7.* The Yard Patrol. *8.* Wet and Dirty. *9.* A Wrench in the Works. *10.* A Drip for Hire. *11.* A Plumber for Hire: Hired. *12.* Rule Number One of Euchre Club. *13.* The Plumber Is Flushed. *14.* Can't Go Home Again. *15.* A New Hope. *16.* Job Snaked Out from Under Me. *17.* Fantabulicious Sex Must Wait. *18.* The Plumber Is a Multi-Tool. *19.* Desperate Encounters Profile:

Plumbing Go D673. *20.* Looking for Love in All the Wrong Toilets.

The Plumber Episodes, 21–46: *21.* Monkeying Around with the Plumber. *22.* You Killed the Monkey. *23.* You Didn't Kill the Monkey. *24.* The Plumber Cleans Up. *25.* Plumbed Out. *26.* Plumber on the Run. *27.* The Plumber's Going Alone. *28.* The Secret Plumber's Other Ball. *29.* The Plumber, the Player. *30.* No Poon for Plumber. *31.* Electrifying Reunion. *32.* Electronically Grounded. *33.* Swing Time. *34.* That Is Why the Plumber Fails. *35.* Fantabulicious Visit. *36.* Going Undercover. *37.* Sucker's Been Euchred. *38.* In Too Ted Deep. *39.* The Boning Sessions. *40.* Plumber's Up for Air. *41.* The Plumber's First Real Battle. *42.* Mail Order Plumber. *43.* Brainwashed and Waterlogged. *44.* Stupidity Saves the Day. *45.* The Plumber Hangs Up His Wrench—for a Wrench. *46.* Unclogging Ronin Force.

986 *Tiki Bar TV.* tikibar.com. 2005–2009.

Patrons of the Tiki Bar receive help in solving their problems from Dr. Tiki (Reginald Hornstein), a physician (Ph D., MD, USB) with a doctorate in Tiki, who prescribes a cocktail as a means to overcome what bothers them. Johnny Johnny (Jonathan J. Jonathan), the bartender mixes the prescribed drink while Lala (Beatrice Fastwater), the bar's entertainer, performs dances. **Cast:** Jeff MacPherson (Dr. Tiki), Kevin Gamble (Johnny Johnny), Lara Doucette (Lala). **Credits:** *Producer:* Tosca Musk. *Director:* Jeff MacPherson. **Comment:** Pleasing Canadian-produced program with good acting, production values and a simple plot (basically just the three regulars conversing) with an added bonus of how to make the drinks used on the program.

2005 Episodes: *1.* Margaritaville. *2.* Suffering Bastard. *3.* The Trap Door. *4.* Hulla Balloo. *5.* Trader Woody. *6.* Interlude. *7.* Checker Challenge. *8.* London Fog Cutter. *9.* Red Oktober. *10.* Drinkbot.

2006 Episodes: *11.* Volcano. *12.* Holiday Mailbag. *13.* Skull and Bones. *14.* Boomerang. *15.* Legal Ease. *16.* Tongue Twister. *17,18.* Space Cadet. *19.* Greeki Tiki. *20.* Son of Internet.

2007 Episodes: *21.* Snake. *22.* Dry Halloween. *23.* Red Handed. *24.* Bunnies. *25.* Blue Hawaiian. *26.* Missionary. *27.* Dingo. *28.* The Play. *29.* The Wedding. *30.* Ice Breaker.

2008 Episodes: *31.* Casino. *32.* Holiday Special. *33.* CCCP. *34.* Mailbag's Revenge. *35.* Conspiracy. *36.* The Roman. *37.* Beatnik. *38.* Apocalypse Tiki. *39.* Backstage Bender.

2009 Episodes: *40.* Drinkbot vs. Robot Box. *41.* Jump the Shark. *42.* Fishbone. *43.* Ghost of the Internet. *44.* Gypsy. *45.* The Commodore.

987 *Til Lease Do Us Part.* youtube.com. 2014.

Believing they can move on to the next stage of their relationship, Mikka (bisexual) and Shannon (lesbian) decide to move into together and share an apartment. It works well at first but as time passes they find that they are not fully compatible and feel it is best to break up. A problem arises when they learn they still need to live together to fulfill the terms of their apartment lease, which still has six months to run. While it appears Shannon has gotten over Mikka, Mikka finds it much more difficult to let Shannon go. The program charts what happens when Mikka and Shannon attempt to find new loves but discover that living together with an ex is not the most inviting of situations when it comes to finding that significant other. **Cast:** Hannah Hogan (Mikka), Joanne Sarazen (Shannon). **Credits:** *Producer:* Adrianna DiLonardo, Sarah Rotella. *Director:* Sarah Rotella. *Writer:* Adrianna DiLonardo. **Comment:** Although it is not related to the series *Rent Controlled*, the plot is similar as it deals with the same situation (lovers breaking up and having to live together). The acting and production values are network television quality and the program worth watching.

Episodes: 6 untitled episodes, labeled "Episode 1" through "Episode 6."

988 *Tilted Straits.* youtube.com. 2013.

It has been six years since four friends (Aiden, Alyssa, Cliff and Jake) graduated from high school. They have remained close and once a week they gather to play a friendly game of poker. The conversations that follow as each friend discusses what is happening in his or her life are related. **Cast:** David Polgar (Aiden), Alyssa Clancy (Alyssa), Brian Flinchbaugh (Cliff), Bill Shannon (Jake). **Credits:** *Writer-Director:* Brian Flinchbaugh. Bill Shannon. **Comment:** Interesting mix of characters in a format that simply has the friends gathering to play poker and talk. As such formats go, the acting and production values are good and the program interesting to see what happens at those gatherings.

Season 1 Episodes: *1.* That's Billy Mays, You Doofus! *2.* We All Know Ted. *3.* Oh, I've Got Jelly. *4.* Fun with Cliff, Right. *5.* Aces and Eights, Man. *6.* Shots for Sal. *7.* Plates, All of Them. *8.* It's Your Time Jake. *9.* Backstabbing Doucheball. *10.* That's Not How It Happened.

Season 2 Episodes: *1.* The Family Feud Guy. *2.* Laugh Your Ass Off Funny. *3.* The Bohemian Rhapsody. *4.* Unknown title. *5.* You Bluffing Bastard. *6.* Swimming in the Tub. *7.* Now, This Is a Party. *8.* His Door Was Locked. *9.* Those Were My Condoms. *10.* To Us!

989 Time for Passion. webserieschannel. com. 2011.

Johnson Roberts, a self-proclaimed star and creator of the Time for Passion method of acting, became famous (in his own mind) through what he believes is the only way to act—by passion (his current script is a movie called *The World* that is totally geared to passion acting). Johnson, a Middle Eastern man, is arrogant, rather ignorant and has taken up residence in Hollywood, California, where he hopes to instill his acting methods into the students in his newly established Time for Passion Acting School. His techniques are rather extreme and the program follows Johnson's misguided students as they attempt to encompass passion as the key element to acquiring roles.

Cast: Amol Shah (Johnson Roberts), Darryl Gibson (Dominic), Alara Ceri (Rachel), Ben Blair (Yorkshire), Natasha Lloyd (Vivienne), Alexandra Grossi (Girl I Meet on the Street), Crystal Marie Denha (Jacqueline), Boyan Deam (Knox), Kaan Gurocak (Jack Ass). **Credits:** *Producer:* Kor Adana, Alara Ceri. *Writer-Director:* Kor Adana. **Comment:** A different approach to programs dealing with acting classes that is very well acted and produced. Amol Shah is especially good as Johnson and he honestly makes you believe that the only way to act is through passion—even though his students try (but fail) to dispute that point.

Episodes: *1.* The Fantom Johnson. *2.* Attack of the Johnson: Judgment Day. *3.* Revenge of the Johnson: Dark Territory. *4.* A New Johnson: Back in the Habitat. *5.* The Umpire Strikes Johnson: Be on Thunderdome. *6.* Return of the Pig in the Sitee.

990 Tiny Apartment. tintapartment.com. 2011.

Jessie and Mike are a young couple stuck in a bad situation: living in a very small rundown Manhattan apartment and surrounded by neighbors who are anything but normal. Lacking the money to move and with their only escape being beer and take-out food, the program follows their efforts to make the best of the situation that surrounds them—made all the more bearable with the help of their best friend Pat.

Cast: Jessie Cantrell (Jessie), Mike O'Gorman (Mike), Pat Driscoll (Pat). **Credits:** *Producer-Writer:* Jessie Cantrell, Mike O'Gorman, Pat Driscoll. **Comment:** While the idea is not totally original, it is a well produced and acted take on a young couple stuck in a miserable situation.

Episodes: *1.* Sexy Night. *2.* Take-Out. *3.* The Wire. *4.* Quiet on the Set. *5.* Flippity Do. *6.* Who Is That? *7.* Roof Party. *8.* Smoking. *9.* Some Air. *10.* Getting Ready. *11.* Brains. *12.* S**t, My Pat Says. *13.* The Doc. *14.* Mikesomnia. *15.* Shakespeare Guy. *16.* Not Roger. *17.* Welcome to the Dollpartment.

991 Tiny Commando. screen.yahoo.com. 2013.

Richard Carlyle was a member of the U.S. Navy's elite SEALs. During a military experiment Richard was exposed to an unnamed something that altered his DNA chemistry and not only ended his military career but left him only four inches in height. But life was not over for Richard. He came to the attention of Mizi McNeil, a computer whiz and private detective who realized the possibilities such a man could mean and made him her partner in Tiny Investigations, where Richard soon became known as Tiny Commando. By incorporating miniature weapons and vehicles, Mitzi and Tiny take on the most dangerous of cases with the program chronicling Tiny's efforts to bring down diabolical villains, especially Cesar Pequino, a madman who seeks to destroy the world but first needs to eliminate his mortal enemy, Tiny Commando.

Cast: Zachary Levi (Tiny Commando), Gillian Jacobs (Mitzi McNeil), Ed Helms (Cesar Pequeno). **Credits:** *Producer:* Jason Berger, Ed Helms, Amy Laslett, Corey Moss, Tiffany Moore. *Director:* Ryan McFaul. *Writer:* Jacob Fleisher, Ed Helms. **Comment:** Television series quality with excellent special effects and superior acting and production values. TV tried similar projects with *The World of Giants* and *The Misfits of Science*, neither of which were a success.

Episodes: *1,2.* Sneak Attack. *3,4.* Tiny Furious. *5,6.* Furry Fury. *7,8.* Red Rover. *9,10.* The Grass Is Meaner. *11,12.* Clash of the Tinies.

992 Tiny Hands. sidereel.com. 2008.

For all intent and purposes Dave Gordon is a seemingly normal-looking man. But like everyone, Dave has certain flaws, his biggest being that he was born with very tiny hands and they have never matured. Dave's struggles to live in a world where incredibly miniature hands make doing everything that much harder are chronicled.

Cast: Jon Glaser (Dave Gordon). **Credits:** *Producer-Writer:* Jon Glaser. **Comment:** The idea does sound intriguing but unfortunately, all episodes (even trailers) have been taken off line.

Episodes: *1.* Glove Shopping. *2.* Back Rub. *3.* Commercial Audition. *4.* Nanny. *5.* Sunday Afternoon. *6.* Palm Reader.

993 Tiny Nuts. webserieschannel.com. 2014.

Walnut is a four-pound Chihuahua and the pet of a young woman named Taylor. Taylor shares an apartment with her college friend Caroline who sometimes finds herself becoming a third wheel when Taylor gets carried away with Walnut and puts her pet above everything else (as she finds Walnut a distraction from the issues that surround her). The program is basically just look at Taylor and Caroline (and Walnut) as they navigate life.

Cast: Taylor Barrett (Taylor), Caroline Goldfarb (Caroline), Walnut Barrett (Walnut). **Credits:** *Producer-Writer:* Taylor Barrett, Caroline Goldfarb. *Director:* Taylor Barrett. **Comment:** On screen the dog receives top billing over Taylor and Caroline. While the show could have followed the path where Taylor's life revolves around the dog, it didn't and does allow for her and Caroline's interactions. The program is not just for dog lovers but anyone interested in seeing a well acted and produced look at young women just coping with life.

Episodes: *1.* Good Morning. *2.* BFF. *3.* Vespa. *4.* Dating. *5.* Rose & Thorn. *6.* Money. *7.* Girlz Night. *8.* Athletic Expertise.

994 *Tiny Office.* youtube.com. 2013.

Kevin and Tom have been promoted to co-managers of the Fiscal Irresponsible Department of their (unnamed) company. The company apparently has no room for them and converts a small janitor's closet into an office which they must now share. With barely any room for their desks, Kevin and Tom manage to adjust to their "Tiny Office" and the program, set in that office, relates the inconveniences they must deal with as they attempt to do their jobs.

Cast: Kevin Etherson (Kevin), Tom Capps (Tom). **Credits:** *Producer:* Emily DeBlasi, Kevin Etherson, Tom Capps. *Writer-Director:* Emily DeBlasi. **Comment:** An amusing, well-done program whose concept plays out very well. The acting is good and the situations being short, makes the whole program work.

Episodes: *1.* Pilot. *2.* The Sign. *3.* The Big Presentation. *4.* Office Antics. *5.* Locked In. *6,7.* Abroad. *8.* Happy Birthday. *9.* Sick Day. *10.* Words with Friend. *11.* Progress Reports. *12.* Separate Ways.

995 *Together.* facebook.com. 2014–2015.

Short (under 60 seconds) glimpses into the lives of a young couple (Greg and Jan) as they tackle a problem together.

Cast: Matthew Stroh (Greg), Jennifer Lenius (Jan). **Credits:** *Writer-Director:* Justin Hillstrom. **Comment:** Well acted and produced program that with appealing leads, could have stretched episodes a minute or two longer and it still would have been just as enjoyable.

Episodes: 4 untitled episodes, labeled "Episode 1" through "Episode 4."

996 *Tony and Miranda: A Therapeutic Video Blog.* webserieschannel.com. 2011.

Tony and Miranda are a married couple with numerous issues, the most prominent being they appear to hate each other. But they have not (yet) divorced. Instead, on the advice of their therapist, they have created a video blog through which they vent their hostilities toward each other. The program chronicles those video blog sessions with Tony and Miranda lashing out against each other for the world to see.

Cast: Patrick De Nicola (Tony Farfaglia), Jessie Stegner (Miranda Farfaglia). **Credits:** *Producer-Writer-Director:* Patrick De Nicola, Jessie Stegner. **Comment:** Tony is so foul-mouthed that his constant cursing will be a turn-off for some viewers. Miranda is his complete opposite and is the only one of the two who is trying to save their faltering marriage. Vulgar language aside, the idea is good and it is complimented by good acting and production values. If you can stand the language, the program is something different to watch.

Episodes: *1.* Chest Hair. *2.* Thanksgiving. *3.* Making Out. *4.* A Farfaglia Christmas. *5.* New Year's Resolutions. *6.* Sh*t Italians Say. *7.* This Isn't a Game. *8.* Oscar Speeches. *9.* Forty Days and Forty Fights.

997 *Top Flight Security.* webserieschannel.com. 2013.

The Linda Park Apartments is a Southern California housing complex patrolled by Top Flight Security of America, a team of officers with a mission: keep the complex safe. Top Flight, however, is anything like its name implies as it is manned by a motley crew: Tre Johnson, a professional slacker and the newest team member (forced by his girlfriend Nicole to get a job); Officer Steve, a failed police academy rookie who is not operating with a full deck and believes he is a military officer; Aabheer, a recruit fresh off the boat from India; Crazy Sherry, the guard who is desperate to steal Tre away from Nicole; and Oscar, the guard with an addiction to snacks, especially chips. All totaled, the team is nuts; the tenants even crazier and what transpires as Top Flight goes into action is presented.

Cast: J.D. Witherspoon (Tre Johnson), Antoinette Mia Pettis (Nicole), Feraz Ozel (Aabheer), James Gill (Officer Steve), Phil Talsky (Oscar), Sayrie (Sherry). **Credits:** *Producer:* Antoinette Mia Pettis, Marquette Williams, Perdell Richardson. *Director:* Perdell Richardson. *Writer:* Ryan Priest. **Comment:** Training for the officers of Top Flight include such crucial instructions as how to use a flashlight. Once understood, Top Flight's new recruits were launched into action in a well presented and acted program.

Episodes: *1.* Pilot. *2.* Training. *3.* Patrolling. *4.* Brownies. *5.* The Date.

998 *Total White Guy Move.* webserieschannel.com. 2013.

Stories, inspired by true events that tackle the subject about "guys dating and heartbreaks in L.A."

Cast: Adam Dobbs, Emily Fitz, Sofia Mattson, Valerie Lucas, Chloe Zak, Ricardo Cisneros, Jennifer Cadena, Jordan Bielsky, Alejandra Morin, Ruben Gomes, Anna Flinchbaugh, Emily Banks. **Credits:** *Producer:* Jordan Bielsky. *Director:* Ricardo Cisneros. *Writer:* Jennifer Cadena. **Comment:** While the title is not explained, it appears to refer to the tactics white guys will use to secure a date (although any other race would try some of the same things). The program is well acted but its dialogue is a bit risqué without any prior warning given.

Episodes: *1.* Are You the Girl of My Dreams? *2.* Wanna Have a Sleepover? *3.* I Don't Date Outside My Zip Code. *4.* So I Have This Groupon. *5.* Need Help with That? *6.* Good Coffee.

999 *Totally Talls.* webserieschannel.com. 2013.

Greta Harrison is a woman so obsessed with tall men that she decides to create a life-style web series about them. "Tall people go by many names. Big Men, Big Boys and Length Men. This show is about tall. It's Totally Tall," says Greta as she opens her show and the program explores the world of tall men as seen through Greta's conversations and interactions with them (who appear as her guests).

Cast: Trish O'Gubbins (Greta Harrison), Matthew C. Vaughan (Matthew), Mitch McTaggart (Mitch), Matthew Drosdowsky (Tuffy Tall), James Arnold Garvey (James), Andrew R. Young (Andrew). **Credits:** *Writer-Producer-Director:* Greta Harrison, Matthew C. Vaughan. **Comment:** Strictly a program with a specific audience in mind as it will not appeal to everyone. The idea is somewhat unusual and not the most interesting to watch as everything is about being tall. The acting and production are just standard for an Internet series.

Episodes: *1.* Histallry. *2.* Tall Sports. *3.* Sorts of Talls. *4.* Tall Solutions. *5.* Scientallogist. *6.* Entalltainment.

1000 *Touch 'N Dix.* youtube.com. 2012.

Christopher Touch and Nathan Dix are musicians who appear to be out of touch with reality. They met on an Internet chat line dealing with vintage dolls and not only did they immediately connect but they started a band called Touch 'N Dix. They were literally going nowhere until they made an appearance on a local Chicago cable access channel fund raiser. Their song, "I Wish We Were Babies," propelled them to the top of the charts for eight straight weeks and made them rich. Unfortunately, they had no concept on handling fame and quickly spiraled downward. They squandered all their earnings, lost track of reality and are now seeking the services of a therapist. They are hoping to restart their band and regain the fame they once had. The program relates what happens as they follow their therapist's sugges-

tions but, being totally lost in a world straight from *The Twilight Zone* are having a hard time just adjusting to everyday life.

Cast: Nate DuFort (Nathan Dix), Chris Pagnozzi Christopher (Touch), Sandy Marshall (Sandy), Susan Messing (Therapist), Ellie Reed (Ellie). **Credits:** *Producer:* Scott Goldstein, Nate DuFort. *Director:* Sandy Marshall. **Comment:** If it were not for a very fast spoken (and difficult to fully comprehend) opening, it would be difficult to figure out what is going on. The program is strange in story and presentation and perhaps only the two stars know what the whole program is really about as on-lookers can become confused.

Episodes: *1.* Introductions. *2.* A New Roommate. *3.* Addiction. *4.* Family. *5.* Relationships. *6.* A New Hope.

1001 *Tough Love.* youtube.com. 2013.

Blaire, a disorganized lesbian in denial, and Steven, her uptight, obsessive best (and gay) friend, are roommates sharing an apartment in Queens, New York. Adapting an "Odd Couple" like format (with Blaire, a female version of untidy Oscar Madison and Steven the perfectionist Felix Unger) the program relates their efforts to not only navigate life but live together without driving each other crazy.

Cast: Steven Bell (Steven), Blaire Mackenzie Wendel (Blaire). **Credits:** *Producer-Writer:* Steven Bell, Blaire Mackenzie Wendel. *Director:* Cody Ball. **Comment:** Well acted and produced program that does a good job of transposing the Oscar and Felix type of characters into a lesbian-gay mix. Each episode is complete in itself and stories most enjoyable.

Episodes: *1.* Weight Loss. *2.* Personal Space. *3.* Meditate on This. *4.* Rage Quilt. *5.* Don't Panic. *6.* Lady Lessons. *7.* Barbie. *8.* Jealousy.

1002 *A Town.* turtledovefilms.tumblr.com. 2014.

Layla, a young woman living in Austin, Texas, is hoping to gain fame as a stand-up comedian. She works as a waitress, has a best friend, Melanie, but little luck in wowing audiences. Layla's stand-up routines are featured in stories that follow her endless trials and tribulations as she seeks that one break that will set her on the road to stardom.

Cast: Elena Weinberg (Layla), Mallory Larson (Melanie), Ivy Koehler (Whitney), Derek Babb (Sex God). **Credits:** *Producer-Director:* Duncan Coe. **Comment:** Nicely acted and produced program that felt it needed foul language and found a way to incorporate it—by playing vulgar rap songs in the background. It has to be assumed that the material Layla uses in her act was meant to be bad as it is simply not funny.

Episodes: *1.* Pilot. *2.* Jobs and Juice. *3.* The Greenbelt. *4.* IMPROVments. *5.* Kayaking Adventure. *6.* Chicks in Pink, Vomit in Sink. *7.* So F***ed Up. *8.* The Breakup Party. *9.* Dunzo. *10.* Best Friends Day.

1003 *Toying with Jerry.* youtube.com. 2012.

As a child Jerry Krinkleman's parent's often neglected him and his only companions were his toys. As he grew, his parents continued in their tradition and Jerry became more and more dependent on his toys. Now, as a man in his forties, Jerry is quite insecure and still turns to those toys for comfort. But to Jerry they are not just toys as they now come to life for him and offer him advice and comfort. The conversations between Jerry and his toys are highlighted and the advice given by them to Jerry is followed as Jerry finds that the only way he can face life is with the help of his childhood toys (here to build up the courage to ask a pretty co-worker [Sam] out on a date).

Cast: David Volin (Jerry). *Character Voices:* Kurt Elftman, Tara Garwood, Greg Crowe, Dave Cooperman. **Credits:** *Producer:* Michael Czogalla, Colin Heichman, Christina Mosser, Rich Volin. *Writer-Director:* Rich Volin. **Comment:** A unique idea that plays well. The coming-to-life toy scenes are very well done and the entire program flows smoothly from episode to episode.

Episodes: *1.* Ask Her Out. *2.* Here's What You Say. *3.* Hi Jerry, I'm Sam. *4.* The Other Friends.

1004 *Tragedy Club.* tragedyclub.com. 2012.

Tragedy Club is a feature film about a suicide prevention group's transformation into a deadly cult. The film is in production but has an extremely limited budget. Encompassing the satiric "mockumentary" approach, the program details all the problems the cast and crew encounter as they use every conceivable means possible to make a movie where buying a cup of coffee could put a serious dent in the budget. Dylan is the movie's creator; Chris, the director; Katie, the female lead; Jonathan, the male lead; Lady Leather, the script supervisor; Blake, the DP (Director of Photography), Stacey, the producer; Tony, second male lead; and Sam, third male lead.

Cast: Dillon Petrillo (Dylan), Chris Blair (Chris), Ellie Macbride (Katie), Daniel Sullivan (Jonathan), Heather Ryan (Lady Leather), Dan Bernstein (Blake), Evangeline Crittenden (Stacey), Marcus Sams (Tony), Paul Cotton (Sam). **Credits:** *Producer:* Danielle Gasbarro, Chris Casilli. *Director:* Chris Casilli. *Writer:* Chris Blair. **Comment:** Well done look behind-the-scenes of the making of a feature film with good acting and production values.

Episodes: *1.* The Pre-Shoot Party. *2.* The First Day. *3.* The Oner. *4.* The Power Struggle.

1005 *Tragic Relief.* youtube.com. 2014.

A series of comedy skits that tackle the nightmarish situations that mostly undeserving people encounter at every turn.

Cast: Jon Marballi, Amber Nelson, Matt Klinman, Pat O'Brien, Matt Hunziker, Matthew Brian Cohen, Alyson Sheppard, Jordan Clifford, Brian Agler, Abby Holland, Kristin Mularz, Sara Cicilian, Sydney Hollis, Megan Stein, Brittany Connors, Julia Wiedeman, Natalie Wetta. **Credits:** *Producer:* Ryan Mazer, Josh Elmets, Michael Goldburg, Nick Mohammed. *Director:* Dan Mirk, Michael Goldburg, Matt Mayer, Matt Klinman. *Writer:* Ryan Mazer, Josh Elmets, Matt Klinman, Adam Sacks, Matt Mayer, Jordan Clifford. **Comment:** Well crafted program that, while stretching things a bit, does present real life situations with good acting and production values.

Episodes: *1.* Event Horizon. *2.* Surprise. *3.* Eat Right. *4.* Surprise II. *5.* The Law of Increasing Poverty. *6.* Twitter Joke.

1006 *Trainers (2012).* youtube.com. 2012.

When John (straight) and Justin (gay), trainers in a corporate gym are fired for misconduct (John for having sex with a patron; Justin for calling a patron fat) they decide to begin their own gym from their apartment on Fulton Avenue. The program charts their mishaps as they try to avoid the situations that caused their termination and run a gym as the experienced trainers they believe themselves to be.

Cast: John Francis O'Brien (John), Justin Mortelliti (Justin), Laura Jean Salerno (L.J.), Adam Meyer (Adam), Kevin Daniels (Kevin), Rebakah Tripp (Elizabeth). **Credits:** *Producer-Writer:* John Francis O'Brien. *Director:* Cameron Thrower. **Comment:** Although only a pilot film has appeared it is well made and acted. While there is foul language it is not possible to tell how the romantic situations that would involve John and Justin would play out. John appears to be a lecherous ladies' man (will go after any girl, no matter how thin or fat) while Justin appears to be a bit classier and will not jump into bed with the first man he sees.

Episodes: *1.* Pilot: Is It Hard?

1007 *Trainers (2013).* trainersshow.com. 2013.

Sweat L.A. Gym is a prestigious Los Angeles gym that sets itself apart from all others as it has a physique building experience called The Technique. But the gym is also on the verge of closing and the program relates the efforts of its staff to somehow save their beloved gym by acquiring paying customers but not kill each other in their efforts to do so.

Reggie is the manager, a man who eats, sleeps and

breathes the gym. Mandy, a trainer, is an actress with an ultimate goal to become a TV star. Al, who wishes people would call her Alexandra, is a trainer who is also a lesbian and conceals her relationship with her girlfriend (Lara). Eddie is the egotistical trainer who believes he is the best trainer he has ever known.

Kaylie is a front desk greeter who wishes she could be more alluring. Samson is the body builder who held the Mr. America and Mr. Universe titles (he pines for Kaylie but his Finnish accent makes everything he says incomprehensible and has Kaylie in a daze). Jin, a Caucasian adopted by Asian parents, is a martial arts expert who believes he is Asian and speaks with an Asian accent. Julio, the Latin lover with the perfect physique (and in love with himself), developed The Technique (he also moonlights as a stripper for Hunks of Hollywood). Scott is Kaylie's front desk associate. Paige is Scott's bitchy girlfriend.

Cast: Jason Kelley (Reggie), Selah Victor (Mandy), Shannon MacMillan (Al), Aubrey Mozino (Kaylie), Michael Onofri (Eddie), Pasi Schalin (Samson), Adam Burch (Jin), Dominic Rains (Julio), Brandon Jones (Scott), Natalie Lander (Paige), Meredith Freen (Lara), Clarke Kohler (Henry), Eileen Fogarty (Rhonda), Kim Kendall (Marie), Alan Blumenfeld (Kleinberg), Allison Summers (Anorexic Allison).

Credits: *Producer:* Selah Victor, Michael Onofri, Alexa-Sascha Lewin, Tony Muscio. *Writer:* Selah Victor, Michael Onofri. *Director:* Alexa-Sascha Lewin. **Comment:** Well developed program with very good acting and production values. There is some vulgar language and brief (blurred) nudity but nothing objectionable. Because of his accent, Samson's dialogue sequences are seen with subtitles.

Episodes: *1.* The Predicament. *2.* Julio. *3.* O.M.G.

1008 Travel Bound. youtube.com. 2010.

Josh is a young man who considers himself just an ordinary guy until he connects with a girl (Claire) on the Internet, falls in love with her and sets his goal to travel to Arizona and propose marriage. The only problem (besides not telling the girl he is coming) is that he has no means of transportation. His solution: Karen, the van of his best friend Bryan. Bryan is not too fond of Claire as he feels she is stealing his best friend but agrees to drive him to meet the love of his life. The program charts the trip Josh and Bryan (and Karen) embark on and what happens along the way when they become involved with a hobo, a baby kidnapping and a crazed ninja.

Cast: Danny Burnette (Josh Quinn), Jason Meagher (Bryan Flett), Dan Maurer (Hobo), Erik Spiller (Ninja), Mike Land (Zadoosh), Anthony Lipuma (Clint), Sarah Labriola (Sam). **Credits:** *Writer-Director:* Jason Meagher. **Comment:** Strange as the concept sounds (and even stranger as you watch) it is a unique idea and well acted and produced. It is all the craziness they encounter along the way that makes the show work.

Episodes: *1.* Point A. *2.* Caring for Karen. *3.* Trouble with Ninjas. *4.* Raising Shaft. *5.* Shiny, Shiny. *6.* Law Ablinding Citizen. *7.* Who's Your Daddy. *8.* Ninjas, Babies and Automobiles.

1009 Trent and Tilly. youtube.com. 2013.

Trent and Tilly are social networking slackers with too much free time on their hands. In its simplistic presentation, what Trent and Tilly do each day as they realize their lives are going nowhere and what they need to do to find a meaningful purpose are depicted.

Cast: Christian Marc (Trent), Tasha Tacosa (Tilly). **Credits:** *Producer-Writer:* Christian Marc, Tasha Tacosa. *Director:* Dave Parker. **Comment:** All episodes have been taken off line thus a comment is not presented.

Episodes: *1.* Take a Picture. *2.* Hipster Football. *3.* Classy Italian. *4.* Poke Her Nickel Back. *5.* Bag Bagging #1. *6.* Totally Pussy. *7.* Puck Sluts.

1010 Tripping. youtube.com. 2013.

For reasons that are not made exactly clear, two morons, Andy and Ben, fake their deaths and now lead a life that constantly has them in hiding, fearing to be caught if they show their faces in public. Andy, a nut collector, has a most unusual hobby: murdering people. Ben, a starving artist, continually drinks milk and, like Andy, survives on what they call "magic mushrooms." It has been three long years since their "demise." They live in squalor, only go out in public if well disguised and their lives are literally as depressing as it can get. Their situation changes drastically when a mysterious woman, called "Temptress," enters their lives and seeks to bring them down even farther than they already are. Temptress can alter thinking (and delights so by tapping into Ben's ultra weak mind) and the program follows what happens as Andy and Ben use what little sense they have to defeat Temptress and return their lives to the misery it once was.

Cast: Lucas McGee (Andy), Paul Haskins (Ben), Lainey Gallenberg (Anna Miller), Carly Wood (Temptress), Xander Toftness (Al Mund), Logan Toftness (Shelley). **Credits:** *Producer-Writer-Director:* Lucas McGee, Paul Haskins. **Comment:** Another of the strange series (see also *Touch 'N Dix*) that becomes more intriguing the longer you watch it. Andy and Ben are totally dysfunctional and live in a world that can only happen on TV. The acting and production, however, are good.

Episodes: *1.* The Anniversary Sack. *2.* Fungal Awakenings. *3.* Dark Temptations. *4.* The Sack Who Came to Dinner. *5.* A Dangerous Dance with Chance. *6.* Milk Terrors. *7.* The Pig Lady Caper. *8.* Once Upon a Swine. *9.* The Start of Something Beautiful. *10.* How to Cleanse a Milk Maid. *11.* Space Rock. *12.* The Return of Something Beautiful.

13. On the Subject of Bees. *14.* Cloudy with a Chance of Jelly. *15.* Cycle of the Sack Master.

1011 *Trivial.* youtube.com. 2014.

Mark and Jason are writers. One day while discussing story ideas, Jason decides to capitalize on one of the ideas and turn it into a TV sitcom, leaving Mark out of the picture. When Mark discovers what Jason has done, he plans to get his revenge by showing Jason up as the fraud he is. While not anything spectacular, Mark arranges for a trivia game night wherein he invites his friends Jaffrey, Jaime and Abby to join him and Jason. Jason is unaware of Mark's intentions until he makes it known that Jason stole his idea and that he (Jason) has no talent. When Jason denies it, Mark challenges him to a story development challenge. With Jaffrey supplying a few facts, Mark and Jason use their laptops to compose a story around it. Jaffrey reads both stories and with Mark being declared the winner, Mark receives his vengeance by proving Jason is a fraud.

Cast: Philip Denver (Jaffrey), Tim Marks (Mark), Vanessa Severo (Jaime), Andy Tyhurst (Jason), Heidi Van (Abby). **Credits:** *Producer-Writer-Director:* Eric Havens. **Comment:** Why Mark only set out to prove Jason was a fraud may enter your mind as you feel he had a possible lawsuit against Jason. While not a laugh-out loud funny program, it does have its humorous moments with good acting.

Episodes: *1.* This Is Going to Be Awkward. *2.* Nerd Fight. *3.* Let the Challenge Begin. *4.* Non Sequitur.

1012 *Troy's Big Break.* youtube.com. 2014.

Troy Lawrence, the director of a theater company for the deaf, is deaf himself and hoping through his workshop to help hearing-impaired, struggling actors find work. Troy has his own issues to deal with and, as he does that, his search to find a leading lady for an upcoming production is chronicled.

Cast: Joseph Ausanio (Troy Lawrence), Fallon Bauer (Trixie), Samantha Shupe (Vivian Pierce), Frances Sorrentino (Flo). **Credits:** *Director:* Taylor Repetski. *Writer:* Joseph Ausanio. **Comment:** A rarity, something that has not really been captured on broadcast or cable TV—a program done totally in sign language. The program begins with a musical opening and then becomes completely silent. The close captioning icon must be turned on to read what is being said to enjoy the program.

Episodes: *1.* Pilot: Flo. *2.* Vivian. *3.* Trixie. *4.* Accept, Reject. *5.* Three Simple Words. *6.* The Ex.

1013 *The True Heroines.* youtube.com. 2011.

Project Paradise Hill, funded by the mysterious Corporation, was a World War I secret experiment intended to breed humans with special abilities (H.S.A.'s). Specific housing units were established with the intent to entice returning soldiers into settling down and unknowingly breed H.S.A.'s. In 1941, with America's entrance into World War II, the government purchased the ability to produce H.S.A.'s from The Corporation. The government, however, misused the ability and enslaved H.S.A.'s, forcing them to work as slaves or soldiers on the front lines in Europe. Though many H.S.A.'s were lost, several escaped and managed to live as regular humans worldwide. The government, however, displeased with that fact, hired agents to find and eliminate fugitive H.S.A.'s. Stories, set in New Paradise Hill in the 1960s, follows a group of female H.S.A.'s (Pearl, Margie and Dottie) as they attempt to uncover the secret of their abilities and who or what they actually are.

Pearl Andrews, an ex-war nurse, is rather uptight and constantly willing to help others with her power of invisibility.

Margie Hepburn is married (her husband is an executive at Milk King Corporation). She is very tidy, possesses the power of super speed and suspects that Milk King is behind what happened.

Dottie Rodriquez is the product of growing up in a tough Cuban neighborhood and, although she possesses super strength, she has also acquired street smarts from her school of hard knocks. Dottie also shares Margie's concerns that something evil lurks behind the doors of Milk King.

Ethel Worthington is a mother-dominated woman who succumbed to a campaign of finding serenity in New Paradise Hill. She works as the Milk King Switchboard operator and considers herself a misfit and knows more than what she lets on about Milk King.

Gordon Fitzgerald, a former soldier, is now a deliveryman for Milk King (he is also heir to the Milk King fortune and has been trained as a military assassin).

Earl Finch is a former delivery man for Milk King whose work as a scientist during the war may hold the key to the questions The True Heroines seek.

Bobby Fitzgerald, the town's mayor, has lived in New Paradise Hill his entire life; it was his father who initiated Project Paradise Hill.

Hugo Rodriquez is married to Dottie (they meet when she worked as a dancer at a USO during the war) and is now a salesman at Milk King.

Calvin Hepburn is Margie's husband, a corporate leader at Milk King.

Percy Andrews is Pearl's husband, a mechanical engineer at Milk King.

Cast: Fiona Vroom (Pearl Andrews), Jovanna Guguet (Margie Hepburn), Paula Giroday (Dottie Rodriquez), Ali Liebert (Ethel Worthington), Fina Chiarelli (Doris Worthington), Joel Sturrock (Gordon Fitzgerald), Denis Simpson (Earl Finch), Peter Benson (Bobby Fitzgerald), Zak Santiago (Hugo Rodriquez), Brendan Penny (Calvin Hepburn), Neil

Grayston (Percy Andrews). **Credits:** *Producer-Writer:* Nicholas Carella, Paula Giroday, Jovanna Guguet, Fiona Vroom. *Director:* Michelle Ouellet. **Comment:** The women are attired in period costumes (1961 is specifically mentioned in one episode) and overall it is an entertaining and well acted and produced series.

Episodes: *1,2.* The Pilot. *3.* For All We Know. *4.* Count Your Blessings. *5.* What'll Do. *6.* Come on a My House.

1014 12 Steps to Recovery. youtube.com. 2010–2012.

Parrish Diaz is a struggling actor who earns extra money by writing jingles. Although not the life he really wants, he is happy mainly because he has a girlfriend (Sheryl, a corporate executive). Life changes drastically for Parrish when Sheryl dumps him and he is left in a daze, so much so that he begins to not only neglect himself, but his work as well. Seeing that an intervention is needed, his best friends Blue and Dani step in and devise a plan to mend his broken heart: set him up on twelve blind dates. Dani and Blue each choose six women for Parrish to meet and the program charts what happens on each of those dates with Parrish learning lessons about friendship, forgiveness and true love.

Cast: Kaleber Soze (Parrish Diaz), Stephen Hill (Blue Garner), Erika Myers (Dani Ulmer), Candice Lenoir (Sheryl Woodson), Malikha Mallette (Bernie Johnson), Celester Rich (Dr. Augusto Fondue), Mario Corry (Anthony Croce), Ashley Paige Allen (Cathy). **Credits:** *Producer:* Tony Clomax, Emelyn Stuart, Danny Weiss. *Writer-Director:* Tony Clomax. **Comment:** Very good acting combined with excellent production values makes for an enjoyable and humorous look at life's ups and downs as faced by Parrish.

Episodes: *1.* Act Like a Man. *2.* Spoken Word. *3.* Tastes Like Kandi. *4.* Chicken and Biscuits. *5.* Out of Your League. *6.* Harlem Nights. *7.* Barack and Michelle. *8,9.* Packed with Secrets. *10,11.* The Method. *12.* Speed Dating. *13.* A Walk in the Park.

1015 Twenty-Five. watchtwentyfive.com. 2013.

Two years after graduating from college and having gone their separate ways, three friends (Beryl, Jimmy and Taylor) reconnect in New York City for a reunion. The journey each has (and will) take as they navigate life as adults is chronicled.

Beryl is an aspiring actress and struggling to make her mark on the world. She has been in a relationship with a man she met in college but is unsure if they have a future together. Jimmy (gay) is an Internet blogger, still single and looking for his significant other. Taylor, a teacher (for the Teach For America program in Missouri) has relocated to Manhattan

hoping to find a better job and a place to call home.

Oakley is the man Taylor meets in Central Park and with whom she begins a relationship. Kyle is Beryl's gay friend (whom she met in yoga class) that Jimmy has a difficult time accepting. Kendall is a bit-off-the-wall girl who becomes Beryl's rival in everything.

Cast: Brennan Caldwell (Jimmy), Jordy Lievers (Beryl), Charles Andrew Callaghan (Kyle), Alex Trow (Taylor), Patrick Barrett (Oakley), Danny Binstock (Patrick), Jessica DiGiovanni (Kendall). **Credits:** *Producer:* Randall Stone, Sam Duboff, Linda Berkeley. *Writer-Director:* Josh Duboff. **Comment:** Enjoyable program with good acting and production values.

Episodes: *1.* The Only Normal Ones. *2.* Cindy and Carl. *3.* Kendall's Party. *4.* I Forgot the Crab.

1016 25 and Married. webserieschannel.com. 2013.

Nicholas and Brittany are a young married couple who love each other but do not always get along with each other or agree with what the other says or thinks. The couple can (and do) get on each other's nerves and the program relates those instances when something enters their lives and they attempt to resolve it.

Cast: Nicholas Mills (Nicholas), Brittany Lauren Djie (Brittany). **Credits:** *Producer:* Nicholas Mills, Brittany Lauren Djie, Chris Tover, Ryan Chan. *Director:* Stephen Wolfe. *Writer:* Nicholas Mills, Brittany Lauren Djie. **Comment:** The acting, as well as the production is very good and the program humorous and enjoyable.

Episodes: *1.* Over and Under. *2.* The Narrator. *3.* Fold. *4.* Going Green. *5.* Not Tonight. *6.* Fireside. *7.* Three Way. *8.* The F Word. *9.* Macho Man. *10.* Dream Spouse. *11,12.* Anniversary.

1017 21 Days of Seaton. 21daysofseaton.com. 2013.

Michael Seaton, now living in Los Angeles but set to begin a job in New York, is a young man who, after a ten year absence from his home town, returns for a three week visit to reconnect with his close-knit group of high school friends: Amber, Shaun, Lucas, Lee and Johnny. Michael is welcomed back, crashes at Shaun's home and finds, like himself, that in a way they are still like their former teenage selves. As the friends reunite, Michael soon finds himself immersed in their culture and back in his old element (and a part of their seemingly care-free lives). Each episode is a look at one day in Michael's life and what happens when, as an old saying goes, "Once you leave, you can never go back" (here to the way things were with Michael realizing that once the initial fun ride is over, he needs to steer his friends in a better direction).

Cast: Harold Littrell (Michael Seaton), Chad Perkins (Shaun Sellers), Kelly Franklin (Amber Green), Kody Kiser (Diesel Washington), Michele Breeze (Alex Parker), Joshia Bentley (Johnny Durbin), Kim Dixon (Jenny Kim), Jenny Wells (Kacie Durance), David Cottingham (Lee Richards). Credits: *Producer:* Chad Perkins, David Cottingham, Russell Johnson, Casey Cooley, Kim Dixon. *Director:* Chad Perkins, David Cottingham, Russell Johnson, Casey Cooley. *Writer:* Chad Perkins, David Cottingham. Comment: A well-developed idea with good acting and production values.

Episodes: *1.* The Arrival. *2.* Our Hangover. *3.* Shower Cam. *4.* Hand Job. *5.* The Ex. *6.* Top Five. *7.* Audition Tape. *8.* Bourbon Night. *9.* The V. *10.* Downloading Diesel. *11.* Ghost Blunders. *12.* The Naping. *13.* My Wingman. *14.* Blue Milk. *15.* Tweet Tweet. *16.* Lucky 12. *17.* Reality Bites. *18.* Closet Case. *19.* Caller IDea. *20.* Sweet Revenge. *21.* The Farewell.

1018　*Two Chairs Two Beers.* 2c2b.tv. 2014.

Dumpsworth, Missouri, is a town that down-on-their luck people call home. There is not much to do but brood over the situation one finds himself in and for excitement the local bar provides a brief escape from misery. Dan Fingerberry is a film maker who has come to the town to document how people here view life. Each episode is a depiction of two of the townspeople and what discussion occurs as they drink their sorrows away.

Cast: Kevin Feehery (Dan Fingerberry), Mark Bisi, Greggory Daniels (All Other Charcaters). Credits: *Producer:* Mark Bisi, Greggory Daniels. Comment: The humor lies in the conversations that are being conducted. There is some comedy, but mostly just talk.

Episodes: *1.* Dolph Turbo & Thomas Weatherington. *2.* Scott Rathfelder & Will Keats. *3.* Lance Blimpton & Vinny Turilli. *4.* Arnie Quick & Glenn Waldinger.

1019　*Two Death.* youtube.com. 2013.

Frank and Francis are minions from Hell who find their lives turned upside down when they are ordered to take a vacation in the above world and live among humans. They choose a flat in London and share it with a female named Saskia. Unknown to Frank and Francis is that their superiors in Hell are using them as guinea pigs in an experiment for Hell Up Top, a program designed to operate a Hell above its lower depths down below. The program is basically a look at how Gabriel, their superior conducts the experiment with Frank and Francis not only attempting to adjust to life above ground and with the living, but how they meet their challenge: disposing a man they kill (Leigh) without exposing the fact that they are actually Death.

Cast: James "Smurf" Dunnell-Smith (Frank), John Woodburn (Francis), Matt Orton (Gabriel), Lucy Evans (Saskia), Rich Spencer (Leigh), John Conway (Humbert), Josh Smith (Quentin). Credits: *Producer:* Emma Moffat, Amber Phillips, Matt Orton. *Director:* Alice Malin, Jack Rose, Harvey Eaton, Matt Orton, Sam Riley, Guen Murroni. Comment: British produced dark comedy that presents an interesting concept and capable acting but the camera work takes some getting use to (as apparently only one camera is used and it pans, too quickly, across the screen to capture what happens with characters, making you a bit dizzy watching it). While Frank and Francis are established as Two Death from the beginning, their wearing the traditional black Reaper outfits makes little sense as they are suppose to just blend in, not stick out and make people wonder why they appear like the Grim Reaper. There is also an abundant amount of vulgar language which certainly was not needed for this concept.

Episodes: 6 untitled episodes, labeled "Episode 1" through "Episode 6."

1020　*Two Doors Down.* twodoorsdowntv. com. 2009.

Kevin Stone (co-owner of a company that creates infomercials) and Jennifer Pierce (a housewife) are divorced but share custody of their son, Daniel. But commuting to be with Daniel has caused problems for Kevin. He solves them by moving into Jennifer's neighborhood and into a house just two doors down from hers in Columbus, Ohio. Kevin and Jennifer have also moved on romantically with Jennifer married to Steven (an English professor) and Kevin involved with Summer, a new-age hairstylist who is much younger than he is. Kevin and Jennifer each have their own ideas about how Daniel should be raised and the program follows the complications that arise as they go about parenting but not always able to do what they would like as they each have to deal with their new love interests and the influence they present on Daniel.

Cast: Louie Cowan (Kevin Stone), Amber Mikesell (Jennifer Pierce), Bill McKinley (Steven Pierce), Jessica Cameron (Summer Perkins), Jaden Montgomery (Daniel Stone), Scott Summitt (Baxter Neugaus). Credits: *Producer:* Louie Cowan, Scott Summitt. *Director:* Louie Cowan. Comment: The catchy opening theme immediately captures your attention and the program, with its excellent acting and production values, flows smoothly from episode to episode; in fact, it is so well done that it can compare to most network sitcoms as being up to their standards.

Episodes: *1.* Home Sweet Home. *2.* Surprise Ingredient. *3.* The House Warming Gift. *4.* Size Matters. *5.* Milk Wars. *6.* Man vs. Nature. *7.* Good Neighbors. *8.* Talk of the Town. *9.* The Cat's Meow.

10. The Cat's Out of the Bag. *11.* Baby Blues. *12.* Hard Times.

1021 Two Dudes and a Van. youtube.com. 2013.

Walker and Brad are the two dudes of the title, enterprising young men who are hoping to launch a career as filmmakers. As they drive the open road in their van and concoct various movie scenarios, most of which are awful, the program explores how such plots would look with Walker and Brad playing out their stories and characters.

Cast: Brad Martocello (Walker), Walker Hare (Brad). **Credits:** *Producer:* Paul Bomba, Walker Hare, Brad Martocello. *Director:* Paul Bomba. *Writer:* Walker Hare, Brad Martocello. **Comment:** As obscure as the plot sounds it does work and watching the dudes becoming the characters their warped minds create is part of the fun. It is also well produced and acted.

Episodes: 4 untitled episodes, labeled "Episode 1" through "Episode 4."

1022 2/8 Life. facebook.com. 2008–2009.

A spin off from the web series *Quarterlife* (see entry) that relates humorous events in the life of Angela Curtis, a vlogger as she and her friends (Rayanne, Jordan and Brian) seek direction now that they are adults.

Cast: Nellie Barnett (Angela Curtis), Dan Campagna (Brian), Jestin Lentz (Jordan), Emily Fox (Rayanne), Bob Wiltfong (Bob). **Credits:** *Producer-Writer:* Marc Campbell, Jamie Flam, Daniel F. Granof. *Director:* Matt Vascellaro. **Comment:** With all episodes taken off line a comment is not possible.

Season 1 Episodes: 5 untitled episodes, labeled "Episode 1" through "Episode 5."

Season 2 Episodes: *1.* The End? *2.* The 23-Year-Old Virgin. *3–5.* The Valley. *6.* Down and Out in the Valley. *7.* Race to the Bottom. *8.* Work It. *9.* What Goes Around. *10.* Home Sweet Home.

1023 Two Girls, One Asian. 2girls1asian.com. 2014.

Caela and Kelliye are best friends and actresses seeking a role that could change their lives forever. They are each half-Asian, share a New York apartment and face the same problems: boyfriend troubles, financial woes, non-rewarding auditions but most importantly, "the social muck of being ethnically ambiguous." But no matter what life throws at them Caela and Kelliye value their friendship the most and the program follows their efforts to deal with all the heartaches they encounter while waiting for their big break and stardom.

Cast: Kelly Coburn (Kelliye), Kaela Mei-Shing Garvin (Caela), Alton Alburo, Tony Vo (Winston Wong), Max Carpenter (Devin the Bro), Travis Baird (Stephen the Bro). **Credits:** *Producer:* Kaela Mei-Shing Garvin, Kelly Coburn, Dorian Carli-Jones, Tyler Byrnes. *Director:* Dorian Carli-Jones. *Writer:* Kelly Colburn, Kaela Mei-Shing. **Comment:** Comedy series featuring Asian-Americans on the Internet are very few but always very good. *2 Girls, 1 Asian* is no different (the title refers to each of the women being half Asian thus 2 make 1 girl). The acting and production is very good and the leads appealing.

Episodes: *1.* Meet Caela and Kelliye. *2.* New Suitors. *3.* The Cousins. *4.* A World of Song and Dance. *5.* Comic Book Knowledge. *6.* Everyone's a Little Bit Racist, Right? *7.* The Road Trip.

1024 Two Guys One Truck. vimeo.com. 2014.

Kenton and Nick are young men with vision: start their own business as furniture movers. With some money and a little bit of luck they manage to buy a truck and establish their business—Two Guys One Truck. The mishaps that occur as Kenton and Nick begin operations—with customers that are, for the most part, anything but normal are chronicled.

Cast: Kenton Remmey (Kenton), Nick Reunhardy (Nick), Lilly Harrison (Jamie Devereaux), Rhys McArthur (Bishop), Jordan Warren (Thad), Jolene Kay (Billie Ryan), Annie Boon (Melissa), Luke Barnett (Nathaniel), Samatha Gangal (Madison). **Credits:** *Producer:* Michelle Maxwell, Francesca Palombo. *Director:* Danny Herb. **Comment** Programs about moving men on television are practically non-existent (several failed pilot films were made) and the subject matter is wide open. Wisely choosing not to become a slapstick comedy but a subtle comedy works here with a situation being established with little or no fanfare then, from out of the blue, the unexpected happening with Kenton and Nick suddenly faced with a problem and what to do. The acting and production values are good and the idea has potential to be further expanded upon and developed into a TV series.

Episodes: *1.* You Were Moveable. *2.* I Could Tell You More About Radishes. *3.* It Is Our Choices Who Show Who We Really Are. *4.* A Thing of Beauty Is a Joy Forever. *5.* Then the Drink Takes You. *6.* More Than Kind (Less Than Kind). *7.* Sic Sempter Tyrannes.

1025 Two Jasperjohns. twohasperjohns.com. 2011.

Believing that Brooklyn, New York, offers them greater opportunities to pursue their life's goals, four of nine gay, red-headed dysfunctional brothers (Joel, Jonas, Joseph and Jude Jasperjohns) leave their home in Ohio and head for what they believe are greener pastures. The brothers are not a bit alike, somewhat eccentric and have yet to adjust to life in a larger city. Each season is an overall look at one of a brothers' eccentricities and how they attempt to either deal with it or overcome it—without killing each other first. The other, not seen brothers are Jenkins, Jebediah, Jim, James and Geoffrey.

Cast: Jim Noonan (Jude Jasperjohns), Vinny Lopez (Joseph Jasperjohns), Tim Harrington (Jonas Jasperjohns), Michael Hartney (Joel Jasperjohns). **Credits:** *Producer-Writer-Director:* Vinny Lopez. **Comment:** While the brothers are eccentric they also like to use foul language. The story arcs are amusing and the acting is very good. The program itself is well done and how they deal with life being gay is only a surface issue and not one that involves sexual situations.

Season 1 Episodes: "White Pants." Deals with Joseph's obsession with a pair of white pants that he believes are mystical and only good things can happen to him when he wears them.

Season 2 Episodes: "It." The problems the brothers face when they attempt to care for a gay dog.

Season 3 Episodes: "Personal Wealth." Jude contemplates his wealth; Joseph begins a quest to discover the meaning of life (his "Forever Love" philosophy) and Joel faces the fact that he is turning 52.

1026 Type Cast. typecastwebseries.com. 2014.

Audrey and Corinne have been friends even before they were born (as their mothers, best friends and pregnant at the same time, planned just that and placed them together in a playpen). It worked. They remained friends through grammar and high schools and when they went their separate ways for college they stayed in touch and visited each other during spring, winter and summer breaks. Audrey and Corinne, now college graduates, have decided to move to New York to pursue their dreams of becoming actresses. Being friends and living apart appeared to be the key to their long lasting friendship as the girls are as different as night and day.

Audrey is temperamental when she doesn't get her way and becomes difficult until she calms down; Corinne has a short fuse when something does not go her way and could "explode" if she doesn't relax. Despite their differences, they choose to live together and stories relate their adventures as they seek those acting careers—made more difficult as they find themselves often competing against each other for the same roles (and what better way to get that role? By sabotaging the other's chances, yet still remain friends?).

Cast: Brisa Freitas (Audrey), Celine Dayan-Bonilla (Connie), Hannah Miller (Rainbow), George A. Redner (Larz), Gavin Eastlack (Tristan). **Credits:** *Producer:* Brisa Freitas. *Director:* Kevin Ralston, Celine Dayan-Bonilla. *Writer:* Celine Dayan-Bonilla. **Comment:** The leads are captivat-

ing, the storyline, while not original, is well updated and amusing and there are numerous situations for the girls to encounter. Add to this good acting and production values and an enjoyable program emerges

Episodes: *1.* Pilot. *2,3.* Rainbow.

1027 U Jelly? webserieschannel.com. 2012.

Detective Dobbs is a veteran police official who has been on the force for over 20 years. He enjoys his morning (and seemingly afternoon and evening) donuts at Jelly Modern Doughnuts and has a serious problem: he has always had partners he could not stand. Dobbs, currently without a partner, suddenly finds his life changing for the better when he is teamed with Detective Sunshine, a very pretty younger woman to whom he finds an immediate attraction. With the doughnut shop as the principal set, the program charts the romance that slowly develops between Dobbs and Sunshine with several episodes devoted to Dobbs struggling to discover if the man Sunshine claims to be her boyfriend (Wendel) is real or just someone she made up.

Cast: Andy Curtis (Det. Dobbs), Nicola Elson (Det. Sunshine). **Credits:** *Director:* Scott Westby, Anna Cooley, Jason Long. *Writer:* Scott Westby, Jason Long, Kevin Doree, Matt Watterworth. **Comment:** With doughnuts and cops being closely associated someone finally had the sense to do a cop show and set it in a doughnut shop. Strange as it may seem, it works due to the acting of its two leads who are, at first like the opposite poles of a magnet and can't connect.

Episodes: *1.* New Partner. *2.* Merry Christmas, Now Shoot Me. *3.* Maybe This Wasn't a Good Idea. *4.* New Year, New Sunshine. *5.* Valentine's Day. *6.* Show Me a Picture. *7.* My Heart Belongs to This Invisible Emu. *8.* Wendel on His Mind. *9.* Kiss Me Beneath the Milky Latte. *10.* Dirty Dueling.

1028 Ugly Love Web Series. youtube.com. 2012.

Just because one may not look like a Marilyn Monroe or Cary Grant that does not mean that someone can't find love. Believing that the unattractive need to find each other, an enterprising entrepreneur named Leonard Love creates The Ugly Love Dating Service for the least desirable singles. The program relates the profiles each of the daters post as they seek that one special person in a world built around the fact that somehow pretty is better.

Cast: Devin Peacock (Leonard Love), Joe Vitale (Mitch Splendor), Sussan Cordero (Margarita Del La Vega), Geoffrey Paydon (Chris Thompson), Kristin Cantwell (Margie Turtleson), Nikki Jenkins (Karisma), Cat Migliaccio (Daisy May). **Credits:** *Producer:* Devin Peacock, David Velesaca. *Director:* David Peacock. **Comment:** The program opens with

Leonard introducing a client who then proceeds to make his or her video profile that he/she hopes will impress another in his/her category. The idea sounds good but focusing entirely on the client making a profile is not always interesting and is, at times, rather boring.

Episodes: *1*. Sh*t Douchey Musicians Say. *2*. Knocked Up in Washington Heights. *3*. Daisy May Loves Doritos. *4*. Karisma Wants You to Make It Rain. *5*. I Work Out. *6*. Southern Charm. *7*. Geeks Need Love Too.

1029 Uncensored Hollywood. webseries channel.com. 2014.

Mark Logan is a conceded acting teacher (at The Mark Logan Theater in Los Angeles) and author of the book *How to Act Like Mark Logan*. Where Mark learned his craft is a mystery as he is literary deranged and his teaching methods anything but rational ("We teach you to act, react and how to act like you're reacting"). Mark's life appears to have been rift with sex, alcohol, drugs and lies and with that "knowledge" he attempts to teach aspiring thespians how to act.

Cast: Mark Lee (Mark Logan), Elena Milinauskyte (Elena), Roxanne Sinclair (Roxanne), Daniel Robertson (B-Roll), Grace Harryman (Grace), Guillermo Lozano, Teferi Seifu (Teferi), Ben Chamberlain (Ben). Credits: *Producer:* Alexandra Guarnieri. *Writer-Director:* Derek Reid. Comment: Mark Lee is quite convincing as the deranged teacher with the overall production well acted and produced.

Season 1 Episodes: SNL Tennessee Williams. *2*. Game of Thrones: The Amateurs. *3*. Sister Act vs. Lethal Weapon. *4*. The King's Speech—Made in Hollywood. *5*. The Quintessential Ne***. *6*. The Witch Doctor. *7*. The Thespian. *8*. The Love Triangle. *9*. I Kissed a Girl. *10*. Arnold Schwarzenegger and Godot. *11*. The Glenn Manners Epic Trailer. *12*. Casting 101. *13*. Assisted Living.

Season 2 Episodes: *1*. Great Show. *2*. I'll Have What She's Having. *3*. Yes and... *4*. The Hollywood Match Maker. *5*. Camera Love. *6*. It Takes 2. *7*. Dead Ringing.

1030 Under the Affluence. youtube.com. 2012.

The Powerball Lottery has a jackpot of $22 million. A young man named Evan becomes its winner but unlike virtually anyone who has won that much money, it doesn't really seem to affect him. His friends, August, Noah and James feel like they have also won the lottery and they have taken it upon themselves to help him find different ways to use the money. As they plan, the unthinkable (and with astronomical odds against it) August also wins the lottery. Now, with two best friends as lottery winners, they become the subjects of a documentary film maker who believes he has an Emmy-winning production waiting to be made—*Luck Buddies*. The program follows the four friends as they first devise ways Evan should spend his money then on Evan and August as they become the stars of a big budget documentary.

Cast: Evan Sheppard, Justin Tyrrell, Nate Gust, Travis Lindner. Comment: Don't expect an episode of the TV series *The Millionaire* or *Lottery* as the program is a rather uneventful look at a lottery winner. There are no plans for Evan to really change his life or any real excitement over the fact at what has happened. It is simply a look at four friends whose lives face little change after what has happened.

Episodes: *1*. Pilot. *2*. The Next Day. *3*. Catfished. *4*. Jew's Clues. *5,6*. Luck Buddies. *7*. James and Evan. *8*. Noah and August. *9*. Evictus. *10*. Finale.

1031 Undergrad. vimeo.com. 2013–2014.

Brooke and Bryce (girls) and their male friend Dillon are facing the next phase in their lives: transitioning from teenager to adult as they begin their junior year as college undergraduates at the University of Arizona. Incorporating improvised dialogue, the program relates what happens as the three friends tackle life head on. The friends are also members of a fictional improvisational group called Second Wind (and in constant confrontations with their rival group Space Wolf, headed by Michael, Bryce's ex-boyfriend). Although the program ends unresolved, it has left the doorway open to continue two storylines: Dillon's efforts to rebound after he is cut off financially from his family (and must now work to sustain himself) and Brooke, after a near-

Undergrad. Dillon Olmanson, Brooke Hartnett, Bryce Villalpando (used by permission of Brooke Hartnett).

death experience from choking on a crouton, to end her status as a virgin (Brooke, while pretty, is a bit awkward when it comes to the opposite sex and it appears that taking advice from her friends regarding dating will further intensify her insecurities).

Cast: Brooke Hartnett (Brooke), Dillon Olmanson (Dillon), Bryce Villalpando (Bryce), Michael Campbell (Michael). **Credits:** *Producer-Writer-Director:* Brooke Hartnett, Dillon Olmanson, Bryce Villalpando. **Comment:** The cast does an excellent job of improvising as it is difficult to tell that it is not a fully scripted program. Network and cable programs have attempted the same premise and in many cases such programs are well done; *Undergrad* falls into the well done category and is not a victim of over acting or improvised dialogue that leads into ridiculous situations (as can be seen on programs like *Whose Line Is it Anyway?*).

Episodes: *1.* The American Dream. *2.* First Day of School. *3.* Identity Crisis. *4.* Cut Off. *5.* Losing It. *6.* Throwing Up or Throwing Down.

1032 Underpaid. webserieschannel.com. 2013.

Northridge, California, is one of many states that sponsor group homes. But The Group Home (as it is called here) is perhaps one a very few that exist where the welfare of the staff is a higher priority over the residents of the home. Frankie, Levi, Rossy, Keke, Rob and Miki are the staffers and while they cover each other's backs at the expense of their charges, they somehow manage to find some spare time to help those who really require guidance. With their own personal issues to contend with, bad pay and a low morale, the program chronicles how a dysfunctional staff not only manages to use drugs and keep their jobs, but how they actually do some good for others.

Cast: Steve Turner (Rob Black), Jeri Wingo (Rossy Oldbert), The Lady Mac (Mikki Wrongmen), Cinderella Graham (Keke Ellis), Levi A. Otis (Levi Hamilton), Dominic Oliver (Frankie Tapatio), Perry Greer (Stainy), Bryan Mathews (Taylor), Malcolm Bowen (Tyler), Raymundo Herrejon (Michael), Kyle Allen (Adonis), Anjie Gallardo (Lisa). **Credits:** *Producer:* Levi A. Otis, Athena Haley. *Director:* Willie Macc. **Comment:** Rather poorly presented program that loses its direction as it is not easy to follow. Dialogue is difficult to understand at times due to room acoustics and the characters are not appealing or even likeable. The rap theme is the most objectionable part as it contains vulgar language.

Episodes: *1.* 'Cause I'm a Lady. *2.* Levi Calls Off. *3.* It's Your Birthday. *4.* Was That My Drank? *5.* The New Client. *6.* Rossy Goes Down. *7.* Uninvited Guests.

1033 The Undrawn. youtube.com. 2012.

SuperCorp is a super hero organization with its pristine as well as its less prestigious members: Jack-Off, Rearview, Iron Gut, Bullet Proof, Thought Whisperer and In & Out. The six enjoy getting drunk and are ineffective when it comes to battling evil but they also realize that they must change their position and make a name for themselves to gain the ultimate recognition: being drawn in a comic book. The bottom feeders, as they are called, are led by a similarly dysfunctional boss and the program charts their sincere (?) efforts to become real super heroes especially when they learn that a movie deal is also pending.

Cast: Graham Kent (Jack-Off), Vittorio Cortese (Rearview), Sara Miller (Thought Whisperer), Tracey Beltrano (In & Out), Scott Goldman (Iron Gut), Damien Gulde (Bullet Proof), Peter Bloch-Hansen (The Boss). **Credits:** *Producer-Writer:* Jason Butler, Brett Butler. *Director:* Jeffrey P. Nesker. **Comment:** The program is rather deceiving in what really transpires during each episode: adult themes, sexual situations and vulgar language. Each episode is dedicated to one of the supposed super heroes and does nothing but focus on some sexual situation. There is no parental warning and one can easily be mislead by what the program's website synopsis does not state.

Episodes: *1.* Rearview from the Hill. *2.* The Pocket Protector. *3.* Recycled Justice. *4.* Gut Check. *5.* Host This!

1034 The Unemployed. unemployedseries. com. 2011.

Dymatic International is a company suffering from the after effects of a poor economy. To make up for lost revenue, it has elected to fire some of its employees, including Oskar (sales representative), Crystal (accounting department) and Kent (tech support). The three are friends but are now faced with unemployment. While they do receive their unemployment benefits, they realize that they need to find new jobs and the program charts their efforts to help each other in their search for work in a time when jobs are scarce and unemployment is rampant.

Cast: Eddie Deirmenjian (Oskar Grant), Justy Hutchins (Crystal Lucena), Mark Valentin (Kent Clark). **Credits:** *Creator-Executive Producer:* Eddie Deirmenjian, Justy Hutchins. *Producer:* Jonathan Suhadolnik. *Director:* Eddie Deirmenjian. **Comment:** A sensitive topic at the time that is well acted and presented.

Episodes: *1.* The Unemployment Mixer. *2.* The Clinic. *3.* Pub Quiz. *4–6.* The Interview. *7.* The Crack House.

1035 The Unemployed Mind. vimeo.com. 2012.

The Unemployed. Series poster art (copyright The Group Collectively).

Patrick and Geoff are unemployed friends looking for jobs (presumably in the entertainment field) that will take them out of the lower depths of poverty. In the meantime, they take what ever jobs they can find until that day when they can realize their dreams and live the good life (or as good as it can get just struggling to make ends meet).

Cast: Timmy Morgan (Geoff Murphis), Luke Custer (Patrick Ladladie). **Credits:** *Producer:* Luke Custer, Josh Long. *Writer:* Josh Long, Luke Custer. *Director:* Josh Long. **Comment:** Well acted and presented program that comically tackles what some people will do to make money.

Episodes: *1.* Party Time. *2.* There's No People Like Show People. *3.* Something's Fishy. *4.* Jeeves and Lester. *5.* Apartment Hunt.

1036 Unicorn Plan-It. unicornplan-it.com. 2011–2014.

A woman named J (who prefers to be called "The Boss Lady") owns Unicorn Plan-It, a Los Angeles-based planning company. She is assisted by her lesbian staff: Keesha, "The emotionally promiscuous girl," Vick, "a lady getter," Bambi, a Lipstick Lesbian (and J's lover); Harmony, a woman who runs a meditation service called "Harmony Om" and the lone gay male of the group, Miguel. Stories follow the relationship each worker has with the other coupled with their individual pursuits to find happiness with that special someone.

Cast: Haviland Stillwell (Harmony), Sarah Croce (Keesha), Sherri D. Sutton (J), Catherine Wadkins (Bambi), Amir Levi (Miguel), Ashley Reed (Vick), Deborah S. Craig (Bree), Alexandra Grossi (Molly), Wendy Guerrio (June), Bruce Dern (Pitch), Idara Victor (Ariel). **Credits:** *Producer-Writer:* Sarah Croce, Ashley Reed, Haviland Stillwell. *Director:* Kim Rocco Shields, Ashley Reed, Haviland Stillwell. **Comment:** The acting is good, the characters like-able and the production values also very good. Veteran movie and TV actor Bruce Dern adds a nice touch to the series as Pitch.

Season 1 Episodes: *1.* VaGchat. *2.* Bang,It.Out. *3.* A Single Ceremony. *4.* #OMmy-God. *5.* Hunting Bambi. *6.* Maybe Not Yet.

Season 2 Episodes: *7.* And So It Is. *8.* Awkward/Awesome. *9.* Kiss Kiss Dang Dang. *10.* Across the YOUniverse. *11.* Dinah Blow Your *Unicorn* Horn. *12.* Come Together. Right Now. Over Me.

1037 Un-Mate. un-mate.com. 2012–2014.

Candy was a very pretty young woman who purchased an anti aging cream over the Internet. On the day it arrives, she quickly opens the box and places the cream on her face. Just then her phone rings and in her rush to answer it, trips and kills herself when her head hits the floor. But she does not die; she resurrects as a zombie. Rufus is a world champion video game player but overly addicted to playing video games, so much so that he vows to play them until they kill him. During one such session, he falls from his chair, hits his head and, like Candy, kills himself. And like Candy, returns as a zombie. Exactly how Candy and Rufus met each other is not shown, but they somehow become a couple and vow to live life as they once did. They begin by purchasing a home that contains Micus, a violently deranged creature that is chained to the walls and lives in an upstairs room. Jo is a young woman, living in Dublin, and seeking an apartment. Rufus and Candy, in their zombie state, are having a difficult time paying bills and just managing to live, and decide to rent out one of their rooms. Several people have answered the ad, but once seeing Rufus have fled for their lives. Jo is an exception. She sees nothing wrong with Rufus, Candy or even the cobwebbed house and agrees to

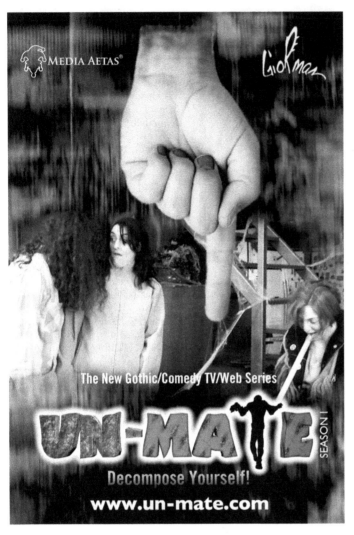

Un-Mate. Series poster art (used by permission).

move in. Rufus and Candy both see her, at first, a threat as she may call the police (or their worst fear, a priest) if she ever realizes that they are zombies. But being zombies makes mobility and speech difficult and they need her to perform things they can no longer do, like buying groceries. A young girl, two zombies, a violent creature and what happens as each tries to live a normal life.

Season two episodes drop the above format to focus on Stan, a skeleton who now lives in the house but doesn't quite realize he is a skeleton and proceeds to live a normal life. Stan is credited as Stan. Season 3 episodes eliminate the Stan character to focus on three nasty puppets (Alpha, Delta and Chevrolet) as they now live in the house and seek a way to terminate the human race. Alpha is the supreme general of the neilA Army; Delta is the chief medical officer of the neilA Army and the

brains behind ways to eliminate the human race. Chevrolet is an intern with the neilA Army and assigned to Alpha for training.

Cast: Giovanna Sanatore (Jo), Cristiana Tirabassi (Candy), Norman Russo (Rufus), Ferrante Orcese (Micus). **Credits:** *Producer-Composer:* Andrea Casagrande. *Director:* Giovanna Senatore, Norman Russo. *Writer:* Giovanna Senatore. **Comment:** The program, produced in Ireland, is filmed in black and white (to give it that eerie feel) with great atmosphere setting gothic music (flashback sequences are seen in color). Season 1 episodes are a pure delight; so well acted and produced that they should play on network or cable TV here in the U.S. Candy and Rufus, unable to talk (they grunt and moan) have their dialogue seen as subtitles. Second and third season episodes are a bit different. The second season features Stan, a plastic skeleton who is made to look human. The puppet creations for the third season are well made and a bit eerie.

Season 1 (2012) Episodes: *1.* Welcome. *2.* The House. *3.* The Room. *4.* Watching TV. *5.* Dinner. *6.* Candy. *7.* Rufus. *8.* Micus. *9.* I Know... *10.* Group Therapy. *11.* Having Fun. *12.* The Greatest Escape.

Season 2 (2013) Episodes: *1.* I Am Stan. *2.* New Job. *3.* Blackout. *4.* Chatting. *5.* Tele-sellers. *6.* Tattoo Time. *7.* I Am Beautiful. *8.* Hamlet. *9.* Sunday Morning. *10.* Super Hero. *12.* The Park.

Season 3 (2014) Episodes: *1.* Protocol neilA. *2.* Communication. *3.* Conquer. *4.* Extermination. *5.* Abduction. *6.* Experiment. *7.* Making Bread. *8.* Human Drone. *9.* Toilet Paper. *10.* Elvis. *11.* Hypnotic Suggestion. *12.* Back Home.

1038 *Unnatural Selection.* webserieschannel.com. 2012.

Percival, Milo, Virgil and Cedric are returning from a two week vacation when they learn that, when they were drunk and partying their lives away, a zombie apocalypse has occurred and destroyed most of the human race. With only pockets of humans remaining, the friends fear for their families in Ottawa, Canada, and set out on a journey to return home. The task is more difficult than just boarding a plane and the program follows what happens as they attempt that mission—with everything that can go wrong happening, including zombies looking for humans on which to feed. **Cast:** Lewis Hill (Percival B. Jacobs), Aaron Hill (Cedric Clark), Jay Carter (Milo Webb), Mike Halucha (Virgil "Doc" Penningsworth). **Credits:** *Producer-Writer:* Mike Halucha, Lewis Hill. **Comment:** The program begins with what looks to be a good idea but then becomes ridiculously silly with the various odd-ball characters (guests) they encounter on their journey. **Episodes:** *1.* Apocalypse How. *2.* Metamorphosis. *3.* Birth or a Villain.

1039 Unpresentable. unpresentable.com. 2014.

Los Angeles has always been the dream of people seeking a career in acting. Adam and Iam, friends who have just moved to the movie capital from Texas, are no exception. They felt that Texas had little opportunity for them and needed to go elsewhere. With what little money they have, they move into a slum of an apartment, enroll in acting class and immediately discover that becoming an actor is no easy task as they are un-presentable as they now stand. The program relates what happens when Adam and Iam befriend Dani, "a hot artsy chick," who helps them navigate the world of acting classes, agent meetings, auditions and just about everything else they encounter along the way to achieving their dreams. **Cast:** David Boswell (Adam Jamison), Levi Packer (Iam Goode), Susan Rhea Lynch (Dani Coulter). **Credits:** *Writer-Director:* Tony Clarno. **Comment:** Although Iam can become a bit annoying when he pronounces his name, the overall production is well acted and presented. Adam and Iam act as the hosts and sort of set up a situation before it is shown. **Episodes:** 10 untitled episodes, labeled "Episode 1" through "Episode 10."

1040 Unsung Heroes. youtube.com. 2012.

In a city beset by crime, a group of citizens, who possess super abilities, join together and form a less-than-desirable band of super heroes led by Phoenix Black. Phoenix, like his team, Annie Gloom, Captain Armstrong, Heather Royale and Revenant Lad, has not made the cut as a real super hero (more like D–List heroes). But each is determined to change that and rise to the status of heroes like Superman, Wonder Woman and Batman. The program charts their battle against the sinister forces of evil, here hoping to stop the deadliest group of villains the world has ever seen.

Phoenix Black is a karate champ who blends his abilities with dancing and the martial arts.

Heather Royale is a glamorous drag queen who possesses the power of super speed but is also very vain and constantly admires herself in mirrors.

Fanboy suffers from ADD (which often interferes with his crime fighting abilities) and has telepathic powers.

Captain Armstrong is the veteran super hero who was forcibly retired from #Heroes of Tomorrow. He is blessed with super strength and cursed with a bad back.

Annie Gloom is a gothic beauty who only became a super hero out of boredom and whose power of boredom causes depression in villains. **Cast:** Devin Peacock (Phoenix Black), Justine S. Harrison (Annie Gloom), Jatin Saraf (Revenant Lad), Nick Searles (Captain Armstrong), Frankie Lapace (Heather Royale). **Credits:** *Producer:* Devin Peacock. *Director:* Sussan Cordero. **Comment:** With only a 55 second trailer available it is difficult to make an accurate evaluation of what the series is actually like. While the comedy aspects can be seen, it also looks to be well-acted and produced.

1041 Untitled MF6: Bring the Rukus. untitledmf6bring-the-rukus.tumblr.com. 2012.

Six characters and the journey each encounters over the course of each episode are presented to the viewer.

Peabody is a "human" puppet (a man dressed in a puppet suit) and has just escaped from prison to reunite his old gang and resurrect his former TV series.

Gunslinger is an old-west-like cowboy determined to avenge the honor of his prostitute girlfriend by finding the men who sought her services.

Zaroot is a tribesman and standup comedian who, after losing at the Habotu of the Mozambique's Last Comic Standing, journeys to America to fulfill that dream.

Grandpa is fulfilling a bucket list of things to do. He is accompanied by his grandson who is filming their journey for a school project.

Bum is a street beggar who, after finding a friend in a dumpster, seeks a way to get out of the urban jungle.

Steven Beacon is, as described, "an incompetent idiot" and leader of a band (The Beaconators) who is seeking to make a name for himself. **Cast:** Adrian Quihuis (Gunslinger/Zaroot/Peabody/Grandpa), Steven Beacon (Himself), Maria Blasucci (Maria), Katie Bogart Ward (Holly). **Credits:** *Producer-Director:* Adrian Quihuis. **Comment:** It is not like the story "Six Characters in Search of an Author" but more of a challenge to figure out what is going on. While there is a short introduction to each of the characters, the acting and production values are not very good and the stories drag somewhat making it a bit confusing to follow as it moves along. **Episodes:** *1.* Peabody in Prison. *2.* Peabody Escapes from Prison. *3.* Gunslinger Proposes to Prostitute Girlfriend. *4.* Zaroot Competes in Habotu's

Last Comic Standing. *5.* Bum in a Dumpster. *6.* Grandpa Decides to Do a Bucket List. *7.* Steven Beacon Wants to Start a Music Career. *8.* Peabody Reunites the Boo Boo Huggingsworth Gang. *9.* Zaroot and Habotu Tribe of the Mozambique. *10.* Gunslinger Fights Back. *11.* Bum Wakes Up. *12.* Peabody and the Gang Start the Rukus. *13.* Grandpa Goes Paint Balling. *14.* Steven Starts His Solo Music Career. *15.* Zaroot Gets Chased By Lions. *16.* Bum Looks for Food. *17.* Peabody Robs an Orphanage. *18.* Grandpa Does Theater. *19.* Steven Gets Other Steven's to Join His Band. *20.* Down a Mountain on a Big Wheel. *21.* Bum Goes Through Dumpster and Trash. *22.* Peabody Goes Raping for Money. *23.* Punching Orphan Kids. *24.* Steven Beacon and the Beaconators Band Rehearsal. *25.* Zaroot Talking to Animals. *26.* Epic Fight: Robot Ladder with Samurai Sword vs. Gunslinger. *27.* The Beaconators Get a Music Manager.

1042 *Untitled Web Series About a Space Traveler Who Can Also Travel Through Time.*
theinsepctor.wix.com. 2014.

B.O.O.T.H. (Bio Organic Omnidirectional Time Helix) is a time ship that allows The Inspector, as he is called, and his companion, Piper, to travel back in time or into the future. The program charts their adventures, most notably those as they battle Boyish the Extraordinary, the mad scientist and The Inspector's most diabolical enemy. See also *What, Doctor?*

Cast: Travis Richey (The Inspector), Carrie Keranen (Piper Tate), Eric Loya (Boyish). **Credits:** *Producer:* Travis Richey. *Director:* Vincent Talenti. *Writer:* Eric Loya, Travis Richey. **Comment:** An obvious parody of the British series *Doctor Who* with very good acting and direction. Here The Inspector has a red time-traveling phone booth while The Doctor had a blue one called T.A.R.D.I.S. (Time and Relative Dimension in Space). It is based on the "Biology 101" episode of the NBC series *Community* wherein a fictional TV series called "Inspector Spacetime" was mentioned but due to copyright that name could not be used for the Internet version.

Season 1 Episodes: *1- 6:* Boyish the Extraordinary.

Season 2 Episodes: *1.* Prequel. Sets up the prem-

Untitled Web Series About a Time Traveler... Piper (left) and The Inspector. Photograph by Philip Martin (used by permission of Travis Richey).

ise for the feature film based on the series: *The Inspector Chronicles: A Motion Picture About a Space Traveler Who Can Also Travel Through Time.* Cast additions include Mayim Bailik (Voice of B.O.O.T.H.), Sylvester McCoy (Uncle Roderick), Robert Picardo (Bernard), and Chase Masterson (Annabelle Wagner). The episode was produced by Golan Ramras and directed by Nicholas Acosta.

1043 *The Unwritten Rules.* the unwritten rulesseries.com. 2012–2014.

Racey Jones is a young African-American woman who, after an exhaustive job search, acquired a position as a manager with *Giant* magazine. Although she has a degree from Brown University she feels that her color has cost her jobs. Now, believing that she has finally found a position wherein she can advance to the head of the company, she discovers that she is a black employee in a predominantly white company and that her manager title is bogus, as everyone in the office has the same status. Although she feels uncomfortable, she knows she has to give the company a chance and the program charts her experiences, mostly with her co-workers as she attempts to become a part of the American workplace (and in later episodes, work with additional black hires).

Cast: Aasha Davis (Racey Jones), Sara Fibley (Kathy), David Lowe (Peter), Kayla Banks (Jessica), Balbinka Korzeniowska (Lisa), Ebenezer Quaye (Craig), Antonio Ramirez (Derek), Gabrielle Christian (Lauren), Adam Muth (Will), Lyn Ross (Kaneisha Jackson), Christina Mendoza Lopez (Anabelle), Donnell Barrett (Westley). **Credits:** *Producer:* Kim Williams, Robert C. Mora, Michelle Clay, Aasha Davis. *Director:* Carlos Hardy, Natasha Gray, Robert C. Mora, Andrew Kowalski, Eric Mofford, Angie Comer, Balbinka Korzeniowska, Michelle Clay, Hilliard Guess, Tamarat Makonnen, David Lowe, Danny Valentine, Kim Williams. *Writer:* Kim Williams, Datra Martindale, Robert C. Mora, Joshua Olatunde. **Comment:** The program is based on the book *40 Hours and an Unwritten Rule: The Diary of a Nigger, Negro, Colored, Black, African-American Woman* and is well acted and produced. Aasha Davis is delightful as Racey and, even though her name sounds a bit racist, she is not as she tries to expel all the stereotypes that exist when it comes to African-Americans as she encounters them first hand and must find a way to deal with the negative (but not meant as degrading) situations—which she accomplishes by directing her comments to the viewer.

Season 1 Episodes: *1.* First Day. *2.* Mmm, That Smells Good. *3.* I Heard It Through the Cubicle. *4.* Let's Talk About Hair. *5.* The Whack Girl. *6.* Let's Dance. *7.* Let's Do Lunch. *8.* Just a Group of Us. *9.* But He's Black. *10.* I Don't Have Twenty on It. *11.* Merry Christmas. *12.* The Redux Episode.

Season 2 Episodes: *1.* A Change Is Comin.' *2.* The Itis. *3.* Lions, Tigers and Pig! Oh, My. *4.* Who Dun It? *5.* Safety in Numbers. *6.* We're Not That Close. *7.* Let's Go to Church. *8.* Let's Play Bingo. *9.* Rumors. *10.* Spooks and Goblins.

Season 3 Episodes: *1.* Trading Places. *2.* The N-Word. *3.* Color Blind. *4.* Guess Who's Coming to the Fundraiser? *5.* Let's Talk About Race. *6.* Let's Talk About a Review. *7.* The 7 Stages of a Decision.

1044 *Upstairs Girls.* blip.tv. 2008–2011.

Short video glimpses into the lives of Taryn, Sandy and DeeDee, twenty-something friends who share an upstairs apartment in Los Angeles as they attempt to navigate life, especially their somewhat hectic romantic lives.

Cast: Erica Rhodes (Sandy), Justine Peacock (DeeDee), Eric Patton (Mutt), Kristien Ortiz (Ashley), Jenny Star Shackleton (Christine), Danielle Vega (Michelle), Adam Sauter (Doug), Dylan Vigus (Kevin), Don Jeanes (Danny), Shawn Richardson (Alex), Drew Garrett (Colin), Andrea Jensen (Danika), Vanessa Born (Taryn), Erica Rhodes (Sandy). **Credits:** *Producer:* Paul Camuso, Al Cash, Rob Cesternino, Tim Pilleri, Scott Zakarin. *Writer-Director:* Rob Cesternino, Scott Zakarin. **Comment:** Although most episodes have been taken off line, it can be seen from those that remain that it was a well acted and produced series.

2008 Episodes, 1–20: *1.* We Are the Upstairs Girls! *2.* Girls Do It Better. *3.* How to Kiss a Girl. *4.* Girls in Bed. *5.* Girls in the Bathroom. *6.* Running Hot. *7.* Taryn's Secret Crush. *8.* Dirty Tricks. *9.* Taryn Opens Up. *10.* Mutt Is Hot for (Sarah) Palin. *11.* Bedroom Crasher. *12.* Sexy Voyeur. *13.* Under the Sheets. *14.* Wetting the Bed. *15.* Mutt Damone Jumps Sarah Palin. *16.* Taryn's Bedroom Confession. *17.* DeeDee All Alone. *18.* Sexy Shower Surprise. *19.* Swinging Ex-Boyfriend. *20.* Strangers Are Watching.

2008 Episodes, 21–40: *21.* Guess Who's Coming Upstairs? *22.* The Anti-Dude Zone. *23.* Sexy Workout. *24.* Sandra Loses It. *25.* I Only Like Her Boobs. *26.* Sex Machine. *27.* Naked Wake-Up Call. *28.* Ashley's Been Naughty. *29.* Lady Elvis. *30.* Doug Makes His Move on Sandy. *31.* The Douche Bowl. *32.* Roller Girl. *33.* Back in Sandy's Bed. *34* Ashley's Seduction. *35.* Sexy Santa Pushes It. *36.* Stuck in DeeDee's Hair. *37.* Bringing Sexy Back. *38.* Wild Aussie Girl. *39.* Catfight. *40.* Showmance Make-Out.

2008 Episodes, 41–60: *41.* Someone's Pregnant? *42.* Drunk & Turned On. *43.* Bathroom Hookup. *44.* Beautiful Hitchhiker. *45.* Back Together in Bed. *46.* Suntan Lotion. *47.* Secret Crush Revealed. *48.* Two Girls and One Town Slut. *49.* L.A. Stories from Bed. *50.* Amish Girl Gone Wild. *51.* Lovers and Fighters. *52.* Mutt Gives It to Sandy. *53.* Kiss and Tell. *54.* High School Musical Halloween. *55.* Big Booty Lover. *56.* Personal Girl Questions. *57.* Big Booty Kiss. *58.* Dirty Dancer. *59.* Girl Stuff in Bed. *60.* Fatal Seduction.

2008 Episodes, 61–80: *61.* Bathing Beauty. *62.* Sexy New Roommate. *63.* Coffee, Tea or Me? *64.* Grilling a Hooker. *65.* Pimp Wants His Money. *66.* Pimp Slappin.' *67.* Looking for Hookers. *68.* Prostitute Love. *69.* Sexy New BFF. *70.* Surprise Girl! *71.* Bikini Battle. *72.* Sex on the Beach? *73.* Three Girls One Bed. *74.* Thanksgiving Drunk Girl. *75.* The Big Blow-off. *76.* Hiding in the Shower. *77.* Sexier Than Band Camp. *78.* Upstairs Bedroom Advice. *79.* Taryn's Shocker. *80.* Pressing Taryn.

2008 Episodes, 81–98: *81.* Sandy's Will Smith Fantasy. *82,83.* Taryn's Love Letter. *84.* DeeDee Gets Her Toe Stuck. *85.* Hot New Lifeguard. *86.* Picking Up Chicks. *87.* Scrubbing Away the Shame.

88. Hung Over Party Girl. *89.* Flirt Lessons. *90.* Too Hot Twister. *91.* Three's a Crowd in Bed. *92.* Leaving for Love. *93.* New Girlfriend for Christmas. *94.* Santa Mutt. *95.* Unmerry Christmas. *96.* Hugging It Out. *97.* Playing the Field. *98.* 2008 Highlights.

2009 Episodes, 1–20: *1.* Bad New Years Eve Kiss. *2.* Hangovers and Massages. *3.* Facebook Foe. *4.* The High School Hottie. *5.* Attack of the Mean Girl. *6.* Dirty Laundry Patrol. *7.* Tease for Two. *8.* Service in the Shower. *9.* Nerds Hide from Bullies. *10.* Revenge of the Nerds. *11.* Dancing with Herself. *12.* Mutt's Bloody Valentine 3D. *13.* Sandy's New Man. *14.* Lost: The Interpretive Dance. *15.* Hot Date. *16.* Late Night Proposition. *17.* Three Girls for One Guy. *18.* Triple Girl Trouble. *19.* How to Dump Your Girlfriend(s). *20.* Pillow Talk.

2009 Episodes, 21–40: *21.* Play-Doh Super Bowl. *22.* Sisters Not Playing Nice. *23.* Yoga Party Crasher. *24.* Spiteful Hookup. *25.* Booty Call or More? *26.* Getting Hot Over Jo-Anne. *27.* Hide and Seek Horror. *28.* Sandy and Jo-Anne Go for Paul Blart Mall Cop. *29.* Bad to the Bone. *30.* Totally Busted. *31.* Not This Time of the Month. *32.* Late Valentine's Day Surprise. *33.* Mutt's Daddy Issues. *34.* A Giant Bowl of Beer. *35.* The Fitting Room. *36.* Ashley in the Shower. *37.* Bachelor Party Rules. *38.* Trying to Get Caught. *39.* Babe of the Week Advice. *40.* Mutt's Sexy Stalker.

2009 Episodes, 41–60: *41.* Switching Partners. *42.* Upstairs Girls Get Too Hot. *43.* Topless Tuesday. *44.* Sex in the Pool? *45.* Terminator Frustration. *46.* Early Morning Party Girl. *47.* Sexy New Sandy. *48.* Olive's Split Personality. *49.* Getting Behind Sandy. *50.* Sandy's Special Father's Day Song. *51.* The Competition Gets Hot. *52.* Upstairs Girls Fire Back. *53.* Chicks Talking About Guys. *54.* Life Guard Your Comments. *55.* What I Hate About Doug. *56.* Sun Screen Surprise. *57.* He Said.... She Said, At the Beach. *58.* House Sitting Girls. *59.* Daddy Issues. *60.* Splashing in the Grotto.

2009 Episodes, 61–77: *61.* Hot Commodity. *62.* Sandy After the Phish Concert. *63.* Melonie's Melon Diet. *64.* Butting In. *65.* Melonie's Harmonic Melody. *66.* Twilight, MJ—Ultimate Halloween Costumes. *67.* Melon Bowling. *68.* Blind Date Secret. *69.* Private Girl Talk By the Pool. *70.* DeeDee Is Back in Town. *71.* DeeDee's Secret Weapon. *72.* Sporty Seduction. *73.* DeeDee Blows Up. *74.* Mutt's Relationship Crisis. *75.* The Last Temptation of Man. *76.* Pool Side Pick-Up Artists. *77.* Upstairs Girls Best of 2009.

2010 Episodes, 1–20: *1.* Christine's Model Ball Coach Stealing Her Away. *2.* Mojo Rising. *3.* Stupid Jim Directs Avatar Video. *4.* Why You Should Keep Your Girlfriend Off Your Computer. *5.* American Idol Auditions. *6.* Amish Girl Gone Wild (Re-Mastered). *7.* Hate on This. *8.* A Seductive Proposition. *9.* Who Farted? *10.* The Ice Princess. *11.* Ow!! What Happened Last Night? *12.* Switching Partners By the Pool. *13.* 3 Hotties Compete for 1 Guy. *14.*

Bathing Beauty. *15.* That '50s Video. *16.* First Reaction to the Lost Finale. *17.* Rachel's Secret Crush. *18.* Father's Day in the Joint. *19.* Sexy Hitchhiker. *20.* The U–Team.

2010 Episodes, 21–39: *21.* Should We Skinny Dip? *22.* A Wookie Hits Light Speed. *23.* Wild Beach Trip. *24.* Sexy Tease for a Backseat. *25.* Nighttime Beach Girls. *26.* Stranded. *27.* Looking for a Free Ride. *28.* How to Pitch a Tent. *29.* Truth or Kiss Dare. *30.* Catching DeeDee Change. *31.* Stupid Jim's Sexy Horror Film. *32.* Day Break-Up. *33.* The Road Taken. *34.* The Upstairs Girls Return. *35.* New Roommate Surprise. *36.* Extreme Santa Babe. *37.* A Wild New Year's Eve. *38.* Sister Fight. *39.* Yoga Dogs.

2011 Episodes: *1.* Girls Playing Rough. *2.* A New Voyeur. *3.* Sex on the Beach (HD Edition). *4.* 2010 Yearbook. *5.* The Ice Princess. *6.* Sandy's Lesbian Friend. *7.* Lesbian Tug of War. *8.* Chakra Treatment. *9.* Would You Rather. *10.* Sandy Makes Her Move on Crystal. *11.* Sneaking in the Bathroom. *12.* New Girls Pressure Sandy. *13.* Sandy and the Hot New Girls. *14.* Female Bonding. *15.* Hot for Michelle. *16.* Poolside Seduction. *17.* Fighting Over a Dude. *18.* The French Kisser. *19.* Upstairs Girls Sexy Halloween Costumes. *20.* Skater Hater. *21.* Upstairs Girls Chicken Fights. *22.* Bed Hopper. *23.* 2011 Video Yearbook. *24.* Girlfriend Surprise!!

1045 *Vag Magazine.* vagmagazine.tv. 2010.

Gemma is a failing feminist magazine purchased by three friends (Bethany [a lesbian], and Fennel and Sylvie [straight]) with money earned from their Etsy business. Felling the name is unsuitable, they change it to *Vag Magazine* and through its pages attempt to teach women how to become better women. The idea sounds good, but accomplishing that goal is not quite as easy and the program charts the comical pitfalls the staff encounters as they go about making a dream come true.

Other Staff Members: Meghan, a former writer for *Gemma*; Heavy Flo, queen of the roller derby circuit; Reba, a legend of feminist pop culture journalism (author of the book *Activities with Celebrities*); and Kit. Their competition is a magazine owned by Jaybird, Bethany's ex-girlfriend.

Cast: Nicole Drespel (Fennel), Sarah Clapsell (Meghan), Jocelyn Guest (Sylvie), Kate McKinnon (Bethany), Leslie Meisel (Reba), Veronica Osorio (Heavy Flo), Morgan Grace Jarrett (Kit), Shannon Coffey (Penny), Shannon Patricia O'Neill (Jaybird). **Credits:** *Producer:* Caitlin Bitzegaio, Leila Cohan-Miccio, Zach Neumeyer, Nicole Shabtai. *Director:* Zach Neumeyer. *Writer:* Caitlin Bitzegaio, Leila Cohan-Miccio. **Comment:** The story, though littered with references to problems faced by women (as well as gutter language for female body parts), is well acted and produced. It is basically the women simply trying to figure out what to do now that they have a magazine to publish.

Episodes: *1.* Fumbling Toward Ecstasy. *2.* Reject All American. *3.* Swamp Ophelia. *4.* Feminist Sweepstakes. *5.* Living in Clip. *6.* Revelling/Reckoning.

1046 Vain. youtube.com. 2013.

Christian Vain is a man with numerous issues, the biggest being that he is, like his last name, extremely vain. Believing he needs guidance, his mother hires a beautiful young woman (unnamed) to watch over and care for him. Christian is an author and self-proclaimed philosopher who believes he has the answers that can fix the human race. Christian's attempts to solve problems through his misguided way of thinking are chronicled.

Cast: Adam Zaka (Christian Vain), Nora May (Christian's Assistant). **Credits:** *Producer:* Adam Zaka. Writer: Connoe McNulty. Director: Kevin McMahon. **Comment:** Although only a pilot was produced, it can be seen that Christian needs psychiatric help for what he does. While well acted, it does contain vulgar language.

Episodes: *1.* Pilot.

1047 Valley Meadows. youtube.com. 2014.

Gary and Tom are substitute teachers who feel they are most often sent to the worst school districts in the city. The work is not always steady and they feel they never get respect. To help overcome their feelings of unimportance, Gary and Tom produce a record album based on their love of Rap music. The CD quickly becomes a no seller, they are sharing an apartment they can't afford, money is tight and anything that can go wrong in their lives does. The program charts Gary and Tom's efforts to cope with life with what little they have (or don't have) and somehow achieve their one big goal—earn respect.

Cast: Chris Knutson (Gary), Zach Coulter (Tom). **Credits:** *Producer:* Joe Filipas, Chris Knutson. *Director:* Joe Filipas. *Writer:* Chris Knutson. **Comment:** The program begins in the middle of nowhere (no real character introduction) and ends in the middle of nowhere (no conclusion). The characterizations are a bit rough (could be a bit more refined) and overall an interesting (but not original) idea about two friends just trying to get by.

Episodes: *1.* Neil Has Had It Up to Here. *2.* South High and Columbia House. *3.* Fat Lards.

1048 Vamped Out. facebook.com. 2010.

Elliot Finke is a filmmaker who believes he has come up with the perfect idea for a documentary: chronicle the life of a real vampire. Alowisus "Al" Hewson is that vampire, a struggling actor who is continually rejected for roles in horror films for actors who look more like vampires. The program relates life as faced by a real vampire in a world where he can function as normal people, but whose abilities appear to be his biggest drawback.

Cast: Kevin Pollak (Elliot Finke), Jason Antoon (Al Hewson), Seana Kofoed (Marie), Samm Levine (Billy Goldborg), Jason McIntyre (Kenneth), Kat Steel (Ginny Lee). **Credits:** *Producer:* Jason Antoon, Amber J. Lawson, Kevin Pollak. *Director:* Kevin Pollak, *Writer:* Jason Antoon, Kevin Pollak. **Comment:** Vampire legends and myths are overlooked to present a vampire that can virtually function as a human. The comedy is quite subtle and the production, while okay, is a bit slow-moving at times.

Episodes: *1.* Al, the Vampire? *2.* Bad Blood. *3.* A New Day. *4.* A Roof with a View. *5.* Billy Saves Elliot. *6.* Hungry Hungry Al.

1049 Vampire Mob. vampiremob.com. 2013.

Mafia hit man Don Grigioni is married (to Annie) and leading a dull life but believes that becoming a vampire will change all that. Through mob connections Don is introduced to a female vampire and allows her to bite him. Annie is not pleased with the news and becomes even more upset when Don "becomes hungry" and bites her, turning her into a vampire. The situation goes from bad to worse when Annie turns her mother (Virginia) into a vampire and Don must now share his home with her also. As Don adjusts to his new life he finds that becoming a vampire was a mistake. He is not more efficient at his job, he can never really be alone with Annie and he must constantly find a source for blood. Don's observations on how tedious life has become since the change are the focal point of the program.

Cast: John Colella (Don Grigioni), Reamy Hall (Annie Grigioni), Marcia Wallace (Virginia Jones), Rae Allen (Carlina Grigioni, Don's mother), Kirsten Vangsness (Laura Anderson, Virginia's sister). **Credits:** *Producer-Writer-Director:* Joe Wilson. **Comment:** The acting and production values are good but there is an abundant use of foul language and none of the blood and gore associated with vampire legends.

Episodes: *1.* We Are All Family to a Few People. *2.* You Can't Choose Your Family. *3.* Castle on the Left. *4.* Through the Tunnel. *5.* Full Nest Syndrome. *6.* An Uneasy Alignment. *7.* Another to Do. *8.* Hit Man's Best Friend. *9.* Back to Rectifying the Situation. *10.* There's a Ying and There's a Yang. *11.* Full Nest Syndrome Plus One. *12.* Dinner for Six. *13.* Massages and Smiles. *14.* Same As the Old Boss.

1050 The Vamps Next Door. youtube.com. 2013.

The Tepes are a modern-day vampire family simply trying to live a normal life in Suburbia. Beverly, the mother is an emergency room nurse whose job not only provides her with a paycheck, but meals (blood). Walter, her husband, is an IRS auditor who can use his power of hypnotism to make taxpayers "pay up." Kate and Jimmy are their children; Emma is their "batty old grandmother" and the family pet (Shadows) is a vampire cat. Stories relate events in the undead lives of a family just trying to be themselves in a world that doesn't exactly see eye-to-eye with them.

Cast: Rachel Bailit (Beverly Tepes), Robert Smokey Miles (Walter Tepes), Daniela Hummel, Polina Frantsena (Kate Tepes), Matt King (Jimmy Tepes), Annette Pascal (Grandma Emma), Olivia Dunkley (Denise), Rae Latt (Nancy Finster), Dexter Elkin (Hal Finster), Antoinette Abbamonte (Dewey), Holly Beavon (Pamela), Jay Denton (Mike), Lynn Manning (Brian), Gabriel Cordell (Miguel). **Credits:** *Producer:* Laura Feig (Van Scotter), Phil Ramuno. *Writer:* Laura Feig (Van Scotter). *Director:* Phil Ramuno. **Comment:** A nice twist on vampire tales that is played more for laughs than horror. The program encompasses handicapped performers, something rare in an Internet series. Here Dewey, Walter's co-worker at the IRS, is deaf and unable to be hypnotized by Walter's voice; Brian is blind (turned into a vampire by Emma) and serves as the family butler; and Miguel is the family's neighbor (uses a wheelchair).

Season 1 Episodes: *1.* Meet the Tepes Family. *2.* IRS Party. *3.* MMM What's for Dinner. *4.* Shadows Runs Away. *5.* All Tied Up. *6.* Eating Dogs for Dinner. *7.* Season Finale.

Season 2 Episodes: *1.* My Nurse Is a Vampire. *2.* Harvey Gets Hypnotized. *3.* Grandma Got Fang. *4.* Neighborhood Watch.

1051 *Vampz!* youtube.com. 2012.

In a world where some people believe the Illuminati rule, one man disagrees believing that it is vampires that secretly rule. Marcus, a psychotic vampire hunter is that man and he has set his goal to destroy them all, beginning with a young woman named Simone, a very pretty Gothic girl who yearns to become a vampire and whom Marcus mistakenly believes is one. Simone is a college student and roommates with her twin brother, Sam, and an exuberant hopeful school cheerleader named Ashlee. Unknown to Simone, at first, is that Ashlee is a good vampire (turned by one of her dates) that will not harm humans (she feeds off dog blood). With the help of his dim-witted assistant Vin, Marcus sets out to destroy Simone not realizing that he is seeking the wrong girl. With Simone's discovery of Ashlee's secret Simone feels that she has, in a way, become a vampire and fulfilled her dream (which began at age 14 when her grandmother took her to see the movie *Bram Stoker's Dracula*). The program chronicles what happens when Marcus kidnaps Sam in an effort to get Simone and Simone and Ashlee's efforts to find Sam and get Marcus.

Cast: Lilly Lumiere (Simone Castillo), Christal

Renee (Ashlee Barnes), Ark Octavian (Marcus Denning), Louis Bacigalupo (Sam Castillo), Guy N. Ease (Vin). **Credits:** *Producer:* Omar Attia, Ramsey Attia, Leonard Buccellato, Jaime A. Guerra. *Director:* Ramsey Attia. *Writer:* Omar Attia, Leonard Buccellato. **Comment:** Simone also believes that because her grandmother was born in Romania she should be a vampire. While there is some vulgar language the program is partly a dark comedy with some humorous vampire-related scenes depicting Ashlee's efforts to remain a good vampire by not feeding on humans.

Episodes: *1.* I Am a Vampire, Duh! *2.* Just One Fix! *3.* All Tied Up. *4.* Let's Make a Deal. *5.* Not So Mexican Standoff.

1052 *The Variants.* youtube.com. 2009–2012.

Zeus Comics Worldwide, a comic book store in Dallas, Texas, is failing and on the verge of closing. Richard, the owner has just about given up hope, but his employees' feel there is a chance that Zeus can be saved. The unique, if not bizarre marketing promotions the staff takes to keep Zeus afloat are chronicled.

Cast: Richard Neil (Richard), Barry Fuhrman (Barry), Ken Lowery (Vlad), Keli Wolfe (Keli), Chris Haley (Terry), Curt Franklin (Svenus). **Credits:** *Producer-Director:* Jason Chinnick, Joe Cucinotti. **Comment:** Although comic book store-themed programs are rare, *The Variants* is unique in that it can sustain the concept as an actual series (as opposed to, for example, such segments on *The Big Bang Theory*). While it is well acted and produced, some story lines are a bit off-the-wall as the employees devise ways to save their jobs.

2009 Episodes: *1.* Pilot. *2.* Dead Man's Comics. *3.* The Upsell. *4.* Passholes. *5.* The Signing.

2010 Episodes: *1.* The Heist. *2.* Tsunami. *3.* Magna Mia. *4.* Power Outage. *5,6.* Serious Business.

2011 Episodes: *1,2.* Think Bigger. *3.* Man Jam. *4.* Roll for Initiative. *5.* Reboot. *6.* Fat Pants. *7.* Where There's a Will, There's a Waid. *8.* The Sellouts.

2012 Episodes: *1.* Zeus Comics Worldwide Baby. *2.* Con Game. *3.* Dicks on Comics. *4.* The Deceivers. *5.* These Boots Are Made for Walking. *6.* Occupy Zeus. *7.* Girl Drink Drunk. *8.* Breaking In. *9.* I Love Money. *10.* Behind the Svenus.

1053 *Vaughan Wylliams: Agent of Lovcraft.* webserieschannel.com. 2012.

Vaughan Wylliams is a man totally down on his luck. Unemployed, broke and hungry, he decides to get a free meal by attending a psychic group's club meeting ("Lovcraft: The League of Valleys and Cardiff Registered Adherents of Felicitous Tuning") with his housemate Zach. Ivor Crowley, the head of the group, sees something in Vaughan and decides to test his psychic abilities through a game of coin tossing. After correctly predicting the outcome of nine out-of-ten flipped coins, Ivor believes he is "The Chosen One" and offers him a position as their Psychic House Detective. Vaughan, with no real psychic powers and only his charm and wits "as his weapons," is followed as he strives to solve cases for Lovecraft, some of which are based in the supernatural.

Cast: Paul Gingell (Vaughan Wylliams), Mat Troy (Zach Ross), Boyd Clack (Ivor Crowley), Kirsten Jones (Gaella Cournaille), Sam Bees (Arthur Bon March), Denis Lennon (Rick Dedalus), Carly Price (Sylvia Rocketman), Helen Couldrey (Mrs. Ross), Gareth King (Soul Crew John), Benjamin Connell (Michael "Buster" Keaton), Ellen Ceri Lloyd (Lana Keaton), Zeljka Whittaker (Denise Kinnock), Mark Woods (Keith O'Suther), Kate Goranka Whittaker (Sam O'Suther), Hugh Griffiths (Kevin Hanson). **Credits:** *Producer:* Hugh Griffiths, Mat Troy, Paul Howard Hunt. *Director:* Hugh Griffiths, Nerys Davies. *Writer:* Mat Troy, Paul Howard Hunt. **Comment:** The program begins rather slowly in the first episode but improves in the episodes that follow. It is a British production that is a bit talkative at times but it does have good acting and production values.

Episodes: *1.* Pilot. *2.* The Lady at Roath Park Lake. *3.* Kinnock's Trade. *4.* An Affair to Forget. *5.* Pie in the Sky. *6.* Things Fall Apart.

1054 *Vegan 101.* youtube.com. 2009–2012.

People who have encompassed a vegan lifestyle but have taken it to extremes are satirized in short comedy skits wherein a group of actors portray different characters. Second season episodes focus on Dr. Eaton Wright, author of the book *Miso Soup for the Soul* (a survival guide on being a vegan) and his wife, Erica, who also co-host a TV show called *Eating Right.* While Eaton's book extols the virtues of being a vegan and provides healthy recipes, he has also created Vegano, a spray that instantly transforms anyone into a vegan. People who thrive on meaty foods but chose to use Vegano, are profiled to show how a healthier life can be achieved by becoming a vegan.

Cast: Joanne Rose (Erica Sprout-Wright), Eric Roberts (Dr. Eaton Wright), Kristina Hughes (Bianca), Brian Vermiere (Ace), Kelly DeSarla (Fan), Laurel Sherwood (Rebecca), Michael Fuller (Boyfriend), Jaime Tintor (Mark), Louisa Kendrick (Trudy), Pam Heffler (Natalie), Will Ryan (Shane), Jackie Loeb (Brenda), Henry (Kerrie-Ann Kettle-Corn), Kelly DeSarla (Fan). **Credits:** *Producer:* Joanne Rose, Eric Roberts. *Director:* John Baumgartner. *Writer:* Joanne Rose. **Comment:** The first and third seasons play like an anthology with different stories and characters involved in a vegan lifestyle. The second season is fine tuned to focus on how one man sets out to change the way people live.

Each episode is very well acted, produced and written and all in all an enjoyable program. Season 1 episodes find Joanne Rose playing Patchouli, Jessica, Girlfriend, Kim, Jane and Lynn. She is Daphne, Jackie and Samantha is the final season.

Season 1 Episodes: *1.* Dating a Vegan. *2.* Veg Book. *3.* Happy Vegan Birthday. *4.* The Raw Experience. *5.* Vegan Potluck. *6.* The Kerrie Anne Kettle Corn Show.

Season 2 Episodes: *1.* Vegano. *2.* Miso Soup for the Soul. *3.* The Book Signing.

Season 3 Episodes: *1.* The Academy of Veganology. *2.* VSI (Vegan Scene Investigation). *3.* Hyptonize.

1055 *Venus Spa.* youtube.com. 2009–2011.

It is the year 1983 and at 63 Norlorne Drive in Winnipeg, Canada stands the Venus Spa (telephone 555-FITT). It has just opened and is facing stiff competition from the other spas that dominate the state. Venus Spa, however, appears to be just a bit different as it incorporates four sexy women (Nancy, Ally, Andrea and Molly; later Jamie) who use sensual dancing coupled with exercise routines. Virtually everything the women do becomes sexy and their efforts to make their spa a success are chronicled.

Cast: Leilanie Girodmaina (Nancy), Danielle Sunley (Ally), Braeley Hobbs (Molly), Amy Simoel (Andrea), Anastasia Furlong (Jamie), Melanie Lynn Nemeck (Tina), Lexi Leibl (Missy), Alex Gancza (Amber). **Credits:** *Producer-Writer-Director:* Chris Greenaway. **Comment:** "Don't try to exercise or other stuff watching this video tape until you first consult a physician. Chad Media assumes no responsibility for any issues, totally scorched corneas or extreme sexual stimulation as a result of watching this video" are the words that are seen before episodes begin. The program is not what you think—a group of girls hustling to keep their spa open; it is very sexy young women, wearing leotards and mostly performing exercise routines. The acting and production is very good and the program is essentially women seducing the viewer.

Season 1 Episodes: *1.* Come and Knock on Our Door. *2.* Hit Me with Your Best Shot. *3.* Hot Sweaty Babes Get Hot Sweaty Dudes. *4.* Don't Stop Believing. *5.* Workout Babes Love Joysticks. *6.* Atari Intervention. *7.* Andrea's Totally Screwed. *8.* Bikini Bottoms Up.

Season 2 Episodes: *1.* Sweat Is Sexy. *2.* Use the Sex Option. *3.* Ally and the Joystick. *4.* Girls Like Playing with Toys. *5.* Bedroom Action. *6.* Thriller Action. *7.* Spandex Makeover. *8.* Take My Trainee, Please. *9.* Posse Eating. *10.* Smurf Molester. *11.* Prank Wars. *12.* Prank Wars 2: Strip and Rip. *13.* Prank Wars 3: The Posse Strikes Back. *14.* Prank Wars 4: Revenge of the Slim. *15.* Locker Confessions. *16.* Train Wreck. *17.* Train Wreck 2. *18.* Kool Aid Man Attacks. *19.* Sweating It Out.

Season 3 Episodes: *1.* Risky Business. *2.* Epic Gamer Girls. *3.* Let's Get Physical. *4.* Spandex Fashion Show. *5.* The Fun's Gonna Fly. *6.* Bananarama. *7.* Exterminate. *8.* Revenge. *9.* Possefield. *10.* Showdown. *11.* Revenge of the Nerd. *12.* Let's Make a Video. *13.* Showtime. *14.* Spandex Stage Fright. *15.* Call on Me. *16,17.* Turning Dreams Into Gold.

1056 *Very Mary-Kate.* collegehumor.com. 2010–2013.

An unofficial biography based on the life of Mary-Kate Olsen, the twin sister of Ashley Olsen (the twins who became known on the ABC TV series *Full House*). Various facts concerning Mary-Kate are used for stories with series star and creator Elaine Carroll embellishing them as Mary-Kate goes about living a life far beyond that of an ordinary college student (as she does attend NYU and acts when time permits). Mary-Kate has recently moved out of the apartment she shared with Ashley to establish her own life and separate herself as one of the Olsen Twins. She rents an apartment in the same building (and floor) as Ashley but is not as bright as Ashley (Ashley is portrayed as the more mature and responsible sister). As their sibling rivalry is explored the program also shows how Mary-Kate now lives and how she manages to navigate life on her own for the first time. Bodyguard, as he is called, is Mary-Kate's bodyguard; Phil Bines, called "Fat Professor" is Mary-Kate's History instructor at NYU; Josh is Mary-Kate's strange acting coach; Limor is a girl in Mary-Kate's class that is called "Jewish Looking Girl"; Woody Allen is the famous actor-writer; and Olivier Sarkozy, is the young man who begins dating Mary-Kate.

Cast: Elaine Carroll (Mary-Kate and Ashley Olsen), Luke Sholl (Bodyguard), Will Hines (Phil Bines), Josh Ruben (Philip Seymour Hoffman), Limor Hakim (Limor), Amir Blumenfeld (Woody Allen), Brandon Scott Jones (Olivier Sarkozy). Credits: *Producer:* Spencer Griffin. *Director:* Sam Reich. *Writer:* Elaine Carroll, Sam Reich. Comment: Exceptionally well done program with good effects showcasing Mary-Kate and Ashley speaking to each other face-to-face. Elaine Carroll does a very good job playing Mary-Kate and Ashley and captures the feel of the real twins.

Season 1 Episodes: *1.* Moving Out. *2.* Moving Day. *3.* Bodyguard. *4.* Baby. *5.* Baby Daddy. *6.* Depressed. *7.* Hangover. *8.* Fight. *9.* Philip Seymour Hoffman. *10.* Cat. *11.* Back to School. *12.* Extension. *13.* Paper. *14.* Crush. *15.* Ashley-Guard. *16.* Nightmare. *17.* Zac Efron. *18.* Hoffman 2. *19.* Gun. *20.* Back. *21.* Clone. *22.* Cheating. *23.* Woody Allen. *24.* Trick or Treat. *25.* Hoffmoween. *26.* Excuses. *27.* Presentation. *28.* Driving. *29.* Woody Allen 2. *30.* Naked. *31.* Fired. *32.* Hired. *33.* Photo Shoot. *34.* Bath. *35.* Presentation 2. *36.* Conference. *37.* Sexy Time. *38.* Sick. *39.* Confession. *40.* Church.

Season 2 Episodes: *1–4.* Vegas. *5.* Gold Rush. *6.* Presentation 3. *7.* Raise Your Hand. *8.* Magazines. *9.* Jetlag. *10.* Santa.

Season 3 Episodes: *1.* Presentation 4. *2.* Jewish Looking Girl. *3.* Layers. *4.* Call My Phon. *5.* Trenta. *6.* Evil Dragon. *7.* Police. *8.* Mug Shot. *9.* Jail. *10.* Dishwasher. *11.* Pillow Talk. *12.* Very Maggie Smith: Sex and Sexuality. *13.* Sleeping in Cars. *14.* Professor's Presentation. *15.* Slumber Party. *16.* Pills.

1057 *The Vessel.* thevesselseries.com. 2012.

Although they are a gay couple, Mike and Rory feel their lives are not complete without a child. To solve their problem, they ask their straight best friend, Kim, to become their surrogate "tummy mummy." The quest begins when they visit a surrogacy consultant and learn that (in England, the series setting) a woman who has not had a child cannot become a surrogate mother. Two solutions are offered: have sex with one of the fathers or "do it yourself" via an ovulation kit and no actual sex. Kim chooses the latter. The program presents what happens as seen through Kim's eyes as she suffers all the traumas of pregnancy while at the same time helping prepare Mike and Rory to become parents.

Cast: Lily Brown (Kim), Philip Whiteman (Mike), Giovanni Bienne (Rory), Louise Jameson (Kim's mother), Robin Soans (Kim's father), Luke Courtier (Luke), Shazia Mirza (Doctor), Daphne Kouma (Midwife), Tim Pritchett (Tim), Rib Ostlere (Rob). Credits: *Producer:* Chloe Seddon, Philip Whiteman. *Director:* Tijmen Veldhuizen. *Writer:* Chloe Seddon, Philip Whiteman, Giovanni Bienne. Comment: Delightful British-produced program that is well acted and uses the clever First Person Singular method of filming that was developed in 1946 for the feature film *Lady in the Lake* (it was also encompassed in the 1951 DuMont TV series *The Plainclothesman*) wherein the camera lens becomes the eyes of a character and everything is seen from that perspective. Here the camera is Kim and, while she is not seen (except in the last episode) characters speak to her by talking directly into the camera.

Episodes: *1.* A Mega Favor. *2.* Not Actual Turkeys. *3.* A Bit Pregnant. *4.* God Didn't Give Either of Them a Womb. *5.* The Teacher's a Psychopath. *6.* The Third Dad? *7.* Damn That's My Ex... . Tim! *8.* Stretch Marks. *9.* Ornithoscelidaphobia! *10.* It Might Feel Like You're Having a Bit of Poo.

1058 *Vexika.* vexika.com. 2010.

During the Earth's formation a meteorite crashed into what is now Arizona and fused with a mineral called Chrysocolla. It remained unknown until the mid–1800s when it was found by gold seekers; but it was only recently that scientists discovered it and found that it can facilitate the biological introduction of nanoid technology when prepared with a specific process and given in exact doses.

Victoria Bloom, a TV reporter for Channel 4 in Arizona, is also Vexika, the only successful test subject of experiments with the newly created nanoid technology (which has endowed her with super abilities). Victoria was coerced by a rogue scientist of what is called the D.A.R.P.A. Project to become a test subject. Believing she would acquire the story of the century, she never dreamed that she would never be able to tell it. Victoria's DNA was altered when the nanoids were introduced into her body and she must now feed off the exotic material that was created to produce the nanoids to survive. It appears that the only source is the failed and now deranged rejects whom she must track and kill (thus absorbing their life-giving force). Events in the life of Victoria are chronicled as she seeks the rejects (especially FR#0) to not only sustain life, but prevent them from causing harm to others. (FR#0, Failed Reject 0, is her ultimate goal. As once she defeats him, she will absorb enough nanoids to last her forever—not the days or weeks she acquires from other rejects. Only her boyfriend [her cameraman], the government, who incorporate her abilities on covert operations, and the failed rejects know of Vexika's existence. FR#0 also creates clones of himself as an army to kill Vexika before she kills him.).

Cast: Miranda Stewart (Victoria/Vexika), Dan Stewart (FR#0/Clones). **Credits:** *Producer-Writer-Director:* Dan Stewart. **Comment:** One of the few Internet series to feature an African-American super hero in the character of Vexika. Miranda Stewart is gorgeous—both as Victoria and Vexika and, even though she plays to the camera (making you know she knows she is being filmed) she pulls it off and makes the program enjoyable as a comic book come-to-life. Dan Stewart, her husband, handles all the other roles and with makeup and trick photography, also makes you believe he is more than just FR#0 and his clones.

Episodes: *1.* Pilot: Get Her. *2.* Get Her: Dark Angel Meets Everybody Loves Raymond. *3.* Get Her: Mortal Kombat Meets Princess Bride. *4.* Vexika Special: Valentine Day Message. *5.* Vexika Holiday Christmas Special *6.* Vexika Prologue.

1059 Vicky and Lysander. vickyandlysander.com. 2012–2014.

Vicky and Lysander are a married couple who live a life of luxury on Manhattan's Upper East Side. Lysander, a wealthy Southerner who inherited his money, is a playboy, known by his signature turtle-neck, who is the life of any party and a standout at art gallery openings. Vicky, born in Houston and the daughter of an oil-rich family, is the woman who landed the flamboyant Lysander and has only one goal in life: climb the New York high society ladder with him. The lives of two people and the incidents that threaten to destroy their happiness as they seek to remain the king and queen of the wealthy New York society scene are charted.

Cast: Damon Cardasis (Lysander), Shannon Walker (Vicky), Elizabeth Neptune (June), John Maybee (Jenny), Caitlin Zvoleff (Cecily), Brian Leider (Phil), Amanda Peters (Misfit), Tamara Daley (Lisa), Amy Driesler (Cass), Elizabeth Gray (Paula), Hillary Hamilton (Nancy), Alex Tonetta (Jethrob Barnaby). **Credits:** *Producer:* Damon Cardasis, Shannon Walker, Roxy Hunt, Lucian Piane, Tony Castle. *Director:* Tony Castle, Roxy Hunt. *Writer:* Damon Cardasis, Shannon Walker. **Comment:** A program that has everything: excellent acting and production values, amusing, well-done stories, non-offensive situations and characters that are absolutely captivating.

Episodes: *1.* Newlyweds. *2.* Jaunt Through Central Park. *3.* Shopping with Jethrob Barnaby. *4.* Drinks with Jenny. *5.* Crosby Street Breakdown. *6.* Downtown. *7.* Graphic Design. *8.* Surprise. *9.* Big News. *10.* Episode 10. *11.* Big News. *12.* Jenny's Fashion Studio. *13.* New Endeavors. *14.* No, No Lie. *15.* My June Lennon. *16.* Give It to Me. *17.* Rise of the Falcon. *18.* The Plot Thickens. *19.* Super Heroes. *20.* Battle Royale. *21.* Back Uptown.

1060 Video Game Reunion. vgr.atom.com. 2014.

It was the 1980s and a time when video games, especially with the introduction of Nintendo that players relished in a world that included characters such as plumbers Mario and Luigi, the heroic blue Mega Man, Princess Peach (Mario's ex-wife) their daughter, Lil P, the sexy, alien-killing Samus and Link, the man who risked all to save the forever-in-peril Zelda. But as time passed, the youth of the era grew up and eventually forgot about the heroes who once amused and entertained them. And the heroes, without inspiration from their human players, fell into a life misery and obscurity. On the occasion of the twenty-fifth anniversary of their "birth," the heroes are invited to Las Vegas for a reunion that will hopefully reignite their careers. But the issues each had in the past are still prevalent now and, through a "mocumentary" style presentation, their efforts to put those issues behind them and become the heroes they were meant to be are related.

Cast: Britain Spellings (Mario), P.J. Marino (Luigi), Courtney Merritt (Lil P), Tonya Kay (Peach), Woody Tondorf (Link), Amy Bloom (Samus), Bonjah Kele (Bowser), Haley Mancini (Zelda), Brendan Bradley (Mega Man), Jeff Sloniker (Kung Fu Guy), Napoleon Ryan (Kid Icarus), Rebecca Ann Johnson (April O'Neil), Craig Frank (Justin Bailey), Kaylyn Slevin (Young Peach), George Anthony Anisimow (Young Mario), Amanda MacKay (Host). **Credits:** *Producer:* Tim Donahue, Matthew Lewis, Aaron Sherry. *Director:*

Matthew Lewis. *Writer:* Brendan Bradley, Dominic Daniel, Tim Donahue, Matthew Lewis, Aaron Sherry, Marie Jach, Andrew Lewis, Alex Lorant, Chris Lorusso, Haley Mancini, Jorge Luis Rivera, Jennifer Losi, Jim Van Over, Aaron Thacker. **Comment:** Interesting and well acted and produced take on programs devoted to video games. Taking the characters out of the past and representing them as human beings makes the concept work and even if you were never a video game fan, you have heard of the characters and curiosity alone should make you want to see what the big fuss was at the time. **Episodes:** 14 untitled episodes, labeled "Episode 1" through "Episode 14."

1061 *The Vines of Sauvignon Blanc.* new onnext.com. 2013.

Eleganza Winery is a wine-producing company owned by a gay man named Doug. He is seated at his desk when his secretary rushes in and tells him, "You have only two minutes and six seconds to live." His family has eagerly waited for this moment but Doug does not want the winery to go to his evil twin brother Duke. Doug's efforts to acquire a new heir by marrying a man he feels will care for his winery—all within the time he has left, are related.

Cast: Reuchen Lemkuhl, Sue Galloway, Stephen Guarino, Jamie Lee, Leslie Meisel, Michael Hartney, Jarvis Derrell. **Comment:** Called a "mini-sudser" as it is styled after a TV soap opera, the program does manage to tell a complete story in the time allotted. It is very fast moving and all episodes can be viewed as one complete story. The acting is very good and the editing expertly executed to prevent a smooth flowing story.

Episodes: 22 six-second episodes that tell the whole story in 132 seconds.

1062 *The Void.* artspear.com. 2013.

The Void is a feature film project under the direction of Gustaf Buganski, considered by all his peers to be the world's worst director. Gustaf has been working on the film for twelve years because "you can't rush a masterpiece." As the head of Gustaf Productions, Gustaf will not reveal what *The Void* is about. He claims that "it is a continually evolving transient phenomena; it defies classification." Also entangled in Gustaf's insane world are a group of filmmakers who were tricked into signing a seemingly never ending contact: Lu, the lead actress (a drama queen); Fex, the editor and special effects nerd; Milly, the down-on-her-luck sound technician; Ed, the grip/camera operator; and Wilton, the gopher who will do anything for a better position on the film. Despite his world-wide, less-than-stellar reputation, Gustaf (called "Satan's gift to filmmaking") has a seemingly endless supply of funding and the program charts what happens to the cast and crew as they work under the direction of a man with little logic to what he does.

Cast: Rob Jenkins (Gustaf), Rita Artmann (Lu), Joe Bauer (Fex), Emily Curtin (Milly), Lawrence Silver (Ed), Isaac Moody (Wilton). **Credits:** *Producer:* Rita Artmann. *Director:* Joe Bauer. **Comment:**

The Void. Series cast (used by permission).

Gustaf may be as far out a director you will ever see but the acting and production are top rate. It is an Australian production and really something different when it comes to a behind-the-scenes look at what might one day become a feature film.

Episodes: *1.* Magnum Octopus. *2.* Contra Zoom Moments. *3.* Brain Squirts. *4.* 3d-001. *5.* Pornoplasty. *6.* Fifth Wheel.

1063 *Voyage Trekkers.* voyagetrekkers.com. 2011–2012.

The Triumph class G.S.V. *Remarkable* is a futuristic space ship commanded by Jack T. Sunstrike. Blake Powell is his First Officer and Elaine Rena is the ship's doctor. Their experiences as they wreck havoc during assignments seeking to further their positions within the Galactic Union are chronicled.

Jack is the grandson of Admiral Reginald P. Sunstrike, the son of Reginald Sunstrike, Jr. (voted "Mr. Handsome Galaxy" three times in a row) and the brother of Captain Reginald Sunstrike III. He is most famous for being the only survivor of the G.S.V. ship *The Montgomery* when it was attached by the Vendrexxi in the Orgo Nullix Nebula (Jack was apparently too drunk to realize what was happening and "was merely sleeping it off in an escape pod"). Jack also has a number of disciplinary actions against him but because of his heritage, he is never brought to trial.

Blake is a lieutenant commander, never questions orders and does what is asked of him. Jack claims there is nothing significant to report about Powell other than "he has good hygiene and above-average punctuality."

Elaine, a lieutenant, "is a troubled soul whose only pleasure seems to be contradicting her handsome captain's authority." Jack thinks she acts like a rebellious teenager who voices her opinion but doesn't stand for anything. Elaine graduated top in her class at Space Academy and first served aboard the Galactic Union's flagship G.S.V. *Republic*

Cast: Adam Rini (Jack Sunstrike), Gabrielle Van Buren (Elaine Rena), Logan Blackwell (Blake Powell). **Credits:** *Producer:* Nathan Blackwell, Craig Michael Curtis. *Writer-Director:* Nathan Blackwell. **Comment:** The program does present laughs along with good acting, special effects and production values.

Episodes: *1.* Rescue from the Lizard Man. *2.* Social Network. *3.* Birthday Surprise. *4.* Language Barrier. *5.* Oh Great Space. *6.* Formal Charges. *7.* The Clutches of General Kang. *8.* Phoning It In. *9.* Fabulous Technology. *10.* Many Paths to Eden. *11.* Welcome Aboard. *12.* Laser Swords at Dawn. *13.* Set Witchcraft to Stun. *14.* Junior Ambassadors of the Galactic Union. *15.* Powell's Last Stand. *16.* The Captain's Ball. *17–20.* Revenge of the Lizard Men.

1064 *Wainy Days.* youtube.com. 2007–2012.

Events in the everyday life of comedian David Wain, an unemployed young man as he tackles the problems of life living in Brooklyn, New York.

Cast: David Wain, A.D. Miles, Zandy Hartig, Matt Ballard. **Credits:** *Producer:* David Wain. *Writer-Director:* David Wain, A.D. Miles, Michael Ian Black, Jonathan Stern, Ian Helfer, Max Spicer, Mat Winkler. **Comment:** Well written and acted program with what happens to Wain becoming the story line for that episode (as in the series *Seinfeld*).

2007 Episodes: *1.* Shelley. *2.* The Date. *3.* My Turn. *4.* Cyrano d'Bluetooth. *5.* Walking Tour. *6.* A Woman's Touch. *7.* The Bank. *8.* Plugged. *9.* Dorvid Days. *10.* The Future. *11.* Zandy. *12.* Happy Endings. *13.* Wainy Nights. *14.* The Pact. *15.* Tough Guy. *16.* The Pickup.

2008 Episodes: *1.* Jonah and the Manilow. *2.* Sublet. *3.* Carol. *4.* Molly. *5.* Nan and Lucy. *6.* Rebecca. *7.* Water Cooler. *8.* The Waindow. *9.* Angel. *10.* Shelly II.

2009 Episodes: *1.* Jill. *2.* Dance Club. *3.* Animator. *4,5.* Rochelle. *6–12.* Kelly and Arielle.

1065 *A Walk in the Park.* webserieschannel.com. 2013.

Walking in a park is the one pleasure a young man named Jonathan has (basically to see a pretty young girl in a tight, sexy outfit, jogging). Once the excitement passes, Jonathan returns to his dull life, which includes working for FeeCease, a company that helps people out of their credit card debts for a monthly fee. He also has a difficult time obeying laws, adjusting to public transportation and dealing with the crazy people that only he seems to encounter. The daily events that often dull the spark that began his day are chronicled.

Cast: Antonio Michaels (Jonathan), Krystle McMullen (Susan), Jay Ronca (Boss), Shelly Dulman (Natalie), Mike Rodriquez (Craig), Rafael Candelaria (Robert), Melvin Cobb (Dreadz), Jess Hollenbach (Justin). **Credits:** *Producer-Writer-Director:* Johnny O (as credited). **Comment:** "This webisode is intended for mature audiences but immature people are also welcome to view it" is seen at the start of the program. Clearly the program has set its goal to attract anyone who stumbles upon it. The concept is different; the acting is good and the overall production is well done (be aware, however, that vulgar language is used on occasion).

Episodes: *1.* First Day at FeeCease, Inc. *2.* Training Day. *3.* Episode 3.

1066 *Walk of Shame.* youtube.com. 2013.

Six very pretty and sexy women (Maggie, Nicole, Sally, Katie, Stella and Anne) and the rather poor

Walk of Shame. Episode title card (used by permission).

choices they make when it comes to the opposite sex. Incorporating an anthology-like presentation, each episode opens with a bed scene (with a woman next to a man) and progresses to show how the woman feels she made a bad choice for a lover and how she goes about extracting herself from that mistake.

Cast: Christiann Castellanos (Maggie), Nikki Limo (Nicole), Trisha Paytas (Sally), Katie Wilson (Katie), Annemarie Pazmino (Stella), Marisha Ray (Anne), Brendan Bradley (Derek), Hunter Davis (Bruce), Courtney Merritt (Katherine), Walker Davis (Harry), Erik Smith (Scotty), Jimmy Wong (Jacob). **Credits:** *Producer:* Ian Andrew Ward, Brendan Bradley. *Director:* America Young, J.C. Reifenberg, Daniel Hanna, Brendan Bradley. *Writer:* Brendan Bradley, Mark Souza. **Comment:** Intriguing look at female sexuality that is well acted and produced. There is vulgar language (pretty as the women may be, they do have potty mouths), suggestive sexual situations and partial (but discreet) nudity.

Episodes: *1.* Not a Working Girl. *2.* How Stella Got Her Shirt Back. *3.* You've Got Males. *4.* Sisterhood of the Traveling Sheets. *5.* When Harry Held Sally. *6.* How to Lose a Guy in 10 minutes.

1067 *Walking in L.A.* blip.tv. 2012.

Keith is a young man with two strikes against him: he has been dumped by his rich girlfriend (Amanda) for being lazy and never taking her out, and fired from his job in the mail room at her father's prestigious law firm. Now, without a job or an income, Keith suddenly faces a crisis as he is forced to fend for himself in Los Angeles. As the days pass Keith hits on an idea to present an Internet vlog to document his life as it is now and how he hopes to improve it. Through an ad placed on Craigslist, Keith hires James, a womanizing cameraman to record what happens as he attempts to re-invent himself. The program chronicles Keith's adventures as he sets out to fulfill his three step plan (find a cool girlfriend, a job and get a car) and what happens when those dreams become nightmares.

Cast: Keith Jordan (Keith), Taryn Southern (Amanda Killroy), Chris Jorie (Mr. Killroy), Christian Calloway (Gary, the Homeless Guy), Edgar Landa (Priest), Laura Siegel (KFC Girl), David Fraioli (Mike the Vampire). **Credits:** *Producer:* Keith Jordan, James Haffner. *Director:* James Haffner. *Writer:* Keith Jordan, Graeme Mullin. **Comment:** The production is well done and the acting on the caliber of a network or basic cable television series.

Episodes: *1.* Pilot: The End. *2.* The Hunger Genie. *3.* Don't Fear the Hipsters. *4.* Beware of D–Bags.

1068 *Wall St. Manor.* youtube.com. 2014.

Wall Street Manor is a home shared by four dysfunctional friends (Garrett, Scott, Hank and Joel). Despite a crazy landlord who threatens to kill if the rent ($2400 a month) is not paid on time, they have agreed to split it. While their lifestyles are different they do have one thing in common: mishap—if anything can go wrong it will. The house was once nice and respectable; it is now the worst residence on the block and stories follow the friends as they just seek a way to survive the concrete jungle.

Cast: Tori Fritz (Whitney), Brad Hill (Garrett), Aaron Van Geem (Hank), Scott Lennard (Scott), Jole Sanchez (Joel). **Credits:** *Director:* Julian Doan, Kevin Hinman. *Writer:* Julian Doan. Kevin Hinman, Jole Sanchez. **Comment:** Typical roommate saga that has been done dozens of times in movies, on TV and even on the Internet. It is only different for its strange mix of characters.

Episodes: *1.* It's Birthday Time. *2.* Dummy Brains. *3.* You Shaved! *4.* Mark Rio. *5.* Aim for the Heart. *6.* Bone Density. *7.* Fear the First. *8.* Love, Passive Aggressive. *9.* My Face. *10.* Guess What I Did Last Night. *11.* My Boozo.

1069 *Wallflowers.* wallflowers.tv. 2013–2014.

Janice, an advice counselor, was a former backup singer on a number of no-name bands. She feels her advice is indispensable and calls herself "a modern master of love" and caters to the hopelessly and eternally single men and women of Manhattan, people who are unable to make a connection. Members of the group feel at ease but once leaving the support group find meeting someone a most difficult endeavor. The program focuses, in particular, on gay relationships, mostly those seen through the experiences of Bryce (and his later steady hookup with Alex).

Bryce, a former child star turned owner of the Hunter Casting Company, is distrustful of people and enjoys drinking and smoking.

Daisy, Bryce's best friend, is also his business partner and has a no-nonsense outlook on life.

Martin, almost 40 years old, is still looking to start a family but doesn't realize that his over-eagerness is preventing him from finding a woman that is compatible with him.

Jane, a recently fired high-powered attorney, has just ended her affair with her married boss and has returned to the center after having successfully graduated.

Rhonda, a fun-loving girl with a positive outlook on life, constantly finds her heart broken by those who continually take advantage of her.

Linus is a bar tender who has aspirations of becoming a comic book artist.

Victoria, raised in a culture where women are seen as subservient, feels the only way she can overcome her upbringing is by dating gay men.

Leslie is the office manager at Hunter Casting; Becca is a casting assistant; Wade is the Hunter Casting receptionist (replaced Todd); Alex is the musician who hooks up with Bryce; Fred is Janice's ex-husband, a band manager; Todd is Daisy's younger brother (a gay who secretly loves Bryce); Tina and Ricky are support group members; and Mark is a filmmaker with whom Daisy seeks to begin a relationship. **Cast:** Sarah Saltzberg (Daisy Loeb), Chad Kimball, Lucas Near-Verbrugghe, Patch Darragh (Bryce Hunter), Gibson Frazier (Martin Parrish), Christianne Tisdale (Janice Ackerman), Susan Louise O'Connor (Rhonda), Ricky Dunlop (Ricky), Tina Hart (Tina), Marcia DeBonis (Leslie), Max Crumm (Linus), Angela Lin (Victoria Pond), Lisa Joyce (Nancy), Jillian Louis (Becca), John Gallbach (Alex), Gideon Glick (Todd), Brooke Davis (Brooke), Matt Dengler (Charlie), Wayne Wilcox, Mark Provencher (Mark), Tina Hart (Tina), Ricky Dunlop (Ricky), Robert Bogue (Fred). **Credits:** *Producer:* David Stoller, Ondine Landa Abramson, Kieran Turner, Michael Canzoniero. *Writer-Director:* Kieran Turner. **Comment:** The acting and production values are very good and stories attempt to make gay characters real, not stereotyped, as they search for love.

Season 1 Episodes: *1.* Square Pegs. *2.* Fridays. *3.* All-American Girl. *4.* Hello, Larry. *5.* The Partridge Family. *6.* The Invaders.

Season 2 Episodes: *1.* The Match Game. *2.* Super Friends. *3.* Misfits of Science. *4.* V. *5.* My Own Worst Enemy. *6.* Roar.

1070 Walter Wants a Woman. youtube.com. 2013.

Walter, a young man who has just declared his independence and moved out of his parents' home, has embarked on a quest: find the girl of his dreams. With a computer that his mother gave him before he left, Walter begins an Internet vlog to relate what happens as he secures a date with a girl and seeks to discover if she is his one true love.

Cast: Callum Butcher (Walter). **Credits:** *Writer-Director:* Rachel Choy. **Comment:** British produced program that is basically Walter presenting his vlog. It is simplistic, well acted and produced.

Season 1 Episodes: *1.* My Quest for Love. *2.* Date One: The Indian Girl. *3.* Thoughts on My Indian Date. *4.* I've Started Online Dating. *5.* Date Two: Jesse. *6.* I Don't Wanna Talk About It. *7.* I've Got a Photo This Time. *8.* Date 3: The Accident. *9.* Milk and Cookies. *10.* A New Week and a New Chance to Find Love. *11.* Date 4: Chinese. *12.* Chinese Food for Two. *13.* Dating Multiple Ladies. *14.* Date 5: The Speed Date. *15.* I Couldn't Leave. *16.* I'm Going to a Party. *17.* Date 6: The Party. *18.* You'll See Me Again.

Season 2 Episodes: *1.* You Won't Believe My Next Date. *2.* The Picnic. *3.* Kiss and Tell. *4.* Mum Thinks I'm Fat. *5.* The Gym. *6.* I Like Girls. *7.* She's Ticking More. *8.* Pizza. *9.* The Break-Up.

1071 Wasted Time. wastedtimeseries.com. 2014.

In life there are situations that go together and there are situations that are totally opposite but sometimes manage to become a part of each other. People encountering such situations are profiled in stand alone stories that show how those seemingly unrelated events affect their lives.

Cast: Adam Jackson, Justin McDonald, Michael Sykora, Gabriela Dizio. **Credits:** *Producer:* Michael Sykora, Adam Jackson, Jesse Collier, Jason Kennedy. *Director:* Michael Sykora. *Writer:* Michael Sykora, Adam Jackson. **Comment:** Well produced and acted stories with adult themes prevalent in some (like "Wine and Porn") although no parental warnings are given.

Episodes: *1.* Get Here Soon. *2.* Wine and Porn. *3.* The Pizza Shop. *4.* So, How Was It? *5.* She's Heading Out. *6.* Death Perception. *7.* Blame Molly. *8.* The Best Man.

1072 We Are Darren and Riley. darrenandriley.com. 2014.

Australian program about two stand-up comedians

(Darren and Riley) and what happens when they become the first human clients of a dog trainer (Wayne Pudding) who promises them the impossible: breaking out of the local comedy circuit for fame on television.

Cast: Darren Low (Darren), Riley Nottingham (Riley), Wayne Bassett (Wayne Pudding), Leah Douglas (Stage Manager). **Credits:** *Producer:* Peter Herbert, Riley Nottingham. *Director:* Henry Boffio. *Writer:* Darren Low, Riley Nottingham, Henry Boffio. **Comment:** Well done program with good acting and, even though it is set in Australia, it can be seen that similar problems are encountered by comics anywhere in the world.

Episodes: *1.* Meet Wayne. *2.* Sausages and Crumpets. *3.* Speed Dating. *4.* The Eddie McGuire Method. *5.* Who Wants to Be a Zen Master.

1073 We Are Wonderful. youtube.com. 2013.

In a land called Wonder City live Bill, Devin and Frasier, friends who appear to be ordinary until it is realized they imagine themselves as heroes who battle evil and solve intriguing mysteries. The imaginary quests the heroes encounter form the basis of the program with it also showing how they explore the meaning of friendship in extra ordinary situations.

Cast: Bill Reinka (Bill), Devin Page (Devin), Alex Fraser (Frasier). **Credits:** *Producer-Writer:* Alex Fraser. *Director:* Brian Leonard. **Comment:** At first glance the program will seem a bit far out, especially with the use of green screen technology to create the fantasy sequences. It will take a few minutes to adjust to the style—even the foul language. Once done you will see that a well-acted but goofy program has emerged.

Episodes: *1.* The Truth Is Cancer. *2.* Not Safe for Work. *3.* Talk. But Who Listens. *4.* A Learned Boy. *5.* The New Neighbor. *6.* I've Got Weed. *7.* Broken Keys. *8.* Billgasm.com. *9.* Finding Four Legs. *10.* Kickin' It. *11.* Job Hunt. *12.* Bestiality. *13.* The Problem with Mice and Sticks. *14.* Chess. *15.* 100 Duck Bet.

1074 We Have to Stop Now. youtube.com. 2009–2010.

Dyna and Kit, a married lesbian couple who are also therapists, have written a book called *How to Succeed in Marriage Without Even Trying.* But since the book was written, they have grown apart and even with the help of their own therapist (Susan) it appears their marriage has ended. Unexpectedly, their book becomes a best-seller and has stirred the interest of Guy, a film-maker who has contracted with them to produce a documentary based on their lives and the contents of their book. A breakup is now out of the question (as it could ruin their reputation and book sales) and the program follows their efforts to remain a couple despite the differences in their relationship.

Kit is not always predictable in what she will do. She is fun to be with, impulsive, honest and openly expresses her feelings.

Dyna prefers intellectual pursuits and her high professional standards make her more sympathetic when it comes to her patients.

Susan is a compassionate woman able to navigate her professional life, but unable to maintain a steady relationship in her personal life.

Cindy, Kit's younger sister, loves to get high or drunk and always finds "a home away from home" by crashing at Kit and Dyna's home.

Guy, the film-maker, soon falls for Cindy and becomes involved in all the awkwardness as Kit and Dyna pretend to be a happy couple.

Cast: Jill Bennett (Kit Janson), Cathy DeBuono (Dyna Cella), Ann Noble (Cindy Janson), Suzanne Westenhoefer (Susan Dyson), John W. McLaughlin (Guy), Meredith Baxter (Judy), Mary Frances Careccia (Dee Dee Cella), Shannan Leigh Reeve (Shauna), Maria Marini (Christy), Maia Madison (Sybil), Catherine O'Connor (Mandy). **Credits:** *Producer:* Jill Bennett, Cathy DeBuono, Ann Noble, Donna Rucks, Libbie Shelton, Robyn Dettman, Rebecca S. Katz. *Director:* Robyn Dettman, Jill Bennett, Cathy DeBuono. *Writer:* Ann Noble. **Comment:** Well-acted and produced program that tries not to be more than it actually is—two lovers trying to understand and overcome the problems that are plaguing their relationship. There are moments of tenderness, but no nudity or vulgar language.

Season 1 Episodes: *1.* Pilot. *2.* The Golden Rules. *3.* The Sock Puppets. *Note:* The following episodes have been taken off line: "A Day at a Time," "Transfererntial," "Whose Side Are You On" and "Carnal Knowledge."

Season 2 Episodes: *1.* The Baby and the Bathwater. *2.* The Grass Is Always Greener. *3.* Sisterhood Winked. *4.* How Sweet It Is. *5.* Celesbianism. *6.* Q&A. *7.* The Truthyness of the Matter. *8.* It's Not a Game.

1075 We Need Girlfriends. youtube.com. 2006–2007.

Following their college graduation three friends since high school (Henry, Rod and Tom) decide to share a New York apartment. All is progressing well until each is dumped by his girlfriend. Instead of wallowing in self pity, they decide to move on and get back into the dating game. Their mishaps as they each seek new girlfriends are the focus of episodes.

Cast: Patrick Cohen (Tom), Seth Kirschner (Henry), Evan Bass (Rod), Olivia Villanti (Sarah), Summer Hagen (Jenny), Brigitte Hagerman (Lucy), Johanna Igel (Laura). **Credits:** *Producer:* Angel L. Acevedo III, Brian Amyot, Steven Tsaoelas, Dennis Erdman. *Director:* Brian Anyot, Steven Tsaoelas, Angel L. Acevedo III. *Writer:* Steven Tsaoelas.

Comment: One of the earliest of Internet comedies with good acting and production values.

Episodes: *1.* Pilot. *2.* Blue Party. *3.* MySpace. *4.* Rod vs. Henry. *5.* First Date Ever. *6.* Game Night. *7.* The Boyfriend. *8.* Future Henry. *9.* The Morning After. *10.* Future Rod. *11.* Goodbye Forever.

1076 Web Therapy. youtube.com. 2008–2010.

Fiona Wallice is a therapist who believes that the shorter the therapy session the better it is for her patients as she will get results much faster than say, sticking with the traditional "50 minute hour." She calls her idea a "modality of therapy" wherein her three minute sessions take place via a web cam over the Internet site iChat.com. As Finoa institutes her new form of dealing with patient problems, hoping to interest investors into backing her conception, the program charts what happens when the viewer can see that a traditional session is needed but Fiona can only see the short end of the stick and is sometimes oblivious to the problems the shorter sessions create. The program was picked up by the Showtime cable network in 2011, where it ran until 2014.

Cast: Lisa Kudrow (Fiona Wallice). *Notable Guest Stars:* Dan Bucatinsky (Jerome Sokoloff), Julie Claire (Robin Griner), Tim Bagley (Richard Pratt), Victor Garber (Kip Wallace), Michael McDonald (Ben Tomlund), Rosie O'Donnell (Maxine De-Maine), Alan Cumming (Austen Clarke), Drew Sherman (Justin Fein), Conan O'Brien (Himself), Natasha Bedingfield (Gemma Pankhurst-Jones), Minnie Driver (Allegra Favreau), Chelsea Handler (Chris Endicott), Matt LeBlanc (Nick Jericho), Lily Tomlin (Putsy Hodge), Megan Mullally (Franny Marshall), Meg Ryan (Karen Sharpe), Jennifer Elise Cox (Gina Spinks), Jane Lynch (Claire Dudek), Courteney Coz (Serena DuVall), Selma Blair (Tammy Hines), Julia Louis Dreyfus (Shevaun Haig), Molly Shannon (Kristine Noble), Meryl Streep (Camilla Bowner). **Credits:** *Producer:* Lisa Kudrow, Dan Bucatinsky, Jodi Binstock, David Codron, Ron Quarshi. *Director:* Don Roos, Dan Bucatinsky. *Writer:* Lisa Kudrow, Don Roos, Dan Bucatinsky. **Comment:** If the TV characters Karen Walker (*Will and Grace*), Samantha Jones (*Sex and the City*) and Lucille Bluth (*Arrested Development*) bring to mind a portrait of a rich, self-absorbed, calculating and insensitive woman then you have already met Fiona Wallice—whether you have seen *Web Therapy* or not (although star Lisa Kudrow puts her own magic touch on such a character). To those that remember such shows as *I Love Lucy* and *I Married Joan*, wherein the day starts off normally but mushrooms into a comical chaos then you also have an idea as to the format of *Web Therapy* (as it has that same setup feeling).

2008 Episodes: *1–3.* An Old Flame. *4–6.* Sibling Ribaldry. *7–9.* The Breakthrough. *10–12.* Psycho Analysis. *13–15.* Exposing the Truth.

2009 Episodes: *1–3.* Gossip Girl. *4–6.* Office Politics. *7–9.* Psychic Friends. *10–12.* Kiss and Tell. *13–15.* Flying High.

2010 Episodes: *1.* Forget Me Knot. *2.* Staff Infection. *3.* Why There Is No Sister's Day. *4.* Mommy Track. *5.* Fiona's Turn. *6.* Mom Always Loved Me Best. *7.* Bringing Up Babies. *8.* Meet the Press. *9.* Maternity Leave. *10.* Dream Girl. *11.* Mistress of the Web. *12.* That Old Pratt Magic. *13.* I Love You, Man. *14.* Breaking Up Is Hard to Do. *15.* Can You Get Up? *16.* Aversion Therapy. *17.* Healing Touch. *18.* Reverse Psychology.

1077 The Webventures of Justin & Alden. mydamnchannel.com. 2010.

Justin and Alden are roommates in the process of checking items off their to-do list. As it nears the end they come across one marked "Become famous." It is an item they continually put off until Justin comes up with a way to become famous: "Make the greatest web series web show on the web computer." But how to get started? Their solution: get Felicia Day, a web series performer to star in their series. When they learn that Felicia is appearing that night at the Streamy Awards Presentation, they set out to find her. The program charts what happens as they begin a five-hour road trip and encounter numerous obstacles that could prevent them from arriving at their destination.

Cast: Justin Tyler (Justin), Alden Ford (Alden). **Credits:** *Producer:* Wilson Cleveland, Dominick Raisch, Sandeep Parikh, Illeana Douglas. *Director:* Sean Becker. *Writer:* Tony Janning. **Comment:** Several short sequences are presented as Justin and Alden plan their web series (from a medieval saga to a hard-boiled private eye series). The program is very well acted and produced and well worth watching.

Episodes: *1.* A Questionable Quest. *2.* 1760. *3.* Back to the Present. *4.* The Streamys. *5.* The Last Episode.

1078 Welcome to Grandpaville. welcome tograndpaville.weebly.com. 2013–2014.

Shelby Elizabeth Lockter is an 11-year-old girl who lives with her mother, Miranda. When Miranda is transferred to the London office of her job, she makes arrangements for Shelby to temporarily live with her grandfather, Desmond Potts, the owner of a toy store called The Toy Pott. Desmond lives in an old Victorian mansion and is cared for by his British butler, Kincaid. At the toy store Desmond is assisted by Old Man Gus, a 70-year-old, hard-of-hearing handyman; Kendall, a book-smart high school student; and Spare Parts, a life size robot. The Toy Pott specializes in unique toys for children and adults, some of which are built by Grandpa Desmond. Shelby is a precocious preteen and computer and electronics wizard who suddenly feels out of place. Her friends are back home and she is surrounded by old people. Desmond too feels out of place as he suddenly has a young girl to care for. The program relates incidents in the lives of Desmond as he accepts new responsibilities and Shelby as she attempts to fit into a world where, she soon discovers, old is cool.

Second season episodes change the format considerably when Shelby leaves Grandpa Desmond to join her mother in England. Kendall and MacKenzie, Shelby's friends (from Samuel Clemens Academy grammar school) are the center of attention as are their activities at school (while Grandpa Desmond, Kincaid and Old Man Gus are still seen, their roles have been cut back dramatically).

Season 1 Cast: Isabella Abreu (Shelby), Dave Wall (Grandpa Potts), Michael T. Lombardi (Kincaid), Deirdre Robins (Kendall), John Swanson (Old Man Gus).

Season 2 Cast: Deirdre Robins (Kendall), Kailyn Kaluna (MacKenzie), Sophie Alter (Cassidy), Abby Rain Heiser (Maya), Jonathan Sartell (Spencer), Eric Murphy (Duncan), Allison Bradshaw (Katie), Jocelyn Vogel (Madison), Hailey Pine (Presley), Hannah Perreault (Brook), Kyra Robins (Gwen), Sima Kasten (Zoe). **Credits:** *Producer-Writer-Director:* Michael T. Lombardi. **Comment:** TV quality production with very good acting and, especially in the first season, very well done stories. The second season loses its charm without Shelby and is literally just a program about grammar school kids and all the mischief they get into.

Season 1 Episodes: *1.* House Guest. *2.* Spare Parts. *3.* Wilderness Adventure Girls. *4.* Runaway Mummy.

Season 2 Episodes: *1.* After Shelby. *2.* Invasion of the Slumber Party Punks. *3.* Monkey See, Monkey Do. *4.* Hallotween.

1079 Welcome to the Neighborhood. wttn. tumblr.com. 2011.

Geoff and Salzo are twenty-something New Yorkers who are not only down-on-their-luck, but struggling with virtually everything else in their lives. The program chronicles their off-the-wall antics as they struggle to get by on what little they have but hopeful that their lives will soon change for the better.

Cast: Geoffrey Grasso (Geoff), John Salzo (Salzo), Evan Roufeh, Chris Salzo. **Credits:** *Producer:* Diego Tovar. *Director:* Matthew Charof. **Comment:** Basically going into a deli and ordering a sandwich plain with no garnishments proves to be one of the biggest problems Geoff has in the only produced episode. The characters are a bit uncouth and the acting and production just standard for an Internet series. Being a pilot, problems are to be expected and would later be worked out had any additional episodes been produced.

Episodes: *1.* Pilot: The Terrorist Sandwich.

1080 Welcome to the X-urbs. vimeo.com. 2014.

Ducksbury is a suburban community and home to Angie, a former writer and filmmaker and now a housewife and mother (of Janie and Jeremiah) who has reached another turning pointing her life: she is now middle-age. Her life in suburbia is dull compared to her time before marriage and to relieve the boredom she decides to make a video diary of her life, as Angie X, for posterity. All is progressing well until Jenny, her best friend from high school, turns up on her doorstep seeking refuge after a bad marriage. Angie is married to Ronnie, the leader of a middle-aged cyber band called The Cove; Jenny is an entrepreneur whose latest effort is a line of lingerie. Also apart of Angie's life are Teddy and Fenton, Ronnie's off-the-wall band mates. As Angie films her documentary a look into Angie's life is presented as she attempts to cope with all the chaos that surrounds her.

Cast: Sims McCormick (Angie), Catherine McCormick (Jenny Dickinson), Rob Knecht (Ronnie), Andrew Corbett (Teddy), Will McCormick (Fenton), Vaughn Knecht (Jeremiah), Ella Knecht (Janie). **Credits:** *Producer:* Rob Knecht, Stefani Gellman. *Writer-Director:* Sims McCormick, Catherine McCormick. **Comment:** Exceptionally well-done program that captures Angie's despair as she attempts to cope with her life. Sims McCormick is not made to look the glamorous middle-aged housewife, but with played-down looks, she fits the role and is very convincing.

Episodes: *1.* Meet Angie X. *2.* Angie & Jenny. *3.* Jeremiah Was. *4.* Jenny's Little Secret. *5.* Mid-Life Crisis. *6.* Old Fish. *7.* Girls' Night Out. *8.* Trailer Park. *9,10.* Intervention. *11.* Air Guitar.

1081 West of Lincoln. webserieschannel. com. 2011.

Frances, called Fanny, is a young waitress not only struggling to make ends meet but find her one true love. She lives on Santa Monica, west of Lincoln Boulevard with her roommate (Krayon) and has a best friend (Ginger). The story follows the events that spark Fanny's life as she copes with her less-than-desirable job, the antics of her overly dramatic friend, her roommate and her own insecurities as she seeks a boyfriend.

Cast: Yukilynn McElvain (Fanny), Elizabeth J. Carlisle (Ginger), David Lloyd Smith (Floyd), Kewon Preston (Krayon), Paul Rackowski (Tyrone). **Credits:** *Producer:* Yukilynn McElvain, Elizabeth J. Carlisle, David Lloyd Smith, Kewon Preston. *Director:* David Lloyd Smith, Paul Rackowski. *Writer:* Yukilynn McElvain, Elizabeth J. Carlisle, David Lloyd Smith, Kewon Preston. **Comment:** As the program opens a young woman is seen on the street dressed like a high-priced call girl and counting money. She is not what she appears as you soon learn that it is Fanny and that she is just returning home from a failed date (that is, she and her date failed to make a connection). Fanny does have a knack for meeting off-the-wall characters and that aspect is cleverly incorporated into the series, which is very well acted and produced.

Episodes: 6 untitled episodes, labeled "Episode 1" to "Episode 6."

1082 *Whacked.* blip.tv. 2010.

Vinny and Tony are low level mobsters with the Chicago Syndicate. While they do perform the jobs assigned to them, they do not always go as planned and cause problems for the Dons who oversee them. Hoping to get their act together and do the job as told, Vinny and Tony set out on a path to rise in the ranks and the program charts those not so successful attempts.

Cast: Tony Rago (Tony), Kirk Diedrich (Vinny). **Credits:** *Producer-Director:* Tony Rago, Kirk Diedrich. *Director:* Tony Rago. **Comment:** Right from the start the program captures the feeling a gangster-themed movie or TV series. The leads are perfect representations of that gangster image and perform their roles quite well. Vinny is the overweight wiseguy while Tony represents the slimmer version of a hired thug. There is some foul language (as can be expected in such themed programs) and the well-produced program flows smoothly from episode to episode.

Episodes: *1.* Weapon of Choice. *2.* Steak Piccata. *3.* Lost. *4.* Two in the Head. *5.* The Out-of Towners. *6.* Going for a Ride. *7.* The Gumar. *8.* Momma's Cooking. *9.* The Sanitation Business. *10.* The Wire. *11.* The Chase.

1083 *What, Doctor?* whatdoctorseries.com. 2013.

The Doctor, as he is called is a traveler in time and space who accomplishes his goal through W.A.T.C.H. (Wide Angle Tele-coordinating Hyperbilator). It resembles an ordinary pocket watch but can transport its possessor to past or future times. The Doctor is assisted by Companion and their adventures are chronicled as they battle the evils of the universe in various times (the watch has a mind of its own and cannot be programmed for a specific time or place and thus they are often at the mercy of the watch). The Doctor often performs missions for U.N.I.Q.U.E. (United Nations Investigations of Queer, Unusual Events), an organization based in the 1970s and to which The Doctor must travel back in time for assignments. Leslie is The Doctor's liaison with U.N.I.Q.U.E. See also *Untitled Web Series About a Space Traveler Who Can Also Travel Through Time.*

Cast: Jerry Kokich (The Doctor), Tosca Minotto (Companion), Nicole Starrett (Leslie). **Credits:** *Writer-Director:* Jerry Kokich. **Comment:** A well-done take off on the British series *Doctor Who* with good special effects and interesting stories. Here Companion does not have an official name and is called various names by The Doctor (Tess, Episode 1; Emma, Episode 3; Tara, Episode 4; and Chloe, Episode 5. Companion did not appear in the second episode).

Episodes: *1.* A Thing to Watch. *2.* What's Not? *3.* Theater at the End of Time. *4.* Outstanding in Their Field. *5.* A Unique Perspective.

1084 *What Exit?* whatexitwebseries.com. 2014.

Tina is a New Jersey girl facing a crisis: She and her fiancé, Gary, have broken up; she has been let go from her job and she has been forced to move back in with her parents (and punk rock sister, Claudia) and work in the family-owned Greek diner. Although it has been six months since the separation, Tina still pines for Gary but with the help of her

What, Doctor? Series poster art (image copyright Ashley Houtz).

girlfriends, Lexi and Krystal, she has been able to move on. The program follows Tina as she seeks to better her life, including a job worthy of her college degree and finding someone to replace Gary.

Cast: Jessica Carollo (Tina), Naamah Harris (Lexi), Lauren Klemp (Claudia), Blanca Harris (Krystal), Shevy Gutierrez (Gary), Judy Bruno Bennett (Connie), Harry Chambarry (George), Ellen Karis (Athena), Mary Orloff-Prastos (Mary), Matthew Knowland (Evan), John Salutare (Marcus), Jessica Pallette (Lisa). **Credits:** *Producer:* Sophia Eptamenitis, Brian Jude. *Writer-Director:* Sophia Eptamenitis. **Comment:** It is best to begin with episode two as the first episode is simply no way to begin a series (here just showing guys drinking at a bar; you have no idea who is who or what is going on). That second episode is not much better but at least you can grasp the story line. There is foul language; Tina does have a very noticeable New Jersey accent (put on?) and overall the program needed character introductions and a story line that could be picked up right away.

Episodes: *1.* Single Gary and the Boys. *2.* Summertime Is Here! *3.* Downsized. *4.* The Pasta Triangle. *5.* The Stalked and the Stifled.

1085 *What's New America?* youtube.com. 2014.

Mickey Armstrong, the host of a live television series called *What's New America?* is hoping to move past his job of selling crazy products via infomercials and get into the ranks of network broadcasting (he previously worked for the Game Show Network as the host of *Card Sharks 2000*). Unfortunately, he appears to be stuck dealing with sponsors and a crew as off-the-wall as the products he sells. As Mickey makes the best of what surrounds him at work, the program also focuses on his efforts to bring some semblance to his private life as well.

Cast: Michael Hartson (Mickey Armstrong), Trudie Petersen (Mel Sharpe), Donn Lamkin (Jack Conrad), Tracy Wiu (Tina Chen), Andrea Canny (Hennie Shultz), A. Ali Flores (Willy Sanchez). **Credits:** *Director:* Joel Kostuch. *Writer:* Michael Hartson. **Comment:** Well done comical spoof of what goes on backstage at home shopping channels, especially when the products are anything but reliable.

Episodes: *1.* Pilot. *2.* The Hood Wink. *3.* The Kwik Kut Show. *4.* The Dog Show. *5.* Meet Mickey's Parents.

1086 *When Life Hands You Lemons.* youtube.com. 2013.

Donovan and Jason are brothers just looking to pay their bills and get by. As children they made money by operating a sidewalk lemonade stand. As adults they make money by operating a lemonade stand. They charge $1 a glass, but purchasing that drink is a health hazard (for example, lemons are stepped on to make the juice and foreign objects can be found in it). The program follows Donovan and Jason as they operate their business with hints that the stand is the cover for something bigger (not exactly made clear in the pilot).

Cast: Donovan Santiago (Donovan), Jason Meyer (Jason). **Credits:** *Producer:* Rebecca Lee, Brendon Schmidt. *Writer-Director:* Jason Meyer. **Comment:** There is also a very short trailer but it is difficult to judge the series based on what is available. There is foul language and the acting and production appear adequate.

Episodes: *1.* Pilot.

1087 *Where the Bears Are.* wherethebearsare.tv. 2012–2014.

In the gay and bisexual culture "Bears" refers to a large hairy man who projects a masculine image. Nelson, Reggie and Wood are gay roommates who fit the description and live in the Silver Lake neighborhood of Los Angeles. Their lives revolve around everything that is gay until circumstances beyond their control involve them in precarious situations that require their ingenuity to overcome and once again return to their comfort zones. Each season involves the roommates, called "bears" in a murder-mystery that they must solve without themselves becoming victims or arrested as the culprits. Season one finds the bears seeking the killer of a man they find dead in their bathtub; solving the murder of a politician becomes their quest in the second season; while the third season follows their efforts to solve a series of murders that appear to be linked to Chunk Studios, a gay porn studio.

Cast: Rick Copp (Reggie Hatch), Joe Dietl (Wood Burns), Ben Zook (Nelson Dorkoff), Ian Parks (Todd "Hot Toddy" Stevens), Chad Sanders (Det. Chad Winters), George Unda (Det. Marcus Martinez), Loretta Fox (Susie Collins), Tim Hooper (Police Chief), Scott Beauchemin (Cyril), George Sebastin (George Ridgemont), Sam Pancake (Alfie Cooper), Mark Powers (Jeremy Richards), Tim Hooper (Capt. Frank Coley), Tuc Watkins (Dickie Calloway), Julio Tello (J Cub), Drew Droege (Oscar Butterfield). **Credits:** *Producer:* Rick Copp, Joe Dietl, Ben Zook. *Director:* Joe Dietl. *Writer:* Rick Copp, Ben Zook. **Comment:** Despite all the silliness and off-the-wall investigations, the program is a light-hearted spoof of straight characters that take it upon themselves to solve crimes. There are some intimate moments, numerous sight gags and very good acting and production values.

Season 1 Episodes: *1.* Bear Down. *2.* Bear in Mind. *3.* Goldicop and the Three Bears. *4.* Bear Essentials. *5.* Bear on a Couch. *6.* Bears of Interest. *7.* A Bear and Honey. *8.* Bears in Heat. *9.* Bear Fan. *10.* Bear Cam. *11.* Bear on Stage. *12.* Bear Reunion. *13.*

Bear on a Date. *14.* Bear Facts. *15.* Bears Undercover. *16.* Mr. Bear Chest. *17.* A Bear in Need. *18.* Bear-napped. *19.* Bears to the Rescue. *20.* Stand Up Bear. *21.* Bear Fight. *22.* Bears in the Desert. *23.* Bear Devil. *24,25.* Bear Trap. *26.* Christmas Special.

Season 2 Episodes: *1.* Party Bears. *2.* Truth or Bear. *3.* Clear the Bear. *4.* Bears in Chains. *5.* Leather Bears. *6.* Go Go Bear. *7.* Bear to Dream. *8.* Blackmail Bears. *9.* Closet Bear. *10.* Bear Movie Night. *11.* Break-in Bears. *12.* Jail Bears. *13.* Bailed Out Bears, *14.* Bear on a Stakeout. *15.* Bear Interrogation. *16.* Rugby Bears. *17.* Wine and Bear. *18.* Bear Audition. *19.* Crazy Bear. *20.* Hunting Bears. *21.* Bears in a Panic. *22,23.* Bears in the Woods.

Season 3 Episodes: *1.* Model Bears. *2.* Bears in the House. *3.* Bad Bear Day. *4.* Dead Body Bears. *5.* Bear on a Table. *6.* County Bear Jamboree. *7.* Bedroom Bears. *8.* Psycho Bear. *9.* Teddy Bear. *10.* Loaded for Bear. *11.* Hollywood Bears. *12.* Killer Bear. *13.* Intensive Care Bears. *14.* Peeping Bears. *15.* Cover Bear. *16.* Bear Scare. *17.* Stripped Bear. *18.* Dungeon Bear. *19–21.* Bears in the Air.

1088 *While Waiting for Godot.* whilewaitingforgodot.com. 2013.

Two people, who appear to be vagrants (Gogo and Pozzo) are first seen sitting on a Manhattan park bench waiting for a wealthy friend (Godot) to join them. But as Godot fails to keep his appointment, Gogo and Pozzo amuse themselves with conversation. Suddenly, a text message is received by Pozzo wherein Godot apologizes for being late and instructs them to meet him at 375 Park Avenue. Gogo and Pozzo, who feel their meeting with Godot will help them find better lives, begin their walk to Park Avenue with the program following their footsteps and all the stumbling blocks they encounter along the way. Based on a re-translated version of Samuel Beckett's 1948 original unpublished manuscript "En Attendant Godot." **Cast:** Ran Shelomi (Gogo), Jenel Moliere (Pozzo), Rudi Azank (Didi), Molly Densmore (Lucky), Stephen Kaiser-Pendergrast (Boy). **Credits:** *Writer-Director:* Rudi Azank. **Comment:** Filmed in black and white with very good acting and outstanding cinematography. It is also a unique presentation for its surreal image of New York City during the winter.

Season 1 Episodes: *1.* Nothing to Be Done. *2.* It's the Only Version They Know. *3.* The Goodness of the Travelers. *4.* You're My Only Hope.

Season 2 Episodes: *1.* That's Worth Waiting for, Isn't It? *2.* You're Not Godot, Are You? *3.* Happy Days. *4.* It's a Scandal. *5.* You Want to Get Rid of Her?

1089 *Whirl Girl.* whirlgirl.com. 1997–2001.

It is the mid–21st century and Zone Werks, an evil media and technology corporation run by Ty Harden, has taken control of mankind. One woman, Morgan Cross, has become a symbol for freedom and became the head of a revolutionary group dedicated to destroying Ty. Morgan's fight ended in her death and her daughter, Kia, was captured and brainwashed to forget what had happened. But as time passed her memory returned and, recalling her mother's actions, picks up where she left off and transforms herself into the super hero Whirl Girl (attired in blue bikini-like top, blue miniskirt and blue boots). With her weapon, the Whirl Blade and her fighting move, the Spin Kick, Kia begins her own battle against Ty to destroy him and return freedom to the world. Stekatta "Kat" Tressner and Sid X assist Kia; Victoria Thalios leads Free Vox, the rebel group opposed to Ty; Axxen Baines is Ty's top agent.

Voice Cast: Kim Campoli, David DiLeo, Betsy Hooper, Jennifer Richards, Kristen Johanssen, Jonathan Ellinghaus, Moe Fischer, Lani Ford, Angela Tweed, Sara Van Beckum. **Credits:** *Producer:* Buzz Potamkin, David B. Williams. *Writer:* Betsy Hooper, George Ostrin. *Director-Creator:* David B. Williams. **Comment:** A pioneering animated series that due to very limited high speed broadband in 1997 used comic strip-like panels to tell a story (using animation with dial-up connections would take several minutes to download). Flexible animation was encompassed the following year when Macromedia introduced Flash 2.0 Animation. Although the entire series cannot be watched the available episode is a good example of how early animation appeared on the Internet.

Episodes: 100 episodes were produced but only one episode and a trailer remains on line.

1090 *Who the F##k Is Nancy?* youtube.com. 2014.

Gay friends Alex and Jo have always gotten along well together until Jo fanaticized about becoming famous as "The Nancy," the one all gays will admire and adore. His endless efforts to achieve that goal have not only upset Alex but an unknown entity (suggested as being an alien) who has sought that prestigious "Nancy" title. When the entity can no longer abide by Jo's attempts to displace it as "Nancy," it decides to rectify the situation by eliminating Jo and Alex in a live web cast execution that will insure it becomes "Nancy." The program follows the entity's efforts (by possessing earthlings) to stop Jo's progression and Jo, Alex and their drag queen friend, Judy, as they attempt to destroy it before it destroys them.

Cast: Alex Josselyn (Alex), Jo Primeau (Jo), Judy Virtago (Judy). **Credits:** *Producer-Director:* Alex Castor, Jo Primeau. **Comment:** "Nancy" is softer terminology for gays who were termed "faggat" or "queer"; "Nance" is a British effeminate variation on the term or slang for a "Nancy Boy." The program is well acted and produced although some scenes that feature Jo and Alex are a bit over acted and just not funny. First season episodes are basically Jo and Alex's efforts to comprehend what is happening as

Jo strives for fame, while the second season parodies horror films to bring Jo, Alex and drag queen Judy into encounters with the alien and a final confrontation wherein Judy literally saves their lives.

Season 1 Episodes: *1.* Celebrite. *2.* Just a Nance! *3.* Call Me Nancy. *4.* 1 Girl, 5 Gaysians. *5.* I Wanna Nance with Somebody. *6.* Mean Gays.

Season 2 Episodes: *1.* Nancy Screams. *2.* Nancy's Nightmare. *3.* Nancy Knows What You Did Last Summer. *4.* The Exorcism of Scarlett Bobo. *5.* Black XXXmas. *6.* Hellbound. *7.* Inside Ivory's Tower. *8.* The Silent Treatment. *9.* Qrafty-ass Queen. *10.* The Evil Web.

1091 *Why I Hate Bitsy Malone.* webseries channel.com. 2010.

Bitsy Malone is a young woman many people simply hate. Not because she is beautiful, outgoing, bubbly and full of life but because their contact with her has, as they say, "obliterated them." For reasons she cannot explain, bad things happen to the people she meets. She loves to associate with people and means well but something always happens that results in a catastrophic situation that leaves people seeking only one thing—revenge. The program follows one such group of people who have formed a support group to cope with what has happened to them and why they hate Bitsy Malone (whose associations with Bitsy are seen in a flashback).

Cast: Natalie Lander (Bitsy Malone), Paula-Anne Sherron (The Professor), Sean Spence (Lenny), Alex Rose (Bobbi-Jo), Linda Kang (Tobi), Christine Horn (Billie), Michael Villar (Big Joel). **Credits:** *Producer:* Genevieve Pearson, Paula-Anne Sherron, Diane Pearson, Iggy Rodriguez, Chip Hale. *Director:* Chip Hale, Iggy Rodriquez. **Comment:** Once Bitsy is introduced you immediately fall in love with her. She is so sweet, pretty and unassuming that you would never suspect that her good intentions to help others would cause such disastrous results. Unfortunately, most information seems to have been taken off line. In addition to the only two episodes that remain on line there is a 66-minute video titled "Why I Hate Bitsy Malone World Premiere and Cast/Crew Q&A" that does contain clips from the well acted and produced series.

Episodes: *1.* Lenny Gets Fingered. *2.* Cheerleaders Become Famous

1092 *W.I.L.D.* webserieschannel.com. 2012.

Wellness. Introspection. Learning. Detox (W.I.L.D. for short) is rehabilitation program that attempts to straighten out teenagers through wilderness lessons. Marcy is the Trip Leader in one such camp and her charges are Karen, Daniel, Lux, Bridget and Cleo, five incorrigible teens who have been enrolled in the program by their parents. The program charts what happens as each teen faces the greatest challenge of his or her life—and hopefully survive Marcy's grueling tactics.

Cast: Taylor Patterson (Marcy), Halle Charlton (Bridget), Simona Kessler (Cleo), A.J. Helfet (Lux), Garrett Baer (Daniel), Matthew Schulman (Leslie). **Credits:** *Producer:* Brandon Baer, Simona Kessler, Robert Axelrod, Jake Monkarsh. *Director:* Brandon Baer. *Writer:* Robert Axelrod, Jake Monkarsh Garrett Baer, Halle Charlton, Mariel Redlin. **Comment:** Despite what the title and what the plot may sound like, it is a comedy with good acting and production values.

Episodes: *1.* Into the W.I.L.D. *2.* Welcome to the Wild W.I.L.D. West. *3.* Walk on the W.I.L.D. Side. *4.* W.I.L.D. Goose Chase. *5.* Where the W.I.L.D. Kids Are. *6.* Kids Gone W.I.L.D. *7.* W.I.L.D. and Out.

1093 Wind City. windcity.com. 2014.

Dylan, a young man with what he believes is great idea, and his girlfriend Kate, pool resources to begin a consulting business. All is progressing well until Kate feels with no profits, it is becoming a nightmare. Dylan believes just the opposite and, with only two options open to him, buying Kate out or proving he can make a success of the company, Dylan sets out to prove the company is worthy with the program also capturing what happens when his principal client becomes Loni Chase, his ex wife. Switch, a pretty young girl who has a fear of addressing people, is Dylan's assistant; Julia is Dylan's sister; and Duke is Dylan's friend from high school.

Cast: Adam Hurtig (Dylan Brady), Rebecca Gibson (Kate), Sierra Noble (Switch), Kyle Nobess (Sam), Sarah Constible (Julia), Trish Cooper (Loni Chase), Ali Tataryn (Morgan), Karl Thordarson (Duke), Abbey Thickson (Olivia). **Credits:** *Producer:* Jeff Peeler, Chris McIvor. *Director:* Darrell Wall. *Writer:* Paul Vieira, Sarah Constible, Rebecca Gibson. **Comment:** Canadian produced program that is very well done with good acting and production values. While the idea has been done before, adding a twist (Dylan's ex) makes for a good story line.

Episodes: 6 untitled episodes, labeled "Episode 1" through "Episode 6."

1094 Wing Women. wingwomenseries. com. 2012.

Sarah and Lauren are best friends just trying to survive the daily hassles of life. Sarah is an accessories fashion designer while Lauren works as an event planner. Each of the women, in their early twenties, is seeking a boyfriend but meeting the right guy seems to be something they cannot achieve. The program follows Sarah and Lauren, there for each other whenever the need be, as they seek those elusive love interests—"looking for love in all the right places and in all the wrong ways."

Cast: Priscilla Kavanaugh (Sarah), Sherz Aletaha (Lauren). **Credits:** *Producer:* Priscilla Kavanaugh, Justin Sharp. *Writer-Director:* Priscilla Kavanaugh. **Comment:** Although it is a comedy, it is also a bit sad at times when Sarah and Lauren fail in their attempt to snare a man. It is also shows that they are human and can be hurt when their hopes are shattered. The acting and production is very good and for something a bit different in the "girl-seeking guy mode" *Wing Women* fills the bill.

Episodes: *1,2.* Flirt. *3.* First Dates Suck. *4.* PSA: First Date Fails. *5.* Giving Him the Slip. *6.* How Come My Boyfriend's So Gay? *7.* Other Couples. *8.* Creepy Parents.

1095 WingMan. wingmanseries.com. 2014.

Scott and Becky are a young couple who unknowingly break a heavenly rule when Scott buys contraceptive pills for Becky and Becky, being of her own free will, takes one. The following morning Wingman (an angel) appears to Scott to tell him that he is angered, that Becky, a Roman Catholic, literally murdered an unborn child and must now pay the consequences: eternal punishment in Hell. Although Scott admits that he bought the pills, it was Becky's decision to use them. Scott does not face the same punishment as Becky, but he can redeem himself and save Becky by righting his wrong: impregnate seven women in seven days. Although reluctant, as he wants to remain faithful to Becky, Scott sees no other choice and sets out on a most unusual quest—with Wingman following his every move and, in a way hoping Scott will fail.

Cast: Victoria Beck (Becky), Guy Edmonds (Scott), Angus King (Wingman). **Credits:** *Producer:* Yingna Lu. *Director:* Steve Anthopoulos. *Writer:* Steve Anthopoulos, Luke Davidson. **Comment:** Well produced and acted Australian program that presents a unique idea and, while the "punishment" may be unusual, does a good job of pulling it off.

Episodes: *1.* The Morning After Pill. *2.* How to Pick Up at a Bar. *3.* How to Seduce a Catholic. *4.* Intermission. *5.* How to Pick Up Women at a Gay Bar. *6.* How to Cheat on Your Girlfriend. *7.* The Breakup. *8.* How to Start a Threesome. *9.* How to Save Your Girlfriend from Hell.

1096 Wingman Purgatory. youtube.com. 2013.

Ralph and Alex are friends and roommates who desperately want girlfriends but like water and oil, the two do not mix and their continual efforts to secure dates always fail. But they are there for each other and have devised a series of rules to live by (to attract women) called "Wingman Rules." The program chronicles what happens when Ralph and Alex put those rules into practice but can't realize they should break those rules and just be themselves.

Cast: Andrew Bachelor (Alex), Alex Salem (Ralph), Danielle Reverman (Courtney), David Dickerson (Merv), Jenny Soo (Krissy), Katie Whol (Tracy). **Credits:** *Producer:* Jolene Bolinger, Brad Simpson, Ben Molyneux. *Director:* Kyle Morrison. *Writer:* Max Kessler. **Comment:** The program while a bit talkative at times, has its comedic moments (especially in the last episode) and is well acted and produced.

Episodes: *1.* Pilot. *2.* Overweight, Alcoholic and an STD. *3.* The Holy Herb. *4.* Naked Car Wash. *5.* Hey Alex! *6.* Toilet Time—4th of July. *7.* Floor Hockey. *8.* Munchies. *9.* Bisexual? *10.* Infestation. *11.* Masturbation 6–500. *12.* Breaking Bad. *13.* Pheromones. *14.* Monogamy. *15.* Robbery. *16.* Live Birth.

1097 *Winners.* youtube.com. 2014.

Dave Van Gogh is the head of Winners Talent, a management company wherein he opens his doors to starving artists and, in turn for free rent, becomes their life coach and takes twenty-percent of what they earn. Dave was once in the position as those he now helps. For fifteen-and-a-half years he too was a starving artist but his big break came when he was chosen to become the commercial spokesman for Stay Strong Condoms and the ad campaign took off and made him wealthy. Feeling a need to help others who are facing the same uphill path, Dave has since opened his home to them, including: Sophia, a less-than talented beauty pageant queen; Ty, a talented but lazy actor; Liz, an awkward comedienne; and Nathan, a science fiction writer and blogger. The program focuses primarily on the people Dave mentors and how they further their plans to make it in Los Angeles (Dave believes that surrounding talents with talent will inspire them and set them on the path to fulfill their dreams). Emily is Dave's ex-girl-friend; Neil is Emily's current husband.

Cast: Paul Carganilla (Dave), Rya Meyers (Sophia), Terry Peay (Ty), Lauren Pritchard (Liz), Stephen Young (Nathan), Eddie Kaulukukui (Porter), Tyler Cole (Connor), Rick Messina (Neil). **Credits:** *Producer:* Paul Carganilla, Terry Peay. *Director:* Jared White. *Writer:* Paul Carganilla, Crystal Hubbard, Jared White, Stephen Young. **Comment:** Well acted and produced program that shows how hidden talent can remain hidden and how, through exposure to other talents, it can be brought forth and make careers.

Episodes: *1.* Pilot. *2.* Pool Party. *3.* Reservoir Dogs. *4.* It's Bad. *5.* The Lesson. *6.* iSandwich. *7.* Big Win. *8,9.* Complementary Valet. *10.* Texter. *11.* Acting Is Hard. *12.* Open Mic Night. *13.* Auld Lang Syne.

1098 *Wise Hit.* youtube.com. 2009–2011.

An American hit man, known only as Wiseguy, works in Shanghai for a local crime boss but yearns to redirect his life, feeling he has a sensitive side, and set up a matchmaking service in New York City. The program follows Wiseguy's last days on the job as he attempts to complete one more assignment: deliver a special package to a mysterious client (Vito) without getting killed along the way as assassins have set their sites on stopping him before he completes his mission.

Cast: Drago Lazetich (Wiseguy), Yuan Chu (Carlos), Jasmine Tse (DJ Honey), Daniel Drescher (The Bull), Karl Dominik (White Glove). **Credits:** *Producer:* Eva Zhou, Jon T. Benn, Drago Lazetich. *Writer-Director:* Drago Lazetich. **Comment:** Filmed on location in Shanghai that incorporates acceptable acting with cornball comedy. The mouth close-up scenes of DJ Honey are a bit annoying (just too close) and due to room acoustical problems, the dialogue is a bit hard to understand at times.

Episodes: *1.* I Have a Sensitive Side. *2.* The White Glove Treatment. *3.* I Needed the Cash. *4.* The Bull. *5.* Lady Number 9. *6.* French Pimp. *7.* The Restroom. *8.* Vampire. *9.* An Expat Named Vito. *10.* Infamous Tea and Honey Show. *11.* Dr. Gropus. *12.* Sidekick: You Never Know Where You Will Get a Helping Hand. *13.* The Way of the Drag Queen. *14.* Fun, Fun on the Band. *15.* Hot 4 Teacher. *16.* From Uranus with Love.

1099 *With Friends Like These.* with-friends-like-these.com. 2014.

Chris is a young corporate executive who believes with a friend like T.J., who needs enemies. T.J. is a twenty-something man child who, according to Chris, is much too social and involves himself in other people's lives (often causing them problems). But, for reasons that are not explained, Chris is stuck with T.J. (they are roommates) and the program follows the sometimes complex situations Chris faces as T.J. involves himself in Chris's business and private affairs.

Cast: Christopher Graves (Chris), T.J. Del Reno (T.J.), Ryan Blackwell (Ryan), Stacee Mandeville (Stacee). **Credits:** *Producer:* Rebecca Soler. *Director:* Matt Scott. *Writer:* Christopher Graves. **Comment:** The program is billed as "a modern-day Odd Couple" and it can be seen in that light as Chris is neat and T.J. is untidy. It is also a bit like the novel *Of Mice and Men* for its dependent factor of one man latching onto another. Although the idea has been done before it still comes off as a good take off on an old subject.

Episodes: *1.* Pilot. *2.* Personal Space. *3.* Wilderness Adventure. *4.* Say Yes. *5.* Susie Kay.

1100 *Woke Up Dead.* webserieschannel.com. 2009.

At a party a young man (Drex) accepts a blue pill

of an unknown substance from a drug dealer and takes it. At home, while taking a bath, the pill's effects put Drex to sleep. Although he is found by his roommate (Matt) after being underwater for 15 minutes, it appears that he is still alive—but as a zombie. The program relates events in Drex's life as he finds romance—first with a pretty nurse (Cassie) then with an equally pretty zombie (Aurora). But romance is not his biggest problem. He soon learns that he is part of something bigger—something that can be attributed to his mother (Marilyn). It appears that when Marilyn was younger, she was in a cult called the Sleepers, wherein members were "trying to awaken their genetic potential." Marilyn knows what is happening to Drex and he is part of that experiment. However, unknown to both Marilyn and Drex, persons unknown are keeping tabs on Drex as he is apparently the key to "The Awakening Underground" and what he possesses others want (unfortunately the program ends unresolved).

Cast: Jon Heder (Drex Greene), Krysten Ritter (Cassie), Josh Gad (Matt), Daniel Roebuck (Shadow Man), Jean Smart (Marilyn Greene), Ella English (Diana Phillips), Wayne Knight (Andrew Batten), Taryn Southern (Debbie), Meital Dohan (Aurora). **Credits:** *Producer:* Brent V. Friedman, Stan Rogow, Jeff Sagansky. *Director:* Tim O'Donnell. **Comment:** Light comedy-horror mix that portrays zombies in a different (less gross) light and even incorporates a zombie romance. Acting and production values are very good and well-known TV personalities Wayne Knight and Jean Smart appear as guests.

Episodes: *1.* Up and At 'Em. *2.* The Walking Dead. *3.* Dead TV. *4.* The Working Dead. *5.* Work It All Out. *6.* The Searching Dead. *7.* Lost and Found. *8.* Dead Man Typing. *9.* Someone Wicked This Way Comes. *10.* Pill of the Dead. *11.* Feeling Groovy. *12.* IM of the Dead. *13.* Hide and Seek. *14.* Date Night. *15.* Warehouse of the Living Dead. *16.* Single Dead Female. *17.* My Gun Is Dead. *18.* Back to School. *19.* Kiss of the Dead. *20.* The Not Bank Job. *21.* Night of the Dead Shark. *22.* Mother's Day.

1101 The Wonder Show. wondershow.com. 2013.

Jim, called "The Radio Guy," Mike, tagged "The Radio Guru" and John, "The Radio Gross" are three friends who appear to have a small Midwest radio station and broadcast and host a program called "The Wonder Show." The program, set mainly at the station focuses on the hosts as they do their daily show, become involved in the antics of their guests and do what it takes to make their show interesting.

Cast: Jim Tudor (Jim), Michael K. Anderson (Mike), John Gross (John), Alexander M. Kelsey (Phil the Vet). **Credits:** *Producer-Writer-Director:* Michael K. Anderson, John Gross, Jim Tudor. **Comment:** Poor man's version of shows like *WKRP in Cincinnati* that uses the radio broadcasting aspect to focus mostly on the station DJ's as they do their daily broadcast. The acting and production values are good but the concept can become tiring after a while.

Episodes: *1.* The Pizza of Doom. *2.* TV Girlfriend. *3.* Competitive Eating. *4.* The Comedy Machine. *5.* The Alien Shirt Saga. *6.* The Toaster Show. *7.* Ghosts. *8.* Wonder Show: CSI! *9.* Going Hollywood.

1102 Work in Progress. wiptheseries.com. 2015.

Four career women (Peyton, Chloe, Paige and Tracey) and their efforts to navigate life by helping each other over the various stumbling blocks they face.

Cast: Marquita Terry (Peyton Nicholson), Kristen Miller (Chloe Grey), Jen Drohan (Paige Turner), Vinessa Antoine (Tracy Grant), Richard T. Jones (R.J. Nicholson), Dawn Joyal (Fern). **Credits:** *Producer-Writer:* Marquita Terry, Kristen Miller. **Comment:** The women are very natural and make you feel you are peeking into their real lives as opposed to them just acting. The overall production is well filmed and acted.

Season 1 Episodes: *1.* Mailman Matt Damon Is Unresponsive. *2.* Sprinkle a Little Joy on a Stinky Situation. *3.* Sit and Breathe. *4.* Different Blondes Mean Different Things. *5.* Purging the Toxicity. *6.* Oh Shoot, I'm Late. *7.* The Vegans Are Coming. *8.* Who Wants Baby Cake? *9.* She Is Wonder Woman Damn It. *10.* It's a Play Date, Not a Real Date.

Season 2 Episodes: *1.* The Fat Knight Returns in Progress. *2.* Challenges in Progress. *3.* Music in Progress. *4.* Hangover in Progress. *5.* Pranks in Progress. *6.* Branding in Progress. *7.* Freaky Friday in Progress. *8.* Advice in Progress. *9.* Paradox in Progress. *10.* Game Show in Progress. *11.* Role Play in Progress.

1103 Workshop. workshoptheseries.com. 2009–2011.

The ups and downs of a group of struggling actors (see cast) as they face the harsh realities of the profession they have chosen—from attending acting classes, to auditions to realizing that fame is a difficult dream to accomplish.

Cast: Nate Golon (Jeff Reynolds), Kimberly Legg (Kaitlyn Murray), Phil Jeanmarie (Adam Saltair), Leanne Wilson (Vivian Smith), Jonathan Schwartz (Matthew Cunningham), Audra Marie (Sarah Clarkson). **Credits:** *Producer:* Nate Golon. *Director:* Andre Welsh. *Writer:* Nate Golon, Kimberly Legg. **Comment:** The program is basically just a look at the actors and what happens to them as they seek their careers. Adobe Flash Player 10 is required to view the program on the official site; it will play normally on YouTube.

Season 1 Episodes: *1.* The Actor's Resource. *2.* The Right Look. *3.* Drink My Sunkist. *4.* The Signature Move. *5.* Something Smells Fishy. *6.* Gas Up the Cadillac. *7.* The Next Big Celebrity. *8.* Somebody's Watchin' Me. *9.* A Little Cocky. *10.* Shake Your Money Maker. *11.* Time to Make Some Moves. *12.* It's All About Connections. *13.* Feel Free to Improv.

Season 2 Episodes: 6 untitled episodes, labeled "Episode 1" through "Episode 6."

Season 3 Episodes: 1 untitled episode, "Season 3, Episode 1."

1104 *The World of Cory and Sid.* funny ordie.com. 2009.

Cory and Sid are best friends, roommates and not the very brightest of young men. They are literally not equipped to handle the responsibilities of being adults. They squander money, never have any to pay the rent and haven't put anything away for emergencies. In another aspect they are resourceful, although not in the brightest of ways. The program charts their harebrained attempts to make ends meet by devising ludicrous schemes (like turning their apartment into a restaurant; selling drug-laced "Speed Brownies"; and taking in borders).

Cast: Pearce Akpata (Sid), David Taylor-Sharp (Cory), Stefon Benson (Cheddar), Marissa Merrill (Semaj), Leigh Jonte (Devon), Rachel Jolley (Gidget), Bridgett Lawrence (Baps). Credits: *Producer:* Caryn K. Hayes. *Director:* Laura Somers, Caryn K. Hayes, Carolyn O. Jacobs. Seth M. Sherwood, Rick Walls. *Writer:* Caryn K. Hayes, Samantha Kern, Seth M. Sherwood. Comment: Only a trailer remains on line and, while it does look a bit corny, it is really not possible to present a fair judgment of the entire series.

Episodes: *1.* Tent Bar. *2.* Tents for Rent. *3.* Brit Rock. *4.* The Secret. *5.* Nazi Juice. *6.* Eyeball. *7.* Speed Brownie. *8.* When the Bell Rings. *9.* Missionary. *10.* Homeless.

1105 *World's Worst Director.* angelwood pictures.com. 2012–2013.

Moses is a film director who believes he does a good job but his peers consider him the world's worst director. Penny is a young woman who will stop at nothing to achieve success. She is also Moses' rival and the two have made a wager to see who can produce the best web series (the outcome to be determined by the number of YouTube hits). With his idea for a series (*Perfect People*) and Penny's (*Pointless Persons*) the contest begins with the program chronicling all the problems Moses faces—from budget problems to acquiring a cast and crew as he seeks to, for the first time in his life, defeat his arch nemesis, Penny. Katie, Rachael and Cherri become Moses' crew while Sharon, Mason, Jennifer, Chris-

tine, Connor, Autumn and Trevor become his cast.

Cast: Seth Chtiwood (Moses), Mary C. Ferrara (Katie), Kristen Sargent Gorman (Carrie), Kia Holiday (Cherri), Theomer Aisha Abramson (Charlie), Gabrielle Cavallaro (Autumn), Paul Kandarian (Mason), Mary Paolino (Sharon), Eva Davenport (Christina), Jennifer Walsh (Jennifer), Thais Vieira (Jess), Evan Clinton (Trevor), Timothy Bonavita (Hector), Michael Kinnane (Eddie), Ryan Legassey (Jacob), Thomas Capuano (Brian), Jessica Kent (Allie), Krystal Hall (Mathilda), Maureen Vlaco (Emma), Heather Conroy (Sadie), Willow Jane Anderson (Bethany). Credits: *Producer:* Seth Chitwood. *Director:* Seth Chitwood, Sophie Kreyssig, Mary C. Ferrara. *Writer:* Seth Chitwood, Eva Davenport, Krystal Hall, January Adams. Comment: It takes a few minutes to adjust to Moses as he doesn't represent the kind of director one pictures in their mind (as he appears timid and someone who does not have the authority to give orders). After adjusting and meeting the spiteful Penny, the program hooks you right in and you do want to see what happens next.

Season 1 Episodes: *1.* Worst Pilot. *2.* Worst Audition. *3.* Worst Creative Team. *4.* Worst Table Reading. *5.* Worst Writer's Meeting. *6.* Worst Photo Shoot. *7.* Worst Filming Day. *8.* Worst Editing. *9.* Worst Interview. *10.* Worst Cast.

Season 2 Episodes: *1.* Worst Rival. *2.* Worst Parents. *3.* Worst Assistant. *4.* Worst Props. *5.* Worst Therapy. *6.* Worst Date Night. *7.* Worst Location. *8.* Worst Father's Day. *9.* Worst Decision. *10.* Worst Stage Mom. *11,12.* Worst Premiere.

1106 *World's Worst Musical.* worldsworst musical.com. 2012.

Guy is a young writer facing what is called the blank page. He has an idea that the world needs another Broadway musical but he faces a serious challenge: what kind? A musical based on zippers? A musical adaptation of *Jurassic Park* or a musical based on learning to drive? These are few of the ideas Guy comes up with until, as the program shows, all his bad ideas are the key to what he has been searching: a musical based on the worst ideas.

Cast: Marty Scanlon (Guy), Jaime Lynn Beatty (Karen). Credits: *Producer:* Kristina Erfe, Bri Maresh, Tim Ortmann, Jacqueline Johnson. *Director-Writer:* Corey Lubowich, Marty Scanlon, Molly Scanlon. Comment: Each episode is a look at one of Guy's ideas with very god acting and mini production numbers.

Episodes: *1.* Not the Best. *2.* Getting Off Track. *3.* Pirated Content. *Roadblock.* 5. Keep It Together. *6.* Hitting the Fan. *7.* Questioning. *8.* Losing It. *9.* Searching. *10.* The Worst.

1107 The Worst Landlord. theworstland-lord.tumblr.com. 2013–2014.

A young man (called only "The Tenant") has just moved into a new apartment (5B). The Landlord (as he is called) is more than just someone you see once a month to collect the rent; he is a pest and totally annoying and feels he must be with his tenants as much as possible. The Tenant would just like to be left alone and enjoy his new home; The Landlord, who appears to have a unique (or magical) way of entering apartments (even when the door is locked) always surprises The Tenant as to how he managed to get in. The Tenant puts up with The Landlord; The Landlord feels he must be an active part of The Tenant's life and the program explores what happens when The Tenant soon realizes that his Landlord is his worst nightmare.

Cast: Kevin Froleiks (The Landlord), Will Carey (The Tenant). **Credits:** *Producer:* Kevin Froleiks, Will Carey. *Writer:* Kevin Froleiks. **Comment:** Short, right to-the-point episodes that quickly establish an annoyance for The Tenant and how he deals with The Landlord. The characters are well defined (especially The Landlord) with good acting, stories and production values.

Season 1 Episodes: *1.* Moving In. *2.* Selling Out. *3.* Noise Complaints.

Season 2 Episodes: *1.* Aftermath. *2.* The Elevator. *3.* Defensive. *4.* A Very Serious Episode.

Season 3 Episodes: *1.* An Introduction Is in Order. *2.* Fast Friends. *3.* Grand Tour. *4.* The Best Roommate.

1108 Wrecked. wreckedtheseries.com. 2012.

The worsening economic economy has cost many people their jobs and Spencer, a young woman who often makes poor life decisions, finds that her company can no longer afford to employ her. With no money and unable to afford rent, Spencer leaves Los Angeles for her home town of Seattle, where she moves in with her brother Peter. Spencer soon reconnects with her best friend, Thomas, and the program chronicles the life of a woman, not always making the right choices, as she seeks to re-invent herself and get back into the work force (although her first job becomes a clerk in an adult video store, which she takes as she knows something better will come along but just needs to wait for that opportunity).

Cast: Bhama Roget (Spencer), Sean Patrick Mulroy (Thomas), Keiko Green (Amina), Ricky Coates (Peter), Robert Bergin (Ted). **Credits:** *Producer:* Liz Ellis, Charley Pope. **Comment:** Very well acted and produced program that is, at times, more dramatic than comedic. The program has all the elements that make for a good broadcast TV series and is quite enjoyable.

Season 1 Episodes: *1.* Wrecked Pilot. *2.* The Story. *3.* Sparkle Toes. *4.* The Plan. *5.* Plug It. *6.* The Wave.

Season 2 Episodes: *1.* Besties. *2.* Four Boobs. *3.* Roomies. *4.* Seattle Freeze. *5.* Kitchen Sink. *6.* The Storm.

1109 Writing Space. webserieschannel.com. 2014.

For Chris and Dan, fledging screenwriters, working together is better than working alone because they believe "writing is a collaborative meeting" while "writing alone is hard." Even with two minds working as one, Dan and Chris have only produced a few non-earth shattering plays, a low budget sketch web series and are currently working on a comedy series pilot they hope to pitch to the networks. To make matters a bit more complicated, Chris and Dan have begun filming their writing sessions and the program showcases those sessions which "record the strenuous work" they put into their scripts.

Cast: Dan Doolan (Dan), Chris Billingham (Chris). **Credits:** *Producer-Writer:* Dan Doolan, Chris Billingham. *Director:* James Watts. **Comment:** Interesting take on the saga of struggling screenwriters with good acting and production efforts. Since the "mocumentary" style of filming is used, the characters also speak directly into the camera to set up or explain scenes.

Episodes: *1.* Where the Magic Happens. *2.* Peaks and Troughs. *3.* The Ginger Conundrum. *4.* Fringe in a Box. *5.* The Wand of Fear. *6.* The Art of Procrastination.

1110 The Wrong Guys for the Job. the wrongguys.com. 2013.

Charlie and Larry are low level criminals who appear to be unable to do anything right. They receive orders from a higher up (possibly mob connected) and all that is asked of them is to complete the assignment without any fanfare or complications. Completing each assignment as asked could bring them closer to higher positions in the world of organized crime but Charlie and Larry are just "The Wrong Guys for the Job." Even if it appears that a job cannot be complicated, Charlie and Larry will find a way to complicate it. It is at this point, when their antics have them fearing what the boss will do that four possible episode endings appear on the screen. The viewer selects the one he feels will best resolve the situation and that conclusion will air.

Cast: Brian Dobski (Larry), Ryan Barry McCarthy (Charlie). **Credits:** *Producer-Writer-Director:* Matthew Tibbenham, Sutton McKee. **Comment:** A good idea that unfortunately only produced four episodes. With the exception of the use of vulgar language (which is used more than needed) the acting and production values are good and viewing all four conclusions is interesting.

Episodes: *1.* The Knockout. *2.* The Hostage. *3.* The Senator. *4.* The Heist.

1111 **X: The Web Series.** xwebseries.com. 2013.

Libby Turner is an unstable young woman who has managed to keep herself under control since she found the love of her life, Brett, the front man for the Journey tribute band "The Wheel and the Guy." But unexpectedly, Brett dumps Libby, causing her borderline psychotic tendencies to manifest once again and sets her on a path to reclaim the love of her life. The program follows Libby as she does what she feels is necessary to achieve her goal and along the way try to understand and accept what has happened to her. Charity is her roommate; Mandi is Brett's new girlfriend, the home wrecker Libby has set her sights on destroying to win back Brett.

Cast: Laura Nargi (Libby Turner), Doug Duke (Brett Foglestein), Paula Schmitt (Charity Lennon), Natalie Camunas (Mandi LaVine). **Credits:** *Producer:* Cali Z. Hayes, Jerry Hayes. *Director:* Jerry Hayes. *Writer:* Cali Z. Hayes. **Comment:** The program's web site exclaims, "Please Note: X is hilarious, dark and not safe for work (or children)." It is nicely performed but it does contain vulgar language.

Episodes: *1.* Separate Ways, Worlds Apart. *2.* After the Fall. *3.* Girl Can't Help It. *4.* Opened the Door. *5.* When You're Alone, It Ain't Easy. *6.* Walks Like a Lady. *7.* Edge of the Blade. *8.* Something to Hide. *9.* Don't Stop Believing. *10.* Troubled Child. *11.* Too Late. *12.* Who's Crying Now?

1112 **Y Life.** youtube.com. 2011–2012.

Andre, Seven and Cici are best friends struggling to cope with the daily frustrations of living in a big city. The world, they find, is progressing faster than they are and the program charts their everyday experiences as they deal with issues virtually everyone faces.

Cast: Andre Diaz (Andre), Charles Nettles (Seven), Cici Valentin. **Credits:** *Producer:* Andre Diaz, Kenny Williams. *Writer-Director:* Andre Diaz. **Comment:** While the acting and production is just standard for an Internet series, it is nothing more than a look at three guys trying to just accept the cards they have been dealt by the hand of Fate.

Season 1 Episodes: *1.* The Date. *2.* After Sex. *3.* The Pants. *4,5.* The Escort.

Season 2 Episodes: *1.* The Lookout. *2.* The Kiss. *3.* The Wanksta. *4.* The Sandman. *5.* Uno Night.

Season 3 Episodes: *1.* The Cheese Dip. *2.* The Print. *3.* Road Rage. *4.* Friend Zone.

1113 **Yes, And?** webserieschannel.com. 2014.

With a dream of becoming a professional actress, a college theater major (Samantha) believes that organizing an improv group may help her and others like her get the experience they need. While she manages to organize a group they are not the ideal actors: Becky, a spoiled girl who only wants fame; Anna Beth, a girl who suffers from extreme stage fright; Stewart, a loud talker; and Mark, a young man who feels joining the group will help him overcome the numerous psychological issues he has. Also a part of the group is Nicky, Becky's manager and, as she says, "her entourage." With the group formed the program charts Samantha's efforts to book gigs while coping with a group of dysfunctional associates.

Cast: Molly Tollefson (Samantha), Krista Curry (Becky), Erin Gunsul (Anna Beth), Damien Charboneau (Stewart), Helen Martin (Nicky), Matthre Rush (Mark). **Credits:** *Producer:* Molly Tollefson, Zac Cain. *Writer-Director:* Adam Boyer. **Comment:** The program is set like an informal gathering with a look at how improvisational comedy works. The characters are believable and the production is well done.

Episodes: *1.* Pilot. *2.* A New Development. *3.* Taxi Driver. *4.* Freeze Tag.

1114 **YOMO (You Only Marry Once).** youtube.com. 2014.

At what age should a woman call it quits and accept the fact that she will be a spinster is the question facing friends Yonah and Moshana. Yo and Mo, as they are called, live in London and are about to turn thirty when the reality of not being married dawns on them. Fearing that they will grow old together with only a cat for company, Yo and Mo begin a quest to change their future by finding a man to marry. The program chronicles their mishaps as they enter the dating scene but seem only to encounter men who are anything but desirable.

Cast: Yonah Odoom (Yo), Moshana Khan (Mo), Ginger Bonsu (Ginger), Lee Barnett (Neil), Angela Aryitey (Auntie O), Joy Isa (Yo's mother), Olivette Cole-Wilson (Auntie Mercy), Ken Smart (Yo's father), Nadim Hanif (Mo's father), Kanchan Raval (Mo's mother). **Credits:** *Producer:* Nana Evans, Nii Odartei Evans. *Director:* James Waterhouse. *Writer:* Yonah Odoom, Moshana Khan. **Comment:** British produced program that although well acted can be difficult to understand at times due to a deep (bass) sound that intensifies the accents.

Episodes: *1.* The African, Asian Persuasion.

1115 **You Are Here.** youtube.com. 2014.

The Panama Red Coffee Company is a small town coffee shop owned by Felix and frequented by Marcus, Toby, Kate, Rodeo Girl and Eric. Due to financial problems, Felix announces that the shop will be closing, leaving his patrons in a state of shock. The program follows what happens on the days before closing as the friends gather to savor what little time is left in their favorite hangout.

Cast: Brandon Rogers (Marcus), Gary Neil (Toby), Riley Krull (Kate), Tabbitha McBride (Rodeo Girl),

Alex Hero (Felix), Dillon Wall (Eric). **Credits:** *Producer:* Dillon Wall, Brandon Fraley. *Writer-Director:* Dillon Wall. **Comment:** A different twist on a bar, diner or restaurant hangout with what happens when such a home to people closes. Very well acted and produced.

Episodes: *1.* Opening and Closing. *2.* HPV and Denial. *3.* Krinto Basi Hahm. *4.* Dreams of Yuma. *5.* Speeches and Caffeine. *6.* Coyote Coats and Erotic Ballet. *7.* Nemesis and the Future. *8.* Neoteny and Super Heroes. *9.* Elizabeth or Ana. *10.* All Good Shops Must Close. *11.* Journeys and Goodbyes. *12.* The End of Panama.

1116 *You Can't Do That on the Internet.*
youcantdothatontheinternet.com. 2010.

Stories of various people addicted to the social media and how they handle their problems as members of the Cyber Addicts Support Group.

Cast: Kate Sargeant (Kate), Nichols Downs (Max), Kelly Huddleston (Cassie), Theresa JunE-Tao (Leslie), Mary Alyce Kania (Becky), Bradley Matthews (Justin), John O'Brien (Chris). **Credits:** *Producer-Writer-Director:* Kate Sargeant. **Comment:** A very well acted and presented program that tackles problems such as texting and Facebook-like addiction in a humorous manner.

Episodes: *1.* TMI. *2.* LilAngel1K*: Skype.It.Out. *3.* LilAngel1K8: Who's That Pickle? *4.* Cassiopia: Totally Almost Maybe Deleted You. *5.* Maxirrific Dude, Where's My Life? *6.* OMG. *7.* Textzilla: Shower Sexting. *8.* Sweet&SourAsian69: Car Wars. *9.* J-Dizzle: The 2010 Post-It. *10.* WTF.

1117 *You've Probably Dated My Mom.*
youtube.com. 2014–2015.

Beth and Jess are sisters, by different fathers, who live with their mother Francine, a woman who has been married three times and is seeking a fourth husband. Francine appears to have no morals when it comes to dating and is a constant source of worry to Beth and Jess who believe her mother "is nuts." Francine is overly flirtatious, pretends to be someone she is not to snare a date and her daughters have little power to stop her from what she is doing. The program charts Beth and Jess's efforts to find a way to control their mother's actions which is made more difficult when she begins an inappropriate dating service that teaches women how to get a man—any man.

Cast: Amy Tolsky (Francine), Jessie Sherman (Jess), Tara Oslick (Beth), Troy Hatt (Trevor). **Credits:** *Producer:* Catherine Roscart, Bruno Wu, Stacee Reich. *Director:* Amy Coughlin. *Writer:* Josh Mosby. **Comment:** TV quality production with excellent acting and production values, although there are adult themes and some foul language is used.

Episodes: *1.* Dress for Success. *2.* All Tied Up. *3,4.* Girls' Night Out. *5,6.* Dating Is Fun.

1118 *Zac and Me.* youtube.com. 2012.

Emma is a very pretty teenage girl who has apparently held onto her imaginary friend, Zac, a crude, rude, heavyset and foul-mouthed twenty-something nightmare of a companion. While it is not really explained, Emma may have been with Zac since she was a pre-teen and just couldn't let him go. He now appears as her less-than-desirable guiding light as he is always by her side and often gives her advice that is anything but helpful. Emma is the only one who can see and hear Zac and her talking to him makes it appear she is talking into thin air. The program follows Emma as she tries to navigate life as a high school girl with a monkey on her back—Zac.

Cast: Jessica Howes (Emma), Zach Dresler (Zac). **Credits:** *Producer:* Paul Komadina, Natalie Lewis, Zach Dresler. *Director:* Paul Komadina. *Writer:* Paul Komadina, Natalie Lewis, Zach Dresler.

Comment: An Australian produced program with a good idea (and acting and production values). Jessica Howes is sweet and adorable as Emma but Zac is crude and uses an abundant amount of foul language. If additional episodes are produced, removing the foul language and adding a parental advisory would make for a more kid-friendly series.

Episodes: *1.* Orange Crush. *2.* Shadow Boxer. *3.* Camp Rick.

1119 *Zoe and Chloe: Private Detectives.*
blip.tv. 2011–2012.

Zoe is a college student majoring in archeology. Chloe, her roommate, is studying criminal justice. While it appears the two have nothing in common as Zoe loves dinosaurs, adventure movies and cats, and Chloe studies the California Penal Code for laughs and dreams of becoming a police officer like her father, they share a love of solving mysteries. They have also started their own campus business, Zoe and Chloe: Private Detectives and stories follow their efforts to solve crimes in a less spectacular way than those seen in movies and on TV. Season one episodes follow the girls as they attempt to help their secretary, Roberta, solve the mystery of who stole the winning secret ingredient from her sister Delilah, a champion baker. Who stole clothes, sent to Zoe from her Nana Dragaboo in Norway, becomes a challenge for the girls in second season episodes.

Cast: Kristin Korsnes (Zoe Jones), Cherrae L. Stuart (Chloe Holmes), Joanna Teris (Roberta), Donald S. Chambers (Off. Horatio Don). **Credits:** *Producer:* Cherrae L. Stuart, Zakareth Ruben. *Director:* C. Shawn, Nelinda Palomino. *Writer:* Cherrae L. Stuart, C. Shawn, Kristin Korsnes, Joanna Teris. **Comment:** Zoe (white) and Chloe (black) are not the cleverest of detectives but they do present themselves as the most unusual private eyes you will ever see. The acting and production values are good and both presented cases are rather intriguing.

Season 1 Episodes: *1.* On the Case. *2.* Secret Ingredient. *3.* Just the Usual. *4.* Winners. *5.* Pristine Cookies. *6.* Just Desserts.

Season 2 Episodes: The Casual Relationship Between Cake and Fun. *2.* Lingonberry Scam. *3.* Guantanamo Garage. *4.* Mail Snail. *5.* Bin-va-oogle. *6.* Dividends. *7.* 3 Girls 1 Troll. *8.* Not Exactly. *9.* SKOAL.

1120 *Zombie Roadkill.* webserieschannel.com. 2010.

While in a national park and driving on an unfamiliar road, a group of college students run over and kill a squirrel. Unknown to them, the road on which they are traveling is cursed and animals such as that squirrel are reanimated as zombies and out to kill the humans who ended their lives. Soon after, when their car crashes, Simon, the only one who is not injured, must find help to save his brother (Greg) and their friends Amber and Trish. As Simon prowls the woods he encounters a park ranger (Chet) who tells him about the murderous animal zombies and together they set out to help Simon's stranded passengers.

Cast: Thomas Hayden Church (Chet Masterson), David Dorfman (Simon), Michael Blaiklock (Greg), Cherilyn Wilson (Amber), Toni Wayne (Trish). Credits: *Producer:* Jim Burns, Sarah J. Donahue, Sam Raimi, Robert Tapert, Aaron Lam. *Director:* Dave Green. *Writer:* Henry Gayden. Comment: An amusing, original idea that plays well and is enjoyable to watch.

Episodes: *1.* An Eye for and Eye. *2.* Smell of Death. *3.* Road Block. *4.* Fur Kills. *5.* Hot Night in Hell. *6.* Dead End.

1121 *Zombie Whisperer.* webserieschannel.com. 2012.

A zombie apocalypse has occurred and changed life on earth: zombies are now a part of society and pose no threat to humans. Tony Mallone is a speech therapist (an expert on undead relations) who has developed PETZ (People for the Esthetical Treatment of Zombies) and realizes there is a whole new market of people, although undead, who need help. He establishes himself as a Zombie Whisperer and the program follows his efforts to train zombies (and humans) how to deal with each other.

Cast: Matt Fowler (Tony Mallone), Lacy Wetmore (Tammy), Kyle Duncan Graham (Bob), Judith McConnell (Jacki), Justin Rupple (Announcer), Matthew Ray Collins (Cujo). Credits: *Producer-Writer-Director:* Matt Fowler. Comment: A different take on the numerous zombie series although the idea can only be stretched so far, thus far dealing with only humans who possess zombies as pets. The program itself makes an over abundant use of the annoying shaky camera coupled with unflattering extreme close-ups of the cast.

Episodes: *1.* Tammy and Bob. *2.* Jacki and Cujo.